PSYCHOPHYSIOLOGY

Systems, Processes, and Applications

PSYCHOPHYSIOLOGY

Systems, Processes, and Applications

EDITED BY

Michael G. H. Coles

Department of Psychology
University of Illinois
Champaign, Illinois

Emanuel Donchin

Department of Psychology
University of Illinois
Champaign, Illinois

Stephen W. Porges

Department of Human Development
University of Maryland
College Park, Maryland

The Guilford Press   New York   London

© 1986 The Guilford Press

A Division of Guilford Publications, Inc.
200 Park Avenue South
New York, New York 10003

Library of Congress Cataloging-in-Publication Data
Psychophysiology : systems, processes, and applications.
    Bibliography: p.
    Includes index.
    1. Psychology, Physiological. 2. Neuropsychology.
I. Coles, Michael G. H. II. Donchin, Emanuel.
III. Porges, Stephen W.
QP360.P785 1986   152   85–17621
ISBN 0–89862–640–4

Contributors

Truett Allison
Neuropsychology Laboratory
Veterans Administration Medical Center
West Haven, Connecticut
    and
Departments of Neurology and Psychology
Yale University
New Haven, Connecticut

Daniel S. Barth
Human Neurophysiology Laboratory
Department of Psychology
University of California, Los Angeles
Los Angeles, California

Theodore R. Bashore
Cognitive Psychophysiology Laboratory
Department of Psychology
University of Illinois
Champaign, Illinois
(Current address:
The Medical College of Pennsylvania at
Eastern Pennsylvania Psychiatric Institute
Philadelphia, Pennsylvania)

John V. Basmajian
Division of Rehabilitation Medicine
Department of Medicine
McMaster University and Chedoke–McMaster Hospital
Hamilton, Ontario, Canada

Jackson Beatty
Human Neurophysiology Laboratory
Department of Psychology
University of California, Los Angeles
Los Angeles, California

Jasper Brener
Department of Psychology
University of Hull
Hull, England

John T. Cacioppo
Department of Psychology
University of Iowa
Iowa City, Iowa

C. Sue Carter
Department of Zoology
University of Maryland
College Park, Maryland

Michael G. H. Coles
Cognitive Psychophysiology Laboratory
Department of Psychology
University of Illinois
Champaign, Illinois

Christopher Davis
Department of Psychology
Simon Fraser University
Burnaby, British Columbia, Canada

Emanuel Donchin
Cognitive Psychophysiology Laboratory
Department of Psychology
University of Illinois
Champaign, Illinois

John A. Edwards
Department of Psychology
University of Reading
Reading, England

Don C. Fowles
Department of Psychology
University of Iowa
Iowa City, Iowa

Nathan A. Fox
Department of Human Development
University of Maryland
College Park, Maryland

John J. Furedy
Department of Psychology
University of Toronto
Toronto, Ontario, Canada

Anthony Gale
Department of Psychology
University of Southampton
Southampton, England

James H. Geer
Department of Psychology
Louisiana State University
Baton Rouge, Louisiana

Gabriele Gratton
Cognitive Psychophysiology Laboratory
Department of Psychology
University of Illinois
Champaign, Illinois

Jonathan C. Hansen
Department of Neurosciences
University of California, San Diego
La Jolla, California

Steven A. Hillyard
Department of Neurosciences
University of California, San Diego
La Jolla, California

J. Richard Jennings
Department of Psychiatry
University of Pittsburgh
Pittsburgh, Pennsylvania

Demetrios Karis
Cognitive Psychophysiology Laboratory
Department of Psychology
University of Illinois
Champaign, Illinois

Marc P. Kaufman
Department of Physiology
University of Texas Health Sciences Center at Dallas
Dallas, Texas

John P. Koepke
Department of Psychiatry
Medical School
University of North Carolina at Chapel Hill
Chapel Hill, North Carolina

Arthur F. Kramer
Cognitive Psychophysiology Laboratory
Department of Psychology
University of Illinois
Champaign, Illinois

Alan W. Langer
Department of Psychiatry
Medical School
University of North Carolina at Chapel Hill
Chapel Hill, North Carolina

Parry B. Larsen
Department of Psychology
University of Miami
Coral Gables, Florida

Peter Levine
Ergos Institute
Flagstaff, Arizona

Kathleen C. Light
Department of Psychiatry
Medical School
University of North Carolina at Chapel Hill
Chapel Hill, North Carolina

Gregory McCarthy
Neuropsychology Laboratory
Veterans Administration Medical Center
West Haven, Connecticut
and
Departments of Neurology and Psychology
Yale University
New Haven, Connecticut

Gregory A. Miller
Cognitive Psychophysiology Laboratory
Department of Psychology
University of Illinois
Champaign, Illinois

Paul A. Obrist
Department of Psychiatry
Medical School
University of North Carolina at Chapel Hill
Chapel Hill, North Carolina

William T. O'Donohue
Department of Psychology
State University of New York at Stony Brook
Stony Brook, New York

Rosemary DeCarlo Pasin
Department of Psychology
University of Miami
Coral Gables, Florida

Richard E. Petty
Department of Psychology
University of Missouri–Columbia
Columbia, Missouri

R. T. Pivik
Department of Psychiatry
School of Medicine
Faculty of Health Sciences and School of Psychology
University of Ottawa
Ottawa, Ontario, Canada

Stephen W. Porges
Department of Human Development
University of Maryland
College Park, Maryland

Francois Richer
Human Neurophysiology Laboratory
Department of Psychology
University of California, Los Angeles
Los Angeles, California

Neil Schneiderman
Department of Psychology
University of Miami
Coral Gables, Florida

Robert H. Schorman
Department of Psychology
State University of New York at Stony Brook
Stony Brook, New York

Gary E. Schwartz
Department of Psychology
Yale University
New Haven, Connecticut

Christopher Wickens
Cognitive Psychophysiology Laboratory
Department of Psychology
University of Illinois
Champaign, Illinois

Charles C. Wood
Neuropsychology Laboratory
Veterans Administration Medical Center
West Haven, Connecticut
and
Departments of Neurology and Psychology
Yale University
New Haven, Connecticut

Theodore P. Zahn
National Institute of Mental Health
Bethesda, Maryland

Preface

Psychophysiologists study behavior from a perspective that emphasizes the biological mechanisms that underlie behavior. The psychophysiologist capitalizes on the fact that the activity of many systems that participate in the control and execution of behavior manifest themselves in signals that can be recorded from awake, behaving humans by means of noninvasive techniques. Psychophysiology fosters, therefore, a symbiotic relationship between psychology and physiology. On the one hand, we seek to understand psychological phenomena by studying the activity of various organ systems: on the other, we seek to evaluate the functional significance of the physiological phenomena by exploring them in psychological contexts. In this volume, we provide a tutorial review of the field.

Since psychophysiology involves the systematic observation of physiological systems, we propose that the psychophysiologist must understand the system under observation. It is particularly important that the relationship between the specific signals that serve as the dependent variables in psychophysiological research and the physiological systems that generate these signals be clearly understood. It is one of the principal assumptions of this volume that the psychophysiological measures are best interpreted within the framework of a detailed knowledge of the systems they manifest. We are equally convinced that the functional significance of the activities we monitor can

only be understood within the framework of a detailed analysis of the psychological context within which recordings are made.

The chapters in Part I of this volume are intended to provide a survey of the organ systems studied by psychophysiologists and of the range of interpretations of the psychophysiological measures that can be made with impunity within the current framework of physiological theories and concepts. The chapters in Parts II and III review the contribution of psychophysiological techniques to the understanding of psychological processes and the usefulness of these techniques in solving a variety of practical problems.

It may appear strange to some psychophysiologists to devote a major section of the volume to the exclusive review of physiological systems. It has been argued that psychophysiological measures can be treated as merely index measures in the same way that the mechanisms underlying the execution of a button press in a reaction time task are generally ignored by researchers in experimental psychology. From this point of view, it does not particularly matter how the individual goes about achieving a button press—the only variable of interest is how long it takes for the button to be pressed. However, we believe that the psychophysiological approach can only be successful if appropriate respect is paid to the knowledge that exists about underlying mechanisms. An aphysiological attitude, such as is evident in some psychophysiological research, is likely to lead to misinterpretation of the empirical relationships that are found between psychophysiological measures and psychological processes and states. We propose that psychophysiological theory can only be enriched if the properties of the underlying physiological systems are acknowledged.

To this end, Part I of this volume contains a series of chapters dealing with each physiological system with which the psychophysiologist has been concerned. We divide the nervous system, along traditional lines, into central and peripheral divisions. The peripheral nervous system is further divided into somatic systems (the musculature) and autonomic nervous systems. For our purposes, the autonomic nervous system is further divided into the cardiovascular system, the pulmonary system, the eccrine system, the pupillary system, and the gastrointestinal system. It should be noted that the pulmonary system is not a "pure" autonomic system, since the somatic nervous system is also involved in its control. We also consider another major system of the body, the endocrine system, because of its known influence on and by the other systems.

In each chapter, the authors describe the basic anatomy and physiology of the system in question. We note that this is not intended to serve as a guide to psychophysiological measurement. Many excellent guides are currently in print. However, in one case, "magnetoencephalography," we have included a chapter devoted mainly to a measurement technique. This is because of its novelty—no existing texts cover this new and exciting technique. In other cases, the description of a function cannot be given without a corresponding description of the technique used to measure the function. In yet other cases, the chapters contain references to sources which provide detailed descriptions of measurement techniques. Thus, the reader should find sufficient guidance from the various chapters to perform the elementary recording procedures associated with psychophysiological measures.

Although we do not devote specific chapters to psychophysiological measurement, we do include a chapter which deals with the analysis of psychophysiological data. We do this for two reasons. First, there is currently no good review of analytical techniques. Second, we believe that there are certain general principles which can be applied to the analysis of psychophysiological signals whatever their source. These are reviewed in the final chapter of Part I.

The basic theme of Part II is that psychophysiological measures can be used to understand psychological processes. It begins with a treatment of those issues normally considered to be the province of experimental or cognitive psychology, such as attention, information processing, and learning. In each case, the authors consider both the actual and potential contribution of a variety of measures to these issues. The next section deals with a set of problems that are more commonly associated with psychophysiology. There is a well-established tradition of research on both stress and emotion, particularly involving measures of the activity of the autonomic nervous system. Similarly, the topics of sleep and sexuality have both received considerable attention from psychophysiologists because of the obvious relevance of our measures. The final section of Part II deals with individual and developmental differences and social processes. To a large extent, these areas have suffered from the misuse of psychophysiological techniques—that is, naive investigators have all too frequently blundered into the research enterprise with little or no understanding of either the methodological or theoretical complexity of psychophysiology. For this reason, the authors of these chapters emphasize the potential as well as actual benefits of the psychophysiological approach. These areas could clearly benefit from a greater appreciation of the basic research findings reviewed in the previous two sections.

Finally, we consider two areas in which psychophysiology may have the potential to provide solutions to applied problems. Lie detection represents probably the most controversial potential application and the chapter airs the issues that have been raised concerning its use and potential use.

The application of psychophysiological methods to the solution of problems in human engineering, such as the measurement of workload, seems destined to be productive. With the increasing reliance of the human on technology, we clearly need as wide a range of tools as possible to match the technology to human capabilities. Psychophysiology may well supply some of these tools.

We should thank the following individuals for their assistance in the preparation of this book: Seymour Weingarten, Editor-in-Chief at The Guilford Press, who encouraged us to embark on the project; Cindy Yee, a graduate student at the University of Illinois, who, with skill and humor, assisted in the onerous but critical task of preparing the subject index; Barb Mullins and Marla Wease, also at Illinois, who were similarly diligent in preparing the author index; and Russell Till, who did the design and production of the book with great care. We encountered many delays and frustrations in the preparation of this book—as have others who have tried to create a handbook of psychophysiology. So we would like to acknowledge those authors who stood by their commitments to participate in the project, particularly those who submitted their chapters on time.

MICHAEL G. H. COLES
EMANUEL DONCHIN
STEPHEN W. PORGES

Contents

Section C: Signal Acquisition and Analysis

PART TWO: PROCESSES

Section A: Attention, Information Processing, and Learning

PART THREE: APPLICATIONS

PSYCHOPHYSIOLOGY

Systems, Processes, and Applications

PART ONE
PHYSIOLOGICAL SYSTEMS AND THEIR ASSESSMENT

SECTION A
The Central Nervous System

Chapter One

The Central Nervous System

Truett Allison
Charles C. Wood
Gregory McCarthy

INTRODUCTION

Psychophysiology shares concepts and methods with both psychology and physiology. With psychology, it shares the conceptual objective of understanding the psychological processes responsible for human behavior and the methodological tools of behavioral experimentation. With physiology, it shares a conceptual emphasis on biological substrates of behavior and a methodological emphasis on dependent variables that reflect activity of parts or components of the organism under study. In our view, what distinguishes the research of investigators who consider themselves "psychophysiologists" from other approaches to the combined study of physiological and behavioral variables is an emphasis on *noninvasive measurement of physiological variables in conscious, behaving human subjects.*

Our purpose in this chapter is to assess the value and limitations of noninvasive measurement of human central nervous system (CNS) activity. We have restricted the broad scope of that question in two ways. First, because of our own experience and research interests, we concentrate on event-related potentials (ERPs) recorded in association with specific stimulus and response events. We do not explicitly address research using the electroencephalogram (EEG) or other noninvasive techniques, such as magnetic recordings of human brain activity. However, many of the issues to be considered apply to all such noninvasive techniques. Second, although applied research using ERPs has resulted in their widespread use as clinical tests in neurology and related fields (e.g., Chiappa & Ropper, 1982; Halliday, 1978; Starr, 1978), our discussion emphasizes the use of ERPs to investigate psychological processes and their biological substrates.

Our assessment of surface ERPs as noninvasive measures of CNS activity begins with a review of how electrical events in the CNS are generated. We then discuss examples of surface ERPs generated by various structures of the somatosensory system. Next we consider the implications of the review and examples for ERP studies, and we conclude with a somewhat irreverent but (we hope) instructive comparison of classical and modern "bumpology."

Truett Allison, Charles C. Wood, and Gregory McCarthy. Neuropsychology Laboratory, Veterans Administration Medical Center, West Haven, Connecticut; Departments of Neurology and Psychology, Yale University, New Haven, Connecticut.

THE NERVE OF LORENTE DE NÓ: SOME FUNDAMENTALS OF NEURONAL ELECTROGENESIS

Ionic current flow across the cell membranes of active neurons gives rise to electrical potential differences between different locations in the extracellular space, which can be recorded between a pair of electrodes located in, or in electrically conductive contact with, that space. Because the brain and its coverings (the meninges, skull, muscle, and scalp) are electrically conductive media, surface ERPs are subject to the same laws and principles of electrical field theory that govern the recording of electrical potentials in any volume conductor (e.g., Freeman, 1975).

Two types of transmembrane current flow (and hence extracellular potentials) are intimately related to information transmission and processing within and between neurons. The first is associated with the all-or-none spike or action potential, which reflects transmission along an axon from the cell body to axon terminals. The second is associated with graded post-synaptic potentials (PSPs), which reflect information transmission from one neuron to another. The latter can be either excitatory (EPSPs) or inhibitory (IPSPs).

First, let us consider the generation of action potentials. During the 1930s and 1940s, many neurophysiologists studied compound action potentials—that is, the summation of many individual action potentials of single nerve fibers—generated by electrical stimulation of peripheral nerves. A classic and still instructive experiment was performed by Lorente de Nó (1947b), which exemplifies many of the fundamental characteristics of extracellularly recorded neuronal electrical activity. His recordings are illustrated in Figures 1-1A and 1-1B, and summarized schematically in Figures 1-1C and 1-1D. When the neuron is at rest (Figure 1-1C, section 1), there is no current flow across the cell membrane, and the extracellular potential is consequently zero. As the region of membrane depolarization associated with the action potential approaches the recording electrode, a positive potential is recorded (Figure 1-1C, section 2). This is seen, for example, in Figure 1-1B at time 1 after the stimulus; at 0 mm the nerve volley has just exited the oil pool and has depolarized the nerve, while 7 mm down the nerve a positive potential is recorded. A negative potential is recorded when the depolarization is adjacent to the recording electrode (Figure 1-1C, section 3). As the action potential passes the electrode (Figure 1-1C, section 4) the potential again becomes positive (e.g., in Figure 1-1B, location 0,0 at time 3), followed by a return to zero potential. Thus, as shown in Figure 1-1B and section 4 of Figure 1-1C, the entire waveform is triphasic: positive, reflecting *outward* current flow toward the approaching region of depolarization; negative, reflecting *inward* current flow in the region of depolarization; and positive again, reflecting a return

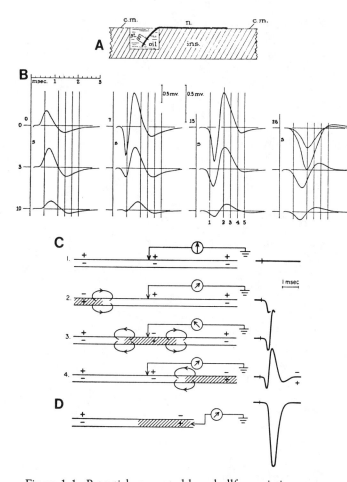

Figure 1-1. Potentials generated by a bullfrog sciatic nerve segment. A. The nerve (n) is laid on insulating material (ins.) covered by a conducting medium (c.m.; a sheet of blotting paper soaked with Ringer's solution). One of the ends of the nerve was submerged in an oil pool in contact with the stimulating electrodes. B. Field potentials produced as the nerve impulses travel from one end of the nerve to the other, recorded from 12 locations. Each column shows the potentials recorded from electrodes located at the indicated distance in millimeters from the point where the nerve exits the oil pool. Each row shows the potentials recorded at a given distance laterally from the nerve. For example, the middle potential in the third column was recorded at a point 15 mm along the nerve and 3 mm lateral to it, which is called location 15,3. The voltage calibration at left is for the top row; the higher gain at right is for the bottom two rows. The reference electrode is on the edge of the blotting paper; negative at the active electrode is upward. The vertical lines note particular times after the stimulus, which in this and following figures is delivered at beginning of trace unless noted otherwise. (Adapted from Lorente de Nó, 1947b.) C, D. Schematic illustration of potentials associated with an action potential traveling along an axon (or compound action potential traveling along a nerve). C. (1) The axon is at rest; there is no current flow, and therefore no potential field. Successive time intervals as the region of membrane depolarization approaches (2), reaches (3), and passes (4) the recording electrode. The complete triphasic positive–negative–positive potential is shown in (4). D. Recording

to *outward* current flow as the depolarization passes. Finally, Figure 1-1B (fourth column) and Figure 1-1D show that an electrode placed at or beyond the end of the nerve records primarily a positive potential. In this case, the region of depolarization approaches but does not reach the electrode. This is an important phenomenon, for it implies that an electrode located beyond the termination of a fiber tract will record primarily a positive potential as a synchronous nerve volley traverses the tract.

Several important generalizations about neuronally generated potential fields are illustrated by Lorente de Nó's recording:

1. Net inward current flow across the cell membrane (often called a current "sink") is associated with a *negative* potential in adjacent regions of the extracellular space.

2. Net outward current flow (often called a current "source") is associated with a *positive* potential in adjacent regions of the extracellular space.

3. Current flow into the active region of the cell is balanced by an equal current flow out of passive regions of the cell.

4. The density of current flow is large in the immediate vicinity of the depolarized region, but decreases rapidly with distance. Since the potential at any point is proportional to the current flow, the amplitude of the potential decreases rapidly as the electrode is moved away from the nerve. For example, at location 15,10, the negativity is only 10% of its amplitude as measured at 15,0. However, the lines of current—and therefore of voltage—extend indefinitely away from the nerve, and under good recording conditions these potentials could be recorded at large distances from the nerve (e.g., 1 m away if the nerve were placed on a large piece of blotting paper or in a bathtub filled with saline).

5. According to Helmholtz's principle of superposition, potentials associated with transmembrane currents of different neurons summate at all locations in the extracellular space. Therefore, potentials of similar latency and morphology from synchronously active cells will tend to summate, producing large-amplitude potentials that can be recorded at considerable distance from their sites or origin. However, the principle of superposition dictates that potentials of opposite polarities also summate, but in this case they tend to cancel rather than reinforce each other. Thus, the instantaneous potential difference between any two

locations is the algebraic sum of the potentials due to all transmembrane currents existing at the instant at which the potential difference is measured.

6. Even in a "simple" recording situation like that depicted in Figure 1-1, ERP morphology and latency are complex functions of electrode and source locations, as well as other factors. In the first column of Figure 1-1B, note that the negative peak increases in latency at locations farther from the nerve. Without any knowledge of the location of the source, one might infer that the depolarization was moving from location 0,0 to 0,10. In this case, we know that the region of depolarization is in fact moving perpendicular to this line. Location 0,0 records primarily the potential generated in the segment of nerve immediately adjacent to it; electrode 0,10, on the other hand, is almost as near the first third of the nerve as it is to point 0,0, and therefore records a space-weighted (and hence time-weighted) average of the negativity along that segment of the nerve. Conversely, at the other end of the nerve (the fourth column of Figure 1-1B), electrode 26,10 sees the approaching source positivity from the last third or so of the nerve; thus the peak latency of the positivity is earlier than at location 26,0.

7. The specific potential recorded under a given set of conditions (or, indeed, whether any net potential is recorded) depends both upon the location of the recording electrodes and the location of the active tissue at any instant in time. In Figure 1-1, for example, the active electrode is near the nerve, and the reference electrode is distant. However, if both electrodes were near the nerve, a more complex waveform would be observed, its exact form depending upon the interelectrode distance.

Thus far we have only considered potentials generated by peripheral nerves, which are structurally simple. However, for neurons in the CNS, the situation is more complex. Individual neurons may be structurally complex, with dendrites and axons of various size, shape, and number proceeding in various directions from the cell body. In addition, the structural relationships between neurons may also be complex. Finally, still further complexity is introduced by the pattern of synaptic contacts between cells. Anatomical studies suggest that afferent input to a group of neurons from a particular source usually makes synaptic contact on the dendrites, or on the cell bodies, but usually not on both to an equal extent. Because of superposition, both the spatial orientation of nerve cells and cell groups and the locus and temporal pattern of synaptic activation of those cells are important determinants of the extracellular potentials that can be recorded in any given case, particularly at large distances from the active cells.

Lorente de Nó (1947) investigated the effects of cell orientation in a series of elegant theoretical and

from the end of the nerve yields only a positivity. (From "Generation of Brain Evoked Potentials" by J. Schlag. In R. F. Thompson and M. M. Patterson [Eds.], *Bioelectric Recording Techniques: Part A. Cellular Processes and Brain Potentials.* New York: Academic Press, 1973. Reprinted by permission.)

experimental studies. First consider a simple case in which cell bodies and their dendrites and axons are aligned in parallel (Figure 1-2, left); examples of such neurons are the pyramidal cells of cortex and hippocampus. As in nerve fibers, most of the extracellular current flow is along the long axis of the neuron. Depolarization of the cell bodies by synaptic excitatory action produces inward current flow and a local negative EPSP, while the large vertically directed dendrites serve as the primary current sources, and hence in their vicinity a positive EPSP is recorded. If the EPSPs are large enough, an action potential will be produced, and the entire waveform will consist of the rapid action potential superimposed on the slower EPSP. When the cell bodies are depolarized at about the same time, as by a synchronous afferent volley, their individual potential fields have the same orientation and therefore summate to produce a large potential. Lorente de Nó called the potential field produced by this arrangement of neurons an "open field." Such potential fields can be recorded at considerable distances from their source.

This distribution of potential approximates that created by a theoretical source called a "dipole," which consists of two electric charges of opposite polarity between which current flows. An open field may be thought of as the summation of the elementary dipole sources produced by each neuron. The degree to which the potential field of this "equivalent dipole" resembles that of a theoretical point dipole depends on the areal extent of the neurons and the degree to which they lie in a plane (as in Figure 1-2, left) or have a more complex shape (e.g., if they extend from the crown into the bank of a gyrus).

In many subcortical nuclei, the arrangement of neurons is less regular. Imagine cells arranged in a sphere as shown in Figure 1-2, center, with their dendrites extending radially outward from an inner core of cell bodies. Depolarization of the cell bodies produces extracellular current that radiates inward from the dendrites, leading to a negative potential throughout the structure with a maximum near the center and a zero potential line near the outer border. Outside the structure, there is no current flow and hence no potential. This "closed field," as Lorente de Nó (1947a) called it, is a neurophysiological black hole, invisible from the outside.

Lorente de Nó (1947a) also considered types of potential fields intermediate between open and closed fields. If a structure contains a mixture of cells whose processes have both parallel and radial orientations, an "open–closed" field is produced (Figure 1-2, right). Llinás and Nicholson (1974) suggest that this may be a common arrangement in nuclei, because an otherwise closed field is punctured by parallel axons entering and leaving the nucleus. It can be imagined that an actual potential field could fall anywhere along the continuum of open and closed fields, but these

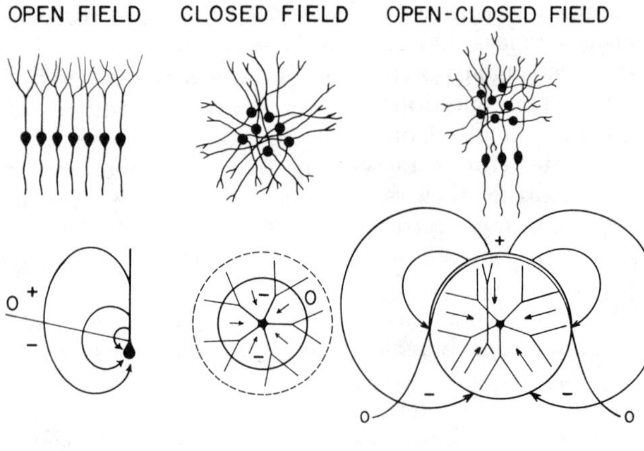

Figure 1-2. Predicted current flow and potential field produced by synchronous depolarization of the cell bodies of a row of neurons with parallel orientation (open field), with cell bodies clustered in the center and with dendrites spreading radially (closed field), and with a combination of radial and parallel elements (open–closed field). (Adapted from Lorente de Nó, 1947a.)

examples will suffice to aid in thinking about potential fields and in developing working hypotheses as to the location and orientation of the neural elements that might generate an observed potential field. For examples of potential fields generated by populations of model neurons that approximate those of certain structures in the mammalian CNS, see Klee and Rall (1977).

FROM THEORY TO PRACTICE: POTENTIALS GENERATED IN THE SOMATOSENSORY SYSTEM BY STIMULATION OF THE MEDIAN NERVE

To illustrate how the principles of electrogenesis reviewed above apply to the interpretation of ERPs recorded from the human body surface, we review the surface ERPs generated in various parts of the somatosensory system. We assume that the median nerve has been electrically stimulated at the wrist (unless noted otherwise), and we follow the resulting afferent volley as it passes up the nerve, enters the spinal cord, and proceeds up the neuraxis. The somatosensory system has been chosen for illustrative purposes because its peripheral portion is accessible to recording, because the neuroanatomy and neurophysiology of the central portion considered here are known in some detail, and because the relationship between surface ERPs and activity of specific anatomical structures has been extensively studied.

Unfortunately, peripheral nerves in a human are not conveniently laid out on a piece of blotting paper, as in Lorente de Nó's demonstration, but are surrounded by muscles and encased in cylinders such as arms and legs. Do compound action potentials produce detectable potentials at the surface of the human body? This question was first answered by Dawson and Scott in 1949; one of their recordings is shown in Figure 1-3 (lower trace). The amplitude of the potential is smaller than those seen in Figure 1-1 because the recording electrodes are farther from the nerve than were Lorente de Nó's electrodes, but otherwise the similarity is striking. Similar recordings can be obtained from an electrode placed on the collarbone overlying the brachial plexus (Figure 1-3, upper trace), where the median and other nerves divide and regroup before entering the spinal cord. The latency of the volley is longer when recorded at the shoulder, the difference corresponding to a nerve conduction velocity of about 60 m/sec.

That a peripheral nerve compound action potential can be recorded from the skin is not a startling result,

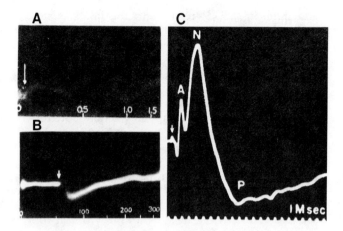

Figure 1-4. Spinal cord recordings. A. Recording of the spike potential evoked by stimulation of a dorsal root in cat. The potential is triphasic positive–negative–positive. B. Similar recording but at a slower speed to show the N and P waves (the N wave is hardly visible). Time is in milliseconds; negative is upward. (From "Potentials Produced in the Spinal Cord by Stimulation of Dorsal Roots" by H. S. Gasser and H. T. Graham. *American Journal of Physiology*, 1933, 103, 303–320. Reprinted by permission.) (C) Potentials recorded from surface of spinal cord in dog to stimulation of a dorsal root. In this recording, the final positivity of the spike potential is obscured by the early portion of the N wave. Stimuli delivered at arrows. (From "Differential Vulnerability of Spinal Cord Structures to Anoxia" by S. Gelfan and I. M. Tarlov. *Journal of Neurophysiology*, 1955, 18, 170–188. Reprinted by permission.)

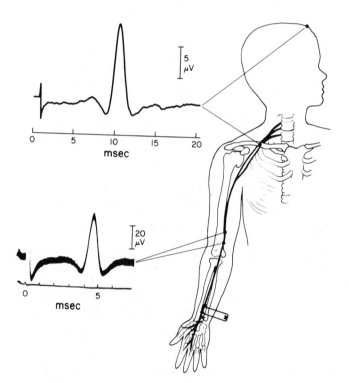

Figure 1-3. Recording of peripheral nerve compound action potentials in humans. Lower tracing: Median nerve volley recorded from the skin just above the elbow. Fifty individual oscilloscope traces were superimposed; negative at distal electrode upward. (From "The Recording of Nerve Action Potentials through Skin in Man" by G. D. Dawson and J. W. Scott. *Journal of Neurology, Neurosurgery and Psychiatry*, 1949, 12, 259–267. Reprinted by permission.) Upper tracing: Median nerve volley recorded from the skin midway along the clavicle overlying the brachial plexus; negative at clavicle electrode upward. Summation of 512 responses.

but for our purposes it allows the important conclusion that surface potentials can be recorded that, in some cases at least, are reasonably faithful reflections of potentials that can be recorded in much closer proximity to their sources within the body. We next follow this nerve volley as it travels through the dorsal roots and enters the spinal cord. In 1933, Gasser and Graham published a remarkable paper. They had set out to study the neural basis of spinal reflexes by recording potentials generated in the spinal cord following stimulation of a dorsal root. For this purpose, they constructed one of the first cathode ray oscilloscopes used for neurophysiological purposes. The tracings they obtained with this instrument were faint and poorly focused (Figures 1-4A, 1-4B); nevertheless, they were able to make a number of important observations when they recorded from the dorsal surface of the cord:

1. They recorded a triphasic positive–negative–positive spike potential, which began about .5 msec after the stimulus and lasted about 1 msec (Figure 1-4A). The spike was immediately followed by slower negative and positive potentials (Figure 1-4B). Figure 1-4C shows a clearer example of these potentials. Gasser

and Graham (1933) referred to the fast and slow portions of the response as the "spike" and "intermediary" potentials. Following Gelfan and Tarlov (1955), we refer to the spike as the "intramedullary primary afferent spike" (A), and the slower potentials as the "N wave" and "P wave."

2. The duration of the A spike was similar to that of a peripheral nerve compound action potential, whereas the N wave has a longer duration.

3. The A spike was resistant to the effects of asphyxia, whereas the N wave was much more sensitive and often disappeared at a time when the spike was unaffected.

4. A conditioning stimulus applied a few milliseconds earlier to the same or a nearby dorsal root had little or no effect on the A spike, but caused a large reduction in the size of the N wave.

5. The N wave was present in deeply anesthetized preparations in which reflex excitation of motoneurons was not possible. In less deeply anesthetized animals, potentials generated by motoneurons in response to dorsal root stimulation occurred later than the N wave.

Gasser and Graham (1933) had little difficulty in concluding that the A spike reflected the afferent volley as it approached and passed the recording electrode. The N wave presented more of a problem, but after reviewing the evidence summarized above, they concluded, "We have presented strong evidence that the prolonged waves in the cord are produced beyond the primary neurone. Motor cell activity alone does not produce them. . . . The burden, therefore, seems to fall on the internuncial neurones" (p. 316).

To determine whether Gasser and Graham were correct, we need several kinds of information. We first need to know the location of the "internuncial neurons," or "interneurons" in current terminology. Wall (1960) recorded from single cells in the dorsal horn of the lumbar cord while touching the animal's hindlimb. He concluded that most of the responsive cells were located in a horizontal band corresponding to laminae IV and V of Rexed (1952) (Figure 1-5A). In this region of the cord, collateral branches of the afferent fibers enter the dorsal horn from the medial side and make numerous synaptic contacts with dendrites of the interneurons (Figure 1-5B). These neurons are aligned in parallel with their dendrites pointing toward the dorsal surface of the cord, their cell bodies situated in laminae IV–V, and their axons proceeding ventrally. Thus we would expect their activation to generate something approximating an open field. However, we cannot directly apply the model of Figure 1-2 (left), which assumes that the *cell bodies* are depolarized, because in the dorsal horn the *dendrites* are depolarized. In this case we would expect to record a negativity in the region of the dendrites and—since the source current necessarily has to come from more

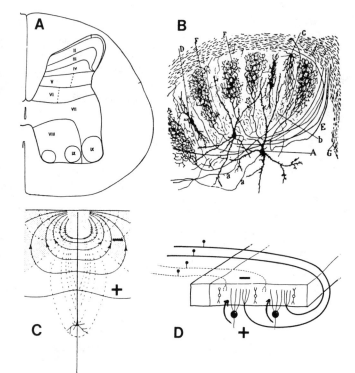

Figure 1-5. Anatomy and electrogenesis of the dorsal horn of the spinal cord. A. The spinal cord is characterized by a number of regions consisting of neurons of particular size, shape, and connectivity. A widely used subdivision is that of Rexed (1952); the example shown is the fifth cervical segment of the cat. B. Collaterals of primary afferent fibers (E) enter the dorsal horn and end in bushy arborizations (F) which make dense synaptic contacts with dendrites of laminae IV–V cells (A) whose axons (a) pass ventrally. (From *Sensory Mechanisms of the Spinal Cord* by W. D. Willis and R. E. Coggeshall. New York: Plenum Press, 1978. [Adapted by Willis and Coggeshall from Ramón y Cajal, 1909.] Reprinted by permission.) C. Theoretical extracellular potential field generated by depolarization of the distal end of a large dendrite of a neuron. Solid lines indicate current flow; broken lines are isopotential lines. For clarity, the most intense parts of the field are omitted. Shading indicates negative potential. (From "Neuronal Basis of EEG-Waves" by O. Creutzfeldt and J. Houchin. In A. Remond [Ed.], *Handbook of Electroencephalography and Clinical Neurophysiology* [Vol. 2C]. Amsterdam: Elsevier, 1974. Reprinted by permission.) D. Schema of the anatomical arrangement of neurons of the dorsal horn and the expected current flow following their excitation by afferent fibers. Large afferent fibers are shown as thick lines terminating in laminae II–III. At stimulus intensities used in human recordings, few if any of the smaller afferent fibers shown would be stimulated. (Adapted from Wall, 1964.)

ventral regions of the neuron, the cell bodies and axons—a positivity ventrally. A quantitative model of this situation is shown in Figure 1-5C, and Figure 1-5D is a summary of the model for dorsal horn neurons. That the experimentally observed dipolar potential field is similar to that predicted by Gasser and

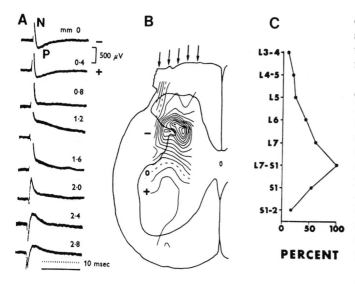

Figure 1-6. Potentials generated in the dorsal horn. A. Potentials recorded in spinal cord at indicated depths from the dorsal surface, to stimulation of cat superficial peroneal nerve. Note polarity inversion of the N wave to a positive potential at a depth of about 2 mm, corresponding to laminae IV–V. (From "Central Pathways Responsible for Depolarization of Primary Afferent Fibres" by J. C. Eccles, P. G. Kostyuk, and R. F. Schmidt. *Journal of Physiology* [London], 1962, 161, 237–257. Reprinted by permission.) B. Isopotential contour map showing the topography of the N wave dorsally and its polarity-inverted counterpart ventrally. C. Longitudinal distribution of N-wave amplitude, plotted as a percentage of maximum. L = lumbar, S = sacral. Both B and C depict stimulation of monkey sural nerve. (From "Spinal Cord Potentials Evoked by Cutaneous Afferents in the Monkey" by J. E. Beall, A. E. Applebaum, R. D. Foreman, and W. D. Willis. *Journal of Neurophysiology,* 1977, 40, 199–211. Reprinted by permission.)

Graham has been demonstrated by many investigators (e.g., Figures 1-6A, 1-6B).

The change in polarity from the region of negative current sinks to positive current sources is called a "polarity inversion," and the point at which the potential changes from one polarity to the other is often regarded as a sign that the electrode is in close proximity to the source. That assumption is correct for potential fields generated by a single localized source, but it can be incorrect in the case of fields generated by multiple sources. In the latter case, the zero potential line is simply the point at which activity from the two sources sums to zero, and it need have no particular spatial significance.

Finally, we need to know the distribution of active neurons longitudinally in the cord. The incoming dorsal root fibers split into ascending and descending branches, which travel some distance while giving off collaterals to the dorsal horn interneurons. Figure 1-6C shows the longitudinal extent of the N wave; while the potential is largest at the level of entry of the

dorsal roots corresponding to the peripheral nerve stimulated, it can be recorded for some distance along the cord. Thus the N wave is generated by a long, narrow sheet of dorsal horn interneurons.

In the cat, the A spike and the N wave produce detectable potentials at the surface of the neck (Figure 1-7A); presumably, corresponding potentials can be recorded from the human neck (Figure 1-7B). The surface potentials are smaller by at least an order of magnitude than those recorded directly from the cord, but signal averaging readily allows their recording. The potential field as recorded from the surface of the head and neck has not been studied in detail, but recordings to date suggest that the field is negative over the posterior neck and scalp and positive over the frontal scalp and neck, in agreement with the postulated field shown in Figure 1-7C.

In the somatosensory system, the dorsal horn neurons are the initial site of generation of PSPs. Graded depolarization of the dendrites spreads into the cell body, and if the magnitude of the EPSP is large enough, a spike is generated. The potential fields generated by action potentials and graded PSPs are not essentially different; in either case, depolarization is associated with a local negative sink and with a positivity near the region of the neuron that provides source current. The N wave (or its positive counter-

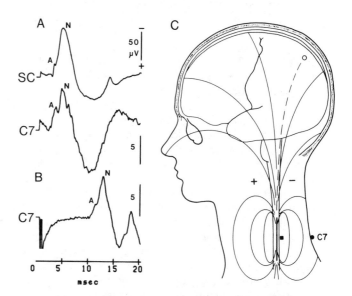

Figure 1-7. Potentials recorded simultaneously in a cat from the surface of the spinal cord (SC, upper trace) and from the surface of the neck over the C_7 vertebra. B. Potentials recorded in a human from the surface of the neck over the C_7 vertebra. For both A and B, reference electrode is on frontal scalp; negative at spinal electrode is upward. C. Postulated potential field produced by excitation of dorsal horn neurons; the field is negative over the posterior neck and scalp and positive over the anterior neck and scalp. For clarity, the most intense parts of the field are omitted.

part in the ventral cord) is thus a summation of EPSPs and action potentials, but the relative contribution of each type of potential to the overall waveform is not known. Most of the primary afferent fibers entering the spinal cord terminate within a few segments, but some of them, particularly the larger ones carrying information from cutaneous receptors, ascend in the ipsilateral dorsal column and terminate in the cuneate nucleus.

The Cuneate Nucleus

The neurons of the cuneate nucleus tend to be oriented vertically with their dendrites extending dorsally. The incoming dorsal column fibers turn ventrally and make dense synaptic contacts with the dendrites (and to a lesser extent the cell bodies) of the relay cells. Hence we might expect the potential field to resemble that generated by dorsal horn neurons. That this is the case has been shown by Andersen, Eccles, Schmidt, and Yokota (1964). Dorsal to the cuneate nucleus, they recorded a negative potential (Figure 1-8A), which they called the "N wave" by analogy with the spinal cord N wave. The N wave polarity is inverted to a positive potential ventral to the nucleus (Figure 1-8B). The extracellular current flow postulated to account for these results is shown in Figure 1-8C; note the similarity to the situation in the dorsal horn. The A spike and N wave of the cuneate nucleus can apparently be recorded from a surface electrode at the base of the skull in cats (Figure 1-9A) and humans (Figure 1-9B); in both species, the potentials are slightly later than their dorsal horn analogues. The potential field of this activity is not known in detail, but may approximate the form postulated in Figure 1-9C. As in the spinal cord, the responsive neurons are located in a narrow strip at least 10 mm long in the rostrocaudal dimension, and thus generate a distributed dipolar field. The cuneate N wave, like its spinal analogue, is a mixture of the EPSPs and action potentials. Because the initial input to the nucleus is highly synchronous, the initial postsynaptic discharge is often recorded as a spike superimposed on the slower EPSPs (Figure 1-9A). In contrast, the dorsal horn N wave often appears as a smooth potential, perhaps because there is more temporal dispersion in the arrival of afferent input from the slowly conducting collaterals of dorsal column fibers. The depolarization of cuneate cell bodies then proceeds into their axons, which constitute the medial lemniscus.

The Medial Lemniscus

An electrode placed in the cat thalamus near the termination of lemniscal fibers records a positive–nega-

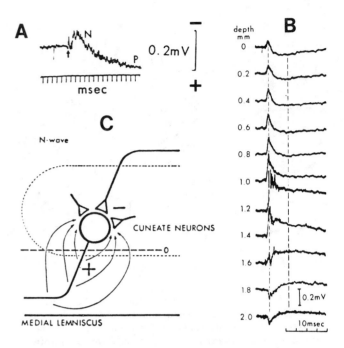

Figure 1-8. Potentials generated in cuneate nucleus. A. Potentials recorded from surface of cat cuneate nucleus to superficial radial nerve stimulation. Arrow indicates afferent volley in dorsal column fibers. B. Potentials evoked by median nerve stimulation at indicated depths from the surface of the cuneate nucleus. C. Postulated basis of N wave recorded in cuneate nucleus to afferent input from dorsal column. Relay neurons are depolarized; the current flowing into this area is indicated by the arrow, and generates a negativity superficially (the N wave) and a deep positivity. Afferent fibers are shown making contact with cuneate cell bodies; the majority of synaptic contacts are probably on the dendrites. In either case the dorsalmost portion of the cell is assumed to be depolarized, producing a negative potential field at and dorsal to the region of depolarization. In this diagram, the back of the neck is upward, and the head is to the left. (Adapted from Andersen, Eccles, Schmidt, and Yokota, 1964.)

tive spike potential (Figure 1-10, upper left, arrow) reminiscent of the A spike in the spinal cord. In humans the surface potential field of the lemniscal volley is not well characterized, but in monkeys it is recorded as a positive potential from the dorsal surface of the brain (Arezzo, Legatt, & Vaughan, 1979). Recall that a compound action potential is recorded at or beyond the termination of the nerve as a positive potential (see Figure 1-1). The same phenomenon has been demonstrated in fiber tracts of the CNS (Schlag, 1973). As a rule, it may be supposed that afferent volleys in ascending sensory pathways will be recorded as positive potentials over most of the scalp. The lemniscal volley now produces a strong depolarization of neurons in the thalamic ventroposterior nucleus.

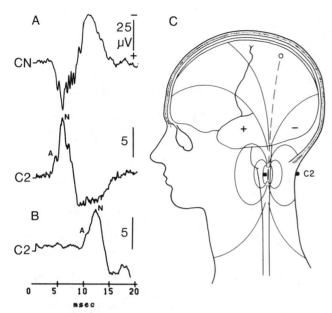

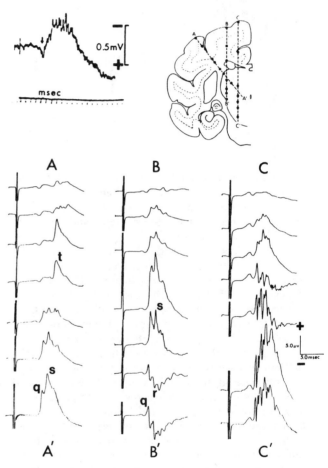

Figure 1-9. Potentials generated in cuneate nucleus. A. Upper trace: Recording 1 mm ventral to cat cuneate nucleus (CN), location indicated by square in human figure at right; dorsal to nucleus, the spike potential was negative and was superimposed on a slower negativity (the cuneate N wave). Lower trace: Simultaneous recording from the skin over the C_2 vertebra illustrating the surface-recorded cuneate N wave. (Adapted from Allison and Hume, 1981.) B. Similar surface recording from human C_2 vertebra showing presumed cuneate N wave. C. Postulated potential field produced by excitation of cuneate neurons. Potential is negative over posterior neck and scalp and positive over anterior neck and scalp. For clarity, the most intense parts of the field are omitted.

The Thalamic Ventroposterior Nucleus

Scheibel and Schiebel (1966) investigated the structure of neurons in the ventroposterior (VP) nucleus of the thalamus (Figure 1-11A). The arborizations of lemniscal afferents terminate on dendrites of the thalamo-cortical relay cells. While there is variation in the arrangement of these cells and their processes, their general orientation may approximate that shown in Figure 1-11B. Depolarization of the dendrites would produce approximately the potential field illustrated.

Andersen, Brooks, Eccles, and Sears (1964) investigated the potentials generated in the VP nucleus by stimulation of peripheral nerves (see Figure 1-10, upper left). The lemniscal volley was followed by a slower negative potential, which they called the "N wave" by analogy with the spinal and cuneate N waves. The N wave reflects the depolarization of VP neurons and would thus correspond to the negative

portion of the field assumed in Figure 1-11B. They did not record the potential field in the thalamus, but Arezzo *et al.* (1979) have done so (see Figure 1-10, lower). In and ventral to the VP nucleus, a lemniscal volley (labeled q in track A-A′ and B-B′) was followed by a negative potential on which a negative spike was superimposed (r in track B-B′). Dorsal to the VP nucleus, a positive spike superimposed on a positive wave is seen at the same latency (s in tracks A-A′ and B-B′). If this activity is assumed to be postsynaptic, the potential field approximates the open field pre-

Figure 1-10. Potentials generated in ventroposterior (VP) thalamus. Upper left: Potentials recorded in VP to cat median nerve stimulation. Diphasic (arrow) and negative lemniscal spike is followed by slower negative potential (VP N wave) with superimposed spikes. (From "The Ventro-Basal Nucleus of the Thalamus: Potential Fields, Synaptic Transmission and Excitability of Both Presynaptic and Postsynaptic Components" by P. Andersen, C. M. Brooks, J. C. Eccles, and T. A. Sears. *Journal of Physiology* [London], 1964, 174, 348–369. Reprinted by permission). Lower: Potentials evoked by monkey median nerve stimulation and recorded along electrode tracks shown at upper right. (Adapted from Arezzo, Legatt, and Vaughan, 1979.)

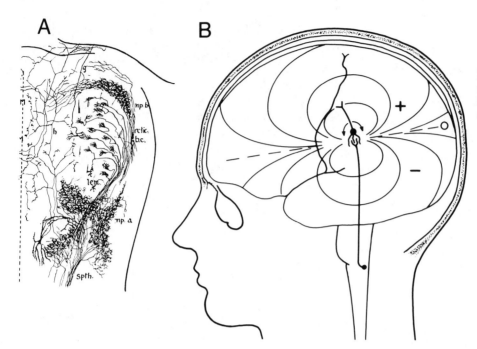

Figure 1-11. Anatomy and electrogenesis of ventroposterior (VP) thalamus. A. Horizontal section showing bushy arborizations of lemniscal (lem) afferents terminating on dendrites of VP relay neurons (g). (From "Patterns of Organization in Specific and Nonspecific Thalamic Fields" by M. E. Scheibel and A. B. Scheibel. In D. P. Purpura and M. D. Yahr [Eds.], *The Thalamus*. New York: Columbia University Press, 1966. Reprinted by permission.) B. Postulated potential field produced by depolarization of VP relay neurons. For clarity, the most intense parts of the field are omitted.

dicted in Figure 1-11B. However, Arezzo *et al.* (1979) interpreted these potentials as being of lemniscal origin, concluded that discharge of VP neurons could not be recorded outside the nucleus, and suggested that the orientation of these neurons leads to the generation of a closed field. The data of Figure 1-11B suggest that the third alternative, an open–closed field, may be the best approximation. Note that an inner core of negativity in and ventral to the VP nucleus is surrounded laterally, dorsally, and medially by a shell of positivity resembling the open–closed field of Figure 1-2 (right). Until detailed three-dimensional plots of the potential field in the region of the VP nucleus are available, it is not possible to choose among these alternatives. The point to be emphasized here is that structures such as thalamic and brain stem nuclei may generate potential fields that are smaller and more complex than the relatively simple open fields considered thus far, and correspondingly more difficult to record at a distance. Whatever the reason, there is as yet no agreement among ERP researchers whether VP and other thalamic potentials can be recorded from the surface of animals or humans. The afferent volley in axons of VP neurons now proceeds via the internal capsule into somatosensory cortex.

Somatosensory Cortex

The thalamo-cortical afferent volley is recorded at or near the cortical surface as a positive potential (Figure 1-10, t in track A-A'), as would be expected from earlier discussion. These fibers terminate mainly in layer IV of somatosensory cortex, where they make synaptic contact on the lower portion of the apical dendrites of pyramidal cells and on the numerous stellate cells that give sensory cortex its characteristic striped appearance. The stellate cells, in turn, are thought to terminate on pyramidal cells. This is a more complicated neuronal connectivity than has been considered previously. However, because the stellate cells have randomly oriented dendrites and axons, their potential fields are usually assumed to cancel. In contrast, the pyramidal cells are oriented in parallel, with their large apical dendrites extending upward into the molecular layer (Figure 1-12A). Depolarization of pyramidal cells approximates Lorente de Nó's open-field model, which assumes that source current is drawn from apical dendrites. But one might wonder whether the axons also serve as current sources in the same manner as the regions on either side of the depolarized portion of an axon serve as sources. Calculations of the potential field generated by a single pyramidal cell indicate that the axon is in fact a weak current source (Figure 1-12B). However, the negative sink potentials are much stronger: for a population of neurons, the algebraic summation of source and sink potentials leads to a net negative potential throughout the region in and ventral to the cell bodies.

An example of this activity in the monkey is shown in Figure 1-13A. The potentials in the latency range of 6–10 msec reflect activity of subcortical structures as discussed above. A few milliseconds later, a positive potential (p) is seen at the surface and superficial layers of cortex, while simultaneously a negative potential (n) is recorded in deeper layers of cortex and white matter. A few milliseconds later still, the potential field reverses, the superficial layers becoming negative and the deeper layers positive. The generally accepted explanation of this sequence of events was provided by Bishop and Clare (1952). Their recordings were made in cat visual cortex, but there is good evidence that the same events also occur in somatosensory and auditory cortex in response to an afferent thalamo-cortical volley (Landau & Clare, 1956, Towe, 1966). Bishop and Clare (1952) concluded that the superficial-positive–deep-negative field is produced by depolarization of pyramidal cells at or near the cell bodies, while the superficial-negative–deep-positive field is produced by slightly later depolarization of the apical dendrites. The earlier field is thus similar to the models of Figure 1-2 (left) and Figure 1-12B, while the later field approximates the model of Figure 1-5C and is similar to the spinal and cuneate N-wave fields.

Figure 1-13B shows recordings from the cortical surface of a human. Location 5 is just posterior to the central sulcus, as in the monkey recording, and sees a positivity (P25) followed by a negativity (N35). This sequence corresponds to the monkey p-n sequence of Figure 1-13A; in both species, the source is thought to be located in area 1 in the crown of the postcentral gyrus (Allison, 1982; Arezzo et al., 1979; see Figure 1-14A). In addition, note that at electrodes 6 and 7 (located a few mm posterior and lateral to 5), P25 is smaller and N35 is not identifiable, while other potentials labeled N20 and P30 are seen. Anterior to the central sulcus, P20 and N30 potentials are seen. To account for the N20–P30 and P20–N30 potentials, it is necessary to postulate at least one source in this region of cortex, in addition to the area 1 source.

One possibility is illustrated in Figure 1-14A. This model assumes a positive–negative sequence analogous to the P25–N35 sequence of area 1, but generated in area 3b and thus tilted by about 90°, due to the location of this area in the posterior bank of the central sulcus. If this is the case, P20–N30 would be recorded at the surface of and anterior to 3b, while posterior to 3b its polarity-inverted deep counterpart

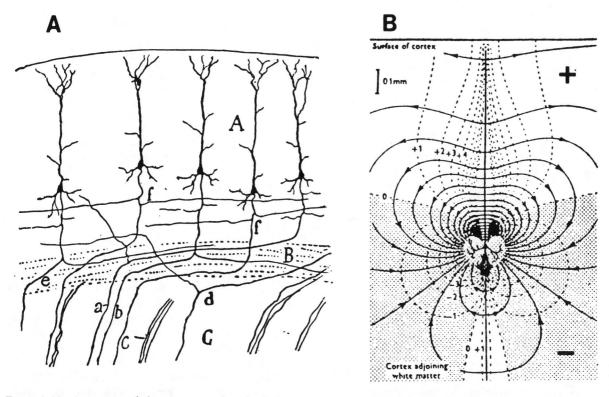

Figure 1-12. Anatomy and electrogenesis of cerebral cortex. A. Cortical pryamidal cells (A) with large dendrites extending to the cortical surface and axons (f) entering white matter (B). (From Neuron Theory or Reticular Theory? by S. Ramón y Cajal. Madrid: Instituto Ramón y Cajal, 1954. Reprinted by permission.) B. Calculated extracellular potential field generated by depolarization of the cell body of a pryamidal cell. Solid lines indicate current flow; broken lines are isopotential lines. For clarity, the most intense parts of the field are omitted. Shading indicates negative potential. Evidence suggests that thalamo-cortical fibers terminate mainly on the basal portion of apical dendrites; if this is the primary source of synaptic input, the region of maximal depolarization would be somewhat higher than shown. (From "Neuronal Basis of EEG-Waves" by O. Creutzfeldt and J. Houchin. In A. Remond [Ed.], Handbook of Electroencephalography and Clinical Neurophysiology [Vol. 2C]. Amsterdam: Elsevier, 1974. Reprinted by permission.)

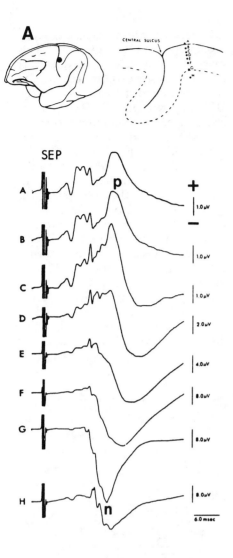

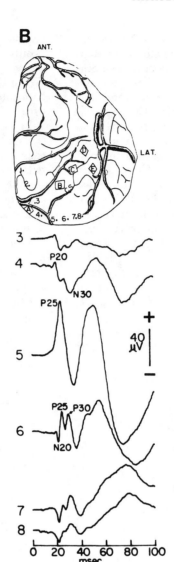

Figure 1-13. A. Potentials generated in monkey somatosensory cortex. Surface positive potential (p) inverts to a negative potential (n) deep in cortex. Earlier potentials are of subcortical origin. Right median nerve stimulation. Adapted from Arezzo, Legatt, and Vaughan, 1979.) B. Potentials recorded from surface of right hemisphere of human somatosensory cortex to left median nerve stimulation. Lettered tickets indicate locations of cortical stimulation: A, wrist and finger flexion; B–E, various mouth movements. CS, central sulcus. (Adapted from Allison, Goff, Williamson, and VanGilder, 1980.)

(N20–P30) would be seen. In other words, all these potentials are postulated to result from the sequential activation of two sources: first, the area 3b source beginning at about 20 msec, then the area 1 source beginning at about 25 msec. Whether or not the details of this model prove to be correct, these recordings illustrate that concurrent activation of nearby cortical regions produce complex potential fields that can be difficult to disentangle, both spatially and temporally.

These potentials are also seen in scalp recordings (Figure 1-14B). Comparison of these recordings with cortical surface recordings of the same activity (see Figure 1-13B) exemplifies the problem that the increased distance from the active tissue and the higher resistivity of the skull degrade scalp recordings in two ways:

1. Scalp potentials are much smaller that their cortical counterparts. Other things being equal, the signal-to-noise ratio of scalp recordings in correspondingly poorer. This is not a major problem, because additional averaging can be used to improve the signal-to-noise ratio.

2. In cortical surface recordings, it is possible to record the area 3b and area 1 potentials in relative isolation at some locations, but scalp recordings show mixtures of both types of activity at most locations. That is, spatial resolution is poorer in scalp recordings. This is a problem because the greater spatial overlap of potentials from different sources decreases the ability to study a source in isolation.

The hypothesized area 3b source should produce an open field, with the zero potential line more or less parallel to the central sulcus and with the major axis of the dipole orthogonal to it. The scalp field shown in Figure 1-14B, plotted at the latency corresponding to the peak of the N30 and P30 potentials, conforms closely to the predicted field. However, the similarity does not by itself prove that the field is generated in area 3b. It is possible that separate generators in

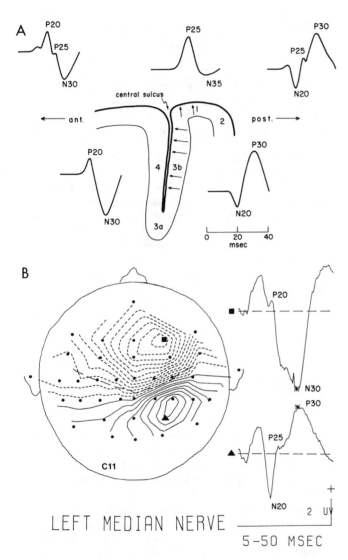

Figure 1-14. A. Location and orientation of sources postulated to account for potential fields recorded from the cortical surface and scalp of humans during initial activation of sensory–motor cortex by median nerve stimulation. Drawing is a sagittal section through the hand area of human sensory–motor cortex in the left hemisphere; note large amount of cortex buried in the central sulcus relative to the amount occupying the surface. B. Potential field recorded from scalp to left median nerve stimulation, plotted at peak (asterisk) of P30 and N30 potentials. Traces are from F₄ (square) and P₄ (triangle); dashed line is approximate location of the central sulcus.

motor cortex and somatosensory cortex independently produce the N30 and P30 potentials, respectively, and indeed some investigators favor this explanation (e.g., Desmedt & Cheron, 1980). In our opinion, the N30–P30 field shown in Figure 1-14B is more plausibly explained by a single somatosensory cortex source than by two simultaneously active sources in motor and somatosensory cortex that produce surface fields of opposite polarity (Allison, 1982). However, it is true that surface recordings alone (whether from the cortex or the scalp) do not provide unambiguous answers regarding the number, location, and orientation of sources contributing to a given surface potential field.

IMPLICATIONS FOR PSYCHOPHYSIOLOGICAL ERP RESEARCH

We can now point, perhaps with equal amounts of pride and alarm, to some generalizations concerning the value and limitations of surface ERPs as measures of human CNS activity. The reader is, we hope, convinced that potential fields generated by neuronal activity and recorded at the surface of the body are not mysterious or unmanageable in any fundamental way. Such potential fields may be described quantitatively and can be accounted for in terms of characteristics of the electrical sources and characteristics of the conductive medium in which they are recorded—that is the number, location, orientation, and synaptic connectivity of the neural elements involved, and the properties of the human brain and body as electrically conductive media.

Nevertheless, as measures of CNS events occurring at a given instant or as measures of changes in such events over time, surface ERPs are limited in a number of important respects that have implications for ERP research:

1. Because of superposition, the extracellular potentials from all neuronal transmembrane currents existing at a given instant summate at every point in and on the surface of the head and body. Thus, surface ERPs are a *statistical aggregate* in which the contribution of the transmembrane currents associated with each active neuron are combined with those from all other active neurons to yield the surface potential field. Moreover, the contribution of each neuron (and each gross anatomical structure) can lose its identity in the summation. Just as there is no way of answering the question "How many different values were added to yield the sum 43, and what are they?", there is no way to determine from the instantaneous potential difference between two electrodes the number of distinct sources that have contributed to that potential

difference and their relative contributions. Note that we are *not* saying that it is in principle impossible to determine the sources of surface ERPs; a number of experimental and theoretical approaches to this problem are being actively investigated (for reviews, see Vaughan, 1982; Wood, McCarthy, Squires, Vaughan, Woods, & McCallum, 1984). Rather, what we wish to emphasize is that neither the number nor the location of sources is directly evident in surface ERPs.

2. Because extracellular potential fields (and hence surface ERPs) depend heavily upon the orientation of active nerve cells and cell groups, the locus of synaptic activation, the degree of temporal and spatial synchronization, and the spatial relationship of the active tissue to the recording electrodes, they are likely to be *incomplete* and *biased* measures of CNS activity. They are incomplete in the sense that not all neural events occurring at any given time contribute significantly to surface potentials. They are biased in the sense that some cells, by virtue of their location, orientation, and other biophysical characteristics listed above, are more likely than other cells to contribute significantly to surface potentials.

3. Because of the aggregate, incomplete, and biased character of surface ERPs, we might anticipate that the mapping between ERP components and psychological processes will not be straightforward. Some of the neural events that mediate a given psychological process may not contribute to surface ERPs, and those that do may contribute to a number of ERP components. Similarly, a given ERP component may be contributed to by neural events that mediate a number of different psychological processes. Even the simplest surface ERP we have discussed, the peripheral nerve volley, is an amalgam of potentials that are generated by afferent neurons from a variety of receptor types in skin, joints, and muscles, and that contribute to a variety of somatosensory functions. The attempt to separate the compound action potential into parts having different functional characteristics won Gasser and Erlanger the Nobel Prize in 1944, but unresolved issues are still being investigated (Dorfman, Cummings, & Leifer, 1981). Since even the simplest surface ERP does not map in a one-to-one manner onto psychological processes, we should be cautious about attributing such one-to-one mappings to more complex ERPs from the CNS. This issue is discussed further in the next section.

4. Even if we knew in exquisite detail both the specific neurons that contribute to a given surface ERP and the relative magnitudes of their contributions, the surface ERP would provide little or no information concerning the information-processing operations at the neuronal level performed by the cells in question. Consider extracellular potentials generated by the lateral geniculate nucleus (LGN) in response to a patterned visual stimulus. Such potentials would be generated by LGN cells having on-center–off-surround receptive fields, as well as those having off-center–on-surround receptive fields. Similarly, extracellular potentials would be generated both by "X-cells" having predominately tonic or sustained responses to visual stimulation, as well as "Y-cells" having predominately phasic or transient responses (Stone, Bogdan, & Leventhal, 1979). ERPs recorded under such conditions (either from the LGN or from the surface) would indicate some form of activity in the cells in question, but they would not indicate the information-processing operations performed by the neurons that contribute to that activity.

On the other hand, useful information can be gained if the generators of surface ERPs are known, even if we cannot specify the cellular information-processing operations being performed. In clinical applications, for example, ERPs are used simply as test signals, in much the same manner that an electronics repairman traces a signal from a phonograph cartridge (receptor) to the movement of a loudspeaker (motor response). Knowledge of the place in the circuit where the signal is absent or distorted is useful even in the absence of a functional understanding of the signal.

5. Implicit in the previous discussion is the conclusion that the polarity of a potential conveys no information about its neurophysiological basis. Even if the orientation of neurons is similar and their activity is recorded in the same manner, the polarity of the potential can differ, depending on the portion of the cell activated. We have seen that dorsal horn and cortical neurons are both arrayed in rows, with their dendrites extending upward and their axons downward. Yet excitation of these neurons by an afferent volley produces initial potentials of opposite polarity when recorded from the surface of these structures. The difference is that the distal portion of the spinal dendrites is depolarized, whereas the proximal portion of the cortical dendrites is depolarized; hence, in the two structures, the spatial relationship of source and sink is reversed. Two conclusions follow:

a. The labels we attach to potentials are arbitrary. It is an accident of spinal anatomy, for instance, that the dorsal surface of the cord is more accessible than the ventral surface, and thus accidental that the excitation of spinal interneurons is recorded as a negativity and is often labeled the "N wave." This is a useful label, but it should not be taken to imply that the negative sink potential is somehow more real or important than the positive source potential that is its necessary counterpart. For this reason, some investigators (e.g., Beall, Applebaum, Foreman, & Willis, 1977) avoid the label "N wave" and use the neutral term "phase" to refer to this activity as recorded with either polarity. In human recordings, it is recommended (Donchin, Callaway, Cooper, Desmedt, Goff, Hillyard, & Sutton, 1977) that peaks of an ERP waveform be labeled according to their polarity and average peak latency in milliseconds (e.g., Figure 1-

14). This is a useful nomenclature—in most respects, it is preferable to other labeling systems—as long as it is kept in mind that the polarity label reflects the particular recording locations used.

   b. Although we have only discussed action potentials and EPSPs, the potential fields produced by IPSPs can be readily understood from the same principles. An IPSP is a *hyperpolarizing* graded potential that is due to an outward flow of current in the vicinity of the synapse and inward current flow over the remainder of the cell (i.e., current source and sink, respectively). IPSPs are accompanied by local extracellular positive potentials and distant negative potentials, just the opposite of EPSPs. In the absence of additional information, such as intracellular recordings, it is not possible to infer whether a positive potential reflects local IPSPs or distant EPSPs. This is unfortunate, because most human ERPs later than the initial afferent volley consist mostly if not entirely of summated PSPs rather than summated action potentials (Goff, Allison, & Vaughan, 1978). For such potentials, ERP and single-unit studies in animals of the presumed counterpart of the human potential are required to determine whether the surface recording reflects excitatory or inhibitory events, or both. This is a major undertaking, but to keep the problem in perspective, consider that the year in which this chapter is being written (1983) marks the 50th anniversary of Gasser and Graham's (1933) study of spinal cord potentials. Despite intense investigation by many excellent neurophysiologists, the excitatory (N wave) and inhibitory (P wave) properties of these potentials are still being clarified (Willis & Coggeshall, 1978).

   6. Extracellular potentials from different sources often overlap in time and space. Gasser and Graham (1933) were aware of this problem in trying to separate the spinal cord N and P waves: "Now, whatever interpretation may be put on the positive wave, the presumption is that the processes producing it do not start at the end of the negative wave but at some time earlier; and from this it follows that the activity producing the negative wave . . . must be in existence longer than the wave itself" (p. 308). Spinal cord neurophysiologists have used several techniques to try to separate the two potentials. One technique is to asphyxiate the animal. Since different neural structures can have different sensitivities to lack of oxygen, it is often possible to eliminate one potential while leaving the other more or less intact. Gelfan and Tarlov (1955), for example, demonstrated that the P wave was abolished before the N wave (Figure 1-15), and it can be seen (at 2′30″, for example) that the N wave has a longer duration than appears to be the case under normal conditions, as Gasser and Graham (1933) surmised. Eccles, Kostyuk, and Schmidt (1962) also assumed that the neural events underlying the N wave outlasted the observable wave itself. In attempting to map the potential field of the P wave in

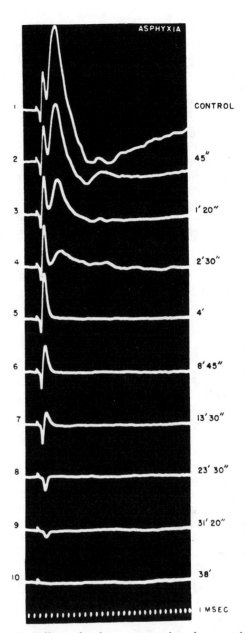

Figure 1-15. Effects of asphyxia on spinal cord potentials in a dog anesthetized with Dial. Recording from the L_7 cord segment to stimulation of the S_1 dorsal root; negative is upward. Note sequential abolition of P wave, N wave, A spike, and positive potential preceding the A spike. (From "Differential Vulnerability of Spinal Cord Structures to Anoxia" by S. Gelfan and I. M. Tarlov. *Journal of Neurophysiology,* 1955, 18, 170–188. Reprinted by permission.)

the cord and hence to infer its origin (see Figure 1-6A), they measured the P wave late in its course "so as to avoid interference by the initial waves" (p. 243).

   In human recordings, it is even more difficult to obtain undistorted measurements of potentials. The manipulation used by Gelfan and Tarlow (1955) is ill-advised, and the method of Eccles *et al.* (1962) can be criticized on the grounds that measuring potential B late in its course to avoid distortion by potential A only increases the distortion due to potential C. Multivariate statistical analysis and other quantitative techniques have been used to attack this problem (e.g., Donchin & Heffley, 1978), but as yet there is no consensus regarding a solution.

7. It is often tempting to assume that the generators of surface ERPs lie in brain structures directly underneath the region where the surface ERP is maximal in amplitude. Such an assumption can be correct, but it need not be. For example, the somatosensory P20–N30 and N20–P30 potentials shown in Figure 1-14 are largest at scalp locations well anterior and posterior to somatomotor cortex. Another example is

the ERP generated in visual cortex by a reversing checkerboard pattern (Figure 1-16). When the pattern is viewed centrally (Figure 1-16A, left), a positive potential (P100) is largest at the midline in the occipital area. With stimulation of the left or right half-fields (Figure 1-16A, center and right, respectively) that project anatomically to visual cortex of the contralateral hemisphere, P100 is largest over the ipsilateral hemisphere rather than the contralateral hemisphere, as might be expected. These results can be explained satisfactorily (Barrett, Blumhardt, Halliday, Halliday, & Kriss, 1976; Blumhardt & Halliday, 1979) by considering the location of human visual cortex in the posterior pole of the occipital lobe and extending into the mesial surface (Figure 1-16B).

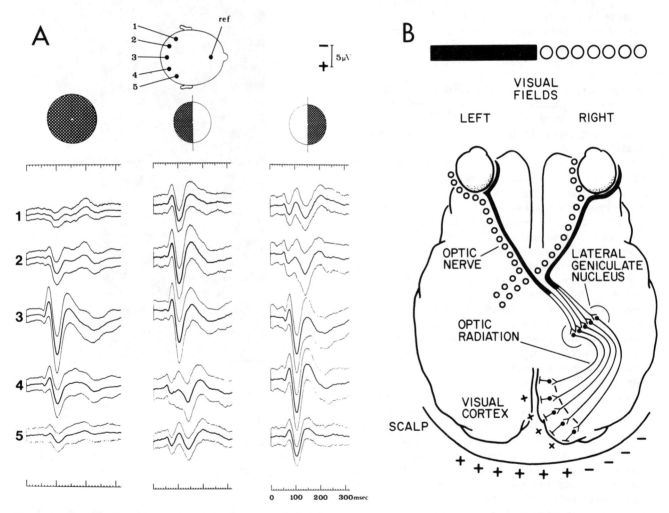

Figure 1-16. Anatomy and electrogenesis of visual cortex. A. Potential fields recorded over human occipital scalp to 2/sec reversal of a checkerboard visual stimulus. Responses to full-field (left), left half-field (center), and right half-field (right) stimulation. Note that largest P100 is recorded at locations ipsilateral to the stimulated half field, with polarity inversion at contralateral locations. Grand average of 50 normal subjects; thick line is mean waveform; thin lines are the standard deviation. (Adapted from Blumhardt and Halliday, 1979). B. Outline of human visual pathway and postulated location of dipole generators in visual cortex to account for the left half field scalp topography in A. Adapted from Barrett, Blumhardt, Halliday, Halliday, and Kriss, 1976 and Kuffler and Nicholls, 1976.)

When a single hemisphere is activated by a visual stimulus in the opposite half-field, the resulting equivalent dipole points toward the opposite hemisphere and thus produces the largest potential over that hemisphere. Full-field stimulation activates both hemispheres and produces the algebraic summation of the two half-field responses. Thus, when the net orientation of active tissue is not perpendicular to the surface of the head, ERP amplitude maxima can occur in scalp regions distant from the active regions of the cortex, including locations over the opposite hemisphere. This has obvious implications for the study of hemispheric function using ERP measures.

8. For additional discussion of neuronal electrogenesis and the recording of extracellular potential fields, see Creutzfeldt and Houchin (1974), Freeman (1975), Goff *et al.* (1978), Klee and Rall (1977), Llinás and Nicholson (1974), Schlag (1973), Vaughan (1974, 1982), Willis and Coggeshall (1978), and Wood and Allison (1981).

CLASSICAL AND MODERN BUMPOLOGY: IT TAKES A LOT OF GALL TO STUDY PSYCHOLOGICAL PROCESSES USING ERPS

In the late 18th century, Franz Joseph Gall became convinced that specific regions of the brain subserve specific psychological functions, and that it might be possible to obtain objective measurements of the amounts of each function by making physical measurements of the skull. His assumptions and methods grew into the 19th-century practice of phrenology, which was ardently accepted by some but viewed with skepticism by others (Figure 1-17). In our opinion, classical "bumpology" provides an instructive example for us modern bumpologists who attempt to study psychological processes and their neural substrates using ERPs. Our purpose in this discussion is not to make invidious comparisons between contemporary ERP research and a 19th-century pseudoscience. Rather, we believe that consideration of certain parallels between them can stimulate a re-examination of some of our tacit, deeply held assumptions.

Gall was a skilled neuroanatomist who wished to establish a science of "organology," which would be "an anatomy and physiology of the brain that would be at the same time a new psychology" (Ackenknecht & Vallois, 1956). Gall's organology was based on four major assumptions:

1. The mind consists of an interacting set of distinct mental functions, or "faculties."
2. Each mental faculty is mediated by a specific, localized region of the brain, which is the "organ" for that faculty.

Figure 1-17. "Bumpology," etching by George Cruikshank, 1826. (Reproduced by permission of the Historical Library, Yale University School of Medicine.)

3. The amount of each faculty is correlated with the physical size of the corresponding region of the brain.
4. The shape of the cranium conforms closely to the shape of the surface of the brain, such that variations in the size of different mental organs are evident as bulges or bumps on the skull (Figure 1-18).

Let us examine each of these assumptions in turn.

1. Many of the mental faculties hypothesized by Gall were characterized only in anecdotal terms, often from his recollection of unusual traits of schoolmates and acquaintances. It should not be surprising that Gall's faculties have, like 19th-century "faculty psychology" in general, not withstood subsequent critical analysis. However, the idea that the mind consists of distinct mental faculties has recently received increased attention in the cognitive sciences (e.g., Chomsky, 1980; Fodor, 1983). Marshall (1980) refers to Chomsky's recent work as the "new organology," emphasizing its similarities to some of Gall's assumptions.

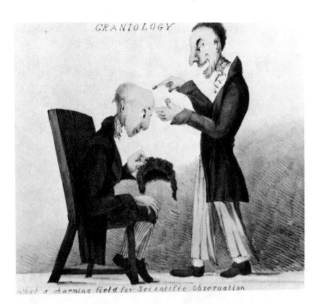

Figure 1.18. "Craniology," anonymous, circa 1840. (Reproduced by permission of the Historical Library, Yale University School of Medicine.)

2. Although functional localization within the brain was a radical notion in Gall's day, the anatomical and neurophysiological discoveries of the 20th century have demonstrated a striking degree of regional specificity in brain structure and physiology. Those discoveries constitute strong evidence for some form of functional localization, but they leave open the key question of how functions defined at the psychological level map onto brain structures and physiological processes (cf. Kaas, 1982). Different regions of the brain have been shown to differ substantially in their anatomical structure and physiological properties, and damage to different regions produces systematic—in some cases, highly specific—patterns of symptoms. However, such evidence does not imply that functions defined at the psychological level (e.g., "long-term memory," "selective attention," etc.) are "localized" in the sense that each such function is mediated by a relatively restricted, contiguous brain region, as Gall hypothesized. The extent to which a given psychological process is or is not "localized" depends both upon the manner in which the process is characterized and distinguished from other processes, and upon the exact sense of the term "localized" under consideration. It is likely that most functions defined at the psychological level are mediated by neural systems of considerable complexity, involving the cooperative activity of a number of different anatomical structures. The herculean task confronting the cognitive and neural sciences is to identify and characterize such systems—that is, to determine the mapping between the abstract processes

hypothesized by cognitive scientists and the structural and functional organization of the brain at the level studied by neuroscientists.

3. Modern neuroscientists rightly balk at Gall's assumption that the amount of a mental faculty is strongly correlated with the size of its corresponding organ in the brain. One reason is that the assumption is untestable unless the neural circuits responsible for a given psychological process are completely specified. Even if such information were available, differences in size of the relevant brain structures are poor predictors of differences in functional capability. Cases do exist, however, in which the size of certain brain structures is strongly correlated with the behavioral capacities to which those structures are thought to contribute. For example, the inferior colliculi of echo-locating bats are large compared to their superior colliculi, and the superior colliculi of birds are, conversely, larger than their inferior colliculi. Closer to home, portions of the human temporal lobe are often larger in the left hemisphere than in the right (Geschwind & Levitsky, 1968), a difference that is reported to be detectable at birth. In nodding assent to such examples, however, we should not lose sight of the fact that many structures other than the inferior colliculi, superior colliculi, and temporal lobes contribute significantly to the capacities for echo location in bats, for visually guided behavior in birds, and for language in humans, respectively.

4. The assumption that variations in the size and shape of the brain are associated with variations in cranial morphology is correct only in the crudest terms. Large regional variations in skull shape and thickness can occur without obvious variations in brain size and shape, and cranial measurements are crude even in reflecting such gross structural differences as the "hypertrophied" structures mentioned above.

Thus, each of Gall's four main assumptions is incorrect in important respects, but some of his ideas have important parallels in the contemporary neurosciences. Two such parallels are particularly instructive for psychophysiological ERP research.

The first, and more superficial, parallel concerns the nature of the dependent variables employed. Whereas Gall measured the size and location of physical bumps on the skull, we measure the size (amplitude), location (distribution over the scalp), and latency of electrical "bumps" in surface ERP recordings. In both cases, there are problems of definition (what is a bump?) and measurement (how do we assign numerical values to the magnitude of a bump uncontaminated by the influences of other bumps?). Whereas the phrenologists had little outside help on these difficult problems, we have the theoretical and practical aid of electrical field theory, as discussed in the bulk of this chapter.

The second, and deeper, parallel is the attempt to investigate human psychological processes and their neural substrates by measuring physical variables related to the brain (skull bumps in one case, electrical bumps in the other) thought to map onto those processes. The psychological constructs used by phrenologists and ERP researchers are very different, but the attempted mapping between physical variables and psychological constructs is similar nonetheless. Phrenologists related their dependent variables to mental faculties such as "acquisitiveness," "self-esteem," and "philoprogenitiveness." ERP researchers, in contrast, typically rely upon the constructs of modern cognitive psychology (e.g., "pattern recognition" and "stimulus classification"—Ritter, Simson, Vaughan, & Macht, 1982; "detection" and "recognition"—Parasuraman & Beatty, 1980; "phonetic processes"—Wood, 1975; "selective attention"—Picton, Campbell, Baribeau, & Proulx, 1978; "stimulus evaluation"—McCarthy & Donchin, 1981). To the extent that these information-processing constructs are more likely to stand the test of time than did the "mental faculties" of the phrenologists, we will have the advantage that one end of the mapping we seek to determine is better established. However, if the constructs in fashion today are found wanting and are replaced, then any mapping relationship involving such constructs is correspondingly weakened (cf. Von Eckardt Klein, 1978).

Assuming that we have been lucky enough to choose valid psychological constructs, an important remaining problem is the nature of the mapping that we assume to exist between psychological processes and surface ERPs. We often conclude that a given ERP component "reflects," "manifests," or "indexes" a given psychological process (e.g., "The results support the hypothesis that NA and N2 reflect sequential stages of information processing, namely, pattern recognition and stimulus classification"—Ritter *et al.*, 1982, p. 909). It is difficult to determine from the literature just how strongly the terms "reflect," "manifest," and "index" are meant to be taken. In their strongest sense, such terms imply the same one-to-one relationship between surface ERPs and information-processing concepts that the phrenologists assumed to exist between bumps on the head and mental faculties.[1]

Having concluded that "ERP measure X reflects psychological process Y," based on experiments in which manipulations thought to influence process Y produce systematic effects on measure X, it seems to be only a small and natural step to conclude that ERP

measure X can now be used as a measure of process Y. But note that such a suggestion involves a subtle but crucial logical shift: From the empirical fact that experimental manipulations thought to influence process Y produce systematic effects on ERP measure X, we do not know *what proportion* of the neural events that mediate psychological process Y in fact contribute to ERP measure X. That proportion could be high, in which case the ERP measure would have considerable value to psychologists as an indicator of properties of the process—for example, its onset, duration, and offset, and its presence or absence and relative magnitude across experimental conditions. However, the same experimental effects could be obtained if the proportion of the neural events relevant to process Y that also contribute to ERP measure X were extremely small. In the latter case, one could be misled by drawing conclusions about the time course or other aspects of the process, because only a small part of the relevant neural events will be observed.

For the reasons discussed in the preceding section—in particular, the aggregate, incomplete, and biased character of surface ERPs—we believe it to be unlikely that more than a relatively small proportion of the neural events that mediate a given psychological process are evident in surface ERPs. We would be delighted, of course, to be proved wrong in this assumption. The problem, however, is that deciding the issue requires knowledge of the mapping between the psychological process in question and the neural events that mediate it, as well as the mapping between those neural events and the surface ERPs said to reflect those processes. That is, it presumes exactly the knowledge that psychophysiological ERP research and other approaches to investigating the neural substrates of mental processes seek to obtain.

In the absence of such information, what type of relationship should we assume to exist between surface ERPs and psychological processes? In other words, how can we relax the excessively strong one-to-one assumption analogous to the one made by Gall, while still attempting to establish relationships between ERPs and psychological processes that have empirical and theoretical value? We have no compelling answers to these questions, merely some biases and hunches. Because it seems unlikely that we will ever know exactly what proportion of the neural events that contribute to a given psychological process are recordable in surface potentials, we believe it prudent to adopt a stance of explicit agnosticism on that issue and to avoid making empirical or theoretical decisions whose validity heavily depends on it. Having adopted such a stance, what contributions to the understanding of psychological processes and their neural substrates can psychophysiological ERP research make? In our opinion, there are three.

The first contribution requires determination of the anatomical structures and neurophysiological pro-

---

1. *Editors' Footnote:* While the authors' critique of the "strong mapping" view may be quite cogent, the view is only one of a number of approaches to the inclusion of psychophysiological tools in the psychologist's armamentarium. For alternative, more positive views see chapters in the Processes and Applications sections of this book (especially, 11, 12, 23 and 26).

cesses that generate the surface ERPs of interest. As noted in the preceding section, that is a difficult but not an intractable problem. Based on such information, modern bumpologists would then be in a position to conduct experiments capable of suggesting that "structure X is involved in psychological process Y," even though such experiments could not establish either the relative magnitude of structure X's contribution or the information-processing operations performed by structure X as its contribution to process Y. Nevertheless, at this stage of the game, even the limited information provided by such experiments would be valuable, both in its own right and in establishing an empirical link to animal experiments in which more extensive neurophysiological investigations can be performed.

The second contribution concerns the use of ERPs as purely psychological tools without attempting to relate psychological processes to the brain. This use of ERPs involves a program of experiments designed to determine the mapping between psychological processes and ERPs, no matter how complex that mapping may be. Such a program would explicitly acknowledge the improbability that any psychological process will map in a one-to-one manner onto a given ERP measure, as well as the possibility that only a small proportion of the neural events relevant to a particular process may be evident in surface ERPs. It should be clear that the likelihood of success of such a program is inversely proportional to the complexity of the mapping. The success of such a program also depends upon solving an important ERP identification and measurement problem. In order to study the effects of different experimental conditions on a particular ERP component, we must be able to identify that component unambiguously in the different conditions. However, because of the principle of superposition and because of the broad time course and scalp distribution of many ERP components, what appears to be the "same" ERP phenomenon in different conditions on morphological grounds (e.g., a broad positivity between 300 and 600 msec, largest at the parietal midline), may not be generated by the same neural events.

The third type of contribution involves the use of ERP measures to discover patterns of organization in the CNS not evident in, or not yet discovered with, other experimental techniques. For example, Regan and Beverley (1973) used ERPs to suggest the existence of a class of cells in the visual system sensitive to direction of motion toward and away from the observer. Once its existence was known, this phenomenon was studied further using psychophysical techniques, but it was originally discovered electrophysiologically.

In conclusion, we believe that the contributions of psychophysiological ERP research can be enhanced by considering explicitly the nature of mapping assumed to exist between surface ERPs and psychological pro-

cesses. Empirical correlations between ERPs and experimental variables thought to be related to psychological processes have been and will continue to be reported. What requires careful consideration is what such correlations imply. We modern bumpologists would be wise to cultivate Gall's mental faculties 10 and 17 ("cautiousness" and "hope").

REFERENCES

Ackenknecht, E. H., & Vallois, H. V. *Franz Joseph Gall, inventor of phrenology, and his collection.* Madison, Wisc.: Published privately, 1956.

Allison, T. Scalp and cortical recordings of initial somatosensory cortex activity to median nerve stimulation in man. *Annals of the New York Academy of Sciences*, 1982, 388, 671–678.

Allison, T., Goff, W. R., Williamson, P. D., and VanGilder, J. C. On the neural origin of early components of the human somatosensory evoked potential. In J. E. Desmedt (Ed.), *Progress in clinical neurophysiology* (Vol. 7, *Clinical uses of cerebral, brainstem and spinal somatosensory evoked potentials*). Basel: Karger, 1980.

Allison, T., & Hume, A. L. A comparative analysis of short-latency somatosensory evoked potentials in man, monkey, cat and rat. *Experimental Neurology*, 1981, 72, 592–611.

Andersen, P., Brooks, C. M., Eccles, J. C., & Sears, T. A. The ventro-basal nucleus of the thalamus: Potential fields, synaptic transmission and excitability of both presynaptic and postsynaptic components. *Journal of Physiology* (London), 1964, 174, 348–369.

Andersen, P., Eccles, J. C., Schmidt, R. F., & Yokota, T. Slow potential wave produced in the cuneate nucleus by cutaneous volleys and by cortical stimulation. *Journal of Neurophysiology*, 1964, 27, 78–91.

Arezzo, J., Legatt, A. D., & Vaughan, H. G., Jr. Topography and intracranial sources of somatosensory evoked potentials in the monkey: I. Early components. *Electroencephalography and Clinical Neurophysiology*, 1979, 46, 155–172.

Barrett, G., Blumhardt, L., Halliday, A. M., Halliday, E., & Kriss, A. A paradox in the lateralisation of the visual evoked response. *Nature*, 1976, 261, 252–255.

Beall, J. E., Applebaum, A. E., Foreman, R. D., & Willis, W. D. Spinal cord potentials evoked by cutaneous afferents in the monkey. *Journal of Neurophysiology*, 1977, 40, 199–211.

Bishop, G. H., & Clare, M. H. Sites of origin of electric potentials in striate cortex. *Journal of Neurophysiology*, 1952, 15, 201–220.

Blumhardt, L. D., & Halliday, A. M. Hemisphere contributions to the composition of the pattern-evoked potential waveform. *Experimental Brain Research*, 1979, 36, 53–69.

Chiappa, K. H., & Ropper, A. H. Evoked potentials in clinical medicine. *New England Journal of Medicine*, 1982, 306, 1140–1150, 1205–1211.

Chomsky, N. *Rules and representations.* New York: Columbia University Press, 1980.

Creutzfeldt, O., & Houchin, J. Neuronal basis of EEG-waves. In A. Remond (Ed.), *Handbook of electroencephalography and clinical neurophysiology* (Vol. 2C). Amsterdam: Elsevier, 1974.

Dawson, G. D., & Scott, J. W. The recording of nerve action potentials through skin in man. *Journal of Neurology, Neurosurgery and Psychiatry*, 1949, 12, 259–267.

Desmedt, J. E., & Cheron, G. Somatosensory evoked potentials to finger stimulation in healthy octogenarians and in young adults: Waveforms, scalp topography and transit times of parietal and frontal components. *Electroencephalography and Clinical Neurophysiology*, 1980, 50, 404–425.

Donchin, E., Callaway, E., Cooper, R., Desmedt, J. E., Goff, W. R., Hillyard, S. A., & Sutton, S. Publication criteria for studies of evoked potentials (EP) in man. *Progress in Clinical Neurophysiology*, 1977, 1, 1–11.

Donchin, E., & Heffley, E. Multivariate analysis of event-related potential data: A tutorial review. In D. Otto (Ed.), *Multidisciplinary perspectives in event-related brain potential research* (EPA-60019-77-043). Washington: U.S. Environmental Protection Agency, 1978.

Dorfman, L. J., Cummings, K. L., & Leifer, L. J. *Conduction velocity distributions: A population approach to electrophysiology of nerve*. New York: Alan R. Liss, 1981.

Eccles, J. C., Kostyuk, P. G., & Schmidt, R. F. Central pathways responsible for depolarization of primary afferent fibres. *Journal of Physiology* (London), 1962, 161, 237–257.

Fodor, J. A. *The modularity of mind*. Cambridge, Mass.: MIT Press, 1983.

Freeman, W. J. *Mass action in the nervous system*. New York: Academic Press, 1975.

Gasser, H. S., & Graham, H. T. Potentials produced in the spinal cord by stimulation of dorsal roots. *American Journal of Physiology*, 1933, 103, 303–320.

Gelfan, S., & Tarlov, I. M. Differential vulnerability of spinal cord structures to anoxia. *Journal of Neurophysiology*, 1955, 18, 170–188.

Geschwind, N., & Levitsky, W. Human brain: Left–right asymmetries in temporal speech region. *Science*, 1968, 161. 186–189.

Goff, W. R., Allison, T., & Vaughan, H. G., Jr. The functional neuroanatomy of event related potentials. In E. Callaway, P. Tueting, & S. H. Koslow (Eds.), *Event-related brain potentials in man*. New York: Academic Press, 1978.

Halliday, A. M. Clinical applications of evoked potentials. In W. B. Matthews & G. H. Glaser (Eds.), *Recent advances in clinical neurology*. Edinburgh: Churchill Livingstone, 1978.

Kass, J. H. The segregation of function in the nervous system: Why do sensory systems have so many subdivisions? *Contributions to Sensory Physiology*, 1982, 7, 201–240.

Klee, M., & Rall, W. Computed potentials of cortically arranged populations of neurons. *Journal of Neurophysiology*, 1977, 40, 647–666.

Kuffler, S. W., & Nicholls, J. G. *From neuron to brain*. Sunderland, Mass.: Sinauer Associates, 1976.

Landau, W. M., & Clare, M.H. A note on the characteristic response pattern in primary sensory projection cortex of the cat following a synchronous afferent volley. *Electroencephalography and Clinical Neurophysiology*, 1956, 8, 457–464.

Llinás, R., & Nicholson, C. Analysis of field potentials in the central nervous system. In A. Remond (Ed.), *Handbook of electroencephalography and clinical neurophysiology* (Vol. 2B). Amsterdam: Elsevier, 1974.

Lorente de Nó, R. Action potential of the motoneurons of the hypoglossus nucleus. *Journal of Cellular and Comparative Physiology*, 1947, 29, 207–287. (a)

Lorente de Nó, R. Analysis of the distribution of action currents of nerve in volume conductors. *Studies of the Rockefeller Institute of Medical Research*, 1947, 132, 384–477. (b)

Marshall, J. C. The new organology. *Behavioral and Brain Sciences*, 1980, 3, 23–25.

McCarthy, G., & Donchin, E. A metric for thought: A comparison of P300 latency and reaction time. *Science*, 1981, 211, 77–80.

Parasuraman, R., & Beatty, J. Brain events underlying detection and recognition of weak sensory signals. *Science*, 1980, 210, 80–83.

Picton, T. W., Campbell, K. B., Baribeau, B., & Proulx, G. B. The neurophysiology of human attention: A tutorial review. In J. Requin (Ed.) *Attention and performance VII*. Hillsdale, N.J.: Erlbaum, 1978.

Ramón y Cajal, S. *Histologie du système nerveux de l'homme et des vertébrés* (Vol. 1). Madrid: Instituto Ramón y Cajal, 1909.

Ramón y Cajal, S. *Neuron theory or reticular theory?* Madrid: Instituto Ramón y Cajal, 1954.

Regan, D., & Beverley, K. I. Electrophysiological evidence for the existence of neurons selectively sensitive to the direction of movement in depth. *Nature*, 1973, 246, 504–506.

Rexed, B. The cytoarchitectonic organization of the spinal cord in the cat. *Journal of Comparative Neurology*, 1952, 96, 415–495.

Ritter, W., Simson, R., Vaughan, H. G., Jr., & Macht, M. Manipulation of event-related potential manifestations of information processing stages. *Science*, 1982, 218, 909–911.

Scheibel, M. E., & Scheibel, A. B. Patterns of organization in specific and nonspecific thalamic fields. In D. P. Purpura & M. D. Yahr (Eds.), *The thalamus*. New York: Columbia University Press, 1966.

Schlag, J. Generation of brain evoked potentials. In R. F. Thompson & M. M. Patterson (Eds.), *Bioelectric recording techniques: Part A. Cellular processes and brain potentials*. New York: Academic Press, 1973.

Starr, A. Sensory evoked potentials in clinical disorders of the nervous system. *Annual Review of Neuroscience*, 1978, 1, 103–127.

Stone, J., Bogdan, D., & Leventhal, A. Hierarchical and parallel mechanisms in the organization of visual cortex. *Brain Research Reviews*, 1979, 1, 345–394.

Towe, A. L. On the nature of the primary evoked response. *Experimental Neurology*, 1966, 15, 113–139.

Vaughan, H. G., Jr. The analysis of scalp-recorded brain potentials. In R. F. Thompson & M. M. Patterson (Eds.), *Bioelectric recording techniques: Part B. Electroencephalography and human brain potentials*. New York: Academic Press, 1974.

Vaughan, H. G. Jr. The neural origins of human event-related potentials. *Annals of the New York Academy of Sciences*, 1982, 388, 125–137.

Von Eckardt Klein, B. Inferring functional localization from neurological evidence. In E. Walker (Ed.), *The biology of language*. Montgomery, Vermont: Bradford Books, 1978.

Wall, P. D. Cord cells responding to touch, damage, and temperature of skin. *Journal of Neurophysiology*, 1960, 23, 197–210.

Wall, P. D. Presynaptic control of impulses at the first central synapse in the cutaneous pathway. In J. C. Eccles & J. P. Schade (Eds.), *Progress in brain research* (Vol. 12, *Physiology of spinal neurons*). Amsterdam: Elsevier, 1964.

Willis, W. D., & Coggeshall, R. E. *Sensory mechanisms of the spinal cord*. New York: Plenum Press, 1978.

Wood, C. C. Auditory and phonetic levels of processing in speech perception: Neurophysiological and information-processing analyses. *Journal of Experimental Psychology: Human Perception and Performance*, 1975, 104, 3–20.

Wood, C. C., & Allison, T. Interpretation of evoked potentials: A neurophysiological perspective. *Canadian Journal of Psychology/Review of Canadian Psychology*, 1981, 35, 113–135.

Wood, C. C., McCarthy, G., Squires, N. K., Vaughan, H. G., Woods, D. L., & McCallum, W. C. Anatomical and physiological substrates of event-related potentials: Two case studies. *Annals of the New York Academy of Sciences*, 1984, 425, 681–721.

Chapter Two

Neuromagnetometry

Jackson Beatty
Daniel S. Barth
Francois Richer
Russell A. Johnson

INTRODUCTION

The movement of ions across the membranes of nerve cells not only generates electrical fields, but produces magnetic fields as well. Both the electrical and magnetic phenomena are necessary consequences of the movement of charge within the brain. In the nervous system, biogenic magnetic fields are not large. Nonetheless, under certain conditions the magnetic fields of a number of simultaneously active neurons may combine to produce fields of sufficient strength to be measured at the surface of the head. Neuromagnetometry is the study of the magnetic fields of the brain; the recording of such fields is termed a magnetoencephalogram (MEG), the magnetic counterpart of the electroencephalogram (EEG). However, the MEG and the EEG reflect somewhat different aspects of neuronal function; for this reason, one may think of magnetoencephalography and electroencephalography as providing complementary images of central nervous system (CNS) activity.

In this chapter, we describe some of the unique properties of the MEG and review the recent application of this technique to the study of both normal human brain function and cases of cerebral pathology.

NEURONAL GENERATION OF THE MAGNETOENCEPHALOGRAM

Direct evidence concerning the cellular mechanisms that generate the MEG is only now becoming available from recent investigations in animal neuromagnetometry (Barth, 1984; Barth, Sutherling, & Beatty, 1984). However, a consideration of the physical properties of CNS neurons is instructive. The magnetic fields recorded from the scalp must reflect the activity of local collections of neurons sharing a similar orientation and pattern of polarization.

It is widely believed that synaptic potentials form the basis of recordable brain magnetic activity. Although magnetic fields have been recorded in isolated nerve fibers, action potentials probably contribute little to the MEG. Despite the large amplitude of these events, their brevity makes synchronous discharge of

Jackson Beatty, Daniel S. Barth, Francois Richer, and Russell A. Johnson. Human Neurophysiology Laboratory, Department of Psychology, University of California, Los Angeles, Los Angeles, California.

many neurons unlikely. Furthermore, the polarizing wavefront of each action potential exhibits a mirror-image symmetry about the momentary locus of propagation; such currents produce opposing magnetic fields that tend to be self-cancelling at a distance. However, the slower synaptic activity in the larger CNS neurons is synchronized more easily.

Not all CNS neurons contribute equally to the recorded MEG. Although stellate and granular cells are very numerous, their contribution to extracranial magnetic fields is probably minimal, due to both their small size and the near random orientation of their dendritic fields. In contrast, populations of similarly oriented pyramidal cells, with their long apical dendrites, can generate substantial magnetic fields when simultaneously activated. Synaptic potentials in groups of parallel pyramidal cells are generally considered to be the most important source of the MEG (Okada, 1983). These extended cell groups form a dipole layer. At typical MEG recording distances imposed by the size of the human cranium and the shape of the magnetometer, such layers often may be modeled as a single equivalent current dipole.

BRAIN MAGNETIC FIELDS ARE SPATIALLY RESTRICTED

The magnetic field produced by the activation of a local population of CNS neurons is restricted to the region of its origin. There are at least two reasons for the highly localized distribution of magnetic fields. First, in an infinite, homogeneous conducting volume, only the intracellular flow of current produces an externally measurable magnetic field; the strength of this magnetic field decreases with the square of the distance from the source. The unique contribution of intracellular currents to the MEG also holds for simple situations in which the conducting medium has a spherical boundary, such as the skull. Second, the skull is virtually transparent to magnetic fields, whereas it behaves as an inhomogeneous highly resistive barrier for the electrical field.

The magnetic field of a biological source that approximates a current dipole describes circles around the source, which at the scalp are measured as magnetic flux emerging from the head on one side of the source and reentering the head on the other side of the source. The field obeys the "right-hand rule" of elementary physics: For a current source oriented in the direction of the thumb of the right hand, the resulting magnetic field will circulate in the direction of the curled fingers. The electrical field is of opposite polarities at the two ends of the source. Figure 2-1 illustrates the orientation of both electrical and magnetic fields about a current dipole. In practice, such ideal

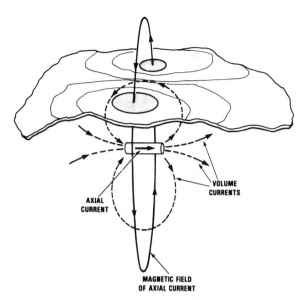

Figure 2-1. Theoretical distributions of electrical and magnetic fields produced on a surface by a current dipole lying tangentially in a conducting medium below the surface. Dotted lines represent the volume currents producing the surface electrical field. The continuous line is the magnetic field produced by the dipole. (Adapted from Kaufman, Okada, Brenner, & Williamson, 1981.)

field patterns are rarely observed. The electrical field of the EEG rarely has such a simple configuration. However, the magnetic field recorded from some cortical sources often does approximate a dipolar field pattern.

THE STRENGTH OF BRAIN MAGNETIC FIELDS

Brain magnetic fields are very weak, particularly when compared with typical magnetic disturbances produced by nonbiological sources in the environment. This may be seen in Figure 2-2. The flux density of brain magnetic fields is on the order of 100–1000 femtotesla. This is at least two orders of magnitude smaller than the fields produced by skeletal or cardiac muscle, six orders of magnitude smaller than the fields produced by large moving metal objects such as automobiles and elevators, and eight orders of magnitude smaller than the magnetic field of the Earth. These considerations pose two requirements for the measurement of magnetic fields of the brain: First, the measurement system must be very sensitive, and second, a substantial signal-to-noise ratio problem must be solved.

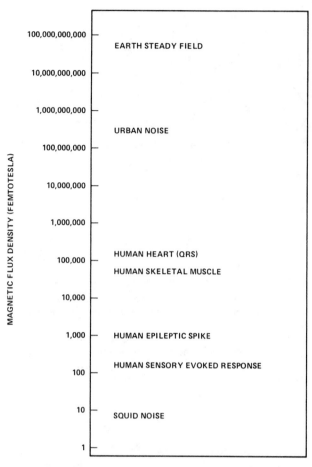

Figure 2-2. Magnetic induction of sources relevant to bio-magnetic measurement.

MEASURING BRAIN MAGNETIC FIELDS

Measuring the weak magnetic fields produced by biological sources is technically quite difficult. Gengerelli, for example, tried unsuccessfully in 1942 to detect the magnetic field produced by stimulation of the frog's sciatic nerve using a detection coil of 30 turns of wire. However, in a second attempt 20 years later, using an improved instrument with a 12,000 turn coil, he was able to measure that magnetic field with success (Gengerelli, Holter, & Glasscock, 1961). In a similar way, Baule and McFee (1963, 1965) recorded the first magnetocardiogram, and Cohen (1968), using a magnetically shielded room to reduce environmental noise, recorded the first MEG. However, this straightforward large-coil approach to magnetic field measurement was not well suited for the study of the CNS.

The reliable measurement of the magnetic fields of the CNS was made possible by the development of a highly sensitive magnetic sensor called the "Supercon-

ductive QUantum Interference Device" (SQUID), developed by J. E. Zimmerman and colleagues in 1970 (J. E. Zimmerman, 1972; J. E. Zimmerman, Thiene, & Harding, 1970). The SQUID may be used to sense magnetic fields directly or may be coupled to specially designed superconducting detection coils, as illustrated in Figure 2-3.

The simplest configuration for the detection coil is a single loop of wire. The single loop design constitutes a magnetometer, sensing the absolute strength of the magnetic field. Although very sensitive, such a design is incapable of rejecting environmental noise and must therefore be operated in a magnetically shielded room or at a remote location. However, input coils can also be given more complex configurations that cancel ambient environmental magnetic noise. One configuration that is widely used is that of a second-order gradiometer, a concentric set of coils sensing the second spatial derivative of the field gradient traversing them (Baule & McFee, 1965; Brenner, Williamson, & Kaufman, 1975). A second-order gradiometer remains selectively sensitive to the steep field gradient of very close sources, but rejects more uniform fields generated by distant sources, even if they are strong. Thus, a second-derivative SQUID gradiometer can achieve a high degree of re-

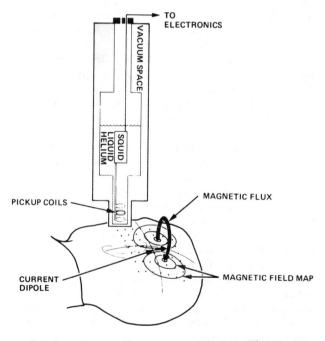

Figure 2-3. Superconductive magnetic sensor. The superinsulated dewar contains liquid helium, which surrounds the SQUID amplifier and the sensing coils, here configured as a second-derivative gradiometer.

jection of background noise. Third-derivative gradiometer configurations have also been used.

In the most commonly used single-channel superconducting gradiometer, the flux transporter and the SQUID are mounted in a superinsulated dewar filled with liquid helium, keeping the sensing apparatus near 4 Kelvin. The dewar (about 1.2 m in length) is mounted on a nonmetallic support structure that allows its precise positioning over specific points on the subject's scalp.

Most commercially available magnetic recording systems in use today are single-channel sensors that are coupled to a gradiometer configured to record the component of the field that is normal to the head. The output voltage of the SQUID control activity is directly proportional to the gradient of magnetic flux and may be amplified and filtered with the same system used to perform EEG measurements.

In a typical recording session, the magnetometer is sequentially positioned through a matrix of closely spaced points thought to encompass the entire extracranial magnetic field produced by a given neural event. This matrix of points is generally referenced to skull landmarks, such as points specified by the International 10–20 EEG recording system (Jasper, 1958), or the orbito–meatal axis, which is used in computerized tomography atlases (e.g., Matsui & Hirano, 1978).

Recently single-channel neuromagnetometers have been replaced in some laboratories by small-array systems. Small-array neuromagnetometers have between five and seven sets of recording coils and SQUIDS encased within a single dewar. These small-array systems speed recording by almost an order of magnitude by obtaining five to seven simultaneous magnetic measurements from adjacent recording locations. Large-array systems with up to 100 recording channels are currently being developed. Large-array neuromagnetometers will permit simultaneous measurement of the exiting and entering magnetic fields over significant portions of the cranium.

Brain magnetic fields may be related to an external event, such as sensory stimulation or voluntary motor activity, or may be produced spontaneously as in the study of epileptiform discharges. In either case, some form of signal averaging is typically performed, time-locked to a series of successive events. Averaging improves both the signal-to-noise ratio and the statistical reliability of the signal. The amplitude of the time series at a particular latency is proportional to the instantaneous magnetic flux density at the recording point. The polarity of the time series represents the direction of the field lines at that point, either entering the head or emerging from the head. The recordings from each point in the matrix may later be reassembled by a computer into topographical maps representing the spatial distribution of the amplitude and polarity of the magnetic fields at selected points in time.

Localization of the source producing a particular magnetic field pattern depends both upon the measured properties of the field and upon the model assumed for the generating source. In the simplest analysis using a current dipole model, the orientation of the underlying source is assumed to be orthogonal to a line connecting the two field extrema. The surface location of the source is assumed to be midway between the field extrema. The direction of the current is determined by applying the right-hand rule to the direction of field circulation.

Finally, the depth of the source is frequently calculated from the distance between the extrema and by making certain assumptions about the volume containing the source. The field pattern produced by a current dipole embedded in a finite conducting volume depends on the geometry of the volume. Cuffin and Cohen (1977) have summarized the derived patterns for the semi-infinite volume, the sphere and other shapes approximating that of the human cranium. In the case of the spherical approximation of the head, Williamson and Kaufman (1981b) have provided an algorithm to estimate the depth of sources. This algorithm depends on the diameter of the head at the surface location of the source and the length of the arc separating the two magnetic extrema obtained at the surface. However, serious deviations from the spherical model may affect the localization derived from the observed field pattern. Such deviations necessitate more complicated analyses to achieve accurate localization of intracranial current sources from measured extracranial magnetic fields.

THE EVENT-RELATED FIELD

The magnetic response of the central nervous system to sensory stimulation has a waveshape similar to that of the event-related potential (ERP), consisting of a sequence of components of differing amplitude and polarity. We have termed this magnetic response the "event-related field" (ERF). By studying the spatial pattern of the magnetic field associated with components of the event-related potential, something may be learned concerning the intracranial source of these phenomena.

THE VISUAL SYSTEM

The neuromagnetic response of visual cortex was first described using steady-state ERFs to rapid stimulation (Brenner, Okada, Maclin, Williamson, & Kaufman, 1981; Brenner *et al.*, 1975). Using a 13-Hz sinusoidally modulated stimulus, Brenner and his colleagues localized the equivalent dipolar source of the response to the occipital cortex on a medial-to-lateral axis, perpendicular to the middle sagittal fissure.

The transient visual ERF to patterned stimulation contains a biphasic response corresponding in latency to the N100–P200 complex of the ERP. This response is restricted to occipital derivations on the cortex (Richer, Barth, & Beatty, 1983) and its distribution is congruent with an equivalent current dipole in mesial occipital cortex that is oriented along the medial-to-lateral axis. (See Figure 2-4.)

The source of the visual ERF to left-hemifield stimulation is generally located to the right of that to right-hemifield stimulation (Brenner et al., 1981; Richer, Barth, & Beatty, 1983). Both sources are, however, very close to midline, and the estimates of their depth below the scalp range between 12 and 25 mm, indicating that their most likely origin is in Brodmann's area 17. One study has found sources of increasing depth in the cortex with increases in the retinal eccentricity of visual stimulation (Maclin, Okada, Kaufman, & Williamson, 1983). This arrangement corresponds with the known retinotopic organization of area 17 in the primate brain.

THE AUDITORY SYSTEM

The transient auditory event related magnetic response to tone, click, and speech stimuli also contains a biphasic complex, which is similar to the N100–P200 components of the event related potential. The exact latencies of these components vary between experiments. The electrical N100–P200 complex is also referred to as the vertex potential, reflecting its characteristic midline maxima. An earlier response, the P50 and its magnetic analog, may also be found in some situations, such as to click stimuli (Reite, Edrich, Zimmerman, & Zimmerman, 1978; Farrell, Tripp, Norgren & Teyler, 1980; Zimmerman, Reite, Zimmerman, & Edrich, 1983). In addition, long-duration tones may elicit a sustained potential shift for several hundred milliseconds after the N100–P200 (Hari, Aittoniemi, Jarvinen, Katila, & Varpula, 1980), as shown in Figure 2-5.

Much neuromagnetic work has been directed toward identifying the source of the vertex response. Bilateral dipolar sources—localized in the superior temporal regions and oriented along a dorsoventral axis, possibly normal to the plane of the Sylvian fissure—have been described for magnetic analogs of the N100, P200, and slow potential (Elberling, Bak, Kofoed, Lebech, & Saermark, 1980; Hari et al., 1980; Aittoniemi, Hari, Jarvinen, Katila & Varpula, 1981). Depth estimates of 2.0–3.5 cm below the scalp place these sources well within the region of Heschl's Gyrus, or primary auditory cortex.

The magnetic auditory responses to both tones and clicks are larger to contralateral than to ipsilateral stimulation (Elberling, Bak, Kofoed, Lebech, & Saermark, 1982; Reite, Zimmerman, & Zimmerman, 1981). The asymmetry between the response of each hemisphere is most pronounced in the case of right ear stimulation, for which the left hemisphere response is larger than the right hemisphere response. Elberling, Bak, Kofoed, Lebech, & Saermark, (1981) also report that contralateral ERF responses occur about 9 msec earlier than corresponding ipsilateral responses. These laterality effects contrast with the widespread nature of the ERP to unilateral stimulation.

There have been reports of systematic differences in the scalp distribution of the ERF to steady-state and transient tones of different frequencies (Elberling et al., 1982; Romani, Williamson, & Kaufman, 1982b). Such spatial differences in the computed source localizations as a function of stimulus frequency suggest a tonotopic organization of the auditory cortex. (See Figure 2-6.)

THE SOMATOSENSORY SYSTEM

The initial work employing somatic steady-state electrical stimulation to the fingers identified a magnetic response which displayed an approximately dipolar field pattern for the hemisphere contralateral to the hand stimulated (Brenner, Lipton, Kaufman, & Williamson, 1978). This, and later studies, argued that the measured field patterns can be accounted for by sources tangential to the scalp, oriented along an approximately anterior–posterior axis, most probably perpendicular to the Rolandic fissure. These sources are strictly contralateral to the side of stimulation, since no responses above noise level were recorded in this region to ipsilateral steady-state stimulation (Okada, Williamson, & Kaufman, 1982).

The somatosensory evoked field (SEF) patterns indicate that cortical sources whose activity pertains to different parts of the body may be noninvasively discriminated. Somatotopic organization of what is proposed to be primary somatosensory cortex is suggested by the arrangement of approximately dipolar field patterns in response to stimulation of the thumb, index finger, little finger, and ankle (Okada, 1983; Okada, Tanenbaum, Williamson, & Kaufman, 1984). The thumb and index fingers map close together on dorsolateral portions of the Rolandic strip, while the little finger and ankle sources are progressively posterior and superior. The average depth of 2.2 cm beneath the scalp would place the putative sources on a bank of the fissure.

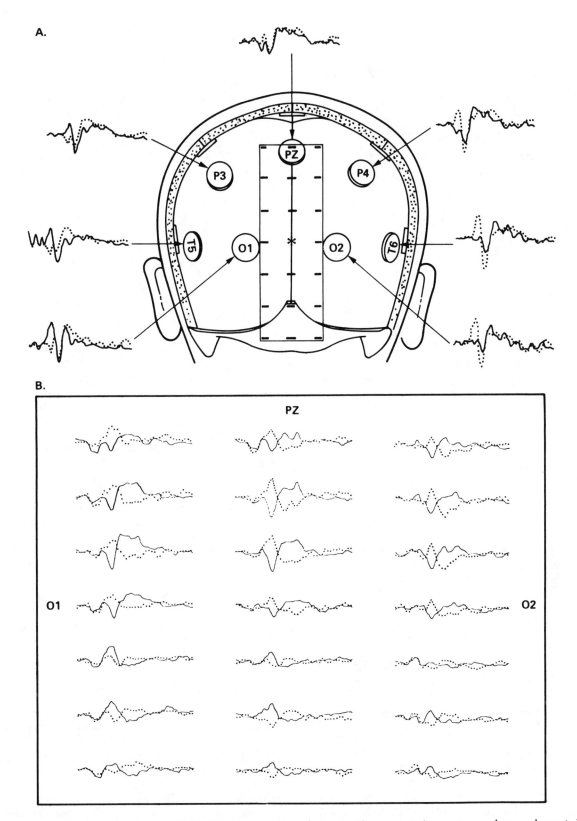

Figure 2-4. A. Matrix of visual evoked field (VEF) measurement locations (2-sm spacing) superimposed on a schematic head diagram, along with representative visual evoked potentials from posterior points of the 10–20 system. B. Grand average VEF waveforms from four subjects. Solid lines represent responses to right-hemifield stimulation, dotted lines are left-hemifield responses to 50-msec flashes of a checkerboard pattern. The 700-msec epoch for each trace includes a 100-msec prestimulus baseline period. (From "Neuromagnetic localization of two components of the transient visual evoked response to patterned stimulation" by F. Richer, D. S. Barth, and J. Beatty. *Il Nuovo Cimento* 1983, 2D, 420–428. Reprinted by permission.)

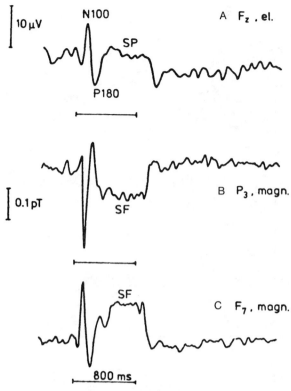

Figure 2-5. A Electrical and B, C magnetic auditory evoked responses to 1-kHz sustained (800-msec duration) tones. The auditory evoked potential A is recorded from an F_z-nose tip derivation. The magnetic analogs of the electrical N100, P180, and Slow Potential (SP) all reverse in polarity between recordings made at the posterior P_3 B and anterior F_7 C locations. (From "Auditory evoked transient and sustained magnetic fields of the human brain" by R. Hari, K. Aittoniemi, M. L. Jarvinen, T. Katila, and T. Varpula. *Experimental Brain Research*, 1980, 40, 237-240. Reprinted by permission.)

In addition to continued work on steady-state responses, there has been extensive investigation of SEFs to transient suprathreshold stimuli, whether delivered to the median nerve, the peroneal nerve, or elsewhere. Transient transcutaneous electric pulses delivered to the palmar skin of the thumb and little finger will elicit a response in the contralateral hemisphere approximately 70–90 msec after stimulus onset (Hari, Hamalainen, Ilmoniemi, Kaukoranta, & Reinikainen, in press). As in the steady-state case, the location of the polarity reversal of the magnetic component, and by implication the location of the source, lies more dorsal for the little finger than the thumb.

Two other components of the transient SEF, at approximately 20 and 30 msec, form an early response complex. These magnetic responses occur to contralateral and not ipsilateral stimulation, and reverse field polarity along a recording track hypothesized to run parallel and posterior to the Sylvian

fissure (Okada *et al.*, 1981). A more detailed topographical mapping examination of the early magnetic complex notes that both components exhibit approximately dipolar patterns of MEG field distributions, suggesting significant but not necessarily exclusive contributions from cortical sources 2.5–3.0 cm below the scalp (Wood, Cohen, Cuffin, Yarita, & Allison, 1985). This early magnetic response bears a close resemblance to the evoked potentials recorded from the pial surface using similar median nerve stimulation (Goff, Williamson, Van Gilder, Allison, & Fisher, 1980). The pial ERP reverses polarity across the central sulcus in an axis that is perpendicular to axis along which the magnetic extrema lie. This would be expected if the same discrete current source normal to the sulcus and tangential to the scalp were generating both electrical and magnetic fields. Area 3b of the somatosensory cortex is suggested as a source for this activity.

Transient responses to ipsilateral somatosensory stimulation have been mapped over temporal scalp areas (Hari, Hamalainen, Kaukoranta, Reinikainen, & Teszner, 1983; Hari, Reinikainen, Kaukoranta, Hamalainen, Ilmoniemi, Penttinen, Salminen, & Teszner; 1984). The components, at 90–95 msec for median nerve shock and 110–125 msec for peroneal nerve shock, exhibit very different field patterns than do their contralateral counterparts which have putative source in primary somatosensory cortex. For example, magnetic flux exits maximally over parietal scalp and enters maximally in frontal locations of the right hemisphere. This leads to the suggestion that this ipsilateral stimulation promotes a change in activity in the secondary somatosensory cortex, in the superior bank of the Sylvian fissure. Furthermore, transient, externally applied stimulation of the tooth pulp of the upper central incisor evokes components at 60–105 msec which also appear to originate from this anterior SII area (Hari, Kaukoranta, Reinikainen, Houpaniemie, & Mauno, 1983).

THE MOTOR SYSTEM

MEG studies involving the initiation of simple ballistic movements of hands and feet have concentrated on the magnetic analog of the slow potential shift, or Bereitschaftspotential (Kornhuber & Deecke, 1965), preceding such movements. The Bereitschaftsmagnetsfeld was first described as a slow magnetic field shift preceding electromyogram (EMG) onset, and hence the beginning of a toe or foot movement, throughout a one second foreperiod (Deecke, Weinberg, & Brickett, 1982). Voluntary plantar flexions of the foot were used in attempts to further characterize the MEG correlate of the slow negative scalp potential (Antervo, Hari, Katila, Poutanen, Seppanen, & Tuomisto,

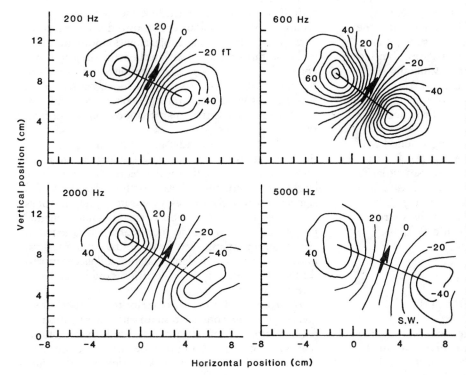

Figure 2-6. Isofield contours for right hemisphere magnetic auditory responses to amplitude-modulated pure tones. The origin of the measurement matrix (0,0) is at the ear canal. The surface location and orientation of the equivalent current dipoles is represented by each arrow, while the calculated depth of each source is related to the length of the line bisected by the arrow, suggesting that source depth increases with increasing frequency of the auditory stimulus. (From "Tonotopic organization of the human auditory cortex" by G. L. Romani, S. J. Williamson, and L. Kaufman. *Science*, 1982, 216, 1339–1340. Reprinted by permission.)

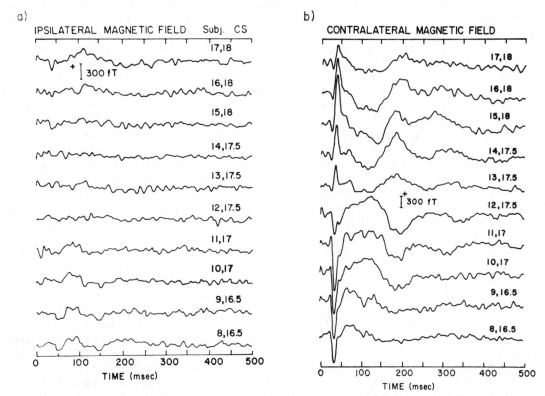

Figure 2-7. Transient somatosensory evoked fields recorded fromt he left hemisphere of one subject to ipsilateral (A) and contralateral (B) median nerve stimulation. Recordings progress from 8 cm (bottom of figure) to 17 cm (top of figure) above the auditory meatus. Notice there is no discernible response to ispilateral stimulation, while two early components (at approximately 20 and 30 msec) to contralateral stimulation reverse polarity along the recording track. (From "On the relation between somatic evoked potentials and fields" by L. Kaufman, Y. Okada, and D. Brenner. *International Journal of Neuroscience*, 1981, 15, 223–239. Reprinted by permission.)

1983; Hari, Antervo, Katila, Poutanen, Seppanen, Tuomisto, & Varpula, 1983). The polarity of the magnetic phenomenon was found to reverse polarity between contralateral frontal and parietal areas, but did not indicate a strictly dipolar source. While the MEG has thus far not proved to localize current sources for the slow field preceding voluntary movements, sufficient patterns of activity have emerged to encourage further investigation.

A more transient component peaking around EMG onset, and corresponding to the motor potential recorded to a voluntary movement, reverses polarity from superior to ventral locations in central regions of the scalp, and its source is oriented frontally (Okada et al., 1981). This would be expected if the source of the motor field were in the dendritic fields of the frontal wall of the Rolandic fissure.

CLINICAL NEUROMAGETOMETRY

The same properties of neuromagnetic recording that permit the localization of current sources within the normal brain may be applied usefully to the study of selected forms of brain pathology. Although clinical neuromagnetometry is still in its infancy, the initial results are encouraging.

The earliest recording of abnormal activity in the human brain was reported by Cohen (1972). A single patient with psychomotor (complex partial) seizures was studied. During hyperventilation, the patient displayed slow delta activity in both the raw EEG and the MEG. The EEG also showed prominent activity in the theta frequency band, although this was not evident in the MEG, reflecting a partial dissociation between the recordable signal of the EEG and the MEG.

The dissociation between EEG and MEG was also noted in a clinical investigation performed several years later in the MIT laboratory by Hughes, Cohen, Mayman, Scholl, and Hendrix (1977). Neuromagnetic measurements were taken of a total of 10 patients with a variety of neurological disorders, including brain tumor, petit mal epilepsy, diffuse abnormalities, and several psychiatric disorders accompanied by prominent slow (delta) waves. In patients where delta activity could be measured in the EEG, an inconsistent appearence of this activity was found in the MEG measured from a number of scalp locations. In the case of 3/sec spike and wave complexes accompanying petit mal absence, the wave was greatly attenuated in the MEG, whereas the spike was easily recorded. These results might reflect different brain sources for each of these phenomena.

Modena, Ricci, Barbanera, Leoni, Romani, and Carelli (1982) have investigated the MEG signals produced by specific categories of seizure disorder. Magnetic fields associated with the 3/sec spike and wave complex of petit mal absence showed a great deal of variability, both among subjects and among different scalp locations recorded within the same subject. Modena et al. (1982) report that the relative amplitude of the spike with respect to the wave changes over brain regions, suggesting separate generators for the two components that differ in spatial location or configuration.

Modena et al. (1982) also measured magnetic fields produced by paroxysmal interictal activity in a series of patients with focal seizure disorders. The largest correspondence between the EEG and MEG signals was found in cases where the epileptic focus was superficial, on the outer cortex. Basal and medial foci produced little or no measurable MEG activity. Although no attempt was made to map the interictal magnetic activity, Modena and his colleagues noted that small changes in scalp location could greatly affect its amplitude.

Neuromagnetic measurements may make their greatest clinical contribution to the investigation of focal (partial) seizure disorders, since localizing information is of primary importance in such cases. The interictal spike characterizing complex partial seizure disorders provides a clear signal of focal origin. Localization of epileptiform current sources is obtained by systematically mapping a series of scalp locations covering points where the field maximally emerges from and reenters the cranium. Averaging is accomplished by using the interictal spike in the EEG as the temporal reference point. An averaged magnetic spike may be computed for each of a series of scalp locations covering the region of the epileptic focus. The magnetic field pattern for each of the components of the spike complex may then be reconstructed and the location of underlying sources determined. This technique has been successfully applied to a number of patients with complex partial seizure disorders (Barth, Sutherling, Engel, & Beatty, 1982).

Figure 2-8 displays an example of a magnetic spike complex recorded from a child with right temporofrontal (Sylvian) spike discharges. In this subject, a dependent contralateral homologous EEG spike focus was also recorded. Averaged magnetic spikes for each of the points within the MEG recording matrices display an orderly amplitude and polarity distribution. The magnetic field from the dependent spike focus in the left hemisphere follows that of the right by 20 msec, probably reflecting its dependence on transcollosal discharge. The morphology of the magnetic spike is very similar to that of the electrical spike averaged from the primary EEG focus. Field maps of the magnetic spike (M1) and sharp wave (M2) of the right hemisphere reveal a common source for these components in the right frontal operculum. Similar field maps localize a common source for the secondary discharge in a homologous region of the left hemisphere. Figure 2-9 presents the data of a second patient with an interictal spike focus located in the left anterior temporal lobe.

The spatial resolution of the spike-averaged MEG in certain cases permits the localization of multiple current sources underlying interictal spiking within a single hemisphere. Sequential analysis of spatial–temporal discharge patterns frequently reveals the magnetic spike complex to be composed of a primary source with activity preceding that of secondary dependent sources (Barth, Sutherling, Engel, & Beatty, 1984). Figure 2-10 displays evidence of multiple sources producing interictal spiking in a patient with complex partial seizures.

Here, a rather extensive measurement matrix was employed to encompass the magnetic field pattern completely, shown marked on an outline of the patient's head. In the matrix of averaged magnetic spikes, two separate pairs of extrema can be discerned (a–a and b–b), differing in both morphology and timing. This suggests the presence of two distinct sources. Magnetic field maps constructed for each of the components of both sources demonstrate an orderly spatial–temporal discharge pattern. The lateral midtemporal focus produces a primary discharge pattern, followed by a biphasic response in the more posterior lateral temporal focus, and concludes with a discharge of opposite polarity, once again in the midtemporal focus. The presence of multiple sources underlying interictal spiking is a more frequent finding than that of single sources.

In these and other cases where the epileptogenic focus is located near the surface of the cortex, three-dimensional localization may be provided by neuromagnetic measures. However, deeper, more mesial interictal discharges may also be recorded. Although the present single-channel systems are inadequate for localizing singular pathological events, such as focal seizure onset, preliminary data indicates that the magnetic fields associated with focal seizures are of sufficient strength to be recorded extracranially without signal averaging. Further analysis of the orientation, polarity, and timing of both interictal and ictal magnetic fields, coupled with histological data, may help resolve a number of issues concerning both the treatment of patients and the understanding of epileptic processes.

SUMMARY

Very often, discoveries in the natural sciences have been the direct result of advances in the technological sciences that provide instruments of measurement. The recently developed capacity to sense weak magnetic fields produced by the human brain is one such instance. Magnetoencephalography is similar in many respects to electroencephalography, but it provides a unique perspective as to the locus of synchronous synaptic activity within the large neurons of the brain. Many events that have been recorded previously by electroencephalograpic methods have also been recorded and localized magnetoencephalographically.

Neuromagnetic sensors, based upon SQUIDs, record the exit and entry of magnetic fields from the head. From such field measurements the position, orientation, and depth of the generating equivalent current dipoles may be modeled. When coupled with other knowledge concerning the anatomy and physiology of the brain, empirically obtained field maps have been remarkably revealing.

The major contribution of neuromagnetometry to the study of ERFs has been the localization of putative sources of brain activity in different cortical systems. To date, anatomically plausible localizations have been obtained for the sources of magnetic fields elicited by visual, auditory, and somatosensory stimuli, as well as for magnetic activity related to movement initiation. Neuromagnetic measurement has permitted the study of the topographical organization of all three perceptual systems and the interhemispheric differences in the responses of these systems. The ERF has also been used to clarify the neuroanatomical basis of electrical measures and to separate temporally overlapping components of the ERP. Further, the ERF is starting to delineate sources of activity related to discrimination and other cognitive processes, and we can expect it to be very helpful in the study of the interaction of multiple cortical systems in human performance.

Although neuromagnetometry has been applied only recently in clinical investigations, the initial results have been quite promising. The electrical disturbances produced by a variety of seizure disorders, including ictal as well as interictal activity, have been shown to produce detectable extracranial magnetic fields. In the case of partial seizure disorders, neuromagnetic measurements have permitted the provisional localization of discrete sources underlying the interictal spike. Analysis of spatial–temporal discharge patterns in many instances show evidence of multiple, interrelated sources producing interictal spike complexes.

Magnetoencephalography has introduced a new and productive phase in the study of the gross electrical signals of the brain. It has provided an initial localization of the sources of many brain signals that have been of uncertain origin. Thus, magnetoencephalography complements electroencephalography; properly used, the MEG may tell where the more easily recordable EEG signals probably originate. In this way, neuromagnetic recording helps one to understand the ways in which brain electrical activity reflects brain anatomy in physiology.

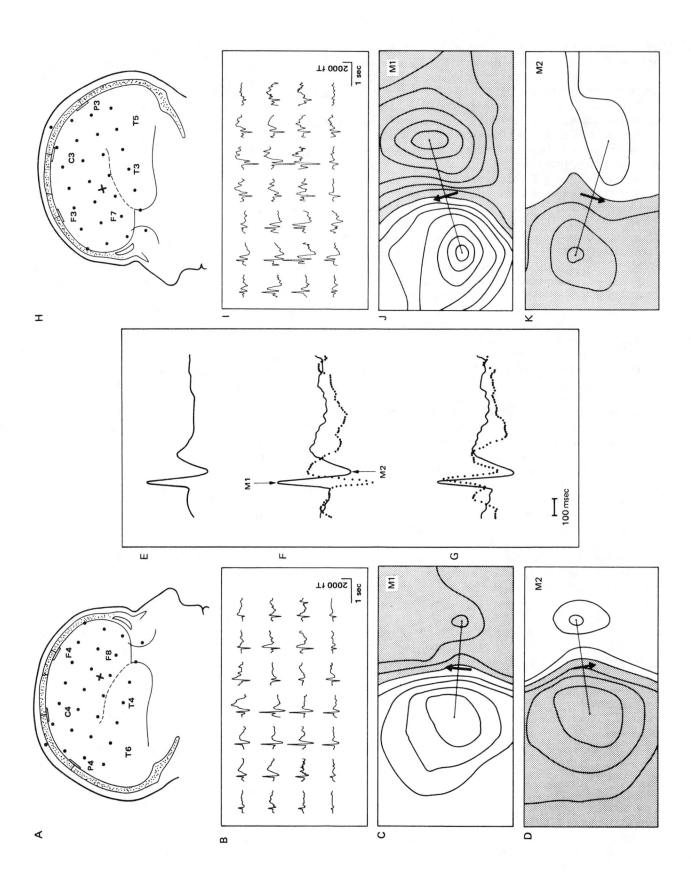

Figure 2-8. Averaged magnetic spike activity measured from the right and left hemispheres of a subject whose interictal spikes were produced by single sources in the bilateral opercular regions. A, H. Rectangular MEG measurement matrices (2-cm spacing) oriented along the temporal axes of both hemispheres. Crosses mark the location of MEG spike foci. B, I. Average magnetic spikes for each point within the right- and left-hemisphere MEG matrices. E. Average EEG spike recorded from the T_4–T_6 derivation over the right hemisphere (90 μV baseline to peak, T_4 negative up; negative spike phase reversed at T_4–F_8). F. Enlargement of two average traces near the extrema of the magnetic fields from the left (solid) and right (dotted) area of the right-hemisphere MEG matrix, demonstrating two reliable temporal components (M1 and M2) and opposing polarity reflecting the magnetic field simultaneously leaving (up) and entering (down) the cortex. G. Magnetic spike from the left hemisphere (dotted, rescaled for comparison) is delayed by 20 msec when compared to that of the right (solid). C, D. Isocontour plots demonstrating the amplitude (750 ft per bar) and polarity (light areas indicates emerging, and shaded area indicates re-entering) distribution of magnetic fields associated with M1 and M2 of the right hemisphere. Straight lines connecting the field extrema demark the orientation of the magnetic fields. Arrows represent the location and polarity of underlying current sources. J, K. Similar contour plots displaying magnetic field distributions of M1 and M2 over the left-hemispheric focus.

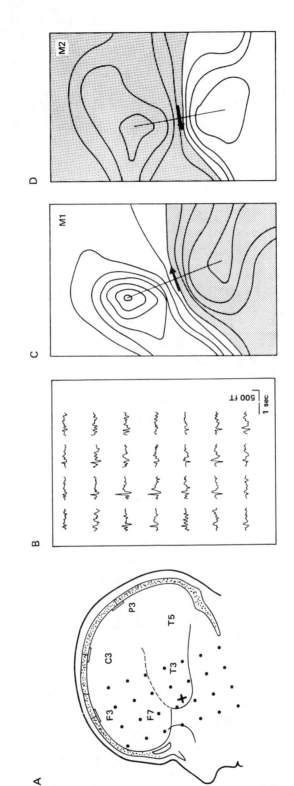

Figure 2-9. Average magnetic spike activity from another subject whose interictal spike complex was produced by a single cortical source in the left anterior temporal lobe. A. Rectangular MEG measurement matrix covering the left anterior temporal region. A cross marks the spot of the MEG spike focus. B. Average magnetic spikes obtained from each point in the matrix. C, D. Isocontour plots (similar to Figure 2-1) displaying the amplitude and polarity distributions of the generators of M1 and M2. The EEG spike was similar in morphology to the MEG spike and maximal at T_1, below and posterior to F_7.

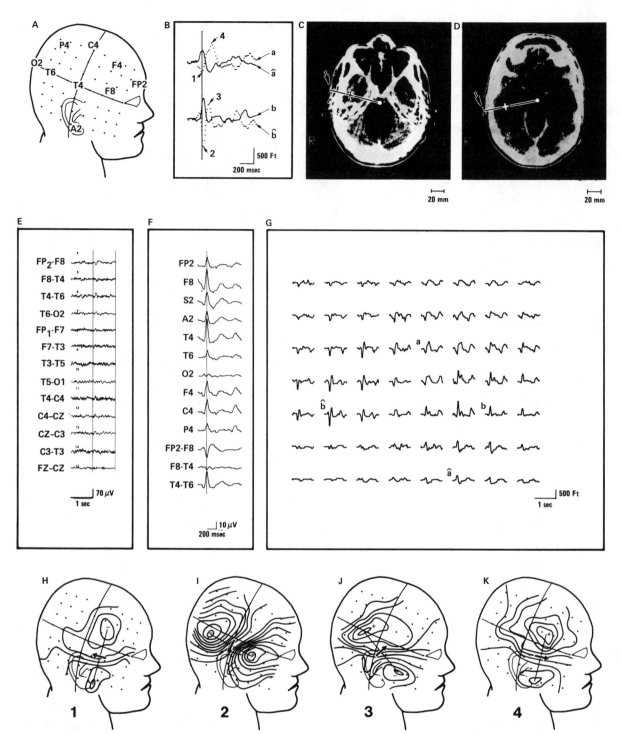

Figure 2-10. Averaged electrical and magnetic spike activity measured from the right hemisphere of a subject whose interictal spike complex was produced by multiple sources in the right midtemporal lobe. A. Rectangular MEG measurement matrix (2-cm spacing) oriented along the temporal axis. EEG electrodes are marked according to the International $_{10-20}$ System. The spenoidal electrode (S2) is not labeled. B. Enlargements of averaged magnetic spikes from separate symmetrical regions ("a" and "b") of the scalp, demonstrating four temporal components (1, 2, 3, and 4) and the opposing polarity reflecting the magnetic field simultaneously emerging from (upward) and re-entering (downward) the cranium. C, D. CT scan sections at the levels of sources "a" and "b," respectively, show the depth of the source (cross) located along a line connecting the surface location of the source marked with a washer (arrow) to the center of the cranium. E. Spike in the raw EEG recorded from both hemispheres. F. Averaged EEG spike from 3 bipolar channels (lower 3 traces) and 10 electrodes referenced to a noncephalic site (upper 10 traces). Line indicates time reference point. G. Averaged magnetic spikes recorded from each position of the MEG matrix with two distinct symmetrical regions of differing morphology marked "a" and "b". H, I, J, and K. Isocontour maps displaying the magnetic fields for each of the four temporal components of the magnetic spike complex (see text for details).

FURTHER READING

A number of excellent reviews of various aspects of neuromagnetic recording are now available. Williamson and Kaufman have provided a detailed overview of a wide range of biomagnetic phenomena (Williamson & Kaufman, 1981a), as well as a review of brain magnetic activity (Williamson & Kaufman, 1981b). Reite and Zimmerman (1978) have written a comprehensive review of the early literature on brain magnetic activity. Issues concerning instrumentation are treated by Romani, Williamson, and Kaufman (1982a) and by Katila (1981).

REFERENCES

Aittoniemi, K., Hari, R., Jarvinen, M. L., Katila, T., & Varpula, T. Localization of neural generators underlying auditory evoked magnetic fields of the human brain. In S. N. Erne, H. D. Hahlbohm, & H. Lubbig (Eds.), *Biomagnetism*. Berlin: Walter de Gruyter, 1981.

Antervo, A., Hari, R., Katila, T., Poutanen, T., Seppanen, M., & Tuomisto, T. Cerebral magnetic fields preceding self-paced plantar flexions of the foot. *Acta Neurologica Scandinavica*, 1983, 68, 213–217.

Barth, D. S. *Neuromagnetic measurements of epileptiform activity in animal and man.* Unpublished doctoral dissertation, University of California, Los Angeles, 1984.

Barth, D. S., Sutherling, W., & Beatty, J. Fast and slow magnetic phenomena in focal epileptic seizures. *Science*, 1984, 226, 855–857.

Barth, D. S., Sutherling, W., Beatty, J., & Engel, J., Jr. Neuromagnetic localization of interictal discharge in partial complex epilepsy. *Society for Neuroscience Abstracts*, 1982.

Barth, D. S., Sutherling, W., Engel, J., Jr., & Beatty, J. Neuromagnetic localization of epileptiform spike activity in the human brain. *Science*, 1982, 218, 891–894.

Barth, D. S., Sutherling, W., Engel, J., Jr., & Beatty, J. Neuromagnetic evidence of spatially distributed sources underlying epileptiform spikes in the human brain. *Science*, 1984, 223, 293–295.

Baule, G. M., & McFee, R. Detection of the magnetic field of the heart. *American Heart Journal*, 1963, 66, 95–96.

Baule, G. M., & McFee, R. Theory of magnetic detection of the heart's electrical activity. *Journal of Applied Physics*, 1965, 36, 2066–2073.

Brenner, D., Lipton, J., Kaufman, L., & Williamson, S. J. Somatically evoked magnetic fields of the human brain. *Science*, 1978, 199, 81–83.

Brenner, D., Okada, Y., Maclin, E., Williamson, S. J., & Kaufman, L. Evoked magnetic fields reveal different visual areas in human cortex. In S. N. Erne, H. D. Hahlbohm, & H. Lubbig (Eds.), *Biomagnetism*. Berlin: Walter de Gruyter, 1981.

Brenner, D., Williamson, S. J., & Kaufman, L. Visually evoked magnetic fields of the human brain. *Science*, 1975, 190, 480–482.

Cohen, D. Magnetoencephalography: Evidence of magnetic fields produced by alpha rhythm currents. *Science*, 1968, 161, 784–786.

Cohen, D. Magnetoencephalography: Detection of the brain's electrical activity with a superconducting magnetometer. *Science*, 1972, 175, 664–666.

Cuffin, B. N., & Cohen, D. Magnetic fields of a dipole in special volume conductor shapes. *IEEE Transactions on Biomedical Engineering*, 1977, BME-24, 372–381.

Deecke, L., Weinberg, H., & Brickett, P. Magnetic fields of the human brain accompanying voluntary movement: *Bereitschaftsmagnetfeld. Experimental Brain Research*, 1982, 48, 144–148.

Elberling, C., Bak, C., Kofoed, B., Lebech, J., & Saermark, K. Magnetic auditory responses from the human brain. *Scandinavian Audiology*, 1980, 9, 185–190.

Elberling, C., Bak, C., Kofoed, B., Lebech, J., & Saermark, K. Auditory magnetic fields from the human cortex: Influence of stimulus intensity. *Scandinavian Audiology*, 1981, 10, 203–207.

Elberling, C., Bak, C., Kofoed, B., Lebech, J., & Saermark, K. Auditory magnetic fields. *Scandinavian Audiology*, 1982, 11, 61–65.

Farrell, D. E., Tripp, J. H., Norgren, R., & Teyler, T. J. A study of the auditory evoked magnetic field of the human brain. *Electroencephalography and Clinical Neurophysiology*, 1980, 49, 31–37.

Gengerelli, J. A. External field of the nerve impulse. *Proceedings of the Society for Experimental Biology and Medicine*, 1942, 51, 189–190.

Gengerelli, J. A., Holter, N. J., & Glasscock, W. R. Magnetic fields accompanying transmission of nerve impulses in the frog's sciatic. *Journal of Psychology*, 1961, 52, 317–326.

Goff, W. R., Williamson, P. D., Van Gilder, J. C., Allison, T., & Fisher, T. C. Neural origins of long-latency evoked potentials recorded from the depth and cortical surface of the brain in man. In J. E Desmedt (Ed.), *Progress in Clinical Neurophysiology*, (Vol. 7). Basel: Karger, 1980.

Hari, R., Aittoniemi, K., Jarvinen, M. L., Katila, T., & Varpula, T. Auditory evoked transient and sustained magnetic fields of the human brain. *Experimental Brain Research*, 1980, 40, 237–240.

Hari, R., Antervo, A., Katila, T., Poutanen, T., Seppanen, M., Tuomisto, T., & Varpula, T. Cerebral magnetic fields preceding voluntary foot movements. *Il Nuovo Cimento*, 1983, 2D, 484–494.

Hari, R., Hamalainen, M., Kaukoranta, E., Reinikainen, K., & Teszner, D. Neuromagnetic responses from the second somatosensory cortex in man. *Acta Neurologica Scandinavica*, 1983, 68, 207–212.

Hari, R., Hamalainen, M., Ilmoniemi, R., Kaukoranta, E., & Reinikainen, K. Magnetoencephalographic localization of cortical activity evoked by somatosensory and noxious stimulation. In *Proceedings of the ENA Satellite Symposium on New Approaches to Pain Measurement in Man (Hamburg, 1983)*, Amsterdam: Elsevier, in press.

Hari, R., Kaukoranta, E., Reinikainen, K., Houpaniemie, T., & Mauno, J. Neuromagnetic localization of cortical activity evoked by painful dental stimulation in man. *Neuroscience Letters*, 1983, 42, 77–82.

Hari, R., Reinikainen, K., Kaukoranta, E., Hamalainen, M., Ilmoniemi, R., Penttinen, A., Salminen, J., & Teszner, D. Somatosensory evoked cerebral magnetic fields from SI and SII in man. *Electroencephalography and Clinical Neurophysiology*, 1984, 57, 254–263.

Hughes, J. R., Cohen, J., Mayman, C. I., Scholl, M. L., & Hendrix, D. E. Relationship of the magnetoencephalogram to abnormal activity in the electroencephalogram. *Journal of Neurology*, 1977, 217, 79–93.

Jasper, H. H. The ten–twenty electrode system of the International Federation. *Electroencephalography and Clinical Neurophysiology*, 1958, 10, 371–375.

Katila, T. Instrumentation for biomedical applications. In S. N. Erne, H. D. Hahlbohm, & H. Lubbig (Eds.), *Biomagnetism*. Berlin: Walter de Gruyter, 1981.

Kaufman, L., Okada, Y., Brenner, D., & Williamson, S. J. On the relation between somatic evoked potentials and fields. *International Journal of Neuroscience*, 1981, 15, 223–239.

Kornhuber, H. H., & Deecke, L. Hirnpotentialanderungen bei Willkurbewegungen und passiven Bewegungen des Menschen: Bereitschaftspotential und reafferente Potentiale. *Pflugers Archiv Geselschaft Physiologie*, 1965, 284, 1–17.

Maclin, E., Okada, Y., Kaufman, L., & Williamson, S. J. Retinotopic map on the visual cortex for eccentrically placed patterns: First noninvasive measurement. *Il Nuovo Cimento*, 1983, *2D*, 410–419.

Matsui, T., & Hirano, A. *An atlas of the human brain for computerized tomography*. Tokyo: Igaku-Shoin, 1978.

Modena, I., Ricci, G. B., Barbanera, R., Leoni, R., Romani, G. L., & Carelli, P. Biomagnetic measurements of spontaneous brain activity in epileptic patients. *Electroencephalography and Clinical Neurophysiology*, 1982, *54*, 622–628.

Okada, Y. Neurogenesis of evoked magnetic fields. In S. J. Williamson, G. L. Romani, L. Kaufman, & I. Modena (Eds.), *Biomagnetism: An Interdisciplinary Approach*. New York: Plenum, 1983.

Okada, Y. C., Kaufman, L., Brenner, D., & Williamson, S. J. Application of a SQUID to measurement of somatically evoked fields: Transient responses to electrical stimulation of the median nerve. In S. N. Erne, H. D. Hahlbohm, & H. Lubbig (Eds.), *Biomagnetism*. Berlin: Walter de Gruyter, 1981.

Okada, Y. C., Tanenbaum, R., Williamson, S. J., and Kaufman, L. Somatotopic organization of the human somatosensory cortex revealed by neuromagnetic measurements. *Experimental Brain Research*, 1984, *56*, 197–205.

Okada, Y. C., Williamson, S. J., & Kaufman, L. Magnetic field of the human sensorimotor cortex. *International Journal of Neuroscience*, 1982, *17*, 33–38.

Reite, M., Edrich, J., Zimmerman, J. T., & Zimmerman, J. E. Human magnetic auditory evoked fields. *Electroencephalography and Clinical Neurophysiology*, 1978, *45*, 114–117.

Reite, M., & Zimmerman, J. Magnetic phenomena of the central nervous system. *Annual Review of Biophysics and Bioengineering*, 1978, *7*, 167–188.

Reite, M., Zimmerman, J. T., & Zimmerman, J. E. MEG and EEG auditory responses to tone, click, and white noise stimuli. *Electroencephalography and Clinical Neurophysiology*, 1981, *53*, 643–651.

Richer, F., Barth, D. S., & Beatty, J. Neuromagnetic localization of two components of the transient visual evoked response to patterned stimulation. *Il Nuovo Cimento*, 1983, 2D, 420–428.

Romani, G. L., Williamson, S. J., & Kaufman, L. Biomagnetic instrumentation. *Review of Scientific Instrumentation*, 1982, 53, 1815–1845. (a)

Romani, G. L., Williamson, S. J., & Kaufman, L. Tonotopic organization of the human auditory cortex. *Science*, 1982, 216, 1339–1340. (b)

Williamson, S. J., & Kaufman, L. Biomagnetism. *Journal of Magnetism and Magnetic Materials*, 1981, 22, 129–202. (a)

Williamson, S. J., & Kaufman, L. Magnetic fields of the cerebral cortex. In: S. N. Erne, H. D. Hahlbohm, and H. Lubbig (Eds.), *Biomagnetism*, Berlin: Walter de Gruyter, 1981. (b)

Wood, C. C., Cohen, D., Cuffin, B. N., Yarita, M., & Allison, T. Electrical sources in human somatosensory cortex: Identification by combined magnetic and potential recordings. *Science*, 1985, 227, 1051–1053.

Zimmerman, J. E. Josephson effect devices and low-frequency field sensing. *Cryogenics*, 1972, 12, 19–31.

Zimmerman, J. E., Thiene, P., & Harding, J. T. Design and operation of stable rf-biased superconducting point-contact quantum devices, and a note on the properties of perfectly clean metal contacts. *Journal of Applied Physics*, 1970, 41, 1572–1580.

Zimmerman, J. T., Reite, M., Zimmerman, J. E., & Edrich, J. Auditory evoked magnetic fields: A replication with comments on the magnetic P50 analog. *Il Nuovo Cimento*, 1983, 2D, 460–470.

SECTION B
The Peripheral Nervous System

Chapter Three
The Pupillary System

Jackson Beatty

INTRODUCTION

Pupillary movements, controlled by the autonomic division of the peripheral nervous system, have served medicine and physiology well as indicators of central nervous system function. In anesthesiology, pupillary diameter provides a primary clinical sign of the depth of surgical anesthesia (Collins, 1966). In neurology, an examination of the pupils and their movements is used to establish the integrity of brain stem nuclei and pathways (Adams & Victor, 1981). In neurophysiology, pupillary movements are employed as indicators of the state of the reticular activating system (Moruzzi, 1972). It is not surprising, therefore, that the primary use of pupillometry in psychophysiology is in the study of brain activation and attention (Beatty, 1982). An excellent series of comprehensive reviews of the physiology of pupillary movements has been published by Loewenfeld (Loewenfeld, 1958; Lowenstein & Loewenfeld, 1962, 1969). It is said that the eye is a window to the soul; however, the pupil provides psychophysiology with a window to the brain.

FUNCTIONS OF THE PUPIL

The pupil provides a variable aperture in the optical system of the eye; pupillary diameter may range between 2 and 8 mm, depending primarily on environmental illumination. Since the amount of light entering the eye is approximately proportional to the area of the pupil, pupillary movements may make adjustments for changes in ambient illumination over a range of about 16 to 1. Such changes are particularly important at extreme luminances, such as night or in very bright sunlight. A second optical effect of changing pupillary diameter is control of the depth of field of the eye: When the aperture of the lens is reduced, depth of field is increased. This is particularly important when the eye is accommodated for viewing near objects. Finally, reducing pupillary diameter serves to reduce aberrations of the eye's optical system. This has the effect of improving visual acuity.

All three primary functions of pupillary movements are optical in nature; thus, it is appropriate that, in the waking organism, optical factors such as

Jackson Beatty. Human Neurophysiology Laboratory, Department of Psychology, University of California, Los Angeles, Los Angeles, California.

luminance levels and lens accommodation are the principal determinants of pupillary diameter. The small pupillary movements reflecting central attentional processes are superimposed upon a pupillary diameter set by these optical factors.

ANATOMY AND PHYSIOLOGY OF THE PUPILLARY SYSTEM

Structure of the Iris

The iris is formed by the ring of pigmented tissue that surrounds the pupil (see Figure 3-1). It is composed of two groups of smooth muscle and various supporting tissues. One muscle group, the dilator pupillae, is oriented radially, like the spokes of a tire. Thus, when the dilator pupillae contract, the iris is retracted and the pupil is opened. The dilator pupillae is principally innervated by sympathetic fibers; noradrenalin is the neurotransmitter substance used at the synapse between the postganglionic sympathetic efferent fibers and the smooth muscle of the dilator pupillae.

The sphincter pupillae is the second muscle group of the iris. Like other sphincter muscles, these fibers are arranged in an annular fashion; contraction of the sphincter pupillae acts to close the pupil by expanding the iris. The sphincter pupillae is innervated by parasympathetic postganglionic fibers; acetylcholine is the neurotransmitter substance at these synapses.

The dilator and sphincter pupillae form an antagonistic pair of smooth muscles, the former acting to expand and the latter to constrict the opening of the pupil. It is usually held that the observed pupillary diameter reflects the balance of activity between these opposing muscular systems. However, there is evidence that the sympathetically innervated dilator muscles play a relatively minor role in the production of pupillary movements; under many circumstances, pupillary diameter is primarily a reflection of activity in the parasympathetically innervated sphincter pupillae (Brodal, 1981).

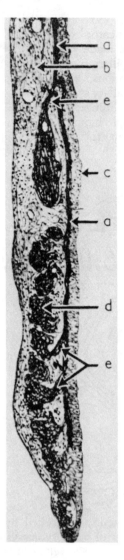

Figure 3-1. A cross-section of the iris, showing the band of dilator pupillae (a), bundle of sphincter pupillae (d), and interconnecting muscle strands (e). (From "Mechanism of Reflex Dilation of the Pupil" by I. E. Loewenfeld. *Documenta Opthalmologica*, 1958, 12, 185. [Adapted by Loewenfeld from Klinge, 1908.] Reprinted by permission.)

Neural Control of Pupillary Movements

The peripheral innervation of the iridic musculature (see Figure 3-2) is relatively straightforward. The parasympathetic innervation of the sphincter pupillae begins at the Edinger–Westphal nucleus in the central core of the midbrain. There, efferent fibers join the third cranial nerve as they exit the brain and synapse near the eye at the ciliary ganglion. The ciliary ganglion projects primarily to the sphincter pupillae, where excitatory synapses are made; there is also evidence of a secondary, inhibitory projection to the dilator pupillae.

The sympathetic innervation of the pupil is more difficult to trace centrally. A number of autonomic influences, including hypothalamic and other diencephalic efferents, project downward to the cilio-spinal center of Budge, which is located in the upper thoracic and lower cervical regions of the spinal cord. Projection fibers from this center leave the spinal cord to synapse the superior cervical ganglion. Sympathetic efferents project directly from the superior cervical ganglion to the dilator pupillae of the iris. This system of innervation, like other sympathetic projections, appears to be less specific than the comparable system of parasympathetic innervation.

Since pupillary movements are used in psychophysiology as an indicator of attentional processes, comment should be made concerning the relationships between the pupillary control system and other, more central brain regions. There are ample connections between the pupillary system and the reticular activating system. The Edinger–Westphal nucleus is the recipient of multiple inputs from specific nuclei of the brain stem reticular formation. It receives known projections from both the nucleus cuneiformis of the

midbrain reticular formation (Edwards & DeOlmos, 1976) and the nucleus pontis oralis of the pontine reticular formation (Graybiel, 1977). The Edinger–Westphal nucleus also receives input from prefrontal cortex (DeVito & Smith, 1964) and from the diencephalon (Lowenstein & Loewenfeld, 1969).

The specificity of the Edinger–Westphal nucleus in the regulation of pupillary movements has been called into question by recent anatomical studies using newly developed fiber labeling methods. Using horse-radish peroxidase to map the central input to the ciliary ganglia, Loewy, Saper, and Yamodis (1978) report that these efferent fibers originate not only in the Edinger–Westphal nucleus, but in surrounding regions of the periaqueductal gray and the ventral tegmentum. Furthermore, the projections of the Edinger–Westphal nucleus are not limited to the ciliary ganglia, but include the dorsal column nuclei, the spinal trigeminal nucleus, and the inferior olive (Loewy & Saper, 1978). The implications of such projections in providing a neurophysiological interpretation of pupillary movements are not fully apparent; however, it would be wise to view pupillary movements not simply as an isolated indicator of ocular–motor response, but also as an index of more complex central events.

Pharmacology of the Pupillary System

The pupillary system behaves in its pharmacology much as would be expected, given knowledge of its innervation. Acetylcholine and related parasympathomimetic substances (e.g., pilocarpine) stimulate the sphincter pupillae and produce extreme pupillary constriction or miosis. The effect of naturally released acetylcholine upon the parasympathetic musculature is also potentiated by compounds that inhibit the action of acetylcholinesterase in inactivating that neurotransmitter; physostigmine is a common substance having this effect. Finally, compounds such as atropine block the action of acetylcholine on the sphincter pupillae by competing for cholinergic receptor sites in that tissue; the effect of such blocking is to inactivate the sphincter and allow the dilator pupillae to dilate the pupil maximally, producing mydriasis (Davson, 1980).

The sympathetic pharmacology of the iris is that of an alpha-adrenergic system. Noradrenalin and its analogues act to dilate the pupil. As is characteristic of an alpha-adrenergic system, this effect may be blocked by agonists such as phenoxybenzene (Davson, 1980).

Pupillary Response to Reticular Stimulation

One reason that pupillary movements may be used in studying attentional processes is that, as noted, there

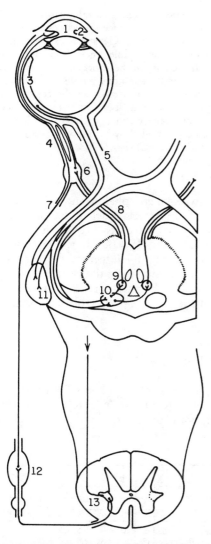

Figure 3-2. The innervation of the iridic musculature and the pathways mediating the light reflex. 1, pupil; 2, iris; 3, retina; 4, short ciliary nerve; 5, optic nerve; 6, ciliary ganglion; 7, opthalmic nerve; 8, third cranial nerve; 9, Edinger–Westphal nucleus of third nerve; 10, pre-rectal area; 11, lateral geniculate nucleus; 12, superior cervical ganglion; 13, cilio-spinal center of Budge. (From "*The Human Central Nervous System: A Synopsis and Atlas*" by R. Nieuwenhuys, J. Voogd and C. van Huijzen. New York: Springer-Verlag. 1978. Reprinted by permission.)

are extensive projections linking nuclei of the brain stem reticular formation with autonomic nuclei controlling pupillary movements. These pathways have been demonstrated not only anatomically (see above), but also physiologically. In the classic series of experiments that established the cortical activating properties of brain stem reticular nuclei, pupillary dilation was utilized as a physiological indicator of successful stimulation of the reticular activating system (Moruzzi, 1972).

The effects of reticular stimulation on pupillary movements have been approached directly by Bonvallet and Zbrozyna (1963), who recorded from both the parasympathetic short ciliary nerves and the cervical sympathetic nerve as electrical stimulation was applied to the reticular formation at the level of the midbrain. Figure 3-3 illustrates their results. Reticular stimulation produced desynchronization of the cortical electroencephalogram (EEG) inhibition of the parasympathetic input to the sphincter pupillae, and facilitation of the sympathetic input to the dilator pupillae. Thus, the pupillary dilation produced by activation of reticular nuclei appears to be mediated by both the sympathetic and parasympathetic branches of the peripheral autonomic innervation.

REFLEXES

The Light Reflex

The principal determinant of pupillary diameter is the "light reflex." This is the characteristic pupillary constriction that results from an increase of illumination. Figure 3-4 illustrates the light reflex as a function of stimulus intensity. Several features of this reflex may be seen. First, the light-induced constriction is relatively rapid; it begins at a latency of several hundred milliseconds and reaches its maximum somewhat later, depending upon the amplitude of the response. Second, the extent of the movement increases with the intensity of the stimulus. By varying the intensity of stimulation, the light reflex can establish a pupillary diameter at any value between 2 and 8 mm, the entire range of pupillary movement. Third, the return of the iridic musculature to the prestimulus state following stimulus offset (the so-called "dark reflex") is relatively slow; thus, the light and dark reflexes show significant differences in their dynamic properties. Finally, both the reflexes are consensual—that is, they occur with equal amplitude and latency in both the stimulated and the unstimulated eye.

Both types of photoreceptors, the rods and the cones, provide input to the light reflex. A small bundle of axons leaves the optic tract and terminates not in the lateral geniculate nucleus of the thalamus, but rather in the pretectal nucleus, which is located at the

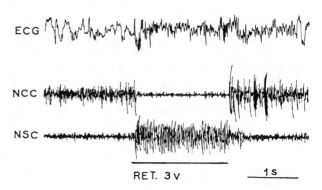

RET. 3 V   1 s

Figure 3-3. The effects of electrical stimulation of midbrain reticular nuclei. The upper trace shows desynchronication of the electrocorticogram (ECG), a classical cortical indication of activation. The middle trace shows inhibition of parasympathetic activity in the short ciliary nerves (NCC), which synapse upon the sphincter pupillae. The lower trace illustrates enhancement of activity in the cervical sympathetic nerve (NSC). (From "Les Commandes Réticulaires du Système Autonome et en Particulier de l'Innervation Sympathique de la Pupille" by M. Bonvallet and A. Zbrozyna. *Archives of Italian Biology*, 1963, 101, 174–207. Reprinted by permission.)

junction between diencephalon and midbrain. It is the neurons of the pretectal nucleus that project to the Edinger–Westphal nucleus to provide input for the light reflex (Davson, 1980). Thus, the light reflex does not depend upon the integrity of either the geniculo-cortical visual system or the visual centers of the superior colliculus. Furthermore, the sympathetic innervation of the pupil plays no role in mediating the light reflex.

The Near Reflex

A second pupillary reflex linked with activity of the ocular–motor system is the "near reflex." In viewing a near object, both convergence of the eyes and accom-

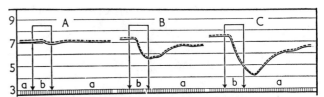

Figure 3-4. The light reflex. Pupillary response to 1-sec periods of light stimulation at (A) visual threshold, (B) four log units over threshold, and (C) eight log units over threshold. The solid line shows the response of the stimulated eye; the dashed line gives the response of the unstimulated eye. (From "The Pupil" by O. Lowenstein and I. E. Loewenfeld. In H. Davson [Ed.], *The Eye* [2nd ed., Vol. 3]. New York: Academic Press, 1969. Reprinted by permission.)

modation of the lenses are produced. Associated with these ocular–motor responses is a marked pupillary constriction. This constriction presumably functions to increase the depth of field of the visual system. Like the light reflex, the near reflex is mediated exclusively by parasympathetic efferent fibers of the third cranial nerve.

The Psychosensory Reflex

The so-called "psychosensory reflex" is particularly interesting, since it forms a bridge between the better-understood light and near reflexes and the more complex pupillary movements that accompany cognitive processing. The psychosensory reflex is a pupillary dilation that may be evoked by either intense or task-relevant stimuli presented in any sensory modality. This dilation depends not so much upon the physical properties of the stimulus, but upon the mental processes that the stimulus elicits in the organism. Figure 3-5 illustrates the psychosensory reflex as observed in a number of species.

The interpretation of the psychosensory reflex has long been controversial, prompting Lowenstein and Loewenfeld (1969) to write: "More than any other pupillary movement, reflex dilation of the pupil has been the innocent butt of endless rounds of argu-ments which left the subject mired in a swamp of conflicting statements, and the unfortunate reader groping about for a solid foothold of fact" (p. 311). Fortunately, much of this confusion has resolved itself in recent years. Both sympathetic and parasympathetic factors are involved in mediating the psychosensory reflex. Lowenstein and Loewenfeld (1969) argue convincingly that the sympathetic pathway is hypothalamic in origin; certainly it is rostral to the midbrain and caudal to the cerebral cortex. Such a pathway has been physiologically traced through the brain stem to the cilio-spinal center of Budge. Activation of this system produces reflex dilatation of the pupil by contracting the dilator pupillae.

However, the sympathetic system is not the only system mediating the psychosensory reflex. A parasympathetic component may be demonstrated under anesthesia or following surgical disruption of the sympathetic pathway (Lowenstein & Loewenfeld, 1969). Thus, the patterning of discharge in the iridic sympathetic and parasympathetic fibers in the psychosensory reflex is like that obtained by electrical stimulation of the midbrain reticular formation. This finding and other evidence suggest tht the psychosensory reflex may reflect an orienting process that is mediated by the reticular activating system of the brain stem (Hobson & Brazier, 1980).

TASK-EVOKED PUPILLARY RESPONSES

It has long been known to neurologists, if not psychophysiologists, that pupillary dilations reliably accompany mental activities. For example, over 70 years ago, the German neurologist Bumke (translated and quoted by Hess, 1975) wrote: "Every active intellectual process, every psychical effort, every exertion of attention, every active mental image, regardless of content, particularly every affect just as truly produces pupil enlargement as does every sensory stimulus" (Hess, 1975, pp. 23–24). The pupillary enlargements that accompany cognitive events are indeed as widespread as Bumke indicated. These dilations, now called "task-evoked pupillary responses," occur at relatively short latencies (300–500 msec) following the onset of cognitive processing and disappear just as rapidly once processing is terminated. Perhaps of greatest importance is that the size of these dilations varies as a function of the processing load or "mental effort" (Kahneman, 1973) that is required to perform the cognitive task (Beatty, 1982). Thus, in many respects, the task-evoked pupillary response may be utilized as a neurophysiological indicator of mental workload (Beatty, 1979).

Figure 3-6 illustrates typical magnitudes of pupillary dilation that are observed during different types of cognitive processing. Notice that these responses

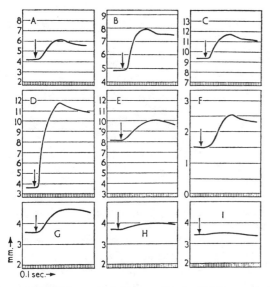

Figure 3-5. The psychosensory reflex in (A) human being, (B) monkey, (C) dog, (D) cat, (E) rabbit, (F) rat, (G) guinea pig, (H) pigeon, and (I) frog. For animals with small eyes, the ordinate of the graph was enlarged, using the ratio of the diameter of each animal's iris to that of the human being as a multiplying factor. (From "Mechanism of reflex dilation of the pupil" by I. E. Loewenfeld, *Documenta Opthalmologica*, 1958, 12, 185–309. Reprinted by permission.)

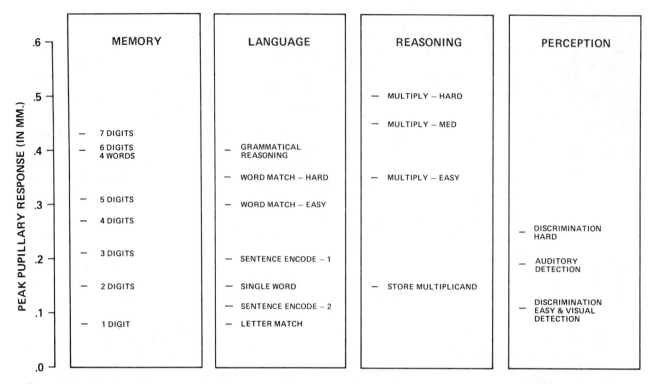

Figure 3-6. Characteristic peak amplitudes of the task-evoked pupillary responses obtained in a range of qualitatively different cognitive tasks, arranged by type of task. (From "Task-Evoked Pupillary Responses, Processing Load, and the Structure of Processing Resources" by J. Beatty. *Psychological Bulletin*, 1982, 91(2), 276–292. Reprinted by permission.)

are much smaller in size than the pupillary movements induced either by accommodation or by modest changes in ambient illumination. Task-evoked pupillary responses must be considered as small perturbations riding upon the discharge of the autonomic nerves innervating the iridic musculature; indeed, under most conditions, these pupillary dilations are not detectable unless special measurement procedures are employed.

Task-evoked pupillary responses bear the same relation to the pupillary record from which it is extracted as event-related brain potentials do to the spontaneous EEG. As with the event-related potential, task-evoked pupillary responses may be averaged with respect to a task relevant temporal marker, or single-trial analyses may be undertaken. Averaged task-evoked pupillary responses have been studied in a wide range of cognitive tasks. When task parameters are varied in a manner expected to increase processing demands, the amplitudes of these responses increase. Furthermore, the task-evoked pupillary responses evoked during complex cognitive processing have been shown to vary inversely with intelligence; apparently, more intelligent individuals process information more efficiently (Ahern & Beatty, 1979). Thus, task-evoked pupillary responses have been shown to

be responsive to within-task, between-task, and between-individual variations in demands for "mental effort" (Beatty, 1982).

MEASURING PUPILLARY RESPONSES

All methods of measuring pupillary diameter are optical in nature; pupillary movements are tracked by processing a series of images of the pupil obtained by one of several techniques. A number of recording schemes have been proposed, but only two are of sufficient accuracy for use in psychophysiology: photographic pupillometry and electronic video-based pupillometry.

Photographic pupillometry is certainly the older of these two recording technologies. It is also the simpler and less expensive, but it is very demanding of both time and labor of the investigator. Photographic pupillometry begins with photographing the pupil of one eye, using a macro-focusing motion picture camera. Typically, the resulting image of the iris fills most of the frame and thus provides satisfactory resolution of pupillary diameter. Both 16-mm film (Hess & Polt, 1964) and 35-mm film (Kahneman & Beatty, 1966) have been employed; the former is less expensive, but the latter offers increased resolution. Frequently infrared film is used, which not only enhances the contrast between iris and pupil, but also permits recording in near-darkness. Photographs of the eye are usually made at intervals of .5 or 1 sec, but more frequent samples are sometimes taken. Absolute calibration is obtained by beginning each roll of film with a photograph of a millimeter rule placed at the exact distance from the camera as the pupil to be measured.

Pupillometric measures are obtained from the developed film are taken by projecting the image of the eye onto a large surface and then measuring the pupil on the selected axis using an ordinary yardstick. After numerical conversion for scale, the data obtained should be sufficiently accurate to serve most purposes.

Electronic video-based pupillometry is the method used in most modern pupillometric laboratories. Figure 3-7 illustrates one such device. These pupillometers employ a high-resolution linear infrared video camera to obtain an image of the iris and the pupil. A series of hardware pattern recognition circuits extracts the boundary separating iris and pupil from the video image. Pupil area or vertical pupillary diameter are then computed electronically. The simpler pupillometers, like the one illustrated in Figure 3-7, require a headrest to fix the position of the eye with respect to the video camera; more complex units utilize eye- and head-tracking systems to permit free head movement. In all electronic pupillometers, momentary estimates of pupillary diameter are continuously available for on-line real-time computer analysis. Using these devices, the same types of computational procedures employed in the analysis of event-related brain potentials may be utilized for pupillometric analysis.

When pupillometric measures are applied to the study of task-evoked pupillary responses, a number of precautions must be taken, since the size of these responses is very small when compared with the dilations and constrictions induced by optical variables. The subject should fixate a distant point that differs little in luminance from the surrounding field. If possible, the subject should be able to initiate each experimental trial; this procedure permits him or her to blink between rather than during periods of pupillary measurement. Finally, if visual stimuli must be utilized, extra care must be taken; adequate control data must be obtained in order to discount any possibility that the observed variations in pupillary diameter may be attributed to either the light reflex or the near reflex.

In computer-based electronic pupillometry, data from individual experimental trials are stored within the computer system for further analysis. Although automatic algorithms exist for detecting artifacts in the pupillometric data, such as those produced by eyeblinks, it is prudent to inspect all raw data visually.

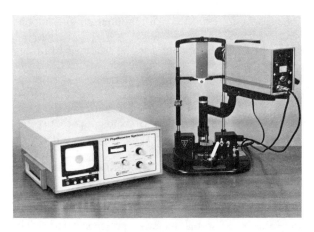

Figure 3-7. An electronic video-based pupillometer. (Developed, produced, and distributed by Applied Science Laboratories, Waltham, Mass.)

This should be done blindly with respect to experimental conditions and trial outcome. Small artifacts may be corrected by linear interpolation, as the frequency response of the pupillary system is very low. Trials containing more major artifacts or artifacts in particularly critical regions of the trial should be discarded. Edited artifact-free data may then be conventionally averaged, backward-averaged, or analyzed by single-trial procedures (Richer, Silverman, & Beatty, 1983). In these respects, pupillometric data are processed in a manner analogous to the analysis of event-related brain potentials.

SUMMARY

Pupillometry has been utilized by psychophysiologists in studying the biological basis of attention, even though the functions of the pupil and the primary determinants of pupillary diameter are optical in nature. The iris, which surrounds the pupil, contains two antagonistic groups of smooth muscle: the sympathetically innervated dilator pupillae and the parasympathetically innervated sphincter pupillae. Pupillary diameter is determined by the balance of activity in these two muscle groups.

The parasympathetic innervation of the pupil may be traced from the Edinger–Westphal nucleus in the midbrain, through the ciliary ganglion, to the sphincter pupillae. The origins of the sympathetic innervation are less well understood, but the efferent pathway includes the cilio-spinal center of Budge and the superior cervical ganglion. The sympathetic neurotransmitter at the dilator pupillae is noradrenalin; the parasympathetic neurotransmitter at the sphincter pupillae is acetylcholine. The pharmacology of these synapses is as expected for cholinergic and alpha-adrenergic systems.

Of primary importance for the study of brain attentional processes are the multiple connections between specific nuclei in the midbrain and pontine reticular formation an the Edinger–Westphal nucleus. Electrical stimulation of the midbrain reticular core produces both suppression of parasympathetic discharge and enhancement of sympathetic discharge to the iridic musculature.

The major determinant of pupillary diameter for the waking organism is the level of ambient illumination. The light reflex receives input from both rods and cones, is mediated through the pretectal area and the Edinger–Westphal nucleus, and is executed solely through the parasympathetic innervation to the iris. Similarly, the near reflex, which accompanies accommodation and convergence movements, is parasympathetically mediated.

The psychosensory reflex, a brief pupillary dilation following presentation of an intense or task-relevant stimulus in any sensory modality, has both sympathetic and parasympathetic components. It may represent a special case of the task-evoked pupillary response, a pupillary dilation that accompanies mental activity. Task-evoked pupillary responses have been measured in a wide variety of mental tasks. The amplitude of these responses varies with the processing load or "mental effort" required by the task. It is sensitive to within-task, between-task, and between-individual factors that control task-processing demands.

Pupillary responses may be measured either photographically or electronically with sufficient precision to study even very small pupillary responses. Photographic methods are both simpler and less expensive, but they are very time-consuming and ill-adapted for computer analysis. Electronic video-based pupillometry permits computer acquisition of pupillometric data, as well as on-line artifact detection and response averaging—all very desirable features for the contemporary psychophysiologist.

ACKNOWLEDGMENT

Compilation of this review was supported in part by the Environmental Physiology Program of the Office of Naval Research on Contract N00014-76-C-0616.

REFERENCES

Adams, R. D., & Victor, M. *Principles of neurology* (2nd ed.). New York: McGraw-Hill, 1981.

Ahern, S. K., & Beatty, J. Pupillary responses during information processing vary with Scholastic Aptitude Test scores. *Science*, 1979, 205, 1289–1292.

Beatty, J. Pupillometric methods of workload evaluation: Present status and future possibilities. In B. O. Harman & R. E. McKenzie (Eds.), *Survey of methods to assess workload*. Neuilly Sur Seine, France: Advisory Group for Aerospace Research and Development, North Atlantic Treaty Organization, 1979.

Beatty, J. Task-evoked pupillary responses, processing load, and the structure of processing resources. *Psychological Bulletin*, 1982, 1(2), 276–292.

Bonvallet, M., & Zbrozyna, A. Les commandes réticulaires du système autonome et en particulier de l'innervation sympathique de la pupille. *Archives of Italian Biology*, 1963, 101, 174–207.

Brodal, A. *Neurological anatomy in relation to clinical medicine* (3rd ed.). New York: Oxford University Press, 1981.

Collins, V. J. *Principles of anesthesiology*. Philadelphia: Lea & Febiger, 1966.

Davson, H. *Physiology of the eye* (4th ed.). New York: Academic Press, 1980.

DeVito, J. L., & Smith, O. A., Jr. Subcortical projections of the prefrontal lobe of the monkey. *Journal of Comparative Neurology*, 1964, 123, 413–424.

Edwards, S. B., & DeOlmos, J. S. Autoradiographic studies of the projections of the midbrain reticular formation: Ascending projections of the nucleus cuneiformis. *Journal of Comparative Neurology*, 1976, 165, 417–432.

Graybiel, A. M. Direct and indirect preoculomotor pathways of the brainstem: An autoradiographic study of the pontine reticular formation of the cat. *Journal of Comparative Neurology*, 1977, 175, 37–38.

Hess, E. H. *The tell-tale eye*. New York: Van Nostrand Reinhold, 1975.

Hess, E. H., & Polt, J. M. Pupil size in relation to mental activity during simple problem-solving. *Science*, 1964, 143, 1190–1192.

Hobson, J. A., & Brazier, M. A. B. *The reticular formation revisited: Specifying function for a nonspecific system*. New York: Raven Press, 1980.

Kahneman, D. *Attention and effort*. Englewood Cliffs, N. J.: Prentice-Hall, 1973.

Kahneman, D., & Beatty, J. Pupil diameter and load on memory. *Science*, 1966, 154, 1583–1585.

Klinge, E. Die inneren Irisschichten der Haussäugetiere. *Anatomische Hefte*, 1908, 36, 601–710.

Loewy, A. D., & Saper, C. B. Edinger–Westphal nucleus: Projections to the brain stem and spinal cord of the cat. *Brain Research*, 1978, 150, 1–27.

Loewy, A. D., Saper, C. B., & Yamodis, N. D. Re-evaluation of the efferent projections of the Edinger–Westphal nucleus of the cat. *Brain Research*, 1978, 141, 153–159.

Loewenfeld, I. E. Mechanism of reflex dilation of the pupil. *Documenta Opthalmologica*, 1958, 12, 185–359.

Lowenstein, O., & Loewenfeld, I. E. The pupil. In H. Davson (Ed.), *The eye* (2nd ed., Vol. 3). New York: Academic Press, 1962.

Lowenstein, O., & Loewenfeld, I. E. The pupil. In H. Davson (Ed.), *The eye* (Vol. 3). New York: Academic Press, 1969.

Moruzzi, G. *Reviews of physiology: Biochemistry and experimental pharmacology*. The sleep–waking cycle. New York: Springer-Verlag, 1972.

Nieuweuhuys, R., Voogd, J., & van Huizen, C. The human central nervous system: A synopsis and atlas. New York: Springer-Verlag, 1978.

Richer, F., Silverman, C., & Beatty, J. Response selection and initiation in speeded reactions: A pupillometric analysis. *Journal of Experimental Psychology: Human Perception and Performance*, 1983, 9(3), 360–370.

Chapter Four

The Eccrine System and Electrodermal Activity

Don C. Fowles

INTRODUCTION

Psychological Significance of Sweat Gland Activity

Response to Psychological Stimuli

Current interest in the activity of the eccrine sweat glands dates from the initial demonstration by Fere (1888) that sensory or emotional stimulation produced a decrease in skin resistance. At that time, the physiological mechanism that produced this electrodermal response was unknown, though Fere proposed that it was due to vascular activity. Since then, various hypotheses have been considered, with the result that evidence rather conclusively points to a contribution by the sweat glands (see reviews by Edelberg, 1972b; Neumann & Blanton, 1970; Venables & Christie, 1973). Other work has attempted to specify the nature of the stimuli that elicit this response: It can be elicited by novel stimuli, emotional stimuli, threatening stimuli, and attention-getting stimuli (e.g., Raskin, 1973). In fact, the stimuli that elicit these responses are so ubiquitous that it has proved difficult to offer a conceptualization of the features common to these stimuli. There is no doubt, however, that the response often occurs to stimuli that depend for their efficacy on their psychological significance, as opposed to their physical intensity.

The Nature of the Psychological Information

Given the assumption of an involvement of the sweat glands in electrodermal activity, the question arises as to whether electrodermal measurements reflect simply the amount of sweat gland activity and nothing more, or whether they may be used to infer something specific about the psychological response of the subject (e.g., anxiety, task orientation, defensiveness, etc.). This question, in turn, can be divided into two approaches. In the first, *characteristics of the electrodermal activity itself* are said to indicate a specific psychological response. In the second, electrodermal activity is assumed only to indicate the occurrence of sweat gland activity, with an inference as to the nature of the subject's psychological response being dependent on the nature of the stimuli being presented (e.g., novel stimuli, threatening stimuli, sexually attractive stimuli, appetitive stimuli, etc.). In the first approach, then, the characteristics of the electrodermal activity are presumed to carry specific psychological significance, whereas in the second approach they are viewed only as noisy manifestations of sweat gland

Don C. Fowles, Department of Psychology, University of Iowa, Iowa City, Iowa.

activity. Much interest in recent years has centered on the possibility that the first approach is valid—so much so that it has dominated the recent literature. Thus, this question of whether the peripheral mechanism codes specific psychological information or is simply a complex and noisy manifestation of nonspecific activity is a major issue to be considered.

Purpose and Organization of the Present Chapter

The purpose of the present chapter is to summarize current knowledge concerning the functioning of the eccrine system and its contribution to the electrodermal activity measured by psychophysiologists.

Since 1970, the major reviews of this topic are those by Edelberg (1971, 1972b, 1973) and Venables and Christie (1973, 1980), as well as one by me (Fowles, 1974). These papers provide summaries of the earlier literature and citations of prior reviews. The major conclusions reached by these authors are discussed in the present review, with an attempt to evaluate them critically and to indicate where there is a consensus or a continuing divergence of opinion. In the interest of brevity, data bearing on those historically important issues that have been resolved to the satisfaction of all are not presented here.

In keeping with the editorial philosophy of this volume, the structure and function of the eccrine system is described first, followed by a discussion of the relation between the activity of the eccrine system and surface measurements of electrodermal activity. Having completed this, I then comment on the psychological significance of electrodermal activity as related to peripheral and central mechanisms.

Definition of Terms

Current Terminology

"Electrodermal activity" (EDA) refers, as the name implies, to the electrical activity of the skin. From the perspective of the psychophysiologist, EDA normally includes surface measurements obtained with three techniques: skin resistance (SR), skin conductance (SC), and skin potential (SP). SR and SC are obtained by applying an external voltage across the skin and measuring the resistance (or conductance) of the skin to the resultant current flow. If a constant-current method is employed, the voltage drop across the skin will be linear with respect to SR. If, on the other hand, a constant-voltage technique is utilized, the current through the skin will be linear with respect to SC and can conveniently be measured as the voltage drop across a small (e.g., 200 Ω) series resistor. Thus the immediate reading obtained will be either resistance or conductance, depending on the method of applying an external voltage. As in any electrical circuit, con-

ductance is simply the reciprocal of resistance, and thus SR and SC are manifestations of the same underlying phenomenon.

In reference to the use of an external voltage source, SC and SR are said to represent "exosomatic" EDA. SP, in contrast, is obtained by recording the endogenous electrical activity of the skin, and is therefore called "endosomatic" EDA. The primary value of the term "exosomatic" is the advantage of being able to refer to both SC and SR measurements in cases where the difference between them is not important, as, for example, when reviewing a number of studies in which one or the other method is used. Otherwise, the more specific terms "SC" and "SR" are quite satisfactory. The use of "endosomatic EDA," as opposed to "SP," is largely dictated by the demand for consistency when the term "exosomatic" is used.

Another important distinction is that between tonic or slowly changing *levels* and phasic or rapidly changing *responses* obtained with each of the techniques. In combination with the distinctions already made, this results in the more specific terms "SR response" (SRR), "SR level" (SRL), "SC response" (SCR), "SC level" (SCL), "SP response" (SPR), "SP level" (SPL), "ED response" (EDR), and "ED level" (EDL). The last two terms can be used if one wishes to include both exosomatic and endosomatic measurements but to specify only phasic or tonic components, respectively. Finally, "exosomatic EDR" can be used to refer to both SCRs and SRRs, whereas "endosomatic EDR" is synonymous with SPR, with similar grouping for levels.

Earlier Terminology

Other widely used terms, particularly in the older literature, are "galvanic skin response" (GSR) and "psychogalvanic response" (PGR). These terms have often been used ambiguously, and little is to be gained by striving to increase the precision of their usage. Consequently, there is little to recommend their continued usage, but the reader should be aware that they are terms referring to EDA. It is probably the case that they most often refer to exosomatic EDRs, but that assumption should be checked in any given case. A helpful summary of changes over time in terminology is provided by Venables and Christie (1973).

THE SKIN

General Features

A thorough description of the complex features of the skin is beyond the scope of the present chapter. Consequently, only a cursory description is provided, with detailed treatment reserved for the sweat glands and the epidermis—those aspects of the skin that are of most relevance to understanding the mechanisms of EDA of interest to psychophysiologists. The reader interested in a more extensive coverage is, therefore, referred to two major references on the skin: the text by Montagna and Parakkal (1974) or the multivolume series edited by Jarrett (1973c, 1973d, 1974, 1977, 1978, 1980b). In addition, Rook, Wilkinson, and Ebling (1979) offer a briefer, but useful, treatment of the topic.

Functions and Gross Anatomy of the Skin

The skin serves numerous functions (Montagna & Parakkal, 1974, Chapter 1). In perhaps the most obvious of these, it serves as a barrier between the internal milieu of the organism and the outside environment. In this capacity, the skin prevents the loss of water and various other constituents of the body, on the one hand, and protects the body from penetration by external fluids in the environment, on the other hand. This protective function also includes protection of the body from injury, as is especially obvious in those cases where the skin is thick and tough, thereby providing protection from abrasion and other mechanical assaults. The skin is also involved in communication with the environment. Its sensitivity to cutaneous external stimuli provides the organism with considerable information about the environment and makes adaptive reactions possible. In many species, the skin has also developed specialized structures that communicate with the environment by secreting substances that attract or repel; serve to protect, warn, or camouflage the organism; and provide stimuli that are important in social and sexual interaction. Finally, the role of the skin in thermal regulation is extremely important. It contains cutaneous thermal receptors, superficial cutaneous vascular beds, and sweat glands, all of which are involved in the regulation and maintenance of body temperature.

The gross anatomy of the skin can be divided into four stratified layers, although one of these is vestigial in humans (Ebling, 1979; Montagna & Parakkal, 1974, Chapter 1). The "stratified epidermis" forms the outer layer. Below this lies a layer of connective tissue known as the "dermis" or "corium." The dermis, in turn, sits on a fatty layer called the "panniculus adiposus." The "panniculus carnosus," a flat sheet of striated (skeletal) muscle, separates the panniculus adiposus from the rest of the body in most mammals, but this layer is vestigial in humans.

Sweat Glands

Although the skin contains many specialized structures, such as sense organs, hair follicles, and sebaceous glands, the one of particular interest in the present context is the eccrine sweat gland (Figure 4-1). This gland is a simple tube consisting of a single or

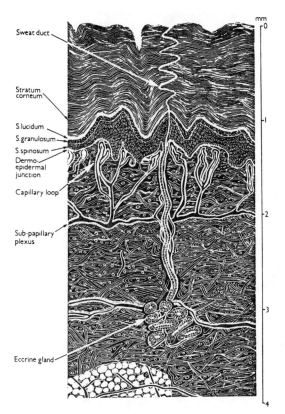

Figure 4-1. Section of glabrous skin of sole. (From "The Normal Skin" by F. J. G. Ebling. In A. Rook, D. S. Wilkinson, & F. J. G. Ebling [Eds.], *Textbook of Dermatology* [3rd ed., Vol. 1]. London: Blackwell Scientific Publications, 1979. Reprinted by permission.)

double layer of epithelial cells opening onto the skin surface (Grice & Verbov, 1977; Montagna & Parakkal, 1974, Chapter 12). This tube can be divided into the secretory segment and the duct. The secretory segment and much of the duct are irregularly coiled into a compact, rounded mass or glomerulus, located either in the lower part of the dermis or extending into the hypodermis, the duct forming approximately one-half of the coiled part. As the duct comes out of the glomerate portion of the gland, it follows a helical or undulating course through the dermis and then "a spiral, inverted, conical course" through the epidermis (Montagna & Parakkal, 1974, p. 371). Three segments of the duct, therefore, are typically distinguished: the coil or glomerate portion, which is continuous with and approximately the same length as the secretory coil; the undulating or helical portion in the dermis; and the spiraling epidermal portion or epidermal sweat duct unit (the acrosyringium), as shown in Figure 4-2.

The eccrine sweat glands just described must be distinguished from apocrine sweat glands, which differ in numerous respects. Eccrine glands open directly onto the surface of the skin and are found

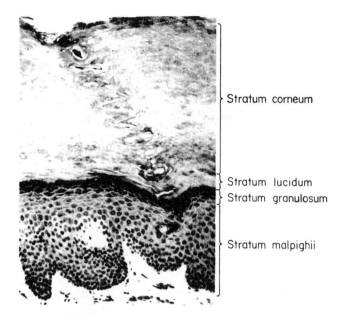

Stratum corneum

Stratum lucidum
Stratum granulosum

Stratum malpighii

Figure 4-2. Epidermis from the palm showing the spiraling duct of an eccrine sweat gland. (From *The Structure and Function of Skin* [3rd ed.] by W. Montagna and P. F. Parakkal. New York: Academic Press, 1974. Reprinted by permission.)

throughout the body surface in humans, the only exceptions being the glans penis and clitoris, labia minora, the inner surface of the prepuce (Montagna & Parakkal, 1974, p. 367), the external ear canal, and the lips (Pinkus, 1971). In contrast, the apocrine glands typically open into hair follicles (Grice & Verbov, 1977) and are found in large numbers in the axilla, the external auditory meatus, the areola region of the breast, and the circumanal area (Sato, 1977, p. 53). Again, in humans, eccrine glands secrete copiously, as opposed to the scant secretions of apocrine glands (Munger, 1971). Although there is some ambiguity concerning the chemical control of both glands (see pp. 62–66 for a discussion of eccrine glands), the dominant influence is adrenergic in apocrine and cholinergic in eccrine glands (Grice & Verbov, 1977; Munger, 1971). Since the apocrine glands lack prominent neural innervation in humans, Grice and Verbov suggest that the adrenergic influence may be exerted via sympathetic nerves that may terminate on nearby blood vessels (the final mode of transmission being vascular) and/or via circulating adrenalin secreted by the adrenal medulla. It is believed that the adrenergic stimulation brings about contraction of the underlying myoepithelial cells, which, in turn, causes the apocrine gland to discharge the previously stored excretory product (Grice & Verbov, 1977; Munger, 1971). The eccrine glands, on the other hand, are innervated by cholinergic fibers from the sympathetic nervous system, with the secretory product itself

being produced in response to the acetylcholine. The contribution of myoepithelial contraction to eccrine secretion is controversial (see page 65), but it appears to be less important than in apocrine glands. At a histological level, only one type of secretory cell is found in apocrine glands, as compared to the so-called "clear" and "dark" secretory cells seen in eccrine glands, the clear cells being unique to eccrine glands (Munger, 1971).

With respect to animals other than humans, eccrine glands are found most consistently on the friction surfaces of many mammals, such as the palms and soles of all primates and the digital pads of many animals (e.g., dog, cat, rat), and on the snouts of others; they are also located on the underside of the prehensile tail found in some New World monkeys and on the knuckle pads of chimpanzees and gorillas (Montagna & Parakkal, 1974, pp. 366–367). Relatively few mammals have eccrine glands on the hairy skin, though they are found in varying degrees among primates, being most abundant (other than in humans) in the great apes (Montagna & Parakkal, 1974). Spearman (1977) relates this scarcity of eccrine glands to the heavy fur covering of most mammals: Wetting by eccrine sweat would reduce the thermal insulation efficiency of the fur, and, in addition, evaporation of sweat from the surface of the fur would be far less effective at lowering body temperature than is the evaporation at the skin surface in humans. Apocrine glands are found in large numbers in several large, hooved species, such as the horse and cattle, where they are able to secrete copiously and are involved in evaporative water loss (Montagna & Parakkal, 1974, p. 367; Munger, 1971; Spearman, 1977).

The reader familiar with research on EDA will already have recognized that it is the eccrine gland that is of interest to psychophysiologists. It is these glands that are found on the sites from which electrodermal recordings are typically taken, such as the palms and soles in humans and other primates and the footpads of nonprimate laboratory animals (e.g., cat, dog, rat).[1] Similarly, it is the eccrine gland response as an index of sympathetic nervous system activity that is most often of interest in psychophysiological studies. In this context, it is to be noted that recordings are customarily obtained from friction surfaces, rather than from the general body surface. In terms of the functions of the skin mentioned in the preceding section, these areas are presumably more concerned with providing protection from abrasion and other mechanical assaults and with tactile sensitivity (at least in

1. EDRs are typically seen only in rather young dogs (Edelberg, 1982). Perhaps this observation is related to the recommendation that one should use only younger cats to study footpad sweat glands, since they are frequently blocked in older cats (Munger & Brusilow, 1961).

humans) than they are with temperature regulation. This regional variation in the function of the skin is discussed further after a description of the epidermis.

The Epidermis

Authoritative discussions of the epidermis can be found in Jarrett (1973a) and Montagna and Parakkal (1974). Earlier references are provided by Venables and Christie (1973). Unless otherwise indicated, the following summary is taken from Jarrett (1973a).

The epidermis is unique in that it shows a progression from dividing, metabolically active cells at its base to dead, keratinized protein at its surface. Keratin—a resistant, nonreactive, fibrous protein—plays an important role in the protective functions of the skin and is shed from the surface of the skin after a period of time (Montagna & Parakkal, 1974, p. 62). In general, then, the epidermis is characterized by cell production at its base, differentiation of these cells as they ascend toward the surface, and eventual death of the cells with subsequent formation of the outer keratin layer. Five strata or layers have been identified in this progression: the basal (or germinating) layer, the prickle cell (or spinous) layer, the granular layer, the stratum lucidum (found only in palmar and plantar epidermis), and the stratum corneum (also called the keratin layer or the horny layer). Four of these layers are shown schematically in Figure 4-3. The basal, prickle cell, and granular layers, together, are sometimes called the "stratum Malpighii" (Montagna & Parakkal, 1974, p. 18).

The "basal layer," only one cell thick, is the lowest layer of cells in the epidermis. A major function of this permanent population of germinating cells is the generation of epidermal keratinocytes (keratin-producing cells) to migrate upward and replace the cells above, which are differentiating and exfoliating. The cells in the basal layer are columnar, with their length perpendicular to the (undulating) dermo-epidermal junction, and have a prominent elongated nucleus. Intercellular cytoplasmic bridges connect the basal cells to each other. These are similar to, but less conspicuous than, those described below for the prickle cell layer.

As the keratinocytes produced by the basal layer move upwards, the cells flatten, the nucleus decreases in size, and other (histochemical) changes occur to create the cells known as the "prickle cell layer" or "spinous layer." Although its thickness varies greatly as a function of site, this layer usually is about five cells thick. In the lowest part of this layer the cells more closely resemble the basal cells, but as they move upward in the prickle cell layer they become flatter and the nucleus becomes smaller. The name derives from the appearance of the intercellular bridges under the light microscope, which are a conspicuous feature of this layer and are associated with

cytoplasmic processes, giving them the appearance of prickles. These prickles or intercellular bridges correspond to the desmosomes identified under electron microscopy as providing cell-to-cell contacts. These bridges are presumed to bind adjacent cells together while, at the same time, providing intercellular spaces for the diffusion upward of oxygen and nutrients needed for cellular nutrition.

Immediately above the prickle cell layer is the "granular layer," in which the cells have lost the nucleus and in which the cytoplasm contains chunks of granular basophilic material that have been called keratohyalin granules. Although they are a prominent feature of these cells, the function of keratohyalin granules is unclear (Jarrett, 1973a; Montagna & Parakkal, 1974, pp. 57–60). The loss of the nucleus in these cells is but one manifestation of the rapid destruction of the cytoplasmic contents that occurs prior to the formation of the stratum corneum or keratin layer.

The fourth layer, the "stratum lucidum," is a poorly staining hyalin layer that can be seen clearly only on the palms and soles and other friction surfaces where the epidermis is very thick (Montagna & Parakkal, 1974, p. 18). It has been suggested that the stratum lucidum represents a stage between the destruction of cells that takes place in the underlying granular layer and the fully developed stratum corneum (Jarrett, 1973a). This layer has been of longstanding interest in the context of electrodermal mechanisms, because it was thought to play an especially important role in the barrier function of the skin (Szakall, 1958). Current thinking, however, places the barrier function largely in the stratum corneum (Montagna & Parakkal, 1974, p. 64; Scheuplein, 1978a, 1978b; Venables & Christie, 1973).

The final layer is variously called the "keratin layer," the "horny layer," or the "stratum corneum." This is the tough outer layer, consisting of layers of flattened, dead cells with thickened keratin membranes. Over most of the body, these cell membranes form a loose "basket-weave" structure containing a mixture of lipids, waxes, sterols, and other products of the destruction of the keratinocytes. These contents of the cells are derived in part from the cellular breakdown and in part from the secretion of the sebaceous glands. In combination with water derived primarily from the secretion of sweat, though to some extent also from epidermal transpiration, this fatty material exists partly as an emulsion (Jarrett, 1973b). The cell walls are not only thicker than those in the lower portions of the epidermis, but they have undergone qualitative changes as well to make them the toughest part of the keratinized cell, and they are said to be firmly cemented together (Montagna & Parakkal, 1974, Chapter 2).

Another aspect of the epidermis deserves mention—its underside, or the dermo-epidermal junction.

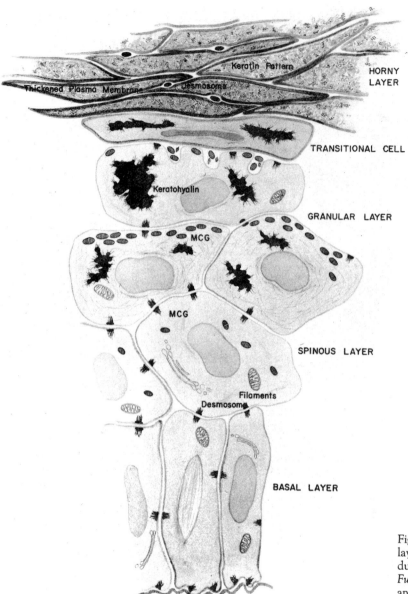

Figure 4-3. Schematic diagram showing the layers of the epidermis. The stratum lucidum is not shown. (From *The Structure and Function of Skin* [3rd ed.] by W. Montagna and P. F. Parakkal. New York: Academic Press, 1974. Reprinted by permission.)

In most areas of human skin, the lower surface of the epidermis and dermis are strongly interdigitated. The actual nature of this complex sculpturing can be seen most clearly in split-skin preparations. Montagna and Parakkal (1974) describe the underside of the epidermis as resembling "a series of branching ridges and mounds of different sizes which enclose channels, valleys, craters, and complex miniature systems of connecting caverns" (p. 32). Pinkus (1971, p. 8) shows fingerlike projections coming up from the dermis (called "dermal papillae"), which fit into cavities in the underside of the epidermis. The portions of the epidermis surrounding the dermal papillae are called "rete ridges." The ducts of glands and the pilary canals (associated with hair follicles) usually enter the epidermis at the nadir of the rete ridges (i.e., the lowest part of the epidermis, having the greatest projection into the dermis). Two possible functions of this complex structure of the dermo-epidermal border are to provide better adhesion between the two layers (Montagna & Parakkal, 1974, p. 3) and to provide a greater rate of production of new cells in the epidermis as a result of the greatly increased basal layer area (Montagna & Parakkal, 1974, p. 36).

Palmar and Plantar Epidermis

The most important of the specialized regional variations in the epidermis to the psychophysiologist are those associated with the palmar and plantar surfaces.

These surfaces show numerous characteristics distinguishing them from other types of skin. In contrasting the glabrous (smooth) skin of the palms and soles with the hairy skin of the general body surface, Ebling (1979) pointed to the absence of hair follicles and sebaceous glands and the presence of encapsulated sense organs on the palms and soles; the opposite pattern is found on hairy skin. The density of eccrine sweat glands is also greatest on the palms and soles in adults (Montagna & Parakkal, 1974, p. 367).

A striking aspect of the palmar and plantar surfaces is the presence of "dermatoglyphics"—the alternating ridges and sulci on the surface of the skin, which are well known for their use in fingerprinting. Dermatoglyphics are found on the friction surfaces of primates and marsupials, in addition to those of humans; these surfaces include the palms and soles, the ventral surface of the prehensile tail in some monkeys, and the knuckle pads of chimpanzees and gorillas (Montagna & Parakkal, 1974, p. 15). Sweat gland pores open at regularly spaced intervals in the center of the epidermal ridges, each of the duct orifices being surrounded by stratum corneum in such a manner that a cup-shaped depression is formed (Montagna & Parakkal, 1974, p. 378).

It has already been noted that one layer of the epidermis, the stratum lucidum, can be seen clearly only in the palms and soles. In addition, in the thicker epidermis from the palms and soles, the prickle cell layer cells show a more gradual differentiation as they ascend from the basal layer (Jarrett, 1973a), and the rete ridges are especially prominent on the palms and soles (Costello & Gibbs, 1967, p. 7; Ebling, 1979). The most dramatic difference from a histological perspective, however, is the 40-fold increase in the thickness of the stratum corneum (Montagna & Parakkal, 1974, p. 63). Scheuplein (1978b) describes the typical corneum as averaging about 19 cells deep with an overall thickness of approximately 10 μm, as compared to palmar and plantar thicknesses of 400–600 μm. In spite of the much greater thickness on the palms and soles, there are only twice as many cell layers, since each cell is over 30 times as thick as those on the rest of the body. In addition to the greater thickness, the horny layer in these areas differs from that in other skin in a number of respects: The cells break off more easily from mechanical trauma, are extremely brittle when dry, show greatly increased permeability to water and chemicals, and show a reduction in water-soluble substances (about half). The cell membranes in the horny layer of the palms and soles are also more soluble in alkali than those in other parts of the body.

From a developmental perspective, the eccrine glands of the palms and soles develop first, those in the axilla second, and those in the rest of the body last, suggesting a threefold classification (Montagna & Parakkal, 1974, p. 369). These developmental differences have led one author to suggest that the eccrine glands on the hairy skin are a later evolutionary development than those on the palms and soles, which are more closely related to those on the friction surfaces of other animals (Ebling, 1979).

These special features of the skin on the palms and soles are presumably related to the need for adaptation to weight bearing, abrasion, gripping, and tactile sensitivity. The greater thickness of the tough horny layer provides protection from the abrasion and mechanical assaults associated with load bearing and heavy work, and the presence of a high density of sweat glands keeps the corneum from becoming dry and brittle. The moisture from these glands also contributes to a better grip, as does the absence of hair and the oil from sebaceous glands (Costello & Gibbs, 1967, pp. 9–10). The increased surface area of the ridges and sulci has been compared with that of the treads on automobile tires by way of noting its importance for grip (Costello & Gibbs, 1967, pp. 23–24; Montagna & Parakkal, 1974, p. 15). This increased surface area also provides room for more tactile sensory organs (Montagna & Parakkal, 1974, p. 15), and the hydration of the corneum by sweat glands would also facilitate tactile sensitivity. Thus the most salient aspect of the skin on the palms is the provision of a thick but well-hydrated stratum corneum designed to promote grip and tactile sensitivity while providing protection from abrasion or other mechanical damage.

The Epidermal Barrier Layer

The role of the skin as a protective barrier has already been stressed. An important aspect of this function is the protection from penetration by various organic and inorganic chemicals. Although perhaps not the only aspect relevant to EDA, it is clearly the penetration of the epidermis by water and inorganic salts that is of central importance. This point is discussed more fully below, but for now it can be noted that SCRs reflect the greater conductivity provided by the sweat in the duct as it passes through the epidermis. It is against the background of a relatively impermeable barrier layer that these sweat gland responses can be seen. Without the barrier layer, there would be no measurable EDA, at least in the sense in which psychophysiologists employ that term. Consequently, the barrier layer constitutes a major aspect of the electrodermal effector system, and one that has been of long-standing interest to psychophysiologists.

Location of the Barrier Layer

In earlier reviews, there was much discussion as to the location of the barrier layer, but it was usually believed to lie between the germinating layer and the upper corneum. The potential sites were said to be the stratum compactum (viewed at the time as the more densely packed lower portion of the corneum), the stratum lucidum, or the granular layer (Edelberg, 1971; Fowles, 1974; Kuno, 1956; Lykken, 1968; Martin & Venables, 1966; Rothman, 1954). In contrast to this, Venables and Christie (1973) gave rather more prominence to Kligman's (1964) view that the entire stratum corneum serves as the barrier. Support for Kligman's view was provided as early as 1944 in experiments by Winsor and Burch (cited in Baker, 1979). Resistance to this view can be attributed to two factors. First, in standard histological preparations, the stratum corneum appeared to be quite porous as a result of (unrecognized) artifacts, creating the erroneous impression that it was far too porous (Baker, 1979; Kligman, 1964; Scheuplein, 1978b). Second, removal of the stratum corneum by adhesive-tape stripping revealed that it was only when the lowermost portion of the horny layer was reached that there was a rapid increase in the rate of water diffusion; this finding was interpreted by Blank (1953) as indicating that the barrier was at the base of the stratum corneum (Jarrett, 1980a). It is now recognized that the hyperbolic function obtained when water diffusion is plotted against the thickness of the remaining horny layer (Blank, 1953, 1965) simply reflects the fact that, with a layer of *uniform* resistance, the resistance is inversely proportional to its thickness (Baker, 1979; Jarrett, 1980a; Scheuplein & Blank, 1971).

It is now well established that the entire stratum corneum—with the exception of the desquamating surface cells—constitutes the barrier layer (Baker, 1979; Grice, 1980; Hurley, 1975; Jarrett, 1980a; Montagna & Parakkal, 1974, p. 64; Scheuplein, 1978a, 1978b, 1978c). The evidence for this derives from numerous sources, but there are two particularly clear findings: (1) When the stratum corneum is divided horizontally into two equal sheets, each half is an excellent permeability barrier (Jarrett, 1980a; Scheuplein, 1978b); and (2) the distribution of radiolabeled penetrants, after a period of diffusion into the corneum, shows decreasing concentration with greater distance from the surface (indicating resistance in the outer layers) (Baker, 1979; Hurley, 1975). There may be some question as to whether the resistance is homogeneous throughout the corneum. A few references suggest a gradient of increasing resistance from the surface to the base of the horny layer (e.g., Montagna & Parakkal, 1974, p. 64), whereas most treatments have accepted the view that the resistance is relatively uniform throughout the corneum (Baker, 1979; Hurley, 1975; Jarrett, 1980a; Scheuplein, 1978b). Scheuplein concludes that there "is little doubt" that resistance is uniform (1978b, p. 1692); in contrast, Grice argues that "the question has not yet been finally resolved" (1980, p. 2134). However, even Grice views the barrier as extending to the outermost keratinized cells. Thus, there is no ques-

tion but that the entire corneum acts as the barrier layer.

Characteristics of the Barrier

The nature of the epidermal barrier has been the object of extensive research. Given the conclusion just stated that the barrier resides in the horny layer, comprised entirely of dead cells, it would be expected that the barrier layer would consist of a passive membrane. This expectation has been confirmed (Baker, 1979; Scheuplein, 1978b). For example, experiments using *in vitro* preparations of the isolated corneum generally show values identical to those obtained for *in vivo* estimates for permeability to water, electrolytes, nonelectrolytes of low molecular weight, and steroids. The permeability characteristics of the isolated corneum, furthermore, last long after the skin is removed from the body. For *in vitro* preparations the diffusion data are the same, regardless of the direction of penetration, again suggesting a passive membrane. Finally, diffusion through the corneum can usually be understood in terms of physiochemical laws.

Scheuplein (1978b) has provided an elegant analysis of skin permeation, focusing particularly on alcohols, which are nonelectrolyte, polar, low-molecular-weight solutes. Although it is somewhat disappointing that little is said about permeability to electrolytes, there is, nevertheless, much to be learned from the discussion of other substances.

Several variables are important in understanding skin permeation. The permeability coefficient (k_p) is a constant, characteristic of a specific diffusing molecule for a given solvent, that has units of velocity (cm/hr). The coefficient of diffusion (D) is the rate of penetration (cm^2/sec) of a given solute through the membrane under specified conditions—that is, the mobility of the diffusing molecules. The membrane-vehicle partition coefficient (K) is defined by the ratio of the solute concentration at the surface of the membrane (C_m) to the solute concentration in the vehicle (C_v) applied to the membrane surface: $K = (C_m)/(C_v)$. This variable, then, refers to the relative solubility of the solute in the stratum corneum versus the solvent in which it is applied. Solutes that are more soluble in the stratum corneum will more readily leave the vehicle and enter the corneum (indicated by a higher value of K). Another important parameter is the thickness of the corneum (δ). With these definitions in mind, the following relationship may be understood:

$$J = \frac{KD(C_1 - C_2)}{\delta} = k_p \Delta c$$

This equation predicts the steady-state flux across the corneum (J) in the units $\mu mol/cm^2 hr$) as a function of the concentration gradient across the corneum ($C_1 - C_2$ or Δc) and the variables already defined. It can also be seen that $k_p = KD/\delta$. Thus the rate of flux across corneum (J) is a function of the permeability coefficient times the concentration gradient. The permeability coefficient (k_p), in turn, is directly proportional to the diffusion coefficient, D, and the membrane/vehicle partition coefficient (K)—indicating that flux, J, increases for solutes that move quickly through the membrane and that leave the vehicle readily—and is inversely proportional to the thickness of the membrane. An analogy to electrical circuits may be helpful here: flux is analogous to current flow, concentration gradient to voltage differences, and k_p to conductance. "Conductance" in this sense is proportional to the ease with which the solute can leave the vehicle and travel through the membrane, and is inversely proportional to the distance it must travel.

The importance of the membrane/vehicle partition coefficient, K, can be illustrated by examining the effects on the permeability coefficient, k_p, of increasing numbers of carbon atoms in alcohols as a function of vehicle. When these alcohols are applied in water as the solvent, there is approximately a 160-fold *increase* in k_p from 1 (methanol) to 10 (decanol) carbons. In the contrast, when the alcohols are applied as pure liquids, there is a 200-fold *decrease* in k_p as a result of increasing molecular size from 1 to 10 carbons. This effect was attributable primarily to the effect of K, which increases dramatically in the water vehicle series as the larger alcohols become less soluble in water and decreases in the pure liquid series. In general, it can be expected that in an aqueous vehicle K will increase as the penetrant becomes increasingly lipophilic, because the vehicle concentration, C_v, decreases markedly. For nonaqueous vehicles, on the other hand, K will generally decrease with increasingly lipophilic solutes. Permeability constants would be independent of carbon chain length if the vehicle's solvent properties were identical to those of the stratum corneum. In this regard, it has been found that butanol is very similar to the stratum corneum, being slightly less polar.

A factor not yet discussed, which has a large effect on the permeability of the skin, is hydration of the corneum. The corneum is extremely hydrophilic. The isolated corneum can absorb up to 600% of its weight if it is immersed in water, and the efficiency of the barrier layer is diminished with hydration (Baker, 1979). Under normal physiological conditions, the corneum is always partially hydrated by the diffusion of water from the body to the surface. This normal degree of hydration increases the permeability of the corneum to water by a factor of 10 compared to the water permeability of completely dry corneum, and with complete hydration there is a further twofold to threefold increase in water permeability (Scheuplein, 1978a). Corneal hydration is, of course, a function of the relative humidity of the air at the outer surface of the skin. At low relative humidities, there will be a gradient of decreasing hydration from the lower to the outer surface of the corneum. With increasing external relative humidity, the gradient decreases, and the corneum becomes more fully hydrated. According to Grice (1980), the hydration of the corneum increases in linear fashion as the relative humidity increases up to about 60–70%, after which it increases exponentially up to a relative humidity of 95%. A similar effect is produced by occlusive dressings, which prevent evaporation of water from the skin surface and eventually results in a well-hydrated corneum.

Another factor influencing barrier function is skin temperature. Using transepidermal water loss to assess permeability to water, Grice (1980) found that water permeability increases exponentially with rising temperature. Within the range of 25–39°C, the permeability to water doubled for an increase in skin temperature of 7–8°C. Since the variation in skin temperature on the palms falls within this range, the effect of skin temperature on water permeability might be a significant factor in electrodermal recordings. Temperature increases also contribute to the impairment of barrier function by occlusive dressings, since the temperature (as well as hydration) increases under such dressings (Baker, 1979).

Role of Lipids in Barrier Function

Given the repeated references to keratin as the major element in the stratum corneum, it might be assumed that keratin constitutes the barrier. However, this appears not to be the case; evidence has been found instead for the contribution of lipids. Nails are strongly keratinized, yet are permeable to water. Agents that alter the kertain molecule have failed to increase permeability appreciably, whereas several manipulations that affect lipids do increase permeability (Grice, 1980; Jarrett, 1980a). For example, organic solvents that extract lipids and proteolipids, such as a mixture of chloroform:methanol (1:1 or 2:1), produce a large increase in permeability to water and to small polar and nonpolar alcohols (Grice, 1980; Jarrett, 1980a; Scheuplein, 1978a). The results obtained from this delipidization imply that the corneum has been changed to a fairly porous, nonselective membrane allowing liquid-like diffusion through water-filled channels (Scheuplein, 1978a).

Other, convergent evidence has led to the hypothesis that essential fatty acids are involved in this contribution of lipids to the barrier function. The two major essential fatty acids found in the skin are linoleic acid and arachidonic acid, which are found in phospholipids within the lipoproteins of the cell membranes and in triglycerides (Baker, 1979). Diets deficient in essential fatty acids cause a great increase in transepidermal water loss in animals and humans. The effect in animals can be readily reversed by feeding them linoleic acid, and in humans topical application of linoleic-acid-rich sunflower seed oil reduces the rate of transepidermal water loss. Arachidonic acid has a deleterious effect (Grice, 1980). Thus it appears that linoleic acid is especially important for the integrity of the water barrier (Baker, 1979; Grice, 1980).

Pathways through the Barrier Layer

It is clear that the horny layer has some affinity for both polar (soluble in water) and nonpolar solutes, raising a question as to the paths by which these two types of solutes traverse the corneum. The two possible pathways are directly through the cells or via the intercelluar spaces. Given the much smaller cross-sectional area, permeability within the intercellular route would have to be substantially greater than for the transcellular route, if the former is to constitute a significant diffusion pathway.

One clue as to the permeability for polar and nonpolar solutes is the distribution of lipids in the corneum. Although this is not fully understood, Scheuplein (1978b) estimates that lipids comprise 80% of the intercellular material, 60% of the cell membranes, and 10% of the intracellular material. There has, nevertheless, been some debate as to the presence of intracellular lipid. In view of the saturation of the intercellular pathway with lipid, the intercellular spaces offer a route for lipid-soluble substances, but they are an unlikely pathway for polar solutes—for instance, low-molecular-weight alcohols (Scheuplein, 1978b, 1978c). The question of the presence or absence of intracellular lipid is important, since the presence of lipids would imply that lipid-soluble substances would encounter little resistance to direct, transcellular diffusion (Scheuplein, 1978b). Thus, if Scheuplein (1978b) is correct in arguing that lipids are present intracellularly, the transcellular route is the major pathway for lipid-soluble substances: Even though they could also diffuse via the intercellular spaces, the greater cross-sectional area would make the transcellular route more important. However, this issue remains somewhat in doubt at present (Scheuplein, 1978c).

Overall, the corneum is more permeable to lipid-soluble than to water-soluble substances, being described as "largely a lipid milieu" (Baker, 1979, p. 297). On the other hand, the stratum corneum shows an affinity for water, as already indicated in the discussion of the ability of the corneum to absorb several times its own weight in water (see "Characteristics of the Barrier," above). Whereas the amount and distribution of lipid largely determines the permeability to water-insoluble nonelectrolytes, the distribution of polar substances that bind water determines the permeability to water-soluble substances (Scheuplein, 1978b). It has already been suggested that polar solutes necessarily traverse the transcellular route, and it is believed that the intracellular material is rate-limit-

ing. Additional evidence in favor of this hypothesis is too complex to summarize fully, but it includes the following in the case of water-soluble nonelectrolytes (Scheuplein, 1978c):

1. When fully hydrated, the horny layer swells intracellularly, the intracellular keratin being mostly water. Thus water-soluble substances should be attracted to intracellular keratin.
2. Water-soluble molecules, such as alcohols from methanol through propanol, show nearly constant k_p's, which are consistent with the assumption that they travel via the aqueous intracellular keratin. If they were limited to the largely lipid intercellular pathway, the k_p's would increase dramatically as a result of rapidly increasing K's (resembling oil–water coefficients).
3. The affinity of intracellular keratin for water is presumed to be attributable to the formation of hydrogen bonds. Water and water-soluble molecules should not, therefore, diffuse freely. The energy required for diffusion has been found to be high—consistent with having to break three or four hydrogen bonds.
4. Molecules with numerous polar groups, permitting more hydrogen bonds, require even greater activation energy for diffusion.
5. The entropy of activation for water-soluble molecules is too large for diffusion through the small portion of the corneum occupied by the intercellular spaces.

In view of this convergent evidence, there is little doubt that water-soluble molecules follow the transcellular route, and it is likely that the binding by intracellular keratin serves as a major permeability barrier.

Appendageal Diffusion and Site Variations

Up to this point, only the pathway for diffusion directly through the horny layer has been considered. This pathway is, indeed, the major diffusion pathway during steady-state conditions with nonelectrolytes. As a result, the bulk of research has focused on the stratum corneum. However, sweat ducts, hair follicles, and sebaceous glands may act as diffusion shunts that are quantitatively important under some conditions. This is particularly the case for sweat glands on the palmar and plantar surfaces and for electrolytes, suggesting that an understanding of diffusion through these appendages is potentially important for electrodermal measurements. A systematic theoretical treatment of this topic has been presented by Scheuplein (1978a), from which the following summary is taken.

Lag Time

The basic question is this: How much do the appendageal diffusion shunts contribute to the total flux across the skin? An argument in favor of a contribution is that the diffusivity of solutes through these appendages is substantially greater than that of the pathway directly through the corneum. On the other hand, the cross-sectional area of the corneum is vastly greater than that of the appendages (by a factor of 1,000 to 100,000). Under *steady-state conditions* of diffusion, the greater cross-sectional area of the corneum more than offsets its lower diffusivity for water and most simple nonelectrolytes, so much so that the contribution of shunt diffusion becomes insignificant.

Prior to the development of steady-state conditions, however, shunt diffusion can be quite important. The reason for this is that there are differences in lag time for the two diffusion routes. "Lag time" refers to the period of time required for the first appreciable entry of the diffusing solute into the viable tissue beneath the corneum (which is highly permeable), and it is defined by the following equation:

$$T = \delta^2 / 6D,$$

where T is lag time, with δ and D defined as before. Since the pathways via the corneum and the appendages are approximately the same length, the greater values for D for the appendages result in substantially shorter lag times. As a result, diffusion occurs via the appendages earlier than it does through the corneum, resulting in a relatively large contribution of the appendageal diffusion shunts during the early phase of penetration. The other point to notice about this equation is that lag time increases as the square of the thickness. This factor tends to result in a longer lag time for the palms and the soles, although this effect is partially offset by the larger values for D. The actual values for lag time in the case of permeability to water are 83 and 106 min for the palm and sole, respectively, as compared to values of 11, 12, 9, 4, 1, and 22 min for the abdomen, volar forearm, back, forehead, scrotum, and dorsal surface of the hand, respectively (Scheuplein, 1978a, Table 1). From this perspective, therefore, the palmar and plantar sweat gland shunt pathway makes a significant contribution to total diffusion for a much longer time than in other areas of the body.

Diffusion of Electrolytes

The second variable of importance for diffusion through the sweat glands is the nature of the diffusing substance. In particular, since electrodermal measurements reflect the flow of electrolytes through the skin, it is the contribution of shunt pathways to the flow of electrolytes that is crucial. Unfortunately, Scheuplein (1978a) does not present data for electrolytes. However, it is clear that the sweat gland pathway is even more important for electrolytes than for nonelectrolytes. Electrolytes are not included in the generalization made in the preceding section concerning the dominance of the corneal pathway for steady-state diffusion. Scheuplein also states, "The permeability of intact stratum corneum to electrolytes is so extremely low that for all practical purposes these bypasses provide the only means of access" (1978b, p. 1679; see also 1978a, p. 1738, for a similar comment). It appears, therefore, that the sweat gland pathway is particularly important for the diffusion of electrolytes. In view of the greater density of sweat glands on the palms and soles than on other areas of the body, this statement is presumably even more applicable to these sites.

A less extreme view of the permeability of the stratum corneum to electrolytes is provided by Edelberg (1971, pp. 515–518), who summarizes evidence that ions can diffuse through the corneum if it is at least moderately hydrated. He also suggests that the current employed in SR measurements may facilitate ionic penetration of the epidermal pathway. Although Edelberg's view does not alter the conclusion reached above that sweat glands are of particular importance in the flow of current through the skin, it does point to a significant role of the corneum and to the importance of corneal hydration for SR.

The Palms and Soles

Given the much thicker corneum on the palms and soles and the conclusion that the corneum acts as the barrier layer, it might be expected that the palms and soles would be less permeable than skin on the rest of the body. In fact, this is not the case. The palmar and plantar surfaces are at least as permeable as the skin on the rest of the body—in spite of the greater thickness of the corneum—because D is much greater. In the case of permeability to water, D is 535.0 and 930.0 for the palms and soles, respectively, whereas it varies from 3.5 to 32.2 for other types of skin (Scheuplein, 1978a, Table 1). The net effect of these two opposing variables (D, δ) is to make the actual water flux through the skin slightly greater for the palms and soles than for most areas of the skin (Scheuplein, 1978a, Table 1): 1.14 (palms) and 3.90 (soles), as opposed to .34 (abdomen), .31 (volar forearm), .29 (back), .85 (forehead), and .56 (back of hand). As already noted, these differences between the palms and soles and the other skin do not cancel each other out in the case of lag time, since the lag time is proportional to the *square* of the thickness and is inversely proportional to only the first power of the D—that is, δ^2/D.

THE ECCRINE SYSTEM

General Characteristics of Sweat Glands

Composition of Sweat in Humans

It is now well established that in humans sweat is formed by the secretion of a plasma-like primary or precursor sweat in the secretory coil, which is then modified as it passes through the ductal portion of the gland. This two-stage hypothesis was first proposed (Thaysen, Thorn, & Schwartz, 1954) for the mammalian salivary gland, but it has been found to apply to other exocrine glands as well, such as the pancreas, sweat glands, and lacrimal glands (Prince, 1977). The most striking feature of the ductal action on the primary sweat is the reabsorption of sodium chloride (NaCl), resulting in a surface sweat of much lower NaCl content than is found in plasma.

An exact analysis of primary and surface sweat has been hampered by the small volume and difficulty of access for primary sweat and by possible evaporation of surface sweat or contamination by chemicals in the corneum. Nevertheless, some estimates have been made. The precursor sweat in humans is believed to contain approximately 147 mM sodium, 122 mM chloride, 5 mM potassium, and probably 10–15 mM hydrogen carbonate plus 15–20 mM lactic anion (Sato, 1977). The composition of surface sweat varies with rate of sweating, presumably reflecting a limited capacity of the duct to reabsorb NaCl; that is, the reabsorption mechanism cannot keep up as the sweat rate increases, allowing the NaCl content of the surface sweat to rise. In surface sweat the sodium varies from 10 to 104 mM, and chloride parallels the sodium concentration but is lower by 10–30 mM. In contrast to sodium and chloride, potassium varies inversely with sweat rate, from a high of 10–35 mM at low rates to a low approximating isotonic values (5 mM) at high rates. Calcium resembles potassium in this respect, declining from a high of 3–10 mM to an asymptote of 1–2 mM as the rate increases (Sato, 1977, p. 103). Sweat also contains very small amounts of numerous other ions.

Distribution of Sweat Glands

The total number of glands is fixed at birth, yet the total surface area of the body increases by a factor of seven from birth to adulthood (Montagna & Parakkal, 1974, p. 367). Consequently, the density of sweat glands decreases proportionately with maturation. Based on studies of cadavers, the total number of sweat glands on the human body ranges from 2 to 5 million (Kuno, 1956, p. 66). The same author reports average densities varying from 143 to 303 glands/cm^2 in adults. Regional variations are also important: The glands are densest on the palm and sole, intermediate

on the head, and least dense on the arms, legs, and trunk (Kuno, 1956, p. 65). Grice and Verbov (1977) report average densities ranging from a low of 120/cm^2 on the thigh to high of 620/cm^2 on the sole. Sato and Dobson (1970) report a similar estimate for the sole, but their lowest density of 64/cm^2 was found on the back.

Species Differences in Sweat Glands

It is mentioned above (see p. 54) that eccrine sweat glands are found on the footpads of many species. The eccrine glands in many of these species differ from those of humans, inasmuch as they lack the capacity for ductal reabsorption of NaCl. For example, the finding that the sweat secreted by the eccrine glands in the cat footpad is isotonic, and the demonstration of differences in the ductal portion of human and cat sweat glands led to the conclusion that sodium is not reabsorbed in the ductal portion of the cat footpad (Munger, 1961; Munger & Brusilow, 1961). In a comparison of different species, Sato (1977, pp. 55–56) found that it is unlikely that the sweat glands in either the cat or the rat reabsorb sodium, but that those from the monkey paw closely resemble human eccrine glands. Consequently, findings from monkey paw glands are most likely to generalize to humans. It is in this context that the *in vitro* preparations of the monkey gland by Sato and his colleagues represent a major advance in research on the functioning of eccrine glands.

Regulation of Sweat Secretion

Cholinergic and Adrenergic Influences

It has long been noted that the sympathetic nervous system fibers that innervate the sweat glands secrete acetylcholine; that the sweat gland responds to acetylcholine and to cholinomimetics; and that sweating is inhibited by the cholinergic blocker atropine. These unmyelinated cholinergic fibers are concentrated around the secretory portion of the sweat gland, but a few are found close to the coiled duct (Sinclair, 1973). There has always been some question as to why acetylcholine should be secreted by sympathetic fibers. The reason for this quite probably lies in the exocrine function of the sweat glands, since cholinergic innervation is common in exocrine glands.

There have, on the other hand, been numerous experiments also indicating an effect of adrenergic stimulation on sweating. The nature of this adrenergic effect—whether direct or indirect, real or artifactual—is unclear. In the past, it was assumed that only cholinergic innervation reached the sweat glands, precluding an adrenergic neural stimulation. More recently, this assumption has been challenged by Uno and Montagna (1975), who reported the presence of catecholamine-containing nerves around the sweat gland in the monkey paw. In view of their finding, direct neural adrenergic stimulation cannot be ruled out. At the same time, this finding of catecholamine-containing nerves in proximity to the sweat glands does not necessarily indicate that the adrenalin acts directly as a sudorific agent (Sato, 1977, p. 63). Of course, circulating catecholamines also may exert an adrenergic effect.

The possible contribution of adrenergic stimulation to sweating has been reviewed in detail by Sato (1977). Intradermal or intra-arterial injections of adrenalin induce sweating in human eccrine glands, but only at 10% of the rate of sweating induced by cholinergic stimulation and only with rather high doses. One hypothesis put forth is that there is an interaction between acetylcholine and adrenalin, the adrenalin potentiating the effects of acetylcholine. Repeating some of the earlier iontophoretic experiments, Dobson and Sato (1972) found that addition of adrenalin to acetylcholine increased sweat rates on the palm but not on the forearm for submaximal cholinergic stimulation. Sato (1977) suggested that this effect on the palm was attributable to a mild vasoconstriction of the dermal blood vessels, which slowed the disappearance of acetylcholine, but which was not severe enough to interfere with the nutrients and oxygen supplied to the gland. Sato (1977) did not, on the other hand, consider all adrenergic effects on sweating to be secondary to vasoconstriction. Specifically, it appears that *circulating* adrenalin increases the sweating induced by exercise. A small dose of systemically administered adrenalin increased sweating during exercise (Terada, 1966). Similarly, a 50% increase in sweating in stump tail macaques during exercise plus heat, as compared to heat alone, was largely eliminated by denervation of the adrenal glands (greatly reducing the exercise-induced release of adrenalin). The effect of denervation could be reversed by infusion of adrenalin.

Additional information has been obtained from Sato's (1977) *in vitro* studies of the isolated monkey sweat gland, which bears many similarities to the human sweat gland. This preparation eliminates the possibility of adrenergic circulatory effects, making it clear that any effects obtained are due to stimulation of the sweat gland. Using doses of epinephrine and Mecholyl (a cholinomimetic) that normally yielded a maximal secretory response, Sato found that most glands showed a stronger secretory response to Mecholyl than to epinephrine, although some of them responded equally to both chemicals. Averaged over all glands, the secretory rate for epinephrine was about half that for Mecholyl. Examining further those glands that initially yielded a poor response to epinephrine, Sato found that a higher dose of epinephrine did not increase the secretory rate, but that prior

stimulation with Mecholyl caused an increased secretory response to epinephrine. This occurred even with repeated changes of the medium to eliminate any residual Mecholyl and the addition of atropine to the medium containing epinephrine (in order to block any cholinergic effects). It was also found that adding epinephrine to a Mecholyl-containing medium did not increase secretion, whereas the addition of Mecholyl to an epinephrine-containing medium increased the secretory rate to the level of Mecholyl stimulation alone. This appears to contradict the hypothesis that epinephrine can potentiate cholinergic stimulation, at least when a concentration range is used that gives a maximal cholingergic response.

Alpha- and Beta-Adrenergic Influences

The effect of epinephrine was further examined by using an alpha-adrenergic (phenylephrine) and a beta-adrenergic (isoproterenol) stimulant to induce secretion. It was found that the beta-adrenergic stimulant was only slightly inferior to epinephrine but was twice as effective as the alpha-adrenergic stimulant. In addition, adding the beta-adrenergic stimulant to the alpha-adrenergic stimulant produced a partial additive effect. Because high concentrations were employed for the alpha- and beta-adrenergic agonists, Sato (1977) interpreted this partial additive effect to imply that there are separate alpha- and beta-adrenergic receptors in the sweat gland, in addition to the cholinergic receptor. The effects of alpha- and beta-adrenergic antagonists on alpha- and beta-adrenergic stimulants were also examined. Considerable specificity was found for the beta-adrenergic stimulant, in the sense that the alpha-adrenergic antagonist was relatively ineffective in inhibiting it. On the other hand, less difference was found between alpha- and beta-adrenergic antagonists for the alpha-adrenergic stimulant, suggesting less specificity in this case.

cAMP as the Second Messenger

Evidence from research on salivary glands, which are also exocrine glands sharing many features with sweat glands, have shown that cyclic adenosine 3,5'-monophosphate (cAMP) may serve as the intracellular mediator of the activation of the beta-adrenergic receptor. This led Sato (1977) to examine the possibility that cAMP is the "second messenger" of adrenergic sweating. Several findings supported this hypothesis. Application of cAMP itself stimulated sweating after a latent period of 15–20 min, the sweat rate being only 10% of that of cholinergic sweating. Application of theophylline, which prevents the destruction of endogenous cAMP, also stimulated sweat secretion, and this effect was not inhibited by either a cholinergic blocker (atropine) or an alpha-adrenergic antagonist (phentolamine). Theophylline was also found to enhance sweating induced by an alpha-adrenergic stimulant (phenylephrine) but not that induced by epinephrine. Recalling that theophylline is presumed to act on cAMP in the beta-adrenergic pathway and that beta-adrenergic stimulants can enhance sweating induced by alpha-adrenergic stimulants (but not by epinephrine, which is both alpha- and beta-adrenergic), these results simply suggest that theophylline added beta-adrenergic secretion to the alpha-adrenergic stimulation produced by phenylephrine. All of these findings point to a contribution of cAMP to beta-adrenergic secretion. The specificity of this association was shown by a failure of cholinergic stimulation to elevate the tissue level of cAMP (Sato, 1977, footnote, page 81). Thus, the evidence quite consistently indicates that cAMP is the second messenger in beta-adrenergic secretion.

Calcium as the Second Messenger

Another factor that plays a major role in the stimulation of secretion is the availability of calcium in the medium around the sweat gland. If calcium is removed by means of a chelating agent, sweating is completely inhibited. Sweating can be restored by reinstating the calcium at a concentration of 5 mM. Variations in magnesium have no effect. Calcium ionophore A23187, which increases the cell membrane's permeability to calcium by acting as a carrier to transfer calcium inside the cell, produces strong and persistent sweating after a delay of 10 minutes. This secretion is blocked by ouabain, an inhibitor of active transport, but it is not blocked either by atropine (a cholinergic blocker) or by propranolol (a beta-adrenergic blocker). On the other hand, removal of periglandular calcium inhibits the secretion of A23187-induced sweat, just as it does that induced by acetylcholine. This indicates that the ionophore A23187 requires extracellular calcium, being unable to mobilize enough cytoplasmic calcium to stimulate secretion, and also that extracellular calcium is essential for sweat gland functioning.

The secretion induced by A23187 is quantitatively similar to that induced by acetylcholine, and the effects of A23187 have been found to resemble the effects of cholinergic stimulation closely in numerous ways. Thus, Sato (1977) concluded that A23187 promotes the passage of calcium into the cell and, more tentatively, that the primary (possibly the only) function of acetylcholine may be to introduce calcium into the cell. That is, he suggested that an influx of calcium into the cell is a crucial initial step following pharmacological stimulation of the gland. It is even possible that acetylcholine itself is a calcium ionophore. On the other hand, another possibility is that acetylcholine causes an influx of sodium into the cell, which, in turn, triggers the influx of calcium. In any event, it seems clear that calcium influx plays a critical role as a second messenger in cholinergically induced secretion.

This finding, and the conclusion above that cAMP serves as a second messenger in beta-adrenergic secretion, are consistent with recent findings in the salivary gland. At present, it appears that in the salivary gland calcium influx into the acinar cell mediates the effect of both cholinergic and alpha-adrenergic stimulations, whereas cAMP is associated with beta-adrenergic stimulation (Sato, 1977, p. 75).

Energy Metabolism and Secretion

Yet another variable that is crucial for adequate secretory activity is the availability of peritubular glucose. Upon removal of glucose from the incubation medium, there is an exponential decline in the rate of secretion over a period of 10–15 min. Upon restoration of the glucose to the medium, secretion recovers rapidly over a 10-min period. If glucose is removed again, the decrease in secretion is even more rapid (5 min). Based on these studies, Sato (1977, p. 86) has concluded that the sweat gland depends exclusively on exogenous sources of energy, such as glucose. Although cellular glycogen does contribute in part to sweat secretion, he has estimated that this source of energy is too small to sustain a vigorously secreting gland for more than a few minutes.

It also appears that glucose is the major source of the metabolic energy for sweat secretion. This conclusion is based on two considerations. First, when the maximal sweat rate for the isolated gland is determined for equal concentrations of glucose, lactate, and pyruvate, it is found that glucose is a considerably more efficient substrate for sweat gland functioning than are lactate and pyruvate. Second, the normal plasma levels of pyruvate ($\ll 1$ mM) and lactate (1–2 mM) are substantially lower than that for glucose (5.5 mM). Thus the decreased efficiency and the much lower available concentrations for lactate and pyruvate make it unlikely that these substances make anything more than a minor contribution to the energy needs of the sweat gland.

With respect to the metabolism of glucose, Sato (1977, pp. 88–90) has summarized evidence that this occurs through the tricarboxylic acid cycle (also called the citric acid cycle or Krebs cycle), preceded by the glycolytic production of pyruvic acid and followed by oxidative phosphorylation to produce adenosine triphosphate (ATP) (see Guyton, 1976, pp. 908–912). The ATP, in turn, provides the energy necessary for secretory activity. The anaerobic metabolism of glucose to lactate is presumed not to make an important contribution to secretory activity.

Although the metabolic pathway just described has been found to be the major route of energy production, evidence has also been found that some glucose is metabolized via the pentose cycle (the phosphogluconate pathway), which provides the precursors nicotinamide-adenine dinucleotide phosphate (NADPH) and ribose for the synthesis of lipid, protein, and nucleic acid. Cholinergic stimulation produces a modest increase in the amount of glucose metabolized through the pentose cycle, but it does not increase the percentage of total glucose utilization attributable to the pentose cycle. In contrast, beta-adrenergic stimulation increases the portion of glucose metabolized by way of the pentose cycle. On this basis, there appears to be a stronger association between beta-adrenergic stimulation and the pentose cycle than is the case for cholinergic stimulation. It is also probable that intracellular cAMP mediates this effect of beta-adrenergic stimulation.

There is no direct evidence concerning the physiological significance of the pentose cycle in the eccrine sweat gland. However, Sato (1977, p. 90) has noted that in the parotid and submaxillary glands beta-adrenergic stimulation is known to induce hypertrophy of the salivary gland, and thus he has suggested that the pentose cycle metabolism of glucose may be involved in the control of glandular growth or hyperplasia. Since these salivary glands have both cholinergic and adrenergic innervation, Sato has suggested that the recently discovered adrenergic nerves around the sweat gland may serve a similar function. Profuse sweating causes morphological changes in the secretory cells (see page 72), and it is possible that beta-adrenergic stimulation provides a mechanism by which the diminished components of the cell may be replenished. Thus Sato appears to suggest that the beta-adrenergic stimulation may be involved in both the immediate restoration of the cell to its normal functioning and the stimulation of grandular growth as a result of continued beta-adrenergic stimulation.

The Role of Myoepithelial Tissue

The possible contribution of the myoepithelial cells to sweating has been a matter of much conjecture. Because of the resemblance of the myoepithelial cells to smooth muscle, it has long been held that preformed sweat is expelled by their contraction (Rothman, 1954). However, Sato (1977) has argued against this hypothesis. Using the isolated monkey eccrine sweat gland, he found that in the secretory coil the lumen was nearly collapsed prior to stimulation, suggesting that there is so little "preformed sweat" that an initial myoepithelial contraction could not expel an appreciable amount of sweat. It was found that the myoepithelial tissue responded to cholinergic stimulation—but not alpha- and beta-adrenergic stimulation—by reducing the length of the secretory coil to approximately two-thirds of its original length. This contraction required a few seconds to reach its maximum, but thereafter the myoepithelial tissue remained tonically contracted for the duration of cholin-

ergic stimulation, the contraction being terminated by the elimination of cholinergic stimulation (either through changing the medium or through the addition of atropine). During the period of cholinergic stimulation, the secretory coil lumen dilated lightly, with a maximum diameter of 10 μm. Equally strong stimulation of secretion could be produced by the calcium ionophore A23187, which resembles cholinergic stimulation in many respects (see "Calcium as the Second Messenger," above), but without contraction of the myoepithelial tissue. It is clear, therefore, that myoepithelial contraction is necessary neither for initiating nor for maintaining the secretion of sweat.

It has been reported that sweat can be seen rising and falling in a cannulating pipette at a frequency of .5–2 cycles per minute during sweating at a low rate, and it has been suggested that myoepithelial contractions may be responsible for this aspect of sweating. Sato (1977, p. 84), following Kuno (1956), argues that this phenomenon is due to variations in neural stimulation rather than to myoepithelial contractions. In particular, Sato stresses that stimulation (at a constant level) with pharmacological agents does not produce pulsatile sweating.

Two other possible functions for the myoepithelial cells, which have not been investigated, are that they provide a supportive structure for the secretory tubule and/or that the contraction of these cells serves to open the intercellular channels, with a resultant increase in the flow of fluid and metabolites to the secretory cells. Montagna and Parakkal (1974, p. 404) conclude that the myoepithelium probably serves as a supportive structure to resist large internal osmotic forces and to ensure the structural integrity of the intercellular canaliculi on whose patency the entire secretory process may depend. According to these authors, then, the myoepithelium may best be regarded as the cytoskeleton of the secretory coil.

Summary

Cholingeric stimulation via fibers from the sympathetic nervous system constitutes the major influence on the occurrence of sweating. Calcium acts as the second messenger in cholinergic stimulation, and its presence in the peritubular fluid is essential. Similarly, an exogenous source of glucose—metabolized via the tricarboxylic cycle—is required for the sustained secretion of sweat.

The contribution of adrenergic stimulation to sweat secretion remains poorly understood. In particular, there is no information concerning the significance of the observation of catecholamine-containing nerves near the sweat gland. Under physiological conditions, the clearest support has been found for a contribution of circulating adrenalin to exercise-induced sweating. *In vitro* studies have demonstrated the presence of both alpha- and beta-adrenergic receptors, with stimulation of the latter being approximately twice as effective as stimulation of the former. In the case of beta-adrenergic stimulation, cAMP has been implicated as the second messenger. Beta-adrenergic stimulation also appears to stimulate the metabolism of glucose via the pentose cycle. Although the functional significance of this adrenergic activation of the pentose cycle is only a matter of speculation at present, it may be associated with the restoration of the gland to normal functioning and the stimulation of glandular growth. Finally, earlier suggestions that adrenergic stimulation may influence sweating via myoepithelial tissue have not been supported.

Exciting though these advances are for the understanding of adrenergic influences, they leave unanswered many fundamental questions, which are raised in the following quotation from Sato (1977):

> Whatever the role of adrenaline, the undisputed fact is that thermal sweating as well as nervously excited sweating (including that induced by electrical nerve stimulation) are completely inhibited by atropine. Such an apparently clear-cut fact naturally leads to a simple but attractive conclusion that there are only cholinergic sudomotor fibers and thus the cholinergic mechanism in the eccrine sweat gland. . . . Nevertheless, lingering questions remain concerning the role of an adrenergic component of the sweat gland. Why is catecholamine present in the periglandular nerve? Why does the sweat gland respond to adrenaline if an adrenergic component is of no use at all? Why does adrenaline exert such a metabolic effect as stimulation of the pentose cycle in vitro? (p. 63)

Microscopic Structure

The microscopic structure of the sweat glands has been described by several authors (Grice & Verbov, 1977; Hashimoto, 1978; Montagna & Parakkal, 1974; Munger, 1971; Sato, 1977). Of these, Hashimoto's treatment is most comprehensive and is followed here except as otherwise noted. The secretory segment and the excretory duct differ in both structure and function, therefore requiring separate treatment. As noted above (page 53), the sweat gland consists of a simple tube made up of a single or double layer of epithelial cells opening onto the skin surface. The secretory segment and the coiled portion of the duct form an irregularly coiled glomerulus, located either in the lower part of the dermis or extending into the hypodermis. Outside of the glomerulus, the duct becomes the "straight duct" and then enters the epidermis, becoming the acrosyringium.

The Secretory Segment

When the secretory portion is viewed in cross-section, the outermost portion is surrounded by the basal lamina (or "basement membrane"), which is seen as a thin sheet surrounding the secretory segment. Above the basal lamina, a layer of myoepithelial cells line the outermost portion of the secretory tubule. These myoepithelial cells do not form a barrier, however, as gaps between them allow contact between the underlying cells and the basal lamina. The structure of myoepithelial cells resembles that of smooth muscle cells, and the bonds between them are similar to those seen between smooth muscle cells (Grice & Verbov, 1977). Between the myoepithelial cells and the lumen of the gland are found one or two layers of secretory cells (see Figure 4-4). The secretory cells are further subdivided into either clear, serous cells or dark, mucous cells. The serous cells either outnumber the mucous cells (Hashimoto, 1978) or occur in approximately equal numbers (Sato, 1977).

The serous cells have often been called "clear cells" because of their appearance under the light microscope. They resemble the epithelial cells seen elsewhere in the body, whose main function is to secrete ions and water, and this is assumed to be their function in the sweat gland as well. Given the assumption that they produce the serous precursor of sweat, these cells are more appropriately called "serous cells." These serous cells are noteworthy for their glycogen content and abundant mitochondria (Sato, 1977). The glycogen and the mitochondria are suggestive of the high rate of metabolic activity presumed to be necessary for the active secretion of sweat by these cells.

The dark or mucous cells contain abundant mucous granules and ribosomes, which appear dark under the light microscope; hence the term "dark

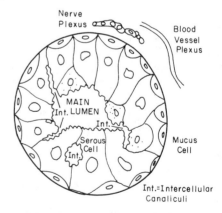

Figure 4-4. Schematic cross-section of the secretory segment showing serous cells, mucous cells, and intracellular canaliculi. (From "The Eccrine Gland" by K. Hashimoto. In A. Jarrett [Ed.], *The Physiology and Pathophysiology of the Skin* [Vol. 5, *The Sweat Glands, Skin Permeation, Lymphatics, and the Nails*]. New York: Academic Press, 1978. Reprinted by permission.)

cell." However, they are similar to the mucin-producing cells seen elsewhere in the body, and, since their main function in the sweat gland is presumed to be the secretion of the mucous granules, the term "mucous cells" is to be preferred. It is widely presumed (e.g., Grice & Verbov, 1977; Hashimoto, 1978; Sato, 1977) that these mucous cells are responsible for the secretion of mucosubstance (mucopolysaccharides).

The serous cells are pyramidal cells that rest on the basement membrane and/or on the myoepithelial cells and extend all the way—or almost all the way—to the lumen. The mucous cells, in contrast, are most clearly seen along the luminal border. However, mucous cells can be seen to extend all the way to the myoepithelial cells or the basal lamina. Montagna and Parakkal (1974) state that both types of cells rest upon the myoepithelial cells and the basement membrane (p. 376) and that the secretory coil consists of only a single layer of cells (p. 378). The mucous cells spread out when they reach the lumen to form a cap over the serous cells, separating them from the lumen. The dark mucous cells are particularly dense in this lining of the lumen, making them appear prominent in this location, and the luminal border of dark cells forms short microvilli. In addition to spreading to form this cap over the serous cells at the lumen, the dark cells tend to be wider at the luminal border and to narrow as they approach the periphery. Thus, they appear as an inverted pyramid with its base near the luminal border and with a cap extending even further in order to cover the serous cells along the lumen.

The serous cells, which are presumed to account for most of the secretory product, are at least partially bordered by the mucous cells on the lumen side and the myoepithelial cells on the periphery. It is not surprising, therefore, that much of the secretory activity occurs at the lateral surfaces where two serous cells abut. In this connection, it is important to distinguish between two intercellular spaces within the secretory gland: the "intercellular channels," which open to the basal interface, and the "intercellular canaliculi," which are extensions of the lumen (see Figure 4-5). Both of these structures can extend from the basement membrane to the lumen, but are separated from each other by a terminal bar or tight junction, which serves as a barrier to the passage of fluids. In addition, a tight junction separates the intercellular channel from the lumen; similarly, the intercellular canaliculi are bounded by a tight junction to prevent contact with the basal lamina. Thus the intercellular channels are open to the interstitial fluid but not the lumen, allowing the absorption of material from the interstitium. The intercellular canaliculi are open to the lumen but not to the interstitial fluid, permitting the secretion of sweat.

The process of absorption and secretion of fluids is facilitated by increasing the surface area provided for this function. To this end, the membrane of the serous

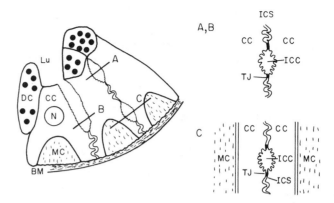

Figure 4-5. Diagrammatic representation of the secretory coil and the intercellular canaliculi. A, B, and C represent the height of the horizontal sections on the left, and on the right the schematic picture of each section is shown. LU, lumen; ICC, intercellular canaliculi; MC, myoepithelial cell; CC, clear cell; DC, dark cell; ICS, intercellular space or channel; TJ, tight junction. (From "The Physiology, Pharmacology, and Biochemistry of the Eccrine Sweat Gland" by K. Sato. *Review of Physiology, Biochemistry, and Pharmacology*, 1977, 79, 51–131. Reprinted by permission.)

cells along the intercellular canaliculus can be seen to be studded with microvilli to facilitate secretion; similarly, the membranes in the intercellular channels can be seen to contain numerous slender projections, which are interdigitated. In addition, the intercellular canaliculi themselves increase the surface area available for secretion. The evidence tends to suggest, therefore, that most—if not all—of the absorption and secretion by the serous cells takes place at their lateral borders, on the intercellular channels and the intercellular canaliculi.

The Coiled Duct

The ductal portion of the sweat gland is divided into three relatively distinct segments: the "coiled duct" intermeshed with the secretory segment in the glomerulus; the "straight duct" running from the glomerulus to the epidermis; and the "acrosyringium," or epidermal sweat duct unit. The sweat gland makes a rather abrupt transition from the secretory segment to the coiled duct. In contrast to the secretory segment, the coiled duct consists of a regular double-cell layer. Since they border the lumen, the cells in the inner layer are called "luminal cells," whereas the cells in the outer layer are referred to as "basal cells" because they are surrounded by the basal lamina. The basal lamina surrounding the duct is thin and inconspicuous (Montagna & Parakkal, 1974, p. 378).

Lanthanum has been used to determine the permeability of the intercellular spaces. With this technique, it has been demonstrated that a tight junction provides a barrier to diffusion at the luminal end of the interspace between the luminal cells. Otherwise, the lanthanum diffuses freely in the interspaces between the basal cells and those between the luminal cells, as well as through the basal lamina. Thus, the major barrier to diffusion across the duct wall is found at the lumen between the luminal cells.

Numerous microvilli on the luminal surface of the luminal cells provide increased surface area. There is also a moderate infolding of the lateral borders of the luminal cells, resembling—though not as great as—that seen in the serous cells of the secretory segment. Villous folds at the base of these cells interdigitate with a similar villous border in the basal cells (Montagna & Parakkal, 1974, p. 389). A distinctive feature of the luminal cells is the presence of a cuticular border surrounding the lumen as described by histologists, which consists of a band of tonofilaments and microfilaments extending from the luminal villi into the cytoplasm along the luminal membrane. There are numerous mitochondria in the luminal cells, though not as many as in the basal cells.

The basal cells are particularly noteworthy for their large number of mitochondria (generally associated with metabolic activity); moderate amounts of glycogen may also be found in these cells. The channels between luminal cells continue between basal cells, which also have interdigitating microvilli along their lateral borders (Montagna & Parakkal, 1974, pp. 387–389).

The Straight Duct

The so-called "straight duct" actually follows an undulating course through the dermis. It closely resembles the coiled duct, inasmuch as the same cell types and configuration are found. There are, nevertheless, a few prominent differences. The lumen is narrower in this portion of the duct than in the other two segments of the duct (Montagna & Parakkal, 1974, p. 378). As already noted, there are fewer mitochondria, less glycogen, and less activity of sodium- and potassium-activated adenosine triphosphatase (Na+K-ATPase) in the basal cells of the straight duct than of the coiled duct, and the basal cells also contain more tonofilaments. There is a greater interdigitation of the lateral membranes of adjacent luminal cells. The cuticular border surrounding the lumen in the luminal cells is more prominent in the straight duct.

One of the most striking differences concerns the tight junctions found at the luminal end of the interspaces between luminal cells. In the straight duct this junction projects into the lumen, whereas in the coiled duct there is no projection. Hashimoto (1978) discusses several possible functions of these projections into the lumen: (1) to serve as a valve to impede the flow of sweat, allowing more time for reabsorption of sodium from the precursor sweat; (2) to contribute a reserve surface area for the lumen wall to keep the lumen open and to facilitate the adjustment of the wall to the deforming forces to which the skin is subjected; and (3) to increase the surface area available for reabsorption. There is little basis for choosing among these alternatives at present, although the assumption that the majority of reabsorption occurs in the coiled duct argues somewhat against the third hypothesis.

The Acrosyringium

The acrosyringium, or intraepidermal sweat duct unit, begins at the point at which the straight duct enters a rete ridge. The inner layer of luminal cells resemble those of the straight duct, continuing to show numerous villi, a somewhat less prominent cuticular border (Montagna & Parakkal, 1974, p. 389), and projections into the lumen at the intercellular junctions. In the human embryo, the luminal cells contain many multivesicular bodies, assumed to represent lysosomes involved in cytoplasmic digestion and lumen formation. Although less dense in the adult acrosyringium, these lysosomes are still prominent. Their presence may reflect a process of lumen formation in new luminal cells similar to that in the embryo. A more interesting hypothesis, however, is that they are associated with the reabsorption of sweat or the absorption of foreign materials in the luminal sweat: Hashimoto (1978) suggests that materials and fluid absorbed from the duct in the epidermis cannot easily be returned to the interstitium, and, consequently, must be digested within the luminal cell lysosomes.

Outside the layer of luminal cells in the rete ridge portion of the acrosyringium, there are two or three layers of cells that separate the luminal cells from the surrounding epidermis. Continuing laterally, one encounters the Malpighian cells, the basal cells, and the basal lamina of the epidermis. There is evidence of mitotic activity, suggestive of the production of keratinocytes, in the basal cells of the straight duct just below the entrance into the epidermis and in the acrosyringium in the lower portion of the rete ridge.

It is believed that the epidermal basal cells do not contribute keratinocytes for the acrosyringium, but that these must come from the mitotic cells just described (Hashimoto, 1978). In general, the process of keratinization is more advanced in the acrosyringium than in the surrounding epidermis. At the level of the epidermal basal cells, the luminal cells already have small keratohyaline granules (characteristic of the granular layer). The number of these granules increases rapidly in the duct at the level of the lower epidermis. Thus the sweat gland pore opening onto the surface of the skin is lined with keratinized cells.

The Production of Sweat

Mechanism of Secretion of Precursor Sweat

The mechanism by which precursor sweat is formed and secreted into the lumen is not well understood. In the mammalian salivary gland, the initial step is thought to be an increased (passive) permeability of the basal membrane, allowing sodium to flow in and potassium to flow out of the cell (Prince, 1977). An electrogenic sodium pump at the apical (luminal) membrane is believed to be responsible for pumping the sodium out of the cell and into the lumen. Electrophysiological measurements show that, when stimulated with acetylcholine, the basal membrane resistance decreases and the potential increases in connection with secretion (Prince, 1977). However, in cells with high resting membrane potentials, there is an initial depolarization followed by the customary hyperpolarization. The luminal membrane also hyperpolarizes during secretion.

Hashimoto (1978) and Morimoto (1978d) have summarized the now traditional view of the secretion of sweat in the secretory coil. As already noted, the primary secretion is isotonic, with the concentration of sodium being the same as that in the incubation medium. The first step in the secretion of sweat is the depolarization by acetylcholine of the infolded basal membranes of the serous cells along the basal lamina and the intercellular channels. This depolarization allows sodium and other interstitial fluids to diffuse into the cell, a process aided by the great surface area provided by the microvilli projecting into the channels. The influx of interstitial fluid stimulates the active transport of sodium at the cell membrane along the intercellular canaliculi, which open into the lumen (it will be recalled that the canaliculi are separated from the intercellular channels by tight junctions). The other constituents of sweat then follow passively. Water is drawn into the canaliculi by the osmotic gradient produced by the active transport of sodium. The active transport mechanism involves Na+K-ATPase with the energy supplied by both aerobic and anaerobic glycolysis.

Sato (1977) summarized his own work on the electrophysiology of the secretory process in the sweat gland, using the isolated monkey gland. The results obtained yield a picture that is not completely consistent with the description above of the assumed functioning of sweat glands, nor do they confirm expectations based on the functioning of salivary glands. The primary problems are that the lumen becomes negative relative to the bathing medium during secretion, and that the basal membrane does not show a decrease in resistance.

Measurements of transepithelial potential (i.e., between the incubating medium and the lumen of the secretory coil) revealed a resting potential very close to zero, which, upon stimulation with Mecholyl or acetylcholine, showed a sharp, spike-like lumen-negative pulse. This was followed by a gradual rise over a period of 1 min to a steady-state lumen-negative potential ranging from 2–10 mV (see Sato's Figure 45). Atropine, cyanide, and ouabain inhibited the development of this potential. Based on studies of the salivary gland, it had been expected that an electrogenic sodium pump (mediated by Na+K-ATPase) would have produced a lumen-positive potential. Consequently, this result suggests that a somewhat different mechanism is involved in the sweat gland.

Using impedance measurements, the length constant of the lumen, measured by moving the luminal current electrode back and forth along the lumen, was found to have a mean of 83 μm. Based on the length constant, it was calculated that the transepithelial impedance was 2.2. Ω-cm^2, an (expected) extremely low value characteristic of epithelia that secrete isotonic fluids.[2] The validity of this analysis was checked by calculating the diameter of the lumen from these values and finding that this estimate agreed with the actual value of 9 μm.

Measurements of the potential difference across the basal membrane of the cells (i.e., between the cell interior and the medium bathing the outside of the gland) revealed two types of cells. One type, assumed to be myoepithelial cells, showed a steady (noiseless) baseline of 50–70 mV (cell interior negative) and an impedance across the cell wall of 50–100 MΩ. In response to cholinergic stimulation, the potential difference slowly increased (in the range of 10–15 mV in the example shown in Figure 47 of Sato, 1977) over a period of several seconds. The second, and more common, type of cell was assumed to be a secretory cell. These cells exhibited a more variable or noisy baseline averaging 63 mV (range 40–80 mV) potential difference with superimposed depolarizing spikes and an impedance of 20–30 MΩ. There was a sharp, transient depolarization (10–20 mV) upon cholinergic stimulation, but no other noteworthy effects on the resting potential; nor was there any effect at all on impedance. Adrenergic stimulation (epinephrine) produced a more gradual but still transient depolarization (5–10 mV). Stimulation of sweating with the calcium ionophore A23187 failed to produce changes in either potential or resistance. Again, these results are contrary to expectations based on the functioning of salivary glands and pancreatic acinar cells. In particular, the failure to find a decreased impedance with cholinergic stimulation is contrary to the usual finding of

2. Although Sato does not define "length constant," I assume that it refers to the length of the secretory tubule required for a change in transmembrane voltage to fall to .37 of the maximum value (cf. "space constant" in Woodbury, 1965, p. 37).

greatly increased permeability of the basal membrane. A possible explanation for this failure to find a decrease in impedance in connection with cholinergic stimulation and the subsequent rapid flux of NaCl across the epithelia is a recently proposed model in which NaCl is transported as a neutral particle through a membrane possessing a very high resistance.

Although the results of these studies do not appear to support a parallelism with the mechanisms seen in other exocrine glands, they do show a clear similarity to other transporting epithelia classified as "leaky" (as opposed to "tight") epithelia (Frömter & Diamond, 1972). The transporting epithelia include such tissues as kidney tubules, urinary bladder, gall bladder, intestinal and gastric mucosa, cornea, and frog skin, in addition to exocrine glands. The characteristics of leaky epithelia include the transport of sodium and water isotonically, high water permeability, and a low transepithelial resistance with a potential near zero (Sato, 1977). The crucial feature of these epithelia is the leakiness of the terminal bar (tight junction) in the intercellular spaces, which separates the lumen from the interstitial fluid. The permeability of the terminal bar to water and small molecules provides a low resistance pathway through the tissue, as a result of which 96% of the transepithelial current passes *around* the cells. Thus this leaky terminal bar provides a paracellular shunt pathway. Sato (1977) has concluded on the basis of his studies that the monkey eccrine gland shows most of the characteristics of leaky epithelia and thus may be assigned to that classification. Presumably, this conclusion generalizes to the human gland, though that remains to be demonstrated directly. Unfortunately, as Sato notes, at present this conclusion does not have any clear implications for the mechanisms of secretion in the sweat gland, since the mechanism of membrane transport in the other leaky epithelia is still not well understood.

In speculating on possible mechanisms for fluid transport in the sweat gland, Sato (1977) has estimated that with a lumen-negative transepithelial potential of 6 mV, approximately one-third of the sodium flux could be attributed to passive diffusion via the paracellular shunt pathway under the influence of the electrochemical gradient for sodium. This still, of course, requires a mechanism for maintaining the secretory potential and for promoting the diffusion of the remaining sodium flux. It is assumed that the lumen negative potential is the result of a 6-mV depolarization of the luminal membrane (i.e., the luminal potential becomes 6 mV less than the basal membrane potential), and that this is the site of some type of active transport mechanism. As already noted, the usual electrogenic sodium pump would be expected to produce a lumen-positive potential. Consequently, Sato considers possible mechanisms involving active transport of chloride ions or bicarbonate ions into the lumen or a neutral sodium–potassium pump accompanied by an increased permeability to chloride. However, none of these models easily fit the available data; nor, for that matter, can they easily be excluded. Consequently, none can be chosen over the others at present.

In spite of this ambiguity, it can be noted that the assumptions common to all of the models are that the initial step in secretion involves an influx of calcium across the basal membrane and that some type of active transport mechanism is located at the luminal (canaliculi) but not at the basal membrane. Calcium is assumed to play a crucial role in cholinergic stimulation (see "Calcium as the Second Messenger," above). Calcium's contribution to adrenergically stimulated sweating is unclear, though it appears to be required in this case as well. Similarly, cAMP clearly plays a role in adrenergic sweating, but its contribution, if any, to cholinergic sweating is unclear (see "cAMP as the Second Messenger," above).

Ductal Reabsorption of Sodium

As noted above, it is now accepted that the primary or precursor sweat is isotonic, whereas the sweat reaching the skin surface is hypotonic in humans and in the monkey palmar sweat gland. Early studies (e.g., Bulmer & Forwell, 1956; Cage & Dobson, 1965) attempted to estimate the sodium content in the primary sweat by extrapolating from the dependence of sodium concentration on rate of sweating. The conclusion from these studies that the primary sweat was approximately isotonic was confirmed by micropuncture studies of the secretory coil of the human sweat gland (Schulz, Ullrich, Frömter, Holzgreve, Frick, & Hegel, 1965, Ullrich, 1967), as well as by direct collection of sweat from the secretory coil of the isolated monkey sweat gland (Sato, 1973). This finding of an isotonic primary sweat, combined with the observation of hypotonic surface sweat, led to the conclusion that NaCl is reabsorbed in the ductal portion of the gland as the sweat passes through on the way to the surface.

The now well-established mechanism proposed for the reabsorption of NaCl in the duct involves the active transport of sodium, as is the case in the transport of ions across a number of epithelial membranes: frog skin, kidney troubles, urinary bladder of the toad, and salivary glands (Ussing, 1960). Current views of the process of sodium reabsorption can be found in Hashimoto (1978), Morimoto (1978d), and Sato (1977). The following summary is indebted to Sato's (1977) treatment unless otherwise noted, as his is the most comprehensive discussion.

An electrical potential, often associated with the active transport of sodium in other epithelial tissues, has been found in the sweat gland as well: Lumen-negative potentials of approximately 50 mV relative to the interstitial fluid have been recorded in human glands (Schulz *et al.*, 1965), and comparable potentials of 70 mV were obtained with an isolated monkey sweat gland (Sato, 1977, p. 106). This potential gradient opposes the passive diffusion of sodium through the duct wall. Similarly, since the luminal concentration of sodium may fall as low as 10 mM, the chemical concentration gradient between the lumen and the interstitial fluid opposes the reabsorption of sodium. Thus, the total electrochemical gradient opposing the reabsorption of sodium can reach 130 mV (Sato, 1977, p. 106), indicating the impossibility of passive diffusion and, consequently, the need for active transport of sodium. The presence of Na+K-ATPase in the duct also suggests the presence of an active sodium pump, as does the finding that ouabain (an inhibitor of active transport) blocks sodium reabsorption. All evidence, therefore, converges to indicate that sodium is actively reabsorbed by the duct.

In contrast to sodium, it is generally accepted that chloride ions diffuse passively down an electrochemical gradient. Although the chemical gradient opposes the passive reabsorption of chloride ions, the electrical potential facilitates it. Since the electrical gradient somewhat exceeds the chemical gradient, on balance the passive diffusion forces favor reabsorption of chloride.

The selective reabsorption of NaCl in the duct implies little or no permeability of the duct to water, which remains in the duct in spite of decreasing electrolyte concentration. Some permeability to water has been demonstrated (Mangos, 1973), but the permeability is low relative to that of sodium and chloride ions.

Aside from these general conclusions, the details of the mechanism of reabsorption remain to be demonstrated directly with sweat glands. Nevertheless, at present the "simplest and most attractive" model is that based on sodium transport in frog skin and in the salivary duct (Sato, 1977, p. 106). The basic elements of this model are the *passive* diffusion of sodium from the lumen to the interior of the luminal cells, combined with active transport via a sodium–potassium exchange pump out of the duct and into the interstitial fluid at the contraluminal (peritubular) cell membrane. The luminal membrane is assumed to be more permeable to sodium than to potassium or chloride, causing it to act as a sodium electrode. Similarly, the peritubular membrane behaves like a potassium electrode because of greater permeability to potassium. The transepithelial potential, then, results from the sum of these passive diffusion potentials (see Fowles & Venables, 1970a, for a more extensive discussion of this model).

The precise location of the sodium pump and the pathway for diffusion through the duct are not clear. Hashimoto (1978) suggests that the influx of sodium and other substances into the luminal cell activates a sodium pump, which then transports them into the intercellular channels (including those between luminal and basal cells). From there, they could either pass directly to the interstitium, or they could be reabsorbed into the basal cells. As noted above, the basal cells resemble ion-secreting cells elsewhere in the body, implying an important contribution of these cells to sodium reabsorption.

In the frog skin model described above, it is assumed that sodium is exchanged with potassium. Such an assumption is consistent with the finding that potassium concentration varies inversely with flow rate; that is, as more sodium is reabsorbed at low rates of sweating, more potassium is exchanged, and the concentration of potassium in the sweat increases. Other speculation, however, has centered on a possible exchange of hydrogen ions for sodium during active transport. As with other aspects of ductal reabsorption, the resolution of this question requires further research.

A recent finding suggests a significant effect of beta-adrenergic stimulation on reabsorption. Based on earlier reports that the beta-adrenergic agonist isoproterenol promoted increased sodium reabsorption in the rat salivary gland (the submaxillary main duct), Sato (1977, p. 110) found that with isoproterenol stimulation the sweat obtained from the open end of the proximal (or coiled) duct showed substantially lower sodium concentrations than expected from cholinergic stimulation (with identical sweat rates). Since isoproterenol stimulation does not affect the concentration of sodium in primary sweat, this result was attributed to increased reabsorption. If this preliminary finding is supported by future work, it suggests that beta-adrenergic stimulation may exert a significant effect on the ductal reabsorption of sodium. It should be noted that this effect was found in the coiled duct, which is readily accessible to neurotransmitters and to circulating adrenalin.

Other Influences on Sweating

Aldosterone and Acclimatization

Aldosterone is a mineralocorticoid, secreted by the adrenal cortex, which promotes increased reabsorption of sodium in the kidney. It is secreted primarily in response to a deficiency of sodium or of fluid volume. The effects of aldosterone on the sweat glands have been detailed by Morimoto (1978b): After a latency of 1 or 2 days, the sodium concentration decreases and remains low until approximately 2 days after aldosterone administration has ceased. The immediate effect of the aldosterone is to stimulate the synthesis of a protein, but the function of the protein is a matter of dispute. The alternative hypotheses are that the aldosterone-induced protein (1) increases the available energy for active transport or (2) promotes the entry of sodium into the cell. Dobson and Slegers (1971) have provided evidence in support of the active transport hypothesis, but the matter cannot be considered resolved at present.

Aldosterone is an important component of the process of acclimation to experimentally induced climatic changes or acclimatization to natural climatic changes (Morimoto, 1978a). The loss of water and salts that is secondary to profuse sweating in response to high environmental temperatures tends to stimulate the secretion of aldosterone. In addition, a cardiovascular adjustment associated with working in heat involves increased blood flow to the skin and a compensatory decrease in the flow of blood to the kidney, which is also a stimulus for aldosterone secretion. As might be expected, the decreased concentration of sweat sodium in the summer (mean value of 45.7 mEq/L) as compared with the winter (77.4 mEq/L) is attributable to greater secretion of aldosterone during the summer.

In addition to the aldosterone-induced reduction in sodium, the eccrine system adapts to high temperatures by increasing the sweat rate (for a given rectal temperature) and by initiating sweating at lower rectal temperatures (Morimoto, 1978a). The increased sweat rate is due to an increased output per gland, since the number of active glands does not increase. This adaptation in glandular function can be produced by numerous methods that continuously activate the sweat glands (e.g., electrical or pharmacological stimulation and local heat as well as high environmental temperatures), suggesting that profuse sweating is the stimulus for morphological changes. Degenerative changes observed after one period of profuse sweating include (among others) cellular atrophy and the depletion of glycogen from both secretory and duct cells (Dobson, 1960). The glands rapidly adapt to this stress, however, as the degenerative changes diminish quickly with repeated daily induction of profuse sweating. The glycogen adaptation is particularly fast: After the initial episode, the cells reacquire the glycogen, which is not depleted by additional periods of profuse sweating.

The finding that heat-adapted subjects begin to sweat at lower rectal temperatures has been attributed by some investigators to changes in the sensitivity of the thermoregulatory center in the hypothalamus. An alternative explanation makes this phenomenon secondary to the increased sweat response: Chen and Elizondo (1974) have proposed that the lower rate of sweating in unacclimatized subjects allow the sweat to be totally reabsorbed in the duct at low rectal temperatures, whereas the greater amount of sweat is acclimatized subjects exceeds the ductal reabsorptive capacity and reaches the surface.

Another, more delayed aspect of adaptation to tropical climates appears to be an ability to decrease sweating with reduced heat stress. Several investiga-

tors have found that long-term residents of the tropics more readily avoid excessive sweating with less severe heat stress (they sweat equally strongly with severe heat stress), and it is possible that this form of adaptation requires as much as 6 years (Morimoto, 1978a).

Antidiuretic Hormone

There has been considerable speculation that antidiuretic hormone-(ADH) might increase water reabsorption in the duct and, consequently, cause a reduction in sweat rate. ADH does increase water permeability in the kidney and in other epithelial tissue (amphibian skin, toad bladder, salivary gland duct). Nevertheless, the results to date indicate that ADH does not affect sweat rate when administered systemically in physiological or pharmacological doses, although topical administration can have a local effect (Morimoto, 1978b).

Demographic Characteristics: Sex, Age, and Race

A lower sweat rate has repeatedly been found for females than for males (Morimoto, 1978e). This difference is found across a wide range of heat stress, but it is larger as the heat stress increases. In addition, females show smaller sweat responses to pharmacological stimuli. These differences have been attributed to a greater gland flow in men, women having been found to have slightly (though not significantly) *more* active glands. Women also showed their maximal glandular flow at a lower level of heat stress than men.

Studies of the effect of increased age on thermal sweating, reviewed by Morimoto (1978e), have consistently shown a decreased response *per gland* for males (e.g., less total sweating for a given heat stress, delayed onset of sweating, failure to show as much variation in sweating with work load changes, and a lower response to Mecholyl stimulation). In sharp contrast, females have not shown declines in sweat response with increasing age. One study of spontaneous *digital* sweating (Silver, Montagna, & Karacan, 1964, 1965) reported that the number of active glands as well as the output per gland decreased with age, but did not find a sex difference in either age group. Sweat chloride concentrations (with the rate of sweating controlled) have been found to rise with age in one study, suggesting a decrease in sodium reabsorption.

Attempts to draw inferences concerning racial differences in sweating are complicated by the difficulty of obtaining data under precisely the same conditions, the small numbers of subjects used in typical studies, and the likelihood that differences are due to acclimatization effects. Morimoto (1978d) suggests that examinations of groups living in different climates show an increase in the number of active sweat glands from northern latitudes to the tropics. Minimal differences have been found, on the other hand, for races studied under the same conditions (e.g., Caucasians vs. Negroes or Japanese vs. Caucasians). It appears, therefore, that racial differences in sweating are difficult to demonstrate, apart from those atrributable to acclimatization. In this context it should be noted that some investigators have argued that the number of active glands is established by 2 years of age, although other investigators have failed to find supporting evidence for this (Morimoto, 1978a).

MECHANISMS OF EDA

Introduction

Complexity of Electrodermal Phenomena

The task of relating the observable electrodermal phenomena seen by psychophysiologists to underlying physiological events is made difficult by the complexity of the electrodermal phenomena themselves. Distinctions have already been made between endogenous and exogenous EDA, as well as between phasic EDRs and tonic EDLs (see page 52). In addition, EDRs have distinctive features that must be considered.

SPRs can show both negative and positive (actually, decreased negativity) components. As a result, SPRs can appear as monophasic negative responses, biphasic responses with a negative component followed by a positive component, or triphasic responses, in which the recovery limb from the positive component of the biphasic response just described achieves a greater negativity than did the initial negative component. This late negative component is often viewed as simply a continuation of the initial negative wave once the effects of the more rapidly recovering positive component have dissipated (Edelberg, 1972b). Finally, under special circumstances, it is possible to see monophasic positive SPRs in which there is either no initial negative component or an extremely small one. The lower two tracings of Figure 4-6A illustrate monophasic SPRs recorded with two

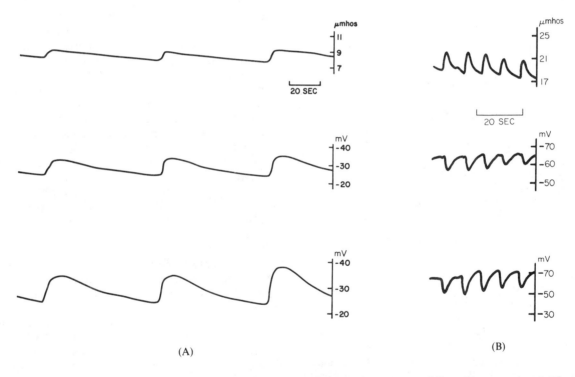

(A)   (B)

Figure 4-6. (A) Slow-recovery SCRs (upper tracing) and monophasic negative SPRs (middle and lower tracings). The upper and middle tracings were recorded with 67 meq/L KCl in Parke–Davis Unibase, as recommended by Lykken and Venables (1971). The lower tracing was recorded with an experimental preparation containing the same concentration of KCl in a mixture of equal parts of Unibase and polyethylene glycol 400. The Unibase–glycol mixture produces less epidermal hydration. (B) Rapid-recovery SCRs (upper tracing) and monophasic positive SPRs (middle and lower tracings), recorded as in Figure 4-6A. Note the difference in scale between the middle and lower tracings. (From "Mechanisms of Electrodermal Activity" by D. C. Fowles. In R. F. Thompson and M. M. Patterson [Eds.], *Methods in Physiological Psychology* [Vol. 1, *Bioelectric Recording Techniques*; Part C, *Receptor and Effector Processes*]. New York: Academic Press, 1974. Reprinted by permission.)

different electrolyte media, and Figure 4-6B shows monophasic positive SPRs using the same preparations. These were recorded with negative deflections upward, as is conventional. The upper tracings of Figures 4-7B and 4-7C illustrate biphasic SPRs. The left half of Figure 4-8 illustrates a triphasic SPR (lower trace) and its resolution into slow negative and rapid positive components.

Exogenous EDRs are simpler than SPRs, inasmuch as they are always unidirectional (i.e., show increased conductance or decreased resistance). They do, nevertheless, vary along a dimension of recovery time—that is, the speed with which they return to baseline. Extreme versions of this are illustrated for SCRs in Figures 4-6A and 4-6B (upper tracings). More continuous gradations can be seen in the lower tracings of Figures 4-7A, 4-7B, and 4-7C. As in the case of SPRs, it has been suggested that these variations in recovery time can be attributed to the combination of two underlying processes, one with a rapid recovery and

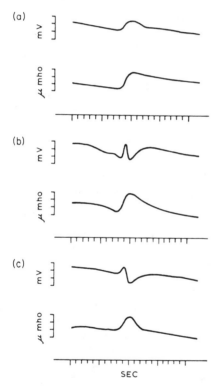

Figure 4-7. SPRs (upper tracings) and SCRs (lower tracings). Negativity (SPR) and increased SC are recorded upward. Note the pairings of (a) a monophasic negative SPR and a slow-recovery SCR; (b) a biphasic SPR with a small positive component and an SCR having a moderate recovery; and (c) a fully biphasic SPR with a fast-recovery SCR. (From "Mechanisms, Instrumentation, Recording Techniques, and Quantification of Responses" by P. H. Venables and M. J. Christie. In W. F. Prokasy and D. C. Raskin [Eds.], *Electrodermal Activity in Psychological Research.* New York: Academic Press, 1973. Reprinted by permission.)

one with a slow recovery, as illustrated in the right half of Figure 4-8.

To summarize, in addition to explaining differences between endogenous and exogenous EDA and between tonic and phasic activity, the attempt to understand the mechanisms of EDA must come to grips with the various components of EDRs. Fortunately, at a theoretical level, it has been assumed that both the endogenous and exogenous EDRs can be resolved into only two components: positive versus negative components for SPRs, and slow versus rapid recovery components for SCRs and SRRs.

Evidence Implicating Sweat Glands in EDA

It has already been stated that the sweat glands are major contributors to EDA (see page 51). Older theories that EDRs might be due to involuntary muscular activity or to vascular activity have received little support, although Edelberg (1972b, p. 385) does report that unpublished studies indicate a possible effect of vasomotor activity on SP measurements. This cautionary note aside, the eccrine sweat gland system is clearly directly involved in EDA and has been the focus of theories of mechanisms.

Numerous lines of evidence have converged to implicate the sweat glands in EDA. Early investigators noted that SCR frequency was greatest in areas where sweat glands were densest (Martin & Venables, 1966). Along the same lines, areas with the greatest sweat gland density, such as the palms and soles, showed higher SCL in spite of the much thicker epidermis found in these regions, a finding attributed to the provision by the sweat glands of high-conductance pathways through the poorly conducting epidermis (Edelberg, 1971). Although it is no longer believed that the greater thickness of palmar and plantar skin makes it less permeable (see page 61), the sweat glands do contribute strongly to the flow of electrolytes (see page 61).

This sweat gland hypothesis has been confirmed by observations of the effects on EDA of either eliminating or stimulating sweat gland activity. When sweat gland activity is eliminated in humans as a result of congenital absence of sweat glands (Richter, 1927; Wagner, 1952) or by peripheral nerve section or sympathetic ganglionectomy (Richter, 1927; Richter & Woodruff, 1941), no SCRs or SPRs (other than a slow positive wave) can be obtained, and SCL is reduced. Along the same lines, elimination of sweat gland activity in the cat footpad by cutting the plantar never reduces SCL and eliminates both SCRs and SPRs (Lloyd, 1960, 1961; Wilcott, 1965), whereas stimulation of the plantar nerve produces SCRs in the cat footpad (e.g., Adams, 1966; Lloyd, 1960). Pharmacological blocking of sweat gland activity with atropine (a cholinergic blocker) yields results paralleling those above for peripheral nerve section: SCRs and

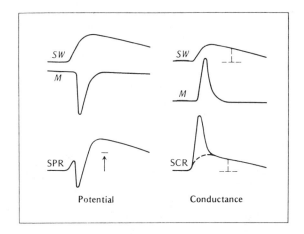

Figure 4-8. Schematic combination of potential components (left) and corresponding conductance components (right). The triphasic SPR (lower left) is resolved into a monophasic negative SPR (upper left) theoretically attributed to filling of the duct with sweat (SW) and a monophasic positive SPR (middle left) theoretically attributed to a membrane potential response (M) by Edelberg. Similarly, the SCR (lower right) is resolved into a hypothetical duct-filling, slow-recovery SCR (upper right) and a rapid-recovery, membrane SCR (middle right). (From "The Electrodermal System" by R. Edelberg. In N. S. Greenfield and R. A. Sternbach [Eds.], *Handbook of Psychophysiology*. New York: Holt, Rinehart & Winston, 1972. Reprinted by permission.)

SPRs are eliminated, and SCL and SPL are reduced (Lader & Montagu, 1962; Venables & Martin, 1967a; Wilcott, 1964).

Another approach to demonstrating a contribution of sweating to EDA is to observe the temporal relation between EDA and the appearance of sweat at the skin surface. Such studies have yielded support for an association between EDA and surface sweating (e.g., Martin & Venables, 1966). For example, a study (Thomas & Korr, 1957) relating intrasubject variations in SCL measured with a *dry* electrode to counts of active sweat glands reported a median product–moment correlation of .91 (range .44–.96), supporting the hypothesis that filled sweat glands provide parallel pathways through the less conductive epidermis.

Studies of EDRs have reported an association with surface sweating that varies as a function of the type of EDR. When there is an association, the SCR (Darrow, 1932, 1964; Wilcott, 1962) and the negative component of the SPR begin approximately 1 sec prior to the appearance of sweat at the surface, with the latency of the negative SPR and the SRR being the same (Goadby & Goadby, 1936; Wilcott, 1958). Examining the conditions under which there is an association with visible sweat, Darrow (1932, 1964) found a strong relationship among rapid-recovery SCRs,

high initial SCLs, surface sweating, and the positive component of the SPR. In contrast, slow-recovery SCRs were associated with a lack of visible sweating. Similarly, Wilcott (1962) found that the positive component of the SPR has a latency indistinguishable from that of visible sweating and is even more closely associated with surface sweat than is the negative SPR. Wilcott (1967) also noted that some SCRs and monophasic negative SPRs are not accompanied by visible sweating. Finally, Edelberg (1970) reported that SCRs accompanied by positive SPRs showed a more rapid recovery than those accompanied by monophasix negative SPRs, further suggesting an association between rapid recovery and the positive component of the SPR.

Taken together, this evidence indicates that the initiation of EDA precedes the appearance of sweat at the surface by about 1 sec, that rapid-recovery SCRs and SPRs containing a positive component tend to be accompanied by surface sweat, and that monophasic negative SPRs and slow-recovery SCRs often occur in the absence of visible sweating. Although some earlier theories attributed these last responses to epidermal events, it is now viewed as more likely that they reflect sweat gland responses in which the sweat does not reach the skin surface (Edelberg, 1972b; Fowles, 1974). More is said at several points below about the theoretical significance of these findings, but for the moment they serve to add to the evidence implicating sweat glands in EDA.

SC: Duct Filling and Corneal Hydration

Duct Filling

The simplest model proposed to account for the effect of sweating on SC is to view each sweat gland as a salt bridge that carries current through the less conducting epidermis, the current ultimately passing through the wall of the sweat gland into the interstitial fluid. Theories differ as a function of assumptions made about the location of the barrier layer in the epidermis and of the path of least resistance through the sweat gland walls (Edelberg, 1971, 1972b; Fowles, 1974), but the essential feature is that it is the sweat passing through the epidermal portion of the duct that produces an increase in SC. Thus the resistance will decrease in proportion to the height of the column of sweat in the duct (e.g., Edelberg, 1968). A corollary assumption is that the slow decline in SCL seen in the absence of SCRs reflects a gradual dissipation of the sweat remaining in the duct, possibly atrributable to a slow rate of reabsorption (e.g., Gordon & Cage, 1966; Lloyd, 1960; Rothman, 1954, p. 190), although the mechanism by which the sweat leaves the duct is still a matter of much conjecture. Because of this central role of sweat in the epidermal portion of the duct, this hypothesis has been known as the duct-filling model.

Hydration of the Corneum

A second possible effect of the sweat glands is to increase SC by hydration of the corneum. An important function of sweating on the palms and soles is to hydrate the corneum, and it is known that wet corneum is a better conductor than dry corneum (Edelberg, 1968, 1971, 1972b; see page 59). Thus, in addition to duct filling, it is possible that sweating increases SC by increasing the conductivity of the corneum. Both of these attractive models appear to represent logical consequences of sweat gland activity. The major difficulty is in determining the extent to which each contributes to any given aspect of EDA.

In addition to demonstrating the correlation between SCL and the number of active sweat glands as described above, Thomas and Korr (1957) estimated the contribution of the nonsudorific (i.e., epidermal) pathway to conductance (by extrapolating to zero active sweat glands). Estimates of the epidermal contribution to SC were higher when sweat gland activity was decreasing than when it was increasing, and both of these estimates were higher than actual values of total SC under conditions of complete rest. These findings were interpreted as reflecting the greater conductance of the epidermis when hydrated by sweat than when completely dry.

A somewhat similar point was made by Adams and Vaughan (1965), using a different technique. Using a wet electrode (Burdick electrode paste), these authors compared recordings of SR in human subjects with the rate of evaporative water loss (EWL) from the skin, an index of eccrine sweat gland activity. Plots of SR versus time and of EWL versus time superimposed on each other clearly demonstrated a substantial correspondence between the two measures. Of particular importance in the present context, the relation between SR and EWL depended on whether sweat gland activity was increasing or decreasing. When activity was increasing, both conductance and EWL increased together. When activity was decreasing, SR remained at a low level while EWL decreased. The authors suggested that water remaining in the corneum around the sweat gland tubules was responsible for maintaining the low SR. As in the Thomas and Korr (1957) study, the Adams and Vaughan (1965) interpretation suggests that one consequence of sweating is to produce a tonic increase in SCL as a result of peritubular hydration of the corneum.

Hydraulic Capacitance of the Skin

Two important studies by Adams demonstrate the existence of what he calls "hydraulic capacitance" in the skin, a term that includes both duct filling and corneal hydration, though presumably the capacitance of the corneum is much greater than that of the duct. Adams (1966) measured EWL by passing dry air over the surface of the cat footpad and measuring the water absorbed by the dry air from the surface of the skin. Starting with the fresh preparation, a period of 25 min was required for the corneum to lose its water and for EWL to reach a minimal level. The hydraulic capacitance of the epidermis was indicated by the fact that there was always a latency for the beginning of increased EWL when starting with a completely unhydrated preparation and stimulating the medial plantar nerves at a constant frequency. Stimulation at frequencies of one pulse every 10 sec or less produced no observable increase in EWL, even if continued for 5 min or more. At frequencies greater than .1/sec, the latency for the beginning of increased EWL was inversely related to frequency of stimulation, as would be expected with a fixed hydraulic capacitance and with the rate of secretion being proportional to the frequency of stimulation. In contrast, if the frequency of stimulation was increased after first producing a steady-state hydration level (by stimulating at a constant frequency over a period of time), there was no latency for the appearance of increased EWL. These results can be explained by assuming that the corneum has a hydraulic capacitance that is unused at the stable-state minimal EWL levels and that must be filled before EWL is visible at the surface of the skin. Under conditions of steady-state EWL well above this minimal level, on the other hand, the hydraulic capacity has already been filled, and any change in rate of sweat secretion is reflected rapidly in surface EWL measurements.

The interpretation of these results involves a number of important conclusions that bear on an understanding of EDA. First, Adams assumes that the minimal level of EWL reached in the absence of stimulation of the sweat glands represents a steady-state passive water diffusion from the subcorneal epidermis through the stratum corneum to the dry air being passed over the surface of the footpad. Second, the failure of low-frequency stimulation (one pulse every 10 sec) to increase EWL above this level is attributed to diffusion into the dry peritubular stratum corneum and reabsorption at the base of the epidermis. Third, the finding that there is always a minimum time required for sweat to reach the surface when starting from a minimally hydrated footpad, but not when starting from an already hydrated corneum, implies that the initial sweat responses serve to fill the sweat ducts and to hydrate the peritubular corneum at levels too low to affect the surface EWL. Only after some degree of duct filling and corneal hydration is achieved does the sweat reach the upper regions of the corneum where an immediate effect on EWL can be seen. Even at that point, it appears that sweat droplets would not necessarily be visible, as Adams says that variations of EWL can be seen in the absence of sweat droplets (microscopic examination). The picture that emerges from this analysis, therefore, is one in which sweat must begin by hydrating the lower levels of the corneum and work its way up to the surface. As Adams says, "only when the sweat ducts are filled and the peritubular areas in the stratum corneum are at a steady-state hydration level does an increase in sweat secretion rate bring about an immediate increase in skin surface EWL rate" (1966, p. 1008).

Although most of these conclusions appear warranted, one might wish to question the necessity of assuming that sweat is reabsorbed at the base of the epidermis. Given that the corneum is drier than the living tissue below it, this assumption necessarily implies an active reabsorption of water. A simple explanation might be that the small amount of sweat entering the corneum at low rates of stimulation is fully absorbed by the deeper corneum and has no effect on evaporation at the surface in the 5 min or so during which the effect was observed. Such an explanation assumes that a small increase in the vapor pressure of the lower corneum would require a longer period of time to affect the surface EWL. The visible effects of more rapid sweat gland stimulation, then, would be attributed to sufficient saturation of the peritubular corneum that sweat is allowed to pass in the duct to the upper levels of the corneum where it can exert an observable effect on EWL. The point here is not that there cannot be active reabsorption of water at the base of the epidermis—only that the results of this experiment do not require such an assumption. The question of whether there is active water reabsorption is discussed further below (see pp. 79–80 and page 83).

This reservation concerning water reabsorption aside, the demonstration of a hydraulic capacitance of the corneum and the conclusion that there may be considerable sweat gland activity that does not result in surface sweat droplets has important implications for EDA. As already noted, both duct filling and corneal hydration are likely to increase SC and thus would appear as an SCR. The evidence above (see "Duct Filling") that slow-recovery SCRs are often seen in the absence of surface sweating fits nicely with this conclusion and indicates that slow-recovery SCRs are likely to be associated with duct filling and hydration of the lower portions of the corneum. At least a portion of the prolonged increase in SC (slow recovery) would be attributable to the prolonged increase in conductance of the corneum as a result of hydration. It is difficult to specify how much of the continuing increase in SC is due to sweat remaining in the duct as a result of a slow rate of reabsorption, but Adams's model appears to argue against this possibility. That is, to the extent that sweat rapidly diffuses into the dry corneum, there is little reason to believe that sweat would remain in the epidermal portion of the duct for long periods of time. On the other hand, if a substantial portion of the hydraulic capacitance resides in the sweat gland itself, these results would

not argue as strongly in favor of rapid diffusion of sweat into the corneum with a subsequent immediate emptying of the ducts. This issue is taken up again below.

More direct evidence of the effects of hydration on both SC and SP is provided by Stombaugh and Adams (1971). Although the focus of the present discussion is on SC, the results for SP are presented for later reference. Again using the cat footpad with controlled stimulation and exposure of the skin to dry air, EDA rather than EWL was recorded from dry metal electrodes (narrow bands of silver conducting paint), allowing evaporation of water from the skin due to their small size. The skin was initially hydrated by stimulation of the medial plantar nerve for 3 min at the rate of 18 impulses per second. Then while the footpad was allowed to dehydrate during exposure to dry air, a standard stimulation (a train of three impulses) was applied at 3- to 10-min intervals over a period of 58 min, allowing an assessment of the effect of the state of corneal hydration on the SCRs and SPRs obtained. The readings just prior to the responses elicited by stimulation were used to monitor changes in SCL and SPL. As would be expected, the SCL was inversely related to hydration—that is, SCL showed a steady curvilinear decrease (from 18.0 to 7.6 μmhos) as dehydration progressed. SPL, on the other hand, showed a rapid increase (in negativity) during the first 10 min, followed by a more gradual increase to a maximum of around 3.3 mV. Of particular interest, the amplitude of the SCR varied with corneal hydration, being minimal (.1–.3 μmhos) at both extremes of hydration and maximal (1.2 μmhos) at the intermediate levels of hydration seen after about 16 min of drying. A similar time course was seen for the slope of the recovery limb measured at the point of maximum rate of recovery. This measure appears to reflect the rate of recovery of the SCR, indicating that the recovery limb is affected by the level of hydration.

Negative SPRs resembled SCRs in showing a peak amplitude (14 mV) at intermediate levels of hydration as compared to dry skin (8.0 mV) or hydrated skin (4.4 mV), but the peak amplitude was seen after approximately 25 min of drying, rather than 16 min as in the case of SCRs. Similarly, the maximum rate of recovery of the negative SPR showed a time course similar to that for SPR amplitude. Roughly 75% of the SPRs showed a positive overshoot during recovery, and it was found that the magnitude of this overshoot increased curvilinearly with drying of the corneum. Finally, the time course of the SPR was much faster than that of the SCR across all hydration levels: The peak of the SPR was reached by the time the SCR just exceeded the value of SCL at the time of stimulation, and the peak of the SCR was reached well after the peak of the SPR.

Stombaugh and Adams (1971) state that this time

lag between the peak of the SPR and that of the SCR is about 2 sec. The data presented (see there Table 1:$t_{c3}-t_{p2}$), however, show an increasing lag with decreasing hydration, reaching an average closer to 3 sec for the later responses, due primarily to an increase in the latency of the SCR (t_{c3}) as hydration decreases. Although the authors report that the changes in the various temporal characteristics of the responses as a function of hydration were not statistically significant, the results just mentioned appear to be quite orderly, and it is possible that the tests employed were not as powerful as they might be (the tests were not specified; possibly a trend analysis of the SCR latency data would be significant). The reason for belaboring this point is that other investigators have reported "sluggish" SCRs when stimuli are presented to resting subjects (Lykken, Miller, & Strahan, 1968), and the apparent increase in the latency with decreasing hydration in the Stombaugh and Adams (1971) study appears to parallel this phenomenon.

Stombaugh and Adams point out that these results reveal a profound influence of corneal hydration on numerous aspects of EDA, including levels and even the amplitudes of SCRs and SPRs elicited by stimulation of the medial plantar nerve. Combined with the conclusions of the earlier study that variations in sweat gland activity will produce different levels of corneal hydration, the present results suggest that uncontrolled, low levels of sweat gland activity during an experiment will affect corneal hydration which will, in turn, influence many aspects of EDA in response to experimental stimulation.

In spite of this emphasis on corneal hydration, Stombaugh and Adams assign an important role to duct filling for SCRs. Like most current theorists, they postulate two resistors in parallel, one representing the sweat gland duct and the other the resistance of the corneum. SCL reflects the additive contribution of the conductance through these two resistors. SCR, on the other hand, is believed to depend on duct filling and thus would primarily reflect decreased resistance in the ducts as a consequence of an increased volume of sweat. The amplitude of the SCR, nevertheless, will vary as a function of the state of the corneum and sweat glands:

> With the stratum corneum and sweat ducts hydrated, both parallel resistances would be small (i.e., conductance would be large) and sweat secretion would cause only small increases in duct filling and footpad conductances, resulting in small SCRs at high levels of epidermal hydration. With the footpad dehydrated, both parallel resistances would be large (i.e., conductance would be small), and secreted sweat would be absorbed into the stratum corneum before filling the duct completely. SCRs elicited during this final phase of dehydration would be relatively small. Between these two limits a level of dehydration exists during which a burst of sweat

secretion would cause the ducts to be filled, producing a path of low electrical resistance through the sweat duct, resulting in a maximal SCR. (Stombaugh & Adams, 1971, p. 1018)

Thus, duct filling is the primary mechanism by which an SCR is produced, but the state of corneal hydration will influence the size of the response.

Distinguishing between Duct Filling and Hydration

Edelberg (1983/1978) has proposed a model resembling the one just described in many respects, but also differing in some of the conclusions reached. Edelberg shares the assumption that the sweat duct and the corneum act as resistors in parallel and that the SCR is due to duct filling. He also adds the further assumption that these parallel resistors are in series with a membrane resistance lower in the epidermis (which has a capacitor in parallel, but this aspect is not of importance in the present context). Edelberg argues that the hydrated corneum will act as a shunt around the sweat duct, and he derives an equation from the simple circuit just described, showing that, as the conductance of the corneum increases with hydration, the contribution of a given increase in sweat gland conductance (duct filling) to the measured (i.e., transepidermal) SCR will diminish.

Edelberg confirmed this prediction with data from the cat footpad, which were produced by starting with a well-hydrated preparation and stimulating the plantar nerve with single pulses at approximately 30-sec intervals. It was assumed that this was sufficient to allow sweat duct emptying to return to the same level each time. The results showed that as the dehydration produced a decline in SCL from 7.3 to 5.5 μmhos, the amplitude of the SCRs increased 69% (change in *log* conductance increased by 118%). Edelberg's results resemble those seen in the early (i.e., hydrated) portion of Stombaugh and Adams's (1971) data, in which SCR amplitude increased as dehydration progressed. It is not clear why Edelberg did not find the decline with further dehydration reported by Stombaugh and Adams. One possibility is that Edelberg used a wet electrode, preventing dehydration of the upper corneum. A second possibility is that Edelberg elicited responses every 30 sec, as opposed to intervals of 3 min or longer in the earlier study. As noted above, Edelberg did this in order to keep the level of duct filling constant at the moment the SCRs were produced.

Quite apart from the effect of corneal hydration, Edelberg found that the initial degree of duct filling at the initiation of a response exerted a profound influence on SCR amplitude. The same electrical circuit described above predicts that the effect on the measured SCR of a given increase in sweat duct conductance (i.e., a duct-filling response) increases as the initial level of duct filling increases (i.e., as the sweat duct conductance at the beginning of the response increases). This prediction was confirmed, again with SCRs from the cat footpad, by producing SCRs during the time period between the scheduled test responses (apparently spaced at 20- to 30-sec intervals). This manipulation produced obvious and large increases in the SCR to the test stimulus. Since the multiple responses during a short time period increased SCL, the effect was quantified by examining the increase in SCR amplitude as a function of the increase in SCL, and it was found that the SCR amplitude tripled with an increase in the initial SCL from 3.87 to 4.00 μmhos. Thus, this presumed manipulation of duct filling had a profound effect on the amplitude of the SCR produced by a single pulse to the plantar nerve.

Edelberg's results provide strong support for the duct-filling model. It would be extremely difficult to subsume these second results under an explanation couched in terms of corneal hydration, since the results were in the opposite direction: The effect of decreasing hydration was to *increase* SCR amplitude, whereas the effect of longer intervals between SCRs in the duct-filling experiment was to *decrease* SCR amplitude. On the assumption that longer intervals between responses should allow more dehydration, the corneal hydration model would predict larger responses with longer intervals, the opposite of Edelberg's results. In addition, the hydration effect was not large enough to account for the duct-filling effect, and the change in SCL was in the opposite direction: In Edelberg's first study, with dehydration there was a *decline* in SCL of 1.8 μmhos associated with an increase in SCR amplitude of 69%, whereas in the duct-filling study an *increase* in SCL of only .13 μmhos was associated with a tripling of the SCR amplitude. It seems reasonable, therefore, to accept Edelberg's assumptions that his procedures manipulated corneal hydration and duct filling separately and his conclusions that both influence SCR amplitude.

These findings regarding duct filling suggest that this variable may contribute significantly to the hydraulic capacity of the skin demonstrated by Adams (1966). In particular, Edelberg's estimate that a period of 30 sec was required for the sweat produced by a single (.5-msec) pulse to the plantar nerve to be reabsorbed implies a relatively slow time course for the ducts to empty. Although it is difficult to extrapolate from this specific estimate to the entire range of duct filling, it would seem that at the least a matter of several minutes would be required to empty completely filled sweat ducts. This perspective would appear to be in some conflict with the model proposed by Stombaugh and Adams (1971)—namely, that diffusion into the corneum is so fast that sweat cannot reach the skin surface if the deeper corneum is not hydrated. A possible resolution of this apparent disagreement would be the possibility that diffusion into the corneum is greatly retarded once the corneum is hydrated and that, therefore, the rate of duct emptying will vary as a function of the hydration of the corneum (see page 88).

Observations of sweat ducts in a condition known as "miliaria" are also relevant to the question of the permeability of the duct walls to the diffusion of sweat. Miliaria results from a plugging of the ducts with keratin, leading to an engorgement and eventual rupture of the ducts. If the plug occurs in the duct near the skin surface, the distention and rupture of the duct occur in the corneum. Edelberg (1972b) notes that this observation perhaps implies that diffusion of the sweat into the corneum meets with considerable resistance, and therefore also implies that the normal route for sweat is to the surface of the skin and thence into the corneum. On the other hand, he suggests that the rupture might be caused by a strong myoepithelial contraction, which produces an increase in pressure too quickly to be dissipated by even an appreciable rate of diffusion into the corneum. Yet a third possibility, as suggested above, is that the corneum becomes so hydrated during the excessive sweating associated with miliaria that it loses its capacity to absorb sweat *rapidly* from the duct (cf. Edelberg, 1979). Consequently, although the engorgement and rupture of the duct in miliaria does at least suggest limitations of the capacity of sweat to diffuse directly into the corneum, it does not necessarily preclude such diffusion. The anatomical observation that the duct passing through the corneum follows a corkscrew path seems to suggest strongly that the increased surface area is there for the purpose of allowing sweat to diffuse into the corneum, and Edelberg (1979) has provided evidence in support of diffusion. On the other hand, the rate at which this diffusion can proceed is still uncertain.

It is perhaps useful to note at this point that diffusion of sweat into the corneum is not the only mechanism proposed by which the filled ducts may be emptied. Numerous authors have assumed that the sweat gland itself reabsorbs water back into the body. For example, Lloyd (1962) believes that sweat is reabsorbed near the base of the gland. Edelberg (1972b) and I (Fowles, 1974), on the other hand, have argued in favor of a more epidermal route of reabsorption. Adams's (1966) assumption that water is reabsorbed at the base of the epidermis even from a relatively dry corneum has already been discussed. Edelberg (1979) proposes both reabsorption from the duct and reabsorption from the lower corneum (by the germinating layer). Taken together, these hypotheses suggest that some type of reabsorption mechanism participates in the emptying of the sweat duct and even, possibly, in the drying out of the corneum.

So far, the focus of this discussion has been on the effects of duct filling and hydration on SCR amplitude, but the conclusions reached have implications for the decline in SCL observed during periods of sweat gland inactivity. At least three possible mechanisms have been proposed that might account for this decline: emptying of the duct through diffusion of sweat into the corneum, emptying of the duct as a result of reabsorption, and dehydration of the corneum as a result of water reabsorption at the base of the epidermis. With dry electrodes, dehydration of the corneum from evaporation of water from the skin surface is a fourth factor. As is obvious from the discussion above, it is difficult to specify the quantitative contribution of each of these factors to declines in SCL, but it is likely that any contribution of corneal dehydration, especially under a wet electrode, would proceed more slowly than would duct emptying.

Hydration beneath the Wet Electrode

It will already have occurred to many experienced psychophysiologists that SC is typically recorded with a wet electrode—that is, with silver/silver chloride electrodes in contact with a chloride salt solution held between the electrode and the skin surface by some type of cream or jelly. The simple act of placing any vapor barrier on the surface of the skin will initiate an increase in corneal hydration, since the water diffusing outward through the corneum from the living tissue below will no longer be able to evaporate from the skin surface, and will therefore eventually produce a highly hydrated corneum (see page 59). Added to this is the consideration that many electrolyte media employed for SC measurements may lose water to the skin themselves, thereby promoting corneal hydration from the surface.

SCRs can be recorded from skin immersed in saline (Edelberg, 1968, 1972b) or from sites hydrated by presoaking for 15 min with distilled water (Fowles & Schneider, 1974). If wet electrodes produce corneal hydration from the living tissue below and from the applied jelly or cream above, it must be asked whether any role can be assigned to corneal hydration under normal recording conditions. The answer to this question appears to be in the affirmative. Edelberg (1968), for example, cites Buettner's (1965) work as indicating that complete hydration of the corneum requires substantially more time than is available in the usual experiment. In addition, Edelberg (1979) has demonstrated that over a period of 10 min a droplet of water on the skin surface produces only superficial hydration of the corneum, and he has also argued that the germinating layer prevents the vapor pressure in the lower corneum from rising above 85% relative humidity (by active reabsorption of water if necessary). The estimates cited above (see page 51) for the lag time required for the first appreciable water to diffuse entirely through the corneum to the living tissue below also show that complete hydration takes time—83 min for the palm and 106 min for the

sole. Furthermore, some wet electrode preparations may not produce rapid hydration of the corneum: For example, it is possible that Parke–Davis Unibase cream does not hydrate the skin as rapidly as does agar jelly (Fowles & Schneider, 1974, 1978).

These observations point to the conclusion that in most experiments corneal hydration is an important—and uncontrolled—variable. In addition to the potentially hydrating effects of simple occlusion and of wet electrode jellies, sweat gland responses probably increase hydration at all levels of the corneum as the sweat passes to the skin surface. The rate of diffusion will be proportional to the vapor pressure gradient between the duct and the corneum, and thus inversely proportional to the level of corneal hydration (Edelberg, 1979).

Hydration and Poral Closure

Yet another consequence of epidermal hydration is relevant to the present discussion. The ability of the corneum to absorb up to 600% of its weight if immersed in water has been discussed above (see page 59). At the same time, the swelling of the corneum with hydration is so great that it produces a simple mechanical obstruction of the sweat duct, as indicated by microscopic observations of the skin surface (Sarkany, Shuster, & Stammers, 1965), preventing the sweat from reaching the skin surface. The evidence for this phenomenon has been reviewed elsewhere (Fowles, 1974; Fowles & Venables, 1970a) and need not be repeated, but it appears that the sweat glands continue to secrete sweat up to a point (Morimoto, 1978c) in spite of this hydration-produced poral closure, presumably requiring increased reabsorption somewhere in the sweat duct.

This aspect of hydration, which can be expected to occur with hydrating electrolyte media, prevents the duct-filling response from reaching all the way to the surface of the skin and interposes a (hydrated) corneal resistance in series between the sweat gland resistance and the electrolyte applied to the skin surface. The maximum conductance for the sweat gland pathway, then, will be somewhat reduced because of this corneal barrier. This attenuation of the duct-filling response will, however, be partially offset by the increased conductance of the well-hydrated corneum, which will facilitate contact with the deeper portions of the sweat gland by way of a volume conduction effect.

Comment

Assuming that most investigators are interested in SCL and SCRs as indices of the amount of neural activity reaching the sweat glands via the sympathetic nervous system, it should be obvious from the preceding discussion that the eccrine system constitutes a noisy transducer between neural activity and changes in epidermal conductance. Presumably, the primary goal of SC measurements is to record some aspect of the response that is directly proportional to the underlying neural activity, and the amplitude of the SCR has traditionally been viewed as the best candidate for this purpose. In view of the demonstrations that the amplitude of the SCR from the cat footpad produced by a standard stimulation of the plantar nerve varies greatly as a function of corneal hydration and the extent of duct filling at the moment, it must be recognized that the SCR is an imperfect index of underlying neural activity. Similarly, the major effect of epidermal hydration on SCL points to the conclusion that this measure only roughly corresponds to the amount of neural activity. In particular, changes in SCL over time may have more to do with changes in corneal hydration than with changes in neural activity (e.g., Bundy & Fitzgerald, 1975).

Skin Potential: Endogenous Potentials, Duct Filling, and Hydration

Sources of Endogenous Potentials

Duct filling and corneal hydration can account for changes in resistance to an applied electrical potential, but they cannot, of course, explain the origin of endogenous potentials. Evidence has already been reviewed suggesting that sweat glands contribute to SPRs, since measures that block sweat gland activity also eliminate SPRs (see pp. 74–75). SPL, in contrast, does not require sweat gland activity: For example, Venables and Martin (1967a) recorded a sizable potential across the human palm even after blocking sweat gland activity with atropine, and a similar potential is obtained during prolonged rest periods in which the absence of sweat gland activity is indicated by the absence of EDRs. These and other observations suggest the presence of an epidermal potential in addition to a sweat gland potential; this hypothesis is supported by many indications that human skin behaves like a membrane with a fixed negative charge, which makes it more permeable to cations than to anions (Edelberg, 1971; Martin & Venables, 1966; Rothman, 1954). Under resting conditions, presumably reflecting the epidermal potential, SPRs in humans result in increased negativity, suggesting that the sweat gland potential contributing to SPRs is of greater magnitude than the epidermal potential. Microelectrode studies on the human palm comparing the potential at the sweat gland pore with those on the surface of the corneum between sweat glands confirm that the sweat gland pore is more negative (Edelberg, 1968).

The source of the large, lumen-negative sweat gland potential almost certainly is the potential of 50 to 70 mV generated in the duct wall in connection with the reabsorption of sodium (Fowles, 1974; Fowles &

Venables, 1970a; Lykken, 1968), as described above (see pp. 70–71). In the micropuncture studies in humans by Schulz and her colleagues (Schulz *et al.*, 1965), potentials of approximately 50 mV were observed in the subepidermal portion of the duct, but decreased as the electrode was pulled out of the duct through the epidermis. The possibility that the potentials came from the secretory coil was ruled out by filling the lower part of the duct with oil without causing any reduction in the measured potential. Inhibiting the sodium pump with subcutaneous injections of ouabain, in contrast, reduced the surface potential and increased the concentration of NaCl in the surface sweat. To this evidence can be added Sato's (1977) findings of a minimal transepithelial potential in the secretory coil (see pp. 69–70), precluding the possibility that the sweat gland potential is due to secretory activity, and a ductal potential of 70 mV in the monkey sweat gland (see pp. 70–71).

An important consideration for later reference is that the eccrine glands in the cat footpad do not reabsorb sodium (see Fowles, 1974; Fowles & Venables, 1970a; see also page 62), differing from human sweat glands in this respect. The SPRs in cats differ dramatically from those seen in humans in that they show only a monophasic negative SPR (e.g., Edelberg, 1973; Shaver, Brusilow, & Cooke, 1962), which reaches its full amplitude very quickly, as discussed above in connection with the Stombaugh and Adams (1971) study. The levels of negativity achieved are also low compared with human SP; for example, Wilcott (1965) referred to an SPL of −8 mV as a "relatively high basal potential." Thus the large, slowly rising, monophasic negative SPRs; the positive component of the SPR; and the large negative SPLs seen in humans all are missing in records from the cat footpad recorded with wet electrodes (Fowles, 1974).

In the case of the sodium reabsorption potential in the duct, it can be assumed that the magnitude of the potential will vary with sweat gland activity. Under resting conditions, the potential will be quite small because the lumen sodium concentration will be low, but the potential will increase sharply with the increase in ductal sodium concentration in connection with a sweat gland response (Fowles, 1974; Fowles & Venables, 1970a). As the rate of sweating declines (or stops), the sodium reabsorption mechanism would slowly lower the concentration of NaCl, with a subsequent slow decline in the potential across the duct wall (recall that one model proposes that the lumen wall acts as a sodium electrode; see page 71). These changes in the sodium reabsorption potential correspond to the phenotypic characteristics of the negative component of the SPR—a moderately fast increase in negativity in connection with the onset of a sweat gland response (but prior to the appearance of sweat at the skin surface), followed by a gradual decrease in the absence of sweating. Thus the negative SPR can be attributed, at least in part, to variations in the generator potential in the dermal portion of the sweat gland duct.

Hydration and Duct Filling: Edelberg's Circuit

Prior to 1968, discussions of SP generally assumed that changes were entirely attributable to variations in the potentials generated by membranes in the skin or sweat gland, such as the model just proposed for the sodium reabsorption potential. A major change in that view followed Edelberg's (1968) presentation of an internal circuit–current model, which emphasizes the contribution of variations in duct filling and hydration of the corneum (Figure 4-9). This model assumes the presence of the various elements already discussed: a surface negative epidermal membrane potential (E), separated from the skin surface by a series resistor due to the resistance of the epidermis (R_e), and a *larger* sweat gland potential (S), separated from the skin surface by a series resistor due to the resistance of the sweat gland duct (R_s). The importance of the model is that it demonstrates that the potential typically measured between the skin surface and the interstitial fluid (i.e., an abraded reference site) will vary as a function of the values of the two resistors. In effect, the voltage difference between S and E will cause a current to flow in the circuit, with the voltage difference being divided between R_s and R_e in proportion to the resistance of each. Since the measured potential reflects the value of S minus the voltage drop across R_s, this conclusion indicates that the measured voltage will increase with duct filling (i.e., there will be a smaller voltage drop across R_s as its resistance decreases relative to that of a fixed R_e). The effect of corneal hydration, on the other hand, is to decrease the measured potential because of the fall in R_e. Edelberg suggests that, in addition to any contribution of variations in the generator potential, the onset of negative SPRs could, therefore, be produced by duct filling, and the recovery portion could be at least partially attributed to emptying of the ducts. Similarly, once the sweat fills the duct to a point at which it diffuses into and hydrates the adjacent corneum, a positive wave is produced. Monophasic negative SPRs seen during a period of relaxation are attributed in this model to duct filling alone, whereas biphasic and monophasic positive SPRs during a reaction time task are (by implication) attributed to sufficient sweat gland activity to promote hydration of the corneum. Yet another implication of this model is that more tonic variations in hydration will influence the SP being measured—that is, hydrated skin will show lower SPs than dehydrated skin (assuming the sweat gland potential remains larger than the epidermal potential). Edelberg confirmed this prediction by comparing SPs recorded with aqueous NaCl versus those obtained with a 90% polyethylene glycol NaCl solu-

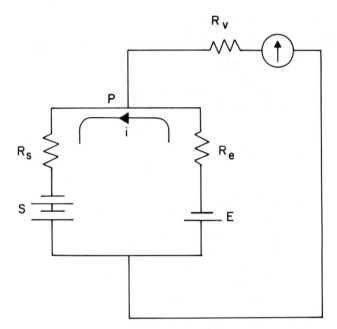

Figure 4-9. Circuit model for origin of transcutaneous potential in human skin as suggested by Edelberg. S and E are potentials across the sweat gland membrane and the epidermal membrane, respectively; R_s and R_e are combined internal and series resistance of the sweat gland and epidermis, respectively; P is the transcutaneous potential; R_v is the input impedance of the voltmeter. (From "Biopotentials from the Skin Surface: The Hydration Effect" By R. Edelberg. *Annals of the New York Academy of Sciences*, 1968, 148, 252–262. Reprinted by permission.)

tion, which has a vapor pressure comparable to air with a relative humidity of 65%.

With this model, it can be seen that the variables found necessary to understand exogenous EDA are also important in understanding endogenous EDA as well. In one sense, this is a simple model of the electrodermal effector system. Even at this level of theoretical simplicity, nevertheless, it is clear that the measured changes in EDA reflect complex interactions of these variables that are beyond the experimenter's control. Unfortunately, this is not the end of the mechanisms story, which may be yet more complicated.

The Epidermal Membrane Response

Limitations of the Duct-Filling Model

Appealing as the duct-filling model is as an explanation of SCRs, it appears to have serious limitations, since membrane-like effects have been demonstrated in SCRs. In a classic paper, Edelberg, Greiner, and Burch (1960) reported that SRRs and SPRs were altered by a number of treatments known to affect membranes. When 1.0-M solutions of different salts were applied at an anodal site, the amplitude of SRRs increased with increasing size of (hydrated) cations— that is, in the order potassium chloride (KC1), NaCl, lithium chloride (LiCl), ammonium chloride (NH$_4$Cl), calcium chloride (CaCl$_2$, and aluminum chloride (AlCl$_3$). Comparisons of SRR amplitudes for each salt at an anodal versus a cathodal site indicated that anodal sites, at which the cations are driven into the skin, much more effectively increased SRR amplitude in the case of large cations (CaCl$_2$ and AlCl$_3$). Conversely, when a salt with a large anion (potassium sulfate, K$_2$SO$_4$) was used, larger responses were obtained at the cathodal site. The effects of the various salt solutions were readily reversed by rinsing the site in tap water for 2–3 min, indicating that the membrane is readily accessible to solutions applied to the surface.

A number of methods known to have a disruptive effect on membranes were also tried. These included anionic and cationic detergents, basic and acidic solutions, and high current densities. As expected, all of these had the effect of reducing both SRR amplitude and SRL. The accessibility of the membrane to surface solutions was demonstrated by the effectiveness of the detergents, regardless of the polarity of the applied voltage. Because of this accessibility, Edelberg et al. (1960) concluded that the membrane must be located in the epidermis. Similar results were said to have been obtained for SPRs, suggesting that they originate in the same membrane, but details of the SPR results were not included.

These experiments, along with other evidence (see Edelberg, 1972b), led to two important conclusions: A membrane is involved in EDRs, and this membrane is located somewhere in the epidermis. It was assumed that this epidermal membrane has a fixed negative charge, which makes it selectively permeable to cations, and that it undergoes a phasic increase in permeability, which is detected as an SCR with surface electrodes (e.g., Edelberg, 1972b, p. 375). Although the findings (see pp. 77–79) that SCR amplitude may be affected by *tonic* changes in duct filling and/or corneal hydration may somewhat weaken the necessity of inferring that the Edelberg et al. (1960) results could not be attributed to *tonic* effects on a membrane in series or in parallel with the duct-filling response, the bulk of the evidence has appeared to support the hypothesis that a membrane response is involved in the SCR. This has resulted in the general assumption that SCRs and SPRs reflect the combined effects of duct filling and an epidermal membrane response (Edelberg, 1972b; Fowles, 1974; Venables & Christie, 1973, 1980).

Duct-Filling versus Membrane Components of EDRs

The active epidermal membrane hypothesis was incorporated into a model of EDA mechanisms by Edelberg (1972b). In this model, the contribution of the duct-filling and membrane components were identified in terms of the recovery limb of the SCRs and the nature of simultaneously recorded SPRs. Specifically, the duct-filling component was said to produce SCRs and monophasic negative SPRs, both of which have slow-recovery limbs, whereas the membrane component was said to produce rapid-recovery SCRs and the positive component of SPR (see also page 75, where these components are paired on other grounds). A key assumption in Edelberg's model was that the diffusion of sweat into the corneum, thereby emptying the sweat duct, is too slow to account for the rapid recovery of many SCRs. In addition, it was stated that these rapid-recovery SCRs are seen particularly during periods of frequent responding when the ducts would be full, thereby minimizing the contribution of duct filling (Edelberg, 1972b, p. 390). In the same article, Edelberg also reported that recent studies had shown that the large potentiation of SPRs by AlCl$_3$ reported in the Edelberg et al. (1960) paper was true only for positive SPRs, suggesting a strong association between this component and the membrane response. It should also be noted that the positive component of SPRs is quite fast, being described as "jet-like" (Edelberg, 1968, p. 253), and thus is difficult to attribute to diffusion of sweat into the corneum as an explanation.

The Water Reabsorption Reflex

Another aspect of Edelberg's (1972b) model was that the epidermal membrane response was believed to be associated with an active reabsorption of water. Using a number of techniques, Edelberg (1966) demonstrated the existence of a water reabsorption reflex by which sweat is reabsorbed from the skin surface; this reflex is always associated with an SCR and strongly associated with the positive component of the SPR. The association of rapid-recovery SCRs with the positive component of the SPR (Edelberg, 1970) completes this picture of the water reabsorption reflex, the positive SPR, and the rapid-recovery SCR as multiple manifestations of the epidermal membrane response (Edelberg, 1970, 1972b).

Location and Innervation of the Epidermal Membrane

Given the accessibility of the membrane to surface electrolytes, Edelberg (1972b) assumed that it must be located in the epidermis and suggested three possible sites. Two of these—the granular layer and the dermo-epidermal layer—were nonsudorific epidermal sites that would control the flow of water (and current) directly through the corneum. The third site suggested was the wall of the epidermal portion of the sweat duct at the level of the Malpighian layer (see page 55). Based on demonstrations by Suchi (1950; cited by Kuno, 1956) regarding the path followed by the ferrous ion driven by electrophoresis, a membrane at this location was assumed to regulate water reabsorption from the duct itself and the flow of current from the skin surface down the filled duct to the Malpighian layer, laterally through the duct wall and intercellular channels of the same layer, and ultimately through the dermo-epidermal junction. A virtue of the granular layer site was that it is close to the barrier layer as Edelberg envisioned it—near the base of the corneum. The sweat duct pathway, on the other hand, was attractive because of the evidence that current flow follows that route, an attractive feature if changes in permeability of the membrane were to influence transepithelial conductance. Elsewhere, Edelberg (1971) argued in favor of the sweat gland pathway—located at the level of the germinating layer—because of the improbability that a nonsudorific epidermal membrane would be accessible to surface electrolytes via the barrier layer and because it appeared that AlCl$_3$ enhanced water reabsorption through the sweat duct wall at this level. (Although this paper bears an earlier publication date, it may well have been written after the 1972b chapter because of an inordinate publication lag for the book in which the 1972b item appeared.)

Edelberg (1972b) made the further assumption that the depolarization of this membrane is initiated either by neural fibers (either intraepidermal fibers or fibers innervating the dermo-epidermal junction) or by a stretching of the duct wall secondary to an increase in sweat pressure. The hypothesis of a separate neural innervation of the epidermal membrane (the dual-innervation–dual-effector model) troubled other reviewers. Venables and Christie (1973) and I (Fowles, 1974) pointed to the strong association between sweat gland activity and *all* EDRs (see pp. 74–75), noted that a separate neural innervation had not been demonstrated, and argued in favor of the sweat duct wall as the membrane locus. I (Fowles, 1974) suggested that either high sodium concentration (with high rates of sweat secretion) or increased ductal hydrostatic pressure might trigger the water reabsorption mechanism, hydrostatic pressure being the more likely mechanism because of its obvious advantage when the sweat pores are blocked. Venables and Christie (1973) cited the sodium and hydrostatic pressure mechanisms and offered two new dual-innervation possibilities for triggering the membrane response: a ductal myoepithelial contraction in response to adrenergic innervation, or a vasodilation response. Both of these events were viewed as secondary to sudomotor activity, accounting for the elimination of membrane responses when sweat gland secretion is blocked. As can be seen, numerous speculations have been offered concerning the triggering mechanism for the membrane response. It is perhaps noteworthy that increased hydrostatic pressure was the only triggering event discussed by all authors.

The Positive Component of the SPR

Given the association between the rapid-recovery SCR and the positive component of the SPR (see page 75), it is natural to extend the membrane hypothesis to account for the positive SPR. Edelberg (1972b, p. 391) proposed that the positive-going wave could be understood as a decrease in the potential of this normally surface-negative (or lumen-negative, in the case of the sweat gland duct wall) membrane. Such a loss of potential is to be expected when a membrane undergoes an increase in permeability and thus a loss of selectivity.

One problem with this explanation for the positive SPR is that it appears to assume that the large lumen-negative sweat gland potential is generated in the epidermal duct wall, whereas the arguments presented earlier (see pp. 81–82) all point to sodium reabsorption in the dermal portion of the duct as the source of this potential. Consequently, I (Fowles, 1974) offered the alternative explanation that the positive SPR reflects the decreased resistance of the epidermal membrane in the duct wall, rather than a decrease in the generator potential. Just as Edelberg (1968) had earlier argued that hydration of the corneum with subsequent decreased corneal resistance could produce a positive component to the SPR by acting as a shunt resistor, a decrease in the resistance of the duct wall in the epidermis below the surface of the skin could short-circuit the dermal duct potential. In effect, the circuit in Figure 4-9 would be viewed as concerned with the potential across the duct wall (rather than across the skin), and the "epidermal pathway" would be through the epidermal duct wall, the germinating layer, and the dermo-epidermal junction. A more complex circuit incorporating this hypothesis is presented below (see page 91). This explanation for the positive SPR also had the attractive feature of being able to account for several features of the exogenous EDA from the cat footpad (Fowles, 1974).

The Psychological Significance of the SCR Recovery Limb

The hypothesis that the recovery limb of the SCR differentiates between duct-filling and membrane responses raised the possibility that this component of the SCR coded valuable information. When coupled with the additional hypothesis of dual innervation, it was proposed that rapid- and slow-recovery SCRs reflect *qualitatively different* psychological information as a result of distinct neural control (Edelberg, 1970, 1972a). The history of this hypothesis, which has been the object of much interest and some controversy in recent years, has been summarized by Edelberg and Muller (1981).

Citing earlier evidence that the water reabsorption reflex was seen more often during cognitive activity than in response to startle stimuli, Edelberg (1970) proposed that the reabsorption response might hold promise as an index of behavioral set and that it could be quantified conveniently in terms of the recovery limb of the SRR or SCR. The recovery limb could be approximated by viewing it as an exponential decay (at least during the early portion of the recovery) and quantified in terms of the time constant—the time required to attain 63% recovery. As a practical convenience, it was shown that recovery half-time, the time taken to reach 50% recovery, was highly correlated with the time constant and could be used in its place. Within-subject correlations between SCR amplitude and the half-time measure on six subjects ranged from −.20 to +.74, indicating substantial independence, but with two of the positive correlations being significant. An examination of the sensitivity of recovery half-time to behavioral state showed faster recovery during an aggressive game than during rest, in response to signal stimuli as opposed to nonsignal stimuli, and in response to reaction time stimuli compared to simple habituation stimuli. Amplitude differences could not account for this discriminating power of recovery half-time. Recovery half-time was also found to increase over trials during a habituation series, and for a few subjects (5/19), there was a significantly faster recovery to execution stimuli than to warning stimuli in a reaction time task. Finally, there was some evidence to suggest that subjects emitting rapid-recovery SCRs during the reaction time task habituated more slowly during the habituation series (in terms of SCR amplitude and finger pulse volume). Although many of these results appear to reflect differences in activation, because substantial bursts of spontaneous SCRs during relaxation periods showed slow-recovery limbs similar to those seen with isolated SCRs, Edelberg concluded that activation per se does not explain recovery time differences. Rather, rapid-recovery responses were seen to "reflect a mobilization for goal-directed behavior" (1970, p. 538).

The 1970 paper was followed by a second paper (Edelberg, 1972a), which documented an attempt to control for activation by comparing activation associated with task performance with the induction of activation by noxious stimulation (cold pressor, threat of shock). The results supported the goal orientation hypothesis, inasmuch as the recovery time was *retarded* during the noxious conditions, leading to the further hypothesis that slow recovery during an arousal situation (in which frequency and amplitude of responses may increase) indicates a defensive orientation. In keeping with the assumed association of slow recovery with the absence of a water reabsorption reflex, the defensive orientation could be seen to have adaptive value, inasmuch as it was implied that more sweat would reach the surface, where it would minimize the susceptibility of the skin to abrasion.

Performance of motor tasks, on the other hand, would be facilitated by intermediate levels of corneal hydration. It was further proposed that the water reabsorption reflex facilitates homeostatic adjustments in the eccrine system by serving as an antagonist to the secretory process.

With these results, it was extremely difficult to account for the discriminating power of the recovery limb in terms of a simple activation hypothesis, thereby greatly increasing the credibility of the "goal-directed behavior versus defensive orientation" interpretation. Couching this hypothesis in the context of a biologically adaptive homeostatic mechanism added to the attractiveness, as perhaps did some degree of similarity to the popular "intake–rejection" theory of cardiovascular functioning (Lacey, 1967). There have been, nevertheless, findings suggesting an alternative hypothesis; the first of these concerned the positive SPR.

In a paper concerned with the effects of corneal hydration on the SPR, Rosenberry and I (Fowles & Rosenberry, 1973) commented that we had been able to produce monophasic negative SPRs by eliciting single SPRs during rest periods and purely or predominantly positive SPRs (especially at unhydrated sites) by eliciting a series of closely spaced SPRs (see also Fowles & Venables, 1970b). That is, the effects of hydration on these two types of responses was investigated simply by controlling the intervals at which subjects took deep breaths. This methodology, which was later extended to eliciting rapid- versus slow-recovery SCRs (Fowles & Schneider, 1974; Schneider & Fowles, 1978, 1979), indicates that the recovery limb is influenced by the history of sweat gland activity, presumably due to the effect of previous sweating on duct filling and, possibly, peritubular corneal hydration. This effect of spacing breaths on SCRs and SPRs can be seen above in Figures 4-6A and 4-6B, which show not only the dramatic effect on SCR recovery limb, but also the theoretically expected reversal of the SPR (from negative to positive). On the basis of these early results with positive SPRs and the older convergent findings that rapid-recovery SCRs and positive SPRs were associated with higher SCLs and surface sweating (see page 75), I (Fowles, 1974) argued in favor of a "primitive" model, in which the epidermal membrane response was attributed to a filling of the ducts, with a subsequent increase in intraductal pressure (pp. 250–251).

Another disconcerting finding for the hypothesis that slow-recovery SCRs reflect a defensive orientation was the report (Raskin, Kotses, & Bever, 1969) that the positive wave of the SPR increased with stimulus intensity in the range of 40–120 dB, and the authors' interpretation of these results as indicating that the positive wave represents the defensive response in the context of orienting reflex theory. Given the association with rapid-recovery SCRs, this finding would imply that rapid-recovery SCRs reflect the defensive response. Although perhaps the concept of a "defensive response" in this context is not the same as Edelberg's "defensive orientation," the similarity is sufficient to be problematic (as noted by Edelberg, 1972b, p. 407).

A major challenge to Edelberg's hypothesis came with the report (Bundy, 1974; Bundy & Fitzgerald, 1975) that recovery half-time could be predicted by an equation summing the ratio of the amplitude to the recency for the two preceding responses, with "recency" defined as the time period between the onsets of the current response and the relevant previous response: Larger and more recent responses would predict more rapid-recovery SCRs. As reported by Bundy and Fitzgerald (1975), the correlation (within subjects) between the predicted and the actual value of recovery half-time ranged from .52 to .91. The amplitude of the current response was also positively associated with recovery half-time (slower recoveries for larger responses), with the correlation varying from .03 to .77 for five subjects. Adding the amplitude of the current response to the predictions based on prior responses, therefore, yielded multiple correlations of .69, .83, .91, .93, and .94. These findings are compatible with the single-innervation, priming or duct-filling peripheral mechanism hypothesis and are hard to reconcile with the dual-innervation, "goal orientation versus defensive orientation" interpretation of recovery limb.

In a recent, elegant series of studies, Edelberg and Muller (1981) tested these alternative views of the SCR recovery limb. Although the results are too extensive to summarize in detail, in general they showed that the "Bundy effect" of prior activity and the amplitude of the present response exert an influence on recovery time that, when partialed out, eliminates the discriminating power of the recovery limb. On this basis, Edelberg and Muller conclude that there is little justification, at present, for the assumption of independent neural control of recovery rate. This conclusion does not negate the discriminating power of recovery half-time, which has been found in numerous studies. Rather, it casts doubt only on the hypothesis that the recovery limb provides unique or qualitatively different information.

This last point is underscored by two recent papers. In the first, Venables and Fletcher (1981) note that Bundy and Fitzgerald's demonstrations of an effect of prior responding on SCR recovery time employed subjects who were highly selected for showing few spontaneous responses and yet for responding to most of the signals presented. These authors then proceed to demonstrate relatively little association between recovery limb and previous responding in a larger number of less carefully selected subjects. Although some of their results should be interpreted cautiously, because spontaneous SCRs during certain time periods were not scored (the data had been collected and analyzed for other purposes, and it was not practical to rescore them for this purpose), the overall results clearly point to a very considerable degree of independence between recovery time and prior responding. Venables and Fletcher also suggest that SCR recovery time may be influenced by factors (e.g., aldosterone) other than amount of previous sweating, thereby adding a theoretical argument to their empirical demonstration that recovery half-time is not redundant with measures of prior activity.

The study described in the second paper (Janes, 1982) demonstrated that recovery half-time was greater for signal stimuli (indicating that the subject would receive 10¢) than for nonsignal stimuli. SCR amplitude discriminated the stimuli as well and was correlated with longer values for recovery half-time, but recovery half-time still discriminated between signal and nonsignal stimuli even with the effect of amplitude controlled (either by regression methods or by selecting SCRs of equal amplitude). Since differences in prior EDA were not seen between the two categories of stimuli, Janes concludes that SCR recovery time conveys information that results from a central mechanism rather than from passive peripheral influences. Prior EDA did affect recovery time within subjects; it just did not account for the discrimination of signal value. Janes also notes that the positive association between SCR amplitude and recovery half-time has not been found in several studies, and that the factors influencing this relationship merit further investigation.

Although Janes argues that these results support Edelberg's (1970) hypothesis that the SCR recovery limb can reflect stimulus meaning, she does concede that the *direction* of this effect is contrary to Edelberg's earlier proposals. That is, as discussed above, goal orientation should be associated with rapid recovery, whereas Janes found that slow recovery was associated with signal stimuli, which surely would involve goal orientation rather than a defensive orientation. Thus, this result cannot be accepted as strong support for the original recovery limb hypothesis.

Comment on the SCR Recovery Limb

The dual-innervation–dual-effector model, in which recovery time serves to index qualitatively different central nervous system processes (e.g., goal orientation versus defensive orientation) conveyed to the sweat glands along distinct neural pathways, has not been strongly supported. The repeated findings that, at least under some circumstances, recovery time is influenced by the amplitude and recency of prior responses, the amplitude of the response being measured, and the initial SCL all point to complex interactions of a peripheral mechanism. Added to this is the absence of any demonstrations of separate neural innervation for the water reabsorption response and the elimination of all EDRs by cholinergic blocking agents. In view of this strong evidence of peripheral interactions, considerable caution should be exercised before interpreting experimental results in terms of a dual-innervation model.

The alternative model—the single-innervation-dual-effector model—is that amplitude, recovery limb, the number of SCRs, and SCL all reflect the amount of sympathetic nervous system activity reaching the sweat glands, but that they do so imperfectly. Not only are they affected by many factors (such as corneal hydration, applied electrolyte, hormonal influences on the skin and sweat glands, number and density of sweat glands, functional capacity of the sweat glands, etc.), but these influences probably interact in complex and poorly understood ways. Assuming the correctness of this model, recovery limb appears to constitute a valuable addition to the assessment of the eccrine system's activity, but demonstrations that its psychological value cannot be totally attributed to measurements of prior activity or to response amplitude do not constitute unequivocal support for a dual-innervation model. In order to demonstrate, for example, that amplitude and recovery limb are not simply unreliable indices of the same underlying neural activity, it is necessary to provide evidence of discriminant validity (Campbell & Fiske, 1959) for these two measures. Different experimental paradigms should be developed to induce the hypothetical psychological attitudes, emotions, or orientations in a variety of ways. It should then be shown that recovery limb, but not amplitude, consistently indexes one of them but not the other, and vice versa. Until this is done, it is parsimonious to retain a single-innervation model.

Having adopted this conservative position, the possibility of a dual-innervation model should be noted. As described in the section on sweat gland functioning, there has been a long-standing question concerning the role of adrenergic stimulation in sweating. The findings in support of this role include a report of catacholamine-containing nerves around the sweat gland in the monkey paw, as well as demonstrations that circulating epinephrine can produce a 50% increase in the amount of sweat secreted during exercise (see page 63). *In vitro* studies with the monkey gland showed a maximal secretory rate to epinephrine averaging about 50% of that produced by the cholinomimetic Mecholyl (see page 63). Strangely, this effect of epinephrine could be increased by prior stimulation with Mecholyl, even though the Mecholyl was carefully removed and/or blocked prior to epinephrine stimulation. These studies also indicated the presence of both alpha- and beta-adrenergic receptors for sweat secretion (see page 63). An apparently entirely different effect of beta-adrenergic stimulation was found in the coiled duct of the monkey gland, where it seems to promote increased sodium reabsorption (see page 71).

Even taking into account the uncertainty as to the significance of these findings (see pp. 65–66), at the very least it is clear that adrenergic influences on EDA are a possibility. At the same time, the difficulty of extrapolating from these observations must be stressed. First, it should be noted that most of these effects are concerned with secretion and would not, therefore, appear to bear on the dual-innervation model discussed above. Second, the proposed effect of beta-adrenergic stimulation on sodium reabsorption in the coiled duct, which might possibly influence permeability to water, may or may not be close enough to the surface to serve as the "epidermal membrane." Thus, while these findings with respect to adrenergic influences point again to the complexity of sweat gland functioning and argue against premature rejection of some form of dual-innervation hypothesis, they do not have obvious implications for interpreting electrodermal data. It remains for future research to determine whether any phenotypic characteristics of electrodermal measurements can be related unambiguously to these still poorly understood adrenergic influences.

Alternatives to the Epidermal Membrane Response

The "Interrupted Decay" Model of Recovery Time

More recently, Edelberg has begun to examine alternatives to the epidermal membrane response as an explanation for differences in the SCR recovery limb. The first of these is the effect of SCL. Edelberg and Muller (1981) have suggested that one can view the recovery limb as falling at some point along a single exponential decay, extending from a maximal (within-subject) vaue down to the level reached after prolonged rest. If the SCR occurs near the upper reaches of the SC range, the recovery will be very rapid (because it falls on the early, rapidly declining portion of the overall exponential decay), but if it falls near the middle of the SC range, the recovery will proceed more slowly. In actual fact, according to this model, the time constant is identical for all responses, but making the (usual) erroneous assumption that the decay is proceeding toward the initial value associated with the onset of the SCR makes it appear that the time constant is shorter for responses initiated at higher SCLs. The authors refer to this as a "black box" approach, based on observations of polygraph records, without any assumption concerning underlying mechanisms, and they report an average correlation of +.41 between SCL and recovery rate (the reciprocal of recovery half-time) in support of the model.

Corneal Hydration

An even stronger attack on the epidermal membrane response hypothesis has been offered by Edelberg (1979). In this paper, he suggests that the active membrane response may not be needed at all in order to understand differences in recovery limb. Indeed, such differences may reflect differences in the rate at which the ducts empty as a function of the state of corneal hydration. The simple assumption that the rate of duct emptying will decrease with increasing relative humidity of the corneum would predict more rapid recovery (due to the reversal of duct filling) with dry corneum. On the further assumption of a natural gradient from approximately 85% relative humidity at the base of the corneum (see page 80) to the relative humidity of air near the surface, this model would predict that responses reaching only the lower portion of the corneum would have slow-recovery limbs, whereas those reaching the drier upper reaches of the corneum would produce rapid-recovery SCRs.

This argument requires the assumption that wet electrodes have minimal effects on the relative humidity of the deeper portions of the corneum, and Edelberg provides supporting evidence. Water drops on the skin surface for 10 min did little to increase the humidity of the corneum at a depth of 22 μm above the initial relative humidity of just over 80%. Similarly, a 20-min exposure to the Schneider–Fowles mixture of Unibase and glycol (moderately hydrating) for 20 min produced a relative humidity of 85% down to a depth of 60 μm but did not reach the drier corneum below that depth. Evidence is also provided to support the assumption that sweat does diffuse into the corneum: Corneal hydration was found to increase at the same time SC was decreasing, presumably as a result of duct emptying into the corneum.

A variation on the corneal hydration theme is briefly mentioned in the same paper. If the duct wall is more permeable in the upper layers of the corneum than in the deeper corneum, then diffusion into the corneum would vary for this reason, quite apart from the state of hydration. As in the other model, large responses or responses occurring with already partially filled ducts would have more rapid-recovery limbs, in keeping with the observations already discussed. This consideration, then, offers yet another possible passive influence on the recovery limb.

Is an Active Membrane Response Needed?

The models just discussed all represent attempts to rethink electrodermal mechanisms to see to what extent one can understand differences in recovery limb without recourse to hypothesizing an active epidermal membrane response. Since Edelberg has not made a general statement on this, it is not clear whether he believes an active membrane response is unnecessary.

One can note, however, that the attack on the active membrane is incomplete on two counts. First, the initial evidence demonstrating membrane-like effects in EDA (Edelberg et al., 1960) has not been reinterpreted in terms of purely passive mechanisms. Second, it has generally been assumed that diffusion of sweat into the corneum is too slow to account for the rising portion of EDRs (e.g., Adams, 1966; Edelberg, 1971, p. 530). If this assumption is valid, it is particularly difficult to interpret the positive wave of the SPR in terms of diffusion into the corneum. While it is quite true that the diffusion model could, as illustrated in Edelberg's (1968) ciruit model (see p. 82), account for decreased negativity of SP, it is difficult to account for the extremely rapid rise time of these responses.

Until such time as these barriers to abandoning the active membrane hypothesis have been overcome, it is best to view it as still a viable model, though not so strongly entrenched as in the past. At the same time, the previously assumed tight coupling between recovery half-time and the operation of a membrane response has been cast in doubt. To the extent that Edelberg's most recent work points to additional factors influencing recovery limb, this measure no longer can be seen simply as an index of the membrane response.

Central Control of EDA

The Neuroanatomical Substrate

Understanding of the neuroanatomical substrate for the central nervous system control of EDA is necessarily incomplete. Nevertheless, a substantial amount is known, and this literature has been reviewed by Edelberg (1972b) and by Venables and Christie (1973). These reviews should be consulted by the interested reader, as only the major points are presented here.

As already indicated, in the periphery the neural control is by way of the sympathetic branch of the autonomic nervous system. In the spinal cord, concentrations of these sympathetic fibers are found in the ipsilateral ventrolateral horn, those for the forelimbs being located at the high thoracic level and those for the hindlimbs at the thoracicolumbar level (Venables & Christie, 1973). In the spinal cat, it is possible to elicit EDRs simultaneously in all four footpads with afferent stimulation, demonstrating the presence of a spinal reflex.

Edelberg (1972b) describes three somewhat independent central pathways that produce EDRs: a premotor cortico-spinal system, a limbo-hypothalamic system, and the reticular formation. The premotor system (which bypasses the hypothalamic system) includes the premotor cortex (area 6 of Brodmann, just posterolateral to the motor area), the pyramidal tract, and the cerebral peduncles. The limbo-hypothalamic system involves an area on the anterior limbic cortex, the tuber cinereum and the lateral portions of the anterior hypothalamus, the prechiasmic area, and probably fibers from the limbic and infralimbic cortex. The amygdala (facilatory), the hippocampus via fornix and mammillary body of the posterior hypothalamus (inhibitory), and the dorsal midline area of the thalamus also appear to contribute to this limbo-hypothalamic system. The ventromedial bulbar reticular formation exerts an inhibitory effect, whereas the lateral portion of the mesencephalic (midbrain) reticular formation and portions of the diencephalic reticular formation exert an excitatory effect on EDRs. The roof nuclei of the cerebellum show inhibitory effects via their activation of the ventromedial bulbar reticular formation. Yet another possible pathway involves the basal ganglia and the pallidum.

Venables and Christie (1973) offer a similar picture of the structures involved in the regulation of EDA, but they stress the importance of cortical control, suggesting that cortical control is likely to be the dominant influence unless otherwise prevented. A second, particularly interesting aspect of their discussion is the role of the reticular activating system in the mediation of the peripheral elicitation of EDRs. Edelberg (1972b) has commented that sensory collateral fibers activate the excitatory mesencephalic reticular formation. Venables and Christie, in addition, cite evidence that this excitatory region, when stimulated, produces electroencephalogram (EEG) signs of wakefulness and facilitates motor activity—that is, the reticular activating system. These same sensory collaterals appear to activate the inhibitory ventromedial bulbar reticular formation, although the inhibitory effect is usually obscured by the excitatory effects via the mesencephalic reticular formation (Edelberg, 1972b).

Biological and Psychological Hypotheses

Although a survey of psychological influences on EDA is the subject of later chapters in this volume, it is appropriate here to mention briefly those theories that are related to the neuroanatomical findings and/or to the biological functions of palmar and plantar EDA. Edelberg (1972b, 1973) has been the foremost advocate of hypotheses combining these two perspectives. These include the importance of sweat glands in thermoregulation, on the one hand, and (for palmar and plantar surfaces) the regulation of the state of corneal hydration, on the other hand.

Even though there is little inherent adaptive need for the palmar and plantar glands to be involved in thermoregulation, Edelberg (1972b) cites evidence of thermoregulatory sweating from these surfaces. He further suggests (1972b, 1973) that a thermoregula-tory response to startling or threatening stimuli may be adpative: The cutaneous vasoconstriction seen in these circumstances has the beneficial effect of delivering more blood to the muscles and reducing bleeding in case of an injury, but it has the disadvantage of reducing heat loss, which may be needed during the ensuing motor activity. The activation of sweat glands serves to shift thermoregulation from the cardiovascular system to evaporative water loss, thereby anticipating the heat load produced by motor activity. This system is viewed as operating via the limbo-hypothalamic pathways (Edelberg, 1973). Edelberg (1973) makes a similar argument that the anticipatory thermoregulatory response would be adaptive in connection with the primary functions of fighting, escape, predatory feeding, and sexual behavior.

Another line of thought focuses on the role of the sweat glands in regulating the hydration of the palmar and plantar corneum. Edelberg (1972b) argues that, among other things, this serves to increase tactile sensitivity, to provide optimal frictional contact with objects being manipulated, and to greatly increase the resistance of skin to abrasion (see also page 53 and pp. 56–57). Edelberg (1973) also distinguishes particularly between EDA that occurs in connection with fine motor control (requiring tactile acuity) and is associated with the premotor cortex, on the one hand, and EDA that occurs in connection with locomotor activity and is mediated by the reticular activating system, on the other. Taken together, these proposals hypothesize the presence of three specialized pathways in the brain that activate EDA in response to (1) fine motor activity, (2) locomotor activity, and (3) thermoregulation. Assuming the validity of Edelberg's analysis, EDA can be expected to accompany a wide range of motor activity, often involving more than one of these three functional systems.

The more psychological conceptualizations of the central control of EDA are not incompatible with the biological functions just described. Edelberg's references to startling or threatening stimuli and to the primary functions of fighting, escape, predatory feeding, and sexual behavior have already been mentioned. Venables and Christie (1973) show a particular interest in the association between EDA and the orienting reflex to novel stimuli. This aspect of EDA appears to involve the reticular formation, limbic structures, and the cortex. These authors do not relate the role of the EDR in orienting to Edelberg's biological functions, but Edelberg (1972b) suggests that explortory behavior would be related to tactile and manipulative activity.

EDA has been related to limbic structures indirectly by another approach. I (Fowles, 1980) have proposed that EDA is reliably elicited by stimuli that elicit activity in what Gray (e.g., 1976a, 1976b, 1978, 1979) calls the "behavioral inhibition system," an aversive motivational system that inhibits behavior in response to cues for response-contingent punishment or frustrative nonreward. According to Gray (1978), the septo-hippocampal system constitutes part of the neurophysiological substrate for the behavioral inhibition system, and thus would be implicated in EDA.

An interesting question concerns the role of emotional motivational stimuli in eliciting EDA, apart from their effect on motor activity. In Gray's model, there is an "appetitive motivational system," which activates behavior in response to cues for reward or relieving nonpunishment (active avoidance). I (Fowles, 1980) have argued that heart rate accelerates in connection with the activity of this system (see also Fowles, 1982; Fowles, Fisher, & Tranel, 1982, and Tranel, Fisher, & Fowles, 1982), but that it is unclear whether EDA does so. It seems quite likely, however, that EDA may be associated with appetitive *behavior*, and that this may reflect the importance of one of the biological functions described by Edelberg. In fact, Edelberg (1973) has reported that the conscious cat shows EDA in connection with appetitive behavior. The question that remains is the degree of association with appetitive versus aversive motivational states, apart from the effects of motor activity per se. One way to approach this question is to compare the effects of appetitive and aversive stimuli in a classical conditioning paradigm, in which adaptive behavior is not possible. More work is needed in this area, but it can be noted that, whereas classical aversive conditioning is routine, classical appetitive conditioning is not (Fowles, 1980). This suggests that *perhaps* EDA is more responsive to increases in aversive as opposed to appetitive motivation.

A second approach is to examine the effects of variations in appetitive or aversive motivation during the performance of a motor task. Although EDA can be expected in connection with the motor activity, there may or may not be an additional effect of motivation. In an experiment with rats using the conditioned emotional response paradigm, in which a conditioned stimulus (CS) previously paired with shock is superimposed on an operant schedule, Roberts and Young (1971) found that the CS elicited an increase in both SCRs and SPRs, in spite of a concomitant decrease in heart rate, lever pressing, and overall movement. Even when the trials were subdivided as a function of whether the CS elicited an increase, a decrease, or no change in overall movement, the electrodermal results were unaffected; that is, increases in EDA were seen to the CS, regardless of the effect on motor activity. These results, along with those of classical aversive conditioning, suggest an effect of aversive motivation quite apart from motor activity per se.

A similar examination of the effects of appetitive motivation by Tranel (1983) yielded negative results. Using a continuous motor task and monetary incentives with college students, Tranel found that EDA, though present in substantial amounts, was not af-

fected by the level of monetary incentive. In contrast, large differences in heart rate were obtained as a function of incentive, as had been found in previous studies (Fowles *et al.*, 1982; Tranel *et al.* (1982). This preliminary finding suggests that EDA is not as responsive to appetitive motivation as to aversive motivation. If these speculations prove to be valid, those aspects of the limbic system involved in aversive motivation should be more closely involved in EDA than should those associated with appetitive motivation.

Hormonal Factors

Another possible influence on EDA is via the endocrine system (see pp. 71–73). On the whole, these hormonal factors are likely to produce effects that are constant or only slowly changing during the typical experimental session, making them unlikely to be the mediating variables in the response to specific experimental manipulations. For that reason, they are not discussed here. The interested reader should consult the excellent review of hormonal influences by Venables and Christie (1973), who make a strong case that sweat gland activity is influenced by such factors as circulating catecholamines, mineralocorticoids, and progesterone. It should be noted that if such influences were greater for some experimental conditions than others, they could affect the results even of experiments employing within-subject manipulations. Thus, depending on the nature of the experiment and the questions being asked, it may be important to consider whether hormonal factors need to be controlled.

Summary and Comment

This summary attempts to apply the various hypotheses that have been reviewed to the description of the sweat gland response as it bears on the measurement of EDRs. In so doing, hypotheses that are still objects of investigation are assumed to be valid in order to describe their role in EDA. Perhaps the most controversial of these is that concerning the epidermal membrane response—or the epidermal duct membrane response, as it is termed here—which is not accepted with as much certainty as it once was. Similarly, it is assumed that this membrane is located in the duct wall and responds to hydrostatic pressure, even though these assumptions are tentative at present.

A major theme of what has gone before is the complexity of the electrodermal effector system and the limitations of our understanding. It would be hard to exaggerate the degree to which each tentative conclusion reached depends on a set of assumptions that, if untrue, weaken the inference drawn. Thus the summary should be taken as my best guess as to the mechanisms of EDA and as an attempt to highlight the issues discussed, not as a set of conclusions to be reified.

Figure 4-10, a simplified model of the electrodermal effector system modified slightly from Fowles (1974), is an expansion of Edelberg's (1968) model that provides a helpful summary of many of the points discussed. R_1 and R_2 are the resistances of the epidermal and dermal portions of the sweat duct, respectively. E_1 and R_4 represent the lumen-negative potential generated across the duct wall in the dermis in connection with sodium reabsorption and resistance of the duct wall. Similarly, E_2 and R_3 represent the lumen-negative potential generated across the duct wall in the epidermis during the epidermal duct membrane response, possibly at the level of the germinating layer, and the resistance to the flow of current out of the lower portion of the duct into the dermis by way of the epidermis (germinating layer?). Taken together, these components illustrate the flow of current down the sweat gland duct and into the interstitial fluid, at which point the resistance becomes negligible, and they also represent the two sources of sweat gland potentials. The remaining components reflect the nonsudorific or epidermal pathway, E_3 being the epidermal potential and R_5 the resistance of the corneum. The epidermal potential is usually surface-negative, though with low concentrations of external cations it can become positive (e.g., Christie & Venables, 1971c). R_v is the input impedance of the voltmeter, which is connected to the palmar surface and an abraded reference site via standard electrodes and electrolyte. An important factor not included in the circuit (out of a desire to keep the circuit as simple as possible) is the pathway from the duct to the skin surface by way of the duct wall and corneum.

For SC recordings, the potentials can be ignored. With a subject at rest and not responding for a period of time, the ducts either are empty or contain only a small residual amount of sweat. The corneum is being hydrated from above by the electrode jelly employed to record SC, but this process progresses rather slowly. The lower portions of the corneum will have varying degrees of hydration—and thus conductivity—depending largely on the recent history of sweating, though in long-term recordings it may become hydrated from the electrolyte medium. Thus, under conditions of prolonged sweat gland inactivity, the resistance to current flow is relatively high in both the sweat duct and the lower portion of the corneum.

With the onset of a sweat response, the sweat rises in the duct, first reducing R_2. The response latency will reflect the time required for sweat to travel through the duct. If the amount of sweat secreted is very small and R_1 and R_5 are very large, the response either may not be seen as an SCR or will be very small because it never reaches the epidermis. With a somewhat larger response, the sweat reaches the lower portion of the corneum, reducing R_1 as well as R_2, and begins to diffuse into the corneum with the effect of reducing R_5. It is not clear what happens at the epidermal duct membrane (E_2 and R_3), but this response probably is not triggered by the moderate sweat response under consideration. Consequently, the observed SCR is primarily attributable to decreases in R_1 and R_2, with a possible contribution from R_5, and this response will not be associated with visible sweating. The recovery will be quite slow, because the hydration-induced decrease in R_5 will continue and the reabsorption of sweat from the duct (increasing R_1 and R_2) proceeds slowly.

In the case of a large sweat gland response—or a moderate one that begins with partially filled ducts—the sweat will reach the skin surface, assuming that the corneal hydration has not produced poral closure. This will effect a considerable reduction in R_1 (in addition to R_2) and will promote diffusion of sweat into the corneum along the entire length of the duct. At the same time, it may generate enough hydrostatic pressure to trigger (depolarize) the epidermal duct membrane, facilitating the flow of current along the R_1–R_3 pathway and producing a more rapid recovery limb because of the rapid repolarization of this membrane. If, on the other hand, hydration has produced poral closure, the sweat cannot reach the skin surface, requiring even the sweat gland portion of the current flow to pass through the duct wall and corneum in order to reach the skin surface. This circumstance is also likely to promote a greater increase in hydrostatic pressure, since the sweat cannot escape to the skin surface, producing a greater depolarization of the epidermal sweat duct.

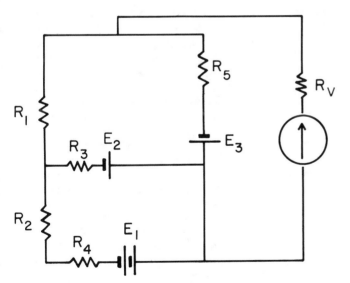

Figure 4-10. A simplified model of the electrodermal effector system. See text for identification of components of the circuit. (Adapted from Fowles, 1974.)

For responses that occur after a period of previous activity, the initial SCL will be higher, the ducts will be at least partially full, and the corneum will be at least partially hydrated along the length of the duct. These changes should decrease the latency of the SCR, while increasing the probability of surface sweating and the epidermal duct membrane response (with the attendant more rapid-recovery limb). It is also possible that the lower vapor pressure gradient between the duct and the partially hydrated peritubular corneum will decrease the diffusion of sweat into the corneum. This effect should be relatively small unless major portions of the corneum are well hydrated. That is, if only the corneum immediately surrounding the duct has been hydrated, the water should continue to diffuse into the drier corneum beyond, reducing the vapor pressure adjacent to the duct. Predictions concerning the effect of this primed condition of the gland on the amplitude of the SCR are difficult, because it may depend on so many variables. It can be noted, nevertheless, that Edelberg found that duct filling increased the SCR amplitude.

If the electrode jelly or the previous sweating have produced poral closure, the sweat cannot reach the surface, and—to the extent that the previous activity may already have filled the ducts—changes in R_1 and R_2 will be small. R_3 is quite another matter: With a blocked pore and a filled duct, a new sweat gland response will cause a large increase in hydrostatic pressure and trigger the membrane response. Also, the peritubular corneum may be well hydrated by the constant presence of sweat in the epidermal portion of the duct, minimizing the reduction of R_5 by further hydration. This may be a condition, therefore, in which rapid-recovery responses are superimposed on a relatively fixed tonic level. It also may be possible for the ducts to become so distended with sweat that tonic depolarization of the epidermal duct membrane occurs or the duct wall itself (i.e., the tight junctions between cells) loses its integrity, in which case further increases in SC with sweating may be minimal. Along the same lines, it is even possible for the buildup in hydrostatic pressure to prevent the further secretion of sweat (Morimoto, 1978c), rendering neurochemical stimulation of the gland ineffective in producing SCRs.

For SP recordings, the sodium reabsorption generator potential in the dermal duct wall will be near zero under (empty-duct) resting conditions, since the sodium will have been removed from the residual sweat in the duct. The potential measured under complete rest probably reflects the potential across the epidermis (E_3) minus the voltage lost across R_5 (Christie & Venables, 1971a, 1971b, 1971c; Fowles, 1974). Any sweat response will push isotonic sweat into the duct, activate the sodium reabsorption mechanism, and thereby generate the large lumen-negative sodium po-

tential. Whether this potential can be seen at the surface will depend, as Edelberg's (1968) analysis showed, on the relative values of R_1, R_2, and R_4 (low values facilitating surface measurement of E_1), on the one hand, and R_5 (low values obscuring surface measurement of E_1), on the other hand. The pathway through the duct wall and into the corneum (not shown in Figure 4-10) acts like R_5—that is, current flow in this pathway contributes to a shunting of the potential, to the extent that it allows the current to flow back toward the epidermis without reaching the skin surface. The significance of this consideration is that the hydration of the lower corneum by sweat from the duct creates such a shunting of the dermal duct potential, which is beyond the experimenter's control.

With small to medium responses in empty ducts with a relatively unhydrated corneum, the increase in the lumen-negative generator potential in the dermal duct and the decrease in R_2 (and, possibly, R_1) all act to produce a monophasic negative SPR. The decreased negativity of recovery will reflect a loss of generator potential (decrease in E_1), emptying of the ducts (increase in R_2 and R_1), and corneal hydration (decrease in R_5). Note that it is assumed here that hydration occurs too slowly to produce a positive component to this response. Should that assumption be incorrect, a hydration-induced positive component would be seen here.

Responses that trigger the epidermal duct membrane response introduce another factor. The rapid decrease in R_3 associated with this response acts in the same way R_5 does to decrease the negative potential measured at the skin surface (Fowles, 1974). Thus large responses or responses initiated with already filled ducts will show a positive component. This will often be preceded by a negative component, due to an increase in E_1 and/or a decrease in R_1 and R_2; however, if the ducts are already full, there may be no further increase in negativity, and the membrane response will appear as a monophasic positive SPR.

Poral closure has the effect of interposing a high resistance between R_1 and the surface, thereby reducing the measured negativity. To the extent that it also contributes to tonic depolarization of the epidermal duct membrane and/or to the loss of integrity of the duct walls, it will also diminish the measured potential (Fowles & Schneider, 1978).

It can be seen from this analysis that many factors can attenuate the negativity of SP measurements: low sodium in the ducts, empty ducts, corneal hydration, depolarization of the epidermal duct membrane, blockage of the duct by swollen corneum, and a loss of integrity of the duct walls. It is only under optimal conditions that the dermal duct potential can be approximated with surface electrodes. These same factors can affect the magnitude, and even the direction, of the SPR. Thus it is important to attempt to control as many of these variables as possible when recording SP.

Clearly, what all of this implies is a need to improve the correlation between our surface measurements and the size of the underlying sweat gland response. Although a great deal has been learned about sources of error in recent years, progress in controlling them has not been impressive. Orderly results with electrodermal measures can be obtained by using large samples, but the ability to increase precision by increasing, for example, the number of trials is severely limited. Not only is this a slow response system, which requires intervals of several seconds to separate responses to different stimuli, but habituation over trials so alters the response as to contaminate the results. What is needed are new developments to improve our assessment of the underlying response. Edelberg's introduction of the recovery limb measure may represent some progress in this direction, as this measure has yielded interesting results, and it appears that it can be used even when the recovery limb is distorted by a second, superimposed response (Fletcher, Venables, & Mitchell, 1982). Another possibility, as yet undeveloped, would be a combination of several measures, such as frequency, amplitude, and recovery time. Until such improvements arise, investigators should be aware of the considerable noise in the electrodermal effector system.

Although the evidence for cholinergic dominance in the activation of the sweat gland response is unequivocal, there continue to be questions about the role of adrenergic stimulation. At this point, it is unclear how important this stimulation is for the volume of sweat secreted, or whether it is largely concerned with the restoration of the cell to its normal functioning and/or the stimulation of glandular growth (see pp. 64–65). Similarly, it is unclear how much adrenergic stimulation may arise from catecholamine-containing nerves around the sweat gland (seen in the monkey paw) as opposed to adrenal medullary secretions (see pp. 62–63).

Finally, the central control of EDA is very complex. A practical, as well as theoretical, problem derives from the pervasiveness of the stimuli that activate EDRs. It seems likely that much of this activity reflects the biological role of sweat glands in thermoregulation, tactile sensitivity, frictional contact, and resistance to abrasion—associated with various aspects of motor activity—as proposed by Edelberg (1972b, 1973). Although this electrodermal–somatic coupling hypothesis has not received as much explicit attention as it deserves, most experimenters implicitly recognize it by investigating the effects of other variables while avoiding or minimizing somatic activity. Nevertheless, a more explicit treatment of these potentially multifactor somatic influences, and their as-sociation with the presumably psychological influences, might lead to a more comprehensive and integrated understanding of the central control of EDA.

APPENDIX: THE MEASUREMENT OF EDA

The discussion of methods for recording EDA faces the conflicting demands of two audiences. There are many investigators who simply wish to record EDA with state-of-the-art techniques for some particular purpose, and who do not wish to become experts in this area. A much smaller number do wish to develop expertise to varying degrees and to understand the rationale behind the choices made. Fortunately, satisfactory coverage from both perspectives is already available and need not be repeated here.

At the request of David Shapiro, the editor of the journal, *Psychophysiology*, a committee was formed to reach agreement on and to write a cookbook presentation of a methodology of recording EDA acceptable to all experts in the area. Such a report was written and circulated to a wider audience; the final draft was published in 1981 (Fowles, Christie, Edelberg, Grings, Lykken, & Venables, 1981). This is an ideal source of information for the first audience. The committee was in strong agreement that, except in unusual circumstances, SC rather than SP is the measure of choice, and detailed recommendations are presented for that technique.

For investigators interested in a deeper understanding of methodology, the most recent comprehensive treatment is that by Venables and Christie (1980). Other major references include Edelberg (1967) and Grings (1974), as well as earlier chapters by Venables and Christie (1973) and Venables and Martin (1967b). The paper by Venables and Sayer (1963) on the measurement of SP is still of interest, as is that by Lykken and Venables (1971) on SC. It is probably most efficient to begin with the chapter by Venables and Christie (1980), and then to read those by Edelberg (1967) and Grings (1974) for the views of other authors and some additional material.

ACKNOWLEDGMENT

I wish to acknowledge my indebtedness to Peter Venables and Robert Edelberg, whose generous contributions to my education on this topic have had a major impact on the present chapter.

REFERENCES

Adams, T. Characteristics of eccrine sweat gland activity in the footpad of the cat. *Journal of Applied Physiology*, 1966, 21, 1004–1012.

Adams, T., & Vaughan, J. A. Human eccrine sweat gland activity and palmar electrical skin resistance. *Journal of Applied Physiology*, 1965, 20, 980–983.

Baker, H. The skin as a barrier. In A. Rook, D. S. Wilkinson, & F. J. G. Ebling (Eds.), *Textbook of dermatology* (3rd ed., Vol. 1). London: Blackwell Scientific Publications, 1979.

Blank, I. H. Further observations on factors which influence the water content of stratum corneum. *Journal of Investigative Dermatology*, 1953, 21, 259.

Blank, I. H. Cutaneous barriers. *Journal of Investigative Dermatology*, 1965, 45, 249–256.

Buettner, K. J. K. The moisture of human skin as affected by water transfer. *Journal of the Society of Cosmetic Chemists*, 1965, 16, 133–143.

Bulmer, M. G., & Forwell, G. D. The concentration of sodium in thermal sweat. *Journal of Physiology* (London), 1956, 132, 115–122.

Bundy, R. S. The influence of previous responses on the skin conductance recovery limb. *Psychophysiology*, 1974, 11, 221–222. (Abstract)

Bundy, R. S., & Fitzgerald, H. E. Stimulus specificity of electrodermal recovery time: An examination and reinterpretation of the evidence. *Psychophysiology*, 1975, 12, 406–411.

Cage, G. W., & Dobson, R. L. Sodium secretion and reabsorption in the human eccrine sweat gland. *Journal of Clinical Investigation*, 1965, 44, 1270–1276.

Campbell, D. T., & Fiske, D. W. Convergent and discriminant validation by the multitrait–multimethod matrix. *Psychological Bulletin*, 1959, 56, 81–105.

Chen, W. T., & Elizondo, R. S. Peripheral modification of thermoregulatory function during heat acclimation. *Journal of Applied Physiology*, 1974, 37, 367–373.

Christie, M. J., & Venables, P. H. Basal palmar skin potential and the electrocardiogram T-wave. *Psychophysiology*, 1971, 8, 779–786. (a)

Christie, M. J., & Venables, P. H. Characteristics of palmar skin potential and conductance in relaxed human subjects. *Psychophysiology*, 1971, 8, 525–532. (b)

Christie, M. J., & Venables, P. H. Effects on "basal" skin potential level of varying the concentration of an external electrolyte. *Journal of Psychosomatic Research*, 1971, 15, 343–348. (c)

Costello, J. J., & Gibbs, R. C. *The palms and soles in medicine*. Springfield, Ill.: Charles C Thomas, 1967.

Darrow, C. W. The relation of the galvanic skin reflex recovery curve to reactivity, resistance level, and perspiration. *Journal of General Psychology*, 1932, 7, 261–272.

Darrow, C. W. The rationale for treating the change in galvanic skin response as a change in conductance. *Psychophysiology*, 1964, 1, 31–38.

Dobson, R. L. The effect of repeated episodes of profuse sweating on the human eccrine sweat glands. *Journal of Investigative Dermatology*, 1960, 35, 195–198.

Dobson, R. L., & Sato, K. The stimulation of eccrine sweating by pharmacologic agents. In W. Montagna, R. B. Stoughton, & E. J. van Scott (Eds.), *Advances in biology of skin* (Vol. 12). New York: Appleton-Century-Crofts, 1972.

Dobson, R. L., & Slegers, J. F. G. The effect of aldosterone on sweating in the cat. *Journal of Investigative Dermatology*, 1971, 56, 337–339.

Ebling, F. J. G. The normal skin. In A. Rook, D. S. Wilkinson, & F. J. G. Ebling (Eds.), *Textbook of dermatology* (3rd ed., Vol. 1). London: Blackwell Scientific Publications, 1979.

Edelberg, R. Response of cutaneous water barrier to ideational stimulation: A GSR component. *Journal of Comparative and Physiological Psychology*, 1966, 61, 28–33.

Edelberg, R. Electrical properties of the skin. In C. C. Brown (Ed.), *Methods in psychophysiology*. Baltimore: Williams & Wilkins, 1967.

Edelberg, R. Biopotentials from the skin surface: The hydration effect. *Annals of the New York Academy of Sciences*, 1968, 148, 252–262.

Edelberg, R. The information content of the recovery limb of the electrodermal response. *Psychophysiology*, 1970, 6, 527–539.

Edelberg, R. Electrical properties of skin. In H. R. Elden (Ed.), *Biophysical properties of the skin* (Vol. 1). New York: Wiley, 1971.

Edelberg, R. Electrodermal recovery rate, goal-orientation, and aversion. *Psychophysiology*, 1972, 9, 512–520. (a)

Edelberg, R. The electrodermal system. In N. S. Greenfield & R. A. Sternbach (Eds.), *Handbook of psychophysiology*. New York: Holt, Rinehart & Winston, 1972. (b)

Edelberg, R. Mechanisms of electrodermal adaptations for locomotion, manipulation, or defense. *Progress in Physiological Psychology*, 1973, 5, 155–209.

Edelberg, R. *More on the mechanism of electrodermal recovery*. Paper presented at the meeting of the Society of Psychophysiological Research, Cincinnati, October 1979.

Edelberg, R. Personal communication, 1982.

Edelberg, R. The effects of initial levels of sweat duct filling and skin hydration on electrodermal response amplitude. *Psychophysiology*, 1983, 20, 550–557. [Portions of this paper were originally presented at the Meeting of the Society for Psychophysical Research in 1978.]

Edelberg, R., Greiner, T., & Burch, N. R. Some membrane properties of the effector in the galvanic skin response. *Journal of Applied Physiology*, 1960, 15, 691–696.

Edelberg, R., & Muller, M. Prior activity as a determinant of electrodermal recovery rate. *Psychophysiology*, 1981, 18, 17–25.

Féré, C. Note sur les modifications de la résistance électrique sous l'influence des excitations sensorielles et des émotions. *Comptes Rendus des Séances de la Société de Biologie*, 1888, 5, 217–219.

Fletcher, R. P., Venables, P. H., & Mitchell, D. A. Estimation of half from quarter recovery time of SCR. *Psychophysiology*, 1982, 19, 115–116.

Fowles, D. C. Mechanisms of electrodermal activity. In R. F. Thompson & M. M. Patterson (Eds.), *Methods in physiological psychology* (Vol. 1, *Bioelectric recording techniques*; Part C, *Receptor and effector processes*). New York: Academic Press, 1974.

Fowles, D. C. The three-arousal model: Implications of Gray's two-factor learning theory for heart rate, electrodermal activity, and psychopathy. *Psychophysiology*, 1980, 17, 87–104.

Fowles, D. C. Heart rate as an index of anxiety: Failure of a hypotheksis. In J. T. Cacioppo & R. E. Petty (Eds.), *Perspectives in cardiovascular psychophysiology*. New York: Guilford Press, 1982.

Fowles, D. C., Christie, M. J., Edelberg, R., Grings, W. W., Lykken, D. T., & Venables, P. H. Committee report: Publication recommendations for electrodermal measurements. *Psychophysiology*, 1981, 18, 232–239.

Fowles, D. C., Fisher, A. E., & Tranel, D. T. The heart beats to reward: The effect of monetary incentive on heart rate. *Psychophysiology*, 1982, 19, 506–513.

Fowles, D. C., & Rosenberry, R. Effects of epidermal hydration on skin potential responses and levels. *Psychophysiology*, 1973, 10, 601–611.

Fowles, D. C., & Schneider, R. E. Effects of epidermal hydration on skin conductance responses and levels. *Biological Psychology*, 1974, 2, 67–77.

Fowles, D. C., & Schneider, R. E. Electrolyte effects on measurements of palmar skin potential. *Psychophysiology*, 1978, 15, 474–482.

Fowles, D. C., & Venables, P. H. The effects of epidermal hydration and sodium reabsorption on palmar skin potential. *Psychological Bulletin*, 1970, 73, 363–378. (a)

Fowles, D. C., & Venables, P. H. The reduction of palmar skin potential by epidermal hydration. *Psychophysiology*, 1970, 7, 254–261. (b)

Frömter, E., & Diamond, J. Route of passive ion permeation in epithelia. *Nature* (New Biology), 1972, 235, 9–13.

Goadby, K. W., & Goadby, H. K. Simultaneous photographic records of the potential and resistance effects of the psychoemotive response. *Journal of Physiology*, 1936, 86, 11P–13P.

Gordon, R. S., Jr., & Cage, G. W. Mechanism of water and electrolyte secretion by the eccrine sweat gland. *Lancet*, 1966, 1, 1246–1250.

Gray, J. A. The behavioral inhibition system: A possible substrate for anxiety. In M. P. Feldman & A. M. Broadhurst (Eds.), *Theoretical and experimental bases of behavior modification.* New York: Wiley, 1976. (a)

Gray, J. A. The neuropsychology of anxiety. In I. G. Sarason & C. D. Spielberger (Eds.), *Stress and anxiety* (Vol. 3). Washington, D.C.: Hemisphere, 1976. (b)

Gray, J. A. The neuropsychology of anxiety. *British Journal of Psychology*, 1978, 69, 417–434.

Gray, J. A. A neuropsychological theory of anxiety. In C. E. Izard (Ed.), *Emotions in personality and psychopathology.* New York: Plenum Press, 1979.

Grice, K. A. Transepidermal water loss in pathological skin. In A. Jarrett (Ed.), *The physiology and pathophysiology of the skin* (Vol. 6, *The mucous membranes, the action of Vitamin A on the skin and mucous membranes, and transepidermal water loss*). New York: Academic Press, 1980.

Grice, K. A., & Verbov, J. Sweat glands and their disorders. In A. Rook (Ed.), *Recent advances in dermatology* (No. 4). New York: Churchill Livingstone, 1977.

Grings, W. W. Recording of electrodermal phenomena. In R. F. Thompson & M. M. Patterson (Eds.), *Methods in physiological psychology* (Vol. 1, *Bioelectric recording techniques*; Part C, *Receptor and effector processes*). New York: Academic Press, 1974.

Guyton, A. C. *Textbook of medical physiology* (5th ed.). Philadelphia: W. B. Saunders, 1976.

Hashimoto, K. The eccrine gland. In A. Jarrett (Ed.), *The physiology and pathophysiology of the skin* (Vol. 5, *The sweat glands, skin permeation, lymphatics, and the nails*). New York: Academic Press, 1978.

Hurley, H. J. Permeability of the skin. In S. L. Moschella, D. M. Pillsbury, & H. J. Hurley, Jr. (Eds.), *Dermatology* (Vol. 1). Philadelphia: W. B. Saunders, 1975.

Janes, C. L. Electrodermal recovery and stimulus significance. *Psychophysiology*, 1982, 19, 129–135.

Jarrett, A. The epidermis and its relations with the dermis. In A. Jarrett (Ed.), *The physiology and pathophysiology of the skin* (Vol. 1, *The epidermis*). New York: Academic Press, 1973. (a)

Jarrett, A. Normal epidermal keratinization. In A. Jarrett (Ed.), *The physiology and pathophysiology of the skin* (Vol. 1, *The epidermis*). New York: Academic Press, 1973. (b)

Jarrett, A. (Ed.). *The physiology and pathophysiology of the skin* (Vol. 1, *The epidermis*). New York: Academic Press, 1973. (c)

Jarrett, A. (Ed.). *The physiology and pathophysiology of the skin* (Vol. 2, *The nerves and blood vessels*). New York: Academic Press, 1973. (d)

Jarrett, A. (Ed.). *The physiology and pathophysiology of the skin* (Vol. 3, *The dermis and the dendrocytes*). New York: Academic Press, 1974.

Jarrett, A. (Ed.). *The physiology and pathophysiology of the skin* (Vol. 4, *The hair follicle*). New York: Academic Press, 1977.

Jarrett, A. (Ed.). *The physiology and pathophysiology of the skin* (Vol. 5, *The sweat glands, skin permeation, lymphatics, and the nails*). New York: Academic Press, 1978.

Jarrett, A. Introduction: The permeability barrier. In A. Jarrett (Ed.), *The physiology and pathophysiology of the skin* (Vol. 6, *The mucous membranes, the action of Vitamin A on the skin and mucous membranes, and transepidermal water loss*). New York: Academic Press, 1980. (a)

Jarrett, A. (Ed.). *The physiology and pathophysiology of the skin* (Vol. 6, *The mucous membranes, the action of Vitamin A on the skin and mucous membranes, and transepidermal water loss*). New York: Academic Press, 1980. (b)

Kligman, A. M. The biology of the stratum corneum. In W. Montagna & W. C. Lobitz, Jr. (Eds.), *The epidermis.* New York: Academic Press, 1964.

Kuno, Y. *Human perspiration.* Springfield, Ill. Charles C Thomas, 1956.

Lacey, J. I. Somatic response patterning and stress: Some revisions of activation theory. In M. H. Appley & R. Trumbull (Eds.), *Psychological stress: Issues in research.* New York: Appleton-Century-Crofts, 1967.

Lader, M. H., & Montagu, J. D. The psycho-galvanic reflex: A pharmacological study of the peripheral mechanism. *Journal of Neurology, Neurosurgery and Psychiatry*, 1962, 25, 126–133.

Lloyd, D. P. C. Electrical impedance changes of the cat's foot pad in relation to sweat secretion and reabsorption. *Journal of General Physiology*, 1960, 43, 713–722.

Lloyd, D. P. C. Action potential and secretory potential of sweat glands. *Proceedings of the National Academy of Sciences USA*, 1961, 47, 351–358.

Lloyd, D. P. C. Secretion and reabsorption in eccrine sweat glands. In W. Montagna, R. A. Ellis, & A. S. Silver (Eds.), *Advances in biology of skin* (Vol. 3, *Eccrine sweat glands and eccrine sweating*). New York: Macmillan, 1962.

Lykken, D. T. Neuropsychology and psychophysiology in personality research: Part II. Psychophysiological techniques and personality research. In E. F. Borgatta & W. W. Lambert (Eds.), *Handbook of personality theory and research.* Chicago: Rand McNally, 1968.

Lykken, D. T., Miller, R. D., & Strahan, R. F. Some properties of skin conductance and potential. *Psychophysiology*, 1968, 5, 253–268.

Lykken, D. T., & Venables, P. H. Direct measurement of skin conductance: A proposal for standardization. *Psychophysiology*, 1971, 8, 656–672.

Mangos, J. A. Transductal fluxes of Na, K and water in the human eccrine sweat gland. *American Journal of Physiology*, 1973, 224, 1235–1240.

Martin, I., & Venables, P. H. Mechanisms of palmar skin resistance and skin potential. *Psychological Bulletin*, 1966, 65, 347–357.

Montagna, W., & Parakkal, P. F. *The structure and function of skin* (3rd ed.). New York: Academic Press, 1974.

Morimoto, T. Acclimatization of sweating mechanism to hot environments. In A. Jarrett (Ed.), *The physiology and pathophysiology of the skin* (Vol. 5, *The sweat glands, skin permeation, lymphatics, and the nails*). New York: Academic Press, 1978. (a)

Morimoto, T. Endocrine function and sweating. In A. Jarrett (Ed.), *The physiology and pathophysiology of the skin* (Vol. 5, *The sweat glands, skin permeation, lymphatics, and the nails*). New York: Academic Press, 1978. (b)

Morimoto, T. The regulation of secretory activity. In A. Jarrett, (Ed.), *The physiology and pathophysiology of the skin* (Vol. 5, *The sweat glands, skin permeation, lymphatics, and the nails*). New York: Academic Press, 1978. (c)

Morimoto, T. Sweat secretion. In A. Jarrett (Ed.), *The physiology and pathophysiology of the skin* (Vol. 5, *The sweat glands, skin permeation, lymphatics, and the nails*). New York: Academic Press, 1978. (d)

Morimoto, T. Variations of sweating activity due to sex, age, and race. In A. Jarrett (Ed.), *The physiology and pathophysiology of the skin* (Vol. 5, *The sweat glands, skin permeation, lymphatics, and the nails*). New York: Academic Press, 1978. (e)

Munger, B. L. The ultrastructure and histophysiology of human eccrine sweat glands. *Journal of Biophysical and Biochemical Cytology*, 1961, 11, 385–402.

Munger, B. L. Histology and cytology of the sweat glands. In E. B. Helwig & F. K. Mostofi (Eds.), *The skin.* Baltimore: Williams & Wilkins, 1971.

Munger, B. L., & Brusilow, S. W. An electron microscopic study of eccrine sweat glands of the cat foot and toepads—evidence for ductal reabsorption in the human. *Journal of Biophysical and Biochemical Cytology*, 1961, 11, 403–417.

Neumann, E., & Blanton, R. The early history of electrodermal research. *Psychophysiology*, 1970, 6, 453–475.

Pinkus, H. Embryology and anatomy of skin. In E. B. Helwig & F. K. Mostofi (Eds.), *The skin.* Baltimore: Williams & Wilkins, 1971.

Prince, W. T. Fluid secretion in exocrine glands. In B. L. Gupta,

R. B. Moreton, J. L. Oschman, & B. J. Wall (Eds.), *Transport of ions and water in animals*. New York: Academic Press, 1977.

Raskin, D. C. Attention and arousal. In W. F. Prokasy & D. C. Raskin (Eds.), *Electrodermal activity in psychological research*. New York: Academic Press, 1973.

Raskin, D. C., Kotses, H., & Bever, J. Autonomic indicators of orienting and defensive reflexes. *Journal of Experimental Psychology*, 1969, 80, 423–433.

Richter, C. P. A study of the electrical skin resistance and the psychogalvanic reflex in a case of unilateral sweating. *Brain*, 1927, 50, 216–235.

Richter, C. P., & Woodruff, B. G. Changes produced by sympathectomy in the electrical resistance of the skin. *Surgery*, 1941, 10, 957–970.

Roberts, L. E., & Young, R. Electrodermal responses are independent of movement during aversive conditioning in rats, but heart rate is not. *Journal of Comparative and Physiological Psychology*, 1971, 77, 495–512.

Rook, A., Wilkinson, D. S., & Ebling, F. J. G. (Eds.). *Textbook of dermatology* (3rd ed.). London: Blackwell Scientific Publications, 1979.

Rothman, S. *Physiology and biochemistry of the skin*. Chicago: University of Chicago Press, 1954.

Sarkany, I., Shuster, S., & Stammers, M. Occlusion of the sweat pore by hydration. *British Journal of Dermatology*, 1965, 77, 101–105.

Sato, K. Sweat induction from an isolation eccrine sweat gland. *American Journal of Physiology*, 1973, 225, 1147–1152.

Sato, K. The physiology, pharmacology, and biochemistry of the eccrine sweat gland. *Review of Physiology, Biochemistry, and Pharmacology*, 1977, 79, 51–131.

Sato, K., & Dobson, R. L. Regional and individual variations in the function of the human eccrine sweat gland. *Journal of Investigative Dermatology*, 1970, 54, 443–449.

Scheuplein, R. Site variations in diffusion and permeability. In A. Jarrett (Ed.), *The physiology and pathophysiology of the skin* (Vol. 5, *The sweat glands, skin permeation, lymphatics, and the nails*). New York: Academic Press, 1978. (a)

Scheuplein, R. The skin as a barrier. In A. Jarrett (Ed.), *The physiology and pathophysiology of the skin* (Vol. 5, *The sweat glands, skin permeation, lymphatics, and the nails*). New York: Academic Press, 1978. (b)

Scheuplein, R. Skin permeation. In A. Jarrett (Ed.), *The physiology and pathophysiology of the skin* (Vol. 5, *The sweat glands, skin permeation, lymphatics, and the nails*). New York: Academic Press, 1978. (c)

Scheuplein, R., & Blank, H. Permeability of the skin. *Physiological Reviews*, 1971, 51, 702–747.

Schneider, R. E., & Fowles, D. C. A convenient, non-hydrating electrolyte for the measurement of electrodermal activity. *Psychophysiology*, 1978, 15, 483–486.

Schneider, R. E., & Fowles, D. C. Unibase/glycol as an electrolyte medium for recording the electrodermal duct filling response. *Psychophysiology*, 1979, 16, 56–60.

Schulz, I., Ullrich, K. J., Frömter, E., Holzgreve, H., Frick, A. & Hegel, U. Mikropunktion und elektrische potential-messung an schweißdrusen des menschen. *Pflugers Archiv*, 1965, 284, 360–372.

Shaver, B. A., Brusilow, S. W., & Cooke, R. E. Electrophysiology of the sweat gland: Intraductal potential changes during secretion. *Bulletin of the Johns Hopkins Hospital*, 1962, 116, 100–109.

Silver, A. Montagna, W., & Karacan, I. Age and sex differences in spontaneous adrenergic and cholinergic human sweating. *Journal of Investigative Dermatology*, 1964, 43, 255–266.

Silver, A., Montagna, W., & Karacan, I. The effect of age on human eccrine sweating. In W. Montagna (Ed.), *Advances in biology of skin* (Vol. 6). Oxford: Pergamon Press, 1965.

Sinclair, D. Motor nerves and reflexes. In A. Jarrett (Ed.), *The physiology and pathophysiology of the skin* (Vol. 2), *The nerves and blood vessels*). New York: Academic Press, 1973.

Spearman, R. I. C. Hair follicle development. In A. Jarrett (Ed.), *The physiology and pathophysiology of the skin* (Vol. 4, *The hair follicle*). New York: Academic Press, 1977.

Stombaugh, D. P., & Adams, T. Skin electrical phenomena, sweat gland activity, and epidermal hydration of the cat footpad. *American Journal of Physiology*, 1971, 221, 1014–1018.

Szakall, A. Experimentalle daten zur klarung der funktion der wasserbarriere in der epidermis des lebenden menschen. *Berufsdermatosen*, 1958, 6, 171–192.

Terada, E. Effects of adrenaline on human sweating. *Journal of the Physiological Society of Japan*, 1966, 28, 176–183.

Thaysen, J. H., Thorn, N. A., & Schwartz, I. L. *American Journal of Physiology*, 1954, 178, 155–159.

Thomas, P. E., & Korr, I. M. Relationship between sweat gland activity and electrical resistance of the skin. *Journal of Applied Physiology*, 1957, 10, 505–510.

Tranel, D. T., Fisher, A. E., & Fowles, D. C. Magnitude of incentive effects on heart rates. *Psychophysiology*, 1982, 19, 514–519.

Tranel, D. T. The effects of monetary incentive and frustrative nonreward on heart rate and electrodermal activity. *Psychophysiology*, 1983, 20, 652–657.

Ullrich, K. J. Introduction. *Modern Problems in Pediatrics*, 1967, 10, 20–22.

Uno, H., & Montagna, W. Catecholamine-containing nerve terminals of the eccrine sweat gland of macaques. *Cell and Tissue Research*, 1975, 158, 1–13.

Ussing, H. H. Transport through epithelial membranes. In H. H. Ussing, P. Kruhoffer, J. H. Thaysen, & N. A. Thorn (Eds.), *The alkali metal ions in biology*. Berlin: Springer-Verlag, 1960.

Venables, P. H., & Christie, M. J. Mechanisms, instrumentation, recording techniques, and quantification of responses. In W. F. Prokasy & D. C. Raskin (Eds.), *Electrodermal activity in psychological research*. New York: Academic Press, 1973.

Venables, P. H., & Christie, M. J. Electrodermal activity. In I. Martin & P. H. Venables (Eds.), *Techniques in psychophysiology*. New York: Wiley, 1980.

Venables, P. H., & Fletcher, R. P. The status of skin conductance recovery time: An examination of the Bundy effect. *Psychophysiology*, 1981, 18, 10–16.

Venables, P. H., & Martin, I. The relation of palmar sweat gland activity to level of skin potential and conductance. *Psychophysiology*, 1967, 3, 302–311. (a)

Venables, P. H., & Martin, I. Skin resistance and skin potential. In P. H. Venables & I. Martin (Eds.), *A manual of psychophysiological methods*. Amsterdam: North-Holland, 1967. (b)

Venables, P. H., & Sayer, E. On the measurement of skin potential. *British Journal of Psychology*, 1963, 54, 251–260.

Wagner, H. N. Electrical skin resistance studies in two persons with congenital absence of sweat glands. *Archives of Dermatology and Syphilology*, 1952, 65, 543–548.

Wilcott, R. C. Correlation of skin resistance and potential. *Journal of Comparative and Physiological Psychology*, 1958, 51, 691–696.

Wilcott, R. C. Palmar skin sweating versus palmar skin resistance and skin potential. *Journal of Comparative and Physiological Psychology*, 1962, 55, 327–331.

Wilcott, R. C. The partial independence of skin potential and skin resistance from sweating. *Psychophysiology*, 1964, 1, 55–66.

Wilcott, R. C. A comparative study of the skin potential, skin resistance and sweating of the cat's foot pad. *Psychophysiology*, 1965, 2, 62–71.

Woodbury, J. W. Action potential: Properties of excitable membranes. In T. C. Ruch & H. D. Patton (Eds.), *Physiology and biophysics*. Philadelphia: W. B. Saunders, 1965.

Chapter Five

The Musculature

John V. Basmajian

MUSCLE MORPHOLOGY

Gross Morphology: General

Muscle is Latin for "little mouse," and it is from the fancied resemblance of some muscles to mice that the name arose in ancient times. There are three types of muscular tissue: (1) "skeletal" (or "striated," or "voluntary"), as in the limbs and body wall; (2) "cardiac" (or "heart"); and (3) "smooth" (or "visceral," or "involuntary"), as in the walls of hollow organs and blood vessels. To contract—and thus to do *work*—is the purpose of all muscles, which therefore also must have a relaxation phase.

Skeletal muscle is also called "striated" because its constituent cells, called "fibers" because they are elongated, are seen under the microscope to have alternating light and dark stripes. However, cardiac muscle is also striped, though it is not directly under voluntary control. Smooth muscle fibers, as their name proclaims, are unstriped.

The distribution throughout the body of the three types of muscle tissue seems to be related to function: Striated muscle is capable of rapid contraction and relaxation, while smooth muscle can give slow sustained contractions without fatigue, as would be required in the blood vessels.

In the remainder of this chapter, only skeletal (striated) muscle is discussed. Skeletal muscles mostly cross from one bone to another across a joint (or joints). By contracting and shortening, a muscle approximates its two ends ("origin" and "insertion") and so moves the intervening joint(s). On other occasions, the contraction of a muscle does not or cannot produce movement because of countervailing forces (e.g., gravity or antagonist muscles); this results in a steadying or a fixing of the joints, as might be needed in the elbow during pushing and the leg and back muscles during standing. Hence the old term "contraction" is a misnomer, because a muscle may perform an important function without actually shortening (i.e., contracting). But the term seems to be embedded in the terminology of muscle physiology.

Architecture

Parts of Muscle

The contractile part of a muscle is its "fleshy belly," which may run from the one attachment to the other.

John V. Basmajian. Division of Rehabilitation Medicine, Department of Medicine, McMaster University and Chedoke–McMaster Hospital, Hamilton, Ontario, Canada.

Most muscles narrow at one or both ends to noncontractile, tough, fibrous cords or bands, called "tendons." The fleshy belly is, of course, the truly dynamic part of a muscle, but it is generally not appreciated that it also contains considerable noncontractile fibrous tissue and many blood vessels. Indeed, it is estimated that all muscle fibers are separated from their neighbors by a network of capillary vessels that nourish the fibers. Being the great motors of the body, the muscle fibers require enormous quantities of glucose and oxygen when they act.

Internal Structure

Muscle fibers are disposed in various geometric arrangements to fulfill specific functions. When the fibers run longitudinally in the muscle, the result is not as powerful as when they run obliquely, because more fibers (hence more power) are packed into the obliquely fibered muscle. When an individual muscle fiber contracts, it shortens to 57% of its resting length. Thus the longer the fleshy belly, generally the longer the range of motion produced by an unresisted contraction.

Muscle Fiber in Its Surroundings

From the description above, it should be apparent that the elongated muscle fibers are loosely packed together in bundles, with many blood capillaries forming a network between and among them. Muscle fibers are wrapped together in bundles by fibrous tissue, which eventually runs into the tendons at the ends of the muscle and hence transmits force to the bones. Coarser collections of bundles are further wrapped in fibrous coverings until finally the whole muscle is enclosed in a fibrous sheath of connective tissue, which separates the muscle from its neighbor.

Fiber Morphology

Each muscle fiber is a long thread-like cell consisting of sarcoplasm, myofibrils, multiple nuclei, and a cell membrane or sarcolemma. Fibers range in length from about 1 mm to more than 40 mm; in cross-section, their diameters vary up to about .2 mm.

Sarcolemma

The "sarcolemma" is the outer plasma membrane of the multinucleated muscle cell. It covers and encloses the sarcoplasm and nuclei. Outside of it is a thicker outer membrane of fibrous tissue elements, the basal lamina. The sarcolemma plays a vital role in the physicochemical and electrical processes of contraction and relaxation.

Sarcoplasm

"Sarcoplasm" is the relatively undifferentiated protoplasm in which the myofibrils are embedded. Sarcoplasm varies in amount and constituents (a variety of special granules and micro-organs) according to function. When there are many such granules and sarcoplasm, a muscle appears darker, and this affects the contraction time and force exerted. A discussion of dark and light (red and white) muscle fibers would take many pages and would not fit the needs addressed by this volume.

Myofibrils

The units of contraction that transmit force to the ends of the muscle fiber are the "myofibrils." These are less than a micrometer (or micron) in diameter and can only be made visible by electron microscopy. They are arranged in bundles within the sarcoplasm. Being cross-striated, they make the whole muscle fiber appear to be striped. Again, details of morphology are available in histology textbooks; here, it is necessary only to emphasize that the cross-striations represent a special spatial arrangement of multitudes of macromolecular filaments. These filaments are made up by either actin or myosin molecules; their chemical interaction results in a longitudinal sliding of the one set on the other to effect an overall shortening of the myofilament during a contraction. Sliding in the opposite directions occurs with a reversal of the electrical and chemical events.

Myoneural Junction

Each mammalian muscle fiber receives the termination of one nerve fiber or motor axon. A special type of synapse occurs at the meeting place. The axoplasm remains separated from the sarcolemma but forms a special depressed and folded area on it, called the "motor end plate." Between the neural and muscular elements, there is a clear zone across which acetylcholine is released by the arrival of a nerve impulse to stimulate the initiation of the electrical and chemical events that culminate in a contraction. It is here, too, that reverse chemical syntheses must occur in preparation for the next impulse's arrival at the end plate. Since contractions occur at frequencies up to 50 Hz, one can appreciate the speed of recovery needed in these transactions.

Motor Units

While the muscle fiber is conceded to be the fundamental substrate of muscle morphology, the motor unit is the functional (neuromotor) one. In normal mammalian striated muscle, muscle fibers never contract as individuals; they are part of a motor unit all of whose fibers contract almost simultaneously during the brief twitch of the motor unit. All the fibers of the motor unit are supplied by terminal branches of one axon that comes from one motoneuron in the ventral horn of the spinal cord (or cranial nerve motor nucleus). A "motor unit" is defined as the motoneuron, its axon and branches, and the muscle fibers they innervate.

From the beginnings of electromyography, we have known that the electromyogram (EMG) is a fairly accurate copy of the electroneurogram and that the electrical responses in the individual muscle fibers should give just as accurate a measure of the nerve fiber frequency as the record made from the nerve itself.

Motor Unit Contraction

Motor units normally contract sharply upon the arrival of each nervous impulse at various frequencies, usually below 50 Hz. This frequency seems to be the upper physiological limit for the frequency of propagation of axonal impulses; apparently, such factors as a necessary recovery period, and the threshold of fatigue in nerves and muscle, must be involved in its determination.

Morphological Arrangement of Motor Units

The number of muscle fibers that are served by one axon varies widely. Generally, muscles that control fine movements and adjustments (such as those attached to the ossicles of the ear and to the eyeball and the larynx) have few muscle fibers per motor unit. Hence, for example, extraocular muscles have small motor units with less than 10 fibers per unit. Large coarse-acting muscles in the limbs have large motor units.

Asynchrony

Complete asynchrony of the motor unit contractions is imposed by asynchronous volleys of impulses coming down the many axons. All the motor units are contracting and relaxing with twitch-like action at differing rates up to 50 Hz. The result of a continuous shower of twitches with different frequencies within a muscle is a smooth pull. In certain disturbances, however, the contractions may become synchronized, resulting in a visible tremor.

MOTOR UNIT POTENTIAL

From histochemical and EMG studies, Buchthal and Rosenfalck (1973) concluded that the intermingling of several motor units means that the individual motor unit is not characterized by a single action potential; rather, a multitude of action potentials can

be picked up separately at different sites within the motor units. They differ in amplitude and shape, according to the grouping of the fibers near the recording multielectrode. The difference in shape of the different potentials is due to the temporal dispersion—as great as 5–7 msec—of the spike components, which, in turn, is caused by the spatial distribution.

When an impulse reaches the myoneural junction or motor end plate, a wave of contraction spreads over the fiber; this results in a brief twitch, followed by rapid and complete relaxation. The duration of this twitch and relaxation varies from a few milliseconds to as much as .2 sec, depending on the type of fiber involved (fast or slow). During the twitch, a minute electrical potential, with a duration of only 1 or 2 (or possibly 4) msec, is generated, which is dissipated into the surrounding tissues. Since all the muscle fibers of a motor unit do not contract at exactly the same time—some being delayed for several milliseconds—the electrical potential developed by the single twitch of all the fibers in the motor unit is prolonged to between 5 and 12 msec. The electrical result of the motor unit twitch, then, is an electrical discharge with a median duration of 9 msec and a total amplitude measured in microvolts—up to about 500 μV—with standard needle electrodes. With surface electrodes, the durations are prolonged as the potentials are "blurred" and rounded out; with bipolar fine wire electrodes, the potentials are considerably shorter, the mean duration being 5 msec (Basmajian & Cross, 1971).

The majority of motor unit potentials seen on a cathode ray oscilloscope (or other display device) are sharp spikes, most often triphasic or biphasic. The larger the motor unit potential, the larger the motor unit producing it, all other things being equal. With changes in muscle tension, there is a change in the signal characteristics of averaged EMG potentials picked up by surface electrodes (number of spikes, amplitude, rise time, and amplitude-rise time).

In rapid isometric contractions, individual motor units initially burst into activity at rates of up to 90 Hz and fall quickly to about 10–20 Hz as maximum tension is achieved (Tanji & Kato, 1972). During slow contractions of the same muscle (abductor digiti minimi), the rates of the same motor units rise to only 40 Hz at about the 70% level of the tension, and fall after that to the same "hold" level of 10–20 Hz. In a study of the effects of changing from one level of voluntary isometric contractions to another, Gillies (1972) found that with gradual (10% per second) increases of force, newly recruited units first discharged at lower rates than those recruited at low force. When ramp increases in force (e.g., 30° per second) were called for, there was a temporary increase in frequencies before new levels were maintained. Discharge frequencies varied from 8 to 35 Hz. Thus both the level of force and its rate of change determine the discharge frequency of motor units in a voluntary isometric contraction. Goldberg and Derfler (1977) found a positive correlation among force of recruitment, spike amplitude, and peak twitch tension.

During voluntary dynamic movements, the myoelectric burst precedes the onset of movement (Maton & Bouisset, 1975). As soon as a motor unit is set into activity at the start of the myoelectric burst, there is a consistent relation between the work to be accomplished and the interval between the two consecutive discharges of this motor unit. Thus, the peak velocity of the movement is preprogrammed when the amplitude of movement is voluntarily limited.

In a study of the mechanisms required for increased force during voluntary contractions, Milner-Brown, Stein, and Yemm (1972) found that during an isometric contraction of increasing magnitude, recruitment of additional motor units is the chief mechanism for raising tension at low forces. At higher force levels, the predominant mechanism is to increase the rates of firing of motor units. Units are recruited in order of increasing strength as the total force output is increased. Also, units with smaller twitch tensions recruited at low forces show smaller fractional increases in their rate of firing when compared with units that start discharging at higher forces (Milner-Brown & Stein, 1975).

In the medial gastrocnemius of the adult cat, Reinking, Stephens, and Stuart (1975) showed that motor units with long contraction times (>45 msec) were nonfatigable and small. In contrast, fast-twitch units (<45 msec) had a broad range of tetanic tension and fatigability, with a tendency to develop more tetanic tensions.

Motor Unit Firing Rates and Recruitment

As noted earlier, the normal upper limit of activation of motor units in man is about 50/sec (Adrian & Bronk, 1929). There is some evidence that higher rates occur in other mammals (e.g., unpublished findings [Basmajian, 1960] suggest a rate of over 100 Hz as a maximum in the lower limb muscles of rabbits). In recruitment, the rate of firing of motor units is increased with stronger contractions.

A motor unit remains active throughout the complete time duration of the constant-force contraction. Near the end of a sustained contraction, the amplitude of the myopotential decreases somewhat, and the time duration tends to increase; however, one-third of the potentials actually show a decreased duration. The generalized firing rate or expected firing rate of a typical motor unit decreases with time, as it does for isometric contractions at lower constant-force levels. The probability of a motor unit firing after a previous firing has occurred increases exponentially with respect to elapsed time (De Luca & Forrest, 1973a).

Motor Unit Recruitment Pattern

Under normal conditions, the smaller potentials appear first with a slight contraction; as the force is increased, larger and larger potentials are recruited, and all motor units increase their frequency of firing (Ashworth, Grimby, & Kugelberg, 1967; Freund, Büdingen, & Dietz, 1975; Grimby & Hannerz, 1974; Henneman, Somjen, & Carpenter, 1965; Olsen, Carpenter, & Henneman, 1968; Thomas, Schmidt, & Hambrecht, 1976). In spite of this, humans can be trained to suppress the small, low-threshold units (Ashworth et al., 1967; Basmajian, 1963, 1979; Basmajian, Baeza, & Fabrigar, 1965); that is, they can reverse the recruitment order of motor units from the normal pattern. However, this reversal cannot be systematized by the subject, except in the form of recruiting larger units in *solo* firing, without the normally earlier-recruited smaller units' firing first.

During a constant-force isometric contraction, a motor unit that is active at the beginning appears to remain active throughout a contraction (De Luca & Forrest, 1973b; Gilson & Mills, 1941; Grimby & Hannerz, 1977; Masland, Sheldon, & Hershey, 1969). The firing rate of motor units decreases monotonically during a sustained constant-force isometric contraction (De Luca & Forrest, 1973b; Person & Kudina, 1971). Hence, the sequential discharge of a motor unit is a time-dependent process. Gurfinkel' and Levik (1976) have presented evidence that the twitch tension of a motor unit increases during sustained stimulation. It is conceivable that these two phenomena complement each other to maintain a constant level of force. Goldberg and Derfler (1977) have presented direct evidence that in the masseter muscle, motor units with high recruitment thresholds tend to have action potentials of large amplitude and twitches with greater peak tensions than motor units recruited at lower force levels.

Fatigue

Investigations of fatigue by EMG are numerous and confusing, probably because there are many types: emotional fatigue, central nervous system fatigue, "general" fatigue, and peripheral neuromuscular fatigue of special kinds. The increasing fatigue of prolonged voluntary periodical contraction is accompanied by reduction of potentials (Loofbourrow, 1948; Seyffarth, 1940). This is exaggerated by ischemia caused by a tourniquet, with diminution and variation in amplitude of the size of the motor unit potential. A constant finding with isometric prolonged contractions is a synchronization of motor unit discharges (Herberts & Kadefors, 1976; Person & Mishin, 1964; Viitasalo & Komi, 1977).

Mortimer, Magnusson, and Petersén (1970) believe that the shift in the EMG frequency spectrum during fatigue is in large part caused by a decrease in the conduction velocity of the muscle fibers, not just the synchronization of the firing of motor units. Stephens and Taylor (1972) find evidence in human physiological studies for the idea that in a maximal voluntary contraction, neuromuscular junction fatigue is important at first, before being superseded by contractile element fatigue. The former is believed to be most marked in high-threshold motor units, while the latter affects low-threshold units.

CONTROL OF MOVEMENT

Coordination, Antagonists, and Synergy

While it is a truism that the brain orders movements of joints and not contraction of muscles, some learned movements are produced by only one or two muscles in isolation. For example, simple pronation of the forearm is usually produced by one muscle alone—pronator quadratus—unless added resistance is offered to the movement; then, more muscles are called upon (Basmajian & Travill, 1961). In elbow flexion, brachialis alone often suffices. Complex movements (such as rotation of the scapula on the chest wall during elevation of the limb) always call upon groups of cooperating muscles.

Many believe that during the movement of a joint in one direction, the muscles that move it in the opposite direction show some sort of antagonism. However, Sherrington's "reciprocal inhibition" is the rule with skilled movements: The so-called antagonist relaxes completely (Travill & Basmajian, 1961) except during a whip-like motion of a hinge joint. The brief terminal activity in antagonists serves a protective function to prevent damage, which such a force in the prime mover could produce. Cohen (1970) has demonstrated that the action of the opposite limb affects the EMG of rhythmic movements in the studied limb in a varying manner. Generally it is agreed that voluntary slow movements in normal humans do not cause stretch-reflex co-contraction of the antagonist; rather, when co-contraction occurs, it does so with rapid movements.

There is a pattern of responses in which low unsustained activity occurs in antagonists at low speeds of voluntary flexion and extension of the elbow; at middle speeds, there are successive activities in the agonist and antagonist, including common electrical silence; at high speeds of flexion and extension, there is partial overlapping of phasic activities in agonist and antagonist (Basmajian, 1979).

In effect, co-contraction of antagonists occurs to a greater or lesser degree in some movements, in some people, at some ages, and under some circumstances.

With increasing age and training at slower speeds, it tends to reduce to nil. When it occurs, it sometimes is due to reflexes and sometimes appears to be extravagant overflow. Because nervous coordination is so fine, there is no need for muscles to act consistently in antagonism to others.

Motor Control and Learning

The best movements are performed with an economy of muscular actions, which is dependent upon impulses' being sent to only one or two muscles or even a localized area of one muscle. What the brain has "learned" is patterning of these actions by means of a progressive inhibition of the inefficient mass responses that are natural to the child. Some movements are extremely economical in the well-trained person. Muscles have several (sometimes many) component parts, which are recruited in different functions at different times (Basmajian, 1979). Local activity is patterned by progressive inhibition of motoneurons until an acceptable performance is achieved. Studies of elbow flexion and thenar muscles (Basmajian & Latif, 1957; Forrest & Basmajian, 1965), which show the interplay of motor unit functions dedicated to specific postures and movements, clearly indicate that the positioning of limbs is predetermined by sets of motor units that are permitted to act for that position. The same appears to be true for well-learned movements. The mosaic of spinal motoneurons is dedicated to the learned response of a specific posture, or of a movement of a joint through space. The ultimately superior performance of a skilled movement depends on the reproducibility of the ideal, an economically spare mosaic of motoneuronal activity (Basmajian, 1977; Payton, Su, & Meydrich, 1976).

Given visual and auditory cues through electronic amplification and feedback, subjects can be quickly trained to activate single motoneurons consciously and with great precision. But conscious activation of single motoneurons in the single-motor-unit training paradigm depends on the same principles as the learning of any other novel task—that is, progressive (and sometimes rapid) inhibition of the motoneuronal activity that adds no useful function in producing a desired motor response (Smith, Basmajian, & Vanderstoep, 1974).

Training, whether it is the unconscious process or the learning of simple social motor responses in childhood or the preparation for specific skilled acts (such as those of a musician or athlete), is a progressive inhibition of many muscles that flood into play when one first attempts to produce the required response (O'Connell, 1958). The athlete's continued drill to perfect a skilled movement exhibits a large element of increasingly successful repression of undesired contractions. The young animal has enormous amounts of overactivity and reactive contractions in muscles that are serving no directed purpose in producing the desired movement or posture. Among others, Janda and Stará (1965) demonstrated in children a high incidence of mass responses in a predictable pattern, even in muscles far removed from those that produce a required movement. As children mature, this overactivity disappears and is absent in normal adults. It reappears in adults under psychological stress, but people can be trained to inhibit it to varying degrees. In patients with diseases and injuries of the central nervous system, the normal inhibition pattern is lacking; mass responses from local interoceptive and exteroceptive bombardments of the motoneurons result in an exaggerated mass response described as "spasticity."

MUSCLE MECHANICS

Protective Muscular Responses

A number of reflex phenomena have been demonstrated with EMGs. Carlsöö and Johansson (1962) showed that when a subject falls to the ground on the outstretched hand, all the muscles that surround the elbow joint are strongly activated some tenths of seconds before the hand touches the surface. Consequently, the musculature is prepared to protect the joint. This is partly a conditioned reflex and partly an unconditioned reflex arising from tonic neck and labryinthine reactions (Basmajian, 1979).

Two-Joint Muscles

A "two-joint muscle" is one that not only crosses two joints but is also known to have an important action on both. Examples include rectus femoris, the hamstrings, gracilis and sartorius, biceps brachii, and the long head of triceps.

The effect of contraction of two-joint muscles is never limited to one joint; whenever a two-joint muscle participates in a monarticular motion, its role shifts in close coordination with the other muscles. In biarticular concurrent motion, the activity of the rectus femoris and the medial hamstrings is inhibited when they are antagonists, especially when the motion of the knee is concerned (Fujiwara & Basmajian, 1975).

Muscle Sparing

Ligaments play a much greater part in supporting loads than is generally thought (Basmajian, 1979). In brief, in many normal postures, even heavy transartic-

ular loading does not recruit muscular activity. Such postures include the normal postures of the shoulder, elbow, and foot, as well as suspension by the hands. Contrary to expectation, the vertically running muscles are not active to prevent the distraction one might expect. During suspensory behavior by apes, muscles in the upper limb that might be expected to act against the force of gravity remain silent in simple hanging (Tuttle & Basmajian, 1974).

There are special inert mechanisms for preventing dislocation. For example, in the shoulder joint, the coracohumeral ligament (a great thickening in the superior capsule of the joint) provides the locking mechanism for the shoulder joint in the normal hanging position of the arm (Basmajian, 1961).

POSTURE

The idealized normal erect posture is one in which the line of gravity drops in the midline between the following bilateral points: (1) the mastoid processes; (2) a point just in front of the shoulder joints; (3) the hip joints (or just behind); (4) a point just in front of the center of the knee joints; and (5) a point just in front of the ankle joints. Muscular activity is called upon to approximate this posture, or, if the body is pulled out of the line of gravity, to bring it back into line.

In humans, the column of bones that carries the weight to the ground constitutes a series of links. Ideally, these links should be so stacked that the line of gravity passes directly through the center of each joint between them. But even in humans, this ideal is only closely approached and never completely reached—and then only momentarily. However, muscular activity of antigravity muscles in standing is slight or moderate. Sometimes it is only intermittent. On the other hand, the posture of quadrupeds, which is maintained by muscles acting on a series of flexed joints, is highly dependent on continuous support by active musclar contraction. Of course, the same is true for the human being in any but the fully erect standing posture.

Shifting from foot to foot in ordinary standing is a relief mechanism according to Carlsöö (1961) who showed that by assuming asymmetric working postures, and using the two legs alternately as the main support, the leg muscles are periodically unloaded and relaxed. Relief to the inert structures is perhaps even more significant (Basmajian, 1979).

SOME REGIONAL MUSCLE GROUPS WITH SPECIAL FUNCTIONS

In this section, only a brief review of individual muscle groups and significant highlights is possible.

Hand and Fingers: Power Grip

An enormous amount of work has been done in studying the movement of hand and fingers. In power grip, the extrinsic muscles provide the major gripping force (Long, Conrad, Hall, & Furler, 1970). All of the extrinsics are involved in power gripping and are used in proportion to the desired force to be used against the external forces. The major intrinsic muscles of power grip are the interossei, used as phalangeal rotators and metacarpophalangeal flexors. The lumbricals, with exception of the fourth, are not significantly used in power grip. The thenar muscles are used in all forms of power grip except hook grip.

Hand and Fingers: Precision Handling

In precision handling, specific extrinsic muscles provide gross motion and compressive forces.

Rotation Motions

In rotation, the interossei are important in imposing the necessary rotational forces on the object to be rotated; the motion of the metacarpophalangeal (MP) joint that provides this rotation is abduction or adduction, not rotation of the first phalanx. The lumbricals are joint extensors as in the unloaded hand, and additionally are first phalangeal abductor–adductors and rotators (Long et al., 1970).

Translation Motions

When translation motions occur toward the palm, the interossei provide intrinsic compression and rotation forces for most efficient finger positioning; the lumbricals are not active. Moving away from the palm, the handled object is driven by interossei and lumbricals to provide intrinsic compression and MP joint flexion and interphalangeal (IP) joint extension (Brandell, 1970; Long et al., 1970).

Trunk Muscles

Perineum

The abdominal and perineal muscles have received sporadic attention and perhaps have been neglected in recent years. The most interesting and practical information concerns the pelvic floor and the urethra in women; these areas are generally misunderstood. Using needle electrodes, Petersén, Franksson, and Danielsson (1955) explored the pubococcyeal part of the levator ani and the urethral sphincter. They concluded that some women are able to relax the sphincter urethrae completely, while others cannot. However, none of the women examined could relax the pubococcygeal part of the levator ani, even though

they were in the "lithotomy position." Vereecken, Derluyn, and Verduyn (1975) do not agree: They find that women have great voluntary control of levator ani.

Petersén, Stener, Seldén, and Kollberg (1962) also proved in women that voluntary complete relaxation of the external sphincter is possible even with a partially filled bladder. Voluntary interruption of micturition results in a rapid closing of the striated external sphincter; only afterwards does the posterior urethra empty relatively slowly in a proximal direction. Diminution or complete cessation of activity in the sphincter urethrae at micturition agrees with our findings in men (Basmajian & Spring, 1955).

Respiration

Jones, Beargie, and Pauly (1953) were the first to make a substantial electromyographic contribution to the knowledge of costal respiration. They countered the old concept that in normal quiet breathing the scalenes anchor or fix the first rib, while the external intercostals elevate the remaining ribs towards the first. Both sets of intercostals in humans are slightly active *constantly* during quiet breathing and show no *rhythmic* increase and decrease. In contrast with this, the scalenes show a rhythmic increase during inspiration.

With forced inspiration, the scalenes, sternomastoid, and internal and external intercostals become markedly active (Jones et al., 1953; Raper, Thompson, Shapiro, & Patterson, 1966). In contrast, with forced expiration, the scalenes are quiescent, while the intercostals are still active. The scalenes are fundamental muscles of inspiration.

Intercostals

The intercostal muscles supply the tension necessary to keep the ribs at a constant distance during inspiration (Jones et al., 1953). The main role in human respiration is performed by the diaphragm, while the intercostals are necessary for markedly increasing the intrathoracic pressure. Jones and Pauly (1957) state that perhaps the intercostal muscles are used in nonrespiratory activity more than in ordinary respiration. (See also Campbell's [1958] monograph for further details.)

In deeper breathing, Koepke, Smith, Murphy, and Dickinson (1958) showed that the lower intercostals, which are noticeably silent in quiet breathing, become progressively recruited in descending order until even the lowest become active on very deep inspiration.

Diaphragm

Petit, Milic-Emili, and Delhez (1960) devised a novel technique for diaphragmatic electromyography in conscious humans. The electrical activity was detected by means of electrodes passed down the esophagus to the level of the diaphragmatic esophageal hiatus. In four normal persons, they found the activity to be synchronous with the respiratory variations of intra-abdominal and intrathoracic pressures. Potentials occurred from the onset of inspiration and increased in intensity. They continued into expiration for a varying length of time with decreasing intensity. During increased ventilation, potentials began immediately before inspiration rather than just at its onset.

TONGUE, MOUTH, AND FACE

There is an observable difference in patterns of swallowing demonstrated by individuals within a group, as well as among the individual swallows of a single subject. A longer period of electrical activity occurs during a saliva swallow than during a water swallow. The type of bolus also seems to affect the pattern of activity in the individual muscles, as well as the length of time that they are working. The geniohyoid muscles do not begin their activity with the genioglossus muscles, but rather lag behind; also, they are not active for as long. Both pairs of muscles remain active during and after the time that the bolus has passed the area of laryngopharynx. A period of electrical silence occurs prior to the characteristic burst of activity associated with a swallow. This appears to be the result of an active inhibition (Cunningham & Basmajian, 1969).

The "tongue-safety" function of the genioglossus muscle has been confirmed by Sauerland and Mitchell (1975) and Sauerland and Harper (1976). More active during inspiration both during working and sleeping hours, the muscle prevents obstruction of the airway. The glossopharyngeal part of the superior pharyngeal constrictor ("myloglossus muscle") acts as an antagonist (Jüde, Dreschsler, & Neuhauser, 1975).

Muscles of Mastication

Temporalis

During end-to-end occlusion (incisor bite), the anterior and middle fibers are active with normal dentition and incomplete dentition with molar support; in edentulous patients, all three parts are active during incisive bite (Vitti, 1970). During molar occlusion, all the fibers of the temporalis are marked by activity in all subjects, as would be expected. This is the chief function of the temporalis.

Masseter

As would be expected, during forceful centric occlusion, the masseter muscle is very active (Vitti & Bas-majian, 1975, 1977). During chewing movements, the maximal acitivity occurs in the masseter about the time the jaw reaches the temporary position of centric occlusion, which accounts for about a fifth of the chewing cycle (Gibbs, 1975). Masseter is not an important muscle in the habitual resting position (Carlsöö, 1952; Vitti & Basmajian, 1975, 1977), though it does show some activity in its superficial part during protrusion (Carlsöö, 1952; Vitti & Basmajian, 1977).

Lip Muscles

A number of investigators have shown that superior and inferior parts of orbicularis oris that circle the mouth are separate muscles (Basmajian & White, 1973; Isley & Basmajian, 1973; Jacob, Haridas, & Ammal, 1971; White & Basmajian, 1973). They act in complex fashions during a multitude of lip positionings. Thus, forceful puffing, pulling the corners of the mouth in different directions, pursing the lips, and curling the lips over the teeth all recruit varying levels of activity, and, again, they vary from subject to subject (Isley & Basmajian, 1973).

REFERENCES

Adrian, E. D., & Bronk, D. W. The discharge of impulses in motor nerve fibres: Part II. The frequency of discharge in reflex and voluntary contractions. *Journal of Physiology*, 1929, 67, 119–151.

Ashworth, B., Grimby, L., & Kugelberg, E. Comparison of voluntary and reflex activation of motor units: Functional organization of motor neurons. *Journal of Neurology, Neurosurgery and Psychiatry*, 1967, 30, 91–98.

Basmajian, J. V. & Spring, W. B. Electromyography of the male (voluntary) sphincter urethrae. *Anatomical Record*, 1955, *121*, 388.

Basmajian, J. V. Weight-bearing by ligaments and muscles. *Canadian Journal of Surgery*, 1961, 4, 166–170.

Basmajian, J. V. Control and training of individual motor units. *Science*, 1963, 141, 440–441.

Basmajian, J. V. Motor learning and control: A working hypothesis. *Archives of Physical Medicine and Rehabilitation*, 1977, 58, 38–41.

Basmajian, J. V. *Muscles alive: Their functions revealed by electromyography* (4th ed). Baltimore: Williams & Wilkins, 1979.

Basmajian, J. V., Baeza, M., & Fabrigar, C. Conscious control and training of individual spinal motor neurons in normal human subjects. *Journal of New Drugs*, 1965, 5, 78–85.

Basmajian, J. V., & Cross, G. L. Duration of motor unit potentials from fine wire electrodes. *American Journal of Physical Medicine*, 1971, 50, 144–148.

Basmajian, J. V., & Latif, A. Integrated actions and functions of the chief flexors of the elbow: A detailed electromyographic analysis. *Journal of Bone and Joint Surgery*, 1957, 39-A, 1106–1118.

Basmajian, J. V., & Travill, A. Electromyography of the pronator muscles in the forearm. *Anatomical Record*, 1961, 139, 45–49.

Basmajian, J. V., & White, E. R. Neuromuscular control of trumpeter's lips. *Nature*, 1973, 241, 70.

Brandell, B. R. An electromyographic–cinematographic study of the muscles of the index finger. *Archives of Physical Medicine and Rehabilitation*, 1970, 51, 278–285.

Buchthal, F., & Rosenfalck, P. On the structure of motor units. In J. E. Desmedt (Ed.), *New Developments in EMG and clinical neurophysiology* (Vol. 1). Basel: Karger, 1973.

Campbell, E. J. M. *The Respiratory Muscles and the Mechanics of Breathing*. London: Lloyd-Luke Medical Books, 1958.

Carlsöö, S. Nervous coordination and mechanical function of the mandibular elevators: An electromyographic study of the activity, and an anatomic analysis of the mechanics of the muscles. *Acta Odontologica Scandinavica*, 1952, 10(Suppl. 11), 1–132.

Carlsöö, S. The static muscle load in different work positions: An electromyographic study. *Ergonomics*, 1961, 4, 193–211.

Carlsöö, S., & Johansson, O. Stabilization of and load on the elbow joint. *Acta Anatomica*, 1962, 48, 224–231.

Cohen, L. Interaction between limbs during bimanual voluntary activity. *Brain*, 1970, 93, 259–272.

Cunningham, D. P., & Basmajian, J. V. Electromyography of genioglossus and geniohyoid muscles during deglutition. *Anatomical Record*, 1969, 165, 404–410.

De Luca, C. J., & Forrest, W. J. Force analysis of individual muscles acting simultaneously on the shoulder joint during isometric abduction. *Journal of Biomechanics*, 1973, 6, 385–393. (a)

De Luca, C. J., & Forrest, W. J. Properties of motor unit action potential trains. *Kybernetics*, 1973, 12, 160–168. (b)

Forrest, W. J., & Basmajian, J. V. Function of human thenar and hypothenar muscles: An electromyographic study of twenty-five hands. *Journal of Bone and Joint Surgery*, 1965, 47-A, 1585–1594.

Freund, H. J., Büdingen, H. J. & Dietz, V. Activity of single motor units from human forearm muscles during voluntary isometric contractions. *Journal of Neurophysiology*, 1975, 38, 933–946.

Fujiwara, M. & Basmajian, J. V. Electromyographic study of two-joint muscles. *American Journal of Physical Medicine*, 1975, 54, 234–242.

Gibbs, C. H. Electromyographic activity during the motionless period of chewing. *Journal of Prosthetic Dentistry*, 1975, 34, 35–40.

Gillies, J. D. Motor unit discharge patterns during isometric contraction in man. *Journal of Physiology* (London), 1972, 223, 36–37.

Gilson, A. S., & Mills, W. B. Activities of single motor units in man during slight voluntary efforts. *American Journal of Physiology*, 1941, 133, 658–669.

Goldberg, L. J., & Derfler, B. Relationship among recruitment order, spike amplitude, and twitch tension of single motor units in human masseter muscle. *Journal of Neurophysiology*, 1977, 40, 879–880.

Grimby, L., & Hannerz, J. Differences in recruitment order and discharge pattern of motor units in the early and late flexion reflex components in man. *Acta Physiologica Scandinavica*, 1974, 90, 555–564.

Grimby, L., & Hannerz, J. Firing rate and recruitment order of toe extensor motor units in different modes of voluntary contraction. *Journal of Physiology* (London), 1977, 264, 865–879.

Gurfinkel', V. S., & Levik, Y. S. [Forming an unfused tetanus]. [*Human Physiology*] (Russian), 1976, 2, 914–924.

Henneman, E., Somjen, G., & Carpenter, D. O. Excitability and inhibitibility of motoneurons of different sizes. *Journal of Neurophysiology*, 1965, 28, 599–620.

Herberts, P., & Kadefors, R. A study of painful shoulder in welders. *Acta Orthopaedica Scandinavica*, 1976, 47, 381–387.

Isley, C. L., & Basmajian, J. V. Electromyography of the human cheeks and lips. *Anatomical Record*, 1973, 176, 143–148.

Jacob, P. P., Haridas, R., & Ammal, P. J. An electromyographic study of the behaviour of orbicularis oris and mentalis muscle. *Journal of Medical Research*, 1971, 59, 311–320.

Janda, V., & Stará, V. The role of thigh adductors in movement patterns of the hip and knee joint. *Courrier* (Centre International de l'Enfance), 1965, 15, 1–3.

Jones, D. S., Beargie, R. J., & Pauly, J. E. An electromyographic study of some muscles of costal respiration in man. *Anatomical Record*, 1953, 117, 17–24.

Jones, D. S., & Pauly, J. E. Further electromyographic studies on muscles of costal respiration in man. *Anatomical Record*, 1957, 128, 733–746.

Jüde, H. D., Drechsler, F., & Neuhauser, B. Elementare elekromyographische Analyse and Bewegungstmuster des M. myloglossus. *Deutsche Zahärztl Zeitschrifte*, 1975, 30, 457–461.

Koepke, G. H., Smith, E. M., Murphy, A. J., & Dickinson, D. G. Sequence of action of the diaphragm and intercostal muscles during respiration. I. Inspiration. *Archives of Physical Medicine*, 1958, 39, 426–430.

Long, C., Conrad, P. W., Hall, E. W., & Furler, S. L. Intrinsic-extrinsic muscle control of the hand in power grip and precision handling. *Journal of Bone and Joint Surgery*, 1970, 52-A, 853–867.

Masland, W. S., Sheldon, D., & Hershey, C. D. The stochastic properties of individual motor unit inter-spike intervals. *American Journal of Physiology*, 1969, 217, 1385–1388.

Maton, B., & Bouisset, S. Motor unit activity and preprogramming of movement in man. *Electroencephalography and Clinical Neurophysiology*, 1975, 38, 658–660.

Milner-Brown, H. S., & Stein, R. B. The relation between the surface electromyogram and muscular force. *Journal of Physiology* (London), 1975, 246, 549–569.

Milner-Brown, H. S., Stein, R. B., & Yemm, R. Mechanisms for increasing force during voluntary contractions. *Journal of Physiology* (London), 1972, 226, 18–19.

Mortimer, J. T., Magnusson, R., & Petersén, I. Isometric contraction, muscle blood flow, and the frequency spectrum of the electromyogram. In E. Spring, T. Jauhianinen, & T. Honkavaara (Eds.), *Proceedings of the First Nordic Meeting on Medical and Biological Engineering*. Helsinki: Society of Medical & Biological Engineers, Publishers, 1970.

O'Connell, A. L. Electromyographic study of certain leg muscles during movements of the free foot and during standing. *American Journal of Physical Medicine*, 1958, 37, 289–301.

Olsen, C. B., Carpenter, D. O., & Henneman, E. Orderly recruitment of muscle action potentials: Motor unit threshold and EMG amplitude. *Archives of Neurology*, 1968, 19, 591–597.

Payton, O. D., Su, S., & Meydrich, E. F. Abductor digiti shuffleboard: A study on motor learning. *Archives of Physical Medicine and Rehabilitation*, 1976, 57, 169–174.

Person, R. S., & Kudina, L. P. Pattern of human motoneuron activity during voluntary muscular contraction. *Neurophysiology*, 1971, 3, 455–462.

Person, R. S., & Mishin, L. N. Auto- and cross-correlation analysis of the electrical activity of muscles. *Medical Electronics & Biological Engineering*, 1964, 2, 155–159.

Petersén, I., Franksson, C., & Danielsson, C.-O. Electromyographic study of the muscles of the pelvic floor and urethra in normal females. *Acta Obstetrica Gynecologica Scandinavica*, 1955, 34, 273–285.

Petersén, I., Stener, I., Selldén, U., & Kollberg, S. Investigation of urethral sphincter in women with simultaneous electromyography and micturition urethro-cystography. *Acta Neurologica Scandinavica*, 1962, 38(Suppl. 3), 145–51.

Petit, J. M., Milic-Emili, G., & Delhez, L. Role of the diaphragm in breathing in conscious normal man: An electromographic study. *Journal of Applied Physiology*, 1960, 15, 1101–1106.

Raper, A. J., Thompson, W. T., Jr., Shapiro, W., & Patterson, J. L., Jr. Scalene and sternomastoid muscle function. *Journal of Applied Physiology*, 1966, 121, 497–502.

Reinking, R. M., Stephens, J. A., & Stuart, D. G. The motor units of cat medial gastrocnemius: Problem of their categorisation on the basis of mechanical properties. *Experimental Brain Research*, 1975, 23 301–313.

Sauerland, E. K., & Harper, R. M. The human tongue during sleep; electromyographic activity of the genioglossus muscle. *Experimental Neurology*, 1976, 51, 160–170.

Sauerland, E. K., & Mitchell, S. P. Electromyographic activity of intrinsic and extrinsic muscles of the human tongue. *Texas Reports of Biology and Medicine*, 1975, 33, 445–455.

Seyffarth, H. *The Behaviour of Motor-Units in Voluntary Contraction*,

Oslo: I. Kommisjon Hos Jacob Dybwad, A. W. Brøggers Boktrykeri A/S, 1940.

Smith, H. M., Jr., Basmajian, J. V., & Vanderstoep, S. F. Inhibition of neighboring motoneurons in conscious control of single spinal motoneurons. *Science*, 1974, 183, 975–976.

Stephens, J. A., & Taylor, A. Fatigue of maintained voluntary muscle contraction in man. *Journal of Physiology* (London), 1972, 220, 1–18.

Tanji, J., & Kato, M. Discharges of single motor units at voluntary contraction of abductor digiti minimi muscle in man. *Brain Research*, 1972, 45, 590–593.

Thomas, J. S., Schmidt, E. M., & Hambrecht, F. T. *Limitations of volitional control of single motor unit recruitment sequence.* Paper presented at the annual meeting of the Society of Neuroscience, Toronto, 1976.

Travill, A., & Basmajian, J. V. Electromyography of the supinators of the forearm. *Anatomical Record*, 1961, 139, 557–560.

Tuttle, R., & Basmajian, J. V. Electromyographic studies of brachial muscles in *Pan gorilla* and hominoid evolution. *American Journal of Physical Antrhopology*, 1974, 41, 71–90.

Vereecken, R. L., Derluyn, J. and Verduyn, H. Electromyography of the perineal striated muscles during cystometry. *Urology International*, 1975, 30, 90–98.

Viitasalo, J. H. T., & Komi, P. V. Signal characteristics of EMG during fatigue. *European Journal of Applied Physiology*, 1977, 37, 111–121.

Vitti, M. Comportamento eletromiográfica do musculo temporal nas mordidas incisiva e molares homo e heterolaterais. *O Hospital* (São Paulo), 1970, 78, 207–214.

Vitti, M., & Basmajian, J. V. Muscles of mastication in small children: An electromyographic analysis. *American Journal of Orthodontics*, 1975, 68, 412–419.

Vitti, M., & Basmajian, J. V. Integrated actions of masticatory muscle: Simultaneous EMG from eight intramuscular electrodes. *Anatomical Record*, 1977, 187, 173–189.

White, E. R., & Basmajian, J. V. Electromyography of lip muscles and their role in trumpet playing. *Journal of Applied Physiology*, 1973, 35, 892–897.

Chapter Six

Physiological Bases of Respiratory Psychophysiology

Marc P. Kaufman
Neil Schneiderman

INTRODUCTION

Mechanisms for the exchange of gases between the organism and the external environment are provided by the respiratory system. The major component of this system is the lung, which serves as the intermediary for the transport of oxygen (O_2) into the blood. By virtue of its interposition between the venous and arterial circulations, metabolic products that are released from bodily organs into the venous circulation must first pass through the lungs before being expelled from the body or transported to a distant organ. Lung tissue can also modify or inactivate substances that come in contact with it (Sackner, 1976).

The respiratory system includes the airways to the lungs and the muscles of respiration, as well as the lungs themselves. Although the system has many functions, including those involved in talking and inactivating or expelling substances from the body, its major life-sustaining functions are to maintain proper concentrations of O_2, carbon dioxide (CO_2), and hydrogen ions (pH) in the body fluids. In order to provide some understanding about how the respira-

tory system accomplishes these functions, we briefly examine the mechanical aspects of pulmonary ventilation, the transport of O_2 and CO_2, and the neural control of the system.

There are numerous reasons why the study of respiratory function has become increasingly important within the field of psychophysiology. First, major respiratory changes are associated with many behaviors (e.g., talking, laughing, exercise, emotional behavior). Second, respiratory function can influence behavioral performance. Third, research into some psychophysiological problems requires experimental animals to be artificially ventilated. In such instances, adequate ventilation procedures are required if behavioral performance is to be properly assessed. Fourth, because the respiratory system is under both voluntary and involuntary control, respiratory performance can be modified by behavioral procedures. Thus, learning to swim properly or to relax can be facilitated by the learning of breathing techniques. A fifth reason for the psychophysiologist to study respiratory function is because of its importance in behavioral medicine. Psychophysiological procedures involving the assessment

Marc P. Kaufman. Department of Physiology, University of Texas Health Sciences Center at Dallas, Dallas, Texas.
Neil Schneiderman, Department of Psychology, University of Miami, Coral Gables, Florida.

or manipulation of respiratory function are important in dealing with health problems as varied as asthma and coronary rehabilitation.

Until recently, psychophysiologists have usually limited themselves to assessing such relatively crude measures as breathing rate and/or amplitude. Typically, the transducers used were a thermocouple, a mercury strain gauge, or an impedance pneumograph. Today a large array of instruments is being used in psychophysiological research to assess respiratory function. These instruments include spirometers for measuring lung volumes; blood gas analyzers to measure acid–base balances (pH), partial pressures of arterial oxygen (pO_2) and carbon dioxide (pCO_2), bicarbonate level (HCO_3), and arterial oxygen saturation (SaO_2); and noninvasive techniques such as the Douglas bag for measuring pO_2 and pCO_2 in adults and transcutaneous electrodes for measuring pO_2 in the neonate. In this chapter, we provide an introduction to the use of such instrumentation.

PULMONARY VENTILATION

Pulmonary Structures

The airways begin at the nose and mouth and include the pharynx, the larynx, and the trachea. The trachea is the first cartilaginous airway and has, in humans, a volume of about 30 cm³ and a diameter of about 1.8 cm. The cartilaginous rings are incomplete, being comprised of smooth muscle on their posterior surfaces. The trachea divides into two main bronchi, which in turn divide into four lobar bronchi, each division having diameters of about .8 cm and .6 cm, respectively. As the lobar bronchi divide, they become less cartilaginous; at the 11th branch, the cartilage disappears completely. At this point, the airway is called a bronchiole, having a diameter of .1 cm. The bronchioles also divide, ending in the terminal bronchioles, which have diameters of approximately .6 cm. The last two branchings of the airways are, respectively, the respiratory bronchioles and the alveolar ducts; both participate in gas exchange. Although a few alveoli arise from the respiratory bronchioles, most alveoli begin at the alveolar ducts. They have diameters of .02 cm, and are the site of most gas exchange with the circulatory system occurring in the lung. The human lung is believed to have about 300 million alveoli.

The respiratory tract contains mucous-secreting cells and cilia-containing cells, whose numbers decrease progressively as the airways divide. Acting together, the glandular cells and cilia protect the respiratory tract by clearing it of foreign bodies. The cilia move the mucous and the foreign bodies trapped into it to the pharynx, where they are either expectorated

or swallowed. This clearance mechanism, unless overloaded, keeps the alveoli almost sterile. There is some evidence suggesting that the clearance mechanism is impaired by cigarette smoke or by alcohol ingestion.

Muscles of Respiration

There are two ways in which the skeletal musculature can expand and contract the lungs to permit ventilation. The first is by downward and upward movement of the diaphragm to lengthen or shorten the chest cavity. Normal quiet breathing is accomplished by inspiratory movement of the diaphragm, which pulls the lower surfaces of the lungs downward. In contrast, during expiration, the diaphragm passively relaxes, with the elastic recoil of the chest wall and abdominal structures thereby compressing the lungs. The second way in which the skeletal musculature can expand and contract the lungs is by elevation and depression of the ribs to increase the anteroposterior diameter of the chest cavity. Because the elastic forces associated with the diaphragmatic breathing are not powerful enough to cause the rapid expiration necessitated by heavy breathing, this is accomplished by having the abdominal muscles actively contract, thereby forcing the abdominal contents upward against the bottom of the diaphragm.

The most important muscle involved in inspiration is the diaphragm. At the outset, it is important to realize that the diaphragm and other respiratory muscles do not have an intrinsic rhythm. Therefore, these muscles do not contract unless they receive a neuronal input. The diaphragm receives such an input from the phrenic nerve. Cell bodies of these nerves are located in the third to fifth cervical segments of the spinal cord. Phrenic nerve neurons discharge during inspiration and are silent during expiration.

When the diaphragm contracts, it enlarges the thoracic cage. Because the lungs are attached via the pleural surfaces to the thoracic cage, they also enlarge when the diaphragm contracts. Enlarging the lungs by contracting the diaphragm decreases pressure in the alveoli below that in the atmosphere. Therefore, air flows into the lungs from the nose and mouth, which are at atmospheric pressure. The process of decreasing alveolar pressure below atmospheric pressure by enlarging the thoracic cavity is called "negative pressure breathing."

The diaphragm is a dome-shaped musculofibrous structure that separates the thoracic from the abdominal cavity. Other muscles that elevate the rib cage during inspiration include the sternocleidomastoid, the anterior serrati, the scaleni, and the external intercostal muscles. The external intercostals, which are innervated by the intercostal nerves, are capable of supporting respiration if the diaphragm is paralyzed (Campbell, 1958). As previously mentioned, the muscles of expiration are normally inactive, because during quiet breathing expiration is a passive process, being dependent upon the elastic recoil of the lungs. The expiratory muscles contract actively during high rates of ventilation. Some important expiratory muscles are in the abdomen and include the rectus abdominis, the internal and external obliques, and the tranversus abdominus (Campbell, 1958; Macklem, 1978). The internal intercostal muscles of the rib cage also play an important role in expiration.

Energy Expenditure during Breathing

During normal quiet breathing, the respiratory muscles contract only during inspiration. The work of inspiration can be divided into two components. First is "compliance," which is proportional to the effort needed to expand the lungs against its elastic forces. Second is pulmonary "resistance," which is proportional to the effort needed to move air into the lungs. Normally, during quiet respiration, only 2–3% of the total energy expended by the body is involved in pulmonary resistance and compliance. Even during heavy exertion, when the energy required for pulmonary ventilation is much increased, this is usually offset by an increase in energy production. Thus, it is primarily with patients having particular pulmonary diseases that the psychophysiologist would be concerned with decreases in pulmonary compliance or increases in airway resistance.

Compliance

Compliance is a measure of the lungs' resistance to distention in response to an applied force. It is measured under static conditions, when no air is flowing into or out of the lungs. Compliance is defined as the ratio of change in volume to a change in pressure, and is expressed as L/cm H_2O.

In measuring compliance in the unanesthetized human, pressure measurements are made from an intraesophageal balloon, which the subject swallows. The air is inspired in steps of 50 to 100 ml, and pressure measurements are made at each step. Then the air is expired in steps of 50 to 100 ml, with pressure again being measured at each step. The intrapleural pressure measure in cm H_2O is then plotted against the lung volume changes expressed in liters.

Resistance

Pulmonary resistance, which refers to the opposition to the movement of air into the lungs, is a dynamic measurement. By contrast, compliance, which refers to the elastic recoil of the lungs, is a static measurement. During quiet breathing, about 65% of the work performed by the inspiratory muscles is used to overcome the elastic recoil of the lungs and thorax. The remaining 35% is used to overcome the frictional resistance to airflow. However, decreasing airway caliber or increasing respiratory rate increases the percentage of muscular work used to overcome frictional resistance (Otis, Fenn, & Rahn, 1950).

The radius of the airways have great importance in determining resistance. In 1846, Poiseuille, using rigid tubes, showed that the pressure required to produce a certain flow varied directly with the length of the tube, but inversely with the fourth power of the radius. The relationship among pressure, flow, and radius is called "Poiseuille's law" and is as follows:

$$\Delta P = \frac{\dot{V}8nL}{\pi r^4}$$

where ΔP is the difference in pressure at the beginning and the end of the tube, $\dot{V}$ is the flow, L is the length of the tube, n is the coefficient of viscosity for the substance flowing through the tube, and r is the radius of the tube.

Pulmonary resistance is defined as the ratio of the transpulmonary pressure to the unit flow change and is measured in cm H_2O/L/sec. Pulmonary resistance has two components, airway resistance and pulmonary tissue resistance. Airway resistance is the frictional resistance produced by air flowing through the airways. Pulmonary tissue resistance is the frictional resistance produced by displacing the tissues of the lungs, rib cage, diaphragm, and abdomen. In the healthy individual, airway resistance comprises 80% of pulmonary resistance.

Nadel and Widdicombe (1962) described an excellent method for determining pulmonary resistance in anesthetized paralyzed animals. To determine pulmonary resistance, two measurements are needed, airflow and transpulmonary pressure. Airflow is obtained with a pneumotachograph, which measures, across a fixed resistance, changes in pressure occurring with each respiratory cycle. The pneumotachograph is connected, in turn, to a differential pressure transducer. Transpulmonary pressure is obtained with a second differential pressure transducer, one side of which is connected to a tracheal cannula. The other side is connected to a catheter, which is inserted between the ribs into the intrapleural space. The outputs of the two differential pressure transducers are connected to the X and Y axes, respectively, of an oscilloscope or X-Y plotter. The slope of the line generated at slow sweep speeds provides the measure of pulmonary resistance. The method described by Nadel and Widdicombe measures both airway resistance and pulmonary tissue resistance.

Airway resistance can be measured independently of pulmonary tissue resistance in unanesthetized humans by means of a body plethysmograph (DuBois, Bothello, & Comroe, 1956). Briefly, the subject is placed in an airtight box, in which airflow is measured with a pneumotachograph. The pressure around the subject is measured continuously. During inspiration, pressure in the box increases; during expiration, it decreases. Using Boyle's law, which states that at constant temperature the volume of a gas varies inversely with the pressure to which the gas is subjected, alveolar pressure is calculated. Airway resistance is then calculated, based upon alveolar pressure and airflow measurements.

Compliance is decreased by contracting the smooth muscle in the alveolar ducts, which in turn decreases lung volume but has little effect on airway resistance. Contraction of the smooth muscle in airways down to and including the terminal bronchioles increases airway resistance, which decreases anatomic dead space and increases the work of breathing. Thus, contraction of the smooth muscle in the airways provides a beneficial action, decreasing dead space, but at the same time provides an undesirable action, increasing the work of breathing. As suggested by Widdicombe (1966), afferent nerves with endings in the airways may provide the feedback necessary for the nervous system to strike the optimal balance between dead space and work.

Pulmonary Volumes and Capacities

During inspiration, air does not travel directly to those parts of the lungs where gas is exchanged with the pulmonary capillary blood. Instead, the air travels through the nose and/or mouth, the pharynx, the larynx, the trachea, the bronchi, and the bronchioles. Those parts of the respiratory system that do not participate in gas exchange are called the "conducting airways"; the volume of the conducting airways comprises the "anatomical dead space." The anatomical dead space can be calculated by a nitrogen washout method in which, after breathing normal room air, the subject inspires pure O_2; changes in nitrogen concentration are then recorded during expiration. A detailed description of the procedure has been provided by Comroe, Forster, DuBois, Briscoe, and Carlsen (1962).

There are several different pulmonary volumes and capacities that are used in the assessment of pulmonary ventilation. The relationship of these volumes and capacities to one another is summarized in Figure 6-1. In the resting individual, for example, the amount of air inspired or expired during each breath ("tidal volume") is considerably less than the maximum amount of air that could actually be inspired ("inspiratory capacity") (see Figure 6-2). Thus, the inspiratory capacity can be said to be made up of both the tidal volume and another volume, called the "inspiratory reserve volume." The inspiratory reserve volume is defined as the maximum volume of air that

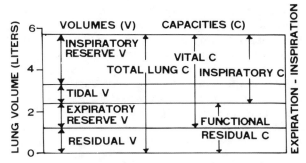

Figure 6-1. Approximate respiratory volumes and capacities in humans and their relationships to one another.

can be inhaled at the end of a normal inspiration ("end-tidal inspiration").

At the end of a normal, passive expiration ("end-tidal expiration"), some air remains in the lungs. This volume of air still in the lungs after end-tidal expiration is defined as the "functional residual capacity." The difference between the volume of air exhaled from the resting end-expiratory position to the maximum volume of air that an individual can exhale is

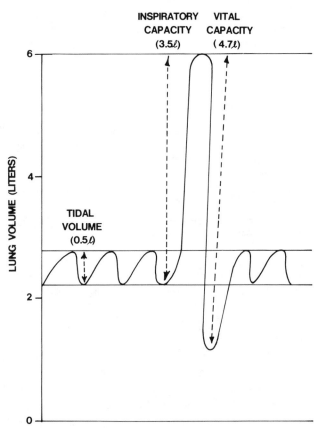

Figure 6-2. Schematic diagram showing respiratory excursions during normal breathing and during maximal inspiration and expiration.

called the "expiratory reserve volume." Because it is impossible to empty the lungs of air completely, even after a maximal expiratory effort, the functional residual capacity after passive end-tidal expiration consists not only of an expiratory reserve volume, but also of a "residual volume." The maximum volume of air that can be exhaled after a maximal inspiratory effort is known as the "vital capacity," which excludes the residual volume. "Total lung capacity," however, which includes the residual volume, is defined as the volume of air in the lungs at the end of a maximal inspiration.

Measurement of Pulmonary Volumes and Capacities

The pulmonary volumes and capacities that do not depend upon residual volume assessment can easily be studied using some form of spirometer. Assessment of residual volume requires procedures such as nitrogen washout (e.g., Comroe *et al.*, 1962). A typical spirometer consists of an air- or O_2-filled drum that is inverted over a chamber of water (see Figure 6-3). The subject is then instructed to breathe into and out of the drum through a valve and connecting tubes. Breathing in and out of the drum causes it to rise and fall, and an appropriate recording can be made on a moving paper, providing measures of rate as well as volumes.

With the type of spirometer shown in Figure 6-3, only a few breaths can be taken during an experimental session because of the buildup of CO_2 and the loss

of O_2 from the gas chamber. For continuous monitoring, a more elaborate spirometer can be used. Such a device chemically removes CO_2 as it is formed, and O_2 can be injected at a rate equal to its consumption. Briefly, the mouthpiece is connected to two rubber tubes. A valve in the tubing from the O_2-filled gas drum opens during inspiration, but closes during expiration. Conversely, the expired air is carried out via a tube containing a valve that only opens during expiration. The expiration tube can be made to pass through a chamber containing pellets of soda lime, which absorb the CO_2 before the expired air is returned to the O_2 chamber.

Depending upon the needs of the investigator, a number of options are available. Some spirometers, for instance, have a second pen, which by moving only in response to inspiration provides a cumulative record of lung volumes over time. Other spirometers have a visual display meter with a needle indicator to provide feedback to the subject. Although wet spirometers such as the one shown in Figure 6-3 are most commonly used, dry spirometers have also been developed. In the dry type of spirometer, a collecting piston that is displaced by respiration is rendered airtight by a silicone rubber seal. As the piston is displaced, it moves the arm of an infinite-resolution potentiometer. The output of the potentiometer can be fed to two high-gain amplifiers. One of these amplifiers produces the direct current (DC) output volume signal; the second amplifier is used in a differentiating circuit to provide an output that is proportional to flow. In comparison with the wet spirometers, the dry spirometers offer less inertia to movement and usually have a better dynamic frequency response.

Other methods of measuring at least some lung volumes are also available. The pneumotachograph, which is a device for measuring airflow, can be used to provide a breath-by-breath record of tidal volume and respiratory rate both in anesthetized animals and in conscious humans. Tidal volume is calculated by integrating airflow for each breath.

For many years psychophysiologists have used a variety of devices, such as thermocouples, electrical impedance plethysmographs, and air pressure pneumographs, to provide measures of absolute respiration rate and relative respiration amplitude. The advantage of an air pressure pneumograph or impedance plethysmograph over the direct methods of obtaining lung volumes is that the former are less intrusive. Unfortunately, attempts to calibrate these measures and correlate them with spirometric measurements have been almost nonexistent in most psychophysiological experiments. Consequently, it has not usually been possible in psychophysiological research to compare the resultant amplitude data, either across subjects or across sessions. It should be pointed out, however, that in instances in which electrical imped-

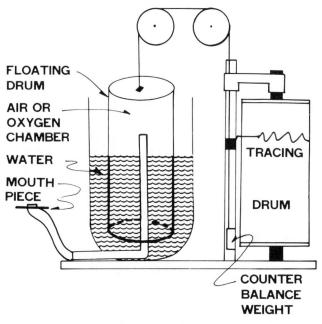

FLOATING DRUM

AIR OR OXYGEN CHAMBER

WATER

MOUTH PIECE

TRACING

DRUM

COUNTER BALANCE WEIGHT

Figure 6-3. A wet spirometer.

ance plethysmography (Allison, Holmes, & Nyboer, 1964) or body surface movements (Mead, Peterson, Grimby, & Mead, 1967) have been correlated with spirometric determinations in normal subjects, the indirect measures have actually fared rather well.

TRANSPORT OF O_2 AND CO_2

Hemoglobin and O_2

If blood was comprised of pure plasma, it would contain .3 ml O_2/100 ml plasma, assuming that alveolar pO_2 was normal (i.e., 100 mm Hg). Considering that the O_2 consumption of a resting person breathing room air is about 250 ml/min, a simple calculation reveals that the heart would have to pump 83 L/min in order to meet the tissue requirements for O_2. Fortunately, a healthy, resting person only needs a cardiac output of 1.3 L/min to satisfy tissue O_2 demands, because blood contains hemoglobin. To put it another way, hemoglobin allows the blood to carry 65 times more O_2 than does plasma at an alveolar pO_2 of 100 mm Hg.

The amount of O_2 that combines with hemoglobin depends on the pO_2 of the blood. A plot of the relationship between pO_2 of the blood and the percentage of hemoglobin saturated with O_2 reveals a sigmoid-shaped curve (see Figure 6-4). Thus, when exposed to an alveolar pO_2 of 100 mm Hg, hemoglobin is almost completely saturated (97%). In addition, between pO_2s of 100 and 60 mm Hg, the percentage of hemoglobin saturated with O_2 decreases from 97% to 91% (Severinghaus, 1966), an effect that allows people to live at high altitudes without much change in the O_2-carrying capacity of the blood. As the pO_2 of the blood decreases from 40 to 10 mm Hg (i.e., pO_2s found in metabolically active tissues), the hemoglobin saturation decreases from 75% to 10%.

The hemoglobin–O_2 dissociation curve is influenced by the temperature and the pH of the blood. Both an increase in temperature and a decrease in pH result in a lower saturation of hemoglobin at any given pO_2. Therefore, in body regions of high metabolic activity, such as exercising muscle, where O_2 demand is great, an elevated local temperature increases the efficiency of O_2 transport by favoring the dissociation of O_2 and hemoglobin. Similarly, body regions, having high rates of metabolic activity, produce higher than usual amounts of CO_2 and metabolic acids, which cause a local decrease in pH. The local decrease in pH, in turn, favors the dissociation of O_2 and hemoglobin, again increasing the efficiency of O_2 transport (called the Bohr shift).

Another molecule that combines with hemoglobin is carbon monoxide. In fact, the affinity of hemoglobin for carbon monoxide is 210 times greater than that for O_2. Equilibrating the blood with alveolar gas containing only .017% of carbon monoxide results in 50% of the hemoglobin being saturated with carbon monoxide. If the entire blood volume is allowed to equilibrate, this condition is fatal. Severe anemia, however, can result in a 50% loss of hemoglobin, a condition that is not fatal. The difference is that exposing hemoglobin to carbon monoxide causes O_2 to be released only at very low tissue pO_2s (see Roughton & Darling, 1944).

The amount of O_2 contained in the blood depends on the blood's pO_2. Similarly, the amount of CO_2 contained in the blood depends on the blood's pCO_2. The shape of the curve describing the dissociation of CO_2 and blood is different from that describing the dissociation of O_2 and blood. Unlike the O_2 curve, the CO_2 curve has no steep portion followed by a flat portion. The CO_2 dissociation curve is dependent on the pO_2 of the blood. Binding of O_2 with hemoglobin tends to displace CO_2 from the blood, a phenomenon that is known as the "Haldane effect" (see Figure 6-5).

Factors Influencing CO_2 Tension

Changes in the volume of air ventilating the lungs affect the CO_2 tension of the arterial blood. Consequently, increasing minute volume (the volume of air inspired per minute) decreases arterial pCO_2, whereas decreasing minute volume increases arterial pCO_2. Because CO_2 diffuses freely from the blood to the alveoli, the pCO_2 in the alveoli equals that in the arterial blood. Moreover, CO_2 in the blood dissociates as follows:

$$CO_2 + H_2O \rightleftarrows H_2CO_3 \rightleftarrows H^+ + HCO_3^-$$

Increases in the arterial pCO_2 drive the equation to the right, which increases the H^+ concentration in the arterial blood, making it more acidic. Conversely,

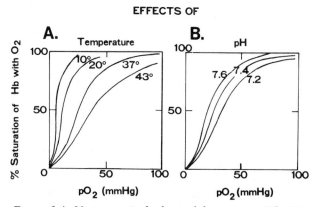

EFFECTS OF

Figure 6-4. Variations in the hemoglobinᴇoxygen (Hb O_2) dissociation curve as a function of changes in (A) temperature and (B) acid–base balance (pH) of the blood.

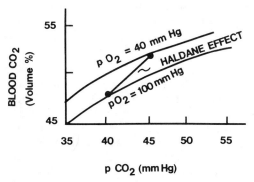

Figure 6-5. Portions of the carbon dioxide (CO₂) dissociation curves at a partial pressure of oxygen (pO_2) of 100 mm Hg and at a pO_2 of 40 mm Hg. The connecting line between the two curves shows the Haldane effect (i.e., the binding of O_2 with hemoglobin tends to displace CO_2 from the blood).

decreases in the arterial pCO_2 drive the equation to the left, which decreases the H^+ concentration in the arterial blood, making it less acidic. The pH of the arterial blood is determined by the Henderson-Hasselbalch equation:

$$pH = 6.1 + \log_{10} \frac{[HCO_3^-]}{.03 p_a CO_2}$$

where $[HCO_3^-]$ is equal to the concentration of HCO_3^- in the arterial blood and $p_a CO_2$ is equal to the partial pressure of CO_2 in the blood.

Measurement of CO₂ Excretion and O₂ Consumption

The development of the Clark and the Severinghaus electrodes has made the measurement of arterial pO_2 and pCO_2 simple. The Clark electrode, which measures arterial pO_2, uses the electrolysis of dilute solutions containing reducible substances, such as O_2, which take up electrons. Thus, to measure the pO_2 of the blood, a voltage is applied to the Clark electrode, which is placed in arterial blood. Because the O_2 in the blood takes up electrons, a current can be measured. The amount of current measured is directly proportional to the pO_2 of the blood.

The Severinghaus electrode is used to measure arterial pCO_2. This electrode consists of a glass membrane, which is permeable to H^+, and an outer surface that is covered by a film of electrolyte. The film of electrolyte is separated from the arterial blood sample by a Teflon membrane, which is permeable to CO_2 but impermeable to H^+. Thus, the CO_2 in the blood sample passes through the Teflon membrane and then reacts with the water in the electrolytic film covering the glass membrane. This reaction results in the formation of $H^+ + HCO_3$. The H^+ ions diffuse through

the glass membrane and are measured in a pH meter, the pH being directly proportional to the pCO_2. Commercially available instruments, such as the Instrumentation Laboratory digital blood gas analyzer, make the accurate assessment of blood CO_2, O_2, and pH a simple matter.

When artifically ventilating the lungs of animals or humans, end-tidal CO_2 is usually monitored to ensure that hypercapnia and acidosis do not occur. Instruments such as the Beckman Medical gas analyzer (Models LB-1 or LB-2) are most frequently used to measure end-tidal CO_2. The Beckman gas analyzer operates on the principle that CO_2 molecules absorb infrared light. Therefore, the alveolar gas to be analyzed for its CO_2 content is pumped into a sample chamber. Infrared light is serially projected through a rotating shutter, then through the sample chamber, and finally through a detector cell containing 100% CO_2. Because carbon dioxide absorbs infrared light, the CO_2 in the detector cell is heated, thereby raising pressure in the cell. The rotating shutter causes the infrared illumination of the detector to be intermittent, which, in turn, causes the pressure changes in the detector cell to oscillate. Any CO_2 present in the sample cell absorbs some of the infrared light, thereby decreasing the amount of infrared light that reaches the detector cell. To compensate for extraneous pressure and temperature changes, a second detector cell is exposed to infrared light, which is projected through a second sample cell. This second sample cell, however, contains no CO_2. The difference in pressure oscillations between the two detector cells is transformed into a voltage, which is directly proportional to the percentage of CO_2 in the alveolar gas.

Changes in O_2 consumption in the behaving human can be accomplished in several different ways. These include use of the Douglas bag technique (Astrand & Saltin, 1961), open-circuit spirometry in conjunction with sampling for gas analysis (Auchincloss, Gilbert, & Baule, 1966), continuous blood flow measurements in conjunction with gas analyses (Cerretelli, Sikand, & Fahri, 1966), and various servo-controlled air circuit instruments that can measure O_2 consumption continuously in real time (Webb & Troutman, 1970).

The Douglas bag procedure typically uses a nose-clip, mouthpiece, and J valve. Following 1- to 3-min timed collections, the Douglas bag is closed, and the mouthpiece is removed from the subject. The volume of expired air in the Douglas bag is then measured with a spirometer. Gas analysis is done by drawing samples from the Douglas bag. These can then be examined using magnetic O_2 and infrared CO_2 analyzers such as those manufactured by Beckman. The gas analyzers are calibrated with gases of known composition.

Although fairly expensive, servo-controlled air circuit instruments such as the Waters MRM-1 O_2 consumption computer have several advantages over the Douglas bag procedure. One of these is simplicity, because measurement and analysis are taken care of by a single device. Another set of advantages is that the subject wears no mouthpiece or noseclip, and there are no valves in the airstream. Therefore, there is no resistance added to breathing, and the measurement procedure is also less obtrusive. Although the servo-controlled O_2 consumption monitor is not suitable for breath-by-breath analyses, it does permit the experimenter to make continuous measurements while the subject is behaviorally engaged. Its one disadvantage as compared to the Douglas bag is that the servo-controlled monitor does not easily allow the simultaneous measurement of CO_2 excretion.

Basically, the Waters MRM-1 computer operates as a closed-loop system. The subject wears a clear plastic facemask through which air is drawn by a blower located on the end of a flexible hose. A polarographic oxygen sensor located in the blower housing serves as a null detector. The blower, which draws ambient air through the facepiece, is servo-controlled from an error signal developed by comparing the output of the polarographic cell with a fixed reference voltage. As the downstream pO_2 decreases, the error signal increases; the blower speeds up, increasing the volume flow, and thereby returning the downstream O_2 content toward that of the ambient air. The servo system maintains a volume flow of air, which is directly proportional to O_2 consumption. Its amplified error signal can then be recorded.

In the case of infants, changes in O_2 saturation can be recorded quite accurately using an ear oximeter in conjunction with spectrophotometric analyses.

Maximal O_2 Consumption

There has been an increased emphasis in behavioral medicine upon studying aerobic fitness, both in the normal individual and in coronary rehabilitation patients. Psychophysiologists are therefore being increasingly asked to estimate the maximal functional capacity of the circulorespiratory system. This maximal functional capacity is best evaluated with a test of the body's capacity to consume O_2 at a maximal rate.

The rate of maximal O_2 consumption per unit of time is abbreviated as $\dot{V}O_2$ max, and represents the greatest difference between the rate at which inspired O_2 enters the lungs and the rate at which expired O_2 leaves the lungs. Assuming that lung and blood characteristics are normal, maximal O_2 uptake or consumption is a function of maximal cardiac output and maximal arteriovenous O_2 difference (max A − V O_2 difference). This A − V O_2 difference merely represents the difference in the content of O_2 between arterial and venous blood. The equation relating $\dot{V}O_2$

max to cardiac output and A − V O_2 difference is expressed as follows:

$$\dot{V}O_{2\ max} = \text{max cardiac output} \times \text{max A − V } O_2 \text{ difference}$$

In the testing of maximal O_2 uptake, treadmill tests produce the highest values for $\dot{V}O_{2\ max}$, when compared with the bicycle or step test (Nagle, 1973). The treadmill test is also least subject to differences in skill and efficiency among subjects. In testing for maximal O_2 consumption on the treadmill, both exercise intensity and duration must be great enough to elicit a maximal response. A minimum of at least 3 or 4 min of running on the treadmill is usually required.

Because O_2 uptake increases linearly with increasing workloads up to the maximal rate, a plateau of O_2 uptake with increasing workload is a sure sign that the person has achieved his or her maximum. Other evidence that would support this conclusion would be a blood lactic acid level above 70–80 mg / 100 ml blood and achievement of a near-maximal heart rate (Astrand & Rodahl, 1970; Nagle, 1973).

During exercise of submaximal intensity, both heart rate and ventilation rate increase approximately in proportion to increases in O_2 consumption. Consequently, numerous attempts have been made to predict O_2 uptake from heart rate, ventilation rate, or other variables during standardized submaximal exercise loads. Although these tests can usually provide a reasonable approximation of maximal O_2 uptake, they are subject to a prediction error of about 10% (Nagle, 1973). Submaximal exercise testing would therefore appear to be justified, primarily in situations in which subject safety is a factor.

NEURAL CONTROL OF VENTILATION

Adjustments in ventilation continually insure that the proper amounts of O_2, CO_2, and H^+ ions are maintained in the blood. Ventilatory activity is extremely sensitive to changes in any of these important factors in the blood, and powerful feedback systems insure that departures from normal are rapidly corrected. Thus, an increase in CO_2 or decrease in pH is sensed by neurons believed to be near the surface of the ventrolateral medulla, which trigger an increase in ventilatory activity (Mitchell, Loeschke, Severinghaus, Richardson, & Massion, 1963). Similarly, a decrease in the pO_2 of the arterial blood stimulates ventilation by a peripheral reflex mechanism based upon receptors strategically located near the carotid sinus and the aorta (Comroe, 1974). Both the stimulating effects on ventilation caused by an increase in pCO_2, or by decreases in pH and pO_2, tend to restore homeostasis.

Reflex Mechanisms

Peripheral Chemoreceptors

Attached to the aortic arch and carotid sinus are chemosensitive areas of tissue known as the aortic bodies and carotid bodies, respectively. Contained within these bodies are afferent nerve endings that project to the nucleus of the solitary tract of the dorsal medulla. Specifically, the afferent endings (i.e., the chemoreceptors) of the carotid bodies send their fibers to the medulla via the carotid sinus branches of the glossopharyngeal nerves; the afferent endings of the aortic bodies send their fibers to the dorsal medulla via the aortic depressor branches of the vagus nerves.

The primary O_2 sensors in humans are the carotid bodies. Although the peripheral chemoreceptors of the aortic and carotid bodies are stimulated by decreases in arterial pO_2, they are also influenced by increases in arterial pCO_2 and by decreases in arterial pH from normal levels (Biscoe, Purves, & Sampson, 1970; Sampson & Hainsworth, 1972). When stimulated, the peripheral chemoreceptors reflexly evoke increases in tidal volume and ventilatory rate. Although stimulation of the chemoreceptors by decreases in arterial pO_2 is more important in causing reflex increases in ventilation than is the stimulation of the receptors by increases in pCO_2 or by decreases in pH, it is important to recognize that if the arterial pCO_2 is maintained at higher than normal levels, a decrease in arterial pO_2 that previously did not evoke a reflex increase in ventilation will now do so (Loeschke & Gertz, 1958). Thus, changes in arterial pO_2, pCO_2, and pH have interactive effects on chemoreceptor discharge, which, in turn, influences ventilation. At normal levels of arterial pCO_2 (i.e., about 36 mm Hg), ventilation does not reflexly increase in humans until the arterial pO_2 reaches 60–80 mm Hg (Loeschke & Gertz, 1958).

Stimulation of the aortic and carotid chemoreceptors have quantitatively different effects on ventilation. In dogs, stimulation of the carotid chemoreceptors evokes an increase in ventilation seven times greater than that evoked by stimulation of the aortic chemoreceptors (Daly & Unger, 1966). Moreover, in humans, removal of the carotid bodies abolishes the increase in ventilation evoked by hypoxemia (Holton & Wood, 1965). In fact, in the absence of carotid bodies, hypoxia of 45 mm Hg reduces ventilation by a direct depressant effect on the respiratory centers (Wade, Larson, & Hickey, 1970).

Although stimulation of either the aortic or carotid chemoreceptors evokes reflex increases in systemic vascular resistance, stimulation of these receptors has qualitatively different effects on the heart. Thus, perfusing the vascularly isolated carotid bodies with hypoxic blood reflexly decreases heart rate (Downing, Remensnyder, & Mitchell, 1962) and myocardial contractility (Hainsworth, Karim, & Sofola, 1979). However, perfusing the vascularly isolated aortic bodies with hypoxic blood has been shown to reflexly increase heart rate and myocardial contractility (Karim, Hainsworth, Sofola, & Wood, 1980).

Vagal Afferents with Endings in the Lung

The vagal afferents innervating the lungs are most frequently categorized into two groups: those with myelinated fibers and those with unmyelinated fibers (Fishman, 1981). The myelinated vagal fibers, and the reflex effects evoked by their stimulation, have been widely studied (Pack, 1981). These myelinated fibers have been further categorized into two subgroups, based on their responses to lung inflation. The first subgroup consists of the "slowly adapting stretch receptors," which were first identified by Adrian (1933). The receptors are believed to be responsible for evoking the Hering–Breuer reflex, which is easily demonstrated in animals by a maintained inflation of the lungs. Reflex effects of this inflation include the termination of inspiratory effort, the prolongation of the expiratory phase of breathing (Clark & von Euler, 1972; Phillipson, Hickey, Graf, & Nadel, 1971), bronchodilation (Widdicombe & Nadel, 1963), and an increase in heart rate (Daly & Scott, 1958). The Hering–Breuer reflex appears to play little role in controlling resting ventilation in conscious humans, because the reflex is only activated at lung volumes of 1.0 L or greater (Clark & von Euler, 1972). Instead, the reflex appears to play a protective role to prevent overinflation of the lung.

The second subgroup of myelinated vagal afferents innervating the lungs consists of the "rapidly adapting stretch receptors," first described by Knowlton and Larrabee (1946). Although these afferents are initially stimulated by lung inflation, they stop or markedly decrease their firing, even though the inflation is maintained. Rapidly adapting receptors have been shown to be stimulated by intravenous histamine, by forced deflation of the lungs (Sampson & Vidruk, 1975), by aerosols of ammonia, by anaphylaxis (Mills, Sellick, & Widdicombe, 1969), and by pneumothorax (Sellick & Widdicombe, 1969). Because these afferents are responsive to noxious stimuli, they have also been called "irritant receptors." There is a considerable amount of correlative evidence that rapidly adapting stretch receptors, when stimulated, reflexly evoke bronchoconstriction and rapid, shallow breathing (e.g., Mills *et al.*, 1969). These receptors, however, are believed to exert little, if any, reflex action on the cardiovascular system.

Unmyelinated (C) fibers comprise the second group of vagal afferents innervating the lungs. These

C fibers were first described by Paintal (1955) in cats, and at that time were believed to be thinly myelinated. Later on, Coleridge, Coleridge, and Luck (1965) found that the conduction velocities of these fibers in dogs were less than 2.5 m/sec. Likewise, Paintal (1969) found that the conduction velocities of these fibers in cats were less than 2.5 m/sec. The lung C fibers found by Paintal (1969) and by Coleridge et al. (1965) were called by these investigators "juxta-pulmonary capillary (J) receptors" and "high-threshold inflation receptors," respectively. Recently, these C fibers have been renamed "pulmonary C fibers" because they are immediately stimulated by injecting chemicals into the pulmonary circulation (Coleridge & Coleridge, 1977).

The most commonly known reflex effects caused by chemical stimulation of pulmonary C fibers are bradycardia, hypotension, and apnea (Coleridge, Coleridge, & Kidd, 1964). However, stimulation of these C fibers also reflexly inhibits skeletal muscle activity (Ginzel, Eldred, Watanabe, & Grover, 1971) and causes reflex bronchoconstriction (Russell & Lai-Fook, 1979). The natural stimulus of pulmonary C fibers is presently unclear, although three likely candidates are lung inflation, pulmonary congestion, and pulmonary edema.

Recently, Coleridge and Coleridge (1977) have described a second population of vagal C fibers with endings in the lung. Unlike pulmonary C fibers, these afferents are stimulated by injection of chemicals into either the systemic or bronchial circulation (Coleridge & Coleridge, 1977; Kaufman, Coleridge, Coleridge, & Baker, 1980) and have therefore been named "bronchial C fibers." Bronchial C fibers are stimulated by histamine and by bradykinin (Coleridge & Coleridge, 1977; Kaufman et al., 1980), substances that are released in the lung in anaphylaxis and in asthma. Furthermore, stimulation of bronchial C fibers has been shown to decrease reflexly airway caliber and heart rate (Roberts, Kaufman, Baker, Brown, Coleridge, & Coleridge, 1981).

Somatosensory Receptors

It has been known for some time that passive movements of the limbs about a joint reflexly increase breathing in cats, dogs, and humans (e.g., Comroe & Schmidt, 1943). The joint afferents responsible for this reflex effect have yet to be identified. In addition, stimulation of thin-fiber (groups III and IV) skeletal muscle afferents, either by exercise or by pain, reflexly increases breathing (Crayton, Aung-Din, Fixler, & Mitchell, 1979; McCloskey & Mitchell, 1972).

Central Chemoreceptors

Section of the nerves supplying the peripheral chemoreceptors of the aortic and carotid bodies does not prevent the increase in ventilation that is evoked by the inhalation of CO_2. Moreover, small increases in arterial pCO_2 (i.e., 2–4 mm Hg) markedly stimulate breathing; yet these increases have little, if any, effect on the firing of peripheral chemoreceptors (Lloyd, Jukes, & Cunningham, 1958). Still other studies have shown that the increase in ventilation evoked reflexly by peripheral chemoreceptor stimulation does not occur until the arterial pCO_2 increases by 10 mm Hg (e.g., Comroe, 1974). Considered together, these findings strongly suggest that the peripheral chemoreceptors play only a small role in regulating arterial pCO_2.

The cells responsible for increasing ventilation in response to an increase in arterial pCO_2, although not located in the aortic and carotid bodies, are believed to be located on the surfaces of the ventrolateral medulla of the brain. These cells have been named the "central chemoreceptors." Perfusion of the ventrolateral medulla with cerebrospinal-fluid-like solutions containing elevated concentrations of either CO_2 or H^+ ions has been shown to increase ventilation markedly (Mitchell et al., 1963), an effect that has been attributed to the stimulation of central chemoreceptors.

The natural stimulus of the central chemoreceptors appears to be an increase in the H^+ ion concentration in the cerebrospinal fluid bathing the ventrolateral medulla. Hydrogen ions, however, do not pass easily from the arterial blood to the cerebrospinal fluid. Therefore, the mechanism that increases the H^+ ion concentration of the cerebrospinal fluid is believed to involve CO_2, which freely diffuses across the blood–brain barrier. Once in the cerebrospinal fluid, CO_2 combines with water to form carbonic acid (H_2CO_3), which, in turn, dissociates into hydrogen (H^+) ions and bicarbonate (HCO_3^-) ions.

Central Generation of a Ventilatory Rhythm

Ventilatory movements do not depend on reflex mechanisms alone, because respiration continues after the vagus, aortic, and carotid sinus nerves are cut. Section of these nerves does, however, result in a pattern of breathing that is slower and deeper than the pattern of breathing seen with intact nerves, an effect attributed to the loss of vagal afferent input from the lungs (Mitchell & Berger, 1975). Thus, the generation of a patterned ventilatory rhythm appears to lie in the central nervous system.

The continuation of ventilatory movements after section of the brain at the border of the pons and medulla demonstrates that the primary pattern generator is located somewhere in the medulla (see Mitchell & Berger, 1975, for a comprehensive review of this work). In the medulla, there are two areas containing neurons that fire with a ventilatory rhythm. The first area is located in the ventrolateral portion of the nucleus of the tractus solitarius and has been termed the "dorsal respiratory group."

Using extracellular recording techniques, Von Baumgarten, Von Baumgarten, and Schaefer (1957) were the first to identify the dorsal respiratory group, which contains two types of neurons that discharge with an inspiratory rhythm of central origin. The two types have been named "I-alpha" and "I-beta" (Mitchell & Berger, 1975). Both are believed to receive inputs from vagal primary afferents, I-alpha cells being inhibited by lung inflation and I-beta cells being excited by this stimulus (Berger, 1977). Moreover, both types have been shown to project, via crossed pathways, to the phrenic nucleus of the cervical spinal cord. In addition, there is evidence that some I-alpha and I-beta cells project to cells in the ventral respiratory group (Merrill, 1975). The findings that neurons in the dorsal respiratory group fire with an inspiratory rhythm of central origin and that these cells project to the phrenic nucleus have given rise to the belief that this group is responsible for causing inspiration.

A third type of cell in the dorsal respiratory group has been described by Berger (1977). These cells do not have a respiratory rhythm of central origin, but are vigorously stimulated by lung inflation. In contrast to the I-alpha and I-beta cells, these cells, which have been named "P cells," do not project to the phrenic nucleus. Berger (1977) has suggested that P cells are interneurons, which function to delay the onset of inspiration.

The ventral respiratory group consists of cells located in the nucleus ambiguus and in the nucleus retroambigualis. In the nucleus ambiguus, there are vagal motoneurons whose axons project to both the larynx and to the airways. Some of these cells fire in inspiration, while others fire in expiration (Merrill, 1970). In the more caudal part of the ventral respiratory group, in the nucleus retroambigualis, there are cells whose axons project, via crossed pathways, to the spinal cord. Some fire in expiration, and their axons are presumed to project to expiratory intercostal and abdominal motoneurons. Others fire in inspiration; their axons also project to expiratory motoneurons, and, in addition, some send collaterals to the phrenic nucleus (Merrill, 1970, 1974). In addition to having inspiratory cells whose axons project to either the spinal cord or to the vagus nerve, the ventral respiratory group also contains cells that fire in inspiration, but that do not project out of the medulla. These are believed to be inhibitory neurons that synapse on expiratory cells, thus causing them to discharge rhythmically (Merrill, 1970). In sum, the ventral respiratory group is generally believed to activate the expiratory muscles involved in ventilation.

There are two other respiratory areas, located in the pons: the pneumotaxic center and the apneustic center. The pneumotaxic center is believed to transmit impulses continuously to the dorsal respiratory group. The major effect of these impulses is to limit inspiratory time and thus to prevent overdistention of the lungs. Because the pneumotaxic center shortens inspiratory time, it has the potential of greatly increasing the ventilation rate. A large amount of input from the pneumotaxic center, for example, can increase the rate of breathing to 30–40 breaths per minute, whereas a small amount of input can decrease the rate of breathing to only a few breaths per minute.

The apneustic center, also in the pons, is believed to transmit impulses to the dorsal respiratory group, which could attempt to prevent the turning off of the inspiratory signal. Provided that the pneumotaxic center is intact, it overrides the influence of the apneustic center. But if the pneumotaxic center is damaged, so that it no longer transmits impulses to the dorsal respiratory group, the apneustic center produces inspiratory spasms.

The anatomical locus and wiring of the central pattern generator that is responsible for generating a ventilatory rhythm has been the subject of much research. The persistence of rhythmic respiration after sectioning of the brain stem at the pontine–medullary border suggests that the central pattern generator is located within the medulla and spinal cord. Mitchell (1980) believes that the central pattern generator actually consists of a hierarchy of generators located in the medulla and spinal cord, each of which is capable of causing a ventilatory rhythm. In addition, the dominant generator, which is possibly the last one to develop on the evolutionary scale, entrains the other generators. However, if the dominant generator is destroyed, other generators take over, producing their own ventilatory rhythm. Some support for this hypothesis has been offered by Speck and Feldman (1982), who showed that ventilation continued after lesioning the dorsal and ventral respiratory groups.

Anesthesia has been known for some time to depress the central pattern generator that is responsible for initiating ventilatory movements. Barbiturates are perhaps the most notorious of the anesthetic agents depressing ventilation. Opioid narcotics, such as morphine, have also been shown to depress the central pattern generator profoundly.

Voluntary Control and Descending Pathways

The available evidence suggests that the voluntary (cortical) drive for breathing descends in the spinal cord by a different pathway from that of the involuntary (medullary) drive for breathing (Plum, 1970). In the cat, the descending cortical pathway travels in the dorsolateral cord, whereas the descending medullary pathway travels in the ventrolateral cord. Thus, section of the ventrolateral pathway may cause the loss of rhythmic involuntary ventilation, but is likely to have no effect upon voluntary ventilation. Conversely, section of the dorsolateral pathway may cause the loss of voluntary ventilation, but is likely to have no effect on involuntary ventilation (Mitchell, 1980). In humans, section of the ventrolateral cord has been found to result in apnea, especially during sleep. This condition has been called "Ondine's curse."

RESPIRATORY ADJUSTMENTS IN HEALTH AND DISEASE

Respiration in the Fetus, Neonate, and Infant

Placental Gas Exchange

Gas exchange in the adult occurs between the lungs and the pulmonary capillaries. Gas exchange in the fetus, however, occurs in the placenta, where the maternal arteries (umbilical) are in close contact with the fetal arteries (cotyledonary). Even though fetal gas exchange oxygenates the fetal blood, the O_2 content of the fetal blood leaving the placenta is less than that of the maternal (umbilical) arterial blood entering this structure. Thus, fetal blood entering the placenta has a pO_2 of about 22 mm Hg, and its hemoglobin is 45–55% saturated; the fetal blood leaving the placenta has a pO_2 of about 30 mm Hg, and its hemoglobin is 65–75% saturated. In contrast, the maternal blood entering the placenta has a pO_2 of about 100 mm Hg, and its hemoglobin is about 98% saturated.

Respiration in the Neonate

There are dramatic changes in a baby's respiration at birth. The fetal lungs contain fluid, which is believed to be secreted by alveolar cells. This fluid expands the lungs to about 40% of the total lung capacity, and thus plays an important role in the first breath taken by the baby. To expand the lungs with the first breath, the baby must overcome large surface tension forces within the alveoli. Because the lungs are partly expanded with fluid, the radii of the alveoli, containing the fluid–air interface, are relatively large, thus decreasing the pressure needed to overcome surface tension (i.e., Laplace's law). Although expansion of the lung is at first uneven, normal functional residual capacity and gas exchange are reached within minutes. Moreover, the liquid within the lungs is removed within minutes by the pulmonary capillaries and lymphatics.

Circulatory Changes in the Neonate

With the first breaths, the pulmonary arteries dilate dramatically. Two major factors appear likely to cause the dilation. The first is the abrupt increase in pO_2 of the blood perfusing the pulmonary arteries, an effect that attenuates the hypoxic vasoconstriction of this arterial bed. The second is the increase in lung volume, which increases the caliber of the pulmonary arteries. Another circulatory change that occurs at this time is that the ductus arteriosus, which connects the pulmonary artery with the aorta in fetal life, constricts at birth when it is exposed to an increased arterial pO_2. The constriction of the ductus arteriosus is probably dependent on the production of prostaglandins.

Sudden Infant Death Syndromes

Approximately 10,000 infants die each year from sudden infant death syndromes (SIDS). The typical victims are generally infants from 2 to 5 months of age, who previously appear to be healthy and then die suddenly during sleep (Irsigler & Severinghaus, 1980). At one time it was thought that these deaths were largely due to mechanical asphyxia, but it now appears more likely that SIDS occur as a function of disordered respiratory control.

The physiological mechanisms involved in SIDS are not well understood, but may well vary with age. Findings of an increased incidence of upper respiratory infection among victims of SIDS (Steinschneider, 1972), for example, is particularly interesting when one considers that rapid eye movement (REM) sleep predominates during the first 2 months of life; it is known that apnea during REM sleep can be triggered by upper airway reflexes (Sutton, Taylor, & Lindeman, 1978). During the third to fifth months of postnatal development, the proportion of time spent in non-REM sleep increases. Instances of centrally induced hypoventilation have been reported to occur during non-REM sleep (Shannon, Marsland, & Gould, 1976), and it appears that at least some SIDS victims previously have impaired ventilatory responses to CO_2 (Shannon, Kelly, & O'Connell, 1977). In conclusion, the available evidence suggests that SIDS occur as a function of disordered respiratory control, and that the full elucidation of the underlying mechanisms involved will require detailed psychophysiological assessment.

Respiration during Exercise

Two major ventilatory adjustments occur during exercise. The first is the increase in ventilation as the metabolic rate of the contracting skeletal muscles increases during mild to moderate exercise (Holmgren & McIlroy, 1964). The second adjustment is the sudden increase in ventilation at the onset of exercise (Dejours, 1967).

Several factors may account for the two ventilatory

adjustments to exercise. One factor may be a reflex mechanism arising from afferent endings in contracting skeletal muscle (McCloskey & Mitchell, 1972). A second factor may arise from the "irradiation" of impulses from areas in the brain that command skeletal muscle contraction toward areas in the medulla controlling ventilation. Thus Eldridge, Millhorn, and Waldrop (1981) have shown that electrical stimulation of locomotor areas in the subthalamus of cats immediately increases ventilation, an effect that is still present even when the cats are paralyzed. Finally, a third factor has been proposed by Wasserman, Whipp, Casaburi and Beaver (1977). They have proposed that ventilatory drive is linked to CO_2 flow to the central circulation. The specific site of the CO_2-sensitive mechanism is unclear, but has been proposed to lie beyond the pulmonary capillaries, possibly in the carotid bodies.

Respiratory Adjustments at High Altitudes

Barometric pressure decreases as one ascends above the surface of the earth. Thus at 18,000 feet, barometric pressure is only half that at sea level (i.e., 380 vs. 760 mm Hg). Because the inspired pO_2 is dependent on the barometric pressure, any decrease in the latter decreases the former. For example, at Pike's Peak, Colorado, which is about 5000 ft above sea level, the barometric pressure is about 400 mm Hg and the inspired pO_2 about 67 mm Hg. However, in spite of the hypoxia associated with initial exposure to high altitudes, humans reside at altitudes as great as 16,000 feet. The following is a brief description of some of the known processes that allow acclimatization to these high altitudes.

Hyperventilation has great adaptive value when humans are exposed to high altitude, because increasing ventilatory minute volume, which reduces alveolar pCO_2, allows alveolar pO_2 to increase. The hyperventilation caused by high altitude is the result of hypoxia-induced arterial chemoreceptor stimulation. Moreover, the chemoreceptor stimulation, in combination with increases in tidal volume and breathing rate, causes cardiac output to increase, which in turn delivers more O_2 to the tissues (Kontos, Levasseur, Richardson, Mauck, & Patterson, 1967). The hypoxia caused by high altitude also results in polycythemia (an increase in the number of red blood cells per cubic millimeter of blood), thereby increasing the O_2-carrying capacity of the blood. The polycythemia is caused by an increase in the rate of secretion by the kidney of erythropoietin, a hormone that increases the production of red blood cells by the bone marrow. Still another adjustment that occurs in response to high-altitude exposure is the growth of new pulmonary capillaries. The new capillaries decrease the distance that oxygen must diffuse from the alveoli to the red blood cells.

Respiration during Sleep

In humans, sleep has been shown to decrease the sensitivity of the respiratory system to increases in arterial pCO_2. Thus in deep sleep, alveolar pCO_2 (and therefore arterial pCO_2) increases from about 40 to 46 mm Hg. However, in sleeping humans, hypoxia is still a powerful stimulus to ventilation (Comroe, 1974). The vagus nerves also appear to play an important role in regulating ventilation during sleep. Thus, Phillipson (1977) has shown that blocking impulse conduction in these nerves in unanesthetized dogs during slow-wave sleep causes a profound decrease in ventilatory rate, an effect that is characterized by expiratory apnea. This finding suggests that vagal afferent impulses arising from pulmonary stretch receptors have an important influence on the central pattern generator, which drives ventilation during sleep.

Respiration and Asthma

Asthma is characterized by the sensation of dyspnea, which is caused by narrowing of the airways. Asthma is believed to be an immunological disease. In response to a foreign antigen, an antibody (immunoglobulin IgE) is formed, which then binds to mast cells in the airways. After this process of sensitization, a second antigen challenge binds the foreign substance, which is often a protein, to the antibody attached to the mast cell. The ensuing antigen–antibody reaction causes the mast cell to release histamine, which in turn directly constricts airway smooth muscle and stimulates afferent vagal endings in the airways. These afferent vagal endings are then believed to bronchoconstrict reflexly (Gold, Kessler, & Yu, 1972). It should be noted that histamine is not the only mediator of asthma; others include bradykinin, prostaglandins, and slow-reacting substances associated with anaphylaxis (Austen & Orange, 1975). Therefore, the bronchoconstriction seen in asthma appears to have two components. The first is a direct contraction of airway smooth muscle caused by mediator release. The second is a vagal reflex arising from afferent endings in the lung. At present, it is controversial which of the two components is dominant.

Because the airways are constricted during asthma, minute volume of ventilation often decreases, resulting in hypoxemia. Hypoxemia, in turn, can cause a further bronchoconstriction, an effect that is due to increased firing from the carotid body (Nadel & Widdicombe, 1962). Thus, asthma represents one of the few instances in which a reflex operates as a positive feedback mechanism, a situation that can be potentially quite harmful to the organism.

CONCLUSIONS

In this chapter, we have discussed some of the basic aspects of pulmonary ventilation, including pulmonary structure, the mechanics of respiration, and the assessment of pulmonary volumes and capacities. Although a knowledge of pulmonary volumes and capacities during behavioral experiments can tell us a good deal about relationships between breathing activity and behavior, knowledge about the consumption of O_2 and the excretion of CO_2 provides a more direct picture of the metabolic changes that occur during behavioral situations. Use of an ear oximeter, the Douglas bag, a servo-controlled O_2 monitor, or a blood gas analyzer can provide important information about metabolic changes occurring during psychophysiological experiments.

As we have seen in this chapter, the human nervous system carefully monitors arterial O_2, CO_2, and H^+ ion concentrations, and uses potent reflexive changes to restore and maintain homeostasis. The manner in which the central nervous system integrates respiratory activity with the metabolic demands produced by various behavioral situations makes the study of these relationships of considerable importance. Finally, there appears to be important work to be done by psychophysiologists in relating respiratory function to stresses imposed by exercise, altitude, and various behavioral challenges. Psychophysiological investigations of health-related issues, including those in the fetus, neonate, and infant, and in asthmatic and emphysematic patients, have begun; these show promise of contributing to the solution of important medical problems.

REFERENCES

Adrian, E. D. Afferent impulses in the vagus and their effect on respiration. *Journal of Physiology* (London), 1933, 79, 332–358.

Allison, R. O., Holmes, E. L., & Nyboer, J. Volumetric dynamics of respiration as measured by electrical impedance plethysmography. *Journal of Applied Physiology*, 1964, 19, 166–172.

Astrand, P., & Rodahl, K. *Textbook of work physiology.* New York: McGraw-Hill, 1970.

Astrand, P., & Saltin, B. Oxygen uptake during the first minutes of heavy muscular exercise. *Journal of Applied Physiology*, 1961, 16, 971–976.

Auchincloss, J. H., Gilbert, R., & Baule, G. H. Effect of ventilation on oxygen transfer during early exercise. *Journal of Applied Physiology*, 1966, 21, 810–818.

Austen, K. F., & Orange, R. P. Bronchial asthma: The possible role of the chemical medicators of immediate hypersensitivity in the pathogenesis of subacute chronic disease. *American Review of Respiratory Disease*, 1975, 112, 423–436.

Berger, A. J. Dorsal respiratory group neurons in the medulla of cat:

Spinal projections, responses to lung inflation and superior laryngeal nerve stimulation. *Brain Research*, 1977, 231–254.

Biscoe, T. J., Purves, M. J., & Sampson, S. R. The frequency of nerve impulses in single carotid body chemoreceptor afferent fibres recorded in vivo with intact circulation. *Journal of Physiology*, 1970, 208, 121–131.

Campbell, E. J. M. *The respiratory muscles and the mechanics of breathing.* Chicago: Year Book Medical Publishers, 1958.

Cerretelli, P., Sikand, R., & Fahri, L. E. Readjustments in cardiac output and gas exchange during onset of exercise and recovery. *Journal of Applied Physiology*, 1966, 21, 1345–1350.

Clark, F. J., & von Euler, C. On the regulation of depth and rate of breathing. *Journal of Physiology* (London), 1972, 222, 267–295.

Coleridge, H. M., & Coleridge, J. C. G. Impulse activity in afferent vagal C-fibers with endings in intrapulmonary airways of dogs. *Respiration Physiology*, 1977, 22, 125–142.

Coleridge, H. M., Coleridge, J. C. G., & Kidd, C. Role of pulmonary arterial baroreceptors in the effects produced by capsaicin in the dog. *Journal of Physiology* (London), 1964, 170, 272–285.

Coleridge, H. M., Coleridge, J. C. G., & Luck, J. Pulmonary afferent fibers of small diameter stimulated by capsaicin and by hyperinflation of the lungs. *Journal of Physiology* (London), 1965, 179, 248–262.

Comroe, J. H. *Physiology of respiration* (2nd ed.). Chicago: Year Book Medical Publishers, 1974.

Comroe, J. H., Forster, R. E., DuBois, A. B., Briscoe, W. A., & Carlsen, E. *The lung: Clinical physiology and pulmonary function tests* (2nd ed.). Chicago: Year Book Medical Publishers, 1962.

Comroe, J. H., & Schmidt, C. F. Reflexes from the limbs as a factor in the hyperpnea of muscular exercise. *American Journal of Physiology*, 1943, 138, 536–547.

Crayton, S. C., Aung-Din, R., Fixler, D. E., & Mitchell, J. H. Distribution of cardiac output during induced isometric exercise in dogs. *American Journal of Physiology*, 1979, 236, H218–H224.

Daly, M. de B., & Scott, M. J. The effects of stimulation of the carotid body chemoreceptors on heart rate in the dog. *Journal of Physiology* (London), 1958, 144, 148–166.

Daly, M. de B., & Unger, A. Comparison of the reflex responses elicited by stimulation of the separately perfused carotid and aortic body chemoreceptors in the dog. *Journal of Physiology* (London), 1966, 182, 370–403.

Dejours, P. Neurogenic factors in the control of ventilation during exercise. *Circulation Research*, 1967, 20–21 (Suppl. 1), I-146-I-153.

Downing, S. E., Remensnyder, J. P., & Mitchell, J. H. Cardiovascular responses to hypoxic stimulation of the carotid bodies. *Circulation Research*, 1962, 10, 676–685.

DuBois, A. B., Bothelo, S. Y., & Comroe, J. H. A new method of measuring airway resistance in man using a body plethysmograph: Values in normal subjects and in patients with respiratory disease. *Journal of Clinical Investigation*, 1956, 35, 327–335.

Eldridge, F. L., Millhorn, D. E., & Waldrop, T. G. Exercise hyperpnea and locomotion: Parallel activation from the hypothalamus. *Science*, 1981, 211, 844–846.

Fishman, A. P. Respiratory physiology. *Annual Review of Physiology*, 1981, 43, 69–71.

Ginzel, K. H., Eldred, E., Watanabe, S., & Grover, F. Drug induced depression of gamma efferent activity. III. Viscero-somatic reflex action of phenyldiguanide, veratridine and 5-hydroxy-tryptamine. *Neuropharmacology*, 1971, 10, 77–91.

Gold, W. M., Kessler, G.-F., & Yu, D. Y. C. Role of vagus nerves in experimental asthma in allergic dogs. *Journal of Applied Physiology*, 1972, 33, 719–725.

Hainsworth, R., Karim, F., & Sofola, O. A. Left ventricular inotropic responses to stimulation of carotid body chemo-receptors in anesthetized dogs. *Journal of Physiology* (London), 1979, 287, 455–466.

Holmgren, A., & McIlroy, M. B. Effect of temperature on arterial blood gas tensions and pH during exercise. *Journal of Applied Physiology*, 1964, 19, 243–245.

Holton, P., & Wood, J. B. The effects of bilateral removal of the carotid bodies and denervation of the carotid sinuses in two human subjects. *Journal of Physiology* (London), 1965, 181, 365–378.

Irsigler, G. B., & Severinghaus, J. W. Clinical problems of ventilatory control. *Annual Review of Medicine*, 1980, 31, 109–126.

Karim, F., Hainsworth, R., Sofola, O. A., & Wood, L. M. Responses of the heart to stimulation of aortic body chemoreceptors in dogs. *Circulation Research*, 1980, 46, 77–83.

Kaufman, M. P., Coleridge, H. M., Coleridge, J. C. G., & Baker, D. G. Bradykinin stimulates afferent vagal C-fibers in intrapulmonary airways of dogs. *Journal of Applies Physiology*, 1980, 48, 511–517.

Kontos, H. A., Levasseur, J. E., Richardson, D. W., Mauck, H. P., & Patterson, J. L. Comparative circulatory responses to systemic hypoxia in man and in unanaesthetized dog. *Journal of Applied Physiology* 1967, 23, 381–386.

Knowlton, G. C., & Larrabee, M. G. A unitary analysis of pulmonary volume receptors. *American Journal of Physiology*, 1946, 147, 100–114.

Lloyd, B. B., Jukes, M. G. M., & Cunningham, D. J. C. The relation between alveolar oxygen pressure and the respiratory response to carbon dioxide in man. *Quarterly Journal of Experimental Physiology*, 1958, 43, 214–227.

Loeschke, H. H., & Gertz, K. H. Einfluss des O_2-Druckes in der Elnatmungszeit auf die Qtemtatigkeit des Menschen, gepruft unter Konstanthaltung des alveolaren CO_2-Druckes. *Pflugers Archiv*, 1958, 267, 460–477.

Macklem, P. T. Respiratory mechanics. *Annual Review of Physiology*, 1978, 40, 157–172.

McCloskey, D. I., & Mitchell, J. H. Reflex cardiovascular and respiratory responses originating in exercising muscle. *Journal of Physiology* (London), 1972, 224, 173–186.

Mead, J., Peterson, N., Grimby, G., & Mead, J. Pulmonary ventilation measured from body surface movements. *Science*, 1967, 156, 1383–1385.

Merrill, E. G. The lateral respiratory neurons of the medulla: Their associations with nucleus ambiguus, nucleus retroambigualis, the spinal accessory nucleus and the spinal cord. *Brain Research*, 1970, 24, 11–28.

Merrill, E. G. Finding a respiratory function for the medullary respiratory neurons. In R. Bellairs & E. G. Gray (Eds.), *Essays on the nervous system*. Oxford: Clarendon Press, 1974.

Merrill, E. G. Preliminary studies on nucleus retroambigualis–nucleus of the solitary tract interaction in cats. *Journal of Physiology* (London), 1975, 244, 54–55.

Mills, J. E., Sellick, H., & Widdicombe, J. G. Activity of lung irritant receptors in pulmonary micro-embolism, anaphylaxis and drug-induced bronchoconstrictions. *Journal of Physiology* (London), 1969, 203, 337–357.

Mitchell, R. A. Neural regulation of respiration. *Clinics in Chest Medicine*, 1980, 1, 3–12.

Mitchell, R. A., & Berger, A. J. Neural regulation of respiration. *American Review of Respiratory Disease*, 1975, 111, 206–224.

Mitchell, R. A., Loeschke, H. H., Severinghaus, J. W., Richardson, J. W., & Massion, W. H. Regions of respiratory chemosensitivity on the surface of the medulla. *Annals of the New York Academy of Sciences*, 1963, 109, 661–681.

Nadel, J. A., & Widdicombe, J. G. Effects of changes in blood gas tensions and carotid sinus pressure on tracheal volume and total lung resistance to airflow. *Journal of Physiology* (London), 1962, 163, 13–33.

Nagle, F. J. Physiological assessment of maximal performance. In J. Wilmore (Ed.), *Exercise and sport sciences reviews* (Vol. 1). New York: Academic Press, 1973.

Otis, A. B., Fenn, W. O., & Rahn, H. J. Mechanics of breathing in man. *Journal of Applied Physiology*, 1950, 2, 592–607.

Pack, A. I. Sensory inputs to the medulla. *Annual Review of Physiology*, 1981, 43, 73–104.

Paintal, A. S. Impulses in vagal afferent fibers from specific pulmonary deflation receptors: The response of these receptors to phenyl diguanide, potato starch, 5-hydroxytryptamine, and nicotine, and their role in respiratory and cardiovascular reflexes. *Quarterly Journal of Experimental Physiology*, 1955, 40, 89–111.

Paintal, A. S. Mechanism of stimulation of type J. pulmonary receptors. *Journal of Physiology* (London), 1969, 203, 511–532.

Plum, F. Neurological integration of behavioural and metabolic control of breathing. In R. Porter (Ed.), *Breathing: Hering-Breuer Centenary Symposium*. London: Churchill, 1970.

Phillipson, E. A. Regulation of breathing during sleep. *American Review of Respiratory Disease*, 1977, 115, 217–224.

Phillipson, E. A., Hickey, R. F., Graf, P. D., & Nadel, J. A. Hering-Breuer inflation reflex and regulation of breathing in conscious dogs. *Journal of Applied Physiology*, 1971, 31, 746–750.

Roughton, F. J. W., & Darling, R. C. The effect of carbon monoxide on the oxyhemoglobin dissociation curve. *American Journal of Physiology*, 1944, 141, 17–31.

Roberts, A. M., Kaufman, M. P., Baker, D. G., Brown, J. K., Coleridge, H. M., & Coleridge, J. C. G. Reflex tracheal contraction induced by stimulation of bronchial C-fibers in dogs. *Journal of Applied Physiology*, 1981, 51, 485–493.

Russell, J. A. & Lai-Fook, S. J. Reflex bronchoconstriction induced by capsaicin in the dog. *Journal of Applied Physiology*, 1979, 47, 961–967.

Sackner, M. A. Pulmonary structures and pathology. In J. Kline (Ed.), *Biological foundations of biomedical engineering*. Boston: Little, Brown, 1976.

Sampson, S. R., & Hainsworth, R. Responses of aortic body chemoreceptors of the cat to physiological stimuli. *American Journal of Physiology*, 1972, 222, 953–958.

Sampson, S. R., & Vidruk, E. H. Properties of 'irritant' receptors in canine lung. *Respiration Physiology*, 1975, 25, 9–22.

Sellick, H., & Widdicombe, J. G. The activity of lung irritant receptors during pneumothorax, hyperpnoea and pulmonary vascular congestion. *Journal of Physiology* (London), 1969, 203, 359–381.

Severinghaus, J. W. Blood gas calculator. *Journal of Applied Physiology*, 1966, 21, 1108–1116.

Shannon, D. C., Kelly, D. H., & O'Connell, K. Abnormal ventilation in infants at risk for sudden infant death syndrome. *New England Journal of Medicine*, 1977, 297, 747–750.

Shannon, D. C., Marsland, D. W., & Gould, J. B. Central hypoventilation during quiet sleep in two infants. *Pediatrics*, 1976, 57, 342–346.

Speck, D. F., & Feldman, J. L. The effects of microstimulation and microlesions in the ventral and dorsal respiratory groups in medulla of cat. *Journal of Neuroscience*, 1982, 2, 744–757.

Steinschneider, A. Prolonged apnea and the sudden infant death syndrome: Clinical and laboratory observations. *Pediatrics*, 1972, 50, 646–654.

Sutton, D., Taylor, E. M., & Lindeman, R. C. Prlonged apnea in infant monkeys resulting from stimulation of superior laryngeal nerve. *Pediatrics*, 1978, 61, 519–527.

Von Baumgarten, R., Von Baumgarten, A., & Schaefer, K.-P. Beitrag zur lokalisationsfrage bulboreticularer respiratorischer Neurone der katze. *Pluegers Archiv*, 1957, 264, 217–217.

Wade, J. G., Larson, C. P., & Hickey, R. F. Effect of carotid endarterectomy on carotid chemoreceptor and baroreceptor function in man. *New England Journal of Medicine*, 1970, 282, 823–829.

Wasserman, K., Whipp, B. J., Casaburi, R., & Beaver, W. L. Carbon dioxide flow and exercise hyperpnea. Cause and effect. *American Review of Respiratory Disease*, 1977, 115, 225–237.

Webb, P., & Troutman, S. J. An instrument for continuous measurement of oxygen consumption. *Journal of Applied Physiology*, 1970, 28, 867–871.

Widdicombe, J. G. THe regulation of bronchial calibre. In C. G. Caro (Ed.), *Advances in respiratory physiology*. London: Edward Arnold, 1966.

Widdicombe, J. G., & Nadel, J. A. Reflex effects of lung inflation on tracheal volume. *Journal of Applied Physiology*, 1963, 18, 681–686.

Chapter Seven

Physiological Bases of Cardiovascular Psychophysiology

Parry B. Larsen
Neil Schneiderman
Rosemary DeCarlo Pasin

INTRODUCTION

The circulatory system has several functions. First, it distributes oxygen (O_2) and other nutrients to the tissues of the body. Second, it returns carbon dioxide (CO_2) to the lungs and other products of metabolism to the kidneys. Third, it plays an important role in the regulation of body temperature. Fourth, it transports hormones and other functional chemicals to target organs. The functions of the circulatory system are dynamic and complex. The need for O_2 in particular tissues continually varies. Transport of hormones depends upon the challenges that the organism must face. Some of the control over the system is autoregulatory, such as the heart's response to changes in the volume of blood flowing into it. In contrast, other aspects of cardiovascular regulation are under the control of the nervous system.

The present chapter describes the basic organization of the circulatory system, its neural and hormonal control, and the electrical and mechanical events associated with the cardiac cycle. We also discuss the manner in which cardiovascular measurements are made, with particular emphasis upon those measures that are of greatest interest to the study of psychophysiology. In general, the measurements of most interest are those cardiovascular changes that reflect activities of the nervous system that are correlated with behavior.

During the course of our discussion, we look at the mechanical aspects of the cardiac cycle that influence the output of blood from the heart, particularly contractility. Contractility is of considerable interest to psychophysiologists, because it is directly under the control of the autonomic nervous sytem (ANS). The extent to which contractility can be reliably assessed noninvasively by the measurement of systolic time intervals (STIs) is examined. We also describe the electrical events of the cardiac cycle, because they provide valuable information about the manner in which the neural and hormonal concomitants of behavior can alter the state of the heart. The vascular system is discussed in terms of blood pressure (BP) changes and redistribution in various vascular beds as a function of the nervous system and behavior.

The effects of behavior on cardiovascular function

Parry B. Larsen. Miami Heart Institute, Miami, Florida.
Neil Schneiderman. Departments of Psychology and Biomedical Engineering, University of Miami, Coral Gables, Florida.
Rosemary DeCarlo Pasin. Department of Psychology, University of Miami, Coral Gables, Florida.

are usually measured by indices of the contractile and electrical states of (1) cardiac muscle, and (2) the smooth muscle cells that are responsible for the "tone" of arteries and veins. Although in substantial part under ANS control, the contractile state of these muscle cells is subject to important modulatory action by adrenocortical, sex, and/or thyroid hormones. Since both the ANS transmitters and other hormones produce their interactive effects upon the receptors in the cell membranes, the assessment of cardiovascular physiological variables as a manifestation of receptor function is important. This is likely to become increasingly central to the field of psychophysiology, because receptors change in number, spatial relations, and affinity for their agonists (i.e., chemicals that stimulate them) as a function of cardiovascular performance. The manner in which behaviorally induced changes in cardiovascular performance can, in turn, influence changes in cardiovascular function by altering receptor processes is potentially of great importance to psychophysiologists. Although the present chapter attempts to provide a comprehensive account of cardiovascular functioning and its assessment, the unifying theme is the neural and hormonal control of the circulation in terms of its relevance to psychophysiology.

ORGANIZATION OF THE CIRCULATORY SYSTEM

The cardiovascular system consists of the heart, which is essentially two pumps in series with each other; a series of distributing (arteries and arterioles) and collecting (venules and veins) tubes; and a system of thin-walled vessels called "capillaries." Capillaries, which consist solely of endothelial cells about 1 μm thick, permit rapid exchanges to occur between the bloodstream and the extracellular fluid outside of the capillaries. Substances leaving the walls of the capillaries enter the extracellular fluid just external to cell membranes. Conversely, substances are removed from the immediate environment of these cells via passage through the capillary walls into the bloodstream.

The cellular elements of the blood consist of red blood cells ("erythrocytes"), white blood cells ("leukocytes"), and platelets ("thrombocytes"). These specialized cells are all suspended in an extracellular liquid medium called "plasma." Plasma contains about 90% water and has as its solutes crystalloids and a heterogeneous group of proteins that makes up about 7% of its weight. The principal protein component is albumin, whose osmotic activity is critical for preventing loss of fluid through the semipermeable membranes of the capillary vessels. Other important proteins include lipoproteins, which are concerned

with the transport of lipids, immunoglobulins (antibodies), the coagulation proteins, and various hormones. Nutrient substances, such as glucose and amino acids, are also transported in plasma. The major cation of plasma is sodium; others include potassium, calcium, and magnesium. Principal inorganic anions are chloride, bicarbonate, and phosphate.

Each 1 mm^3 of blood contains about 5 million erythrocytes, each about 8 μm in diameter. Some 95% of the dry weight of each erythrocyte consists of hemoglobin, which is responsible for the cellular transport of O_2. The affinity of hemoglobin for O_2 is a nonlinear function, the parameters of which are modified by local CO_2 concentration and pH so that hemoglobin is 95% saturated in the lungs and gives up 25–65% of its oxygen content in the tissues, depending on local requirements (Spivak, 1980).

The leukocytes are larger and more heterogeneous than the erythrocytes. Their principal functions involve defense against infectious agents and foreign cells, and repair of damaged tissues (Quastel, 1979). The three major types of white cells are the granulocytes, lymphocytes, and monocytes. Of these, the granulocytes and monocytes are capable of engulfing bacteria and other particles. This phenomenon is known as "phagocytosis" (Gabig & Babior, 1981). Lymphocytes, on the other hand, are part of the immune system.

The smallest of the three major types of blood cell is the platelet. The 150,000 to 300,000 platelets per cubic millimeter of blood each have an average diameter of about 2 μm. In response to endothelial damage, platelets instantly adhere to the injured surface in large numbers. They release substances that accelerate coagulation, produce vasoconstriction (e.g., serotonin), and incite smooth muscle proliferation in damaged vessel walls (R. T. Wall & Harker, 1980).

There are aspects of blood composition that are of interest to psychophysiologists. The viscosity of blood is one of the elements that provides frictional resistance to flow. Only erythrocytes and the larger plasma proteins (especially the coagulation protein, fibrinogen) contribute significantly to viscosity. During exercise, crystalloid fluid translocation can raise the concentration of both of the components, producing an important increase in viscosity. The minimally invasive test of venous hematocrit is a reasonable index of this alteration.

Also, the cellular elements are emerging as communicators, just as did hormones over half a century ago. Adrenoreceptors are prominent components of the plasma membranes of many of the cellular elements of blood (Lefkowitz, 1979). Clues to their function are only beginning to emerge (Peterson, Gerrard, Glover, Rao, & White, 1982). Apparently, the adrenoreceptors' density and activity on lymphocytes are regulated by natural or iatrogenic exposure to adrenergic agonists or antagonists (Butler, O'Brien,

O'Malley, & Kelly, 1982; Fraser, Nadeau, Robertson, & Wood, 1981). Even more intriguing is the discovery that lymphocyte adrenoreceptor density is closely correlated with cardiac sensitivity to isoproterenol (Fraser *et al.*, 1981). This relationship may provide a minimally invasive, albeit complex, test of chronic cardiac adrenoreceptor status.

The circulating blood, including plasma and cells, traverses through two systems in succession. One of these is the "systemic circulation," which supplies the tissues of the body. The second of these systems is the "pulmonary circulation," which carries the blood through the lungs.

From a functional standpoint, the heart may be described as two pumps. Each of these pumps has two chambers: an "atrium" and a "ventricle." During the filling period of each heart chamber, the cardiac muscles relax. In contrast, during the emptying period, the cardiac muscles contract. Unidirectional flow of blood into and out of the heart's chambers is maintained by a series of one-way valves that are operated by pressure differentials. The right ventricle in this pumping system may be considered as a volume pump that sends relatively unoxygenated blood throughout the lungs. This pulmonary circuit is a low-pressure, low-resistance system. In contrast, the left ventricle is a pressure pump that transmits oxygenated blood throughout the relatively high-resistance systemic circulation.

The superior and inferior vena cava supply the right atrium with relatively unoxygenated blood. This blood passes through an atrioventricular (tricuspid) valve into the right ventricle. When the right ventricle contracts, blood passes through the pulmonary valve into the pulmonary artery. After blood is oxygenated in the lungs, it is transported back to the left atrium via the pulmonary vein. The oxygenated blood passes from the left atrium through an atrioventricular (bicuspid, mitral) valve into the left ventricle.

The efficiency of the heart as a pump largely depends upon a sequential pattern of excitation and contraction. This pattern proceeds in an orderly and coordinated manner from the atria to the ventricles. Contraction of the atria is followed by contraction of the ventricles ("ventricular systole"). During "diastole," all four chambers are relaxed. Specialized structures that form the cardiac conduction system are responsible for coordinating the rhythmic contraction and relaxation of the heart. These structures include the sinoatrial (SA) node, the atrioventricular (AV) node, the bundle of His, and the Purkinje system (Figure 7-1).

The basic principle of coordination involved is that the cardiac conduction system discharges at a more rapid rate than cardiac muscle. Normally, the SA node discharges most rapidly, and hence serves as the cardiac pacemaker. The rate of discharge of this node normally determines the rate at which the heart beats.

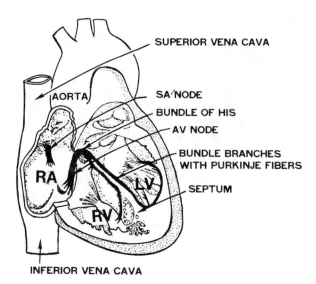

Figure 7-1. The conduction system of the heart includes the sinoatrial (SA) node and the atrioventricular (AV) node in the right atrium (RA), the AV bundle of His, and the left and right bundle branches of Purkinje fibers in the right ventricle (RV) and left ventricle (LV).

Impulses generated in the SA node are transmitted through the atrial muscle to the AV node, and thence through the bundle of His and the Purkinje system to the ventricular muscle.

During contraction of the left ventricle, blood is forced through the aortic valve into the aorta and is distributed throughout the systemic circulation via the arterial tree. As blood leaves the heart, its flow is pulsatile, moving through the major arteries with a pulse rate velocity. The resistance of the smaller arteries and arterioles, however, causes a relatively large decrease in pressure. Also, by the time blood flow reaches the smaller arterioles and the capillary bed, these vessels essentially act as a low-pass frequency filter, and blood flow becomes steady.

NEURAL CONTROL OF THE CIRCULATION

The regulation of cardiovascular activity requires coordination of local, reflexive, and central nervous systems (CNS) command activities. Impulses initiated in visceral and other receptors are relayed to the CNS, integrated within it at various levels of the neuraxis, and transmitted via efferents out to the cardiovascular effectors. The outflows are both neuronal and hormonal and ultimately are determined by CNS regulatory activities, negative feedback, and cellular metabolic factors. In this section we discuss the efferent pathways innervating the heart and vasculature, afferent pathways and reflexive adjustments, and the CNS pathways and mechanisms that integrate cardiovascular activities with other bodily functions. Although brief mention of the electrical and mechanical events of the cardiac cycle is necessarily made in this section, more rigorous definitions of such terms as "contractility," "cardiac output," and "total peripheral resistance" are presented in subsequent sections.

Efferent Pathways and Mechanisms

Overview

Efferent transmission within the ANS occurs via the sympathetic and parasympathetic divisions. Sympathetic efferent nerves originate from the thoracic and lumbar segments of the spinal cord. In contrast, parasympathetic nerves originate from the brain and the sacral region of the cord. In general, the ANS pathways from the CNS to particular organs consist of "two-neuron" chains. The cell body of the first-order neuron lies within a ganglion. In the parasympathetic division, the ganglion is close to or within the innervated organ. In the sympathetic division, the synapse between the first-order and second-order neuron is typically located within a sympathetic ganglion chain that runs outside of and parallel to the vertebral column.

A conspicuous exception to the arrangements described above occurs in the case of the adrenal medulla, which is part of the sympathetic division. The first-order neurons innervating the adrenal medulla synapse directly onto cells that secrete epinephrine (E) and norepinephrine (NE) directly into the circulation. These secretory cells are embryologically derived from nervous tissue, however, and are analogous to postganglionic neurons.

The first-order neurons in both the parasympathetic and sympathetic divisions (including fibers projecting to the adrenals) release acetylcholine (ACh). Therefore ACh and ACh-like substances, when applied to the ganglia, will excite both sympathetic and parasympathetic postganglionic neurons. Although second-order neurons of the parasympathetic division also release ACh, the receptor sites on postganglionic neurons and on parasympathetic effector cells are different. At sympathetic and parasympathetic ganglia, the primary postganglionic cholinergic receptor site is said to be nicotinic, because the receptor can also be activated by nicotine but not by muscarine (see Table 7-1). In contrast, the cholinergic receptor site on the parasympathetically innervated effector cell membrane is considered to be muscarinic, because the receptor cell can be activated by muscarine but not by nicotine.

Some drugs, such as hexamethonium, are referred to as "ganglion-blocking agents," because they are able to functionally block the ANS by antagonizing nicotinic postsynaptic receptors at both sympathetic and parasympathetic ganglia. In contrast, drugs such as atropine and scopolamine primarily exert their influence by blocking receptor sites on parasympathetic effector cells.

Unlike the parasympathetic division, in which all of the postsynaptic neurons liberate ACh, most postganglionic sympathetic neurons release NE. Sympathetic postganglionic neurons innervating the sweat glands as well as a few blood vessels are cholinergic, however, and the adrenal medulla liberates both NE and E. The effectors on which NE and E act can also be subdivided on the basis of receptor properties (Ahlquist, 1948). In general, alpha-adrenergic receptors mediate vasoconstriction, whereas beta-adrenergic receptors mediate such actions as increases in cardiac rate and the strength of cardiac contractions. Adrenergic receptors have been further subdivided on the basis of their selective properties. Table 7-1 briefly lists some prototypical autonomic agonists and antagonists.

Neural and Hormonal Control of the Heart

The rate and contractile force of the heart are under the control of the parasympathetic and sympathetic divisions of the ANS. In the normal adult at rest, the heart rate (HR) is approximately 70 beats per min

Table 7-1
Autonomic Agonists and Antagonists

Normal Transmitter	Receptor Location	Prototypical Agonist	Prototypical Antagonist
ACh	Postganglionic neuron	Nicotine	Hexamethonium
ACh	Parasympathetic effector (e.g., heart)	Muscarine	Atropine
NE	Alpha-adrenergic effector (e.g., arteriole)	Phenylephrine	Phentolamine
NE, E	Beta-adrenergic effector (e.g., heart)	Isoproterenol	Propranolol

(bpm). During sleep, this HR may be diminished by 10 to 20 bpm; during emotional excitement or muscular exercise, it may exceed 150 bpm. These rates, which are influenced by neural and hormonal factors, are referred to as "control rates." Under most conditions the SA node, which is the normal pacemaker of the heart, is under the tonic influence of both the sympathetic and the parasympathetic divisions of the ANS. The former facilitates the rhythmicity of the pacemaker, whereas the latter inhibits it. In contrast, in the absence of neural or hormonal influences, the young adult human heart has an invariant "intrinsic rate" of about 105 bpm.

The sympathetic division influences the heart neuronally via cardiac sympathetic fibers and hormonally via the adrenal medulla. First-order neurons of the cardiac sympathetic nerves originate in the intermediolateral columns of the upper five thoracic segments of the spinal cord. These neurons, which liberate ACh at their terminals, synapse with postganglionic neurons located at the same level within the paravertebral sympathetic ganglion chain and in the cervical ganglion. In humans, the postganglionic fibers project to the heart as the superior, middle, and inferior cardiac nerves from the superior, middle, and inferior cervical ganglia. The transmitter that is liberated by these postganglionic fibers is NE. Distribution of fibers at the heart is primarily in the vicinity of the SA and AV nodes as well as in the ventricles. In general, the sympathetic cardiac nerves originating from the right side of the spinal cord predominantly influence HR, and the nerves from the left side of the cord mostly influence contractility, but there is considerable overlap in their distributions (Randall, Priola, & Ulmer, 1963).

The first-order neurons that arise in the intermediolateral columns of the spinal cord and synapse in the paravertebral ganglia give rise when stimulated to a rapid excitatory postsynaptic potential (fast EPSP), which generates action potentials as well as a prolonged inhibitory postsynaptic potential (slow IPSP), followed by a prolonged excitatory postsynaptic potential (slow EPSP). The slow IPSP and slow EPSP appear to modulate transmission through the ganglion (e.g., Flacke & Gillis, 1969).

The preganglionic neurons release ACh, which elicits, in postganglionic neurons, fast EPSPs via action upon nicotinic receptors and slow EPSPs via action upon muscarinic receptors (see Figure 7-2). Sympathetic ganglia also contain small, intensely fluorescent (SIF) cells that serve as interneurons between pre- and postganglionic neurons. These SIF cells, which have muscarinic receptors and are intrinsic to the ganglia, are activated by the release of ACh from preganglionic neurons. The SIF cells have a catecholamine, usually dopamine, as a transmitter. Activation of the SIF cell produces slow IPSPs in the postganglionic neurons

(Libet, 1977). Transmission in sympathetic ganglia has been extensively studied, and it now appears that activating the dopamine receptor on the postganglionic neuron is mediated intracellularly by cyclic adenosine monophosphate (cAMP) (Greengard, 1978). In addition to the effects produced upon postganglionic sympathetic neurons that are attributable to the release of ACh (see Figure 7-2), stimulation of the presynaptic neuron apparently also causes the release of a polypeptide, possibly luteinizing hormone-releasing hormone (LHRH), which produces a very slow EPSP lasting several minutes (Jan, Jan, & Kuffler, 1979).

Sympathetic activation of the heart does not occur only neuronally via the sympathetic cardiac nerves, but also hormonally by the release of E and to a much lesser extent NE into the bloodstream by the adrenal medulla (Weiner, 1980). First-order neurons originating within the intermediolateral column of thoracic segments 5–9 project to the adrenal medulla as part of the greater splanchnic nerves. The secretion of catecholamines from the adrenal medulla is regulated transsynaptically by the presynaptic release of ACh acting upon the nicotinic receptors located on the membrane of chromaffin cells of the adrenal medulla (Guidotti & Costa, 1974).

As previously mentioned, alpha-adrenergic receptors mediate vasoconstriction, whereas beta-adrenergic receptors mediate such actions as increased HR ("positive chronotropic effect") and increased strength of ventricular contraction ("positive inotropic effect"). The development of increasingly selective agonist and antagonist drugs that act at adrenergic receptors has allowed for further subclassification. Lands, Arnold, McAuliff, Luduena, and Brown (1967) made the important distinction between beta-1- and beta-2-adrenoceptors. Beta-1-adrenergic receptors predominate in cardiac and adipose tissues; beta-2-adrenergic receptors are found primarily in arteriolar smooth muscles and lung tissues.

Although NE released by the sympathetic cardiac nerves on the one hand, and NE and E released by the adrenal medulla on the other, each activate beta-1-adrenoceptors at the heart, the effects of neuronal (sympathetic cardiac nerves) and hormonal (adrenal medulla) release upon heart function are not identical. This occurs because the distribution of the beta-adrenoceptors in the heart does not precisely follow the noradrenergic innervation of the heart by the sympathetic nerves (Baker, Boyd, & Potter, 1980). Instead, the distribution of adrenoceptors appears to be similar to that of the coronary blood flow, with most receptors located in the ventricles, which are much less neuronally innervated than the right atrium. Baker and Potter (1980) have concluded, therefore, that most cardiac adrenoceptors are not at nerve endings, but are localized where they can respond optimally to circulating E. In addition, Baker and Potter

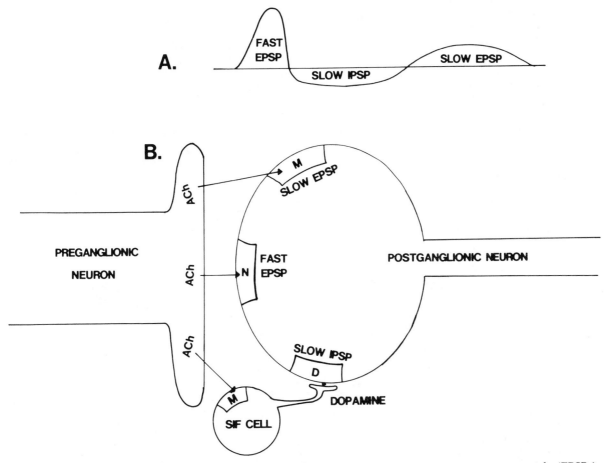

Figure 7-2. Synaptic actions in a sympathetic ganglion. A. Sequences of excitatory postsynaptic potentials (EPSPs) and inhibitory postsynaptic potentials (IPSPs). B. The preganglionic neuron releases acetylcholine (ACh), which elicits fast EPSPs by nicotinic (N) action (shown in A) and slow EPSPs by muscarinic (M) action (also shown in A) upon the postganglionic neuron. Release of ACh from the preganglionic neuron also activates muscarinic receptors on the membrane of small, intensely fluorescent (SIF) cells that are intrinsic to the ganglion, which in turn release dopamine (D), producing the slow IPSP shown in A. The effect of a polypeptide upon the postganglionic neuron (not shown) produces a very slow EPSP lasting several minutes.

(1980) found that circulating levels of NE rarely approach concentrations likely to influence most cardiac adrenoceptors.

The adrenoceptors in the vicinity of nerve endings in the heart appear to be preferentially activated by neuronally released NE during exercise; the increase in plasma NE found during exercise also reflects the release of NE at nerve endings innervating vasoconstrictor vessels. In contrast, during life-threatening situations (e.g., hemorrhage, severe acidosis, hypoglycemia, hypoxia, or the discharge of pheochromocytomas), circulating plasma levels of E reach concentrations that are adequate for this catecholamine to activate beta-adrenoceptors throughout the heart. Some forms of psychological stress, including public speaking (Dimsdale & Moss, 1980) and competition with harassment (Glass, Krakoff, Contrada, Hilton,

Kehoe, Mannucci, Collins, Snow, & Elting, 1980), also result in the preferential release of E.

In contrast to the sympathetic division, which exerts positive chronotropic and inotropic effects upon the heart (see Table 7-2), activation of the parasympathetic division produces a decrease in HR ("negative chronotropic effect") and a decrease in the force of cardiac contractions ("negative inotropic effect"). The cardiac parasympathetic fibers originate in the dorsal vagal nucleus (Ellenberger, Haselton, Liskowsky, & Schneiderman, 1983; Schwaber & Schneiderman, 1975) and/or the nucleus ambiguus (McAllen & Spyer, 1976, Ellenberger *et al.*, 1983) of the medulla and project to the heart via the vagus nerves.

Unlike the sympathetic division, in which the ganglia are typically situated along the nerves, parasympa-

Table 7-2
Autonomic Responses in the Cardiovascular System

Effector	Cholinergic Response	Adrenergic	
		Response	Receptor
Heart			
SA node	− Chronotropic	+ Chronotropic	Beta-1
Atria	− Inotropic	+ Inotropic	Beta-1
		+ Dromotropic	Beta-1
AV node	− Dromotropic	+ Dromotropic	Beta-1
His–Purkinje system	—	+ Dromotropic	Beta-1
Ventricles	− Inotropic	+ Inotropic	Beta-1
		+ Dromotropic	Beta-1
Arterioles			
Coronary	Dilation	Constriction	Alpha
		Dilation	Beta-2
Skin and Mucosa	Dilation	Constriction	Alpha
Skeletal muscle	Dilation	Constriction	Alpha
		Dilation	Beta-2
Mesentery	—	Constriction	Alpha
		Dilation	Beta-2
Cerebral	Dilation	Constriction (slight)	Alpha
Pulmonary	Dilation	Constriction	Alpha
		Dilation	Beta-2
Renal	—	Constriction	Alpha
		Dilation	Beta-2
Veins (systemic)	—	Constriction	Alpha
		Dilation	Beta-2
Kidney			
Juxtaglomerular cells	—	Renin secretion	Beta-2

thetic ganglia are located within the organs that they innervate. Most cardiac ganglion cells are located near the SA node and AV node. Cardiac ganglion cells are also found in atrial muscle, and to a much lesser extent in the ventricular myocardium.

At the SA node, the release of ACh from the postganglionic neuron slows the HR by decreasing the rate of spontaneous depolarization of pacemaker cells, thereby delaying the triggering of action potentials. Vagal innervation of the AV node slows conduction ("negative dromotropic effect") and increases the refractory period of action potentials. The increase in vagal tone tends to enhance the electrical stability of the ventricles and reduces the incidence of spontaneous ventricular fibrillation (Kent & Epstein, 1976).

Increased vagal activity in atrial muscle decreases strength of contraction, slows the conduction of action potentials, and shortens the refractory period. The combination of these factors can actually facilitate atrial fibrillation arising from an ectopic focus (Taylor, 1980). Increased vagal activity also normally decreases slightly the strength of contraction of the left ventricle (DeGeest, Levy, Zieske, & Lipman,

1965). This is most apparent when contractility has been enhanced by adrenergic stimulation.

Many of the nerve terminals of the sympathetic and parasympathetic divisions are in close proximity to one another at the heart. This allows for complex interactions to occur. The most conspicuous of these is the inhibitory influence of terminal vagal fibers on postganglionic sympathetic neurons and on the myocardium itself (Figure 7-3). Numerous studies have indicated that the greater the background level of sympathetic activity, the more profound is the depressant effect of vagal activity (Levy, 1977). This phenomenon is known as "accentuated antagonism," and appears to apply to myocardial contractility as well as to HR.

Accentuated antagonism depends in part upon a muscarinic inhibition of NE release and in part upon a reduced cardiac response to a given quantity of NE. The reduced cardiac response to NE in particular appears to involve the intracellular activities of the cyclic nucleotides (see Figure 7-3).

It is thought that the NE released at sympathetic nerve endings produces its effects by elevating intra-

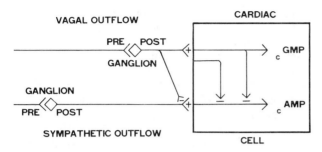

Figure 7-3. The neuronal and intracellular mechanisms responsible for accentuated antagonism between the cardiac sympathetic and vagal nerves. These include changes of cyclic guanosine monophosphate (cGMP) and cyclic adenosine monophosphate (cAMP) within the effector cardiac cell. (Modified from Levy, 1977.)

cellular levels of cAMP (Epstein, Levey, & Skelton, 1971; Sutherland, Robison, & Butcher, 1968). When cAMP has been increased by adrenergic stimulation, however, ACh can profoundly depress the intracellular levels of cAMP by elevating cyclic guanosine monophosphate (cGMP) (Glaviano, Goldberg, & Pindo, 1975; Watanabe & Besch, 1975). This could be accomplished in two ways. First, the cGMP produced by cholinergic stimulation is known to have a profound inhibitory effect upon the elevation of cAMP. Second, the raised level of cGMP produced by vagal stimulation could accelerate the hydrolysis of cAMP. In any event, the strong coactivation of the sympathetic and parasympathetic inputs to the heart leads to a pronounced bradycardia and at least slightly decreased myocardial contractility.

Cardiac receptor populations should not be thought of as fixed and invariant. The phenomenon wherein the response of intact tissues or organs to beta-adrenergic receptor agonists decreases after exposure to the agonist is called "desensitization." This phenomenon appears in large part to be due to a decrease in the number of beta-adrenergic receptors as a function of the concentration and duration of exposure to agonists (Fraser *et al.*, 1981; Watanabe, Jones, Manalin, & Besch, 1982). It is conceivable that the diminished contractility associated with ventricular hypertrophy related to neurogenic hypertension may in part be due to a decreased population of beta-adrenergic receptors or to a functional uncoupling of the receptors to adenylate cyclase.

Receptor populations may increase as well as decrease as a function of hormonal influences. Hyperthyroidism, for example, is associated in the heart with an increased number of beta-adrenergic receptors and a decreased number of presynaptic alpha-adrenergic receptors (Ciaraldi & Marinetti, 1977), as well as with a decreased number of muscarinic receptors (Sharma & Banerjee, 1977). Interestingly, systolic hypertension is often seen in otherwise un-

complicated hyperthyroidism (Strong, Northcutt, & Sheps, 1977).

Neural and Hormonal Control of the Vasculature

The innervation of the arterioles and small arteries by alpha-adrenergic receptors (see Table 7-2) allows sympathetic activity to increase "peripheral resistance" (i.e., total resistance to blood flow in the systemic circulation), and thereby to increase systemic arterial pressure and the rate of blood flow through tissues. In some vascular beds, such as the skin and mucosa, neurogenically induced vasoconstriction is the main contributor to increases in resistance; in the coronary and cerebral vessels, however, such factors as metabolic autoregulation are far more important.

Whereas vasoconstriction in arteriolar vessels tends to increase arterial pressure by increasing peripheral resistance, sympathetic constriction of the veins and venules does not significantly change the overall peripheral resistance. Instead, the major effect of sympathetic stimulation of the postcapillary vessels is to decrease their capacity. Hence, a sympathetically induced increase in venous tone (i.e., reduced venous compliance) moves blood from the venous reservoir into the heart, lungs, and systemic arteries. The increased venous return to the heart, in turn, increases cardiac output in accordance with "Starling's law of the heart," thereby elevating systemic arterial pressure (see below, "Mechanical Events of the Cardiac Cycle").

Although the release of NE at the heart and blood vessels plays an important role in increasing BP, the most potent pressor agent known is the peptide angiotensin II. The strong pressor effect of angiotensin II is due to a number of factors, including direct stimulation of vascular and cardiac muscle receptors, presynaptic facilitation of sympathetic transmission, and stimulation of CNS pathways controlling sympathetic outflow (Douglas, 1980).

Whenever blood flow through the kidneys is decreased, the juxtaglomerular cells of the kidney, which are located in the walls of the arterioles, release the enzyme renin into the blood. Renin works upon renin substrate to produce angiotensin I. Angiotensin I, in turn, is acted upon by a converting enzyme in the small vessels of the lungs to produce angiotensin II.

Angiotensin II has several effects that can elevate BP. First, constriction of the arterioles increases peripheral resistance and thereby restores systemic arterial BP back toward normal. Second, mild constriction of the veins increases venous return to the heart and thereby increases cardiac output. Third, angiotensin II has a direct effect upon the kidneys to cause decreased excretion of sodium and water. And fourth, angiotensin stimulates the secretion of aldosterone by the adrenal cortex, which in turn also causes decreased excretion of sodium and water.

There are basically three ways in which systemic arterial BP can be raised, and increased sympathetic activity can selectively or jointly contribute to all of them. The manner in which sympathetic nervous system activity can influence each of these three ways—increased cardiac output, total peripheral resistance, and/or fluid volume—is diagrammed in Figure 7-4.

Although Figure 7-4 provides a reasonable descriptive summary of the means by which sympathetic activity can lead to increases in arterial pressure, the actual situation is somewhat more complex. Figure 7-5, for example, shows some of the factors that appear to influence transmission. Note, for example, that angiotensin II not only sensitizes the effector cell, but also potentiates vasoconstrictor responses as a result of presynaptic facilitation of NE release (Zimmerman, Gomer, & Liao, 1972). Note also that circulating E may enhance NE secretion by presynaptic activation of beta-2-adrenergic receptors (Stjarne & Brundin, 1976), and that ACh—at least in the heart—may activate muscarinic receptors on presynaptic nerve terminals as well as on innervated cells (Levy & Martin, 1979).

Of considerable importance in NE transmission is the autoinhibition of NE secretion, which is mediated via presynaptic alpha-2-adrenergic receptors (Berthelson & Pettinger, 1977; Langer, 1977). Virtually all NE neurons that have been studied possess this autoinhibitory mechanism, which quantitatively dominates local control of NE transmission. Other substances that influence NE transmission include prostaglandin E_2 (PGE_2), ACh, substance P, and perhaps dopamine.

The basic principles of peripheral vascular control include not only the maintenance of an adequate pressure head within the systemic arterial circulation, but also the adequate distribution of blood flow through various tissues in order to meet various bodily needs. This distribution of the blood flow is under the control of neurogenic, myogenic, and local metabolic factors. In some vascular beds, such as the skin and mucosa, neurogenic factors are preeminent. In other beds, such as the cerebral vasculature and coronary arteries, neurogenic factors are important, but they play a secondary role to local autoregulatory processes. The skeletal musculature, offers a good example of a vascular bed in which neurogenic factors and local autoregulatory factors are both extremely important.

The blood vessels supplying skeletal muscles are innervated by the sympathetic nervous system.

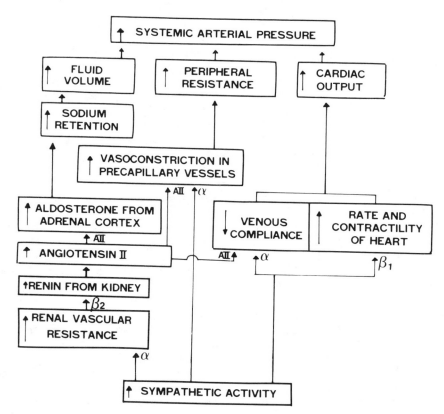

Figure 7-4. Control of systemic arterial blood pressure by the sympathetic nervous system involves neuronal influences upon the heart, kidney, adrenal cortex, precapillary vessels, and postcapillary vessels.

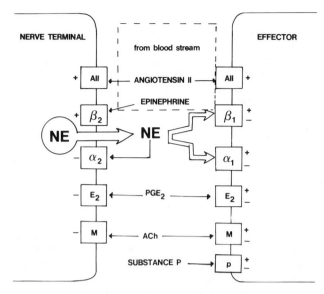

Figure 7-5. The action of various biologically active substances that can influence the release of the neurotransmitter norepinephrine (NE) and its postsynaptic effect upon the effector cell. Notice that the release of NE can produce negative (−) feedback effects upon the presynaptic terminal, which are mediated by alpha-2 (α_2) adrenergic receptors. Other substances such as angiotensin II (AII), epinephrine, prostaglandin E (PGE$_2$), acetylcholine (ACh), and substance P can modify the release of NE and or its action upon effector cells via their activation of appropriate receptors (e.g., muscarinic [M] receptors for ACh and beta-2 [β_2] adrenergic receptors for epinephrine). The type of effect is shown as (+) for augmentation and (−) for diminution.

Alpha-adrenergic receptors mediate vasoconstriction, whereas beta-2-adrenergic receptors mediate vasodilation. The sympathetic vasoconstrictor fibers tonically help to support systemic arterial BP. Also, during circulatory shock and other emergency situations in which it is desirable for blood to be preferentially shunted from the periphery to the brain and heart, sympathetically mediated vasoconstriction can reduce blood flow in this vascular bed to approximately one-fourth of normal.

Under exercise conditions, increases in local metabolism cause muscle cells to consume nutrients rapidly and vasodilator substances to be released. Although the exact nature of these local autoregulatory vasodilators is not fully known, adenosine appears to be a likely candidate. Extremely small quantities of adenosine produce vasodilation in skeletal muscle. Resting skeletal muscle contains adenosine, and the amount increases during flow-restricted exercise in skeletal muscle (Belloni, Phair, & Sparks, 1979).

While the prolonged vasodilation accompanying exercise, and the "reactive hyperemia" (i.e., increased blood flow to a body part) following temporary occlusion of a limb, appear to be attributable to metabolic vasodilator substances being released under local control, the increase in muscle blood flow that occurs during behavioral challenges not requiring physical exertion (e.g., Brod, Fencl, Hejl, & Jirka, 1959) seems likely to be mediated by sympathetic vasodilator fibers activating beta-2-adrenergic receptors. During physical exercise, plasma NE increases; however, during emotional challenges requiring active coping, plasma E increases (Dimsdale & Moss, 1980; Glass *et al.*, 1980). Interestingly, NE does not activate beta-2-adrenergic receptors, but E does. The E released during emotional stress thereby provides a mechanism for neurogenically induced vasodilation.

Cardiovascular Reflexes

In our discussion of the neural control of the circulation, we have thus far focused upon the efferent pathways innervating the heart and vasculature. With this information as background, we can now turn to a discussion of the afferent pathways and reflexive adjustments involved in the neural control of the circulation.

Arterial Baroreceptors

Information about changes occurring in different parts of the cardiovascular system are provided by arterial, pulmonary, atrial, and ventricular mechanoreceptors. Mechanoreceptors sensitive to arterial pressure are known as "baroreceptors." Major groups of these stretch receptors lie within the walls of the carotid sinus and aortic arch. Some receptors are also located along the thoracic aorta as well as along the subclavian, common carotid, and mesenteric arteries (e.g., J. H. Green, 1967).

An increase in baroreceptor stimulation (i.e., increase in systemic arterial BP) leads to pronounced reflexive decreases in HR and BP unless the reflex is "gated" within the CNS. These reflexive decreases in HR and BP help to stabilize arterial pressure (Korner, 1971). The reflexive "bradycardia" (i.e., HR slowing) is mediated by the cardiac branches of the vagus nerves. Systemic injections of atropine methylnitrate, which blockade the cholinergic output of the vagus nerves of the heart and therby abolish the bardycardia response, do not eliminate the reflexive, systemic hypotension. Thus, the decrease in BP appears to be largely due to an inhibition of sympathetic vasoconstrictor activity.

The first-order neurons of the baroreceptor reflex terminate within the nucleus of the solitary tract in the medulla. CNS efferents for the reflex consist of (1) vagal preganglionic cardioinhibitory motoneurons originating in the dorsal vagal nucleus (Ellenberger *et al.*, 1983; Schwaber & Schneiderman, 1975) and/or nucleus ambiguus (Ellenberger *et al.*, 1983; McAllen & Spyer, 1975) of the medulla, and (2) preganglionic sympathetic neurons originating in the intermediolateral horn of the thoracic spinal cord (Chung, Chung, & Wurster, 1975). Barosensory information is transmitted not only to the medulla and spinal cord, but also to the pons, midbrain, and diencephalon (e.g., Kaufman, Hamilton, Wallach, Petrick, & Schneiderman, 1979). This permits a good deal of circulatory control to be integrated at supramedullary levels. The baroreceptor reflex, for example, can be attenuated or abolished by neuronal activity initiated at least as far rostral as the hypothalamus (Gebber & Snyder, 1970; Hilton, 1963) with the central inhibition of the reflex occurring at either the input to the nucleus of solitary tract (Adair & Manning, 1975) or the outflow to vagal preganglionic cardioinhibitory motoneurons (Jordan, Khalid, Schneiderman, & Spyer, 1979).

The baroreceptors play an important role in stabilizing BP when relatively abrupt changes in cardiac output, peripheral resistance, or blood volume occur. In contrast, more long-term control of BP is determined by the balance between fluid intake and output. The most important organ in this control of body fluid volume is the kidney.

Reflexive Control of the Blood Volume

Changes in blood volume are sensed by mechanoreceptors in the vena cava, pulmonary artery, and atria. Paintal (1953) divided the atrial receptors into A and B types. The B receptors are activated by an increase in atrial volume, whereas the A receptors are activated by an increase in atrial tension, but not by an increase in volume per se. Increases in atrial volume are sensed by the vagal sensory B receptors and transmitted to the brain, where they reflexively produce increased urinary output by the kidneys and decreased secretion of antidiuretic hormone by the pituitary (Paintal, 1973). In addition to cardiac vagal afferents, cardiopulmonary afferents also project to the CNS via sympathetic nerves (Weaver, 1977).

Chemoreceptor Reflexes

The chemoreceptors consist of relatively small, highly vascular bodies found in the vicinity of the aortic arch and carotid sinus. The aortic and carotid chemoreceptors are particularly sensitive to a reduction in arterial blood oxygen tension (pO_2) and to increased arterial blood carbon dioxide tension (pCO_2). Although these aortic and carotid chemoreceptors are primarily concerned with the regulation of respiration, and the respiratory adjustments can obscure chemoreceptor influences upon the circulation, the circulatory influences can be easily seen when respiration is controlled. In this case, stimulation of the chemoreceptors cause (1) bradycardia and decreased cardiac output due to increased vagal activity; (2) increased

BP due to increased sympathetic activity associated with constriction of the resistance vessels in skeletal muscle, splanchnic bed, and kidney, as well as in splanchnic capacitance; and (3) dilatation of the coronary vessels due to the activation of vagal fibers (Donald & Shepherd, 1980).

Diving Reflex

When the face is immersed in water, the sensory endings of the trigeminal nerve become activated. This leads to an increase in BP due to constriction of systemic vessels in the splanchnic region, skeletal muscles, and cutaneous capacitance vessels. The reflex also includes bradycardia and a cessation of breathing ("apnea"). Although the apnea is rapidly followed by a decrease in pO_2 and an increase in pCO_2 in the arterial blood, the sensory input from the trigeminal nerve overrides the action of the chemoreceptors on the respiratory center (Daly, Korner, Angell-James, & Oliver, 1978). In contrast, the vasoconstriction and bradycardia associated with the chemoreceptor reflex augment those of the trigeminal nasopharyngeal reflex. Reflex dilatation of the coronary vessels mediated by the vagus nerves also occurs. In this manner, arterial BP is maintained, and maximum amounts of blood are made available to the heart and brain.

Cerebral Ischemic Reflex

The global cerebral ischemia that occurs during cardiopulmonary arrest or severe hypotension elicits a constellation of responses that is quite similar to the diving reflex. This cerebral ischemic reflex includes (1) an increase in systemic arterial pressure associated with vasoconstriction in renal, mesenteric, and femoral beds; (2) bradycardia associated with decreased cardiac output; and (3) apnea (Dampney, Kumada, & Reis, 1979). Studies in which the brains of rabbits have been made ischemic by occlusion of the vertebral and common carotid arteries have indicated that the reflex is organized in the medulla, since it persists after ponto-medullary transection. In these studies, section of the carotid sinus and aortic nerves had no effect upon the reflexive BP or peripheral resistance changes and only partially diminished the bradycardia response. Lesions in the ventromedial part of the rostral ventrolateral medulla selectively abolish the BP increase, whereas injection of glutamate to this region increases BP. This suggests that the ischemic response results from activation of neurons in the medulla.

Although the evidence is convincing that the cerebral ischemic response is organized within the medulla, the extent, if any, to which forebrain ischemia may activate pathways to the site(s) of reflex integration within the medulla is presently unknown. Neurons have been found, however, in the periventricular regions (e.g., subfornical organ; organum vascularis laminae terminalis) of rats and cats (Ishibashi & Nicolaidis, 1981; Nicolaidis, 1970), which increase their discharge rates to even small decreases in BP. The areas in which these neurons have been found are of particular interest, because the region also appears to contain receptor sites for the pressor action of angiotensin II (Mangiapane & Simpson, 1980).

Reflexive Control of Body Temperature

When body temperature begins to rise, neurons in the hypothalamus initiate reflexive changes in regional blood flow favoring heat exchange (Crawshaw, 1980). Two important processes are involved (Hales, Iriki, Tsuchiya, & Kozawa, 1978). First, neuronal influences increase blood flow through cutaneous arteriovenous anastomoses. Second, the increased flow through these anastomoses increases local tissue temperature, which facilitates capillary blood flow by the direct effects of heat upon local vessels. When core temperature begins to fall, reflexive, sympathetically mediated vasoconstriction occurs in the skin; shivering is initiated; and stimulation of the thyroid gland increases cellular metabolism.

Orthostatic Reflex

When a person shifts to an erect position, the force of gravity results in the pooling of 300–800 ml of blood in the legs (Sjostrand, 1952). Normal people, however, engage powerful compensatory mechanisms that permit BP to be maintained. The baroreceptors respond immediately to the fall in pressure and trigger hemodynamic responses that begin in a second or two. Sympathetically mediated arteriolar and venous vasoconstriction occur, vagal restraint upon the heart is inhibited, and the sympathetic cardiac nerves exert both positive chronotropic and positive inotropic effects (Ziegler, 1980).

Although HR increases substantially, a small decrease in the total output of the heart actually occurs because of a pronounced decrease in the amount of blood ejected with each beat. Peripheral resistance increases slightly, however, and this is sufficient to maintain mean arterial BP.

Normal individuals typically double their plasma NE levels after standing for 5 or 10 min and triple their levels after moderate exercise. Thus, care must be taken in psychophysiological experiments monitoring catecholamines to insure that postural effects are not confounded with other behavioral variables under study. It should also be noted that patients with idiopathic orthostatic hypotension, who have isolated autonomic impairment, show a pronounced depletion of NE in blood vessels innervated by sympathetic nerves (Kontos, Richardson, & Norvell, 1975). In diabetics, orthostatic hypotension can develop due to autonomic neuropathy and/or volume depletion caused by renal salt and albumin wasting and by protein leakage through diseased capillaries (Ziegler, 1980).

Bainbridge Reflex and Normal Sinus Arrhythmia

Bainbridge (1915) found that infusions of blood or saline produced cardiac acceleration, provided that venous pressure rose sufficiently to distend the right atrium. The effect was abolished by bilateral transection of the vagus nerves. Bainbridge therefore postulated that increased cardiac filling reflexively elicited tachycardia, and that the afferent projections to the brain were conducted by the vagus nerves.

Rhythmic variations in heart rate that occur at the frequency of respiration are referred to as "respiratory sinus arrhythmia." This sinus arrhythmia is observable in most people, and is particularly marked in children. Generally, the HR accelerates during inspiration and decelerates during expiration. The vagus nerves appear to be primarily responsible for producing the sinus arrhythmia, and the extent of the arrhythmia varies with the degree of vagal tone (Levy, Ng, & Zieske, 1968).

The extent of sinus arrhythmia appears to be influenced by both reflexive and central (i.e., CNS) factors. First, during each respiratory cycle, negative intrapleural pressure increases and decreases, thereby influencing venous return. This produces a waxing and waning of the Bainbridge reflex. Second, baroreceptors and volume receptors are alternately loaded and unloaded during the cardiac cycle, causing reflexive decreases and increases in HR. Third, direct brain stem projections from respiratory centers to cardiac centers also exert an influence (Levy, DeGeest, & Zieske, 1966; Lopes & Palmer, 1976).

Since the extent of sinus arrhythmia varies with the degree of vagal activity, Katona and Jih (1975) suggested that sinus arrhythmia can be used to estimate parasympathetic control of HR. They found that the magnitude of sinus arrhythmia was correlated .97 with parasympathetic control.

Although the range of HR variability provides a reasonable estimate of parasympathetic control in an anesthetized, immobilized preparation, this may not be the case in freely moving, behaving individuals. Consequently, Porges, Bohrer, Cheung, Drasgow, McCabe, and Keren (1980), and Porges, McCabe, and Yongue (1982) have suggested that by examining the spectral densities for heart period in relation to respiratory frequencies, nonrespiratory contributions can be partialed out. They have suggested that in the behaving individual, isolation of heart period variability in relation to respiratory rhythms can provide a better estimate of vagal control of HR than does simple variance, which provides a more global measure of variability.

Central Neural Control of the Circulation

Central regulation of the cardiovascular system involves neuronal integration at every level of the CNS from the neocortex to the spinal cord. Progress has been made in examining control of the circulation during exercise, emotional behavior, and quiet inactivity.

H. D. Green and Hoff (1937) observed that following electrical stimulation of the motor cortex in cats or monkeys, cardiovascular responses occurred that included an increase in arterial BP accompanied by renal vasoconstriction and vasodilation in skeletal limb muscles. Typically, electrical stimulation of the motor cortex elicits both limb movement and muscle vasodilation (Clarke, Smith, & Shearn, 1968). The vasodilation in muscle apparently does not occur, however, unless muscle contraction takes place or behavioral concomitants of the defense reaction such as piloerection are evident (Hilton, Spyer, & Timms, 1975). Thus the descending pathway from the motor cortex involved in circulatory regulation appears to be activated in exercise as opposed to agonistic behavior. Cardiovascular changes that are similar to those elicited during exercise have also been elicited by stimulating a discrete area of the subthalamus (Smith, Rushmer, & Lasher, 1960).

Another important CNS pathway involved in the regulation of the circulation is associated with the defense reaction (*Abwehrreaktion*) described by Hess and Brügger (1943). These investigators stimulated the perifornical region of the hypothalamus in the unanesthetized cat and elicited a constellation of behavioral responses now known to include piloerection, pupillary dilation, retraction of the nictitating membrane, arching of the back, baring of the teeth, unsheathing of the claws, hissing, spitting, and ultimately fight-or-flight behavior. Stimulation of the perifornical hypothalamus in anesthetized cats leads to piloerection, pupillary dilation, and retraction of the nictitating membrane, as well as "tachycardia" (i.e., increased HR), increased systemic arterial BP, vasoconstriction in the skin and intestine, and vasodilation in skeletal muscle (Abrahams, Hilton, & Zbrozyna, 1960; Eliasson, Folkow, Lindgren, & Uvnas, 1951). The pathway extends from at least as far rostral as the amygdala and descends to the hypothalamus via the ventral amygdalo-fugal pathway (Hilton & Zbrozyna, 1963). From the hypothalamus, the pathway descends between the substantia nigra and the cerebral peduncles, maintaining a ventral course throughout the brain stem to the medulla (Abrahams et al., 1960; Coote, Hilton, & Zbrozyna, 1973; Eliasson et al., 1951).

A third pattern of cardiovascular responses that can be elicited by intracranial electrical stimulation includes a depressor response and bradycardia (Kabat, Magoun, & Ranson, 1935). Such changes

elicited by stimulation of the orbito-frontal cortex have been traced to a reduction in vasoconstrictor tone, an augmentation of vagal tone, and an inhibition of catecholamine secretion by the adrenal medulla (Goldfein & Ganong, 1962; Kaada, Pribram, & Epstein, 1949; von Euler & Folkow, 1958). Depressor responses have also been elicited by stimulating the temporal cortex, pyriform lobe, septal region, and amygdala (Ban, 1966; Reis & Oliphant, 1964; P. D. Wall & Davis, 1951). Electrical stimulation of the anterior hypothalamus elicits bradycardia and a depressor response (Folkow, Langston, Oberg, & Prerovsky, 1964; Gellhorn, 1964; Hilton & Spyer, 1971). These responses are partially due to descending influences upon the hypothalamus, since they are diminished by degeneration of cortico-fugal fibers from the frontal lobe (Magoun, 1938). However, stimulation of the anterior hypothalamus can also potentiate the effects of baroreceptor afferent stimulation (Gimpl, Brickman, Kaufman, & Schneiderman, 1976; Hilton & Spyer, 1971; Klevans & Gebber, 1970).

The functional organization of the hypothalamus with regard to cardiovascular responses and behaviors elicited by intracranial electrical stimulation show some differences among species. Whereas Hess (1957) found that the feline hypothalamus was organized into an anterior zone concerned with quiescent, parasympathetic-like functions and a posterior one concerned with aroused, sympathetic-like functions, Ban (1966) provided evidence that the rabbit hypothalamus reveals a mediolateral functional organization. According to Ban's schema for the rabbit, the medial hypothalamus mediates sympathetic, and the lateral hypothalamus parasympathetic, activity.

Research in our own laboratory with rabbits has confirmed and expanded Ban's (1966) schema. In one study, for example, we found that microstimulation of the medial hypothalamus, particularly the ventromedial hypothalamic nucleus, elicited tachycardia and a pressor response associated with circling movements, hindlimb thumping, and other responses usually associated with aggressive behavior (Gellman, Schneiderman, Wallach, & Le Blanc, 1981). In contrast, stimulation of an intermediate zone, including the anterior and posterior hypothalamus, elicited pronounced primary bradycardia (nonreflexive) and a pressor response as well as other manifestations of sympathetic arousal (e.g., pupil dilation). The rabbits tended to remain immobile except for rather slow, orienting-like movements of the head. A third pattern of responses, identified by microstimulation of the far lateral hypothalamus, elicited profound bradycardia, a depressor response, and quiet inactivity.

Of considerable importance in our work were the findings that although the medial and intermediate hypothalamic zones both elicit sympathetic activity (e.g., BP increases and pupil dilation), stimulation of the medial region elicits tachycardia and an inhibition of vagal cardioinhibitory motoneurons (Jordan *et al.*, 1979); however, stimulation of the intermediate region elicits bradycardia (Gellman *et al.*, 1981). In preliminary work we have also observed that stimulation of the ventromedial hypothalamus but not the intermediate zone leads to a significant increase in plasma E, as well as damage to the endothelium of the aorta that is observable under the electron microscope. Our findings concerning the ventromedial hypothalamus are consistent with the results of Sudakov and Yumatov (1978), who also observed that stimulation of the ventromedial hypothalamus of rabbits produced a pressor response and an increase in plasma E.

Several of our experiments using intracranial stimulation, coagulation lesions, horseradish peroxidase histochemistry, and extracellular single-neuron recording techniques have indicated that the bradycardia elicited by stimulation of the far lateral hypothalamus involves a pathway originating at least as far rostral as the central nucleus of the amygdala (Gellman *et al.*, 1981). This pathway descends polysynaptically through the lateral hypothalamus (Wallach, Ellenberger, Schneiderman, Liskowsky, Hamilton, & Gellman, 1979), lateral zona incerta of the caudal diencephalon (Kaufman *et al.*, 1979), parabrachial nucleus (Hamilton, Ellenberger, Liskowsky, Gellman, & Schneiderman, 1981), and cardioinhibitory vagal preganglionic motoneurons in dorsal vagal nucleus (Schwaber & Schneiderman, 1975) and nucleus ambiguus (Ellenberger *et al.*, 1983).

In recent years there has been increasing recognition that several antihypertensive drugs, including clonidine (Schmitt, 1977), alpha methyldopa (Henning & Robinson, 1971), and propranolol (P. J. Lewis, 1976), may act principally through their actions on the CNS. Clonidine, for example, stimulates both central and peripheral alpha-adrenergic receptors, but the peripheral effects clearly cannot account for its potent antihypertensive action. Chan and his coworkers (Chan & Koo, 1978; Chen & Chan, 1978) have localized an area in the medial medullary reticular formation that plays a crucial role. In addition to this region, the nucleus of the solitary tract in the medulla and the ventral surface of the lower brain stem also appear to be important. Transection experiments indicate that the medulla plays a key role in regulating clonidine's actions upon tonic levels of BP (Schmitt & Schmitt, 1969).

Clonidine also exerts an influence upon the anterior hypothalamus, where microinjections of this agent produce a depressor response and bradycardia. The effects appear to be mediated by alpha-adrenergic receptors, since localized prior injection of an alpha-adrenergic agonist (phentolamine) abolishes the depressor and bradycardia effects otherwise induced by NE or clonidine (van Zwieten, 1973). Current thinking is that in addition to regulating tonic levels of BP

via its medullary action, clonidine facilitates phasic depressor and bradycardia adjustments, including the baroreceptor reflex. This appears to be accomplished via alpha-adrenergic influence upon neurons in the anterior hypothalamus, and perhaps also upon the nucleus of the solitary tract in the medulla.

In contrast to clonidine, propranolol exerts its effects via beta-adrenergic blockade. The major peripheral action of propranolol is an immediate decrease in HR and cardiac output, which is due to beta-adrenergic blockade of the heart. Reduction in BP requires days to weeks of chronic drug administration, suggesting that the hypotensive effect of propranolol may be due to central beta-adrenergic blockade. In support of this hypothesis, P. J. Lewis (1976) has shown that intracerebroventricular administration of propranolol in conscious rabbits results in decreased sympathetic splanchnic activity and hypotension. The delayed hypotensive effect of propranolol when administered peripherally may have to do with changes in the affinity or population of central beta-adrenergic receptors.

MECHANICAL EVENTS OF THE CARDIAC CYCLE

Overview

In the preceding section, we have seen how the nervous system influences the heart and blood vessels in order to adjust the flow of blood to various tissue beds. This section provides a more detailed look at the role of the heart in the bulk transport of blood. At this point, it would be well to emphasize that the O_2-for-CO_2 exchange that takes place in blood is so vital that the total mass of hemoglobin is directly proportional to that of the lean tissue, and the bulk rate at which hemoglobin is circulated is directly related to tissue O_2 demand. This bulk rate of the circulation is called the "cardiac output" ($\dot{Q}$).

Although the ultimate determinant of $\dot{Q}$ is tissue demand (Guyton, 1981; Shepherd & Vanhoutte, 1981), there are proximate limitations on the heart's ability to satisfy those demands. On the one hand, there are the strength of the heart muscle and its ability to obtain and transduce chemical energy resources; on the other, there are frictional resistances to flow, which chiefly are due to (1) viscous blood passing through small-caliber arteries and arterioles, and (2) the relationship between blood volume and the capacitance of the heart and blood vessels.

The pump that propels $\dot{Q}$ is phasic, the ventricle ejecting with each systole an amount of blood called the "stroke volume" (SV). Cardiac output, which is usually quantified as a minute volume, is necessarily the sum of all of the stroke volumes in that period. If one disregards the minor alteration in SV in the respiratory cycle (or, better, averages several SV determinations), then

$$\dot{Q} = SV \times HR$$

While successive resting SVs are nearly equal, at the onset of heavy exercise every ventricular systole for a minute or more may involve different conditions of ventricular filling, outflow resistance, interbeat interval (1/HR), availability of O_2 and nutrients, and interaction among the membrane-bound receptors of the ANS. Not surprisingly, the SV that results from the integratation of these influences will vary on a beat-to-beat basis. Each heart beat results from the sequential repetition of electrical and mechanical events known as the "cardiac cycle" (Wiggers, 1921a, 1921b).

The Cardiac Cycle

The cardiac cycle begins with the opening of the atrioventricular valves at the completion of the previous systole and proceeds in a series of stages, through ventricular filling, electrical activation, contraction, and relaxation (Figure 7-6). In principle, the right and left sides of the heart have different cycles; for our purposes, however, the conventional consideration of only the left-sided cycle is sufficient. The mechanical events have quite variable relationships among themselves, and the electrocardiogram (ECG) has variable coupling to the mechanical events (see section on STIs). The cardiac cycle flow diagram (Figure 7-6) should be extensively consulted during the reading of the sequential description that follows. It is important to be familiar with the electrical and mechanical events that occur in each period.

At the opening of the mitral valve, the increased pressure exerted by the accumulated venous return and the elastic recoil of the left ventricle (Hori, Yellen, & Sonnenblick, 1982) combine to promote a phase of rapid filling, the first component of ventricular diastole. During diastasis, the passive filling slows and nearly ceases before atrial systole completes the final 15–25% of ventricular filling. Note that the valves are mechanically rather than electrically operated.

The onset of ventricular contraction (systole) and closure of the mitral valve are followed by the "isovolumic contraction" phase, during which ventricular pressure rapidly rises. At this stage, the valves into and out of the ventricle are closed, and the ventricle is contracting, but no ejection occurs. Adjustments made in the geometry of the ventricular cavity during this phase make "isometric" a less appropriate label than "isovolumic." This period is of great interest to those who feel that its duration, or the velocity of pressure development during it, is a measure of contractility. This is discussed in detail later.

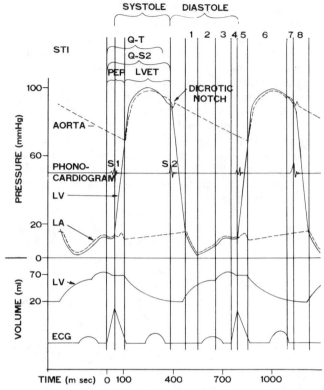

Figure 7-6. Events of the cardiac cycle include changes in the electrocardiogram (ECG), left ventricular (LV) volume, left atrial (LA) pressure, phonocardiogram, and aortic (aorta) pressure. The cardiac cycle begins with a period of relaxation, "diastole," followed by a period of contraciton called "systole." The onset of stage 1 begins with the opening of the atrioventricular valve. Subsequent stages are (2) diastisis, (3) atrial systole, (4) electromechanical delay, (5) isovolumic contraction, (6) ejection, (7) protodiastole, and (8) isovolumic relaxation. Note that the diagram shows two successive cardiac cycles so that the first heart sound, S_1, which reflects closure of the atrioventricular valves, and the second heart sound, S_2, which reflects closure of the semilunar (e.g., aortic) valves, each occur twice. Q-T, Q-S_2, pre-ejection period (PEP), and left ventricular ejection time (LVET) refer to systolic time intervals (STIs). See text for description of cardiac cycle and STIs.

During the ejection phase, the ventricular contents are propelled into the ascending aorta. Usually about 50–80% of the end-diastolic volume (EDV) is ejected. Resistance to outflow changes as a curvilinear function throughout this phase. At the end of ventricular contraction, during protodiastole, the myocardial fibers transiently hold their shortened state. Ventricular pressure falls below aortic pressure, but ejection continues due to the momentum of the blood. The duration and volume of ejection following cessation of ventricular contraction tends to increase in situations with low systemic vascular resistance (Sagawa, 1981). The paradoxical flow, which occurs even after contraction has ceased, is the basis of the controversy over end-ejection versus end-systole, which assumes some importance in the pressure–volume model of contractility, to be discussed later. The ejection phase ends when the blood kinetic energy is converted into aortic hydrostatic pressure and the aortic valve closes, creating the dicrotic notch on the aortic pressure trace. Finally, there is the stage of isovolumic relaxation to the point at which ventricular pressure falls below atrial pressure and the mitral valve opens again. Various aspects of the cardiac cycle are emphasized in many invasive and noninvasive measures of cardiac function.

Cardiac Output

Cardiac output ($\dot{Q}$) is the sum of local tissue flows throughout the body. Demand regulates local perfusion to the extent that long-term surplus flow is resisted (Guyton, 1981), and prolonged flow deficits are avoided by local modulation or override of central adrenergic influences (Shepherd & Vanhoutte, 1981). Indeed, resting $\dot{Q}$ so precisely satisfies O_2 demand that artificially elevating systemic flow produces little increase in O_2 consumption, while decreases in $\dot{Q}$ cause progressive reduction in oxidative capacity (Figure 7-7). Flow autoregulation at the tissue level is a continuous function, but $\dot{Q}$ should be considered in terms of the discontinuous mode of the cardiac cycle as well.

The determinants of $\dot{Q}$ at the cardiac level are preload, afterload, myocardial contractility, and HR. Each of these affects the events of the cardiac cycle differently. In the case of preload, afterload, and contractility, the effects are on SV and the time required for its ejection.

Briefly stated, the heart has a tendency to pump into the arteries all the blood that returns to it (Levy, 1979; Nixon, Murray, Leonard, Mitchell, & Blomqvist, 1982), so that, under steady-state conditions, venous return equals $\dot{Q}$. When venous return increases, myocardial autoregulatory mechanisms are brought into play, which enable the heart to adjust $\dot{Q}$ without hormonal or neural stimulation. Indeed, the first of these mechanisms was elucidated by Patterson, Pipe, and Starling (1914) on an isolated heart experimental preparation. They found that the stretch of ventricular muscle caused by increased diastolic filling led to stronger contraction, so that nearly all of the augmented venous return was expelled. This relationship between ventricular filling and SV has been restated many times as "Starling's law of the heart."

The cardiac cycle segments the continuous venous return into aliquots that fill the ventricle during diastole. Each aliquot, with the pressure that it generates as it stretches the elastic myocardium, constitutes the preload of the ensuing systole. The output of that contraction is, of course, the SV. Thus a succinct paraphrasing of Starling's law of the heart might be that SV is determined by preload. This form of autoregulation is called "heterometric" because there must be a change in length of myocardial fiber for it to occur. Preload is satisfactorily evaluated in terms of either end-diastolic pressure or EDV in the left ventricle. However, it is, perhaps, best described in terms of end-diastolic wall stress, which may be calculated as follows:

$$\text{Stress} = \frac{\text{Wall tension}}{\text{Mean wall thickness}}$$

where tension is the product of instantaneous chamber volume and pressure (Rackley, 1980), and mean wall thickness, likewise, is measured at precisely end-diastole.

Coming into play after 30 sec or so is a poorly understood homeometric autoregulation that restores the myocardial fibers nearly to their former length while their increased work output continues. Finally, stretching of the fibers in the SA node causes a 15–20% increase in rate of pacemaker firing. It should be emphasized that this particular increase in HR is autoregulatory (i.e., not the result of cardioaccelerator nerve activity). Autoregulatory control of SV is brought into play nearly continuously. This contrasts with the relatively few exercise episodes that invoke

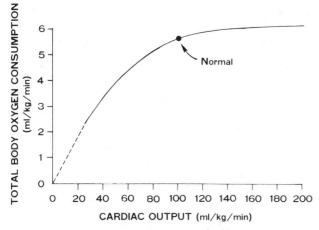

Figure 7-7. Total body oxygen consumption as a function of cardiac output. The normal cardiac output is at a level barely high enough to provide almost maximum oxygen consumption by the body, yet using the least pumping energy of the heart to achieve this result. The figure is based upon data obtained from dogs and includes corrections for excess oxygen consumed by the heart at the high cardiac outputs. (From "The Relationship of Cardiac Output and Arterial Pressure Control" by A. C. Guyton. *Circulation*, 1981, 64, 1079–1088. Reprinted by permission of the author and the American Heart Association.)

the cardioaccelerator system, and the rare life-threatening emergencies or perceived threats that elicit pronounced sympathetic neural and adrenomedullary responses.

Afterload is usually defined as total resistance to flow, in which case mean systolic pressure (MSP)—or, less satisfactorily, mean arterial pressure (MAP)—is a good index (see section on BP for discussion). Afterload has also been described as peak systolic stress (Rackley, 1980). The determinants of afterload are systemic vascular resistance (R), blood viscosity and volume, and vascular compliance. Even when there is no neurohumoral influence on arterial smooth muscle, the number–caliber–length relationships of the peripheral arterial bed produce significant resistance to flow. During exercise, the algebraically additive effects of auto- and neuroregulatory influences on arteriolar smooth muscle decide distribution of flow, since the pressure increase is more related to constriction of capacitance vessels than increase in R (Guyton, 1981). However, during emotional states, major increases in R may result when neurally excited vasoconstriction is not balanced by demand-mediated dilation in some vascular beds.

The volume component of afterload has two aspects. First, there is the relationship of blood volume to vascular capacity. Obviously, higher blood volumes will fill a given closed vascular system to a higher pressure than lower volumes (Levy, 1979). The distribution of blood within the vessels is also important. If adrenergic influences cause shifting of blood from the capacitance vessels to resistance vessels, the BP will rise (Rutlen, Supple, & Powell, 1981). This is a major factor in the increased BP of exercise. On a long-term basis, increased blood volume is thought to be critical in the development of clinical hypertension (Guyton, 1981). The initial action of the hypervolemia is to increase $\dot{Q}$ but widespread tissue autoregulation quickly sets in. $\dot{Q}$ returns to normal, but R, and with it BP, are increased. Although the R increase is reversible at first, secondary organic changes may render it permanent. When afterload increases, the initial effect is a reduction in SV (Reichek, Wilson, Sutton, Plappert, Goldberg, & Hirshfeld, 1982). The EDV increases (preload), increasing the strength of contraction so that SV returns to the previous level, but at the expense of increased preload.

The effect of HR on $\dot{Q}$ is twofold. There is the obvious multiplicative effect on SV, but simply increasing HR (e.g., by pacing) does not make $\dot{Q}$ larger unless venous return is augmented as well (Braunwald, Sonnenblick, Ross, Glick, & Epstein, 1967; J. Ross, Linhart, & Braunwald, 1965). Less evident is the effect of HR on the events of the cardiac cycle. Diastole, especially the phase of passive filling, tends to be shortened much more than systole. Thus, atrial contraction makes a relatively greater contribution to ventricular filling. Tachycardia is said to produce a secondary increase in contractility (Sonnenblick, 1962), but recent evidence (Boudoulas, Geleris, Lewis, & Leier, 1981; Boudoulas, Geleris, Lewis, & Rittgers, 1981) suggests that, at least with pacing-induced tachycardia, the excitation–contraction coupling relation is not characteristic of increased contractility (see also section on STIs).

The direct effects of contractility on $\dot{Q}$ are quite complex. As with HR, simply augmenting contractility does not increase $\dot{Q}$ unless HR is increased as well (see also the section on contractility).

Because $\dot{Q}$ is so extensively autoregulated, it is not a good index of cardiac function taken by itself. Nevertheless, evaluation of $\dot{Q}$ is necessary if R is to be assessed (see section on BP). Therefore, access to good measures of $\dot{Q}$ is well worthwhile.

Measurement of Cardiac Output

We can measure $\dot{Q}$ in two basic ways: (1) as the volume of dilution of an indicator substance; or (2) as the product of HR and SV as determined by a variety of methods. If a known quantity (A) of an indicator substance is added to (or removed from) an unknown volume of diluent (V), then

$$V = \frac{A}{C_a - C_b}$$

where C_b and C_a are the concentrations of indicator before and after its total amount is changed. This relationship is often used to measure relatively static volumes (e.g., blood volume).

In principle, flowing volumes also may be calculated as a volume of dilution. For the classical Fick method, V is a minute volume ($\dot{Q}$), A is the amount of O_2 *removed* from the blood in 1 min, and $C_a - C_b$ is the mean arteriovenous difference in blood O_2 content:

$$\dot{Q}\,(\text{L/min}) = \frac{O_2 \text{ consumed (ml/min)}}{\text{arteriovenous } O_2 \text{ difference (ml } O_2/\text{L of blood)}}$$

O_2 consumption is usually determined by the gas volume change after 15 min of rebreathing from a closed circuit in which CO_2 is removed by passing the expired air through soda lime. The arterial and venous O_2 contents are measured by volumetric techniques on three samples of blood obtained from systemic and pulmonary arterial catheters over the same time span. When meticulously performed, this is the standard against which other techniques of $\dot{Q}$ measurement are judged. However, if assumptions are made regarding

O_2 consumption, arterial O_2 content, and/or the relationship between volume of O_2 in blood and other, more easily determined blood O_2 parameters, or if the position of sampling catheters is compromised, the accuracy will be affected in unpredictable ways.

The classical Fick technique is limited in its application because pulmonary and arterial blood samples are required. In contrast, an indirect Fick method based upon the measurement of CO_2 has been developed. In this indirect Fick method, ventilation and mixed expired CO_2 are measured for the calculation of CO_2 output (V_{CO_2}) using a spirometer and CO_2 gas analyzer. In individuals with normal lung function the arterial CO_2 content may be estimated from the end-tidal pCO_2 (Jones, Robertson, & Kane, 1979). Measurement of venous CO_2 content depends upon having the subject rebreathe a mixture of CO_2 in O_2 from a 5 L bag (Collier, 1956). CO_2 is continuously sampled at the mouthpiece and examined for equilibrium; if not reached in 3 to 4 breaths a bag of different CO_2 concentration is substituted. Once the V_{CO_2}, estimated arterial pCO_2 (p_aCO_2), and estimated venous pCO_2 (p_vCO_2) have been determined, $\dot{Q}$ is calculated as:

$$\dot{Q} = \frac{V_{CO_2}}{p_aCO_2 - p_vCO_2}$$

Commercial systems are available for making the necessary measurements with computer assistance.

Methods in which indicators are injected (dye, cold solution) are nearly as time-honored as the classical Fick technique. As is the case with mixed venous O_2, the indicator must be thoroughly mingled with the venous return by passage through at least one ventricle between the injection and sampling sites. If the rapid injection mode is employed, and the concentration of indicator is continuously recorded beyond the mixing chamber, a curve will be inscribed, the area under which can be used to calculate the mean concentration of the indicator during the curves registration. The curve morphology first is mathematically corrected to remove the effects of recirculation. The area under the curve is determined by planimetry or, more commonly, by computer integration. Then

$$\dot{Q}(\text{ml/min}) = \frac{\text{milligrams of dye injected} \times 60 \text{ (sec)}}{\text{mean concentration of dye} \times \text{duration of curve (sec)}}$$

There are many commercially available, microprocessor-based units for automatic calculation of $\dot{Q}$ from dye dilution or thermodilution curves. Although the ear densitometer has been used for recording of dye concentration, the curves are often too prolonged and gradual to correct accurately for recirculation. Generally, the best results are obtained with central injection and sampling sites (e.g., superior vena cava) for injection of cold solution and pulmonary artery thermistor position, as in the commercial Swan–Ganz catheters. If repeated outputs are to be measured, dye dilution is impractical because of accumulation of indicator. Thermodilution is safe and relatively artifact-free in these circumstances. If the double-lumen Swan–Ganz catheter is passed from a peripheral vein, the indicator dilution technique is the safest of the invasive methods of measuring $\dot{Q}$. However, three determinations are usually averaged for each recorded value, so that this method may be unsuitable if rapid fluctuations of $\dot{Q}$ are to be assessed.

As previously mentioned, $\dot{Q}$ also can be assessed as $SV \times HR$. Almost all of the methods for directly determining SV involve separate calculations of EDV and end-systolic volume (ESV), so that

$$SV = EDV - ESV.$$

The most extensively documented techniques for SV determination is "angiocardiography," in which the geometry of left ventricular contraction is demonstrated by rapid, serial X-ray filming of the radiopaque-dye-filled chamber (Rackley, 1980). In calculating the volumes, the ventricular cavity is assumed to be a prolate ellipsoid with volume V:

$$V = \left(\frac{4}{3}\pi\right)\left(\frac{L}{2}\right)\left(\frac{D_1}{2}\right)\left(\frac{D_2}{2}\right),$$

where L is the maximum distance from mitral valve to apex, and D_1 and D_2 are minor chamber diameters obtained from the simultaneously filmed anteroposterior and lateral projections. The diameters (D_1 and D_2) are calculated using planimetric measurement of the opaque cavity (A) and L:

$$D = \frac{4}{\pi} \cdot \frac{A}{L}.$$

Although high-resolution quantitative research requires biplane filming for separate determination of D_1 and D_2, single-plane delineation in anteroposterior or right anterior oblique projections yields values that correlate well with biplane calculations, especially if corrective regression equations are employed. Naturally, this means that $D_1 = D_2$, and

$$V = \frac{\pi}{6}\left(LD^2\right).$$

With appropriate sensing devices, particular X-ray frames may be related to simultaneously recorded intraventricular pressure and ECG. When the pressure and volume changes are graphically related, one can quantitate left ventricular work and can obtain a good index of contractility. Ventricular wall thickness can also be measured for calculation of stress.

SV and $\dot{Q}$ assessed by angiocardiography correlate highly with those from direct Fick and indicator dilution techniques. According to simultaneous hemodynamic evaluation, ventricular function is unaltered by the injection of contrast material if ventricular arrhythmias are avoided. However, if studies are to be repeated, adequate time (minutes to tens of minutes) must be allowed for adjustment to the increased blood volume induced by the concentrated contrast medium. Equipment expense is high, and the technical skill of the operator is at a premium. The radiation exposure and the risk of the catheterization to the subject preclude investigative use of this technique except as a by-product of clinically indicated studies.

Ventricular volume can also be determined using radionuclide-labeled blood components as contrast medium and by computer processing of scintillation data from high-resolution gamma cameras. The same geometric methods used in angiocardiography may be applied to the images thus obtained, or else nongeometric radioactive-counts-based analysis may be used (Massie, Kramer, Gertz, & Henderson, 1982; Strauss & Boucher, 1982). The geometric techniques are based on films of the first transit of the radionuclide through the heart. Only a short period of time can be sampled, and because of radiation hazard from repeated radionuclide injection, sampling can be repeated only three times at most. The nongeometric, counts-based method samples a much longer period of time (minimum of 100 beats to a practical maximum of about 1000), during which circulatory dynamics should be in equilibrium. Moreover, only one peripheral injection is required, and many studies can be repeated over a period of hours. Comparison with angiographic data shows that the counts-based method would have 95% confidence limits of 120–185 ml for a hypothetical 150-ml chamber volume, versus 115–225 ml for the best of the geometric methods (Massie *et al.*, 1982). In view of the long time interval during which studies can be performed following injection, collaborative studies in patients injected for clinical reasons would seem to be feasible.

"Echocardiography" uses the reflection of pulsed ultrasound to provide information about the movement of cardiac structures or blood. In the case of M-mode echocardiography (Figure 7-8) and biplane examinations, the sound is reflected from interfaces between substances of different acoustic impedance (e.g., blood–myocardium or lung–myocardium). The time for return of the emitted sound to the transducer is proportional to the distance from the target. Since temporal resolution is high, both the distance a structure moves and the time required may be measured. Thus changes in the minor axis (D) of the left ventricle can be determined with fair accuracy (Popp, 1982). Unfortunately, the long axis (L) of the chamber cannot be directly evaluated because the lung overlying the apex of the heart does not transmit the

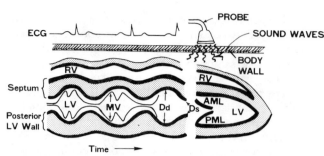

Figure 7-8. M-mode echocardiography. The right-hand side of this figure shows a transducer receiving reflected sound after a sound beam is directed through the chest body wall. This beam passes through the right ventricle (RV) and left ventricle (LV) to intersect the anterior mitral leaflet (AML) and posterior mitral leaflet (PML). The left hand side of the figure shows the motion pattern (M-mode) of echoes across time depicted upon photographic paper. Changes correlated across time with the electrocardiogram (ECG) can be seen in the thickness of the septum, right ventricular (RV), and posterior left ventricular (LV) walls. Changes across time can also be seen in the left ventricle (LV) and mitral valve (MV). Also shown are maximal end-diastolic dimension (Dd) and minimal systolic dimension (Ds).

ultrasound. Consequently, the additional geometric assumption is made that $L = 2D$; then

$$V = \frac{\pi D^3}{3}$$

There is great controversy over the validity of SV calculated by this technique (Linhart, Mintz, Segal, Wawai, & Kotler, 1975; Pombo, Bart, & Russell, 1971; Teichholz, Kreulen, Herman, & Gorlin, 1976). Error in the range of 10–15% is a reasonable expectation in individuals with normal hearts when compared to angiocardiographic studies. This dispute is important not only with regard to the measurement of $\dot{Q}$ but also because the noninvasive assessment of ventricular contractility may employ echocardiographic volumes (see "The Pressure-Volume Diagram," below). Although biplane echocardiography may improve accuracy of SV determination, it has not yet been tested thoroughly (Henry, 1982).

The equipment for M-mode echocardiography is not excessively expensive, but expertise in its use requires special training. Although the broad field of echocardiography is quite complex, there is no reason why, with a trained technician and consultation with a clinical echographer, the measurements required for volume determinations cannot be made in laboratories that lack broad clinical expertise. The procedure is intrusive only to the extent that the subject must remain quiet while recordings are in progress (Sugashita & Koseki, 1979). One drawback of the method is that 10–20% of echocardiographic examinations must be discarded for technical reasons.

M-mode echocardiography provides a good noninvasive measure of instantaneous ventricular wall thickness (Devereux & Reichek, 1977), which correlates well with the value obtained during angiocardiography. This is important if wall stress is to be used as a measure of preload or afterload (Reichek *et al.*, 1982). Whereas M-mode echocardiography measures the time for a pulsed sound to be reflected, ultrasonic Doppler echocardiography employs the measurement of frequency shift to assess $\dot{Q}$. Thus, using Doppler echocardiography, the linear velocity of a particle (i.e., red blood cell) of blood is determined by measuring the frequency shift in the sound reflected from it (Darsee, Mikolich, Walter, & Schlant, 1980; Magnin, Stewart, Meyers, von Ramm, & Kissle, 1981; Pearlman, 1982). The mean systolic velocity of flow is then multiplied by diameter of the conduit involved. The velocity of flow is measured with a hand-held probe directed toward the ascending aorta from the suprasternal notch. The area under the systolic velocity curve is then electronically integrated and divided by systolic time to obtain mean systolic velocity. Assumptions are made that the probe is in the axis of flow and that the sample of the flow plane is representative of the whole. The probability that the probe is in the axis of flow is enhanced by manipulating the probe so that the velocity reading is maximized. The second assumption, however, has been held to be invalid both theoretically and empirically (Histand, Miller, & McLeod, 1973). The good agreement between $\dot{Q}$ as measured by the ultrasonic Doppler technique and $\dot{Q}$ as measured by the indicator dilution technique thus provides only correlative support for the technique. Still another problem with the technique is the constant variation in aortic orifice diameter throughout systole. At present, the mean aortic orifice is measured nonsynchronously by M-mode echocardiography (but see Magnin *et al.*, 1981). The technique has been employed both at rest and during upright and supine exercise (Loeppky, Greene, Hoekenga, Caprihan, & Luft, 1981). In view of the theoretical problems involved, ultrasonic Doppler echocardiography appears to offer no advantages over the M-mode method, particularly in view of the versatility of M-mode echocardiography in assessing other contractility indices.

A highly invasive method of flow measurement, which also makes use of the velocity multiplied by conduit-area principle, is the electromagnetic flow meter. A probe is operatively placed around the ascending aorta. The flow velocity is proportional to the current induced by movement of red blood cells in the conduit (i.e., aorta) interrupting the lines of force of the magnetic field in the probe. The flow velocity is then multiplied by the known corrected cross-sectional area of the probe. The ascending aortic probe never measures total $\dot{Q}$ because coronary flow exits more proximally. Many relatively inexpensive commercial units are available, some of which have soft probes suitable for chronic implantation in animal experiments.

"Impedance cardiography" has been used to measure SV with varying degrees of success (Kubicek, Karnegis, Patterson, Witose, & Matson, 1966; Miller & Horvath, 1978). The method depends on thoracic impedance changes being proportional to pulsatile blood flow. The thorax is assumed to be a cylinder of length L, constant cross-sectional area A, and homogeneous resistivity ρ. These assumptions are approximate at best, but are considered to introduce an intrasubject error that is constant over time (Miller & Horvath, 1978).

The volume conductor equation for mean thoracic impedance (Zρ) is

$$Z\rho = \frac{L}{A}$$

where Zρ is the mean thoracic impedance, L is the distance between recording electrodes (which is the equivalent of the thoracic cylinder mentioned above), and ρ is the resistivity constant.

If an electrical field is set up (Figure 7-9) between two electrodes (E_1, E_2), the impedance can be measured between two electrodes (M_1, M_2) within that field and the time course (T) recorded. During the

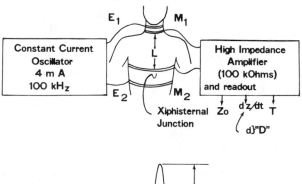

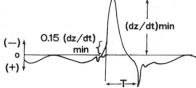

Figure 7-9. The top portion of the figure depicts the typical electrode and apparatus configuration used in impedance cardiography. When an electrical field is set up between electrodes E_1 and E_2, the impedance can be measured between recording electrodes M_1 and M_2 within that field. The bottom portion of the figure depicts the pulsatile thoracic impedance wave form across the length of systolic ejection time (T), where (dz/dt) min is the first derivative of the minimum negative rate change in impedance across the thorax during a cardiac cycle. (Redrawn from Kubicek, Karnegis, Patterson, Witose, & Matson, 1966.)

cardiac cycle, $Z\rho$ changes .10–.15 ohms (Ω) from a mean Z_o of about 2.5 Ω for a normal adult. To obtain SV, the minimum value of the first derivative of the time course of (dz/dt) is used in the equation:

$$SV = \rho \left(\frac{L^2}{Z_o^2} \right) T \left(\frac{dZ}{dt_{max}} \right)$$

The value for ρ has been taken as 150 Ω-cm, but should be corrected for measured hematocrit during exercise, in view of the known resistivity changes due to hemoconcentration (Y. Kobayashi, Andoh, Fujinami, Nakayama, Takada, Takeuchi, & Okamato, 1978).

The extent of deviation of SV measured by this technique from that measured by invasive techniques is not yet completely worked out (Miller & Horvath, 1978), and the assumptions regarding thoracic cross-sectional area and resistivity may not be valid. The model that projects (dz/dt_{max}) throughout systole also is open to serious question (Ito, Yamakoshi, & Togawa, 1977). The ejection curve that is assumed does not correspond to the empirical form. Waveform is apparently sensitive to electrode placement. This could greatly alter (dz/dt_{max}).

Despite these drawbacks, impedance cardiography has been valuable in measuring $\dot{Q}$ at rest and during moderate exercise (Denniston, Maher, Reeves, Cruz, Cymerman, & Grover, 1976; Kinne, 1970; Y. Kobayashi et al., 1978). It has been found recently that correction for respiration does not reduce variability, but does considerably reduce the number of beats that can be evaluated (Doerr, Miles, & Frey, 1981). If the sources of error and drawbacks are recognized and the technique is validated in the investigator's own hands, it may be useful in within-subject comparisons of response to various circulatory challenges.

Various techniques of SV measurement have employed analysis of arterial pulse wave form (Warner, Swan, Connolly, Tompkins, & Wood, 1953). In view of the marked change in pulse contour as the wave proceeds distally in the arterial tree, only the aortic root curve has even a slight chance of providing valid information. Even here, differences in aortic mural elasticity and outflow impedance make interpretation almost impossible.

Contractility

"Contractility" is by far the most difficult determinant of $\dot{Q}$ to define and to quantify adequately. It is also of considerable interest to psychophysiologists because it is altered by the interaction of myocardial autonomic receptors with sympathetic and parasympathetic neurotransmitters, by blood-borne catecholamines released by the adrenal medulla, and by neuropharmacological analogue drugs.

Contractility, which is also sometimes referred to as the "inotropic activity" of the heart, has been defined in terms of the heart as a pump or as a muscle. When the heart is considered as a pump, a change in contractility is said to occur when there is an alteration in the amount of work performed by each contraction without a corresponding change in preload (Wallace, Skinner, & Mitchell, 1963). Alternatively, when the heart is considered in terms of muscle properties, contractility is said to be altered when velocity of fiber shortening changes. The different models of contractility (i.e., heart as pump vs. heart as muscle) have led to divergent approaches to measurement. These have consisted of (1) pressure–volume relations and rate of pressure development or fiber shortening, which are discussed in this section; and (2) measurement of the duration of the contractile phases of the cardiac cycle (i.e., STIs), which are described following our discussion of the ECG. In any event, the ideal measure of contractility would be one that is totally unaffected by changes in preload and afterload.

The Pressure–Volume Diagram

The cardiac cycle can be characterized simply, but no less rigorously, with much less information than is recorded in the comprehensive description shown in Figure 7-6. The pressure–volume diagram portrays the heart as a pump (Figure 7-10). The loop can be derived from the comprehensive description by extracting the simultaneous values of intracavitary pressure and volume at a large number of instants in time and plotting them as the (x,y) coordinates of points on the graph. However, for most purposes, the loop is determined by only four points, which correspond to (1) the opening and closing of the mitral value, (2) opening of the aortic valve, (3) cessation of ventricular contraction, followed shortly by (4) closure of the aortic valve (Sagawa, 1978, 1981).

One can obtain a family of pressure–volume loops (Figure 7-10) by systematically changing resistance to outflow (afterload) under conditions in which extrinsic alteration of the myocardial state is precluded (e.g., the isolated heart preparation or total beta-adrenergic receptor blockade). Two significant relationships are defined by these loops. First, the points at the end of diastolic filling may be connected to form a nonlinear pressure–volume curve, which describes the passive response of the ventricular wall to stretch (preload). Secondly, there is a linear relationship between end-systolic pressure (ESP) and ESV. The figure shows that the ESP-ESV relationship is independent of ventricular preload. Also, the slope of the ESP-ESV line is independent of afterload, even though it is determined by alterations in afterload. This merely says that the slope of the line, as determined at low afterloads, is the same as that found at

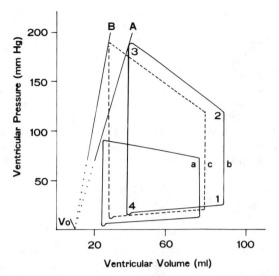

Figure 7-10. The pressure–volume diagram portrays a family of pressure–volume loops in which resistance to outflow (afterload) systematically changes under conditions in which extrinsic alteration of the myocardial state is precluded (e.g., beta-adrenergic blockade). Each loop is derived by extracting the simultaneous values of intracavitary pressure and volume and plotting them on the graph. The pressure–volume diagram includes 1, end-diastole; 2, opening of the aortic valve; 3, end-systole; 4, opening of the mitral valve. Loops a and b determine the slope of line A, which in turn defines the particular contractile state. Note that when contractility increases (line B), there is a lower end-systolic volume and higher ejection fraction with the same work load (i.e., blood pressure and stroke volume). Extrapolations of lines A and B meet at V_0, the theoretical ventricular volume at zero pressure. Since V_0 is not known, end-systolic volume must be obtained at two different afterloads (end-systolic pressures) to determine a contractility slope.

high afterloads. Now, if contractility is defined as the slope of the ESP-ESV line, we have a function that is insensitive to preload and afterload. Notice that contractility is defined in terms of *strength* rather than *velocity* of contraction.

A change in contractility is shown by a change in slope of the ESP-ESV line. For example, increase in slope indicates increased contractility. At a given resistance (ESP), the more contractile heart is able to eject more blood (lower ESV). This is what we would expect intuitively.

Needless to say, determination of the ESP-ESV line requires more than one point. One cannot use one point plus the origin, because all studies show that the ESP-ESV line intercepts the zero pressure line at a volume (V_0) that would determine a slope quite different from that of a line through the origin. V_0 is a functionally dead volume agianst which the ventricle can generate no supra-atmospheric pressure (Sagawa, 1978, 1981). Even more to the point, V_0 apparently varies from person to person and can be quite large in

diseased hearts. The problem is that the two ESP-ESV data points must be obtained at two different afterloads. As this involves a time lapse, the two consecutive points may actually lie on different ESP-ESV lines in conditions of rapidly changing contractility.

There are two methods that are said to predict isovolumic peak pressure and that would supply the additional point. One of these would be to measure ESP in an experimental paradigm in which afterload is so high that the ventricle cannot achieve ejection (Shroff, Janicki, & Weber, 1980). Since one cannot use this sort of resistance in humans, a means of predicting this value is from the isovolumic contraction and relaxation slopes of a pressure tracing from an ejecting beat (Sunagawa, Yamada, Senda, Kikuchi, Nakamura, Shibahara, & Nose, 1980). The second procedure, which uses beta-blockade to preclude contractility change (Mehmel, Stockins, Ruffman, von Olshaussen, Schuler, & Kubler, 1981), is satisfactory if the blockade does not interfere with the experimental design. Alternatively, one might comment on directional change in contractility with a single point if either pressure or volume remained constant while the other changed.

The ESP-ESV relationship satisfies a widely accepted model of cardiac function (Sagawa, 1978, 1981). The well-designed experimental (Piene & Covell, 1981) and clinical (Mehmel *et al.*, 1981) studies that support this model have shown the independence of contractility, as so defined, from preload and afterload influence. Also, Piene and Covell have cast great doubt on definitions of contractility in the pressure-time frame (dp/dt) at constant volume), since they were measured simultaneously and found wanting.

The methods described so far are highly invasive. Recently steps have been taken toward a totally non-invasive approach (Borow, Neumann, & Wynne, 1982; Marsh, Green, Wynne, Cohn, & Grossman, 1979; Nivatpumin, Katz, & Scheuer, 1979; Reichek *et al.*, 1982; Sasayama & Kotura, 1979). The echocardiographically measured ESV or end-systolic dimension (ESD) is related to ESP or peak-systolic pressure (PSP). Substitution of ESD for ESV is not theoretically appealing; however, in the physiological range, ESD and ESV have been demonstrated empirically to be linearly related (Suga & Sagawa, 1974). Also, the well-designed study of Borow *et al.* (1982) shows that slopes constructed from ESP-ESD relations are nearly as sensitive to inotropic changes as those from ESP-ESV. Although some have found PSP to be just as valid as ESP (Nivatpumin *et al.*, 1979; Sasayama & Kotura, 1979), the simultaneous comparisons of Borow *et al.* (1982) clearly show that ESP, as measured by their technique, is the only reliable parameter. Of course, all methods that measure pressure and volume at different points in the cardiac cycle violate the model in an as yet unevaluated way (Sagawa, 1981).

Thus far, we have looked at the heart as a *pump*; this conception is best characterized by the mechanical events during one of its cycles. As resistance to outflow increases, the amount of blood remaining in the pump chamber at the end of force application (i.e., ESV) also increases as a linear function to the point at which any ejection is impossible (ESP-ESV line). The output that the pump is able to produce against a given resistance can be increased only by changing the characteristic of the pump that is defined by the ESP-ESV slope, which is called "contractility."

Velocity of Fiber Shortening

Heart is also *muscle*. In a classic series of experiments, Sonnenblick (1962) related myocardial contraction to the skeletal muscle mechanics of A. V. Hill (cited in Sonnenblick, 1962). Since "the most fundamental mechanical property of muscle is the inverse hyperbolic relation between the velocity of muscle shortening and the load carried" (Sonnenblick, Parmley, Urschel, & Brutsaert, 1970, p. 450), it was thought that this should be true of the myocardium as well. Within the limitations of Sonnenblick's experimental paradigm, it was demonstrated that this was the case, by extrapolating the load–velocity curve back to zero load. The theoretical *velocity* of fiber shortening at zero load was labeled V_{max} and termed a measure of contractility.

One of the problems with generalization from this work was the narrowness of experimental design—isolated papillary muscle contracting at constant afterload. Major criticisms involve the model itself (Pollack, 1970), the probability that the response of the elastic element that is in series with the muscle is nonlinear (Parmley, Chuck, & Sonnenblick, 1972), and the noncomparability of myocardial twitch to skeletal muscle tetany.

The transfer of V_{max} to the intact heart and organism has taken two courses. One approach involves the assumption that dL/dt at zero load ($P = 0$) and dP/dt at zero change in muscle length ($dL = 0$) measure the same quality (Mason, Braunwald, Covell, Sonnenblick, & Ross, 1971; Sonnenblick et al., 1970). Various formulas (Falsetti, Mates, Greene, & Bunnell, 1971; Mason et al., 1971) were devised to use dP/dt (rate of pressure development) during the isovolumic contraction phase of the cardiac cycle as an index of contractility, but they never were able to avoid exquisite sensitivity to preload and afterload. The accurate measurement of dP/dt during the very short isovolumic contraction phase requires equipment of extraordinary frequency response of the type that is ordinarily present only in micromanometer-tip catheters (Falsetti et al., 1971; Sonnenblick et al., 1970). With this requirement in mind, the futility of attempting to extrapolate to dP/dt measurements from the externally recorded carotid pulse tracing becomes obvious (Obrist, Lawler, Howard, Smithson, Martin, & Manning, 1974; Obrist & Light, 1980; Heslegrave & Furedy, 1980). A more promising approach has been the direct measurement of mean velocity of circumferential fiber shortening (VCF) by angiocardiography (Karliner, Gault, Eckberg, Mullins, & Ross, 1971) and echocardiography (Cooper, O'Rourke, Karliner, Peterson, & Leopold, 1972; Paraskos, Grossman, Saltz, Dalen, & Dexter, 1971). The echocardiographic measure has been shown to be highly correlated ($\pm 6\%$) with the angiocardiographic findings (Cooper et al., 1972) and quite insensitive to preload changes (Nixon et al., 1982).

Although V_{max} and other measurements involving dP/dt are currently out of favor (Abel, 1976), VCF appears quite promising. Also, intensive work is being done on time considerations in the pressure–volume loop (Strobeck, Krueger, & Sonnenblick, 1980), so that the time–pressure paradigm may yet stage a comeback.

At this point, it is important to recapitulate the versatility of echocardiographic studies. SV, pressure–volume loops, VCF, and STIs (which are discussed in detail later) all can be measured noninvasively. Both resting and exercise studies may be obtained (Kraunz & Kennedy, 1970). Of the methods discussed in detail in this section, echocardiography would appear to be perhaps the most promising future addition to the psychophysiologist's armamentarium.

ELECTRICAL EVENTS OF THE CARDIAC CYCLE

Overview

The ECG provides a noninvasive recording of the bioelectrical activity produced by the heart muscle during the cardiac cycle. Traditionally, psychophysiologists have monitored HR in response to behavioral manipulations. The ECG, however, offers considerably more extensive information about the state of the heart than a simple rate count. This section therefore discusses (1) the conduction system of the heart, (2) characteristic waveforms of the ECG, (3) some common cardiac arrhythmias, and (4) basic principles of ECG recording.

Conduction System

The heart is comprised of three types of muscle: atrial fibers, ventricular fibers, and specialized fibers that make up the conduction system. Whereas atrial and ventricular muscles are striated and contract in a manner similar to skeletal muscle, the muscle of the conduction system contracts very little, because it contains few contractile fibers. As previously mentioned (see Figure 7-1), impulse formation normally occurs in the SA node; from there the impulse is conducted to both atria and the AV node, down the bundle of His and the Purkinje system, to the ventricular muscle.

Within the conduction system there are three types of cells. These are the "pacemaker" (P) cells, transitional cells, and Purkinje cells. The P cells are found in the SA node, AV node, and internodal pathways, but are most numerous in the SA node (James & Sherf, 1978). Transitional cells are found predominantly within the nodes, but also extend into adjacent regions of the atria. The Purkinje cells extend from the margins of the SA node throughout the conduction system.

The P cells, sometimes referred to as "automatic cells," slowly and spontaneously depolarize themselves until they reach a critical threshold. At this point they depolarize completely, producing a conducted impulse. Rate of impulse formation in P cells depends upon the intrinsic rate of the cell and upon various factors influencing it (e.g., neurotransmitters). The highest rate of intrinsic impulse formation, which is about 105–110/min, occurs within the SA node. P cells at the AV junction have intrinsic rates of 40–60 impulses/min, and P cells in the ventricular Purkinje system can fire 20–40 impulses/min (Marriott & Myerburg, 1978). The decreasing rate of impulse formation usually prevents regions distal to the SA node from usurping the heart's pacemaking function inappropriately. At the same time, this hierarchy provides a safety mechanism whereby a more distal conduction region can take over the pacemaking function should the more proximal region fail.

Once the pacing impulse is formed in the SA node, it is transmitted via the conduction system through the myocardium in an orderly sequence. Beginning at the SA node, the impulse is conducted radially through the atrial muscle and internodal tracts. The impulse is delayed at the AV node, which provides time for the atria to fill. It then proceeds through the slowly conducting AV node tissue before traversing the rapidly conducting His bundle–Purkinje branch system to the cells of the ventricular myocardium.

Characteristic ECG Waveforms

The ECG provides a noninvasive record of the electrical properties and rhythmicity of cardiac muscle. As the impulse or muscle action potential is conducted across the myocardium, electrical currents spread to the tissue surrounding the heart and to the surface of the body. Electrodes properly placed on the limbs or body surface are able to pick up the changing electrical currents and record them as the ECG.

The normal ECG is composed of waves and intervals (Figure 7-11). Waveforms are given letter designations for uniform identification. Intervals can be identified by the waves that mark their beginning and end: (1) P wave, (2) QRS complex, (3) T wave, and (4) U wave. Actually, the QRS complex is made up of three separate waves, Q, R, and S. The intervals are (1) P-R interval, (2) Q-T interval, and (3) S-T interval. Each Q-T interval is further subdivided into QRS duration and S-T segment. Duration and configuration of waves, as well as duration of intervals or segments, offer clinically relevant information regarding the metabolic state of the myocardium and/or the conduction system.

The P wave of the ECG is produced by the electrical currents generated by atrial depolarization and occurs prior to atrial contraction. Likewise, the QRS complex signifies the electrical depolarization of the ventricles prior to contraction. Although the QRS complex describes the normal occurrence of three successive waves, not all QRS complexes actually have all three waves. According to conventional usage, the form representing ventricular depolarization is known as the QRS complex, regardless of its configuration. The Q wave is defined as the first negative deflection in the complex. The first upright deflection is an R wave, regardless of whether or not it is preceded by a Q. A negative deflection following the R wave is an S wave. Subsequent excursions above the line are labeled R' or R". Likewise, negative excursions are labeled S' or S".

The T wave is a repolarization wave. It is generated by the electrical current produced as the ventricles return to the polarized state. Configuration and height are clinically important features of the T-wave form, but T-wave amplitude has been repudiated as an index

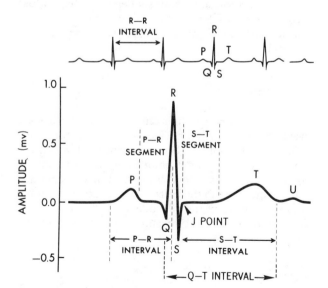

Figure 7-11. The normal electrocardiogram is composed of waves, intervals, and the QRS complex.

of myocardial performance or sympathetic tone (Bunnel, 1980). The U wave is a low-voltage wave sometimes seen following the T wave. The significance of this wave is unclear.

The P-R interval incorporates both atrial depolarization and the length of delay of the impulse at the AV node. It is measured from the beginning of the P wave and ends with the occurence of the R-wave complex (ventricular depolarization). The Q-T interval includes ventricular depolarization (QRS) through ventricular repolarization (T wave). Within the Q-T interval are three important points of information. The first is the QRS duration. It is measured from the first deflection of the complex to the end of the S wave. If the QRS is "splintered" by R' or S' waves, or prolonged in duration, it indicates abnormal conduction in the His–Purkinje system. A second important item of information within the Q-T interval is the S-T segment, which connects the QRS with the T wave. The S-T segment "takes off" from the QRS at the junction or "j" point and normally ends by flowing gently into the T wave. Features of the S-T segment that are clinically relevant are its level relative to the baseline (i.e., elevated or depressed) and its shape. Depression of the S-T segment, especially the j point, is indicative of muscle ischemia (low oxygen availability), while S-T segment elevation almost always signifies injury. Chronic pain at rest associated with reversible S-T segment elevation is characteristic of "variant angina," and has been attributed to coronary spasm (Prinzmetal, Kannamer, Merliss, Wada, & Bor, 1959). The shape of the T wave is most often influenced by potassium levels, the wave becoming peaked when serum potassium is high and flattened when it is low. Finally, the total duration of the Q-T interval is attracting increasing attention because of the association of its prolongation with sudden death (e.g., Moss & Schwartz, 1979). Horizontality or a sharp angle formed with the T wave is suggestive of myocardial ischemia.

Arrhythmias

Abnormal cardiac rhythms can be produced in several ways. First, the rhythmicity of the SA node pacemaker can be normal. Second, transmission can become blocked at some point along the conduction system. Third, abnormal impulses can be generated almost anywhere in the heart. Fourth, pacemaker function can shift from the SA node to another part of the heart. Fifth, abnormal transmission pathways can develop.

Sinus Rhythms

The HR of the normal human adult while seated is approximately 70 bpm. Under certain circumstances,

the SA node can remain as the pacemaker, but very high or very low HR may occur. Increased body temperature, conditions that are toxic to the heart, or pronounced catecholaminergic activity associated with exercise or emotional excitement can produce "tachycardia" (i.e., elevated HR). Conversely, the aerobic training of the athlete, which may be associated with an increase in SV, thereby improving the efficiency of heart work, can produce "bradycardia" (i.e., HR slowing). Bradycardia is also observed in behavioral states associated with increased vagal activity. A pathological condition known as "carotid sinus syndrome" is also associated with pronounced bradycardia. In this condition, the carotid sinus is extremely sensitive to mechanical stimulation, so that even tight collars or rapid turning of the neck can lead to an exaggerated baroreceptor reflex, with hypotension and bradycardia leading to syncope. Carotid atherosclerosis or other local pathology is often responsible for the sensitivity.

Changes in HR can readily be seen on a polygraph tracing by using a "cardiotachometer." This device detects the duration of intervals between successive QRS complexes, and produces deflections that are proportional to the size of the interval. By simply inverting the signal output, the polygraph operator can easily interpret upward deflections as increases and downward deflections as decreases in HR from some precalibrated baseline value.

Impulse Conduction Blocks

Although the condition is rare, the impulse from the SA node can be blocked even before it enters the atrial muscle. This phenomenon, known as "SA nodal block," is reflected by a sudden cessation of P waves, resulting in atrial standstill. Usually, under these circumstances, the ventricles pick up an AV nodal rhythm so that the QRS complexes and T waves are unaltered, but there may be a dangerously long period of total asystole before the AV node takes over. In a relatively few sensitive subjects, vagal stimulation can suppress SA nodal function, but most instances of SA block appear to be due to structural disease or to the toxicity of such drugs as digitalis (Marriott & Myerburg, 1978).

A more common conduction defect is AV block, which is usually classified into three degrees. In first-degree AV block, the AV conduction time is prolonged. This is reflected in an increased P-R interval, but all impulses are conducted from the SA node to the ventricles. In contrast, in second-degree AV block, some impulses are blocked and do not reach the ventricles. Often the impulse is transmitted to the ventricles following one atrial contraction, but an impulse is not transmitted following the next one or two atrial contractions. In such instances of alternating conduction and nonconduction, the atria beat at a faster rate than the ventricles, and "dropped beats" of the ventricles are observed. First- or second-degree AV block can be caused by vagal stimulation or by drug toxicity. It can also be produced by coronary (ischemic) heart disease (CHD) or by myocardial infarction.

In third-degree or complete AV block, no impulse is transmitted from the atria to the ventricles. The P waves are completely dissociated from the QRS complex and T waves, with the P waves, of course, being produced at a much faster rate. Most cases of complete AV block are due to fibrosis of the cardiac muscle or to primary disease of the specialized conduction tissue (Zoob & Smith, 1963), but post-myocardial-infarction block is becoming increasingly important. The impulse-generating and conducting tissues are extremely vulnerable to acute perturbations, such as viral infections or excessive caffeine or alcohol intake, so that most individuals will experience arrhythmias during their lifetime. This is compounded by cell dropout and increasing fibrosis in these specialized tissues as a function of aging. Often this leads to "sick sinus node syndrome," which is characterized by a variable combination of sinus node arrest or exit block, atrial fibrillation, circus re-entry or ectopic tachycardias, and slow response of AV-nodal P cells to arrest of higher pacemakers (Ferrer, 1974).

Ectopic Beats

In some instances, a small region of the heart becomes more excitable than usual. This can cause an abnormal impulse to be generated, which can result in a wave of depolarization spreading outward and initiating an aberrant beat. The focus at which the impulse is generated is called an "ectopic focus." Ectopic foci can be caused by localized myocardial ischemia or scarring, and, in susceptible individuals, are often activated by emotional upheaval or the excessive use of stimulants.

Sometimes an ectopic focus is sufficiently irritable that it establishes a rhythmic contraction of its own at a faster rate than that of the SA node and becomes an "ectopic pacemaker." The most common points for the development of an ectopic pacemaker are in the AV node or atrial wall. This can give rise to bursts of rapid heart beats in a condition known as "atrial or AV-nodal paroxysmal tachycardia." Although generally considered benign, the condition can frighten the individual and cause weakness during the paroxysms.

Circus Re-entry

Under certain conditions, a cardiac impulse may reexcite some region through which it had passed previously. The phenomenon is known as "circus re-entry" and can produce arrhythmias. In order for re-entry to occur, an area of slow conduction combined

with unidirectional block must be present. Figure 7-12 provides a schematic example. In A, conduction in a bundle continues down two branches. Impulses conducted more slowly across a muscle bridge collide, canceling each other out. In B, conduction in a bundle also continues down two branches. However, conduction down one of the branches is blocked in the descending direction. This allows the collateral impulse from the other branch to conduct relatively slowly across the muscle bridge and descend as a "normal" impulse. It also allows the impulse conducted across the bridge to ascend and re-enter the conduction pathway. Re-entry pathways may involve pathways in the AV-nodal region involving atrial muscle, or pathways in specialized ventricular conduction tissue and a ventricular muscle bridge. Re-entry loops may also occur entirely within conduction tissue or around scars (Wit, Cranefield, & Hoffman, 1972).

Premature Beats

A premature beat ("extrasystole") is related to and dependent upon the preceding beat. Such beats, arising in ectopic foci in the atria, are benign and can be triggered by fatigue, emotion, alcohol, tobacco or coffee. A premature atrial beat is manifested in the ECG

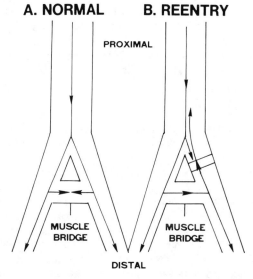

Figure 7-12. Normal conduction and circus re-entry. In panel A, an excitation wave traveling down a conduction pathway branches. When the depolarization wave gains entry to a muscle bridge from both ends, it cancels at the point of collision. In panel B, the excitation wave is blocked as it travels down one of the branches. The depolarization wave therefore gains entry from only one end of the muscle bridge. When the depolarization wave reaches the blocked branch, it conducts in both anterograde and retrograde directions. The retrograde transmission passes through the zone of unidirectional block, resulting in re-entry.

as a premature, abnormal P wave. The cycle following one of these atrial premature beats is usually longer than the dominant sinus cycle.

Premature ventricular contractions (PVCs) are a common form of rhythm disturbance and are often found in otherwise asymptomatic individuals (Hinkle, Carver, & Stevens, 1969). Because the impulse of a ventricular extrasystole originates in an ectopic focus within a ventricle and spreads anomalously, the QRS complex is usually wide and distorted as well as premature. Most PVCs do not disrupt the sinus rhythm and are therefore followed by a compensatory pause. They can, however, simply be interpolated between two consecutive sinus beats, or can be manifested with a less than compensatory pause. Although PVCs are frequently found in asymptomatic individuals, and can be precipitated by emotional stimuli or exercise, they are prognostic in patients with left ventricular hypertrophy or previous myocardial infarction. In both cases, they convey increased mortality risk.

Ventricular Tachycardia

When three or more ectopic beats occur at a rate of 100 bpm or more, this is said to define a run of ventricular tachycardia. These paroxysms usually begin with a PVC, which may be perpetuated by the rapid firing of a single ectopic focus or by circus re-entry. Ventricular tachycardia is almost never manifested in a normal heart, but is very commonly seen in diseased ones. The most commonly associated types of disease are CHD and rheumatic heart disease. In susceptible individuals, exercise or emotional upheaval may precipitate ventricular tachycardia.

Fibrillation

Under certain circumstances, the contractions of cardiac muscle can become completely uncoordinated. The part of the heart affected becomes entirely ineffectual in propelling blood. Such an arrhythmia is known as "fibrillation" and may involve either the atria or the ventricles. Although atrial fibrillation is compatible with life and with almost full activity, ventricular fibrillation is usually a terminal event unless the victim can be resuscitated. That is, the continuous, irregular, uncoordinated twitchings of the ventricular muscle fail to result in the pumping of blood, and the individual dies.

A common precipitator of ventricular fibrillation in a diseased heart is for a PVC to occur during the downslope of the T wave. During this so-called vulnerable period, there is some variability in the excitability of cardiac cells. Because some fibers are still in their refractory period while others have begun to recover their excitability, impulses may be propagated in multiple wavelets over circuitous paths at varying conduction velocities. The circus re-entry patterns precipi-

tated in the ischemic heart may then tend to become self-sustaining.

Recording the ECG

The ECG lead system consists of five electrodes. One is placed on each of the four limbs. Another is placed at specific sites on the precordium (chest). During the cardiac cycle, each lead can provide a continuous recording of changes in electrical potential between two of the electrodes, or between one electrode and the others combined.

The three standard limb leads (I, II, III) are shown in Figure 7-13A. Lead I records the potential difference between the left arm and right arm; lead II, that between the right arm and left leg; and lead III, that between the left arm and left leg. Because the standard limb leads provide recordings that are similar to each other, it matters relatively little which lead is recorded when one wishes to diagnose cardiac arrhythmias. In general, lead II provides the best single record for psychophysiological recordings of HR or R-R intervals, because it provides the largest R wave, and the sum of the voltages in leads I and III equals the voltage in lead II ("Einthoven's law").

Although it matters relatively little which lead is recorded when one wishes to examine HR or look at cardiac arrhythmias, it matters considerably when one wishes to evaluate cardiomyopathies or CHD. When recording from precordial leads, an exploring electrode is placed at each of six predesignated places on the chest (V_1 through V_6) and connected to the positive terminal of the electrocardiograph. The negative or so-called "indifferent" electrode is connected to the central terminal of Wilson (Figure 7-13B). This terminal is constructed by connecting the right-arm, left-arm, and left-leg electrodes through 5000-Ω resistors in order to largely cancel out the potentials from these three points. In practice, the cancellation is incomplete (Lipman, Massie, & Kleiger, 1972).

Augmented unipolar limb leads are also widely used in clinical diagnoses. In this system of leads, the central terminal of Wilson constitutes the indifferent electrode, and the exploring electrode is one of three active limb electrodes. As shown in Figure 7-13C, lead aVR uses the right-arm electrode as the active electrode, lead aVL uses the left-arm electrode, and lead aVF uses the left-leg electrode. The reason this system is called "augmented unipolar limb lead recording" is that by disconnecting the input to the central terminal of Wilson from the extremity with the active electrode, and by connecting the latter to the wire used for recording the precordial lead, the resulting unipolar limb lead recording can be augmented by a voltage as much as 50% greater than that obtained using a standard unipolar lead. This type of recording is particularly useful because it records the

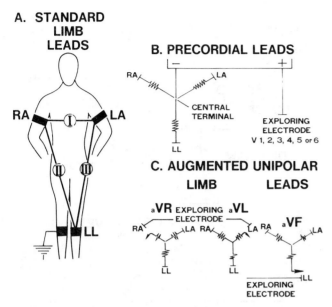

Figure 7-13. Recording the electrocardiogram. The standard limb leads shown in panel A are placed on the right arm (RA), the left arm (LA), and the left leg (LL), and potential differences are recorded between pairs of leads. When recording from precordial leads, shown in B, an exploring electrode is placed at 6 predesignated places on the chest (V_1–V_6) and connected to the positive (+) terminal of the electrocardiograph. The negative (−) electrode is connected to the central terminal of Wilson (see text). When recording from augmented unipolar leads, as shown in panel C, two limbs are connected electrical resistances to the negative terminal of the electrocardiograph, while the third limb is connected to the positive terminal. In recording aVR, the positive terminal is connected to the right arm; in aVL, the left arm; and in aVF, the left leg.

potentials of the heart on the side nearest to the respective limb, especially aVF and the inferior surface of the heart.

Ambulatory Monitoring of the ECG

Prolonged ECG monitoring in patients engaged in normal daily activities was initially reported by Holter (1961). Holter monitoring provides a sensitive method for detecting spontaneously occurring arrhythmias, and for relating ECG changes (including arrhythmias) to behavior. Briefly, the monitor provides a method of recording the ECG on magnetic tape. The tape recorder is battery-powered and runs at a slow (3.75 in./min) tape speed. It is small enough to be suspended by a strap over the shoulder or around the waist. In recent years, input signals to the recorder have typically been obtained from four signal electrodes and one ground electrode. This allows one channel to record simultaneously one standard limb

lead and one unipolar precordial lead. The monitor is also equipped with a digital clock, synchronized to the tape recorder, to permit accurate time marking. By pushing an event marker, the person being monitored provides a time marking on the ECG record that later can be correlated with a diary, which the person also keeps. In this way, symptoms and behaviors can be related to the ECG record.

Because each 24-hr monitoring period contains over 100,000 cardiac cycles, playback and analyses must be accomplished much faster than real time. In recent years, computer scanning techniques have been developed that can summarize HR, frequencies of premature atrial beats and PVCs, runs of tachycardia, and variations in QRS, S-T, or T patterns during any time period.

SYSTOLIC TIME INTERVALS (STIs)

Overview

We have considered in some detail the mechanical events that occur during the phases of the cardiac cycle, ways in which each can be measured, and the limitations of each as an indicator of cardiac function. There is a growing body of evidence that the relative durations of those mechanical events (i.e., STIs) contain reliable information about the contractile state of the heart. This impression has been a long time maturing (Wiggers, 1921a, 1921b; see also Weissler, Stack, & Sohn, 1980, for other historical references), but it now appears that the relationship between electrical and mechanical systole may be one of the simplest and best indices of adrenergic influence on the heart.

Onset of ventricular systole is signaled by the initial deflection of the QRS complex of the externally recorded ECG. The entire QRST complex is the vectorial sum of the action potentials of the individual myocardial cells. The rate and quantity of transmembrane flow of Na^+, K^+, and Ca^{2+} ions determine the contour and time course of the action potentials, and the Ca^{2+} couples the electrical impulse with myocardial contraction (Nayler & Seabra-Gomes, 1975; Reuter, 1974). The duration of the action potential is directly related to the duration of the slow inward Ca^{2+} current, which is known to be prolonged by adrenergic agents (Reuter, 1974). On the other hand, the time course of contraction is related to the rapidity of movement of Ca^{2+} between the sarcoplasmic reticulum and the space surrounding the myofilaments. Rapid movement in response to Beta-adrenergic stimulation has been shown to increase both rate of force development and rate of relaxation, thus shortening contraction (Winegrad, 1982), in addition to increasing the total amount of force produced (Reuter, 1974). Thus, there is reason to expect changes in length of the phases of the cardiac cycle in response to adrenergic stimulation.

Before we begin to discuss the STIs in detail, it is appropriate to consider the relationship between HR and the R-R interval of the ECG. It seems more logical to use the R-R interval in discussing circulatory control, since the control mechanisms can only act by changing the shape of the spontaneous sinus node P-cell depolarization curve between two consecutive action potentials. Also, duration (in milliseconds) is the currency of all of the other STIs. Nevertheless, much of the literature is reported in terms of regressions against HR. So long as we realize that rate and interval are related as an inversion that plots as a hyperbola, not as a straight line, the proper interpretations will be made (however, see Boudoulas, Geleris, Lewis, & Leier, 1981, for some theoretical considerations).

Methods for Measuring STIs

The three basic STIs are the pre-ejection period (PEP), the left ventricular ejection time (LVET), and total electromechanical systole (Q-S_2), as shown in Figure 7-14. These measurements are obtained from simultaneous high-speed recordings of the ECG, a noninvasively monitored carotid pulse tracing, and a phonocardiogram (R. P. Lewis, Rittgers, & Boudoulas, 1980; R. P. Lewis, Rittgers, Forester, & Boudoulas, 1977; Van de Werf, Piessens, Kesteloot, & DeGeest, 1974; Weissler, 1974). Apparatus with high-frequency response and paper speed are required, since changes are in terms of 10s of milliseconds. For best results, several cycles are averaged. Although manual measurements are the standard, computer readouts are being evaluated and are obviously desirable if large numbers of readings must be processed.

The ECG lead employed should be the one that shows the longest Q-T interval—most often a vertical lead, such as II or aVF. The phonocardiogram pickup should be positioned for highest fidelity recordings of the aortic component of the second heart sound (S_2). There should be no compromise of S_2 fidelity to obtain recordings of the mitral portion of the first heart sound (S_1), since this sound is often difficult to identify on high-speed tracings, and the intervals that employ it are correspondingly imprecise (Metzger, Chough, Kroetz, & Leonard, 1970). Satisfactory records of the Q-T and Q-S_2 intervals can be obtained in a high percentage of cases, regardless of subject position, even during mild exercise.

The use of carotid pulse tracing to determine LVET has been subject to some criticism (Luisada, Bhat, & Knighten, 1980). It is true that the contour of the arterial pulse changes markedly as the pulse moves distally, but this does not alter the time between up-

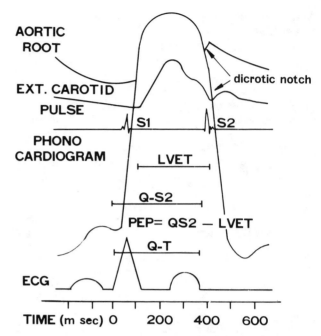

Figure 7-14. Systolic time intervals. In this figure, the external carotid pulse is displayed against a background of internally recorded pressure. Note that the upstroke and dicrotic notch of the carotid pulse are *both* delayed about 30–36 msec after the corresponding events in the ascending aorta, so that time from upstroke to dicrotic notch remains a good index of left ventricular ejection time (LVET). In practice, electrical systole (Q-T), mechanical systole (Q-S_2), LVET, and the pre-ejection period (PEP = Q-S_2 − LVET) can be assessed noninvasively using the electcrocardiogram, the phonocardiogram, and an externally recorded pulse tracing of the carotid artery (EXT. CAROTID PULSE). (From "Neurogenic influences upon the heart" by N. Schneiderman, P. M. McCabe, & K. Hausman. In J. A. Herd & S. M. Weiss (Eds.), *Cardiovascular instrumentation: Applicability of new technology to biobehavioral research.* DHHS Publication: NIH-84-1654, 1984. Reprinted by permission.)

stroke and dicrotic notch (R. P. Lewis *et al.*, 1977), except, perhaps, at high HR (Van de Werf *et al.*, 1974). This has been documented repeatedly by simultaneous carotid pulse tracings and intra-aortic recordings using catheter-tip micromanometers (Lewis *et al.*, 1977; Martin, Shaver, Thompson, Reddy, & Leonard, 1971; Van de Werf *et al.*, 1974). However, care must be taken to use the same type of air-coupled manometer employed by the documenting authors. The LVET is probably somewhat less accurate than the Q-S_2 because of rounding of the upstroke and incisura, but it has withstood intense testing.

Ear densitometry (Lance & Spodick, 1977), echocardiography (Kahn, 1980), thermistor plethysmography (Ferro, Maione, Tari, Guinta, Chiarello, & Condorelli, 1980), and Doppler flow measurement (Rothendler, Schick, & Ryan, 1981) have been used to determine the LVET but have not been documented outside of the originators' laboratories. Ear densitography, thermistor plethysmography, and Doppler recording may have uses in exercise and 24-hr ambulatory situations where respiratory excursions may distort the carotid pulse (K. Kobayashi, Kotilainen, Haffty, Moreau, Bishop, & Spodick, 1978; Spodick, Haffty, & Kotilainen, 1978). Ear densitography has its pulse pickup rather distal in the arterial tree for high-fidelity tracings, especially for conditions in which skin circulation may be reflexively decreased, and use of the derivative of the curve is open to theoretical objections (Rothendler, Schick, & Ryan, 1982). The difficulty in accurately defining the upstroke and dicrotic notch in the carotid pulse tracing appears to be reasonably solved by using a thermistor pulse transducer positioned over the neck region superficial to the carotid artery (Ferro, *et al.*, 1980). Using this procedure, the PEP as measured by STIs correlated well with the fractional shortening of the left ventricle as measured by an echocardiogram. Also a good correlation was found between LVET corrected for HR and SV as determined by echocardiography.

An intriguing study by Boudoulas, Geleris, Lewis, and Leier (1981) omitted using a carotid tracing at all and still provided provocative data concerning increased adrenergic drive upon the heart. Briefly, they looked at changes in electrical systole (Q-T) in comparison with mechanical systole (Q-S_2) as a function of isoproterenol (beta-adrenergic agonist) infusion before and after oral propranolol (beta-adrenergic antagonist). During atrial pacing over the physiological range of HRs (80–140), Q-T is usually shorter than but parallels the duration of Q-S_2. What Boudoulas and colleagues found was that for any given HR during isoproternol infusion, Q-S_2 became shorter than Q-T. This reversal was blocked by propranolol. Thus, a reversal of the normal relationship between Q-T and Q-S_2 may provide a simple index of increased adrenergic activity of the heart that cannot be accounted for by changes in HR. Whether or not the reversal of Q-T and Q-S_2 will be useful in assessing increased adrenergic drive during various behavioral situations remains to be determined.

Interpretation of STIs

Electromechanical systole (Q-S_2) is the most reliable of the STIs; its main drawback is the question of whether the aortic valve closure sound is a totally reliable indicator of end-systole (see the discussion above of the left ventricular pressure–volume relationship). There is also some preload and afterload sensitivity (Weissler, 1974). As has been discussed, the carotid pulse tracing provides an accurate measure of LVET. However, LVET is highly sensitive to both preload and afterload, and therefore is fairly useless as a single index (R. P. Lewis *et al.*, 1977).

The PEP, on the other hand, is a derived figure, obtained by subtracting LVET from Q-S_2. Since this algebraically combines the errors of Q-S_2 and LVET measurement in an unpredictable way, the net error in PEP may be quite large. PEP is a composite of the electromechanical delay and the isovolumic contraction time (ICT). Of course, the true ICT, as recorded with intracavitary micromanometers, is a highly significant period in assessing contractility, since it relates to the rate of force development. Although the ICT can be measured noninvasively (S_2-S_1 minus LVET), the result is often inaccurate because of uncertaity regarding the point of onset of the mitral component of S_1 (Metzger *et al.*, 1970). Indeed, it turns out that PEP is a more accurate indication of true ICT than is the externally measured ICT. For this reason, ICT is not considered further here.

All of the intervals require correction for HR if comparison is to be made between different subjects or within the same subject at different HR assessments. The correction factors are those determined by the regression of STI versus HR (Weissler, 1974). It will be noticed that PEP requires little correction. The PEP:LVET ratio has been advocated as an index of contractility that does not require rate correction. However, considering the number of factors involved, the chance for error should be high (but see R. P. Lewis *et al.*, 1977).

Both Q-T and Q-S_2 have linear inverse relationships to HR at rest or when artificially controlled by atrial pacing (Ahnve & Vallin, 1982; Boudoulas, Geleris, Lewis, & Leier, 1981; Boudoulas, Geleris, Lewis, & Rittgers, 1981; Ferro, Ricciardelli, Sacca, Chiarello, Volpe, Tari, & Trimasco, 1980b; Johnson, Meeran, Frank, & Taylor, 1981; Van de Werf *et al.*, 1974). The regression lines are nearly parallel, and Q-S_2 is consistently greater than Q-T. When the beta-adrenergic agonist isoproterenol is administered, the decreases in Q-T are only those that are consistent with the increase in HR (Boudoulas, Geleris, Lewis, & Leier, 1981). The effect of isoproterenol on Q-S_2 is much more marked. There is shortening of the interval, far beyond what one would expect to see from HR increase alone (Boudoulas, Geleris, Lewis, & Leier, 1981; Johnson *et al.*, 1981). This is thoroughly consistent with animal experimental work on the effect of adrenergic stimuli on development and relaxation of contraction (Winegrad, 1982). Most importantly, Q-S_2 becomes shorter than Q-T even at the relatively moderate isoproterenol infusion rates employed in this study. Another important feature of this relationship is that no correction needs to be made for HR. Unfortunately, there has been no attempt to quantify the adrenergic effect.

Rate-related shortening of the Q-S_2 during atrial pacing is almost entirely due to decrease in LVET

(Johnson et al., 1981), whereas PEP shortening contributes heavily to the Q-S_2 decrease due to beta-adrenergic-sympathetic agonists (Ahmed, Levinson, Schwarz, & Ettinger, 1972; Harris, Schoenfeld, & Weissler, 1967; Johnson et al., 1981). This should mean that PEP is a good index of contractility, and so it is, but its usefulness is limited because of its extreme sensitivity to preload and afterload (R. P. Lewis et al., 1977; Martin et al., 1971). Studies, however, have shown good correlation of PEP:LVET with left ventricular ejection fraction and dP/dt normalized for afterload (Ahmed et al., 1972).

Although the pulse transit time (PTT) has received criticism as a pure index of either myocardial contractility or blood pressure (Newlin & Levenson, 1979), it deserves examination as an STI. It comprises the interval between the Q and the arrival of the peak systolic pressure wave at the external carotid recording site (Obrist, Light, McCubbin, Hutcheson, & Hoffer, 1979). As such, it includes the electromechanical delay, ICT, the time from beginning ejection to peak ventricular pressure (PVP time), and the true transit time of the pressure wave from the aortic valve to the recording site. Two of these intervals, ICT and time to development of peak pressure, are identical to the PVP time, which Abel (1976) found to be the most sensitive to adrenergic stimulation and least sensitive to preload and afterload among a large number of evaluated contractility indices. If it can be documented that PTT and PVP time are highly correlated, the PTT may have some real value.

In summary, the STIs provide reasonably good indices of myocardial contractility. The relationship between Q-T and Q-S_2 is easy to measure noninvasively, and equipment costs are not great. If continuous BP readings are obtained, the effects of afterload can be accounted for in forming interpretations. Preload is more difficult to handle. LVET and its relationship to PEP may be helpful here, particularly if a measure of cardiac output is not available. Measurements are repeatable as often as desired, but there is some variation in values in the same subject on an hour-to-hour (Boudoulas, Geleris, Lewis, & Rittgers, 1981) and day-to-day (Johnson et al., 1981; Weissler, 1974) basis.

A major problem with STIs is that, as yet, no effort has been made to quantify the changes in sympathetic activation. This should be approachable by bioassay. Drugs such as isoproterenol (pure beta-adrenergic agonist), propanolol (beta-adrenergic antagonist), methoxamine (alpha-adrenergic agonist), and phentolamine (alpha-adrenergic antagonist) are being given regularly in cardiac catheterization laboratories and can even be given safely experimentally, so that quantitative information should be forthcoming. Also, safe manipulations of preload (amyl nitrite, postural alterations) and afterload (isometric exercise) can be accomplished without autonomic manipulation. The

clinical syndrome of sympathetic sensitivity associated with thyrotoxicosis and propranolol withdrawal are both known to be characterized by higher than normal beta-adrenergic receptor populations (Hoffman & Lefkowitz, 1982; Watanabe et al., 1982). Both clinical situations have been investigated with STIs, showing another way in which quantification may be approached (Boudoulas, Geleris, Lewis, & Leier, 1981; Boudoulas, Lewis, Kates, Dalamangas, & Beaver, 1980; Parisi, Hamilton, Thomas, & Mazzaferri, 1974).

THE VASCULAR SYSTEM

Blood Pressure

Blood pressure (BP) is measured so frequently, by everything from intra-arterial pressure transducers to drugstore coin-operated sphygmomanometers, that the accuracy of its evaluation and the significance of the reported levels are rarely questioned. But the true situation is not that simple. Systemic arterial BP is usually reported as a maximum (systolic) and minimum (diastolic) value (SP/DP), with pulse pressure being the difference between the two. Unfortunately, neither SP nor DP is of basic physiological importance. Rather, mean systolic pressure (MSP) and mean arterial pressure (MAP) are the salient values to be assessed. MSP is the integral of the aortic root pressure tracing during the ejection phase of the cardiac cycle divided by the ejection time. As mentioned earlier (see "Cardiac Output," above), MSP is the best estimate of cardiac afterload. MAP is the integral of the pressure curve of the entire cardiac cycle divided by the interbeat interval (1/HR). It is one of the two determinants of tissue perfusion (local R is the other), and is a good index of the vascular traumatic effects of hypertension. As we shall see, reliable estimates of MSP and MAP are not easy to obtain.

In the major arteries, the pressure contour is a complex interaction between true wave and pulsatile displacement of fluid (Bruner, Krenis, Kunsman, & Sherman, 1981a). Even within the aortic arch and its brachiocephalic branches, the wave component undergoes phase shift (R. P. Lewis et al., 1977). More distally, impedance mismatch at the small-artery–arteriolar level causes a reflected wave to reascend the artery (Bruner et al., 1981a). Progressive increases in arterial caliber increases impedance to flow, so that the pulsatile displacement component of the pressure pulse is also attenuated. The net effect of these distorting influences is that directly measured SP tends to rise while DP remains nearly the same as the recording site is moved distally (e.g., radial artery SP is considerably higher than that in the ascending aorta). Since pulse contour and timing are important in assessing MSP, a direct high-fidelity recording of the pressure within the aortic root is required. With MAP, on the other hand, the situation is not so critical. Integration of the simultaneous pressure curves from various arterial levels apparently yields essentially the same MAP as that in the ascending aorta (Bruner *et al.*, 1981a). Moreover, the conventional rule of thumb that

$$MAP = DP + \frac{SP - DP}{3}$$

applies fairly well to intra-arterial tracings at all levels. The difference between MSP and MAP increases with age, due to loss of resiliency in the large proximal arteries. Once MAP and $\dot{Q}$ are known, R may be calculated as follows:

$$R = \frac{MAP}{\dot{Q}}.$$

The reflected wave augmentation of SP is proportional to the degree of peripheral impedance mismatch, which, in turn, is a function of R (Bruner *et al.*, 1981a). So far as the propulsion of blood is concerned, the reflected wave is lost energy. Thus, the difference between proximal and distal directly recorded pressure pulses contains information about R and the efficiency of cardiac energy utilization. As yet, this sort of information can be evaluated only qualitatively.

Since neither momentary SP nor DP is physiologically important in terms of cardiovascular regulation, it is not worthwhile to list their determinants separately. In the broadest sense, MAP is directly proportional to $\dot{Q}$ and R (Guyton, 1981; Levy, 1979):

$$MAP = \dot{Q} \times R.$$

However, as discussed in the section on $\dot{Q}$, neither $\dot{Q}$ nor R is an independent variable (i.e., they are the integrals of the locally and neurohumorally regulated flows and resistances in all of the tissues of the body). The ideal MAP is that which is barely high enough to permit local tissue blood flow to be independently autoregulated in all parts of the body (Guyton, 1981). (See the discussion of $\dot{Q}$ for the interrelation of blood volume, compliance changes in capacitance vessels, and central and peripheral regulation of R in the determination of MAP.)

Measurement of BP

The same equipment problems that limit the high-fidelity recording of intraventricular pressures affect assessment of the arterial system as well. The damping and resonance characteristics of the hydraulic system that connects arterial lumen and transducer surface can greatly influence the fidelity of pressure pulse reproduction (Bruner *et al.*, 1981a). Excessive damping, chiefly by small-caliber cannulae and connecting tubing, removes the high-frequency components of the pulse. Conversely, underdamping combined with external circuit resonance frequency close to that of the pressure pulse results in a gross amplification of the SP called "overshoot." This problem is not easily addressed by making improvements in the frequency response of the system or tampering with the filtration parameters of the recording apparatus (Bruner, Krenis, Kunsman, & Sherman, 1981b). Only intra-arterial micromanometers entirely avoid distortion, but these are impractical in many situations. For the present, most intra-arterial pressure traces must be considered to have significant artifact.

Systolic overshoot is particularly a problem in radial artery tracings in which the reflected wave component is maximized. This makes these recordings unsuitable for calculation of MAP from SP and DP, and probably for calculation by electronic integration as well. Brachial artery cannulation partially avoids this problem, but is much more difficult and dangerous to perform.

All noninvasive BP techniques require a method of producing occlusion of the artery by application of a known external pressure and a means of detecting minimal flow or wall motion in the artery when the intraluminal pressure barely exceeds that which is externally applied. Pressure applied to the tissues surrounding an artery tend to constrict it. If the arterial wall is normally compliant, the artery occludes and flow ceases when tissue pressure exceeds arterial pressure. Usually the pressure is applied with an inflatable cuff, and cuff pressure equals tissue pressure equals arterial pressure at the point of occlusion.

For flow detection, the methodology is more diverse. In classical sphygmomanometry, the stethoscope is used to detect Korotkoff (K) sounds in the artery below the cuff. As the cuff is slowly deflated from a totally occlusive pressure, the first rushing sound occurs at the systolic pressure. With further deflation, diastolic pressure is recorded at the point of sudden decrease or disappearance of pulsatile, thumping sounds (Bruner *et al.*, 1981a). Also, flow may be sensed with Doppler flow probes proximal or distal to the point of occlusion.

In view of the artifactual nature of many arterial (especially radial) pressure recordings, it is not surprising that correlations of BP obtained between intra-arterial and external methods have only been fair to poor (Bruner *et al.*, 1981a; Bruner, Krenis, Kunsman, & Sherman, 1981c). SP comparisons have had somewhat higher correlations than DP comparisons, but even SP loses its precision at very high or low pressures or in vasoconstrictive states. For the present, it is impossible to tell whether the direct or indirect value is the more accurate. The pressure cuff may be aggravating or even painful, particularly with repeated inflations. Since cuff deflation must be slow, pressure sampling is intermittent and low in frequency. Thus, conventional sphygmomanometry is unsuitable if the expected changes are rapid. A major advantage of classical sphygmomanometry, however, is its good correlation with clinical status in hypertension over decades of widespread use.

Microphonic sensing of K sounds is the basis of several automatic BP recording devices used in both stationary and ambulatory situations. The ambulatory systems permit around the clock sampling at intervals as short as 6.0 min, the values being recorded on tape. Many of the devices have provision for subject-initiated pressure recordings so that response to specific situations may be assessed. This feature is especially useful in real-life conditions when accompanied by a diary (Pickering, Harshfield, Kleinert, Blank, & Laragh, 1982). Validation studies show a high degree of correlation with manual sphygmomanometric determinations of SP and adequate correlation for DP (Harshfield, Pickering, & Laragh, 1979; Sheps, Elveback, Close, Kleven, & Bissen, 1981). In one of the stationary systems (Borow et al., 1982), there is extremely high correlation between automatically recorded BP and simultaneous tracings from the aortic root (1% mean error for SP and 2% mean error for DP).

Another modification of standard sphygmomanometry is the tracking-cuff system (Shapiro, Greenstadt, Lane, & Rubinstein, 1981). Using a servo system, cuff pressure is readjusted upward or downward after each beat, depending on whether or not a sound is detected. Continuous recordings are obtained for 1 min with rest periods of cuff deflation. Cuff-related discomfort is said to be minimal. However, the system does have several disadvantages. Most importantly, only one pressure can be recorded, so that one system on each arm is required if DP as well as SP is to be recorded. MAP must then be estimated. At present there is no allowance for avoiding cuff pressure change if the blood pressure remains unchanged. Finally, there is significant hysteresis in the system, because cuff pressure only changes by 2–3 mm Hg per beat, so that rapid, large pressure swings can only be followed with considerable lag. Nevertheless, the system is a real advance and produces good information about the direction and magnitude of short-term BP changes.

Special occlusion cuffs permit BP to be determined in the earlobe and finger (Man-i & Imachi, 1981). Only the SP can be evaluated. Correlation with intra-arterial pressures is only fair. The probes are fairly unobtrusive and can be used in the exercising individual. Much more documentation is needed, before this approach can be used with confidence.

A promising method for continuous BP recording involves Doppler flow detection and a servo mechanism that permits the pressure in an arm cuff to track arterial pressure continuously (Aaslid & Brubaak, 1981). The pressure in the arm cuff is servo-adjusted so that instantaneous transmural pressure (arm tissue to arterial lumen) is nearly zero, as reflected by a constant, low, reference flow velocity in the underlying artery. Using this technique, a pulsatile tracing is obtained (Figure 7-15) that closely replicates the simultaneously recorded brachial intra-arterial pulse contour from the opposite arm, and there is extremely close correlation for SP, DP, and electronically damped MAP (Figure 7-16). Recording is semicontinuous. Observation periods of 2 min each are interspersed with 5- to 15-sec periods of cuff deflation to permit venous return to adjust. The pulsatile cuff is said to be less uncomfortable than the slowly deflated cuff used in conventional sphygmomanometry. Pain occurs only when obstruction to venous return is unduly prolonged. Motion artifact, particularly due to contraction of the muscles underlying the cuff, is avoidable in most experimental paradigms if the subject is properly instructed.

The determination of BP by oscillometry has been reported to be highly accurate (Ramsey, 1979; Yelderman & Ream, 1979), but has its detractors as well (Aaslid & Brubaak, 1981; Bruner et al., 1981a, 1981c). The degree of oscillation may be detected visually or by a microprocessor-based system. MAP is recorded as the lowest cuff pressure at which maximum cuff oscillation occurs. Ramsey (1979) and Yelderman and Ream (1979) found good correlation between oscillometrically determined MAP and the results of intra-arterial tracings. Bruner et al. (1981a, 1981c) could not confirm this, although they used an admittedly less standardized technique of evaluating magnitude of oscillation.

Pulse wave velocity (Gribbin, Steptoe, & Sleight, 1976) and pulse transit time (Weiss, Bo, Reichek, & Engelman, 1980), have been advocated as indices of BP change. While correlation of these measures with MAP change is fairly high, the correlation with myocardial contractility seems just as good (Obrist, 1981; Obrist et al., 1979). Thus the velocity of pulse wave transit seems more related to sympathetic tone than to BP per se (see section on STIs). The unpredictable effects of change in arterial wall structure and the inability to calibrate the method contribute further to dissatisfaction with the procedure.

The combination of externally monitored carotid pulse tracings and manual or automatic recording of brachial sphygmomanometric pressures has been used to assess MAP accurately (Stefadouros, Dougherty, Grossman, & Craige, 1973) or the pressure at the dicrotic notch (Borow et al., 1982; Marsh et al., 1979). SP and DP are determined by sphygmomanometry and assigned to the zenith and nadir of the

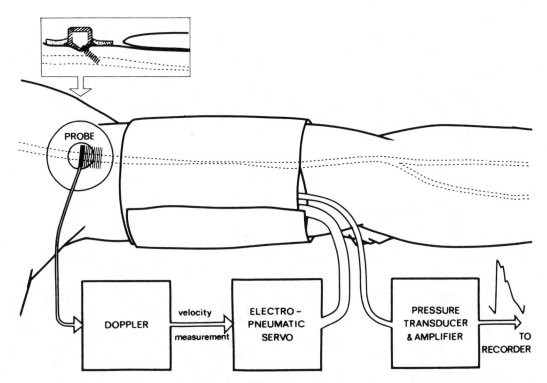

Figure 7-15. Schematic of the ultrasonic Doppler servo method for the noninvasive recording of instantaneous arterial blood pressure. (From "Accuracy of an Ultrasound Doppler Servo Method for Non-Invasive Determination of Instantaneous and Mean Arterial Blood Pressure" by R. Aaslid and A. O. Brubaak. *Circulation*, 1981, 64, 753–759. Reprinted by permission.)

carotid trace. MAP is then determined by using the planimetered area of the curve divided by the R-R interval and adding this to the DP. The level of the dicrotic notch is found by linear interpolation between SP and DP. In view of the vagaries of carotid pulse morphology and noninvasive measures of BP, the technique requires validation from another laboratory. The initial validation (Stefadouros *et al.*, 1973) loses a bit of its glow when one realizes that the noninvasive arterial pressures and the invasive studies with which they were compared were measured 24 hr apart. Also, the new technique yielded no better data than could be obtained from SP and DP alone. The use of the technique for dicrotic notch pressure determination has received separate validation, albeit by the same group (Marsh *et al.*, 1979).

There are several commercially available automatic BP measuring devices that have received validation studies. Of these, the Del Mar Avionics (sphygmomanometric) system (Harshfield *et al.*, 1979) and the Dinamap (oscillometric) system (Borow *et al.*, 1982) appear quite useful. However, the most promising approach may well be the Doppler system of Aaslid and Brubaak (1981), which still needs independent confirmation of its validity.

Flow in Various Vascular Beds

Coronary Circulation

In recent years, psychophysiologists have increasingly begun to work with physicians to study behavioral factors that may be involved in the etiology and pathogenesis of cardiovascular disease. Since approximately one-third of all deaths in the United States result from CHD, it is not surprising that increasing interest has developed in measuring coronary function and assessing coronary artery damage.

The left and right coronary arteries arise from the aortic root just after the aorta leaves the left ventricle. The left coronary artery immediately divides into a left anterior descending branch and a left circumflex branch. These supply the left atrium and ventricle. In contrast, the right coronary artery largely supplies the right atrium and ventricle.

The performance of the heart is measured in terms of the heart as pump (i.e., $\dot{Q}$). The efficiency and, indeed, the viability of that pump depend on the constant integrity of its blood supply. Short periods of deficiency in coronary blood flow (CF), whether global or regional, can produce dangerous arrhyth-

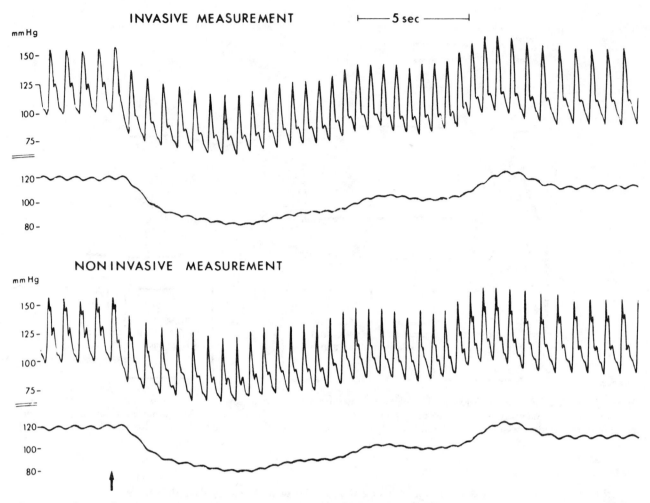

Figure 7-16. Simultaneous invasive and noninvasive recordings of arterial blood pressure. The lower trace in each of the panels represents the mean pressure obtained by electronic damping of the waveform. At the time indicated by the arrow, the blood pressure was suddenly lowered by deflating occluding cuffs around both legs. (From "Accuracy of an Ultrasound Doppler Servo Method for Non-Invasive Determination of Instantaneous and Mean Arterial Blood Pressure" by R. Aaslid and A. O. Brubaak. *Circulation*, 1981, 64, 753–759. Reprinted by permission.)

mias and pump failure. The clinical diseases that cause so much of the heart disease in the Western world are thought to act regionally, although the deprived regions may coalesce to compromise the whole heart when all of the coronary arteries are diseased.

There are some important questions that are of interest to psychophysiologists. Can CNS-mediated coronary vasomotor activity (1) aggravate regional, organic (i.e., arteriosclerotic) coronary artery disease, or (2) cause global or regional flow deficiency in the absence of organic coronary arteriosclerosis (Buja, Hillis, Petty, & Willerson, 1981)? CF amounts to about 225 ml/min, or 5% of $\dot{Q}$ at rest and barely keeps pace with increased O_2 demand during the increased flow and pressure work of exercise. Of more interest are situations where psychogenically generated pressure/work may increase metabolic demand without increasing CF. The demand for CF can be expressed as the time–tension index, which is the product of area under the left ventricular pressure curve and HR. This can be assessed noninvasively as the rate–pressure product, which is expressed as HR × SP. The rate–pressure product is felt to be "highly correlated with" the time–tension index. Much of coronary flow occurs during diastole, and in hypertension and CHD the flow is almost entirely during that period. The opportunity for flow can be assessed in terms of diastolic time (DT). In this case DT is calculated from the STI by subtracting Q-S_2 from the R–R interval. Since this DT has a nonlinear relationship to HR, small changes in HR can produce important differences in opportunity for flow (Boudoulas et al., 1980). Thus a good way exists for assessing CF demand, but, unfortunately, there is no easy method of measuring CF.

Coronary artery flow in humans has been measured in several ways. These include (1) the nitrous oxide (N_2O) breathing technique; (2) ^{84}Rb uptake in conjunction with coincidence counting over the chest; and (3) measurement of the clearance rate of a radioactively labeled inert gas (e.g., ^{133}Xe, ^{85}Kr).

In the N_2O breathing technique (Eckenhoff, Hafkenschiel, Harmel, Goodale, Lubin, Bing, & Kety, 1947), the subject suddenly begins to breathe nitrous oxide at a steady concentration. Samples of arterial blood are removed from a peripheral artery, while samples of venous blood are obtained from the coronary sinus through a venous catheter. The concentrations of N_2O in the artery and in the venous sinus are plotted for 10 min. From these data, a proportionality factor that has been derived in experiments on the isolated heart, and an estimate of total heart mass, CF can be calculated by the Fick equation:

$$CF = \frac{\text{Amount of } N_2O \text{ taken up by heart during time } (T_2 - T_1)}{\text{Arteriovenous } (A - V) \text{ differences of } N_2O \text{ across heart during time } (T_2 - T_1)}.$$

The cannulation of the coronary sinus is not as hazardous as coronary arterial catheterization and is fairly easy to perform. Additionally, the cannula may be left in place for prolonged periods. The subject may change position or even exercise. Obviously, to the extent that the N_2O concentration produces psychological effects, the technique is compromised for use by psychophysiologists. Xenon, however, is a good substitute for N_2O.

A less invasive but also less versatile method involves external measurement of rubidium uptake by the heart (Bing, Bennish, Bluemchen, Cohen, Gallagher, & Zaleski, 1964). Rubidium is taken up by myocardium because it is freely exchangeable with intracellular potassium (K). If a radioactive isotope (rubidium-84) is administered by continuous intravenous injection, its rate of uptake (dK/dt) by myocardium can be measured by appropriate external scintillation detectors. With simultaneous measurement of the concentration of radioactive material in arterial blood (A), we can calculate the clearance (C) as follows:

$$C = \frac{dK/dt}{A} = \frac{dK/dt}{(A-V)/A}.$$

Clearance is, then, the amount of blood flow that would be required if the indicator were totally removed from the blood in a single pass through the heart. Of course this does not happen, but the extraction ratio $(A-V)/A$ may be empirically determined as a constant, using isolated nonhuman hearts. The assumption of similarity of extraction ratios of humans and other mammals is probably correct, but, as with the N_2O method, has never been tested. CF then becomes the quotient of clearance divided by extraction ratio. As with other measures of CF, the value is relative (i.e., expressed in clearance equivalents). Also, the assumption must be made that the particular portion of myocardium being monitored is representative of the whole. An intricate arrangement of scintographic equipment permits subtraction of lung and chest wall uptake and limitation of field by bilateral coincidence counting. The equipment is expensive and the radiation hazard significant. Also, as with the N_2O technique, several minutes of counting are required, so that short-term changes in CF will not be reflected. Finally, the patient must remain in one position throughout the examination.

Flow in single coronary arteries may be measured with direct single injections of the radioisotopes of xenon or krypton via an intracoronary catheter (R. W. Ross, Ueda, Lichtlen, & Rees, 1964). The rate of loss of radioactivity from the myocardium is then proportional to blood flow. Since either gas is 90% expired in a single passage through the lungs, there is minimal distortion of the curve by recirculation. There is little advantage to this technique, however, since it is inherently more dangerous and less versatile than the N_2O method.

The techniques described above measure global CF. However, no consistent deficiency in global CF has been demonstrated in any disease state including severely obstructive coronary artery disease (R. S. Ross, 1974). Although regional CF deficiency is not within the scope of this discussion, it should be mentioned that ECG stress testing (Diamond, Hirsch, Forrester, Staniloff, Vas, Halpern, & Swan, 1981) and myocardial imaging (Okada, Boucher, Kirschenbaum, Kushner, Strauss, Block, McKusick, & Pohost, 1980), usually with radioactive thallium, are reliable detectors of local myocardial perfusion discrepancies. In general, measures of CF seem beyond the reach of the psychophysiologist. However, the questions to be answered are of major importance, so that collaborative studies with cardiac physiologists should be worthwhile.

The standard by which all other methods of diagnosing coronary atherosclerosis are measured in the human patient is coronary arteriography. This procedure provides an anatomic map of the coronary arteries, including the site and extent of stenotic lesions. The procedure is used for diagnosing coronary occlusive disease and for evaluating the results of coronary bypass surgery. Using this cinefluoroscopic procedure, it is possible to determine the number, location, degree of narrowing, and length of coronary occlusions. Because coronary collateral circulation is often quite good, stenoses or even occlusions do not always signify regional flow deficiency.

Coronary arteriography involves introducing a specially constructed catheter into a peripheral artery (e.g., brachial, femoral), then selectively catheterizing the coronary artery orifices and individually injecting them with a radiopaque contrast medium. Meanwhile, a 35-mm cine camera is used to record the fluoroscopic visualization of the coronary arteries. Several methods of quantitative artery analysis have been proposed, but none has yet achieved universal acceptance.

Blood Flow in Skeletal Muscle

As previously noted, $\dot{Q}$ is the product of HR and SV. At rest $\dot{Q}$ is approximately 5 L/min, whereas during heavy exercise, $\dot{Q}$ may exceed 25 L/min. Not only does $\dot{Q}$ vary as a function of exercise or other behavioral states, but the distribution of $\dot{Q}$ to the vascular beds serving various organs also shows pronounced changes. Thus, for example, at rest about half of $\dot{Q}$ goes to the renal and mesenteric beds, with only 15% going to skeletal muscle. In contrast, during vigorous exercise, more than 80% of $\dot{Q}$ may go to skeletal muscle. Increased flow to skeletal muscle has been associated with the defense reaction (Abrahams et al., 1960; Adams, Baccelli, Mancia, & Zanchetti, 1968) and with behavioral tasks not usually associated with physical exertion, such as "mental arithmetic" (Brod et al., 1959).

Blood flow to a limb is made up of blood flow to muscle, skin, and bone. Under resting conditions, the proportion of limb blood flow distributed to muscle is about 70–80%. This proportion increases with exercise. Invasive experiments conducted upon anesthetized animals undergoing intracranial stimulation in the cerebral defense pathway have sometimes measured outflow from a deep femoral vein after the paw circulation has been excluded by a tight ligature around the ankle, the leg has been skinned, and the calf muscle has been isolated (Djojosugito, Folkow, Kylstra, Lisander, & Tuttle, 1970). In practice, the skin contributes little to the total flow in the limb, and the change in flow to bone is negligible. Consequently, there appears to be some justification for the use of venous occlusion plethysmography of a limb in humans to provide a noninvasive estimate of changes in muscle blood flow.

In venous-occlusion plethysmography a mercury-in-rubber or silastic strain gauge transducer is placed around the largest circumference of a limb such as the forearm (Whitney, 1953). At this placement the ratio of muscle to skin and bone is maximal. Two occlusion cuffs are used in conjunction with the strain gauge. The distal cuff, which is located at the wrist is inflated to greater than systolic pressure, thereby excluding circulation in the hand and fingers from measurement. This is done because blood flow to the hand is more to skin than to muscle. The proximal cuff is rapidly inflated to a pressure that is above venous pressure but below diastolic arterial pressure (e.g., 40–50 mm Hg). Arterial inflow to the arm is unimpaired, but venous outflow is prevented.

As the arm becomes engorged with blood, the mercury-in-rubber strain gauge, which circumscribes the forearm between the two occlusion cuffs, detects an increase in electrical resistance that is proportional to the circumferential change. Based upon this information, a percentage change in arm volume (dV) against time after venous occlusion (dt) can be calculated, and forearm blood flow (F) can be expressed as

$$F = \frac{dV}{dt}.$$

This is expressed in cc/100 cc of limb/min. When MAP is concurrently measured or calculated, vascular resistance in the limb can be calculated as

$$R = \frac{MAP}{F}.$$

Venous occlusion plethysmography provides a noninvasive measure of absolute limb flow in humans that has proven useful in psychophysiological experiments (Williams, Lane, Kuhn, Melosh, White, & Schanberg, 1982). Care must be taken in using this measure, however, because it is subject to numerous artifacts. Ischemic pain caused by the distal cuff as well as changes in ambient temperature, limb position above or below the heart, sympathetic tone, and circulating vasoactive substances all can influence the results, and need to be controlled.

Cutaneous Blood Flow

Circulation through the skin has two major functions: nutrition of skin tissue, and regulation of body temperature. Because most changes in cutaneous blood flow are related to temperature regulation, and because temperature regulation is controlled by the nervous system, most changes in skin blood flow reflect neural mechanisms rather than local autoregulation. This differs from the cardiovascular regulation that occurs in most parts of the body. The transmitters that most affect skin blood vessels are NE, which is secreted by sympathetic vasoconstrictor fibers, and circulating E, which is released by the adrenal medulla.

Psychophysiologists seem to have become attracted to the measurement of skin blood flow for two major reasons. The first of these is because cutaneous blood flow is susceptible to influence by the sympathoadrenomedullary system, and hence to emotional behavior. The second reason appears to be that relatively simple, inexpensive, noninvasive methods have long been available for the indirect measurement of relative changes in skin blood flow.

One of these methods is photoelectric plethysmography. The basic principle involved here is that light reflectance of skin varies primarily as a change in blood volume with each heart beat. Thus, a photocell can be employed to measure the reflected light provided by a separate light source, thereby providing an indirect measure of blood flow. Because the temperature on the skin surface varies as a function of blood flow through the skin, monitoring of skin temperature with a thermistor has also been used to provide an indirect measure of skin flow. A detailed description of the procedure and issues involved in the noninvasive measurement of peripheral vascular activity has been provided by Jennings, Tahmaush, and Redmond (1980).

Behavioral scientists have begun to use noninvasive measurement of peripheral vascular activity in the treatment of migraine and vascular headaches as well as Raynaud disease. Several studies have reported that migraine and other vascular headaches can be treated successfully by increasing hand temperature by means of biofeedback (e.g., Blanchard, Theobald, Williamson, Silver, & Brown, 1978), but there appears to be no clear relationship between changes in hand temperature and regional cerebral blood flow (Largen, Mathew, Dobbins, Meyers, & Claghorn, 1978). Instead, it appears that any procedure that can cause a reduction in sympathetic nervous system activity may be beneficial to migraine patients. From the point of view of psychophysiology, reliability, validation, and quantitation studies will need to be performed before meaningful relationships can be documented between noninvasive measures of cutaneous blood flow and specific biobehavioral functions.

pear promising for the noninvasive assessment of vagal influences upon the heart. Similarly, the use of STIs has contributed substantially to our ability to assess left ventricular function noninvasively. It also appears, that the reversal of the normal relationship between Q-T and Q-S$_2$ described by Boudoulas, Geleris, Lewis, and Leier (1981) may even provide a simple index of increased adrenergic activity of the heart that cannot be accounted for by changes in HR.

The past decade has witnessed increased collaboration between research physicians interested in the etiology, pathogenesis, and treatment of cardiovascular diseases and behaviorally trained psychophysiologists who share similar interests. This has been facilitated by research implicating the nervous system and behavior in CHD (Schneiderman, 1983), and the development of instrumentation that has permitted detailed noninvasive cardiovascular assessments to be made in the behaving individual. The development of ambulatory HR and BP monitoring has allowed cardiovascular activity and behavior to be correlated in real-life situations. Procedures such as coronary angiography have also become of interest to cardiovascular psychophysiologists because they offer hard clinical endpoints for studies relating behavior to CHD in living patients. Impedance cardiography, echocardiography, and evaluation of STIs should permit more in depth study of relationships between cardiac function and behavior to take place within the psychophysiology laboratory. Finally, such clinical tools as radionuclide angiography should lend themselves to collaborative psychophysiological investigations, since the duration of radionuclide activity in which interesting and important relationships between the cardiovascular system and behavior can be explored often lasts far longer than the time needed for clinical diagnosis.

CONCLUSIONS

It is an interesting paradox that while our understanding of neurogenic influences upon the cardiovascular system has become increasingly detailed and complex during the past several years, the assessment of neurogenic and psychophysiological influences upon the circulatory system has become more manageable. The neurogenic influences upon the heart, for example, have turned out to be extremely complex. Interactions between sympathetic and parasympathetic innervations, effects of E as opposed to NE, and changes that occur in receptor populations and affinities need to be taken into account when attempting to understand the autonomic control of the heart. At the same time, progress has been made in assessing parasympathetic and sympathetic influences upon the heart using relatively simple noninvasive measures. Procedures developed by Akselrod, Gordon, Ubel, Shannon, Barger and Cohen (1981) and by Porges *et al.* (1982) for examining the spectral densities for heart period ap-

REFERENCES

Aaslid, R., & Brubaak, A. O. Accuracy of an ultrasound Doppler servo method for non-invasive determination of instantaneous and mean arterial blood pressure. *Circulation*, 1981, 64, 753–759.

Abel, F. L. Comparative evaluation of pressure and time factors in estimating left ventricular performance. *Journal of Applied Physiology*, 1976, 40, 196–205.

Abrahams, V. C., Hilton, S. M., & Zbrozyna, A. Active vasodilation produced by stimulation of the brain stem: Its significance in the defense reaction. *Journal of Physiology* (London), 1960, 154, 491–513.

Adair, J. R., & Manning, J. W. Hypothalamic modulation of baroreceptor afferent unit activity. *American Journal of Physiology*, 1975, 229, 1357–1364.

Adams, D. B., Baccelli, G., Mancia, G., & Zanchetti, A. Cardiovascular changes during naturally elicited fighting behavior in the cat. *American Journal of Physiology*, 1968, 216, 1226–1235.

Ahlquist, R. P. Study of adrenotropic receptors. *American Journal of Physiology*, 1948, 153, 586–600.

Ahmed, S. S., Levinson, G. E., Schwarz, C. J., & Ettinger, P. O. Systolic time intervals as measures of the contractile state of the left ventricular myocardium in man. *Circulation*, 1972, 52, 559–571.

Ahnve, S., & Vallin, H. Influence of heart rate and inhibition of autonomic tone on the QT interval. *Circulation*, 1982, 65, 435–439.

Akselrod, S. O., Gordon, D., Ubel, F. A., Shannon, D. C., Barger, A. C., & Cohen, R. J. Power spectrum analysis of heart rate fluctuations: A quantitative probe of beat-to-beat cardiovascular control. *Science*, 1981, 213, 220–222.

Bainbridge, F. A. The influence of venous filling upon the rate of the heart. *Journal of Physiology* (London), 1915, 50, 65–78.

Baker, S. P., Boyd, H. M., & Potter, L. T. Distribution and function of β-adrenoceptors in different chambers of the canine heart. *British Journal of Pharmacology*, 1980, 68, 57–63.

Baker, S. P., & Potter, L. T. Biochemical studies of cardiac β-adrenoceptors, and their clinical significance. *Circulation Research*, 1980, 46 (Suppl. I), 34–42.

Ban, T. The septo-preoptico-hypothalamic system and its autonomic function. In T. Tokizane & J. P. Schade (Eds.), *Correlative neurosciences: Part A. Fundamental mechanisms*. Amsterdam: Elsevier, 1966.

Belloni, F. L., Phair, R. D., & Sparks, H. V. The role of adenosine in prolonged vasodilation following flow restricted exercise in canine skeletal muscle. *Circulation Research*, 1979, 44, 759–766.

Berthelson, S., & Pettinger, W. A. A functional basis for classification of alpha-adrenergic receptors. *Life Sciences*, 1977, 21, 595–606.

Bing, R. J., Bennish, A., Bluemchen, G., Cohen, A., Gallagher, J. P., & Zaleski, E. J. The determination of coronary flow equivalent with coincidence counting technic. *Circulation*, 1964, 29, 833–846.

Blanchard, E. B., Theobald, D., Williamson, D., Silver, B., & Brown, B. Temperature feedback in the treatment of migraine headaches. *Archives of General Psychology*, 1978, 35, 581–588.

Borow, K. M., Neumann, A., & Wynne, J. Sensitivity of end-systolic pressure dimension and pressure–volume relations to the inotropic state in humans. *Circulation*, 1982, 65, 988–997.

Boudoulas, H., Geleris, P., Lewis, R. P., & Leier, C. V. Effect of increased adrenergic activity on the relationship between electrical and mechanical systole. *Circulation*, 1981, 64, 28–33.

Boudoulas, H., Geleris, P., Lewis, R. P., & Rittgers, S. E. Linear relationships between electrical systole, mechanical systole, and heart rate. *Chest*, 1981, 80, 613–617.

Boudoulas, H., Lewis, R. P., Kates, R. E., Dalamangas, G., & Beaver, B. M. Usefulness of the systolic time intervals in the study of beta-blocking agents. In W. F. List, J. S. Gravenstein, & D. H. Spodick (Eds.), *Systolic time intervals*. New York: Springer-Verlag, 1980.

Braunwald, E., Sonnenblick, E. H., Ross, J., Glick, G., & Epstein, S. F. An analysis of the cardiac response to exercise. *Circulation Research*, 1967, 20–21 (Suppl. 1), I44–I54.

Brod, J., Fencl, V., Hejl, Z., & Jirka, J. Circulatory changes underlying blood pressure elevation during acute emotional stress (mental arithmetic) in normotensive and hypertensive subjects. *Clinical Science*, 1959, 18, 269–279.

Bruner, J. M. R., Krenis, L. J., Kunsman, J. M., & Sherman, A. P. Comparison of direct and indirect methods of measuring arterial blood pressure: Part I. *Medical Instrumentation*, 1981, 15, 11–21. (a)

Bruner, J. M. R., Krenis, L. J., Kunsman, J. M., & Sherman, A. P. Comparison of direct and indirect methods of measuring arterial blood pressure: Part II. *Medical Instrumentation*, 1981, 15, 97–101. (b)

Bruner, J. M. R., Krenis, L. J., Kunsman, J. M., & Sherman, A. P. Comparison of direct and indirect methods of measuring arterial blood pressure: Part III. *Medical Instrumentation*, 1981, 15, 182–186. (c)

Buja, L. M., Hillis, L. D., Petty, C. S., & Willerson, J. T. The role of coronary arterial spasm in ischemic heart disease. *Archives of Pathology and Laboratory Medicine*, 1981, 105, 221–226.

Bunnel, D. E. T-wave amplitude and the P-Q interval: Relationships to non-invasive indices of myocardial performance. *Psychophysiology*, 1980, 17, 592–597.

Butler, J., O'Brien, M., O'Malley, K., & Kelly, J. G. Relationship of β-adrenoreceptor density to fitness in athletes. *Nature*, 1982, 298, 60–62.

Chan, S. H. H., & Koo, A. The participation of medullary reticular formation in clonidine-induced hypotension in rats. *Neuropharmacology*, 1978, 17, 367–373.

Chen, Y. H., & Chan, S. H. H. Clonidine-induced hypotension in cats: The role of medial medullary reticular α-adrenoceptors and vagus nerve. *Neuroscience Abstracts*, 1978, 4, 47.

Chung, J. M., Chung, K., & Wurster, R. D. Sympathetic preganglionic neurons of the cat spinal cord: Horseradish peroxidase study. *Brain Research*, 1975, 91, 126–131.

Ciaraldi, T., & Marinetti, G. V. Thyroxine and propylthiouracil effects in vivo on alpha and beta adrenergic receptors in rat heart. *Biochemistry and Biophysics Research Communications*, 1977, 74, 984–991.

Clarke, N. P., Smith, O. A., & Shearn, D. W. Topographical representation of vascular smooth muscle of limbs in the primate motor cortex. *American Journal of Physiology*, 1968, 214, 122–129.

Collier, C. R. Determination of mixed venous CO_2 tension by rebreathing. *Journal of Applied Physiology*, 1956, 91, 25–29.

Cooper, R. H., O'Rourke, R. A., Karliner, J. S., Peterson, K. L., & Leopold, J. R. Comparison of ultrasound and cineangiographic measurements of the mean rate of circumferential fiber shortening in man. *Circulation*, 1972, 46, 914–923.

Coote, J. H., Hilton, S. M., & Zbrozyna, A. W. The ponto-medullary area integrating the defense reaction in the cat and its influence on muscle blood flow. *Journal of Physiology* (London), 1973, 229, 257–274.

Crawshaw, L. I. Temperature regulation in vertebrates. *Annual Review of Physiology*, 1980, 42, 473–491.

Daly, M. de B., Korner, P. I., Angell-James, J. E., & Oliver, J. R. Cardiovascular–respiratory reflex interactions between carotid bodies and upper-air-ways receptors in the monkey. *American Journal of Physiology*, 1978, 234, H293–H299.

Dampney, R. A. L., Kumada, M., & Reis, D. J. Control neural mechanisms of the cerebral ischemic response: Characterization, effect of brainstem and cranial nerve transections, and stimulation by electrical stimulation of restricted regions of medulla oblongata in rabbit. *Circulation Research*, 1979, 45, 48–62.

Darsee, J. R., Mikolich, J. R., Walter, P. F., & Schlant, R. C. Transcutaneous method of measuring Doppler cardiac output: I. Comparison of transcutaneous and juxta-aortic Doppler velocity signals with catheter and cuff electromagnetic flowmeter measurements in closed and open chest dogs. *American Journal of Cardiology*, 1980, 46, 607–612.

DeGeest, H., Levy, M. N., Zieske, H., & Lipman, R. I. Depression of ventricular contractility by stimulation of the vagus nerves. *Circulation Research*, 1965, 17, 222–235.

Denniston, J. C., Maher, J. T., Reeves, J. T., Cruz, J. C., Cymerman, R., & Grover, R. F. Measurement of cardiac output by electrical impedance at rest and during exercise. *Journal of Applied Physiology*, 1976, 40, 91–95.

Devereux, R. B., & Reichek, N. Echocardiographic determination of left ventricular mass in man. *Circulation*, 1977, 55, 613–618.

Diamond, G. A., Hirsch, M., Forrester, J. S., Staniloff, H. M., Vas, R., Halpern, S. W., & Swan, H. J. C. Application of information theory to clinical diagnostic testing: The electrocardiographic stress test. *Circulation*, 1981, 63, 915–921.

Dimsdale, J. E., & Moss, J. M. Plasma catecholamines in stress and exercise. *Journal of the American Medical Association*, 1980, 243, 340–342.

Djojosugito, A. M., Folkow, B., Kylstra, P. H., Lisander, B., & Tuttle, R. S. Differential interaction between the hypothalamic defence reaction and baroreceptor reflexes. *Acta Physiologica Scandinavica*, 1970, 78, 376–385.

Doerr, B. M., Miles, D. S., & Frey, M. A. B. Influence of respiration on stroke volume determined by impedance cardiography. *Aviation and Space Environmental Medicine*, 1981, 52, 394–398.

Donald, D. E., & Shepherd, J. T. Autonomic regulation of the peripheral circulation. *Annual Review of Physiology*, 1980, 42, 429–439.

Douglas, W. W. Polypeptides—Angiotension, plasma kinins and others. In A. G. Goodman, L. S. Goodman, & A. Gilman (Eds.), *Goodman & Gilman's: The pharmacological bases of therapeutics* (6th ed.). New York: Macmillan, 1980.

Eckenhoff, J. E., Hafkenschiel, J. H., Harmel, M. H., Goodale, W. T., & Lubin, M., & Bing, R. J., & Kety, S. S. Measurement of coronary blood flood by the nitrous oxide method. *American Journal of Physiology*, 1947, 152, 356–364.

Eliasson, S., Folkow, B., Lindgren, P., & Uvnas, B. Activation of sympathetic vasodilator nerves to the skeletal muscle in the cat by hypothalamic stimulation. *Acta Physiologica Scandinavica*, 1951, 23, 333–351.

Ellenberger, H., Haselton, J. R., Liskowsky, D. R., & Schneiderman, N. The location of chronotropic cardioinhibitory vagal motoneurons in the medulla of the rabbit. *Journal of the Autonomic Nervous System*, 1983, 9, 513–529.

Epstein, S. E., Levey, G. S., & Skelton, C. L. Adenyl cyclase and cyclic AMP: Biochemical links in the regulation of myocardial contractility. *Circulation*, 1971, 43, 437–450.

Falsetti, H. L., Mates, R. E., Greene, D. G., & Bunnell, I. L., V/Max as an index of contractile state in man. *Circulation*, 1971, 43, 467–479.

Ferrer, M. I. *The sick sinus syndrome*. Mount Kisco, N.Y.: Futura, 1974.

Ferro, G., Maione, S., Tari, M. G., Guinta, A., Chiarello, M., & Condorelli, M. Non-invasive evaluation by thermistor plethysmography of left ventricular performance during dynamic exercise. *Japanese Heart Journal*, 1980, 22, 335–343.

Ferro, G., Ricciardelli, B., Sacca, L., Chiarello, M., Volpe, M., Tari, M. G., & Trimasco, B. Relationship between systolic time intervals and heart rate during atrial or ventricular pacing in normal subjects. *Japanese Heart Journal*, 1980, 21, 765–771.

Flacke, W., & Gillis, R. A. Impulse transmission via nicotine and muscarinic pathways in the stellate ganglion of the dog. *Journal of Pharmacology and Experimental Therapeutics*, 1969, 163, 266–276.

Folkow, B., Langston, J., Oberg, B., & Prerovsky. Reactions of the different series-coupled vascular sections upon stimulation of the hypothalamic sympatho-inhibitory area. *Acta Physiologica Scandinavica*, 1964, 61, 476–483.

Fraser, J., Nadeau, J., Robertson, D., & Wood, A. J. J. Regulation of human leukocyte beta receptors by endogenous catecholamines. *Journal of Clinical Investigation*, 1981, 67, 1777–1784.

Gabig, T. G., & Babior, B. M. The killing of pathogens by phagocytes. *Annual Review of Medicine*, 1981, 32, 313–336.

Gebber, G. L., & Snyder, O. W. Hypothalamic control of baroceptor reflexes. *American Journal of Physiology*, 1970, 218, 124–131.

Gellhorn, E. Motion and emotion: The role of proprioception in the physiology and pathology of the emotions. *Psychological Reviews*, 1964, 71, 457–472.

Gellman, M. D., Schneiderman, N., Wallach, J. H., & Le Blanc, W. Cardiovascular responses elicited by hypothalamic stimulation in rabbits reveal a medio-lateral organization. *Journal of the Autonomic Nervous System*, 1981, 4, 301–317.

Gimpl, M. P., Brickman, A. L., Kaufman, M. P., & Schneiderman, N. Temporal relationships during barosensory attenuation in the conscious rabbit. *American Journal of Physiology*, 1976, 230, 1480–1486.

Glass, D. C., Krakoff, L. R., Contrada, R., Hilton, W. F., Kehoe, K., Mannucci, E. G., Collins, C., Snow, B., & Elting, E. Effect of harassment and competition upon cardiovascular and plasma catecholamine responses in Type A and Type B individuals. *Psychophysiology*, 1980, 17, 453–463.

Glaviano, V. V., Goldberg, J., & Pindo, M. T. Acetylcholine and norepinephrine interactions on cardiac lipids and hemodynamics. *American Journal of Physiology*, 1975, 1678–1684.

Goldfein, A., & Ganong, W. F. Adrenal medullary and adrenal cortical responses to stimulation of the diencephalon. *American Journal of Physiology*, 1962, 202, 205–211.

Green, H. D., & Hoff, E. C. Effects of faradic stimulation of the cerebral cortex on limb and renal volumes in the cat and monkey. *American Journal of Physiology*, 1937, 118, 641–652.

Green, J. H. Physiology of baroreceptor function: Mechanism of receptor stimulation. In P. Kezdi (Ed.), *Baroreceptors and hypertension*, Oxford: Pergamon Press, 1967.

Greengard, P. *Cyclic nucleotides, phosphorylated proteins and neuronal function*. New York: Raven Press, 1978.

Gribbin, B., Steptoe, A., & Sleight, P. Pulse wave velocity as a measure of blood pressure change. *Psychophysiology*, 1976, 13, 86–90.

Guidotti, A., & Costa, E. A role for nicotinic receptors in the regulation of the adenylate cyclase of adrenal medulla. *Journal of Pharmacology and Experimental Therapeutics*, 1974, 189, 665–675.

Guyton, A. C. The relationship of cardiac output and arterial pressure control. *Circulation*, 1981, 64, 1079–1088.

Hales, J. R. S., Iriki, M., Tsuchiya, K., & Kozawa, E. Thermally-induced cutaneous sympathetic activity related to blood flow through capillaries and arteriovenous anastomoses. *Pfluegers Archiv*, 1978, 375, 17–24.

Hamilton, R. B., Ellenberger, H., Liskowsky, D., Gellman, M. D., & Schneiderman, N. Parabrachial area as mediator of bradycardia in rabbits. *Journal of the Autonomic Nervous System*, 1981, 4, 261–281.

Harris, W. S., Schoenfeld, C. D., & Weissler, A. M. Effects of adrenergic receptor activation and blockade on the systolic pre-ejection period, heart rate, and arterial pressure in man. *Journal of Clinical Investigation*, 1967, 46, 1704–1714.

Harshfield, G. A., Pickering, T. G., & Laragh, J. H. A validation study of Del Mar Avionics ambulatory blood pressure system. *Ambulatory Electrocardiography*, 1979, 1, 7–12.

Henning, M., & Robinson, A. Evidence that the hypotensive action of methyldopa is mediated by central actions of methyl-noradrenaline. *Journal of Pharmacy and Pharmacology*, 1971, 23, 407–413.

Henry, W. L. Evaluation of ventricular function using two dimensional echocardiography. *American Journal of Cardiology*, 1982, 49, 1319–1323.

Heslegrave, R. J., & Furedy, J. J. Carotid dP/dt as a psychophysiological index of sympathetic myocardial effects: Some considerations. *Psychophysiology*, 1980, 17, 482–494.

Hess, W. R. *Functional organization of the diencephalon*. New York: Grune & Stratton, 1957.

Hess, W. R., & Brügger, M. Das subkorticale zentrum des affektiven abwehrreaktion. *Helvetia Physiologica Acta*, 1943, 1, 33–52.

Hilton, S. M. Inhibition of baroreceptor reflexes on hypothalamic stimulation. *Journal of Physiology* (London), 1963, 165, 56.

Hilton, S. M., & Spyer, K. M. Participation of the anterior hypothalamus in the baroreceptor reflex. *Journal of Physiology* (London), 1971, 218, 271–293.

Hilton, S. M., Spyer, K. M., & Timms, R. J. Hind limb vasodilation evoked by stimulation of the motor cortex. *Journal of Physiology* (London), 1975, 252, 22–23.

Hilton, S. M., & Zbrozyna, A. W. Amygdaloid region for defense reactions and its efficient pathway to the brain stem. *Journal of Physiology* (London), 1963, 165, 160–173.

Hinkle, L. E., Carver, S. T., & Stevens, M. The frequency of asymptomatic disturbances of cardiac rhythm and conduction in middle-aged men. *American Journal of Cardiology*, 1969, 24, 629–637.

Histand, M. B., Miller, L. W., & McLeod, F. D. Transcutaneous measurement of blood velocity profiles and flow. *Cardiovascular Research*, 1973, 7, 703–712.

Hoffman, B. B., & Lefkowitz, R. J. Adrenergic receptors in the heart. *Annual Review of Physiology*, 1982, 44, 475–484.

Holter, N. J. New method for heart studies: Continuous electrocardiography of active subjects over long periods is now practical. *Science*, 1961, 134, 1214–1216.

Hori, M., Yellin, E. L., & Sonnenblick, E. H. Left ventricular diastolic suction as a mechanism of ventricular filling. *Japanese Circulation Journal*, 1982, 46, 124–129.

Ishibashi, S., & Nicolaidis, S. Hypertension induced by electrical stimulation of the subfornical organ (SFO). *Brain Research Bulletin*, 1981, 6, 135–139.

Ito, H. I., Yamakoshi, K., & Togawa, T. A. A model study of stroke volume values calculated from impedance and their relation to wave form of blood flow. *IEEE Transactions in Biomedical Engineering*, 1977, 24, 489–491.

James, T. N., & Sherf, L. Ultrastructure of the myocardium. In J. W. Hurst, R. B. Logue, R. C. Schlant, & N. K. Wenger (Eds.), *The heart, arteries and veins* (4th ed.). New York: McGraw-Hill, 1978.

Jan, L. Y., Jan, Y. N., & Kuffler, S. W. A peptide as a possible transmitter in sympathetic ganglia of the frog. *Proceedings of the National Academy of Sciences*, 1979, 76, 1501–1505.

Jennings, J. R., Tahmaush, A. J., & Redmond, D. T. Non-invasive measurement of peripheral vascular activity. In I. Martin & P. H. Venables (Eds.), *Techniques in psychophysiology*. Chichester, England: Wiley, 1980.

Johnson, B. F., Meeran, M. K., Frank, A., & Taylor, S. H. Systolic time intervals in measurement of inotropic response to drugs. *British Heart Journal*, 1981, 46, 513–521.

Jones, N. L., Robertson, D. G., & Kane, J. W. Difference between end-tidal and arterial PCO_2 in exercise. *Journal of Applied Physiology*, 1979, 47, 954–960.

Jordan, D., Khalid, M., Schneiderman, N., & Spyer, K. M. The inhibitory control of vagal cardiomotor neurons. *Journal of Physiology* (London), 1979, 301, 54.

Kaada, B. R., Pribram, K. H., & Epstein, J. A. Respiratory and vascular responses in monkeys from temporal pole, insula, orbital surface and cingulate gyrus. *Journal of Neurophysiology*, 1949, 12, 347–356.

Kabat, H., Magoun, H. W., & Ranson, S. W. Electrical stimulation of points in the forebrain and midbrain: The resultant alteration in blood pressure. *Archives of Neurology and Psychiatry*, 1935, 34, 931–955.

Kahn, A. H. Systolic time intervals: Comparison of echocardiographic and conventional methods. In W. F. List, J. S. Gravenstein, & D. H. Spodick (Eds.), *Systolic time intervals*. New York: Springer-Verlag, 1980.

Karliner, J. S., Gault, J. H., Eckberg, D., Mullins, C. B., & Ross, J., Jr. Mean velocity of fiber shortening: A simplified measure of left ventricular myocardial contractility. *Circulation*, 1971, 44, 323–333.

Katona, P. G., & Jib, F. Respiratory sinus arrhythmia: Noninvasive measure of parasympathetic cardiac control. *Journal of Applied Physiology*, 1975, 39, 801–805.

Kaufman, M. P., Hamilton, R., Wallach, J. H., Petrick, G., & Schneiderman, N. Lateral subthalamic area as mediator of bradycardia responses in rabbits. *American Journal of Physiology*, 1979, 236, H471–H479.

Kent, K. M., & Epstein, S. E. Neural basis for the genesis and control of arrhythmias associated with myocardial infarction. *Cardiology*, 1976, 61, 61–74.

Kinne, E. Cardiac output from transthoracic impedance variations. *Annals of the New York Academy of Sciences*, 1970, 170, 747–756.

Klevans, L. R., & Gebber, G. L. Facilitory forebrain influence on cardiac component of baroreceptor reflexes. *American Journal of Physiology*, 1970, 219, 1235–1241.

Kobayashi, K., Kotilainen, P. W., Haffty, B. G., Moreau, K. A., Bishop, R. I., & Spodick, D. H. Cardiac responses during uninterrupted treadmill exercise and recovery: Measurement of systolic time intervals. *Chest*, 1978, 74, 265–270.

Kobayashi, Y., Andoh, Y., Fujinami, T., Nakayama, K., Takada, K., Takeuchi, T., & Okamato, M. Impedance cardiography for estimating cardiac output during submaximal and maximal work. *Journal of Applied Physiology*, 1978, 45, 459–462.

Kontos, H. A., Richardson, D. W., & Norvell, J. E. Mechanisms of circulatory dysfunction in orthostatic hypotension. *Transactions of the American Clinical Climatology Association*, 1975, 87, 26–35.

Korner, P. I. Integrative neural cardiovascular control. *Physiological Review*, 1971, 51, 312–367.

Kraunz, R. F., & Kennedy, J. W. Ultrasonic determination of left ventricular wall motion in normal man. *American Heart Journal*, 1970, 79, 36–43.

Kubicek, W. G., Karnegis, J. N., Patterson, R. P., Witose, D. A., & Matson, R. H. Development and evaluation of the impedance cardiac output system. *Aerospace Medicine*, 1966, 37, 1208–1212.

Lance, V. Q., & Spodick, D. H. Systolic time intervals utilizing ear densitography: Advantages and reliability for stress testing. *American Heart Journal*, 1977, 94, 62–66.

Lands, A. M., Arnold, A., McAuliff, J. P., Luduena, F. P., & Brown, T. G. Differentiation of receptor systems activated by sympathomimetic amines. *Nature*, 1967, 214, 597–598.

Langer, S. Presynaptic regulation of catecholamine release. *Biochemical Pharmacology*, 1977, 23, 1793–1800.

Langer, S. Z. Presynaptic receptors and their role in the regulation of transmitter release. *British Journal of Pharmacology*, 1977, 60, 481–497.

Largen, J. W., Mathew, R. J., Dobbins, K., Meyers, J. S., & Claghorn, J. L. Skin temperature self-regulation and non-invasive regional cerebral blood flow. *Headache*, 1978, 18, 203–210.

Lefkowitz, R. J. Direct binding studies of adrenergic receptors: Biochemical, physiologic, and clinical implications. *Annals of Internal Medicine*, 1979, 91, 450–458.

Levy, M. N. Parasympathetic control of the heart. In W. C. Randall (Ed.), *Neural regulation of the heart*. New York: Oxford University Press, 1977.

Levy, M. N. The cardiac and vascular factors that determine systemic blood flow. *Circulation Research*, 1979, 44, 739–747.

Levy, M. N., DeGeest, H., & Zieske, H. Effects of respiratory center activity on the heart. *Circulation Research*, 1966, 18, 67–78.

Levy, M. N., & Martin, P. J. Neural control of the heart. In R. M. Berne, N. Sperelakis, & S. R. Geiger (Eds.), *Handbook of physiology: The cardiovascular system*. Baltimore: Williams & Wilkins, 1979.

Levy, M. N., Ng, M. L., & Zieske, H. Cardiac responses to cephalic ischemia. *American Journal of Physiology*, 1968, 215, 159–175.

Lewis, P. J. Propranolol—An antihypertensive drug with a central action. In D. Davies & J. L. Reid (Eds.), *Central action of drugs in blood pressure regulation*. Baltimore: University Park Press, 1976.

Lewis, R. P., Rittgers, S. E., & Boudoulas, H. A critical review of systolic time intervals. In A. Weissler (Ed.), *Reviews of contemporary laboratory methods*. Dallas: American Heart Association, 1980.

Lewis, R. P., Rittgers, S. E., Forester, W. F., & Boudoulas, H. A critical review of systolic time intervals. *Circulation*, 1977, 56, 146–158.

Libet, B. The role SIF cells play in ganglionic transmission. *Advances in Biochemistry and Psychopharmacology*, 1977, 16, 541–546.

Linhart, J. W., Mintz, G. S., Segal, B. L., Wawni, N., & Kotler, M. N. Left ventricular volume measurement by echocardiography: Fact or fiction? *American Journal of Cardiology*, 1975, 36, 114–118.

Lipman, B. S., Massie, E., & Kleiger, R. E. *Clinical scalar electrocardiogram* (6th ed.). Chicago: Year Book Medical Publisher, 1972.

Loeppky, J. A., Greene, E. R., Hoekenga, D. E., Caprihan, A., & Luft, U. C. Beat-by-beat stroke volume assessment by pulsed Doppler in upright and supine exercise. *Journal of Applied Physi-*

ology: Respiratory, Environmental, and Exercise Physiology, 1981, 50, 1173–1182.

Lopes, O. V., & Palmer, F. J. Proposed respiratory gating mechanism for cardiac slowing. *Nature*, 1976, 264, 454–456.

Luisada, A. A., Bhat, P. K., & Knighten, V. The systolic time intervals: A new method of study. In W. F. List, J. S. Gravenstein, & D. H. Spodick (Eds.), *Systolic time intervals*. New York: Springer-Verlag, 1980.

Magnin, P. A., Stewart, J. A., Meyers, S., von Ramm, O., & Kissle, J. A. Combined Doppler and phased-array echocardiographic estimation of cardiac output. *Circulation*, 1981, 63, 688–692.

Magoun, H. W. Excitability of the hypothalamus after degeneration of corticofugal connections from the frontal lobe. *American Journal of Physiology*, 1938, 112, 530–532.

Mangiapane, M. L., & Simpson, J. B. Subfornical organs: Forebrain site of pressor and dipsogenic action of angiotensin. II. *American Journal of Physiology*, 1980, 239, R382–R389.

Man-i, M., & Imachi, Y. Effect of training on blood pressure and heart rate measured continuously during exercise. *Journal of Sports Medicine and Physical Fitness*, 1981, 21, 97–112.

Marriott, H. J. L., & Myerburg, R. J. Recognition and treatment of cardiac arrhythmias and conduction disturbances. In J. W. Hurst, R. B. Logue, R. C. Schlant, & N. K. Wenger (Eds.), *The heart, arteries, and veins* (4th ed.). New York: McGraw-Hill, 1978.

Marsh, J. D., Green, L. H., Wynne, J., Cohn, P. F., & Grossman, W. Left ventricular end-systolic pressure–dimension and stress–length relations in normal human subjects. *American Journal of Cardiology*, 1979, 44, 1311–1317.

Martin, C. E., Shaver, J. A., Thompson, M. E., Reddy, P. S., & Leonard, J. J. Direct correlation of external systolic time intervals with internal indices of left ventricular function in man. *Circulation*, 1971, 419–431.

Mason, D. T., Braunwald, E., Covell, J. W., Sonnenblick, E. W., & Ross, J., Jr. Assessment of cardiac contdractility: The relation between the rate of pressure rise and ventricular pressure during isovolumic systole. *Circulation*, 1971, 44, 47–58.

Massie, B. M., Kramer, B. L., Gertz, E. W., & Henderson, S. G. Radionuclide measurement of left ventricular volume: Comparison of geometric and counts-based methods. *Circulation*, 1982, 65, 725–730.

McAllen, R. M., & Spyer, K. M. The location of cardiac vagal preganglionic motoneurons in the medulla of the cat. *Journal of Physiology* (London), 1976, 258, 187–204.

Mehmel, H. C., Stockins, B., Ruffman, K., von Olshaussen, K., Schuler, G., & Kubler, W. The linearity of the end-systolic pressure–volume relationship in man and its sensitivity for assessment of left ventricular function. *Circulation*, 1981, 63, 1216–1222.

Metzger, C. Z., Chough, C. B., Kroetz, F. W., & Leonard, J. J. True isovolumic contraction time: Its correlation with two external indices of ventricular performance. *American Journal of Cardiology*, 1970, 25, 434–442.

Miller, J. C., & Horvath, S. M. Impedance cardiography. *Psychophysiology*, 1978, 15, 80–91.

Moss, A. J., & Schwartz, P. J. Sudden death and the idiopathic long Q-T syndrome. *American Journal of Medicine*, 1979, 66, 6–7.

Nayler, W. G., & Seabra-Gomes, R. Excitation-contraction coupling in cardiac muscle. *Progress in Cardiovascular Disease*, 1975, 18, 75–88.

Newlin, D. B., & Levenson, R. W. Pre-ejection period: Measuring beta-adrenergic influences upon the heart. *Psychophysiology*, 1979, 16, 546–553.

Nicolaidis, S. Mise en évidence de neurons barosensibles hypothalamegues antérieur et médian chez le chat. *Journal de Physiologie* (Paris), 1970, 62, 199–200.

Nivatpumin, T., Katz, S., & Scheuer, J. Peak left ventricular systolic pressure/end-systolic volume ratio: A sensitive detector of left ventricular disease. *American Journal of Cardiology*, 1979, 43, 969–974.

Nixon, J. V., Murray, R. G., Leonard, P. D., Mitchell, J. H., &

Blomqvist, C. G. Effect of large variations in preload on left ventricular performance characteristics in normal subjects. *Circulation*, 1982, 65, 698–703.

Obrist, P. A. *Cardiovascular psychophysiology: A perspective*. New York: Plenum, 1981.

Obrist, P. A., Lawler, J. E., Howard, J. L., Smithson, K. W., Martin, P. L., & Manning, J. Sympathetic influences on cardiac rate and contractility during acute stress in humans. *Psychophysiology*, 1974, 11, 405–427.

Obrist, P. A., & Light, K. C. Comments on "Carotid dP/dt as a psychophysiological index of sympathetic myocardial effects: Some considerations." *Psychophysiology*, 1980, 17, 495–498.

Obrist, P. A., Light, K. C., McCubbin, J. A., Hutcheson, J. S., & Hoffer, J. L. Pulse transit time: Relationship to blood pressure and myocardial performance. *Psychophysiology*, 1979, 16, 292–301.

Okada, R. D., Boucher, C. A., Kirschenbaum, H. K., Kushner, F. G., Strauss, H. W., Block, P. C., McKusick, K. A., & Pohost, G. M. Improved diagnostic accuracy of thallium-201 stress test using multiple observers and criteria derived from interobserver analysis of variance. *American Journal of Cardiology*, 1980, 46, 619–624.

Paintal, A. S. A study of the right and left atrial receptors. *Journal of Physiology*, 1953, 120, 596–610.

Paintal, A. S. Vagal sensory receptors and their reflex effects. *Physiological Reviews*, 1973, 53, 159–227.

Paraskos, J. A., Grossman, W., Saltz, S., Dalen, J. E., & Dexter, L. A non-invasive technique for the determination of velocity of circumferential fiber shortening in man. *Circulation Research*, 1971, 29, 610–615.

Parisi, A. F., Hamilton, B. P., Thomas, C. N., & Mazzaferri, E. L. The short cardiac pre-ejection period: An index to thyrotoxicosis. *Circulation*, 1979, 49, 900–904.

Parmley, W. W., Chuck, L., & Sonnenblick, E. H. Relation of Vmax to different models of cardiac muscle. *Circulation Research*, 1972, 30, 3–9.

Patterson, S. W., Piper, H., & Starling, E. H. The regulation of the heart beat. *Journal of Physiology* (London), 1914, 48, 465–513.

Pearlman, A. S. Evaluation of ventricular function using Doppler echocardiography. *American Journal of Cardiology*, 1982, 49, 1324–1330.

Peterson, D. A., Gerrard, J. M., Glover, S. M., Rao, G. H. R., & White, J. G. Epinephrine reduction of heme: Implication for understanding the transmission of an agonist stimulus. *Science*, 1982, 215, 71–73.

Pickering, T. G., Harshfield, G. A., Kleinert, H. D., Blank, S., & Laragh, J. H. Blood pressure during normal daily activities, sleep, and exercise. *Journal of the American Medical Association*, 1982, 247, 992–996.

Piene, H., & Covell, J. W. A force–length–time relationship describes the mechanics of canine left ventricular wall segments during auxotonic contractions. *Circulation Research*, 1981, 49, 70–79.

Pollack, G. H. Maximum velocity as an index of contractility in cardiac muscle. A critical evaluation. *Circulation Research*, 1970, 26, 111–127.

Pombo, J. F., Bart, L. T., & Russell, R. O., Jr. Left ventricular volumes and ejection fraction by echocardiography. *Circulation*, 1971, 43, 480–490.

Popp, R. L. M-mode echocardiographic assessment of ventricular function. *American Journal of Cardiology*, 1982, 49, 1312–1318.

Porges, S. W., Bohrer, R. E., Cheung, M. N., Drasgow, F., McCabe, P. M., & Keren, G. A new time-series statistic for detecting rhythmic co-occurrence in the frequency domain: The weighted coherence and its application to psychophysiological research. *Psychological Bulletin*, 1980, 88, 580–587.

Porges, S. W., McCabe, P. M., & Yongue, B. G. Respiratory–heart rate interactions: Psychophysiological implications for pathophysiology and behavior. In J. J. Cacioppo & R. E. Petty (Eds.), *Focus on cardiovascular psychophysiology*. New York: Guilford Press, 1982.

Prinzmetal, M., Kannamer, R., Merliss, R., Wada, T., & Bor, N. Angina pectoris: I. A variant form of angina pectoris. *American Journal of Medicine*, 1959, 27, 375–388.

Quastel, M. R. *Cell biology and immunology of leukocyte function.* New York: Academic Press, 1979.

Rackley, C. E. Quantitative evaluation of left ventricular function by radiographic techniques. In A. M. Weissler (Ed.), *Review of contemporary laboratory methods.* Dallas: American Heart Association, 1980.

Ramsey, M., III. Non-invasive automatic determination of mean arterial pressure. *Medicine, Biology, Engineering, and Computers*, 1979, 17, 11.

Randall, W. C., Priola, D. V., & Ulmer, R. H. A functional study of distribution of cardiac sympathetic nerves. *American Journal of Physiology*, 1963, 205, 1227–1231.

Reichek, N., Wilson, J., Sutton, M. S., Plappert, T. A., Goldberg, S., & Hirshfeld, J. W. Non-invasive determination of left-ventricular end-systolic stress: Validation of the method and initial application. *Circulation*, 1982, 65, 99–108.

Reis, D. J., & Oliphant, M. C. Bradycardia and tachycardia following electrical stimulation of the amygdaloid region in the monkey. *Journal of Neurophysiology*, 1964, 27, 893–912.

Reuter, H. Localization of beta adrenergic receptors and effects of noradrenaline and cyclic nucleotides on action potentials, ionic currents, and tension in mammalian cardiac muscle. *Journal of Physiology*, 1974, 242, 429–451.

Ross, J., Jr., Linhart, J. W., & Braunwald, E. Effects of changing heart rate in man by electrical stimulation of the right atrium. *Circulation*, 1965, 32, 549–558.

Ross, R. S. Myocardial perfusion: Historical perspectives and future needs. In: H. W. Strauss, B. Pitt, & A. E. James (Eds.), *Cardiovascular nuclear medicine.* St. Louis: C. V. Mosby, 1974.

Ross, R. W., Ueda, K., Lichtlen, P. R., & Rees, J. R. Measurement of myocardial blood flow in animals and man by selective injection of radio-active inert gas into the coronary arteries. *Circulation Research*, 1964, 15, 28–41.

Rothendler, J. A., Schick, E. C., Jr., & Ryan, T. J. Derivation of systolic time intervals from Doppler measurement of temporal arterial flow. *American Journal of Cardiology*, 1981, 47, 68–72.

Rothendler, J. A., Schick, E. C., Jr., & Ryan, T. J. Reply. *American Journal of Cardiology*, 1982, 49, 1378,

Rutlen, D. L., Supple, E. W., & Powell, W. J. Adrenergic regulation of total systemic distensibility. *American Journal of Cardiology*, 1981, 47, 579–588.

Sagawa, K. The ventricular pressure–volume diagram revisited. *Circulation Research*, 1978, 43, 677–687.

Sagawa, K. The end-systolic pressure–volume relation of the ventricle: Definition, modifications and clinical use. *Circulation*, 1981, 63, 1223–1227.

Sasayama, S., & Kotura, H. Echocardiographic approach for the clinical assessment of left ventricular function: The analysis of end-systolic pressure (wall stress)–diameter relation and force-velocity relation of ejecting ventricle. *Japanese Circulation Journal*, 1979, 43, 357–366.

Schmitt, H. The pharmacology of clonidine and related products. In F. Gross (Ed.), *Handbook of experimental pharamacology* (Vol. 39, *Antihypertensive agents*). Berlin: Springer-Verlag, 1977.

Schmitt, H., & Schmitt, H. Localization of the hypotensive effect of 2-(2-6-dichlorophenylamine)-2-imidazoline hydrochloride (St 155, Catapresan). *European Journal of Pharamacology*, 1969, 6, 8–12.

Schneiderman, N. Behavior, autonomic function and animal models of cardiovascular pathology. In T. M. Dembroski, T. H. Schmidt, & G. Blumchen (Eds.), *Biobehavioral bases of coronary heart disease.* Basel, Switzerland: Karger, 1983.

Schwaber, J., & Schneiderman, N. Aortic nerve activated cardioinhibitory neurons and interneurons. *American Journal of Physiology*, 1975, 229, 783–789.

Shapiro, D., Greenstadt, L., Lane, J. D., & Rubinstein, E. Tracking-cuff system for beat-to-beat recording of blood pressure. *Psychophysiology*, 1981, 18, 129–136.

Sharma, V. K., & Banerjee, S. P. Muscarinic cholinergic receptors in rat hearts: Effect of thyroidectomy. *Journal of Biological Chemistry*, 1977, 252, 7444–7446.

Shepherd, J. T., & Vanhoutte, P. M. Local modulation of adrenergic neurotransmission. *Circulation*, 1981, 64, 655–666.

Sheps, G. G., Elveback, L. R., Close, E. L., Kleven, M. K., & Bissen C. Evaluation of the Del Mar Avionics automatic ambulatory blood pressure-recording device. *Mayo Clinic Proceedings*, 1981, 56, 740–743.

Shroff, S., Janicki, J. S., & Weber, K. T. Prediction of peak isovolumetric pressure in ejecting left ventricle. *Circulation*, 1980, 62(Suppl. III), III-68. (Abstract)

Sjostrand, T. Regulation of the blood distribution in man. *Acta Physiologica Scandinavica*, 1952, 26, 312–320.

Smith, O. A., Rushmer, R. F., & Lasher, E. P. Similarity of cardiovascular responses to exercise and to diencephalic stimulation. *American Journal of Physiology*, 1960, 198, 1139–1142.

Sonnenblick, E. H. Implications of muscle mechanics in the heart. *Federation Proceedings*, 1962, 21, 975–993.

Sonnenblick, E. H., Parmley, W. W., Urschel, C. W., & Brutsaert, D. L. Ventricular function: Evaluation of myocardial contractility in health and disease. *Progress in Cardiovascular Diseases*, 1970, 12, 449–466.

Spivak, J. L. *Fundamentals of clinical hematology.* Hagerstown, Md.: Harper & Row, 1980.

Spodick, D. H., Haffty, B. G., & Kotilainen, P. W. Non-invasive ambulatory monitoring of physiologic data: Recording systolic time intervals. *Medical Instrumentation*, 1978, 12, 343–345.

Stefadouros, M. A., Dougherty, M. J., Grossman, W., & Craige, E. Determination of systemic vascular resistance by a non-invasive technique. *Circulation*, 1973, 47, 101–107.

Stjarne, L., & Brundin, J. Beta-adrenoceptors facilitating noradrenaline secretion from vasoconstrictor nerves. *Acta Physiologica Scandinavica*, 1976, 97, 88–93.

Strauss, H. W., & Boucher, C. A. Radionuclide angiography. *American Journal of Cardiology*, 1982, 49, 1337–1340.

Strobeck, J. E., Krueger, J., & Sonnenblick, E. H. Load and time considerations in the force–length relation of cardiac muscle. *Federation Proceedings*, 1980, 39, 175–182.

Strong, C. G., Northcutt, R. C., & Sheps, S. G. Clinical examination and investigation of the hypertensive patient. In J. Genest, E. Kosws, & O. Kuchel (Eds.), *Hypertension: Physiopathology and treatment.* New York: McGraw-Hill, 1977.

Sudakov, K. V., & Yumatov, E. A. Acute psychosocial stress as the cause of sudden death. In *USA-USSR First Symposium on Sudden Death, Yalta, USSR* (DHEW Publ. No. NIH 78-1470). Washington, D.C.: U.S. Government Printing Office, 1978.

Suga, H., & Sagawa, K. Assessment of absolute volume from diameter of the intact canine left ventricular cavity. *Journal of Applied Physiology*, 1974, 36, 496–499.

Sugashita, Y., & Koseki, S. Dynamic exercise echocardiography. *Circulation*, 1979, 60, 743–752.

Sunagawa, K., Yamada, A., Senda, Y., Kikuchi, Y., Nakamura, M., Shibahara, T., & Nose, Y. Estimation of hydromotive source pressure from ejecting beats of the left ventricle. *IEEE Transactions in Biomedical Engineering*, 1980, 27, 299–305.

Sutherland, E. W., Robison, A., & Butcher, R. W. Some aspects of the biological role of adenosine 3′,5′-monophosphate (cyclic AMP). *Circulation*, 1968, 37, 279–306.

Taylor, P. Cholinergic agonists. In: A. G. Gilman, L. S. Goodman, & A. Gilman (Eds.), *Goodman and Gilman's: The pharmacological basis of therapeutics* (6th ed.). New York: Macmillan, 1980.

Teichholz, L. E., Kreulen, T., Herman, M. V., & Gorlin, R. Problems in echocardiographic volume determinations: Echocardiographic–angiographic correlations in the presence or absence of asynergy. *American Journal of Cardiology*, 1976, 37, 7–11.

Van de Werf, F., Piessens, J., Kesteloot, H., & DeGeest, H. A comparison of systolic time intervals derived from the central aortic pressure and from the external carotid pulse tracing. *Circulation*, 1974, 51, 310–316.

van Zwieten, P. A. The central action of antihypertensive drugs, mediated via central α-receptors. *Journal of Pharmacy and Pharmacology*, 1973, 25, 89–95.

von Euler, U. S., & Folkow, B. The effect of stimulation of autonomic areas in the cerebral cortex upon adrenaline and noradrenaline secretion from the adrenal gland of the cat. *Acta Physiologica Scandinavica*, 1958, 42, 313–320.

Wall, P. D., & Davis, G. D. Three cortical systems affecting autonomic functions. *Journal of Neurophysiology*, 1951, 14, 507–517.

Wall, R. T., & Harker, L. A. The endothelium and thrombosis. *Annual Review of Medicine*, 1980, 31, 361–371.

Wallace, A. G., Skinner, N. S., & Mitchell, J. Hemodynamic determinants of maximum rate of rise of left ventricular pressure. *American Journal of Physiology*, 1963, 205, 30–36.

Wallach, J. H., Ellenberger, H., Schneiderman, N., Liskowsky, D., Hamilton, R., & Gellman, M. Preoptic–anterior hypothalamic area as mediator of bradycardia responses in rabbits. *Neuroscience Abstracts*, 1979, 5, 52.

Warner, H. R., Swan, J. H. C., Connolly, D. C., Tompkins, R. G., & Wood, E. H. Quantitation of beat-to-beat changes in stroke volume from the aortic pulse contour in man. *Journal of Applied Physiology*, 1953, 5, 495.

Watanabe, A. M., & Besch, H. R. Interaction between cyclic adenosine monophosphate and cyclic guanosine monophosphate in ventricular myocardium. *Circulation Research*, 1975, 37, 309–317.

Watanabe, A. M., Jones, L. R., Manalin, A. S., & Besch, H. R. Cardiac autonomic receptors: Recent concepts from radiolabeled ligand-binding studies. *Circulation Research*, 1982, 50, 161–174.

Weaver, L. C. Cardiopulmonary sympathetic afferent influences on renal nerve activity. *American Journal of Physiology*, 1977, 233, H592–H599.

Weiner, N. Norepinephrine, epinephrine, and the sympathomimetic amines. In A. G. Gilman, L. S. Goodman, & A. Gilman (Eds.), *Goodman and Gilman's: The pharmacological basis of therapeutics* (6th ed.). New York: Macmillan, 1980.

Weiss, T., Bo, A. D., Reichek, N., & Engelman, K. Pulse transit time in the analysis of autonomic nervous system effects on the cardiovascular system. *Psychophysiology*, 1980, 17, 202–207.

Weissler, A. M. *Noninvasive cardiology*. New York: Grune & Stratton, 1974.

Weissler, A. M., Stack, R. S., & Sohn, Y. H. The accuracy of systolic time intervals as a measure of left ventricular function. In W. F. List, J. S. Gravenstein, & D. H. Spodick (Eds.), *Systolic time intervals*. New York: Springer-Verlag, 1980.

Whitney, R. J. The measurement of volume changes in human limbs. *Journal of Physiology (London)*, 1953, 121, 1–27.

Wiggers, C. J. Studies on the consecutive phases of the cardiac cycle: I. The duration of the consecutive phases of the cardiac cycle and the criteria for their precise determination. *American Journal of Physiology*, 1921, 56, 415–438. (a)

Wiggers, C. J. Studies of the consecutive phases of the cardiac cycle: II. Laws governing the relative durations of ventricular systole and diastole. *American Journal of Physiology*, 1921, 56, 439–459. (b)

Williams, R. B., Lane, J. D., Kuhn, C. M., Melosh, W., White, A. D., & Schanberg, S. M. Type A behavior and elevated physiological and neuroendocrine responses to cognitive tasks. *Science*, 1982, 218, 483–485.

Winegrad, S. Calcium release from cardiac sarcoplasmic reticulum. *Annual Review of Physiology*, 1982, 44, 451–462.

Wit, A. L., Cranefield, P. F., & Hoffman, B. F. Slow conduction and reentry in the ventricular conducting system. *Circulation Research*, 1972, 30, 11–20.

Yelderman, M., & Ream, A. K. Indirect measurement of mean blood pressure in the anesthetized patient. *Anesthesiology*, 1979, 50, 253–256.

Ziegler, M. G. Postural hypotension. *Annual Review of Medicine*, 1980, 31, 239–245.

Zimmerman, B. G., Gomer, S. K., & Liao, J. C. Action of angiotensin on vascular nerve endings: Facilitation of norepinephrine release. *Federation Proceedings*, 1972, 31, 1344–1350.

Zoob, M., & Smith, K. S. The aetiology of complete heart-block. *British Medical Journal*, 1963, 2, 1149–1154.

Chapter Eight
The Gastrointestinal System

Christopher Davis

INTRODUCTION

Psychologically, we tend to think of the entrance and exit of the gastrointestinal (GI) tract, the mouth and anus, as orifices guarding entry to our insides. Food may be beautiful—until the first chew; saliva is fine inside the mouth, but outside it is spit. Similar distinctions obtain at the other end of the system. Biologically, however, the distinction between inside and out is not nearly so clear. The inner surface of the GI system is lined with epithelial tissue, the same type of cell that forms skin. Since the GI system is continuous, the lumen uninterrupted from mouth to anus, the human form may be viewed as having a hole through it. The inside of the lumen is, in a real biological sense, outside the surface of the body. We are formed, it seems, as a kind of anatomical doughnut. Now the hole is, in fact, a tube of approximately 3 m in length that occupies much of the abdominal cavity. Functionally, the system is specialized for digesting and absorbing nutrients and fluids from the contents of the lumen.

Psychophysiologists would seem to have reason to include GI behavior in their views of human function. The function of all bodily systems is affected by what

has or has not been consumed. A considerable portion of human behavior involves appetite, thirst, food seeking, and food preparation and consumption. Furthermore, except during prolonged fasting, one or another part of the system is working with food and liquids ingested earlier. Indeed, appetitive influences are put near the top of most hierarchies of motives (Hull, 1943; Maslow, 1965). Also, since the GI system is well supplied with afferent nerve fibers, conditions in the system, whether recognizable or not, can be expected to influence the behavior of other systems. What we think, say, and feel may indeed be affected by what we eat and when. Conversely, activity elsewhere in the body may influence GI function.

For all of that, the GI system has been little studied by psychophysiologists. Textbooks devoted to psychophysiology seldom concern themselves with the behavior of the GI tract (e.g., Andreassi, 1980). Venables and Martin (1980) omitted a chapter on recording from the GI system that had been part of their 1967 book. The pages of *Psychophysiology* reflect greater interest in secretory functions of the skin and perturbations within the cardiovascular system than in GI action. Speculations about reasons for these omissions (the kinds of questions psychophysiolo-

Christopher Davis. Department of Psychology, Simon Fraser University, Burnaby, British Columbia, Canada.

gists ask, traditions, the equipment available, etc.) pale before an obvious obstacle: Except at its two ends, the GI tract is buried deep within the body, apparently safe from the probing instruments of noninvasive surface recording. Whether or not transducers swallowed or inserted through the anus are invasive becomes, in light of the earlier point, an interesting question to be considered in a later examination of measurement techniques. For the point at issue, it is enough that experimenters and subjects have treated inserted devices as invasive and have used them sparingly, aside from attempts to use biofeedback as a treatment for GI disorders.

Nevertheless, electrical events of GI origin can be recorded from the surface of the abdomen, using electrodes and amplification techniques common to our discipline. The technique has been little used since its introduction to psychologists (R. C. Davis, Garafolo, & Gault, 1957; R. C. Davis, Garafolo, & Kveim, 1959). Since that time, knowledge of the genesis of electrical potentials within the GI tract and their relation to surface-recorded potentials has been pursued mainly by gastroenterologists and physiologists researching the biology of digestion (Brown, Smallwood, Duthie, & Stoddard, 1975; Kohatsu, 1968, 1970; Nelsen, 1967; Nelsen & Kohatsu, 1968; Smout, Van Der Schee, & Grashuis, 1980). The technique may well provide psychophysiologists with a means for examining GI motility that is analogous to recording the electrocardiogram (ECG), the motor action of the heart recorded from surface electrodes.

Anatomically, the long hollow of the GI system is divided into sections specialized for various parts of the digestive process and separated from one another by muscular sphincters. The mouth is the organ of entry, the intake receptacle. Though they are not usually so considered, the lips form the first muscular sphincter of the system. Following mastication and some initial digestion of carbohydrate, small amounts of ingested substances are passed through the second sphincter (the upper esophageal sphincter) by the swallowing reflex and are reflexly conducted down the esophagus through the lower esophageal sphincter into the stomach. The esophagus is really an active tube connecting mouth and stomach; no digestion or other treatment of its contents is seen. The stomach is a hopper where a quantity of food and liquid is temporarily stored, mixed, and partially digested before being passed in small squirts through the pyloric sphincter into the duodenum, the initial section of the small intestine. In the small bowel, the "chyme" (as the intestinal contents are termed) is mixed with enzymes, which break down fats, proteins, and carbohydrates into the forms in which they are transported from the lumen into the intestinal circulation. All vital digestion and absorption (except water) take place in the small intestine. The remaining chyme is moved through the ileo-cecal sphincter to the large

intestine. Here water is absorbed along with some electrolytes and vitamins. The chyme is moved toward the rectum very slowly (about 5 cm/hr, normally). The chyme, now termed "feces," accumulates in the rectum where it meets the final sphincters in the system: the internal and external anal sphincters, the guardians of excretion.

The journey from mouth to anus (which may take from 1 to 5 days) requires muscular and secretory coordination within and between units along the way. Control and coordination are provided mainly by the autonomic nervous system. Interestingly, motor action at the entrance and exit to the system, where it interacts with the outer environment, is entirely served by the peripheral somatic nervous system. The mouth, the upper half of the esophagus, and the external anal sphincter are supplied by somatic motor neurons. In between, the smooth muscles and glands are controlled by their own rhythmic transmembrane potentials, and by local reflex circuits that are influenced by centrally originating parasympathetic and sympathetic activity. It is notable that the human GI system, deprived of central nervous system (CNS) innervation, is quite capable of coordinated digestion, mobility, secretion, and absorption (Davenport, 1978).

STRUCTURE AND FUNCTION

Anatomically, the GI system is a hollow tube, the inside of which is constituted of several tissue layers, collectively termed the "mucosa." The mucosa includes supportive and secretory cells, as well as a thin smooth muscle layer arranged so that its contractions adjust the secretory layers and perhaps influence the efflux of digestive juices from their origin to the lumen (Schofield, 1968). Outside the mucosa and another layer of soft tissue lie two (or, in the stomach, three) more powerful muscle layers. Fibers in the outer layer, the "longitudinal layer," lie parallel to the lumen. This layer is continuous through the lower tract (esophagus caudally), though in the stomach fibers do not completely surround the hollow. Inside the longitudinal layer, the fibers of the "circular layer" are arranged at or nearly at right angles to the lumen, forming rings around it. In the stomach the third muscle layer, the "oblique layer," incompletely covers the rostral areas, the fundus and body. In the upper half of the esophagus and at the anal sphincter, the fibers of the muscle coats are striate muscle, functionally isolated from one another and from the smooth muscle fibers with which they are intermixed. They are dependent for their action on efferent neural activity originating in the CNS.

The smooth muscle fibers are organized in bundles. Unlike striate cells, the fibers within a bundle are connected through small gap junctions that permit cells of a unit to influence one another. Individual cells do not have motor end plates, and some cells do not receive direct neural input.

Some of the smooth muscles, particularly those in the stomach, small intestine, and colon, exhibit a periodic variation in transmembrane electrical potential. This variation, termed "electrical control activity" (ECA), is a property of the cells themselves. Local and CNS influences may affect the frequency of the rhythm and the size of the variation. These variations reflect alternate depolarizations and hyperpolarizations of the cells.

ECA is generated in bundles of cells in the longitudinal layer, but spreads to underlying bundles in the circular layer electrotonically and over smooth muscle fibers that reach into the circular layer. A group of fibers oscillating in this way may influence adjacent groups, depending on the phase of their ECA. Such a system of interdependent cell groups has been described as "linked oscillators" (Nelsen, 1971). In a system of oscillators, the one with the highest frequency will control the phase of other oscillators within a range frequency. Oscillators with very different frequencies will not be controlled, since they will be out of phase with the driver. In the stomach, ECA originates high on the greater curvature, from whence it successively drives bundles in the caudal direction at a frequency of about 3.0 cm/min. The ECA proceeds at about 1 cm/sec over the body, faster near the antrum. It is this "sweep" of control activity that results in peristalsis (Nelsen, 1971).

When a depolarization reaches a threshold value, an action potential is produced that spreads over the entire surface of the cell, and, through the gap junctions, to the other cells of the bundle. The entire bundle then contracts. Thus, contraction of smooth muscle of the gut is controlled by ECA and preceded by electrical response activity (ERA). This electrical activity may include one or more spikes superimposed on the ECA, as well as a second slow potential. Both ECA and the combined ECA and ERA can be recorded from the abdominal surface over the stomach, as well as from electrodes aspirated or surgically affixed to the serosal wall (Nelsen, 1968; Smout et al., 1980). Surface records of stomach ECA and ERA are termed "electrogastrograms" (EGGs) and are discussed in detail below.

The innervation of the smooth muscles of the tract is unique and invites functional comparison to the action of other organ systems. The tract has, in effect, its own nervous system. Between the muscle layers there are plexuses, groups of cell bodies, receiving input from chemoreceptors and mechanoreceptors within the system and delivering motor impulses to muscular and glandular cells of the tract (Davenport, 1978). The organization of this intrinsic nervous system coordinates digestive and motile functions of the tract so well, and so completely, that CNS influences are not required for reasonable GI function:

> [T]he most important point to understand about the function of these structures is that they are provided with a nervous system of their own which is capable of executing the functions of the gut without any extrinsic innervation whatever. The extrinsic innervation this nervous system receives from the sympathetic and parasympathetic nerves modulates but does not command its activity. (Davenport, 1978, p. 19)

The spinal cord provides a similar coordination of the somatic musculature, where muscle afferents influence coordinated muscle action, though its normal function is dependent on descending CNS input. Nevertheless, the smooth muscle of the gut is supplied with neural input from the CNS. This arrives as autonomic outflow, preganglionic parasympathetic fibers traveling via the vagus nerve, and postganglionic and some preganglionic sympathetic fibers traveling along blood vessels (Schofield, 1968). The parasympathetic neurons end on ganglion cells within the intrinsic plexuses. They are mainly cholinergic and excitatory, though relaxation of sphincters and the relaxation of the body of the stomach are partially parasympathetically controlled. However, it has been estimated that 80% of vagal fibers are visceral afferents, not preganglionic outflow to the muscles and glands of the tract (Davenport, 1978). There are neither motor end plates nor motor units within the smooth muscles. Rather, efferent fibers originating in the plexuses lie along and among muscle fibers of the longitudinal muscle layer. Transmitter substance (usually acetylcholine) is released along the terminal portions of the neuron and diffuses to the muscle cells, causing the transmembrane potential to be altered (decreased in the case of excitation and increased in inhibition). The threshold of bundles of cells in the circular layer is influenced by electrotonic spread from the longitudinal layer.

Sympathetic innervation is preganglionic to the outlying ganglia of the gut, the celiac ganglia, the superior mesenteric ganglia, and the superior and inferior hypogastric ganglia. Postganglionic fibers terminate on ganglion cells of one or another of the enteric plexuses, or at smooth muscle cells of the vascular blood vessels. Within the enteric nervous system, the sympathetic effect is usually inhibitory, though stimulation of sympathetic efferents excites muscles of the sphincters. Additionally, sympathetic neurons reach some secretory cells.

The striated muscles of the mouth, pharynx, and upper esophagus are arranged in the usual somatic organization of motor units, each muscle cell served by a branch of a somatic motor neuron. Afferents from these muscles reach the cord and brain stem, where, in addition to reflex connections, they diverge to other CNS areas.

INTEGRATED ACTION IN DIGESTION

In integrated action, the GI system appears completely specialized for digestion. It is physically well hidden from the vagaries of the external environment; it is protected at its entrance and exit by sphincters under voluntary control; between these two points, it is controlled by a local nervous network that is more dependent on the location, size, and constitution of its luminal contents than on conditions elsewhere in the body. When the system is not actively involved in digestion, it is mostly quiet, or is slowly acting (the colon) on the remains of prior meals. Aroused by a meal, it is both slow to respond and slow in its action; smooth muscle does not twitch as does striate muscle. Nevertheless, secretory and motile activity of the tract is influenced by reflexes involving the extrinsic neural fibers with origins in the CNS. By this route, and by circulating epinephrine and norepinephrine, extrasystemic conditions may affect the activity of the GI system.

THE STOMACH, THE INTESTINES, AND THE ELECTROGASTROGRAM

History

In 1922 Alvarez reported the first electrogastrograms (EGGs), as he termed them—smoked-drum kymographs of electrical variations recorded from a herniated portion of the abdominal surface of a single subject. The source of the signals and their relationship to stomach motility were not in doubt, since movements of the stomach could be seen under the hernia and related to the kymograph tracings. The technique was introduced to psychophysiologists in 1957 by R. C. Davis, Garafolo, and Gault. Recording from electrodes over abdominal quadrants, they reported amplitude and frequency variations related to external stimulation, as well as to physical parameters (e.g., body position). That some of the recorded variations were associated with gastrointestinal activity was shown by simultaneously recording the EGG and pressure variations exerted on an ingested balloon. The correlations were apparent, not calculated. Moreover, some surface-recorded potential variations occurred in the absence of recordable stomach pressure changes. Techniques for scoring the polygraph records were arbitrary, reflecting the authors' aim of exploring the potentials rather than focusing on a particular waveform or rhythm (R. C. Davis et al., 1957). However, an "atypical case" was reported in which regular waves (3/min) were found in a subject who had fasted for at least 8 hours (R. C. Davis et al., 1959). Despite attempts to relate surface records to electrical and secretory GI events, the early psychophysiological research was premature, in the sense that it was not certain what the researchers were looking for. The electrical behavior of visceral sources was not well understood in the 1950s and early 1960s, when most of the psychophysiological surface recording was attempted.

Current Status

Rhythmic waves of depolarization of gastric smooth muscle should be observable from surface electrodes. Successive depolarization and repolarization of bands of smooth muscle linked as already described would produce a moving dipole involving extracellular current flow (Smout et al., 1980). This source is analogous to the wave of depolarization that sweeps around the heart preceding ventricular contraction. Correspondence of potential variations from the abdominal surface to those taken directly from stomach tissue (the mucosa and serosa) has been repeatedly found. Nelsen and Kohatsu (1968) reported that ECA was continually present in both sersosal and surface leads of humans. Brown et al. (1975) found a significant 3/min component in frequency analysis of 88% of their samples of surface records in both fasted and fed subjects. Smout et al. (1980) reported ECA activity in the surface records of over 91% of the 17/min blocks of EGG data from dogs. The fundamental frequency of the surface record was the same as that of ECA recorded from electrodes attached to the serosal musculature and so "proved the gastric origin of the electrogastrogram" (Smout et al., 1980, p. 181).

The finding that ECA is continually present in surface records from fasted and postprandial subjects both expands the possibilities of surface recording and complicates its interpretation. Both ECA and ERA contribute to the EGG (Nelsen & Kohatsu, 1968; Smout et al., 1980). Brown et al. (1975) found that, following a meal, the surface record was greatly increased in amplitude (by 150%), but they attributed the increase to the increased proximity of the stomach muscle to the surface electrode. Since ERA, indicative of gastric motility, is time-locked to ECA, the inability to distinguish the two electrical events means that one cannot know when stomach contractions are present. Smout et al. (1980) found that both ECA and ERA contributed to the EGG, but that the amplitude of the surface record was greater during ERA than during ECA alone. This difference occurred when the stomach was empty, suggesting that the increased amplitude of EGG during contraction was not an artifact of stomach distention. However, Smout et al. (1980) were unable to find an amplitude criterion for the EGG that reliably distinguished between ECA and ERA. The Smout *et al.* analysis was based on the assumption that at the surface of the abdomen both ECA and ERA are sinusoidal; they generated a formal model to predict its character.

Figure 8-1 is the untreated EGG from two sites of the abdomen of a human subject before (Figure 8-1A) and after (Figure 8-1B) a meal (C. Davis, 1981). In the fasted record, a 3/min rhythm is clearly discernible in the lower trace (electrode over the body of the stomach). Though the form of the waves from the body is generally sinusoidal, postprandial ECA plus ERA waves are not (Figure 8-1B). Rather, each major voltage change in the 3/min range includes a fast-changing slope, a plateau, and a ramp of varying steepness, depending on the site of the electrode. The postprandial wave is about 150% of the fasting wave (ECA, presumably), as reported by Smout *et al.* (1980). Careful examination of the waveforms in addition to their amplitude should permit ECA to be distinguished from contractile activity from surface electrodes.

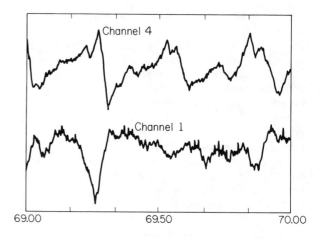

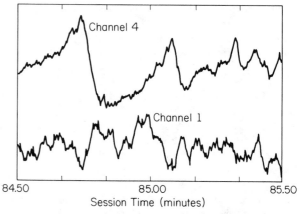

Figure 8-2. Continuous EGGs from abdominal surface over the body of the stomach (Channel 1) and the antrum (Channel 4); same subject as in Figure 8-1. (A) 30 min postprandial; (B) 45 min postprandial. (From Variations in pre- and post-prandial human surface electrogastrograms, by C. Davis. Unpublished manuscript, 1981. Used by permission.)

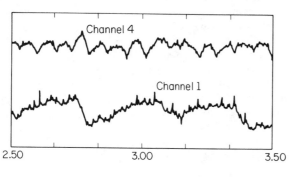

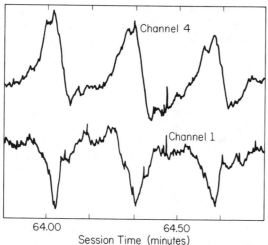

Figure 8-1. Continuous EGGs from abdominal skin over the body of the stomach (Channel 1) and the antrum (Channel 4). (A) Subject fasted for 18 hours; (B) 25 minutes postprandial. (From Variations in pre- and post-prandial human surface electrogastrograms, by C. Davis. Unpublished manuscript, 1981. Used by permission.)

Moreover, recording from multiple sites may facilitate the distinction of ECA from ECA and ERA together. The fasted stomach (Figure 8-1A) reveals ECA from over the body (where it probably originates; see Nelsen, 1971) but not from an electrode over the antrum (the upper trace in Figure 8-1A). The higher rate of about 13/min is probably of duodenal origin (Smout *et al.*, 1980). Postprandially, both sites exhibit a large-amplitude 3/min rhythm, often with reversed polarity (Figure 8-1B). The polarity reversal is consistent with the presence of a dipole moving away from one site and toward the other, as would be the case if the dipole represented ECA originating caudal to the body (Figure 8-1B, lower trace) and successively depolarizing smooth muscle bands in the direction of the antral electrode (Figure 8-1B, upper trace). The EGGs from the two sites are more than different views of the same activity. In both the resting state (Figure 8-1A) and 30 and 45 min following a meal (Figures 8-2A and 8-2B, respectively; recordings taken from the same subject and the same electrode sites), independence of the traces is clear. In the fasting record (Figure 8-1A), the ECA is prevalent in the electrode over the body but not from the electrode over the antrum. Postprandially (Figure 8-2), independence and correlation of records from the two sites is clear but not presently interpretable.

Whatever the relationship of ECA, ERA, and the surface record, the EGG varies in rate from 2.3 to 3.4/min (Kohatsu, 1970). The often-cited 3/min rhythm has been found to be characteristic of the fasting record (actually 2.9/min). Following a meal, there is an immediate drop averaging 8%, followed by an increase to above resting rate within half an hour and a gradual return to the resting rate. The sorts of influences on gastric activity looked for by earlier researchers (R. C. Davis *et al.*, 1957, 1959; Walker & Sandman, 1977) might be found in variations of the rate of ECA-ERA. Indeed, given the omnipresence of the control rhythm and its observability from surface electrodes, it is appropriate to consider the stomach rate in the same way as heart and respiratory rates are viewed. Extrasystemic events do influence gastric activity (e.g., Steinbach & Code, 1980), so it would not be surprising to discover that food-related stimuli and unrelated psychological conditions result in acute or chronic alterations in stomach rate. The linkage between ECA and ERA may also be affected and discernible (as described above).

TECHNIQUES FOR RECORDING FROM THE GI SYSTEM (THE EGG)

Seen from the abdominal surface, the EGG is a fairly large potential (up to 1 mV) and therefore does not require great amplification. However, the voltage changes are sufficiently slow that direct current (DC) or near-DC treatment is required. Additionally, some filtering of large higher-frequency signals from the heart and from the striate muscles of the abdomen is necessary. There are very slow potential variations (some around .3/min) as well, some of them larger than the 3/min gastric activity. While the genesis of these very slow potentials is unknown, they may arise from ECA and ERA in the transverse colon, which crosses the gut just under the stomach, or possibly from secretory or very slow stomach potentials. Interesting, and unexplored in their own right, these variations introduce a range sensitivity problem for DC recording of gastric ECA-ERA. Some form of resetting or balancing may be required.[1]

1. Locally designed (H. Gabert, P. Eng) resetting DC amplifiers used in our laboratory may be reset to zero either manually or automatically under computer (Nova 2) when the EGG nears control system limits.

There are as yet no standard electrode locations for the EGG, as befits the rudimentary knowledge of its genesis. However, sites to the left of and above the navel (but below the rib) are over the body of the stomach, while those along the midline of the body just above the navel and the right of it are closer to antral stomach. Most often, surface records are monopolar (e.g., referred to an ankle lead), though bipolar arrangements may be used.

REFERENCES

Alvarez, W. C. The electrogastrogram and what it shows. *Journal of the American Medical Association*, 1922, *79*, 1281–1284.

Andreassi, J. L. *Psychophysiology: Human behavior and physiological response*. New York: Oxford University Press, 1980.

Brown, B. H., Smallwood, R. H., Duthie, H. L., & Stoddard, C. J. Intestinal smooth muscle electrical potentials recorded from surface electrodes. *Medical Biological Engineering*, 1975, *13*, 97–103.

Davenport, W. W. *A digest of digestion*. Chicago: Year Book Medical Publishers, 1978.

Davis, C. M. Variations in pre- and post-prandial human surface electrogastrograms. Unpublished manuscript, 1981.

Davis, R. C., Garafolo, L., & Gault, F. P. An exploration of abdominal potentials. *Journal of Comparative and Physiological Psychology*, 1957, *50*, 519–523.

Davis, R. C., Garafolo, L., & Kveim, K. Conditions associated with gastrointestinal activity. *Journal of Comparative and Physiological Psychology*, 1959, *52*, 466–474.

Hull, C. L. *Principles of behavior*. New York: Appleton-Century-Crofts, 1943.

Kohatsu, S. A study of the human electrogastrogram using cutaneous electrodes. *Japanese Journal of Smooth Muscle Research*, 1968, *4*, 148–150.

Kohatsu, S. Human electrogastrography. *Japanese Journal of Smooth Muscle Research*, 1970, *6*, 129–132.

Maslow, A. H. A theory of human motivation. *Psychological Review*, 1943, *50*, 370–396.

Nelsen, T. S. Use of phaselock techniques for retrieval of the electrogastrogram from cutaneous and swallowed electrodes. In *Digest of the Seventh International Conference on Medical Electronics and Biological Engineering*. Stockholm: 1967.

Nelsen, T. S. A theory of integrated gastrointestinal motor activity based on the chain oscillator model. *American Journal of Digestive Diseases*, 1971, *16*, 543–547.

Nelsen, T. S., & Kohatsu, S. Clinical electrogastrography and its relationship to gastric surgery. *American Journal of Surgery*, 1968, *116*, 215–222.

Schofield, G. C. Anatomy of muscular and neural tissues in the alimentary canal. In C. F. Code (Ed.), *Handbook of physiology* (Section 6, *Alimentary Canal*, Vol. 4, *Motility*). Washington, D.C.: American Physiological Society, 1968.

Smout, A. J., Van Der Schee, E. J., & Grashuis, J. L. What is measured in electrogastrography? *Digestive Disease and Science*, 1980, *25*, 179–187.

Steinbach, J. H., & Code, C. F. Increase in the period of the interdigestive myoelectric complex with anticipation of feeding. In J. Christensen (Ed.), *Gastrointestinal motility*. New York: Raven Press, 1980.

Venables, P. H., & Martin, I. (Eds.). *Techniques in psychophysiology*. New York: Wiley, 1980.

Walker, B. E., & Sandman, C. Physiological response patterns in ulcer patients: Phasic and tonic components of the electrogastrogram. *Psychophysiology*, 1977, *14*(4), 393–400.

Chapter Nine

The Reproductive and Adrenal Systems

C. Sue Carter

INTRODUCTION

Fundamental to psychophysiology is the integration of behavioral and physiological processes. Electrochemical events coordinate these functions by regulating intra- and interorganismic phenomena at many levels. The most compelling evidence for specific endocrine–behavioral interactions is available for the reproductive glands (ovaries or testes) and the adrenal glands. These organs and their regulatory systems are capable of coordinating environmental factors (e.g., resource availability, photoperiod, social influences, stress, etc.) with appropriate biobehavioral events (e.g., egg or sperm production, sexual and parental behaviors, energy mobilization, etc.).

The purposes of this chapter are (1) to describe basic concepts in endocrine–behavioral interactions; (2) to describe the essential components of the reproductive and adrenal systems, the endocrine organs, the neural–pituitary regulatory systems, and other target organs, including neural sites influenced by the hormones of these systems; and (3) to present a brief survey of some behavioral functions attributed to these endocrine systems. Emphasis is directed to hypotheses regarding human behavior where feasible. In

addition, a few applications of psychophysiological techniques to behavioral–endocrine questions are discussed in the context of the reproductive system. The chapters by Geer, O'Donohue, and Schorman (Chapter 19) and by Levine (Chapter 16) in Part II of this volume should be consulted for additional information on the functions of the reproductive and adrenal systems. The references used in this chapter also provide more detailed background for the interested reader.

BASIC CONCEPTS

The history of experimental endocrinology is often said to have begun with a classic study of the importance of the testes in the maintenance of male reproductive characteristics. In 1849, A. A. Berthold demonstrated that transplanted testes were capable of supporting both male sexual behavior and comb size in previously castrated male chickens. The invention of the hypodermic needle followed, and in 1889 a prominent physiologist, Brown-Sequard, reported a remarkable reversal of the effects of aging after self-

C. Sue Carter. Department of Zoology, University of Maryland, College Park, Maryland.

injection with aqueous extracts from dog or guinea pig testes: ". . . a radical change took place in me . . . I had regained at least all the strength I possessed a good many years ago" (p. 106). Although most of his claims were not replicated by subsequent investigation, the reports by Brown-Sequard nonetheless initiated the modern era of experimental endocrinology. (A booming business in "monkey glands," marketed for their rejuvenating and aphrodisiac powers, also arose from the response to Brown-Sequard's claims, in spite of the fact that natural forms of testicular hormones are not water-soluble and would have no hormonal actions if ingested.)

Endocrinology was formally born in 1905. The work of Bayliss and Starling (1902–1905) offered clear evidence for the presence of biochemical regulators, "hormones" (from the Greek *hormon*, to arouse or excite), produced in one organ and capable of being carried by the bloodstream to their site of action in a distant target organ. These investigators also developed the classical paradigms that continue to be used in the analysis of endocrine functions (Beach, 1981; Carter, 1974; Turner & Bagnara, 1971).

There are a number of other classes of biochemical agents with physiological action that are not considered to be hormones. Although distinctions among these classifications have become less marked as understanding of the systems has improved, hormones are characterized by the fact that they must be transported (usually through the circulation) to another tissue in order to act. Neurotransmitters, in contrast, are biochemical substances that need only move across a neuronal synapse or neuromuscular junction in order to be effective. A number of substances have been discovered that satisfy both the criteria for neurotransmitters and hormones. In general, however, hormones act slowly and have broad-ranging effects. They may cordinate or regulate a variety of diverse activities. Neurotransmitters tend to act more locally and to influence discrete physiological functions.

Both hormones and neurotransmitters function by acting on receptors. Typically, a "receptor" is believed to be a molecule essential for the transport and/or mediation of hormonal or neurotransmitter effects. For hormones, at least two types of receptor functions have been identified, which may be categorized according to the chemical structures of the hormones involved.

Steroid hormones (produced by the gonads and adrenal cortex) pass through cell membranes and form an intracellular hormone–receptor complex. This hormone–receptor complex is responsible for the cellular effects of steroids, which are believed to be directly involved in such processes as protein synthesis. New proteins formed under the influence of steroids may have relatively slow but long-lasting physiological effects.

Hormones that are derived from amino acids, including polypeptides and proteins (e.g., the products of the adrenal medulla or pituitary gland), interact with cell surface receptors and thus indirectly trigger cellular events leading to the production of a so-called "second messenger" (e.g., cyclic adenosine monophosphate [cAMP]). In turn, cAMP can influence cellular metabolism. The physiological actions of hormones derived from amino acids tend to be more rapid and less long-lasting than those observed for steroids.

Hormone levels and hormone actions are regulated by feedback mechanisms, thus forming homeostatic systems. Feedback may either be negative (resulting in declines in production) or positive (yielding increased synthesis and/or release and increases in hormone levels). Some hormones regulate their own production through direct feedback mechanisms, while others rely on a chain of hormonal events.

Among the factors that influence hormone levels are the rates of synthesis, release, and metabolism. An active hormone may be directly secreted by an endocrine organ; alternatively, a precursor or "prohormone" may be released, which is then converted into a functional form in another tissue, such as adipose tissue or the liver, or at the target organ. (There is, for example, evidence that the sex steroid testosterone can be converted into an estrogen in brain tissue and elsewhere in the body.)

The function of a given hormone also can be influenced by the presence or absence of hormone-binding proteins (globulins or albumin). For example, steroid hormone availability may vary according to whether a hormone is "free," tightly "bound" to binding globulins, or more loosely bound to albumin. Loosely bound or free hormones are believed to be those most readily available to initiate physiological changes.

To demonstrate that a given organ has endocrine functions, it is necessary to document changes following the removal of that organ. In addition, viable transplants ought to reinstate the physiological conditions seen before organ removal. Organ extracts (in appropriate solvents) should substitute for the missing organ. At present, many hormones have been successfully extracted, identified biochemically, and synthesized. Thus it is possible to inject, and study the effects of, specific chemicals following organ removal.

THE CENTRAL NERVOUS SYSTEM AND THE PITUITARY

It has become obvious in the last two decades that the brain plays a pivotal role in the regulation and integration of virtually all endocrine events (reviewed in Frohman, 1980; Ganong, 1979). Central nervous system (CNS) tissues contain receptors for each of the hormones to be discussed in this chapter. In some cases, agents manufactured in a so-called "endocrine organ," such as the adrenal gland, may be identical to those produced in the brain. For example, norepinephrine is produced by the CNS and by the adrenal medulla. The pituitary gland (also known as the "hypophysis") and peripheral target organs and tissues of the various endocrine systems are under the hormonal influence of neuroendocrine factors from the hypothalamus and limbic system of the brain. The hypothalamus and limbic system, in turn, provide connections between external sensory events (such as light cycles, temperature, stressors, and behavioral stimuli from other organisms) and internal regulatory adjustments (including endocrine secretions).

The secretions of the anterior pituitary gland are controlled by releasing or inhibiting hormones (sometimes called "factors"), which reach the anterior pituitary through a direct vascular link, known as the portal vessels. Hypothalamic hormones are secreted into the portal vessels, are carried to the anterior pituitary, and function there to inhibit or stimulate the release and synthesis of anterior pituitary hormones.

Among the hormones secreted by the anterior pituitary gland are adrenocorticotropic hormone (corticotropin, or ACTH), prolactin (luteotropic hormone), follicle-stimulating hormone (FSH), and luteinizing hormone (LH, also known as interstitial-cell-stimulating hormone or ICSH). (FSH and LH are known collectively as "gonadotropins.")

Each of these pituitary hormones is under the regulation of hypothalamic hormones, of which the best known are corticotropin-releasing hormone (CRH), dopamine (believed to be a prolactin-inhibiting factor), and gonadotropin-releasing hormone (GnRH, also known as luteinizing-hormone-releasing hormone or LHRH). Debate exists at present regarding the existence of separate releasing hormones that may be involved in the control of LH and FSH, but GnRH is capable of stimulating the release of both LH and FSH.

The anterior pituitary and posterior pituitary are functionally very different organs. Embryologically, the anterior pituitary arises from tissue in the roof of the mouth and is not neural tissue. The posterior pituitary, in contrast, is true neural tissue and can properly be considered as an extension of the brain.

The posterior pituitary hormones are manufactured in the brain, carried to the posterior pituitary through long neuronal processes (rather than through the bloodstream), and at the posterior pituitary are liberated into the general circulation. Oxytocin and vasopressin are posterior pituitary hormones with roles in reproduction and fluid regulation.

Anterior pituitary hormones tend to be large molecules (proteins), which are relatively resistant to breakdown on their journey through the circulatory system to their sites of action. Hormones produced in neural tissues, including the hypothalamus and posterior pituitary, tend to share biochemical properties with neurotransmitters and are often small molecules (polypeptides).

THE REPRODUCTIVE SYSTEM

The endocrine organs responsible for reproductive functions ("gonads") include the testes in the male and ovaries in the female. Both males and females are capable of manufacturing identical steroid hormones; however, the concentrations and the patterning of hormone secretions during the mammalian life cycle differ between the sexes and thus account for many of the recognized differences in genital anatomy and reproductive physiology. Sex steroids can influence almost every tissue in the body, although steroid hormone receptors seem to be concentrated in the genitalia, the internal reproductive organs, the secondary sex tissues, the pituitary gland, and the limbic hypothalamic areas of the brain (McEwen, 1981).

Male Hormone and Sperm Production

Male sex steroids are synthesized in the Leydig cells of the testes. The primary testicular androgen is testosterone. The testes may also secrete a variety of other androgens (including dihydrotestosterone) and estrogens (estradiol or estrone).

The biosynthesis of testosterone is regulated by pituitary LH acting on Leydig cell membrane receptors. These in turn influence the production of cAMP, protein kinase, and the subsequent conversion of steroid precursors into androgens. Androgens alternately suppress and then increase LH release, creating relatively constant blood levels of androgen in normal adult males. Androgens are essential to the development and maintenance of a masculine genital anatomy, sperm production (Bardin & Catterall, 1981; Wilson, George, & Griffin, 1981), and male sexual behavior (Davidson, Camargo, & Smith, 1979).

Estrogen production in males can occur through both testicular secretion and the extratesticular conversion of testosterone into estrogen (a biochemical process known as "aromatization"). The functional significance of estrogen in the male human remains incompletely known. However, animal research suggests that estrogens may play a critical role in the activation of male sexual behavior (McEwen, 1981).

FSH secretion in males is believed to be under the inhibitory control of a nonsteroidal testicular factor (or factors) described as "inhibin." Inhibin may also play a minor role in the regulation of LH production (Bardin, 1980).

An additional pituitary hormone, prolactin, has

been implicated in male reproduction. The role of prolactin is complex and includes the ability to potentiate the effects of LH on Leydig cells. Recent clinical evidence suggests that hyperprolactin secretion is associated with reproductive dysfunction and impotence (Kirby, Kotchen, & Rees, 1979).

A role has been suggested for dopamine as a prolactin-inhibiting factor. Dopamine (a catecholamine), in turn, is apparently a psychoactive neurotransmitter, which has been implicated in the activation of male sexual behavior (reviewed in Carter & Davis, 1976). Because of the intimate interaction of dopamine and prolactin, it has not yet been possible to determine whether prolactin has direct behavioral effects, although this possibility remains open. Dopamine agonists, including bromoergocryptine, can be used to reverse hyperprolactinemia, and both testicular infertility and sexual dysfunction are reportedly reversed by these treatments. In the presence of high prolactin levels, testosterone treatments are not effective in restoring sexual function (Tolis, 1980).

Male Genital Anatomy and Physiology

Erection

The capacity to elicit penile tumescence is under psychogenic (cognitive) and reflexogenic (tactile) control. Cognitively induced erections are mediated in part by spinal nerves from the thoraco-lumbar area of the spinal cord. Reflexive erections depend on neural input into the sacral spinal cord (S_2, S_3, S_4). Light touch and friction are transmitted through the pudendal nerve, while pressure and tension in the penis and pelvic organs are transmitted along the pelvic splanchnic nerve (Bancroft, 1980; Tarabulcy, 1972).

It is usually assumed that psychogenic erections depend on an intact spinal cord (Verkuyl, 1977). However, this view is complicated by reports that psychogenic erections can occur after complete upper motor neuron lesions (Higgins, 1979).

A successful erection depends on the interaction of autonomic (sympathetic and parasympathetic) fibers leading to penile vasocongestion. During sexual stimulation, arterial blood flow increases. Additional mechanisms responsible for erection presumably depend on sphincters and valvules that prevent venous return (Tordjman, Thierre, & Michel, 1980). Parasympathetic dominance and sympathetic inhibition are thought to regulate erection. However, as discussed by Bancroft (1980), it is likely that both active parasympathetic (arteriolar dilatation) and sympathetic (venous valve constriction) influences are necessary for a normal erection.

Reflexive erections are believed to be under the inhibitory control of the CNS (Hart, 1978). In primates, electrical stimulation of parts of the limbic system (including areas of hippocampus, mammillary bodies, and thalamus), probably traveling through the medial forebrain bundle and periventricular system (and eventually the spinal cord), may elicit penile erection (MacLean & Ploog, 1962).

Nocturnal erections in humans are often correlated with rapid eye movement (REM) sleep episodes. Plethysmographic measurement of nocturnal erections has been used to differentially diagnose cases of organogenic or reflexive, as opposed to psychogenic, impotence (Karacan, Salis, Ware, Dervant, Williams, Scott, Attia, & Beutler, 1978).

Ejaculation

The ejaculatory reflex is spinally mediated and can be divided into emission, in which semen enters the urethra, and ejaculation, during which semen is released (Tarabulcy, 1972). Emission depends on the sympathetic nervous system and the integrity of the upper thoraco-lumbar spinal cord and involves contraction of the vas deferens and seminal vesicles. The ejaculatory reflex is integrated in the sacral spinal cord and is dependent on rhythmic contractions of the bulbocavernosa muscle and on the integrity of sacral and pudendal nerves.

Orgasm

The subjective component of male orgasm is highly variable (Kinsey, Pomeroy, & Martin, 1948). Physiological changes during sexual arousal and orgasm have been described by Masters and Johnson (1966). Dramatic increases in heart rate and blood pressure routinely accompany orgasm. It has been shown that blocking the increase in blood pressure does not prevent orgasm (Fox, 1970). A relatively long postorgasmic refractory period is common, but not inevitable, in males (Kinsey et al., 1948) and is not clearly related to the subjective experience of orgasm.

The destruction of one specific brain region, the preoptic area, usually eliminates male sexual behavior (Hart, 1978). The effect of preoptic area lesions has been replicated in a variety of laboratory animals, including the rhesus monkey (Slimp, Hart, & Goy, 1978). In monkeys, although sexual interest was apparently disturbed, masturbation continued following preoptic area lesions, indicating that this area is not essential for the reflexive components of erection and ejaculation.

The hypothesis that male sexual behavior is normally under inhibitory neural control has been supported by studies in which apparent increases or facilitations followed lesions. For example, following temporal lobe lesions, male monkeys may show high levels of mounting behavior, directed in some cases toward inappropriate objects. This phenomenon, termed the "Kluver–Bucy syndrome," may be related to the apparent "hypersexuality" that has been reported in epileptic patients following temporal lobe surgery (Blumer, 1970). However, there are also indications from animal research that temporal lobe lesions may interfere with the ability to discriminate appropriate objects for sexual interactions. Additional research is needed to describe the physiology of both sexual motivation and sexual performance more precisely.

Female Reproductive Function

The ovaries are responsible for production of eggs (ova) and also for the secretion of steroid hormones. Ovarian function is regulated by the gonadotropins, FSH and LH, and may be influenced by prolactin (Yen, 1980). The physiologically active steroids secreted by the ovary include the estrogens and progestins. The primary estrogens are estradiol, estrone, and estriol. Progesterone and 17-OH progesterone are classified as progestagens.

The Menstrual Cycle

The female primate reproductive cycle (see Figure 9-1) is characterized by the periodic loss of the inner (endometrial) lining of the uterus (i.e., menstruation). The average length of the menstrual cycle is 28–29 days, although variations between 20 and 40 days may not be unusual. The first day of menstrual bleeding is considered day 1 of the cycle. In a 28-day cycle, ovulation occurs on approximately day 14. The portion of the cycle between the end of menstrual bleeding and ovulation is termed the "follicular phase." The follicular phase is characterized by increasing levels of estrogen, released from the ovarian follicle. At about the time of ovulation, progesterone levels increase, and the follicle from which an ovum has been expelled is transformed into the corpus luteum. The postovulatory portion of the cycle, preceding menstruation, is termed the "luteal phase" and is characterized initially by high levels of progesterone (primarily secreted by the corpus luteum) and estrogens. Estrogens and progestagens are necessary for the maintenance of the endometrial (uterine) lining, and menstrual bleeding occurs when the levels of these hormones decline.

The precise timing of ovulation is regulated by a surge of LH, which is believed to be preceded by a pulse of hypothalamic GnRH. Steroid hormones, in turn, influence the release of both GnRH and LH. Oral contraceptives, composed of synthetic steroids, block ovulation primarily through inhibitory effects in the hypothalamo-pituitary system. In addition, it is well known that the timing of ovulation, like the length of a given cycle, may be quite variable (creating problems for the rhythm method of contraception).

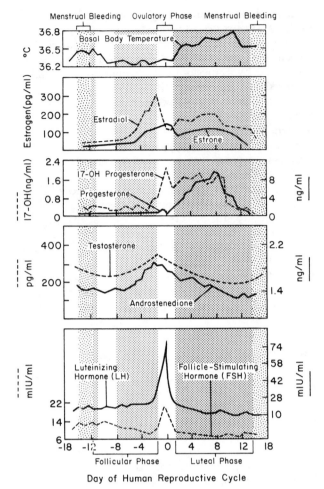

Figure 9-1. Hormonal fluctuations in the female human reproductive cycle. Adapted from Yen (1980) with permission.

High levels of stress, for example, may induce or inhibit ovulation, presumably acting through effects on the hypothalamo-pituitary axis.

Female Genital Anatomy and Physiology

In the female, the developmental homologue of the male penis is the clitoris. The detailed anatomy of the clitoris is described elsewhere (Lowry & Lowry, 1976). Like the penis, the clitoris is a richly innervated, erectile organ. Erection in this tissue also depends on the autonomic control of blood flow.

It has been shown in animal research that the clitoris (and presumably the penis as well) has sensory input that varies according to whether the organ is engorged or not. During tumescence, genital tactile corpuscles convey sensations that are usually labeled with sexual significance, and sensitivity may be altered. In the nonaroused state, the clitoris has a "general cutaneous sensibility that differs little from that of the surrounding skin areas, except perhaps a distinctly richer bed of end-organs" (Campbell, 1976, p. 60).

The vascular control of clitoral erection has been described by Danesino and Martella (1976). Major differences from penile function have not been described, although this literature is very limited (reviewed in Lowry & Lowry, 1976).

The vagina is a well-vascularized muscular tube with a mucous membrane lining. During the early part of sexual arousal, vaginal lubrication occurs, due to transudation or "sweating" of fluids from the vaginal walls (Masters & Johnson, 1966). Production of this vaginal fluid may be estrogen-dependent (Perl, Milles, & Shimozato, 1959). The cervix also produces a mucous discharge, which may be used in some women to monitor ovulation (Billings, Billings, Brown, & Burger, 1972).

During sexual stimulation the labia and vaginal walls, like the clitoris, undergo vasocongestion. This response is presumably similar to erection in the male and involves a net inflow of arterial blood with a subsequent reduction in venous return, leading to engorgement.

The nature of female orgasm and optimal methods for its elicitation have long been a subject of controversy (Fisher, 1973; Lowry & Lowry, 1976; LoPiccolo & LoPiccolo, 1978; Masters & Johnson, 1966).

Psychophysiological Measurements

Vaginal vasocongestive responses have been monitored using photoplethysmography (see Geer *et al.*, Chapter 19, this volume). The direct current (DC) signal from the vaginal photoplethysmograph has been interpreted as reflecting blood pooling, and the amplitude of the alternating current (AC) signal has been used as a measure of the vaginal pressure pulse.

The effects of exposure to erotic stimuli on regional vaginal blood flow are usually rapid (within seconds) and large (involving a doubling or more of pulse amplitude) and have tended to occur in most young women. However, vaginal pulse amplitude may be attenuated in women considered to be sexually dysfunctional (Wincze, Hoon, & Hoon, 1976).

In an early study, Palti and Bercovici (1967) reported that vaginal pulse amplitude showed menstrual cycle variations, with a periovulatory peak that paralleled the presumed cyclic release of estrogen. The same study reported that noncycling (postmenopausal or amenorrheic) women had dramatically attenuated vaginal pulse amplitudes. A more recent study by Schreiner-Engel, Schiavi, Smith, and White (1981) has also reported cyclic changes in vaginal pulse amplitude but found a different pattern from that reported by Palti and Bercovici (1967). Schreiner-Engel *et al.* (1981) exposed young women to erotic stimuli during the "follicular, ovulatory and luteal" phases of

their menstrual cycles and found the lowest level of pulse amplitude change in the ovulatory (midcycle) phase. In this study, correlations with blood levels of estradiol were low and negative. Plasma progesterone and testosterone also were not clearly correlated to measures of vaginal pulse amplitude, although Schreiner-Engel *et al.* did report indications of a weak relationship between serum testosterone levels and "maximum degree of vaginal vasocongestion" as well as the duration of time that vasocongestion remained at "30% above baseline." It is likely that any correlation that exists between changes in vaginal pulse amplitude and phase of the menstrual cycle is relatively weak, considering the discrepancies between the reports by Schreiner-Engel *et al.* (1981) and Palti and Bercovici (1967), and considering the fact that other recent reports incorporating relatively similar methods have failed to detect any evidence of menstrual cyclicity in measures of vaginal pulse amplitude (Hoon, Bruce, & Kinchloe, 1982; Morrell, Dixen, Carter, & Davidson, 1984).

These findings cannot be interpreted as suggesting that hormones play no role in vasomotor responsivity, however. For example, we have recently observed (Morrell *et al.*, 1984) that vaginal pulse amplitude changes in response to visual erotic stimuli are less pronounced in acyclic postmenopausal women as compared to cycling women of a relatively similar age. In addition, in a pilot study with a woman who was receiving high levels of androgen treatment in preparation for transsexual surgery, we observed an exceptionally high vaginal pulse amplitude response. A number of methodological problems remain to be resolved before generalities can be drawn from this research (Cook, 1974; Hatch, 1979).

In spite of these problems, investigations of the physiology of sexual arousal or arousability deserve the attention of the psychophysiologist. Although menstrual cyclic variations in sexual functions (including sexual behavior) have not been consistently observed, it remains possible that hormonal modulation may be of clinical consequence. For example, exogenous hormone treatments, such as those used for contraception, the alleviation of menopausal symptoms, or other medical purposes, present circumstances in which hormones may influence sexual behavior and/or physiology.

ADRENAL GLAND

Adrenal Medulla

The adrenal gland is divided anatomically into two organs: adrenal medulla and adrenal cortex. (For reviews, see Ganong, 1979; I. C. Jones & Henderson, 1980; Kopin, 1980; Lightman, 1979.) The adrenal medulla is neural tissue and is an extension of the sympathetic branch of the autonomic nervous system. The cells of the adrenal medulla are capable of synthesizing and excreting epinephrine (also called adrenalin) and norepinephrine (also called noradrenalin) into the bloodstream. The hormones epinephrine and norepinephrine are amino acid derivatives and, based on their structures, are classified as catecholamines. Epinephrine is formed by the addition of a methyl group to norepinephrine; the enzyme phenylethanolamine-N-methyltransferase (PNMT), which catalyzes this conversion, is found in the adrenal medulla. Tissues in other neural structures, including the brain, are capable of norepinephrine production, but high concentrations of PNMT and thus epinephrine production are generally limited to the adrenal medulla. In humans, about 80% of the catecholamine output from the adrenal medulla is epinephrine (Ganong, 1979).

The neurotransmitter acetylcholine initiates the release of catecholamines from adrenal cells. Acetylcholine, in turn, is secreted by the preganglionic nerves of the sympathetic nervous system. Catecholamines are released and degraded rapidly. Thus adrenal medullary functions are well suited to respond to acute stresses (Selye, 1976).

The general actions of adrenal medullary hormones on the metabolic and cardiovascular systems result in increases in blood pressure, free fatty acids, blood glucose, and body temperature. Norepinephrine tends to cause vasoconstriction, and increases both systolic and diastolic blood pressure. However, norepinephrine also stimulates vagal activity, and thus the net effect of norepinephrine action is a drop in heart rate (reflex bradycardia). Epinephrine tends to cause vasodilation, as well as increases in systolic blood pressure, cardiac output, and heart rate. (The effects of epinephrine on blood pressure are not sufficient to induce reflex bradycardia.) Epinephrine is particularly active in stimulating the release of glucose from liver and muscle and inducing hyperglycemia. Blood glucose thus generated also provides available energy and promotes increased metabolism and heat production. Both norepinephrine and epinephrine mobilize free fatty acids, which also provide fuel for an increase in metabolic rate.

Behavioral effects of adrenal hormones can be detected following injection. However, catecholamines do not readily penetrate the blood–brain barrier (Vernikos-Danellis, 1972). Thus effects of these hormones on the CNS may be primarily indirect, resulting from peripheral or nonneural actions of the catecholamines. In spite of uncertainty regarding the mechanisms through which catecholamines affect behavior, it has been known for some time that the effects of epinephrine injections can be detected and can influence emotional responses (Schachter & Singer, 1962).

Adrenal Cortex

The adrenal cortex is embryologically related to the gonad and, like that organ, also produces steroid hormones. Glucocorticoids, mineralocorticoids, and sex steroids are secreted in varying concentrations by the cells of the adrenal cortex.

The precursor of the adrenal steroids is cholesterol (Brooks, 1979). The basic steroid molecule formed from cholesterol can, through modifications in its side chains, be converted into mineralocorticoids or glucocorticoids. Both types of hormones have 21 carbon atoms and share certain functional properties. Removal of side chain carbons can result in androgenic (19-carbon) and estrogenic (18-carbon) steroids.

In humans, the primary glucocorticoids are cortisol and corticosterone. In the bloodstream, these hormones may be bound to proteins (corticosteroid-binding globulin and albumin). Corticosteroid-binding hormone levels play an important role in stabilizing glucocorticoid availability, and only unbound glucocorticoids are active.

The principal metabolic effects of the glucocorticoids are to increase blood glucose through effects on the liver and on the breakdown (catabolism) of proteins. Glucocorticoids also interact with the catecholamines to produce glucose from free fatty acids. Glucocorticoids are anti-inflammatory and play an important role in the response to stress and disease. Because of these effects, synthetic glucorcorticoids have numerous medical applications and may be applied either systemically or topically (e.g., cortisone cream) (Brooks, 1979; Ganong, 1981).

The primary mineralocorticoid is aldosterone. Mineralocorticoids increase sodium reabsorption and promote the loss of potassium and other ions from the kidney, intestinal mucosa, salivary glands, and sweat glands. Aldosterone secretion increases in the face of stress. If mineralocorticoid secretion is inadequate, plasma volume and blood pressure falls. Shock may develop if treatment is not provided.

Sex hormones of adrenal origin include dehydroepiandrosterone, androstenedione, and 11 beta-hydroxy-androstenedione. The most potent of these is the androgen, androstenedione, which has only about 1/10th the androgenic activity of testosterone. However, since relatively large amounts of these hormones are produced, they can be biologically relevant (Brooks, 1979). For example, adrenal androgens regulate axillary and pubic hair growth in females at puberty and may influence female sexuality.

Hypothalamo-Pituitary Regulation of Adrenal Cortex Secretion

The anterior pituitary secretes ACTH. ACTH is composed of 39 amino acids, of which the first 23 are active in regulating adrenal cortical secretion. ACTH is capable of stimulating glucocorticoid release within minutes (M. T. Jones, 1979).

ACTH secretion is under the regulatory control of CRH, which is found in the hypothalamus (and probably other CNS areas as well). The polypeptide structure of CRH has recently been identified (Vale, Spiess, Rivier, & Rivier, 1981), and it has been shown that CRH may stimulate the release not only of ACTH but also of beta-endorphins. Complex interactions among the adrenal system and the endogenous opiates (including the endorphins) may explain a number of phenomena, including certain forms of stress-induced analgesia (MacLennan, Drugan, Hyson, Maier, Madden, & Barchas, 1982; Miczek, Thompson, & Shuster, 1982; Rossier, Bloom, & Guillemin, 1980).

It is well documented that ACTH levels increase in the presence of stressors and other emotional events. Hypothalamic CRH presumably enters the portal vessel system and integrates CNS–sensory input with subsequent pituitary–adrenal stress responses. Neural and chemical influences from other CNS regions (such as the amygdala) converge on the hypothalamus and thus provide pathways for adrenal responses to various emotionally labeled events, including those of learned or experiential origins (deWied, 1980; M. T. Jones, 1979). (See Levine, Chapter 16, this volume, for additional discussion of the role of the adrenal in stress responses.)

Aldosterone secretion is regulated by the renin-angiotensin system. This system is influenced by the sympathetic input to the kidney (M. T. Jones, 1979).

Hormones associated with the adrenal system, and particularly the adrenal cortex, show marked circadian rhythms. ACTH may cycle even when adrenal steroids are held relatively constant. Animal research suggests that the suprachiasmatic nucleus of the hypothalamus functions to integrate photoperiodic and neural events with biological rhythms, including those of the adrenal system (Rusak & Zucker, 1979).

Adrenal size and function are also under the influence of neural inputs (Dallman, Engeland, & McBride, 1977). Studies of the CNS regulation of adrenal function and the reciprocal effects of adrenal hormones on CNS function constitute an active research area (Vernikos-Danellis & Heybach, 1980).

SUMMARY

This chapter is restricted to a description of the reproductive and adrenal systems. The relevance of these systems to psychophysiology is well documented.

Other endocrine systems of course influence psychophysiological events, although in less well-defined ways. For example, endocrine organs that regulate energy balance and metabolism (pancreas, thyroid, etc.) must function properly for normal health. Metabolically related processes have often been seen as too nonspecific to be of interest to or amenable to psychophysiological investigation. This assumption deserves re-examination. Endocrinologically determined processes, such as glucose regulation, obviously influence behavior. The endocrine systems are simply one aspect of the chemical mediation that integrates intraorganismic (and in some cases interorganismic) functions, such as behavioral and physiological homeostasis.

REFERENCES

Bancroft, J. Psychophysiology of sexual dysfunction. In H. M. van Praag (Ed.), *Handbook of biological psychiatry.* New York: Marcel Dekker, 1980.

Bardin, C. W. The neuroendocrinology of male reproduction. In D. T. Krieger & J. C. Hughes (Eds.), *Neuroendocrinology.* Sunderland, Mass.: Sinauer Associates, 1980.

Bardin, C. W., & Catterall, J. F. Testosterone: A major determinant of extragenital sexual dimorphism. *Science,* 1981, *211,* 1285–1294.

Beach, F. A. Historical origins of modern research on hormones and behavior. *Hormones and Behavior,* 1981, *15,* 325–376.

Berthold, A. A. Transplantation der hoden. *Archiv fur Anatomie und Physiologie,* 1849, *16,* 42–46.

Billings, E. L., Billings, J. J., Brown, J. B., & Burger, H. G. Symptoms and hormonal changes accompanying ovulation. *Lancet,* 1972, *1,* 282–284.

Blumer, D. Hypersexual episodes in temporal lobe epilepsy. *American Journal of Psychiatry,* 1970, *126,* 83–90.

Brooks, R. V. Biosynthesis and metabolism of adrenocortical steroids. In V. H. T. James (Ed.), *The adrenal gland.* New York: Raven Press, 1979.

Brown-Sequard, D. The effects produced on man by subcutaneous injections of a liquid obtained from the testicles of animals. *Lancet,* 1889, 105–106.

Campbell, B. Neurophysiology of the clitoris. In T. P. Lowry & T. S. Lowry (Eds.), *The clitoris.* St. Louis: W. H. Green, 1976.

Carter, C. S. (Ed.). *Hormones and sexual behavior.* Stroudsburg, Pa.: Dowden Hutchinson & Ross, 1974.

Carter, C. S., & Davis, J. M. Effects of drugs on sexual arousal and performance. In J. K. Meyer (Ed.), *Clinical management of sexual disorders.* Baltimore: Williams & Wilkins, 1976.

Cook, M. R. Psychophysiology of peripheral vascular changes. In P. Obrist, A. Black, J. Brener, & L. DiCara (Eds.), *Cardiovascular psychophysiology.* Chicago: Aldine, 1974.

Dallman, M. F., Engeland, W. C., & McBride, M. H. The neural regulation of compensatory adrenal growth. *Annals of the New York Academy of Sciences,* 1977, *297,* 373–392.

Danesino, V., & Martella, E. Modern conceptions of corpora cavernosa function in the vagina and clitoris. In T. P. Lowry & T. S. Lowry (Eds.), *The clitoris.* St. Louis: W. H. Green, 1976.

Davidson, J. M., Camargo, C. A., & Smith, E. R. Effects of androgen on sexual behavior in hypogonadal men. *Journal of Clinical Endocrinology and Metabolism,* 1979, *48,* 955–958.

deWied, D. Pituitary-adrenal system hormones and behavior. In H. Selye (Ed.), *Selye's guide to stress research.* New York: Van Nostrand Reinhold, 1980.

Fisher, S. *The female orgasm.* New York: Basic Books, 1973.

Fox, C. A. Reduction in the rise of systolic blood pressure during human coitus by the β-adrenergic blocking agent, propranolol. *Journal of Reproduction and Fertility,* 1970, *22,* 587–590.

Frohman, L. A. Neurotransmitters as regulators of endocrine function. In D. T. Krieger & J. C. Hughes (Eds.), *Neuroendocrinology.* Sunderland, Mass.: Sinauer Associates, 1980.

Ganong, W. F. *Review of medical physiology.* Los Altos, Calif.: Lange, 1979.

Hart, B. L. Hormones, spinal reflexes and sexual behavior. In J. B. Hutchison (Ed.), *Biological determinants of sexual behavior.* Chichester, England: Wiley, 1978.

Hatch, J. P. Vaginal photoplethysmography: Methodological considerations. *Archives of Sexual Behavior,* 1979, *8,* 357–374.

Higgins, G. E., Jr. Sexual response in spinal cord injured adults. A review of the literature. *Archives of Sexual Behavior,* 1979, *8,* 173–196.

Hoon, P. W., Bruce, K., & Kinchloe, B. Does the menstrual cycle play a role in sexual arousal? *Psychophysiology,* 1982, *9,* 21–27.

Jones, I. C., & Henderson, I. W. *General, comparative and clinical endocrinology of the adrenal cortex.* New York: Academic Press, 1980.

Jones, M. T. Control of adrenocortical hormone secretion. In V. H. T. James (Ed.), *The adrenal gland.* New York: Raven Press, 1979.

Karacan, I., Salis, P. J., Ware, J. C., Dervant, B., Williams, R. L., Scott, F. B., Attia, S. L., & Beutler, L. E. Nocturnal penile tumescence and diagnosis in diabetic impotence. *American Journal of Psychiatry,* 1978, *135,* 191–197.

Kinsey, A. C., Pomeroy, W. P., & Martin, C. E. *Sexual behavior in the human male.* Philadelphia: W. B. Saunders, 1948.

Kirby, R. W., Kotchen, T. A., & Rees, E. D. Hyperprolactinemia—a review of most recent clinical advances. *Archives of Internal Medicine,* 1979, *139,* 1415–1419.

Kopin, I. J. Catecholamines, adrenal hormones and stress. In D. T. Krieger & J. C. Hughes (Eds.), *Neuroendocrinology.* Sunderland, Mass.: Sinauer Associates, 1980.

Lightman, S. Adrenal medulla. In V. H. T. James (Ed.), *The adrenal gland.* New York: Raven Press, 1979.

LoPiccolo, J., & LoPiccolo, L. (Eds.) *Handbook of sex therapy.* New York: Plenum, 1978.

Lowry, T. P., & Lowry, T. S. (Eds.). *The clitoris.* St. Louis: W. H. Green, 1976.

MacLean, P. D., & Ploog, D. W. Cerebral representation of penile erection. *Journal of Neurophysiology,* 1962, *25,* 29–55.

MacLennan, A. J., Drugan, R. C., Hyson, R. L., Maier, S. F., Madden, J., IV, & Barchas, J. D. Corticosterone: A critical factor in an opioid form of stress-induced analgesia. *Science,* 1982, *215,* 1530–1532.

Masters, W. H., & Johnson, V. E. *Human sexual response.* Boston: Little, Brown, 1966.

McEwen, B. S. Neural gonadal steroid actions. *Science,* 1981, *211,* 1303–1311.

Miczek, K. A., Thompson, M. L., & Shuster, L. Opioid-like analgesia in defeated mice. *Science,* 1982, *215,* 1520–1522.

Morrell, M. J., Dixen, J. M., Carter, C. S., & Davidson, J. M. The influence of age and cycling status on sexual arousability in women. *American Journal of Obstetrics and Gynecology,* 1984, *148,* 66–71.

Palti, Y., & Bercovici, B. Photoplethysmographic study of the vaginal blood pulse. *American Journal of Obstetrics and Gynecology,* 1967, *97,* 143–153.

Perl, J. I., Milles, G., & Shimozato, Y. Vaginal fluid subsequent to panhysterectomy. *American Journal of Obstetrics and Gynecology,* 1959, *78,* 285–289.

Rossier, J., Bloom, F. E., & Guillemin, R. Endorphins and stress. In H. Selye (Ed.), *Selye's guide to stress research.* New York: Van Nostrand Reinhold, 1980.

Rusak, B., & Zucker, I. Neural regulation of circadian rhythms. *Physiological Reviews,* 1979, *59,* 449–?.

Schachter, S., & Singer, J. E. Cognitive social and physiological determinants of emotional states. *Psychological Review,* 1962, *69,* 379–399.

Schreiner-Engel, P., Schiavi, R. C., Smith, H., & White, D. Sexual arousability and the menstrual cycle. *Psychosomatic Medicine,* 1981, *43,* 199–214.

Selye, H. *The stress of life.* New York: McGraw-Hill, 1976.

Slimp, J. C., Hart, B. L., and Goy, R. W. Heterosexual, autosexual and social behavior of adult male rhesus monkeys with medial preoptic-anterior hypothalamic lesions. *Brain Research,* 1978, *142,* 105–122.

Tarabulcy, E. Sexual function in the normal and paraplegia. *Paraplegia,* 1972, *10,* 201–208.

Tolis, G. Prolactin: Physiology and pathology. In D. T. Krieger & J. C. Hughes (Eds.), *Neuroendocrinology.* Sunderland, Mass.: Sinauer Associates, 1980.

Tordjman, G., Thierre, R., & Michel, J. R. Advances in the vascular pathology of male erectile dysfunction. *Archives of Sexual Behavior,* 1980, *9,* 391–398.

Turner, C. D., & Bagnara, J. T. *General endocrinology.* Philadelphia: W. B. Saunders, 1971.

Vale, W., Spiess, J., Rivier, C., & Rivier, J. Characterization of a 41-residue ovine hypothalamic peptide that stimulates secretion of corticotropin and β-endorphin. *Science,* 1981, *213,* 1394–1397.

Verkuyl, A. Some neuromotor syndromes and their sexual consequences. In J. Money & H. Musaph (Eds.), *Handbook of sexology.* Amsterdam: Elsevier/North-Holland Biomedical Press, 1977.

Vernikos-Danellis, J. Effects of hormones on the central nervous system. In S. Levine (Ed.), *Hormones and behavior.* New York: Academic Press, 1972.

Vernikos-Danellis, J., & Heybach, J. P. Psychophysiologic mechanisms regulating the hypothalamic–pituitary–adrenal response to stress. In H. Selye (Ed.), *Selye's guide to stress research.* New York: Van Nostrand Reinhold, 1980.

Wilson, J. D., George, F. W., & Griffin, J. E. The hormonal control of sexual development. *Science,* 1981, *211,* 1278–1284.

Wincze, J. P., Hoon, P. W., & Hoon, E. F. Physiological responsivity of normal and sexually dysfunctional women during erotic stimulus exposure. *Journal of Psychosomatic Research,* 1976, *20,* 445–451.

Yen, S. S. C. Neuroendocrine regulation of the menstrual cycle. In D. T. Krieger & J. C. Hughes (Eds.), *Neuroendocrinology.* Sunderland, Mass.: Sinauer Associates, 1980.

SECTION C
Signal Acquisition and Analysis

Chapter Ten

Principles of Signal Acquisition and Analysis

Michael G. H. Coles
Gabriele Gratton
Arthur F. Kramer
Gregory A. Miller

INTRODUCTION

This chapter describes various techniques that can be used to analyze psychophysiological measures. We approach this description with the assumption that there is a general set of principles that can be applied to any psychophysiological measure, regardless of its origin. We justify this assumption by the observation that all psychophysiological signals are reducible through appropriate measurement techniques to voltage × time functions. Note that we are distinguishing between measurement procedures and analytic procedures. The former may be peculiar to a specific function. For example, the measurement of the electroencephalogram (EEG) requires the use of two electrodes and amplifiers to derive voltage × time functions, where the voltage represents some simple transformation of the voltage difference between the two electrodes. Measurement of electrodermal activity (skin conductance), on the other hand, requires not only the use of two electrodes and an amplifier, but also some kind of bridge circuit to translate the variations in skin conductance beneath the electrodes into a voltage × time function.

Although measurement procedures may be "special" in the sense that each psychophysiological function has its own procedure, analytic procedures need not be special because they are all applied, in the end, to a voltage × time function. Of course, some functions have traditionally been associated with specific types of analyses. In some cases, this tradition is understandable because of the special characteristics of the psychophysiological function in question. For example, for most measurements of the cardiovascular system, data are available only at each heart beat, and not continuously. This creates some special problems when appropriate values for parameters of cardiovascular functioning in real, rather than cardiac, time are derived (e.g., Graham, 1978).

In spite of occasional esoteric factors that tie particular analytic techniques to particular measures, we propose that, in general, such ties are based on little more than historical accident. Adherence to a technique for the sake of history may be constricting, and part of the aim of this chapter is to encourage a break with tradition. We hope that investigators will consider enriching their analytic repertoires by including techniques that are either customarily employed in

Michael G. H. Coles, Gabriele Gratton, Arthur F. Kramer, and Gregory A. Miller. Cognitive Psychophysiology Laboratory, Department of Psychology, University of Illinois, Champaign, Illinois. The order of authors is alphabetical. No ranking is implied.

other branches of psychophysiology or not currently in use. In this way, the range of questions that can be answered with respect to a given psychophysiological function can be extended.

Our emphasis on the potential generality of analytical techniques should not be taken to mean that we think that specific measurement techniques are unimportant. Other chapters in this volume discuss the measurement techniques that are typically used in the recording of different psychophysiological functions. Furthermore, for the sake of completeness, we briefly review different approaches to psychophysiological measurement in the next section. However, the bulk of this chapter is devoted to a review of analytic techniques. We present, in detail, two classes of analytic techniques: time domain and frequency domain. Selection between these two classes, and among the different techniques within each class, is dictated by the questions asked by the investigator. Thus, we not only describe the different techniques, but also point to those questions that the techniques are best suited to answer.

DERIVING VOLTAGE × TIME MEASUREMENT FUNCTIONS

In this section, we consider the sequence of events that transpires between variations in the activity of a physiological system in a human subject, and the derivation of the voltage × time functions that represent this activity. This is a brief review. More detailed treatments can be found in other chapters in this volume, and also in Brown (1967), Martin and Venables (1980), Stern, Ray, and Davis (1980), and Venables and Martin (1967a).

Attachments to the Subject

We may distinguish here between two classes of attachments. First, there are those used when the investigator is interested in the activity of a physiological function that manifests itself in variation in electrical activity that can be measured on the surface of the skin. Secondly, there are those used when the activity of the function of interest is manifested in a nonelectrical fashion. We consider these two separately.

Electrodes

Electrodes are used when the activity of the psychophysiological function of interest can be detected in the form of electrical activity at the surface of the skin. Measures of the EEG, the electromyogram (EMG), the electro-oculogram (EOG), the electrocardiogram (ECG or EKG), and EDA all require the use of electrodes. In most cases, the electrodes merely constitute an interface between the subject and amplification equipment (see below), although for some measures of EDA (skin conductance and resistance) the electrodes are used to apply small, constant voltages or currents to the skin in order to quantify properties other than surface voltage.

Electrodes customarily are small metallic discs or disc shapes that are attached to the surface of the subject's skin. Placement depends on the function of interest. Attachment to the subject is generally accomplished through the use of double-adhesive collars that stick to both the electrode and the subject. However, if the electrodes are to be placed on an area that is hairy (e.g., the scalp), then either a glue (e.g., collodion) or a rubber cap may be needed to hold the electrodes in place.

The most critical aspect of the electrode is that it is electrically stable. It should be both inert (i.e., have no inherent electrical activity) and nonpolarizable (i.e., be unaffected by continued exposure to current flow). For all functions, the electrode material of choice is currently silver/silver chloride (silver chloride surface surrounding a solid silver base).

Prior to electrode attachment, the skin is generally cleaned with a mild solvent, such as acetone. With EDA, however, the measure itself can be influenced by the method of cleaning. Venables and Martin (1967b) report that, while acetone, ether, and distilled water do not affect EDA, soap and water lower conductance and raise resistance. To eliminate the possibility of between-subjects variations due to the method of cleaning, these authors advise standardizing procedures across subjects.

Contact between electrodes and skin is maintained by a jelly or paste. For all functions, it is desirable that the jelly be chemically compatible with the skin. For this reason, electrolytes containing sodium chloride (NaCl) or potassium chloride (KCl) are generally used, preferably in concentrations that correspond to those found on the skin. Although commercially available electrolytes do not always satisfy this last requirement, they are usually judged to be acceptable for most recording applications. The primary requirement is that there should be chemical overlap among electrolytes at each interface of material. Silver chloride on the electrode surface plus NaCl in the jelly creates an appropriate sequence of electrolytes between metal electrode and skin. As noted above, measurement of EDA presents a special set of problems, since the behavior of the system itself can be influenced by the electrolyte. Venables and Christie (1980) present a detailed discussion of the problems of electrolyte, with special reference to the measurement of EDA.

The particular characteristics of electrodes, skin preparation, and electrolyte are chosen for one reason—that is, to provide faithful transmission of the electrical activity manifested at the skin to an amplifying system (in a polygraph) where the electrical activity can be magnified. The selection of these characteristics is based on the requirement that whatever reaches the amplifying system should consist of no less and no more than what actually exists at the skin. Note that the activity at the skin may not always represent the activity of interest. Electrodes cannot discriminate among brain electrical activity, muscle electrical activity, or the electrical activity associated with eye movements. For this reason, care must be exercised in ascribing a cause to the electrical activity recorded using electrodes. We consider how this activity is treated by the polygraph after we have discussed the second type of subject attachment.

Transducers

Many physiological functions of interest are not directly manifested in electrical activity at the skin surface. The activity may appear in a number of different ways. First, it may appear directly as mechanical activity. The respiration belt and the strain gauge plethysmograph both rely on the fact that mechanical changes occur with variations in the activity of the function. Respiration may also be measured using a less direct mechanical procedure, the respiratory spirometer, which converts the changes in airflow that occur during respiration into mechanical changes. In other cases, the fact that the function is manifested in changes in the optical quality of tissue is used (e.g., the photoplethysmograph).

The task of the transducer is to convert the mechanical or optical manifestation of the function into an electrical function. With primary and secondary mechanical systems, the conversion can be made to electrical resistance using a strain gauge. The prototypical strain gauge is a plastic tube filed with mercury. Variations in the length and cross-section of the tube, resulting from stretching, are associated with changes in resistance of the tube. Appropriate placement of the strain gauge ensures that variations in the resistance of the strain gauge are due to variations in the function of interest. Using a suitable bridge circuit (see below), these changes in resistance are then converted into changes in voltage.

Other functions that can be monitored using the resistance principle include temperature. In this case, a thermistor is used whose resistance changes with temperature.

With optical systems, the need is to convert variations in the optical properties of tissue that are associated with vascular events into electrical activity (see Jennings, Tahmoush, & Redmond, 1980). In all optical systems, there are two elements, a light source and a receiver. Activity at the receiver depends either on the amount of light transmitted (if source and receiver are on opposite sides of the tissue) or on the amount of light backscattered (if source and receiver are on the same side). Depending on the characteristics of the receiver, variations in the amount of transmitted

or backscattered light are converted into variations in electrical current or electrical resistance. In the latter case, a bridge circuit must be used to convert resistance change to voltage change.

In this section, we have considered devices that are used to convert the activity of physiological functions into electrical activity. Note that the transducer can only operate on that aspect of the function it is designed to detect. The function may have many manifestations, only one of which can be detected by the transducer. Furthermore, the transducer will not differentiate between activity that is caused by the function of interest and activity that is caused by extraneous events. For example, respiration strain gauges will be sensitive to all forms of movement—not just those attributable to respiration. Thus, however well a transducer is designed and positioned, it will be blindly faithful in converting what it "sees" into electrical activity. With these caveats in mind, we can now turn to the system that scales these diverse voltage $\times$ time functions to a common format.

The Polygraph

"Polygraph" is a generic name for a device that amplifies, shapes, and records psychophysiological functions. Although polygraphs come in different shapes and sizes, they have a number of common features: amplifiers, bridge circuits, integrators, rate devices, analog filters, and a graphic readout facility. The increasing use of computers in psychophysiological research has made the last item redundant for many investigators. The polygraph is interfaced directly with a computer, thus making scoring of polygraph records by hand unnecessary.

The connection between subject and polygraph is achieved via wires or cables (leads). Their function is merely to transmit electrical activity to and from the subject (electrodes) or to and from the transducers. Each psychophysiological measure is processed by a separate channel of the polygraph. Each channel contains a device that is directly connected to the subject or transducer (sometimes called a "coupler") and an amplifying system. The amplifying system is generally the same for all channels. Most manufacturers of polygraphs supply a variety of couplers, each of which is specific for the measurement of a particular psychophysiological function. Below, we review some general characteristics of these couplers and amplifiers.

Amplifiers

The most elementary function of the polygraph is to magnify psychophysiological signals. Amplifiers fulfill this function by increasing the magnitude of the input voltage by a factor of up to 500,000. Following amplification, the signal should have an amplitude on the order of about ±1 V to be compatible with either the graphic readout system of a polygraph or the analog-to-digital converter of a computer (see below).

The size of the amplification factor will depend on the size of the input signal. For example, the magnitude of the ECG signal is about 1 mV, while that of the EEG is about 50 μV. Thus, the amplification factor for these two measures might be 1000 and 20,000 times, respectively.

To ensure that the amplifier is performing the appropriate magnification, it is important to pass calibration voltages of known amplitude through the amplification system.

Bridge Circuits

As we have seen, most transducers represent psychophysiological activity in the form of resistance changes. For this reason, a critical function of the polygraph is to measure resistance change and to convert it to voltage change. This is accomplished through the use of a bridge circuit, which can be as simple as a few resistors arranged in a special way (Malmstadt, Enke, & Crouch, 1974). A bridge circuit provides constant current to the transducer. As the resistance of the transducer changes, so the voltage across the transducer changes. This voltage change is then amplified (see above).

Bridge cricuits are also used in the measurement of two complementary forms of EDA, skin conductance and skin resistance. In this case, either a constant voltage or a constant current is imposed on the subject, and the bridge measures variations in current or voltage that correspond, respectively, to variations in conductance or resistance. Because this procedure involves the imposition of external electrical activity on the subject, safety is a critical factor. However, the procedure is now reasonably standardized (see Fowles, Chapter 4, this volume).

Analog Filtering

As we have mentioned, the task of the electrodes and transducers is to convey to the polygraph a faithful representation of the electrical or other activity associated with a psychophysiological function. In some cases, the signal so conveyed may be filtered by the polygraph, either because it contains artifacts or because it contains aspects of the psychophysiological signal that are of no interest to the investigator.

For the purposes of describing the principles of signal modification or "signal conditioning," the signal is considered as being comprised of different frequencies. Thus, some of these frequencies may be artifactual (due to sources outside the subject or to activity of other, irrelevant functions), while others may simply be of no interest.

For example, a common source of artifact in psychophysiological measurement is 60-Hz (or 50-Hz) activity from standard electrical equipment. This artifact can be minimized by the use of a "notch" filter set at 60 or 50 Hz, which attenuates activity at this frequency while permitting activity at higher or lower frequencies to pass.

Other filters attenuate activity above or below specified frequencies (low-pass and high-pass filters). For example, in EEG recording, the investigator is generally interested only in activity below 40 Hz. Thus, a low-pass filter set at 40 Hz can be used. The ECG consists of frequency components between .05 Hz and 80 Hz (Strong, 1970). If the investigator merely wants to detect the R wave (e.g., to measure interbeat interval), a high-pass filter set at 10 Hz can be used. The high-pass filter attenuates slow shifts in the ECG signal that may be due to EDA or some other unwanted activity.

The various types of electronic circuitry that typically serve as filters can be characterized by their "time constant." The value of the time constant of a high-pass filter is the time for a given sustained input to the circuit to be attenuated to 63% of its original value. While all analog filtering circuits have a time constant characteristic, in practice the concept is associated primarily with that portion of a circuit that serves as the high-pass filter. Some correspondences between time constant and filter cutoff frequency (-3 dB) are as follows ($F = 1/[2*\pi*TC]$, where F = frequency, TC = time constant):

Time Constant (sec)	Frequency (Hz)
10.00	.016
5.00	.032
1.00	.159
.30	.531
.01	15.915

Of course, it is imperative that great care be taken in the use of filters. The investigator does not want to distort the signal of interest (see, for example, Duncan-Johnson & Donchin, 1979). Filters are useful when the characteristics of the unwanted aspects of the signal do not overlap the wanted aspects. The problems that occur when there is overlap, and the solutions to these problems, are discussed below (see "Data Analysis in the Time Domain").

The "analog" filters briefly discussed here are electronic components placed in-line during initial recording of continuous signals, often within the amplifier chassis. Their chief advantages are simplicity and speed. Their disadvantages are that they introduce a phase shift into the signal and that in a particular polygraph they are typically limited to a few settings. Analog filters must be distinguished from digital filters, which are algebraic manipulations of discrete (digitized) signals after recording is complete. Digital filters, discussed below (see pp. 195–196), can be constructed without phase shift and with any desired filter characteristics.

Analog Integration

For some physiological signals, particularly EMG, the investigator is not so much interested in the frequency characteristics of the signal as in the overall amplitude–frequency activity in the signal. Analog integrators provide this measure by first rectifying the signal and then converting the area under the rectified record into a smoothed analog voltage (rectification involves removing or inverting either the positive or negative portion of an alternating current [AC] signal). The resulting voltage × time function will depend on both the amplitude and the frequency of the input signal at any point in time. Because analog integration is normally accomplished with an in-line electronic circuit that is essentially a low-pass filter (smoothing out rapid peaks but preserving average amplitude), different integrators are appropriate for different physiological signals, depending on the frequency characteristics of the signal and the time constant of the integration circuit. Furthermore, the output of such an analog circuit lags the input, again introducing the issue of phase shift. When the frequencies of interest are high in relation to the time resolution needed, as in EMG recording, this lag is inconsequential.

Rate Devices

With some physiological functions, the measure of interest is the rate at which some event occurs, rather than the level of activity. For example, with heart rate (HR), the investigator is concerned with the rate at which R waves are observed in the ECG, rather than with voltage characteristics of the ECG waveform itself.

To accomplish this measurement, most polygraph manufacturers offer rate devices (cardiotachometers), which convert inter-event intervals into an analog signal whose amplitude varies with rate. In some implementations, the conversion is made through a circuit that first detects an R wave, then allows a capacitor to be charged until the next R wave is detected, at which time the capacitor is discharged. The voltage discharged by the capacitor will vary as a function of the duration of the charging period and hence will be proportional to the interbeat interval (and inversely proportional to the rate). Note that the level of the output of the rate device (a voltage × time function) will depend on the previously completed interbeat interval. Thus, the output will lag the input.

Computer Access to Voltage × Time Functions

Digital Input and Analog-to-Digital Conversion

With the development of computers, automatic scoring of physiological data has become a reality. But, before a digital computer can apply the appropriate scoring algorithms, the data must be presented in a palatable form—a set of digitized (i.e., discrete) values. However, the voltage × time functions we have described are inherently analog (i.e., continuous) functions. The requirement, then, is to convert these analog functions into digital representations. Some types of physiological activity are easily represented digitally. For example, while the ECG is a continuous voltage, the occurrence of its R-wave component is easily approximated digitally as a "1" in a series of "0's." Simple electronic circuitry between polygraph and computer, such as Schmitt trigger, readily converts the analog ECG input signal to such a digital output signal. Thus, a continuous voltage × time signal is converted to a discrete voltage × time signal. This method is more accurate than, and obviates the need for, a cardiotachometer rate device, described above.

More elaborate conversion circuitry is required when more information about the continuous input function, besides the mere occurrence of an event, must be represented in the discrete output function. The term "analog-to-digital" (A/D) converter is normally reserved for such circuitry, which produces a series of numerical values that are discrete samples of voltage level from a continuous input. Rather than merely one bit of information (0 or 1), the output has a large number of possible values. For example, a 12-bit A/D converter can output 4096 different values, depending on the voltage input at the time of sampling. Such resolution is essential for measurement of signal amplitude. The sampling intervals used vary as a function of the particular measure. For example, for the auditory brain stem response the intervals are typically 20 μsec (sampling rate of 50 kHz), while for respiration the intervals may be as long as 1 sec (1 Hz). Choice of sampling interval (or sampling rate) is dictated by the expected period or frequency characteristics of the measure in question. The slowest acceptable sampling rate is twice the highest frequency present in the data. A slower sampling rate will provide a distorted digital representation of the analog input (this issue is elaborated further in the section by Porges). A good rule of thumb, then, is to err on the conservative side and sample at least two to five times the highest expected frequency.

The output of the A/D converter, now a discrete voltage × time function, is fed directly to the computer. While logically distinct from the computer itself, pieces of circuitry such as Schmitt triggers, digital input interfaces, and A/D converters are typically integrated electronically into the computer enclosure.

Distributed Processing: Remote Data Acquisition

Given the low price and small size of current microprocessors, laboratory equipment manufacturers have begun to offer "smart" laboratory products that perform the continuous-to-discrete conversion external to the computer and its associated A/D converters and other circuitry. Data are then passed to the computer in highly palatable form—as the same 8-bit characters that video display terminals send. Thus, the traditional configuration of "dumb" equipment plus a dedicated laboratory computer (with central A/D converter, etc.) can be replaced with "smart" equipment plus a simpler, general, multipurpose computer.

The investigator should, of course, consider the growing variety of configuration options in laboratory equipment when developing a new measurement capability. The point is that across these diverse options all psychophysiological data, whether written on polygraph paper or handled by the most elaborate microprocessor network, can be treated as a voltage × time function, a series of voltage levels in time—a voltage "time series."

DATA ANALYSIS IN THE TIME DOMAIN

Introduction

This section of the chapter distinguishes analytic techniques applied to data in the time domain from those applied in the frequency domain (see the section by Porges). Psychophysiologists intend to monitor the activity of some internal structure manifested as a "signal" conveyed to the body surface by some functional channel. This signal is combined with "noise" coming from other internal and external sources. In many cases, the extraction of the signal from the background noise is a very challenging task.

In the case of data in the time domain, the signal is typically a phasic, nonrepetitive feature of the time series recorded at the surface; this feature is assumed to reflect the activity of a specific internal structure. Important characteristics of the feature commonly include its restriction to a particular time epoch in the record and its variability in latency. Since the signal of interest contributes only part of the variability observed in the time domain, we refer to it as a "component." This component constitutes the target of the signal extraction procedure.

Since signal components are in most cases embedded in noise, the first task for the data analyst is to extract the signal from its background. To accomplish this task, the signal must be defined.

Signal extraction techniques differ in the way in which they define components. The choice of an extraction technique implies a model of the signal, including a specification of its distinctive features and the ways in which these interact to produce the waveforms (time series) that are actually recorded. For instance, a model of event-related potentials (ERPs) could define a component as a deflection of the EEG

trace time-locked to a stimulus, with a specific latency and scalp distribution, that "summates" with other components and with noise to produce the waveforms recorded at the scalp. Alternatively, EDA components are deflections of the skin conductance trace, with some shape and latency following an eliciting stimulus. A cardiac cycle can be identified by means of a distinctive feature (R wave), or by its general waveshape, referred to the spatial location used for the recording. Analogous definitions can be given for any component of interest for the psychophysiologist. Specific component models are often highly controversial. Nevertheless, the procedure adopted to extract the signal from the noise in which it is embedded necessarily depends on some kind of model. Therefore, in the present discussion, we pay particular attention to models of signal and noise implicit in different signal extraction techniques.

Once the signal component is defined, the amplitude, latency, or spatial distribution of the raw data can be quantified. These quantification techniques depend on the definition of "components" used for extracting the signal. In many cases, these two stages of data analysis (signal extraction and quantification) constitute a single process. However, the logical distinction between signal extraction and quantification should be kept in mind throughout this section.

Signal Extraction Techniques

The remainder of this section provides a brief sample of the many ways to process the basic voltage × time function. This review is divided into techniques for signal extraction, for data reduction, and for spatial analysis. In fact, since a given technique may serve several such functions, such a division is necessarily somewhat arbitrary.

Signal Averaging

Since the psychophysiological signal is often obscured by noise, many techniques have been proposed to amplify selectively the information of interest for the psychophysiologist. A number of techniques assume that the signal can be differentiated from the noise on the assumption that only the signal is temporally related to an external marker event. Such procedures therefore define the signal as eveything in the recording that is time-locked to an external event. All other variability, not time-locked to the external event, is considered noise. This definition is particularly useful when studying perceptual and motor processes. In this case, the relevant external events are readily identifiable, and the temporal relationship of the external event and the internal process is assumed to be constant. The basic procedure consists of the repetition of a large number of essentially identical trials.

Through superimposition or averaging of the single trials, the constant psychophysiological response (signal) to the stimulus remains constant, while variability not consistently related to the external event averages to zero.

The superimposition technique consists simply of overlapping the trace for each of the single trials on a plotter. It can be also obtained with a storage oscilloscope by triggering the display sweep at each presentation of the stimulus. Since superimposition does not require high-speed computing facilities or A/D conversion, it was extensively imployed in the 1950s. An advantage of superimposition is that it portrays the range of variability of the single trials. However, it is fairly difficult to detect small potentials, or small differences in amplitude between conditions, by means of this technique. Thus, superimposition is more appropriate when measuring latency than when measuring amplitude. However, in recent years it has been replaced by averaging techniques.

In averaging, the values obtained at each time point are averaged across trials. To employ this algebraic technique, it is, of course, necessary to transform the signal obtained from the amplifier from analog to digital format.

The advantage of averaging over superimposition is the "cleaner" waveform that averaging produces. This expresses the "central tendency" of the sample of trials examined and corresponds to the best statistical estimate of the signal. It is easy to compute the point-by-point standard deviation or range in parallel with the averages, in order to have more complete information about the data.

In principle, averaging can extract an arbitrarily small signal relative to background noise amplitude, if a large number of invariant trials are averaged. The noise will be reduced as a function of the square root of the number of trials. For example, the brain stem auditory ERP, typically less than $1.0\ \mu V$, may require several thousand trials.

However, averaging is vulnerable to violations of its assumptions of specifiable external stimulus and invariant response latency and morphology. Particularly when the investigator suspects cross-trial inconsistency in the signal, averages must be interpreted cautiously.

Removing Systematic Noise

Most signal extraction techniques have been developed in order to deal with the problem of *random* noise. Consequently, they are often insufficient in the case of *systematic* noise. In fact, these techniques generally assume that "noise" is that part of the variance that is not systematically related to the experimental variables. Of course, this corresponds to the definition of random noise. However, some of the noise present in the data can be systematically related to the experimental variables. We label this "systematic noise."

In the presence of systematic noise, two important points must be kept in mind. First, the signal must be defined in a more restricted way than simply as "everything related to experimental variables." An example is provided by brain ERPs, where, for a component to be considered a signal, it is not sufficient that it is systematically related to the eliciting event. It is also necessary that it be generated by the brain. Therefore, a systematic ocular potential, recorded at the scalp, does not constitute a brain ERP component, but systematic noise. This kind of systematic noise is commonly called an "artifact."

A second important point concerns the difficulty of dealing with systematic noise by means of traditional signal extraction techniques. A procedure usually adopted to reduce artifact in recording is filtering. There are many ways of filtering data, the most common being frequency filtering. This kind of filtering is discussed elsewhere in this chapter (see pp. 186–187 and pp. 195–196). However, frequency filters are sometimes insufficient for handling artifacts in the data. This is especially the case when signal and artifact have similar frequencies. Eye movement artifact in brain ERPs is an example of this problem.

Fortunately, artifacts are sometimes recognizable by their specific features. These features may be evident in the data themselves or in a recording from electrodes placed near the source of the artifact. In either case, the artifact can be detected (by visual inspection or by some automatic procedure) and the associated record discarded from subsequent analysis. However, although this is a common procedure, such loss of data is not always affordable (Gratton, Coles, & Donchin, 1983).

For this reason, procedures have been developed in order to compensate for artifacts. They are based on the possibility of inferring the effect of an artifact on the records at a certain spatial location from data obtained from a location close to the source of artifact. Data of the latter type may be considered "pure" measures of the activity of the "artifact generator." The remainder of this section describes a recently developed procedure of this type.

This procedure, proposed by Gratton *et al.* (1983), represents an example of an artifact compensation technique. It assumes that the effect of an eye movement on the potential recorded at any scalp location (EEG) can be inferred from activity recorded at a location close to the eyeball (EOG). In order to make this inference, it is sufficient to know how much a signal recorded at the ocular electrode "propagates" to the scalp location under study. Previous researchers (e.g., Corby & Kopell, 1972; Overton & Shagass, 1969; Weerts & Lang, 1973) have demonstrated that not all ocular potentials propagate to the scalp in the same way. In particular, potentials generated by eyeblinks propagate less than potentials generated by saccadic eye movements.

Accordingly, the proposed eye movement correction procedure (EMCP) distinguishes between time points in the record during which eyeblinks occur (detected by means of a pattern recognition technique; see "Pattern Recognition," below) and time points in which saccadic eye movements occur. Separate propagation factors are then computed for blinks and saccades.

The propagation factors are computed by means of a least-squares-regression technique. However, as noted above, ocular artifacts can be consistently related to some external events. Since brain ERPs can also be elicited consistently by external events, spurious relationships can affect the computation of the correction factors. Therefore, the averaged EOG and EEG traces are subtracted from the single-trial records before the correction factors are computed. In this way, the propagation factors are computed on that portion of the variance of the EOG and EEG recordings that is not related to the external event. The propagation factors are then applied to the original data to correct for the ocular artifact. A schematic representation of EMCP is presented in Figure 10-1.

Although some inaccuracy is present (involving mainly the invariance in time of the EEG and EOG

response to the external event, and the difference between the propagation factor for upward and downward eye movements), tests presented by Gratton et al. (1983) indicate that EMCP effectively compensates for the ocular artifact.

Pattern Recognition

INTRODUCTION
Signal-averaging techniques (see pp. 188–189) are particularly useful in separating small signals that are time-locked to an external event from background noise that is not time-locked to the external event. However, in many cases, the assumption of invariance of latency of the signal over trials is untenable, even as a first approximation. In other cases, it is impossible to establish an external event to which the psychophysiological signal can be time-locked. Thus, straightforward signal averaging is not always possible. Pattern recognition techniques can be helpful in these cases. The general assumption underlying such techniques is that the signal is distinguishable from the background noise on the basis of specific features, typically aspects of its waveshape. Two types of pattern recognition techniques may be distinguished: those in which the characterizing features are established *a priori* on the basis of previous data or conceptualizations, and those

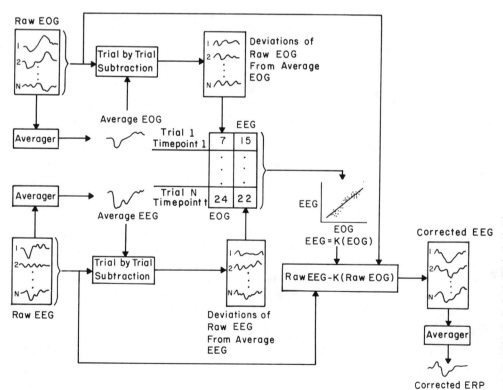

Figure 10-1. Schematic representation of the eye movement correction procedure (EMCP). (From "A New Method for Off-Line Removal of Ocular Artifact" by G. Gratton, M. G. H. Coles, and E. Donchin. *Electroencephalography and Clinical Neurophysiology*, 1983, 55, 468–484. Reprinted by permission.)

in which the characterizing features are established *a posteriori* on the basis of characteristics of the data to be processed.

Examples of the first type are the techniques used in psychophysiology to detect the R wave of the ECG, the phasic electrodermal response, or blinks in the EOG trace. Procedures of this type are specific for a particular psychophysiological measure and are not easily generalizable to other measures. Note also that many of these pattern recognition techniques are used to recognize artifacts (see also the discussion of EMCP, above). Although pattern recognition may be performed simply by visual inspection of the records, for reasons of reliability it is preferable to automate the procedure using hardware devices (e.g., Schmitt triggers) or software algorithms.

Pattern recognition techniques based on standard statistical procedures (e.g., cross-correlational techniques, discriminant and canonical analyses, etc.) usually require the use of high-speed computing devices, since they involve large amounts of computation. However, they have the advantage of being generalizable to many different measurement domains; they can also sometimes be applied without any previous knowledge of the "pattern" of "feature" to be recognized. Two examples of this kind of technique (cross-correlation and discriminant analysis) are discussed below in some detail.

CROSS-CORRELATION

A fundamental assumption of the cross-correlational approach (Friedman, 1968) is that the waveshape of the signal component to be detected is constant over trials, while the shape of the noise varies randomly from trial to trial. Thus, that portion of the variance that is constant over trials will contribute to the correlation between trials. Because cross-correlational techniques do not assume invariance of the interval between external event and internal process manifested by the signal component of interest, they are applicable even in the absence of any identified external event and are potentially more versatile than signal averaging, which assumes signal invariance in both morphology and latency.

Cross-correlational techniques involve the computation of a "cross-correlational series" between a "template" (predetermined pattern of consecutive points) and any single trial. A cross-correlational series is an array of correlation values between two time series (or within the same series), where one of the time series is progressively shifted by a certain interval ("lag"). For example, the first correlation index is computed between the elements $a(1)$, $a(2)$, $a(3)$, . . . , $a(n)$ of the template and the elements $b(1)$, $b(2)$, $b(3)$, . . . , $b(n)$ of a given trial. In this case, the lag between the elements of the template and of the trial is 0. Then a second correlation index is computed between the elements $a(1)$, $a(2)$, $a(3)$, . . . , $a(n)$ of

the template and the elements $b(1 + \text{lag})$, $b(2 + \text{lag})$, $b(3 + \text{lag})$, . . . , $b(n + \text{lag})$. A series of correlation values is computed by progressively increasing the size of the lag. This procedure is limited only by the number of the elements of the trial array (a correlation involving too small a number of elements would not be reliable). Then, the maximum value in the series of cross-correlations is selected. The lag corresponding to this maximum value is the one at which the trial maximally "looks like" the template. According to the pattern recognition approach, this is the lag at which the signal is "detected." In most cases, if for a given trial some minimal correlation value cannot be reached with any lag, the "signal" is considered to be absent on that trial.

Cross-correlation is vulnerable to two problems. First, the maximum cross-correlation for a particular trial may be unacceptably low. To accept such a trial is to assume that the signal is whatever in the data is least dissimilar to the template. Second, cross-correlation cannot easily handle the presence of multiple components differing in latency. This would constitute a violation of the assumption of invariance of shape of the signal. Cross-correlational techniques should not replace signal-averaging techniques in the case of components with fixed latency, particularly when the signal-to-noise ratio is very small.

Notwithstanding these limitations, cross-correlation techniques have the advantage of utilizing the information provided by the *whole* time series, thereby increasing the power of the analysis. They are particularly useful in identifying components having variable latencies embedded in large amounts of noise.

THE WOODY ADAPTIVE FILTER

The Woody adaptive filter (Woody, 1967) is a particular kind of cross-correlational technique. The term "adaptive" refers to the fact that the template is not established *a priori*, but is extracted by means of an iterative procedure from the data themselves. Each iteration serves to refine the template. This method was originally proposed to identify particular patterns of variation of the EEG recorded in epileptic patients.

Typically, the template used for the initial iteration is the half-cycle of a sine or triangular wave, or the average of the unfiltered single trials. Cross-lagged covariances or correlations are computed between each trial and this template. A new template is obtained by aligning the single trials at the lag that gives the maximum cross-correlation. This procedure is then repeated, using the new average as the template, until the maximal values of cross-correlation become stable. Trials where correlations with the template do not reach a criterion (e.g., .30–.50) at any lag are not used in subsequent template construction and may be discarded entirely from subsequent analysis.

Several studies have been conducted to test the power and reliability of the Woody filter (Nahvi,

Woody, Ungar, & Sharafat, 1975; Wastell, 1977; Woody & Nahvi, 1973). They have concluded that the Woody filter method is often superior to a simple peak detection technique (see pp. 196–198). However, the use of multiple iterations has been questioned (Wastell, 1977). In fact, Wastell reports a decline in validity of the procedure when several iterations are used. Therefore, in contrast with signal averaging, the Woody filter (like most autocorrelation techniques) is not able to improve the signal-to-noise ratio over a definite limit. Therefore, its reliability under conditions of very low signal-to-noise ratio is questionable.

DISCRIMINANT ANALYSIS

Introduction. Discriminant analysis provides a method of discriminating between two or more groups on the basis of systematic differences in the data set. A case classification rule is derived from data whose group membership is known ("training set data"). This rule is then applied to new data of unknown group membership ("test set data"). Thus, discriminant analysis requires that the investigator specify *a priori* the groups into which the data are to be classified. Groups may refer to distinct samples of subjects or to distinct classes of events that vary within subjects.

In addition to providing a method of discriminating among groups, discriminant analysis also provides a means by which to reduce the dimensionality of the data. Such a reduction serves to increase the stability of the discriminant composite. Data reduction is accomplished by selecting a subset of the original variables that best discriminates among the groups. These variables are then used in computing a linear combination of weighting coefficients $\times$ variables to produce a discriminant score. The pattern of weighting coefficients provides information concerning the contribution of each variable to the differentiation between the groups. The function employed in the computation of the discriminant score is referred to as the "discriminant function." The purpose of the function is to provide optimal separation between two or more groups by maximizing the between-group variance while minimizing the within-group variance. In the case of psychophysiological data, when the investigator wishes to discriminate between sets of voltage $\times$ time functions, the discriminant function consists of a linear combination of time points $\times$ weighting coefficients.

As has been discussed above (see pp. 188–189), signal averaging can serve as a relatively simple method of pattern recognition and signal classification. One might doubt the necessity of employing more complex, multivariate techniques, such as discriminant analysis, to accomplish the same goal. In many situations, averaging is adequate. In some situa-

tions, however, signal averaging will produce misleading results. For example, averaging is inappropriate when substantial, uncontrolled variation in the amplitude of a component occurs. In such cases, discriminant analysis provides a clear advantage over signal-averaging procedures, since the differential amplitude of the psychophysiological component can become the basis for group classification. In addition to supplementing the signal-averaging procedure, discriminant analysis also provides a technique that can be employed in the analysis of single-trial data. This is clearly advantageous when the investigator is interested in the trial-to-trial variation in both psychophysiological and performance measures. For example, the use of discriminant analysis procedures in the evaluation of single-trial ERPs has had important theoretical implications. Squires, Wickens, Squires, and Donchin (1976) employed it to construct a quantitative expectancy model of the P300 component of the ERP (see pp. 194–195).

Linear Stepwise Discriminant Analysis. The most commonly used discriminant analysis procedure for the assessment of psychophysiological data is linear stepwise discriminant analysis (LSDA) (Donchin & Herning, 1975; Horst & Donchin, 1980; McGillem, Aunon, & Childers, 1981; Squires & Donchin, 1976). The goal of the LSDA procedure is the selection of a subset of variables that maximizes the between-group separation. The process is analogous to stepwise multiple regression, except that in LSDA the predicted criterion can be a multilevel nominal variable.

The first step is to identify the variable that accounts for the largest proportion of between-group variance. A second variable is then selected that accounts for the maximum proportion of between-group variance not already accounted for by the first variable. This successive selection of variables constitutes the stepwise portion of the LSDA procedure. The between-group difference at each step in the procedure is measured by a one-way analysis of variance (ANOVA) F statistic, and the variable with the largest F is chosen. Several LSDA computer programs permit the deletion of variables that no longer provide a substantial contribution to group separation as other variables are added (Dixon, 1979; Jennrich, 1977). These variables may later be re-entered if their F value is again adequate. The process of variable selection is terminated when some specified criterion has been met. Criteria commonly employed include the number of variables already entered, the amount of variance accounted for, or the point at which no further improvement occurs in some criterion (e.g., the U statistic in the BMDP package, see Dixon, 1979).

A separate vector of weighting coefficients will be derived for each of $n - 1$ discriminant functions, n

being the number of groups. The discriminant criterion value provides a measure of group differentiation for each discriminant function. The first discriminant function has the largest discriminant criterion value, indicating the dimension of maximal group differentiation. The second discriminant function represents the largest group difference not accounted for by the first dimension. Thus, the discriminant criterion value and hence the group differentiation accounted for by each discriminant function decreases with successive functions.

Although $n - 1$ discriminant functions can be calculated, they might not all contribute significantly to group differentiation. Several procedures are available to test the incremental significance of successive discriminant functions (see Tatsuoka, 1970, 1971). Eliminating discriminant functions that do not contribute significantly to group differentiation serves further to reduce the dimensionality of the data set.

As mentioned above, one of the main functions of discriminant analysis is to provide a classification rule that correctly identifies a high proportion of cases. However, the usefulness of the discriminant function is not determined solely on the basis of its classification accuracy with the original data set (training set). Cross-validation is necessary to establish the validity of the discriminant function. When the investigator has a large number of cases available, the most direct procedure is to divide the data set in half, calculate the discriminant function with one half of the data, and validate it on the other half. This procedure can also be carried out on a new data set collected under the same general experimental paradigm. If, on the other hand, the investigator has an insufficient quantity of data to perform this procedure, there are several alternative techniques. One method, commonly called the "jackknife procedure," removes one case from the training set, computes the discriminant function, and then classifies the case that has been omitted. This procedure is repeated until a discriminant function has been calculated for each of the cases in the data set. Overall classification accuracy is determined by dividing the number of single cases misclassified by the total number of cases contained in the data set. Although the jackknife procedure provides a check on the efficiency of the discriminant function, it does not usually produce results that vary greatly from the original computation. Another cross-validation procedure, the "randomization test," is applied to the entire training set. In this instance, however, the cases in the training set are randomly assigned to two groups. A new discriminant function is then computed for these randomly assigned groups. This process is repeated several times, and a distribution of discriminant functions is compiled. The distribution provides an indication of the classification results that can be expected with random data, thereby providing the investigator

with a basis against which to compare the performance of the original discriminant function.

The LSDA procedure outlined above assumes that the covariance across groups is equal and that noise or error in the data conforms to a normal distribution. In cases in which these assumptions are violated, LSDA will provide less than optimal group discrimination performance. A useful alternative in some of these cases is the quadratic discriminant analysis (QDA) technique. The QDA procedure is similar in function to the LSDA technique and has been used successfully in a number of studies (Aunon, McGillem, & O'Donnell, 1982; McGillem, Aunon, & O'Donnell, 1981; Sencaj, Aunon, & McGillem, 1979).

Applications of LSDA. The standardized weighting coefficients obtained in the discriminant analysis procedure can provide valuable information concerning the relative importance of the variables employed in the discriminant function. Examination of the weighting coefficients enables the investigator to assess the contribution of each variable in the discriminant function. Large weights, in either a positive or a negative direction, denote a substantial contribution of their respective variables to group differentiation. In psychophysiological experiments in which the investigator wishes to classify voltage $\times$ time functions into two or more groups, the magnitude of the weighting coefficients identifies those features or time points that best differentiate between groups. For example, Horst and Donchin (1980) found that the ERP time points that best differentiated between two pattern reversal conditions were within the region of the voltage $\times$ time functions that were predicted to change as a function of experimental manipulations. Furthermore, these time points were consistent with the components derived in a principal-components analysis (PCA) of the data (see pp. 198–202).

Discriminant analysis also provides a classification rule that best differentiates between the training groups. This classification rule can be applied to other data sets collected in similar paradigms. In this case, the investigator is interested in classifying new data according to probability of group membership.

Although the primary purpose of the discriminant function is the correct classification of the greatest possible proportion of cases, useful information may also be obtained from the misclassified cases. This point has been illustrated by several studies that have employed discriminant analysis to assess the group membership of single-trial ERPs. In one such study, subjects were asked to count covertly the total number of high-pitched tones from a Bernoulli series of high- and low-pitched tones. High tones occurred with a probability of .20, while low tones occurred with a probability of .80. The common finding in this general paradigm is that counted, low-probability events produce larger P300 components than uncounted, high-probability events. Replicating this design, Squires and Donchin (1976) then employed discriminant analysis for the purpose of classifying each single-trial ERP as either a high- or low-probability event. The discriminant function was able to classify 81% of the single-trial ERPs correctly. An examination of the averages of correctly and incorrectly classified ERPs (see Figure 10-2) indicated that the misclassified events resembled the category into which they were classified more closely than they resembled their correct category. These results suggest that some rare stimuli evoked a response characteristic of frequent stimuli, and vice versa. That is, rather than erring in its classification of waveforms, discriminant analysis may have identified trials in which the subject erred in classifying stimuli. This example illustrates the heuristic value of the technique in revealing the fine structure of the subject's behavior, which can be obscured by cross-trial signal-averaging techniques.

Another example of the use of discriminant analysis in the detailed examination of subjects' behavior is found in tree diagrams of discriminant scores. Figure 10-3 depicts the discriminant scores obtained from ERP waveforms in a two-tone discrimination task (Squires *et al.*, 1976). The investigators calculated discriminant scores for fifth-order sequential stimulus patterns to demonstrate the effect of sequence on the amplitude of several components in the ERP waveform. As can be seen from the figure, the discriminant scores obtained in the experiment closely paralleled the sequential structure of the task. Thus, the discriminant tree diagram provides another

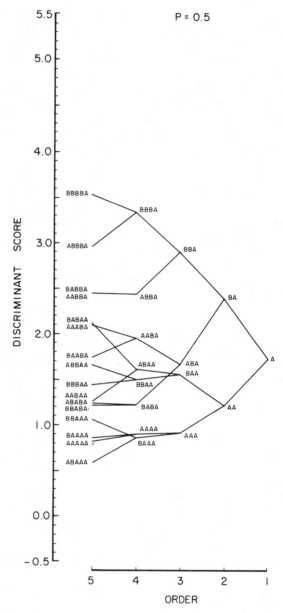

Figure 10-3. Tree diagram of discriminant scores calculated for ERPs elicited by high- and low-pitched tones. The discriminant scores are plotted as a function of stimulus sequence. (From "The Effect of Stimulus Sequence on the Waveform of the Cortical Event-Related Potential" by K. C. Squires, C. D. Wickens, N. C. Squires, and E. Donchin. *Science*, 1976, 193, 1142–1146. Copyright 1976 by the American Association for the Advancement of Science. Reprinted by permission.)

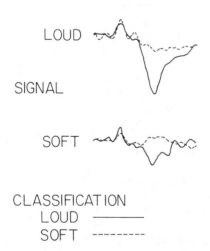

Figure 10-2. Average ERPs sorted by discriminant function classification and type of stimulus. The waveforms represent an average of 16 subjects. (From "Beyond Averaging: The Use of Discriminant Functions to Recognize Event-Related Potentials Elicited by Single Auditory Stimuli" by K. C. Squires and E. Donchin. *Electroencephalography and Clinical Neurophysiology*, 1976, 41, 449–459. Reprinted by permission.)

means of analyzing the fine structure of subjects' behavior.

Discriminant analysis may also be employed to evaluate the degree of resemblance of a single trial to the average of one group or another. In the case of voltage × time functions collected in a psychophysiological experiment, the investigator may wish to know how well a single function resembles the average of one of several groups. This information is provided by the discriminant score.

Evaluation of Discriminant Analysis. As with other statistical techniques, there are both advantages and disadvantages associated with using discriminant analysis procedures in the evaluation of psychophysiological data. Discriminant analysis provides an objective, quantifiable method of assessing differences in single voltage × time functions, both within the training set and across other data sets collected under the same general experimental paradigm. In addition to providing classification information, discriminant analysis also provides an alternative to signal averaging in situations in which the amplitude and latency of the voltage × time components vary across trials. The weighting coefficients derived in the process of discriminant analysis provide information that can be interpreted in terms of the voltage × time components. Thus, components derived in the PCA procedure can be compared with the time points selected in the discriminant analysis procedure to give the investigator an indication of the important features in the data set. Although the initial calculation of the discriminant function is computationally costly, its application is relatively simple. In most cases, it requires only the multiplication and summation of a few variables × weighting coefficients.

There are also several disadvantages to discriminant analysis. The need for an independent basis for grouping voltage × time functions can be problematic in some cases, particularly during exploratory data analysis, in which hypotheses are weak or nonspecific. A second problem is that a useful discriminant function can be calculated only if the groups differ significantly. Finally, the need for cross-validation of the discriminant function imposes additional requirements on the investigator. It is preferable that sufficient data be collected so that the discriminant function can be computed with one set of data and validated on another.

As with other analytic techniques discussed in the present chapter, discriminant analysis cannot be profitably employed without consideration of its limitations and assumptions. However, correct application of the discriminant analysis procedure can produce valuable information for the psychophysiologist.

Digital Filtering

Digital filters have been little used explicitly in psychophysiology. They constitute an interesting contrast with analog filters (see pp. 186–187). A digital filter is most easily described by example. Conceptually, perhaps the simplest digital filter consists of replacing each value in a time series with the average of that number, the number preceding it, and the number following it. Such a common smoothing operation is a rudimentary low-pass filter, in that high-frequency components are reduced.

Specific digital filters vary along several dimensions, which determine the bandpass characteristics and computational speed of each filter. In the example above, three weights are used, each having a value of ⅓. Somewhat less smoothing is accomplished if a different set of weights is used: ¼, ½, ¼. Alternatively, smoothing is also altered if the number of weights (the "window width") is changed to 5, each weight perhaps being ⅕. If the number and values of the weights are held constant but the time interval between data points is changed, the filter will again have different characteristics. A final choice is whether to apply the weights recursively—that is, after applying the filter at point T, does the filter applied to point $T + 1$ employ the unfiltered T (nonrecursive) or the filtered T (recursive) in computing the filtered $T + 1$?

Clearly, psychophysiologists routinely manipulate their data algebraically in ways that constitute digital filtering. Even the computation of a mean of n values can be seen as (1) assigning each value a weight of $1/n$, (2) applying the filter to the midpoint value in the time series by summing the weighted values, and (3) discarding all but the "filtered" midpoint value in the time series. What are typically not discussed when simple digital filters are used are the bandpass characteristics of the filter procedure. Ruchkin and Glaser (1978) describe simple digital filters and present their characteristics. More generally, Cook (1981) has developed a Fortran program, based on the methods of Ackroyd (1973), which determines the optimal values for a set of weights for a nonrecursive filter, given sampling interval, bandwidth, and number of weights desired. Glaser and Ruchkin (1976) present a mathematical discussion of digital filters oriented to the psychophysiologist.

A more elaborate digital method for filtering voltage × time function is Wiener filtering (Walter, 1968; Wiener, 1964). Naitoh and Sunderman (1978) outline the application of this method to ERP data. As they describe it, an estimate of the frequency characteristics of background noise is made from a comparison of the spectra of the average ERP with the average of the spectra of single-trial ERPs, the spectra being obtained via Fourier analysis. This noise estimate is then used to correct the single-trial spectra. Finally, the original ERPs are regenerated via inverse Fourier transforms of the corrected spectra. Naitoh and Sunderman (1978) review evidence that Wiener filtering does not adequately preserve high-frequency information. Furthermore, they suggest that as a technique for general use the slight improvement in signal-to-noise ratio is not worth the trouble (see also Carlton & Katz, 1980; Ungar & Basar, 1976). However, they describe special circumstances for which it might be very appropriate.

Other than for simple smoothing, digital filters are perhaps most commonly employed prior to a pattern recognition procedure such as the Woody filter (see pp. 191–192). However, they are potentially appropriate for any voltage $\times$ time function. They deserve serious consideration in the laboratory, particularly given the continually decreasing cost of additional computation.

Data Reduction Techniques

Introduction

Although the headings "Signal Extraction Techniques" and "Data Reduction Techniques" serve to illustrate the fact that these are distinct processes to which psychophysiological signals are subjected, they are not mutually exclusive. One technique included under the heading of "Signal Extraction Techniques" that would also fit under the present heading is LSDA. Discriminant analysis techniques serve both to provide a method of signal extraction and pattern recognition and, at the same time, to reduce the magnitude of the data set to a much smaller subset of variables. Another technique, PCA, which is discussed under the present heading, could have been included under "Signal Extraction Techniques." As with discriminant analysis, the PCA procedure serves to reduce the size of the data base from numerous dimensions to a relatively few "components." In addition, the PCA technique does not require the restrictive, *a priori* assumptions of group membership that characterize the discriminant analysis procedure. Thus, we do not wish to assert that any of the techniques illustrated in this chapter fit into a single category, but instead that there are distinct stages in the process of data analysis.

A major problem in the analysis and interpretation of psychophysiological data is the determination of the specific criteria by which a signal is defined. For example, if one averages single-trial data, one makes certain assumptions about the signal and noise distributions that underlie the data: That portion of the voltage $\times$ time function that is temporally invariant over repeated presentations of a stimulus is defined as the "signal," while other, randomly varying portions of the epoch that are reduced as a result of averaging are defined as the "noise." Even if we adopt the signal–noise model implied by the averaging procedure, the problem of determining the important features of this "signal" remain. One commonly employed procedure for subdividing the average signal is to define its features on the basis of their relationship to the experimentally induced variance. In this case, the important features of the signal become identical with the components of variance in the data set. This type of definition of features or components of the

voltage $\times$ time function requires not only the proper use of signal extraction and data reduction techniques, but also the exercise of tight experimental control. Since components of the signal are defined in terms of their relationship to experimentally manipulated variance, poor experimental design can lead to spurious components. Thus, another point to be emphasized is that the proper use of methods of analysis can provide the investigator with useful information only within the framework of good experimental design.

As mentioned above, the signal extracted from the raw or average voltage $\times$ time function is typically subdivided into features or components that are related to the experimentally induced variance. Each of these derived components can be thought of as a linear combination of weighting coefficients $\times$ time points. The problem with this approach, however, lies in the fact that there are an infinite number of possible linear representations for a vector of voltage $\times$ time values. Therefore, criteria must be adopted to aid in the selection of a subset of possible linear combinations. The determination of these weighting coefficients and their application to the voltage $\times$ time signal constitute the primary topic of the remainder of this section.

Peak Measurement

The identification of a peak in a voltage $\times$ time vector is perhaps one of the oldest measurement procedures in psychophysiology. The procedure is relatively simple, and it provides both amplitude and latency information. Although there are several methods of defining the peak of a component, they all involve a simple linear combination rule that assumes a weighting coefficient for each time point. This rule typically involves setting all of the weighting coefficients to zero, except for the one weighting coefficient $a(x)$ that corresponds to the time point $t(x)$ at which either the largest or smallest voltage is observed within a prespecified temporal window. This coefficient is set to one. Thus, in the case of peak measurement, the component derived from the voltage $\times$ time vector is defined as a single point. The principal advantages of this measurement procedure are its intuitive appeal and computational simplicity. Peak measurement algorithms represent a direct analogue of the visual inspection of voltage $\times$ time data, with the added advantage of an easily standardized selection procedure.

A few representative procedures for peak measurement are presented here. The identification of "peaks" (single-point events) as zero crossings along the voltage $\times$ time function was proposed in the mid-1960s (Ertl, 1965; Ertl & Schafer, 1969). The method was suggested for peak identification in average ERPs and provides a reliable means for determining latency information. However, amplitude information is not available, since the peak has been defined as the zero point. Another method of peak identification that has been widely employed involves selecting either the largest or smallest voltage within a prespecified temporal window and defining it as the peak. Amplitude information can be obtained from a base-to-peak difference, with the baseline usually being defined as some relatively inactive portion of the voltage × time function, such as that for some period prior to stimulus presentation. Alternatively, a peak-to-peak difference can be derived. In both cases, latency information is provided by the time point $t(x)$ at which the largest or smallest voltage is obtained. The peak or peaks of the voltage × time function can also be defined in terms of the intersection of the tangents of their positive and negative slopes. Amplitude and latency information is also provided by this method.

All of the peak measurement techniques outlined above provide latency information, and, with the exception of the zero-crossing technique, all give amplitude information. Note that each of the procedures makes the assumption that the psychophysiological component of interest can be defined as a single point in the voltage × time vector. When measuring a well-delineated peak with a large signal-to-noise ratio (either the single trial or the average), this assumption would appear to be appropriate. Examples of psychophysiological signals that would meet these criteria include the cardiac R wave, the skin conductance response, and the systolic and diastolic peaks in the blood pressure cycle. However, even peaks that normally are sharply defined can easily become obscured by nonsystematic variance, producing spurious measurements. Another disadvantage of defining a component in terms of a single point is the loss of information concerning the morphology of the voltage × time function. This information, which may be of benefit to the investigator, is discarded prior to analysis of the peak measurement. In effect, all information other than a single point in the voltage × time function is defined as noise in the peak measurement procedure.

Other signal extraction and data reduction techniques also make assumptions about the nature of the signal and noise distributions. However, a subset of these provide information that is similar to that given by the peak measurement techniques, while also retaining some morphological information. For example, the polarity histogram is one measurement technique that provides amplitude information in the form of probability instead of voltage (Callaway & Halliday, 1973; Kubayashi & Yaguchi, 1981). The procedure is performed by incrementing a frequency count whenever an individual time point in the voltage × time function is above or below a zero baseline. A component is then defined whenever the time × probability histogram exceeds some criterion value.

The advantages of the technique include its computational simplicity and relative insensitivity to random fluctuations in the voltage × time signal. Some morphological information is also retained in the form of probability values.

Another procedure that provides amplitude as well as morphological information (symmetry and peakedness) has been proposed by Callaway, Halliday, and Herning (1983). In this procedure, called PEAK, a grand average template is computed. The important features (peaks and troughs) of the template are defined by means of a standard algorithm. Lagged correlations are then computed between the template and the individual voltage × time vectors. Components in the voltage × time vectors are defined as the maximum lagged correlations between the template and the individual vectors. A series of measurements are then made on the features, such as amplitude, latency, peakedness, and symmetry. Other component measurement techniques, such as area measurement and PCA, that also provide alternatives to traditional peak measurement procedures are discussed below.

Another disadvantage of the peak measurement methodology is the difficulty encountered in defining the peak of a relatively slow component. Can a single time point accurately represent a slow component—and, even if it could, which point would be selected? Several psychophysiological signals would qualify as slow components (e.g., respiration, skin conductance response, contingent negative variation [CNV]). Such techniques as area measurement and PCA may provide a more appropriate representation of these components.

In addition to the limitations mentioned above, peak measurement techniques also fail to provide information concerning component overlap. The measurement of a single point does not permit the assessment of the actual number of temporally overlapping components that may jointly be responsible for the voltage recorded at the specific time point. Several examples of this particular problem have been addressed in the ERP literature (Donchin, Tueting, Ritter, Kutas, & Heffley, 1975; Squires, Donchin, Herning, & McCarthy, 1977). While carefully designed factorial experiments can alleviate this problem to some degree, a better solution lies in the application of a procedure that will permit a direct evaluation of the overlapping components.

A final problem concerns independence among peaks when several peaks are measured in the voltage × time function. This is particularly important if statistical inference techniques are to be applied to the data, since most of these techniques assume independence among measures.

In summary, peak measurement procedures must be applied with caution when they are used to define a psychophysiological component. It must be realized that data reduction may result in the loss or distortion of relevant information. However, the techniques outlined above can provide useful information in situations in which the psychophysiological signals are relatively fast, are well delineated, and possess a high signal-to-noise ratio.

Area Measurement

Like peak measurement, the measurement of the area of a psychophysiological component can also be conceptualized in terms of a linear combination of n time points. In this case, however, the weighting coefficients that correspond to the temporal region of the component are set to $1/n$, while the rest of the weighting coefficients are set to zero. Thus, unlike the peak measurement procedures, area measurement defines the component of interest in terms of a range of contiguous time points. These points are then integrated relative to a baseline to produce the area measurement of the component. The assumption underlying the use of area measurement is that the psychophysiological component is most accurately represented by the area of some specific epoch along the voltage $\times$ time function. This appears most reasonable in the case of slow components, such as the skin conductance response, respiration, and CNV.

The measurement of the area or amplitude of a component is performed relative to some baseline. In most cases the baseline is defined as that portion of the voltage $\times$ time vector that occurs prior to stimulus presentation. It is assumed that the baseline represents an inactive portion of the vector. However, this is not always the case. In some situations, anticipatory activity is present (e.g., CNV). In this case another method of defining an inactive baseline is required. One such method is the use of "trimmed" averages, which are relatively insensitive to extreme deviations in the data (see Donchin & Heffley, 1978).

Like peak identification, area measurement also possesses a good deal of face validity, since many psychophysiological signals extend over more than a few time points. The need for elaborate computational algorithms is also minimized by area measurement. Furthermore, area measurements are less susceptible to modest amounts of latency jitter in the component, as well as less sensitive to random amplitude variations in a few time points, than is peak measurement. The degree of insensitivity to random fluctuations is a function of both the number of points included in the area and the temporal range of the latency variability.

Although area measurement presents a distinct advantage over peak identification in some cases, it still fails to deal adequately with several measurement issues. The determination of integration limits is often difficult and/or arbitrary, due to the poor resolution of component limits in the raw or average voltage $\times$ time function. The issue of the establishment of reliable integration limits becomes less of a problem with components that are easily recognized. The issue of component overlap is also not addressed by the area measurement procedures: It is difficult to assess the relative contribution of overlapping components to the voltage measured at either one or several time points. As has been mentioned above, one way to lessen this problem is to control the experimental variables that are known to affect the amplitude and latency of the overlapping components. Finally, as with peak measurement, area measurement techniques may fail to provide the investigator with a clear, detailed picture of the morphology of the voltage $\times$ time function.

In summary, although area measurement procedures alleviate some of the problems encountered with peak identification techniques, there still remain unresolved issues. Area measurement would appear to be most appropriate when nonoverlapping, slow components are evaluated.

PCA

INTRODUCTION

Unlike discriminant analysis, PCA does not require that the subclasses be known *a priori*. Thus PCA makes less restrictive assumptions about the number of relevant categories into which the data will be subdivided. This is particularly useful to the investigator when the nature and number of subclasses are unknown prior to the analysis. In addition to the pattern recognition information garnered from PCA, the technique also provides a means by which a huge data base is reduced to a few components that most parsimoniously describe the experimental variance. Although the PCA procedure has been employed most frequently in the analysis of ERP data, it is clearly relevant to the analysis of other psychophysiological signals.

Like peak and area measurement techniques, PCA can also be conceptualized in terms of a linear combination of time points. To reiterate, the peak measurement procedure defines the psychophysiological component as a single time point in the voltage $\times$ time function. The other time points are discarded prior to analysis. In the case of the area measurement, the psychophysiological component is defined as the integration of equally weighted values at several time points. Area measurement represents a distinct improvement over peak measurement procedures in the assessment of slow components. However, neither procedure addresses the issues of the selection of optimal weighting coefficients or the effects of component overlap on the observed voltages.

Unlike the peak and area measurement techniques, the PCA procedure employs the complete voltage $\times$ time data matrix to determine the weighting coefficients. In the present case, we describe the R-PCA procedure, which involves the computation of a time point × time point input matrix. Other investigators (John, Ruchkin, & Villegas, 1964; John, Ruchkin, & Vidal, 1978) have suggested the usefulness of the Q-PCA procedure, which involves the computation of a waveform × waveform input matrix. In the former case, the interest is in the relationship among time points across the voltage × time function. In the latter case, the analysis provides information concerning the relationship among individual waveforms in the data matrix. Although the present discussion is concerned with the R-PCA procedure, its general points also apply to the Q-PCA technique.

In terms of providing optimal weighting coefficients for the determination of components, PCA is clearly preferable to the methods employed in peak and area measurement. In the case of the PCA procedure, the weighting coefficients (component loadings) represent the contribution of the derived component to the variance at each time point in the voltage × time function. Another advantage of the component extraction procedure employed in PCA is that the weighting coefficients associated with each component are uncorrelated with the weighting coefficients associated with each of the other components. Thus, the component scores computed from the linear combination of time points × weighting coefficients are orthogonal. Therefore, in contrast to peak and area measurements, PCA permits the investigator to assess the independent effects of the experimental manipulations on temporally overlapping components (Donchin *et al.*, 1975; Glaser & Ruchkin, 1976).

As with the peak and area measurement procedures, the method of determining the weighting coefficients in the PCA procedure implies a particular definition of the psychophysiological component. The PCA procedure defines a component in terms of the covariation between time points in the voltage × time function. A pattern of high covariation among time points implies that a specific component (source of variance) can be assumed to be influencing them jointly. These derived components are represented in terms of the variance in the data. The component score produced by the linear combination of the time points × weighting coefficients provides a measure of the magnitude of a specific component in a specific voltage × time function. Thus, for each PCA component a separate weighting coefficient is obtained for each of the time points, and a separate component score is derived for each voltage × time function in the data matrix. An example of a component loading plot is presented in Figure 10-4. This figure displays four sets of component loadings and the grand mean waveform from an ERP experiment. There are 128 component loadings, which correspond to the 128 time points in the waveform. A separate set of loadings is calculated for each of the four components.

Several assumptions underlie the PCA model. It is

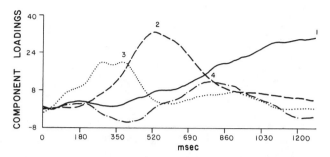

Figure 10-4. Plot of four sets of component loadings derived from a principal-components analysis (PCA) of an ERP data set. Each of the component loading vectors is composed of 128 points corresponding to 128 time points (100-Hz digitizing rate) in the waveforms.

a linear model, and thus assumes that the derived components simply sum together to produce the voltage × time function without interaction. A second assumption concerns the sources of variability in the data. It is assumed that the sources of variance in the data are orthogonal. Although there is no foolproof method of assuring that this assumption is met, good experimental design (in terms of the factorial manipulation of experimental variables that are believed to influence the major sources of variance) is one way to minimize intercomponent correlation (Donchin & Heffley, 1978). Techniques are also available for testing the assumption of orthogonality (Harman, 1967). In cases in which two or more sources of variance are highly correlated across voltage × time functions, PCA will yield a set of weighting coefficients and a single component score, which represent a composite of these correlated components. The interpretation of this composite component in terms of the voltage × time data set will be misleading (Roessler & Manzey, 1981; Wastell, 1981a). A third assumption of the PCA model concerns the domain of component variability. PCA can reliably and efficiently handle variability in the amplitude of the component. On the other hand, variability in the latency of the component over voltage × time functions can cause substantial problems in the interpretation of the derived components. The PCA procedure does not discriminate between variance in the data that is due to variations in amplitude of the underlying component and variance that is due to variations in latency of the underlying component. Therefore, if both the amplitude and latency of a component are changing over trials, PCA will not be able to distinguish the two dimensions. In the case of latency variability, some attempt needs to be made to decrease the variability over trials prior to the use of the PCA technique (Picton & Stuss, 1980). One such procedure, which is described in the present chapter (see pp. 191–192), is the adaptive filter for the analysis of variable-latency neuroelectric signals (Nahvi *et al.*, 1975; Woody, 1967;

Woody & Nahvi, 1973). Callaway *et al.* (1983) demonstrate the improvement in PCA results that latency correction can provide.

APPROPRIATE EXPERIMENTAL DESIGN

The assumptions of the PCA model that are outlined above, and the ease with which they can be violated, suggest that PCA cannot be blindly employed in the analysis of psychophysiological data. The exercise of good experimental design, as well as sensitivity to the assumptions of the PCA model, is of paramount importance if the technique is to provide valid information. The PCA technique represents a multistep procedure for the analysis and interpretation of psychophysiological data. Each step in the procedure requires forethought about the assumptions of the model and the design of the experiment. The initial step, and perhaps the most important, concerns the design of the experiment. There are several issues that must be considered prior to the design of an experiment destined for PCA.

The first issue concerns the second assumption of the PCA model mentioned above—that the major sources of variance are orthogonal. One method to minimize intercomponent correlation is the factorial manipulation of the major sources of variance. A second issue to be considered during the design of the experiment is that the number of cases (typically, subjects × conditions) should exceed by a factor of 10 or more the number of variables (typically, number of time points) in the voltage × time function (Picton & Stuss, 1980). As the number of cases decreases relative to the number of variables, the stability of the component structure will also decrease. In terms of a practical example, this means that a voltage × time vector with 60 time points (variables) would require 600 separate cases to insure stability. A third issue to be considered during the design of the experiment concerns the requirement of the PCA model that the number of variables be of sufficient quantity to determine a stable component structure. For many psychophysiological data sets, this mathematical precondition is usually not a problem, since a large number of variables produce relatively high loadings on each component. However, if underdetermination of the component structure is suspected (too few variables having high loadings on a specific component), there are several techniques that permit the investigator to assess the resulting instability (Mulaik, 1972; Thurstone, 1935; Tucker, 1973).

SELECTION AND COMPUTATION OF THE INPUT MATRIX

Once the investigator has designed the experiment and collected the data, the next step is to decide on the type of input matrix to be employed in the PCA solution. This selection has important implications for the interpretation of the resulting component structure. The input matrices that are accepted by most PCA programs include mean cross-products, covariance, and correlation matrices.

Calculation of the mean cross-products matrix involves summing the products of cross-multiplication of the voltage values for all time points with all other time points. Note that in this case all of the experimental variance is analyzed, since neither the mean nor the variance at each time point is removed from the data set before analysis. The fact that the mean is not subtracted from the cross-products matrix has certain implications for the component structure. To begin with, the loadings of the first derived component usually duplicate the grand average voltage × time function. Second, large base-to-peak deflections in the voltage × time function will produce components even when they are not influenced by the experimental manipulations (Donchin & Heffley, 1978). The use of the cross-products matrix would appear to be most appropriate when the investigator wishes to retain information about the absolute variations in amplitude, as well as the polarity of the corresponding component in the raw data (see Ruchkin, Sutton, & Stega, 1980; Squires *et al.*, 1977).

The calculation of the covariance matrix is similar to that of the cross-products matrix, with the exception that the grand average voltage × time vector is subtracted from the individual voltage × time functions prior to the computation of the cross-products. Thus, the portion of variance that is contributed by the differences between the variable (time point) means is removed in the process of calculating the covariance matrix. In terms of the component structure that will be derived from the covariance matrix, the important issue will be the degree to which the individual voltage × time functions differ from the grand average, not the absolute amplitude or polarity, as is the case for the cross-products matrix. Thus, component scores will reveal relative rather than absolute differences in the component. The covariance matrix has been used most frequently in the analysis of ERPs, since the differences among ERPs relative to the grand mean waveform are usually of primary importance (see Isreal, Chesney, Wickens, & Donchin, 1980; Ruchkin *et al.*, 1980).

The correlation matrix is another option in the selection of the input matrices for the extraction of principal components. The calculation of the correlation matrix requires that the mean of each variable be subtracted (as in covariance), and, additionally, that the difference be divided by the variable's standard deviation. Thus, in the case of the correlation matrix, the variance attributed to the differences between the time point means, as well as the variance due to differences in time point variability, is removed during the process of calculation of the matrix. Essentially, each time point value is converted prior to PCA to a standard z score, based on that point's mean and variance across voltage × time functions. The components extracted from the correlation matrix will be similar to those derived from the covariance matrix, with the exception that the loadings will be more uniform across the length of the component, due to the standardization of the variables (Donchin & Heffley, 1978). Thus, in the case of the correlation matrix, the loadings will not reflect the component morphology as well as when the covariance matrix is employed. This standardization also serves to obscure the magnitude of differences in variance across time points. This may result in the assignment of relatively high loadings to time points at which differences are small.

As can be seen from the preceding discussion, the choice of an input matrix for the PCA procedure constrains the conclusions that can be drawn from the derived component structure. Thus, the investigator must take a careful look at the specific questions that are to be addressed with the PCA, prior to the selection of the input matrix.

EXTRACTION OF PRINCIPAL COMPONENTS

The third step in the PCA process involves the extraction of the weighting coefficients to be used in the linear combination of time points. The extraction procedure, consisting of a sequence of standard matrix manipulations normally performed by packaged statistical software, produces one vector of weighting coefficients for each of the derived components. A separate weighting coefficient is derived for each of the time points in the voltage × time function. Thus, if six components are extracted from a series of voltage × time functions, each composed of 60 time points, there would be six sets of 60 weighting coefficients derived in the PCA procedure. As has been mentioned above, a vector of weighting coefficients represents the contribution of the derived component to the variance at each time point in the voltage × time function. The weighting coefficients associated with each component are uncorrelated with the weighting coefficients associated with each of the other components.

The orthogonality of the components produced by the PCA technique represents a distinct advantage over the peak and area measurement procedures in terms of later inference testing. Univariate ANOVAs can be performed on the component scores for each of the components. On the other hand, computation of separate ANOVAs for each peak or area measurement is of doubtful validity, due to the possible correlation between measures in different parts of the voltage × time function.

The first component extracted in the PCA accounts for the largest proportion of systematic variance in the data matrix. The second derived component accounts for the largest possible percentage of residual variance and is orthogonal to the first component. This process of component extraction continues until all possible components have been derived.

It must be noted that the components derived via PCA need not reflect the physiological generators underlying the recorded voltage changes in a one-to-one fashion. Instead, the components represent merely one summary of the systematic variance present in the data. Theoretical inferences and converging measurement operations are required to verify the relationship of PCA components and physiological components.

One of the goals of the PCA technique is the reduction of the data base to a subset of meaningful components. That is, the hope is that a few orthogonal dimensions (components) will be able to account for most of the variability in the raw data, or that most of the information in the raw data can be more simply represented. Intuitively, this is possible to the extent that the original observation time points are redundant. Determination of the number of components to retain is usually based on such criteria as the amount of variance accounted for and the parsimony of interpretation of the component structure. Several statistical methods have been suggested to assess the number of components to retain (Cattell, 1966; Humphreys & Montanelli, 1975; Kaiser, 1960; Montanelli & Humphreys, 1976; Tucker, 1973).

One point that is specifically relevant to component extraction with psychophysiological data concerns the temporal range of the components in the voltage × time function (Wastell, 1981b). The PCA procedure initially selects components associated with relatively slowly varying regions of the voltage × time function, since these components typically encompass a large amount of the variance. Somewhat faster components, such as the P300, are then selected. Components that extend over a relatively limited temporal range will be extracted much later in the PCA procedure. Therefore, by virtue of the component extraction procedure employed in PCA, some fast components will not constitute a sufficient amount of variance to produce a component that will meet the selection criteria. This point is especially important if the voltage × time functions consist of both slowly and quickly varying components.

ROTATION OF COMPONENT LOADINGS

Once the desired number of components has been extracted from the input matrix, the next step usually involves trying to simplify the component structure. In most cases the component loadings for each derived component vary across the entire voltage × time function, because of a nonzero correlation among time points. The purpose of the rotation procedure is to simplify the pattern of loadings so as to localize each component to a portion of the voltage × time function.

The varimax rotation procedure has been frequently used with ERP data and provides one method by which the interpretability of the component structure can be enhanced. The procedure retains an orthogonal component space while maximizing the variance of the component loadings by attempting to drive the high loadings to unity and the low loadings to zero. Thus, the varimax rotation maximizes the association between each component and a few time points and minimizes the association at all other time points for each component. The rotation redistributes the component variance among the time points, but does not alter the goodness of fit of the component model. Note that the PCA extraction procedure provides the component structure while the rotation temporally localizes the components, thereby permitting the evaluation of the components in terms of the original voltage × time functions. In terms of psychophysiological data, the varimax procedure emphasizes the peak of the signal and is therefore analogous to a base-to-peak measurement.

Following the completion of the rotation procedure, the next step is to compute the linear combination of time points × weighting coefficients for each component. This transformation will produce a separate component score for each voltage × time function in the input matrix. The component score represents a measure of the magnitude of a specific component in a specific voltage × time function.

The majority of psychometric studies that employ the PCA technique terminate prior to the calculation of component scores. In many cases, investigators are only interested in the association between the principal components and the observed data. Component loadings are sufficient to provide this information. The psychophysiologist, on the other hand, is also concerned with the effect of experimental manipulations on the components derived from the voltage × time data. In this case, the component scores as well as the loadings are of interest. Calculation of the component scores permits the investigator to locate the observed voltage × time functions in a simpler and presumably more meaningful component space. Differences among the component scores reflect the effect of experimental manipulations on the principal components and may be subjected to inference-testing procedures (see "Inference Testing," below).

Summary Comparison of Data Reduction Techniques

At this point it is appropriate to summarize the advantages and disadvantages of PCA in the analysis of psychophysiological data, relative to simpler data reduction techniques. To begin with, PCA provides an objective and statistically based method for identifying and computing linear combinations of time points × weighting coefficients. This serves to reduce experimenter bias in the selection and definition of the psychophysiological components. Another advantage of the PCA procedure concerns the method of calculating the weighting coefficients. In the peak and area measurement procedures, weighting coefficients are set to either zero or one. The PCA technique permits the assignment of graded weighting coefficients on the basis of the contribution of the derived component to the variance at each time point in the voltage × time function. Thus, the entire data set is employed in the calculation of component scores, rather than a few time points. This serves to increase the sensitivity of the experimental procedures, as it attenuates the effects of noise and sampling fluctuations on the components. Furthermore, unlike the peak and area measurement techniques, PCA provides information about both the amplitude variability and the morphology of the voltage × time functions. Amplitude information is available in the form of component scores. The morphological characteristics of the component are provided by the weighting coefficients. PCA also gives the investigator information about the degree of component overlap, provided that the underlying components are not highly correlated. Since the components derived from the PCA are orthogonal, univariate tests of significance may be appropriately applied to the component scores. Finally, PCA provides an efficient summary of a very large data base by providing a simpler and therefore more readily interpretable data structure.

Although PCA presents numerous advantages over some traditionally employed psychophysiological analysis techniques, it has some limitations that should be mentioned. For example, the PCA model assumes that the components embedded in the voltage × time function are temporally invariant over trials. In cases in which this assumption is not met, PCA confounds the amplitude and latency variability of the components and provides a component structure that is difficult to interpret. There are, however, several techniques that can be employed as preprocessors to reduce the latency variability prior to employing the PCA technique (e.g., the Woody filter or other autocorrelation measures). The transformation process employed in the PCA is certainly not as intuitively clear as that used in peak or area measurements. This may sometimes lead to confusion when raw voltage × time functions are compared with the reduced component structure. Another point to consider is that components in the voltage × time functions that span a relatively few time points may not constitute sufficient variance to meet the component selection criteria prior to rotation. Finally, since PCA does in fact employ the entire time point × time point data matrix, substantial computing power is required to carry out the transformations.

Spatial Analysis

Introduction

Although some psychophysiological signals can be treated as reflecting the activity of a single structure (as in the case of heart rate), in other cases the signal reflects the activity of what are functionally multiple generators (e.g., EEG). Furthermore, the signal produced by these generators, propagated through space to the body surface, can vary as a function of the spatial characteristics of the generators and the conductivity characteristics of the structures interposed between the operators and the skin. As a result, the signal recorded at the surface will depend on the location of the electrode or other transducer.

In some cases the variability due to electrode location is not of interest to the psychophysiologist but constitutes merely a source of error to be eliminated. For example, ECG morphology depends greatly on electrode location. However, the psychophysiologist might only be interested in interbeat interval. Thus, variation in the morphology of the ECG waveform with electrode position can be ignored. Of course, when variation due to location is ignored in this way, the psychophysiologist is assuming that a single "channel" or "generator" is of interest and that the variability observed at different locations on the body surface is irrelevant. This model is more often adopted for measures of autonomic activity than for EEG or EMG. However, by ignoring the spatial distribution over the body surface of the psychophysiological signal, we may miss a relevant part of the information provided by the signal.

Although there are serious problems in making inferences about location of the ERP component generators from the scalp distribution, measures derived from multielectrode recordings can still be very useful as an empirical method for defining components (see Donchin, 1978). In fact, if a component recorded at the scalp represents the sum of many fields generated by the activity of neurons functionally linked together (although not necessarily localized in a specific brain structure), the scalp distribution of a component will reflect its spatial properties. If we accept this basic model, and if we use scalp topographical information merely to infer functional, not physical, generators, the actual relationship between anatomical generators and their scalp manifestations need not be known. To this end, it is only necessary to record from those locations that allow us to discriminate among functional systems.

The remainder of this section is concerned with a brief description of some procedures devised to study the spatial distribution of psychophysiological measures. Although these procedures have been devised for analyzing brain ERPs, they can be applied to any other measure that can be recorded simultaneously from multiple locations.

Isopotential Maps

Isopotential maps are one way of expressing the values of a psychophysiological variable at different locations on the body surface. They involve recording at a large number of locations in order to obtain an accurate description of the similarities in voltage between different points of the body surface at a particular time point. Isopotential maps have been most frequently used for the EEG.

In an isopotential map (e.g., Ragot & Remond, 1978), the body surface is schematically represented on paper in the same way that terrain is represented in topographical maps. Voltage values observed at any location on the body are presented at the corresponding points of the map. Values of the intervening points are extrapolated by means of algorithms that typically rely on values at adjacent points. Points with equal values are then connected by lines, and a convention is adopted to distinguish positive and negative values.

Isopotential maps constitute only a graphical representation of the data and do not therefore imply any particular assumptions (beyond those concerning interpolation). However, they do not simplify the structure of the data, and therefore they do not qualify as signal extraction techniques. Rather, they are a preliminary tool for investigating the spatial distribution of the psychophysiological variable, where no assumptions about signal and noise are made.

A particular kind of isopotential map is the spatiotemporal map (Remond, 1962). In this map, one of the axes is given by time. Therefore, the spatial information is restricted to a line, but information about the variation over time of the spatial distribution is included. As indicated above, this kind of map is more a data description technique than a signal extraction procedure. The problem of defining the signal remains unsolved.

Another kind of spatial map is the significant probability map (Duffy, Bartels, & Burchfiel, 1981). This kind of map plots z or t statistics obtained by the comparison of pairs of values from two data sets. Maps for different time points are compared. A signal is defined as those aspects of the distribution which differentiate significantly between two sets of data. Note that this kind of definition yields a signal that is specific to the data sets used, and comparisons between data obtained in different experiments are problematic.

Univariate and Multivariate Approaches to Spatial Analysis

An isopotential map is essentially a graphical way of representing the information obtained with a multiple-electrode recording. Because it does not make any distinction between signal and noise, it does not qualify as a signal extraction technique. However, signal extraction from an isopotential map can be accomplished in at least two ways. A peak detection algorithm (see pp. 196–198) can define a signal. Alternatively, the signal may be defined on the basis of a pattern in point-by-point t tests between what are understood to be signal-present and signal-absent conditions (see the discussion of significant probability mapping, above).

However, the use of typical univariate techniques to test inferences about data from multiple-electrode recordings is unsatisfactory for two reasons. First, the large number of resulting significance tests greatly inflates experiment-wise error rate. Standard adjustment of the alpha level is likely to undercorrect for this problem, because error variance is likely to be correlated across recording sites. Second, univariate analysis provides little information about effects or patterning at different sites. A further limitation of standard methods of signal extraction and inference testing with isopotential maps is the inability to distinguish between overlapping sources of activity at each time point.

The remainder of this section is concerned with a description of vector analysis (VA), a multivariate approach to representing the spatial distribution of a psychophysiological variable. The procedure is both powerful (in that all the available information is used) and efficient (in that signal and noise are clearly distinguished).

Multivariate Approach to Spatial Analysis

Vector Analysis (VA) is a multivariate procedure proposed by Gratton, Coles, and Donchin (1985) to quantify information about the spatial distribution of a psychophysiological variable. "Spatial distribution" is here defined as the polarity and relative amount of activity observed at any number of electrode sites, independent of the absolute size of this activity. VA estimates the portion of the activity recorded at several different electrode locations that can be attributed to one or more components, defined in terms of spatial distribution. Therefore, VA defines the signal as one or more components characterized by a specific spatial distribution, and the noise as the remaining variance.

VA treats the voltage values of the electrode locations at a given time point as being the elements of a vector (the data vector). Thus, there is one vector for each time point, and within each vector there is a value for each recording site. This voltage × electrode arrangement contrasts with the usual voltage × time representation. The data vector can be represented geometrically in a space (the vector space) having one dimension for each recording site. Any vector may be characterized by its length and its orientation when plotted in the Euclidean space defined by the dimensions.

VA uses a specific multivariate approach to data reduction, such that a univariate approach to inference testing may be employed. The length of the data vector is a measure of the total activity recorded at all the electrode locations, independent of their relative value or sign. The orientation of the data vector rela-

tive to the dimension axes (recording sites) is determined by the relative amplitude and polarity at the different electrode sites, independent of the total activity recorded. Therefore, when a polar notation is adopted to describe the data vector, the information concerning the spatial distribution at each time point can be isolated and expressed by a series of angles between the vector and arbitrary reference axes. Figure 10-5 shows an example of this notation.

This approach yields two important benefits: Information about the spatial distribution at any given time point can be quantified, and any imaginable spatial distribution can be represented by an orientation in the vector space. In other words, a combination of angles (with the reference axes) in the vector space defines a given spatial distribution.

It is therefore possible to measure the degree to which the spatial distribution observed at a given time point compares with a distribution defined *a priori*. This relationship is described by the cosine of the angle between the observed data vector and the vector representing the hypothesized distribution. A first application of VA to the analysis of spatial distribution consists of establishing the vectors of interest in the vector space, computing the angle with the observed data vectors, and testing the differences. In such an analysis, the same time point from different trials could enter as a replication factor into a one-sample significance test. The difference between two or more observed spatial distributions can also be tested.

Given the usual rules of vector arithmetic, an observed data vector can be viewed as the sum of two or

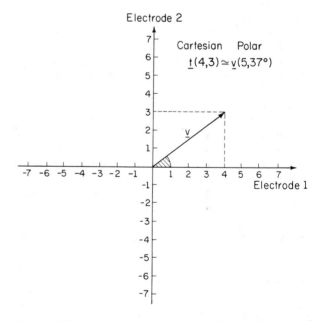

Figure 10-5. Vector analysis: Geometrical representation of a two-element vector (v). Values of the corresponding Cartesian and polar coordinates are also shown.

more component vectors, one of which can be considered as an error vector. Each component vector will be characterized by its own orientation in the space (corresponding, as shown above, to a specific spatial distribution) and its own length (which is a measure of the weight of each component vector in determining the data vector). The "contribution" of each component to the data vector is equal to the length of the component vector. Several different procedures to estimate either the length of the component vectors, their orientation, or both, are available (Gratton *et al.*, 1985). These procedures can be labeled as "vector decomposition." In the simplest case (the vector filter, or VF), a single component, with known spatial distribution, is considered responsible for the spatial distribution observed at a given time point, and discrepancies between this expected distribution and the observed distributions are attributed to sampling error or noise. A brief description of this procedure is given here.

The purpose of the VF technique (Gratton *et al.*, 1985) is to determine the amount of the activity recorded with a multiple-electrode montage at a given time point that can be attributed to a particular target component, defined *a priori* by the investigator. The target component is defined in terms of a spatial distribution that can be represented as a vector in a multidimensional space. All the activity that cannot be attributed to the target component is defined as error. Orthogonality between the orientations of the target vector and of the error vector is postulated (i.e., at each time point, signal and error are uncorrelated). Therefore, the model adopted by VF assumes that the data vector at each time point is given by the sum of a target vector, with given orientation and unknown length, and of an error vector, with orientation orthogonal to the signal vector and unknown length. A statistical test such as Hotelling's one-sample T-square can be used to test the hypothesis that the discrepancies between the observed vector (equal to the mean vector of a sample of vectors) and the theoretical vector may or may not be attributed to chance.

The task of the VF procedure is to estimate the length of the target vector, which, as shown above, corresponds to its contribution to the observed distribution. This can be accomplished by projecting the data vector onto the target vector. This operation is equivalent to rotating the vector space to align one of the axes with the target vector, thus projecting the data vector onto the new axis (see Figure 10-6). The length of the target vector is equal to the length of the data vector multiplied by the cosine of the angle between the observed and the target vectors. Therefore, the length of the target vector will depend on its orientation. This orientation can be chosen *a priori*, on the basis of knowledge of the spatial distribution of the target component, or of some standard experimental procedure known to elicit the target compo-

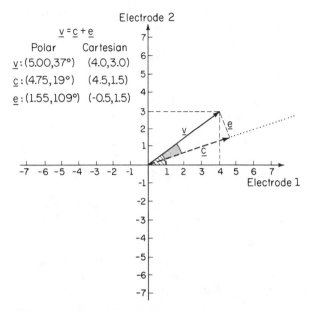

Figure 10-6. Vector filter: Projection of the observed vector (*v*) on the target component vector (*c*). Values of the Cartesian and polar coordinates for observed, target, and error (*e*) vector are also shown.

nent. An alternative procedure is to select the orientation of the signal vector on the basis of some post hoc statistical procedure (e.g., discriminant analysis, PCA, etc.).

The lengths of the target vectors obtained at each time point can be directly submitted to standard inferential procedures. The practical result of VF is to "filter" the data for the component of interest (defined by the spatial distribution expressed in the target vector), with the filter output proportional to the goodness of fit between data vector and target vector. Therefore, VF qualifies as a signal extraction technique. A series of filter output values, one for each time point, constitutes a time series, whose values refer to the estimated contribution of the target component to each time point. This time series can be submitted to the analytical and inferential procedures described elsewhere in this chapter.

VF has several advantages in comparison with the traditional procedures of spatial analysis. First, it involves a small amount of computation. Second, it makes use of all the information available at any given time point. Third, it provides a tool for testing hypotheses concerning spatial distribution.

Since the distribution of the target component is established *a priori*, VF needs no cross-validation. Actually, VF itself can be considered as a test for the distribution of the target component. VF does not make use of the information obtained at different time points in determining the target component. While this can be in some cases disadvantageous (as the analysis is conducted separately for each time point), it is useful when the latency of the components is variable.

Another limitation is that VF is not able to distinguish between the overlapping contribution of several components to the same time point, unless their distributions correspond to orthogonal vectors in the vector space. In the latter case, for each time point, the independent contributions of as many components as the number of recording sites can be assessed. Note that, since the vector space is defined by the recording sites used, an appropriate choice of the electrode sites can greatly improve the resolution of the effects of overlapping components by the VF technique. However, components with different spatial distribution will be differently amplified, or filtered out, by a VF. On the other hand, the general approach of VA allows the investigator to distinguish between overlapping components. Procedures particularly devised to solve this problem are presented in Gratton *et al.* (1985).

DATA ANALYSIS IN THE FREQUENCY DOMAIN (by Stephen W. Porges)

The Description and Partitioning of Variance

The description of physiological activity in terms of both dependent and independent variables is difficult. Physiological activity is seldom in a "binary" state that can be described as either being "on" or "off." Moreover, changes in level or frequency seldom are complete descriptors of physiological activity. The physiological systems of interest to psychophysiologists are continuously changing, reflecting the dynamic regulatory function of the nervous system. It would, of course, be naive to believe that these systems are sensitive solely to those variables we choose to manipulate in our experiments. Thus, we are faced with a series of paradoxical problems. For example, we may be interested in monitoring the central nervous system during manipulations of "mental effort" or "information processing." However, the dimensions of physiological activity that may be the most sensitive to the "neural mediation" of information processing may also be the most sensitive to the "neural mediation" of basic homeostatic function.

In the psychophysiological literature, two methodological procedures have been employed to deal with the problems of partitioning the impact of "stimulus processing" from the background "neurophysiological regulation." Both procedures reside within the time domain (i.e., the stimulus and the physiological activity are indexed by time). The first procedure is characterized by indexing the changes in mean level or variance produced by an experimental event. Implicit

in this type of procedure is the notion of a "statistically significant" response. This notion is based upon a model that assumes that the variance of the physiological process associated with the experimental manipulation is conveyed by the mean level of the physiological process.

The second procedure is characterized by averaging across repeated trials. This procedure is based upon the view that physiological signals reflect neurally mediated responses to stimuli and are superimposed on the background regulatory neurophysiological function. The averaging model assumes that the statistical distribution of the background activity is not influenced by the stimulus and that the background activity is identically and independently distributed. This means that the background activity is assumed to be distributed randomly. Thus, the two prevalent quantitative strategies of decomposing physiological response variance are insensitive both to the possibility that the "signal" is encoded in a parameter other than level and to the possibility that the "signal" is encoded in the background "noise."

Although all voltage $\times$ time functions are "time series," few psychophysiologists have used time series statistics (applied to the frequency domain) as analytic tools. Instead, most psychophysiological researchers have attempted to describe responses via more traditional descriptive statistics. For example, the experimental designs that have been prevalent in psychophysiology have involved traditional, repeated-measures ANOVAs, which test effects of stimulus manipulations on the descriptive statistic of mean level. In a few instances, the pattern of the physiological response as a voltage $\times$ time function has been estimated with measures of variability such as the standard deviation (e.g., heart period variability). However, in most cases, pattern is described by directional or polarity shifts in the voltage $\times$ time function (e.g., HR deceleration or P300).

The repeated-measures ANOVA design tends to evaluate "pre-," "during," and "post-" stimulation periods. By partitioning the variance in this manner, the variance is divided into "treatment" or "time" (repeated measures) and error effects. The error tends to include the variance associated with individual differences among the subjects. To reduce the variance associated with individual differences (i.e., error variance in the analysis of variance design), potent manipulations are used. The objective of this strategy is to enhance the signal-to-noise ratio by maximizing the difference between the "baseline" spontaneous activity and the "response" elicited by the stimulus manipulations.

Ironically, massive treatments often violate the homogeneity-of-variance assumption of ANOVAs. Although the ANOVA is viewed as a "robust" test and is relatively insensitive to violations of the homogeneity of variance assumption in between-groups designs, slight variations in the variance between re-peated measures in the repeated-measures design will produce difficulties in interpretation (see page 214; see also Porges, 1979).

An alternative method of describing voltage $\times$ time functions is to incorporate "time series statistics" into the experimental and quantitative strategies. Time series methods may be used to detect changes in the voltage $\times$ time functions in response to an event by describing the pattern of the function during baseline or stimulus conditions. Time series methods may be classified into two broad categories: time domain and frequency domain. As a general rule, all time series may be represented in either domain. However, certain data may be more easily or more appropriately described in one domain than in the other. One domain may lead to a more natural interpretation. For example, the frequency domain is often used to describe the periodic characteristics of spontaneous EEG and fits nicely into our conceptualization of rhythmic generators in the central nervous system.

Time Series Analysis: Definitions and Methods

The Definition of a Time Series

Although most psychophysiological data are presented in terms of mean levels within or across subjects, the sequential pattern, on which the mean is based, may contribute important information. Time series statistics provide methods to describe and evaluate these patterns. A set of sequential observations, such as the circumference of the chest sampled every second or the time intervals between sequential heart beats, constitutes a time series. Mathematically, a time series may be described as a string of variables that are sequentially indexed—for example, X_t, X_{t+1}, X_{t+2}, $\ldots$, X_{t+n}. In this example, the index t represents time.

Time Domain and Frequency Domain Methods: An Overview

There are two basic approaches that may be used to describe and analyze a time series. The series may be represented and analyzed in the time domain or in the frequency domain. Time domain representations plot data as a function of time (see the "Data Analysis in the Time Domain" section). Those time domain methods that are most closely related to the frequency domain are based on autocorrelation and cross-correlation measures. As their names imply, the techniques are mathematical extensions of traditional correlational techniques. An autocorrelation is the correlation of one time series with a time-shifted version of itself. If the time series is periodic, the plot of the autocorrelations (the autocorrelogram) at different time lags will be periodic. Similarly, a cross-correlation is the correlation of one time series with a time-shifted version of a second time series. The cross-correlation function provides information regarding the statistical dependence of one series on another. If the two time series are identical, the peak value of the cross-correlation function will be unity at the lag that makes the two series identical and less than unity at all other lags. In most cases, since the second series is not simply a time-shifted version of the first series, the peak value of the cross-correlation will be less than unity.

Autocorrelation techniques are effective in detecting periodicities only when the series are characterized by a relatively pure sinusoid, uncontaminated by other influences. Cross-correlation techniques lose their effectiveness and sensitivity to assess the communality between two series when the difference between the series is more than a temporal displacement.

Autoregression techniques are more commonly used in developing models of baseline activity and using the model to forecast into the future. These techniques consist of predicting the value of a time series function at a particular time on the basis of previous values of that function. In a multiple-regression sense, each previous time point serves as an independent predictor variable to which a weight is assigned. Stock market forecasting "systems" are dependent upon this type of modeling. Once the model is generated, confidence intervals can be calculated for the forecasted values. In the case of psychophysiological research, one can define a significant response in any physiological system, on any trial, for any subject, by evaluating whether the stimulus manipulation produces a physiological response that occurs outside the confidence intervals of the forecasted values. Autoregression models may be as simple as a linear forecast (i.e., projecting best linear fit from the baseline) or may involve higher-order models. Individuals interested in applying time domain forecasting and prediction models to detect the impact of an intervention are encouraged to study the Box and Jenkins models (Box & Jenkins, 1976) and to be familiar with the interrupted time series model described by Campbell and Stanley (1966).

If the goal is to describe a periodic signal that represents only a small percentage of the total variance of the series, then the successful application of time domain techniques will be limited to the experimenter's ability to filter the data by removing trend and periodicities other than the one of interest (see pp. 186–187 and pp. 195–196). This requires *a priori* knowledge of the underlying periodic structure of the process.

In contrast to time domain techniques, frequency domain techniques are those based upon the spectral density function, which describes how the periodic variation in a time series may be accounted for by cyclic components at different frequencies. The procedure estimates the spectral densities at various frequencies and is called "spectral analysis." For bivariate series, the "cross-spectral" density function measures the covariances between the two series at different frequencies.

Spectral technology decomposes the variance of a time series into constituent frequencies or periodicities. There is a mathematical relationship between the time domain correlation procedures and spectral analysis. The spectral density function is the Fourier transform of the autocovariance (unstandardized correlation) function, and the cross-spectral density function is the Fourier transform of the cross-covariance function. (The Fourier transform is an algebraic method of decomposing any time series into a set of pure sine wave of different frequencies, with a particular amplitude and phase angle for each frequency.)

Other Frequency Domain Methods

There are other frequency domain techniques. A simple and often visually appealing method is "zero crossing." This method quantifies the frequency with which a waveform crosses an arbitrary baseline. It provides a relatively accurate estimate of the frequency of the process if, and only if, the process contains only one periodic component and is not contaminated by background noise. The periodogram is effective at finding periodic components and may be efficiently calculated using the fast Fourier transform. However, the periodogram has poor statistical characteristics and should not be used without appropriate frequency domain smoothing (see Bohrer & Porges, 1982).

Periodic covariation may be described with "cross-spectral analysis." Cross-spectral analysis generates a coherence function, which is a measure of the best linear association of each observed rhythm in one variable with the same rhythm in a second variable. The coherence is the square of the correlation between the sinusoidal components of the two processes at a specific frequency. The coherence at any specific frequency is the square of the cross-spectral density divided by the product of the spectral densities of each series at the specified frequency. Note the similarity of this equation with the calculation of a squared correlation coefficient; the cross-spectral density parallels the squared cross-products, and the spectral density parallels the variances. Conceptually, the coherence may be thought of as a time series analogue of Ω^2 (see Hays, 1981), or as the proportion of variance accounted for by the influence of one series on the other at each specific frequency. Since physiological processes are not perfect sinusoids, but occur over a band of frequencies, we have developed a summary statistic that describes the proportion of shared variance between two systems over a band of frequencies (see Porges, Bohrer, Cheung, Drasgow, McCabe, & Keren, 1980). We have labeled this statistic the "weighted coherence" (C_w). In our laboratory, C_w has been used primarily to describe the relationship between heart period and respiration. However, the application of C_w is not limited to the assessment of the coupling between respiration and heart period activity, but may also be used to determine the proportion of shared variance between any two processes that fit the statistical assumptions for spectral analysis.

Spectral analysis is based upon a model that assumes that the constituent periodic components of a time series are statistically "independent" and linearly additive. There are situations in which one frequency component in a system could trigger a faster frequency. For example, consider a physiological system in which four breaths occur before there is a general shift in blood pressure. Both frequencies will be manifested in the spectrum of blood pressure. Using traditional spectral analysis, one would assume that the periodic components are independent. However, by using a spectral technology called "polyspectral" (see Brillinger, 1975), it is possible to identify potential "coherences" between two frequency components within one physiological process, or between two different frequency components represented in two different physiological processes.

Time Series Statistics: Methods to Partition Variance

By viewing psychophysiological variables as a time series (i.e., voltage $\times$ time functions), and by viewing experimental procedures as a method of partitioning variance, we may arrive at two insights into the construct of "variance." First, the variance associated with the "treatment" must be partitioned from the variance associated with the background physiological activity. This procedure is necessary, since physiological activity is omnipresent and physiological responses must be evaluated against a varying, rather than a constant, baseline. Second, the variance of any physiological process is not uniquely determined by any one specific physiological mechanism. Virtually all physiological response systems represent the actions of antagonistic mediators that reflect the organism's quest to maintain dynamic homeostasis. Therefore, the variance of the physiological process contains "component" variances representing potentially independent mechanisms. Thus, time series methods may be useful in partitioning the variance of the complex physiological response patterns into components. Moreover, it is possible that the statistical behavior of the components will be different; that is, different components will be differentially sensitive to various manipulations.

The discussion above leads to a revised conceptualization of the physiological response pattern in the psychophysiological experiment. Most physiological response patterns may be conceptualized as the sum of two uncorrelated processes: a baseline trend, and an ensemble of rhythmic influences that are superimposed on the baseline trend. The impact of a stimulus or psychological state may reliably influence either or both "component" physiological processes. To complicate matters, the constituent rhythmic components may be manifestations of different underlying neurophysiological processes. For example, in HR there are two obvious rhythms: One is modulated at the respiratory frequency (i.e., respiratory sinus arrhythmia); the second, an oscillation at a slower frequency, appears to represent the influence of the rhythmic oscillation of blood and cerebrospinal fluid, since the same rhythm is observed in vasomotor activity, blood pressure, and cerebrospinal fluid.

Time domain approaches focus on evaluating changes in trend as an indicator of the impact of the stimulus manipulation. These methods tend to remove the background rhythmic activity by averaging across trials. The averaging method assumes that the phase relationship between the underlying rhythmic background activity and the stimulus is identically and independently distributed. Thus, when the data are averaged across trials, the rhythmic background activity will average to zero. This assumption, of course, is only tenable in experiments in which the timing of stimulus presentation is independent of the physiological process. In self-paced experiments, it is highly unlikely that a rhythmic component of the background physiological activity is not phase-related to the self-initiated trial onset, since behavior is neurophysiologically mediated.

In contrast, frequency domain approaches tend to focus on describing the rhythmic components of the background physiological activity that are superimposed on the trend. Thus, it appears that the frequency domain approach tends to evaluate the component of variance that is treated as "error" variance in the time domain approach. Moreover, appropriate implementation of many frequency domain techniques requires that the trend be removed prior to partitioning of the variance into frequency-specific components. Frequency domain approaches tend to be associated with spectral analysis technology. The theories underlying the spectral technology have been, for the most part, developed for "stationary" data sets (Chatfield, 1975). (A time series is said to be stationary when the mean, variance and autocovariance function are independent of time.) Application of the spectral technology to nonstationary data will result in potentially unreliable and uninterpretable spectral density estimates.

Although any data set that is described in the frequency domain may be represented in the time domain, or vice versa, the two approaches do not provide identical information. For example, in the discussion above, I have described the primary emphases of time domain (i.e., the description of trend) and frequency domain (i.e., the description of rhythmic activity) approaches. In both approaches, the data set typically is modified prior to analysis. In the time domain approach, the data have been "smoothed" to remove the variance associated with background activity. In the frequency domain approach, the data have been "detrended" to provide a stationary data set with a constant baseline. However, any time series, which in the examples given here would be voltage $\times$ time functions, could be described via frequency domain spectral technology in terms of the sum of spectral density estimates and could be "reconstituted" into the original time series with knowledge of the spectral density estimates and the phase relationships among the constituent frequency components. The time domain autocorrelation approach and the frequency domain spectral approach are merely transformations of each other, although time domain models are more likely to be used to describe changes in trend and frequency domain models to describe changes in the constituent frequency components.

The discussion above is relevant, since most physiological systems monitored by psychophysiologists tend to have both aperiodic (i.e., trend) and periodic (i.e., rhythmic) components. For example, with HR, we have the basic problem of the directional HR responses associated with motor and cognitive function being superimposed on the naturally occurring respiratory sinus arrhythmia. In the case of HR, most psychophysiological investigations attempt to maximize the impact of the stimulus or psychological state on the trend. This is done by averaging and treating the rhythmic oscillations as background "error." Similarly, averaging across trials minimizes the background oscillations in EDA. However, in the case of EEG recordings, it is the periodic characteristics that are emphasized, and it is the trend that is filtered from the data set and treated as "error." In both situations, the assumption is made that the physiological response "component" (i.e., trend or periodic) is a sensitive index of the psychological process being monitored. However, it is conceivable that there may be situations in which the "level" of the output of the physiological system manifested in a change in "trend" may be unresponsive to the manipulation, while the treatment effect may be easily observed in a change in the pattern—or vice versa.

Constraints and Limitations of Sampling Procedures

Physiological Activity: Continuous Processes

Sensitive evaluations of physiological activity must necessarily include sophisticated techniques to evaluate pattern and change. The quantification strategy that the researcher employs in psychophysiological research must rely on an *a priori* definition of the response parameters being investigated. In most psychological research, background spontaneous activity is considered unimportant. Meaningful responses can be easily identified as a discrete change in the ongoing activity of the system. However, in the investigation of physiological processes, it is clear that most physiological systems function continuously. Although we can easily identify the occurrence of many discrete behavioral responses, meaningful physiological responses are often much more difficult to define and isolate. One must assume that virtually every physiological system is continuous, even though the measurable datum is manifested at discrete times (e.g., heart beats).

Physiological Activity: Discrete Processes

Although the underlying physiological processes are assumed to be continuous, the prevalent quantification strategies necessitate estimates of the physiological activity at discrete points in time. There are two reasons for this procedure: First, most analytic methods are based upon statistical models in which the continuous process is sampled at sequential points in time; and second, the prevalent quantification techniques associated with digital computers necessitate time-dependent sampling. Thus, although many physiological processes are continuous, the statistical and computer technologies generally force the researcher into quantifying and analyzing the voltage × time functions as discrete processes sampled at sequential points in time.

How fast should one sample continuous processes? The sampling rate or "time window" must be fast enough to describe the variance of the process accurately. The decision regarding sampling rate requires an *a priori* understanding of the physiological response system being monitored. If relevant information is encoded in a periodic component of the physiological process with a duration shorter than twice the sampling interval, then the sampled data set will not convey the relevant information. For example, if peripheral vasomotor activity is being sampled from a finger at a rate slower than the HR, the variance in vasomotor activity associated with the beating of the heart will be "aliased" or "folded back" on a slower periodicity. The fastest frequency about which we can derive meaningful information from a data set is called the "Nyquist" frequency. The Nyquist frequency is one-half the sampling frequency.

To illustrate the impact of sampling too slowly, consider sampling a 60-Hz pure sine wave 30 times/sec. Because the signal would always be at the same point in the cycle when sampled, the samples would all have the same value, implying that no signal is present. Sampling this signal 60 times/sec would still yield a flat line. Sampling slightly faster than that would mean measuring successive portions of the cycle, implying a very slowly changing sine wave. For example, sampling a 60-Hz signal 70 times/sec would yield a time series of discrete values resembling a pure 10-Hz signal. Indeed, the investigator could not distinguish true 10-Hz activity from "aliased" 60-Hz activity. Only if the 60-Hz signal were sampled 120 or more times/sec would the 60-Hz signal not be distorted.

As a more complex example, imagine that three physiological variables (i.e., HR, respiration rate, and finger vasomotor activity) are being sampled at a rate of 1 time/sec. In this example, the heart is beating at 90 beats/min (i.e., 1.5 beats/sec, or 1.5 Hz), and the breathing frequency is 15 times/min (i.e., one breath every 4 sec, or .25 Hz). If each variable is sampled 1 time/sec, the fastest periodic process we can evaluate in each of the variables is a process that is slower than one oscillation every 2 sec, or .5 Hz. This does not cause any serious problems with the respiration series, since the breathing is slower than the Nyquist frequency of .5 Hz. Similarly, in the cardiac system, the fastest periodic activity is the respiratory sinus arrhythmia at the frequency of breathing. However, although vasomotor activity exhibits rhythmic processes at the respiratory frequency and at even slower frequencies, it also oscillates at the frequency of the heart beat, since the flow of blood to the periphery is changing on each systole and diastole. Therefore, the peripheral vasomotor activity should exhibit a rhythm of approximately 1.5 Hz (i.e., 90/min), concordant with the average HR. However, if the vasomotor activity is sampled only 1 time/sec, what happens to the variance associated with this fast oscillation? The variance associated with the fast oscillation will be "folded back" and added to the variance of frequencies slower than the Nyquist frequency (which in this case is one-half the 1-Hz sampling rate, or .5 Hz). These lower frequencies are said to be "aliased." The same problem will exist if these variables are sampled every 500 msec when the average HR is about 90 beats/min. In this example, the frequency decomposition (spectrum) of the vasomotor time series will result in a periodic component at a frequency slower than breathing, a second "peak" at the breathing frequency, and a third "peak" at a frequency faster than breathing. This faster frequency does not represent a true neurophysiological process, but rather the impact of an inappropriate sampling rate. In this example it would be necessary to sample at 3 Hz or faster (at least twice the 1.5-Hz HR) to prevent aliasing. To decompose the rapidly changing vasomotor waveform into frequency components accurately, or to be sensitive to short-latency changes in amplitude, it would be preferable to sample more than 3 times/sec.

The dangers of inappropriate sampling rates are clear, but how does one avoid these problems? If one were interested in the relationship among various physiological variables, such as HR and respiration, it would be necessary to sample the activity of all variables at a frequency that is at least twice the frequency of the fastest variable. Note that the problem of aliasing is not problematic solely in the frequency domain: One can see the inappropriate interpretations or loss of relevant information in the time domain, if slow sampling results in not detecting the response component that is sensitive to the stimulus. Fundamentally, sampling a "continuous" process necessitates an understanding of the periodic components and response latencies of the physiological system being studied.

Physiological Activity: Point Processes

Some physiological processes are, by their nature, events that may be characterized as "binary"—categorized as "occurring" or "not occurring." These processes are called "point processes." For example, the beating of the heart may be operationalized as a "binary" event indicated by the occurrence of the R wave. Similarly, single-unit activity in the central nervous system is characterized by "spikes" and "interspike intervals." Point processes pose special statistical problems. The primary problem arises when attempting to sample a point process at equal intervals in time (e.g., second by second). Time series texts (e.g., Gottman, 1981) deal primarily with equal time sampling of continuous processes. Fortunately, this is not problematic with many physiological processes, since they may be represented as continuous voltage $\times$ time functions. However, how does one deal with such processes as heart period and the ensemble of processes temporally determined by the beating of the heart? Although blood pressure changes are time locked to the beating of the heart, is it legitimate to view blood pressure as a continuous process and to sample it at equal time intervals? Moreover, how would one estimate the duration of any specific cardiac cycle component (e.g., the P-R interval) across time? These questions have never been adequately discussed in the psychophysiological literature and can be reduced to two points: First, how does one sample event-related physiological data in equal time intervals; second, how frequently must one sample event-related physiological data?

Although Bartlett (1963) provides a method for performing spectral analysis on the "interval" characteristic of binary data, it is of little use to the psychophysiologist. The reasons are self-evident, since the data are assumed to be stationary for this analysis. Recall the arguments given above that the spectral analysis of "nonstationary" time series provides uninterpretable estimates of the spectral densities and that physiological processes tend to be "nonstationary" time series. It is, therefore, necessary to "detrend" the interval time series to generate a data set that is at least

weakly stationary. (A process is called "weakly stationary" if its mean is constant and its autocovariance function depends only on lag; see Chatfield, 1975.) Moreover, even in the time domain, equal time interval estimates are necessary for assessing trends. Since most methods of detrending data to produce "stationary" time series for frequency domain analyses are actually time domain methods that have been developed for equal time sampling of continuous process, it is necessary to generate an estimate of the point process at equal points in time.

There are a variety of methods that may be used to generate an estimate of a point process at equal points in time, such as interpolation, weighting, and sampling. Each method has its own unique characteristics. An important requirement is to make the "time window" short enough to map into the temporal variability of the process. If the time window is longer than twice the shortest inter-event interval, then the time window may smooth or alias a component of the variance of the process. In the case of heart period, it is necessary to estimate the heart period in sequential intervals of approximately one-half the duration of the fastest heart period. By estimating the heart period process at sequential intervals that are shorter than half the duration of the fastest heart period, the variance of the heart period process will be preserved in the transformed data set. Moreover, the transformed data set will now be amenable to time domain detrending and filtering techniques, as well as spectral analysis techniques.

Conclusion

The investigator should consider the relative assumptions, advantages, and disadvantages of time domain and frequency domain techniques. Attention to periodicities in a time series, rather than to trends alone, can enhance our understanding of psychophysiological processes.

INFERENCE TESTING

Introduction

"Inference testing" involves procedures that evaluate the probable validity of statements about one set of phenomena, where those statements are based on knowledge about a second set of phenomena. The inference being tested may be "inductive" (one knows real-world event X, which appears to be generalizable to principle Y), "deductive" (one entertains theory Y, which predicts real-world event X), or some elaborate combination of these.

Both inductive and deductive inferences typically contribute to a psychophysiological experiment. First, a general concern or hypothesis is stated, and a highly specific instance of it is studied (deduction). Straightforward algebraic manipulations might then be performed on the resulting voltage × time functions to evaluate whether the claim of the hypothesis was manifested in the data obtained. These manipulations produce "descriptive statistics," merely summarizing the data in some highly specified way. Within the confines of a particular experiment, the validity of a hypothesis is tested by inspection of the data; inferential statistical tests are unnecessary. The discussions of time domain and frequency domain data analysis in this chapter catalog such algebraic procedures, ranging from the computation of a sample mean to PCA.

The investigator is rarely content merely to evaluate the validity of the hypothesis in the specific case alone, however, because the purpose is to confirm the original generalization or to derive new generalizations from initial ones. Thus, the experimenter is likely to attempt to apply one set of concepts to a real-world procedure (deduction), the results of which can then be used to infer new concepts (induction). "Inferential statistics" are those used in this way to evaluate the generalizability of the findings of a particular experiment. Such statistics address the extent to which findings in a specific case can be expected to hold for some superset of similar cases, versus the alternative that specific results are merely the result of variations in the phenomena not accounted for by the theory under consideration.

As noted earlier in this chapter, the algebraic manipulations that raw data often endure are not easily localized in a single stage of analysis. Just as it is artificial to distinguish between signal extraction and data reduction, so it is artificial to segregate data analysis and inference testing. However, while particular techniques straddle such boundaries, the logical distinction between description and inference is essential. The investigator's statistical options become severely curtailed when moving from descriptive and/or exploratory analysis to inferential analysis.

There are numerous texts on the general use of inferential statistics (e.g., Hays, 1981; Myers, 1979; Winer, 1971). Rather than a complete user's guide to statistical inference, the remainder of this section provides a sampling of issues of particular relevance to the psychophysiologist, highlighting assumptions of statistical tests, common violations of those assumptions, and remedial solutions.

Univariate ANOVA

Two issues arise when the traditional ANOVA as an inferential process is applied to psychophysiological data. One issue concerns the need to study phenomena independently of pre-existing basal levels.

The use of analysis of covariance (ANCOVA) and of change scores has been particularly controversial. The other issue, the assumption of homogeneity of covariance, derives from the special constraints on ANOVA when repeated measures are used, either alone or crossed with between-subjects variables (mixed-model ANOVA).

Both issues arise because the psychophysiologist typically studies the time course of voltage × time functions in the context of changing inputs from independent variables. If one wishes to measure acute, event-related responses, variations in average or basal level may contribute a major source of statistical noise (variance not controlled by factors in the ANOVA table appearing in the error term). Alternatively, such variance may constitute the main phenomenon of interest if one studies slower, homeostatic actions.

Clearly, it is valuable (though not always possible) for the investigator to determine, *a priori*, the likely sources of variance in the dependent measure. Gaining experimental control over variance is inherently preferable to attempting to assert post hoc statistical control.

ANCOVA

The ANCOVA is commonly the method of choice for post hoc removal of undesired sources of variance. Unfortunately, it is often difficult to achieve such statistical control over undesired sources of variance without systematically distorting the data of interest. For example, it has been argued that ANCOVA is not valid in the very situation for which it is intuitively most appealing (see Chapman & Chapman, 1973, pp. 82–83; Lord, 1967). These authors claim that ANCOVA is legitimate only if two requirements are met: The regression slopes of the dependent variable on the covariate must be the same for each level of the independent variable, and the mean value of the covariate must be the same for each level of the independent variable. As an illustration, assume an experiment in which HR during imagery is believed to vary systematically as a function of imagery ability, a between-subjects factor. To complicate matters, however, some of the subjects are athletes having resting HR levels as much as 40% below those of other subjects. Relative to the hypothesis of the experiment, this source of variance in HR is merely statistical noise. The investigator wishes to employ resting HR as the covariate in an ANCOVA. In order to permit the use of ANCOVA in this case, the investigator would have to show that, for each level of imagery ability in the design, (1) the regression slopes of imagery HR on resting HR are equal and (2) the mean resting HR levels are equal. It is the second requirement that is most likely to disappoint the investigator, since it is often such hypothetically irrelevant, *a priori* group differences that tempt the use of ANCOVA. The former requirement, on the other hand, is less constraining: Differences in regression slopes amount to an interaction of experimental variables with the covariate, which may be a meaningful, if unanticipated, result (see pp. 215–216).

Opinion on the second requirement is not uniform (see Benjamin, 1967; Cohen & Cohen, 1975; Lubin, 1965; Overall & Woodward, 1977). It has been argued that ANCOVA may be permissible despite group differences on the covariate, depending on the reason for the difference. Overall and Woodward (1977) have argued in favor of ANCOVA in the case where experimental treatments do not affect the covariate and subjects are assigned to experimental groups either randomly, or nonrandomly but on the basis of scores on the covariate.

In the case of nonrandom group assignment, Cohen and Cohen (1975) suggest that the issue be considered in terms of causality. When it is believed (for theoretical—not statistical—reasons) that the covariate is causally dependent on the independent variable, ANCOVA would not be legitimate. Specifically, if covariate C shares variance with independent variable X because X affects C, then removing their shared variance from X unfairly robs X of variance with which X may actually affect dependent variable Y. Thus, ANCOVA in this case would distort the experimental effect of X on Y. On the other hand, if C is causally prior to X, then any shared variance with which they jointly affect Y properly belongs to C, not X. Y would be affected by that source of variance whether or not X were present, so X should not be credited with that variance. In the example above of imagery and HR, in which group assignment is nonrandom (based on imagery ability), it can be argued that there is no theoretical basis for basal HR determining imagery ability. Thus, the use of ANCOVA in the face of group differences on the covariate can be defended.

In the case of random assignment to groups, Cohen and Cohen (1975) are quite comfortable with ANCOVA. They reason that, although two random samples may by chance differ on the covariate, what matters is the population they represent, about which inferences will be drawn. Randomization assures that the expected (population) differences between samples will be zero, regardless of actual sample differences. Thus, C and X share no variance in the population, even though they may do so by chance in the samples selected. Although the groups differ on C, they will tend to regress toward their population mean (i.e., no difference on C) when they are observed in order to measure Y. Of course, this tendency will be realized only for large samples.

We do not attempt here to advocate one or the other of these positions on the validity of ANCOVA in the face of group differences on the covariate. Clearly, the investigator should evaluate whether the two assumptions are met in a given data set and should consider whether violation of the assumptions will pose an interpretative problem. Perhaps the important lesson to be drawn from such debates is that what constitutes a proper use of inferential statistics is partially a function of the experimental purpose and the conceptual framework. Just as a given statistical model is developed under certain assumptions, the importance of a violation of those assumptions rests on the use made of the statistic. Furthermore, particular assumptions differ with respect to the consequences of violation. However, the confidence intervals of traditional statistics are not the only means of testing inferences. Repeated sampling from the superset of cases to which one's first experiment belongs—known as "replication" and "cross-validation"—is a respectable alternative.

Change Scores and the Law of Initial Values

Wilder (1957) first formulated the "law of initial values" (LIV), which states that response amplitude is a function of prestimulus level. Assuming an implicit ceiling effect, the prediction is that higher prestimulus levels will be associated with smaller responses. A number of early papers report confirmatory data (e.g., Hord, Johnson, & Lubin, 1964; Lacey, 1956; Sternbach, 1960). The LIV has serious implications for the most popular metric in psychophysiology, the change score. Specifically, the size of the change score may be partially a function of initial level. Clearly, the LIV phenomenon can affect change score data in ways that are unrelated to the experimental manipulation, generally reducing statistical power. To deal with this problem with autonomic measurs, where the LIV problem is most widely acknowledged, Lacey (1956) proposed the autonomic lability score (ALS) transformation. While the ALS was intended to take account of the LIV by standardizing the effect of the homeostatic influence on response amplitude scores, it was later shown (Benjamin, 1963) that the ALS actually removes LIV effects completely. Essentially, the ALS method is a customized elaboration of ANCOVA. As such, it is vulnerable to the same constraints and debates as ANCOVA (see the discussion of ANCOVA, above). When the investigator is satisfied that the ALS method is statistically acceptable in a particular data set, it can be useful for standardizing data that consist of multiple dependent measures having different measurement scales, variances, and the like. It is particularly appropriate for a close examination of response pattern across situations and measures (e.g., Lacey, 1956; cf. the discussion of coefficient of concordance, page 217). However, the ALS is rarely used in current research.

The validity of change scores is still arguable (e.g., Benjamin, 1973; Etaugh & Etaugh, 1972; Harris, 1963; Lubin, 1965). We are in sympathy with Benjamin (1973), who has argued that one's metric achieves validity because of its theoretical appropriateness, not its statistical purity. Thus, if one's theory actually makes predictions about change scores, one should measure change scores.

The Assumption of Homogeneity of Covariance

"Homogeneity of covariance" means that the covariance between each pair of repeated-measures factor levels is constant. The assumption of homogeneity of covariance in ANOVA is perhaps less controversial than the requirement for ANCOVA, but it is still frequently violated. For example, Jennings and Wood (1976) reported that 84% of the articles using repeated-measures ANOVA designs in Volume 12 of *Psychophysiology* (1975) appeared to have ignored the assumption. Violations of the assumption generally bias the F test toward a Type I error (Myers, 1979; Winer, 1971).

Violations of the assumption are possible in any repeated-measures design, but almost inevitable in psychophysiological studies analyzing voltage $\times$ time functions. Neighboring time points tend to be highly correlated, but samples that are more widely spaced in time will generally be less tightly coupled. The problem is exacerbated when periodicities exist in the signal, such as sinus arrhythmia in HR, producing systematic irregularities in the covariance among sample points. Thus, the covariances among pairs of points in a time series will vary as a function of their temporal separation. This problem is clearly larger when "time" is measured in milliseconds between digitized samples than in minutes between trial blocks or days between sessions. Of course, the critical issue is not the absolute time scale but the stability of the psychophysiological function relative to the sampling interval and the total sample epoch. Neighboring 10/sec samples of skin conductance level are likely to be much more closely intercorrelated than 10/sec samples of EEG.

Two ways of coping with heterogeneity of covariance have been proposed. Jennings and Wood (1976) apprised psychophysiologists of Box's (1954) solution as developed by Geisser and Greenhouse (1958; see also Games, 1975, 1976; Keselman & Rogan, 1980; Keselman, Rogan, Mendoza, & Breen, 1980; McCall & Appelbaum, 1973; Richards, 1980; R. S. Wilson, 1974). This method reduces the degrees of freedom used for evaluation of the significance of the F statistic. The reduction is proportional to the amount of heterogeneity among the covariances. Assuming K treatment levels and n subjects, the maximum possible reduction is from $(K - 1)$ and $(K - 1) \times (n - 1)$ to (1) and $(n - 1)$ degrees of freedom. Jennings and Wood (1976) and Myers (1979) provide a formula for calculating the correction factor, known as ϵ or λ.[1] These writers point out that the F can first be evaluated using the most conservative $[(1), (n - 1)]$ and the most liberal $[(K - 1), (K - 1)$

$\times (n - 1)]$ limits; if the F is significant in the first case or nonsignificant in the second case, there is no need to calculate the correction factor.

To illustrate the potential impact of the Geisser–Greenhouse correction factor, consider a standard CNV paradigm (Simons, Ohman, & Lang, 1979). The EEG was digitized at 30 Hz, and sets of 15 consecutive points were averaged to one value every .5 sec. One of us computed the correction factor for this data set to be .19. Thus, using the correction factor would have cost the investigators 80% of their degrees of freedom in analyses using the .5-sec data points. Using median HR data obtained during sequential 30-sec periods of an imagery experiment (Lang, Kozak, Miller, Levin, & McLean, 1980), the correction factor was computed to be .35. This higher value (i.e., less heterogeneity) reflects the much longer interobservation interval in this study than in the CNV example, though about two-thirds of the degrees of freedom would still have been lost had the correction been made.

In sum, the Geisser–Greenhouse correction factor can take a very serious toll on the apparent statistical power of a psychophysiological experiment (though, of course, it merely reclaims the inflated "power" caused by heterogeneity of covariance). In addition, Davidson (1972) has pointed out that with small sample sizes there may be inadequate statistical power in the procedure to detect a violation of the homogeneity assumption. Finally, it has been suggested that the product of the correction factors for the separate main effects be used for testing interactions of repeated-measures factors, but this application has not been fully validated (Jennings & Wood, 1976). These factors together undoubtedly explain how rarely the correction factor is used in published research.

The second way to cope with violations of the homogeneity-of-variance assumption, advocated by Richards (1980), is to do multivariate analysis of variance (MANOVA), rather than the usual repeated-measures, univariate ANOVA. The different levels of the repeated-measures factor in ANOVA become separate dependent variables analyzed simultaneously in MANOVA (see pp. 216–217).

Power of the F Test in ANOVA

Statistical power is generally well understood conceptually but is rarely considered quantitatively in the design or evaluation of psychophysiological studies. "Power" may be defined as the ablty to find an effect that actually exists. More formally, if β is the probability of a Type II error (failure to reject a false null hypothesis), then power is $1 - \beta$.

Cohen and Cohen (1975) discuss statistical power as a joint function of three other parameters, such that power is increased when any of the following is increased: sample size, effect size, and α (the probability of a Type I error, rejection of the null hypothesis

---

1. There is a typographical error in the formula given in Jennings and Wood (1976). The penultimate parenthesis should be deleted.

when it is true). Fixing the values of any three of these parameters determines the fourth. Conversely, the appropriate value for any of them, such as sample size, cannot be determined without knowing the other three. Effect size is often most difficult to deal with in experimental design. The magnitude of an experimental effect can intuitively be understood as the value of an equivalent correlation coefficient. Although the investigator's hypotheses may not specify the effect size anticipated, prior experience with a given paradigm often implicitly guides the decision, with sample size and α level set accordingly.

However, in our opinion, statistical power is frequently too low in many psychophysiological studies. While it may be argued that power is low only for weak effects and that perhaps we should normally confine ourselves to seeking strong effects, the issue is rather that investigators too rarely consider the questions of effect size and power explicitly when designing experiments.

As an illustration of low power levels prevalent in psychophysiological research, effect size and power were calculated for a subset of data published in Lang *et al.* (1980). For a simple between-subjects main effect, with 16 subjects in each of two groups—a relatively large sample size for a psychophysiological study—the effect sizes actually obtained for two dependent measures were equivalent to correlations of .43 and .35. These were conceptually important effects and were statistically significant. Assuming an α level of .05 and an effect size of .40 (Cohen & Cohen, 1975, suggest .30 as "moderate" and .50 as "large" effect sizes when one has no basis for estimate), a total sample size of 32 provides a power level of .64. In other words, Lang *et al.* could expect to find such an effect, upon replication, in only two experiments out of every three attempts. If sample size were reduced to 24, power would fall to .51, or only an even chance of replication.

The point of this illustration is that statistical power is surprisingly low in many psychophysiological studies. Cohen and Cohen (1975) provide an enlightening discussion of power and a straightforward method for its computation. They recommend .80 as a reasonable target value for power in many situations. Koele (1982) discusses the relative power of different types of ANOVA designs and emphasizes the simplicity of determining power. A more detailed treatment is available in Cohen (1977).

Multiple Regression/Correlation

Traditionally, the correlational approach in psychology has been associated with psychometric test construction and with studies of individual differences and clinical phenomena. In these cases, independent variables generally vary between subjects and are typically difficult to manipulate experimentally, due to logical, practical, and ethical constraints. Although causality is more difficult to demonstrate with correlational than with experimental designs, there is much to recommend multiple regression/correlation (MRC) as a general data-analytic strategy that subsumes ANOVA and ANCOVA (Cohen, 1968; Cohen & Cohen, 1975, especially Section 8.7 and Chapters 9 and 10).

In fact, correlational methods are increasingly used in the processing of psychophysiological data prior to the stage of inference testing. EMCP, Woody filtering, discriminant analysis, PCA, and a number of techniques in the frequency domain employ correlational calculations (see the discussions of these techniques earlier in this chapter).

Several factors have probably contributed to the underutilization of MRC for inference testing in psychophysiology. First, investigators are usually interested in establishing whether a "significant" relationship exists between two variables, rather than in estimating the strength of the relationship, or predicting the exact value of one variable given the other. More conceptually, the specific prediction of a physiological variable on the basis of a psychological variable would be meaningful only given a level of theorizing beyond what is often available. Third, the traditional association of correlational techniques with correlational designs (and their limitations) unnecessarily constrains appreciation of the MRC approach. Fourth, when used for inference testing, MRC is not conveniently adapted for use in repeated-measures or mixed-model designs. Fifth, most computer packages do not include in their MRC routine an easy facility for accomplishing an ANOVA-type analysis, especially with nominal independent variables. Finally, MRC normally requires the investigator to make explicit choices about error terms, interactions, and the priority among independent variables. ANOVA programs typically deny the investigator these often difficult choices, with the benefit of convenience but at the cost of flexibility and, sometimes, statistical power.

The last point bears expansion. It must be understood that, both conceptually and algebraically, MRC is a superset of ANOVA. Indeed, such ANOVA complexities as trend analysis, ANCOVA, planned comparisons, continuous independent variables and their interactions, and unequal cell sizes can be handled very routinely within MRC. For example, nonparallel regression slopes that preclude ANCOVA (see pp. 212–213) amount to an analyzable interaction effect in MRC—that is, a problem becomes a significant finding. Similarly, complex planned comparisons are easily tested using appropriate "dummy coding" of the levels of the independent variable(s).

As one gains experience in the use of MRC to accomplish inference testing of data collected in a traditional ANOVA-type experimental design, one realizes the extent to which most ANOVA packages encourage the investigator to ignore certain basic statistical questions. Specifically, the inclusion or exclusion of particular interaction terms in the statistical model, and the pairing of independent variables and error terms, involve difficult scientific questions with which the investigator should struggle. Typically, in ANOVA, all possible interactions are included in the statistical model and the source table. However, in principle the investigator is free to select, on conceptual grounds, which interactions should be included and which ones should be left in the error term. Use of an incomplete design is particularly appropriate when an interaction term has little theoretical meaning and when its associated degrees of freedom could be put to better use reducing the mean square error. Similarly, ANOVA generally forces the testing of the significance of each factor against an error term, which is the residual after all available sources of variance have been removed (i.e., with a minimum of both error sum of squares and error degrees of freedom—a mixed blessing); MRC permits one to use any of several estimates of error, with potentially greater statistical power—consistent with the original Fisherian emphasis on hierarchical (sequential) rather than simultaneous analysis. Again, the choice among these options should be consciously made, not delegated to an ANOVA program. As an example, consider an experiment in which subjects' autonomic response to snake exposure is measured. Should the effect of subject gender be tested before or after the snake fear questionnaire score has been partialed out of the autonomic measure, and/or partialed out of the gender variable? The converse question can also be raised. ANOVA normally tests each effect after all other effects have been removed from the dependent variable. In other words, each factor is evaluated with all other factors treated as covariates. The investigator may not always find this to be theoretically appropriate.

In sum, MRC is potentially of great use to the psychophysiologist as a general, conceptually stimulating method of inference testing. The highly readable text by Cohen and Cohen (1975) is recommended to the ANOVA-oriented investigator seeking to employ the more general methods of MRC, particularly when considering ANCOVA.[2]

Multivariate Techniques

Multivariate Analysis of Variance

Although most inferential statistics used in psychophysiology involve multiple variables, multivariate analysis of variance (MANOVA) is a term normally

reserved for a technique that is the extension of the typical univariate ANOVA (multiple independent variables but a single dependent variable) to the simultaneous analysis of multiple *dependent* variables. MANOVA appears to be highly appropriate for inference testing in psychophysiological research, because measurement of multiple dependent measures is routine. MANOVA has been especially advocated as an alternative to univariate ANOVA when repeated measures are involved (Davidson, 1972; Richards, 1980). In the MANOVA approach to such a design, the levels of the repeated-measures variable(s) in the ANOVA become separate dependent variables.

A particular advantage of MANOVA over ANOVA is that while both assume homogeneity of covariance (see page 214), studies have shown MANOVA to be very robust to violations of this assumption, especially if cell sizes are equal (Hakstian, Roed, & Lind, 1979; see Richards, 1980). Furthermore, MANOVA is more sensitive than ANOVA to certain types of small but reliable effects (Davidson, 1972). MANOVA is clearly in a better position to control experiment-wise error rate and to test hypotheses involving several response systems.

Despite these advantages, MANOVA is rarely used in published psychophysiological research. Besides the lack of familiarity most investigators have with the technique, two obstacles probably account for this neglect. A practical obstacle is the greater difficulty of computation and statistical interpretation of MANOVA than of ANOVA, including continuing disputes over choice of test statistic (e.g., Olson, 1976, 1979; Stevens, 1979). Standard statistical packages appear to be improving in this regard. However, a conceptual obstacle is the lack of theory to specify the relationship among multiple physiological dependent variables. On what common scale should HR and skin conductance be quantified? How readily can one interpret a multivariate F indicating significant systematic variability somewhere among 100 digitized samples from each of eight EEG sites? Thus, even though the basic phenomena of interest are fundamentally multivariate, psychophysiologists have preferred the narrower, univariate ANOVA approach. It is difficult to evaluate how this understandable restriction of vision constrains the hypotheses proposed and the inferences made. The interested reader may consult Cooley and Lohnes (1971), Press (1972), Tatsuoka (1971), Van Egeren (1973), R. S. Wilson (1974), Winer (1971), or Woodward and Overall (1975) for basic discussions of MANOVA.

Canonical Correlation Analysis

The traditional Pearson product–moment correlation coefficient, a measure of linear association between variables x and y, may be generalized in two stages. If variable x is replaced by set X consisting of several

2. The content of this section owes much to Cohen and Cohen (1975). As the present chapter is being written, a new edition of their book is in press.

variables, MRC can evaluate the association between y and set X. If variable y is then replaced by set Y of several variables, it is canonical correlation that measures the association between set X and set Y. Specifically, canonical correlation analysis seeks a linear combination of the variables in set X and a linear combination of the variables in set Y such that a maximum correlation between these two linear combinations is achieved—in other words, such that set X controls a maximum amount of the variance in set Y. Cohen and Cohen (1975, Chapter 11) and Knapp (1978) demonstrate that canonical correlation subsumes a wide variety of common univariate and multivariate parametric methods of inference testing, including ANOVA, ANCOVA, MRC, MANOVA, MANCOVA (MANOVA with covariance), and discriminant analysis. Given the common practice of quantifying several types of physiological phenomena from multiple recording sites, this technique appears highly appropriate for psychophysiological inference testing. It combines the benefits of MRC and MANOVA (see above) over traditional ANOVA. However, it faces the same interpretative difficulties described for MANOVA.

In general, multivariate statistics have not been widely adopted in psychophysiology, probably because investigators have not felt the need to go beyond what ANOVA will do for them. When the questions asked and the hypotheses tested no longer fit within such strictures, multivariate methods will have to be dealt with. Conversely, once they become routine, they will undoubtedly influence the questions that are asked.

Nonparametric Tests

Given the frequency with which psychophysiological data violate the assumptions of parametric statistics, nonparametric statistics would seem a highly appropriate alternative. They typically require fewer assumptions, though they do so at some cost of statistical power. However, nonparametric approaches have not been developed adequately to accommodate the complex experimental designs often used in psychophysiology. One-way and two-way analogues of standard parametric ANOVA have been described and occasionally appear in the literature (Kruskal–Wallis one-way ANOVA by ranks and Friedman two-way ANOVA by ranks; Siegel, 1956). Methods for testing post hoc comparisons following these analyses exist (Levy, 1979; Marascuilo & McSweeney, 1967). K. V. Wilson (1956) offered a more general nonparametric ANOVA analogue, which is computationally more cumbersome and has not generally been used.

Several other nonparametric statistics deserve consideration when the design is appropriate. The well-known Spearman rank–order correlation (Rs) has

been generalized to the coefficient-of-concordance statistic (W; Siegel, 1956). Where Rs reflects the agreement between two sets of rankings, W reflects the agreement among multiple sets of rankings. For example, W can reflect the degree of agreement among judges ranking a series of responses. Intuitively, W is the average of the pairwise Rs values in the data set. Siegel (1956) presents a test of significance for W. This statistic is highly suitable as a summary statistic computed for individual subjects across multiple physiological dependent measures in multiple situations, providing a measure of response stereotypy. Thus, it is potentially useful as a means of classifying subjects. However, it is not so readily applicable to hypothesis testing about relatively homogeneous populations of subjects, the more common goal in experimental design. Some early studies of response patterning did use W (e.g., Schnore, 1959), but it has received little attention since then.

Dependent variables in psychophysiological studies are usually quantified as continuous variables. However, when the dependent variable in a repeated-measures design is dichotomous (e.g., responses might be scored as present or absent, as is sometimes done for skin conductance responses), the usual parametric ANOVA is not in general appropriate (Marascuilo & McSweeney, 1977; Winer, 1971). The nonparametric Q statistic (Cochran, 1950) is recommended instead, although under some conditions (including a sufficiently large number of observations), the F of ANOVA approximates Q (D'Agostino, 1971; Lunny, 1970). Q is easily computed and follows a chi-square distribution. Q is vulnerable to heterogeneity of covariance in a manner analogous to the F statistic, and the Box/Geisser–Greenhouse correction factor for degrees of freedom in the F test is appropriate for Q (Bhapkar & Somes, 1977; Myers, DiCecco, White, & Borden, 1982). Methods for testing post hoc comparisons following the Q analysis exist (Levy, 1979; Marascuilo & McSweeney, 1977). Although developed for a simple subjects $\times$ conditions design, Q has been extended to certain cases of interaction (Marascuilo & Serlin, 1977). However, Q has not been extended adequately to cover the complex designs typical of much of psychophysiology.

A Few More Caveats

The use of change scores pervades data analysis in psychophysiology. Nevertheless, change scores are notorious for having low reliability. Furthermore, if treatment means and variance in true scores are held constant, statistical power is directly related to the reliability of the dependent variable (i.e., inversely related to variance in error scores). Thus, change scores seem poor candidates for inference testing. However, Nicewander and Price (1978) have demonstrated that high reliability is not necessarily optimal for inference testing, largely because variance in true scores is often *not* held constant in experiments. They show, in fact, that under certain conditions statistical power is paradoxically maximized when the reliability of dependent measures is minimized. They conclude that the optimal level of reliability depends on the nature of the hypothesis being tested. One caveat would be that the investigator should consider carefully whether, on conceptual grounds, change scores are appropriate in a given study.

A related issue includes the direction of statistical inference and the relative reliability of different measurements. Though more often discussed in the clinical realm, this issue arises in psychophysiological research as well. Chapman and Chapman (1973) provide a clear example: "If schizophrenics are as inferior to normal subjects on one ability as on another, but the test that is used to measure one of the abilities is more reliable than the test for the other, a greater deficit will be found on the more reliable measure" (p. 67). In psychophysiology, a number of examples can be given. If two conditions produce equal real changes from a third condition, the measured change will be larger for the condition measured with greater reliability. Similarly, if one quantifies HR with greater reliability than finger pulse volume, genuinely equal changes in both will yield data indicating a larger change in HR than in finger pulse volume. As a final example, if P300 in the brain ERP can be measured more reliably (in a statistical sense) at the parietal than at the frontal electrode placement, it will be easier to find same-size effects at the parietal than at the frontal location. A second caveat, then, would be that investigators should evaluate the statistical reliability of psychophysiological measures and, in making statistical inferences, should be careful not to confound differences in genuine effects with differences in reliability of measurement.

CONCLUSION

In this chapter, we have reviewed techniques that can be used to analyze psychophysiological functions result in a voltage × time function. For this reason, all analytic techniques can, at least in principle, be applied to any psychophysiological function. Selection of which technique to use must be guided in part by the particular question the investigator seeks to answer and in part by the nature of the underlying physiological system. We have attempted to indicate the advantages and disadvantages of each technique. By doing this, we hope that investigators will look beyond those techniques that have traditionally been associated with a particular function. We also hope that, in spite of space limitations, we have given enough

guidance to enable the interested researcher to make an intelligent selection of a technique. The references we have provided should ensure that users go beyond a "cookbook" approach.

We should emphasize that analytic techniques are, in some sense, only as good as the data to which they are applied. There is clearly no substitute for careful recording procedures and appropriate experimental design.

ACKNOWLEDGMENTS

The preparation of this chapter was supported in part by the Air Force Office of Scientific Research (Contract No. F49620-79-C-0233); the Environmental Protection Agency (Contract No. EPA CR 808974-02); the School of Aerospace Medicine, Brooks Air Force Base (Contract No. F33615-82-C-0609); and the Defense Advanced Research Projects Agency (Contract No. MDA903-83-C-0017).

The preparation of Porges's section was supported, in part, by Research Scientist Development Award K02-MH-0054 from the National Institute of Mental Health and by Grant No. HD 15968 from the National Institutes of Health.

REFERENCES

Ackroyd, M. *Digital filtering.* London: Butterworth, 1973.
Aunon, J. I., McGillem, C. D., & O'Donnell, R. D. Comparison of linear and quadratic classification of event-related potentials on the basis of their exogenous or endogenous components. *Psychophysiology,* 1982, 19, 531–537.
Bartlett, M. S. The spectral analysis of point processes. *Journal of the Royal Statistical Society* (Series B), 1963, 25, 264–280.
Benjamin, L. S. Statistical treatment of the law of initial values (LIV) in autonomic research: A review and recommendation. *Psychosomatic Medicine,* 1963, 25, 556–566.
Benjamin, L. S. Facts and artifacts in using analysis of covariance to "undo" the law of initial values. *Psychophysiology,* 1967, 4, 187–206.
Benjamin, L. S. Remarks on behalf of change scores and associated correlational statistics: A response to the Etaughs. *Developmental Psychology,* 1973, 8, 180–183.
Bhapkar, V. P., & Somes, G. W. Distribution of Q when testing equality of matched proportions. *Journal of the American Statistical Association,* 1977, 72, 658–661.
Bohrer, R. E., & Porges, S. W. The application of time-series statistics to psychological research: An introduction. In G. Keren (Ed.), *Statistical and methodological issues in psychology and social sciences research.* Hillsdale, N.J.: Erlbaum, 1982.
Box, G. E. P. Some theorems on quadratic forms applied in the study of analysis of variance problems: II. Effects of inequality of variance and covariance between errors in the two-way classification. *Annals of Mathematical Statistics,* 1954, 25, 484–494.
Box, G. E. P., & Jenkins, G. M. *Time series analysis, forecasting and control.* San Francisco: Holden Day, 1976.
Brillinger, D. R. *Time series: Data analysis and theory.* New York: Holt, Rinehart & Winston, 1975.
Brown, C. C. (Ed.). *Methods in psychophysiology.* Baltimore: Williams & Wilkins, 1967.
Callaway, E., & Halliday, R. A. Evoked potential variability: Effects of age, amplitude and methods of measurement. *Electroencephalography and Clinical Neurophysiology,* 1973, 34, 125–133.
Callaway, E., Halliday, R. A., & Herning, R. I. A comparison of

methods for measuring event-related potentials. *Electroencephalography and Clinical Neurophysiology*, 1983, 55, 227–232.

Campbell, D. T., & Stanley, J. C. *Experimental and quasi-experimental designs for research.* Chicago: Rand McNally, 1966.

Carlton, E. H., & Katz, S. Is Wiener filtering an effective method of improving evoked potential estimation? *IEEE Transactions in Biomedical Engineering*, 1980, 27, 187–192.

Cattell, R. B. The scree test for the number of factors. *Multivariate Behavioral Research*, 1966, 1, 245–276.

Chapman, L. J., & Chapman, J. P. *Disordered thought in schizophrenia.* New York: Appleton-Century-Crofts, 1973.

Chatfield, C. *The analysis of time series: Theory and practice.* London: Chapman & Hall, 1975.

Cochran, W. G. The comparison of percentages in matched samples. *Biometrika*, 1950, 37, 256–266.

Cohen, J. Multiple regression as a general data-analytic system. *Psychological Bulletin*, 1968, 70, 426–443.

Cohen, J. *Statistical power analysis for the behavioral sciences.* New York: Academic Press, 1977.

Cohen, J., & Cohen, P. *Applied multiple regression/correlation analysis for the behavioral sciences.* Hillsdale, N.J.: Erlbaum, 1975.

Cooley, W. W., & Lohnes, P. R. *Multivariate data analysis.* New York: Wiley, 1971.

Cook, E. C. FWTGEN—An interactive FORTRAN II/IV program for calculating weights for a non-recursive digital filter. *Psychophysiology*, 1981, 18, 489–490.

Corby, J. C., & Kopell, B. S. Differential contribution of blinks and vertical eye movements as artifacts in EEG recording. *Psychophysiology*, 1972, 9, 640–644.

D'Agostino, R. B. A second look at analysis of variance on dichotomous data. *Journal of Educational Measurement*, 1971, 8, 327–333.

Davidson, M. L. Univariate versus multivariate tests in repeated-measures experiments. *Psychological Bulletin*, 1972, 77, 446–452.

Dixon, W. T. *BMDP biomedical computer programs.* Los Angeles: University of California at Los Angeles, 1979.

Donchin, E. Use of scalp distribution as a dependent variable in event-related potentials studies: Excerpts of preconference correspondence. In D. Otto (Ed.), *Multidisciplinary perspectives in event-related brain potential research* (EPA-600/9-77-043). Washington, D.C.: U.S. Government Printing Office, 1978.

Donchin, E., & Heffley, E. Multivariate analysis of event-related potential data: A tutorial review. In D. Otto (Ed.), *Multidisciplinary perspectives in event-related brain potential research* (EPA-600/9-77-043). Washington, D.C.: U.S. Government Printing Office, 1978.

Donchin, E., & Herning, R. I. A simulation study of the efficacy of stepwise discriminant analysis in the detection and comparison of event-related potentials. *Electroencephalography and Clinical Neurophysiology*, 1975, 38, 51–68.

Donchin, E., Tueting, P., Ritter, W., Kutas, M., & Heffley, E. On the independence of the CNV and the P300 components of the human average evoked potential. *Electroencephalography and Clinical Neurophysiology*, 1975, 38, 449–461.

Duffy, F. H., Bartels, P. H., & Burchfiel, J. L. Significance probability mapping: An aid in the topographical analysis of brain electrical activity. *Electroencephalography and Clinical Neurophysiology*, 1981, 51, 455–462.

Duncan-Johnson, C. C., & Donchin, E. The time constant in P300 recording. *Psychophysiology*, 1979, 16, 53–55.

Ertl, J. P. Detection of evoked potentials by zero crossing analysis. *Electroencephalography and Clinical Neurophysiology*, 1965, 18, 630–631.

Ertl, J. P., & Schafer, E. W. P. Brain response correlates of psychometric intelligence. *Nature*, 1969, 223, 421–422.

Etaugh, E. F., & Etaugh, C. F. Overlap: hypothesis or tautology? *Developmental Psychology*, 1972, 6, 340–342.

Friedman, D. H. *Detection of signal by template matching.* Baltimore: Johns Hopkins University Press, 1968.

Games, P. A. Computer programs for robust analyses in multifactor analysis of variance designs. *Educational and Psychological Measurement*, 1975, 35, 147–152.

Games, P. A. Programs for robust analyses of ANOVA's with repeated measures. *Psychophysiology*, 1976, 13, 603.

Geisser, S., & Greenhouse, S. W. An extension of Box's results on the use of the F distribution in multivariate analysis. *Annals of Mathematical Statistics*, 1958, 29, 885–891.

Glaser, E. M., & Ruchkin, D. S. *Principles of neurobiological signal analysis.* New York: Academic Press, 1976.

Gottman, J. M. *Time-series analysis.* New York: Cambridge University Press, 1981.

Graham, F. K. Constraints on measuring heart rate sequentially through real and cardiac time. *Psychophysiology*, 1978, 15, 492–495.

Gratton, G., Coles, M. G. H., & Donchin, E. A new method for off-line removal of ocular artifact. *Electroencephalography and Clinical Neurophysiology*, 1983, 55, 468–484.

Gratton, G., Coles, M. G. H., & Donchin, E. A vector analysis of ERPs. Manuscript in preparation, 1985.

Hakstian, A. R., Roed, J. C., & Lind, J. C. Two-sample T2 procedure and the assumption of homogeneous covariance matrices. *Psychological Bulletin*, 1979, 86, 1255–1263.

Harman, H. H. *Modern factor analysis* (Rev. ed.). Chicago: University of Chicago Press, 1967.

Harris, C. W. (Ed.). *Problems in measuring change.* Madison: University of Wisconsin Press, 1963.

Hays, W. L. *Statistics.* New York: Holt, Rinehart & Winston, 1981.

Hord, D. J., Johnson, L. C., & Lubin, A. Differential effect of the law of initial value (LIV) on autonomic variables. *Psychophysiology*, 1964, 1, 79–87.

Horst, R. L., & Donchin, E. Beyond averaging II: Single trial classification of exogenous event-related potentials using stepwise discriminant analysis. *Electroencephalography and Clinical Neurophysiology*, 1980, 48, 113–126.

Humphreys, L. G., & Montanelli, R. G. An investigation of the parallel analysis criterion for determining the number of common factors. *Multivariate Behavioral Research*, 1975, 10, 193–206.

Isreal, J. B., Chesney, G. L., Wickens, C. D., & Donchin, E. P300 and tracking difficulty: Evidence for multiple resources in dual-task performance. *Psychophysiology*, 1980, 17, 259–273.

Jennings, J. R., Tahmoush, A. J., & Redmond, D. P. Non-invasive measurement of peripheral vascular activity. In I. Martin & P. H. Venables (Eds.), *Techniques in psychophysiology.* Chichester, England: Wiley, 1980.

Jennings, J. R., & Wood, C. C. The epsilon-adjustment procedures for repeated-measures analyses of variance. *Psychophysiology*, 1976, 13, 277–278.

Jennrich, R. I. Stepwise discriminant analysis. In K. Enslin, A. Ralston, & H. S. Wief (Eds.), *Statistical methods for digital computers.* New York: Academic Press, 1977.

John, E. R., Ruchkin, D. S., & Villegas, J. Experimental background: Signal analysis and behavioral correlates of evoked potential configurations in cats. *Annals of the New York Academy of Sciences*, 1964, 112, 362–420.

John, E. R., Ruchkin, D. S., & Vidal, J. J. Measurement of event-related potentials. In E. Callaway, P. Tueting, & S. H. Koslow (Eds.), *Event-related brain potentials in man.* New York: Academic Press, 1978.

Kaiser, H. F. The application of electronic computers to factor analysis. *Educational and Psychological Measurement*, 1960, 20, 141–151.

Keselman, H. J., & Rogan, J. C. Repeated measures F tests and psychophysiological research: Controlling the number of false positives. *Psychophysiology*, 1980, 17, 499–503.

Keselman, H. J., Rogan, J. C., Mendoza, J. L., & Breen, L. J. Testing the validity conditions of repeated measures F tests. *Psychophysiological Bulletin*, 1980, 87, 479–481.

Knapp, T. R. Canonical correlation analysis: A general parametric significance-testing system. *Psychological Bulletin*, 1978, 85, 410–416.

Koele, P. Calculating power in analysis of variance. *Psychological Bulletin*, 1982, 92, 513–516.

Kubayashi, H., & Yaguchi, K. A statistical method of component identification of average evoked potentials. *Electroencephalography and Clinical Neurophysiology*, 1981, 51, 213–214.

Lacey, J. I. The evaluation of autonomic responses: Toward a general solution. *Annals of the New York Academy of Sciences*, 1956, 67, 123–164.

Lang, P. J., Kozak, M. J., Miller, G. A., Levin, D. N., & McLean, A. Emotional imagery: Conceptual structure and pattern of somatovisceral response. *Psychophysiology*, 1980, 17, 179–190.

Levy, K. J. Nonparametric large-sample pairwise comparisons. *Psychological Bulletin*, 1979, 86, 371–375.

Lord, F. M. A paradox in the interpretation of group comparisons. *Psychological Bulletin*, 1967, 68, 304–305.

Lubin, A. [Book review of *Problems in measuring change*, C. Harris, Ed.]. *American Journal of Psychology*, 1965, 78, 324–327.

Lunny, G. H. Using analysis of variance with a dichotomous dependent variable: An empirical study. *Journal of Educational Measurement*, 1970, 4, 263–269.

Malmstadt, H. V., Enke, C. G., & Crouch, S. R. *Electronic measurements for scientists.* Menlo Park, Calif.: W. A. Benjamin, 1974.

Marascuilo, L. A., & McSweeney, M. Nonparametric post hoc comparisons for trend. *Psychological Bulletin*, 1967, 67, 401–412.

Marascuilo, L. A., & McSweeney, M. *Nonparametric and distribution free methods for the social sciences.* Monterey, Calif.: Brooks/Cole, 1977.

Marascuilo, L. A., & Serlin, R. Interactions for dichotomous variables in repeated measures design. *Psychological Bulletin*, 1977, 84, 1002–1007.

Martin, I., & Venables, P. H. (Eds.). *Techniques in psychophysiology.* Chichester, England: Wiley, 1980.

McCall, R. B., & Appelbaum, M. I. Bias in the analysis of repeated-measures designs: Some alternative approaches. *Child Development*, 1973, 44, 401–415.

McGillem, C. D., Aunon, J. I., & Childers, D. G. Signal processing in evoked potential research: Applications of filtering and pattern recognition. *Critical Reviews in Bioengineering*, 1981, 6, 225–265.

McGillem, C. D., Aunon, J. I., & O'Donnell, R. D. Computer classification of single event-related potentials. *Psychophysiology*, 1981, 18, 192. (Abstract)

Montanelli, R. G., & Humphreys, L. G. Latent roots of random data correlation matrices with squared multiple correlations on the diagonal: A Monte Carlo study. *Psychometrika*, 1976, 41, 341–347.

Mulaik, S. A. *The foundations of factor analysis.* New York: McGraw-Hill, 1972.

Myers, J. L. *Fundamentals of experimental design* (3rd ed.). Boston: Allyn & Bacon, 1979.

Myers, J. L., DiCecco, J. V., White, J. B., & Borden, V. M. Repeated measures on dichotomous variables: Q and F tests. *Psychological Bulletin*, 1982, 92, 517–525.

Nahvi, M. J., Woody, C. D., Ungar, R., & Sharafat, A. R. Detection of neuroelectric signals from multiple data channels by optimum linear filter method. *Electroencephalography and Clinical Neurophysiology*, 1975, 38, 191–198.

Naitoh, P., & Sunderman, S. Before averaging: Preprocessing slow potential data with a Wiener filter. In D. Otto (Ed.), *Multidisciplinary perspectives in event-related brain potential research* (EPA-600/9-77-043). Washington, D.C.: U.S. Government Printing Office, 1978.

Nicewander, W. A., & Price, J. M. Dependent variable reliability and the power of significance tests. *Psychological Bulletin*, 1978, 85, 405–409.

Olson, C. L. On choosing a test statistic in multivariate analysis of variance. *Psychological Bulletin*, 1976, 83, 579–586.

Olson, C. L. Practical considerations in choosing a MANOVA test statistic: A rejoinder to Stevens. *Psychological Bulletin*, 1979, 86, 1350–1352.

Overall, J. E., & Woodward, J. A. Nonrandom assignment and the analysis of covariance. *Psychological Bulletin*, 1977, 84, 588–594.

Overton, D. A., & Shagass, C. Distribution of eye movement and eye blink potentials over the scalp. *Electroencephalography and Clinical Neurophysiology*, 1969, 27, 544–549.

Picton, T. W., & Stuss, D. T. The component structure of human event-related potentials. In H. H. Kornhuber & L. Deecke (Eds.), *Motivation, motor and sensory processes of the brain: Electrical potentials, behavioral and clinical use.* Amsterdam: North-Holland Biomedical Press, 1980.

Porges, S. W. Developmental designs for infancy research. In J. D. Osofsky (Ed.), *Handbook of infant development.* New York: Wiley, 1979.

Porges, S. W., Bohrer, R. E., Cheung, M. N., Drasgow, F., McCabe, P. M., & Keren, G. New time-series statistic for detecting rhythmic co-occurrence in the frequency domain: The weighted coherence and its application to psychophysiological research. *Psychological Bulletin*, 1980, 88, 580–587.

Press, S. J. *Applied multivariate analysis.* New York: Holt, Rinehart & Winston, 1972.

Ragot, R. A., & Remond, A. EEG field mapping. *Electroencephalography and Clinical Neurophysiology*, 1978, 45, 417–421.

Remond, A. Construction et ajustment des enregistrement cartographiques et spatio-temporals des EEG. *Revue Neurologique*, 1962, 106, 135–136.

Richards, J. E. *Multivariate analysis of variance of repeated physiological measures.* Paper presented at the annual convention of the Society for Psychophysiological Research, Vancouver, British Columbia, October 1980.

Roessler, F., & Manzey, D. Principal components and varimax-rotated components in event-related potential research: Some remarks on their interpretation. *Biological Psychology*, 1981, 13, 3–26.

Ruchkin, D. S., & Glaser, E. M. Simple digital filters for examining CNV and P300 on a single-trial basis. In D. Otto (Ed.), *Multidisciplinary perspectives in event-related potential research* (EPA-600/9-77-043). Washington, D.C.: U.S. Government Printing Office, 1978.

Ruchkin, D. S., Sutton, S., & Stega, M. Emitted P300 and slow wave event-related potentials in guessing and detection tasks. *Electroencephalography and Clinical Neurophysiology*, 1980, 49, 1–14.

Schnore, M. M. Individual patterns of physiological activity as a function of task differences and degree of arousal. *Journal of Experimental Psychology*, 1959, 58, 117–128.

Sencaj, R. W., Aunon, J. I., & McGillem, C. D. Discrimination among visual stimuli by classifications of their single evoked potentials. *Medical and Biological Engineering and Computing*, 1979, 17, 391–396.

Siegel, S. *Nonparametric statistics for the behavioral sciences.* New York: McGraw-Hill, 1956.

Simons, R. F., Ohman, A., & Lang, P. J. Anticipation and response set: Cortical, cardiac, and electrodermal correlates. *Psychophysiology*, 1979, 16, 222–233.

Squires, K. C., & Donchin, E. Beyond averaging: The use of discriminant functions to recognize event-related potentials elicited by single auditory stimuli. *Electroencephalography and Clinical Neurophysiology*, 1976, 41, 449–459.

Squires, K. C., Donchin, E., Herning, R. I., & McCarthy, G. On the influence of task relevance and stimulus probability on event-related potential components. *Electroencephalography and Clinical Neurophysiology*, 1977, 42, 1–14.

Squires, K. C., Wickens, C. D., Squires, N. K., & Donchin, E. The effect of stimulus sequence on the waveform of the cortical event-related potential. *Science*, 1976, 193, 1142–1146.

Stern, R. M., Ray, W. J., & Davis, C. M. *Psychophysiological recording.* New York: Oxford University Press, 1980.

Sternbach, R. A. Some relationships among various "dimensions" of autonomic activity. *Psychosomatic Medicine*, 1960, 22, 430–434.

Stevens, J. P. Comment on Olson: Choosing a test statistic in multivariate analysis of variance. *Psychological Bulletin*, 1979, 86, 355–360.

Strong, P. *Biophysical measurements*. Beaverton, Oregon: Tektronix, 1970.

Tatsuoka, M. M. *Discriminant analysis: The study of group differences*. Champaign, Ill.: Institute for Personality and Ability Testing, 1970.

Tatsuoka, M. M. *Multivariate analysis: Techniques for educational and psychological research*. New York: Wiley, 1971.

Thurstone, L. L. *The vectors of mind*. Chicago: University of Chicago Press, 1935.

Tucker, L. R. *Note on number of attributes in a battery to support a given number of common factors*. Unpublished manuscript, 1973.

Ungar, P., & Basar, E. Comparison of Wiener filtering and selective averaging of evoked potentials. *Electroencephalography and Clinical Neurophysiology*, 1976, 40, 516–520.

Van Egeren, L. F. Multivariate statistical analysis. *Psychophysiology*, 1973, 10, 517–532.

Venables, P. H., & Christie, M. J. Electrodermal activity. In I. Martin & P. H. Venables (Eds.), *Techniques in psychophysiology*. Chichester, England: Wiley, 1980.

Venables, P. H., & Martin, I. (Eds.). *A manual of psychophysiological methods*. Amsterdam: North-Holland, 1967. (a)

Venables, P. H., & Martin, I. Skin resistance and skin potential. In P. H. Venables & I. Martin (Eds.), *A manual of psychophysiological methods*. Amsterdam: North-Holland, 1967. (b)

Walter, D. O. A posteriori "Wiener filtering" of average evoked responses. *Electroencephalography and Clinical Neurophysiology*, 1968, (Suppl. 27), 59–70.

Wastell, D. G. Statistical detection of individual evoked responses: An evaluation of Woody's adaptive filter. *Electroencephalography and Clinical Neurophysiology*, 1977, 42, 835–839.

Wastell, D. G. On the correlated nature of evoked brain activity: Biophysical and statistical considerations. *Biological Psychology*, 1981, 13, 51–69. (a)

Wastell, D. G. PCA and varimax rotation: Some comments on Roessler and Manzey. *Biological Psychology*, 1981, 13, 27–29. (b)

Weerts, T. C., & Lang, P. J. The effects of eye fixation and stimulus and response location on the contingent negative variation (CNV). *Biological Psychology*, 1973, 1, 1–19.

Wiener, N. *Extrapolation, interpolation, and smoothing of stationary time series*. Cambridge, Mass.: MIT Press, 1964.

Wilder, J. The law of initial values in neurology and psychiatry: Facts and problems. *Journal of Nervous and Mental Disease*, 1957, 125, 73–86.

Wilson, K. V. A distribution-free test of analysis of variance hypotheses. *Psychological Bulletin*, 1956, 53, 96–101.

Wilson, R. S. CARDIVAR: The statistical analysis of heart rate. *Psychophysiology*, 1974, 11, 76–85.

Winer, B. J. *Statistical principles in experimental design* (2nd ed.). New York: McGraw-Hill, 1971.

Woodward, J. A., & Overall, J. E. Multivariate analysis of variance by multiple regression methods. *Psychological Bulletin*, 1975, 82, 21–32.

Woody, C. D. Characterization of an adaptive filter for the analysis of variable latency neuroelectric signals. *Medical and Biological Engineering*, 1967, 5, 539–553.

Woody, C. D., & Nahvi, M. J. Application of optimum linear filter theory to the detection of cortical signals preceding facial movement in the cat. *Experimental Brain Research*, 1973, 16, 455–465.

PART TWO
PROCESSES

SECTION A
Attention, Information Processing, and Learning

Chapter Eleven

Attention: Electrophysiological Approaches

Steven A. Hillyard
Jonathan C. Hansen

INTRODUCTION

In recent years, the term "attention" has been expanded in scope to denote any or all of those perceptual and cognitive mechanisms responsible for the selectivity of human information processing (Kinchla, 1980). It has become more of a chapter-heading word, encompassing a diverse set of processes and paradigms, than a precisely defined theoretical construct. Roughly speaking, an attentional process may be inferred whenever a person chooses to analyze some kinds of information more effectively than others. Thus, attended stimuli generally exert greater control over motor responses, are detected and discriminated more accurately, are better remembered, and elicit reports of awareness more readily than unattended stimuli.

A number of competing theories of attention have arisen over the years, providing different views about the locus of stimulus selections (early or late), the number and type of processing structures involved, and the extent to which stimulus analyses are carried out automatically. A major theoretical development within the past decade has been the distinction between "automatic" signal analyses, which are accomplished rapidly and with little effort or conscious intent, and a slower, "controlled" processing, which is applied to actively attended stimuli (Posner & Snyder, 1975; Schneider & Shiffrin, 1977). While automatic analyses are performed in parallel and do not interfere with other processing activities, the controlled systems operate serially and draw on resource pools of limited capacity (Kahneman, 1973; Norman & Bobrow, 1975). Theoretical models have been developed that show how allocations of attention between concurrent tasks can be optimized (Navon & Gopher, 1979), and patterns of interference between different kinds of tasks have provided evidence for functionally distinct resource pools (Wickens, 1980).

Most of our knowledge about mechanisms of attention in humans has been derived from behavioral investigations. While observations in brain-injured patients have identified the general brain regions that seem important in attentional processes (Heilman & Valenstein, 1979), little is known of the anatomical structures and pathways that are involved. Even less is known about the neurophysiology of attention in humans, since invasive experiments are rarely possible. Studies of attention in animals have yielded much information about the critical brain structures and

Steven A. Hillyard and Jonathan C. Hansen. Department of Neurosciences, University of California, San Diego, La Jolla, California.

associated neural processes (e.g., Pribram & McGuiness, 1975), but the comparability of human and animal attention mechanisms remains questionable.

New sources of information about human attention and cognition have been developed in recent years through noninvasive physiological recordings of central nervous system (CNS) and autonomic nervous system activity. The processing of sensory signals in the brain is reflected in characteristic patterns of voltage oscillations that can be detected in the scalp-recorded electroencephalogram (EEG), and stimuli that are significant or novel elicit changes in a wide range of autonomic responses as well. The phasic brain potentials that are elicited in conjunction with sensory, cognitive, or motor events have been collectively termed "event-related potentials" (ERPs); they are generally considered to be reflections of the synchronous activity within large neuronal populations. While ERPs occur in close temporal proximity to the actual processing of information in the brain, the peripherally mediated autonomic responses represent delayed manifestations of CNS activity. Both types of measures provide converging operations (Garner, Hake, & Eriksen, 1956) for classifying attentional processes and differentiating them from one another. In general, qualitative differences in physiological response patterns may be taken as *prima facie* evidence for distinctive psychological operations, while physiological similarities provide converging evidence for common modes of processing (Sutton, 1969).

ERPs and Information Processing

The main emphasis of this chapter is on the contributions that ERP evidence can make to our understanding of attention mechanisms in humans. The scalp-recorded ERPs elicited by stimuli in different modalities (traditionally known as "evoked potentials") have waveforms that can be described as a series of components or peaks and troughs that occur at characteristic latencies (Figure 11-1). Certain components of shorter latency have been identified with neural activity in specific structures of the sensory pathways (Goff, Allison, & Vaughan, 1978). For example, the auditory ERP components occurring between 1 and 10 msec (labeled I–VI in Figure 11-1) arise from activity in the eighth nerve and brain stem relay nuclei. Since most early components are sensitive to variations in physical stimulus parameters and show little change as a function of processing demands, they have been termed "exogenous" (Donchin, Ritter, & McCallum, 1978).

Some of the longer-latency components occurring after 50 msec also appear to be exogenous, but others can only be elicited when the stimulus is being processed in a particular way. These "endogenous" components presumably occur in conjunction with inter-

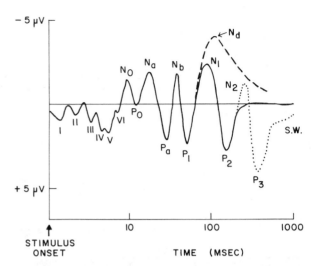

Figure 11-1. Idealized waveform of the auditory ERP. Exogenous components, represented by solid tracing, include the brain stem responses (waves I–VI), the midlatency components (waves No, Po, Na, Pa, Nb), and the long-latency "vertex potential" (waves P1, N1, P2, N2). Endogenous components (dashed and dotted tracings) are elicited by sounds that are selectively attended (the Nd wave) or are task-relevant and improbable (the N2–P3–slow wave complex), respectively. Note logarithmic time base. (Adapted from Picton, Hillyard, Krausz, & Galambos, 1974.)

mediate stages of information processing, and much research has been directed at identifying ERP indices of specific perceptual and cognitive processes (Donchin *et al.*, 1978; Hillyard, Picton, & Regan, 1978). Two types of endogenous ERPs that figure prominently in selective information processing are shown in Figure 11-1. The broad Nd component is elicited at about the same latency as the exogenous N1 wave (60–80 msec), but only by auditory signals that belong to an attended source or channel of information. The P3 component (also called P300) and the associated N2 and slow wave tend to be elicited together as the "P3 complex" by stimuli that both are relevant to the task at hand and occur unpredictably. Since the P3 complex depends upon the identification and classification of relevant stimuli, Hillyard and Picton (1979) have argued that P3 must in part reflect attentional mechanisms.

In seeking relationships between ERPs and psychological processes, it is certainly an oversimplification to consider an ERP as a linear sequence of discrete components. Each peak or valley in the ERP probably reflects the activity of many different neural systems operating in parallel, and there is no reason to suppose that these peaks reflect more important neural events than do intermediate time points. In any case, the size and shape of the scalp-recorded voltage excursions are determined by such factors as intracranial generator orientations, neural synchrony, and process overlap, all of which may be extraneous to their psychological relevance.

Indeed, the pattern of neural events that represents even the simplest cognitive process is probably dispersed widely in space and in time. This makes it difficult to decide which aspects of an ERP ought to be measured in relation to psychological variables. Donchin *et al.* (1978) have made the excellent suggestion that a "component" in the ERP should be defined as the entirety of the waveform change, no matter how complex, brought about by an experimental variable. These components of variation may be isolated by principal-components analysis (Donchin & Heffley, 1978) or visualized by taking "difference waves" between the ERPs recorded under different experimental conditions.

The study of ERPs can contribute to the analysis of attention mechanisms on both physiological and psychological levels. As the neural generators of the attention-related ERPs are characterized more fully, our understanding of the brain structures and pathways mediating selective information processing will grow accordingly. Furthermore, the timing of ERP changes during attention allows us to make inferences about the structure of the underlying processing systems. As described below, ERP evidence can illuminate such traditional issues in attention research as early versus late levels of selection, serial versus parallel analyses, and automatic versus controlled processing. The fact that ERP changes can be recorded independently of motor activity makes them particularly suitable for studying stimulus interactions in rapid temporal sequences and moment-to-moment allocations of attention, without the limitations normally imposed by response bottlenecks.

Methodological Considerations

In order to demonstrate that an ERP is associated specifically with selective attention, a number of experimental design criteria need to be fulfilled (Hillyard & Picton, 1979; Karlin, 1970; Naatanen, 1975). In general, ERPs must be recorded in response to two or more classes of stimuli (attended and unattended) presented in unpredictable order within the same session. This prevents the subject from anticipating the attended stimuli and developing a "differential preparatory state" (e.g., of arousal or alerting) that could alter the ERPs. During different sessions or trials, the subject's attention must then be switched to the previously unattended stimuli. If the same ERP configuration is seen in the attended versus unattended comparison for all stimuli, then that ERP may be considered a physiological sign of that particular type of selection. ERP changes that behave in this fashion cannot be attributed to changes in nonselective states

or to differences in the difficulty of processing the stimulus classes.

Another important consideration in all attention experiments, particularly those involving ERPs, is physical stimulus control. Any systematic change in physical input between attention conditions (e.g., due to receptor orienting acts) could alter exogenous components and/or the endogenous processing of the altered sensory data. Either type of change could erroneously be ascribed to a stimulus selection process.

Acoustic stimulus constancy can usually be achieved by presenting identical stimuli in different experimental runs through earphones. This does not rule out the possibility of ERP modulation by middle-ear muscle contractions, but it has yet to be demonstrated that humans have the capability of voluntarily contracting these muscles in such a way as to attenuate input from one source and mimic a central selection process. Middle-ear muscle effects may be minimized by choosing sound frequencies that are relatively insensitive to their contractions (Lukas, 1981; Moller, 1974), by monitoring peripheral acoustic transmission in the brain stem evoked potentials (Picton & Hillyard, 1974), or by showing that the pattern of ERP changes is inconsistent with simple input attenuation (Schwent & Hillyard, 1975). Stimulus control is also critical in studies of visual attention, since the visual ERPs can be highly sensitive to small changes in fixation or accommodation (Regan, 1972).

It is also important to document associations between ERPs and attentional processes by obtaining behavioral measures of the latter concurrently with recordings of the former. The behavioral measures should demonstrate that the attentional manipulation is effective in producing a preferential processing of one stimulus class over another, or otherwise reveal the allocation of attentional resources. This can be achieved, for example, by comparing signal discrimination or reaction time (RT) on primary versus secondary input channels (e.g., Bookbinder & Osman, 1979), or by assessing divided attention decrements in single-task versus dual-task conditions. A further refinement is to examine ERPs separately according to the perceptual outcome for each individual stimulus (K. C. Squires, Squires, & Hillyard, 1975; Sutton, 1969). This allows for trial-to-trial variations in attentional efficiency to be correlated with ERP changes.

LEVELS OF STIMULUS SELECTION

One of the longest-running controversies in attention research has been between proponents of "early" versus "late" models of selection. Theories of early selection (Broadbent, 1971; Treisman, 1964) propose a rapid rejection of irrelevant stimuli after as little information is analyzed from them as possible; overall processing efficiency is thereby increased. The early selection is achieved by a hypothetical "filter" or "stimulus set" stage (Broadbent, 1970), which selects stimuli for further analysis based on rapidly analyzable attributes common to relevant stimuli (typically, simple physical characteristics such as pitch or location). Models of late selection, on the other hand, propose relatively full analyses of all stimulus attributes prior to any selections' taking place (Deutsch & Deutsch, 1963; Norman, 1968). This now-classic controversy still forms the backdrop for much current research in attention (e.g., Bookbinder & Osman, 1979; Johnston & Heinz, 1979; Rollins & Hendricks, 1980). While many studies have obtained evidence for early selection on the basis of physical attributes, others have failed to find such effects. A number of theorists have concluded that early and late selections may be invoked separately or in concert according to task demands (e.g., Keele & Neill, 1978; Johnston & Heinz, 1979; Posner, 1978).

It seems likely that the early–late distinction will turn out to be more of a continuum than a dichotomy (Keren, 1976). As discussed below, current ERP data suggest that information about various attributes of stimuli becomes available to attentional mechanisms at different times, depending on the characteristics and modalities of the stimuli, as well as the task requirements. By revealing the timing of stimulus selections, ERPs can delineate the various steps in the processing of stimuli and provide evidence about the parallel, serial, or hierarchical structure of the analyses.

Peripheral Efferent Gating

The notion of a peripherally situated filter capable of modulating sensory input has had considerable currency in physiological theories of attention. On the basis of animal studies, Hernandez-Peon (1966) concluded that sensory transmission in unattended pathways is gated or filtered at peripheral levels such as the cochlear nucleus. Early experiments supporting this concept were effectively criticized for lack of control over stimulus input and motivational states (Worden, 1966), but recent animal experiments provide more convincing evidence for the selective gating of peripheral transmission as a function of stimulus relevance (Gabriel, Saltwick, & Miller, 1975; Oatman, 1976; Oatman & Anderson, 1977; Olesen, Ashe, & Weinberger, 1975). It is important to note, however, that Broadbent's *psychological* concept of an attentional filter need not be embodied in a peripherally situated *physiological* filter of the sort Hernandez-Peon proposed (Hillyard, 1981). Broadbent's filter, defined functionally in terms of a rapid selection prior to full analysis, may or may not entail peripheral inhibitory gating as its mechanism.

The possibility of peripheral sensory modulation

as an attention mechanism in humans can be investigated via recording the short-latency ERPs. Several experiments have failed to find any change in the auditory evoked brain stem potentials to clicks as a function of whether or not the clicks were attended (Picton, Campbell, Baribeau-Braun, & Proulx, 1978; Picton & Hillyard, 1974; Picton, Hillyard, Galambos, & Schiff, 1971; Woods & Hillyard, 1978). It appeared that simple forms of auditory attention (e.g., counting clicks) were not associated with gross peripheral modulation of auditory transmission. The midlatency components between 10 and 50 msec were similarly found to be insensitive to various attentional manipulations, both for auditory and for somatosensory stimuli (Desmedt & Robertson, 1977).

More recently, however, Lukas (1980, 1981) has reported that both wave I (auditory nerve) and wave V (midbrain) of the auditory evoked potential to tone pips showed increased amplitudes and shorter latencies when attention was directed toward the tones. The changes in auditory nerve activity were ascribed to inhibitory modulation of the hair cells under the influence of the olivo-cochlear pathway. The high tone frequency used (8000 Hz) made it unlikely that the middle-ear muscles could play a role. Lukas has suggested that the olivo-cochlear pathway, under the control of higher centers, "may tonically inhibit rather discrete portions of the basilar membrane during selective attention" (1980, p. 144). These promising results need to be followed up to determine whether these early ERP changes actually reflect the operation of a true stimulus selection mechanism.

Early somatosensory evoked components between 10 and 30 msec have also been localized rather precisely to specific structures in the afferent pathways and to the primary sensory cortex (Desmedt & Cheron, 1980; Goff *et al.*, 1978). Several studies have reported that the primary cortical response remains stable during shifts of attention toward and away from the eliciting shock stimuli (Desmedt, Debecker, & Manil, 1965; Desmedt & Robertson, 1977; Velasco & Velasco, 1975).

ERPs and Levels of Selection

An ERP correlate of early auditory selection was reported by Hillyard, Hink, Schwent, and Picton (1973) in a design that employed randomized presentation of tones to the two ears at short intervals (200–400 msec). Subjects attended selectively to tones in one ear at a time, striving to detect occasional "target" tones of a slightly higher pitch. Under these high-load conditions, attended-ear tones elicited an enhanced negativity after stimulus onset, which augmented the measured amplitude of the N1 peak above that elicited by the same tones when unattended (Figure 11-2). Rather than a simple enlargement of the exogen-

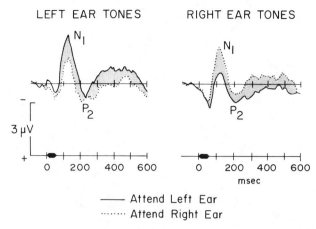

LEFT EAR TONES   RIGHT EAR TONES

—— Attend Left Ear
········· Attend Right Ear

Figure 11-2. Auditory ERPs to standard tones in a selective listening task, in which attention was switched between tones in the two ears. Left-ear tones were 1800 Hz and right-ear tones were 2800 Hz, all at 45-dB SL and 75-msec durations. Shaded differences between attended and unattended ERPs for each ear represent the Nd component. (Grand average data over 10 subjects from Knight, Hillyard, Woods, & Neville, 1981.)

ous N1 peak, however, this attention effect seems to consist of a broader negativity beginning at 60–80 msec that is superimposed upon the N1 wave and may outlast it considerably (Hansen & Hillyard, 1980; Naatanen & Michie, 1979). Since this attention-sensitive component is defined as the ERP difference between conditions of attention and inattention, we refer to it here as the "negative difference" (Nd) wave, shaded in Figure 11-2. The later phases of Nd seem to be entirely endogenous, while the early portion has a scalp distribution similar to that of the N1 itself.

Since the Nd component appears to be largely endogenous, these results provide no evidence for a physiological filter or gate as a mechanism of early selection. Nonetheless, the properties of the Nd effect do resemble those of the Broadbent–Treisman early selection (stimulus set) in a number of respects. First, its short onset latency (as early as 50 msec) suggests that it manifests a tonic set to process attended and unattended material differentially prior to full analysis and recognition. Second, the same ERP patterns were observed when the attended and unattended "channels"[1] were distinguished either by pitch or localization cues (Schwent, Snyder, & Hillyard, 1976) or by sound intensity cues (Figure 11-3). According to Broadbent's (1971) proposals, any rapidly analyzable attribute distinguishing attended from unattended tones could form the basis for a stimulus set selection. Finally, the Nd was found to be elicited equivalently

1. Here the term "channel" is simply being used to designate a common cue characteristic of the attended stimuli that is used as the basis for the selection.

by all stimuli that belonged to the attended channel, whether or not they were relevant to the task (Hink & Hillyard, 1976; Hink, Hillyard, & Benson, 1978). Together, these findings suggest that Nd reflects the preferential processing of relevant stimuli following an early selection on the basis of a physical attribute or "channel cue."

The functional properties of the early selection indexed by Nd are still in need of clarification. The most likely interpretation seems to be that Nd is a sign of a postselection processing that extracts additional information (e.g., concerning the target cues) from attended-channel stimuli. This fits with evidence that larger Nd components are associated with more accurate target detections (Parasuraman, 1978; Parasuraman & Beatty, 1980; Schwent et al., 1976). The prolonged duration of the Nd suggests that this stimulus analysis may be carried out over an extended period, or, alternatively, that this ERP may reflect a kind of short-term memory store for attended events. The suggestion has also been made that Nd is simply a sign of the accumulation of "internal evidence" that a stimulus shares the channel cue with the attended targets (Naatanen, 1975).

The selection of targets within an attended channel in these experiments was associated with a different ERP configuration, which included the late positive P3 or P300 wave arising well after the Nd onset. The P3 was elicited only by the infrequent targets in the attended channel, and not by comparable stimuli in the unattended channel. This pattern of data (illustrated in Figure 11-4) suggests that the Nd and P3 waves reflect two hierarchically ordered levels of selection (Hillyard et al., 1973). According to this hypothesis, the Nd reflects the between-channel (stimulus set) selection based on rapidly discriminable cues, whereas the P3 reflects processes subsequent to target

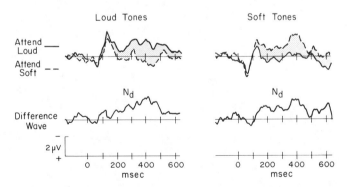

Figure 11-3. Auditory ERPs in an attention task where subjects listened selectively to either loud (60-dB SL) or soft (40-dB SL) tones, which were presented binaurally in a randomized sequence. All tones were 700 Hz, delivered at random interstimulus intervals (ISIs) from 200 to 500 msec. The shaded areas are Nd components associated with stimulus selection on the basis of the intensity cue. (Data from one subject in unpublished study by Hansen.)

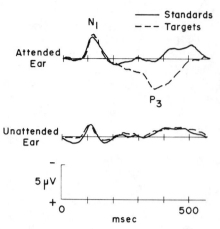

Figure 11-4. ERPs to syllables ("ba," "da," "ga," "ja") presented in random order to one ear in a male voice and to the other in a female voice. The subject's task was to listen selectively to syllables in one ear and press a button upon detecting one of them, designated the target, which was varied across runs. ERPs are averaged separately for the three nontarget syllables and for the target syllables in both attended and unattended ears. (Data from Hink, Hillyard, & Benson, 1978.)

identification and depends upon a more detailed analysis of stimulus features in the attended channel.

Hillyard *et al.* (1973) suggested that the P3 in this type of task was dependent upon the subject's "response set" (Broadbent, 1970) to detect the targets. As elaborated by Keren (1976), response set selection involves a higher level of cognitive processing, whereby stimuli are classified according to acquired categories of meaning rather than by simple physical attributes. In some cases, the P3 is clearly elicited by targets defined in terms of cognitive categories (e.g., Chapman, 1973; Kutas, McCarthy, & Donchin, 1977); however, for targets that deviate slightly in a physical attribute, such as pitch or duration, it is not clear that a cognitive categorization is mandatory.

A number of questions remain to be answered about the interpretation of these ERP effects. The absence of the P3 to targets in the irrelevant channel is in accordance with the Broadbent–Treisman view that stimuli rejected by a stimulus set are not processed as fully as those that are accepted. However, P3 waves are generally elicited only by unexpected (improbable) stimuli that require a cognitive or motor response. If the P3 reflects the "closure" of the subject's decision process (Desmedt, 1980), occurring only upon completion of stimulus evaluation (Kutas *et al.*, 1977; McCarthy & Donchin, 1981) or the postdecision updating of expectancies (Donchin *et al.*, 1978), the lack of a P3 would not necessarily rule out a full perceptual analysis of the stimuli from the irrelevant channel.

More definitive evidence for hierarchical dependencies among processing events comes from experiments involving multidimensional stimuli (detailed in a later section), which utilize the finding that the latency of Nd onset is delayed as the "channel" discrimination is made more difficult (Hansen, 1981). The delay in Nd as a function of cue difficulty suggests that information about stimulus attributes becomes available to attention mechanisms at different times.

Further study of attention-related ERPs associated with increasingly complex types of cues should help to determine how many qualitatively distinct levels of attention we are dealing with and how they interact. Keren (1976) has suggested that the stimulus set (simple cue) versus response set (cognitive categorization) distinction forms a continuum rather than a dichotomy. To get at this question, we have recently recorded ERPs during a selective listening task in which the attended and unattended channels were defined by the more complex cues that distinguish the syllables "pa" versus "ba" and "da" versus "ga." The subjects task, for example, was to listen to the "pa's" and ignore the "ba's" that were presented in a random sequence and to try to detect occasional longer-duration "pa's" (targets). As seen in Figure 11-5, similar

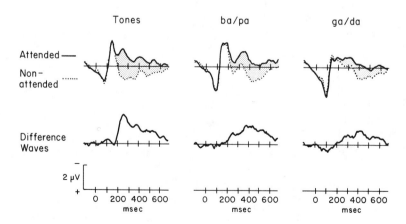

Figure 11-5. ERPs during selective listening to channels designated by tones differing in frequency (300 vs. 375 Hz) or by different syllables ("pa" vs. "ba" and "da" vs. "ga"). ERPs were to shorter-duration (51-msec) nontarget sounds, delivered at random ISIs of 250–550 msec in all three conditions. The selections between the two computer synthesized syllables were based on voice onset time in the case of "pa"/"ba," and direction of formant transition for "da"/ "ga." (Grand average data over 12 subjects from Hansen, Dickstein, Berka, & Hillyard 1983.)

Nd waves were associated with selections between pairs of syllables and between pairs of tones, but the Nd to the syllables was delayed in onset by about 100 msec; this probably reflected the time required for the more complex syllable discrimination. These qualitative similarities in Nd waveforms suggests that similar processing systems are engaged for selections between simple physical cues and between syllables. Further experiments could test whether an Nd would accompany more "cognitive" selections, and if not, whether extensive training to the point where the cue discriminations became "automatic" would result in an Nd. Such a result would suggest that Nd accompanies selections by any rapidly discriminable cue.

Signal Detection Experiments

Converging evidence for ERP indices of distinct processing stages comes from signal detection experiments where subjects tried to detect threshold level tones. K. C. Squires, Hillyard, and Lindsay (1973) found that the N1 and P3 components to correctly detected tones increased in amplitude and decreased in latency as a function of the subject's rated confidence in the detection. They proposed that the N1 amplitude (which might include Nd) reflects the amount of signal information that is utilized in the decision process, while the P3 reflects the certainty of the decision based on that information.

In a design where subjects had to discriminate the tones' frequency as well as detect them, Purasuraman and Beatty (1980) found that the N1 amplitude was proportional to the confidence of detection, regardless of whether or not the tone was identified correctly, whereas the P3 was larger for the correctly identified tones. Their data suggest that trial-to-trial fluctuations in N1 amplitude reflect a more effective intake of information, which leads to more accurate signal identification. Parasuraman, Richer, and Beatty (1982) concluded that the process of detection, associated with N1, begins before the process of identification, reflected in the P3. These signal detection results reinforce the differential roles of early negativity and late positivity that were seen in the two-channel selective listening experiments.

Modality-Specific Effects

The ERPs recorded during selective attention to somatosensory stimuli are also suggestive of a hierarchically organized sequence of selections. Desmedt and Robertson (1977) applied random sequences of shocks to the index and middle fingers of both hands while subjects attended to one finger at a time. They found that all shocks to the attended hand elicited an enlarged N130 component (resembling the auditory Nd), while the P3 (P400) wave was only elicited by shocks to the attended finger. Thus, the N130, which was found to be lateralized over the contralateral somatosensory cortex, appeared to index the early selection of input from the relevant body region.

Visual selective attention is associated with changes in a series of ERP components beginning at about 80 msec, which vary in waveform and scalp distribution according to what types of cues are being attended. In experiments where attention was shifted between different spatial locations in the right and left visual fields, attended flashes showed enhancement of occipital P1 (90–110 msec) and N1 (160–180 msec) waves, as well as N1 and P2 (200–240 msec) components at the vertex (Eason, Harter, & White, 1969; Van Voorhis & Hillyard, 1977). Eason (1981) has suggested that these early occipital changes, which are largest over contralateral cortical areas, may reflect an attenuation of input from irrelevant spatial locations prior to its arrival at the primary visual cortex.

Harter, Aine, and Schroeder (1982) reported that the ERPs associated with color or form selections within a visual field had a longer latency than the early "geniculostriate" ERPs associated with the between-field selection. Moreover, a later component associated with spatial selections (N272) predominated over the right cerebral hemisphere, whereas the ERPs correlated with color–form selections (N222–N272) were larger over the left; this is consistent with other evidence that the processing of these stimulus dimensions is lateralized in this fashion. Harter *et al.* interpret the series of negative ERPs between 100–300 msec as reflecting "a functional hierarchy of premotor selection processes" that are initiated in series but continue to operate in parallel. Based on the latencies of these temporally overlapping ERPs, Harter and associates have suggested that different types of cues are selected in the following order: location, contour, color, spatial frequency, orientation and conjunction of features (Harter & Guido, 1980).

In conclusion, ERP data have pointed to clear distinctions among stimulus selection processes, which vary according to stimulus modality, discrimination difficulty, and stimulus complexity. The findings so far are supportive of multiple levels of stimulus selection, which operate in parallel in some cases and show hierarchical dependencies in others. It seems likely that ERP data like these will be used more and more for dissecting the intricate structure of complex processing sequences.

PROPERTIES OF ATTENTIONAL CHANNELS

Closely linked with the hypothesis of early selection is the concept of an attentional "channel." The term "channel" has been used in different ways in the sensory processing literature, which has led to some misunderstandings and intensive discourse (e.g., Donchin, 1984). Channels have traditionally been defined rather loosely in terms of specific sources of stimuli in the environment, zones of receptor surface, or regions in sensory "input space" (e.g., Moray, 1969). From a neurophysiological standpoint, a channel can be considered as the set of neurons that are selectively responsive to some aspect of a stimulus, presumably because of their receptive field organization (Blakemore & Campbell, 1969).

An *attentional* channel, on the other hand, can be defined in terms of the set of stimuli that is processed more effectively when a member of that set is attended. That is, focusing attention on a particular stimulus results in enhanced processing not only of that specific locus in sensory space, but also of a range of loci that are (usually) adjacent along some sensory dimension. In this vein, Shiffrin, McKay, and Shaffer (1976) suggested that an attention channel is "a class of sensory loci within which no selective attention occurs" (p. 15); that is, if paying attention to sensory locus A produces "benefits" in the processing of both loci A and B while incurring "costs" in the processing of locus C, then A and B would belong to the same channel and C to another. This definition of a channel as "that which is selected by attention" is *not* circular; rather, it is descriptive of how narrowly focused or cue-specific a particular selective act happens to be.

Attentional channels can be studied effectively using ERPs, since a wide range of stimuli both within and outside of the presumptive channel may be given in rapid succession without the necessity of making overt behavioral responses. Using an ERP criterion, a channel would be defined as that set of stimuli that elicits an equivalent ERP effect when attention is focused on any member of the set. The decline in ERP amplitude with distance from the attended locus would define the "bandwidth" of the attentional channel. Harter and Previc (1978) performed an experiment of this type for the dimension of visual–spatial frequency (check size in a checkerboard). Nine different-sized checkerboards were flashed in random order while the subject attended to one particular size and pressed a button each time it occurred. Harter and Previc found that a broad negative ERP (latency 100–300 msec) was elicited over the occipital scalp by the attended stimulus. There was a progressive decline in the amplitude of this attention-related negativity for checks that were increasingly disparate in size from the attended value. This ERP amplitude versus stimulus size function defined an attentional channel that had the same bandwidth (about one octave) as did the physiological "size channels" defined in an interocular interaction paradigm. Harter and Previc suggested that selective attention in this case operated by influencing the size-specific neural channels that normally process patterned visual input.

Another approach to recording the properties of attentional channels is to record ERPs to a range of irrelevant "probe" stimuli that are superimposed on a stream of stimuli being attended. We (Woods, Hillyard, & Hansen, 1984) recently used this technique to investigate the specificity of selective attention to natural speech messages. Subjects listened to a male voice reading a novel in one ear and ignored a female voice telling a different story in the other ear (or vice versa). Superimposed on each voice were four different kinds of probes occurring in random order: (1) a tone pip at the fundamental frequency of the speaker's voice, (2) a tone pip at the second-formant frequency of the speaker's voice, (3) the word "ah," and (4) the word "but"; the latter two were spoken by the actual voices in each ear and digitized for repeated presentation. The subject's task was simply to remember the story in the attended ear for a later questionnaire.[2]

The effects of attention on the ERPs to the probes are shown in Figure 11-6. The ERPs to the two sinusoids, fundamental and second-formant, showed little difference in the attended versus unattended ears. In contrast, the ERPs to the two natural speech sounds showed strong effects of attentional selection, with a broad Nd following attended-ear sounds. This indicates that the human speech selection system is a highly sophisticated "filter" that is specifically tuned to the higher-order, patterned characteristics of the attended voice. The attentional channel so created appears to admit sounds based not on the constituent frequencies of the speech, but on the entire acoustic pattern.

Processing of the Irrelevant Channel

Theories of early and late selection make different predictions about the extent to which stimuli are evaluated in irrelevant channels. Early experiments using the dichotic speech paradigm generally supported the filter theory, in that little of the contents of the message in the unattended ear could be reported (reviewed in Moray, 1969). Several more recent studies, however, have shown that at least some semantic information in the rejected ear is analyzed and can interfere with processing on the attended-ear message (reviewed in Traub & Geffen, 1979). There is still some doubt, however, as to how fully the irrelevant channel is analyzed when attention is sustained to continuous streams of stimuli (Treisman, Squire, & Green, 1974).

Because of the inherent difficulty in obtaining behavioral measures of the processing of stimuli that are expressly not to be attended, this question is particu-

2. In another condition, the subject softly shadowed (repeated aloud) the message in one ear. This produced attention effects on the ERPs similar to those produced by simply monitoring the message.

larly amenable to the nonintrusive ERP approach. In the experiment illustrated in Figure 11-6, for instance, it appeared that pure tones were processed similarly (using an Nd criterion) in the attended and rejected channels of speech; this result corresponds well with previous behavioral findings to this effect (Lawson, 1966; Treisman & Riley, 1969; Zelnicker,

Rattok, & Medem, 1974). For the actual speech sounds, however, it was clear that the processing was more selective, again confirming behavioral studies that show reduced detectability of spoken targets in an irrelevant message (Bookbinder & Osman, 1979; Treisman & Geffen, 1967).

The P3 component can also serve as an indicator of the processing of irrelevant material. As discussed above, infrequent targets belonging to a rejected channel generally elicit much smaller P3 waves than do attended-channel targets. There is some evidence, however, that strongly deviant events belolnging to a presumably irrelevant channel do elicit P3 waves (Ritter, Vaughan, & Costa, 1968; Smith, Donchin, Cohen, & Starr, 1970; N. K. Squires, Donchin, Squires, & Grossberg, 1977). N. K. Squires *et al.* (1977) presented sequences of simultaneous auditory and visual stimuli while subjects reacted to infrequent targets in one of the modalities. They found that the deviant events in the irrelevant modality not only elicited P3 waves, but also retarded the subjects' responses to the relevant-channel targets. This behavioral verification of interference from irrelevant events suggests that the P3 indexes the extent to which attention is shifted toward them and away from the primary task.

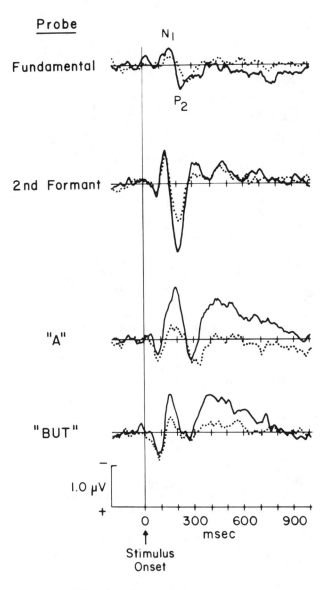

Figure 11-6. ERPs to four types of computer-generated probe stimuli that were superimposed at random (mean ISI of about 1 sec) upon the male voice in one ear and the female voice in the other. Subject monitored one voice at a time. ERPs are grand-averaged over 12 subjects and both ears, comparing attended versus unattended channels. (Data from Woods, Hillyard, & Hansen, 1984.)

MULTIDIMENSIONAL STIMULUS PROCESSING

Several theories of perception have dealt with the question of how the separate attributes or dimensions of a stimulus are integrated into compound percepts. While "analytic" theories assert that perceptual wholes are formed by combining the results of separate feature analyses, "synthetic" (e.g., Gestalt) theorists have argued that perception of the whole precedes analysis of the parts (reviewed in Miller, 1978; Treisman & Gelade, 1980). This debate has direct implications for theories of selective attention. If the analytic view is correct, it would be possible for an attention mechanism to select for particular stimulus attributes independently of one another without necessarily registering the whole configuration. The question being posed is this: "Do we first attend to attributes or to objects?"

On the basis of some visual search experiments, Treisman and associates (Treisman & Gelade, 1980; Treisman, Sykes, & Gelade, 1977) have put forth a two-stage model they call the "feature integration" theory of attention. They propose that simple stimulus features such as colors are registered automatically and in parallel across the sensory field, whereas the identification of an object (a conjunction of attributes) requires an additional stage of focal attention. This hypothesis would allow for an early, fast selection of simple attributes, while the selection of conjunctions would entail the slower, serial process of focal attention.

By recording ERPs to multidimensional stimuli in a task where the target stimuli are defined by a conjunction of attributes, it is possible to get at the question of whether two attributes are selected and processed independently of each other. (This may well depend on whether the attributes in question are integral or separable in Garner's [1974] sense.) One paradigm for doing this would involve the presentation (in random order) or four stimuli, comprised of two levels of two different attributes, A and B (i.e., A_1B_1, A_2B_1, A_1B_2, A_2B_2). The subject's attention would be directed toward one of these compounds, and ERPs to stimuli that did or did not share specific attributes with the attended stimulus would be compared.

If, for example, stimulus A_1B_1 was being attended and the selection process extracted information about each attribute independently of the other, then the ERP associated with the selection of attribute A should not differ as a function of what level of B the stimulus had. In terms of ERP difference waves, the following relationship should hold:

$$A_1B_1 - A_2B_1 = A_1B_2 - A_2B_2$$

where A_1B_1 is the ERP to the attended stimulus, and so forth. This type of relationship has considerable generality for testing whether two processes occur independently, occur in parallel, or interact.[3] Such an independence of attribute selection would also imply that the total attention effect in the ERP is equal to the sum of the attention effects due to selection of each individual attribute; that is,

$$A_1B_1 - A_2B_2 = (A_1B_2 - A_2B_2) + (A_2B_1 - A_2B_2)$$

This is simply a rearrangement of the equation above. On the other hand, if selective processing is accorded only to the conjunction of attended attributes, then the ERP to A_1B_1 would be expected to differ distinctly from the other three ERPs, which would be similar to one another.

We applied this type of analysis to an auditory attention experiment where pitch and location were the attributes that defined the attended channel (Hansen, 1981; Hansen & Hillyard 1983). The tones were either high or low in pitch and right or left in location; these four stimuli were presented in random order, while the subjects attended to one pitch–location combination at a time and detected occasional target tones of longer duration in that "channel." Hypothetical ERP waveforms are shown in Figure 11-7, under the assumption that the attention-sensitive component is a broad Nd wave. If, for example, the

3. For example, using this criterion of ERP independence, Kutas and Hillyard (1980) showed that the differential processing of words according to whether they were semantically congruous or incongruous did not interact with whether the words were printed in normal or unexpectedly larger print.

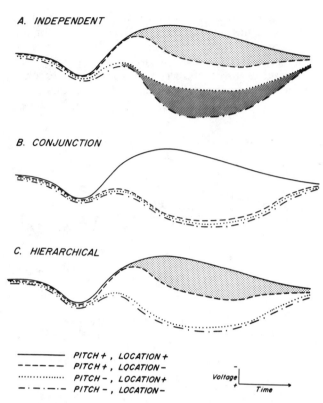

Figure 11-7. Idealized ERP waveforms in dual-attribute selective listening task under three different hypotheses. The four superimposed tracings in each case are ERPs to standard (51-msec) tones that shared (+) or did not share (−) the pitch and/or location attributes with the attended channel. Four types of tones (all 50-dB SL) were presented in random order to ISIs of 200–500 msec. In A and B, the pitch and location "channel cues" were equally discriminable, while in C pitch was more discriminable than location. (From "Selective attention to multidimensional auditory stimuli" by J. C. Hansen and S. A. Hillyard. *Journal of Experimental Psychology: Human Perception and Performance*, 1983, 9, 1–19. (Copyright 1983 by the American Psychological Association. Reprinted by permission of the author.)

location and pitch attributes are selected independently (Figure 11-7A), then the ERP difference wave between attended and unattended locations should be identical, whether the tones have the attended pitch (upper shaded area) or the unattended pitch (lower shaded area). On the other hand, if the selection process reflected in Nd is specific to the conjunction of attributes, then only those tones would elicit a substantial negativity (Figure 11-7B). Tones that do not have the attended value of one attribute would not be processed differentially on the basis of the other. Another possible outcome might be that an early pattern like that of Figure 11-7A would transform into a pattern like that of Figure 11-7B, suggestive of an early parallel selection followed by a later selection of the conjunction.

PITCH EASY, LOCATION EASY
RAW WAVEFORMS (F_z)

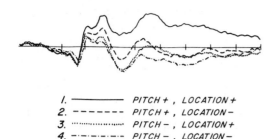

    1. ───────── PITCH + , LOCATION +
    2. ─ ─ ─ ─ ─ PITCH + , LOCATION −
    3. ············· PITCH − , LOCATION +
    4. ─·─··─··─ PITCH − , LOCATION −

DIFFERENCE WAVES (F_z)

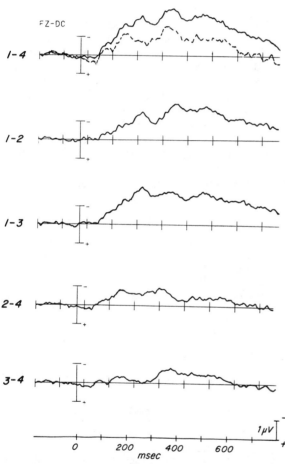

Figure 11-8. Grand average ERPs in dual-attribute selective listening experiment. Overlapped tracings at top are ERPs to each of the four pitch–location combinations, averaged separately according to whether the tones shared (+) or did not share (−) the indicated attribute with the attended channel. Difference waves below (solid lines) show the effects of selecting for both attributes together (1–4), for location when pitch was (1–2) and was not (3–4) fulfilled, and for pitch when location was (1–3) and was not (2–4) fulfilled. (Based on data from Hansen, 1981).

The actual ERPs to the four attribute combinations in this experiment are shown in Figure 11-8. Since the attention effects were equivalent for each attribute combination, the ERPs are collapsed according to whether they shared (+) or did not share (−) the attended level of each attribute. This pattern of data appears most consistent with a selection on the basis of the attribute conjunction, although the fit is not perfect. It is clearly inconsistent with a hypothesis of independent processing of the two attributes. This can also be seen in the subtracted difference waves shown in Figure 11-8; the ERP difference wave associated with selection of the location attribute was much larger for tones of the attended pitch (wave 1–2) than for tones of the unattended pitch (wave 3–4).

Evidence for hierarchical selections of attributes was seen in other conditions of this experiment, where one of the two attributes was made more difficult to discriminate (the two frequencies or the two locations were moved closer together), while the other was left "easy." In this case the pattern of data closely resembled the ERPs shown in Figure 11-7C. At about 70 msec after stimulus onset, there was an early Nd associated with selection of the easy dimension (pitch, in this case); about 100 msec later, additional negativity was elicited to tones having the proper location (the hard dimension). Most importantly, tones that were rejected on the basis of the easy attribute were not processed any further on the basis of the more difficult attribute. Thus, these results are strongly suggestive of a hierarchical selective process and seem concordant with the Broadbent–Treisman hypothesis of a rapid early selection based on easily discriminable features (Hansen & Hillyard, 1983).

Additional results from this experiment provided evidence that these auditory attribute analyses are initiated and proceed in parallel. The latencies of the P3 waves and RTs to the infrequent, longer-duration targets were not delayed when the pitch or location cues were made more difficult to discriminate. This implies that the analysis of tone duration did not await the completion of the selections for pitch and location. In the framework of an "analytic" processing model, this pattern of results suggests that analyses of all three dimensions (pitch, location, and duration) begin and proceed in parallel until it is determined that any attribute has the wrong (unattended) value, whereupon all processing of that stimulus is terminated.[4] Should the stimulus possess the proper levels of all three attributes (i.e., be a target), processing continues until target recognition, signaled by the P3 complex of waves. Since stimuli can be rejected more rapidly when they differ from the targets along an

4. It is also possible to interpret these ERP data in terms of holistic processing models (Lockhead, 1972; Miller, 1978). In this case, parallel analysis would be made of the attribute ensembles, and speed of selection would depend upon the time taken to evaluate differences between ensembles.

easily discriminable dimension, a hierarchical pattern of selection ensues. This interpretation closely follows parallel self-terminating models of processing (Hawkins, 1969; Snodgrass & Townsend, 1980) and suggests a mechanism by which the early–late selection hierarchy proposed by Broadbent and Treisman could occur.

TEMPORAL ASPECTS OF ATTENTION

The speed with which attention can be focused upon or switched between different kinds of stimuli has been estimated using a variety of behavioral techniques (Moray, 1969). Treisman *et al.* (1974), for example, investigated how rapidly perceptual selectivity develops when attention is focused on verbal material in one ear during dichotic presentations. Using the inter-aural semantic interference paradigm of Lewis (1970), they found that words in the irrelevant channel were not fully excluded until after several words had been presented. Evidently some time was required before the "filter" became effective.

This same question can be addressed using ERP techniques. Donald and Young (1980) required subjects to listen to tones in one ear and ignore tones in the opposite ear in a variation of the task developed by Hillyard *et al.* (1973). By averaging ERPs over many blocks of trials, it was possible to examine the ERP to each successive tone in both attended and unattended channels. It was found that the Nd component associated with the interchannel selection developed rapidly, within the first few tones. This approach should prove useful for assessing how rapidly attentional filtering develops in a variety of situations.

One explanation for why it takes time to build up attentional selectivity is that the subject has to establish or refresh internal representations of the pertinent sensory cues that guide the selection. That is, it may be more difficult to attend to (or to reject) an "empty" channel than one that has recently been cued. If this is the case, we might expect to see enhanced selectivity for stimuli that are delivered at short interstimulus intervals (ISIs); such an effect might well account for the dependence of the Nd effect upon rapid rates of stimulus delivery. If the recency of cue presentation were found to enhance Nd amplitudes, this would be the exact opposite of the refractory effects that normally accompany shortened ISIs. However, such a result would be consistent with reports that endogenous ERPs can show very rapid recovery at short ISIs (Woods, Hillyard, Courchesne, & Galambos, 1980).

Appropriate experimental designs could also be devised to determine how rapidly attention can be switched from one channel to another. In principle, ERP recordings can reveal a good deal about the temporal dynamics of attentional processes, since the consequences of rapid deployments of attention can be tested without interference from motor response requirements.

The time course of the facilitation of processing brought about by a prior "priming" stimulus can also be studied with ERPs. In tasks developed by Posner and associates, a priming cue instructs the subject where in space to expect a subsequent visual stimulus (Posner, 1978; Posner, Nissen, & Ogden, 1978). They found that subjects responded more quickly in a simple RT task to flashes occurring at expected locations than at unprimed locations; this selectivity developed within 200 msec after the prime. ERPs could be very helpful here to ascertain whether the speeded RT is accomplished by an early "pathway facilitation" or by a later surprise or incongruity effect. The physiological evidence may be important here, since Duncan (1981) has argued that behavioral evidence does not settle the question of early–late selection in such priming experiments. Preliminary evidence from our laboratory (Figure 11-9) suggests that flashes at primed locations elicit ERPs with earlier "P2" components, paralleling the speeded RTs; however, the enhancement of N1 and other waves that occurs during sustained attention (e.g., Van Voorhis & Hillyard, 1977) is not obvious. This suggests that attending to a recurring sequence of events may involve a different atten-

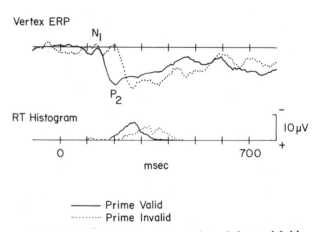

Figure 11-9. ERPs to flashes in the right or left visual field, averaged separately according to whether a preceding "prime" cue indicated their correct (valid) or incorrect (invalid) location. Prime was an arrow pointing right or left, which preceded the target flash by 1.2 sec. Subjects made a simple RT response to both valid (80%) and invalid (20%) flashes. (Data of one subject from unpublished study by Van Voorhis & Hillyard.)

tional system than does the trial-by-trial precueing of each stimulus.

ALLOCATIONS OF ATTENTIONAL RESOURCES

Current "economic" models of attention use the concept of resource allocation to account for the selectivity of human information processing (e.g., Navon & Gopher, 1979). In this framework, "paying attention" implies the allocation of appropriate processing resources from their limited-capacity pools, resulting in "benefits" to performance on the attended task and/or "costs" to capabilities on the secondary task. It seems likely that different information-processing structures, such as input and output modalities, stages of processing, and hemisphere of processing, have their own separate resource pools (Wickens, 1980). Two tasks will interfere with each other when performed at the same time to the extent that they draw on common processing structures and resources.

Allocations of attention can be evaluated by the nonintrusive recording of ERPs, as well as by the traditional method of examining performances costs and benefits. The Nd component, for example, appears to index the distribution of processing resources among different channels of input during divided attention. As shown in Figure 11-10, the Nd amplitudes elicited by events in either channel during divided attention are intermediate in amplitude between those elicited by attended and unattended stimuli during focused attention (Hink, Van Voorhis, Hillyard, & Smith, 1977; Okita, 1979; Parasuraman, 1978). The Nd amplitude here (measured as the N1 peak) is plotted in a format analogous to the "attention operating characteristic" (Kinchla, 1980), which shows the ERP costs and benefits associated with shifts of attention. The total Nd elicited in both channels remains nearly constant during focused and divided attention, suggesting a resource drawn from a limited-capacity pool.[5]

Several other dynamic properties of Nd are consistent with its being a measure of resource allocation. The amplitude of Nd is increased when stimulus intensities are reduced, when a masking background noise is added, and when ISIs are shortened (reviewed

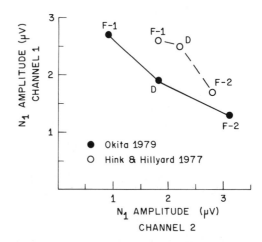

Figure 11-10. "Allocation" function for Nd during focused and divided attention. Mean amplitude of the N1 peak (a measure that includes Nd) to sounds delivered in two channels during conditions of focused attention to one channel and divided attention to both channels. In the study by Hink, Van Voorhis, Hillyard, and Smith (1977), the channels were the two ears, while in Okita (1979) the channels differed in pitch and spatial location and had to be tracked as they changed continuously.

in Hillyard & Picton, 1979). All of these changes would tend to increase the processing load and would require the allocation of more resources to the attended-channel inputs. Thus, there is good reason to believe that the Nd reflects the operation of an auditory analysis system having a fixed capacity, which receives input from channels selected by a stimulus set. Further experiments on allocations of ERP amplitudes during intermodal divided attention would also be of interest, to test the proposal (Treisman & Davies, 1973; Wickens, 1980) that stimulus analyses show less interference when attention is divided between modalities than within a modality. Comparisons of the scalp distributions of the associated ERPs would also help to get at the question of modality-specific resource pools.

P300 and Workload Assessment

A recently developed approach for assessing allocations of attention involves recording the late endogenous ERPs to a secondary ("probe") task while varying the difficulty of a primary sensory–motor task (Isreal, Chesney, Wickens, & Donchin, 1980a). The idea is that increasing the utilization of resources by the primary task will be reflected in changes of ERPs that draw on that same resource pool. This method provides a relatively unobtrusive probe of resource allo-

---

5. Näätänen and Michie (1979) have cautioned, however, that quantitative ERP comparisons between focused and divided attention conditions may be suspect, because the subject's general state (e.g., of arousal) may not remain constant. This is a valid point for both ERP and behavioral studies of divided attention. Not only could altered arousal levels affect ERPs in a nonselective manner, but changes in arousal associated with overall task difficulty could well influence the total available processing resources.

cation by minimizing response interference with the primary task.

In experiments of this type, (Isreal *et al.*, 1980a; Isreal, Wickens, Chesney, & Donchin, 1980b) recorded the P300 component to occasional "oddball" tones (frequency shifts in a repetitive sequence) concurrently with performance of primary tasks, such as tracking a moving visual target with a joystick or detecting shifts in the trajectories of moving targets on a display. They found that P300 amplitudes were reduced when the "perceptual load" of these tasks was increased (e.g., more visual elements in the display), but that P300 was relatively insensitive to variations in the "response load" (e.g., tracking on one versus two dimensions). These results were taken as supporting multiple-resource models of attention. Further, since RTs to tones in such a secondary task were found to be sensitive to *both* perceptual and motor loading, it appeared that the P300 yielded more precise information about the type of resources being engaged by the primary task. The interaction of P300 with perceptual load is consistent with hypotheses that the P300 is dependent upon processes of stimulus identification and classification, rather than response selection and execution.

In some cases, the topography of ERPs to probes may give an indication not only of the type of resources that are being utilized, but also of the general brain regions that are engaged. For example, Shucard, Shucard, and Thomas (1977) found that the late components of the auditory ERP were reduced over the left cerebral hemisphere during a verbal task and were smaller over the right hemisphere when music was played. This can be interpreted as a sign of differential engagement of the two hemispheres in these tasks. As we learn more about the perceptual and cognitive processes that are indexed by the different ERP components, they will become increasingly useful in assessing the utilization of processing resources.

CLINICAL APPLICATIONS OF ERPs

Deficits in selective attention have been implicated in a number of different clinical syndromes, including schizophrenia, hyperactivity, learning disability, and senile dementia, and, to a lesser extent, in normal aging. There have been numerous studies of altered exogenous and endogenous ERPs in these clinical populations (reviewed in Begleiter, 1979; Callaway, Tueting, & Koslow, 1978), but most experiments have not utilized paradigms that isolated selective from nonselective influences on the ERPs. By studying ERPs that are specifically related to attention, it may be possible to characterize more precisely the nature of the processing deficiencies in these patients.

An attenuated Nd component, for example, would be suggestive of a problem with the early selection of relevant from irrelevant inputs. Such a result was obtained for hyperactive children in an auditory selective attention task, where both the Nd and P3 waves were found to be substantially reduced in comparison with those of normal children (Loiselle, Stamm, Maitinsky, & Whipple, 1980; Zambelli, Stamm, Maitinsky, & Loiselle, 1977). These ERP reductions were correlated with lower scores on behavioral tests of attention and vigilance. Loiselle *et al.* (1980) proposed that hyperactivity is associated with deficiencies in both stimulus set and response set attention.

The Nd during selective listening to dichotic tones was also found to be attenuated in neurological patients with frontal lobe damage (Knight, Hillyard, Woods, & Neville, 1981). This suggests a role for the frontal cortex in the control of early stimulus selections (but not necessarily in the actual generation of the Nd wave). On the other hand, Ford, Hopkins, Roth, Pfefferbaum, and Kopell (1979) found that the Nd effect was just as large in a group of elderly women (mean age 80 years) as in a younger control group (mean age 22). This result runs counter to proposals that the frontal cortex shows an accelerated involvement in the normal aging process (e.g., Smith, Michalewski, Brent, & Thompson, 1980) and suggests that its attentional control functions remain relatively intact.

It has been widely reported that the P3 component in various tasks shows a progressive increase in latency with advancing age (Beck, Swanson, & Dustman, 1980; Ford *et al.*, 1979; Goodin, Squires, Henderson, & Starr, 1978). Older persons showing signs of senile dementia exhibit an even greater retardation of P3 latencies (Goodin *et al.*, 1978). This ERP delay implies a slowing of stimulus evaluation and classification processes or of subsequent decision making that is dissociated from any slowing of motor control that may be present. In future work, it would be important to find out whether older persons have a diminished ability to divide attention among different tasks or to make rapid sequential decisions (e.g., Woods *et al.*, 1980).

There is wide agreement that schizophrenics suffer from deficiencies of attention, but whether the impact is more upon early or late stages of processing has not been established (for reviews, see Hemsley & Zawada, 1976; McGhie, 1971). While no studies have reported on the presence or absence of the Nd effect or other indices of early selection, the P3 component is reported to be attenuated in schizophrenics (Roth, Horvath, Pfefferbaum, & Kopell, 1980). This result suggests a definite problem with stimulus evaluation, and future studies of both early and late ERP components should help to specify the level(s) of the information-processing deficit.

REFERENCES

Beck, E. C., Swanson, C., Dustman, R. E. Long latency components of the visually evoked potential in man: Effects of aging. *Experimental Aging Research*, 1980, 6, 523–545.

Begleiter, H. (Ed.). *Evoked brain potentials and behavior*. New York: Plenum Press, 1979.

Blakemore, C., & Campbell, F. W. On the existence in the human visual system of neurons selectively sensitive to the orientation and size of retinal images. *Journal of Physiology* (London), 1969, 203, 237–260.

Bookbinder, J., & Osman, E. Attentional strategies in dichotic listening. *Memory and Cognition*, 1979, 7, 511–520.

Broadbent, D. E. Stimulus set and response set: Two kinds of selective attention. In D. I. Mostofsky (Ed.), *Attention: Contemporary theory and analysis*. New York: Appleton-Century-Crofts, 1970.

Broadbent, D. E. *Decision and stress*. New York: Academic Press, 1971.

Callaway, E., Tueting, P., & Koslow, S. (Eds.). *Event-related brain potentials in man*. New York: Academic Press, 1978.

Chapman, R. M. Evoked potentials of the brain related to thinking. In F. J. McGuigan (Ed.), *The psychophysiology of thinking*. New York: Academic Press, 1973.

Desmedt, J. E. P300 in serial tasks: An essential postdecision closure mechanism. In H. H. Kornhuber & L. Deecke (Eds.), *Progress in brain research* (Vol. 54, *Motivation, motor and sensory processes of the brain electrical potentials, behavior and clinical use*). Amsterdam: Elsevier/North-Holland, 1980.

Desmedt, J. E. Scalp-recorded cerebral event-related potentials in man as point of entry into the analysis of cognitive processing. In F. O. Schmitt, F. G. Worden, G. Adelman, & S. D. Dennis (Eds.), *The organization of the cerebral cortex*. Cambridge, Mass.: MIT Press, 1981.

Desmedt, J. E., & Cheron, G. Central somatosensory conduction in man: Neural generators and interpeak latencies of the far-field components recorded from neck and right or left scalp and earlobes. *Electroencephalography and Clinical Neurophysiology*, 1980, 50, 382–403.

Desmedt, J. E., Debecker, J., & Manil, J. Mise en évidence d'un signe électrique cérébral associé à la détection par le sujet d'un stimulus sensoriel tactile. *Bulletin of the Royal Academy of Medicine* (Belgique), 1965, 5, 887–936.

Desmedt, J. E., & Robertson, D. Differential enhancement of early and late components of the cerebral somatosensory evoked potentials during forced-paced cognitive tasks in man. *Journal of Physiology* (London), 1977, 271, 761–782.

Deutsch, J. A., & Deutsch, D. Attention: Some theoretical considerations. *Psychological Review*, 1963, 70, 80–90.

Donald, M. W., & Young, M. Habituation and rate decrements in the auditory vertex potential during selective listening. In H. H. Kornhuber & L. Deecke (Eds.), *Progress in brain research* (Vol. 54, *Motivation, motor and sensory processes of the brain, electrical potentials, behavior and clinical use*). Amsterdam: Elsevier/North-Holland, 1980.

Donchin, E. (Ed.). *Cognitive psychophysiology*. Hillsdale, N.J., Lawrence Erlbaum, 1984.

Donchin, E., & Heffley, E. F., III. Multivariate analysis of event-related brain potential data: A tutorial review. In D. Otto (Ed.), *Multidisciplinary perspectives in event-related brain potential research* (EPA-600/9-77-043). Washington, D.C.: U.S. Government Printing Office, 1978.

Donchin, E., Ritter, W., & McCallum, W. C. Cognitive psychophysiology: the endogenous components of the ERP. In E. Callaway, P. Tueting & S. H. Koslow (Eds.), *Event-related brain potentials in man*. New York: Academic Press, 1978.

Duncan, J. Directing attention in the visual field. *Perception and Psychophysics*, 1981, 30, 90–93.

Eason, R. G., Harter, M., & White, C. Effects of attention and arousal on visually evoked cortical potentials and reaction time in man. *Physiology and Behavior*, 1969, 4, 283–289.

Eason, R. G. Visual evoked potential correlates of early neural filtering during selective attention. *Bulletin of the Psychonomic Society*, 1981, 18, 203–206.

Ford, J. M., Hopkins, W. F., III, Roth, W. T., Pfefferbaum, A., & Kopell, B. S. Age effects on event-related potentials in a selective attention task. *Journal of Gerontology*, 1979, 34, 388–395.

Gabriel, M., Saltwick, S. E., & Miller, J. D. Conditioning and reversal of short-latency multiple-unit responses in the rabbit medial geniculate nucleus. *Science*, 1975, 189, 1108–1109.

Garner, W. R. Attention: The processing of multiple sources of information. In E. C. Carterette & M. P. Friedman (Eds.). *Handbook of perception* (Vol. 2). New York: Academic Press, 1974.

Garner, W. R., Hake, H. W., & Eriksen, C. W. Operationism and the concept of perception. *Psychological Review*, 1956, 63, 149–159.

Goff, W. R., Allison, T., & Vaughan, H. G., Jr. The functional neuroanatomy of event-related potentials. In E. Callaway, P. Tueting, & S. Koslow (Eds.). *Event-related brain potentials in man*. New York: Academic Press, 1978.

Goodin, D. S., Squires, K. C., Henderson, B. H., & Starr, A. Age-related variations in evoked potentials to auditory stimuli in normal human subjects. *Electroencephalography and Clinical Neurophysiology*, 1978, 44, 447–458.

Hansen, J. C. Electrophysiological correlates of selective auditory attention in man. Unpublished doctoral dissertation, University of California at San Diego, 1981.

Hansen, J. C., Dickstein, P. W., Berka, C., & Hillyard, S. A. Event-related potentials during selective attention to speech sounds. *Biological Psychology*, 1983, 16, 211–224.

Hansen, J. C., & Hillyard, S. A. Endogenous brain potentials associated with selective auditory attention. *Electroencephalography and Clinical Neurophysiology*, 1980, 49, 277–290.

Harter, M. R., Aine, C., & Schroeder, C. Hemispheric differences in the neural processing of stimulus location and type: Effects of selective attention on visual evoked potentials. *Neuropsychologia*, 1982, 20, 421–438.

Harter, M. R., & Guido, W. Attention to pattern orientation: Negative cortical potentials, reaction time, and the selection process. *Electroencephalography and Clinical Neurophysiology*, 1980, 49, 461–475.

Harter, M. R., & Previc, F. H. Size-specific information channels and selective attention: Visual evoked potential and behavioral measures. *Electroencephalography and Clinical Neurophysiology*, 1978, 45, 628–640.

Hawkins, H. L. Parallel processing in complex visual discrimination. *Perception and Psychophysics*, 1969, 5, 56–64.

Heilman, K. M., & Valenstein, E. (Eds.). *Clinical neuropsychology*. New York: Oxford University Press, 1979.

Hemsley, D. R., & Zawada, S. L. Filtering and the cognitive deficit in schizophrenia. *British Journal of Psychiatry*, 1976, 128, 456–461.

Hernandez-Peon, R. Physiological mechanisms in attention. In R. W. Russell (Ed.), *Frontiers in physiological psychology*. New York: Academic Press, 1966.

Hillyard, S. A. Selective auditory attention and early event-related potentials: A rejoinder. *Canadian Journal of Psychology*, 1981, 35, 159–174.

Hillyard, S. A., Hink, R. F., Schwent, V. L., & Picton, T. W. Electrical signs of selective attention in the human brain. *Science*, 1973, 182, 177–180.

Hillyard, S. A., & Picton, T. W. Event-related brain potentials and selective information processing in man. In J. Desmedt (Ed.), *Progress in clinical neurophysiology* (Vol. 6, *Cognitive components in cerebral event-related potentials and selective attention*). Basel: Karger, 1979.

Hillyard, S. A., Picton, T. W., & Regan, D. M. Sensation, perception and attention: Analysis using ERPs. In E. Callaway, P. Tueting, & S. Koslow (Eds.), *Event-related brain potentials in man*. New York: Academic Press, 1978.

Hink, R. F., & Hillyard, S. A. Auditory evoked potentials during selective listening to dichotic speech messages. *Perception and Psychophysics*, 1976, 20, 236–242.

Hink, R. F., Hillyard, S. A., & Benson, P. J. Event-related brain potentials and selective attention to acoustic and phonetic cues. *Biological Psychology*, 1978, 6, 1–16.

Hink, R. F., Van Voorhis, S. T., Hillyard, S. A., & Smith, T. S. The division of attention and the human auditory evoked potential. *Neuropsychologia*, 1977, 15, 597–605.

Isreal, J. B., Chesney, G. L., Wickens, C. D., & Donchin, E. P300 and tracking difficulty: Evidence of multiple resources in dual-task performance. *Psychophysiology*, 1980, 17, 259–273. (a)

Isreal, J. B., Wickens, C. D., Chesney, G. L., & Donchin, E. The event-related brain potential as an index of display-monitoring workload. *Human Factors*, 1980, 22, 211–224. (b)

Johnston, W. A., & Heinz, S. P. Depth of nontarget processing in an attention task. *Journal of Experimental Psychology: Human Perception and Performance*, 1979, 5, 168–175.

Kahneman, D. (Ed.). *Attention and effort*. Englewood Cliffs, N.J.: Prentice-Hall, 1973.

Karlin, L. Cognition, preparation and sensory-evoked potentials. *Psychological Bulletin*, 1970, 73, 122–136.

Keele, S. W., & Neill, W. T. Mechanisms of attention. In E. C. Carterette & M. P. Friedman (Eds.), *Handbook of perception* (Vol. 9). New York: Academic Press, 1978.

Keren, G. Some considerations of two alleged kinds of selective attention. *Journal of Experimental Psychology: General*, 1976, 105, 349–374.

Kinchla, R. A. The measurement of attention. In R. S. Nickerson (Ed.), *Attention and performance III*. Hillsdale, N.J.: Erlbaum, 1980.

Knight, R. T., Hillyard, S. A., Woods, D. L., & Neville, H. J. The effects of frontal cortex lesions on event-related potentials during auditory selective attention. *Electroencephalography and Clinical Neurophysiology*, 1981, 52, 571–582.

Kutas, M., & Hillyard, S. A. Event-related brain potentials to semantically inappropriate and surprisingly large words. *Biological Psychology*, 1980, 11, 99–116.

Kutas, M., McCarthy, G., & Donchin, E. Augmenting mental chronometry: The P300 as a measure of stimulus evaluation time. *Science*, 1977, 197, 792–795.

Lawson, E. A. Decisions concerning the rejected channel. *Quarterly Journal of Experimental Psychology*, 1966, 18, 260–265.

Lewis, J. Semantic processing of unattended messages during dichotic listening. *Journal of Experimental Psychology*, 1970, 85, 225–228.

Lockhead, G. R. Processing dimensional stimuli: A note. *Psychological Review*, 1972, 79, 410–419.

Loiselle, D. L., Stamm, J. S., Maitinsky, S., & Whipple, S. C. Evoked potential and behavioral signs of attentive dysfunctions in hyperactive boys. *Psychophysiology*, 1980, 17, 193–201.

Lukas, J. H. Human attention: The olivo-cochlear bundle may function as a peripheral filter. *Psychophysiology*, 1980, 17, 444–452.

Lukas, J. H. The role of efferent inhibition in human auditory attention: An examination of the auditory brainstem potentials. *International Journal of Neuroscience*, 1981, 12, 137–145.

McCarthy, G., & Donchin, E. A metric for thought: A comparison of P300 latency and reaction time. *Science*, 1981, 211, 77–80.

McGhie, A. Attention and perception in schizophrenia. In B. A. Maher (Ed.), *Progress in experimental personality research*. New York: Academic Press, 1971.

Miller, J. Multidimensional same–different judgements: Evidence against independent comparisons of dimensions. *Journal of Experimental Psychology: Human Perception and Performance*, 1978, 4, 411–422.

Moller, A. R. The acoustic middle ear muscle reflex. In W. D. Keidel & W. D. Neff (Eds.), *Handbook of sensory physiology* (Vol. 5/I). Berlin: Springer-Verlag, 1974.

Moray, N. *Attention: Selective processes in vision and hearing*. London: Hutchinson Educational, 1969.

Naatanen, R. Selective attention and evoked potentials in humans—A critical review. *Biological Psychology*, 1975, 2, 237–307.

Naatanen, R., & Michie, P. T. Early selective attention effects on the evoked potential: A critical review and reinterpretation. *Biological Psychology*, 1979, 8, 81–136.

Navon, D., & Gopher, D. On the economy of the human processing system. *Psychological Review*, 1979, 86, 214–255.

Norman, D. A. Toward a theory of memory and attention. *Psychological Review*, 1968, 75, 522–536.

Norman, D. A., & Bobrow, D. G. On data-limited and resource-limited processes. *Cognitive Psychology*, 1975, 7, 44–64.

Oatman, L. C. Effects of visual attention on the intensity of auditory evoked potentials. *Experimental Neurology*, 1976, 51, 41–53.

Oatman, L. C., & Anderson, B. W. Effects of visual attention on tone burst evoked potentials. *Experimental Neurology*, 1977, 57, 200–211.

Okita, T. Event-related potentials and selective attention to auditory stimuli varying in pitch and localization. *Biological Psychology*, 1979, 9, 271–284.

Olesen, T. D., Ashe, J. H., & Weinberger, N. M. Modification of auditory and somatosensory system activity during pupillary conditioning in the paralyzed cat. *Journal of Neurophysiology*, 1975, 38, 1114–1139.

Parasuraman, R. Auditory evoked potentials and divided attention. *Psychophysiology*, 1978, 15, 460–465.

Parasuraman, R., & Beatty, J. Brain events underlying detection and recognition of weak sensory signals. *Science*, 1980, 210, 80–83.

Parasuraman, R., Richer, F., & Beatty, J. Detection and recognition: Concurrent processes in perception. *Perception and Psychophysics*, 1982, 31, 1–12.

Picton, T. W., Campbell, K. B., Baribeau-Braun, J., & Proulx, G. B. The neurophysiology of human attention: A tutorial review. In J. Requin (Ed.), *Attention and performance VII*. Hillsdale, N.J.: Erlbaum, 1978.

Picton, T. W., & Hillyard, S. A. Human auditory evoked potentials: II. Effects of attention. *Electroencephalography and Clinical Neurophysiology*, 1974, 36, 191–200.

Picton, T. W., Hillyard, S. A., Galambos, R., & Schiff, M. Human auditory attention: A central or peripheral process? *Science*, 1971, 173, 351–353.

Picton, T. W., Hillyard, S. A., Krausz, H. I., & Galambos, R. Human auditory evoked potentials: I. Evaluation of components. *Electroencephalography and Clinical Neurophysiology*, 1974, 36, 179–190.

Posner, M. I. *Chronometric explorations of mind*. Hillsdale, N.J.: Erlbaum, 1978.

Posner, M. I., Nissen, M. J., & Ogden, W. C. Attended and unattended processing modes: The role of set for spatial location. In H. L. Pick & E. Saltzman (Eds.), *Modes of perceiving and processing information*. Hillsdale, N.J.: Erlbaum, 1978.

Posner, M. I., & Snyder, C. R. Attention and cognitive control. In R. Solso (Ed.), *Information processing and cognition*. Hillsdale, N.J.: Erlbaum, 1975.

Pribram, K. H., & McGuiness, D. Arousal, activation and effort in the control of attention. *Psychological Review*, 1975, 82, 116–149.

Regan, D. *Evoked potentials in psychology, sensory physiology, and clinical medicine*. London: Chapman & Hall, 1972.

Ritter, W., Vaughan, H. G., & Costa, L. D. Orienting and habituation to auditory stimuli: A study of short term changes in averaged evoked responses. *Electroencephalography and Clinical Neurophysiology*, 1968, 25, 550–556.

Rollins, H. A., Jr., & Hendricks, R. Processing of words presented simultaneously to eye and ear. *Journal of Experimental Psychology: Human Perception and Performance*, 1980, 6, 99–109.

Roth, W. I., Horvath, T. B., Pfefferbaum, A., & Kopell, B. S. Event-related potentials in schizophrenics. *Electroencephalography and Clinical Neurophysiology*, 1980, 48, 127–139.

Schneider, W., & Shiffrin, R. M. Controlled and automatic human information processing: I. Detection, search, and attention. *Psychological Review*, 1977, 84, 1–66.

Schwent, V., & Hillyard, S. A. Auditory evoked potentials and multi-channel selective attention. *Electroencephalography and Clinical Neurophysiology*, 1975, 38, 131–138.

Schwent, V. L., & Hillyard, S. A. Auditory evoked potentials and potentials during multichannel selective listening: Role of pitch and localization cues. *Journal of Experimental Psychology: Human Perception and Performance*, 1976, 2, 313–325.

Shiffrin, R. M., McKay, D. P., & Shaffer, W. O. Attending to forty-nine spatial positions at once. *Journal of Experimental Psychology: Human Perception and Performance*, 1976, 2, 14–22.

Shucard, D. W., Shucard, J. L., & Thomas, D. G. Auditory evoked potentials as probes of hemispheric differences in cognitive processing. *Science*, 1977, 197, 1295–1298.

Smith, D. B. D., Donchin, E., Cohen, L., & Starr, A. Auditory average evoked potentials in man during binaural listening. *Electroencephalography and Clinical Neurophysiology*, 1970, 28, 146–152.

Smith, D. B. D., Michalewski, H. J., Brent, G. A., & Thompson, L. W. Auditory averaged evoked potentials and aging: Factors of stimulus, task and topography. *Biological Psychology*, 1980, 11, 135–151.

Snodgrass, J. G., & Townsend, J. T. Comparing parallel and serial models: Theory and implementation. *Journal of Experimental Psychology: Human Perception and Performance*, 1980, 6, 330–354.

Squires, K. C., Hillyard, S. A., & Lindsey, P. L. Vertex potentials evoked during auditory signal detection: Relation to decision criteria. *Perception & Psychophysics*, 1973, 14, 265–272.

Squires, K. C., Squires, N. K., & Hillyard, S. A. Decision-related cortical potentials during an auditory signal detection task with cued observation intervals. *Journal of Experimental Psychology: Human Perception and Performance*, 1975, 104, 268–279.

Squires, N. K., Donchin, E., Squires, K. C., Grossberg, S. Bisensory stimulation: Inferring decision-related processes from the P300 component. *Journal of Experimental Psychology: Human Perception and Performance*, 1977, 3, 299–315.

Sutton, S. The specification of psychological variables in average evoked potential experiments. In E. Donchin & D. B. Lindsley (Eds.), *Averaged evoked potentials: Methods, results and evaluations* (NASA SP-191). Washington, D.C.: U.S. Government Printing Office, 1969.

Traub, E., & Geffen, G. Phonemic and category encoding of unattended words in dichotic listening. *Memory and Cognition*, 1979, 7, 56–65.

Treisman, A. M. Selective attention in man. *British Medical Bulletin*, 1964, 20, 12–16.

Treisman, A. M., & Davies, A. Divided attention to ear and eye. In S. Kornblum (Ed.), *Attention and performance IV*. New York: Academic Press, 1973.

Treisman, A. M., & Geffen, G. Selective attention: Perception or response? *Quarterly Journal of Experimental Psychology*, 1967, 19, 1–17.

Treisman, A. M., & Gelade, G. A feature-integration theory of attention. *Cognitive Psychology*, 1980, 12, 97–136.

Treisman, A. M., & Riley, J. G. Is selective attention selective perception or selective response?: A further test. *Journal of Experimental Psychology*, 1969, 79, 27–34.

Treisman, A. M., Squire, R., & Green, J. Semantic processing in dichotic listening?: A replication. *Memory and Cognition*, 1974, 2, 641–646.

Treisman, A. M., Sykes, M., & Gelade, G. Selective attention and stimulus integration. In S. Dornic (Ed.), *Attention and performance*. VI Hillsdale, N.J.: Erlbaum, 1977.

Van Voorhis, S. T., & Hillyard, S. A. Visual evoked potentials and selective attention to points in space. *Perception and Psychophysics*, 1977, 22, 54–62.

Velasco, M., & Velasco, F. Differential effect of task relevance on early and late components of cortical and subcortical somatic evoked potentials in man. *Electroencephalography and Clinical Neurophysiology*, 1975, 39, 353–364.

Wickens, C. D. The structure of attentional resources. In R. S. Nickerson (Ed.), *Attention and performance*. VIII Hillsdale, N.J.: Erlbaum, 1980.

Woods, D. L., & Hillyard, S. A. Attention at the cocktail party: Brainstem evoked responses reveal no peripheral gating. In D. Otto (Ed.), *New perspectives in event-related potential research* (EPA-600/9-77-043). Washington, D.C.: U.S. Government Printing Office, 1978.

Woods, D. L., Hillyard, S. A., Courchesne, E., & Galambos, R. Electrophysiological signs of split-second decision-making. *Science*, 1980, 207, 655–657.

Words, D. L., Hillyard, S. A., & Hansen, J. C. Event-related potentials reveal similiar attention mechanisms during selective listening and shadowing. *Journal of Experimental Psychology: Human Perception and Performance*, 1984, 10, 761–777.

Worden, F. G. Attention and auditory electrophysiology. In E. Stellar & J. M. Sprague (Eds.), *Progress in physiological psychology* (Vol. 1). New York: Academic Press, 1966.

Zambelli, A. J., Stamm, J. S., Maitinsky, S., & Loiselle, D. L. Auditory evoked potentials and selective attention in formerly hyperactive adolescent boys. *American Journal of Psychiatry*, 1977, 134, 742–747.

Zelnicker, T., Rattok, J., & Medem, A. Selective listening and threshold for tones appearing on a relevant and on an irrelevant input channel. *Perception and Psychophysics*, 1974, 16, 50–52.

Chapter Twelve

Cognitive Psychophysiology and Human Information Processing

Emanuel Donchin
Demetrios Karis
Theodore R. Bashore
Michael G. H. Coles
Gabriele Gratton

INTRODUCTION

In this chapter, we describe how information obtained by recording event-related potentials (ERPs) can prove valuable to the experimental psychologist, and can help elucidate processes that are difficult to understand using traditional performance and subjective measures. To understand the meaning of variation in ERP components, and the ways in which this variation is related to processes of interest to the experimental psychologist, we discuss the cognitive psychophysiological paradigm, as well as the procedures necessary to gain an understanding of ERP components. Our focus is on the P300 component of the ERP, and we review research on the necessary antecedent conditions and possible functional significance of this component. We then demonstrate how recording ERPs during cognitive tasks can aid in solving seemingly intractable problems by allowing a more precise chronometric analysis of information processing. ERPs have proved particularly valuable in the study of selective attention, and are now showing great promise in the assessment of workload. The

chapters in this volume by Hillyard and Hansen (Chapter 11) and by Donchin, Kramer, and Wickens (Chapter 26) review the research in these areas, and they are not discussed here. Other late components, particularly the contingent negative variation (CNV) and slow wave, can also provide valuable information, but are not reviewed in detail here (see Rohrbaugh & Gaillard, 1983; Ruchkin & Sutton, 1983).

THE COGNITIVE PSYCHOPHYSIOLOGICAL PARADIGM

The data we discuss here are obtained by placing electrodes on a person's head and recording electroencephalographic (EEG) activity while the person is engaged in a task. Using the technique of signal averaging, we then extract from the EEG (a voltage $\times$ time function) estimates of the portion of the voltage (the ERP) that is time-locked to some event of interest. We assume that these ERPs represent the synchronized activity of multiple units whose fields

Emanuel Donchin, Demetrios Karis, Theodore R. Bashore, Michael G. H. Coles, and Gabriele Gratton. Cognitive Psychophysiology Laboratory, Department of Psychology, University of Illinois, Champaign, Illinois. (Current address for Bashore: The Medical College of Pennsylvania at Eastern Pennsylvania Psychiatric Institute, Philadelphia, Pennsylvania.)

are so aligned that they summate to produce recordable potentials.

A distinction is usually made between "exogenous" components, which occur early (within the first 100 msec) and "endogenous" components, which occur later (Donchin, Ritter, & McCallum, 1978). Exogenous components reflect early neural processing of the features of the stimuli presented. They are obligatory responses to stimuli whose amplitude and latency are responsive to changes in the physical characteristics of the stimulus, and whose scalp distribution is determined by the sensory system activated. In experiments designed to investigate these early components, subjects typically lie passively while stimuli are presented, often at very high rates (10 times/sec is common in auditory paradigms). In contrast, cognitive psychophysiological paradigms often challenge the subject with complex tasks, and the subject always has some task to perform. Several attributes of the task are manipulated and serve as the independent variables of the study. Systematic changes in brain activity measured at the scalp are considered representative of the engagement of different neural processes, and serve as the dependent variables. The complex brain response is analyzed for patterns of activity that are characterized by a *distinct* scalp distribution and by a *consistent* relation to task variables. These are defined as the endogenous components of the ERP. Such components are distinguished by the fact that they are *not* obligatory responses to physical stimuli; whether they will or will not be elicited depends on the nature of the information processing required of the subject. The endogenous components that follow a warning stimulus and precede an imperative stimulus, for example, are believed to be manifestations of intracranial processes that are involved in the subject's processing of the warning stimulus and preparation for a forthcoming stimulus. Endogenous components that follow a task-relevant stimulus depend more on the processing demands imposed by the task than on the physical nature of the eliciting stimulus (Donchin, 1979, 1981). In contrast to the exogenous components, they can also occur long after the stimulus (often between 500 and 1000 msec).

Although the endogenous components of the ERP can be recorded with reliability, the source of these components is not known. Evidence has begun to accumulate that suggests that some of these components may *not* be generated in the cortex (Halgren, Squires, Wilson, Rohrbaugh, Babb, & Crandall, 1980; Wood, Allison, Goff, Williamson, & Spencer, 1980). There is a hint from this work that we may be observing neural activity generated, in part, from archicortex (the hippocampal formation) and/or the subcortical amygdaloid nuclear complex. Some of the more compelling data, obtained in studies of patients with indwelling electrodes, have led McCarthy, Wood, Allison, Goff, Williamson, and Spencer

(1982) to conclude that one endogenous component, the P300, may not reflect the activity of a unitary generator. They suggest that this component represents the summed activity of multiple sources with multiple orientations (see also Okada, Kaufman, & Williamson, 1983).

Our aim is to demonstrate that ERPs provide a rich class of responses that may, within the appropriate research paradigm, allow the study of processes that are not readily accessible to experimental psychologists by other means. The key assumption of cognitive psychophysiology is that ERP components are manifestations at the scalp of the activity of specific intracranial processors. Our reference is not to specific neuroanatomical entities, but rather to specific functional processors. While networks of nuclei may be involved in a dynamic fashion in the activity represented by each ERP component, our current understanding of the underlying neuroanatomy is insufficient to generate meaningful neuroanatomical hypotheses. Yet, the available data, regarding the consistency with which certain components measured at the scalp behave, permit us to hypothesize that these components do signal the activation of internal "subroutines."

The discussion above should not be construed as implying that the electrical activity recorded at the scalp is itself of functional significance. For our purposes, the ERPs may be due solely to the fortuitous summation of electrical fields that surround active neurons. Although some have argued that EEG fields do have functional significance (especially persuasive is Freeman, 1975), we can remain agnostic on this issue. For our purposes it is sufficient that we elucidate the functional role, in information-processing terms, of the subroutines manifested by the ERP components. It will, of course, be of considerable interest to obtain a detailed neurophysiological description of the neural implementation of the subroutine. However, a description of the subroutine as a processing entity is of interest independently of the neurophysiological description.

Once we identify the existence of a component, we deploy the essential tools of the cognitive psychophysiological paradigm to identify the subroutine it manifests and to articulate its parameters. This search and analysis require that (1) we elucidate the antecedent conditions under which the component is elicited, from which (2) we derive a model of its subroutine that (3) we test by predicting the consequences of calling the subroutine (i.e., of engaging the processes whose activation is manifested at the scalp). Our attempt in this chapter is to show how this paradigmatic procedure is likely to provide the data that are needed if the endogenous components are to serve a useful function in providing valuable information to the experimental psychologist, and to cognitive scientists in general.

COGNITIVE MODELS AS ANCHORS OF SPECIFICITY

A research enterprise needs an anchor of specificity. In any investigation, some aspects of the puzzle must be known with a degree of certainty so that the data and the questions they raise can be interpreted within the framework of some well-established principles. In the study of exogenous components, neuroanatomy serves as the anchor. However, we cannot use neuroanatomy as an anchor of specificity in the study of the endogenous components. A different anchor must, therefore, be found. We submit that, given our current knowledge base, an appropriate anchor can be established by developing an understanding of the functional significance of the ERP components. Until we know the intracranial origins of the components and their underlying neuroanatomy, we must seek a different anchor of specificity. We suggest that the anchor must be *psychological*. It is this logic that leads to the adoption of the cognitive psychophysiological paradigm.

Our assumptions and the underlying model have been presented elsewhere (Donchin, 1979, 1981). In brief, the basic assumptions made in interpreting an ERP component are that (1) the appearance of the component implies that, somewhere inside the head, populations of neurons are activated synchronously; and that (2) these neurons (subsequently referred to as "units") have an appropriate geometry to allow fields that are generated by the individual units to summate and produce a potential recordable at the scalp during a relatively fixed time period. The activity thus observed is an expression, an appearance on the scalp, of the activity of some functionally unified piece of the brain's processing machinery. We are not suggesting that an ERP component reflects the activity of a specific nucleus, or that the tissues whose activity is monitored are related in a neuroanatomical sense (e.g., have reciprocal connections). We simply do not know. We do claim that *if* there is systematic control of the units whose activation is observed, then these units probably perform, or are associated with the performance of, elements of the algorithmic activity of the nervous system. (We call to the reader's attention the need to distinguish between statements about the neural activity and statements about the ERPs. One can derive and test from the ERPs hypotheses about neural processes, but the ERPs are treated here merely as index responses.) We are assuming that proper description of the brain's operation, from a psychologist's point of view, is as a sequence of multiple, parallel, interacting processing activities (e.g., see Eriksen & Schultz, 1979; Grice, Nullmeyer, & Spiker, 1982; McClelland, 1979; Miller, 1982; Turvey, 1973). Stimuli impinge on this stream of activities. They trigger processing activities that chain and cascade. Occasionally some such processing unit has physical properties that allow its activity to be manifested on the scalp. We can then see, in relationship to a particular algorithmic element, the appearance of an ERP component. Our task, then, as noted above, is to elucidate the functional significance of the elements of the algorithm manifested by the ERP component.

In seeking a description of the functions of the process manifested by the component, we are not seeking specifications of such constructs as "attention" or "arousal." It is important to realize that such constructs do not refer to specific pieces of the computing machinery in the brain. They are, rather, descriptions of the entire system and of its mode of operation. In this sense, audition or hearing is a construct pertaining to the entire system, while selective sensitivity to pitch is a construct that pertains to specific components of the system. It is to the latter class of constructs that we need to relate the ERP components. There is no question, for example, that the activity producing auditory brain stem potentials is crucial for hearing, but it is not a manifestation of hearing. Hearing is accomplished by the structures and connective pathways that are referred to collectively as the auditory system; it is not located in the cochlea or in the auditory cortex. We can say that a person hears, but not that the inner ear or the inferior colliculus hear. Thus, the amplitudes of wave IV and V of the brain stem potential are not manifestations of hearing or "correlates" of hearing. Rather, they are manifestations of activity in specific stations of the auditory brain stem. The components indicate that information is being transmitted from one point to another in the brain stem—no more and no less.

In the same sense, we are not trying to correlate the ERP with such concepts as "attention," "decision," or "surprise." Rather, we are assuming that some very specific processes are activated every time we see, say, a P300. Elsewhere we have used the metaphor of the "subroutine" (Donchin, 1981) or of a "special-purpose processor" (Donchin, Kubovy, Kutas, Johnson, & Herning, 1973) to refer to the functional entities manifested by the ERP component. The view implied by such metaphors is best explained within the context of the general approach to the study of human information processing that characterizes contemporary cognitive science. The cognitive scientist accepts as the primary object of study an information-processing system that is describable primarily in terms of the algorithms it applies to information (Marr, 1982). An "algorithm" is a collection of transformation rules that determine the relationship among input data, state parameters, and data appearing at the output of the algorithm. The descriptions may take the form of block diagrams, narrative descriptions, or formal statements such as production systems (Newell & Simon, 1972). It is the cognitive scientist's task to develop algorithmic descriptions that, in a sense, serve as theories of cognition.

Description, in this domain, is taken to involve a specification of the transformations that the algorithm as a whole or its elementary constituents apply to the information. Thus, for example, most theories of cognition include the assertion that a memory is an element in the information-processing algorithm. Theorists then differ in the manner in which they describe this component. The differences are essentially in the details of the transformations that the memory applies to the information it stores and the manner in which the information is retrieved. Theorists vary in the time constant they attribute to the memory, in the number of different memories they postulate, in the characteristics of the retrieval process, and in the relationship they perceive between the data entered into the memory and the nature of the representation created in the memory. The point is that all these descriptive details refer to the transformations that the memory establishes between its input and the outputs it supplies to other components of the algorithm.

We emphasize this point because, in our view, the entities manifested by ERP components may be describable in the same sense. We assume that the consistency displayed by an ERP component in its relation to experimental manipulations is due to the fact that the activity it manifests is generated by the invocation of a distinct component of the information-processing system. A description of the component —if it is to bear meaning for the cognitive scientist— must identify the transformations that the algorithmic component, or the "subroutine," performs. The description, to be adequate, will have to identify the conditions under which the subroutine is invoked, the domain of data to which the subroutine is applied, and the transformation applied by that routine to the data.

There is, of course, another level at which the information system can (and should ultimately) be described. The specific manner in which the algorithms are implemented in the neural hardware must be described if we are to have a complete understanding of biological information-processing systems. The cognitive scientist may choose to focus on the algorithmic description, ignoring the fact that the system is implemented by means of specific hardware. Yet the implementation is real enough, and for the neuroscientist its description is the true challenge. The cognitive neuroscientist, or psychophysiologist, indeed hopes that the detailed description of the cognitive algorithms will ultimately lead to fruitful studies that will identify which neural structures embody specific subroutines, as well as describe the mechanism whereby the routine is executed by neurons. It seems, however, that a careful description of the functional nature of the algorithms must precede, or at least accompany, the study of neural implementations.

What, then, do we need in order to arrive at a functional description of the subroutine that may underlie a given ERP component? If our target is a description of the transformation applied by our processor to its input, then there are at least three phases to the research paradigm. We begin with what is under our control as experimenters. We need to ascertain the conditions that govern the subroutine's invocation. We must search among the bewildering diversity of variables that control the external manifestation of the subroutine's action (the ERP) for consistencies that will allow us to reduce the multiplicity of conditions and variables to a tractable collection of descriptors. Our goal is to arrive at a parsimonious summary of the antecedent conditions that control the elicitation of the subroutine. This description would allow sound, testable theorizing regarding the functional role of the routine.

It is important to emphasize at this point that in this first phase of the research we are not studying the relationship between the inputs and the outputs of the subroutine. We study the effect of external conditions and of experimental manipulations on the amplitude, latency, and scalp distribution of an ERP component. We do not consider the electrical activity recorded on the scalp to be the output of the subroutine. (For the unfortunate consequences of the failure to observe that distinction, see Schwartz & Pritchard, 1981, 1982. These authors' critique of Donchin & Lindsley, 1965, and Donchin, 1982, is based largely on a confusion between statements about the ERP and statements about the underlying neural processes.) Rather, the ERP is a manifestation of the subroutine's activity. We may assume, as we often do, that the amplitude of the ERP reflects the degree of activation of the routine. We can infer the duration of all the processes that must transpire before the routine is invoked from the latency of the onset of the electrical activity manifesting the subroutine. We can also regard the scalp distribution as a source of useful hints regarding the structure of the intracranial events. But in no event can we consider these variables to be the target variables of the subroutine—its outputs, so to speak. That is, we do not believe that the intracranial source reflected in an ERP component is activated in order to generate the potentials we are recording. The subroutine must have outputs framed in the internal code of the information-processing system—a code interpretable by the elements of a system that receive as inputs our subroutine's output as the critical target variable.

An example may clarify the point. When we record wave V of the brain stem ERP, we are observing the activity of a relay station in the auditory pathway. It is unclear whether we are observing axonal volleys or intraganglionic interactions. But, in any event, it is the case that the component is a manifestation of activity in the pathway that moves data about acoustic inputs from the cochlea to the inferior colliculus and points beyond. In terms of an algorithmic description of the auditory pathway, it is not quite clear whether this relay station transforms the information in some specific way, or acts, rather, as a signal enhancer in a noisy pathway. Of course, no one would suggest that the function of the station is to produce a voltage that can be recorded as wave V. It is assumed that the function of the tissue generating wave V is to transform, or transmit, the acoustic data in a manner that in some way affects the subsequent stations in the auditory pathway.

If the ERP is not the critical output of the subroutine, then it is clear that a description of the relationship between the variables that control attributes of the ERP cannot in itself constitute an adequate description of the subroutine. The transformations we seek to describe are between the proper input and the proper output of the subroutine. Therefore, the study of the antecedent conditions can only provide clues from which one must derive hypotheses regarding the functional significance of the routine. These hypotheses must be stated in terms of the effect the activation of the subroutine has on subsequent functional elements. Clearly, to be of value, the output of the processor must act as input to some other stage of the system. A theory specifying the function of the subroutine should therefore specify the effect its activation will have on the recipients of its output. This analysis underlies our assertion that theories of ERP components should specify the *consequences* of the component's activation.

We return to this point below. However, it may be useful to illustrate here the distinction among descriptions of the antecedent conditions for a component, theories about its functional significance, and tests of hypotheses regarding its consequences derived from these theories. Thus, statements about the effect of subjective probability or workload on the P300 are discussions of its antecedent conditions. The suggestion that the P300 reflects the activation of a response set (Hillyard, Hink, Schwent, & Picton, 1973) or the switch from automatic to controlled processing (Rosler, 1983) are general statements about the functional significance of the component. These hypotheses suffer from a lack of specificity, in that they fail to articulate the transformation applied by the component to its inputs, and therefore do not generate testable predictions of the consequences of the component. More specific are assertions that the P300 is related to equivocation (Ruchkin & Sutton, 1978), or that it reflects a closure registration process (Desmedt, 1981), or that it is—as we suggest below—involved in the updating of working memory (Donchin, 1981). These latter models, vague as they are at this time, do yield specific predictions regarding the

consequences of the P300. Predictions take the form of statements regarding difference in the recall of items that elicit P300 of certain attributes, or regarding the confidence subjects will display with regard to their reports. Of course, the predictions may not be confirmed, and this will trigger a cycle of theory revision and new predictions. However, it is only by determining the consequences of an ERP component that the cognitive psychophysiological paradigm will achieve its full fruition.

In the course of our research within the cognitive psychophysiological paradigm, even at the early stage in which we endeavor to specify the antecedent conditions of a component, data are acquired on the attributes of the ERP. These data can be used to derive tools for the study of cognitive function (Donchin, 1979). Thus, an advantage of the cognitive psychophysiological paradigm is that even before a complete understanding of the ERP is achieved, it yields useful applications.

In the remainder of this chapter, we illustrate the manner in which cognitive psychophysiological paradigms can be utilized in developing practical applications of ERP components and solving problems within experimental psychology. We begin with a detailed review of the data currently available on the antecedent conditions of the P300, and then discuss the manner in which these data can be used to develop tools for assessing cognitive studies. The implications of these data for developing hypotheses about the subroutine manifested by P300, and a test of one hypothesis, are touched upon.

THE P300 COMPONENT: THE ROLE OF SUBJECTIVE PROBABILITY

The following discussion focuses on the P300 component of the human ERP, which was first observed and reported by Sutton, Braren, Zubin, and John (1965). Since this initial report, the P300 has been observed in a wide variety of different circumstances. The diversity of the conditions in which this component can be elicited are, however, often variants of what is known as the "oddball" paradigm. In an oddball task, the subject is presented with two stimuli, one rare and one frequent, that occur in a Bernoulli sequence (i.e., on any given trial, one of two stimuli can occur, and their probability is complementary). Stimuli are typically presented every 1–2 sec, and the subject is instructed to keep a mental count of the rare stimulus. Almost invariably, the rare stimulus elicits a P300. That the ERP elicited across the various oddball tasks is a P300 is implied by the observation that the scalp distribution of the component is largely invariant; it is largest at the parietal electrode, somewhat smaller at the central electrode, and minimal at the frontal electrode. Johnson and Donchin (1982), for example, presented the subject with a sequence of tones of two different frequencies, 33% of which were of one pitch and 67% of the other pitch. Furthermore, every 40–80 trials the probabiliy of the stimuli was reversed, unbeknownst to the subject. The subject was instructed to count the number of times the low-pitched tone was presented. Presentation of the rare tone elicited a large, positive-going ERP whose peak amplitude occurred approximately 300 msec after the tone, the P300. Thus, the rare, counted stimulus elicited a large P300. It was of particular interest in this study that when the probabilities were reversed, the larger P300 was elicited by the rarer of the two tones, rather than by the counted tone. Thus, each of the two tones elicited the larger P300 in different segments of the series, depending on the probability of the tone, rather than on its specific physical characteristics. It should be noted that even though probability appeared to be the prime factor controlling P300 amplitude, the counted stimulus, when rare, elicited a larger P300 than was elicited by the uncounted stimulus when *it* was rare. This "target" effect points out that the amplitude of P300 depends (1) on the probability of occurrence of a stimulus and (2) on the task relevance of that stimulus. In fact, it is becoming increasingly clear that while, under certain circumstances, the subjective probability of a stimulus exercises a powerful effect on P300 amplitude, there are conditions in which the amplitude of P300 is quite insensitive to stimulus probability (Heffley, Wickens, & Donchin, 1978).

The effect of stimulus probability on P300 amplitude has been confirmed frequently. Indeed, in a parametric study by Duncan-Johnson and Donchin (1977), it was shown, using randomly presented tones, that the amplitude of P300 depends more on the probability of the stimulus than on its role as a specific target to be counted. These investigators showed that as the relative probability of the counted (target) tone decreases, the associated P300 increases; and that as the probability of the uncounted (nontarget) tone decreases, the amplitude of the P300 it elicits increases. This is the "probability" effect; that is, low-probability stimuli produce a large P300, whether or not they are counted. A moderate target effect was also observed. At equal probabilities, target stimuli generally elicit a larger P300 than do nontarget stimuli. The importance of task relevance to the elicitation of P300 is demonstrated in this experiment by the fact that when the subject was solving a word puzzle, and was not counting either of the tones, no P300 was evident. Similar results were obtained by Hillyard and his associates (N. K. Squires, Squires, & Hillyard, 1975), and by Picton and his coworkers (Campbell, Courchesne, Picton, & Squires, 1979; Stuss & Picton, 1978). For a comprehensive review, see Pritchard (1981). The "target" effect is, of course,

of considerable power. It is always the case that the more task-relevant the stimulus, the larger the P300 it elicits. Johnson and Donchin (1978) have shown that the P300 amplitude increases if the subject relies increasingly on the information conveyed by a stimulus in performing the task.

Although the early work by Sutton's group demonstrated that probability is an important variable in determining the amplitude of P300 (an antecedent condition in our terminology), it was not quite clear whether it is the objective, prior probability of the stimulus events or their subjective probability as determined by the *subject's* perception of the situation that is critical (though see Tueting, Sutton, & Zubin, 1971, for an early indication that it is the subjective probability that is critical in P300 elicitation).

The manner in which this issue has been addressed is illustrative of the approach taken to resolve issues within the cognitive psychophysiological paradigm. The challenge posed by the paradigm is that first we elucidate the antecedent conditions for the elicitation of P300. These conditions must be described with as much precision as possible. Thus, knowing the variables that actually control P300 is crucial. Determining, in each case, the variables that control the P300 dictates a choice between quite different models of the component. For example, if the amplitude of the P300 is controlled by the prior probability of a stimulus, determined solely by the environment in which the stimulus is triggered, then the subroutine that we seek is probably lodged in the periphery, controlled more by the nature of the physical stimuli than by the structure of the psychological situation in which they are embedded. If, on the other hand, the *subjective* probability is critical, then we are probably observing quite a different class of subroutines, anchored in deeper levels of psychological processing.

Subjective probability was demonstrated to be a crucial variable in a series of experiments by K. C. Squires, Wickens, Squires, and Donchin (1976), illustrated in Figure 12-1. The ERPs shown were elicited by the same physical stimulus, and this stimulus had the same objective prior probability throughout—namely, .50. The subject's task was to count the number of times one of two tones of different frequencies was presented. Experimental trials were sorted so that in one group counted tones were preceded by uncounted tones, while in another group counted tones were preceded by other counted tones. By sorting trials in this way, K. C. Squires *et al.* (1976) were able to show that a larger P300 was produced when the preceding stimulus differed from the counted stimulus. The longer the sequence of different stimuli that preceded the counted stimulus, the larger the P300 that was elicited by that stimulus. The longer the sequence of similar stimuli (i.e., those that were also counted) preceding a counted stimulus, the smaller the P300 elicited by that stimulus. Thus,

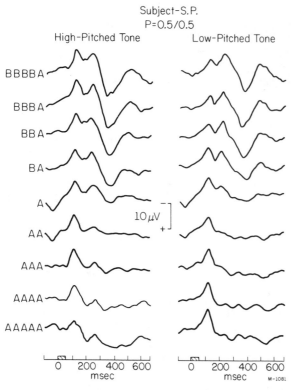

Figure 12-1. The ERPs in each column were elicited by the same physical tone; high-pitched tones were used for the left column and low-pitched tones for the right column. Both were presented in a Bernoulli series in which the probability of the two stimuli were equal. In the middle of each column (labeled "A") is the ERP elicited by all the presentations of the stimulus. The curve labeled "AA" was obtained by averaging together all the tones of one frequency that were preceded on the previous trial by tones of the same frequency. On the other hand, the curves labeled "BA" were elicited by stimuli preceded on the previous trial by the tones of different frequency. Similar sorting operations were applied to all other curves in this figure. It can be seen that the same physical tone elicited quite different ERPs, depending on the events that occurred on the preceding trials. Whenever a tone terminated a series of tones from the other category, a large P300 was elicited, and its magnitude was a function of the length of the stimulus series. (From "Effect of Stimulus Sequence on the Waveform of the Cortical Event-Related Potential," by K. C. Squires, C. D. Wickens, N. K. Squires, and E. Donchin. *Science*, 1976, 193, 1142–1146. Copyright 1976 by the AAAS. Reprinted by permission.)

there is an exquisitely sensitive relationship between the precise structure of the sequence preceding a stimulus and the amplitude of the P300 that it elicits.

Another example of the importance of subjective factors in determining P300 amplitude is provided by Horst, Johnson, and Donchin (1980). Subjects in this study memorized associations between pairs of nonsense syllables. On each trial, they typed in a nonsense

syllable in response to a syllable displayed on a screen by the computer. The subjects also indicated how confident they were that their response was correct. Each trial was terminated by the presentation of the correct syllable. The ERPs shown in Figure 12-2 were elicited by this "feedback" stimulus. These ERPs are sorted according to a subject's confidence in his or her response, as well as by the actual accuracy of the response. The interesting aspect of these data is that the largest ERPs were elicited by stimuli that "surprised" a subject. These are presumably the stimuli that showed subjects they were wrong when they were sure they were right, and those that confirmed their response when they were certain that they erred.

Karis, Chesney, and Donchin (1983; see also Donchin, 1979) have demonstrated that while the overt responses in a prediction paradigm may be strongly affected by the subject's expectations of reward, the P300 amplitude continues to reflect the probability of the eliciting events. Their subjects were instructed to predict which of three digits (1, 2, or 3) would appear next in a sequence of random trials. The prior probability of the events remained the same in all experimental conditions: $p(1) = p(3) = .45$, and $p(2) = .10$. However, by varying the reward schedule, subjects could be made to choose 2's with greater or lesser frequency. The 2's, however, elicited the largest P300 in all experimental conditions, regardless of the reward structure.

How Specific Must the Eliciting Stimuli Be?

In the experiments we have cited, the stimuli constituting the Bernoulli series can be specified on the basis of relatively simple physical or semantic attributes. But how important is it that stimuli be physically distinct and easily discriminable in physical terms or easily categorized on semantic dimensions? That is, can stimuli that differ on complex semantic dimensions elicit a P300? Again, the answer is very important in delineating the nature of the subroutine. The answer to this question is unequivocal. There is absolutely no need for these stimuli to be distinct physical events or simple semantic stimuli. Stimuli that differ in physical attributes but share meaning in the context of a task do elicit a P300 if the task requires that the stimuli be categorized, and if items from one category occur less often than do items from the other category. We have shown this, for example, using a Bernoulli series consisting of names of males and females that are used frequently in the American culture and are readily recognizable as names (Kutas, McCarthy, & Donchin, 1977). Our subjects were instructed to count male names, the rare stimulus event. Thus, the subject had to read the word on each trial, interpret and code it, and then determine whether a male or a female name was shown. Only then, after this categor-

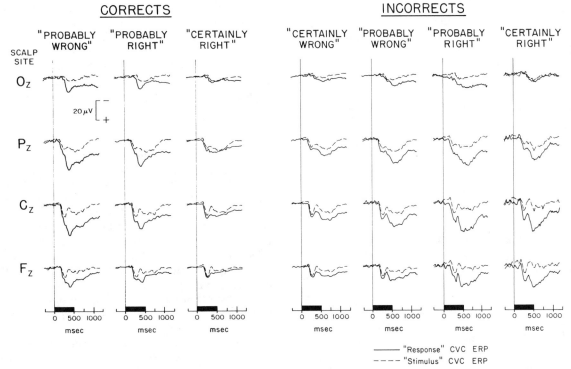

Figure 12-2. The ERPs indicated by solid lines were elicited by nonsense syllables that told the subject whether his or her response, in a paired-associate learning experiment, was correct. Subjects also reported their confidence in their report prior to the appearance of the eliciting syllables. The largest P300s were elicited either when subjects believed they were wrong and turned out to be correct, or when subjects believed they were correct and turned out to be wrong. (From "Event-Related Brain Potentials and Subjective Probability in a Learning Task" by R. L. Horst, R. Johnson, and E. Donchin. *Memory and Cognition*, 1980, 8, 476–488. Reprinted by permission.)

ization, could the probability of the item be determined. A large P300 was elicited by the rare items (i.e., male names) and a rather small P300 by the frequent items.

Another example is provided by Towle, Heuer, and Donchin (1980). Their subjects were presented a sequence of magazine covers, 20% of which contained pictures of politicians while the rest did not. They were instructed, for example, to count the number of magazine covers that fell into a predefined category. In one condition, they counted the number of times politicians were shown. In other runs, the subjects counted the number of entertainment figures. Covers containing politicians elicited a P300 only when politicians were counted. Thus the magazine covers did, or did not, elicit a large P300, depending on the categorization rule imposed by the instructions. Clearly, the P300s observed in these three experiments could not have been elicited without *previous* categorization of the stimulus.

The Latency of P300

Stimuli that elicit the P300 can be defined at rather elaborate levels of abstraction. Further, the level of

abstraction may be reflected in the latency to the peak amplitude of the P300. If the P300 is elicited by stimuli in one of two categories, the P300 cannot be elicited until the system "knows" the category membership of the event. Hence, we can delineate even further the nature of the P300 subroutine. The routine is elicited *after* stimuli have been categorized and their probability has been determined. These data also bear on the problem of the dissociation between reaction time (RT) and P300 latency. Donchin *et al.* (1978) have suggested that the "disturbing" failure of RT and P300 latency to correlate may be explained by assuming that the relationship between the two variables depends on the strategy of the subject. While many different processes determine RT, only a subset of these processes determines P300 latency. Thus, the coupling between the P300 and RT depends on the relationship between the processes that determine P300 latency and those that determine RT. Kutas *et al.* (1977) have demonstrated that if the subject is instructed to respond accurately, so that the stimuli must be processed before responding, the correlation between P300 latency and RT is high, and the P300 precedes RT. However, when the subject is trying to respond as quickly as possible, and may not be processing the stimuli completely before responding, the response is faster and, on many occasions, precedes P300. On those trials in which an incorrect response is made, RT typically precedes P300.

These data suggested that P300 latency is determined largely by the duration of categorization processes, and not by response selection and execution processes. Support for this hypothesis has been provided in several recent studies. McCarthy and Donchin's (1981) work illustrates the strategy used to test this hypothesis. In this experiment, both stimulus discriminability and response selection processes were manipulated. On each trial the subject saw one of four stimulus matrices, in each of which either the word "LEFT" or "RIGHT" appeared. Stimulus discriminability was influenced by surrounding the target word with either # (number) signs (the "no-noise" condition) or with letters chosen randomly from the alphabet (the "noise" condition). Embedding the target word in a matrix of random letters made it far more difficult to discriminate (see Figure 12-3A). Response selection was influenced by making the response either compatible or incompatible with the target word. That is, in the compatible condition, the word signaled a response with the same hand (e.g., "RIGHT"—right-hand response), whereas in the incompatible condition the word signaled a response with the opposite hand (e.g., "RIGHT"—left-hand response). McCarthy and Donchin (1981) found that RT increased when other letters were presented in the matrix and when an incompatible response was executed.

It turned out that there was no interaction between the effect of "noise" and the effect of "response compatibility" on RT. The two factors were additive, each increasing the average RT by a certain number of milliseconds. Such additivity implies that the two variables, noise and compatibility, affect two different stages of processing (Sternberg, 1969, 1975). Evidence reviewed by McCarthy (1980) suggests that discriminability affects categorization and that response incompatibility affects response selection. McCarthy and Donchin (1981) thus predicted that the latency of P300 would be delayed when the target stimulus was more difficult to discriminate, but would not be changed when response selection was more difficult. This is exactly what happened. The P300s recorded in this experiment are shown in Figure 12-3B.

In a subsequent experiment, Magliero, Bashore, Coles, and Donchin (1984) were able to show that the latency of P300 can be modulated by varying the "amount" of noise in the matrices (see Figure 12-4). Noise increased P300 latency as it did RT; response incompatibility had a large effect on RT but a much smaller effect on P300 latency. Magliero et al. (1984) also presented subjects with an "oddball" task based on a series constructed from the matrices shown in

Figure 12-4. They varied which of the commands (right or left) was the target. It turned out that the component whose latency was increased by the addition of noise to the series had a larger amplitude when the eliciting stimulus was the target. This result confirms McCarthy and Donchin's (1981) assertion that the delayed positive peak they studied is indeed the P300.

Complications in the Probability Story

From parametric analyses of amplitude changes in P300, we now know that task-relevant, improbable stimuli elicit the largest P300; that the subjective, rather than objective, probability of these stimuli is critical for the elicitation of P300; and that these stimuli can be defined at rather deep levels of abstraction. Further, at this point we know with considerable confidence that the P300 reflects cerebral processes engaged by stimulus evaluation components in the stream of human information processing. Before these assertions can be integrated into a model that attempts to specify the functional significance of P300, we must review studies indicating that the effects of probability on the P300 depend on the circumstances in which it is elicited. Evidence of this complexity has emerged from studies by Heffley (1985). In an earlier study (Heffley et al., 1978), subjects viewed stimuli—triangles and squares, with squares designated as targets—that moved from left to right on a screen in a random, straight-line trajectory. Every 4–8 sec, one of the shapes was brightened for 200 msec; the subjects were instructed to count enhancements in the brightness of the squares and to ignore those of the triangles. Thus, the subjects' task was to monitor changes in the intensity of one stimulus and to report at the end of the session how many such changes occurred. Hence, one stimulus was task-relevant and the other was irrelevant. It was found that the relevant stimuli elicited a larger P300 than did the irrelevant stimuli (Heffley et al., 1978). These data are, of course, quite similar in intent and message to the data reported in Donchin and Cohen (1967).

While these data confirmed the importance of task relevance in controlling P300 amplitude, they presented a puzzling challenge to the model that attributes the variance in P300 amplitude to variance in the subjective probability of the eliciting stimuli. Heffley (1985) varied the number of targets on the screen and the probability with which each of the targets flashed. There could be two, five, or eight targets, and the probability of one target's flashing could be .20, .50, or .80. P300 latency increased as the probability of a target flash decreased (and as the number of stimuli in the display increased), but changes in target probability had *no* effect on the amplitude of P300. This latter finding was inconsistent with the assertion that the

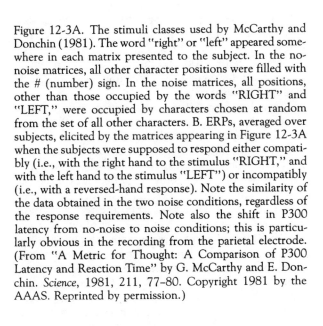

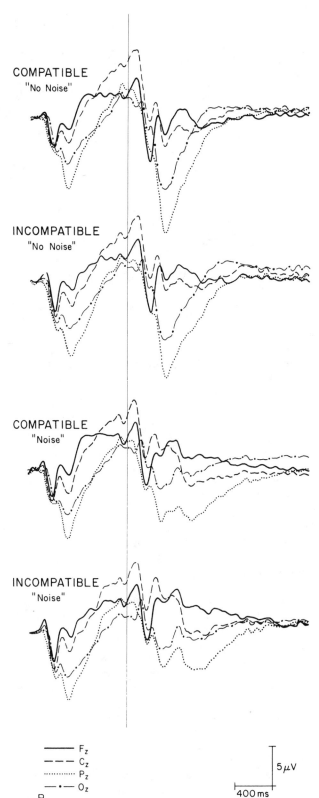

Figure 12-3A. The stimuli classes used by McCarthy and Donchin (1981). The word "right" or "left" appeared somewhere in each matrix presented to the subject. In the no-noise matrices, all other character positions were filled with the # (number) sign. In the noise matrices, all positions, other than those occupied by the words "RIGHT" and "LEFT," were occupied by characters chosen at random from the set of all other characters. B. ERPs, averaged over subjects, elicited by the matrices appearing in Figure 12-3A when the subjects were supposed to respond either compatibly (i.e., with the right hand to the stimulus "RIGHT," and with the left hand to the stimulus "LEFT") or incompatibly (i.e., with a reversed-hand response). Note the similarity of the data obtained in the two noise conditions, regardless of the response requirements. Note also the shift in P300 latency from no-noise to noise conditions; this is particularly obvious in the recording from the parietal electrode. (From "A Metric for Thought: A Comparison of P300 Latency and Reaction Time" by G. McCarthy and E. Donchin. *Science*, 1981, 211, 77–80. Copyright 1981 by the AAAS. Reprinted by permission.)

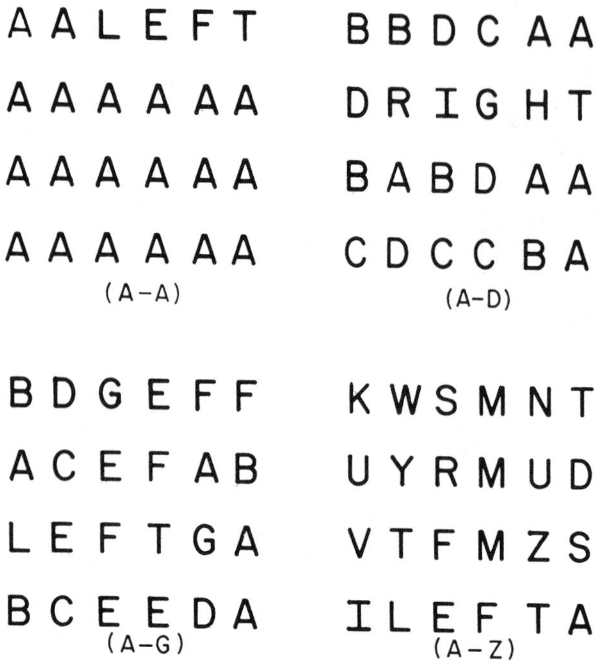

A A L E F T   B B D C A A

A A A A A A   D R I G H T

A A A A A A   B A B D A A

A A A A A A   C D C C B A

(A–A)   (A–D)

B D G E F F   K W S M N T

A C E F A B   U Y R M U D

L E F T G A   V T F M Z S

B C E E D A   I L E F T A

(A–G)   (A–Z)

Figure 12-4. Noise matrices used by Magliero, Bashore, Coles, and Donchin (1981). Note that these are identical in principal to the noise matrices in Figure 12-3A, except that the characters used to fill in the nonstimulus positions were drawn from the set of characters indicated under each matrix. In this way, four different levels of noise were created. (Copyright © 1984, The Society for Psychophysiological Research. Reprinted with permission of the publisher from A. Magliero, T. R. Bashore, M. G. H. Coles, and E. Donchin. "On the Dependence of P300 Latency on Stimulus Evaluation Processes." *Psychophysiology*, 1984, 21, 171–186.)

lower the probability of a target stimulus, the larger the P300. One possible explanation was that inasmuch as both the relevant and irrelevant stimuli were always on the screen, the subjects could selectively attend to the relevant stimuli; as a result, the probability of the target was of little consequence.

Another experiment was run to test this notion. In this second experiment, subjects viewed either a continuous display, similar to that used in the first experiment, or a periodic presentation of the same display. In the periodic display, the screen was kept blank until such time as a stationary stimulus array was presented. Every 4–8 sec, an array was shown, with the positions of all target and nontarget stimuli varied across trials. So, instead of a continuously displayed array of moving squares and triangles, the subjects viewed a periodic display of variously located but stationary squares and triangles. Both the continuous and periodic display contained two squares (targets) and eight triangles (nontargets); the probability of a brighter target stimulus appearing on a given trial was .20, .50, or .80. Note that presentation of a periodic display is equivalent, procedurally, to the oddball paradigm. The only apparent differences between this monitoring task and the visual oddball task were that the target and nontarget stimuli did not appear at the center of the screen and that they were embedded in a display with multiple figures. It was likely, therefore, that the probability effect would emerge with a periodic display. This prediction was not confirmed. Both target and nontarget stimuli elicited substantial P300s; the larger P300 was elicited by the target stimulus, but the probability effect did not emerge. The P300 invoked by the nontarget stimulus presumably indicates that this stimulus must be processed in the periodic display and cannot be selectively ignored.

Another difference between Heffley's task and the studies in which the probability effect was demonstrated is that the mean interval between intensity changes in his study was 6.0 sec—much longer than the interval used in the oddball studies. Typically, in the oddball task, the stimuli are presented every 1.0–2.0 sec. The effect of the interstimulus interval (ISI) was assessed in a third experiment. In this experiment, the periodic display was used, and the ISI was either 1.3 or 3.0 sec. The results were clear: The ISI is a significant determinant of the probability effect. At the 3.0-sec ISI, there was only a small effect of target probability on P300 amplitude; at an ISI of 1.3 sec, however, the probability effect reappeared.

The results of this series of experiments are summarized in Figure 12-5. They indicate that selective attention, stimulus probability, and ISI interact to produce significant effects on P300 amplitude. The target effect predominates at the long ISI, and there is little effect of stimulus probability on P300 amplitude. The probability effect reappears when the ISI is reduced. At an ISI of 1.3 sec, the target effect is small, and the probability effect predominates. It is also important to note that, unlike the sequential dependency effects reported by K. C. Squires *et al.* (1976), the amplitude of P300 to a target flash was independent of the relevance of the preceding flash with both displays at the long ISI.

These data force a further definition of the nature of the P300 subroutine. We are evidently monitoring the activity of a routine whose elicitation is strongly related to stimulus probability, but only over relatively short intervals. This, of course, suggests that the effect of stimulus probability may depend on the existence of stimulus representations in memory. It appears that a P300 is elicited when the representation in working memory of the incoming stimulus is weak. Stimulus representations presumably decay with the passage of time. With rapid stimulus presentations, the stimulus representation may persist, and therefore a P300 is not elicited. If the interval between stimuli is long, then the representation may decay, and presentation of either the rare or frequent stimulus will elicit a P300. Campbell *et al.* (1979) have presented data that are consistent with this position. This interpreta-

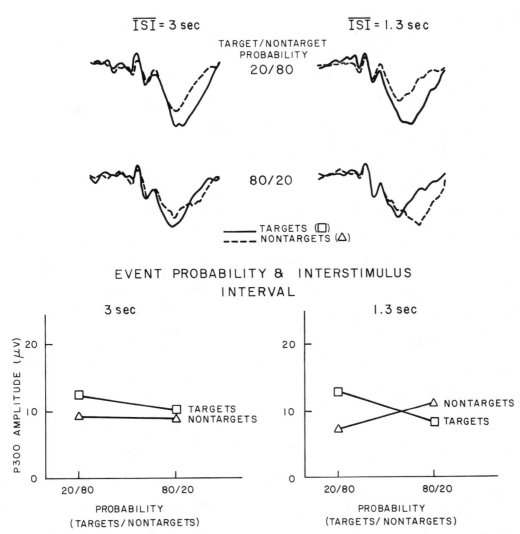

Figure 12-5. A summary of the experiments demonstrating that the effect of event probability on the amplitude of P300 depends on the interval between stimuli. Data were obtained in a classic oddball paradigm in which stimuli could be either triangles or squares. Subjects always counted squares. The probability of squares and triangles was varied, as was the interstimulus interval (ISI). Note that when the ISI was 1.3 sec, the improbable event elicited a larger P300, regardless of what the subject was counting. When the ISI was extended, a larger P300 was elicited by the counted stimulus, regardless of the probability of the eliciting event. (From *Elements of a Neural Theory of Human Information Processing Derived from an Analysis of Cognitive Event-Related Potentials* by E. F. Heffley. Manuscript in preparation, 1985. Used by permission.)

tion would also account for the sequential effects described above. When the memory representation is maintained for short intervals for the frequent events, the subroutine represented by the P300 is not elicited. When the intervals are long and the memory decays, both frequent and rare events call forth the P300 subroutine.

This interpretation of P300 suggests that rather than attempting to explain why a rare event elicits a large P300, it may be more useful to ask why a frequent event *fails* to elicit a P300. It has heretofore been assumed that stimuli normally do not elicit a P300, unless they are rare. But it may be more appropriate to assume that the P300 is always elicited when a task involves a certain form of processing. The call for the P300 subroutine may be inhibited, however, when the nontarget stimulus is presented frequently at short intervals. Hence, the answer to the newly formulated question may be that when the irrelevant stimulus is frequent and appears relatively rapidly, the P300 subroutine is not necessary because representations of that stimulus exist in the short-term memory buffer; when a memory search is required, a P300 is elicited. This leads us to a consideration of the consequences of the elicitation of a P300.

Preliminary Observations on the Consequences of the P300

From studies of the antecedent conditions of the P300 reviewed here and elsewhere (Donchin, 1981; see also Donchin, 1984; Naatanen, 1982; Pritchard, 1981), a data base emerges that permits some preliminary speculations concerning the functional significance of the subroutine manifested by the P300. To recapitulate, the P300 is elicited by important events—"important" in the sense that knowledge regarding the event affects the performance of tasks in which the subject is engaged. The routine is engaged only after the stimulus has been adequately categorized, and its invocation appears to play a role in the perceptual domain, rather than in the domain of response selection and execution. Moreover, the evidence indicates that the subroutine is not crucial for the immediate response to stimuli. A possible implication of this view of the P300 is that the process it manifests is related to some "housekeeping" activities that are triggered by the stimulus. The notion is that the information processing reflected by the P300 is strategic, rather than tactical, as discussed by Donchin et al. (1978). Strategic processing is used to determine the manner in which the system will respond to future events, rather than the present event. The nature of this processing is suggested by the strong relation between P300 and probability, on the one hand, and the abolition of this relation when the interval between stimuli is longer than 3000 msec. The importance of probability has been interpreted, ever since Sutton et al.'s (1965) original report, as triggering a mismatch between a model of the environment and the actual environmental events.

Donchin and his coworkers have suggested that the function of the P300 process is to update the mental model (or schema) that humans maintain of the environment. The dependence of the process on the interval between stimuli is consistent with a view that the P300 subroutine performs tasks that are required in the maintenance of working memory. The specific details of this model are less important to our purpose here than the manner in which such a set of speculations is integrated into the study of ERPs. The chain of reasoning must incorporate into the hypothesis regarding P300 as much as is known about the antecedent conditions as is possible. This process of logical derivation cannot base its strength either on the force of logic, or on the completeness with which the antecedent conditions are used, or from the plausibility of the emerging model. All of these are post hoc arguments that are only as good as the predictions

they generate regarding the consequences of the P300. It is only in the confirmation of such predictions that we can find adequate support for any model of ERP components.

Research designed to test the model we describe may be illustrated by the study reported by Karis, Fabiani, and Donchin (1984). These investigators tested the hypothesis that the larger the P300 elicited by a stimulus, the more likely the subject is to recall this stimulus. Note the critical feature of the hypothesis: It predicts *future* behavior from the amplitude of a P300 elicited *prior* to the time recall is tested. This is quite a different analysis of the process than is required when one tests the hypothesis, say, that P300 is larger when stimuli are rare. In this latter case, we specify the conditions that may influence the occurrence of P300, but we have no way of determining how these conditions actually affect the performance of the task. The memory prediction asserts nothing about the conditions that will cause P300 amplitude to vary. Instead, it suggests that some aspects of the subject's future behavior will covary with the amplitude of P300. Of course, we cannot argue causality from these data. But, the observations we make are of postelicitation, rather than of concurrent, performance.

To test this hypothesis, Karis et al. (1984) used the von Restorff effect. This effect was first reported by von Restorff (1933). She demonstrated that when a few items in a series that must be learned are different from others, they tend to be better recalled. The "isolates," as these different items are called, can stand out in any number of physical or semantic dimensions. In the Karis et al. study, subjects were presented with 40 series of 15 words each. They were to recall the items in each series immediately after they were presented. In 30 of the series, one item (always in one of the positions in the middle third of the series) was displayed in a larger, or a smaller, font. As expected, these isolates elicited a prominent P300 that varied in amplitude from trial to trial. The prediction was that isolates that elicited a larger P300 would be recalled more often than isolates that elicited a small P300.

This prediction was confirmed, but only in part. It turned out that there are substantial individual differences, hitherto unreported, in the von Restorff effect. The subjects could be clustered into three categories: one group showing a very strong von Restorff effect, another showing virtually no effect, and a third group showing the effect to an intermediate degree. The groups also differed in the strategies they used for recalling the words. Subjects showing the strong von Restorff effect tended to use rote memorization, while low-effect subjects (who generally recalled many more words) used various semantic elaboration procedures to assist in recall. A striking relation was observed between these group classifications and the degree to which recall and P300 amplitude were related. The pattern can be seen in Figure 12-6. The high-effect, rote memorizes confirmed the hypothesis. The P300 elicited at the initial presentation of a word that was subsequently recalled was clearly larger than the P300 elicited by a word that was not recalled. In contrast, the low-effect, semantic organizers showed a P300 as large for the recalled words as for those that were not recalled. The isolates elicited large P300s in all subjects, and Karis *et al.* (1984) argue that the initial processing of isolates was similar across subjects.

Isolated words have a distinct orthography, and this will be represented in memory. Karis *et al.* (1984) propose that during retrieval individuals who rely on rote memorization will use orthographic distinctiveness as an aid in recall, while individuals who engage in semantic elaboration will make use of more effective retrieval strategies based on associative linkages. They argue that if the "activation" of representations of orthographically distinct words is related to the size of the P300 these words initially elicit, then when recall depends on the representations of individual words, as when rote strategies are used, P300 will be related to recall. When recall depends on word combinations or elaborations, however, the relationship between P300 and recall will not emerge, because P300 does not predict the extent to which individuals will engage in these elaborations. This depends on idiosyncratic associations to each particular word, and so will vary unpredictably from person to person.

The memory data reported by Karis *et al.* are of course preliminary. If the hypothesis concerning the relationship between mnemonic strategies and the P300–recall relationship is true, then several predictions can be made. First, to the extent that mnemonic strategies are minimized, the relationship between P300 amplitude and recall should be strong for all subjects. Fabiani, Karis, Coles, and Donchin (1983) demonstrated this using an oddball paradigm composed of male and female names with instructions to count names of one gender. They followed this oddball with an unexpected free recall and found a more consistent relationship between P300 and recall than in the previous study. This was expected, because in incidental paradigms there will generally not be extensive processing after the primary task is accomplished (count the number of male or female names; on an individual trial, increase an internal count by one, or do nothing). A more direct, and powerful, approach would be to manipulate strategy within a session for each subject and to examine the P300–recall relationship. If complex, associative strategies that continue after the time frame reflected by P300 aid later retrieval, and thus recall, then when a subject is instructed to use these strategies there should be little or no relationship between P300 amplitude and recall. On the other hand, when the same subjects use simple rote strategies that, in effect, limit associative process-

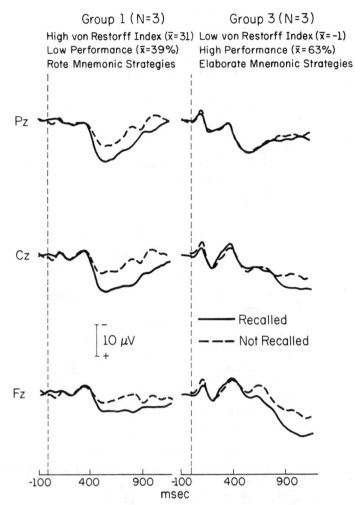

Figure 12-6. ERPs elicited by words that the subject was expected to memorize and recall at the end of a series. All ERPs shown in this figure were elicited by "isolates." These are words that were of a different size than all other words in the series. The ERPs represented by a solid line were elicited by isolates that were subsequently recalled; the dashed line are isolates that were not recalled. In Group 1 were included subjects who showed a strong von Restorff effect and who utilized rote memory strategies. In Group 3 were subjects who showed little or no von Restorff effect and who used various organizational strategies. Note that in the average for Group 1, words that were subsequently recalled elicited a larger P300 than words that were not subsequently recalled. Group 3 did not show this effect (for P300). Group 2 (which is not shown) was intermediate in all respects. (From "P300 and Memory: Individual Differences in the von Restorff Effect" by D. Karis, M. Fabiani, and E. Donchin. *Cognitive Psychology*, 1984, 16, 177–216. Reprinted by permission.)

ing, then P300 should predict later recall. An assumption must be made, of course, that with appropriate instructions, and practice, subjects will be able to adopt radically different strategies (see the discussion by Jennings, Chapter 14, this volume, on inducing rote rehearsal by the addition of noise). This experiment is now under way in our laboratory. Preliminary data are encouraging, although it appears that some subjects may be unable to suppress their preferred strategies effectively.

The specific nature of the relationship between memory and P300 remains a matter for future research. The point for the present discussion is the process by which we derive hypotheses about the functional significance of a component and test these hypotheses by means of predictions about consequences. From this process, there may develop a comprehensive understanding of the component. These analyses will converge, one hopes, with data on the intracranial origins of the components to produce a coherent picture. The hints, and they are no more than that, of a P300-like process in the limbic system (McCarthy et al., 1982; Okada et al., 1983) are rather consistent with the context-updating hypothesis we have described here. But this work is still in its initial stages; furthermore, it is complicated by studies of patients whose hippocampus was unilaterally excised, which provide conflicting data (Wood et al., 1980).

The current state of affairs, with respect to the P300, is that its antecedent conditions are sufficiently well known to allow their use in the assessment of cognitive function in the manner illustrated in our studies of mental workload (see Chapter 26, this volume). A deeper understanding that would support even more penetrating applications is emerging. We emphasize that P300 is only one of the endogenous components that can be analyzed in this manner. The reader is referred to Naatanen's (1982) analysis of processing negativity, and to work on the N200 and similar negative waves (Kutas & Hillyard, 1980a, 1980b, 1980c, 1982; Ritter, Simson, Vaughan, & Friedman, 1979; Ritter, Simson, Vaughan, & Macht, 1982). A review is presented by Hillyard and Kutas (1983), and the book by Gaillard and Ritter (1983) contains a number of papers presenting recent research.

We now have sufficient specificity to begin utilizing this ERP in the assessment of human cognition, even though we do not know, at this stage, either the generating source of the P300 or its precise functional significance. On the other hand, we do know at this point, with considerable confidence, that the latency of the P300 provides a measure of mental processing time that is relatively unaffected by response selection and execution processes. So, if one is interested in dissecting the flow of information processing into its response-related and stimulus-related components, then the P300 can serve as a useful scalpel with which to begin the dissection (see Duncan-Johnson & Donchin, 1982).

It is in this way that the cognitive psychophysiological paradigm uses psychological models as anchors of specificity. We anchor our interpretation of the data in the literature and the methodology of human experimental psychology. We gain support from, among other sources, the extensive investigations of additive factors (e.g., Sternberg, 1975) and from the detailed analyses of RT that derive from a variety of contexts (Eriksen & Schultz, 1979; Grice et al., 1982; McClelland, 1979; Miller, 1982; Posner, 1982; Schneider & Shiffrin, 1979; Shiffrin & Schneider, 1977). With this anchor, we can now make forays into other realms, using our interpretation of the signals to illuminate new issues. Elsewhere (Donchin & Bashore, in press), we have discussed the use of the cognitive psychophysiological paradigm in the study of the schizophrenia. We focus here on experimental psychology, the very domain from which we derive the anchor of specificity.

ERPS IN COGNITIVE PSYCHOLOGY

We now illustrate how information derived from ERPs can help solve problems in cognitive psychology. Once again, we should note that we do not review the exciting work on attention or the assessment of workload, for these areas are discussed in Chapters 11 and 26 of this volume. Our focus is on the P300, but it should be kept in mind that other ERP components can also provide valuable information.

The Locus of Word Frequency Effects

It is well known that people process words faster if the words occur frequently in the language. That is, words that are used often in literature, in speech, or in writing are responded to faster than other words. We refer to the frequency of words in a language as their "global probability." It is also known that when a subject responds to two kinds of stimuli presented in a series, those that occur more frequently are responded to more quickly; that is, RT is faster to those stimuli that have a higher local probability. It is of interest to know whether the speeding of the response to frequent, globally probable words is the same as the speeding of the response to locally probable words. In other words, we want to determine whether the response to globally probable words is faster because people are better able to encode these words or because they are simply more ready to emit responses to them. This issue was addressed in a study by Polich and Donchin (1985). Subjects were presented with a series of character strings, some of which were words in the English language, others of which were not words. Half of the words were frequently used in the language; the other half were infrequently used. In any given series, words could be more or less probable (i.e., words were presented with either an .80 probability, a .50 probability, or a .20 probability). The subject's task was to determine whether the character string on the screen was, or was not, a word. The RTs, the P300 latencies, and the error rates for these judgments are shown in Figure 12-7. As expected, subjects responded faster to frequent words ("Common" in Figure 12-7), and they responded even faster to words if they were probable than if they were improbable. It is interesting to note that the latency of P300 was affected only by the frequency of the word in the language, while RT varied with both variables. The ERPs recorded during performance of this task are shown in Figure 12-8. An analysis of these data shows that the amplitude of the P300 elicited by words was inversely proportional to the probability that a word would be included in the series. The latency of P300, however, was affected by the frequency of words in the language, rather than by the probability of words in the sequence.

Given the anchor of specificity we have derived from our previous findings, it is possible to interpret these data as evidence that while the speeding of the

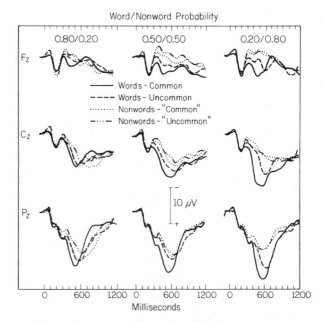

Figure 12-8. ERPs elicited in the word frequency experiment. For details, see Figure 12-7. (From *P300 and the Word Frequency Effect* by J. Polich and E. Donchin. Manuscript in preparation, 1985. Used by permission.)

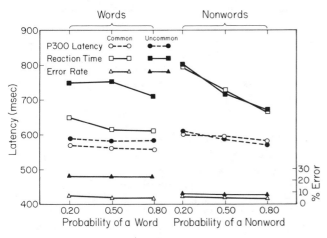

Figure 12-7. Reaction time (RT) and P300 latencies as well as error data from a study in which subjects had to judge whether character strings that appeared on the screen were or were not words in the English language. The probability that a string would be a word was varied as indicated on the abscissa. Furthermore, half of the words in each series were commonly used words in English, while the other half were uncommon words. (Nonwords were produced by changing at least one vowel from another set of common or uncommon words; the results for both types of nonwords are presented.) Note that RT and P300 latency varied with the frequency of the word in the language, while there was no effect of the probability of a word in the series on the latency of the P300. (From *P300 and the Word Frequency Effect* by J. Polich and E. Donchin. Manuscript in preparation, 1985. Used by permission.)

response to common words operates at the encoding stage, the speeding of the response to words that are more prevalent in the sequence is probably due to response bias. Duncan-Johnson and Donchin (1982), however, did find P300 latency changes to probable stimuli, but this can be explained by differences in the paradigms used. Duncan-Johnson and Donchin did not use words, and did not present a series of items, with a response required to each. They used a warned RT paradigm in which the conditional probability of the imperative stimulus (H or S), given the warning stimulus (H, S, or *), was varied. They recorded P300 and RT to probable stimuli and to stimuli that matched the previous stimulus. Probability here was not given by the number of occurrences in a string of stimuli, but by a single warning stimulus. For example, the subjects were told in one condition that when an H was presented as a warning stimulus, the probability of an S appearing as the imperative stimulus was .80, while the probability of another H would be .20. Duncan-Johnson and Donchin found that when a probable stimulus occurred, there was a speeding of both stimulus evaluation (P300 latency was faster) and response selection, while facilitation of response selection alone was responsible for the increased speed of responses to matching stimuli. In this paradigm, unlike that of Polich and Donchin, subjects could prepare for a specific, highly probable stimulus. When it occurred, stimulus encoding and evaluation were speeded, as indexed by P300 latency. When the improbable imperative stimulus occurred, however, P300 latency increased, indicating a slowing of these processes.

P300 latency has also been used to investigate the interaction between orthography and phonology during word processing (Polich, McCarthy, Wang, & Donchin, 1983), while late negativities ("N400") have been postulated to reflect semantic incongruity (Kutas & Hillyard, 1980a, 1980b, 1980c, 1982) and used to support models of sentence comprehension (Fischler, Bloom, Childers, Roucos, & Perry, 1983) (see also Stuss, Sarazin, Leech, & Picton, 1983). A recent review on the use of ERPs in studies of language processing is provided by Rugg, Kok, Barrett, and Fischler (in press).

A Continuous-Flow Model of Information Processing

Traditionally, it has been proposed that information processing involves the transformation of input data by processes that proceed sequentially (Donders, 1868/1969; Sternberg, 1966, 1969, 1975). In recent years, these discrete models have been challenged by those who propose that information can be transmitted from one structure to another before the process performed by the first is completed (Eriksen & Schultz, 1979; McClelland, 1979; Grice et al., 1982; Miller, 1982). Thus, continuous models imply that several processes can occur simultaneously (or in parallel) and that a given process can operate on the partial information provided by another process. (See Miller, 1982, for a discussion of the difference between discrete and continuous models.)

The measurements taken by cognitive psychologists (RT, percent correct, etc.) are seriously limited in terms of their ability to test continuous theories, principally because they represent a single output measure that is determined by many intervening processes and their interactions. Thus, a particular experimental manipulation may affect not only the duration of a mental process, but also the rate of transmission between processing structures and/or the criterion level at which the output is emitted. Changes in RT that result from a manipulation might be the result of any of these factors. Thus, cognitive psychologists are faced with a serious problem if they wish to use RT measures to make inferences about the nature of the effect of a particular experimental manipulation. Psychophysiological measures may prove to be extremely useful in dealing with this problem, because they can provide information about the processes that intervene between input and behavioral output. In this sense, they can be considered as adjuncts to traditional measures of RT and accuracy.

We now review an experiment in which we used the psychophysiological approach to evaluate

Eriksen's continuous-flow model (Coles, Gratton, Bashore, Eriksen, & Donchin, 1985). The particular setting we chose for a test of the approach was an apparently simple one. Twelve male subjects were required to make a discriminative response as a function of the center letter (target) in a five-letter stimulus array. There were four arrays: HHHHH, SSSSS, HHSHH, and SSHSS. The responses we required of the subjects were slightly unusual—a squeeze with the left or right hand of zero-displacement dynamometers at 25% of maximum force.

This particular task has been used often by Eriksen. In a variety of studies, his laboratory has found a consistent difference in RT between compatible and incompatible arrays (Eriksen & Schultz, 1979). In accordance with his continuous-flow model, his explanation for the difference goes as follows: Incompatible arrays contain information about the incorrect response. As stimulus evaluation proceeds and before it is completed, this incorrect information is passed to the response activation system. Thus, the incorrect response is activated. Although the correct response may ultimately be given, the activation of the incorrect response will interfere with the execution of the correct response (through the process of response competition), thereby prolonging RT for incompatible arrays.

Thus, the first mission in this experiment was to determine whether the RT difference between compatible and incompatible arrays is indeed due to response competition effects. As we note below, we believed that we could assess the response competition process by evaluating electromyogram (EMG) and squeeze responses on the incorrect side. An alternative hypothesis would be that it takes subjects longer to evaluate incompatible arrays, thus prolonging RT. This hypothesis could be tested by using P300 latency as a measure of stimulus evaluation time.

A second question in this experiment concerned the effects of a noninformative tone stimulus that preceded array presentation. We knew from previous research that provision of such a warning stimulus speeds reaction time. We were interested in confirming Posner's claim that the alerting effect of a noninformative warning stimulus in this type of situation is due to a change in response-related processes (Posner, 1978). We proposed that this claim could be investigated by using P300, EMG, and squeeze measures, as well as the CNV, an evoked potential measure of preparatory processes.

A critical aspect of the continuous-flow model is that it proposes that the activation of the incorrect response interferes with the execution of the correct response, thereby postponing RT. To analyze this process of response competition, we used measures of EMG activity and squeeze activity on the incorrect side to classify trials in terms of their degree of error. The following classification was used:

N = Activity only on the correct side in EMG and squeeze channels.

E = Activity on the correct side of EMG and squeeze channels; activity also present for EMG on the incorrect side.

S = Activity on the correct side for EMG and squeeze channels; activity also present for both EMG and squeeze channels on the incorrect side.

Error = Activity on the incorrect side for EMG and squeeze channels. EMG activity on the correct side may or may not be present.

We first review evidence concerning the nature of the compatibility effect. The upper part of Figure 12-9 illustrates that S and Error trials (where the wrong squeeze response was produced) occurred more often when the arrays were incompatible. The lower part of Figure 12-9 illustrates two main points. First, the latency of activity on the correct side increased as the degree of activity on the incorrect side increased— that is, correct responses were longer when there was activity on the incorrect side (E and S categories). Second, the time between the manifestation of response initiation (by the EMG) and response completion (the squeeze) increased with the degree of error. This can be seen most clearly by comparing (within compatible or incompatible conditions) the difference between EMG and squeeze onset for S trials with the comparable differences for N or E trials. The difference is significantly greater for S trials. Thus, with incompatible arrays there were more trials in which the subject squeezed the incorrect dynamometer (S), and on these trials the interval between EMG onset and squeeze onset *for the correct dynamometer* was longer than for the other conditions (N, E). There was evidence of response competition when EMG activity occurs on the incorrect side (E and S), and when force was also applied to the incorrect dynamometer (S), response competition was greatest. Taken together, these findings support the hypothesis that at least one reason for the longer incompatible RTs is the fact that response competition (especially in the S category) occurs more often when the array is incompatible, and RT is prolonged by response competition.

This is not the whole story, however. When we look at the latency data for compatible and incompatible displays within the different error categories, we note that, in all cases, both P300 latency *and* RT were prolonged. (P300 latency is presented in the middle of Figure 12-9.) Thus, the effect of incompatibility on RT appears to be due *both* to a greater incidence of response competition for incompatible trials and to the generally longer stimulus evaluation time. If we combine all correct trials (N, E, S), then responses to incompatible trials were approximately 47 msec[1]

longer than responses to compatible trials. We can explain about 53% of this difference (25 msec) by the change in stimulus evaluation (indued by P300 latency), while the other 47% (22 msec) can be explained by response competition. There is also a relationship between P300 latency and the degree of error: The longer the stimulus evaluation time, the more likely it was that the subject would activate the incorrect response.

Our second question concerned the effect of the non-informative warning tone (noninformative in terms of response choice). Why does the warning stimulus speed up responses?

The relevant data are shown in Figure 12-10. First, note that for all response classes, both EMG and squeeze latencies were shorter for the warned condition. Second, note that P300 latency (that is, stimulus evaluation) was not affected by the warning. Third, note that warned trials were associated with a slightly higher incidence of incorrect activity. This was most evident for the S category.

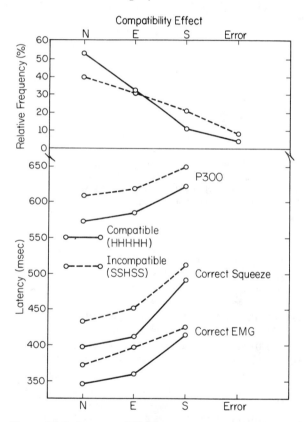

Figure 12-9. Latency of EMG, squeeze response onset, and P300 for correct trials in a study on the effect of incompatible displays on the speed of perceptual processing. Four different response classes are reported on the abscissa. Solid lines indicate responses to compatible displays; dashed lines indicate responses to incompatible displays. The frequency of each response class is shown in the upper part of the figure. (Copyright 1985 by the American Psychological Association. Reprinted by permission of the publisher.)

---

1. This and subsequent values were computed on means weighted by the number of trials in each class.

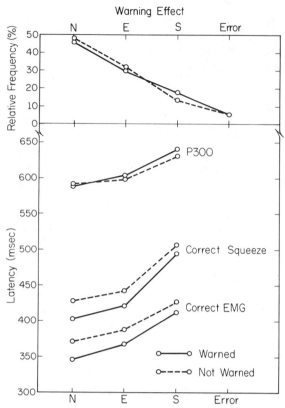

Figure 12-10. Latency of EMG, squeeze response onset, and P300 for correct trials with and without a warning stimulus. Four different response classes are reported on the abscissa. Solid lines indicate responses in the warned condition, dashed lines indicate responses in the unwarned condition. The frequency of each response class is shown in the upper part of the figure. (Copyright 1985 by the American Psychological Association. Reprinted by permission of the publisher.)

Thus, the effect of the warning stimulus was to decrease response latency by about 30 msec, and to increase the incidence of incorrect activity (S) by about 3%. At the same time, the warning stimulus did not affect the latency of P300 (stimulus evaluation time). These findings are most parsimoniously interpreted in terms of the speed–accuracy tradeoff function. The warning tone led the subjects to adopt a less conservative strategy.

We believe that this strategy is best considered in terms of an ''aspecific activation'' process—that is, activation of the response channels can occur independently of the specific nature of the stimulus. In the case of the warning, this activation occurs during the foreperiod and may be manifested by the large CNV that is present. Variations in the level of aspecific activation are also responsible for the presence of incorrect activity on compatible trials—that is, errors occur even when there is nothing in the stimulus to trigger an incorrect response.

Our data, then, suggest that the compatibility effect on RT is due to both greater incidence of response competition and slower stimulus evaluation for incompatible arrays. The warning effect is due to greater aspecific activation on warned trials. This manifests itself in the form of a change in response bias toward a less conservative strategy. Since activation of both correct and incorrect responses can occur on the same trials, some sort of continuous-flow conception (as proposed by Eriksen) is warranted. However, since incorrect activity can occur even when there is nothing in the stimulus array to call for the incorrect response, it seems likely that we must also infer that some form of aspecific activation can occur (as proposed by Grice et al., 1982).

The combined use of P300 and EMG response measures have allowed us to make inferences about the cognitive locus of the Eriksen effect. Similarly, information provided by the P300 has enabled us to say something about the locus of the warning effect. Beyond this, we have several indications of how, with some modifications, the psychophysiological approach might be even more useful. First, if the hypothesis that the CNV is a manifestation of aspecific activation is correct, then a more detailed analysis of the CNV will help us understand this process in more detail. For example, the late CNV is lateralized as a function of the response channel (left or right) that is activated prior to overt response (Rohrbaugh & Gaillard, 1983). Thus, lateral CNV measures derived on individual trials will provide a description of processes that occur during the foreperiod at a time when no overt behavior is available. Second, we can obtain a precise description of the stimulus evaluation process by looking at speed–accuracy tradeoff functions for trials with different P300 latencies. This will enable us to describe in detail the differences in evaluation between compatible and incompatible displays. Together, these two psychophysiological approaches should provide us with a detailed description of two processes that are determinants of the final overt response—stimulus evaluation and aspecific activation—and their interrelationship.

Sternberg's Memory-Scanning Paradigm

Sternberg (1966, 1969, 1975) developed a simple choice RT task that has generated enormous interest and research over the past 15 years (e.g., see Lachman, Lachman, & Butterfield, 1979). There are many variations, but in a typical experiment a subject is presented with a "memory set" of one to six items (typically numbers or letters) followed by a single probe. Subjects indicate whether or not the probe is a member of the memory set (probability is generally set at 50%), and RT is recorded.

In contrast to the approaches presented above,

Sternberg developed a serial model of the information-processing stages required to perform this task. The model consists of four stages: stimulus encoding, serial comparison, binary decision, and response organization and execution. Sternberg argued that the slope of the RT function (when RT is plotted against set size) represents the time required to scan each item in the memory set, while the intercept represents the summation of encoding time plus time necessary for response organization and execution. There have been both alternative theoretical interpretations of the basic results, and results inconsistent with Sternberg's model (McClelland, 1979; Pieters, 1983). We present here ways in which the model can be clarified by the addition of P300 latency data. Most of these results are interpreted within the general framework of Sternberg's original model. Exactly how interpretations would change under different models has not been addressed, but we argue that enough is now known about P300 so that the additional ERP data may prove useful in choosing between competing models.

The interpretations that follow have been presented in papers by several investigators (e.g., see Callaway, 1983; Ford, Pfefferbaum, Tinklenberg, & Kopell, 1982; Ford, Roth, Mohs, Hopkins, & Kopell, 1979; Pfefferbaum, Ford, Roth, & Kopell, 1980). P300 latency is taken to be a relative index of the time necessary to reach a decision on whether a probe belongs to the memory set. This involves encoding the probe and evaluating it against memory set items. The time interval between P300 and RT will then reflect processes occurring after stimulus evaluation, such as motor preparation and execution. The intercept of this function (RT minus P300) will represent response-processing time alone (unaffected by memory set size).

It is argued that the slope of the P300 latency function is better than the RT slope as a measure of the time necessary to evaluate the probe against each item in the memory set. The RT slope is generally steeper than that of P300. One argument is that the difference between these two slopes results from an increase in RT (but not P300 latency) as set size increases due to a gradual reduction in decision confidence (Ford, Roth, Mohs, Hopkins, & Kopell, 1979).

The RT intercept is generally assumed to represent encoding time plus response-processing time. We have stated above that the intercept of the RT minus P300 latency function is a measure of response-processing time alone. Therefore, if we subtract this index from the RT intercept, we are left with a pure measure of encoding time. This will equal, of course, the intercept of the P300 latency function. P300 latency reflects both encoding and the evaluation process with memory set probes; the intercept can be thought of as being associated with a memory set size of 0, and therefore will reflect encoding alone, without any comparison process.

These interpretations form a coherent picture, but we should emphasize that we are not arguing here for their validity. On the contrary, preliminary data from our laboratory (using a Sternberg paradigm with multiple probes) call some of these interpretations into question. We present this research as yet another example of how the use of ERP data can increase the precision with which we relate our data to models of information processing.

Changes in Information Processing with Age

In research on aging, there is one very general but well-supported conclusion: With advancing age, almost everything gets slower, and "everything" ranges from simple RT to complex decision making. The precise explanation for this slowing, however, or for its locus, is not clear. ERP experiments can be especially valuable in these studies, because behavioral measures may be particularly vulnerable to disruptions produced by loss of precision in motor control that is independent of cognitive functioning. In other cases, successful task completion may require several subprocesses. Failure in the task will thus not be informative in locating the subprocess (or processes) responsible for the decrement in performance. This was evident in a study by Ford, Hopkins, Pfefferbaum, and Kopell (1979) using the attention paradigm described in detail in Chapter 11, Hansen & Hillyard. Elderly subjects listened to tones presented to each ear and were asked to count, or respond (Ford & Pfefferbaum, 1980), to target tones in one ear that were slightly higher in pitch than the common (standard) tones. The performance of these subjects was very poor (they missed over half of the targets), but there was still a strong selective attention effect on "N1." Ford and Pfefferbaum (1980) were thus able to conclude that "elderly subjects can focus attention on a selected channel of input, even though they cannot always perform the discrimination task accurately or quickly within that channel" (p. 122). Using behavioral measures alone, it would have been impossible to reach this conclusion.

Using the Sternberg paradigm described above, Ford, Hopkins, Pfefferbaum, and Kopell (1979) found that young and old subjects had both different slopes and intercepts for RT. For P300 latency, however, the intercepts were different, while the slopes were the same (see, however, Ford *et al.*, 1982, and Pfefferbaum *et al.*, 1980, who did *not* find an increase of P300 latency with set size). Ford, Hopkins, Pfefferbaum, and Kopell (1979) concluded from these data that although the old subjects encoded stimuli more slowly, they scanned memory at the same speed. As Ford and colleagues pointed out, these conclusions are contrary to those of Anders and Fozard (1973), who used only RT, but are more convincing because the addition of P300 latency permits greater precision in the dissection of processing stages.

When the correlations between P300 latency and RT in this experiment were calculated by Pfefferbaum et al. (1980), they found age-related differences in strategies. Young subjects had high correlations between P300 latency and RT. For old subjects, on the other hand, the correlation decreased with memory set size. For these subjects, the P300–RT correlations were low in the largest memory set and there were many false alarms, suggesting a speed–accuracy trade-off weighted more toward speed. When correlations were high, there were more omissions (RTs greater than 2000 msec were counted as omissions), suggesting a strategy weighted more heavily toward accuracy. These are brief examples of how ERPs can be used with behavioral measures to study changes in information processing with aging. The use of ERPs with aging populations will almost certainly increase (for reviews, see Klorman, Thompson, & Ellingson, 1978; Smith, Thompson, & Michalewski, 1980; K. C. Squires, Chippendale, Wrege, Goodin, & Starr, 1980).

Callaway (1983) has investigated changes in information processing as a function of both age and various drugs, using a Sternberg paradigm in both cases. As Callaway points out, there is very little specific knowledge about how psychopharmacological agents influence cognitive processes. At what stages of information processing do various drugs exert their effects? Callaway's ERP data suggest that stimulants such as methylphenidate (Ritalin) affect response execution but not stimulus evaluation, whereas barbiturates may slow stimulus evaluation.

The Stroop Task

In the Stroop (1935) task, a subject is typically asked to name the color of ink used to print a word. When the word is a color name that differs from the color of the ink (e.g., the word "green" printed in red ink), there is massive interference, and the subject takes longer to report the color. Does this interference originate at an early stage of stimulus encoding (the color word influences the speed of processing the color), or at later response stages (where there is response competition when word and color do not match)? Recording ERPs elicited by the words, Warren and Marsh (1979) and Duncan-Johnson and Kopell (1981) were able to identify response competition as the primary source of Stroop interference. In both investigations P300 latency remained constant across word–color pairings, unlike RT, which exhibited the classic increase for incongruent color–word pairs. Warren and Marsh (1979) also recorded preresponse motor potentials, and found differences between congruent and noncongruent color–word pairs. This is in accord with the response competition explanation, although the specific relationships between premotor activity recorded at the scalp and motor processes remains unclear (see Chiarenza, Papakostopoulos, Giordana, & Guareschi-Cazzullo, 1983).

The von Restorff Effect in Free Recall: The Use of P300 Amplitude

In the preceding sections, we have focused primarily on P300 latency. P300 amplitude is also often useful, although it has been used less frequently than latency. We expect the use of P300 amplitude to expand greatly as the functional significance of amplitude variability becomes more clearly understood. Amplitude was of primary concern in the study by Karis et al. (1984) on the von Restorff effect, described above. Isolated items in a list (words of different size) elicited larger P300s than nonisolated items in comparable positions. This was the case for all subjects, including those who did not show any von Restorff effect (defined as an increase in the recall of isolated items). On the basis of these P300 data, we can thus rule out explanations of the von Restorff phenomenon based solely on "surprise" or arousal (e.g., Green, 1956; Roth, 1983), or an explanation based primarily on the initial encoding of the isolated items (or in any initial reaction to them). Such an explanation is probably incorrect, because the P300 data indicate that there was no variation between extreme groups of subjects in the initial processing of the isolated items, and yet there was large variation in the size of the von Restorff effect. Isolated items elicited large P300s in all subjects, but not all subjects exhibited a von Restorff effect in their free-recall data. As presented above, consideration of subjects' mnemonic strategies, along with the ERP data, clarifies this situation considerably.

Conclusions

In the experiments presented above, we have tried to show that the cognitive psychophysiological paradigm can complement traditional experimental methods. P300 latency, used as a measure of the duration of stimulus evaluation and categorization, has been very useful in the chronometric analysis of information-processing tasks. The information from ERPs may become even more helpful when a full range of traditional measures is not available. For example, when studying cognitive processing in infancy, behavioral measures are very limited indeed, and ERP paradigms are now being adapted for use with young infants (Hofmann & Salapatek, 1981; Hofmann, Salapatek,

& Kuskowski, 1981; see also Petrig, Julesz, Kropfl, Baumgartner, & Anliker, 1981). We have focused primarily on the P300 component of the brain ERP, although we have noted that similar chronometric applications have been made of other ERP components. Noteworthy is the manner in which the behavior of an early negativity is used to illuminate processes of selective attention (Hansen & Hillyard, 1980; Hillyard *et al.*, 1973; Hillyard & Hansen, Chapter 11, in this volume; for a review, see Naatanen, 1982). Another useful chronometric approach is exemplified in the work of Ritter and his associates on the N200 (Ritter *et al.*, 1979, 1982). Work is also progressing on long-duration "slow-wave" components, and by examining changes in several components simultaneously we can often gain greater insight into the cognitive activity that is occurring. We expect, and hope, that the cross-fertilization between cognitive psychology and cognitive psychophysiology will continue to grow, and that the fruits of this collaboration will benefit both fields.

ACKNOWLEDGMENTS

Sections of this chapter were presented by Emanuel Donchin as a Fellow's Address to Division Six of the American Psychological Association (Los Angeles, 1980). Other sections were used in a Didactic Lecture at the International Congress of EEG Societies (Kyoto, 1981), and in two papers:

Donchin, E., & Bashore, T. R. Clinical versus psychophysiological paradigms in the study of event-related potentials. *Brain and Behavioral Sciences*, in press.

Coles, M. G. H., & Gratton, G. Psychophysiology and contemporary models of human information processing. In D. Papakostopoulos & I. Martin (Eds.), *Clinical and experimental neuropsychophysiology*. Beckenham, England: Croom Helm, in press.

The research at the Cognitive Psychophysiology Laboratory (CPL) described was supported variously by the Air Force Office of Scientific Research (AFOSR) Contract F49620-79-C-0233; by Defense Advanced Research Projects Agency (DARPA) Contract N000-14-76-C-0002; and by contracts with Air Force Aerospace Medical Research Laboratory (AFAMRL) (F33615-79-C-0512), the U.S. Environmental Protection Agency (R 808974-02), and National Aeronautics and Space Administration (US NASA SBC California Institute of Technology #955610). The support of Al Fregly, Craig Fields, Robert O'Donnell, David Otto, and John Hestenes is appreciated. Of course, without the help of our colleagues at the CPL, and of the technical and secretarial staff of the CPL, none of this would have been accomplished. We are indebted to Art Kramer for helpful comments on an earlier draft.

REFERENCES

Anders, R. R., & Fozard, J. L. Effects of age upon retrieval from primary and secondary memory. *Developmental Psychology*, 1973, 9, 411–416.

Callaway, E. The pharmacology of human information processing. *Psychophysiology*, 1983, 20, 359–370.

Campbell, K. B., Courchesne, E., Picton, T. W., & Squires, K. C. Evoked potential correlates of human information processing. *Biological Psychology*, 1979, 8, 45–68.

Chiarenza, G. A., Papakostopoulos, D., Giordana, F., & Guareschi-Cazzullo, A. Movement-related brain macropotentials during skilled performances: A developmental study. *Electroencephalography and Clinical Neurophysiology*, 1983, 56, 373–383.

Coles, M. G. H., Gratton, G., Bashore, T. R., Eriksen, C. W., & Donchin, E. A psychophysiological investigation of the continuous flow model of human information processing. *Journal of Experimental Psychology: Human Perception and Performance*, 1985, 11, 529–553.

Desmedt, J. E. Scalp-recorded cerebral event-related potentials in man as point of entry into the analysis of cognitive processing. In F. O. Schmitt (Ed.), *The organization of the cerebral cortex*. Cambridge, Mass.: MIT Press, 1981.

Donchin, E. Event-related brain potentials: A tool in the study of human information processing. In H. Begleiter (Ed.), *Evoked potentials and behavior*. New York: Plenum, 1979.

Donchin, E. Surprise! . . . Surprise? *Psychophysiology*, 1981, 8, 493–513.

Donchin, E. The relevance of dissociations and the irrelevance of dissociationism: A reply to Schwartz and Pritchard. *Psychophysiology*, 1982, 19, 457–463.

Donchin, E. (Ed.). *Cognitive psychophysiology* (Vol. 1). Hillsdale, N.J.: Erlbaum, 1984.

Donchin, E., & Bashore, T. R. Clinical versus psychophysiological paradigms in the study of event-related potentials. *Brain and Behavioral Sciences*, in press.

Donchin, E., & Cohen, L. Averaged evoked potentials and intramodality selective attention. *Electroencephalography and Clinical Neurophysiology*, 1967, 22, 537–546.

Donchin, E., Kubovy, M., Kutas, M., Johnson, R., Jr., & Herning, R. I. Graded changes in evoked response (P300) amplitude as a function of cognitive activity. *Perception and Psychophysics*, 1973, 14, 319–324.

Donchin, E., & Lindsley, D. B. Visual evoked response correlates of perceptual masking and enhancement. *Electroencephalography and Clinical Neurophysiology*, 1965, 19, 325–335.

Donchin, E., Ritter, W., & McCallum, W. C. Cognitive Psychophysiology: The endogenous components of the ERP. In E. Callaway, P. Tueting, & S. Koslow (Eds.), *Event-related brain potentials in man*. New York: Academic Press, 1978.

Donders, F. C. [On the speed of mental processes.] In W. G. Koster (Ed. and trans.), *Attention and performance II*. Amsterdam: North-Holland, 1969. (Originally published, 1868)

Duncan-Johnson, C. C., & Donchin, E. On quantifying surprise: The variation of event-related potentials with subjective probability. *Psychophysiology*, 1977, 14, 456–467.

Duncan-Johnson, C. C., & Donchin, E. The P300 component of the event-related brain potential as an index of information processing. *Biological Psychology*, 1982, 14, 1–52.

Duncan-Johnson, C. C., & Kopell, B. S. The Stroop effect: Brain potentials localize the source of interference. *Science*, 1981, 214, 938–940.

Eriksen, C. W., & Schultz, D. W. Information processing in visual search: A continuous flow conception and experimental results. *Perception and Psychophysics*, 1979, 25, 249–263.

Fabiani, M., Karis, D., Coles, M. G. H., & Donchin, E. P300 and recall in an incidental memory paradigm. *Psychophysiology*, 1983, 20, 439. (Abstract)

Fischler, I., Bloom, P. A., Childers, D. G., Roucos, S. E., & Perry, N. W., Jr. Brain potentials related to stages of sentence verification. *Psychophysiology*, 1983, 20, 400–409.

Ford, J. M., Hopkins, W. F., III, Pfefferbaum, A., & Kopell, B. S. Age effects of brain responses in a selective attention task. *Journal of Gerontology*, 1979, 34, 388–395.

Ford, J. M., & Pfefferbaum, A. The utility of brain potentials in determining age-related changes in central nervous system and cognitive functioning. In L. W. Poon (Ed.), *Aging in the 1980s: Psychological issues*. Washington, D.C.: American Psychological Association, 1980.

Ford, J. M., Pfefferbaum, A., Tinklenberg, J. R., & Kopell, B. S.

Effects of perceptual and cognitive difficulty on P3 and RT in young and old adults. *Electroencephalography and Clinical Neurophysiology*, 1982, 54, 311–321.

Ford, J. M., Roth, W. T., Mohs, R. C., Hopkins, W. F., & Kopell, B. S. Event-related potentials recorded from young and old adults during a memory retrieval task. *Electroencephalography and Clinical Neurophysiology*, 1979, 47, 450–459.

Freeman, W. *Mass action in the nervous system.* New York: Academic Press, 1975.

Gaillard, A. W. K., & Ritter, W. (Eds.). *Tutorials in event related potential research: Endogenous components.* Amsterdam: North-Holland, 1983.

Green, R. T. Surprise as a factor in the von Restorff effect. *Journal of Experimental Psychology*, 1956, 52, 340–344.

Grice, G. R., Nullmeyer, R., & Spiker, V. A. Human reaction time: Toward a general theory. *Journal of Experimental Psychology: General*, 1982, 111, 135–153.

Halgren, E., Squires, N. K., Wilson, C. L., Rohrbaugh, J. W., Babb, T. L., & Crandall, P. H. Endogenous potentials generated in the human hippocampal formation and amygdala by infrequent events. *Science*, 1980, 210, 803–805.

Hansen, J. C., & Hillyard, S. A. Endogenous brain potentials associated with selective auditory attention. *Electroencephalography and Clinical Neurophysiology*, 1980, 49, 277–290.

Heffley, E. F. *Elements of a neural theory of human information processing derived from an analysis of cognitive event-related potentials.* Manuscript in preparation, 1985.

Heffley, E., Wickens, C. D., & Donchin, E. Intramodality selective attention and P300-reexamination in a visual monitoring task. *Psychophysiology*, 1978, 15, 269–270.

Hillyard, S. A., Hink, R. F., Schwent, V. L., & Picton, T. W. Electrical signs of selective attention in the human brain. *Science*, 1973, 182, 177–180.

Hillyard, S. A., & Kutas, M. Electrophysiology of cognitive processing. *Annual Review of Psychology*, 1983, 34, 33–61.

Hofmann, M. J., & Salapatek, P. Young infants' event-related potentials (ERPs) to familiar and unfamiliar visual and auditory events in a recognition memory task. *Electroencephalography and Clinical Neurophysiology*, 1981, 52, 405–417.

Hofmann, M. J., Salapatek, P., & Kuskowski, M. Evidence for visual memory in the averaged and single evoked potentials of human infants. *Infant Behavior and Development*, 1981, 4, 401–421.

Horst, R. L., Johnson, R., & Donchin, E. Event-related brain potentials and subjective probability in a learning task. *Memory and Cognition*, 1980, 8, 476–488.

Johnson, R., Jr., & Donchin, E. On how P300 amplitude varies with the utility of the eliciting stimuli. *Electroencephalography and Clinical Neurophysiology*, 1978, 44, 424–437.

Johnson, R., & Donchin, E. Sequential expectancies and decision making in a changing environment: An electrophysiological approach. *Psychophysiology*, 1982, 19, 183–200.

Karis, D., Chesney, G. L., & Donchin, E. ". . . 'twas ten to one: And yet we ventured . . .": P300 and decision making. *Psychophysiology*, 1983, 20, 260–268.

Karis, D., Fabiani, M., & Donchin, E. P300 and memory: Individual differences in the von Restorff effect. *Cognitive Psychology*, 1984, 16, 177–216.

Klorman, R., Thompson, L. W., & Ellingson, R. J. Event-related potentials across the life-span. In E. Callaway, P. Tueting, & S. H. Koslow (Eds.), *Event-related brain potentials in man.* New York: Academic Press, 1978.

Kutas, M., & Hillyard, S. A. Event-related brain potentials to semantically inappropriate and surprisingly large words. *Biological Psychology*, 1980, 11, 99–116. (a)

Kutas, M., & Hillyard, S. A. Reading between the lines: Event-related brain potentials during natural sentence processing. *Brain and Language*, 1980, 11, 354–373. (b)

Kutas, M., & Hillyard, S. A. Reading senseless sentences: Brain potentials reflect semantic incongruity. *Science*, 1980, 207, 203–205. (c)

Kutas, M., & Hillyard, S. A. The lateral distribution of event-related potentials during sentence processing. *Neuropsychologia*, 1982, 20, 579–590.

Kutas, M., McCarthy, G., & Donchin, E. Augmenting mental chronometry: The P300 as a measure of stimulus evaluation time. *Science*, 1977, 197, 792–795.

Lachman, R., Lachman, J. L., & Butterfield, E. C. *Cognitive psychology and information processing: An introduction.* Hillsdale, N.J.: Erlbaum, 1979.

Magliero, A., Bashore, T. R., Coles, M. G. H., & Donchin, E. On the dependence of P300 latency on stimulus evaluation processes. *Psychophysiology*, 1984, 21, 171–186.

Marr, D. *Vision.* San Francisco: W. H. Freeman, 1982.

McCarthy, G. *The P300 and stages of human information processing: An additive factors study.* Unpublished doctoral dissertation, University of Illinois at Urbana–Champaign, 1980.

McCarthy, G., & Donchin, E. A metric for thought: A comparison of P300 latency and reaction time. *Science*, 1981, 211, 77–80.

McCarthy, G., Wood, C. C., Allison, T., Goff, W. R., Williamson, P. D., & Spencer, D. D. Intracranial recordings of event-related potentials in humans engaged in cognitive tasks. *Neuroscience*, 1982, 8, 976. (Abstract)

McClelland, J. L. On time relations of mental processes: A framework for analyzing processes in cascade. *Psychological Review*, 1979, 86, 287–330.

Miller, J. Discrete versus continuous stage models of human information processing: In search of partial output. *Journal of Experimental Psychology: Human Perception and Performance*, 1982, 8, 273–296.

Naatanen, R. Processing negativity: An evoked-potential reflection of selective attention. *Psychological Bulletin*, 1982, 92, 605–640.

Newell, A., & Simon, H. *Human problem solving.* Englewood Cliffs, N.J.: Prentice-Hall, 1972.

Okada, Y. C., Kaufman, L., & Williamson, S. J. The hippocampal formation as a source of the slow endogenous potentials. *Electroencephalography and Clinical Neurophysiology*, 1983, 55, 417–426.

Petrig, B., Julesz, B., Kropfl, W., Baumgartner, G., and Anliker, M. Development of stereopsis and cortical binocularity in human infants: Electrophysiological evidence. *Science*, 1981, 213, 1402–1405.

Pfefferbaum, A., Ford, J. M., Roth, W., & Kopell, B. S. Age differences in P3-reaction time associations. *Electroencephalography and Clinical Neurophysiology*, 1980, 49, 257–265.

Pieters, J. P. M. Sternberg's additive factor method and underlying psychological processes: Some theoretical considerations. *Psychological Bulletin*, 1983, 93, 411–426.

Polich, J., & Donchin, E. *P300 and the word frequency effect.* Manuscript in preparation, 1985.

Polich, J., McCarthy, G., Wang, W. S., and Donchin, E. When words collide: Orthographic and phonological interference during word processing. *Biological Psychology*, 1983, 16, 155–180.

Posner, M. I. (Ed.). *Chronometric explorations of the mind.* Hillsdale, N.J.: Erlbaum, 1978.

Posner, M. I. Cumulative development of attentional theory. *American Psychologist*, 1982, 37, 168–179.

Pritchard, W. S. Psychophysiology of P300. *Psychological Bulletin*, 1981, 89, 506–540.

Ritter, W., Simson, R., Vaughan, H. G., & Friedman, D. A brain event related to the making of a sensory discrimination. *Science*, 1979, 203, 1358–1361.

Ritter, W., Simson, R., Vaughan, H. G., & Macht, M. Manipulation of event-related potential manifestations of information processing stages. *Science*, 1982, 218, 909–911.

Rohrbaugh, J. W., & Gaillard, A. W. K. Sensory and motor aspects of the contingent negative variation. In A. W. K. Gaillard & W. Ritter (Eds.), *Tutorials in event related potential research: Endogenous components.* Amsterdam: North-Holland, 1983.

Rosler, F. Endogenous ERPs and cognition: Probes, prospects and pitfalls in matching pieces of the mind–body puzzle. In A. W. K. Gaillard & W. Ritter (Eds.), *Tutorials in event related potential* research: *Endogenous components*. Amersterdam: North-Holland, 1983.

Roth, W. T. A comparison of P300 and skin conductance response. In A. W. K. Gaillard & W. Ritter (Eds.), *Tutorials in event related potential research: Endogenous components*. Amsterdam: North-Holland, 1983.

Ruchkin, D. S., & Sutton, S. Equivocation and P300 amplitude. In D. Otto (Ed.), *Multidisciplinary perspectives in event-related brain potential research*. Washington, D.C.: U.S. Government Printing Office, 1978.

Ruchkin, D. S., & Sutton, S. Positive slow wave and P300: Association and disassociation. In A. W. K. Gaillard & W. Ritter, (Eds.), *Tutorials in event related potential research: Endogenous components*. Amsterdam: North-Holland, 1983.

Rugg, M., Kok, A., Barrett, G., & Fischler, I. ERPs associated with language and hemispheric specialization. *Electroencephalography and Clinical Neurophysiology* (Supplement, *Proceedings of the Seventh International Conference on Event Related Potentials of the Brain*), in press.

Schneider, W., & Shiffrin, R. M. Controlled and automatic human information processing: I. Detection, search and attention. *Psychological Review*, 1979, 84, 1–66.

Schwartz, M., & Pritchard, W. S. AERs and detection in tasks yielding U-shaped backward masking functions. *Psychophysiology*, 1981, 18, 678–685.

Schwartz, M., & Pritchard, W. On the language and logic of psychophysiology: A reply to Donchin. *Psychophysiology*, 1982, 19, 464–466.

Shiffrin, R. M., & Schneider, W. Controlled and automatic human information processing: II. Perceptual learning, automatic attending and a general theory. *Psychological Review*, 1977, 84, 127–190.

Smith, D. B. D., Thompson, L. W., & Michalewski, H. J. Averaged evoked potential research in adult aging—status and prospects. In L. W. Poon (Ed.), *Aging in the 1980s: Psychological issues*. Washington, D.C.: American Psychological Association, 1980.

Squires, K. C., Chippendale, T. J., Wrege, K. S., Goodin, D. S., & Starr, A. Electrophysiological assessment of mental function in aging and dementia. In L. W. Poon (Ed.), *Aging in the 1980s: Psychological issues*. Washington, D.C.: American Psychological Association, 1980.

Squires, K. C., Wickens, C. D., Squires, N. K., & Donchin, E. The effect of stimulus sequence on the waveform of the cortical event-related potential. *Science*, 1976, 193, 1142–1146.

Squires, N. K., Squires, K. C., & Hillyard, S. A. 1980. Two varieties of long-latency positive waves evoked by unpredictable auditory stimuli in man. *Electroencephalography and Clinical Neurophysiology*, 1975, 38, 387–401.

Sternberg, S. High-speed scanning in human memory. *Science*, 1966, 153, 652–654.

Sternberg, S. The discovery of processing stages: Extensions of Donders' method. *Acta Psychologica*, 1969, 30, 276–315.

Sternberg, S. Memory scanning: New findings and current controversies. *Quarterly Journal of Experimental Psychology*, 1975, 27, 1–32.

Stroop, J. Studies of interference in serial verbal reaction. *Journal of Experimental Psychology*, 1935, 18, 643–662.

Stuss, D. T. & Picton, T. W. Neurophysiological correlates of human concept formation. *Behavioral Biology*, 1978, 23, 135–162.

Stuss, D. T., Sarazin, F. F., Leech, E. E., & Picton, T. W. Event-related potentials during naming and mental rotation. *Electroencephalography and Clinical Neurophysiology*, 1983, 56, 133–146.

Sutton, S., Braren, M., Zubin, J., & John, E. R. (1965) Information delivery and the sensory evoked potential. *Science*, 1965, 155, 1436–1439.

Towle, V., Heuer, D., & Donchin, E. On indexing attention and learning with event-related potentials. *Psychophysiology*, 1980, 17, 291. (Abstract)

Tueting, P., Sutton, S., & Zubin, S. Quantitative evoked potential correlates of the probability of events. *Psychophysiology*, 1971, 7, 385–394.

Turvey, M. On peripheral and central processes in vision: Inferences from an information-processing analysis of masking with patterned stimuli. *Psychological Review*, 1973, 80, 1–52.

von Restorff, H. Uber die Wirkung von Bereichsbildungen im Spurenfeld. *Psychologische Forschung*, 1933, 18, 299–342.

Warren, L. R., & Marsh, G. R. Changes in event related potentials during processing of Stroop stimuli. *International Journal of Neuroscience*, 1979, 9, 217–223.

Wood, C. C., Allison, T., Goff, W. R., Williamson, P., & Spencer, D. C. On the neural origin of P300 in man. *Progress in Brain Research*, 1980, 54, 51–56.

Chapter Thirteen

Bodily Changes during Attending

J. Richard Jennings

Every student of information processing has heard of the cocktail party problem. How can conversations be heard in the overwhelming din and confusion of a cocktail party? The answer usually given focuses on the selection of sensory signals (e.g., filtering, early and late selection). A psychophysiologist is not satisfied with this answer, since it ignores body state. After all, what is the central feature of a cocktail party? Aren't the effects of alcohol and noise on bodily state important? Might the partygoers drink in order to facilitate selective attention or even be driven to drink by the effort of selective attending?

This chapter discusses the relation of bodily states and responses to attention processes. From a psychological perspective, we can ask what bodily responses can tell us about attention. Common views would suggest that bodily responses would have little to do with attention unless emotion or motivation is involved. The autonomic nervous system is viewed as the effector system for emotional expression or as a convenient source of validating measures for degree of motivation. However, short of extreme bodily states, such as illness or starvation, cognitive processing is thought to be independent of the muscles and viscera.

Such common views may, however, be incomplete. All cognitive processing has action on the environment as its ultimate result, and maintenance of the biological organism as a goal. Not long ago, in fact, behaviorists believed that even the most advanced mental processes could be traced to muscular and glandular responses. Furthermore, in the last few years, a phenomenal amount of information has accumulated concerning the neural control of visceral and motor functions. In general, this information suggests that reflexive, nonspecific reactions of the autonomic and skeletal nervous system to psychological events are the exception, not the rule. Detailed relations between task requirements and autonomic responses are now being sought. In this chapter, I examine such evidence as it relates to attention and discuss interpretations based on physiological arousal and alternative concepts.

Three levels of relationship between attention and bodily response are discussed. I use these levels as an organizational framework rather than attempting to prove that one level is "correct." Chapter 14 is organized similarly. Electromyographic and autonomic indices are related to thought and memory in that

J. Richard Jennings. Department of Psychiatry, University of Pittsburgh, Pittsburgh, Pennsylvania.

chapter. In this chapter, I focus on attention and autonomic—particularly cardiovascular—change.

The first level of relationship is autonomic change as an *indicator* of attention. For example, a shift in salivary pH may occur whenever attention is focused on spatial images. If this change occurs during no other psychological process, then pH shift would be an excellent indicator of attending to spatial images. Such an index would be of great use to the experimental or clinical psychologist, even in the absence of any knowledge or interest in salivary pH as such. No assumptions are made about the functional significance of salivary pH for attention. A good deal of the research in psychophysiology can be characterized as seeking this level of relationship. Such relationships may not be very interesting to a physiologist. Good indices must not be demeaned, however, for few relationships between psychological and physiological processes have been convincingly established.

The second level of the relationship is autonomic change as a *facilitator* of attention. To pursue our example, salivary pH change prior to mental imaging may facilitate attention during spatial imaging. The bodily state acts directly on the cognitive process. Note that changes in pH may not be necessary for imaging or attention—it only facilitates (or interferes) with the psychological process. More generally, physiological arousal is often said to facilitate or interfere with performance.

The final level is autonomic change as a *regulator* of attention. Salivary pH may show an endogenous biological rhythm. If attention to imaging shows identical changes, and manipulation of pH consistently alters attention to imaging, then we can say that the regulation of pH also regulates attention. This level of relationship goes beyond the second (facilitator) level in two ways. First, the bodily change is necessary to the psychological process; second, the change in psychological process is a consequence of biological regulation.

The three levels of relationship have been chosen because data and theory in psychophysiology are available at each level. Other relationships can be imagined as well, but they are not discussed here. Furthermore, data discussed at one level may in fact be applicable to another. In short, the levels of relationship provide an organizational framework. The chapter only discusses normal states and responses. Extreme conditions such as starvation and critical illness show obvious effects on cognitive functioning (e.g., brain anoxia produces giddiness and lack of attention prior to death). These are not discussed, although their potential relevance is not denied. Even within studies of normal function, it is impossible to cover all bodily responses and all attentional processes. Thus, I only discuss good examples of psychophysiological responses that are related to attention.

So far, I have repeatedly referred to "attention" without defining it. In the next section of the chapter, I attempt to do so. My purpose is, first, to identify attention processes that may be related to bodily response, and, second, to provide a conceptual rationale for the relationship between attention and bodily response. The questions are complex and space is limited, so I primarily take a stance on these issues and refer to other authors for detailed discussions.

CONCEPT OF ATTENTION

Attention, like digestion, normally takes place outside of our conscious awareness. Attention determines which events are observed and acted upon. At any instant, many sensory experiences and motor responses are possible. We are unable to perform all of them. Thus, our continued performance of some implies that selection has occurred. This selection is the basic phenomenon of attention.

"Attention" refers to multiple processes related to selection—not to a single process. This is illustrated in Figure 13-1, which schematizes the course of attending to a particular event. Relative to some resting state, attending to an event may be initiated by an environmental event (e.g., a loud sound) or endogenously (e.g., attempt to recollect a phone number). The initiating event and the person's intention then determine whether attention is directed at enhancing perceptual, cognitive, or motoric function. Regardless of this choice, attention may then become focused further as the event is processed. For example, attention to perceptual events would be expected to facilitate object definition and recognition (e.g., Kahneman, 1973; Posner, 1978). The course of attending will be terminated either when the event is processed or when processing is interrupted by an event of greater importance to the person. Initiation, focusing, and termination of attention may be viewed as different attentional processes. Not all processes may be related to bodily responses. For example, psychophysiological indices may be useful in identifying the initiation and termination of attention, but not focusing processes.

Figure 13-1 also lists a number of functional properties of attending. Once attention is initiated, it can be characterized as showing a certain *intensity* and *duration*. Over time, it will show varying degrees of *temporal consistency*. A fourth property, *breadth of attention*, ranges from a generalized alertness to any event to fixation on one aspect of a perceptual display or a motor act. Finally, attending to an event will depend on the interaction of the event with the current *structural and functional limitations* on the person's capacity to attend. For example, attending will be hampered if an auditory event occurs in masking

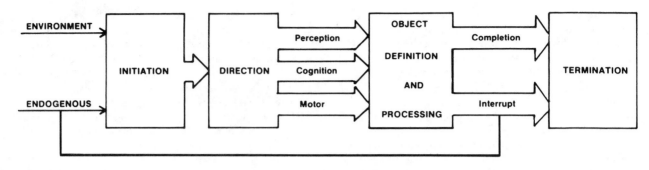

PROPERTIES

1. Intensity
2. Duration
3. Temporal Consistency
   (Distractibility)
4. Breadth
5. Structural and functional
   limitations

Figure 13-1. The course of attending to a particular event. Initiation is shown as either environmental or endogenous. Subsequent stages are shown in order to suggest that attention may be conceived as a set of separable processes. The diagram also shows five properties characteristic of any episode of attending.

noise (a structural interference) or during performance on a complex task (functional interference) (see Kahneman, 1973). Psychophysiological variables will be unlikely to contribute to the understanding of structural limitations (or to the understanding of cognitive structure in general). Autonomic response in combination with performance measures may, however, be useful in assessing the remaining properties.

Why are autonomic responses related to some attention processes? So far, this descriptive treatment of attention has not answered this question. In his early writing, Broadbent (1953) considered attention a passive sensory filter that was tuned to selected physical characteristics by the organism. In contrast, Neisser (1967) suggested that the organism constructed a schema of the environment that was adjusted only as necessary by sensory input. The setting of a passive sensory filter and its subsequent operation would seem unlikely to be related to bodily response. The continual construction of the environment by the organism might be expected to be related to bodily response. Bodily responses do not seem to be ever-present in routine, automated information processing, however. Thus, I adopt a midway position that identifies attention with processes that can be flexibly allocated to facilitate information processing at a variety of stages and levels (cf. Johnston & Heinz, 1978; Kahneman, 1973; Posner, 1978; Shiffrin & Schneider, 1977). Frequently, attention processes will be consciously experienced as effort (Kahneman, 1973). Intuitively, effort corresponds to the processes I am referring to as facilitating processing. As Schiffrin and Schneider (1977) have pointed out, such processes will be more important during early acquisition of a performance task than during later "auto-

mated" performance (Broadbent, 1977). As defined, attention is related not only to sensory experience, but also to cognitive and motoric (response selection) processes. Attention is closely linked to the "executive" function of choice between alternatives, temporal scheduling, and thus priority assignments. These "executive" functions are necessary because of our inability to process all available information simultaneously.

Any physiological explanation of attention must consider mechanism. How does attention facilitate information processing? For the psychophysiologist, energy regulation may link attention and autonomic nervous system responses. The autonomic nervous system regulates metabolism, and thus the energy expenditure of the body. Following Kahneman (1973), I suggest that some attentional processes (see Figure 13-1) allocate energy or effort (using Kahneman's terms) to support the currently selected information processing. Attention provides the resource of energy (greater blood flow and enhanced metabolic rate) to "attended" events and denies it to other events (see Kahneman, 1973; Navon & Gopher, 1979). This process of regulation may be detected in changes in cardiac function and regional blood flow (Roy & Sherrington, 1890; Williams, Poon, & Burdette, 1977), as well as in specific metabolic activity of brain regions (e.g., Phelps, Kuhl, & Mazziotta, 1981). This evidence is only suggestive, however, and we know very little about energy regulation (strictly defined) and attention.

In a general sense, however, I suggest that bodily measures provide information about the energy aspect of attention. Referring to Figure 13-1, we can identify this energy aspect with the property of the intensity of attention and its temporal expression in duration and consistency. As I indicate later, autonomic measures are also of use in examining the initiation and direction of attention. Most other attention processes (i.e., primarily selective processes) must be left to the performance psychologist or the electroencephalographer.

The concept of attention I have developed has some implications for the evidence that will be most important for establishing a relationship between attention processes and bodily responses. First, the attention processes of primary relevance have been defined as an optional allocation of energy by the organism. Thus, attention cannot be studied without evidence of this allocation. A tone may produce a galvanic skin response, but this response cannot be attributed to attention unless a separate measure (or, preferably, converging measures) also indicates that the tone has altered attention. Attention can be convincingly inferred from a performance measure only when performance change cannot be explained by a change in environmental stimulation or cognitive activity (e.g., change in learned association). Second, although any task should produce some autonomic or motoric responses, physiological responses directly relevant to the psychological task are most likely to relate to attention (e.g., examination of electromyographic activity from the tongue during verbal problem solving or muscle blood flow during a perceptual–motor task). Finally, the biological function of the physiological responses must be understood in order to see whether and why they may be relevant to attention.

I can now consider the three levels of autonomic attention relationship developed previously: autonomic change as an *indicator* of attentive processes, as a *facilitator* of attention, and as a *regular of attention*. Throughout the discussion, I consider whether the evidence establishes the presence of an attentional process and whether the evidence contributes to a general understanding of how bodily responses contribute to attention.

BODILY CHANGE AS AN INDICATOR OF ATTENTION

A wealth of evidence suggests that changes in autonomic function are correlated with changes in attention. More precisely, autonomic change has frequently been shown to occur during environmental changes presumed to alter attention. Less frequently, performance indices of attention have been shown to correlate with autonomic change. My aim in this and the next two sections is not to review all pertinent studies exhaustively. Rather, studies from a restricted area are chosen. This strategy is designed to permit a

discussion of conceptual issues with clarity gained from a restricted focus. Heart rate changes observed in two simple situations—orienting after an unexpected event, and anticipation of an expected event—constitute the focus of this section.

It is commonly known that unexpected environmental events cause behavioral orientation and physiological response. However, research has been necessary to define the conditions producing such reactions and to enumerate the physiological systems involved. Much of this work centers on the "orienting response"—most recently associated with the work of the Soviet psychophysiologist Sokolov (1963).

The argument that the orienting reflex is an attentional process can be made from the evidence presented by Sokolov (1963). In his influential book, *Perception and the Conditioned Reflex*, Sokolov (1963) emphasizes the importance of the orienting response for perception. Perception is viewed as the matching of sensory input to a neuronal model of the environment. Whenever the input fails to match the model, an orienting response occurs. The functional role of this response is to enhance the sensitivity of sensory analysers and facilitate the adjustment of the neuronal model. In our terms, the intensity and focus of attention are enhanced by the orienting response. The orienting response has been shown to be independent of stimulus energy. This finding and related evidence suggest that the orienting reflex is a central phenomenon, rather than a reflex solely determined by physical changes at the receptor. Secondly, perceptual performance seems to be enhanced by the reflex. Thus, some converging evidence of attention has been combined with evidence questioning a sensory reflex position. Berlyne (1960) has drawn heavily on Sokolov's work and has discussed four stimulus attributes related to orienting—novelty, uncertainty, conflict, and complexity. He has related these attributes to the elicitation of exploration (curiosity) and ultimately to the development of knowledge about the environment.

The important claims made by Sokolov and Berlyne have been investigated over the last 25 years. This work is summarized in a recent volume (Kimmel, Van Olst, & Orlebeke, 1979) and is reviewed only briefly here. A second line of research is also reviewed to some extent in the Kimmel et al. (1979) volume. Early psychophysiologists such as Darrow (1929) and Freeman (1948) were interested in the physiological changes that accompany information-processing tasks. Darrow (1929), in particular, suggested that the slowing of heart rate might characterize sensory as opposed to "ideational" stimuli. More recently, the Laceys (e.g., J. I. Lacey, Kagan, Lacey, & Moss, 1963) have suggested that the direction of heart rate change indexes the organism's intent to input or reject environmental stimuli. The evaluation of this hypothesis has centered on the examination of heart rate just before an expected event, as opposed to orienting reflex research, which has examined similar change just after an unexpected event (see reviews, Elliott, 1972; Hahn, 1973; B. C. Lacey & Lacey, 1974). An influential review by Graham and Clifton (1966) has pointed out the convergence between physiological results from orienting reflex and Lacey-type paradigms. Indeed, it seems reasonable that the organism should be in a similar state of attentiveness, irrespective of whether the state is elicited by an unexpected environmental event or by an expected one.

Figure 13-2 illustrates typical physiological responses preceding and following significant environmental events. In these two sample records from a polygraph tracing, the timing of light illumination and mild shock are indicated by the lines drawn through the records and by event marks on the two bottom channels. Both before and after events, we see examples of decreases in skin resistance (top channel), speeding and slowing of heart rate (seen as the rise and fall of a cardiotachometer voltage in the second channel from the top), and bursts of muscle tension (seen in the electromyograph record in the third channel from the top). Further detail is noted in the figure caption. The figure illustrates the occurrence of physiological events surrounding significant events; it also shows that responses to these events occur not in one system, but in a large number of physiological response systems. For the purposes of this section, I am focusing on one system, the cardiovascular system. Other response systems, particularly skin conductance, show evidence of relating to attention. For further information on these response systems, the interested reader should refer to Kimmel et al. (1979) and to recent papers by Dawson, Schell, Beers, and Kelly (1982) and Dawson and Schell (1982). Öhman (1979) presents an information-processing account of the orienting reflex, based in part on skin conductance data. For now, though, let us examine heart rate changes in humans during simple information-processing and orienting reflex paradigms.

The Basic Phenomenon

Either before an anticipated event or following a significant but unexpected event, the heart rate slows for a few seconds. The same events typically induce a psychological state of focused alertness. Thus, an active psychological state is associated with a slowing of heart rate. Other active states, such as exercise or the experience of anger, are typically associated with a speeding of heart rate. Thus, the direction of heart rate change seems to distinguish between two active states—states not distinguished by other physiological measures, such as skin conductance and muscle tension. In Chapter 14, the speeding of heart rate during information processing is examined. Here, I examine

the slowing of heart rate. Thus far, I have suggested that heart rate deceleration may be a specific indicator of the onset of attention in orienting and anticipation tasks. Examining further characteristics of cardiac deceleration should help us define the precise attention process indicated by deceleration.

What characteristics of a situation influence cardiac deceleration?

1. The inducing event must be significant to the individual. Deceleration in response to even strong stimuli quickly disappears or habituates (see Graham, 1973), and deceleration does not develop prior to events having no significance for the individual. This point has been made most forcefully by Bernstein (e.g, Bernstein & Taylor, 1979), who has shown that stimulus change per se is not sufficient to elicit orienting (cf. Sokolov, 1963). Bernstein's arguments are based on skin conductance data, but they are equally applicable to heart rate change. Stimulus-related conditions, such as the collative variables of Berlyne (1960), do not seem sufficient to predict all events that will elicit orienting. Siddle and Spinks (1979) suggest that the problem may be an inappropriate emphasis on the stimulus for orienting. Their experiment suggests that orienting response amplitude is not determined by the stimulus, but by the complexity of the information processing signaled by the stimulus.[1] This viewpoint suggests the similarity of the orienting response and the anticipatory response. In the literature on the anticipatory response, little emphasis has been placed on the stimulus characteristics of the anticipated cue. Rather, significance of the event has been altered by varying incentive and the task emphasis within a multitask setting (Coles, 1974; Coles & Duncan-Johnson, 1975; Jennings, Schrot, & Wood, 1980; J. I. Lacey, 1972; Lawler & Obrist, 1974). Significance, as defined by these manipulations, generally increases the depth of the deceleration response.

2. Cardiac response to unexpected stimulus depends on stimulus intensity and onset. A rapid-onset, transient stimulus will produce startle and transient cardiac acceleration; in contrast, an intense, noxious stimulus will elicit a sustained (greater than 2 or 3 sec) heart acceleration. Outside of these extremes, cardiac deceleration is expected (Graham, 1979).

3. Anticipatory cardiac deceleration depends on a relatively precise estimation of the time of occurrence of the event. As reviewed in Bohlin and Kjellberg (1979), deceleration is maximal with an 8-sec anticipation and is less at shorter or longer intervals. Deceleration may be difficult to detect with an interval as long as 20 sec and a temporal uncertainty of greater than 5–10 sec. Changes over trials in this paradigm are

---

1. The findings suggesting that cardiac deceleration is part of the orienting response have recently been challenged by Barry. A chapter reviewing his argument with commentary by various authors is available in Ackles, Jennings, and Coles (in press).

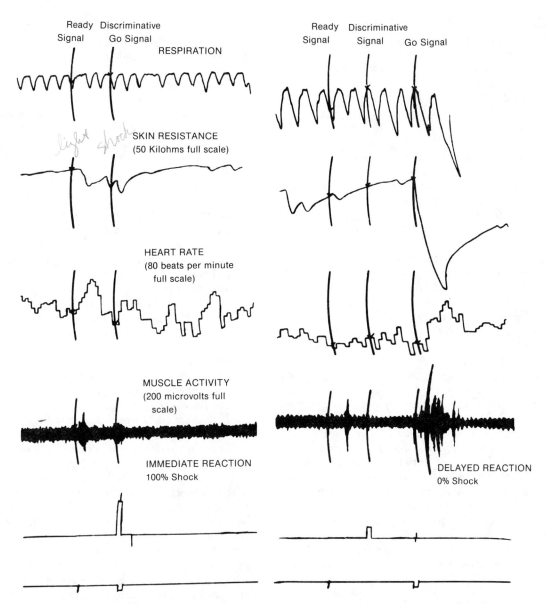

Figure 13-2. Typical psychophysiological reactions before and afer significant events. The top channel shows respiration. Changes in rate and amplitude of breathing movements frequently occur in psychological tasks. The second channel shows skin resistance; a drop in resistance is a typical response to significant events. The third channel shows heart rate. The height of each column (flat place in the record) reflects the speed of the heart rate in this cardiotachometer reading. Episodes of heart rate speeding and slowing are clear in the record. The fourth channel shows electromyographic data; the abrupt widening of the trace indicates a burst of muscle tension. The two bottom traces indicate experimental events. A fixed foreperiod reaction time task is performed with three significant events. A ready signal is followed in 10 sec by a "Discriminative" signal indicating which of two buttons to press. A "Go" signal releasing the press occurs immediately in the condition shown on the left and after 10 sec in the condition on the right. In addition, a mild electric shock occurs along with the "Discriminative" signal for the left panel. (The data are drawn from an experiment reported by Jennings, Averill, Opton, & Lazarus, 1971.)

small, but they tend toward increased deceleration, suggesting a fine tuning of temporal expectation. The omission of an expected event is known to lead to the continuation of deceleration beyond the expected time of occurrence, and deceleration will occur coincident with a time interval estimated by a volunteer in

the absence of external cues (see Bohlin & Kjellberg, 1979).

4. As suggested by the preceding sentence, termination of anticipation seems to terminate deceleration. Deceleration is terminated by the response in reaction time (RT) tasks (Jennings & Wood, 1977;

J. I. Lacey, 1972) and by target identification in search tasks (Lewis & Wilson, 1970). Thus, given a short-term, temporally focused anticipation, the termination of deceleration seems to index the termination of anticipatory attention.

5. Amplitude of deceleratory change is weakly, but significantly, correlated to perceptual and perceptual–motor performance. Sokolov's (1963) volume makes and supports to some extent the claim that the orienting reflex serves to tune sensory analyzers and thus to improve perceptual performance. Given the importance of this claim, the dearth of subsequent evidence on this point is surprising (see Siddle & Spinks, 1979). Indirect measures such as strength of conditioning and intelligence do seem, however, to be related to deceleration (e.g., Putnam, Ross, & Graham, 1974) as well as to electrodermal indices of orienting (e.g., DeBoskey, Kimmel, & Kimmel, 1979; Zeiner, 1979). The relation of anticipatory heart rate deceleration to perceptual–motor and perceptual performance has been examined reasonably well. Depth of deceleration shows a very small (.10–.20), but consistent, correlation to performance (Bohlin & Kjellberg, 1979; Jennings & Hall, 1980).

6. Stimulus detection difficulty enhances orienting and anticipatory changes, but stimulus probability does not significantly alter anticipatory deceleration. Sokolov (1963) presents evidence that stimuli close to sensory thresholds produce greater physiological change than those above threshold. A number of studies have shown that anticipatory deceleration is greater when the anticipated stimulus must be identified as one of two similar stimuli (see Bohlin & Kjellberg, 1979). In contrast, anticipatory deceleration does not appear to separate signals that are readily discriminable but vary in their cue value (Bohlin & Kjellberg, 1979). In particular, deceleration prior to reaction cues does not differ between simple and choice RT.

Interpretations of Cardiac Deceleration

A number of interpretations have been placed on the findings outlined above. Most, but not all, of these interpretations would fit under the general heading of attention. Some early interpretations (e.g., Jennings, Averill, Opton, & Lazarus, 1971) suggested wide-ranging relations between attention and decelerations. Current hypotheses, however, are more specific. Each hypothesis to be discussed here suggests a psychological (or physiological process) that causes cardiac deceleration. Three positions are examined: the Laceys' and related hypotheses; the position of Graham, arising from orienting response studies; and finally, Obrist's somatic–motor hypothesis. Two of these (the Laceys' and Graham's) relate attention processes (in the sense of the term as used here) to deceleration,

while the third, at least partially, questions the importance of attention. Except as noted, all provide a reasonable account of the experimental findings just reviewed.

The current position of the Laceys (B. C. Lacey & Lacey, 1980) is consistent with their earlier formulations. In their words, "intention to note and detect external stimuli results in slowing of the heart" (B. C. Lacey & Lacey, 1980, p. 100), and the "decreased heart rate (and blood pressure) seen in attentive states might serve the function of improving both the organism's receptivity to afferent stimulation and the organism's readiness to make effective responses to such stimulation" (J. I. Lacey, 1972, p. 183). This latter statement is relevant to the next section, where the possibility that physiological response facilitates performance is considered; however, it is also relevant here if we interpret the statement in a less causative sense—the attentional state that induces heart rate slowing facilitates both sensory and response efficiency. A closely related interpretation has been offered by Coles and Duncan-Johnson (1975): "[C]ardiac decelerative responses reflect preparatory activity, and their magnitude is dependent on the detection and response requirements inherent in the anticipated event" (p. 426).

The Laceys' hypothesis is consistent with much of the empirical literature, but it has been criticized in two important ways. First, the phrasing of the hypothesis has consistently involved subjective terms, such as the "intention to" (Carroll & Anastasiades, 1978; Hahn, 1973). This has led to vagueness because of the uncertainty in determining the moment-by-moment intent of a volunteer. Secondly, the Laceys' hypothesis suggests a direction of attention to the sensory environment. Cardiac deceleration has, however, been consistently observed in time estimation tasks (see review in Carroll & Anastasiades, 1978), in which any cues must be generated by the volunteer and not by the environment. As Carroll and Anastasiades (1978) note, attempts by the Laceys to use "intention to respond" as an explanatory concept considerably complicate their hypothesis.

My colleagues and I (Jennings, Lawrence, & Kasper, 1978) attempted to deal with both problems by introducing the notion of processing capacity from the field of experimental psychology (e.g., Posner, 1978). "Processing capacity" refers to a hypothetical central stage of processing whose information handling capacity is limited. Thus, this stage is the locus of selection of input and output (defining attention). We (Jennings et al., 1978) suggested that the holding of available processing capacity produces cardiac deceleration. To use a computer analogy, the central processing unit is cleared (or partially cleared) of ongoing processing so that any input can be recognized and acted upon. This input can be from any source outside of the central processing unit, be it "internal" clock or "external" input. This "held available" capacity must be measured in order to test this viewpoint and avoid vagueness. Processing capacity can be assessed (albeit with some difficulty) using a dual-task methodology in which performance on a secondary task assesses the moment-by-moment state of capacity devoted to a primary task (see Kerr, 1973). Relatively efficient performance on the secondary task would indicate capacity available for immediate processing of input. As such, performance on the secondary task should correlate with cardiac deceleration. An example of such an approach is found in Jennings *et al.* (1978). I return subsequently to some of the strengths and weaknesses of this approach.

A somewhat different approach to interpreting cardiac deceleration has been taken by Graham (1979). She has outlined three systems controlling the processing of phasic events. Figure 13-3, reprinted from her work, illustrates this interpretation. The interpretation is clearly focused on the processing of environmental stimuli, as opposed to the more general orientation of the Laceys. Our current concern is with Graham's treatment of orienting and heart rate deceleration. In contrast to the Laceys' position, cardiac deceleration is viewed as solely associated with the enhancement of input. Although the emphasis is in keeping with available evidence, little work is available to show directly that deceleration is associated with enhanced perceptual clarity or stimulus discriminability (see discussion in Jennings & Hall, 1980).

The probe startle evidence illustrated in Figure 13-3 is an interesting form of evidence for Graham's position. Startle to a sudden stimulus can be modified by the prior occurrence of a weak stimulus. As noted, the different forms of stimuli result in either inhibition or facilitation of the effect of the weak or probe stimulus. The effect related to orienting, selective facilitation, is particularly interesting. As reviewed in Graham (1979), if a volunteer is anticipating an event in the same sensory modality as the startle stimulus (or expecting the startle stimulus itself), cardiac deceleration occurs (as expected) and is associated with a facilitation of probe startle. If, however, an event in a different sensory modality is anticipated, deceleration occurs, but probe startle is inhibited. Presumably, startle facilitation indicates that attention has heightened the sensory impact of the startle stimulus. When attention is directed elsewhere, sensory input is reduced. This result suggests that cardiac deceleration is associated with attention narrowly focused on any expected sensory input (see Bohlin, Graham, Silverstein, & Hackley, 1981, and later discussion). These effects may, however, need to be replicated and extended.

In a paradigm somewhat similar to Graham's, Del-Pezzo and Hoffman (1980) reported that instructing volunteers to attend to the occurrence of a probe

STIMULUS

	TRANSIENT CHANGE	INFORMATION	SUSTAINED INTENSITY INCREASE
RESPONSE ELICITED	STARTLE: Short-Latency HR ↑ Flexor-Contraction	ORIENTING: Prolonged HR ↓	DEFENSE: Long-Latency HR ↑
CONTROL SYSTEM ELICITED	INTERRUPT	INPUT-ENHANCING	OUTPUT-ENHANCING
EFFECT ON PROBE STARTLE	INHIBITION	SELECTIVE FACILITATION	FACILITATION

Figure 13-3. Graham's (1979) schematic representation of relations between stimulus characteristics and their phasic effects. From "Distinguishing among Orienting, Defense, and Startle Reflexes" by F. K. Graham. In H. D. Kimmel, E. H. Van Olst, and J. F. Orlebeke [Eds.], *The Orienting Reflex in Humans.* Hillsdale, N.J.: Erlbaum, 1979. Reprinted by permission of the author and publisher.)

stimulus at a particular visual angle led to heightened inhibition, not facilitation. Further support for reflex facilitation during anticipatory cardiac deceleration is found in studies of Hoffman and Achilles tendon reflexes from the legs (these studies do not involve a modifying probe stimulus). Brunia (1979) reviews work showing that both reflexes are facilitated during a 4-sec preparatory interval. Furthermore, the facilitation does not depend on whether or not responses are performed with the arms or legs. These studies show facilitation, even though the reflex-eliciting stimulus is not relevant to the volunteer's task. Probe startle results are not, however, directly comparable to leg reflex changes.[2] Thus, reflex modifications are involved in orienting, although considerably more needs to be learned about their exact roles and how they relate to cardiac deceleration. Graham's (1979) suggestion that modification of probe startle reflexes is related to orienting seems supported. In contrast, the emphasis on sensory enhancement seems questionable. The evidence just reviewed seems to point directly to major motoric effects of orienting.

The third position to be discussed, that of Obrist (e.g., Obrist, 1981; Obrist, Howard, Lawler, Galosy,

2. In a personal communication, Dr. Graham (1982) commented upon a number of the points raised. She points out that Hoffman and Achilles tendon reflexes are monosynaptic reflexes and that results from polysynaptic startle reflexes would be expected to differ. Regarding the DelPezzo and Hoffman findings, she notes that the critical difference is that their work directed attention at the lead stimulus not the startle stimulus. These points are well taken and serve to illustrate my general conclusion that further understanding of the complexities of reflex modification will contribute to our understanding of attention and its relation to cardiac change.

Meyers, & Gaebelein, 1974), has emphasized the primacy of motor activity in the control of heart rate. Research from his laboratory as well as others has demonstrated that cardiac deceleration is frequently accompanied by a motoric quieting (e.g., reduced electromyographic activity of muscles irrelevant to the task, reduced eye blinks, and reduced general activity). A strong form of Obrist's view suggests that the motor changes cause the heart rate change, while a weaker form suggests that both cardiac deceleration and motor quieting are usual peripheral expressions of a central attentional state (see Jennings et al., 1971; Obrist et al., 1974). Evidence obtained in Obrist's laboratory, as well as in experiments such as those with leg reflexes, questions the necessary or causal relationship between motor activity and heart rate (see Obrist, 1981). There is no question that major motor changes such as exercise induce heart rate change, but brief changes in heart rate are not necessarily a side effect of a change in motor activity. The weaker form of the Obrist hypothesis is well supported. Motor changes are a frequent component of the preparatory or orienting state that we also associate with cardiac deceleration. In a more general sense, Obrist's work has emphasized the physiological context of the cardiac decelerative response. His motor hypothesis can be viewed as an attempt to understand the biological role of cardiac deceleration. Motor activity as a major determinant of metabolic rate provides an explanation of heart rate that is consistent with commonly accepted concepts of biological functioning (cf. the Laceys' view as presented on p. 283). Motor quieting reduces metabolic demand, which permits a fall in heart rate—a fall that presumably indicates a drop in cardiac output. This formulation, despite its failure to explain all the data, does suggest an important goal for a psychophysiological description of attention. That is, the description should be reasonable from both psychological and physiological perspectives.

Interpretive Summary

This section has described concepts and results suggesting that the initiation of attention consistently produces certain physiological responses (see Figure 13-1). The particular response discussed at length is brief, stimulus-related heart rate slowing (cardiac deceleration). Responses before expected stimuli (anticipation paradigm) and after unexpected stimuli (orienting) have been discussed, although cardiac deceleration can be observed in complex situations as well (see Chapter 14). Cardiac deceleration, relative to other responses (e.g, skin conductance), seems to be rather specifically related to attention. Although an interpretation in terms of attention is not completely accepted (Obrist, 1981), the evidence is clear that

situations including expectancy or orienting are associated with cardiac deceleration. Three positions have been reviewed that attempt to specify the process causing cardiac deceleration: (1) the Laceys' hypothesis of the intention to note and detect environmental events; (2) Graham's view of a control system for the enhancement of phasic stimulus events; and (3) Obrist's hypothesis of the inhibition of motor activity.

Heart rate deceleration thus seems to be a valid indicator of the initiation and termination of attention to the input of information. Heart rate deceleration is not solely an effect of attention, however. For example, various breathing maneuvers can produce cardiac slowing. Thus, attention cannot be inferred solely from the occurrence of deceleration. Task demands must also be known. Given appropriate task demands, deceleration provides information on whether or not attention to input information is initiated. The hypotheses I have reviewed are consistent with this view, although the exact attentional process indicated by cardiac deceleration can be questioned. Even the strong form of Obrist's hypothesis does not question the value of deceleration as an index—only its interpretation as a direct effect of attention rather than an indirect effect mediated by motor activity.

Additional Questions

Three conceptual questions arise from this discussion that go beyond the question of deceleration as an indicator. These questions bear upon our concept of attention, its measurement, and finally suggestions for its functional role. A consideration of these questions leads us to the next level of relationship—bodily change as a facilitator of attention. The following three questions can be raised: First, is cardiac deceleration specific to the enhancement of sensory or motor function? Second, what is the biological role of cardiac deceleration? Finally, is cardiac deceleration associated with attention to a single input channel or with a generalized alerting?

From the perspective of our view of attention (see also Kahneman, 1973), the question of sensory versus motor function appears to pose an artificial dichotomy. Attention may facilitate both sensory or motor processes. Indeed, the heart rate literature shows that deceleration can occur without any sensory input (e.g., B. C. Lacey & Lacey, 1974) or without any motor output (e.g., Coles & Duncan-Johnson, 1975). Such evidence led us (Jennings et al., 1978) to emphasize access to central processing capacity rather than direction of attention or sensory–motor enhancement. Deceleration occurs when ongoing activity is inhibited, and processing capacity is held available for expected input. Sensory scanning (and thus probability of stimulus detection) might be enhanced by such a state, but no direct effect on sense organs is necessary.

The question of biological relevance is particularly important, given our concerns with both Obrist's motor position and the cardiac afference viewpoint of the Laceys (see p. 283). Unless proven otherwise, we can assume that cardiac deceleration is adaptive—that is, that it aids or at least does not interfere with efficient performance. Superficially, deceleration just prior to an input requiring action seems biologically anomalous. Why should the heart supply blood to the body at a slower rate just prior to action? The access viewpoint we have taken leads to the possibility that deceleration is one aspect of the coordination of sensory, motor, and autonomic (respiration, digestion) functions necessary to optimize both stimulus detection and subsequent action. To use a mechanical analogy, the clutch in an automobile disengages the gears so that they can respond appropriately to new adjustments. Cardiac deceleration may be part of a similar bodily function.

In a general sense, we can make two assumptions. The first of these is that information processing as well as bodily regulation are organized in time; that is, input and action are sequenced in order to avoid interference. This sequencing may even be cyclic and regular (cf. the clock driving a computer). Second, we assume that new input will require a temporal resequencing so that the expected information can be processed; that is, a new temporal organization is required. A state of inhibition might facilitate such resequencing. The Laceys have, of course, previously suggested that deceleration may facilitate sensory–motor integration. I am suggesting that this may be so because the heart beat is one of a set of brain and bodily functions that must be temporally in synchrony to optimize performance. Suggestive evidence for such a position can be seen in the tendency for cardiac deceleration and respiration to be synchronized and in the termination of deceleration by the onset of action (Jennings & Wood, 1977; Porges, Bohrer, Cheung, Drasgow, McCabe, & Keren, 1980). This speculation is also relevant to investigations of regional blood flow correlates of deceleration (Williams *et al.*, 1977), and of motor inhibition states that facilitate performance (Brunia, 1979).

The question of whether deceleration is related to a broad or narrow focus of attention points to difficulties with dual-task measures of attention that should be discussed. Although little evidence is available on the breadth of attention associated with deceleration, a relatively precise temporal expectation is required to initiate anticipatory deceleration. Thus, anticipatory deceleration in a multistimulus environment suggests the formation of a relatively precise temporal expectation. Once deceleration is initiated, however, are all inputs equally likely to be detected quickly, or only the expected input? If deceleration is initiated by an unexpected stimulus, rather than an anticipated one, are the results the same? (See Bohlin *et al.*, 1981.) How modality-specific are effects? (See Posner, 1978.)

Methodologically, answering these questions will require multiple tasks or multistimulus single tasks. In such paradigms, the interaction between task events is currently a topic of some interest (Israel, Chesney, Wickens, & Donchin, 1980; Navon & Gopher, 1979; Wickens, 1976, 1980). The dual-task paradigm used to assess attention (the allocation of processing capacity) assumes that capacity is undifferentiated—that is, that it may be equally well added to a perceptual as to a motor task. If this assumption is true, tasks in the dual-task paradigm are interchangeable. A secondary RT task and a secondary memory task will produce similar estimates of capacity. Unfortunately, this assumption does not seem to be warranted (see Navon & Gopher, 1979; Wickens, 1980). Thus, a single estimate of processing capacity cannot be justified, and specialized pools of capacity must be considered (e.g., memory capacity or motor coordination). The existence of specialized pools of capacity may not be surprising, given the work on heart rate change and information processing. If a task induces deceleration and a readiness for input, secondary tasks requiring input detection will be processed efficiently. Secondary tasks requiring memory maintenance may not fare so well. Thus, a concept of the control of processing capacity derived from heart rate studies may have implications for task compatibility and capacity assessment. Note, however, that this argument depends on the association of cardiac deceleration with a relatively broad focus of attention.

A broad focus of attention has been questioned by the reflex inhibition results of Graham (1979), reviewed above. Probe startle was facilitated during deceleration only when the startle stimulus was also the anticipated (deceleration-inducing) stimulus. If not, startle inhibition was found. If startle facilitation is equated with attention, then the results suggest a narrowly focused attention. What, however, is the logical status of startle as a probe of attention? The reflexes involved are presumed to be controlled by brain stem mechanisms. Higher cortical influence is thought, with some reason, to be unlikely (e.g., Leitner, Powers, Stitt, & Hoffman, 1981). Yet these reflexes are sensitive to the demands of the anticipation tasks. The amount of attention allocated in such tasks has frequently been studied in dual-task experiments. These experiments presume that a central information-processing capacity exists and that this capacity (attention) can be allocated to one or more ongoing activities (e.g., Kahneman, 1973). As mentioned above, the logic of the dual-task paradigm suggests that (1) a primary task will use the majority of the capacity available and (2) a secondary task will use whatever is left over. Variations in performance on the secondary task reflect capacity (attention) allocated to the primary task. Note, however, that *both* tasks must require central processing capacity. It is doubtful whether theorists would consider the reflexes we are discussing to require central processing capacity; nontheless, the experimental results mimic those obtained in the dual-task paradigm. For example, consider the predictions if an RT probe were to replace the startle probe in the experiments reviewed by Graham (1979). When the stimulus for the RT is also the stimulus to be anticipated, facilitation of RT would be expected. When, however, RT is made a secondary task by shifting the primary anticipation elsewhere, RT would be slowed (inhibited). Startle seems to act like a task requiring central capacity. A secondary task should also be shown sensitive to the variations in capacity demanded by the secondary task. To date, however, startle used as a secondary task has not been shown to be sensitive to varying capacity demands of a primary task. Recently Bohlin *et al.* (1981) have discussed the conceptual status of probe startle and have suggested that orienting to a novel stimulus elicits a broad focus of attention (as shown by probe facilitation). Thus, evidence is emerging that will determine whether or not cardiac deceleration is uniquely related to a broad or narrow focus of attention.

In summary, a number of interesting issues remain, but cardiac deceleration seems to respond to the initiation of attention by unexpected and expected stimuli. A conceptual account relating cardiac deceleration to access of input to processing capacity has been suggested. A more convincing and more interesting argument could be made if bodily change could be shown to facilitate attention. I have already reviewed research suggesting a correlation of heart rate change and performance, but such evidence confounds the central state (i.e., attention and bodily reaction). In the next section, I consider evidence showing that the induction of bodily change produces changes in attention. As in other sections of this chapter, I restrict my purview to normally occurring as opposed to pathological bodily changes.

CHANGE IN BODILY STATE AS A FACILITATOR OF ATTENTION

This section examines changes in attention during periods of biological adaptation to temporary conditions, such as exercise, drug states, or periods of anxiety. These temporary conditions may induce a psychophysiological state that facilitates (or interferes with) attention. The best known example of such a relationship is the Yerkes-Dodson law relating performance to arousal. This law posits an inverted-U relationship in which low and high arousal are associated with poorer performance than midlevel arousal. Dif-

ferent theorists have used a number of terms synonymous with "arousal": "drive," "motivation," "effort," or "activation." A large number of variables have been used experimentally to alter arousal; a partial list would include stimulus strength, drugs, noise, anxiety, social pressure, and crowding. In much of this work, "arousal" is used as an explanatory construct, but measurement of arousal is not attempted. In short, arousal has been widely used as an explanatory concept, but rather infrequently defined or measured. (A useful historical collection of articles on arousal and performance is found in Porges & Coles, 1976.) Furthermore, the inverted-U relationship permits the facile interpretation of both increases and decreases of performance as due to arousal. Such critiques are hardly novel (e.g., Duffy, 1962; Hamilton, Hockey, & Rejman, 1977; Hockey, 1979; Kahneman, 1973), but the inverted-U concept of arousal and performance continues to be used—even by its detractors. The reason for this is not surprising. Positive findings as well as personal experience provide some support for the concept. We, therefore, may well hesitate to discard the concept when no other guiding concept exists. In this section, I examine some instances in which the inverted-U hypothesis fails to adequately explain the results and attempt to develop alternative explanations. As a first step, however, we must examine the concept of general arousal.

Arousal is a hypothetical state that energizes behavior. The state varies on a continuum from sleep to extreme excitement. Arousal is a general state that can be observed in behavior, elicited by self-report, and measured using both autonomic and electrocortical indices of physiological activity. Duffy (1962) provides an excellent review of the psychological aspects of arousal, while Lindsley (1960) develops its neurophysiological activity. Lindsley (1970) provides a particularly appropriate discussion of arousal in the nonspecific reticular–thalamic–cortical system as a control system for attention. His discussion is interesting because it shows the progressive refinements of the concept from a general system of arousal to specific systems. The initial appeal of the theory of general arousal is, however, that a small number of measures can index a state that (1) alters a wide range of behavior and (2) can be characterized neuroanatomically and neurophysiologically.

Arousal theorists such as Duffy and Lindsley have recognized specific arousal as well as general arousal, but the general state has been emphasized. Critiques of arousal reverse the emphasis. J. I. Lacey's (1967) well-known critique is typical: If arousal is a general state, then autonomic, behavioral, and cortical measures should all vary concomitantly. Literature reviewed in J. I. Lacey (1967) shows, however, that high autonomic "arousal" can be present during drowsiness as indexed by electrocortical changes. Furthermore, quantitative relations between simultaneous measures of arousal are typically low, even within a given type of measure (e.g., autonomic measures). In short, a single, general arousal system may not exist. Physiological regulatory systems do interact, and it may well be that increased activity in one will raise the probability of increased activity in another. If so, then a statistical relationship between "arousal" indices will arise. Such a relationship depicts an important property of the organism, but it does not establish a single arousal system. Indeed, the multiplicity of arousal states rather than unitary arousal seems to be generally accepted among psychophysiologists.

If we reject general arousal, however, we must assume the burden of providing an alternative guiding concept. A simple, preliminary step may be to examine psychophysiological responses relative to the goals of the organism. Behavior and physiological support for that behavior presumably optimize goal attainment. For example, in an RT task, the goal is to produce the fastest response possible after stimulus detection. A variety of motoric and autonomic changes occur that appear to optimize the probability of early stimulus detection and rapid coordinated response. This process of optimization is interesting because it is nontrivial. For example, a speeded response to a visual stimulus might be optimized in part by tensing appropriate muscle groups and perfusing these with an ample blood supply. This occurs, but only momentarily: Biological constraints limit the amount of time this readiness is maintained. The task of psychophysiology is to describe and understand these constraints—constraints that are most probably related to energy regulation, when we consider autonomic and motoric systems. In a relative sense, we know a great deal about the biological function of the end organs influenced by the autonomic and peripheral nervous system. For example, autonomic regulation of the blood vessels has one functional goal of maintaining tissue perfusion. As psychophysiologists, awareness of these biological functions permits us to ask why the nervous system regulates these functions differently in support of psychological processes. In contrast, cortical electrophysiology works with less knowledge of the functions served by the tissue measured.

Noise, Arousal, and Attention

As I return to the question of arousal and performance, I must change from the focus on second-by-second adjustments and task-induced change. Rather, I am now presuming a relatively sustained arousal state that precedes and alters task performance. In this discussion of the literature, however, I consider the alternative proposal that task demands induce both "arousal" and performance changes. "Arousal" states specific to the task can be considered relative to per-

formance. As in the previous section, I review only one area—the influence of noise on attention as mediated by arousal. In doing so, I must temporarily ignore the problems of the concept of general arousal. After noting further background of the inverted-U relationship, I ask two questions: (1) Does intermittent or continuous noise induce sustained physiological change? (2) Does noise alter attention in paradigms permitting an independent index of attention?

In an influential review, Easterbrook (1959) reformulated the inverted-U hypothesis. Easterbrook suggested that increasing emotional arousal leads to progressive narrowing of the range of cues utilized during task performance (i.e., a narrowing of attention). Thus, for simple tasks with few critical cues, performance generally improves during emotional arousal; however, with complex tasks, performance peaks with minimal emotional arousal and then decreases—that is, performance shows the inverted-U relationship with arousal. Callaway, among others (Callaway, 1959; Callaway & Dembo, 1958; Callaway & Thompson, 1953), provided evidence for this view by inducing arousal with drugs and observing a reduced use of cues in perceptual tasks. Similar arguments were made by Hebb (1955), but he suggested that performance decrements might be due to the energizing of competing responses, not to the narrowing of attention. Tecce and Cole (1976) again reviewed much of the same work and suggested that arousal induces distraction. "Distraction" was defined as a process that directs attention to irrelevant cues (not to irrelevent responses, as Hebb suggested). In sum, by 1976, independent reviews of the literature had resulted in conceptually discrepant views of the relationship of "overarousal" and attention: Overarousal was said to (1) narrow attention or broaden attention; (2) facilitate irrelevant responses; or (3) facilitate the processing of irrelevant stimuli. Such a state of affairs requires more detailed examination of the available data. It is appropriate at this point to examine the specific relation of noise-induced arousal to attention. This example illustrates some difficulties with the inverted-U concept.

Noise and Arousal

A necessary first step is to ask whether noise does indeed induce arousal (an assumption widely made in this area). Both continuous and intermittent noise produce transient changes in autonomic indices. Kryter's (1970) review of the literature (see also Miller, 1974) suggests, however, that adaptation occurs within minutes. Thus, noise even in the range of 80–100 dBA does not induce sustained autonomic increases. Self-reports of arousal after continuous noise similarly fail to suggest any sustained changes (e.g., Thayer & Carey, 1974). Thus, in agreement with many authors (e.g., Glass & Singer, 1972), I doubt whether noise per se induces a sustained arousal state in humans.

Two other possible noise–arousal relationships should be considered, however. First, the endocrine system seems adapted for hour-by-hour regulation, as opposed to the second-by-second regulation characteristic of the nervous system. Perhaps we should be looking for endocrine rather than neural indicators of a sustained arousal. This possibility is seriously questioned, however, by Follenius, Brandenberger, Lecornu, Simeoni, and Reinhardt (1980). These authors found essentially no changes in catecholamines, adrenocorticotropic hormone (ACTH), or cortisol during 3 hr of intermittent 45-dBA and 95-dBA pink noise—a combination judged highly unpleasant by the volunteers. Thus with the possible exception of salivary gland output (Corcoran & Houston, 1977), no physiological measure seems to show sustained arousal in humans due solely to experimental exposure to noise.

Second, noise may have a catalytic action; that is, whenever combined with a performance task, it may induce heightened and sustained arousal. Poulton (1979) takes such a position and cites some suggestive support from a neuroendocrine study. Reasonably good support for this position can also be found in autonomic indices. Investigations of learned helplessness have frequently used noise in conjunction with task performance and have compared this with a no-noise control. Task involvement is usually manipulated by conditions that either suggest or actually change a performance–reward contingency. Systolic and diastolic blood pressure, skin conductance level, skin conductance responses, and vasoconstriction have all been shown to be higher or more frequent during performance in noise, particularly when noise level is perceived as contingent on performance (Gatchel, McKinney, & Koebernick, 1977; Gatchel & Proctor, 1976; Glass, Krakoff, Contrada, Hilton, Kehoe, Mannucci, Collins, Snow, & Elting, 1980; Glass & Singer, 1972; Lovallo & Pishkin, 1980; Weidner & Matthews, 1978). The studies do not, however, show that any one index is consistently elevated. Blood pressure and vasoconstriction seem to be relatively consistent, while heart rate has generally failed (see previous section) to show a sustained acceleration. Furthermore, the relationship may be sensitive to additional variables, such as success on the task and task difficulty (e.g., Lovallo & Pishkin, 1980). Thus, these results do not support a simple arousal position, but they do suggest that multiple physiological indices may show sustained changes during task performance that are heightened by the presence of high-intensity (at least 70-dBA) noise.

This conclusion partially justifies the widespread practice of adding noise to tasks to create an arousal manipulation. Conceptually, however, noise does not simply "turn on" arousal; it interacts with the demands of task performance. The proposition that arousal alters attention is difficult to test if the arousal is dependent on the task used to assess attention. This difficulty in independently manipulating arousal is yet another factor reducing the utility of the inverted-U hypothesis. Later, I argue that this problem is not specific to the use of noise to manipulate arousal.

Arousal and Attention

Again ignoring the limitations of the arousal concept, we can proceed to the next question: Does noise alter attention via arousal? More specifically, we can ask whether noise alters the breadth of attention (narrows or broadens the focus of attention) or the intensity of attention as measured in dual-task paradigms.

Two experiments by Hockey (1970a, 1970b) are illustrative of recent work. After reviewing research supporting the Easterbrook (1959) hypothesis, Hockey devised a performance task complex enough to yield decrements due to noise. The volunteer performed both a primary pursuit-tracking task and a secondary light detection task. Six lights were arranged in a semicircle facing the volunteer, with three on either side of the tracking display. In two separate sessions, volunteers performed the dual task in either 75-dBA or 100-dBA broadband continuous noise. Through its arousing effect, the higher noise level was expected to facilitate performance on the primary tracking task and reduce performance on the secondary detection task. This, in fact, occurred. Light detection was only reduced, however, for the lamps that were peripheral to the tracking display. Lamps next to the display were detected slightly better in the high-noise condition. The second experiment replicated this effect *when* the probability of lamp illumination was biased to the more central lamps. In this experiment, the lamps remained on until detected; therefore, peripheral lamps could not simply be missed, as they could have been in the first experiment. Detection latencies were shorter for the central lamps when lamp illumination was biased toward these lamps, but not when illumination of the peripheral lamps was equally as likely as the illumination of the central lamps. Thus, Hockey (1970a, 1970b) concludes that noise through its arousal effect leads to an "enhancement of attention paid to sources already being given priority, with a resulting withdrawal of attention from the low priority sources" (1970a, p. 41).

This interpretation essentially supports Easterbrook's (1959) position. A variety of performance effects have been found, however, during noise exposure. Some of these question the completeness of the Easterbrook position. The following six effects have been reported or replicated relatively recently.

1. Continuous noise alters the confidence of detection responses in experimental designs in which

the "narrowing" of attention also produces selectivity effects (Hockey, 1979; review in Broadbent, 1971). The frequency of unsure confidence judgments declines after noise exposure.

2. Continuous noise broadens spatial response generalization (Thayer & Carey, 1974). After training on a center light, responses to adjacent test lights increase in noise.
3. Continuous noise improves color naming speed on the interference card of the Stroop test (e.g., Houston, 1969; Houston & Jones, 1967; cf. Hartley & Adams, 1974). In noise, volunteers can more quickly name the ink color of a color word (e.g., the word "red" printed in blue ink), and may also simply name colors more quickly (Broadbent, 1981).
4. Continuous noise increases the use of salient cues in complex judgment (e.g., Siegal & Steele, 1980) and memory tasks (e.g., Hamilton *et al.*, 1977). The use of less salient cues or incidental cues decreases. Some of these effects may occur in memory rather than attention, as they are not found with a simultaneous presentation of cues (e.g., Houston, 1968; see Chapter 14).
5. Intermittent and continuous noise in combination with a task produces aftereffects on Stroop, proofreading, and problem-solving tasks (see reviews in Broadbent, 1979; Cohen, 1980). At the end of noise exposure, volunteers exposed to noise perform more poorly on these tasks than volunteers not exposed to noise.
6. Continuous noise frequently improves performance in long-term vigilance studies, particularly those with a relatively high frequency of signal presentation (see Broadbent, 1971; Corcoran, Mullin, Rainey, & Frith, 1977; Parasuraman, 1979).

Two current theoretical positions suggest a major but conflicting role for arousal in explaining these results. The Broadbent–Hockey position (Broadbent, 1971, 1978; Hockey, 1970a, 1970b, 1978) suggests that arousal induces attentional selectivity, lapses in performance (errors and long-latency responses), and an increase in high-certainty responses.[3] The first effect is clearly on attention, while it is an interpretive issue whether or not the remainder are also due to a similar mechanism. Broadbent (1978) suggests that all of the effects are due to selectivity induced by arousal. Selectivity implies a narrow focus of attention. If this focus is temporarily directed away from a task, then lapses occur. Failure to perceive secondary cues due to selectivity is said to eliminate cues that might produce unsure responses. The aftereffect data do not seem to be directly integrated in his view.

The second position is that of Poulton (1979). He suggests that noise-induced arousal has a consistently

beneficial effect. In a 30-min session, noise is said to induce arousal that decreases slowly over time and rebounds to a decreased level at noise offset. Performance would follow this function exactly, except for a masking effect that is also induced by noise. Masking induces consistent decrement in performance throughout noise. Arousal and masking effects combined lead to performance that briefly falls at noise onset, then improves above baseline as enhanced arousal aids adaptation. As arousal falls over the session, however, adaptation fails to maintain performance. At noise offset, performance will briefly improve and then succumb to the effect of the lowered arousal level. Masking is a reasonably straightforward explanation of performance deficits on auditory tasks, but most investigators have used visual detection tasks. Poulton suggests that masking acts on auditory feedback cues from experimental equipment and on inner speech, which is said to be useful in such tasks. Poulton (1977, 1979) provides a clever analysis of the literature supporting his position. The arousal part of his argument is largely unchallenged (see indirect critique in Cohen, 1980, for discussion of arousal and aftereffects), and it explains the aftereffects not conceptualized by Broadbent (1978). The masking argument is controversial. Broadbent (1978) cites evidence questioning this aspect of Poulton's view and supporting the attentional selectivity view. Poulton's view vis-à-vis psychophysiology would correspond to a nonspecific view of arousal, in which efficiency of all processes is enhanced by arousal. Broadbent's view suggests a specific attentional effect of arousal. Although the interested reader should judge for himself or herself, Broadbent seems to provide sufficient evidence to support the viability of the attentional view; that is, not all the evidence for a performance decrement seems to be handled by a decrement due to masking.

A number of important issues remain, however, some of which are applicable to both Broadbent's and Poulton's positions. Both positions dismiss an effect of arousal on the ease of elicitation of irrelevant or competing responses. Broadbent (1971; see also Bacon, 1974) cites evidence against such a position and analyzes its roots in Hullian psychology. Nonetheless, the evidence of Thayer and Carey (1974) seems to support such a heightened response generalization during noise, as does evidence presented by Tecce and Cole (1976) and Hamilton *et al.* (1977). Although one can fault this evidence, it may be wise at present to accept more than one mechanism by which noise can alter performance.

A major problem with most of the research is that noise effects are attributed to arousal, but arousal is not measured. As we have seen, general arousal may only express a statistical tendency for the coactivation of different response systems. The effects of noise on performance are, however, superficially similar to the effects of incentive, stimulant drugs, and anxiety (Broadbent, 1971). A unifying concept such as

3. I would like to thank Drs. Broadbent, Forster, and Poulton for responding to an inquiry about their current (1982) work relating noise and arousal.

arousal would be theoretically desirable. Investigations continuing to use the simple arousal concept would, however, seem obligated to provide either a physiological or a self-report measure of arousal within their experiments, or to replicate results across "arousal-inducing" manipulations. This need is particularly acute, given the ease of post hoc formulations based on the inverted-U relationship.

One other question can be raised about the explanation of noise effects as due to general arousal. The influence of task performance on tonic and phasic physiological measures has been largely ignored. As discussed above, noise must be combined with task performance to elicit physiological response consistently. Thus, the influence of the task on physiological state becomes a critical variable. This has been recognized indirectly in the literature (e.g., Broadbent, 1971; Hockey, 1970a) by statements that performance decrements only occur in difficult tasks. Here again, we see a need for either a measure of "arousal" or an index of task difficulty independent of performance. A second aspect of this problem is that phasic or momentary changes in physiological indices are known to occur as a function of task performance (see above and Kahneman, 1973). These changes may be closely tied to attention and should be incorporated in concepts of the noise–arousal–attention relationship. Interactions between phasic and longer-term tonic physiological changes may be particularly important in interpreting the effects of noise on vigilance (see Mackworth, 1969; Parasuraman, 1979). Individual differences in the adaptation of physiological responses to sensory stimuli (Crider & Augenbraun, 1975), as well as phasic responses at the time of signals to detect (Blakeslee, 1979) seem to be important predictors of vigilance performance. In short, even in the context of a simple arousal view, phasic arousal responses as well as tonic or sustained arousal during a task should be considered.

These interpretive problems are rather well illustrated in a series of papers focused on problems in replicating Hockey's (1970a, 1970b) findings. Forster and Grierson (1978) reported four experiments, two of which closely followed the methods of Hockey (although the lamps appear to have consistently been illuminated until the volunteer responded). The experiments failed to support either the attentional deficit on peripheral lamps reported by Hockey or the masking interpretation of Poulton. The interchange following this report (Forster, 1978; Hockey, 1978) emphasizes (1) the task difficulty factor—in particular, the exact difficulty level of the tracking task; (2) uncertainty as to whether the task and noise produced the expected arousal (i.e., whether noise would improve the specific tracking performance assessed); and (3) difficulties in establishing the subjective salience of task and task elements. Hockey's (1978) reply maintains that noise does induce selectivity, but that

this effect on particular events is difficult to predict. Although Forster and Grierson's (1978) findings weaken the attentional selectivity position, the support for the position is considerably more extensive than the Hockey experiments (see Broadbent, 1971, 1978). The results of Hockey (1970a, 1970b) have also recently been replicated using a large sample and similar methodology (Hartley, 1981). The controversy does illustrate my contention that testing a hypothesis is essentially impossible when measurement of its major construct is not included in experiments. I have no idea of whether "arousal" was manipulated the same way in Hockey's and in Forster and Grierson's work.

Conclusions

Finally, this review of noise, arousal, and attention needs to be placed into the context of what it tells us about the relation of bodily to attentional functioning. The first rather obvious point is that because of its simplicity, the inverted-U relationship has outlived its utility. Neither arousal nor performance is a unidimensional concept that can be directly related to the other in a single function. Such a position is hardly unique and is similar to the current position of Hockey and colleagues (Hamilton et al., 1977; Hockey, 1978). At present, a conservative interpretation of available data may be that bodily response (arousal) has no direct effect on any aspect of performance. Using our noise example, we can suggest that (1) noise alters attentional selectivity and (2) noise combined with a task yields increases in certain physiological variables. If noise is considered as but one of a number of task demands, then we can simply ask whether noise specifically alters information processing and physiological response patterns. For example, phasic cardiac deceleration to visual displays may be altered by the addition of noise (Gibson & Hall, 1966). If so, possible relations of deceleration to task performance and, theoretically, to processing capacity would allow a more comprehensive theoretical account than that provided by an inverted-U hypothesis. Both suggestions are supported by the literature reviewed. At present, little or no evidence directly supports arousal as a causal (facilitator or inhibitor) influence on breadth of attention. Although "arousal" seems to summarize similar effects due to induced muscle tension, anxiety, noise, incentive, and drug manipulation, most of these manipulations create added possibilities of distraction (Naatanen, 1973). Squeezing a dynamometer may easily distract one from an RT task, and the same may be true of the worrying of the anxious individual. Drug effects are a possible exception to this argument. The interpretation of drug effects, however, is complicated by the usual presence of multiple central and peripheral effects, as well as by interactions with ongoing psychological state (e.g., see Tecce & Cole, 1976). A second reason for the continued use of the arousal concept is the integration of results from studies of low arousal. Although data are sparse, states such as sleep deprivation may induce attentional selectivity effects that are the inverse of those associated with high arousal (see review in Broadbent, 1971). All and all, however, we can conclude that arousal is not a proven cause of attentional selectivity.

In an earlier section, I have suggested that brief cardiovascular changes are important in preparing for the integration of sensory and motor function or for divorcing central integration from input–output activities. These formulations imply a facilitory role for these bodily changes. Thus, although I have questioned the interpretation of arousal states, I am unwilling to state that bodily responses are solely epiphenomenal indicators of attentional processes. The facilitory role imagined is, however, integral to the psychological processes—not an antecedent, as in the arousal–performance view. Thus, manipulations such as noise are expected to produce changes in both performance and physiology. Evidence for such a position should show that conditions facilitating (interfering with) physiological responses appropriate to the task should facilitate (interfere with) performance. Such experiments are difficult. Human beings seem well adapted for efficient performance. Decrements in performance due even to such gross manipulations as sleep deprivation have proven difficult to detect. Compensatory mechanisms seem readily available to offset losses in efficiency. Differences may be best detected in the way in which the organism achieves a behavioral endpoint, not in a scoring of whether or not that endpoint is achieved. Hockey (1978) provides an interesting discussion paralleling this one on the need to relate, and difficulty of relating, patterns of physiological response to patterns of performance.

BODILY CHANGE AS A REGULATOR OF ATTENTION

The most tantalizing possibility for the psychophysiologist is that the processes of bodily regulation also alter attention. This section first examines a historical and a current example of research suggesting that blood pressure regulation alters attention. Then, the less well-defined regulation of the diurnal (24-hr or sleep–wake) rhythm is examined. The implication of these examples is that some necessary substrate for attention is being regulated either by the blood pressure or by the sleep–wake regulatory system.

Biological regulation has the goal of adapting the organism to its current external and internal milieu.

Since the time of Bernard, this regulation has been conceptualized in terms of feedback systems designed to maintain constancy in the face of changing conditions. The operation of such systems and their relation to biological rhythmicity was elegantly reviewed in the classic text of Sollberger (1965). Biological regulation is evident not only in the relative constancy of regulated functions, such as body temperature, but also in oscillatory behavior due to the short-term regulation of such functions as blood pressure (e.g., Korner, 1971). The complexity of regulated systems with inherent feedback lag, reasonably high gain, and delayed error correction leads to characteristic oscillatory behavior. These oscillations are among those that may be classified as biological rhythms. These rhythms occur over a wide range of frequencies— short-term oscillations of the cardiovascular and respiratory systems, 24-hr oscillations of body temperature, the menstrual cycles of the female reproductive system.

The nervous and endocrine systems comprise the regulatory apparatus for most of these functions, and thus may induce the oscillations. These integrative actions of the nervous and endocrine systems may, however, influence psychological functioning as well as the biological function specifically regulated. For example, blood pressure shows a well-known homeostatic regulation based on efferent signals from the baroreceptors. Transient increases in blood pressure induce baroreceptor firing that is transmitted to the brain stem. The ultimate result is a lowering of blood pressure accomplished through autonomic efferents. An additional effect of baroreceptor activity (reviewed in J. I. Lacey, 1972) is, however, an inhibition of higher cortical functioning. In short, the possibility exists that normal biological regulation may alter psychological functioning. This section reviews two such possibilities. Neither has been established, but both have sufficient support to be of current interest. Recent physiological discussions of rhythmic control of the cardiovascular system may be found in the symposium chaired by Manning (1980).

Blood Pressure Regulation and Attention

Defining a biological constraint on our ability to attend is of obvious importance. Some of the earliest workers in psychology sought such a relationship. Like current psychophysiologists, they first sought correlated performance and physiological changes, and then attempted to show that the biological regulation of the physiological change induced the change in performance.

In the early 1900s, American psychologists, such as Angell and Pillsbury, studied "attention waves" using psychophysiological techniques. These investigators were interested in the cognitive rather than the environmental determinants of attention. Thus, the student of attention examined situations in which the stimulus field was constant but the perception of that field changed. For example, a barely perceptible gray ring (i.e., a Masson disk) will appear and disappear in rhythmic fashion if it is visually fixated. Similar "attention waves" can be observed in the auditory and tactile senses (Woodworth, 1938). Given that receptor adaptation and movement had not completely explained the waves, one hypothesis of the time was that a central attentional state modulated the efficiency of the sensory apparatus. Early speculation had suggested that rhythmic variations in blood pressure, the so-called Traube–Hering waves, might cause variation in perfusion of the brain and thus variation in perceptual efficiency (e.g., Roy & Sherrington, 1890). Angell and Thompson (1899) and Pillsbury (1903) brought this speculation to psychology and initiated work in their laboratories. A number of reports ensued, suggesting that vascular waves measured by a plethysmograph were relatively synchronous with the "attention waves" (e.g., Bonser, 1903; Slaughter, 1901). Considerable interest in this explanation of the phenomenon continued until the controlled study of Griffitts and Gordon (1924). These investigators showed that extraneously induced changes in stimulus intensity would induce vasomotor rhythmicity. Thus, the perceptual experience seemed to induce the physiological change, rather than vice versa. Although interesting and relevant to modern concerns (e.g., Porges et al., 1980), this finding refutes the claim that vascular events determine the perceptual experience.

In recent times, a different mechanism has been proposed for cardiovascular effects on attention. Over the last 20 years, Bea and John Lacey (B. C. Lacey & Lacey, 1978) have developed and supported a hypothesis concerning the significance of heart rate for behavior. Earlier sections of this chapter have mentioned psychological aspects of this hypothesis; this section focuses on its physiological aspects. The Laceys suggest that the frequency of neural input from the baroreceptors to the brain stem influences the efficiency of sensory–motor function (B. C. Lacey & Lacey 1978). Neuroanatomical and physiological data (see Larsen, Schneiderman, & Pasin, Chapter 7, this volume) are cited to show that baroreceptor firing inhibits sensory and motor nuclei in the brain stem, as well as electroencephalographic indices of activation. The Laceys suggest that such modulation of the brain will be observed in fluctuations in human performance—fluctuations that would fit the present definition of attention.

The testing of Laceys' hypothesis requires some connecting arguments. Subsequent to the initiation of the heart beat at the sinus node, an orderly sequence of events occurs that can be termed the "cardiac cycle"—electrical impulses spread to the ventricle; the

ventricle contracts and then relaxes during diastole. The baroreceptors (primarily located in the aortic arch and carotid sinus) will be stretched (stimulated) when the systolic pulse reaches them and relaxed thereafter during diastole. Thus, measuring from the P wave of the electrocardiogram in humans, we could expect baroreceptor activation to occur during the middle one-third of the cardiac cycle. Returning to the hypothesis, one can predict that sensory–motor efficiency will be higher during the first and last thirds of the cycle, relative to the middle third. I term this the "cardiac cycle prediction" of the hypothesis. A second prediction is based on the fact that the baroreceptors will be activated less frequently during a period of slow heart rate than during a period of high heart rate (and futhermore baroreceptor sensitivity may also be frequency dependent). Thus, during naturally occurring or induced periods of heart rate deceleration, sensory–motor efficiency should be enhanced.

What is the current status of the evidence on these two predictions? A series of thorough reviews are available to answer this question (Carroll & Anastasiades, 1978; Elliott, 1972; Hahn, 1973; B. C. Lacey & Lacey, 1974), and thus I can summarize here. Neither prediction has been conclusively proven or disproven. Tests of the cardiac cycle time prediction were initially supportive; RT and signal detection were altered by a cardiac cycle time. Subsequent evidence was, however, largely negative. The Laceys' response (e.g., J. I. Lacey & Lacey, 1974) was basically to point out that they proposed a working hypothesis about a complex mechanism. Their work was seeking to define those complexities, rather than to defend any general or literal meaning of their hypothesis. Recent work of the Laceys (B. C. Lacey & Lacey, 1978, 1980) has shown that cardiac cycle effects are influenced at least by (1) average length of the cardiac cycle; (2) temporal location of both stimuli and responses in the cycle; and (3) changes in the cardiac cycle itself due to the temporal location of stimuli and responses. We (Jennings & Wood, 1977) verified the last point, as well as noting respiratory influences on the effects. At present, it seems fair to suggest, first, that the presence of cardiac cycle time effects has been revealed, largely due to the influence of the Laceys' hypothesis; second, that the early hypothesis is now largely irrelevant to the emerging number of complex relations observed. Further investigations and a new conceptual integration will be necessary before a relationship between the cardiac cycle and attention can be claimed. Current evidence has not proven that cardiac cycle events alter attentional processes.

The second prediction, relating episodes of cardiac slowing to attentive efficiency, likewise does not have enough support to claim an influence of biological regulation on attention. Episodes of cardiac deceleration occur regularly and have been related to the regulation of respiration and blood pressure. Given that these variations alter baroreceptor firing, such spontaneoous slowing should be related to efficient performance. As with the previous prediction, both positive and negative evidence is available. Consistent support for the prediction is found *if* deceleration induced by a psychological task is related to performance (see "Bodily Change as an Indicator of Attention"). Reaction times and perceptual judgments are very weakly but consistently related to the depth of cardiac deceleration. Such findings do not, however, directly support an influence of biological regulation on performance. As in the case of the "attention waves," the task performance may be inducing the physiological change, rather than vice versa.

In sum, the biological constraints on attention proposed by the Laceys remain unproven. The ideas remain of interest, and the findings of some laboratories have consistently supported predictions based on the hypothesis (Cacioppo, Sandman, & Walker, 1978; McCanne & Sandman, 1974; Sandman, McCanne, Kaiser, & Diamond, 1977), and have even extended it to the modulation of evoked potentials and cerebral blood flow (Walker & Sandman, 1979). Dworkin, Filewich, Miller, Craigmyle, and Pickering (1979) have used notions derived from the Laceys in developing hypotheses concerning the etiology of hypertension. The amount of negative evidence clearly suggests, however, that the Laceys' hypothesis is either wrong or, more likely, only one facet of a multifaceted relationship between cardiovascular function and attention.

Diurnal Rhythms and Attention

Biological regulation occurs over minutes and hours, as well as over the brief time spans we have considered so far. The sleep–wake cycle is an obvious fact of our existence. Such gross state changes alter attention, and less dramatic changes may similarly affect attention. Many physiological measures in humans show 24-hr rhythms, although the mechanisms for their rhythms remain controversial (Mills, 1966; Surowiak, 1978). Among the measures showing these variations are heart rate, metabolic rate, and body temperature. Heart rate, for example, is usually highest in late afternoon, decreases throughout the night, and rises in the morning. In this respect, heart rate change is correlated in time with body temperature (Orr, Hoffman, & Hegge, 1976). These circadian rhythms, although influenced by environmental events, do not appear to be directly caused by them; that is, the rhythm is endogenous (Hockey & Colquhoun, 1972; Mills, Minors, & Waterhouse, 1977; Scheving, Halberg, & Pauly, 1974). Thus, like the cardiac cycle, the 24-hr rhythm is a biological cycle that might alter psychological function.

Performance on challenging, continuous tasks can be reliably shown to vary as a function of time of day (see the reviews of Hockey & Colquhoun, 1972; Lavie, 1980). These performance variations have been attributed to diurnal variations in physiological function. Kleitman (1963), for example, found that performance on eight tasks varied with diurnal variations in heart rate and body temperature. His interpretation suggested that body temperature altered the metabolic processes that influence performance. Clearly, his hypothesis directly expresses the possibility that normal biological regulation alters psychological function. As reviewed in Hockey and Colquhoun (1972), Kleitman's results have been reasonably well supported in subsequent investigations. His interpretation is controversial, however.

Kleitman's hypothesis continues to be relevant to circadian rhythm research, although its verification may seem even more distant than it did when it was proposed. First, however, we should consider why the findings are relevant to our concern with attention. The tasks used in these experiments have typically been simple performance tasks, such as serial RT tasks, card sorting, and letter cancellation. As such, the tasks do not require extensive learning or problem solving. In addition, diurnal variations related to temperature have been found across tasks, not within a single task. Finally, performance failures have typically been due to lapses (i.e., temporary failure interspersed with relatively optimal performance). Taken together, these observations suggest that specific sensory, motor, or cognitive impairments have not been produced. Thus, it seems reasonable to suggest that circadian state may have prevented the continuous supply of attention or effort to the processing of these tasks.

Such a conclusion must be highly tentative, however, since neither the available evidence or the conceptual state of biorhythm research allows us to conclude that the diurnal rhythm directly regulates attention. First, independent measures of attention were not used in available studies, and the designs of the studies did not permit an assessment of moment-by-moment covariance of physiology and performance. Furthermore, exact diurnal variations in performance have not always been replicated (Hauty & Smith, 1972; Hockey & Colquhoun, 1972). Individual differences in diurnal rhythms and differences in rhythm among physiological measures are also complicating factors (see discussions in Eysenck & Folkard, 1980; Humphreys, Revelle, Simon, & Gilliland, 1980; Revelle, Humphreys, Simon, & Gilliland, 1980). Finally, exactly what diurnal rhythms regulate remains unclear. Kleitman's hypothesis is a bold speculation about what is regulated. In order to test the hypothesis, however, metabolic rate or temperature would have to be varied while holding psychological factors constant. The rather extreme measures necessary to perturb metabolic rate or temperature would seem to preclude holding psychological factors constant. In conclusion, Kleitman's hypothesis and biorhythmic influences in general constitute at present an interesting possibility, but little more.

SUMMARY

"Attention" in this chapter has been used as a general term referring to a set of separable processes. Some of these processes are usefully studied with autonomic measures. Heart rate change has been shown to detect increments in attention relative to a resting state (termed in Figure 13-1 the "initiation of attention"). Furthermore, the direction of heart rate change indicates the direction of attention to or away from current input. The validity of such bodily changes as indicators of attention is seen as relatively well established. At present, experimental work is directed at defining precisely which attention processes are related to heart rate change.

Theoretical accounts suggest further, however, that physiological change may facilitate or interfere with attention (i.e., may play a functional role in the maintenance of attention). In particular, general physiological arousal induced by noise has been said to induce a narrowing of attention. Problems with the concept of general arousal and its measurement have led to questioning of this claim. Facilitating or inhibiting functions of bodily change are probably better demonstrated by examining physiological responses to task demands rather than general arousal. Little current evidence (outside of pathology), however, seems to establish that bodily change per se facilitates or inhibits attention.

Finally, the possibility has been considered that bodily system regulation also regulates attention. No strong evidence for this possibility has been found in studies of blood pressure and diurnal regulation. As a general orientation, the utility of considering attention as a regulator of energy is suggested. The tantalizing evidence that is available may encourage investigators to unravel the complex interactions of biological and psychological control systems. An increased emphasis must, however, be placed on the intricacies of the regulation. Bodily energy regulation and transformation may be more comparable to that performed by a modern large-scale integrated circuit than to that performed by the single potentiometer envisaged by theories of general arousal.

ACKNOWLEDGMENT

Kay Jennings's and Steve Manuck's assistance in reading early drafts of this chapter is gratefully acknowledged.

REFERENCES

Ackles, P. K., Jennings, J. R., & Coles, M. G. H. *Advances in psychophysiology, Vol. 2.* Greenwich, Conn.: JAI Press, in press.

Angell, J. R., & Thompson, H. B. A study of the relations between certain organic processes and consciousness. *Psychological Review*, 1899, 6, 32–53.

Bacon, S. J. Arousal and the range of cue utilization. *Journal of Experimental Psychology*, 1974, 102, 81–87.

Berlyne, D. E. *Conflict, arousal, and curiosity.* New York: McGraw-Hill, 1960.

Bernstein, A. S., & Taylor, K. W. The interaction of stimulus information with potential stimulus significance in eliciting the skin conductance orienting response. In H. D. Kimmel, E. H. Van Olst, & J. F. Orlebeke (Eds.), *The orienting reflex in humans.* Hillsdale, N.J.: Erlbaum, 1979.

Blakeslee, P. Attention and vigilance: Performance and skin conductance response changes. *Psychophysiology*, 1979, 16, 413–419.

Bohlin, G., Graham, F. K., Silverstein, L. D., & Hackley, S. A. Cardiac orientation and startle blink modification in novel and signal situations. *Psychophysiology*, 1981, 18, 603–611.

Bohlin, G., & Kjellberg, A. Orienting activity in two stimulus paradigms as reflected in heart rate. In H. D. Kimmel, E. H. Van Olst, & J. F. Orlebeke (Eds.), *The orienting reflex in humans.* Hillsdale, N.J.: Erlbaum, 1979.

Bonser, F. G. A study of the relations between mental activity and the circulation of the blood. *Psychological Review*, 1903, 10, 100–138.

Broadbent, D. E. *Perception and communication.* Oxford: Pergamon Press, 1953.

Broadbent, D. E. *Decision and stress.* London: Academic Press, 1971.

Broadbent, D. E. Levels, hierarchies, and the locus of control. *Quarterly Journal of Experimental Psychology*, 1977, 29, 181–201.

Broadbent, D. E. The current state of noise research: Reply to Poulton. *Psychological Bulletin*, 1978, 85, 1052–1067.

Broadbent, D. E. Is a fatigue test now possible? *Ergonomics*, 1979, 22, 1277–1290.

Broadbent, D. E. The effects of moderate levels of noise on human performance. In J. V. Tobias & E. D. Schubert (Eds.), *Hearing: Research and theory, Vol. 1,* New York: Academic Press, 1981.

Brunia, C. H. M. Some questions about the motor inhibition hypothesis. In H. D. Kimmel, E. H. Van Olst, & J. F. Orlebeke (Eds.), *The orienting reflex in humans.* Hillsdale, N.J.: Erlbaum, 1979.

Cacioppo, J., Sandman, C., & Walker, B. The effects of operant heart rate conditioning on cognitive elaboration and attitude change. *Psychophysiology*, 1978, 15, 330–339.

Callaway, E. The influence of amobarbital and methamphetamine on the focus of attention. *Journal of Mental Science*, 1959, 105, 382–392.

Callaway, E., & Dembo, D. Narrowed attention: A psychological phenomenon that accompanies a certain physiological change. *Journal of Neurology and Psychiatry*, 1958, 79, 74–90.

Callaway, E., & Thompson, S. V. Sympathetic activity and perception, an approach to the relationship between autonomic activity and personality. *Psychosomatic Medicine*, 1953, 15, 443–455.

Carroll, D., & Anastasiades, P. The behavioral significance of heart rate: The Laceys' hypothesis. *Biological Psychology*, 1978, 1, 249–275.

Cohen, S. Aftereffects of stress on human performance: A review of research and theory. *Psychological Bulletin*, 1980, 88, 82–108.

Coles, M. G. H. Physiological activity and detection: The effects of attentional requirements and the prediction of performance. *Biological Psychology*, 1974, 2, 113–125.

Coles, M. G. H., & Duncan-Johnson, C. C. Cardiac activity and information processing: The effects of stimulus significance and detection and response requirements. *Journal of Experimental Psychology*, 1975, 1, 418-428.

Corcoran, D. W. J., & Houston, T. G. Is the lemon test an index of arousal level? *British Journal of Psychiatry*, 1977, 68, 361-364.

Corcoran, D. W. J., Mullin, J., Rainey, M. T., & Frith, G. The effects of raised signal and noise amplitude during the course of vigilance tasks. In R. Mackie (Ed.), *Vigilance*. New York: Academic Press, 1977.

Crider, A., & Augenbraun, C. B. Auditory vigilance correlates of electrodermal response habituation speed. *Psychophysiology*, 1975, 12, 36-40.

Darrow, C. W. Differences in the physiological reaction to sensory and ideational stimuli. *Psychological Bulletin*, 1929, 26, 185-201.

Dawson, M. E., & Schell, A. M. Electrodermal responses to attended and nonattended significant stimuli during dichotic listening. *Journal of Experimental Psychology: Human Perception and Performance*, 1982, 8, 315-324.

Dawson, M. E., Schell, A. M., Beers, J. R., & Kelly, A. Allocation of cognitive processing capacity during human autonomic classical conditioning. *Journal of Experimental Psychology: General*, 1982, 111, 273-295.

DeBoskey, D., Kimmel, E., & Kimmel, H. D. Habituation and conditioning of the orienting reflex in intellectually gifted and average children. In H. D. Kimmel, E. H. Van Olst, & J. F. Orlebeke (Eds.), *The orienting reflex in humans*. Hillsdale, N.J.: Erlbaum, 1979.

DelPezzo, E. M., & Hoffman, H. S. Attentional factors in the inhibition of a reflex by a visual stimulus. *Science*, 1980, 210, 673-674.

Duffy, E. *Activation and behavior*. New York: Wiley, 1962.

Dworkin, B. R., Filewich, R. J., Miller, N. E., Craigmyle, N., & Pickering, T. G. Baroreceptor activation reduces reactivity of noxious stimulation: Implications for hypertension. *Science*, 1979, 205, 1299-1301.

Easterbrook, J. A. The effect of emotion on cue utilization and the organization of behavior. *Psychological Review*, 1959, 66, 183-201.

Elliott, R. The significance of heart rate for behavior: A critique of Lacey's hypothesis. *Journal of Personality and Social Psychology*, 1972, 22, 398-409.

Eysenck, M. W., & Folkard, S. Personality, time of day, and caffeine: Some theoretical and conceptual problems in Revelle et al. *Journal of Experimental Psychology*, 1980, 109, 33-41.

Follenius, M., Brandenberger, G., Lecornu, C., Simeoni, M., & Reinhardt, B. Plasma catecholamines and pituitary adrenal hormones in response to noise exposure. *European Journal of Applied Physiology*, 1980, 43, 253-261.

Forster, P. M. Attentional selectivity: A rejoinder to Hockey. *British Journal of Psychiatry*, 1978, 69, 505-506.

Forster, P. M., & Grierson, A. T. Noise and attentional selectivity: A reproducible phenomenon? *British Journal of Psychiatry*, 1978, 69, 489-498.

Freeman, G. L. *The energetics of human behavior*. Ithaca, N.Y.: Cornell University Press, 1948.

Gatchel, R. J., McKinney, M. E., & Koebernick, L. F. Learned helplessness depression, and physiological responding. *Psychophysiology*, 1977, 14, 25-31.

Gatchel, R. J., & Proctor, J. D. Physiological correlates of learned helplessness in man. *Journal of Abnormal Psychology*, 1976, 85, 27-34.

Gibson, D., & Hall, M. K. Cardiovascular change and mental task gradient. *Psychonomic Science*, 1966, 6, 245-246.

Glass, D. C., Krakoff, L. R., Contrada, R., Hilton, W. F., Kehoe, K., Mannucci, E. G., Collins, C., Snow, B., & Elting, E. Effect of harassment and competition upon cardiovascular and plasma catecholamine responses in Type A and Type B individuals. *Psychophysiology*, 1980, 17, 453-463.

Glass, D. C., & Singer, J. E. *Urban stress: Experiments on noise and social stressors*. New York: Academic Press, 1972.

Graham, F. K. Habituation and dishabituation of responses innervated by the autonomic nervous system. In H. V. S. Peeke & M. J. Herz (Eds.), *Habituation: Behavioral studies and physiological substrates*. New York: Academic Press, 1973.

Graham, F. K. Distinguishing among orienting, defense, and startle reflexes. In H. D. Kimmel, E. H. Van Olst, & J. F. Orlebeke (Eds.), *The orienting reflex in humans*. Hillsdale, N.J.: Erlbaum, 1979.

Graham, F. K., & Clifton, R. K. Heart rate change as a component of the orienting response. *Psychological Bulletin*, 1966, 65, 305-320.

Griffitts, C. H., & Gordon, E. I. The relation between the Truabe-Herving and attention rhythms. *Journal of Experimental Psychology*, 1924, 7, 117-134.

Hahn, W. W. Attention and heart rate: A critical appraisal of the hypothesis of Lacey and Lacey. *Psychological Bulletin*, 1973, 79, 59-90.

Hamilton, P., Hockey, B., & Rejman, M. The place of the concept of activation in human information processing theory: An integrative approach. In S. Dornic (Ed.), *Attention and performance VI*. Hillsdale, N.J.: Erlbaum, 1977.

Hartley, L. R. Noise, attentional selectivity, serial reactions and the need for experimental power. *British Journal of Psychology*, 1981, 72, 101-107.

Hartley, L. R., & Adams, R. G. Effects of noise on the Stroop test. *Journal of Experimental Psychology*, 1974, 102, 62-66.

Hauty, G. T., & Smith, F. L. Psychological correlates of physiological circadian periodicity. In W. P. Colquhoun (Ed.), *Aspects of human efficiency: Diurnal rhythm and loss of sleep*. London: English Universities Press, 1972.

Hebb, D. O. Drives and the C.N.S. (conceptual nervous system). *Psychological Review*, 1955, 62, 243-254.

Hockey, G. R. J. Effect of loud noise on attentional selectivity. *Quarterly Journal of Experimental Psychology*, 1970, 22, 28-36. (a)

Hockey, G. R. J. Signal probability and spatial location as possible bases for increased selectivity in noise. *Quarterly Journal of Experimental Psychology*, 1970, 22, 37-42. (b)

Hockey, G. R. J. Attentional selectivity and the problems of replication: A reply to Forster and Grierson. *British Journal of Psychiatry*, 1978, 69, 499-503.

Hockey, G. R. J. Stress and the cognitive components of skilled performance. In V. Hamilton & D. M. Warburton (Eds.), *Human stress and cognition*. Chichester, England: Wiley, 1979.

Hockey, G. R. J., & Colquhoun, W. P. Diurnal variation in human performance: A review. In W. P. Colquhoun (Ed.), *Aspects of human efficiency: Diurnal rhythm and loss of sleep*. London: English Universities Press, 1972.

Houston, B. K. Inhibition and the facilitating effect of noise on interference tasks. *Perceptual and Motor Skills*, 1968, 27, 947-950.

Houston, B. K. Noise, task difficulty, and Stroop color-word performance. *Journal of Experimental Psychology*, 1969, 81, 403-404.

Houston, B. K., & Jones, T. M. Distraction and Stroop color-word performance. *Journal of Experimental Psychology*, 1967, 74, 54-56.

Humphreys, M. S., Revelle, W., Simon, L., & Gilliland, K. Individual differences in diurnal rhythm and multiple activation states: A reply to M. W. Eysenck and Folkard. *Journal of Experimental Psychology*, 1980, 109, 42-48.

Israel, J. B., Chesney, G. L., Wickens, C. D., & Donchin, E. P300 and tracking difficulty: Evidence for multiple resources in dual-task performance. *Psychophysiology*, 1980, 17, 259-273.

Jennings, J. R., Averill, J. R., Opton, E. M., & Lazarus, R. S. Some parameters of heart rate change: Perceptual versus motor task requirements, noxiousness, and uncertainty. *Psychophysiology*, 1971, 7, 194-212.

Jennings, J. R., & Hall, Jr., S. W. Recall, recognition, and rate: Memory and the heart. *Psychophysiology*, 1980, 17, 37-46.

Jennings, J. R., Lawrence, B. E., & Kasper, P. Changes in alertness and processing capacity in a serial learning task. *Memory and Cognition*, 1978, 6, 45–63.

Jennings, J. R., Schrot, J., & Wood, C. C. Cardiovascular response patterns during choice reaction time. *Physiological Psychology*, 1980, 8, 130–136.

Jennings, J. R., & Wood, C. C. Cardiac cycle time effects on performance, phasic cardiac responses, and their intercorrelation in choice reaction time. *Psychophysiology*, 1977, 14, 197–307.

Johnston, W. A., & Heinz, S. P. Flexibility and capacity demands of attention. *Journal of Experimental Psychology*, 1978, 107, 420–435.

Kahneman, D. *Attention and effort*. Englewood Cliffs, N.J.: Prentice-Hall, 1973.

Kerr, B. Processing demands during mental operations. *Memory and Cognition*, 1973, 1, 401–412.

Kimmel, H., Van Olst, E. H., & Orlebeke, J. F. (Eds.). *The orienting reflex in humans*. Hillsdale, N.J.: Erlbaum, 1979.

Kleitman, N. *Sleep and wakefulness*. Chicago: University of Chicago Press, 1963.

Korner, P. I. Integrative neural cardiovascular control. *Physiological Review*, 1971, 51, 312–367.

Kryter, K. D. *The effects of noise on man*. New York: Academic Press, 1970.

Lacey, B. C., & Lacey, J. I. Studies of heart rate and other bodily processes in sensorimotor behavior. In P. A. Obrist, A. H. Black, J. Brener, & L. V. DiCara (Eds.), *Cardiovascular psychophysiology: Current issues in response mechanisms, biofeedback and methodology*. Chicago: Aldine-Atherton, 1974.

Lacey, B. C., & Lacey, J. I. Two way communication between the heart and the brain. *American Psychologist*, 1978, 33, 99–113.

Lacey, B. C., & Lacey, J. I. Cognitive modulation of time-dependent primary bradycardia. *Psychophysiology*, 1980, 17, 209–221.

Lacey, J. I. Somatic response patterning and stress: Some revisions of activation theory. In M. H. Appley & R. Trumbull (Eds.), *Psychological stress: Issues in research*. New York: Appleton-Century-Crofts, 1967.

Lacey, J. I. Some cardiovascular correlates of sensorimotor behavior: Example of visceral afferent feedback? In C. H. Hockman (Ed.), *Limbic system mechanisms and autonomic function*. Springfield, Ill.: Charles C Thomas, 1972.

Lacey, J. I., Kagan, J., Lacey, B. C., & Moss, H. A. The visceral level: Situational determinants and behavioral correlates of autonomic response patterns. In P. H. Knapp (Ed.), *Expression of the emotions in man*. New York: International Universities Press, 1963.

Lacey, J. I., & Lacey, B. C. On heart rate responses and behavior: A reply to Elliott. *Journal of Personality and Social Psychology*, 1974, 30, 1–18.

Lavie, P. The search for cycles in mental performance from Lombard to Kleitman. *Chronobiologica*, 1980, 7, 247–256.

Lawler, J. E., & Obrist, P. A. Indirect indices of contractile force. In P. A. Obrist, A. H. Black, J. Brener, & L. V. DiCara (Eds.), *Cardiovascular psychophysiology: Current issues in response mechanisms, biofeedback and methodology*. Chicago: Aldine-Atherton, 1974.

Leitner, D. S., Powers, A. S., Stitt, L. L., & Hoffman, H. S. Midbrain reticular formation involvement in the inhibition of acoustic startle. *Physiology and Behavior*, 1981, 26, 259–268.

Lewis, M., & Wilson, C. O. The cardiac response to a perceptual cognitive task in the young child. *Psychophysiology*, 1970, 6, 411–420.

Lindsley, D. B. Attention, consciousness, sleep and wakefulness. In H. W. Magoun (Ed.), *Handbook of physiology: Section 1, Neurophysiology* (Vol. 3). Washington, D.C.: American Physiological Society, 1960.

Lindsley, D. B. The role of nonspecific reticulo-thalamo-cortical systems in emotion. In P. Black (Ed.), *Physiological correlates of emotion*. New York: Academic Press, 1970.

Lovallo, W. R., & Pishkin, V. A psychophysiological comparison of Type A and B men exposed to failure and uncontrollable noise. *Psychophysiology*, 1980, 17, 29–36.

Mackworth, J. F. *Vigilance and habituation*. Baltimore: Penguin, 1969.

Manning, J. W. Central integration of cardiovascular control: Central cardiovascular control: A distributed neural network. *Federation Proceedings*, 1980, 39, 2485–2486.

McCanne, T. R., & Sandman, C. A. Instrumental heart rate responses and visual perception: A preliminary study. *Psychophysiology*, 1974, 11, 283–287.

Miller, J. D. Effects of noise on people. *Journal of the Acoustical Society of America*, 1974, 56, 729–764.

Mills, J. M. Human circadian rhythms. *Physiological Review*, 1966, 46, 128–171.

Mills, J. M., Minors, D. S., & Waterhouse, J. M. The physiological rhythms of subjects living on a day of abnormal length. *Journal of Physiology*, 1977, 268, 803–876.

Naatanen, R. The inverted U relationship between activation and performance: A critical review. In S. Kornblum (Ed.), *Attention and performance IV*. New York: Academic Press, 1973.

Navon, D., & Gopher, D. On the economy of the human processing system. *Psychological Review*, 1979, 86, 214–255.

Neisser, U. *Cognitive psychology*. New York: Appleton-Century-Crofts, 1967.

Obrist, P. A. *Cardiovascular psychophysiology: A perspective*. New York: Plenum, 1981.

Obrist, P. A., Howard, J. L., Lawler, J. E., Galosy, R. A., Meyers, K. A., & Gaebelein, C. J. The cardiac–somatic interaction. In P. A. Obrist, A. H. Black, J. Brener, & L. V. DiCara (Eds.), *Cardiovascular psychophysiology: Current issues in response mechanisms, biofeedback and methodology*. Chicago: Aldine-Atherton, 1974.

Ohman, A. The orienting response, attention and learning: An information processing perspective. In H. D. Kimmel, E. H. Van Olst, & J. F. Orlebeke (Eds.), *The orienting reflex in humans*. Hillsdale, N.J.: Erlbaum, 1979.

Orr, W. C., Hoffman, H. J., & Hegge, F. W. The assessment of time dependent changes in human performance. *Chronobiologica*, 1976, 3, 293–305.

Parasuraman, R. Memory load and event rate control sensitivity decrements in sustained attention. *Science*, 1979, 205, 924–927.

Phelps, M. E., Kuhl, D. E., & Mazziotta, J. C. Metabolic mapping of the brain's response to visual stimulation: Studies in humans. *Science*, 1981, 211, 1445–1449.

Pillsbury, W. B. Attention waves as a means of measuring fatigue. *American Journal of Psychology*, 1903, 14, 277–288.

Porges, S. W., Bohrer, R. E., Cheung, M. N., Drasgow, F., McCabe, P. M., & Keren, G. New time-series statistic for detecting rhythmic co-occurrence in the frequency domain: The weighted coherence and its application to psychophysiological research. *Psychological Bulletin*, 1980, 88, 580–588.

Porges, S. W., & Coles, M. G. H. (Eds.). *Psychophysiology*. Stroudsberg, Pa.: Dowden, Hutchinson, & Ross, 1976.

Posner, M. I. *Chronometric explorations of mind*. Hillsdale, N.J.: Erlbaum, 1978.

Poulton, E. C. Continuous intense noise masks auditory feedback and inner speech. *Psychological Bulletin*, 1977, 84, 977–1001.

Poulton, E. C. Composite model for human performance in continuous noise. *Psychological Review*, 1979, 86, 361–375.

Putnam, L. E., Ross, L. E., & Graham, F. K. Cardiac orienting during "good" and "poor" differential eyelid conditioning. *Journal of Experimental Psychology*, 1974, 102, 563–573.

Revelle, W., Humphreys, M. S., Simon, L., & Gilliland, K. The interactive effect of personality, time of day, and caffeine: A test of the arousal model. *Journal of Experimental Psychology*, 1980, 109, 1–31.

Roy, C. S., & Sherrington, C. S. On the regulation of the blood supply of the brain. *Journal of Physiology*, 1890, 11, 85–108.

Sandman, C. A., McCanne, T. R., Kaiser, D. N., & Diamond, B. Heart rate and cardiac phase influences on visual perception.

Journal of Comparative and Physiological Psychology, 1977, 91, 189–202.

Scheving, L. E., Halberg, F., & Pauly, J. E. *Chronobiology*. Tokyo: Igaku Shoi, 1974.

Shiffrin, R. M., & Schneider, W. Controlled and automatic human information processing: II. Perceptual learning, automatic attending, and a general theory. *Psychological Review*, 1977, 84, 127–140.

Siddle, D. A. T., & Spinks, J. A. Orienting response and information processing: Some theoretical and empirical problems. In H. D. Kimmel, E. H. Van Olst, & J. F. Orlebeke (Eds), *The orienting reflex in humans*. Hillsdale, N.J.: Erlbaum, 1979.

Siegal, J. M., & Steele, C. M. Environmental distraction and interpersonal judgments. *British Journal of Social and Clinical Psychology*, 1980, 19, 23–32.

Slaughter, J. W. The fluctuations of the attention in some of their psychological relations. *American Journal of Psychology*, 1901, 12, 313–334.

Sokolov, E. N. *Perception and the conditioned reflex*. Oxford: Pergamon Press, 1963.

Sollberger, A. *Biological rhythm research*. Amsterdam: Elsevier, 1965.

Surowiak, J. F. Circadian rhythms. *Medical Biology*, 1978, 56, 119–127.

Tecce, J. J., & Cole, J. O. The distraction–arousal hypothesis, CNV, and schizophrenia. In D. I. Mostofsky (Ed.), *Behavior control and modification of physiological activity*. Englewood Cliffs, N.J.: Prentice-Hall, 1976.

Thayer, R. E., & Carey, D. Spatial stimulus generalization as a function of white noise and activation level. *Journal of Experimental Psychology*, 1974, 102, 539–542.

Walker, B. B., & Sandman, C. A. Human visual evoked responses are related to heart rate. *Journal of Comparative and Physiological Psychology*, 1979, 93, 717–729.

Weidner, G., & Matthews, K. A. Reported physical symptoms elicited by unpredictable events, and the Type A coronary-prone behavior pattern. *Journal of Personality and Social Psychology*, 1978, 36, 1213–1220.

Wickens, C. D. The effects of divided attention on information processing in manual tracking. *Journal of Experimental Psychology*, 1976, 2, 1–13.

Wickens, C. D. The structure of attentional resources. In R. S. Nickerson (Ed.), *Attention and performance VIII*. Hillsdale, N.J.: Erlbaum, 1980.

Williams, R. B., Poon, L. W., & Burdette, L. J. Locus of control and vasomotor response to sensory processing. *Psychosomatic Medicine*, 1977, 39, 127–133.

Woodworth, R. S. *Experimental psychology*. New York: Holt, 1938.

Zeiner, A. R. Individual differences in orienting response magnitude related to academic performance. In H. D. Kimmel, E. H. Van Olst, & J. F. Orlebeke (Eds.), *The orienting reflex in humans*. Hillsdale, N.J.: Erlbaum, 1979.

Chapter Fourteen

Memory, Thought, and Bodily Response

J. Richard Jennings

INTRODUCTION

Bodily correlates of memory and thought have had a more central role in psychological theory than the bodily correlates of attention considered in Chapter 13. For example, the learning theorists Hull and Tolman held differing views about the role of motor responses in mediating learned behavior. Hull (1943) suggested that learning could be explained by an associative chain of stimuli and responses (motoric, glandular or autonomic), whereas Tolman (1932) asserted that a concept of the task—a cognitive map—was developed. Thus, for Hull, ideation was ultimately based on motor action. Humphrey (1963) provides an excellent account of early arguments over motor theories of thought.

The organization of this chapter parallels that of Chapter 13. Three possible relations between bodily change and memory or thought are considered: (1) bodily change as an indicator of memory or thought; (2) bodily change as facilitating or inhibiting memory or thought; and (3) bodily regulation as a necessary condition for memory or thought. In addition, the chapter asks whether bodily change is related to a general process, such as attention, or to processes specific to memory or problem solving. Rather than attempt an exhaustive review, I have selected paradigms and response measures that are best suited to answer the questions posed. I hope, however, that conclusions drawn from this focused examination will have application to other paradigms and response measures.

BODILY CHANGE AS AN INDICATOR OF MEMORY AND THOUGHT

Relative to a resting state, an increase in physiological activity is observed during problem-solving and memory tasks (see review in Duffy, 1962). While this observation is commonplace, its interpretation is controversial. Arousal theorists, such as Duffy (1962, 1972) and Hebb (1955), identify these changes as increases in nonspecific energy, drive, or motivation elicited by the task. As such, any task should elicit physiological change in proportion to its motivational significance for the organism. However, drive state does not directly predict physiological change (e.g., Bartoshuk, 1971); and as we have seen in Chapter 13,

J. Richard Jennings. Department of Psychiatry, University of Pittsburgh, Pittsburgh, Pennsylvania.

some variables, such as heart rate, seem to respond to task demands rather than motivational demands. In particular, tasks requiring attentive observation initiate heart rate slowing rather than the speeding expected by arousal theorists. These heart rate findings raise the logical possibility that each psychological process may produce a different bodily response. For example, memory storage might be uniquely related to heart rate speeding and cognitive transformation to forearm muscle tension. Thus, specific cognitive processes, not an unspecific drive state, would induce physiological change.

Heart Rate, Memory, and Thought

How closely are memory and thought processes related to bodily change? To answer this question, I examine relevant data from the heart rate literature. This choice is based on the availability of data and the evidence (presented in Chapter 13) that heart rate is responsive to attentional aspects of information-processing tasks. The same studies that led the Laceys (B. C. Lacey & Lacey, 1974) to relate cardiac deceleration to environmental intake led them to relate cardiac acceleration to the rejection of environmental information and cognitive elaboration. One such study was reported by J. I. Lacey, Kagan, Lacey, and Moss (1963). Heart rate and skin conductance were measured as volunteers performed a battery of tasks. The tasks ranged from listening to white noise to solving anagrams. Little control was exerted over stimulus materials or response requirements. A regular pattern of results emerged, however: Two anagram-like tasks, mental arithmetic, and a cold pressor test produced cardiac acceleration, while listening to an emotional drama, noise, or watching flashing lights produced deceleration. An intermediate response (little change) occurred while volunteers listened to the rules of a fictitious game in preparation for a later quiz. In contrast, skin conductance increased in all tasks. The Laceys' conceptual summary of these results is the hypothesis that cardiac acceleration is related to rejection of environmental input or cognitive elaboration.

Subsequent research on the Laceys' hypothesis has been widely reviewed (e.g., Carroll & Anastasiades, 1978; Elliott, 1972; Hahn, 1973; B. C. Lacey & Lacey, 1974, 1978; J. I. Lacey & Lacey, 1974). The relation of cardiac acceleration to cognitive elaboration has not been as thoroughly studied as the relation of cardiac deceleration to information input. In the absence of further data, arousal theorists could claim that general arousal, not "rejection of the environment," induces cardiac acceleration. Thus, cardiac deceleration has been of greater interest than acceleration, because deceleration during information processing clearly challenges an arousal interpreta-

tion. There have, however, been studies that have questioned the association of cardiac acceleration with "rejection of environmental input." These studies examined heart rate change during the viewing of unpleasant scenes—for example, gruesome slides of auto accidents (Hare, Wood, Britain, & Frazelle, 1971). Many volunteers, although they emotionally "rejected" the slides (found them distasteful), nonetheless observed them closely. The deceleration of the heart rate that occurred was consistent with the attentive observation. Rejection was subsequently redefined as "motivated inattention" (B. C. Lacey & Lacey, 1978) because it referred to the control of input, not to the affective acceptance or rejection of a percept. Otherwise, the interpretation of cardiac acceleration has not been critically discussed (see Chapter 13 for general critiques of the Laceys' position).

A small literature exists, however, that does relate cardiac acceleration and information processing from the perspective of the Laceys' hypothesis. I examine these studies here in order to see whether cardiac acceleration is a reliable index of "cognitive elaboration," "motivated inattention," or some specific cognitive process. A number of early studies examined complex information-processing tasks that would be expected to require both information input (presumably eliciting deceleration) and information retention and manipulation (presumably eliciting acceleration). These early studies established that acceleration to anagram and mental arithmetic tasks (1) occurred in children and adults; (2) was a function of task difficulty; and (3) was enhanced when performance occurred in distracting noise (Adamowicz & Gibson, 1968; Costello & Hall, 1967; Gibson & Hall, 1966; Steele & Koons, 1968; Steele & Lewis, 1968). Furthermore, degree of heart rate acceleration seemed related to intelligence and developmental level of functioning (Jennings, 1971; Lacey *et al.*, 1963; Steele & Lewis, 1968). Using two Piagetian tasks, I (Jennings, 1971), for example, demonstrated that developmentally more mature children showed greater cardiac acceleration than less mature children exposed to identical tasks. The interpretation of such results, however, is not precise. Even within a Piagetian framework, the developmentally advanced children could be either divorcing themselves from the perceptual display, maintaining a representation of the display, cognitively transforming the input, or developing logical reasons for their judgments. Any or all of these factors might be associated with cardiac acceleration.

In other experiments (e.g., Jennings, 1975; Kahneman, Tursky, Shapiro, & Crider, 1969; Tursky, Schwartz, & Crider, 1970), an attempt was made to separate different aspects of the information processing required and to relate these to changes in heart rate. Kahneman *et al.*, (1969), for instance, asked volunteers to add 0, 1, or 3 to four integers that were subsequently presented. A 1-sec pause then preceded paced responding. Thus, volunteers in the +0 condition only had to remember the four integers as they were presented, while in other conditions the integers had to be memorized and transformed. Heart rate accelerated minimally during input with the +0 transform, accelerated an intermediate amount for the +1 transform, and accelerated most for the +3 transform. A decelerative recovery followed during the response interval. Cardiac acceleration seemed responsive to the difficulty of cognitive manipulation; however, attentive listening to the input items was also required. Therefore, might not deceleration have been expected? This concern was addressed by the simple manipulation of placing the transformation instruction *after* the input of the items (Tursky *et al.*, 1970). The influence of attentive listening could then be examined, albeit with a small (four-item) memory load. Under these conditions, cardiac deceleration (relative to the acceleration seen at task onset) was observed during item input. Acceleration was subsequently observed while items were maintained in memory and transformed. Thus, different processes required by a single task were associated with different directions of heart rate change. At a descriptive level, the Laceys' distinction between environmental intake and cognitive elaboration was supported. Going beyond this description, the experiment suggested that both maintenance in memory and cognitive transformation influenced cardiac acceleration.

The question of whether cardiac acceleration was related to any specific cognitive process was further pursued (Jennings, 1975). Holding stimulus and response requirements essentially constant, the relative influence on cardiac acceleration was examined for memory, transformation, and energy demands. As in the Tursky *et al.* (1970) study, the tasks were paced in time in order to separate information input and cognitive requirements. Each task began with a 5-sec presentation of 6 one- to two-digit numbers. This was followed by a task instruction stipulating further silent reading of the input, memory maintenance, addition with the numbers visually available, addition from memory, or discovery of the transformation that made column 1 of the display equal to column 2. Thus, relative to the Tursky *et al.* (1970) experiment, memory difficulty was increased (6 one- to two-digit numbers vs. 4 integers), items were visually presented in a single display, and cognitive transformation and stimulus availability were varied. In contrast to the Tursky *et al.* (1970) results, the initial period of information input and memorization produced a strong cardiac acceleration. Presumably, the relatively greater memory load induced acceleration that masked deceleration due to information input (see below).

Figure 14-1 shows the results from the task performance period. Silent reading and rule discovery tasks produced a deceleration relative to the input response. Maintaining items in memory ("Store") re-

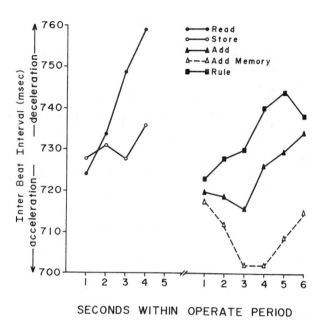

SECONDS WITHIN OPERATE PERIOD

Figure 14-1. Second-by-second changes in interbeat interval during the performance of five tasks. Responses during the "Read" and "Store" tasks are shown on the left, while those for the "Add," "Add Memory," and "Rule" tasks are shown on the right. Average interbeat interval in a comparable interval prior to task initiation was 740 msec; the average during the input and memorization of the items was 725 msec. (From "Information Processing and Concomitant Heart Rate Changes in the Overweight and Underweight" by J. R. Jennings. *Physiological Psychology*, 1975, 3, 290–296. Reprinted by permission of the Psychonomic Society.)

sulted in heart rates continuing at about the same level as during input. Mental arithmetic produced cardiac acceleration that was brief when items were visually available ("Add"), but more sustained when items were added from memory ("Add Memory"). The most surprising result is the deceleration in the "Rule" task. Volunteers judged this task to be difficult, and solution of the task typically required multiple attempts at "fitting" the two sets of numbers. In the "Rule" as well as the "Read" and "Add" tasks, however, the availability of visual display seemed to induce decelerative change. On the other hand, the requirement to maintain items in memory seemed to prevent any decelerative change. The requirement to transform ("Add") items from memory produced the clearest acceleration.

These results (Jennings, 1975) suggest that either memory or "motivated inattention" (the Laceys' position) controls cardiac acceleration. Cognitive manipulation seems capable of augmenting, but not initiating, acceleration. Subjective ratings of "energy required," however, correlated well with cardiac acceleration. In order to decide whether memory load, motivated inattention, or energy demand initiated cardiac acceleration, an additional experiment was performed. This experiment (Jennings & Hall, 1980) explicitly manipulated memory load and collected self-reports of energy demand. During a 5.6-sec input period, a set varying between 5 and 10 items was visually presented. A 5.6-sec retention period followed, which was terminated by a recognition test (Experiment 1) or a recall test (Experiment 2). Set size effectively manipulated performance and self-reports of difficulty. Thus, if memory load and acceleration were directly linked, cardiac acceleration would be positively related to set size. This did not occur, although cardiac acceleration was present in both the input and retention periods. Furthermore, ratings of task difficulty (energy demand) were also unrelated to cardiac acceleration. The failure of memory load or self-reported difficulty to predict acceleration indirectly supported the Laceys' direction-of-attention hypothesis.

Thus, attempts to relate cardiac acceleration to a specific cognitive process other than the direction of attention were unsuccessful. Although this negative evidence is hardly conclusive, it is supplemented by positive evidence. Information-processing tasks that produce accelerative responses include mental arithmetic, anagrams, memorizing, retention, logical reasoning (see Jennings & Hall, 1980), decision making (Coles & Duncan-Johnson, 1975), response selection (Coles & Duncan-Johnson, 1975), and cognitive imaging (Schwartz & Higgins, 1971). Acceleration is not found in tasks primarily requiring attention to input. Other investigations of memory and psychophysiology (Silverstein & Berg, 1977) have also interpreted their results as due to an attention process, not to memory processes per se. Thus, we return to the Laceys' formulation that deceleration is related to sensory intake and acceleration to sensory rejection or motivated inattention (Lacey et al., 1963; B. C. Lacey & Lacey, 1978). This formulation of the Laceys has, however, been rightfully criticized for vagueness (Carroll & Anastasiades, 1978; Hahn, 1973; see Chapter 13). Can the Laceys' viewpoint be stated so that it is both more precise and also more relevant to current views of information processing?

Processing Capacity and Heart Rate Changes

Although not without its own problems, a concept of attention in terms of information-processing capacity suggests measures that may be useful in redefining the "motivated inattention" related to cardiac acceleration. Information-processing concepts have previously been related to psychophysiology by Kahneman (1973). Obvious limitations exist on humans' capability to process information. Most particularly, we are frequently unable to perform two tasks simultaneously and well, even though we are quite able to perform each task well individually. If we know, how-

ever, that one task is more important than the other, we can perform it well and allow performance on the other to suffer. Thus, some resource (i.e., attention) can be committed to improve performance on selected activities. The quantity of this resource may be fixed or flexible, and its effectiveness in enhancing performance may or may not depend on the activity supported (see Kahneman, 1973; Navon & Gopher, 1979; Wickens, 1980). The assumptions most useful for measurement purposes are that attention (the resource) has a fixed capacity and that its facilitative effects apply to any process. A physiological expression of such a resource might be metabolic energy. Over brief periods, at least, energy available may be fixed, and all physiological processes are potential consumers. Given these assumptions, a dual-task methodology provides a measure of attention. Two tasks are selected that, when performed together, exceed the fixed processing capacity. One task is then defined as primary, so that performance on it is equal to that obtained when it is performed alone. Performance of the second task then becomes a function of the capacity "left over" from the primary task. When performance on the secondary task is good, the capacity demands of the primary task are assumed to be low (see Kerr, 1973). When performance on the secondary task is poor, the demands of the primary task are assumed to be high.

What are the implications for the Laceys' hypothesis? First, such a concept of attention suggests that cardiac acceleration, as well as deceleration, would be associated with attention. The resource of attention will presumably be committed as readily to tasks inducing deceleration (e.g., a fixed-foreperiod reaction time [RT] task) as to tasks inducing acceleration (e.g., mental arithmetic). Direction of attention, not attention–inattention, determines whether acceleration or deceleration occurs. Second, a secondary-task measure of attention should correlate well with cardiac acceleration during a cognitive task, such as mental arithmetic. Attention directed to ongoing cognitive processing would presumably induce cardiac acceleration. If a secondary-task measure also indexes attention allocated to the processing, cardiac acceleration and secondary-task performance should be correlated. As discussed below, however, the association of attentional processes with both acceleration and deceleration complicates this prediction.

The relation of cardiac acceleration and secondary-task performance was examined in a serial learning task (Jennings, Lawrence, & Kasper, 1978). A learning task was used that compared the retention of randomly selected (experimental) and ordered (rote) two-digit numbers. Dependent measures were performance on a secondary RT task and heart rate (expressed as interbeat interval [IBI]). Differences between rote and experimental trials, learning and retention periods, and seconds within the trials all supported an inverse relation between IBI and RT (the secondary task). These relations are illustrated in Figure 14-2. The top panel, from left to right, indicates that RT increased progressively between ROTE: LEARNING and EXPER: ANTICIPATION. "ANTICIPATION" refers to the retention test, which required the volunteer to verbalize the number that would appear next as list items were sequentially presented. The bottom panel indicates that IBI decreased progressively between ROTE: LEARNING and EXPER: ANTICIPATION. An interpretation of these results might be that the processing capacity (attention) required by the primary task increased between ROTE: LEARNING and EXPER: ANTICIPATION, and thus secondary RT was lengthened and IBI was shortened (or, equivalently, heart rate increased). In contrast to the convergence of RT and IBI results, subjective ratings of effort failed to relate to either RT or IBI. Thus, the results questioned a simple arousal interpretation and supported the association of heart rate acceleration and processing capacity.

A processing capacity orientation has the virtue of providing a theoretical mechanism for heart rate change and a measurement paradigm for independently assessing "attention." Not all problems have been surmounted, however. The most critical problem is that of the multiple factors influencing both secondary task measures and heart rate. For example, we (Jennings et al., 1978) found that IBI and RT were not inversely related between trials (see Figure 14-2). Post hoc analyses suggested that RT was influenced by time on task. Only early in the experimental session was IBI change over trials inversely related to RT. During later trials, volunteers may have withdrawn capacity from both the primary and secondary tasks. Thus, late in the task, an assumption of the dual-task paradigm may have been violated: Total capacity may not have been solely devoted to the performance of the two tasks.

Details of the heart rate results also suggest a complication in the relation of heart rate and attentional capacity. We (Jennings et al., 1978) asked whether either secondary-task or cardiac measures of attention were related to subsequent memory performance. Presumably, greater attention to the memory task (i.e., poorer RT performance and greater cardiac acceleration) would result in enhanced memory. In fact, relative cardiac deceleration, not acceleration, was associated with the learning of items subsequently anticipated correctly (probe RT was relatively slow, as expected). The finding can be explained if relative deceleration reflects heightened perceptual attention to these items—a factor that would be expected to enhance performance. This interpretation raises the problem. If both heart rate acceleration and deceleration are associated with impaired secondary-task performance, then the vagueness of the Laceys' hypothesis has not been eliminated. Gradations of processing

capacity may be detected, but we have not separated intention to note and detect input from motivated inattention. Such a separation would be possible if deceleration were associated with broad rather than with focused attention (see discussion in Chapter 13). If deceleration predominantly indexes a broad focus of attention (generalized alertness to input), then deceleration to a primary task should actually enhance performance of a secondary input detection task. In this case, facilitation of detection would relate to deceleration, and inhibition of detection would relate to acceleration. The current finding of deceleration associated with slowed secondary-task RT suggests, however, that deceleration may sometimes reflect focused attention (see other evidence discussed in Chapter 13). Thus, further work may be needed to find an objective index of direction of attention, or, in the Laceys' terms, "motivated inattention" and intention to note and detect input. Such work seems likely, however, to build upon the framework of secondary- or probe-task measures of attention.

This discussion has indirectly led to a problem with the dual-task paradigm—the comparability of different secondary tasks. I have implied that a secondary input detection task might yield different results from those of a secondary task not involving detection (e.g., a finger-tapping or memory task). Indeed, such results have been found (see Navon & Gopher, 1979; Wickens, 1980). These results imply that processing capacity is not a simple, undifferentiated resource that can facilitate any cognitive process. Rather, interference between primary and secondary tasks may depend on the degree of specific resources (e.g., memory transformation) momentarily shared by the two tasks. The complexity implied by such an assumption is thoroughly developed in Navon and Gopher (1979). At present, however, I hesitate to adopt the full complexity of their model; instead, I pursue the distinction made by the heart. Tasks may be classified on the basis of whether they produce cardiac acceleration or deceleration. Following Jennings et al. (1978) or B. C. Lacey and Lacey (1978), we might suspect that sharing attention between two tasks producing deceleration might be more efficient than shifting between a task producing acceleration and one producing deceleration. Facilitation of a secondary detection task might even occur during deceleration initiated by a primary task. Although this suggestion is speculative, it can be empirically tested and it provides an alternative to the Navon and Gopher (1979) account of why all secondary tasks do not yield uniform results.

Interpretive Summary

In this section, I have asked whether complex information processing is associated with reliable bodily

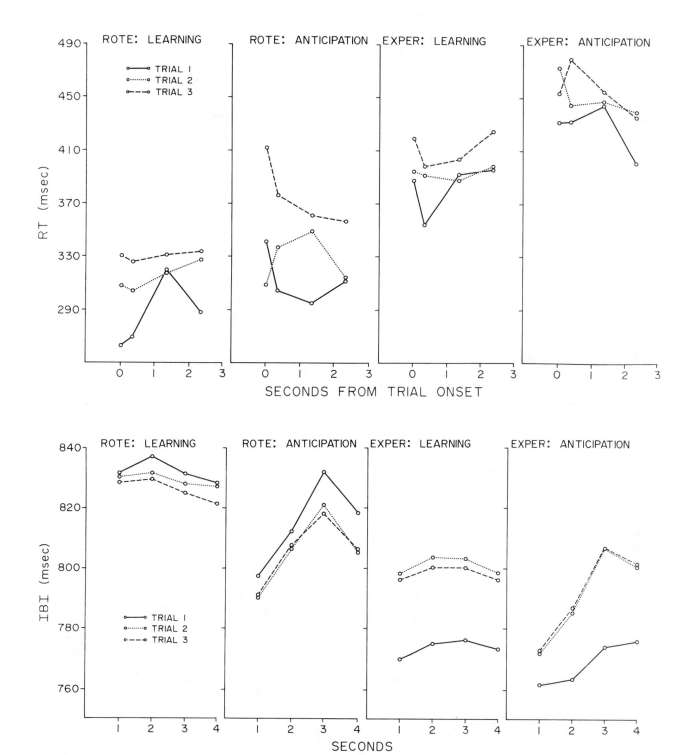

Figure 14-2. Secondary-task performance (reaction time, RT) and interbeat interval (IBI) during the performance of a serial learning task with either randomly ordered numbers (experimental condition) or serially ordered numbers (rote or control condition). Three trials of learning and anticipation are shown. The top panel (A) shows the RT results, and the bottom panel (B) shows the IBI results. If both secondary-task and IBI measures reflect attention to the primary task, RT and IBI should be inversely related. (From "Changes in Alertness and Processing Capacity in a Serial Learning Task" by J. R. Jennings, B. E. Lawrence, and P. Kasper. *Memory and Cognition*, 1978, 6, 45–63. Reprinted by permission of the Psychonomic Society.)

responses. Noting the wealth of data suggesting a positive answer (e.g., Duffy, 1962), I have sought to characterize this relationship more specifically. To do so, the relation of heart rate change to information processing has been examined. Cardiac deceleration appears to be related to anticipation and detection to information input, and cardiac acceleration seems related to further processing of that information (i.e., storage, transformation). There is little evidence to suggest that cardiac acceleration is related to a specific cognitive process, such as mental transformation. Rather, heart rate acceleration seems related to the directing of attention to cognitive processing, to the exclusion of further input. Furthermore, cardiac acceleration during information processing appears unrelated to gradations of reported arousal. Measurement issues related to the Laceys' hypothesis and its revisions have been discussed.

In conclusion, direction of attention within complex information processing is reflected in heart rate change. Furthermore, performance in complex tasks seems weakly correlated with heart rate change (Jennings & Hall, 1980). Thus, we may conclude that heart rate is an acceptable indicator of cognitive processing, given that other factors, such as motoric demands, are controlled.

BODILY CHANGE AS A FACILITATOR OF MEMORY AND THOUGHT

This section examines evidence that has been put forth to answer the question of whether bodily state facilitates or inhibits complex information processing. This question presumes that the bodily state is not caused by the information processing itself, but rather by an external influence (e.g., environmental noise), or an aspect of the task (e.g., its emotional impact), independent of information processing per se. Work in this area has typically been conceptualized as the effect of general arousal on performance. Chapter 13 discusses this use of the concept of general arousal. Briefly, general arousal is presumed to be a state indicated by the concurrent activation of behavioral, subjective, and physiological symptoms. Experiments using the "arousal" concept are discussed, although I am critical of the concept. These experiments manipulate a number of factors, such as stimulus meaning, drug state, and noise. These manipulations are presumed to alter arousal and thus complex information processing.

Perhaps the most well-known experiment on arousal and memory is that of Kleinsmith and Kaplan (1963). These investigators measured skin conductance responses during one slow-paced, paired-associate learning trial. Word–number pairs were used

with some words such as "Rape," chosen to elicit arousal. A word was presented first for 4 sec; then the word–number pair was presented, followed by a filler task (8 sec of naming colors from a display). This sequence was repeated for the eight items tested. Retention was tested in the same manner, but omitting the word–number pair slides. Different groups of subjects were tested for retention at 2 min, 20 min, 45 min, 24 hr, and 1 week. High-arousal items were defined by the amplitude of skin conductance responses to initial word presentation. At the 2-min interval, 45% of the low-arousal items were correctly paired with numbers, but only 8% of the high-arousal items were correct. Retention of high- and low-arousal pairs was equal at 20 min, but by 45 min and subsequently, some 40% of high-arousal items were retained, in contrast to only some 12% of the low-arousal items. Note that a clear reminiscence effect occurred between groups: High-arousal items were unlikely to be retained at 2 min, but were likely to be retained after 45 min. Thus Kleinsmith and Kaplan (1963) reported strong arousal effects on memory and demonstrated a reminiscence effect—a relatively rare finding in memory research.

Kleinsmith and Kaplan (1963) interpreted these results as showing that a bodily state of arousal alters cognitive processes. Arousal was said to facilitate long-term memory by improving a consolidation process. Short-term memory (defined in the 2-min vs. 1-week time frame) was impaired by the same process. High arousal induced lengthier consolidation than low arousal, and memory traces were said to be unavailable during the process of consolidation. Thus item-induced arousal apparently acted both to facilitate and to inhibit memory.

Two reviews (Craik & Blankstein, 1975; Eysenck, 1976) have examined the Kleinsmith and Kaplan (1963) effects in detail, so my discussion of subsequent work is brief. The results have been replicated a number of times. The effect is found when nonsense syllables rather than words have been used, and during both incidental and intentional learning. Arousal during retention tests (as opposed to learning) seems unrelated to memory. The free-recall (item memory) paradigm seems to produce different results from paired-associate memory. Free-recall experiments have in general shown that arousal (i.e., skin conductance change) is positively related to recall at all time intervals; no decrease in immediate recall of high-arousal items is observed. The paired-associate paradigm of Kleinsmith and Kaplan has, however, repeatedly produced results replicating the original findings. The differences between paradigms in the facilitation versus inhibition of immediate memory is interesting. The free-recall paradigm, in contrast to the paired-associate paradigm, requires only recollection of the items presented, not recollection of the associations between items. Thus, the presence of the reminiscence effect in the paired-associate task and its absence in the free-recall task suggests that associations between items are initially unavailable and later strengthened due to high arousal. The difference between the results from the two paradigms seems to support the original interpretation of Kleinsmith and Kaplan.

Studies based on the Kleinsmith–Kaplan design have generally used only skin conductance response to index arousal. The use of several converging measures of arousal has not been attempted. At least two studies employing heart rate rather than skin conductance (Jennings & Hall, 1980; Jennings *et al.*, 1978) failed to find item-related suppression of recognition, free recall, or serial learning. Small, but significant, correlations in these studies suggested that deceleration during item input and acceleration during rehearsal was related to improved memory performance. This finding is consistent with the results relating skin conductance changes to free recall. Unfortunately, no one seems to have studied heart rate change in the paired-associate paradigm used by Kleinsmith and Kaplan.

In their discussion, Craik and Blankstein (1975) discuss major problems with the acceptance of the Kleinsmith–Kaplan interpretation, but no alternative explanation is offered. The Kleinsmith and Kaplan explanation requires consolidation processes in memory; however, little if any evidence, other than their study, supports the existence of such processes. Subsequent work has sought different paradigms in which arousal could be readily manipulated and its effect on a variety of memory tasks observed. One approach uses environmental noise to manipulate arousal. Chapter 13 reviews the background and assumptions for this approach. Most investigations using this approach do not measure physiological responses. Noise combined with performance of a task can generally be assumed, however, to induce physiological change. Early work using noise-induced arousal rather than stimulus-induced arousal (see Craik & Blankstein, 1975; Eysenck, 1976) found results similar to those of Kleinsmith and Kaplan (1963), but the association of arousal with enhanced long-term retention was more consistent than association with a short-term retention decrement. More recent work has reported effects of noise on only certain aspects of memory. We can now turn to this work in hopes of finding an alternative to the arousal–consolidation interpretation of Kleinsmith and Kaplan.

A recent surge of interest in the influence of moderately intense noise (70–90 dBA) on memory has, indeed, resulted in a proliferation of research and interpretations. The impact of this work has largely been to emphasize the complexity of noise-induced (implicitly, arousal-induced) effects on memory. Despite the complexity, specific hypothesis are being considered in an orderly examination of noise-induced influences on memory. A brief review of three of these hypotheses will illustrate a promising research strategy, as well as review current evidence relevant to the facilitation or inhibition of memory processes by bodily processes.

The first hypothesis suggests that noise facilitates the learning of item order or sequence. Hamilton, Hockey, and Quinn (1972) examined paired-associate learning in noise and quiet. Two procedures for retention testing were used: testing with pairs in the same serial order as learning, and testing with a randomized order. According to Hamilton *et al.* (1972), the latter test procedure was used by Kleinsmith and Kaplan (1963). The results showed that noise ("arousal") improved short-term retention with the fixed order of testing, but not with the randomized order. A nonsignificant difference between noise and quiet in the randomized condition suggested that noise impaired short-term retention. Hamilton *et al.* (1972) interpret their results by suggesting that noise strengthens retention of ordered information. Recall of order, however, is of little benefit for the randomized retention test. Thus, noise may have induced inappropriate learning. This, then, is a partial explanation of the decrement in short-term retention reported by Kleinsmith and Kaplan: Noise biases learning strategies in favor of order information. Different aspects of learned material are acquired in noise relative to quiet; consequently, retention over time is different for items learned in noise relative to those learned in quiet.

Two studies (Daee & Wilding, 1977; A. P. Smith, Jones, & Broadbent, 1981) have reported extensive tests of a particular version of the hypothesis relating noise and item order learning. In both studies, lists of items were presented in a free-recall task. List items, although randomly ordered, were members of specific categories (e.g., animal names, household objects, military ranks). The specific hypothesis suggested that noise would induce recall of item order, and thus would decrease recall based on categories. Typically, categorized lists lead to recall in which all the items of a category are recalled together in clusters. Both studies showed that under certain conditions noise reduced the amount of clustering in recall and increased recall by sequence or order. Weakly categorical items or items from exhaustive categories (e.g., military ranks) were not altered by noise. Furthermore, manipulations that specifically induced recall by category or order eliminated the noise effect. Noise did not seem necessarily to facilitate or interfere with one form of learning; rather, it biased the learning strategy of the individual. Daee and Wilding (1977) specifically examined the strategy used to recall the order of items. Their results showed an enhancement of strategy to remember order at the expense of category membership. A. P. Smith *et al.* (1981) failed, however, to find strong evidence of recall of order interfering with recall by category. Overall, these two reports have refined the conditions necessary to see a noise effect, and have generally supported the Hamilton *et al.* (1972) suggestion that noise may induce a strategy of learning the order of item input.

A second hypothesis suggests that noise induces a lower order of information processing. Assume first that items can be processed to different depths. For example, an item may be superficially processed on the basis of its physical characteristics, such as size or brightness, or processed more deeply on the basis of its meaning. Processing based on item order may then be defined as less deep than processing based on meaning (e.g., category membership). This view has been expressed by Eysenck (1976, 1977) and Dornic (1973). The evidence of both Daee and Wilding (1977) and A. P. Smith *et al.* (1981), however, questions this attractive hypothesis. Furthermore, A. P. Smith and Broadbent (1981) report a direct test of the hypothesis that fails to support it. Thus, it seems that the general framework of level of processing is not a useful explanation.

Finally, Hamilton and Hockey (Hockey, 1979; Hamilton, Hockey, & Rejman, 1977) have suggested the hypothesis that noise alters emphasis on working storage in favor of faster throughput in item processing. They examined the influence of noise on running-memory span and working memory. The running-memory task presented a continuous visual series of letters. At unpredictable points, a recall cue required the sequential recall of the last eight letters. In noise, the last three or four letters presented were better recalled than in quiet. The first three or four letters were, however, more likely to be forgotten in noise. Seemingly, "here and now" processing was favored at the expense of long-term retention. If this is true, then cognitive transformation of recent times should be performed well in noise—but only if the memory load required by the transformation is low. This interpretation was tested by combining a letter transformation task factorially with a memory load factor. In noise, performance on combinations with high transformation requirements and low memory loads was better than on combinations with high memory loads and low transformation requirements. Taken together, the two studies clearly support the hypothesis that noise increases emphasis on the "here and now" throughput to the neglect of storage of less recent items. This interpretation is attractive and accords well with results showing that noise induces selective attention to salient, high-probability events (see Chapter 13), and with results showing that memory span improves as arousal decreases (due to sleep deprivation) (Hamilton, Wilkinson, & Edwards, 1972). The interpretation suggests, however, that noise reduces working memory for ordered items and implicitly thereby reduces long-term storage. The Hamilton *et al.* (1972) results reviewed above question any noise-induced reduction in working memory, while any noise-induced reduction in long-term memory is questioned by the bulk of research on the Kleinsmith–Kaplan effect (which shows increased long-term retention with arousal). In short, this hypothesis is not consistent with previous findings in the area.

These recent studies of noise and memory retain, to differing extents, the hypothesis that noise influences memory by altering physiological arousal. The results do not demand such an interpretation, however. Noise does seem to shift learning strategies away from coding by associative meaning and toward coding by order (or spatial cues; see Broadbent, 1981). This shift might be due to a specific interference of noise with strategies using acoustic processing (e.g., verbal rehearsal; see Broadbent, 1981). Alternate strategies, such as coding by spatial location or order, would be free of such interference. If this account is true, arousal would not directly facilitate or interfere with memory. Arousal during noise might well be due to the effort involved in changing learning strategies, not to noise per se. Noise may lead, for example to a greater use of spatial strategy, but there would be no reason to suggest that arousal induces spatial strategies. Physiological change would thus be a function of task demands, rather than an independent state altering subsequent information processing. Any conclusion is premature, however. The noise studies, in general, have not measured any physiological index of arousal and have not shown that other arousal-inducing agents (e.g., drugs, social presence) produce effects similar to noise. Arousal has not truly been tested in the recent experiments using noise. Thus, we may turn to other approaches relating arousal and complex processes.

Arousal, Direction of Attention, and Complex Processes

Two further experiments are discussed that are relevant to the question of whether bodily change facilitates memory or complex information processing. These experiments are discussed because they examine complex processes—that is, achievement test performance and reading comprehension, rather than laboratory memory tasks. In addition, the first experiment illustrates problems with the concept of general arousal, and the second shows facilitation of processing without employing general arousal as a guiding concept.

Revelle, Humphreys, Simon, and Gilliland (1980) examined achievement test performance as a function of three factors all presumably influencing general arousal: personality (introversion–extraversion), stimulant drug (caffeine), and time of day (morning vs. evening). Their report is an important attempt to define arousal by converging operations. If arousal is a unitary concept, as is implied by the concept of general arousal, one would expect individual differences in arousal to be additive with exogenously induced arousal. The individual difference dimension of introversion–extraversion was assumed to represent an overaroused–underaroused dimension. Revelle *et al.* (1980) reported seven separate experiments involving single and multiple sessions over 1 or 2 days of testing. Their results did not support the notion of a unitary concept: The three factors did not show simple additive effects. Revelle *et al.* (1980), however, attempted to modify the arousal concepts to fit their results.

The Revelle *et al.* (1980) interpretation shows how complex the concept of general arousal must become in order to fit the data even partially. In their results, arousal due to caffeine interacted with individual differences, but the relationship was modulated by time of day. Conceptually, differing times of day represent differing arousal states as determined by the 24-hr rhythm of the sleep–wake cycle. High-impulsive individuals (individuals high in the impulsive component of extraversion) were thought to be underaroused relative to low-impulsive individuals. Thus high impulsives had been expected to improve their performance when stimulated by caffeine or tested in the afternoon. In fact, the results were not this simple. Impulsivity seemed to be expressed in timing of arousal, not level of arousal. High impulsives were postulated to show peak arousal after noon, while low impulsives were postulated to show peak arousal before noon. Given this revision, caffeine was expected to reduce morning performance in low impulsives and evening performance in high impulsives (the overaroused effect). Conversely, caffeine was expected to assist the morning performance of high impulsives and the evening performance of low impulsives. The results of Revelle *et al.* (1980) showed precisely this pattern for Day 1 performance. Day 2 data were inconsistent, however, and no clear explanation for this is offered by the authors.

The interpretation of general arousal offered by Revelle *et al.* (1980) is not convincing. The intended arousal manipulations are either influencing arousal in a very complex manner or are, in fact, influencing not one but a variety of processes. Eysenck and Folkard (1980) further discuss problems with Revelle *et al.*'s (1980) interpretation of general arousal. In their critique, they cite physiological data questioning the assumption that the timing of peak arousal could differ by several hours between high and low impulsives. In short, Eysenck and Folkard (1980) use a physiologically based concept of arousal to question the Revelle *et al.* (1980) interpretation. Logically, arousal could be (following Revelle *et al.*, 1980) a hypothetical construct defined by similar effects of a variety of (arousal-altering) agents. The complex interpretation required by the Revelle *et al.* (1980) Day 1 results weakens this logic, however, as does the failure to explain the Day 2 results. A physiological concept seems demanded, although this concept must be more complex than the concept of general arousal (cf. Eysenck & Folkard, 1980; Revelle, Simon & Gilliland, 1980).

Given the conceptual problems with arousal, it is not surprising that some recent work has examined bodily states and mental processing without employing the concept of arousal. Cacioppo (1979) provides a striking example of a change in performance induced by a specific physiological change, heart rate acceleration. Arguing from the Laceys' hypothesis, Cacioppo (1979) suggested that the induction of cardiac acceleration should facilitate mental elaboration. In order to test this suggestion, heart rate was altered in patients with cardiac pacemakers. Heart rate could be altered between 72 and 88 beats per minute (bpm) by placing a capped or uncapped magnet over the pacemaker. As in the Revelle *et al.* (1980) study, complex performance tasks were used—reading comprehension, and sentence and argument generation. The results showed enhanced performance on all these tasks when the heart was paced at 88 bpm rather than 72 bpm. Bodily change seemed to facilitate performance rather directly. The experiment had a number of interesting features. First, although the experimenter knew which magnet was used, the patients were not able to perceive differences in heart rate level. Second, when uncapped, the pacemaker only prevented heart rate from falling below 72 bpm (i.e., cardiac pacing only occurred when a normal rate failed to be maintained). Thus, heart rate acceleration induced by the task in the uncapped condition may have, in some cases, exceeded 72 bpm. Actual heart rates were not reported.

Although Cacioppo's results were clear, they need to be replicated. Other studies manipulating heart rate have failed to find differences in mental performance. Neither Cacioppo (1979) nor other investigators (e.g., Westerhaus, Jensen, Steinberg, Callahan, Maslang, & Stern, 1976) have been able to demonstrate consistently enhanced performance in college students due to physiological maneuvers that change heart rate, such as postural change or exercise. Thus, either the pacemaker manipulation is uniquely effective, or performance facilitation is not a reliable effect of heart rate change. Furthermore, at least one group of investigators (Nowlin, Eisdorfer, Whalen, & Troyer, 1971) previously failed to find clear effects of cardiac pacing on RT performance. Thus, the results of Cacioppo (1979) are an important demonstration that heart rate acceleration in the absence of other significant bodily change can enhance complex cognitive performance. Complete acceptance of a facilitative effect of heart rate change must, however, await replication of this study.

Interpretive Summary

This section has examined the possibility that exogenously induced changes in bodily response might facilitate or interfere with memory or cognitive functioning.

First, the literature suggesting that general physiological arousal during learning alters short- and long-term memory has been examined. Of central interest is the Kleinsmith and Kaplan (1963) finding that items associated with relatively large skin conductance response were not recalled at short delays (2 min) but were recalled at long ones ($\geq$45 min). A number of theoretical psychophysiological concepts might be described to explain the effect on long-term retention. Such speculations do not, however, explain the decrements in short-term memory. As argued well by Craik and Blankstein (1975), Kleinsmith and Kaplan's original explanation seems unsatisfactory. A renewed empirical attempt to understand this phenomenon might focus on combining psychophysiological measures with the noise paradigm that has succeeded a number of times in conceptually replicating the Kleinsmith–Kaplan result. This strategy may be particularly potent, given the success of Hockey, Broadbent, and others in demonstrating the effect of noise on specific memory strategies. At present, we can only point to fascinating but unexplained effects of arousal-related manipulations on memory.

Methodologically, in many of the studies reviewed, the concept of general arousal has been used without any measure of arousal. Ideally, arousal should be established by converging measures of physiology, self-report, and behavior. None of the studies in this area appear to have provided adequate measures of the construct according to these criteria.

The limitations of the concept of arousal have also been discussed. Unfortunately, ample external evidence exists to question the existence of a unitary dimension of general arousal (see Chapter 13). One study that made a reasonably complete attempt to establish the arousal construct has been reviewed—that of Revelle et al. (1980). The complex results of this study suggest that interpretation in terms of general arousal is less justified than interpretation in terms of more situationally specific arousal processes modified by individual differences.

Finally, one study has been examined that did not use arousal changes as an explanation of an induced change in complex information processing. Cacioppo (1979) suggested that accelerative heart rate change,

when exogenously induced, may facilitate complex information processing. Interpretively, acceleration was seen as supporting attention to cognitive processes (see the preceding section). Considerable work needs to be done, however, in replicating and identifying which specific information processes are influenced (if any) and in understanding the exact physiological changes induced by cardiac pacing. All in all, a moderate amount of support has been found for the proposition that bodily change may facilitate memory and complex information processing. Our understanding of how such facilitation might occur is, however, rudimentary.

BIOLOGICAL REGULATION AS A REGULATOR OF MEMORY AND THOUGHT

In this section, I examine the possibility that the physiological regulation of bodily functions places limits on cognitive performance. In extreme states, this proposition is obviously true—for example, during illness or starvation. I restrict my focus, however, to the day-to-day functioning of the normal individual. In previous sections, bodily changes have been discussed that occur concomitantly with cognitive functioning and that might be facilitory or inhibitory. Such relationships do not imply logical necessity, however. Consider, for example, the effect of a mnemonic strategy, such as visualizing, on the recall of unconnected words. Visualizing may facilitate recall, but recall can occur without visualizing. Visualizing is thus facilitative but not logically necessary for recall. The possibility is now considered that bodily changes may be necessary for basic cognitive functions.

Two areas of research are examined to provide a focused answer to this query. First, biological rhythms seem to be endogenous cycles related to bodily regulation. Kleitman's (1963) observation of cyclicities over time in performance led him to suggest that the cyclic regulation of cerebral blood flow or body temperature causes the cycles of performance efficiency. Second, overt and covert muscular responses have been considered since antiquity as a potential mechanism for thought (see McGuigan, 1978). Such theories as Watson's motor theory of thought (see Humphrey, 1963) suggest that thought is no more than chains of previously learned autonomic and motor responses. This is, of course, a direct claim that bodily responses are necessary for cognitive function.

Circadian Rhythm and Memory

Over a period of 24 hr, most of us experience a cycle of sleep and wakefulness that is graded between deep sleep and periods of full alertness. The changes in performance associated with this cycle are discussed in Chapter 13. Performances on a broad range of tasks (e.g., RT and problem solving) seem roughly to follow the 24-hr rhythm of body temperature. Performance is lowest in the depths of the night and then improves, gradually peaking in the late afternoon. A major exception to this trend is performance on memory tasks. These tasks seem to be performed as well or better in early morning than in early or midafternoon.

Folkard and Monk (1980) briefly review the literature and present two experiments on circadian effects on human memory. Part of the current theoretical interest relates to the Kleinsmith–Kaplan effect on short- and long-term memory. The 24-hr (circadian) cycle is sometimes conceptualized as a cycle of general arousal, with core body temperature being used as an index of arousal. Given such a stance, the Kleinsmith–Kaplan effect suggests that memory performance should differ among times of day differing in arousal level. The low arousal of morning should produce relatively good short-term memory performance ("short-term" meaning "within 2 min") but relatively poor long-term retention. The high arousal of late afternoon should produce the opposite effect. Evidence from studies of diurnal rhythms largely supports this generalization from the work of Kleinsmith and Kaplan. Folkard and Monk (1980) review several studies of short-term digit span and recall tests that show improved performance between 10 A.M. and 12 noon relative to other times. Further, two additional studies support enhanced long-term retention due to presentation during periods of relatively high arousal (see also Hockey & Colquhoun, 1972). Thus, the effect of time of day on memory seems to mimic that of item-induced arousal in the Kleinsmith–Kaplan paradigm.

Folkard and Monk (1980) report two experiments replicating previous work and also testing alternative explanations for the effect of time of day on memory. The first experiment asked whether the recall of complex prose passages would show time-of-day effects similar to those found for simple tasks. At six times throughout the day, volunteers were asked to read a passage from the *New Scientist* and then to complete a multiple-choice test of memory for the passage. Practice with the task was unconfounded from time of day by starting testing at different times for different groups of volunteers. Figure 14-3, reproduced from Folkard and Monk (1980), shows the results. The figure also shows oral temperatures taken at the time of testing, and data from a similar study done by Laird in 1925. The trend is clear: Arousal as measured by oral temperature is inversely related to short-term memory performance.

The second study reported by Folkard and Monk (1980) used shift workers to examine alternate explanations of the memory effects. One theory of memory

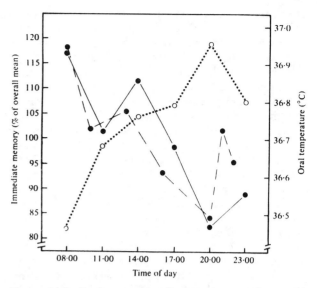

Figure 14-3. Decline in immediate memory performance over the course of a day (black dots, solid lines); the accompanying increase in body temperature (open dots, dotted lines); and data from a similar study done by Laird in 1925 (black dots, dashed lines). (From "Circadian Rhythms in Human Memory" by S. Folkard and T. H. Monk. *British Journal of Psychology*, 1980, 71, 295–307. Reprinted by permission of the British Psychological Society.)

suggests that most forgetting is due to interference between and among similar items in memory; that is, we don't forget, we only recall the wrong things. Such a theory predicts better memory when interference is low between learning and testing (e.g., during sleep). Another possible explanation is based on similarity in states between learning and testing. Animal work has frequently demonstrated state-dependent learning. Animals taught a task during a drug state frequently are able to "recall" the task (i.e., to perform it) only when that drug state is present. Folkard and Monk reasoned that these alternatives to the arousal interpretation could be tested in shift workers (1) by placing memory tests at the same time of day but after 8 hr of sleep or after 8 hr of work (interference theory test); and (2) by testing 28 days later at either the same or different times of day, and therefore the same or different arousal state (state-dependent test). The results of this study showed no evidence for either the interference or state-dependent interpretation. The arousal interpretation for both short- and long-term retention was supported. Arousal state at the time of learning was predictive of memory performance. The relationship between oral temperature and memory was, however, influenced by the degree to which a volunteer was adapted to the shift work schedule. These findings question a general arousal view, since memory performance and body temperature indicate different rates of adjusting to shift work. In addition, these findings question the notion that biological regulation regulates memory. Indeed, the evidence that performance adapted to new shift schedules more quickly than physiology suggests that performance rhythms may alter physiology rather than vice versa (see Hockey & Colquhoun, 1972, for discussion of the multiplicity of biological rhythms). The possibility that biological rhythms alter performance cannot be completely dismissed; however, a portion of the data from animals supports this view. For example, Tapp and Holloway (1981) showed that rats that were shifted to a new cycle of light and dark failed to recall a recently learned behavior.

The consistent association between time of day and memory encourages us to specify the memory processes altered by time of day. If well-defined psychological processes can be identified, it may become easier to relate these processes to bodily change. Broadly speaking, memory can be separated into storage and retrieval processes. The experiments I have reviewed assessed both processes, because the material to be remembered was both stored and retrieved during the experiment. Retrieval can be assessed by asking the recall of well-learned materials (e.g., names of the states of the United States or category names). Arousal might only influence retrieval processes, not storage processes. Eysenck (1977) reviews the literature on this question and suggests that high arousal due to noise or individual differences enhances retrieval from long-term memory. Folkard and Monk (1980), however, report a failure to replicate this finding when amount retrieved was measured (see also Broadbent, 1981). Work by Millar, Styles, and Wastell (1980) attempted to clarify the reason for this difference. They showed that *latency* of recognition was directly related to arousal (time of day), in a task similar to that of Folkard and Monk (1980). Thus, speed but not completeness of retrieval may increase throughout the day, presumably following increasing arousal. In this respect, retrieval from long-term memory is more similar to speeded perceptual tasks than to short-term memory.

Such results (in combination with studies reviewed in Eysenck, 1977) suggest a focus on the influence of arousal on short-term storage and recall strategies. A number of studies are available with this focus. Folkard (1979b) imposed storage and recall strategies on groups of volunteers at 10:30 A.M. (low arousal) and 7:30 P.M. (high arousal). If strategy differences accounted for the effect of time of day (arousal) on memory, imposing a single strategy would presumably eliminate any differences. Indeed, instructions to recall recent items first eliminated all time-of-day effects. This recall strategy had its effect irrespective of the storage strategy used by the volunteer. In addition, instructions to group and rehearse items during storage eliminated time-of-day effects when recall strategies were relatively unrestrained. Paradoxically, the same storage instructions produced a time-of-day effect when combined with strict serial recall. Thus, strategy showed potent but perplexing interactions with time of day. Folkard (1979b) designed these experiments to test the hypothesis that arousal reduces the strategy of covert verbal rehearsal of items (see also Jones, Smith, & Broadbent, 1979). Experiment 1 of his report (Folkard, 1979b) reported that elimination of verbalization produced memory deficits similar to those induced by arousal—in this case, maintenance of muscular tension in the legs. Induced muscle tension, however, produced a different memory deficit from that produced by arousal due to time of day: Muscle tension effects were on early list items, while time-of-day effects were on middle to late list items. Again we see a failure of *a priori* defined arousal manipulations to yield similar psychological effects. A better approach would be to avoid the assumption that arousal is a causative factor. Then, we can ask whether the manipulation influences task processing in such a way that bodily respones during the task are altered. Strategy may influence physiological response, rather than vice versa. In general, the examination of diurnal influences on memory has failed to support a necessary relation between arousal state and memory capabilities. Rather, diurnal state seems to alter strategies and directly or indirectly to influence bodily response.

Motor Activity and Thought

Folkard's (1979a) suggestion that arousal reduces covert verbalization is interesting, because it partially conflicts with other claims that thought processes are dependent on motor activity. Similar claims relating thought and motor action date back to the foundations of modern psychology and even before—for example, to Titchener's claim that recognition of a shade of gray was a quiver of the stomach. The motor response was thought to add meaning to the visual sensation. Related views of early structuralists, reviewed in Humphrey (1963), identified consciousness with motoric action. Though stated in different language, such views show some continuity with those of recent authors (e.g., Cacioppo & Petty, 1981a; Keele, 1973; McGuigan, 1978). More direct roots can, however, be found in the writings of early behaviorists and information-processing psychologists. Their early viewpoints and their subsequent empirical tests provide an important background to this discussion. Since the discussion here is brief, interested readers may wish to consult reviews in Boring (1957), Duffy (1962), and Humphrey (1963). A number of important early papers are reprinted in McGuigan (1966).

The structuralists' interest in mental contents made it important for early behaviorists to provide an alternate account of thinking. Such an account of necessity had to be based on observable responses. Thus, Watson (1958) suggested first that both verbal behavior and a wealth of bodily responses become associated with environmental stimuli. These "habits" can then be re-enacted to perform what is commonly termed "thinking." Particular emphasis was placed on speech habits; in Watson's words, "thought is in short nothing but talking to ourselves" (p. 238). In terms of the question posed by this section, talking is not a typical form of biological regulation, but the claim that thought is reducible to the peripheral motoric responses of speech (and related behaviors) is clearly an example of a necessary relation between bodily processes and information processing. It is interesting that Watson and the structuralists both expected covert motor changes during thought. For Watson, however, the changes were both the content and process of thought; for the structuralists, they were only the content. Both views, however, suggested that covert motor processes might be necessary for thought.

Empirical support for these positions showed that various forms of thought are reliably associated with covert motor activity—particularly covert action of the speech musculature. As amply reviewed in Duffy (1962), Humphrey (1963), and McGuigan (1978), three types of motoric responses are related to thought. First, general muscle tension increases during task performance. Second, certain patterns of muscle excitation–contraction seem to characterize different tasks. For example, tension in the right arm may be characteristic of mental arithmetic but not memory tasks. Finally, certain spatial–temporal patterns of muscle contactions characterize specific cognitive activity. In particular, covert electromyogram (EMG) patterns during the reading of a syllable may mirror the pattern present during the articulation of the syllable.

Most empirical work has focused on the last type of motor response—EMG patterns specific to certain thought processes. Early problems with this postulated relationship between thought and motor processes were revealed by the failure to find covert motor indices for all images and thoughts. Early and current evidence does, however, show specific relations between EMG patterns and some relatively well-defined cognitive processes. Current examples of such work may be found in McGuigan (1978) and in studies cited in Garrity (1977a) and Cacioppo and Petty (1981a). Cacioppo and Petty (1981a), for example, review their studies in which an adjective was classified as possessing or not possessing a certain attribute. Classification was indicated by a "yes–no" button press, but the dependent measure was covert lip or forearm EMG amplitude. Their hypothesis was that classifications that required relatively "deep" levels of processing would yield relatively higher lip EMG tension. Lip tension did order the classifications task by showing increasing tension from classification

by volume, rhyme, and association through classification by self-reference and evaluation. Recognition confidence ordered the classifications similarly, but forearm tension produced little discrimination among classifications. Cacioppo and Petty (1981a, 1981b) argue that the results follow depth-of-processing requirements much more closely than the affective characteristics of the items. A theoretical, behavioral context for such results is provided by McGuigan (1978). His well-developed model suggests that those covert motor responses are at least facilitative if not necessary for the thought processes elicited.

Such studies suggest that covert motor processes index certain thought processes, but they do not establish the necessity of these motor processes for thought. A substantial literature ranging from historical to current times questions the necessity of covert motor processes. Jacobsen (1938) provided an early demonstration linking covert motor processes to thought. Using his progressive relaxation technique, he claimed that complete relaxation eliminated psychological processes. We find, he said, "the experience of muscular tension a sine qua non of imaging, attention, and thought processes" (Jacobsen, 1938, p. 186). Relaxation may, however, induce a central inhibition of thought as well as muscular relaxation. Thus, other investigators examined the presence of thought when motor responses were pharmacologically blocked. In the late 19th century, Dodge (cited in Humphrey, 1963) anesthetized his lips and tongue and reported no impairment in thought or speech. In a more dramatic demonstration, S. M. Smith, Brown, Toman, and Goodman (1947) reported unimpaired thought when motor activity was blocked with curare. Similar results may be found in the animal literature. The classic animal demonstration, however, comes from the controversy between the learning theories of Hull and Tolman (e.g., see Humphrey, 1963). Hull claimed that specific stimulus–response connections mediated learning, while Tolman and Lashley suggested that a cognitive representation was formed independently of the specific responses made during learning. The Tolman–Lashley position was supported when rats continued to exhibit learned responses despite surgical denervation of limbs and transfer between running a maze and swimming through a maze. Finally, more recent work has systematically removed motor afferent connections in order to see whether feedback from the limbs is necessary for behavior. These results (e.g., Taub, Williams, Barro, & Steiner, 1978) suggest that such feedback is not a necessary prerequisite of motor control. Thus, substantial converging evidence questions the necessity of motor responses for thought.

Two other important, if not completely necessary, roles for covert motor activity in thought can be suggested. First, feedback from motor responses may provide useful, but redundant, information that normally facilitates thought (see McGuigan's comments on pp. 380–381 in McGuigan & Schoonover, 1973, and in McGuigan, 1978). Second, motor responses and motor organization may be critical during initial learning (i.e., early in development and/or during performance in adverse conditions). At least two influential cognitive/information-processing psychologists have suggested such hypotheses. Piaget (e.g., 1952) has suggested that the organization of sensory-motor reaction in the child becomes progressively internalized and divorced from environmental control. More particularly, biological regulations form a basic organization of thought that is then freed from physical constraints by development of logical operations such as reversibility and compensation. Sensory–motor schemas are often observed to reappear when a child faces developmental challenges. The developmentally prior "cognitive" organization appears when difficulty is experienced. A markedly similar argument is made by Bartlett (1958). In his volume *Thinking: An Experimental and Social Study,* Bartlett suggests that thought is a form of skilled performance. Again, thought is viewed as internalized action. As such, Bartlett presents evidence that thought and skilled performance show similar characteristics. Essential characteristics are timing, stationary phases, a point of no return, and direction. Successful performance and thought are characterized by a sense of knowing when to act or consider the next piece of information (timing), pauses to evaluate information (stationary phases), a point at which an action or train of thought is unshakably adopted (point of no return), and an overall direction or goal that influences the whole process (direction). Thus, both Piaget and Bartlett suggest (1) the relevance of motor activity as a model for thought processes and (2) the possibility that motoric action may be observed during information processing in children or during information processing by adults performed in adverse circumstances.

Unfortunately, these theoretical notions have not been actively pursued in psychophysiology. There has, however, been interest in the area of subvocalization during reading and recall tests. Studies in this area provide us with an illustration of research on EMG activity and thought.

Subvocal EMG, Reading, and Memory

We can return to Folkard's (1979b) suggestion that time-of-day effects on memory may be due to an inhibition of subvocal speech. Folkard's argument was based on the following findings. First, induced muscle tension facilitated rejection of distracting stimuli when salient, but irrelevant, information was presented in a card-sorting task. Second, induced muscle tension also facilitated rejection of distracting stimuli in a color–word interference task (Folkard & Gree-

man, 1974). Third, induced muscle tension produced memory decrements that mimicked the effect of blocking subvocal speech (Folkard, 1979a). Folkard's (1979b) interpretation of these three findings was that induced arousal inhibited subvocal speech. We have previously seen, however, that arousal defined in terms of time of day failed to influence memory in the same way as induced muscle tension. Another problem with Folkard's interpretation is that contradictory findings are available from other studies. For example, prior work (see Duffy, 1962) had suggested that induced muscle tension could aid rote memorization. Furthermore, the work of Hockey and Broadbent (see Chapter 13 and "Bodily Change as a Facilitator of Memory and Thought," above) with noise-induced arousal suggested increased, not decreased, attention to salient events. Finally, measurements of subvocal speech have usually revealed an increase in amplitude during stress (a presumably arousing condition) (see McGuigan, 1978). Again, these problems indicate difficulties with the arousal concept that occur when an investigator systematically tries to apply the concept across different experimental situations. Enticing experimental effects appear relatively task-specific rather than general. Furthermore, in Folkard's case, an explanation that could be verified with physiological measures was proposed, but these measures were not collected.

Can we gain any clarification from studies that have employed physiological measures of subvocal speech? Physiologically oriented studies first sought to answer the old question of whether and when subvocalization aids reading comprehension and speech. Humphrey (1963) discusses in detail an experiment by Karn done in the late 1920s. Normal children between the ages of 9 and 11 were asked to read silently, and movement of the vocal apparatus was observed. Vocal movements were negatively related to intelligence: The brighter children showed less subvocalization. Within each gradation of intelligence, however, comprehension was higher in children showing subvocalization. Subsequent work reviewed by McGuigan (1978; McGuigan & Schoonover, 1973) and Garrity (1977a) supports these early interpretations. In addition, the difficulty of reading in a foreign language or in a noisy environment seems to increase subvocalization. Developmentally, subvocalization appears early and declines as adult proficiency in reading is achieved. Programs to increase reading rate seem to also increase subvocalization. In a well-known report, Hardyck and Petrinovich (1970; see also Hardyck, Petrinovich, & Ellsworth, 1966) found that subvocal speech could be readily suppressed using a feedback technique, but that such suppression lead to decreased comprehension of difficult material. Overall, these results suggest that subvocal speech movements facilitate comprehension, but that, perhaps due to the effort required, these movements disappear whenever such facilitation is unnecessary. Implicitly, the possibility is raised that subvocal speech is necessary for the comprehension of high-difficulty prose. Even in the early studies reviewed, intelligence, difficulty of reading material, and environmental condition were found to alter subvocalization. Clearly subvocalization is a variable that must be measured rather than implied in the fashion of Folkard (1979a&b).

Recent work on a subvocalization has refined the techniques employed and the experimental tasks used. Earlier work left some doubt as to whether the physiological measures taken were indices of general motoric activity or of specific speech movements. A series of studies by Locke and Fehr (e.g., 1970; see Garrity, 1977a) showed the specificity of the measurements by comparing the memorization of words with labial and nonlabial phonemes. The pronounciation of labial phonemes, relative to nonlabial phonemes, produces substantial EMG activity. Nonlabial phonemes should, however, be subject to any nonspecific changes in the speech musculature. Thus, EMG changes above those produced by the nonlabial phonemes should be due to subvocalization of the labial phonemes. Locke and Fehr (1970) were able to show that the learning and maintenance of labial picture labels was associated with increases in EMG beyond those exhibited by nonlabial items. Thus, support for EMG patterns as an index of specific processing was supported.

Two issues somewhat tangential to the present question have motivated studies relating EMG to item learning and retention. These studies have moved away from reading comprehension toward rote learning and recall of verbally coded items. Some of these studies are relevant because they identify processes specifically altered by subvocalization. The first issue is whether verbal labeling "mediates" the learning and retention of nonverbal items. This issue was explored developmentally to see whether proficient object learning and subvocalization emerged concomitantly. Evidence favoring this hypothesis is reviewed in Garrity (1977b). EMG evidence in particular has suggested that children, when shown an object, initially subvocalize its verbal label but do not rehearse the label subvocally during retention. Later in development, the children subvocalize both during presentation and retention intervals. This data supports a facilitative role for subvocalization, but does not establish its necessity for information processing.

The second issue of recent interest in the area of EMG and information processing is more relevant. Short-term maintenance of an item has been posited to require an articulatory representation or code (as opposed to an acoustic representation; e.g., see Glassman, 1972). Such an articulatory code may involve the subvocalization of relevant phonemes. If so, the hypothesis can be tested by observing the effect on memory of suppressing subvocalization. Glassman

(1972) compared the memory performance of groups with and without EMG suppression. The memory task was either a set of acoustically similar or a set of dissimilar word triads. The results showed that acoustic confusion errors were substantially reduced when EMG was suppressed. In contrast, Cole and Young (1975) provided better measures of EMG suppression and failed to find any memory effects. Serial memory for sequences of six consonant–vowel syllables was tested. No attempt was made to manipulate acoustic similarity, but acoustic errors were assessed. EMG suppression had the general effect of increasing errors, but no specific effect on acoustic errors.

The results of these two experiments seem consonant with our interpretation of the early work on EMG and thought. Motoric changes are only associated with processing efficiency when the task is difficult or conditions adverse. At least the high-similarity condition of Glassman (1972) would qualify as a difficult task in which subvocalization might assist item encoding. If this strategy was adopted, acoustic confusion errors would be expected (due to errors in subvocalization). Cole and Young's (1975) task may not have been difficult enough to induce subvocalization, and thus acoustic confusion errors would be unlikely. Unfortunately, this can only be a speculative explanation, as Glassman (1972) does not provide EMG data to compare to Cole and Young's (1975). Recently, Milberg, Whitman, Rourke, and Glaros (1981) suggested that suppression of subvocalization may alter more than acoustic coding. Short-term recall of dichotically presented syllables was studied with and without EMG suppression. Suppression of EMG did not have a clear effect on acoustic confusion, but it dramatically altered the typical advantage of input to the right ear in this task. With EMG suppression, presentation to the left ear produced fewer errors than presentation to the right ear. Milberg *et al.* (1981) suggest that subvocalization may be related to the hemispheric dominance induced by a task. Considerable work will be necessary, however, to relate this phenomenon empirically to previous work.

We have now briefly examined the question of whether bodily responses required by speech are necessary for efficient silent reading and memorization of verbal material. It is clear that speech-related muscle responses often occur during reading and memorization. Reading and memorization, however, seem possible without these covert motor responses. Thus, we must conclude that, at least in adults, subvocal speech movements do not also regulate thought and memory. Available evidence suggests that covert speech movements may be necessary to maintain efficiency in adverse environmental settings or when processing difficult items (e.g., acoustically similar items). Further work should specify the processes that aid efficiency, and thus should define more clearly the situations in which facilitation is required. Available data suggest complex interactions among subvocalization, task difficulty, and different "arousal"-inducing manipulations. Further work would be aided by a heuristic concept of why the activation of speech musculature should influence information processing. It is not clear why the involvement of more of the organism's physiology should facilitate comprehension or memory. McGuigan's (1978) concepts may be useful in this regard, although he seems to place a greater emphasis on the necessity of covert speech than is currently warranted.

In sum, the regulation of diurnal rhythms and subvocal speech have not been shown to control thought or memory. A number of interesting situations have been described in which altering diurnal rhythms or subvocal speech movements affect thought or memory. Each situation has, however, been complex. Simple concepts such as "general arousal" and "performance" have not been adequate to explain the diversity of the findings.

SUMMARY AND CONCLUSIONS

What have we found out about the relation of bodily response to memory and complex information processing?

First, it has been noted that many bodily functions are altered during memorizing or complex information processing. Can such bodily changes be used to index the occurrence of these cognitive processes? Any bodily response used as an index would need to show direct relationship with its cognitive process; for example, changes in attention would need to parallel changes in heart rate. There are limitations, however, to how closely changes in bodily response can mirror changes in cognitive processes. All bodily responses are altered by multiple psychological and biological factors. Thus, psychophysiological indicators are only useful as one of a number of converging indices suggesting the occurrence of a cognitive process. The specific literature reviewed here suggest that heart rate changes reliably during memory storage and complex transformations of stored information. Heart rate change is, however, not specific to a particular cognitive process, but rather indexes the unavailability of processing capacity for further input. In general, it is suggested that bodily response during information processing can indicate the volunteer's responsivity to task demands. More specifically, heart rate change may relate to demands for access to limited processing capacity. Subvocal speech movements may be a special case in which the content of thought may be indexed by a bodily response. Complex memorizing and verbal processing tasks, at least, appear to be reliably associated with subvocal speech movements.

Selection of appropriate stimulus materials and EMG electrode placements may permit an index of the processing of specific items.

The second question asked is whether bodily responses facilitate information processing. This question implies that in certain conditions appropriate bodily responses contribute to efficiency of information processing. Evidence has been presented that induced heart rate change can facilitate reading comprehension, while induced EMG suppression can impair reading comprehension of complex material. The complexity of both the manipulations and tasks used in these demonstrations suggests, however, that the processes involved should be stipulated in some detail. To date, follow-up work has failed to identify specific mechanisms. Work relating skin conductance and memory is at a similar stage. Initially, it was shown that a high-amplitude skin conductance induced by an item predicted a short-term memory decrement and a long-term increment in recall of that item. Other so-called "arousal" manipulations, such as performance in noise conditions, reproduced this phenomenon to a certain extent. Again, however, when memory tasks were simplified and "arousal" manipulations varied, conflicting results were obtained; the validity of the concept of general arousal must therefore be questioned. Future work must focus on the relationship of specific task-induced bodily responses to specific strategies of information processing. A particularly puzzling and promising area is the effect of noise on bodily response, attention, and memory strategies (see Chapter 13). In sum, bodily responses seem to have facilitative (and interfering) effects on memory and comprehension. These effects are complex and may be mediated by information processing strategies. Definitive interpretation awaits careful experimental work.

Finally, this chapter has asked whether bodily regulation processes involved in biorhythms and speech production might have necessary implications for complex information processes. No convincing evidence for this supposition has been found. Changes in biorhythms and subvocal speech do have facilitative or interfering effects on memory or comprehension. Neither memory nor reading comprehension, however, seems to be impossible in the absence of bodily change.

Perhaps, the biggest need in the area is for a theoretical framework to replace the concept of general arousal. The Laceys' emphasis on task demands and current concepts of the influence of subvocal speech on memory may be promising starting points for such an endeavor.

ACKNOWLEDGMENT

I would like to thank Kay Jennings for her comments on early drafts of this chapter.

REFERENCES

Adamowicz, J. K., & Gibson, D. *Cue screening, cognitive elaboration and heart rate change.* Paper presented at the annual meeting of the Canadian Psychological Association, 1968.

Bartlett, F. *Thinking: An experimental and social study.* London: Unwin University Books, 1958.

Bartoshuk, A. K. Motivation. In J. W. Kling & L. A. Riggs (Eds.), *Experimental psychology.* New York: Holt, Rinehart & Winston, 1971.

Boring, E. G. *A history of experimental psychology.* New York: Appleton-Century-Crofts, 1957.

Broadbent, D. E. The effects of moderate levels of noise on human performance. In J. V. Tobias & E. D. Schubert (Eds.), *Hearing: Research and theory,* Vol. 1. New York: Academic Press, 1981.

Cacioppo, J. T. Effects of exogenous changes in heart rate on facilitation of thought and resistance to persuasion. *Journal of Personality and Social Psychology,* 1979, 37, 2181–2199.

Cacioppo, J. T., & Petty, R. E. Electromyograms as measures of extent and affectivity of information processing. *American Psychologist,* 1981, 36, 441–456. (a)

Cacioppo, J. T., & Petty, R. E. Electromyographic specificity during covert information processing. *Psychophysiology,* 1981, 18, 518–523. (b)

Carroll, D., & Anastasiades, P. The behavoral significance of heart rate: The Laceys' hypothesis. *Biological Psychology,* 1978, 1, 249–275.

Cole, R. A., & Young, M. Effect of subvocalization on memory for speech sounds. *Journal of Experimental Psychology,* 1975, 1, 772–774.

Coles, M. G. H., & Duncan-Johnson, C. C. Cardiac activity and information processing: The effects of stimulus significance and detection and response requirements. *Journal of Experimental Psychology,* 1975, 1, 418–428.

Costello, C. G., & Hall, M. Heart rate during performance of a mental task under noise conditions. *Psychonomic Science,* 1967, 8, 405–406.

Craik, F. M., & Blankstein, K. R. Psychophysiology and human memory. In P. H. Venables & M. J. Christie (Eds.), *Research in psychophysiology.* Chichester, UK: Wiley, 1975.

Daee, S., & Wilding, J. M. Effects of high intensity white noise on short-term memory for position in a list and sequence. *British Journal of Psychiatry,* 1977, 68, 335–349.

Dornic, S. Order error in attended and non-attended tasks. In S. Kornblum (Ed.), *Attention and performance IV.* New York: Academic Press, 1973.

Duffy, E. *Activation and behavior.* New York: Wiley, 1962.

Duffy, E. Activation. In N. S. Greenfield & R. A. Sternbach (Eds.), *Handbook of psychophysiology.* New York: Holt, Rinehart & Winston, 1972.

Elliott, R. The significance of heart rate for behavior: A critique of Laceys' hypothesis. *Journal of Personality and Social Psychology,* 1972, 22, 398–409.

Eysenck, M. W. Arousal, learning, and memory. *Psychological Bulletin,* 1976, 83, 389–404.

Eysenck, M. W. *Human memory: Theory, research, and individual differences.* Oxford: Pergamon Press, 1977.

Eysenck, M. W., & Folkard, S. Personality, time of day, and caffeine: Some theoretical and conceptual problems in Revelle et al. *Journal of Experimental Psychology,* 1980, 109, 33–41.

Folkard, S. Changes in immediate memory strategy under induced muscle tension and with time of day. *Quarterly Journal of Experimental Psychology,* 1979, 31, 621–633. (a)

Folkard, S. Time of day and level of processing. *Memory and Cognition,* 1979, 7, 247–252. (b)

Folkard, S., & Greeman, A. L. Salience induced muscle tension, and the ability to ignore irrelevant information. *Quarterly Journal of Experimental Psychology,* 1974, 26, 360–367.

Folkard, S., & Monk, T. H. Circadian rhythms in human memory. *British Journal of Psychology,* 1980, 71, 295–307.

Garrity, L. I. Electromyography: A review of the current status of subvocal speech research. *Memory and Cognition,* 1977, 5, 615–622. (a)

Garrity, L. I. A review of short term memory studies of covert speech in young children. *Journal of Psychology,* 1977, 95, 249–261. (b)

Gibson, D., & Hall, M. K. Cardiovascular change and mental task gradient. *Psychonomic Science,* 1966, 6, 245–246.

Glassman, W. E. Subvocal activity and acoustic confusions in short term memory. *Journal of Experimental Psychology,* 1972, 96, 164–169.

Hahn, W. W. Attention and heart rate: A critical appraisal of the hypothesis of Lacey and Lacey. *Psychological Bulletin,* 1973, 79, 59–70.

Hamilton, P., Hockey, G. R. J., & Quinn, J. G. Information selection, arousal, and memory. *British Journal of Psychiatry,* 1972, 63, 181–189.

Hamilton, P., Hockey, B., & Rejman, M. The place of the concept of activation in human information processing theory: An integrative approach. In S. Dornic (Ed.), *Attention and performance VI.* Hillsdale, N.J.: Erlbaum, 1977.

Hamilton, P., Wilkinson, R. T., & Edwards, R. A study of four days' partial sleep deprivation. In W. P. Colquhoun (Ed.), *Aspects of human efficiency.* London: English Universities Press, 1972.

Hardyck, C. D., & Petrinovich, L. F. Subvocal speech and comprehension level as a function of the difficulty level of reading material. *Journal of Verbal Learning and Verbal Behavior,* 1970, 9, 647–652.

Hardyck, C. D., Petrinovich, L. F., & Ellsworth, D. W. Feedback on speech muscle activity during silent reading: Rapid extinction. *Science,* 1966, 154, 1467–1468.

Hare, R., Wood, K., Britain, S., & Frazelle, J. Autonomic responses to affective visual stimulation. *Journal of Experimental Research in Personality,* 1971, 5, 14–22.

Hebb, D. O. Drives and the C.N.S. (conceptual nervous system). *Psychological Review,* 1955, 62, 243–253.

Hockey, G. R. J. Stress and the cognitive components of skilled performance. In V. Hamilton & D. M. Warburton (Eds.), *Human stress and cognition.* Chichester, England: Wiley, 1979.

Hockey, G. R. J., & Colquhoun, W. P. Diurnal variation in human performance: A review. In W. P. Colquhoun (Ed.), *Aspects of human efficiency: Diurnal rhythm and loss of sleep.* London: English Universities Press, 1972.

Hull, C. L. *Principles of behavior.* New York: Appleton-Century-Crofts, 1943.

Humphrey, G. *Thinking: An introduction to its experimental psychology.* New York: Wiley, 1963.

Humphreys, M. S., Revelle, W., Simon, L., & Gilliland, K. Individual differences in diurnal rhythms and multiple activation states: A reply to M. W. Eysenck and Simon Folkard *Journal of Experimental Psychology: General,* 1980, 109, 42–48.

Jacobsen, E. *Progressive relaxation.* (Rev. ed.). Chicago: University of Chicago Press, 1938.

Jennings, J. R. Cardiac reactions and different developmental levels of cognitive functioning. *Psychophysiology,* 1971, 8, 433–450.

Jennings, J. R. Information processing and concomitant heart rate changes in the overweight and underweight. *Physiological Psychology,* 1975, 3, 290–296.

Jennings, J. R., & Hall, S. W., Jr. Recall, recognition, and rate: Memory and the heart. *Psychophysiology,* 1980, 17, 37–46.

Jennings, J. R., Lawrence, B. E., & Kasper, P. Changes in alertness and processing capacity in a serial learning task. *Memory and Cognition,* 1978, 6, 45–63.

Jones, D. M., Smith, A. P., & Broadbent, D. E. Effects of moderate intensity noise on the Bakan vigilance task. *Journal of Applied Psychology,* 1979, 64, 627–634.

Kahneman, D. *Attention and effort.* Englewood Cliffs, N.J.: Prentice-Hall, 1973.

Kahneman, D., Tursky, B., Shapiro, D., & Crider, A. Pupillary, heart rate and skin resistance changes during a mental task. *Journal of Experimental Psychology,* 1969, 79, 164–167.

Keele, S. W. *Attention and human performance.* Pacific Palisades, Calif.: Goodyear, 1973.

Kerr, B. Processing demands during mental operations. *Memory and Cognition,* 1973, 1, 401–412.

Kleinsmith, L. J., & Kaplan, S. Paired associative learning as a function of arousal and interpreted interval. *Journal of Experimental Psychology,* 1963, 65, 190–194.

Kleitman, N. *Sleep and wakefulness.* Chicago: University of Chicago Press, 1963.

Lacey, B. C., & Lacey, J. I. Studies of heart rate and other bodily processes in sensorimotor behavior. In P. A. Obrist, A. H. Black, J. Brener, & L. V. DiCara (Eds.), *Cardiovascular psychophysiology: Current issues in response mechanisms, biofeedback and methodology.* Chicago: Aldine-Atherton, 1974.

Lacey, B. C., & Lacey, J. I. Two way communication between the heart and brain. *American Psychologist,* 1978, 33, 99–113.

Lacey, J. I., Kagan, J., Lacey, B., & Moss, H. A. The visceral level: Situational determinants and behavioral correlates of autonomic response patterns. In P. H. Knapp (Ed.), *Expression of the emotions in man.* New York: International Universities Press, 1963.

Lacey, J. I., & Lacey, B. C. On heart rate responses and behavior: A reply to Elliott. *Journal of Personality and Social Psychology,* 1974, 30, 1–18.

Locke, J. L., & Fehr, F. S. Young children's use of the speech code in a recall task. *Journal of Experimental Child Psychology,* 1970, 10, 367–373.

McGuigan, F. J. *Thinking: Studies of covert language processes.* New York: Appleton-Century-Crofts, 1966.

McGuigan, F. J. *Cognitive psychophysiology: Principles of covert behavior.* Englewood Cliffs, N.J.: Prentice-Hall, 1978.

McGuigan, F. J., & Schoonover, R. A. *The psychophysiology of thinking: Studies of covert processes.* New York: Academic Press, 1973.

Milberg, W. P., Whitman, R. D., Rourke, D., & Glaros, A. G. Role of subvocal motor activity in dichotic speech perception and selective attention. *Journal of Experimental Psychology,* 1981, 7, 231–239.

Millar, K., Styles, B. C., & Wastell, D. G. Time of day and retrieval from long term memory. *British Journal of Psychology,* 1980, 71, 407–414.

Navon, D., & Gopher, D. On the economy of the human processing system. *Psychological Review,* 1979, 86, 214–255.

Nowlin, J. B., Eisdorfer, C., Whalen, R., & Troyer, W. G. The effect of exogenous changes in heart rate and rhythm upon reaction time performance. *Psychophysiology,* 1971, 7, 186–193.

Piaget, J. *The origins of intelligence in children.* New York: Norton, 1952.

Revelle, W., Humphreys, M. S., Simon, L., & Gilliland, K. The interactive effect of personality, time of day, and caffeine: A test of the arousal model. *Journal of Experimental Psychology,* 1980, 108, 1–31.

Schwartz, G. E., & Higgins, J. D. Cardiac activity preparatory to over and covert behavior. *Science,* 1971, 173, 1144–1145.

Silverstein, L. D., & Berg, W. K. *Repetition and distribution effects on memory: A psychophysiological analysis.* Paper presented at the annual meeting of the Society for Psychophysiological Research, October 1977.

Smith, A. P., & Broadbent, D. E. Noise and levels of processing. *Acta Psychologica,* 1981, 47, 129–142.

Smith, A. P., Jones, D. M., & Broadbent, D. E. The effects of noise on recall of categorized lists. *British Journal of Psychiatry,* 1981, 72, 299–316.

Smith, S. M., Brown, H. O., Toman, J. E. P., & Goodman, L. S. The lack of cerebral effects of d-tubocurarine. *Anesthesiology,* 1947, 8, 1–14.

Steele, W. G., & Koons, P. B. Cardiac response to mental arithmetic order quiet and white noise distraction. *Psychonomic Science,* 1968, 11, 273–274.

Steele, W. G., & Lewis, M. A. A longtitudinal study of the cardiac response during problem solving task and its relationship to general cognitive function. *Psychonomic Science,* 1968, 11, 275.

Tapp, W. N., & Holloway, F. A. Phase shifting circadian rhythms produces retrograde amnesia. *Science,* 1981, 211, 1056–1058.

Taub, E., Williams, M., Barro, G., & Steiner, S. S. Comparison of the performance of differential and intact monkeys on continuous and fixed rate schedules of reinforcement. *Experimental Neurology,* 1978, 58, 1–13.

Tolman, E. C. *Purposive behavior in animals and man.* New York: Century, 1932.

Tursky, B., Schwartz, G. E., & Crider, A. Differential patterns of heart rate and skin resistance during a digit-transformation task. *Journal of Experimental Psychology,* 1970, 83, 451–457.

Watson, J. B. *Behaviorism.* Chicago: University of Chicago Press, 1958 (reissue of 1930 revised edition).

Westerhaus, M. D., Jensen, P. D., Steinberg, W., Callahan, M., Maslang, J., & Stern, R. M. Effects of postural change on reaction time. *Psychophysiology,* 1976, *13,* 179.

Wickens, C. D. The structure of attentional resources. In R. S. Nickerson (Ed.), *Attention and performance VIII.* Hillsdale, N.J.: Erlbaum, 1980.

Chapter Fifteen

Operant Reinforcement, Feedback, and the Efficiency of Learned Motor Control

Jasper Brener

INTRODUCTION

The development of more efficient behavior implies the elimination of those components of the organism's response that are not demanded by the prevailing reinforcement contingencies. As unnecessary motor activities are extinguished, the behavioral residue progressively comes to approximate the minimal response required for reinforcement. Consequently, the energy costs of each goal unit decline, and the behavior is rendered more efficient. Although this tendency to maximum energy efficiency is assumed in most theories of motor learning, its validity has seldom been tested, and the processes by which it occurs have not been comprehensively described.

These matters, which seem fundamental to the understanding of motor learning, are considered in this chapter. It is argued that in many cases, the acquisition of motor control may be understood in terms of a learning process in which stimuli gain access to those pre-established responses that may be effectively deployed in the learning situation. Such instances of learning do not imply motor reorganization and are not characterized by increased behavioral efficiency with continued training. However, in other cases, ap-

propriate responses do not exist in the organism's repertoire, and here successful behavioral adaptation requires the reformulation of motor plans. It is argued that such motor planning depends on the interaction of internal and external feedback processes, and that the mechanisms governing their interaction lead automatically to plans for more efficient behavior.

LEARNING AND BEHAVIORAL EFFICIENCY

It is conventional to distinguish the motivational or incentive functions of operant reinforcers from their informational or learning functions. Although there is no generally agreed upon system for identifying reinforcing stimuli independently of their effects, they are usually selected on the basis of their perceived biological value. This implicit acceptance of a homeostatic criterion has been associated with considerable progress in developing theories to account for variations in performance. For example, the "matching law" (Herrnstein, 1970) accounts for more than 80% of variance in the results of experiments on choice be-

Jasper Brener. Department of Psychology, University of Hull, Hull, England.

tween concurrently available schedules of reinforcement (De Villiers, 1977). This "law," which states that organisms distribute their activities between behavioral options in proportion to the rewards offered by those options, is compatible with the energy maximization premise on which ethological theories of energy foraging ("optimal foraging theories") are based.

The biological axioms that underpin these successful theories of performance also provide a basis for assuming that the function or evolutionary rationale of learning is to increase behavioral efficiency. By decreasing the costs of fulfilling some behavioral functions, learning frees resources to deal with other functions and thereby confers a survival advantage on the individual. Much evidence indicates that instrumental behavior becomes more efficient with practice, even when this is not explicitly demanded by the reinforcement contingencies. Thus on successive exposures to the same demand conditions, organisms tend to meet the behavioral requirements in less time or by a shorter path or by selecting a less effortful response (Lewis, 1965; Solomon, 1948).

The biofunctional relation between learning and performance is clarified by viewing behavioral efficiency in quantifiable energetic terms (Goldspink, 1977): as a ratio of the energy consumed in performing a behavioral function to the energy value of the work achieved by the behavior. Thus if an organism forages inefficiently, it necessarily follows that it will have to spend more time gathering food and will therefore have less time for attending to other survival functions. For example, a failure to recognize more profitable types of prey (Krebs, 1973) may result in a decrease in the net rate of energy gain by decreasing the gross rate of energy input. On the other hand, if the organism does recognize more profitable types of prey, but chases, subdues, or ingests them inefficiently by engaging in redundant or excessive motor activities, the gross energy costs will increase, and thereby the net energy gain of the activity will decline. In either case, the organism will have to spend additional time foraging for the extra energy reserves depleted by its excessive activities (Norberg, 1977). Such considerations have led Hughes (1979) to the view that learning processes by which perceptual and motor activities are refined must be taken into account by optimal foraging theories (Krebs, 1978). Although, unlike foraging, most behavior does not result in energy capture, efficient performance always confers an advantage on the organism by freeing resources to cope with competing survival demands.

In the context of traditional theories of instrumental learning, these arguments suggest that increased behavioral efficiency is somehow reinforced by the biological utility of its consequences. Where food reinforcement is used, one might argue that more efficient behavior reduces the costs of obtaining food

and hence augments the net calorific value of the reinforcer. Thus, more efficient behavioral variants result in greater rewards and are therefore preferentially strengthened. However, the argument seems implausible, since it implies that net energy gain is computed in real time; this would require the continuous on-line monitoring of the calorific values of food ingested and work done. Furthermore, since systematic increases in behavioral efficiency are also observed in situations involving aversive reinforcers (Brener, Phillips, & Connally, 1980; Sherwood, Brener & Moncur, 1983), they cannot be explained simply by an increase in the biological value of the goal object. Even if a common intrinsic property of operant reinforcers could be identified, the problem of accounting for *how* that property leads to the development of more efficient behavior would remain.

Because the informational or learning properties of operant reinforcers are poorly understood, their modes of action are not clearly distinguished from motivational properties. As a consequence, explanations of learning in terms of operant reinforcement often appear to entail a teleological problem, in which current behavior is attributed to the incentive properties of future events. This criticism gathers strength from the absence of mechanistic explanations of how operant reinforcement serves to modify behavior. However, specific roles have been attributed to internal (kinesthetic) and external (e.g., reinforcing) response-contingent feedback in the study of motor control. It therefore seems reasonable that since that area of study shares a common interest with learning theory in understanding the regulation of behavior, it may provide insights into the mechanisms by which operant reinforcement achieves its effects. From a motor control point of view, the problem of how learning produces more efficient behavior resolves to the question of how striate muscular control is replanned to meet prevailing survival demands more precisely. In the context of this perspective, it is argued here that the refinements of motor control implied by increases in behavioral efficiency during learning are an automatic product of the movement-planning functions of response-contingent reinforcement.

The striate musculature through which organisms interact with their environments is the largest effector system. In mammals, it comprises approximately 50% of the total body mass, and variations in the rate of striate muscle activity are by far the most conspicuous sources of variations in overall energy expenditure. At rest, this effector system consumes about 20% of the total oxygen uptake. However, under conditions of heavy exercise, in which overall energy expenditure may increase by 25 times, striate muscle activity accounts for over 90% of the total oxygen uptake (Brown, 1973). At maximum efficiency, the striate muscles consume at least 4 times as much energy as the calorific value of the work they perform, and usually their efficiency is far lower than this. It therefore follows that achieving the fundamental survival functions associated with energy foraging, defense, and reproduction depends heavily on the precision of striate muscular control.

In view of these considerations, it is not surprising that a capacity for learning very precise striate muscular control has evolved. For example, Basmajian (1963) found that when provided with exteroceptive feedback, individuals rapidly learn to control the rates of firing of single motor units. Phylogenetic comparisons reveal that the muscle systems employed by different species for fine-grain manipulation of their environments are provided with the most conspicuous central sensory–motor projections (Paillard, 1960). This observation is compatible with the proposal that the programmability of effectors is related to the informational input (feedback) they provide to the central motor control circuits. It is argued that this information may be employed to construct motor plans that serve as behavioral templates for appropriate responses to the prevailing survival demands.

The behavioral implications of particular survival demands are usually signaled by stimuli arising from the environment. Through previously established pathways, these stimuli selectively activate motor programming processes that generate appropriate responses. The first learning process to assert itself may be attributed to classical conditioning or "feedforward learning," by which stimulus aspects of the new environment gain access to motor plans that have been genetically and experientially preformulated. It is argued that the experiential mechanisms by which these plans are formulated and updated involve the development of associations between the internal kinesthetic consequences of the act and its environmental consequences (operant conditioning or "feedback learning"). The process of behavioral refinement generally implied by the revision of motor plans proceeds as an automatic consequence of feedback learning and continues until some limiting factor constrains further modification of the plan.

FEEDFORWARD AND FEEDBACK CONTROL

The distinction between "feedforward" and "feedback" control is adopted here as an analytical convenience. These concepts have a high currency in the analysis of motor control, and they embody the fundamental distinction that is drawn between classical (feedforward) and operant (feedback) conditioning processes. However, the distinction is not absolute: It depends to some extent on how a response is defined, and on the time frame of the analysis. It is also worth noting that, as an expression of theoretical taste, the same behavioral processes may be represented in terms of either feedforward or feedback models (see the exchange between Kugler & Turvey, 1979, and Roland, 1979). Even if one is committed to a feedback model of behavioral regulation, it is sometimes fruitful to view one limb of a feedback circuit in isolation, in which case it appears as a feedforward process. Thus, Fromm and Evarts (1978) refer to cortical responses evoked by kinesthetic stimuli as "reflexes," even though they propose that these processes are components of a feedback loop concerned with the regulation of the intensive and spatial characteristics of muscular activity.

Feedforward control is inferred from instances of motor control where there is little or no chance of participation by feedback processes. For example, Desmedt and Godaux (1978) describe data indicating that in rapid ballistic movements, muscular contractions cease before the limb movement has achieved midamplitude. This temporal arrangement obviously reduces the possible contribution of kinesthetic feedback processes to movement regulation. Nevertheless, those authors conclude that feedback processes are involved in formulating plans for generating ballistic movements, and McCloskey (1978) has proposed that feedback information available prior to the initiation of a ballistic movement is likely to be important in framing the commands for that instance of the response.

Complex behavioral sequences, which are usually of the genetically preprogrammed variety and which depend on feedback for their coordination, may also be viewed as the targets of feedforward control. Examples of such activities were described by Sechenov (1863/1965), who, in the first chapter of *Reflexes of the Brain*, catalogued the complex adaptive behavioral repertoire of the decapitated frog. After a frog has recovered from the initial shock of having its head cut off, it adopts a normal standing posture and will leap away from a noxious stimulus, with the magnitude of the leap being related to the intensity of the stimulus. If the animal is now suspended and pricked on the belly, the leg ipsilateral to the prick will knock the offending pin away, whereas if acid is applied to the skin, the leg will wipe at the stimulated skin area. If the leg ipsilateral to the location of the stimulus is now amputated, the animal will execute the same defensive actions by directing the contralateral leg to the stimulated skin locations. These examples indicate that many of the complex processing tasks imputed to the brain are, in fact, performed by hard-wired spinal neural structures. This local organization considerably reduces the informational load on higher centers. Feedback processes involved in the performance of such responses are seen as intrinsic properties of the coordinative structure that embodies the response and on which the feedforward-eliciting stimulus acts (Easton, 1972).

Despite these complications, the term "feedforward" control is employed here to denote the triggering of an integrated behavioral act by events that arise independently of its performance, and the term "feedback" is used to denote the short- and long-term regulation of an act by its consequences. Much experimental evidence indicates that any interoreceptive or exteroceptive sensory source may serve either feedforward or feedback functions. While the general validity of this point is not questioned, it is argued that interoceptive and exteroceptive feedback processes serve different functions in motor learning.

Experimental evidence of learning is usually if not always constituted by the observation that a stimulus or set of stimuli (conditioned or discriminative stimulus, or CS) has come to control a response or set of responses (conditioned responses, or CR). Such observations imply, *inter alia*, that the brain circuits responsible for detecting the CS have acquired the capacity to activate the motor circuits responsible for generating the CR. Pavlov believed that this occurred by the development of links between the sensory centers responsible for analyzing the CS on the one hand and the unconditioned stimulus (UCS) on the other. His theory may be expressed by a neurophysiologically plausible model in which the sensory centers activated by the CS gain access to the reflex pathway by which the unconditioned response (UCR) is controlled.

Although the stimulus substitution theory does not have universal application even in accounting for the phenomena of classical conditioning, it does appear to apply in certain cases, such as autoshaping. Jenkins and Moore (1973) observed that in pecking at a lighted key that signals the response-independent delivery of food, pigeons exhibit a response topography that resembles eating movements. On the other hand, when they peck at a key that signals water, the CR resembles drinking. Such cases illustrate that visual signals may acquire the capacity to activate morphogenetically preprogrammed maintenance activities (Altman, 1966), which are expressed through particular patterns of muscular responses. This learned feedforward control is a predominantly open-loop process that is markedly uninfluenced by its environmental consequences. Thus in their "negative autoshaping" experiments, Williams and Williams (1969) found that pigeons continued to peck at a key that signaled noncontingent food delivery, even when the experimental protocol prevented food delivery if the pigeon performed that response. Although apparently maladaptive in the context of this artificial experimental arrangement, it may be assumed that the "sign-tracking" behavior reflected by autoshaping (Hearst & Jenkins, 1974) carries significant survival advantages in more usual circumstances.

Tolman's (1932) theory that instrumental learning also involves the development of stimulus associations persists in the currently popular ideas expressed by Mackintosh (1974) and Dickinson (1981). However, the stimulus association model appears to be less satisfactory when it is applied to instrumental learning. These theories hold that learned stimulus associations comprise "cognitive maps." The "knowledge" contained in these maps is then employed to guide behavior toward its goals. According to the interesting arguments presented by O'Keefe and Nadel (1979), the hippocampus is the brain structure through which cognitive mapping functions are realized. However, this localization of cognitive maps in the nervous system does not resolve the fundamental problem of how the knowledge they contain is translated into appropriate motor activities (Semjen, 1977). Hence the theory is not wholly successful in accounting for the behavioral manifestations of instrumental learning.

The essence of instrumental behavior is that it is influenced by its programmed external consequences. As such, it seems appropriate to model instrumental learning in terms of an adaptive servo mechanism. In this connection, a distinction is frequently drawn between short-term feedback regulations, which occur during the conduct of an act, and long-term feedback adaptations, in which the success or otherwise of a particular instance of the act modifies the algorithm for its future production. The short-term regulations relate to the intrinsic processes by which the servo mechanism tracks its set point. The hypothesis adopted here is that these regulatory processes rely on internal (kinesthetic or central) feedback information. The long-term adaptations, on the other hand, relate to processes responsible for resetting the servo mechanism's set point, and it is argued that these processes require the integration of information carried in both the internal and external feedback pathways. In the short term, feedback is employed to gauge and correct the execution of ongoing acts so as to generate motor responses that conform to previously formulated plans.

That data from the kinesthetic pathways are employed in the programming of movements according to previously formulated plans is strongly suggested by observations such as those recently reported by Bonnet and Requin (1982). This investigator elicited stretch reflexes in forearm muscles by rapid mechanical disturbances of wrist position at various times during the foreperiod of a precued two-choice reaction time experiment. On experimental trials, a warning stimulus informed subjects about whether on that trial they had to rotate their wrists to the right or to the left when an imperative stimulus occurred. At various times following the onset of the warning stimulus, a torque pulse was applied to the wrist. This stimulus produced three sequential muscular reflexes. The shortest-latency muscular response, which reflects activity in the monosynaptic reflex pathway, did not differentiate trials on which the subject was precued to move the wrist right or left. In other words, planning for the direction of the forthcoming movement was not manifested at this level of the nervous system. However, the longer-latency responses (particularly the third component), attributed to transcortical loops and involving a number of higher structures, exhibited increasing reflex gain when the recorded muscle served as the agonist of the forthcoming movement and decreasing gain when it served as the antagonist.

How motor plans might operate in generating the specific patterns of muscular activity required to meet prevailing environmental demands has been described by Requin (1980) in his neuropsychological theory for preparation for action. Current models of motor control consider that when activated, motor plans supervise the programming of relevant activities through a series of sequential processing stages. The first stage involves identifying an action project that meets the requirements of the demand situation. Then through further stages, this general behavioral specification is decomposed into the specific patterns of efference that will activate the striate musculature. Target effectors must be specified and their force, timing, and sequential parameters must be set before the derived pattern of efference is relayed to the involved muscles. Requin points out that the information-processing stages employed by psychologists to describe how environmentally signaled demands for behavior are translated into appropriate motor activities are mirrored by the sequence of nervous system events revealed by parallel neurophysiological experiments in the area of motor control.

Since they specify the informational processes by which appropriate behavior is generated, accounts of motor programming are highly relevant to the analysis of motor learning. However, these accounts do not deal in any detail with the fundamental question of how the motor plans themselves originate. In fact, with few exceptions (e.g., Adams, 1971; Schmidt, 1975), the articulation of models that describe how feedback processes operate in long-term behavioral adaptation has received relatively little attention. Evidence presented below suggests that although motor plans may be genetically prewired, they may also have been elaborated through the long-term, calibrating functions of external feedback (feedback learning or operant conditioning). In relation to the mechanisms by which external feedback achieves its motor planning functions, Paillard (1980) makes reference to the "pretuning" of regulatory feedback loops to be employed in guiding the movement. This may involve defining the program structure by identifying relevant sources of kinesthetic information to be tapped and setting the program's operating characteristics by selecting appropriate gain levels in the implicated pathways. As a function of continued practice with external feedback, these parameters may be set and stored, and thereby a motor plan is constituted. Evidence suggests that once external feedback has achieved this calibrating function, its involvement in motor control and learning is substantially reduced.

The processing of external feedback entails a commitment of nervous system resources that may be lessened by a reversion to an open-loop, feedforward mode of control once a motor plan has been formulated. This process is illustrated by the work of Flowers (1978) on predictive control of tracking behavior. He found that in tracking a predictably moving visual target, subjects learned to simulate the movements of the target with the pointing limb. He observed that when sight of the target was briefly eliminated, the movement of the tracking limb continued to reflect the position of the unseen target. This supported the inference that feedforward processes had come to play an important role in controlling "tracking" performance. However, when the target's movements were made unpredictable, thereby precluding the development of an appropriate motor plan, subjects continued to rely on visual guidance. As Flowers points out, the additional time lag and information-processing load implied by employing the visual feedback mode of pointing renders this a less efficient means of achieving the target. Relevant experimental data have also been presented by Hay (1978), who found that at the age of 7 years, children start to use visual feedback during the course of target pointing. Use of this information offers advantages by permitting adjustments to be in the course of a movement. However, while children are learning to employ information from this source, they exhibit a temporary decrease in open-loop pointing accuracy, and their movement times increase.

Such a temporary reliance on feedback may apply not only to external sources of information about the conduct of behavior, but to internal sources as well. Many researchers (e.g., Keele, 1981) have reiterated the point of view that a primary function of kinesthetic feedback is the updating of motor programs, and it would seem that our understanding of how instrumental learning contributes to variations in behavioral efficiency may be improved by a more detailed specification of this function. The experimental study of deafferentation provides a major source of relevant information.

DEAFFERENTATION

The conventional servo control view of motor regulation implies a logical necessity for the brain circuits responsible for controlling an effector to receive information about the state of activity of that effector. Mott and Sherrington's (1895) early demonstration that monkeys cease to use a limb voluntarily when it is unilaterally deafferented did much to reinforce this view. Subsequent observations that if the normal limb is physically restrained or if both limbs are deafferented, then deafferented limbs are used fairly normally (Taub, 1976), are mentioned less often. Nevertheless, the deafferentation experiments reported by Taub and his colleagues have been pivotal in shaking the belief that effector-produced peripheral feedback is essential for motor control. Following an extensive series of experiments involving total and partial unilateral and bilateral dorsal rhizotomy in fetal, infant, and mature monkeys, Taub (1976) concluded that "the central nervous system of the motorically mature monkey is capable of autonomously generating movements of almost any type in the absence of guidance either from the environment or from sensory cues originating in the organism's body" (p. 676).

These dramatically counterintuitive findings have tended to deflect attention away from the deficits in motor performance that were found and that constrain the implications of Taub's conclusion. In assessing the effects of deafferentation, it is important to take account of the level of behavioral analysis on which interferences about the effects of the procedure have been drawn. Thus, while much data confirms Taub's general conclusion, there is also clear evidence of specific motor deficits. Bossom and Ommaya (1968), Taub (1976), Vierck (1978), and Brinkman and Porter (1978), among others, have reported that deafferentation leads to impairments of fine-grain control of the fingers, movement timing, the regulation of force, tactile discriminations, and the location of targets on the basis of tactile information.

Many of the behaviors examined in deafferented animals are drawn from the class of phylogenetically preprogrammed responses; as mentioned earlier, such activities are largely prewired and controlled as coordinative structures by feedforward processes. For example, Fentress (1972) observed that following amputation of a forelimb at 1 day of age, mice displayed normal grooming behavior. The movement patterns exhibited by these animals involved a complex sequence of postural adjustments, and incorporated muscular activation patterns in the stumps of amputated limbs that were indistinguishable from those recorded from the normal limbs of unoperated mice. A similar phenomenon has been reported by Provine (1979) for "wing-flapping" in chicks that have had their wings amputated. It seems clear that neither kinesthetic feedback from the involved effectors nor knowledge of the results of the programmed actions is important in regulating these activities. In confirmation of the latter point, Bolles and Woods (1964) observed that at 5 days of age, normal rats will go through all the motions of scratching without the limb making any contact with the body. These abortive "scratching" bouts are incorporated in grooming sequences that terminate with animals licking the "scratching foot" and then their fur. In each of these cases, the sequencing and coordination of the activities described are largely independent of their immediate effects.

It is probable that most behaviors are built on such genetically preprogrammed cores, which may be elaborated or resequenced by experience but which are not amenable to downward modification. Thus, Nottebohm (1970) found that unilateral deafferentation of the vocal apparatus in birds led to their developing songs that lacked certain features, but that nevertheless displayed correct timing. It is interesting to note that a similar effect is obtained by preventing chaffinches from hearing birdsong during a sensitive period of their early development (Hinde, 1970). In the latter case, the birds were deprived of an appropriate auditory model for the motor plan, whereas in the former case, although the model was available, the elimination of kinesthetic feedback prevented the animals from developing an appropriate motor plan.

Thus it would appear that although the prewired framework of behavior is impervious to experience and uninfluenced by deafferentation, the experiential elaboration of the motor framework requires kinesthetic feedback from the involved effectors. This hypothesis seems to be compromised by observations that although movement in the affected limbs is severely impaired following deafferentation, normal motor control is gradually reacquired over a period of months. However, Taub (1976) presents a good case in favor of the proposition that this restoration of function is attributable, not to learning, but to recovery from the shock of spinal surgery, which enables previously acquired motor processes to re-emerge.

In fact, deafferented animals require significantly more time than normal animals to learn new sensory-motor coordinations. For example, comparisons of avoidance conditioning between normal and deafferented monkeys revealed that acquisition of avoidance responses took three times as long, and extinction of responses four times as long, in operated as in nonoperated animals (Taub & Berman, 1963). Where tonic rather than phasic muscular responses are required, the effects of deafferentation are more pronounced. Thus, Rodin and Berman (1981) found that rats were unable to acquire a tonic flexion avoidance response in a deafferented limb unless they had previously acquired the response in the other, normal limb. One of the implications of this finding is that movement algorithms formed on the basis of kinesthesia from one source may be applied to generating movements in effectors that are remote from that source of information.

Another illustration of the contribution of kinesthetic feedback to the learning process is contained in a report by Polit and Bizzi (1978), who taught monkeys to point at illuminated targets with their unseen forearms for food rewards. On some trials, the starting position of the forearm was changed immediately prior to the movement (within the reaction time), but this did not affect pointing accuracy. Furthermore, accuracy under normal conditions and conditions in which the forearm position had been disturbed was not degraded by bilateral deafferention of the arms. During the course of the experiment, a series of trials was given in which the body positions of normal and deafferented animals were altered relative to the target lights. This postural disturbance required pointing movements (elbow angles) to be adjusted in order to achieve accurate target location. Although normal animals rapidly made such adjustments, deafferented animals did not modify their behavior and persisted with their inaccurate preoperative pointing movements. This led Polit and Bizzi to conclude that "in the performance of visually evoked, learned movements, one of the major functions of afferent feedback is in the adaptive modification of learned motor programs" (1978, p. 1237).

Finally, in evaluating the effects of deafferentation, consideration must be given to arguments that lesions of the dorsal columns do not unequivocally exclude the contribution of peripheral effector feedback. Following such surgery, two alternative internal routes may continue to provide information about effector activity. Coggeshall (1980) has pointed out that the law of separation of afferent and efferent functions at the spinal level (the "Bell–Magendie law") is an oversimplification: A significant proportion of fibers entering the ventral roots are sensory in function. Secondly, there is a great deal of redundancy in the information transmitted within and between sensory systems. An example of redundancy within the visual channel is provided by evidence that cats can still perform complex visual discriminations following lesions of the optic tract that are 98% complete (Galambos, Norton, & Frommer, 1967). Also relevant is the report by Weiskrantz, Warrington, Sanders, and Marshall (1974) that an individual with cortical lesions that prevented conscious vision in part of the visual field was still able to discriminate objects instrumentally in the blind area.

Such redundancy is also characteristic of information transmitted through the feedback channels. Thus Frommer (1981) found that tactile discriminations were relearned by cats and rats following lesions in midbrain afferent (lemniscal) pathways from which responses to tactile stimulation had been previously recorded. Furthermore, evoked responses to tactile stimulation in higher somatosensory areas were virtually unchanged following the lesions. These phenomena were attributed both to fibers traveling outside of the main afferent tracts and to some residual fibers that were spared by the lesions. Frommer concluded that normal performance may be sustained by a small fragment of the feedback information normally available.

The possibility of sensing effector action through relatively remote peripheral pathways is another route through which effector activity may be assessed following deafferentation. This point is recognized by Duysens and Loeb (1978), who have remarked, "A complete description of the physical events accompanying a behavioral task is virtually impossible; some change is affected in virtually every muscle, joint, skin surface and metabolic and circulatory pathway in the body" (p. 149). Thus, if a preferred source of regulatory information is blocked, alternative sources may be tapped. Consequently, the possibility that activity is being regulated by peripheral feedback is not excluded by dorsal column lesions.

The results of experiments involving deafferentation permit several conclusions. Fine-grain activities, particularly those involving tactile discriminations, are most dependent on feedback from the involved effectors for their regulation. Desmedt and Godaux (1978) have concluded that the results of deafferentation experiments "do not really question the view that smooth and precise skilled movements in intact man could not be made without kinesthetic feedback" (p. 37). Nevertheless, many other activities appear to be controlled independently of feedback in an open-loop fashion. These are frequently genetically pre-wired and are not modifiable by experience. Since well-established learned acts are also relatively uninfluenced by kinesthetic feedback impairments, it may be inferred that they too are controlled in an open-loop fashion. However, following deafferentation, learned acts become resistant to further modification and persist in their preoperative state even if situational changes render them ineffective. This supports the view that internal effector-produced feedback is implicated in formulating and updating motor plans responsible for generating adaptive movements. In order to employ feedback for this purpose, the nervous system must deal with the formidable task of selecting relevant kinesthetic information from the constant stream of afference with which it is continuously bombarded. It is suggested below that this filtering function is performed by central neural processes involved in driving the target effectors.

AFFERENT-FILTERING, INFORMATIONAL, AND COMPARATOR FUNCTIONS OF CENTRAL MOVEMENT PROCESSES

One of the more vexing problems posed by the deafferentation experiments concerns how operated animals learn new sensory–motor coordinations. A suggested solution is that although feedback is necessary for the formulation of motor plans, once a plan has been established it may be executed without feedback, and it may also come under the control of new stimuli through feedforward learning processes. In order to examine this hypothesis, Taub (1976) deafferented fetal monkeys in the final third of their gestation periods and reimplanted them in their mothers' uteri. This treatment should prevent the initial formulation of motor plans and lead to intractable impairments in motor control and learning. Although somewhat retarded in their motor development, the two subjects on which this procedure was successful developed relatively normal patterned movements. Perhaps fibers spared by the lesions, or ventral root afferents, supported motor learning in these subjects. The alternative favored by Taub in accounting for this surprising result is that efferent outflow from the motor control centers provided adequate information for formulating motor plans.

The concepts of a "sense of innervation," "corollary discharge," and "central efferent monitoring," referred to here as "central movement processes," have come to play an increasingly important role in models of behavioral regulation. The idea that the brain monitors its own output was introduced by von Helmholtz (1866/1964) in order to explain the observation that the apparent motion of the visual world produced by externally imposed eye movements was absent when the eye movements were triggered by the brain. This implied that the visual system takes account of movement commands to the eyes in assessing afference from the retina. In other words, the nervous system has the capacity to utilize information flowing from the motor generators in interpreting information from the peripheral sensory receptors.

The wide adoption of this concept in neuropsychological models is due largely to the classic experiments of von Holst and Mittelstaedt (1950/1971) on optokinetic reflexes in flies. Their data provided a strong basis for inferring that when the nervous system generates and transmits a pattern of efference to the effectors, it retains a copy for comparison with the sensory consequences of the motor activity produced. Two interrelated functions are attributed to the efference copy. It serves a "comparator" function in providing a standard against which reafferent stimuli can be evaluated and response corrections made if necessary. In the process, it serves a gating or "afferent-filtering" function that distinguishes response-contingent (reafferent) stimuli from response-independent (exafferent) stimuli.

Central movement processes have also been implicated in perception by Festinger, Ono, Burnham, and Bamber (1967). These investigators have provided an experimental case in favor of the hypothesis that motor outflow is a powerful determinant of how sensory input will be interpreted. Although their analysis emphasized the informational content of efferent outflow, this "motor theory of perception" (Metzger, 1974) may be viewed as an expression of the afferent-filtering function. Another influential interpretation of this function applied to perception has been proposed by Held (1965), who argued that since adapta-

tion to displacement prisms occurred more markedly under conditions of active than passive movement, central movement processes must be responsible for gating afferent inputs into the associative ("correlational") circuits that are responsible for sensory-motor recalibration. In agreement with the original formulation of von Holst and Mittelstaedt (1950/ 1971), Held's view implies that the comparator and afferent-filtering functions of central feedback are combined. The residue (exafference) that results from subtracting the information contained in the efference copy from the information contained in the reafference constitutes perception.

A considerable body of relatively direct evidence supports the view that central processes related to movement serve the function of filtering and routing afferent input to appropriate neural analyzers. For example, Dyhre-Poulsen (1978) observed that responses in the medial lemniscus evoked by peripheral tactile stimuli are suppressed immediately prior to a movement. This structure forms an intermediate section of the pathway from the dorsal columns to the motor cortex. During the period of this depression, tactile discrimination is also relatively impaired (see also Coquery, 1978). Since here the depression of central nervous system responses to peripheral stimulation is accompanied by a discriminative performance deficit, it may be inferred that the filtering processes active in the period surrounding a movement influence not only data transmission but also information transmission. This effect is more marked for stimuli applied to the limb to be moved than to the contralateral limb.

Similar effects at the spinal level are described by Bonnet, Requin, and Semjen (1981), who found that prior to a movement, and over approximately the same time course as that recorded by Dyhre-Poulsen (1978), myotatic reflexes are more depressed in the limb to be involved in the forthcoming movement than in the contralateral limb. They have attributed this monosynaptic reflex depression to presynaptic inhibition of stretch receptor outputs at the spinal level. The postulated function of this process is to provide unfettered access by the higher brain centers to the alpha motoneuron pools to be involved in a forthcoming movement. Thus, during the time surrounding a movement, monosynaptically linked peripheral sensory inputs to the target effectors are disabled. Although information from the intrafusal receptors to their direct spinal motoneuron targets is suppressed in the period preceding a movement, these sensory sources may continue to feed information to higher levels. This is illustrated in experiments by Coquery (1978), where the effects of movement on the amplitudes of evoked responses to tactile stimulation were recorded from three consecutive locations along the peripheral–central afferent pathway in cats. He concluded that "motor commands appear to inhibit the first (more peripheral) relay of the lemniscal pathway and possibly to facilitate the thalamic relay" (p. 168).

Further evidence of the selective nature of movement-related afferent-filtering processes is provided by the observation of Fromm and Evarts (1978) that precentral cortical evoked responses to kinesthetic inputs (a torque pulse applied to the responding limb) were enhanced in preparation for an accurate placing or fine-grain movement, but depressed prior to a ballistic movement. This finding, which is compatible with the view that peripheral feedback is not implicated in the regulation of ballistic movements (Kornhuber, 1974), indicates that the nature of the movement being planned or executed may determine the pathways through which reafferent information will flow. When the motor cortex transmits signals down the spinal cord to produce motor activity, collaterals from the pyramidal tract also deliver strong signals to the basal ganglia, the brain stem, and the cerebellum. These pathways may well be involved in afferent-filtering processes. In this connection, Tsumoto, Nakamura, and Iwana (1975) have described data indicating that, although at rest the ventrobasal relay cells preferentially transmit cutaneous over kinesthetic stimuli, this bias is reversed by pyramidal tract facilitation during voluntary movements.

These data suggest that in achieving their function of activating the effectors, efferent processes serve essential intermediate functions. At central and peripheral levels, they appear to be responsible for filtering afferent input and routing sensory data to those structures that require it for regulating effector activity in accordance with the demands of the prevailing conditions. Such filtering functions may not be the exclusive domain of central movement processes; similar functions have been attributed to exteroceptive (Graham, 1975), peripheral kinesthetic (Coquery, 1978), and cardiovascular afference (Lacey & Lacey, 1974). However, this does not appear to compromise the implication that there is a strong compatibility among the "languages" in which the nervous system represents goals, effector activity, and reafference. The comparator function ascribed to central movement processes is critical to this analysis. In order to evaluate reafference, the comparator must retain a template of the intended action. It is argued below that the templates or motor plans are themselves constructed from information contained in kinesthetic afference.

FUNCTIONS OF FEEDBACK IN TARGET IDENTIFICATION

Bizzi, Polit, and Morasso (1976) studied neck movements in monkeys that had been deprived of their vestibular apparatus. Subjects had to rotate their heads to different extents and in different directions so as to point at illuminated visual targets. At the inception of each movement, the target light was extinguished, thereby preventing animals from employing visual guidance to achieve target position. Unpredictably, on some trials an inertial load was applied to head movements, resulting in target overshoot with subsequent correction. On other trials, a spring arrangement increased the muscular force required to achieve target position. This resulted in target undershoot, which was corrected as soon as the spring was released. The accuracy and topography of movements observed on normal trials and on trials in which these disturbances were introduced were not affected by deafferentation of the neck muscles. This indicated that the pointing movements were driven in an open-loop, feedforward fashion. Furthermore, the topographies of movements recorded on trials in which the inertial and spring loads were introduced implied that the movements were programmed to achieve particular muscular endpoints. This section considers the possibility that such motor goals are specified on the basis of information contained in kinesthetic afference.

The results of this and other experiments (e.g., Kelso & Holt, 1980; Polit & Bizzi, 1978) are consistent with Feldman's (1966a, 1966b) hypothesis that the brain codes limb target positions in terms of length–tension coordinates in the agonist–antagonist muscle pairs moving a joint. Other data (e.g., Bizzi, Accornero, Chapple, & Hogan, 1982) suggest that the representation of movements solely in terms of their terminal muscular states may apply only to a restricted class of responses. However, if some variant of the endpoint hypothesis is accepted, and if it is acknowledged that visually specified target locations may be associated with appropriate muscular endpoints, a mechanism is implied whereby the nervous system may use a single algorithm to generate accurate pointing movements, regardless of the limb's starting position. Obviously, movements directed at the same target from different starting positions will have different topographies. Therefore, the hypothesis suggests a physiologically comprehensible way of generating as many functionally equivalent pointing movements as there are starting positions. In so doing, it provides an option to the implausible alternative that is gratuitously and frequently attributed to "stimulus–response" learning theory: that the nervous system retains a copy of each response variant that an organism exhibits.

The endpoint programming hypothesis provides a potentially powerful concept in the analysis of motor learning when it is assimilated with William James's (1890/1950) ideomotor theory of voluntary control. This theory, which continues to command a substantial following among researchers concerned with modeling the processes of motor learning, proposes that the stored sensory consequences of previous occurrences of a response provide the motor template for future occasions on which the response is required. It therefore suggests that the endpoint representations are constructed from information contained in response feedback (Kimble & Perlmuter, 1970). An attempt to apply this model to account for instances of learned visceral–motor control has been described previously (Brener, 1974a, 1974b, 1977a, 1977b, 1982). These ideas provide a basis for the view that the eliciting conditions for learned actions may be physiologically isomorphic with the sensory goals of those actions.

The experimental basis on which one might claim that motor plans are based upon motor memories is illustrated in an experiment by Liu (1968). This investigator required subjects on one occasion to press a plunger 3.5 cm against a load of either 500 or 1000 g. On a second occasion, the subject was presented with the same task (press the plunger 3.5 cm), but the force required for the response was altered. Invariably, subjects who had to press against a lighter load on the second occasion overshot the extent criterion, and subjects who had to press against a heavier load undershot it. These results indicate that following the first trial, subjects planned the force of the response in addition to its extent. Although this procedure did not yield data on the sources of information employed to identify the required force of the movement, other procedures do yield relevant data.

Following a thorough review of kinesthesia, McCloskey (1978) concluded that central efferent sources provide a preferred basis for judging heaviness or response force over more accurate information derived from the sense organs in the involved effectors. For example, subjects report great effort in trying to contract curarized muscles (Goodwin, McCloskey, & Matthews, 1972). It is also relevant that as a function of the time that a subject has to support a weight, the weight appears to get heavier. This is unlikely to be due to changes in tactile, joint, or tendon sensations, which reflect the actual state of the involved receptors. Therefore, by default, central efferent processes are implicated; since maintaining the same work output in a fatigued muscle requires greater central motor outflow ("effort"), it may also be assumed that fusimotor drive and hence stretch receptor output will be augmented. However, it has been shown that stimulation of the stretch receptors by mechanical vibration leads to a decrease in the sense of effort accompanying the contraction of the vibrated muscle (Hagbarth & Eklund, 1966), and not an increase. Hence the increased effort associated with fatigue may be attributed to central efferent monitoring.

Because of the great redundancy in feedback information, it is possible to sense a given movement parameter through many different channels, and this makes it difficult to draw firm general conclusions about the sources of information contained in a motor plan. For example, after having trained rats to press a lever with a criterion force in order to obtain food reinforcement, Notterman and Mintz (1965) anesthetized the front (lever-pressing) paws of subjects, thereby eliminating tactile feedback. Under these conditions, force increased, suggesting that in this case the motor plan specified a peripheral tactile endpoint rather than a particular level of central efferent output. Other experiments indicate that force may also be specified on the basis of stretch receptor feedback.

Roland (1978) has provided relevant information in an interesting series of experiments concerned with the sources of afference employed in constructing movement targets and with the kinesthetic cues required to guide movements to those targets. Subjects were required to match either the force or the extent of a squeezing movement in one hand (the reference hand) with a similar movement of the other hand (the indicator hand). Sources of information that could logically permit the performance of this task were then successively eliminated. In principle, subjects could regulate movements of the reference or the indicator hand by feedback derived from joint receptors, from tactile pressure receptors, from central efferent processes, or from muscle and tendon organs sensitive to stretch.

It was found that following local anesthetization of the joints and tactile receptors, subjects were still able to match the force and extent of responses by the reference hand with responses by the indicator hand. Such matching could be supported either by stretch receptor feedback or by central feedback processes. In order to eliminate the latter possibility, Roland partially blocked myoneural transmission in the involved muscle of the reference hand by the local administration of gallamine triethiodide, a curare-like substance. This reduced the effectiveness of central commands to the muscle fibers and hence required a greater "central effort" to achieve the same muscular contraction. Under these conditions, and following elimination of tactile and joint sensations in both hands, force and extent matching of the partially paralyzed reference hand with the indicator hand was observed. This leads to the conclusion that force and extent targets can be set on the basis of stretch receptor or tendon organ output. Hence any of the sensory sources that may code response force will perform this function under the appropriate conditions.

Furthermore, sensory sources that enable the coding of one movement parameter, such as force, may also provide information for the coding of other parameters, such as extent or position (Stein, 1982). For example, the value of information from active movement receptors in locating the position of a limb has been demonstrated by Paillard and Brouchon (1968). Blindfolded subjects were required to touch the finger tips of the two hands together. It was found that if a subject actively moved the reference hand to the target location, its position was identified more accurately than if the reference hand was moved to the target position passively. This advantage, which lasted for a few seconds, may have been due to the greater activation by active movement of peripheral stretch receptors, which are sensitive to movement change. These receptors may provide trajectory information from which an endpoint can be computed. Alternatively, through afferent-filtering processes, central neural activities related to active but not passive movement may have served to identify the states of static joint and/or muscle receptors associated with the achievement of the target endpoint. These accounts are further complicated by consideration of data from a subsequent experiment by Paillard, Brouchon-Viton, and Jordan (1978). They found that a cutaneous stimulus (an unpainful 1-msec electric shock) delivered to the pointing finger of the reference hand significantly improved localization of the finger by the other hand if it had been displaced by passive movement to its target position. This could imply that location information from the phasic joint and muscular receptors activated during transport of the reference hand to its target location, or from the static receptors on achieving target position, was "gated" into memory by the cutaneous stimulus. This explanation attributes a similar afferent-filtering role to the cutaneous stimulus as that previously attributed to central movement processes.

The results of experiments involving mechanical vibration of tendons strongly suggest that the sensations produced by the phasic stretch receptors of muscles acting at one joint may serve as *movement* targets for muscles moving the contralateral joint. Goodwin et al. (1972) required subjects to "track" the movements of an unseen vibrated arm with the contralateral arm. Tracking performance indicated that muscular vibration, which activates Ia afferent pathways (Roll, 1981), gave rise to sensations of stretching of the vibrated muscle. Thus if the biceps were vibrated while the vibrated limb was mechanically restrained from moving, subjects tracked a path with the contralateral limb that indicated elbow extension in the vibrated arm. In principle, it should be possible to teach a subject a movement pattern by stimulating the kinesthetic afferent pathways in the absence of any actual movement.

The feasibility of this proposal is supported by experiments reported by Roll (1981), in which tendon vibration was examined as a method for muscular rehabilitation of the legs. The studies were carried out on patients whose legs had been immobilized in plaster casts for long periods of time following bone or joint injuries. Following removal of the plaster casts, a control group received traditional physiotherapy, whereas an experimental group received tendon vibration in the affected limb, followed by traditional physiotherapy. After five daily sessions of tendon vibration, experimental patients were found to have achieved a significantly greater improvement in angular rotation in the affected joint. This advantage was maintained when the patients in this group were transferred to the traditional methods received by control subjects from the outset of therapy. In a further study, patients received tendon vibration through holes cut in the plaster casts while their legs were still immobilized. It was found that on removal of the casts, physiotherapy was unnecessary for four of the five patients studied. It is possible that these therapeutic effects were due to informational functions of Ia afference in maintaining movement plans.

These data are consistent with the view that kinesthetic information provides the machine "language" of the motor control system. This is the language in which motor programs are written and their performance is evaluated. it is argued below that learning assembles environmental commands, which are conveyed through the exteroceptive modalities, into motor commands, which are written in kinesthetic language.

SENSORY–MOTOR CALIBRATION

The processes by which organisms learn to achieve external goals must entail the acquisition of selective movement-controlling properties by exteroceptive stimuli. As in the case of autoshaping, feedforward learning may contribute to these processes by providing goal-predicting signals with access to established pathways through which goal responses are activated. However, if a maturing organism is to maintain efficient performance in a changing environment, the algorithms for generating goal-directed movements must be amenable to continuous revision on the basis of their consequences. It would seem that the mechanisms underlying such revisions have much in common with the learning functions of operant reinforcement.

The achievement of external goals implies, *inter alia*, the need for a mechanism that translates goal stimuli into positions in egocentric space. At the moment that a goal is actually reached, its exteroceptively sensed location coincides with the kinesthetically sensed location of the reaching limb. This correlation provides a readily available means of identifying goal-directed kinesthetic information. Evidence has been presented to indicate that motor plans may be formu-lated on the basis of such kinesthetic information. It is now proposed that learning serves to develop associations between exteroceptive goal stimuli and the kinesthetic stimuli produced by goal-directed responses. By so doing, learning provides goal stimuli with access to motor plans that generate movements leading to the capture of the goal object. This associative process may provide a physiologically plausible route through which stimulus–stimulus learning can mediate instrumental behavior.

The complex informational functions of exteroceptive goal stimuli in this process have been illuminated by Paillard's (1980) interesting experimental analyses of the functions served by two anatomically distinguishable visual pathways that are involved in directing movements toward external targets. The "positional" pathway that runs from the center of the retina through the lateral geniculate bodies to the striate cortex is capable of high resolution and is concerned with identifying the position and shape of the target. During the movement, and while the target is "grasped" by the fovea, data from the "movement" pathway, which runs from the peripheral retina to the collicular structures, provides information that can be used to regulate the trajectory of the reaching limb relative to the visual axis. It may be argued that these anatomically distinct pathways serve distinguishable functions in generating plans for movements that are appropriate to the environmental circumstances signaled through vision.

The processes of exteroceptive–kinesthetic association have been studied most comprehensively in relation to the sensory–motor adjustments that occur when individuals are required to wear displacement prisms for protracted periods. It is well established that these conditions give rise to predictable disturbances in sensory–motor coordination. Thus a person wearing prisms that displace the visual world 10° to the left will initially point 10° to the left of the real location of visual targets. Such inaccuracies wane more or less rapidly, depending on the conditions that prevail while the subject is wearing the prisms. If the prisms are removed when adaptation has taken place and accurate pointing has been re-established, then errors will be committed in the opposite direction to the displacement of the prisms: In this case, the subject will point to the right of the target.

Prism adaptation may be attributed to the recalibration of cues employed by the nervous system to calculate the egocentric position of the target (Kornheiser, 1976). Apart from the controversial results generated by experiments that have examined adaptation to inverting prisms (e.g., Stratton, 1896), there is no evidence that individuals learn to reinterpret the positional significance of localized patterns of retinal stimulation (Crawshaw & Craske, 1974). On the other hand, a considerable body of evidence does show that adaptation may influence the interpretation of kinesthetic cues related to eye position, head position, or the position of any of the joints involved in the pointing movement. Recalibration of head and eye kinesthesia serves to alter the perceived locations of external objects with respect to the body. By redefining the positional significance of these visual–motor cues, the subject's visual axis with respect to the target is redefined; this results in straight-ahead visual targets being seen, for example, 10° to the right. On the other hand, recalibration of kinesthesia from the pointing limb serves to redefine the position of the limb with respect to the body; in this case the adapted limb will be felt to be, for example, 10° to the right of its actual location. Adaptation either of eye and head position or of limb position will enable the subject to point accurately at prismatically displaced targets. However, different loci of adaptation have different behavioral consequences, and there is some evidence that different neural pathways may be involved in recalibrating head and eye kinesthesia on the one hand and limb kinesthesia on the other.

Following an excellent review of the prism experiments, Kornheiser (1976) concluded that adaptation can best be understood in terms of processes by which conflicts in information regarding location are resolved. If a situation leads the subject to rely on one source of feedback to guide a movement, then information from that source will be employed to define the body coordinates of target position, and data from other potential sources of body position will be realigned with it (Canon, 1971; Cohen, 1967). This hypothesis is supported by evidence that the adaptation procedure employed is a significant determinant of which source of kinesthesia will be recalibrated.

The positional significance of eye and head cues tends to be modified under conditions in which subjects are required to point at a prismatically displaced visual target with an unseen arm and are given information about their accuracy only when the movement is completed (terminal feedback condition). Under this "knowledge of results only" condition, guidance of the limb toward the apparent location of the target must be accomplished ballistically or on the basis of kinesthetic cues. Here, relevant visual information is only available through the central "positional" visual pathway and not through the peripheral "movement" pathway. Adaptation effects generated by these constraints transfer to limbs that were unseen during the adaptation procedure; on this basis, recalibration of head and eye kinesthesia may be inferred. By biasing the position of the visual receptors, the subject's body axis with respect to the target is maintained, and this adaptation thereby avoids the need to update visual–motor transformations for each potential pointing limb.

On the other hand, if subjects are required to point at a prismatically displaced target under conditions where sight of the pointing limb is not restricted (continuous feedback), visual guidance plays a stronger part in directing movement to the target; here limb kinesthesia is recalibrated, rather than head and eye cues. In such conditions, which permit visual guidance through the peripheral channel during the course of the movement, adaptation effects are restricted to the reaching limb and do not transfer to other limbs (Kornheiser, 1976). Thus the motor consequences of this form of adaptation are more localized than those produced by the terminal feedback condition. However, the contribution of the peripheral visual channel to the more specific recalibration observed under continuous feedback conditions remains unclear, since, in either case, adaptation need involve nothing more than redefinition of the kinesthetic (either of the eye and head or of the limb) equivalents of visually sensed locations (endpoints).

The fact that adaptation occurs under terminal feedback conditions and under conditions of passive movement (Kornheiser, 1976) suggests that endpoint programming may provide an adequate basis for generating coordinated movement patterns. However in real life, reaching responses are often directed at moving targets; in such cases, the desired endpoint cannot be specified independently of movement velocity. Furthermore, since the masses of different limbs vary, they require different muscular impulses in order to achieve the same trajectory. Thus it might be expected that information delivered through the peripheral visual channel, which is only sensitive to movement cues, is necessary for updating algorithms that determine the dynamic properties of movements transporting the pointing limb from its starting position to its endpoint.

By this hypothesis, movement (as opposed to position) recalibration should be prevented by restricting visual input through stroboscopic illumination. This technique, which necessarily excludes visual input of movement, has been shown not to impair prism adaptation (Moulden, 1971), which presumably proceeds through the same pathways that account for adaptation under terminal feedback conditions. However, the hypothesis appears to be severely compromised by results showing that kittens that had been reared under conditions of regular stroboscopic illumination (2 Hz) exhibited normal visual–motor coordination (Paillard, 1980). This implies either that exteroceptive information available through the central visual channel is adequate for developing dynamic movement programs, or that the algorithms for transporting a limb from its starting point to its endpoint are hardwired. The former possibility has been considered by Paillard, who has suggested that in the case of regular stroboscopic illumination, limb velocity may be computed from changes in position on successive flashes. This interpretation is supported, and the hypothesis of movement programming through the peripheral

visual channel is sustained by the observation that rearing kittens under conditions of irregular stroboscopic illumination (.5–3.5 Hz) led to greatly impaired visual–motor coordination as measured in a pointing task.

SYNOPSIS

Refinements in motor control that characterize learning may be attributed to the calibration functions of reinforcing stimuli. Although it may be reasonably inferred that increases in behavioral efficiency carry survival advantages, it has been suggested that such biological advantages cannot easily account for the phenomena of improved behavioral efficiency. The alternative view taken here is that the calibration of kinesthetic stimuli by exteroceptive feedback occurs as an automatic consequence of the organism's interaction with its environment. This process leads to the incorporation of kinesthetic information that is most reliably associated with the achievement of an exteroceptively sensed goal into the motor plans activated by signals that predict this goal. As a result, motor responses that are more precisely attuned to prevailing environmental conditions develop naturally, and behavioral efficiency increases. In other words, increases in behavioral efficiency are understood in terms of the informational functions of response-contingent stimulation, and not in terms of their incentive functions. Thus, although the survival chances of organisms are enhanced by more efficient motor control, the nervous system only realizes this in its genetically prestructured features, and not through real-time evaluations of biological value.

The same hard-wired features also limit the extent of recalibration and thereby place ceilings on the levels of behavioral refinement and efficiency that may be achieved. These limits seem to be imposed in accordance with a principle of minimizing informational load. Judging from the resistance to learning exhibited under a variety of conditions, it may be inferred that reprogramming of the nervous system entails a substantial biological cost. This is particularly evident in learning that occurs in situations that release genetically preprogrammed responses, such as autoshaping, avoidance conditioning (Bolles, 1970), and omission training (Sheffield, 1965), as well as in the phenomena of instinctive drift (Breland & Breland, 1961). But it is also clear that learned behavioral variations are differentially amenable to alteration according to the conditions under which they have been acquired and maintained (Staddon, 1975). For example, McCulloch (1934) found that rats only acquired a more efficient strategy for getting food if the already unfavorable costs of their current strategy were greatly augmented. He found that the length of time that animals had maintained an unfavorable strategy and the intrinsic costs of this preprogrammed strategy were both positively related to its resistance to modification.

Perhaps this tendency has evolved because learning absorbs a significant proportion of the organism's information-processing capacity, and, as such, it diverts these resources from other more immediate survival demands. In other words, a survival penalty may be incurred by individuals who are more absorbed in learning, because this puts them at an immediate competitive disadvantage and makes them more subject to predation. Nevertheless, it is clear that a balance must be struck, since unmodifiable behaviors also carry survival penalties in a changing environment. A compromise between the needs for flexibility and short-term efficiency may be achieved by providing feedforward control with a higher priority than feedback control. This arrangement would result in the motor-programming functions of operant reinforcement only entering the learning process at a relatively advanced stage of behavioral adaptation to a novel situation.

It is obvious that before an operant reinforcer may exert a feedback influence, the reinforcer must be produced by the response on which it is contingent. At least on the first occasion, the response must be produced open-loop with respect to the reinforcing stimulus—through feedforward control exerted by features of the situation. It is likely that when the reinforcing stimulus does occur, and before its feedback-programming functions begin to be realized, it will further restrict the organism's behavioral repertoire through feedforward pathways. In addition, via classical conditioning or feedforward learning, exteroceptively sensed features of the novel environment that predict the reinforcing stimulus will act in concert with the reinforcing stimulus to further narrow the range of behaviors exhibited by the organism. This focusing of behavior may be expected to influence the frequency of reinforcement-producing responses, and therefore the extent to which feedback learning will occur.

The primacy of feedforward learning and the late emergence of feedback learning is illustrated by the results of an experiment reported by Wahlsten and Cole (1972). Leg flexion responses were conditioned in some dogs using a classical conditioning schedule, in which an auditory CS preceded an unavoidable shock delivered to the foreleg by 2 sec. In other dogs, an avoidance schedule was used in which a flexion response during the tone served to avoid the shock. Following stabilization of performance under the initial training procedure, subjects were shifted to the other procedure. Although leg flexion CRs were made on significantly more trials under the avoidance procedure than under the classical conditioning procedure, both procedures gave rise to an appreciable rate of

CRs. It was also observed that CR latencies recorded under both conditions were similar until the terminal stages of conditioning. This supports Wahlsten and Cole's conclusion that the feedforward properties of the avoidance procedure initially predominated in controlling performance. Presumably, classical conditioning processes operated by providing the auditory warning signal with access to the subjects' leg flexion reflexes, which were elicited polysynaptically by peripheral electric shock.

However, immediately upon achieving a performance criterion of 10 successive avoidances, some subjects showed a dramatic decrease in response latency that clearly distinguished their performance from that recorded during the classical conditioning procedure. This abrupt shift in performance was only shown by dogs that exhibited a low initial rate of general activity, little intertrial responding, and relatively long-latency flexion responses. On the other hand, dogs that initially displayed a high rate of activity, much intertrial responding, and short-latency flexion responses did not manifest any clear influence of the avoidance contingency and exhibited similar CR latencies under both the avoidance and classical conditioning procedures.

These results suggest that in the case of the active animals, the acquisition of avoidance CRs was based exclusively on feedforward learning in which the CS gained access to preformulated short-latency flexion responses. This early adaptation pre-empted the operation of the feedback-programming functions of the reinforcing stimulus. On the other hand, in the slow subjects, the rate of avoidance produced by feedforward processes resulted in a relatively high rate of shocks. This enabled the feedback functions of the procedure to be realized, thereby leading to the specification of more efficient motor plans for shock avoidance. The fact that more successful responses led to the nonoccurrence of electric shocks does not raise special problems for the calibration hypothesis, since, by this account, continuous variations in the values of kinesthetic parameters (e.g., response force, extent, direction and frequency) were associated with variations in the frequency of electric shocks. The extent to which such correlations (Baum, 1973) are learned determines the range of responses that may be generated by the plan, and hence the degree to which performance principles may select behavioral variants that optimize the organism's adjustment to the prevailing circumstances.

The abrupt shift in response latencies displayed by the slow subjects suggests that although the reprogramming of motor responses may require protracted feedback experience, the adoption of a more efficient behavioral variant occurs rapidly when some threshold is passed. This threshold may depend jointly on the extent to which the behavioral set produced by the prevailing feedforward control processes permits the emergence of more efficient behavioral variants, and on the extent to which the prevailing conditions of feedback sustain the preprogrammed response. A useful analysis of factors that may influence resistance to behavioral change has been provided by Staddon (1975), who has modeled the processes of behavioral adaptation in terms of the evolutionary mechanisms of variation and selection.

Where the compatibility between the preprogrammed adaptation elicited by the situation and the optimal behavior defined by the situation is either very high or very low, operant reinforcement contingencies tend to have relatively little effect in modifying behavior. In neither of these conditions does the occurrence of the reinforcing stimulus reduce uncertainty (convey information) about the kinesthetic state of the motor system. They therefore deny a calibrating role to the reinforcing stimuli. By this argument, it may be expected that conditions that generate variability in the organism's initial reaction to the situation will promote the effects of feedback learning. Notterman and Mintz (1965) found that the discontinuation of reinforcement during extinction was followed by a significant although transitory increase in response force. Extinction also leads to significant increases in the variability of other response parameters (Catania, 1979).

Like energetic processes, informational processes also have a tendency toward maximum efficiency. As suggested by the data of Egger and Miller (1963) and Kamin (1968), organisms do not acquire or work for (Hendry, 1969) redundant information. If an individual is able to predict the occurrence of a biologically significant event on the basis of one signal, it does not learn that other signals also predict that event unless the other signals offer some predictive advantage. This principle also seems to apply to motor replanning. To the extent that an organism complies with the demands of a situation by using existing elements of its behavioral repertoire, it will be resistant to acquiring additional behavioral means of meeting those demands. Only when its preformulated adaptation fails to meet the requirements of the situation does behavioral variability increase and establish the conditions for recalibration.

CONCLUSIONS AND SPECULATIONS

It has been argued that the degree to which motor adaptations will come to conform to the requirements of demand situations depends on the informational functions of response-contingent stimuli. In particular, the refinement of motor acts is determined by the extent to which external feedback associated with the achievement of situational goals operates to calibrate internal, effector-produced feedback produced by

goal-related activities. However, the operation of this process is constrained by environmental, ontogenetic, and phylogenetic factors, which frequently prevent the energy efficiency of behavior from being maximized. It has been suggested that the evolutionary basis of these constraints on energetic efficiency is that they function to minimize the information-processing load associated with fulfilling the behavioral demands implied by the situation. The behavior that emerges therefore reflects a compromise between energetic and informational efficiency.

Thus, it is expected that in a given demand situation, there will be a negative relationship between the information-processing load entailed by a behavior and its metabolic load. Such a relationship is consistent with the hypothesis that improvements in the energetic efficiency of behavior must be bought at the cost of a greater commitment of information-processing resources. Reference has been made to Davis's (1943) finding that children comply with instructions to engage in specific movements with a far more generalized motoric response than do adults. In order to overcome the energetic inefficiency implied by a child's nonspecific responding, information derived from response-produced feedback must be processes so as to permit more refined motor plans to develop. This occurs throughout the period of development. Data discussed by Paillard (1980) on the acquisition of pointing strategies in children suggest that the time required to employ such information to develop new motor plans may be considerable. Between the ages of 7 and 9 years, when children are learning to use feedback information from the peripheral visual channel to guide movements toward a target, their pointing accuracies are significantly lower than those of adults.

Such reduced efficiency is probably a general feature of behavior during the process of motor replanning. And since this reduction in efficiency carries additional metabolic costs, it must be taken into account in specifying the energy value of replanning a behavior. In order for motor learning to offer an energy advantage, the energy costs of the new response must be less than the sum of the energy costs of the old response and the costs of replanning. Clearly, such calculations should take account of both temporal and energetic factors. For example, if a situation changes only temporarily, the long-term energy efficiency of behavior may be optimized by the organism's retaining its old response, although this response is inefficient in the context of the temporarily altered conditions. However, the extent to which this conservative strategy is optimal will depend on the difference between the energy costs of the old and new responses in the new situation.

Since the nervous system cannot estimate the energy efficiency of behaviors that have yet to be implemented, or predict the duration of changes in reinforcement contingencies, it is unable to make decisions on these bases about whether or not to replan a movement. Therefore, it has been argued that the principles that govern whether and when motor learning will take place have evolved as permanent attributes of the nervous system. In particular, the conditions for replanning are those in which the prevailing contingencies fail to maintain behaviors generated by existing motor plans. Under such conditions, behavioral variability increases, thereby creating the conditions for motor replanning by the processes of recalibration. This suggests that experimental explorations of the conditions that give rise to alterations in behavioral variability may help to identify the processes by which behavioral efficiency is controlled.

Despite the hypothesis that motor replanning is an automatic by-product of the calibrating functions of exteroceptive feedback acting on increased behavioral variability, the relationship between energetic and informational efficiency remains an important issue that is amenable to experimental examination. In this connection, Harvey and Greer (1982) have discussed the regulation of muscle stiffness in the legs. If subjects encounter mechanical shocks to the legs (as in walking across rough terrain), they exhibit an increase in the tonic level of leg muscle stiffness. This adaptation protects the legs by absorbing the shocks. It has been experimentally demonstrated that if the shocks occur at preditable intervals, muscle stiffness increases prior to, and decreases immediately following, such shock. They argue that muscle stiffness is not maintained at a high level between shocks, because this would entail a useless expenditure of energy. The question is posed as to what would happen if the mechanical shocks were made unpredictable. If the protective function has a higher priority than the efficiency function, it would be anticipated that under these conditions, a constant tonic level of muscle stiffness would be maintained. However, there are many levels of uncertainty between predictability and unpredictability, and exploration of the relationship between the uncertainty of shock presentation and muscle stiffness may provide a useful vehicle for exploring the tradeoff between informational and energetic efficiency.

Finally, it must be recognized that limitations in the information-processing capacities of the nervous system may prevent motor replanning in the face of either gross energetic inefficiency or high levels of behavioral variability. Such a limitation probably accounts for the nonspecific compliance subjects exhibit in response to instructions to alter their visceral activity. Instructions to increase heart rates generally lead to ergotropic responses that have pronounced striate muscular and respiratory components. These undemanded motor elements entail substantial metabolic costs that degrade the efficiency of fulfilling the experimental requirements. That cardiac-specific control does not emerge indicates that motor plans are not formed on the basis of cardiac afference, but, rather, that feedforward learning processes provide the heart rate instructions with access to preformulated ergotropic response plans (Lacroix, 1981). This could imply that the nervous system is explicitly unable to employ cardiac or other visceral afference in the same way that employs afference from the striate muscles.

Alternatively, a failure to demonstrate visceral-specific control could imply a more general limitation associated with the calibration of internal afferent signals that have relatively low signal-to-noise ratios. Variations in visceral activity are generally accompanied by highly correlated variations in striate muscular activity, and afference from the latter source may overshadow afference from target visceral effectors. Such considerations have led to the intensive study of the relationship between visceral response discrimination and control. Although these studies have not yielded conclusive evidence regarding the viability of an afferent process theory of motor learning, they have resulted in the development of a number of methods for assessing and training response discrimination and examining its relationship to response control. It would seem that these methods could be usefully applied to examining the processes by which kinesthetic processes contribute to the development of striate muscular control. This subject has only recently begun to attract experimental attention. For example, Laszlo and Bairstow (1983) have shown that training in kinesthetic discrimination leads to significant improvements in the drawing skills of children.

ACKNOWLEDGMENTS

This chapter was prepared during the academic year 1981–1982, while I was at the Centre Nationale de la Recherche Scientifique, Marseille, France. I am deeply grateful to Jean Requin, Andras Semjen, and Michel Bonnet and their colleagues at INP 3 for providing a congenial and stimulating environment, and to the Royal Society for the award of a European Science Exchange Fellowship.

REFERENCES

Adams, J. A. A closed-loop theory of motor learning. *Journal of Motor Behavior*, 1971, 3, 486–504.

Altman, J. *Organic foundations of animal behavior.* New York: Holt, Rinehart & Winston, 1966.

Basmajian, J. V. Control and training of individual motor units. *Science*, 1963, 20, 662–664.

Baum, W. M. The correlation-based law of effect. *Journal of the Experimental Analysis of Behavior*, 1973, 20, 137–153.

Bizzi, E., Accornero, N., Chapple, W., & Hogan, N. Arm trajectory formation in monkeys. *Experimental Brain Research*, 1982, 46, 139–143.

Bizzi, E., Polit, A., & Morasso, P. Mechanisms underlying achievement of final head position. *Journal of Neurophysiology*, 1976, 39, 435–444.

Bolles, R. C. Species-specific defense reactions and avoidance learning. *Psychological Review*, 1970, 77, 32–48.

Bolles, R. C., & Woods, P. J. The ontogeny of behaviour in the albino rat. *Animal Behaviour*, 1964, 12, 427–441.

Bonnet, M., & Requin J. Long loop and spinal reflexes in man during preparation for intended directional hand movements. *Journal of Neuroscience*, 1982, 2, 90–96.

Bonnet, M., Requin, J., & Semjen, A. Human reflexology and motor preparation. *Exercise and Sports Sciences Reviews*, 1981, 9, 119–157.

Bossom, J., & Ommaya, A. K. Visuo-motor adaptation (to prismatic transformation of the retinal image) in monkeys with bilateral dorsal rhizotomy. *Brain*, 1968, 91, 161–172.

Breland, K., & Breland, M. The misbehavior of organisms. *American Psychologist*, 1961, 16, 681–684.

Brener, J. Factors influencing the specificity of voluntary cardiovascular control In L. V. DiCara (Ed.), *The limbic and autonomic nervous systems: Advances in research*. New York: Plenum, 1974. (a)

Brener, J. A general model of voluntary control applied to the phenomena of learned cardiovascular control. In P. A. Obrist, A. H. Black, J. Brener, & L. V. DiCara (Eds.), *Cardiovascular psychophysiology*. Chicago: Aldine, 1974. (b)

Brener, J. Sensory and perceptual determinants of voluntary visceral control. In G. E. Schwartz & J. Beatty (Eds.), *Biofeedback: Theory and research*. New York: Academic Press, 1977. (a)

Brener, J. Visceral perception. In J. Beatty & H. Legewie (Eds.), *Biofeedback and behavior*. New York: Plenum, 1977. (b)

Brener, J. Psychobiological mechanisms in biofeedback. In L. White & B. Tursky (Eds.), *Clinical biofeedback: Efficacy and mechanisms*. New York: Guilford Press, 1982.

Brener, J., Phillips, K., & Connally, S. R. Energy expenditure, heart rate and ambulation during shock-avoidance conditioning of heart rate increases and ambulation in freely-moving rats. *Psychophysiology*, 1980, 17, 64–74.

Brinkman, J., & Porter, R. Movement performance and afferent projections to the sensorimotor cortex in monkeys with dorsal column lesions. In G. Gordon (Ed.), *Active touch*. Oxford: Pergamon Press, 1978.

Brown, A. C. Energy metabolism. In T. C. Ruch & H. D. Patton (Eds.), *Physiology and biophysics*. Philadelphia: W. B. Saunders, 1973.

Canon, L. K. Directed attention and "maladaptive" adaptation to displacement of the visual field. *Journal of Experimental Psychology*, 1971, 88, 403–408.

Catania, A. C. *Learning*. Englewood Cliffs, N.J.: Prentice-Hall, 1979.

Coggeshall, R. E. Law of separation of function of the spinal roots. *Physiological Reviews*, 1980, 60, 716–755.

Cohen, M. Continuous versus terminal visual feedback in prism aftereffects. *Perceptual and Motor Skills*, 1967, 24, 1295–1298.

Coquery, J. M. Role of active movement in control of afferent input from skin in cat and man. In G. Gordon (Ed.), *Active touch*. Oxford: Pergamon Press, 1978.

Crawshaw, M., & Craske, B. No retinal component in prism adaptation. *Acta Psychologica*, 1974, 38, 421–423.

Davis, R. C. The genetic development of patterns of voluntary activity. *Journal of Experimental Psychology*, 1943, 33, 471–486.

Desmedt, J. E., & Godaux, E. Ballistic skilled movements: Load compensation and patterning of the motor commands. In J. E. Desmedt (Ed.), *Progress in clinical neurophysiology* (Vol. 4, *Cerebral motor control in man: Long loop mechanisms*). Basel: Karger, 1978.

De Villiers, P. Choice in concurrent schedules and a quantitative formulation of the law of effect. In W. K. Honig & J. E. R. Staddon (Eds.), *Handbook of operant behavior*. Englewood Cliffs, N.J.: Prentice-Hall, 1977.

Dickinson, A. Conditioning and associative learning. *British Medical Bulletin*, 1981, 37, 165–168.

Duysens, J., & Loeb, G. Precortical processing of somatosensory information. *Behavioral and Brain Sciences*, 1978, 1, 149–150.

Dyhre-Poulsen, P. Perception of tactile stimuli before ballistic and during tracking movements. In G. Gordon (Ed.), *Active touch*. Oxford: Pergamon Press, 1978.

Easton, T. A. On the normal use of reflexes. *American Scientist*, 1972, 60, 591–599.

Egger, M. D., & Miller, N. E. When is reward reinforcing?: An experimental study of the information hypothesis. *Journal of Comparative and Physiological Psychology*, 1963, 56, 132–137.

Feldman, A. G. Functional tuning of the nervous system with control of movement of maintenance of steady posture: II. Controllable parameters of the muscle. *Biophysics*, 1966, 11, 565–578. (a)

Feldman, A. G. Functional tuning of the nervous system with control of movement or maintenance of steady posture: III. Mechanographic analysis of the execution by man of the simplest motor tasks. *Biophysics*, 1966, 11, 766–775. (b)

Fentress, J. C. Development and patterning of movement sequences in inbred mice. In J. Kiger (Ed.), *The biology of behavior*. Cornvallis: University of Oregon Press, 1972.

Festinger, L., Ono, H., Burnham, C. A., & Bamber, D. Efference and the conscious experience of perception. *Journal of Experimental Psychology Monographs*, 1967, 74, (4, Pt. 2).

Flowers, K. A. The predictive control of behaviour: Appropriate and inappropriate actions beyond the input in a tracking task. *Ergonomics*, 1978, 21, 109–122.

Fromm, C., & Evarts, E. V. Motor cortex responses to kinesthetic inputs during postural stability, precise find movement and ballistic movement in the conscious monkey. In G. Gordon (Ed.), *Active touch*. Oxford: Pergamon Press, 1978.

Frommer, G. P. Tactile discrimination and somatosensory evoked responses after midbrain lesions in cats and rats. *Experimental Neurology*, 1981, 73, 775–800.

Galambos, R., Norton, T. T., & Frommer, G. P. Optic tract lesions sparing pattern vision in cat. *Experimental Neurology*, 1967, 18, 8–25.

Goldspink, G. Muscle energetics. In R. M. Alexander & G. Goldspink (Eds.), *Mechanics and energetics of animal locomotion*. London: Chapman & Hall, 1977.

Goodwin, G. M., McCloskey, D. I., & Matthews, P. B. C. The contribution of muscle afferents to kinesthaesthesia shown by vibration induced illusions of movement and by the effects of paralyzing joint afferents. *Brain*, 1972, 95, 705–748.

Graham, F. K. The more or less startling effects of weak prestimulation. *Pschophysiology*, 1975, 12, 238–248.

Hagbarth, K. E., & Eklund, G. Motor effects of vibratory muscle stimuli in man. In R. Granit (Ed.), *Muscular afferents and motor control*. Stockholm: Almgvist & Wiksell, 1966.

Harvey, N., & Greer, K. Force and stiffness: Further consideration. *Behavioral and Brain Sciences*, 1982, 5, 547–548.

Hay, L. Accuracy of children on an openloop pointing task. *Perceptual and Motor Skills*, 1978, 47, 1079–1082.

Hearst, E., & Jenkins, H. M. *Sign-tracking: The stimulus-reinforcer relation and directed action*. Austin, Texas: The Psychonomic Society, 1974.

Held, R. Plasticity in the sensorimotor system. *Scientific American*, 1965, 213, 84–92.

Hendry, D. P. Concluding commentary. In D. P. Hendry (Ed.), *Conditioned reinforcement*. Homewood, Ill.: Dorsey Press, 1969.

Herrnstein, R. J. On the law of effect. *Journal of the Experimental Analysis of Behavior*, 1970, 13, 243–266.

Hinde, R. A. *Animal Behavior: A synthesis of ethology and comparative psychology*. New York: McGraw-Hill, 1970.

Hughes, R. N. Optimal diets under the energy maximization premise: the effects of recognition time and learning. *American Naturalist*, 1979, 113, 209–221.

James, W. *Principles of psychology*. New York: Dover, 1950. (Originally published, 1890)

Jenkins, H. M., & Moore, B. R. The form of the autoshaped response with food and water reinforcers. *Journal of the Experimental Analysis of Behavior*, 1973, 20, 163–181.

Kamin, L. J. Attention-like processes in classical conditioning. In

M. R. Jones (Ed.), *Miami Symposium on the Prediction of Behavior: Aversive stimulation*. Miami: University of Miami Press, 1968.

Keele, S. W. Behavioral analysis of movement. In V. B. Brooks (Ed.), *Handbook of physiology: The nervous system. Volume II*, Baltimore: American Physiological Society, 1981.

Kelso, J. A. S., & Holt, K. G. Exploring a vibratory systems analysis of human movement production. *Journal of Neurophysiology*, 1980, 43, 1183–1196.

Kimble, G. A., & Perlmuter, L. C. The problem of volition. *Psychological Review*, 1970, 77, 361–384.

Kornheiser, A. S. Adaptation to laterally displaced vision: A review. *Psychological Bulletin*, 1976, 83, 783–816.

Kornhuber, H. H. Cerebral cortex, cerebellum and basal ganglia: an introduction to their motor functions. In F. O. Schmitt & G. Worden (Eds.), *The neurosciences: Third study program*. Cambridge, Mass.: MIT Press, 1974.

Krebs, J. R. Behavioral aspects of predation. In P. P. G. Bateson & P. H. Klopfer (Eds.), *Perspectives in ethology*. New York: Plenum Press, 1973.

Krebs, J. R. Optimal foraging: Decision rules for predators. In N. B. Davies & J. R. Krebs (Eds.), *Behavioral ecology: An evolutionary approach*. Oxford, Blackwell Scientific Publications, 1978.

Kugler, P. N., & Turvey, M. T. Two metaphors for neural afference and efference. *Behavioral and Brain Sciences*, 1979, 2, 305–307.

Lacey, B. C., & Lacey, J. I. Studies of heart rate and other bodily processes in sensorimotor behavior. In P. A. Obrist, A. H. Black, J. Brener, & L. V. DiCara (Eds.), *Cardiovascular psychophysiology*. Chicago: Aldine, 1974.

Lacroix, J. M. The acquisition of autonomic control through biofeedback: The case against an afferent process and a two-process alternative. *Psychophysiology*, 1981, 18, 573–587.

Laszlo, J. I., & Bairstow, P. J. Kinaesthesia: Its measurement, training and relationship to motor control. *The Quarterly Journal of Experimental Psychology*, 1983, 35A, 411–421.

Lewis, M. Psychological effect of effort. *Psychological Bulletin*, 1965, 64, 183–190.

Liu, L. M. Effects of repetition of voluntary response: From voluntary to involuntary. *Journal of Experimental Psychology*, 1968, 76, 398–406.

Mackintosh, N. J. *The psychology of animal learning*. London: Academic Press, 1974.

McCloskey, D. I. Kinesthetic sensibility. *Physiological Reviews*, 1978, 58, 763–820.

McCulloch, T. L. Performance preferentials of the white rat in force-resisting and spatial dimensions. *Journal of Comparative Psychology*, 1934, 18, 85–111.

Metzger, W. Consciousness, perception and action. In E. C. Carterette & M. P. Friedman (Eds.), *Handbook of perception* (Vol. 1). New York: Academic Press, 1974.

Mott, F. W., & Sherrington, C. S. Experiments upon the influences of sensory nerves upon movement and nutrition of the limbs. *Proceedings of the Royal Society* (London), 1895, 57, 481–488.

Moulden, B. Adaptation to displaced vision: Reafference is a special case of the cue-discrepancy hypothesis. *Quarterly Journal of Experimental Psychology*, 1971, 23, 113–117.

Norberg, R. A. An ecological theory on foraging time and energetics and choice of optimal food search method. *Journal of Animal Ecology*, 1977, 46, 511–529.

Nottebohm, F. The ontogeny of bird songs. *Science*, 1970, 176, 950–956.

Notterman, J. M., & Mintz, D. E. *The dynamics of response*. New York: Wiley, 1965.

O'Keefe, J., & Nadel, L. [Précis of O'Keefe & Nadel's *The hippocampus as a cognitive map*.] *Behavioral and Brain Sciences*, 1979, 2, 487–533.

Paillard, J. The patterning of skilled movement. In J. Field, H. W. Magoun, & V. E. Hall (Eds.), *Handbook of physiology* (Section I, Neurophysiology). Washington, D.C.: American Physiological Society, 1960.

Paillard, J. The multichanneling of visual cues and the organization of a visually guided response. In G. E. Stelmach & J. Requin (Eds.), *Tutorials in motor behavior*. Amsterdam: North-Holland, 1980.

Paillard, J., & Brouchon, M. Active and passive movement in the calibration of position sense. In S. J. Freedman (Ed.), *Neurophysiology of spatially-oriented behavior*. Homewood, Ill.: Dorsey Press, 1968.

Paillard, J., Brouchon-Viton, M., & Jordan, P. Differential encoding of location cues by active and passive touch. In G. Gordon (Ed.), *Active touch*. Oxford: Pergamon Press, 1978.

Polit, A., & Bizzi, E. Processes controlling arms movements in monkeys. *Science*, 1978, 201, 1235–1237.

Provine, R. R. "Wing-flapping" develops in wingless chicks. *Behavioral and Neural Biology*, 1979, 27, 233–237.

Requin, J. Toward a psychobiology of preparation for action. In G. E. Stelmach & J. Requin (Eds.), *Tutorials in motor behavior*. Amsterdam: North-Holland, 1980.

Rodin, B. A., & Berman, D. Influence of dorsal rhizotomy on a sustained avoidance response in rats. *Experimental Neurology*, 1981, 73, 465–476.

Roland, P. E. Sensory feedback to the cerebral cortex during voluntary movement in man. *Behavioral and Brain Sciences*, 1978, 1, 129–171.

Roland, P. E. Degrees of freedom between somatosensory and somatomotor processes; or, one nonsequitur deserves another. *Behavioral and Brain Sciences*, 1979, 2, 307–312.

Roll, J. P. *Contribution de la proprioception musculaire à la perception et au controle du mouvement chez l'homme*. Unpublished doctoral dissertation, The University of Aix-Marseille I, 1981.

Schmidt, R. A. A schema theory of discrete motor skill learning. *Psychological Review*, 1975, 82, 225–260.

Sechenov, I. M. *Reflexes of the Brain*. Cambridge, Mass.: MIT Press, 1965. (Originally published, 1863)

Semjen, A. From motor learning to sensorimotor skill acquisition. *Journal of Human Movement Studies*, 1977, 3, 182–191.

Sheffield, F. D. Relation between classical conditioning and instrumental learning. In W. F. Prokasy (Ed.), *Classical conditioning: A symposium*. New York: Appleton-Century-Crofts, 1965.

Sherwood, A., Brener, J., & Moncur, D. Information and states of motor readiness: Their effects on the covariation of heart rate and energy expenditure. *Psychophysiology*, 1983, 20, 513–529.

Solomon, R. L. The influence of work on behavior. *Psychological Bulletin*, 1948, 45, 1–40.

Staddon, J. E. R. Learning as adaptation. In W. K. Estest (Ed.), *Handbook of learning and cognitive processes*. Hillsdale, N.J.: Erlbaum, 1975.

Stein, R. B. What muscle variable(s) does the nervous system control in limb movements? *Brain and Behavioral Sciences*, 1982, 5, 535–577.

Stratton, G. Some preliminary experiments in vision without inversion of the retinal image. *Psychological Review*, 1896, 3, 611–617.

Taub, E. Motor behavior following deafferentation in the developing and motorically mature monkey. In R. M. Herman, S. Grillner, P. S. G. Stein, & D. G. Stuart (Eds.), *Neural control of locomotion*. New York: Plenum Press, 1976.

Taub, E., & Berman, A. J. Avoidance conditioning in the absence of relevant proprioceptive and exteroceptive feedback. *Journal of Comparative and Physiological Psychology*, 1963, 56, 1012–1016.

Tolman, E. C. *Purposive behavior in animals and men*. New York: Century, 1932.

Tsumoto, T., Nakamura, S., & Iwana, K. Pyramidal tract control over cutaneous and kinesthetic sensory transmission in the cat thalamus. *Experimental Brain Research*, 1975, 22, 281–294.

Vierck, C. J. Interpretations of the sensory and motor consequences of dorsal column lesions. In G. Gordon (Ed.), *Active touch*. Oxford: Pergamon Press, 1978.

von Helmholtz, H. *Physiological optics*. New York: Dover, 1964. (Originally published, 1866) von Holst, E., & Mittelstaedt, H. The principle of reafference: interactions between the central nervous system and the peripheral organs. In P. C. Dodwell (Ed. and trans.), *Perceptual processing: Stimulus equivalence and pattern recognition.* New York: Appleton-Century-Crofts, 1971. (Originally published, 1950)

Wahlsten, D. L., & Cole, M. Classical and avoidance training of leg flexion in the dog. In A. H. Black & W. F. Prokasy (Eds.), *Classical conditioning II: Current research and theory.* New York: Appleton-Century-Crofts, 1972.

Weiskrantz, L., Warrington, E. K., Sanders, M. D., & Marshall, J. Visual capacity in the hemianopic field following a restricted occipital ablation. *Brain,* 1974, 97, 709–728.

Williams, D. R., & Williams, H. Auto-maintenance in the pigeon: Sustained pecking despite contingent nonreinforcement. *Journal of the Experimental Analysis of Behavior,* 1969, 12, 511–520.

SECTION B
Stress, Emotion, Sleep, and Sexuality

Chapter Sixteen

Stress

Peter Levine

THEORIES OF STRESS

Overview

The term "stress," like "sin," has been used flexibly to suit a wide variety of purposes; sometimes as stimulus, other times as response, consequence or process. "Stress" is used in biology, medicine, and the social sciences without precise or even consistent definition. This situation could occur only because of a need to describe significant groups of phenomena that are not covered adequately by other generic terms or concepts. This has led to a great deal of confusion. For example, the three-phase biochemical "general adaptation syndrome" (GAS) of alarm, resistance, and exhaustion (Selye's "stress" response) has been loosely applied to psychological processes such as anxiety, depression, or "burnout," to which it has only an indirect relationship.

Stress has been widely considered in its relationship to disease. It is indicated as a contributory or primary factor in hypertension, ulcers, depression, asthma, immunocompetence, and various neoplastic tumorous growths (see Riley, 1981). Emotional stress components are now acknowledged widely in the medical profession. Unfortunately, there have been few systematic means to define and study stress factors and their cumulative effects, or to clarify differences between potentially beneficial and detrimental effects of stress.

This chapter traces some of the broad historical developments in stress theory and measurement. It is also oriented toward more circumscribed and speculative views of stress not covered by general reviews. Particularly, this chapter sets out to show that confusion can be reduced by an appreciation of fundamental differences between static (i.e., open-loop) and active (i.e., closed-loop) systems. In the former, deleterious effects of stress are seen to arise from a gradual eroding of tissue and cellular integrity, leading toward pathology, by a series of stressors that act cumulatively on a passive organism. In Hans Selye's analogy of a bank account ledger, consequences of stress occur additively as the result of continually overdrawing one's "energy resources" ("the rate of wear and tear in the body"). However, the physiological mechanisms in mediating good "eu-stress" and bad "distress," proposed by Selye, are not clear. The closed-loop systems view offers some insight in this regard. Complex dynamic feedback patterns govern a wide

Peter Levine. Ergos Institute, Flagstaff, Arizona.

spectrum of behaviors and reflect the organism's capacity for order and stability, which may be influenced differentially in stress.

The systems approach recognizes phenomena as qualitatively different from the analytical sum of their parts. Rather, it emphasizes the interrelationships among elements that organize function. Prigogine (1976) has demonstrated, for example, how stressors that perturb nonequilibrium dissipative systems (the central nervous system [CNS] may be such a system) can not only lead to disintegrative outcomes, but can also trigger reordering to higher levels of complexity and efficiency. (See Jantsch, 1980, for a readable review.) In an attempt to apply a nonequilibrium analysis to healing, Cahn (1982) has examined finite discontinuities in Van Der Pool's equations for neuroendocrine and perineural systems, suggesting that provoked perturbations can lead to new, more stable, states. I (P. Levine, 1977) have made a similar analysis of the healing process using catastrophe theory.

There has been a growing recognition that "emotion" plays a role and is a legitimate if not an essential component in stress measurement and theory. Subjective ghosts of William James are discreetly being exhumed and hold promise of integrating the realm of subjective experience into an emerging cybernetic model.

Stress and Activation Theory: History and Unresolved Issues

Theory and measurement in psychophysiology have developed mutually with stress research, though it has not always been clear which is progenitor and which is offspring. An early relationship stems from the association of the concept of arousal with W. B. Cannon's (1914, 1929) sympathetic–adrenal stress response. But even before this, it had become possible to measure electrical activity generated by the heart, brain, and skin. (See Porges & Coles, 1976, for a review.) Objective measurements could now be made in what was formerly the province of introspection and behavior. Investigators looked at arousing stimuli that would evoke sizable reactions in the hope of developing a physiological psychophysics. This enthusiasm peaked in the 1950s with the influential writings of Duffy (1957) and Malmo (1959), and also with the growing capability of measuring hormone levels in urine and blood. It was hoped that with more refined measurement, the construct of arousal would become quantifiable.

However, even by the early 1930s, investigators—notably Wilder—were coming to realize that the state of autonomic activity during stimulation had a significant effect on psychophysiological measures. In 1931 Wilder formulated the "law of initial values" in an attempt to quantify some of these relationships. The

fundamental differences between the behavior of open- and closed-loop systems were not known to him; they were established later, during World War II, when new technologies demanded analysis of complex feedback systems. Wilder's analysis was thus confined to static measures. Later it was acknowledged, although not quantified, that autonomic effector outputs reflect a dynamic and nonlinear combination of sympathetic and parasympathetic effects generated by interaction between the two branches of the autonomic nervous system (see Gellhorn, 1957, 1967). Darrow and coworkers (e.g., Darling & Darrow, 1938) responded to this challenge and devised a matrix of cardiovascular and galvanic skin measures to separate the two autonomic components. Unfortunately, most of their assumptions were incorrect. At about this time, Wenger (1941) attempted to address this problem with a factor analysis of several physiological variables. Later the Laceys (e.g., Lacey, 1967) examined the behavioral significance of feedback from even small changes in autonomic effector outputs on the CNS. Psychophysiologists still tend to overlook the importance of dynamic analysis of psychophysiological data.

Important unresolved issues have emerged from the first four or five decades of psychophysiological stress research. Physiological arousal, measured from autonomic effector systems or hormonal levels, does not provide an unambiguous quantitative measure of the intensity of the eliciting stimulus, since intervening variables cannot be partitioned from the raw electrophysiological data. Further, because human physiological measurements are usually noninvasive, it is difficult to separate complex nonlinear relationships of innervations. Dynamic state variables, which describe internal organization in closed-loop systems, are required to adequately define the relationship of the autonomic nervous system and psychophysiology. This chapter discusses methodologies from systems theory that may facilitate the development of a quantitative model of activation to define and measure states of stress.

The idea that stress is a closed-loop process while arousal is an open-loop process is developed here. Unfortunately, the terms "stress" and "arousal" are used somewhat interchangeably. J. W. Hennessy and S. Levine (1979), for example, regard stress under the umbrella of an activation/arousal construct. They view "stress" in Selye's sense—as the response to physical injury. "Arousal" is taken more generally to be synonymous with psychosocial stress. Both are important concepts in specific areas of activation psychophysiology and have been measured primarily by autonomic effector activity and adrenocorticotropic hormone (ACTH) (and corticosteroid) levels. I (P. Levine, 1977) have suggested that "stress" and "arousal" be differentiated by their potentially progressive effects on the disorganization of CNS functioning. When an organism is stressed, there exists the possibility that preactivation equilibrium will not be re-established. Stress is thus distinguished as being "resolved" or "unresolved" (i.e., accumulated). If equilibrium is not restored, unstable or maladaptive states develop; stress here is said to be unresolved or accumulated. If activation is sufficient for the potential of accumulation, but there is instead a return to equilibrium, then stress is said to be resolved. Under certain conditions, suitable activation can trigger resolution of previously accumulated stress and thereby can enhance function. "Arousal" is defined as that form of stress in which activation is *necessarily* resolved, following termination of the stressor. Arousal, as used in this sense, is a subset of stress activation and does not impair function. The rationale for these distinctions is developed in the following sections, which provide a conceptual framework to eliminate some confusion in stress research.

Selye and the Psychosomatic View: An Open-Loop Approach

In the open-loop, wear-and-tear view of stress, pathology is seen to arise from erosion due to accumulation of biochemical substrates released by stressors, or from depletion of these substrates. Mann (1895) noted histological changes in sympathetic, motor, and sensory neurons during prolonged activity. Crile (1915) extended these observations and demonstrated that stained cells in the brain and in the adrenals showed first hyperchromatism and then chromatolysis when rats were subjected to fear, rage, and injections of foreign agents or production of anaphylactic reactions. From crossed perfusion experiments, Crile proposed that changes in brain cell staining were secondary to those in the adrenal medulla and cortex. Twenty years later, Hans Selye (1936) published a one-page article entitled "A Syndrome Produced by Diverse Nocuous Agents," in which he reported that when rats were exposed to nonspecific nocuous agents, quite similar to those used by Crile, a typical, stereotyped response occurred. The nature of this reaction appeared to be independent of the inciting agent and represented what Selye argued was a nonspecific response to damage. He coined the term "general adaptation syndrome" (GAS) for this, and concluded that this three-phase response (alarm, resistance, and exhaustion) represents "the usual response of the organism to stimuli—to which inurement can occur" (1936, p. 32). The responses he described were similar to those studied by Crile and included adrenal enlargement, thyroid, and liver changes, as well as exophthalmos and loss of muscular tone in the alarm stage.

Mann, Crile, and Selye viewed stress as the effect of external stimuli acting on the organism to stimulate internal secretions: "The syndrome as a whole seems to represent a generalized effect of the organism to adapt itself to [these] new conditions" (Selye, 1936, p. 32). The general role of Selye's syndrome has been difficult to establish, and more specific functions have been speculated by a number of authors. According to Christian (1959), for example, pituitary–adrenocortical activation is a response to increasing population density, serving to limit population growth by reducing fertility and interfering with healing. Brain and Poole (1974) see the evolutionary advantage of ACTH in enhancing conditioned responses; and Leshner and Politch (1979) argue that its adaptive value may be in establishing dominance hierarchies. They found that in mice ACTH decreased aggressiveness, while corticosterone increased submissiveness. The adaptive significance of the GAS still remains to be established.

The possibility of a single response to stimuli having very different homeostatic requirements has caused concern (e.g., J. W. Mason, 1975). J. W. Mason (1968a, 1968b, 1971, 1975) disputes Selye and regards the response to stress stimuli as a diverse and somewhat variable set of neuroendocrine reactions, which is evoked almost exclusively by stimuli having a strong "psychological" meaning to the organism. The particular hormonal pattern of response, he argues, is related more to the behavioral and metabolic context in which it occurs than to the nature of the physical stimulus. The pituitary–adrenal axis of Selye is activated within an integrated reaction of catabolic and anabolic hormones, including Cannon's adrenomedullary secretion. Mason takes the concept of "stress" full circle, back to the notion of "mental strain" that Selye sought arduously to avoid, and poses the issue of how psychosocial stressors are received and processed through the rational–intellectual, cerebro-cortical centers. Burchfield, Elich, and Woods (1977) have termed this a "cognitive mediator" theory of stress. The complex set of neural interactions—by which the neocortex transmits the psychosocial stress impulse to the hypothalamic final common pathway, in translating psychological to pituitary–endocrine reactions—has become a major focus to modern psychosomatic medicine. The mind–body duality of the previous century, wherein "body stress" was thought to be caused by "mental strain," has been replaced by an analysis of hierarchical neural circuits. These pathways relate the "highest" order of brain function in the neocortex to the activity of primitive brain centers in the brain stem and diencephalon, and thence to the hormonal outputs of the "master" (pituitary) gland. The transforming of psychological inputs into biochemical and autonomic outputs becomes a basic psychosomatic paradigm.

Selye's approach minimizes the role of specific CNS mechanisms and opts for an undefined primary mediator. J. W. Mason, in his psychosomatic approach, has taken a hierarchical view and makes the assumption that sensory stress information is processed at the level of the neocortex and has endocrine and visceral effects by descending circuits onto the hypothalamo-pituitary unit. Both are basically open-loop approaches (see Figure 16-1).

J. W. Mason (1975) argues, with respect to Selye's principle of nonspecificity, that from the perspective of homeostasis, the existence of a single response (pituitary–adrenocortical GAS) to stimuli that have diametrically opposite metabolic needs, such as heat versus cold, simply does not make sense. Mason reasons that the only bodily response that might be appropriate under both conditions would be a behavioral response of emotional arousal or hyperalerting preparatory to flight, which would serve to eliminate the source by removing the subject from its presence. However, the GAS may not be adaptive even in this restricted sense, since diminished muscular tone (demonstrated by Selye, in the "alarm" stage) is maladaptive where mobilization is required. Thus, if on no other basis, it is clear that while both Selye and Mason (after Cannon) use the same word "stress," they are referring to very different processes with basically different functions. It is unfortunate, indeed, that the same term has been employed by both authors. Still, it is possible that the two responses have some integrative relationship. The more slowly acting adrenocortical response might, for example, function to reinforce negative avoidance conditioning subsequent to aversive situations.

Overview

Depending on which model of stress has been accepted, different measures of stress have been taken. Early measurement of stress, following Cannon's work, emphasized level of sympathetic–adrenal activity. Selye's followers have measured corticosteroid and ACTH levels. J. W. Mason's later work has encouraged the measurement of combinations of neuroendocrine responses.

When an individual experiences difficulty or threat, he or she may exhibit a variety of homeostatic changes, including those that are preparations for fight or flight. The history of psychophysiology has many examples of parallelisms among autonomic (sympathetic-like) changes (e.g., galavanic skin response [GSR], heart rate, blood pressure), electrocortical activity (i.e., electroencephalogram [EEG], activity), skeletal muscle tensions (i.e., electromyogram [EMG] activity), and neurochemical outflow (e.g., catecholamine levels). The covariation of these classes of response systems gradually has become known as "activation/arousal." The writings of Duffy, Darrow, Lindsley, and Malmo (e.g., Duffy, 1932, 1957; Darrow, Jost, Solomon, & Mergener 1942; Lindsley, 1951; Malmo, 1959) have been particularly influential in propagating this "activation/arousal" view. "Arousal" is viewed as a continuum ranging from coma and deep sleep to the most disorganized behaviors in extreme stress. Metabolic adjustments have also been incorporated into autonomic stress theory. Obrist, Howard, Lawler, Galosy, Meyers, and Gaebelein (1974), Brener (1974), and Elliott (1974) have looked at change in autonomic activity in terms of homeostatic response to metabolic demands.

Stress versus Arousal

Lacey (e.g., 1967) disagrees with activation theory, admitting that there is much evidence of generalized arousal, but adding that science is not based on polls. He argues that EEG, autonomic, motor, and other behavioral systems are imperfectly coupled, complex, interacting systems. Lacey cites various dissociations produced pharmacologically or by lesions in the CNS. He also points to the partial dissociations reported by Elliott (1964) in the responses of young adults and kindergarten children in reaction time experiments. Both children and adults responded to positive incentives with decreased reaction time. The adults showed a parallel and significant activation in all physiological functions measured; however, the children showed changes only in heart and respiratory rates. Lacey concludes that the belief that autonomic, EEG, and EMG activation simultaneously covary may be related to the limitation of experimental conditions. He suggests that aversive stimuli, demanding tasks, and anxiety-producing stimuli are used perhaps too often at the expense of nonaversive stimuli and pleasant tasks.

A problem here, again, is variance in the definition of "stress." If "stress" is used in Cannon's sense, then nonaversive or pleasant stimuli are *not* stressful, though they may be arousing. They do not evoke neurobehavioral emergency preparedness for "fight or flight," even though similar levels of catechol-

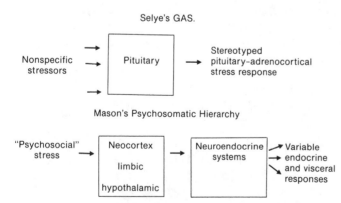

Figure 16-1. Schematic representation of Selye's general adaptation syndrome (GAS) and J. W. Mason's psychosomatic hierarchy.

amines may be released (Levi, 1965). Obrist, Lawler, and Gaebelein (1974) suggest that perhaps two subsystems exist. One involves sympathetic influences on the sudomotor and vasomotor–constrictor responses that are evoked by *novel* stimuli, which are not necessarily stressful. This system appears to be response-stereotypic, in agreement with Lacey's observations. The second system, in contrast, is evoked by more intense activation, where the subject attempts to cope. It involves not only sudomotor and vasomotor activity, but cardiac and vasodilatory processes as well. This second subsystem is consistent with Cannon's emergency sympathetic function. Cannon (1914) articulated that the adrenal response occurs primarily when an animal is behaviorally aroused to fight or rage, and *not* by the stimuli of fear, pain, cold, or immobilization in themselves. Also, maximal ACTH secretion occurs during limbic stimulation too weak to evoke an emotional reaction (J. W. Mason, 1959). So, as Cannon (1914) first suggested and J. W. Mason (1959) and Obrist, Lawler, and Gaebelein (1974) later elaborated regarding stress in contrast to arousal, the organism must be responding, or set to respond. The stress reaction (of Cannon) requires an organized involvement of autonomic and somatic responses, integrated by the CNS. Gellhorn (1964, 1967) adds that patterned proprioceptive somatic feedback is important in maintaining a central excitatory state appropriate to fight or flight.

Even large and organized stress responses do not preclude the possibility of individual differences, and particularly of dynamic, complex, and somewhat variable patterns of autonomic relationships and somatic coupling. Correlations even among autonomic measures themselves, as well as of autonomic measures with EEG and EMG, have not always been impressive. Lacey's criticism of stress research while confusing "stress" and "arousal," does show the need for more precise and dynamic analysis of autonomic stress data.

Biochemical and Endocrine Levels

The other main measurement in the open-loop view of stress is that of endocrine levels. The availability of sensitive fluorimetric methods in the mid-1950s made it possible to infer increased sympathetic activity from adrenal secretion in different states, including emotional stress. For example, von Euler and Lundberg (1954) showed that urinary catecholamines increased in both Air Force pilots and passengers during flight. Elmadjian and his associates Elmadjian, 1963; Elmadjian, Lamson, Maschouf, & Gibson, 1960) studied boxers, hockey players, and psychiatric patients appearing at staff meetings. They all were shown to have similarly increased levels of epinephrine. Levi (1965) presented the first systematic human data on catecholamine levels. By monitoring levels in individ-

uals who were exposed to industrial and office stress, or who viewed films of neutral, negative, and positive emotional content, Levi arrived at the following conclusions:

1. The different stressors were all capable of evoking increased catecholamine excretion, sometimes approaching very high levels.
2. Moderately anxious individuals as a group did *not* excrete more catecholamines than did normals, either during control conditions or during stress.
3. There was considerable interindividual variability in catecholamine excretion, but intraindividuality levels roughly paralleled the degree of emotional arousal.
4. An individual's catecholamine excretion rates during corresponding periods of different experiments were positively correlated.
5. Stimuli evoking responses of calmness and equanimity reduced the catecholamine excretion below control levels.
6. Pleasant stimuli evoking amusement were nearly as potent as unpleasant ones in provoking a catecholamine increase, though unpleasant films resulted only in the excretion of noradrenalin, while pleasant films evoked both adrenalin and noradrenalin.
7. The physical characteristics of a stress situation (i.e., noise, light, the task to be accomplished) influenced the excretion levels *less* than did the subject's attitude to the entire experimental or life situation.

The last finding particularly acknowledges "psychological state" as an important variable. Stress measured solely by open-loop (i.e., input–output), Weber–Fechner psychophysics would therefore not be appropriate.

Human studies of corticosteroids began at about the same period and in the same sorts of situations as studies involving catecholamines. Hill, Goetz, Fox, Muravski, Krakauer, Reifenstein, Gray, Reddy, Hedberg, Marc, and Thorn (1956) looked at competitive sports; Franksson and Gemzell (1955) examined anticipation of surgery; emotional disturbances were studied by Board, Wadeson, and Persky (1957) and Hetzel, Schottstaedt, Grace, and Wolff (1955). In the following decade, the idea began to emerge that the pituitary–adrenal system reflected arousal rather than any specific emotional state (J. W. Mason, 1968a; Oken, 1967). J. W. Hennessy and S. Levine (1979) and J. W. Mason, Harwood, and Rosenthal (1957) showed that in animals the initial exposure to the experimental setting evoked large elevations in plasma cortisol. In human studies, the increased adrenocortical activity in response to the novelty of the test situation was shown to be as large as to the presumably greater intensity of the test stimulus (e.g., shock) (Bassett, Cairncross, & King, 1973; Friedman &

Ader, 1967; Friedman, Ader, Grota, & Larson, 1967; S. Levine & Treiman, 1964). For many subjects, introduction to the experimental situation for the first time was a more effective method of increasing plasma or urinary steroid levels than anything the experimenter could devise (Davis, Morrill, Fawcett, Upton, Bondy, & Spiro, 1962). It was concluded that levels of corticosteroids thus primarily reflect a response to novelty, uncertainty, and conflict, rather than to the complex of emotional and survival-related behaviors. Moreover, when any disturbing situation is long-lasting most individuals adjust to it, and persistently increased levels of adrenocortical activity occur only in a minority of subjects (Gibbons, 1968). This may be true even for some of the most severe affective-emotional pathologies, such as psychosis and schizophrenia (Brambella & Penti, 1978).

The early work on catecholamines and adrenocortical release gave the impression of somewhat parallel responses for the two classes of hormones. However, the "stressful" situations studied were vaguely defined, and average data often took little, if any, account of large interindividual differences. J. W. Mason's pioneering studies (1968a, 1968b) marked the beginning of a more refined era in psychoneuroendocrine research. Mason found that cortisol responses became dissociated from catecholamine release and increased sharply when behavior that was previously successful was thwarted and become disorganized. The recent work of Lundberg (1980), Frankenhaeuser (1980), Henry and Stephens (1977), Henry (1980), M. B. Hennessy, Heybach, Vernikos, and S. Levine (1979), J. W. Hennessy and S. Levine (1979), and Ursin (1980) has begun to establish a basis for understanding certain differences in the psychoendocrine responses in humans and in animals. Frankenhauser and Lundberg make the generalization that in humans, effort without "distress" is accompanied by sympathetic-adrenal activation. Distress, produced by feelings of helplessness and passivity even in the absence of effort, is associated with increased excretion of cortisol but not catecholamines.

In a study during training of parachutists, Ursin (1980) looked at three endocrine factors. Changes in catecholamine, cortisol, and testosterone levels were found to be independent of one another. Differences were related to "psychological type." Repressed fear was positively correlated most strongly with elevated cortisol levels and negatively with performance. Catecholamine release, on the other hand, characterized persons exhibiting "Type A" behavior (i.e., persons who have a constant need for activity and competition, and who display general impatience). Finally, parachutists psychologically characterized by thrill-seeking behaviors responded to jumping only by elevated testosterone and free fatty acids. Henry (1980) and Henry and Stephens (1977) showed, in animal experiments, that sympathetic-adrenal activation was associated with aggressive behavior, while pituitary-adrenocortical activation related more to submissive or passive behavior. These sympathetic-medullary and pituitary-cortical adrenal responses were reversed when the social position of animals in the colony became reversed. Henry and Meehan (1981), reviewing a wide range of both animal and human studies, have proposed the existence of distant subcortical systems for "conservation/withdrawal" and for "defense/action." A hippocampal system is linked primarily to the pituitary-ardenocortical system and operates, from a behavioral point of view, by signaling the disruption of expectancies about the environment. The sympathetic-adrenal system is involved primarily with aggressive behaviors. Henry and Meehan cite experiments on humans that show a *decrease* of 170H corticosteroid, even in high-stress situations, where there is a sense of enjoyment, social support, and skilled control.

Henry and Meehan (1981) conceptualize stress behaviors as organized along orthogonal coordinates. The amygdaloid/sympathetic-adrenomedullary axis has "effort" (fight-flight, aggression, and territorial control) as one polarity and "relaxation" as an opposing force. A second axis—the hippocampal-adrenocortical system—has as its endpoints "distress" (helplessness, depression, loss of control, submission) and "euphoria" (security, control, reproduction, and parenting). Studies of CNS pathways regulating the hypothalamo-pituitary-adrenal response to stress are consistent with this view. Catecholamines, particularly norepinephrine and dopamine, appear to inhibit cortiocotropin-releasing factor (CRF). (See Hodges, 1976, and Danellis & Heybach, 1980, for general reviews.)

The work of Flynn, Vanegas, Foote, and Edwards (1974) and Adamec (1978) suggests, however, more of a functional interdependence of amygdala and hippocampal circuits, at least with respect to attack and defensive behaviors. It may be that an animal's first reaction to threat is arousal, interpreted as fight or flight. If the situation cannot be resolved by mobilization, then inhibition or freezing might have survival value. Prolonged or chronic stress might lead to biasing toward the hippocampo-pituitary response, and to distress. The hippocampo-pituitary system may also be central in human depression (Carroll, 1976).

Seligman (1975) has suggested that learned helplessness (where escape from shock is prevented) may be an essential element of depression. Blocking septal input to the hippocampus seems to relieve or reverse learned helplessness in animals (Weiss, 1972). Another system that may be involved in stress and learned helplessness is endorphin-mediated analgesia. Grau *et al.* (1981) has found that development of learned helplessness is also associated with analgesia in the same animal. This analgesia is naloxone-reversible, implicating the endogenous opioids. The relationship of endogenous opioids to stress-produced analgesia is also suggested, since anxiety is one of the few predictors of response to an analgesic placebo (J. D. Levine, Gordon, & Fields, 1978). A close neuroendocrine link between beta-endorphin and corticosteroids is supported by the recent finding that they are both controlled by hypothalamic CRF (Vale, 1981). MacLennan, Drugan, Hyson, Maier, Madden, and Barchas (1982) propose, in addition, that corticosterone is critical in an endogenous stress-induced analgesia. "Long-term analgesia," which is blocked by dexamethasone and hypophysectomy, was also blocked in MacLennan et al.'s experiments by adrenalectomy and restored by corticosterone injections. Also, Miczek, Thompson, and Shuster (1982) have reported analgesia in defeated mice that appears to be mediated by endogenous opioids, since it is blocked by nalaxone.

THE SYSTEMS VIEW

Early Attempts

One of the underlying problems in the open-loop measurement of stress, by catecholamine or pituitary-adrenocortical axis hormone levels, is that adrenalin, ACTH, and cortisol appear to function primarily as nonspecific facilitators and inhibitors of neuroelectric activity (e.g., Gellhorn, 1967; J. W. Hennessy & S. Levine, 1979). As modulators, only limited information is provided regarding the organized function of the CNS in stress. In terms of a cybernetic analysis, the amount of information that can be determined from average levels is small compared with the information that could theoretically be extracted from dynamic analysis of autonomic function.

In the closed-loop or cybernetic model of stress, the key concept is the maintenance of equilibrium (stability) by continuously and dynamically organized responses. Change, in response to disturbance in either the external or internal environment, requires the organized expenditure of energy. An observation reported by Cannon (1914) supported, even then, a systems view of stress. He and his collaborators found that the appearance of the adrenal response depended on the animal's emotional reaction to its experience: "Neither pain, cooling nor being bound . . . was a factor—the essential element was the fight or rage of the animal" (1914). Over 50 years later, J. W. Mason (1971, 1975) re-evaluated Selye's adrenocortical response and concluded similarly that when experiments were properly controlled, only stimuli with a strong "psychosocial" component evoked the GAS.

Cannon, drawing on the tradition of Darwin, Bernard, and Sherrington, viewed sympathetic activation and adrenal secretion as part of an integrated behav-

ioral response: "The pattern of the reaction in these as in other reflexes is deeply inwrought in the workings of the nervous system, and when the appropriate occasion arises, typical organic responses are evoked through inherent automatisms" (Cannon, 1914). It was not until 1925, however, that W. R. Hess demonstrated the intimate interrelation between the autonomic and somatic nervous systems in integrating defensive behavior. Hess later (1949) coined the terms "ergotropic" and "trophotropic" to describe these neurobehavioral patterns organized at the level of the hypothalamus. The ergotropic syndrome, in Hess's view, is characterized by sympathetic discharges associated with a pattern of increased somatic activity in skeletal and respiratory muscles, preparing the animal for defensive action (Cannon's "fight or flight"). The trophotropic pattern consists of parasympathetic effects associated with a decreased activity and responsiveness in the somatic system. These syndromes, which range from maximal excitation in aggressive states to inertness and sleep, are also associated with profound alterations in cortical and subcortical activity. Gellhorn (e.g., 1967) also adds that proprioceptive feedback is essential in maintaining and organizing these patterns. The terms "ergotropic" and "trophotropic" have largely been disregarded, in part because pure invariant sympathetic and parasympathetic responses rarely occur. The ergotropic-trophotropic concept does, however, underscore the principle that behavioral and functional systems tend to be linked throughout various physiological systems.

Measurement

Darrow (Darling & Darrow, 1938) made one of the earliest attempts at a systems analysis of the autonomic nervous system and suggested that investigation of the autonomic nervous system is difficult because, in the intact organism, activity ordinarily may be inferred from the effector outputs. He pointed out that such measurement is not useful because the activity of autonomic effectors is the resultant of two generally opposed innervations, by sympathetic and parasympathetic divisions of the autonomic system (Darling & Darrow, 1938). To derive separate measures, Darrow assumed linear additivity between the two branches in GSR and heart rate. Two equations representing these relationships were solved simultaneously. Unfortunately, his basic assumptions were not correct and were based only on open-loop analysis of average levels. It is known, for example, that vagal influence can be overriding on heart rate (e.g., Rosenblueth & Simeone, 1934). Also, an aroused individual may shift in sympathetic (dominant) direction. This manifest sympathetic response also corresponds to an increased probability of parasympathetic rebound. Obrist (1976), for example, described in reactive subjects a depressor response that was initiated 5–6 sec after sympathetic influences were manifested and terminated while heart rate was still elevated. This depressor response was particularly pronounced where heart rate increases were greatest. Gellhorn (1957, 1967) demonstrated that nonreciprocal, nonlinear, and concomitant activation of the sympathetic and parasympathetic systems generally characterizes higher levels of activation.

Autonomic responses in humans that are generally measured by noninvasive techniques generate, then, complex, overlapping, and essentially average indices of both innervation pathways. For example, decreased heart rate may be due to facilitated parasympathetic tone, to inhibited sympathetic tone, or to both. Katona and Jih (1975) proposed that since respiratory sinus arrhythmia is mediated primarily by the vagus nerve, it could be used as a quantitative and noninvasive means of measuring parasympathetic control of heart rate. Using data on sympathetic and parasympathetic neural control of heart rate of anesthetized dogs (Rosenblueth & Simeone, 1934; Warner & Russell, 1969), Katona and Jih developed a model for inferring steady-state vagal efferent activity.

I (P. Levine, 1977) extracted dynamic (non-steady-state) sympathetic and parasympathetic components of blood pressure responses in human subjects. I simulated an autonomic test based on the rate and course of return to baseline blood pressure after the administration of peripheral hypertensive and hypotensive agents (Funkenstein, Greenblatt, Soloman, 1950) by solving a set of differential equations describing cardiovascular function. Funkenstein and his coworkers were able to sort a population of psychiatric patients into six autonomic response categories that corresponded with their response to treatment. They were not, however, able to make a priori predictions about relative effectiveness of treatment or spontaneous remission.

My dynamic closed-loop systems analysis of the cardiovascular system for these data (P. Levine, 1977) generated a set of blood pressure response curves that, upon comparison, fit the data curves with the groups categorized by Funkenstein et al. (1950). Sympathetic and parasympathetic components (gain and set point) were then plotted on the control surface of a "catastrophe model." (See review of this branch of typology by Zeeman, 1976.) Catastrophe theory predicts the properties of systems that have, in a mechanical analogy, frictional forces. In this three-dimensional representation, I defined the "control surface" by sympathetic and parasympathetic vectors, while the dependent variable, on the "behavior surface," represented a motility variable. This model exhibits discontinuous and divergent behavior in a fold region called the "cusp." Prognoses for Funkenstein et al.'s groups were predicted accurately by position on the

fold surface, even though no such prediction had been possible from the raw data. Those individuals whose response to injected pharmacological agents resulted in a shift on the behavior surface to a metastable region had a better prognosis than those whose responses moved to an unstable region. Prognoses of those shifting deeply to the area of the "cusp" were the worst. This latter group would be most representative of those manifesting a severely diminished adaptational capacity.

The catastrophe (systems-analytic) model is thus able to portray proximate and distant causes of stress-induced pathology due to progressive accumulation of unresolved stress. It can also predict abrupt catastrophic changes, such as manic–depressive behaviors, that occur following only small shifts in autonomic balance. However, there are two major problems with this model. First, it requires several assumptions about the complex interconnectedness of the cardiovascular central systems, and gain and set point parameters are extrapolated from a variety of experiments. Second, the pharmacological perturbations (the Mecholyl and noradrenalin tests) are invasive and cumbersome. Nevertheless, the model demonstrates the possibility of deriving complex information on the functioning of the CNS by dynamic cybernetic systems analysis of peripheral autonomic effectors.

Porges (1976) has proposed a general rationale for assessing central states and behavioral tendencies from autonomic effector systems. In formalizing the "continuity theory," he has proposed mathematical strategies to extract certain operations of the CNS from discrete patterns of effector outputs. The model looks at autonomic outputs encoding specific periodic information on the organization and functioning of the CNS. Porges, Bohrer, Cheung, Drasgow, McCabe, and Keren (1980) point out that research assessing the validity of a general arousal theory has usually consisted of describing central tendencies, such as mean or variability of specific physiological response systems, and then correlating these variables. Descriptive statistics of mean and variance are, however, insensitive to a number of important organizational characteristics of the nervous system. Porges et al. (1980) note that the conclusions of earlier important studies may have been more a function of the statistical methodology than of the principles underlying neural and behavioral organization: "Specifically, mean and variance statistics are insensitive to rhythmicity, and the correlations among descriptive statistics are insensitive to rhythmic co-occurrence."

One of the tools employed by Porges and collaborators is cross-spectral analysis. This analysis generates a coherence statistic that describes shared rhythmic covariation. In some cases, the stimulus is provided by the organism itself. For example, Porges et al. (1980) have described autonomic (cardiovascular) activation gating by the pulmonary stretch receptors.

Estimates of medullary brain stem gains can also be made noninvasively and without specific knowledge of internal interconnectivity, opening the way to modeling closed-loop state parameters from autonomic effector outputs. Porges has used spectral analysis in assessing attention (Porges & Coles, 1982), hyperactivity in children (Porges, 1976; Porges & Smith, 1980), and fetal and neonatal competence (Porges, 1979, 1983). The application of these methods in the area of accumulated versus resolved stress is promising, since it may make it possible to quantify the periodic variation and covariation of sympathetic and parasympathetic systems at high levels of arousal where there is complex interaction.

The continuity approach represents a conceptual complement to and point of departure from the open-loop, psychosomatic view of J. W. Mason and others. The continuity approach models the organization of central autonomic states from rhythmicity and coherence of autonomic effectors, assuming an isomorphic relationship with central autonomic systems rather than the hierarchical relationship set forth in the psychosomatic view. Continuity analysis describes the *organization* of CNS processes, involving operations occurring in primitive as well as phylogenetically more recent portions of the CNS. The existence of direct sensory pathways to the hypothalamus and limbic system, via the midbrain reticular system, is well known (Fortier, 1966; Mangili, Motta, & Martini, 1966; Yates & Maran, 1974). Stress research, however, has placed an unbalanced emphasis on the more "refined," downward neocortical role, ignoring almost completely the more primitive effects ascending directly from the brain stem medulla, and hypothalamus. This bias is expressed by J. W. Hennessy and S. Levine (1979): "The terms psychological stress and arousal are essentially synonymous."

THE NEURAL STRATA

Anatomical and Conceptual Basis

The psychosocial view of stress traces chains of cause and effect, attempting to describe open-loop sequences that may lead to pathology. The systems view looks at homeostatic responses to internal and external fluctuation. Under the persistence of stress, in the systems view, the organism goes through processes of adaptation until new, relatively stable states are achieved. Prolonged "loading" of adaptive neural circuitry by unresolved stress will, however, limit the organism's capacity to regulate other functions, thus reducing its flexibility. Extreme adaptations that have occurred early in an organism's development and have altered neurohormonal organization at primitive neural strata (i.e. the brain stem–hypothalamus region

and the limbic system) may have more pervasive consequences on resilience to stress than those acting primarily through neocortical systems.

The importance of the "lower" brain—autonomic function—in governing overall behavior was first introduced as a clinical concept by Eppinger and L. Hess in 1915 and then experimentally by the work of W. R. Hess (1925) and Gellhorn (1957, 1967). Yakovlev (1948) proposed that CNS structure, and behavior, have evolved from within outward: The innermost and evolutionarily most primitive brain structures regulate internal states through autonomic control of the viscera. The most primitive system, Yakovlev argued, forms the *matrix* upon which the remainder of the brain, as well as behavior, is elaborated. Next (in terms of evolution and location) is a system related to posture, locomotion, and external (e.g., facial) expression of the internal visceral states in the form of emotional drives and affects. The outermost development, an outgrowth of the middle system in Yakovlev's schema, allows for control, perception, and manipulation of the external environment.

Yakovlev emphasized that these spheres are not independent, but are overlapping and integrated parts of the organism's total behavior. It was his contention that the appearance of more complex neural apparatus and even the tendency toward encephalization are *refinements* of the evolutionarily primitive needs of visceral function and are not new and independent processes. This contrasts with the hierarchical view that vital regulation by "lower" centers frees the "higher" ones for independent conscious activity (e.g., Cannon, 1929). While less sympathetic to the human's emerging ego consciousness, this evolutionary perspective focuses on integrative survival function as a primary substrate of neural organization. The matrix, Yakovlev's sphere of visceration, is in the reticular formation of the mammalian nervous system. This innermost core—a diffuse brain stem network of short neurons—provides the most primitive basis for integrating internal–external sensory, paleocortical, and neocortical inputs in forming the outflow of the sympathetic and parasympathetic effector systems.

MacLean (1955) proposed that the hypothalamus is nodal in these relations—a driver at the wheel of the brain stem, regulating autonomic nervous system outflow. He argued that the hypothalamus organizes alternative courses of behavior and directs the behavior of the organism as a whole. Similarly to Yakovlev, MacLean (1962, 1964, 1969) divided the mammalian brain into three more or less distinctly organized strata, corresponding roughly to the reptilian, the paleomammalian, and the neomammalian epochs of evolutionary development. Although these fundamental brain types show great differences in structure and chemistry, all three intermesh and function together as a unitary ("triune") brain.

Gellhorn (1957, 1967) studied the relationship of the hypothalamus to a wide spectrum of normal and abnormal behaviors. Pivotal in his work was the concept of autonomic reciprocity, as well as states of relative sympathetic or parasympathetic dominance, whereby the normal reciprocity breaks down and one branch becomes "tuned" at the expense of the other. Gellhorn concluded, in accord with W. R. Hess, that in arousal an integrative response is organized at the level of the hypothalamus to meet, in a unitary way, the continuous biological needs of the animal. In taking this one step further, he proposed that "the alterations in autonomic balance are not merely reflections of changes in overall behavior but are causally related to them." This assertion does not deny the downward contribution of neocortical and limbic influences on the hypothalamus. Rather, it recognizes a two-way interaction integrated at the level of the hypothalamus. Here balance and stability of vital regulations occur and can exert compelling effects on autonomic, somatic, and CNS behavioral reactions at all levels.

Routtenberg (1978), while studying the hypothalamic reward ("pleasure") system, has added to the integrative view by pointing out that both norepinephrine and dopamine systems send their axons into the cerebral cortex. Routtenberg views this as important because it relates the cerebral cortex to primitive structures deep within the midbrain and hindbrain, raising the possibility that highly complex intellectual activity in the cortex is influenced by the evolutionarily primitive catecholamine systems. Penfield (1938), on the basis of probing the brains in conscious patients, came to a similar conclusion: "The realization that the cerebral cortex, instead of being on the top, the highest level of integration, was an *elaboration level* . . . came to me like a bracing wind." Penfield viewed cognition, in hierarchical terms, not as a top-down process (as in the psychosomatic model) but as a bottom-up process. In general systems theory, microlevel events that produce macrolevel effects are called "emergence phenomena." It is the cyclic influence of microlevel and macrolevel events that characterizes self organization and that may relate "lower" feeling states to the formation of cognitive Gestalts (see La Violette, 1979).

The idea that behavior and consciousness itself are organized throughout the brain's evolutionary strata poses a series of important questions: What are the differential effects of stress acting at these levels, and how may they be modified by responding to extreme or chronic demands throughout the organism's development? What behavioral consequences may this have upon the organism as a whole? How can a measurement (continuity) approach be applied that differentially assesses levels at which stress has become accumulated? Finally, what are the implications of

stress strata for rational prophylaxis and treatment of stress disorders?

Hypothalamic and Autonomic Mechanisms

A primitive stratum suggesting altered function by stress is the hypothalamic region. In a series of experiments employing electrical and physiological stimulation of posterior hypothalamic nuclei, Gellhorn found that when strong excitation of the sympathetic (erogotropic) system is followed by sudden parasympathetic (trophotropic) rebound, arousal subsides quickly and normal conditions are restored. Brief stimuli favor this process (2–6 sec, in cats). The homeostatic capability to be rapidly mobilized (cf. W. R. Hess's and Cannon's emergency defensive "fight-or-flight" reaction) and then to be actively restored to prearousal levels may be a central mechanism for mammalian survival in an ever-changing and often hostile environment. If ergotropic stimulation is more prolonged (16–20 sec), even at relatively low levels of activation, then simultaneous ergotropic and trophotropic discharges often occur. Under these conditions, a heightened level of ergotropic excitation remains after stimulation. Gellhorn has used the term "tuning" to describe this phenomenon. Tuning is a possible mechanism underlying unresolved (accumulated) stress (P. Levine, 1977).

For animals in the wild, intense excitation is virtually always followed immediately by certain species-specific behaviors that tend to restore homeostasis. For example, following shock, pairs of rats will engage in a characteristic fighting behavior. Conner, Vernikos-Danellis, and S. Levine (1971) showed that ACTH secretion was much reduced in animals that were shocked in pairs (and fought), compared to those that received shocks individually. In terms of Gellhorn's hypothalamic concepts, the intense and brief afferent proprioceptive feedback evoked by short bouts of species-specific fighting behavior (itself an ergotropic stimulus) may trigger ergotropic discharge into trophotropic rebound, resetting autonomic balance. Where motor activity is blocked or escape is not possible, experimental neurosis occurs frequently. Both ergotropic and trophotropic discharges have been found to occur simultaneously in these states (Gellhorn, 1967).

Richter (1957) confined wild Norway rats in glass jars filled with water and kept them from surfacing by water jets. The animals soon became passive, ceased to struggle, and died. If, however, rats were exposed and freed several times beforehand, they remained aggressive and were able to withstand the stress for as long as 40 to 80 *hr*, compared with sometimes less than 15 *min* without the pretreatment! Richter also observed that the first response to stress was an accelerated heart rate, which subsequently, with prolongation of the stress situation, was followed by slowing of heart rate and death due to intense vagal discharge. Gellhorn (1960) noted a similar phenomenon in asphyctic clamping (suffocation) of anesthetized cats. He showed in addition that sectioning of the sympathetic cardiac nerve eliminated the later heart rate slowing; this demonstrated that *both* the sympathetic and parasympathetic systems were concurrently active in the prolonged asphyctic stress. Gellhorn (1967) also found this concurrent activation to be a characteristic of experimental neurosis and of chronic activation generally.

In an understanding of stress disorders, active phenomena like tuning may be helpful where passive, erosion-by-arousal mechanisms have been of limited value. As an example, the wild Norway rats used in Richter's experiment are, when compared with their domesticated laboratory strain, characterized by large adrenals and small thymus glands. Selye's theory would predict a chronic GAS, and the expectation was that these animals would succumb earlier to the effects of stress. This indeed was the case—except that when submerged and freed beforehand, the wild rats remained alive much longer (often longer than even the domestic strain with "normal" adrenals and thymus). Richter's serendipitous observation of this increased viability in the pre-exposed rats demands a more complex explanation, and points again to the problems of overgeneralizing Selye's simple biochemical GAS from host–pathogen relationships to complex neurobehavioral responses.

MacLean (1960) stated that it has not been demonstrated in animals or humans that emotional states have an immediate effect of inducing lesions in previously healthy tissue. This assertion was directed at Selye's (1950) proposal that psychological stress could precipitate widespread lesions by activation of the pituitary–adrenocortical system. Selye's argument was based on observations of animals maintained on a high-sodium and high-protein diet and "sensitized" by unilateral nephrectomy. These animals evidenced widespread changes of connective tissue, arthritis, ulcers, and hypertension, following long exposure to a "stressful" agent such as cold. Similar effects occurred if a synthetic adrenocorticoid was administered in lieu of the physical stressor. From this evidence, Selye proposed that the strains and stresses of normal life can act upon the organism and that when unduly prolonged and severe bring about diseases of adaptation. There are, however, alternative explanations that do not require such extreme "sensitization" procedures. Folkow (1978) has studied how physiological shifts in equilibrium due to increased sympathetic tone can lead to heart attack, arteriosclerosis, and stroke. Gutstein, Harrison, Parl, Kiu, and Avitable (1978) have demonstrated atherogenesis by lateral

hypothalamic stimulation. These findings are consistent with tuning-like mechanisms for accumulating stress.

There are difficult points to accept in Gellhorn's interpretation of tuning (e.g., 1964, 1970). He categorizes disorders such as depression and stomach ulcer as instances of parasympathetic tuning; he also views certain psychoneurotic states that are accompanied by a fall in blood sugar as evidence of parasympathetic tuning. Such explanations are contradicted by clinical observations: The coexistence of essential hypertension with peptic ulcer, of cold hands with bradycardia, and of tachycardia with increased urinary secretion is known by observant physicians. By "explaining" depression as a tuned parasympathetic dominance, Gellhorn virtually equates it with sleep and relaxation. This is somewhat bewildering, because Gellhorn has shown that under prolonged stress dual activation of the sympathetic and parasympathetic systems often occurs. In accumulated stress, sympathetic signs can be "masked" by concurrent parasympathetic effects, and small autonomic shifts may be expressed in abrupt "catastrophic" behavioral changes, such as the sudden onset of depression subsequent to chronic anxiety states (P. Levine, 1977; see also Nelson & Gellhorn, 1958, and Roessler, 1973).

Gellhorn's concept of hypothalamic tuning has been to a large extent ignored by neurobiologists and stress researchers. This is due in part to the increased trend toward specialization and molecularizing, but also to the lack of direct evidence that tuning is anything more than an interesting hypothalamic phenomenon without fundamental physiological and behavioral significance. Animal studies on the relationship of the limbic to the ergotropic hypothalamic system help to clarify the role of the paleomammalian strata in regulating autonomic, endocrine, and behavioral states.

Limbic Mechanisms

Limbic function related to survival behavior was studied by Egger and Flynn (1963), Flynn *et al.* (1974), and Stokman and Glusman (1970). Stimulation of the dorsolateral amygdala facilitated hypothalamic attack, whereas the medial portions actively suppressed it. Defensive behaviors, on the other hand, were facilitated by basolateral stimulation. A similar summating mechanism for defense was found by Flynn *et al.* (1974) to be mediated in hippocampal structures. Facilitation resulted from stimulating ventral portions, while suppression resulted from stimulating dorsal areas.

Stock, Schlor, Heidt, and Buss (1978) demonstrated in the cat that two distinctly different behavioral–autonomic patterns were elicited by stimulating different regions in the amygdaloid nuclear complex. Stimulation of the basal nuclei elicited a reaction in which the cat growled, hissed, pulled in its ears, and retracted its head. This defensive behavior was described earlier by Leyhausen (1960) from ethological observations. Stock *et al.* contrast this with a pattern that was evoked by stimulating regions in the central amygdala. More aggressive behavior was elicited, similar to what Leyhausen referred to as preparatory to attack. This differed from the "defensive" posture, in that the cat did not flatten its ears or retract its head. In the former (the basal amygdaloid defense or fear response), there was cholinergic vasodilation of skeletal muscles and only a small increase of heart rate and blood pressure (possibly this reflected concomitant sympathetic and parasympathetic activation, and not merely a nonreactive cardiovascular response). In contrast, stimulation of the central amygdaloid attack or fight response resulted in a sharp increase in heart rate, blood pressure, and peripheral resistance. Hypothalamic ergotropic "fight-or-flight" behaviors, then, appear to be elaborated by the limbic system.

The existence of subcortical mechanisms that are modified by stress experience could thus affect basic tendencies toward aggression and defensiveness. The amygdala is also central in behaviors relating to the preservation of the species. Deprivation, rewards, threats, and sexual opportunities energize specific response systems organized through the amygdala, medial forebrain bundle, and brain stem (Isaacson, 1972).

An interesting mechanism for the "storage" and wide effects of stress was suggested by the clinical observations of Heath, Monroe, and Mickle (1955). Stimulation of the amygdala in human patients elicited behavioral responses that intensified with repeated exposure. Initially, interest or amusement (or rage at high intensities) was evoked; later, stimulation caused intense fear with an impulse to run (at both intensities of stimulation). Stevens, Mark, Erwin, Pacheco, and Suematsu (1969) reported a case in which a single stimulation of the amygdala resulted in mood change, restlessness, and galloping mental activity that lasted for many hours. Though their subjects were disturbed and anxious patients, these observations point to the possibility that unresolved stress or anxiety, once fixed, can be a stimulus toward maintaining limbic activation. In addition, Lesse, Heath, Mickle, Munroe, and Miller (1955) have reported limbic spindle activity upon recollection of stressful experiences. Chronic (repeated) activation of the subcortical strata involved in emergency responses (i.e., fight or flight) might initiate processes that may sensitize rather than habituate and thus may be resistant to extinction.

The effects of limbic stimulation were first systematically explored in experimental animals by Goddard (1967, 1969). He coined the term "kindling" to describe a chain of long-lasting neurochemical events that were set into motion by daily, weekly, or even monthly stimulation of limbic structures in rats with single, brief, low-intensity currents. Initially, after the first few administrations, afterdischarges occur and are then paralleled progressively by chains of behavioral automatisms. The amygdala is particularly sensitive to kindling. Later, on continued daily or weekly stimulation, waves of electrical activity spread bilaterally and into the frontal cortex. These effects are highly resistant to extinction and are often considered a permanent restructuring of organization. Convulsions may occur in this final phase, though animals higher on the phylogenetic scale tend not to develop the final generalized convulsive motor seizures (Wada, 1978).

Neurobehavioral Models

Behavioral automatisms and anxiety states occur frequently in neurosis and psychosis. According to Antelman and Caggiula (1980), an almost universal response to moderate or prolonged stress, found throughout the animal kingdom and having a component in a number of human behavioral disorders, is the emergence of stereotypies. These authors differentiate between dopaminergic behaviors mediated by the nigro-striatal system and those mediated by the mesolimbic system. The former appears to mediate *acute* behavioral responses to stress, while the latter is more affected by prolonged or repeated stress. The mesolimbic system involves the limbic structures most sensitive to kindling. The nigro-striatal system, on the other hand, may be more related to passive arousal phenomena. Situations of overwhelming emotional affect or chronic stress may lead toward kindled or "prekindled" states. In this way, unresolved stress may contribute to and interact with symptoms in diverse psychopathologies and with stress diseases in general.

Mechanisms like kindling and tuning, though speculative, illustrate difficulties in viewing stress solely in stimulus terms. The history of the organism with respect to previous alterations by severe or chronic stress, or even by normal developmental variables, may have significant if not predominant effects. Adamec (1978) has suggested that kindling be viewed as a more general phenomenon, which he terms "emotional biasing." He has studied the behavior of cats partially kindled, by amygdaloid stimulation, to the afterdischarge (preconvulsive stage) and demonstrates a continuum from normal balanced limbic emotional function, through hyperfunctional states to excessively hyperfunctional (dysfunctional) states and flattened affect. Adamec suggests that these phenomena are important in understanding normal as well as abnormal biasing of affective states. Of particular interest is the developmentally permanent shaping of fearful and defensive reactions. (See also Adamec, Stark-Adamec, & Livingston, 1980a, 1980b, 1980c.)

If amygdaloid activation plays a role in reinforcing and "storing" fight-or-flight (Cannon's stress) behaviors through kindling-like phenomena, identification of functional amygdaloid connections with other portions of the brain may be important in understanding the nature and consequences of accumulated stress. The amygdala receives information from the hypothalamus below and from the neocortex above. Cullen and Goddard (1975) have shown that the amygdala can be kindled by stimulating posterior, anterior, and ventromedial hypothalamic nuclei corresponding closely with the stria terminalis. The amygdala receives downward connections from temporal, insular, and parietal opercular neocortex. These projections appear to synapse upon amygdal *outputs*, which in turn terminate primarily in the ventromedial hypothalamus (Gloor, 1978). Cortical afferents thus stimulate the amygdala only indirectly, via the ascending stria terminalis. The hypothalamus may, in this regard, be a nodal point to the limbic system, spanning brain stem to neocortical inputs.

Stress "stored" in the primitive neural strata could lead eventually to disorganization of behavior, such as stereotypy and altered affect, as well as to neuroendocrine changes. These primitive effects may make at least as compelling a contribution to health and disease as "psychosocial" (i.e., primarily neocortical) ones. Perhaps such a distinction is even basically artificial, diverting attention away from the study of classes of situations that are potent activators of the limbic and hypothalamic circuits. Closed-loop limbic interactions, for example, with the prefrontal cortex via specific (i.e., prefrontal dorsomedial thalamic) and diffuse (thalamo-cortical) projection systems are well known (e.g., see Skinner & Lindsley, 1973).

STRESS IN HEALTH AND DISEASE

Wolff and his colleagues, in studies of thousands of patients, found that certain types of life events clustered prior to the onset of disease; (Wolff, Wolf, & Hare, 1950). Holmes and Rahe (1967) systematized these events in a rating scale that was validated in cross-cultural studies, suggesting that these life events ("life change units," or LCUs) are objectively and universally stressors. The LCU is a logical endpoint of the "wear-and-tear" view of stress, which does not consider the developmental interrelationship of the organism with its environment. Rahe later (1974) departed from this strictly open-loop view by stating that only in dealing with quite large samples can these mean LCU values be used. With small groups of subjects, individual variation in LCU scaling assumes much more importance. Paykel, Prusoff, and Uhlen-

huth (1971), who are strong adherents of the LCU concept, have examined the standard deviations of these scores; they caution that scores will not be reliable with single individuals, since the usual variance of two standard deviations on either side of the mean spans a moderate range. Rahe (1974) has proposed a subjective LCU scaling system in which the ratings are based upon the amount of adjustment needed to handle life stresses. There is less variability with this method, which Rahe describes conceptually as "the past experience filter" (Rahe, 1978). The problem with this approach is that it shows that people may be aware that certain events affect them more than others do, but it does not suggest why or how—that is, what biological, developmental, and psychosocial mechanisms comprise the filter.

Lazarus (1966, 1968, 1981), Lazarus, Cohen, Folkman, Kanner, and Schaefer (1980), and Caplan (1981) have emphasized the role of coping mechanisms and cognitive appraisal in dealing with stressful situations. From preliminary studies, Lazarus (1981) suggests that little day-to-day hassles may be more injurious to health than the major stressful events. He even argues that major changes exert much of their harm as a consequence of the "pile-up" of little problems that arise as sequelae of major change or loss. Because we are embedded in networks of social relationships, our own experiences are compounded by those of many other individuals, and our reactions to some degree depend on theirs (Antonovsky, 1979). Thus support is an important factor. Berkman and Syme (1979) showed that individuals who lacked social and community ties were more likely to die prematurely from various causes than were those with fuller social contact. Kobasa, Hilker, and Maddi (1979), Antonovsky (1979), McClelland (1976), and Pine (1980) have identified a subgroup of persons labeled "stress-resistant." They seem little harmed by stresses that might overwhelm most persons and are characterized by openness to change, a feeling of involvement in whatever they are doing, and a sense of control. Reasons for this hardiness have not yet been explored systematically.

Animal studies shed some light on factors that may account for stress resiliency by allowing manipulations that could not practically or ethically be controlled with human subjects. In perhaps the earliest description of learned helplessness, Miller (1948) demonstrated that in an aversive situation where escape was prevented, rats showed considerable agitation. If a treadmill was then activated that allowed the rats to escape, the signs of strong fear were greatly reduced. One of the provocative issues brought out in Seligman's work (e.g., 1975) is a developmental aspect of learned helplessness. Female rats experiencing learned helplessness *before* becoming pregnant somehow pass "susceptibility" to this condition on to their offspring.

DEVELOPMENTAL STRESS: THE PERINATAL CONTINUUM

The earliest stresses an organism may be exposed to occur during its gestation. For humans, it is quite difficult to isolate effects of the intrauterine environment, such as maternal stress, in shaping subsequent behavior and particularly later resiliency to stress in offspring. There has been a tendency to view the neonate as *tabula rasa* (a blank tablet). Brazelton (1978) and others, however, raise a note of caution:

> Too often in our approach to the newborn, we deal with him as if he is exactly that—"brand new"—and we are neglectful of the fact that the neonate is really the culmination of an amazing developmental experience. . . . By looking at the neonate as if he had "sprung full blown from the brain of Zeus," we are missing the opportunities that the history of the newborn as a fetus can provide.

Several lines of evidence converge on the importance of such early developmental events in sequelae later in life. A substantial animal literature exists on prenatal psychosocial stress. Archer and Blackman (1971) have reviewed much of this literature, which shows detrimental effects on viability and behavior. Joffe (1969) also looked at effects of prenatal hypoxia and concluded that animals exposed to stress or hypoxia in gestation are generally less emotional and relatively hyperactive. Joffe characterized them as somatically energized under stress and sluggish in familiar surroundings.

The effects of maternal stress in human populations are not as easy to interpret. Recent evidence does suggest significant consequences of maternal stress on neurological development and pathological behaviors. Demographic studies (Campbell, Hardesty, & Burdock, 1978) indicate a very high incidence of childhood autism associated with complications of pregnancy. Campbell *et al.* also found that autistic children tended to have had during infancy frequent upper respiratory infections, febrile seizures, excessive burping, constipation, and loose bowel movements; these findings suggest autonomic instability as an underlying factor. In a preliminary study of 59 mothers of autistic children, Ward (1978) found that 32% had experienced family discord while pregnant (compared with under 3% in the control group). Since autism is considered by some to have a hereditary component, the population studies of Stott (1957, 1973) and Stott and Latchford (1976) are important. They found that stresses involving severe, continuing personal tensions (in particular, marital discord) were closely associated with child morbidity in the form of ill health, neurological dysfunction, developmental lag, and behavior disturbance. In addition, Stott found little correlation between child morbidity and physical illness, accidents or dental operations in the pregnant mothers—in other words, more or less isolated (i.e., resolvable) stresses.

Carlson and Barba (1979) have reviewed data supporting a relationship between maternal emotionality and outcome of pregnancy. The clearest links with emotional stress were found with habitual abortion, hyperemesis, gravidarum, toxemia, and birth complications. An argument could be made that some genetically transmittable characteristic makes such mothers more apt to have birth complications and be in conflict; however, the general agreement with animal studies (e.g., Seligman's "transmittable learned helplessness"), where these factors can be controlled, implies stress effects. Sontag's (1966) pioneering studies on infants followed into young adulthood suggest basic personality influences due to maternal stress. Sontag assessed fetal activity in response to sound stimulation and found correlations with later personality factors. High maternal anxiety also correlated strongly with many somatic problems in offspring.

A possible mechanism for "transmittable stress" in animals was examined by Keeley (1973). Injecting pregnant mice with epinephrine resulted in offspring's being less emotional at maturity. Injecting them with norepinephrine and hydrocortisone biased offspring to be hyperemotional; they were more readily frightened and more prone to autonomic disturbances in adulthood. Systematic investigations of the actual *in vivo* mechanisms of stress transmission have not been carried out. Recent technical advances, such as sonography, have provided refined tools that may make it possible to study the effects of maternal stress upon fetal neurological development. It has been established that rhythmic breathing movements, accompanied by primitive EEG activity and rapid eye movement (REM), occur *in utero* during much of gestation. These cyclic activities are influenced by small changes in blood gas levels (see Boddy & Dawes, 1975; Dawes, 1973, 1974).

The existence of critical periods for functional neurological development has been demonstrated by Hubel and Wiesel's (1970) electrophysiological experiments of pattern recognition in newborn kittens. The logical extension of these concepts to the developmental role of stimulation *in utero* is suggested by the work of the Bergstroms (L. Bergstrom, 1966; R. M. Bergstrom, 1969) and Stenberg (1967). They have shown that electrical stimulation to the fetal brain stem increases the rate of reflex development, as well as augmenting coherency of the primitive EEG. Baker and McGinty (1977) exposed newborn kittens to moderate hypoxia, which decreases the spontaneous electrical activity in the fetal lamb brain (Boddy, Dawes, Fischer, Pinter, & Robinson, 1974). Both respiration and heart rate became variable and disorganized, suggesting that basic neural stability requires sufficient rhythmic spontaneous activity. If this does not occur, it may dispose the organism to instability and lack of coherence, resulting eventually in potential distress and pathology (Porges, 1979, 1983; Prechtl, 1969; Rubin, 1962).

If fetal brain stem activity is a foundation for later stability, neurological development, and the emergence of behaviors that develop in infancy and into childhood, then it becomes important to identify maternal factors that can influence *in utero* electrical activity. Workers in fetal breathing find that fetal EEG and respiratory activity in sheep are highly dependent upon the level of oxygen available to the fetus and on blood gas carbon dioxide levels. A very mild degree of hypoxia (a fall of 5–7 mm Hg) in fetal carotid oxygen tension inhibits spontaneous EEG and fetal respiration for several hours, even after normal conditions are re-established. Hypercarbia is an extremely potent activator of the fetal CNS, its stimulatory effect also lasting several hours (Boddy & Dawes, 1975).

Normally, it is assumed that fetal oxygenation is constant and that the fetus is protected against maternal hypoxia through placental buffering. It is, in addition, protected by its own sympathetic nervous system through oxygen-conserving circulatory adjustments (Purves, 1974; Saling, 1968). However, two issues about "fetal protection" need to be considered. First, a responsive autonomic nervous system exists in the fetus (Nuwayhid, Brinkman, Su, Bevan, & Assali, 1975; Purves, 1974). If it is activated for protracted periods of time (even at low levels), then conditions may be set for progressive levels of stress to accumulate through tuning-like mechanisms. Although there is no general agreement, some authors (e.g., Cheek & Rowe, 1969; Isabel, Towers, Adams, & Gyepes, 1972) have suggested that a predisposing factor of respiratory distress at birth is an overactive sympathetic nervous system. Autonomic mechanisms by which fetal nutrition and oxygenation may be compromised were first suggested by Toth, McEwen, and Shabanah (1964) in studying placental circulation. Marshal (1970) summarized the work on autonomic control of uterine blood vessels and concluded that stimulation of the adrenergic nerves to the uterus in the intact animal usually causes a profound decrease in uterine blood flow. Toth *et al.* (1964) pointed out that the placental hypoxia caused by diminished circulation (due to sympathetic vasoconstriction) may also precipitate a vicious circle by decreasing tissue permeability of the uterine–placental transfer barrier.

If a situation of chronic stress exists, then increased maternal pelvic sympathetic tone could result in significant fetal blood gas alternations (Boddy & Dawes, 1975). By interfering with spontaneous fetal neural activity, this could set into motion neurodevelopmental sequelae influencing later autonomic patterns of excitability, stability, and balance. In this way, fetal hypoxia/hypercarbia may be a final common pathway by which diverse factors—such as certain pharmacological agents, smoking, alcohol, toxemia, uterine-placental insufficiency, and maternal stress—may act deleteriously upon the developing fetus. A chance observation by Boddy *et al.* (1974) suggests another way in which the fetus may be vulnerable to maternal anxiety factors. These workers noted that in a few ewes that were hyperventilating, the resulting low partial carbon dioxide pressure (30–32 mm Hg) in the fetuses was associated with a low incidence of fetal breathing and EEG (mean 15%), compared to about 40% at normal partial pressure (40 mm Hg). The fetal nervous system may be sensitive to maternal carbon dioxide and may not be protected, even in physiological ranges, from a drop in its level. Boddy *et al.* also reported an inverse relation between maternal ACTH levels and fetal breathing and EEG.

The developing fetus, if subjected *chronically* to even low-grade demands on its autonomic protective mechanisms, may preserve vital function, but perhaps does so at the expense of retarded development, CNS instability, and later diminished capacity to resolve stress. Fetal protection (against maternal hypoxia by placental buffering) focuses attention away from maternal mechanisms—such as chronic sympathetic tone in the pelvic region, circulating hormones, chronic hyperventilation, and abnormal myometric activity—that may compromise fetal oxygenation and alter carbon dioxide levels. While physiological mechanisms have not yet been directly established, both animal and human studies point toward maternal stress transmission as a significant phenomenon.

The birth process itself is also a possible source of stress, particularly if hypoxic complications arise. Birthing practices have attracted considerable interest among the general public, and many physicians (e.g., Kimball, 1974) have advocated a re-evaluation of prevailing medical practice. While experimental verification of the impact of the birth process on later development is another difficult research area, some provocative work has been conducted. Windle (1971) exposed monkey infants to births simulating "routine hospital deliveries." This included supine position, cutting of the cord, and the use of standard anesthetic procedures. These monkeys were shown later to have marked developmental lag, as well as histological signs of damage (asphyxia neonatorum at autopsy). Spontaneous births in the same colony showed none of these deficits. Rutt and Offord (1970) studied a group of 33 schizophrenic children and adolescents, and found a 40% rate of birth complications. Mednick (1970) followed a group of 172 youngsters who were classified as high-risk because their mothers were schizophrenic. By school age, 20 children in this group, who later became schizophrenic, were labeled as "troublemakers" by their teachers. Of this group, 70% had suffered at least one complication at birth or during gestation. Of the high-risk children who did *not* develop schizophrenia, only 15% had had any kind of complication during gestation of birth. Mednick also noted greater autonomic instabilities in the preschizophrenic population. On the other hand, in the "Kaui study" cited by Prescott (1976), the effects of even severe "birth trauma" appeared to be mitigated by close infant–parent interaction. There was little correlation between "birthing difficulties" and later development with follow-up until the sixth grade. Similarly, recent preliminary findings by Field, Dempsey, and Shuman (1983) do not show any clear correlation between birthing difficulties, including Caesarian section, and development and adjustment. This is an area needing more research, including sophisticated autonomic measurements, as well as more subtle assessment of behavior, particularly under stress.

Various psychoanalytic schools (e.g., those of Freud, Rank, and Reich) have posited that birth experiences are significant to personality development, particularly in susceptibility to undifferentiated anxiety states. As difficult as this is to substantiate, Cheek (1974, 1975), Johnson (1972), and Grof (1976) claim to have demonstrated reconstruction of "birth recall," catalyzed by the therapeutic use of hypnosis and psychotropic drugs. They argue that a relationship exists between perinatal experience and later anxiety states, phobias, neurosis, psychosis, schizophrenia, and behavioral disorders in general. Grof's work, employing serial LSD-25 sessions, was analytically and "transpersonally" oriented. Johnson administered a single large dose (750–1000 mg) of methylphenidate (Ritalin), followed by weekly (nondrug) "reporting" sessions. Cheek (1974, 1975), an obstetrician, hypnotized a few young adults whom he had delivered. He claimed that their recollections of "birth memories" via hypnosis, which included the spontaneous positioning of head, neck, and shoulders, were corroborated by detailed notes taken at the time of their delivery. Cheek's subjects were able to relate birth experiences to pervasive moods and behavior patterns, particularly those that occurred under stress. While these reports are only anecdotal, better-controlled studies (Chamberlain, 1980) have confirmed and extended Cheek's results. This work has far-reaching social implications for the medical management of delivery and needs to be verified by systematic prospective studies.

The time shortly after birth is another potentially significant period in molding later stress behaviors. Lorenz (1960) first used the term "imprinting" (*Praegung*) to describe the permanent and time-critical type of behavior he observed in newly hatched goslings. The most relevant observations of time-critical bond formation in primate animals come from the pioneering isolation studies of the Harlows and their students and colleagues (e.g., Harlow, 1958, 1964; Harlow & Harlow, 1965; Harlow, Harlow, & Hansen, 1963; Hinde, 1975; Mitchell, 1968, 1970, 1975). In these studies, infant monkeys reared in isolation, but in a room where they could see, hear, and smell other monkeys, later developed severe emotional and social pathologies. Symptoms included depression, withdrawal, and "autistic-like" behaviors; movement stereotypes; self-mutilation; abnormal sexual behaviors; and pathological violence. W. A. Mason (1968) reported the dramatic finding that vestibular stimulation provided by a mechanical swinging mother surrogate helped to prevent most of these abnormal socioemotional behaviors in the isolates.

A criticism of the studies of primates reared in isolation has been that the conditions of isolation employed are rather complete and severe, compared to conditions for human infants. The studies of Spitz (1946) on anaclitic depression in orphans suggest that humans are subject to similar behavioral disorders as a consequence of severe contact deprivation. However, Rutter (1965), reviewing the human literature on the consequences of maternal deprivation, points out an array of uncontrolled variables and difficulties in drawing definite conclusions on the specific role of the mother–child relationship to later problems, such as depression, delinquency, and retardation. In an analysis of the National Institutes of Health (NIH) file of anthropological studies from primitive cultures throughout the world, Prescott (1975) found a very high negative correlation ($-.96$) existing between the degree of physical contact and intimacy during infancy and adolescence and the prevalence of adult violence in these societies. The high incidence of child abusers in contemporary Western culture who were themselves abused also attests to this view (Prescott, 1975). Prescott's study is perhaps unique in that the societies examined (now virtually extinct) were less encumbered by the complex veneers of modern culture and presented a picture that more closely parallels the experimental primate work.

In human endocrine studies, abnormalities, particularly deficient growth hormone response associated with deficient parental contact ("deprivation dwarfism"), characteristically normalize with provision of a close relationship and a more stable environment (Imura, Yoshimi, & Ikekubo, 1974; Powell, Brasel, & Blizzard, 1967). This applies to younger children as well as infants, suggesting that deprivation of emotional needs generates sufficient stress to disrupt basic neuroendocrine processes. If interactions between infants/children and "caretakers" can be so profound as to regulate growth, then other effects would not be surprising. Recent animal studies by Hofer (1970, 1973, 1976) with rats and by Reite and colleagues (Reiter, Kaufman, Pauley, & Stynes, 1975; Reite & Short, 1978) with primates have demonstrated a basic similarity in responses in maternal separation across species. The effect of acute isolation in 6-month-old animals is an initial agitation with elevated heart rate. This is generally followed by a slowly developing locomotor retardation, with diminished play and a characteristic slouched posture. In 2-week-old separated rats and monkeys, acute separation resulted in a decrease in heart rate and body temperature, disrupted sleep, insomnia, and marked reduction in REM sleep. Reite and Hofer found that many of the autonomic changes persist into adulthood and may be related to immunological weaknesses. Reite and his coworkers view their results as related to organismic stress states induced by maternal separation, while Hoffer sees his findings more in terms of the loss of specific regulatory actions.

The immature nervous system may be molded by perinatal stress, predisposing it to later maladaptive responses. For example, amygdaloid circuits are critical not only in aggressive behaviors, but in forming the social bonds that develop out of the mother-infant relationship (Kling & Steklis, 1976). Thus if the perinate's primitive nervous system is strained beyond its developmentally delicate homeostatic capabilities, this could have subtle and pervasive effects on many later social behaviors. Extreme or even low-grade chronic maternal stress could predispose the neonate to difficulty with the primary maternal bond (compounded by the mother's frustration from her perceived inability to alleviate her infant's distress) and with later social relationships. It could even lay the groundwork for violent and self-destructive behaviors, as well as a wide spectrum of "psycho-"somatic problems. To implicate stress in the perinatal period as the cause of many serious health and social problems would not be scientifically justified. At the same time, it would be irresponsible to dismiss the implications of a picture that is beginning to emerge from both animal and human studies, and that calls into question many prevalent medical and cultural assumptions.

STRESS MANAGEMENT

The preceding section has suggested that early developmental periods may be critical in developing later resiliency to handling stress and social behaviors. Awareness of this relationship may foster the growth of more responsible practices that serve to prevent distress and pathology.

Though the best treatment is always prevention, there is a great need for development of other approaches in the art/science of stress management. Some lesser-studied "somatic" avenues related to the systems view are discussed here.

"Emotional stress" (after Cannon and Bard) is pictured as centrally generated and acting downward upon autonomic and somatic (muscular) effectors, via autonomic nerves and gamma efferents. In an earlier "peripheralist" view (that of James and Lang; see James, 1884), bodily (visceral and somatic) changes

experienced during such states as fear, anger, or joy were viewed as the initial events; they were seen as precluding emotional experience and as necessary for its perception. Gellhorn (1964, 1967, 1970) has used portions of each view and has speculated on the role of proprioceptive feedback in maintaining hypothalamically tuned states and mediating emotional behaviors. Since high-frequency group I spindle afferents bias sympathetic, ergotropic dominance, while low-frequency activity on the same pathways mediate parasympathetic, trophotropically tuned states, posture and bodily attitudes may be related to the closed-loop regulation of stress behaviors. Gellhorn's observations suggest the possibility of access to central excitatory states (accumulated stress) and emotional affective processes directly, via somatic alteration. The use of muscle relaxation techniques (e.g., Jacobson's [1938] progressive relaxation) is an obvious application of tuning principles. The role of proprioceptive feedback on specific affect is suggested by the experiments of Pasquarelli and Bull (1951). If a certain emotional state (e.g., joy) was suggested in hypnotic trance and the concomitant body state was "locked" by suggestion, then a contrasting mood (e.g., depression or sadness) could not be produced unless the previous postured setting was first changed (in trance).

Little is known in this area, but certain facts suggest that the neck and respiratory muscles may play a special role in sympathetic–parasympathetic balance and emotion (Gellhorn, 1970). Similarly, relaxation of the neck muscles, which occurs in the paradoxical phase of sleep, is associated with the most marked fall in blood pressure (Rossi, 1963). The effects of neck immobilization were studied in a series of interesting but little-known experiments by Zubek, Aftanas, Kovach, Wilgash, and Winocur (1963). A group of adult faculty members at a university took part in an experiment where their heads were fixed in neck halters. The experience was reported as "stressful" by 85% of the participants. Vision and hearing were not interfered with, and the subjects were free to converse with each other and engage in any activity they wished as long as their heads remained in the halters. Zubek *et al.* found that restriction of neck movement alone resulted in "intellectual inefficiency, bizarre thoughts, exaggerated emotional reactions, and unusual bodily sensations" (1963).

The powerful effects of general immobility have also been mentioned by Prescott. Infants and children immobilized in bed for the treatment of bone fractures often develop emotional disturbances, marked by hyperactivity and outbursts of rage and violence.

Although these are extreme situations, they demonstrate possible consequences of altered proprioception in maintaining states of accumulated stress. Hunt (1980) has shown in preliminary studies with free-moving EMG telemetering equipment that individuals experiencing moderate anxiety or frustration exhibit an overlapping pattern of *sustained* agonist–antagonist EMG activity. In Hunt's anxious subjects, movement was generated by a shifting dominance between co-contracted flexor and extensor activities. This was compared with a reciprocal, rhythmic pattern, which seems to categorize younger children, many dancers, some athletes, and a group of Polynesians Hunt tested. Thus, stress patterns may reinforce themselves by a type of closed-loop, self-imposed immobilization.

Relationships of static body tension and behavior were presaged by various unorthodox schools of therapeutic work, including F. M. Alexander, A. T. Stills and W. G. Sutherland (osteopathy), W. Reich, M. Feldendreis, I. Rolf, and others. Reich, for example, developed a system therapy in the 1930s and 1940s, which proposed that muscular rigidity was the expression of a chronic disturbance of the autonomic nervous system. (See Boadella, 1974, for a historical review.) F. M. Alexander, in the early 1900s, also recognized the intimate role of bodily tension patterns in behavior. His work consisted of very gentle manipulation, first exploratory and then corrective, in a re-education of the entire muscular system. Treatment started with the head and neck, and all body areas were subsequently worked with. Tinbergen (1974) reported, in his Nobel Prize acceptance address, the beneficial effects on sleep, blood pressure, cheerfulness, alertness, and resilience to general stress that he and his family experienced when they underwent Alexander treatment. Other prominent scientists and educators have also written of the benefit of this treatment. Tinbergen mentions John Dewey, Aldous Huxley, and scientists like G. E. Coghill, Raymond Dart, and even Sir Charles Sherrington. While admiration from such prominent individuals is provocative, it hardly constitutes rigorous scientific inquiry. It is unlikely, on the other hand, that men of such intellectual rigor have all been duped.

There have been clinical trials in various manipulative muscle approaches. Korr (e.g., 1978) has published some interesting observations based on osteopathic work. Most of these studies, however, are poorly designed, and controls are often inadequate (Haldeman, 1978). In a publication on the Rolf Method of Structural Integration, Silverman, Rappaport, Hopkin, Ellman, Hubbard, Belleza, Baldwin, Griffin, and Kling (1973) have shown a wide range of interesting myographic, evoked potential, psychological, and biochemical changes. The myographic work of Hunt (1980) suggests a more efficient patterning of neuromuscular energy after Rolf processing, and Silverman found an openness to change such as might characterize Kobasa *et al.*'s (1979) stress-resistant population.

The use of systems-oriented stress paradigms for detection of accumulating stress (even before symptoms develop) and the utilization of somatic disciplines in prevention and treatment could be a most exciting and rewarding area in future multidisciplinary and health care research. With few exceptions, the academic and medical community is unaware of these somatic approaches. Some recent programs, however, are attempting to encourage the "networking" necessary to foster the emergence of a somatics field (e.g., "The Body and The Person—Toward a Somatic Model of Health," University of California Extension, Berkeley School of Public Health, May 1982).

SUMMARY

Studies in the psychophysiology of stress have been hampered by lack of consistant definitions. In this review, stress behaviors are broadly divided into open- and closed-loop phenomena.

The open-loop type of model is typified by Hans Selye's GAS and by the earlier psychosomatic views in general. In these views, stressors are seen to act on a relatively passive organism by eroding tissue and cellular integrity, leading toward pathology.

In the closed-loop or systems model, dynamic feedback patterns govern a wide spectrum of behaviors and reflect the organisms capacity for order and stability. The "stress response" is contingent in a complex, nonlinear way on previously developed neurobehavioral modes of adaptation. Patterns become structured within the CNS as a result of severe or chronic activation, particularly during developmentally sensitive periods.

In the systems view, stress susceptibility, resiliency, and specificity have a complex ontogenetic basis. In this approach, appropriate methodologies of measurement employing sophisticated analytical techniques may be necessary, particularly with human populations. The systems view also suggests that stress patterns might be therapeutically restructured by altering somatic afferents to the CNS. In this way, it may be possible to re-establish greater adaptational capacity (resiliency) to stress.

REFERENCES

Adamec, R. E. Normal and abnormal limbic system mechanisms in emotive biasing. In K. E. Livingston & O. Hornykiewicz (Eds.), *Limbic mechanisms: The continuing evolution of the limbic system concept.* New York: Plenum Press, 1978.

Adamec, R. E., Stark-Adamec, C., & Livingston, K. E. The development of predatory aggression and defense in the domestic cat (*Felis catus*): 1. Effects of early experience on adult patterns of aggression and defense. *Behavioral and Neural Biology,* 1980, 30, 389–409. (a)

Adamec, R. E., Stark-Adamec, C., & Livingston, K. E. The development of predatory aggression and defense in the domestic cat (*Felis catus*): 2. Development of aggression and defense in the first 164 days of life. *Behavioral and Neural Biology*, 1980, 30, 410–434. (b)

Adamec, R. E., Stark-Adamec, C., & Livingston, K. E. The development of predatory aggression and defense in the domestic cat (*Felis catus*): 3. Effects on development of hunger between 180 and 365 days of age. *Behavioral and Neural Biology*, 1980, 30, 435–447. (c)

Antelman, S. M., & Caggiula, A. R. Stress induced behavior. In J. Davidson & R. J. Davidson (Eds.), *Psychobiology of consciousness*. New York: Plenum, 1980.

Antonovsky, A. *Health, stress and coping: New perspectives on mental well-being*. San Francisco: Jossey-Bass, 1979.

Baker, T. L., & McGinty, D. J. Reversal of cardiopulmonary failure during active sleep in hypoxic kittens: Implications for sudden infant death. *Science*, 1977, 198, 419.

Bassett, J. R., Cairncross, K. D., & King, M. G. Parameters of novelty, shock predictability, and response contingency in corticosterone release in the rat. *Physiology and Behavior*, 1973, 10, 901–907.

Bergstrom, L. Fetal development of mesencephalic motor functions in the guinea-pig. *Acta Physiologica Scandinavica*, 1966, 68(Suppl. 227), 22.

Bergstrom, R. M. Electrical parameters of the brain during ontogeny. In R. J. Robinson (Ed.), *Brain and early behavior*. New York: Academic Press, 1969.

Berkman, L. F., & Syme, S. L. Social networks, host resistance and mortality. *American Journal of Epidemiology*, 1979, 109, 186–204.

Boadella, D. *Wilhelm Reich: The evolution of his work*. London: Vision Press, 1974.

Board, F., Wadeson, R., & Persky, H. Depressive affect and endocrine functions: Blood-levels of adrenal cortex and thyroid hormones in patients suffering from depressive reactions. *Archives of Neurology and Psychiatry*, 1957, 78, 612.

Boddy, K., & Dawes, G. S. Foetal breathing. *British Medical Bulletin*, 1975, 31, 3.

Boddy, K., Dawes, G. S., Fischer, R. L., Pinter, S., & Robinson, J. S. Foetal respiratory movements, electrocortical and cardiovascular responses to hypoxaemia and hypercapnea in sheep. *Journal of Physiology*, 1974, 243, 599.

Brain, P. F., & Poole, A. E. The role of endocrines in isolation-induced intermale fighting in albino laboratory mice: I. Pituitary–adrenocortical influences. *Aggressive Behavior*, 1974, 1, 39–69.

Brambella, F., & Penti, G. Schizophrenia: Endocrinological review. In F. Brambella, P. K. Bridges, E. Endroczi, & G. Hensen (Eds.), *Perspective in endocrine psychobiology*. New York: Wiley, 1978.

Brazelton, T. B. (1978). The remarkable talents of the newborn. *Birth and the Family Journal*, 5, 187–191.

Brener, J. A general model of voluntary control applied to the phenomena of learned cardiovascular change. In P. A. Obrist, A. H. Black, J. Brener, & L. V. DiCara (Eds.), *Cardiovascular psychophysiology: Current issues in response mechanisms, biofeedback, and methodology*. Chicago: Aldine, 1974.

Burchfield, S. R., Elich, M. S., & Woods, S. C. Geophagia in response to stress and arthritis. *Physiology and Behavior*, 1977, 19, 265–267.

Cahn, H. A. *Beyond homeostasis: An unexplored domain of wellness*. Unpublished manuscript, 1982.

Campbell, M., Hardesty, A. S., & Burdock, E. I. Demographic and perinatal profile of 105 autistic children: A preliminary report. *Psychopharmacology Bulletin*, 1978, 14(23), 36.

Cannon, W. B. The emergency function of the adrenal medulla and the major emotions. *American Journal of Physiology*, 1914, 33, 356–372.

Cannon, W. B. *Bodily changes in pain, hunger, fear, and rage*. New York: Appleton, 1929.

Caplan, G. Mastery of stress: Psychosocial aspects. *American Journal of Psychiatry*, 1981, 138, 413–420.

Carlson, D. B., & LaBarba, R. C. Maternal emotionality during pregnancy and reproductive outcome: A review of the literature. *International Journal of Behavioral Development*, 1979, 2(4), 343–376.

Carroll, B. J. Limbic system adrenal cortex regulation in depression and schizophrenia. *Psychosomatic Medicine*, 1976, 38, 106–121.

Chamberlain, D. *Reliability of birth memories: Evidence from mother and child pairs in hypnosis*. Paper presented at the 23rd Annual Scientific Meeting of the American Society of Clinical Hypnosis, Minneapolis, November 15, 1980.

Cheek, D. B. Sequential head and shoulder movements appearing with age regression, in hypnosis to birth. *American Journal of Clinical Hypnosis*, 1974, 16, 261–266.

Cheek, D. B. Maladjustment patterns apparently related to birth. *American Journal of Clinical Hypnosis*, 1975, 18, 75–82.

Cheek, D. B., & Rowe, R. D. Aspects of sympatehtic activity in the newborn. *Pediatric Clinics of North America*, 1969, 13(3), 863.

Christian, J. J. Hormonal control of population growth. In B. E. Elftheriou & R. L. Sprott (Eds.), *Hormonal correlated behavior*. New York: Plenum, 1975.

Conner, R. L., Vernikos-Danellis, J., & Levine, S. Stress, fighting and neuroendocrine function. *Nature*, 1971, 234, 564–566.

Crile, G. W. *The origin and nature of the emotions*. Philadelphia: W. B. Saunders, 1915.

Cullen, N., & Goddard, G. U. Kindling in the hypothalamus and transfer to the ipsilateral amygdala. *Behavioral Biology*, 1975, 15(2), 119–131.

Danellis, J. V., & Heybach, J. P. Psychophysiologic mechanisms regulating the hypothalamic–pituitary adrenal response to stress. In H. Selye (Ed.), *Selye's guide to stress research* (Vol. 1). New York: Van Nostrand Reinhold, 1980.

Darling, R., & Darrow, C. W. Determining activity of the autonomic nervous system from measurements of autonomic change. *Journal of Psychology*, 1938, 7, 85–89.

Darrow, C. W., Jost, H., Solomon, A. P., & Mergener, J. C. Autonomic indications of excitatory and homeostatic effects on the electroencephalogram. *Journal of Psychology*, 1942, 14, 115–130.

Davis, J., Morrill, R., Fawcett, J., Upton, V., Bondy, P. K., & Spiro, H. M. Apprehension and elevated serum cortisol levels. *Journal of Psychosomatic Research*, 1962, 6, 83–86.

Dawes, G. W. Revolutions and cyclical rhythms in pre-natal life: Fetal respiratory movements rediscovered. *Pediatrics*, 1973, 51(6), 965.

Dawes, G. W. Breathing before birth in animals and man. *New England Journal of Medicine*, 1974, 290(10), 557.

Duffy, E. The measurement of muscular tension as a technique for the study of emotional tendencies. *American Journal of Psychology*, 1932, 44, 146–162.

Duffy, E. The psychological significance of the concept of "arousal" or "activation." *Psychological Review*, 1957, 64(5), 265–275.

Egger, M. D., & Flynn, J. P. Effects of electrical stimulation of the amygdala on hypothalamically elicited attack behavior in cats. *Journal of Neurophysiology*, 1963, 26, 705–720.

Eliott, R. Physiological activity and performance: A comparison of kindergarten children with young adults. *Psychological Monographs*, 1964, 78(10, Whole No. 587).

Elliott, R. The motivational significance of heart rate. In P. A. Obrist, A. H. Black, J. Brener, & L. V. DiCara (Eds.), *Cardiovascular psychophysiology: Current issues in response mechanisms, biofeedback, and methodology*. Chicago: Aldine, 1974.

Elmadjian, F. Excretion and metabolism of epinephrine and norepinephrine in various emotional states. In *Proceedings of the 5th Pan American Congress of Endocrinology, Lima, 1963*.

Elmadjian, F., Lamson, E. T., Maschouf, C., & Gibson, N. Aldosterone excretion in behavioral disorders. *Acta Endocrinologica*, 1960, 34 (Suppl. 51–53), 165.

Eppinger, H., & Hess, L. Vagotonia. *Journal of Nervous and Mental Disease*, 1915 (Monograph Series 20).

Field, T., Dempsey, J., & Shuman, H. H. Five year follow-up of preterm respiratory distress syndrome and post-term postmaturity syndrome infants. In T. Field & A. Sostek (Eds.), *Infants born at risk: Physiological, perceptual, and cognitive processes*. New York: Grune & Stratton, 1983.

Flynn, J. P., Vanegas, H., Foote, W., & Edwards, S. Neural mechanisms involved in a cat's attack on a rat. In R. E. Whalen, R. F. Thompson, M. Verzeano, & N. M. Weinberger (Eds.), *The neural control of behavior*. New York: Academic Press, 1974.

Folkow, B. Cardiovascular structural adaptation: Its role in the initiation and maintenance of primary hypertension. *Clinical Science and Molecular Medicine*, 1978, 55, 322.

Fortier, C. Nervous control of ACTH secretion. In G. W. Harris & B. T. Donovan (Eds.), *The pituitary gland* (Vol. 2). Berkeley: University of California Press, 1966.

Frankenhaeuser, M. Psychobiological aspects of life stress. In S. Levine & H. Ursin (Eds.), *NATO Conference Series III: Human factors* (Vol. 12, *Coping and health*). New York: Plenum Press, 1980.

Franksson, C., & Gemzell, C. A. Adrenocortical activity in the preoperative period. *Journal of Clinical Endocrinology*, 1955, 15, 1069.

Friedman, S. B., & Ader, R. Adrenocortical response to novelty and noxious stimulation. *Neuroendocrinology*, 1967, 2, 209–212.

Friedman, S. B., Ader, R., Grota, L. J., & Larson, T. Plasma corticosterone response to parameters of electric shock stimulation in the rat. *Psychosomatic Medicine*, 1967, 29, 323–328.

Funkenstein, D. H., Greenblatt, M., & Soloman, H. J. Autonomic nervous system changes following electric shock treatment. *Journal of Nervous and Mental Disease*, 1950, 114, 1–118.

Gellhorn, E. *Autonomic imbalance and the hypothalamus*. Minneapolis: University of Minnesota Press, 1957.

Gellhorn, E. The tuning of the autonomic nervous system through the alteration of the internal environment (asphyxia). *Acta Neurologica*, 1960, 20, 515–540.

Gellhorn, E. Motion and emotion. *Psychological Review*, 1964, 71, 457–472.

Gellhorn, E. *Principles of autonomic–somatic integrations: Physiological basis and psychological and clinical implications*. Minneapolis: University of Minnesota Press, 1967.

Gellhorn, E. The emotions and the ergotropic and trophotropic systems. *Psycholosche Forschung*, 1970, 34, 48–94.

Gibbons, J. L. The adrenal cortex and psychological distress. In R. P. Mitchell (Ed.), *Endocrinology and human behavior*. London: Oxford University Press, 1968.

Gloor, P. Inputs and outputs of the amygdala: What the amygdala is trying to tell the rest of the brain. In K. E. Livingston & O. Hornykiewicz (Eds.), *Limbic mechanisms: The continuing evolution of the limbic system concept*. New York: Plenum Press, 1978.

Goddard, G. V. Development of epileptic seizures through brain stimulation at low intensity. *Nature*, 1967, 214, 1020–1021.

Goddard, G. V. Analysis of avoidance conditioning following cholinergic stimulation of amygdala in rats. *Journal of Comparative and Physiological Psychology* (Monograph), 1969, 63(No. 2, Pt. 2), 1–18.

Grau, J. W., Hyson, R. L., Maier, S. F., Madden, J., & Barchas, J. D. (1981). Long-term stress-induced analgesia and activation of the opiate system. *Science*, 213, 1409–1411.

Grof, S. *Realms of the human unconscious: Observations from LSD research*. New York: Bobbs-Merrill, 1976.

Gutstein, W. H., Harrison, J., Parl, F., Kiu, G., & Avitable, M. Neural factors contribute to atherogenesis. *Science*, 1978, 199, 449–451.

Haldeman, S. The clinical basis for discussion of mechanisms of manipulative therapy. In I. Korr (Ed.), *The neurobiologic mechanisms in manipulative therapy*. New York: Plenum Press, 1978. Pp. 53–75.

Harlow, H. F. The nature of love. *American Psychologist*, 1958, 13, 673–685.

Harlow, H. F. Early social deprivation and later behavior in the monkey. In A. Abrams (Ed.), *Unfinished tasks in the social sciences*. Baltimore: Williams & Wilkins, 1964.

Harlow, H. F., & Harlow, M. K. The affectional systems. In A. M. Schrier, H. F. Harlow, & F. Stollnitz (Eds.), *Behavior of nonhuman primates* (Vol. 2). New York: Academic Press, 1965.

Harlow, H. F., Harlow, M. K., & Hansen, E. W. The maternal affectional system of rhesus monkeys. In H. L. Rheingold (Ed.), *Maternal behaviors in mammals*. New York: Wiley, 1963.

Heath, R. G., Monroe, R. P., & Mickle, W. A. Stimulation of the amygdaloid nucleus in a schizoprhenic patient. *American Journal of Psychiatry*, 1955, 111, 862–863.

Hennessy, J. W., & Levine, S. Stress, arousal and the pituitary-adrenal system: A psychoendocrine hypothesis. In J. M. Sprague & A. N. Epstein (Eds.), *Progress in psychobiology and physiological psychology* (Vol. 8). New York: Academic Press, 1979.

Hennessy, M. B., Heybach, J. P., Vernikos, J., & Levine, S. Plasma corticosterone concentrations sensitively reflect levels of stimulus intensity in the rat. *Physiology and Behavior*, 1979, 22, 821–825.

Henry, J. P. Present concept of stress theory. In E. Usdin, R. Kvetnansky, & I. J. Kopin (Eds.), *Catecholamines and stress* (Proceedings of the Second International Symposium on Catecholamines and Stress, September 12–16, 1979, Smolenice Castle, Czechoslovakia). New York: Elsevier/North-Holland, 1980.

Henry, J. P., & Meehan, J. P. Psychosocial stimuli, physiological specificity and cardiovascular disease. In H. Weiner, M. A. Hofer, & A. J. Stunkard (Eds.), *Brain, behavior and bodily disease*. New York: Raven Press, 1981.

Henry, J. P., & Stephens, P. M. *Stress, health, and the social environment: A sociobiologic approach to medicine*. New York: Springer-Verlag, 1977.

Hess, W. R. *Uber die Wechselbeziehungen zwischen psychischen und vegetativen Funktionen* (Vol. 3). Zurich: Fussli, 1925.

Hess, W. R. *Das Zwischenhirn*. Basel: Schwabe, 1949.

Hetzel, B. S., Schottstaedt, W. W., Grace, W. J., & Wolff, H. G. Changes in urinary 17-hydroxycorticosteroid excretion during stressful life experiences in man. *Journal of Clinical Endocrinology*, 1955, 15, 1057.

Hill, S. R., Goetz, F. C., Fox, H. M., Muravski, B. J., Krakauer, L. J., Reifenstein, R. W., Gray, S. J., Reddy, W. J., Hedberg, S. E., Marc, J. R. S., & Thorn, G. W. Studies on adrenocortical and psychological response to stress in man. *Archives of Internal Medicine*, 1956, 97, 269.

Hinde, R. A. Mother/infant relations in rhesus monkeys. In N. F. White (Ed.), *Ethology and psychiatry*. Toronto: University of Toronto Press, 1974.

Hodges, J. R. The hypothalamic pituitary–adreno-cortical system. *Journal of Pharmacy and Pharmacology*, 1976, 28, 379–382.

Hofer, M. A. Physiological responses of infant rats to separation from their mothers. *Science*, 1970, 168, 871–873.

Hofer, M. A. The effects of brief maternal separation on behavior and heart rate of two weak old rat pups. *Physiology and Behavior*, 1973, 10, 423–427.

Hofer, M. A. The organization of sleep and wakefulness after maternal separation in young rats. *Developmental Psychobiology*, 1976, 9, 189–206.

Holmes, T. H., & Rahe, R. H. The Social Readjustment Rating Scale. *Journal of Psychosomatic Research*, 1967, 11, 213–218.

Hunt, V. Personal communication, 1980.

Huxley, A. *Ends and means*. London: Chatto & Windus, 1937.

Hubel, D. H., & Wiesel, T. N. The period of susceptibility to the physiological effects of unilateral eye closure in kittens. *Journal of Physiology*, 1970, 206, 419.

Imura, H., Yoshimi, T., & Ikekubo, K. Growth hormone secretion in a patient with deprivation dwarfism. *Endocrinologia Japonica*, 1971, 18, 301–304.

Isaacson, R. L. Neural systems of the limbic brain and behavioral inhibition. In R. A. Boakes & M. S. Halliday (Eds.), *Inhibition and learning*. London: Academic Press, 1972.

Isabel, J. B., Towers, B., Adams, F. H., & Gyepes, M. T. The effects of ganglionic blockade on tracheobronchial muscle in fetal and newborn lambs. *Respiration Physiology*, 1972, 15, 255.

Jacobson, E. *Progressive relaxation* (2nd ed.). Chicago: University of Chicago Press, 1938.

James, W. What is emotion? *Mind*, 1884, 9, 188–205.

Jantsch, E. *The self organizing universe*. New York: Pergamon Press (Pergamon International Library), 1980.

Joffe, J. M. Prenatal determinants of behavior. Oxford: Pergamon Press, 1969.

Johnson, V. *The schiz experience: A learning and feedback model for schizophrenic and schizoid process*. Houston, Texas: Society for Neuroscience, 1972.

Katona, P. G., & Jih, F. Respiratory sinus arrhythmia: Non-invasive measure of parasympathetic cardiac control. *Journal of Applied Physiology*, 1975, 39(5), 801–805.

Keeley, J. Prenatal influences on the behavior of crowded mice. In J. Stone (Ed.), *The competent infant*. New York: Basic Books, 1973.

Kimball, C. D. Applied ethology in clinical obstetrics. In *Transaction of the Pacific Coast Obstetrical and Gynecological Society*, Vol. 42. St. Louis, Mosby, 1974.

Kling, A., & Steklis, H. D. A neural substrate for affiliative behavior in non-human primates. *Brain, Behavior, and Evolution*, 1976, 13, 216–238.

Kobasa, S. C., Hilker, R. J., & Maddi, S. R. *Journal of Occupational Medicine*, 1979, 21, 595–598.

Korr, I. Sustained sympathicotonia as a factor in disease. In I. Korr (Ed.), *The neurobiologic mechanisms in manipulative therapy*. New York: Plenum Press, 1978.

Lacey, J. I. Somatic response patterning and stress: Some revisions of activation theory. In M. H. Appley & R. Trumbell (Eds.), *Psychological stress: Issues in research*. New York: Appleton-Century-Crofts, 1967.

LaViolette, P. A. Thoughts about thoughts: The emotional–perceptive cycle theory. *Man–Environment Systems*, 1979, 9, 15–47.

Lazarus, R. S. *Psychological stress and the coping process*. New York: McGraw-Hill, 1966.

Lazarus, R. S. Emotions and adaptation: Conceptual and empirical relations. In W. J. Arnold (Ed.), *Nebraska Symposium on Motivation* (Vol. 16). Lincoln: University of Nebraska Press, 1968.

Lazarus, R. S. Little hassles can be hazardous to health. *Psychology Today*, July 1981, pp. 58–62.

Lazarus, R. S., Cohen, J. B., Folkman, S., Kanner, A., & Schaefer, C. Psychological stress and adaptation: Some unresolved issues. In H. Selye (Ed.), *Selye's guide to stress research* (Vol. 1). New York: Van Nostrand Reinhold, 1980.

Leshner, A. I., & Politch, J. A. Hormonal control of submissiveness in mice: Irrelevance of the androgens and relevance of the pituitary–adrenal hormones. *Physiology and Behavior*, 1979, 22, 531–534.

Lesse, H., Heath, R. G., Mickle, W. A., Munroe, R. R., & Miller, W. H. Rhinencephalic activity during thought. *Journal of Nervous and Mental Disease*, 1955, 122, 433–440.

Levi, L. Emotional stress; physiological and psychological reactions, medical industrial, and military implications. In L. Levi (Ed.), *Proceedings of an International symposium arranged by the Swedish Delegation for Applied Medican Defense Research*. New York: Elsevier, 1967.

Levine, J. D., Gordon, N. C., & Fields, H. L. Naloxone dose dependently produces analgesia and hypralgesia in postoperative pain. *Nature*, 1978, 278, 740–741.

Levine, P. *Accumulated stress reserve capacity and disease*. (Doctoral dissertation, University of California, Berkeley, 1976.) Ann Arbor: University of Microfilms No. 77-15, 760.

Levine, S., & Treiman, D. M. Differential plasma corticosterone response to stress in four inbred strains of mice. *Endocrinology*, 1964, 75, 142–144.

Leyhausen, P. Verhaltensstudien an Katzen. *Zeitschrift fur Tierpsychologie*, 1960 (Suppl. 2).

Lindsley, D. B. Emotion. In S. S. Stevens (Ed.), *Handbook of experimental psychology*. New York: Wiley, 1951.

Lorenz, K. Z. Imprinting. In R. C. Birney & R. C. Teevan (Eds.), *Instinct: An enduring problem in psychology: Selected readings*. Princeton, Van Nostrand, 1960.

Lundberg, U. Catecholamine and cortisol excretion under psychologically different laboratory conditions. In E. Usdin, R. Kvetnansky, & I. J. Kopin (Eds.), *Catecholamines and stress* (Proceedings of the Second International Symposium on Catecholamines and Stress, September 12–16, 1979, Smolenice Castle, Czechoslovakia). New York: Elsevier/North-Holland, 1980.

MacLean, P. D. The limbic system ("visceral brain") and emotional behavior. *Archives of Neurology and Psychiatry*, 1955, 73, 130–134.

MacLean, P. D. Psychosomatics. In J. Field, H. W. Magoun, & V. E. Hall (Eds.), *Handbook of physiology* (Vol. 3, Section I, Neurophysiology). Washington, D.C.: American Physiological Society, 1960.

MacLean, P. D. New findings relevant to the evolution of psychosexual functions of the brain. *Journal of Nervous and Mental Disease*, 1962, 135, 289–301.

MacLean, P. D. Man and his animal brains. *Modern Medicine*, 1964, 32, 95–106.

MacLean, P. D. *A triune concept of the brain and behavior: Lecture I. Man's reptilian and limbic inheritance: Lecture II. Man's limbic brain and the psychoses; Lecture III. New trends in man's evolution*. Clarence Hincks Memorial Lectures presented at Queen's University, Kingston, Ontario, 1969.

MacLennan, J. A., Drugan, R. C., Hyson, R. L., Maier, S. F., Madden, J., & Barchas, J. D. Corticosterone: A critical factor in an opioid form of stress induced analgesia. *Science*, 1982, 215, 1530–1532.

Malmo, R. B. Activation: A neuropsychological dimension. *Psychological Review*, 1959, 66, 367–386.

Mangili, G., Motta, M., & Martini, L. Control of adrenocorticotropic hormone secretion. In L. Martini & W. F. Ganong (Eds.), *Neuroendocrinology*. New York: Academic Press, 1966.

Mann, G. Histological changes induced in sympathetic, motor and sensory nerve fibers by functional activity. *Journal of Anatomy and Physiology*, 1895, 29(9), 100–108.

Marshal, J. M. Regulation of uterine blood flow. *Ergebnissader Physiologie*, 1970, 62, 1.

Mason, J. W. Psychological influences on the pituitary–adrenal cortical system. In G. Pincus (Ed.), *Recent progress in hormone research*. New York: Academic Press, 1959.

Mason, J. W. A review of psychoendocrine research on the pituitary–adrenal cortical system. *Psychosomatic Medicine*, 1968, 30, 576–607. (a)

Mason, J. W. A review of psychoendocrine research on the sympathetic–adrenal medullary system. *Psychosomatic Medicine*, 1968, 30, 631–653. (b)

Mason, J. W. A re-evaluation of the concept of "non-specificity" in stress theory. *Journal of Psychiatric Research*, 1971, 8, 323–333.

Mason, J. W. Confusion and controversy in the stress field. *Journal of Human Stress*, 1975, 1, 6–35.

Mason, J. W., Harwood, C. T., & Rosenthal, N. R. Influence of some environmental factors on plasma and urinary 17-hydroxy-corticosteroid levels in the rhesus monkey. *American Journal of Physiology*, 1957, 190, 429–433.

Mason, W. A. Early social deprivation in the non-human primates: Implications for human behavior. In D. E. Glass (Ed.), *Environmental influences*. New York: The Rockefeller and Russell Sage Foundations, 1968.

McClelland, D. C. Sources of stress in the drive for power. In G. Sherban (Ed.), *Psychopathology of human adaptation*. New York: Plenum Press, 1976.

Mednick, S. A. Breakdown in individuals at high risk for schizophrenia. *Mental Hygiene*, 1970, 54, 50–61.

Miczek, K. A., Thompson, M. L., & Shuster, L. Opioid-like analgesia in defeated mice. *Science*, 1982, 215, 1520–1522.

Miller, N. E. Studies of fear as an acquirable drive: 1. Fear as motivation and fear reduction as reinforcement in the learning of new responses. *Journal of Experimental Psychology*, 1948, 38, 89–101.

Mitchell, G. D. Persistent behavior pathology in rhesus monkeys following early social isolation. *Folia Primatology*, 1968, 8, 132–147.

Mitchell, G. D. Abnormal behavior in primates. In L. A. Rosenblum (Ed.), *Primate behavior: Developments in field and laboratory studies*. New York: Academic Press, 1970.

Mitchell, G. D. What monkeys can tell us about human violence. *The Futurist*, April 1975, pp. 75–80.

Nelson, R., & Gellhorn, E. S. The influence of age and functional neuropsychiatric disorders on sympathetic and parasympathetic function. *Journal of Psychosomatic Research*, 1958, 3, 12–26.

Nuwayhid, B., Brinkman C. R., III, Su, C., Bevan, J. D., & Assali, N. S. Development of autonomic control of fetal circulation. *American Journal of Physiology*, 1975, 228, 2.

Obrist, P. A. The cardiovascular–behavioral interaction as it appears today. *Psychophysiology*, 1976, 13, 95–107.

Obrist, P. A., Howard, J. L., Lawler, J. E., Galosy, A., Meyers, K. A., & Gaebelein, C. J. The cardiac-somatic interaction. In P. A. Obrist, A. H. Black, J. Brener, & L. V. DiCara (Eds.), *Cardiovascular psychophysiology: Current issues in response mechanisms, biofeedback, and methodology*. Chicago: Aldine, 1974.

Obrist, P. A., Lawler, J. E., & Gaebelein, C. J. A psychobiological perspective on the cardiovascular system. In L. V. DiCara (Ed.), *Limbic and autonomic nervous systems research*. New York: Plenum Press, 1974.

Oken, D. The psychobiology and psychoendocrinology of stress and emotion. In M. H. Appley & R. Trumbull (Eds.), *Psychological stress: Some issues in research*. New York: Appleton-Century-Crofts, 1967.

Pasquarelli, B., & Bull, N. Experimental investigation of the body-mind continuum in affective states. *Journal of Nervous and Mental Disease*, 1951, 113, 512–521.

Paykel, E. S., Prusoff, B. A., & Uhlenhuth, E. H. Scaling of life events. *Archives of General Psychiatry*, 1971, 25, 340–347.

Penfield, W. The cerebral cortex in man: The cerebral cortex and consciousness. *Archives of Neurology and Psychiatry*, 1938, 40, 417–422.

Pine, M. Psychological hardiness: The role of challenge in health. *Psychology Today*, December 1980, pp. 34–98.

Porges, S. W. Peripheral and neurochemical parallels of psychopathology: A psychophysiological model relating autonomic imbalance and hyperactivity, psychopathy, and autism. In H. W. Reese (Ed.), *Advances in child development and behavior* (Vol. II, pp. 35–65) New York: Academic Press, 1976.

Porges, S. W. The application of spectral analysis for the detection of fetal distress. In T. M. Field, A. M. Sostek, S. Goldberg, & H. H. Shuman (Eds.), *Infants born at risk*. New York: Spectrum, 1979.

Porges, S. W. Heart rate patterns in neonates: A potential diagnostic window to the brain. In T. M. Field & A. M. Sostele (Eds.), *Infants born at risk: Physiological, perceptual, and cognitive processes*, New York: Grune & Stratton, 1983.

Porges, S. W., Bohrer, R. E., Cheung, M. N., Drasgow, F., McCabe, P. M., & Keren, G. New time series for detecting rhythmic co-occurrence in the frequency domain: The weighted coherence and its application to psychophysiological research. *Psychological Bulletin*, 1980, 88(3), 580–587.

Porges, S. W., & Coles, M. G. H. (Eds.). *Psychophysiology*. Stroudsberg, Pa.: Dowden, Hutchinson & Ross, 1976.

Porges, S. W., & Coles, M. G. H. Individual differences in respiratory-heart period coupling and heart period responses during two attention-demanding tasks. *Physiological Psychology*, 1982, 10, 215–220.

Porges, S. W., & Smith, K. M. Defining hyperactivity: Physiological and behavioral strategies. In C. K. Whalen & B. Henker (Eds.), *Hyperactive children: The social ecology of identification and treatment*. New York: Academic Press, 1980. pp. 75–104.

Powell, G. F., Brasel, J. A., & Blizzard, R. M. Emotional deprivation and growth retardation stimulating idiopathic hypopituitarism. *New England Journal of Medicine*, 1967, 276, 1271–1288.

Prechtl, H. F. R. Neurological findings in newborn infants after pre- and paranatal complications. In J. H. R. Jonxis, H. K. A. Visser,

& J. A. Troelstra (Eds.), *Aspects of prematurity and dysmaturity: A Nutricia Symposium*. Leider: Stenfert Kroese, 1968.

Prescott, J. C. Body pleasure and the origins of violence. *Bulletin of the Atomic Scientists*, November 1975, pp. 20–26.

Prescott, J. C. Somatosensory deprivation and its relationship to the blind. In Z. S. Jastrzembska (Ed.), *The effects of blindness and other impairments on early development*. Washington, D.C.: U.S. Department of Health, Education and Welfare, 1976.

Prigogine, I. Order through fluctuation: Self organizing and social systems. In E. Jantsch & C. Waddington (Eds.), *Evolution and consciousness: Human systems in transition*. Reading, Mass.: Addison-Wesley, 1976.

Purves, M. J. Onset of respiration at birth. *Archives of Diseases in Childhood*, 1974, 49, 333.

Rahe, R. H. The pathway between subjects' recent life changes and their near future illness reports. In B. Dohrenwend & B. Dohrenwend (Eds.), *Stressful life events: Their nature and effects*. New York: Wiley, 1974.

Rahe, R. H. Editorial: Life change measurement clarification. *Psychosomatic Medicine*, 1978, 40, 95–98.

Reite, M., Kaufman, I. C., Pauley, J. D., & Stynes, A. J. Depression in infant monkeys: Physiological correlates. *Psychosomatic Medicine*, 1974, 36, 363–367.

Reite, M., & Short, R. Nocturnal sleep in separated monkey infants. *Archives of General Psychiatry*, 1978, 35, 1247–1253.

Richter, C. D. On the phenomenon of sudden death in animals and man. *Psychosomatic Medicine*, 1957, 19(3), 191–198.

Riley, V. Psychoneuroendocrine influences on immunocompetence and neoplasia. *Science*, 1981, 212, 1100–1109.

Roessler, R. Personality, psychophysiology and performance. *Psychophysiology*, 1973, 10, 312–325.

Rosenblueth, A., & Simeone, F. A. The interrelations of vagal and accelerator effects on the cardiac rate. *American Journal of Physiology*, 1934, 110, 42–55.

Rossi, G. F. Sleep-inducing mechanisms in the brain stem. *Electroencephalography and Clinical Neurophysiology*, 1963, 24 (Suppl.), 113–132.

Routtenberg, A. The pleasure systems of the brain. *Scientific American*, 1978, 239(5), 154.

Rubin, L. S. Patterns of adrenergic–cholinergic imbalance in the functional psychoses. *Psychological Review*, 1962, 69, 501–519.

Rutt, C. N., & Offord, D. R. Prenatal and perinatal complications in childhood schizophrenics and their siblings. *Journal of Nervous and Mental Disease*, 1970, 152, 321–324.

Rutter, M. *Infantile autism*. London: Methuen, 1965.

Saling, E. *Foetal and neonatal hypoxia in relation to clinical obstetric practicee*. London: Edward Arnold, 1968.

Seligman, M. E. P. *Helplessness: On depression, development and death*. San Francisco: W. H. Freeman, 1975.

Selye, H. A syndrome produced by diverse nocuous agents. *Nature*, 1936, 138, 32.

Selye, H. *Stress: The physiology and pathology of exposure to stress; a treatise based on the concepts of the general adaption syndrome and the disease of adaptation*. Annual report on stress. 1950.

Sherrington, C. S. *The endeavor of Jean Fernel*. Cambridge: Cambridge University Press, 1946.

Silverman, J., Rappaport, M., Hopkin, K., Ellman, G., Hubbard, R., Belleza, T., Baldwin, T., Griffin, R., & Kling, R. Stress stimulus intensity control, and the structural integration technique. *Confinia Psychiatrica*, 1973, 16, 201–219.

Skinner, J., & Lindsley, D. The non-specific mediothalamic-frontocortical system. In K. Pribram & A. Luria (Eds.), *Psychophysiology of the frontal lobes*. New York: Academic Press, 1973.

Sontag, L. W. Implications of fetal behavior and environment for adult personalities. *Annals of the New York Academy of Sciences*, 1966, 134, 782.

Spitz, R. Hospitalism: A follow-up report. *The Psychoanalytic Study of the Child*, 1946, 2, 113–117.

Stenberg, D. The ontogenesis of the spontaneous electrical activity of the lower brain stem. *Acta Neurologica Scandinavica*, 1967, 43(Suppl. 31), 162.

Stevens, J. R., Mark, V. H., Erwin, F., Pacheco, P., & Suematsu, K. Deep temporal stimulation in man: Long latency, long lasting psychological changes. *Archives of Neurology*, 1969, 1, 157–169.

Stock, G., Schlor, K. H., Heidt, H., & Buss, J. Psychomotor behavior and cardiovascular patterns during stimulation of the amygdala. *Pfluegers Archiv*, 1978, 376, 177–184.

Stokman, C. L. J., & Glusman, M. Amygdaloid modulation of hypothalamic flight in cats. *Journal of Compartive and Physiological Psychology*, 1970, 71, 365–375.

Stott, D. H. Physical and mental handicaps following a disturbed pregnancy. *Lancet*, 1971, 1, 1006.

Stott, D. H. Follow-up study from birth of the effects of prenatal stresses. *Developmental Medicine and Child Neurology*, 1973, 15, 770.

Stott, D. H., & Latchford, S. A. Prenatal antecedents of child health development and behavior. *Journal of the American Academy of Child Psychology*, 1976, 15.

Tinbergen, N. Ethology and stress diseases. *Science*, 1974, 185, 20–27.

Toth, A. R., McEwen, R., & Shabanah, E. H. Role of the autonomic nervous system in the nutrition of the products of conception: Effects of pelvic parasympathectomy on uterine and sub-placental decidual blood flow. *Fertility and Sterility*, 1964, 15, 263.

Ursin, H. Personality, activation and somatic health: A new psychosomatic theory. In S. Levin & H. Ursin (Eds.), *NATO Conference Series III: Human factors* (Vol. 12, *Coping and health*). New York: Plenum Press, 1980.

von Euler, U. S., & Lundberg, U. Effect of flying on the epinephrine excretion in Air Force personnel. *Journal of Applied Physiology*, 1954, 6, 551.

Wada, J. A. The clinical relevance of kindling: Species, brain sites and seizure susceptibility. In K. E. Livingston & O. Hornykiewicz (Eds.), *Limbic mechanisms: The continuing evolution of the limbic systems concept*. New York: Plenum Press, 1978.

Ward, A. J. Behavior uptake. *Brain Mind Bulletin*, 1978, 3(4), 82.

Warner, H. R., & Russell, R. O. Effect of combined sympathetic and vagal stimulation on heart rate in the dog. *Circulation Research*, 1969, 24, 567–575.

Weiss, J. M. Influence of psychological variables on stress-induced pathology. In R. Porter (Ed.), *Physiology, emotion, and psychosomatic illness* (Ciba Foundation Symposium No. 8). Amsterdam: Associated Scientific Publishers, 1972.

Wenger, M. A. The measurement of individual differences in autonomic balance. *Psychosomatic Medicine*, 1941, 3(4), 427–434.

Wilder, J. The "law of initial values": A neglected biological law and its significance for research and practice . *Zeitschrift fuer die Gesamte Neurologie und Psychiatrie*, 1931, 137, 317–324, 329–331, 335–338.

Windle, W. *The physiology of the fetus: Relation to brain damage in the perinatal period*. Springfield, Ill.: Charles C Thomas, 1971.

Wolff, H. G. (Ed.), *Stress and disease*. Springfield, Ill.: Charles C Thomas, 1968.

Wolff, H. G., Wolf, S. G., Jr., & Hare, C. C. (Eds.). *Life stress and bodily disease*. Baltimore: Williams & Wilkins, 1950.

Yakovlev, P. I. Motility, behavior and the brain. *Journal of Nervous and Mental Disease*, 1948, 107, 313–335.

Yates, F. E., & Maran, J. W. Stimulation and inhibition of andrenocorticotropin release. In E. Knobil & W. H. Sawyer (Eds.), *Handbook of physiology* (Vol. 4, Part 2, *Endocrinology*). Washington, D.C.: American Physiological Society, 1974.

Zeeman, E. C. Catastrophe theory. *Scientific American*, 1976, 234(4), 65–83.

Zubek, J. P., Aftanas, M., Kovach, K., Wilgash, L., & Winocur, G. Effect of severe immobilization of the body on intellectual and perceptual processes. *Canadian Journal of Psychology*, 1963, 17, 118–133.

Chapter Seventeen

Emotion and Psychophysiological Organization: A Systems Approach

Gary E. Schwartz

INTRODUCTION AND OVERVIEW

The topic of emotion is one of the most fundamental and confusing areas in psychophysiology. It is a common belief among psychophysiologists (as well as laypersons) that bodily processes are related to emotional experiences and expressions, and that this relationship is fundamental to biological, psychological, and social well-being. However, the nature of the relationship between bodily processes and emotional experience and expression is not well understood. The literature suffers from conceptual and methodological problems that inadvertently encourage continued confusion rather than clarity. The purpose of this chapter is not only to provide a selective review of the recent research on the psychophysiology of emotion, but also to propose a conceptual framework having direct methodological implications that promises to bring light and clarity to this fundamental area.

In Greenfield and Sternbach's (1972) *Handbook of Psychophysiology*, the chapter on emotion emphasized that "in human subjects, emotional behavior includes responses in three expressive systems: verbal, gross motor, and physiology (autonomic, cortical, and neuromuscular)" (Lang, Rice, & Sternbach, 1972,

p. 624). Lang *et al.* further emphasized that "the responses of no single system seem to define or encompass an 'emotion' completely." In the 13 years that have passed since this important chapter was written, some progress has been made in describing the empirical relationship among these "three expressive systems" (e.g., see Lang, Miller, & Levin, 1983). However, little progress has been made in clarifying the conceptual relationship among these three expressive systems (Schwartz, 1978, 1982).

I propose that general systems theory (deRosnay, 1979; von Bertalanffy, 1968) provides a framework for understanding the relationship between the concept of emotion and the various measurable components presumed to reflect the presence of emotion. As becomes clear as the chapter unfolds, the concept of emotion is an inferred concept, not unlike inferred concepts from modern physics. The concept of emotion is evoked to explain why it is that subjective experience, overt behavior and physiology are at times *organized* and *coordinated* to achieve particular organism–environmental interactions. In fact, it is reasonable to propose that the concept of emotion, appropriately defined, can be a fundamental organizing principle in psychophysiology. Simply stated, emo-

Gary E. Schwartz. Department of Psychology, Yale University, New Haven, Connecticut.

tion may be the process whereby the three expressive systems (or more appropriately stated, subsystems) are organized in order to achieve specific biopsychosocial goals (Schwartz, 1984).

The central thesis of this chapter is that emotion reflects a fundamental mechanism whereby biopsychosocial processes are organized to achieve specific adaptive goals. After considering various theories of emotion from a systems perspective, I review recent research on patterns of subjective experience, patterns of skeletal muscle activity, patterns of autonomic activity, and patterns of central nervous system activity. The relationship of emotion to personality and to disease is also considered. Finally, implications of viewing emotion as an organizing concept for research methods in psychophysiology and emotion are discussed.

EMOTION FROM A SYSTEMS PERSPECTIVE: THE IMPORTANCE OF ORGANIZED PATTERNING AND EMERGENT PROPERTIES

A fundamental tenet of systems theory is that a system is a "whole" composed of a set of "parts" (i.e., subsystems). The parts interact in novel ways to produce unique properties or "behaviors" of the system as a whole. Therefore, the behavior of a system is said to "emerge" out of the interaction of its parts. The concept of the behavior of a whole system being qualitatively different from the simple sum of the behavior of its parts, yet being dependent upon the interaction of its parts for its unique properties as a whole, is very general. This concept can be applied to any system, be it living or nonliving, be it at a micro level (such as the atom) or at a macro level (such as the social group) (von Bertalanffy, 1968).

Although the general concept of emergent property is by no means fully understood or free from controversy (Phillips, 1976), it is nonetheless considered by most philosophers of science to be fundamentally true. Emergent phenomena are found at all levels in nature, from mathematics and physics, through chemistry and biochemistry, to biology and psychology, sociology, political science, and beyond (e.g., ecology and astronomy).

One difficulty in thinking across levels of complexity (and, therefore, across disciplines) is that one discipline's "system" often turns out to be another discipline's "part." For example, for the physiologist the "system" is "physiology," which itself is composed of parts (organs are composed of cells), whereas for the psychologist the "physiology" becomes the parts that comprise a person or lower animal (organisms are composed of organ systems). We can apply this issue to the relationship between physiology and emotion.

From a systems point of view, emotion at the organism level emerges out of the interaction of biological parts at the physiological level. From this perspective, the "behavior" of the physiology is not a "correlate" of the "emotion," regardless of where the physiology is measured (peripherally or centrally). Rather, the physiology should be viewed and described as being a "component" of the "emotion" in the same way that a cell is considered to be a component (rather than a correlate) of an organ.

Thinking in systems terms can be confusing, because words such as "behavior" and "level" must be carefully redefined. The systems theorist would argue that it is as reasonable to speak of the behavior of a nerve, or the behavior of a muscle, as it is to speak of the behavior of a person, or the behavior of a group. "Behavior" is an abstract concept that applies to any level in any system. Consequently, when a person "behaves" at a psychological level, he or she is also "behaving" at a physiological level (and every level below this). In systems terms, it is imprecise to say that tensing the muscles in one's arm is a "correlate" of overt movement behavior; rather, it is a "component" of the overt behavior, and furthermore, it is itself a behaving process! The reason why *Behavioral Science*, the journal of the Society for General Systems Research, publishes selected articles in physics and physiology as well as in psychology and sociology is that it adopts the concept of behavior as being very general—a concept that can be applied to any system at any level. To use the term "behavior," then, requires that it be carefully qualified regarding the level of analysis (see Table 17-1). How this applies to the psychophysiology of emotion is explained shortly.

There is a tricky problem in defining levels, because different levels occur *within* disciplines as well as *across* disciplines. For example, in psychology, one can speak of complex cognitive processes as being composed of underlying component cognitive processes (Sternberg, 1977) in the same way that in physiology one can speak of complex cardiovascular processes as being composed of underlying component physiological processes (Miller, 1978; Schwartz, 1983). Note that specifying such sublevels *within* a given discipline does not eliminate the concept of unique properties (behaviors) emerging out of components interacting with one another. Rather, the need to specify levels within a given discipline (as well as across disciplines) requires that we think more clearly about what is really a component of what.

The implications of levels and emergent properties for the psychophysiology of emotion are important. Although it was an essential first step to describe emotion as consisting of three basic components (subjective experience, overt behavior, and physiological activity; reviewed in Lang *et al.*, 1972), it is a mistake to think that these three categories operate at the same level of analysis, and therefore to treat the three cate-

Table 17-1
Levels of Complexity in systems and Associated
Academic Disciplines

Level and complexity of the system	Academic discipline associated with the level of the system
Beyond earth	Astronomy
Supranational	Ecology
National	Government, political science, economics
Organizations	Organizational science
Groups	Sociology
Organism	Psychology, ethology, zoology
Organs	Organ physiology, (e.g., neurology, cardiology)
Cells	Cellular biology
Biochemicals	Biochemistry
Chemicals	Chemistry, physical chemistry
Atoms	Physics
Subatomic particles	Subatomic physics
Abstract systems	Mathematics, philosophy

Note. According to systems theory, in order to understand the behavior of an open system at any one level, it is essential to have some training in the academic disciplines below that level, plus have some training in the relevant discipline at the next highest level as well.
From "A Systems Analysis of Psychobiology and Behavior Therapy: Implications for Behavior Medicine" by G. E. Schwartz, *Psychotherapy and Psychosomatics*, 1981, 36, 159–184. Copyright 1981 by *Psychotherapy and Psychosomatics*. Reprinted by permission.

gories as if they were relatively independent parts. First of all, from a systems point of view, subjective experience and "overt" behavior (note that the word "behavior" is qualified here as required by systems theory) are both categories of behavior at the organism level, each of which is comprised of patterns of physiological processes. Physiological processes are therefore not independent of these two categories. On the contrary, physiological processes are the building blocks of both of these processes, and must therefore be conceptualized and researched from this perspective.

Moreover, from a systems perspective, subjective experience and overt behavior are themselves not at the same level. Whereas subjective experience is completely personal (private at the organism level), overt behavior is fundamentally social (i.e., it allows the organism to communicate and interact with the environment of which the organism is a part). Hence, a systems approach leads to the suggestion that emotion is truly a biopsychosocial process (e.g., Engel, 1977; Leigh & Reiser, 1980; Schwartz, 1983) or a social psychobiological process (e.g., Cacioppo & Petty,

1983), depending upon whether one views the process from the micro to the macro levels (biopsychosocial) or from the macro to the micro levels (social psychobiology). In both cases, subjective experience and cognitive processing become the "middle" processes between one's biology (at the micro level) and one's social interactions (at the macro level).

Note that from a systems perspective, patterns of processes can occur at each level (biological, psychological, and social). Interactions at each level should lead to emergent properties at the next level (e.g., physiological patterns should contribute to unique subjective experiences, and subjective patterns should contribute to unique social interactions). From a systems perspective, not only does psychology emerge out of physiology, and social behavior emerge out of psychology, but physiology, psychology and social behavior represent different levels on analysis *of the same, ultimate, whole system.* It should be clear that according to systems theory, analyzing the physiological parts in relative isolation, or analyzing the subjective or social parts in relative isolation, will not lead to a complete understanding of emotion as a whole process. Emotion takes on its unique holistic properties as a result of complex *interactions* and *organizations* of its component processes *at each level.* This is why an analysis of emotional processes from a systems point of view requires that the investigator measure patterns of variables across levels and search for unique *interactions* or *emergents* between and among the variables across levels.

One point needs to be underscored here before we move to empirical findings. A fundamental question that needs to be addressed is this: "How is it that biological, psychological, and social processes are ever organized?" Where does the apparent order come from? Clearly, there are instances where physiological, subjective, and behavioral responses are relatively dissociated (e.g., Weinberger, Schwartz, & Davidson, 1979). However, implicit in the concept of emotion is the notion that a fundamental organization does exist and has evolutionary, adaptive significance for survival (Darwin, 1872; Plutchik, 1980). If there was no order, no organization of biological, psychological, and social processes, the study of emotion would ultimately be impossible. Moreover, there would be no empirical utility or scientific justification for having a concept of emotion.

Systems theory encourages psychophysiologists to look for organized patterns of processes, within and across levels of nature. The concept of emotion, when viewed from the perspective of systems theory, has the potential to clarify the growing literature indicating that organized patterns of processes can and do occur within and across the biological, psychological, and social levels. Moreover, the concept of emotion, when viewed from the perspective of systems theory, has the potential to clarify and stimulate new methods for measuring emotion at physiological, subjective, and social levels.

It is difficult to discuss research on human emotion without beginning in the middle—that is, at the psychological level. Researchers and laypersons alike often begin with their own subjective experience, and then look for relationships among their subjective experience, biology, and overt behavior. Although a systems approach to emotion encourages us to take a comprehensive, biopsychosocial approach to emotion, this chapter focuses primarily on the relationship between the psychological and biological levels, and, within the biological level, primarily on the physiological (organ) level (excluding the cellular and biochemical—e.g., neurohumoral and neuroendocrine—levels). Since this volume is concerned with human psychophysiology, the present chapter reviews representative empirical findings in psychology first and then considers relationships between psychology and physiology.

Most modern theorists of emotion believe that different emotions reflect different organizations or patterns of processes at psychological and physiological levels of analysis (e.g., Izard, 1977; Lang *et al.*, 1972; Leventhal, 1980; Plutchik, 1980; Tompkins, 1980), though some modern theorists focus primarily on the psychological level (e.g., Zajonc, 1980). It is important to recognize that the concept of patterning of psychological and biological processes is explicitly made in many classic theories of emotion (Darwin, 1872; James, 1884) and is implicitly made in more recent social psychobiological theories of emotions (e.g., Schachter & Singer, 1962).

Schachter and Singer (1962) proposed that emotional experience and emotional social behavior reflect an interaction of the nature of the social situation (e.g., an experimenter makes jokes), the way in which the social situation is interpreted by the subject (e.g., the subject perceives the jokes as humorous), and the subject's level of general physiological arousal (e.g., the subject is aroused by an injection of epinephrine, and, moreover, the subject is not told that the specific physiological side effects of injection are related to the injection itself). Though Schachter and Singer (1962) did not emphasize patterning of processes *within* each of the levels (e.g., they assumed that physiological patterning played little, if any, role in emotional experience and expression), they did emphasize patterning of processes *across* levels. The concept of patterning, be it within and/or between levels of processes, is implicit if not explicit in all theories of emotion.

Before we can meaningfully consider patterning of physiological processes, it is essential to examine some of the recent data on patterning of subjective experience. As becomes clear below, it is possible to measure reliable patterns of subjective experience when the appropriate theoretical and associated methodological considerations are adopted.

PATTERNING OF SUBJECTIVE EXPERIENCE AND EMOTION

Few researchers have systematically examined subjective experience closely to uncover possible distinct patterns *within* the experience as a function of different emotions. The pioneering research of Izard (1972) is very important in this regard. Not only did Izard assess simultaneously multiple emotional experiences to different affective situations using the Differential Emotions Scale (DES), but he proposed that a subset of emotions, such as anxiety and depression, are themselves composed of different combinations of underlying fundamental emotions. Izard has essentially proposed that *within* the psychological level, it is possible to uncover levels of emotional experience, where higher levels of subjective experience presumably represent emergent combinations or patterns of lower levels of subjective experience. In systems terms, what Izard has proposed is that anxiety and depression are each unique emotional states that emerge out of the interaction of patterns of fundamental emotions. At least six different fundamental emotions (happiness, sadness, anger, fear, surprise, and disgust) have been found to exist cross-culturally and to be linked to specific facial expressions of emotion (Ekman, Friesen, & Ellsworth, 1972; Izard, 1971).

As part of a research program at Yale University examining affective imagery and the self-regulation of emotion, we decided to determine whether it was possible to discover standardized situations that college students could imagine that would evoke consistent patterns of subjective experience. In the process of conducting the research to address this basic methodological question, we attempted to replicate and extend Izard's (1972) research on the relationship between the hypothesized higher-order emergent emotions of anxiety and depression, and patterns of fundamental emotions, using an abreviated DES scale (Schwartz & Weinberger, 1980).

Initially, 55 subjects filled out a questionnaire asking them to "give a one-sentence statement or a single phrase about a situation that either happened in the past, or could happen in the future, that would make you feel one of the following: happy, sad, angry, fearful, anxious, depressed." Subjects were further told to note that "for each emotion, three separate situations are requested that reflect three different intensities of emotion: strong, moderate, and weak." Therefore, each subject was required to generate 18 emotional situations.

From this sample, 20 of the questionnaires (from 10 males and 10 females), which were complete and did not contain highly idiosyncratic or redundant answers, were chosen to be validated in a second questionnaire. The items were edited into complete sentences. Then, the 18 items from each of the 20 questionnaires were combined to create a pool of 360 statements. These statements were randomly sorted into four forms of 90 items each, with each emotional category and intensity represented by 5 items per form. A total of 216 subjects filled out one of the forms of the questionnaire, using the following instructions:

> For each of the following statements, *imagine* that they are happening to you, and rate *how you would feel*. Note that each statement has *six* emotions to be *separately* rated—happiness, sadness, anger, fear, depression, and anxiety. Since it is not uncommon for people to experience more than one emotion in a given situation, you should rate each statement on all six emotions. Use the numbers 1–5 for your ratings, with 1 meaning very little, 3 meaning moderate, and 5 meaning very strong. Numbers 2 and 4 should also be used to reflect intermediate categories between very little and moderate, and moderate and very strong, respectively.

As can be seen in Figure 17-1, the average ratings (across the three intensities of items) yielded highly distinct patterns of subjective experience for the four fundamental emotions (Part A of the graph) and similar yet distinct patterns of response comparing sad-

ness with depression and anxiety with fear (Part B of the graph). The richness of these data should not go unnoticed. For example, it can be seen that anger situations elicited more feelings of depression than did either fear or anxiety situations. Also, note that fear situations elicited more feelings of anxiety than anxiety situations elicited feelings of fear.

Figure 17-2 presents the mean ratings for happiness situations subdivided by intensity (high, moderate, low). This figure illustrates not only that the situations reliably elicited primarily feelings of happiness that vary with intensity, but that the *higher* the happiness, the *lower* the sadness, depression, and anger, but *not* the fear and anxiety. In fact, high happiness was accompanied by moderately high feelings of anxiety!

These results can be compared with those obtained for the mean ratings for anxiety situations subdivided by intensity. Figure 17-3 shows not only that these situations reliably evoked primarily feelings of anxiety, but that the *higher* the anxiety, the *higher* the fear, depression, and sadness, while the relationship with happiness and anger is less clear. Happiness items and anxiety items clearly differed in the *patterns* of emotions that they elicited.

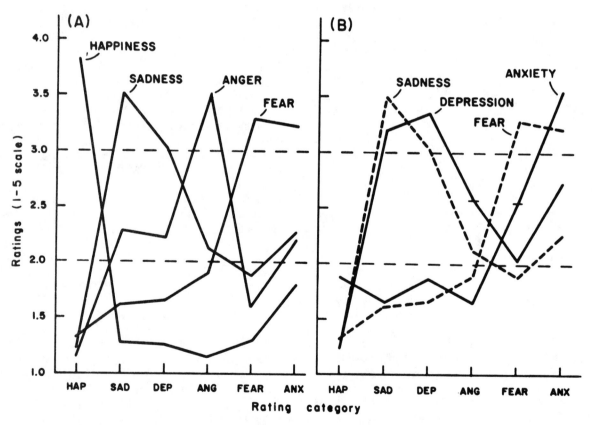

Figure 17-1. Mean ratings of happiness (HAP), sadness (SAD), depression (DEP), anger (ANG), fear (FEAR), and anxiety (ANX) separately for happiness, sadness, anger, and fear situations (1A) and for depression and anxiety situations (1B) (with sadness and fear situations redrawn for comparsion). (From Schwartz and Weinberger, 1980.)

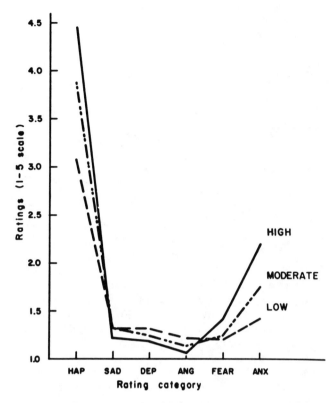

Figure 17-2. Mean ratings for happiness situations subdivided by intensity (high, moderate, low). (From Schwartz and Weinberger, 1980.)

Apparently, at least for a sample of college students, specific classes of affective situations evoked specific patterns of subjective experience. This does not mean that all subjects gave (or give) identical responses to the average items in a given category or to specific items. On the contrary, individual differences in response to standardized situations are of fundamental importance for basic research and clinical applications, and should be assessed carefully. The question of individual differences is discussed later in the context of relating patterns of subjective experience to patterns of physiological activity. The important point to remember here is that distinct patterns of subjective experience to specific classes of affective situations can be assessed and reveal rich complexity and organization in the psychological structure of emotional experience.

The most surprising and informative aspects of findings are uncovered when patterns of responses to individual items are examined (from Schwartz, 1982). It turns out that specific items evoke particular blends or patterns of subjective experience. As shown in Table 17-2, when college students imagined that "Your dog dies," high ratings occurred primarily in sadness and depression (high ratings are in italics in the table), whereas when they imagined that "Your

girlfriend/boyfriend leaves you for another," high ratings now occurred in anger and anxiety as well as in sadness and depression. Whereas the former item might be globally labeled as a "sadness" or "depression" item, the latter item (having the same sadness rating) might be globally labeled either as a "sadness" or "depression" item, or as an "anger" item, or as an "anxiety" item (if one views the data in either–or categories). Note that in response to the question "You realize that your goals are impossible to reach," college students rated this situation highly in all of the five negative emotions assessed in the study. Clearly, this particular situation is a complex, highly negative, patterned emotional state. Its relevance to social/political problems facing children, adolescents, and adults in modern society (with the increased societal recognition that fundamental limits do exist and that one's life style must be limited accordingly if society is to survive) should be self-evident. We should not be surprised that the general mood in modern societies today is conflicted, since the pressing social problems probably elicit complex, yet organized blends of fundamental emotions.

These particular patterns of subjective experience are not necessarily unique to Yale University students. It is conceivable that the relative differences in patterns observed among the different situations may

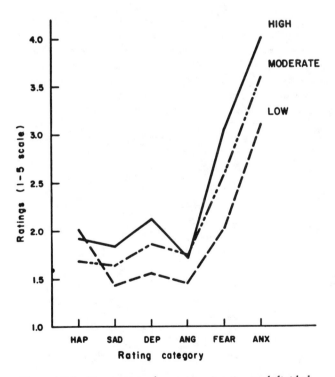

Figure 17-3. Mean ratings for anxiety situations subdivided by intensity (high, moderate, low). (From Schwartz and Weinberger, 1980.)

Table 17-2

Ratings on an Abbreviated DES for Yale University Students

Item	Happiness	Sadness	Anger	Fear	Anxiety	Depression
Your dog dies	1.09	<u>4.08</u>	2.08	1.38	1.93	<u>3.34</u>
Your girlfriend/boyfriend leaves you for another	1.13	<u>4.13</u>	<u>3.41</u>	2.11	<u>2.72</u>	4.09
You realize that your goals are impossible to reach	1.15	<u>3.64</u>	<u>3.00</u>	2.48	3.08	3.67

Note. Underlined entries indicate high ratings.

apply to various age groups and may even apply to various modern cultures. Table 17-3 presents the average self-reports of 23 Italian physicians and psychologists to the same questions. The items were presented in Italian by a translator at a scientific meeting in Rome, Italy, in the spring of 1983; the data reflect the percentage of subjects giving a 4 or 5 rating for a given emotion to a given question. The summary data were collected with the aid of the translator at the meeting itself, prior to my presenting the theory and findings obtained in the United States (see Schwartz & Weinberger, 1980). Depsite the differences in age, academic background, culture, and mode of administration, the relative pattern of differences among the three items is preserved. It is conceivable not only that the meaning of these particular situations was similar for the two samples of subjects, but that the two samples of subjects interpreted the meanings of the emotional words in a similar fashion. One could hypothesize that American college students and Italian professionals would show comparable patterns of physiological responses differentiating among the various emotional situations. However, cross-cultural research comparing subjective and physiological patterns of response to different fundamental emotions and blends of emotions has yet to be reported in the literature.

The value in assessing blends or patterns of subjective experience in the study of emotion should be emphasized for its methodological as well as its theoretical implications. Consider the following ratings on two items that might both be globally described as "high-happiness" items for students at Yale: "You are accepted at Yale" and "You have just graduated from Yale." As shown in Table 17-4, the first item evoked high ratings not only in happiness but also in anxiety. Hence, from an either–or perspective, one could conclude that this item was an "anxiety" item rather than a "happiness" item; clearly, the situation evoked both anxiety and happiness—a blended/patterned emotion. Note that in contrast, the second item evoked moderate to high ratings in sadness, fear, and depression, as well as in happiness and anxiety. Clearly, both situations evoked high "happiness" (and high anxiety) in the average Yale student, but the patterning of emotions in the second item is even more complex than the relatively "pure" happiness of the first item.

This difference in patterns of emotional experience between being admitted to a university versus graduating from a university is apparently not unique to Yale students. As illustrated in Table 17-5, similar differences in relative patterns of emotional experiences were reported by Italian professionals when they compared beginning versus completing their grad-

Table 17-3

Ratings on an Abbreviated DES for Italian Professionals

Item	Happiness	Sadness	Anger	Fear	Anxiety	Depression
Your dog dies	0	<u>52</u>	13	0	17	<u>26</u>
Your girlfriend/boyfriend leaves you for another	0	<u>70</u>	<u>61</u>	13	<u>43</u>	<u>70</u>
You realize that your goals are impossible to reach	0	<u>61</u>	<u>61</u>	30	<u>70</u>	74

Note. Each entry represents the *percentage* of subjects giving a 4 or 5 rating for a given emotion to a given question. Underlined entries indicate high percentages.

Table 17-4

Ratings on an Abbreviated DES for Yale University Students

Item	Happiness	Sadness	Anger	Fear	Anxiety	Depression
You are accepted at Yale	<u>4.18</u>	1.14	1.04	1.96	<u>3.04</u>	1.09
You have just graduated from Yale	<u>4.09</u>	<u>2.74</u>	1.38	<u>2.57</u>	<u>3.40</u>	<u>2.36</u>

Note. Underlined entries indicate high ratings.

uate training (implying that the findings generalize across undergraduate and graduate schooling, as well as across age, academic background, and culture).

It is fascinating how what at first glance might appear to be minor differences in wording can dramatically change the pattern of subjective experience elicited by an item. As can be seen in Table 17-6, in response to the item "You feel loved," a pure emotion of happiness was generated in Yale college students, whereas in response to the item "You meet someone with whom you fall in love," the more complex pattern of happiness and anxiety was elicited (a more "stressful" situation). Interestingly, as can be seen in Table 17-7, similar relative patterns of subjective experience were reported for the Italian professionals (with the Italians giving less of a pure happiness rating for the second item compared to the first). The shift in wording from feeling loved to meeting someone with whom you fall in love seems to have had similar significance for the two samples of subjects.

There are numerous conclusions that can be drawn from data such as these. It appears that different situations can evoke different combinations of emotions as assessed through self-report. Therefore, if only a single emotion is assessed (a still reasonably common research practice), this will lead to an incomplete if not an erroneous description of the emotional state of the person. The fact that combinations of emotions can be elicited reliably by affective imagery and can be

assessed reliably using a simple self-report DES procedure indicates that future research should adopt a pattern approach to assessing and interpreting the subjective dimensions of emotion. Statistical techniques for assessing patterns of physiological activity using multivariate pattern recognition and classification procedures (Fridlund, Schwartz, & Fowler, 1984; Schwartz, Weinberger, & Singer, 1981), to be discussed later in the sections on patterning of skeletal and autonomic muscle activity, can be similarly applied to assessing patterns of subjective experience. From a systems point of view, the conceptual approach to assessing patterns of responses should be sufficiently general to apply to all levels and disciplines.

Are different patterns of subjective experience associated with different patterns of physiological responses? Are the weak and often inconsistent findings in the psychophysiological literature linking subjective experience to patterns of physiological activity due, at least in part, to the fact that patterns of subjective experience have not been assessed? If patterns of subjective experience are assessed, will we find that certain situations are better than others in eliciting relatively pure emotions? Do emotions actually occur simultaneously in patterns, or do fundamental emotions shift from one to another, whereas the subjective impression is that they occur concurrently? These questions and many others are stimulated when one

Table 17-5

Ratings on an Abbreviated DES for Italian Professionals

Item	Happiness	Sadness	Anger	Fear	Anxiety	Depression
You are accepted at school	<u>83</u>	0	4	13	<u>26</u>	4
You have just graduated from school	<u>61</u>	<u>26</u>	0	<u>39</u>	<u>70</u>	22

Note. Each entry represents the *percentage* of subjects giving a 4 or 5 rating for a given emotion to a given question. Underlined entries indicate high percentages.

Table 17-6

Ratings on an Abbreviated DES for Yale University Students

Item	Happiness	Sadness	Anger	Fear	Anxiety	Depression
You feel loved	<u>4.78</u>	1.28	1.13	1.19	1.57	1.19
You meet someone with whom you fall in love	<u>4.58</u>	1.20	1.04	2.00	<u>3.06</u>	1.33

Note. Underlined entries indicate high ratings.

begins to adopt a systems perspective and applies the perspective to the study of patterns of biopsychosocial responses in emotion.

SKELETAL MUSCLE PATTERNING AND EMOTION

If any single physiological system is designed to express different emotions, it is the skeletal muscle system. The skeletal muscles can be finely regulated by the brain to produce delicate, precise, and highly complex patterns of activity across muscles and over time. The face, with its high ratio of single motor units to muscle mass, and its rich neural innervation, is a muscular system anatomically and neurally capable of reflecting different fundamental emotions and patterns of emotions (Ekman & Friesen, 1978).

Whether one chooses to label facial expression as "psychological" behavior or "physiological" behavior is more a reflection of the orientation of the observer than it is a true psychophysiological distinction (Schwartz, 1978). In systems terms, what we observe overtly as facial expression *is* an indirect indicator of complex patterns of facial muscle activity. This is the basis of the comprehensive, anatomically derived visual rating system for scoring overt facial expression developed by Ekman and Friesen (1978).

Subtle and fast-acting changes in muscle activity can be readily quantified by attaching miniature silver/silver chloride electrodes to the surface of the skin over relative muscle regions (see Figure 17-4). More precise measurements can be made using fine wire needle electrodes inserted through the skin to monitor the activity of single motor units (Basmajian, 1978). Both of these electromyogram (EMG) methods are relatively obtrusive. EMG methods restrict the subject's freedom of movement and often increase the subject's attention to his or her facial behavior. Consequently, EMG recordings may influence the affective processes being measured. A recent chapter by Fridlund and Izard (1983) provides an excellent review of the facial EMG literature and discusses the methodological difficulties involved in conducting such research and interpreting the findings. Despite these complications, important basic and clinical information can be obtained using EMG (so long as the restrictions of the method are kept firmly in mind).

It should be recognized that research on patterns of facial muscle activity (and other skeletal muscle activity) has not been restricted to the study of emotion per se. For example, in the program of research conducted by McGuigan and colleagues (reviewed in McGuigan, 1978) and Cacioppo and Petty (reviewed in Cacioppo & Petty, 1981), different patterns of facial EMG have been associated with different cognitive and social information-processing tasks.

In a series of studies, my colleagues and I have documented the sensitivity of facial EMG patterning in differentiating low to moderate intensity emotional states elicited by affective imagery (Schwartz, Fair,

Table 17-7

Ratings on an Abbreviated DES for Italian Professionals

Item	Happiness	Sadness	Anger	Fear	Anxiety	Depression
You feel loved	<u>100</u>	0	0	22	<u>34</u>	0
You meet someone with whom you fall in love	<u>96</u>	0	0	30	<u>70</u>	0

Note. Each entry represents the *percentage* of subjects giving a 4 or 5 rating for a given emotion to a given question. Underlined entries indicate high percentages.

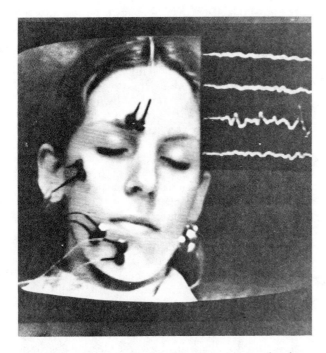

Figure 17-4. Photograph of a videoscreen showing the placement of four pairs of EMG electrodes and, superimposed electronically next to the face, the oscilloscope tracings of the amplified electromyographic activity from the four facial regions. (From Schwartz *et al.*, 1976b.)

Salt, Mandel, & Klerman, 1976a; Schwartz, Fair, Salt, Mandel, & Klerman, 1976b; Schwartz, Ahern, & Brown, 1979; Schwartz, Brown, & Ahern, 1980). Some of the major results of these studies can be briefly summarized as follows:

1. Different patterns of facial muscle activity accompany the generation of happy, sad, and angry imagery, and these patterns are not typically noticeable in the overt face.
2. Instructions to re-experience or "feel" the specific emotions result in greater EMG changes in relevant muscles than instructions simply to "think" about the situations (see Figure 17-5).
3. Depressed patients show a selective attenuation in the generation of facial EMG patterns accompanying happy imagery, but show a slight accentuation in the facial EMG response to sad imagery (see Figure 17-5). The biggest facial EMG difference between depressed and nondepressed subjects occurs when subjects imagine what they do in a "typical day," with nondepressed subjects generating miniature happy facial EMG pattern and depressed subjects generating a miniature mixed sadness–anger facial EMG pattern.
4. Changes in clinical depression following treatment with active drug medication or placebo are accom-

panied by relevant changes in facial EMG. Also, higher initial resting levels of facial EMG appear to be predictive of subsequent clinical improvement.
5. Females (compared to males) tend to:

a. Generate facial EMG patterns of greater magnitude (relative to rest) during affective imagery, and report a corresponding stronger subjective experience to the affective imagery.
b. Show greater within-subject correlations between the experience of particular emotions and relevant facial muscles.
c. Show somewhat higher corrugator levels during rest (possibly reflecting more sadness and/or concern) and lower masseter levels during rest (possibly reflecting less anger).
d. Generate larger facial EMG patterns when instructed to voluntarily produce overt expressions reflecting different emotions.

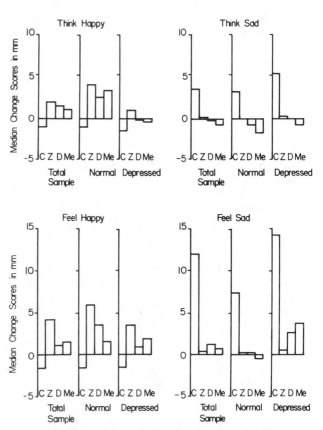

Figure 17-5. Change from baseline for muscle activity from the corrugator (C), zygomatic (Z), depressor annuli oris (D), and mentalis (Me) regions during two affective imagery (happy, sad) and two instructional (think, feel) conditions. Data are displayed separately for the total sample ($N = 24$), the normal subgroup ($N = 12$), and a depressed subgroup ($N = 12$). A 1 mm change score equals 45 µV/30 sec. (From Schwartz *et al.*, 1976b.)

Taken together, these data strongly support the hypothesis not only that affective imagery results in reliable self-report of different patterns of subjective experience (reviewed in the previous section), but that these self-reports are *preceded* by the generation of unique patterns of facial muscle activity that vary both in pattern and intensity with the subsequent self-reports. Since the facial EMG situation are usually not visible to an observer, and also are not typically perceived by the subject (whose attention during imagery is largely focused on the images and associated feeling states rather than on his or her face per se), it is reasonable to hypothesize that the self-reports and the facial patterns are reflecting two different aspects of the same, underlying neuropsychological system. This is not to say that self-report and facial activity need always covary or be synonymous. On the contrary, according to systems theory, self-report is an emergent process dependent upon the interaction of multiple processes in addition to facial feedback (both central and peripheral), just as facial behavior is itself an emergent process dependent upon the interaction of multiple neuropsychological processes in addition to the expression of emotion. In systems terms, the concept of a "single" response is an oversimplification, since any "behavior" reflects a composite or pattern of underlying processes. This fundamental point is directly related to the whole–part–emergent concept presented at the beginning of the chapter.

Until discrete patterns of facial EMG are discovered that reflect relatively pure fundamental emotions, it is not possible to address the more complex and intriguing question regarding blends or combinations of different emotions and their relationship to complex patterns of facial EMG. In a recent experiment, we (Polonsky & Schwartz, 1984) attempted to determine whether images designed to evoke a *combination* of happiness and sadness would elicit a *combination* of facial muscle responses previously found to be reliably associated with happiness and sadness. Prior research (e.g., Schwartz et al., 1980) has documented that zygomatic activity increases reliably in happiness, while corrugator activity may simultaneously decrease below resting levels in happiness. This pattern is virtually reversed for sadness: Corrugator activity increases reliably in sadness, while zygomatic activity typically remains at baseline. We (Polonsky & Schwartz, 1984) predicted that items selected to elicit a *combination* of happiness and sadness should be accompanied by relative increases in *both* zygomatic and corrugator activity, though the magnitude of each increase would be less than that found in response to relatively pure emotion items reflecting happiness versus sadness.

In the experiment, a standard pure happy item was "You feel loved"; a standard pure sad item was "Someone close to you dies"; and a standard mixed happy–sad item was "You feel that you are finally separated from your family and are really a tremendous sense of

freedom about that, but at the same time you miss the closeness that you had or potential closeness that you could have had." The data indicated that as predicted, the combined happy–sad item generated moderate increases in both zygomatic and corrugator activity, whereas the happy item generated large increases in zygomatic activity unaccompanied by increases in corrugator activity, and the sad item generated large increases in corrugator activity unaccompanied by increases in zygomatic activity. It is important to note that the moderate levels of zygomatic and corrugator activity observed in the combined happy–sad item corresponded to moderate levels of perceived intensity as indicated by self-report for the combined happy–sad item (compared to the happy and sad items, respectively).

These are the first data documenting that discrete emotional blends of affective subjective experience can be associated with discrete blends of physiological activity (i.e., facial EMG). Whether or not more complex blends of affective experience can be mapped onto more complex blends of skeletal muscle activity remains to be determined in future research. Also, the precise timing and synchrony of the blended emotions (e.g., do the emotions actually occur simultaneously in real time as measured by facial EMG, or do they flip back and forth in some cyclic fashion?) remain to be investigated. It is clear that the potential now exists for addressing such questions by taking advantage of advances in the measurement of self-report patterns and EMG patterns.

As discussed elsewhere (Fridlund & Izard, 1983; Schwartz, 1982), the previous research has used relatively simple (i.e., univariate) and therefore conservative statistical procedures for quantifying patterns of responses (be they self-report or physiological). A systems approach to pattern data proposes that more complex, sensitive multivariate statistical analyses should be performed. We (Fridlund et al., 1984) have recently demonstrated how multivariate pattern classification strategies can be applied to facial EMG data (see Figure 17-6). Within this general framework, multiple physiological variables are recorded and digitized by computer (transduced); particular components of each variable are selected for analysis (e.g., means, standard deviations, peaks, time to peaks, etc.); and then a statistical iterative process is performed, whereby specific features are derived that maximally discriminate among sets of variables (feature extraction) and show maximal hit rates on these sets of variables (classification). Using this approach, the reliability of classification hit rates can be used to index the success of the pattern recognition procedure, thereby demonstrating the degree of discriminability of the organization of the input variables.

In the Fridlund et al. (1984) experiment, 12 females were administered 48 counterbalanced 20-sec trials of affective imagery, using items preselected for

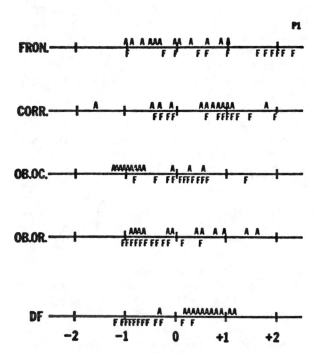

Figure 17-6. Steps used for pattern classification from a systems perspective. (From Fridlund *et al.*, 1984.)

relative purity along the dimensions of happiness, sadness, anger, and fear (from Schwartz & Weinberger, 1980). Facial EMG was recorded from the lateral frontalis, corrugator, orbicularis oculi, and orbicularis oris regions. The findings documented the superiority of statistical strategies that were sensitive to patterns of multiple physiological responses over traditional univariate methods. Moreover, the degree of facial EMB discriminability across emotions within subjects was correlated with the subjects' perceived vividness of their affective imagery.

By using a large number of trials (48) within subjects, it became possible to apply the pattern classification procedures to individual subjects. Figure 17-7 shows a single subject's data comparing anger and fear items for the four separate muscles individually and the composite results of linear discriminant analysis combining the four muscles. This figure illustrates how the multivariate analysis can pull out an anger–fear difference that is not readily apparent in any single muscle.

These multivariate pattern analysis procedures can be applied to patterns of any "input variables," be they self-reports, facial EMG, autonomic responses, electrocortical responses, or patterns across these classes of response systems. The integration of these procedures with research on the psychophysiology of emotion promises to resolve prior confusions and reveal new organized patterns. Unfortunately, to do so requires that we develop new statistical skills and learn new ways of thinking about patterning in systems terms.

One conclusion seems justified from the EMG data available to date: The face is a system that is exquisitively sensitive to underlying affective processes. It therefore provides an excellent window for studying the relationship between subjective experience and physiological activity.

AUTONOMIC PATTERNING AND EMOTION

At one time, it was generally believed that responses innervated by the autonomic nervous system were highly intercorrelated and involuntary, and therefore only capable of reflecting overall levels of arousal and/or alertness (from deep sleep to states of awake excitement). However, it is now well known that the sympathetic and parasympathetic branches of the autonomic nervous system are each capable of very fine regulation of specific peripheral organs. Moreover, this regulation is quite selective and can be brought under voluntary control using such techniques as biofeedback (Schwartz & Beatty, 1977).

Figure 17-7. Plots of standard EMG scores for 12 anger and 12 fear responses of subject P1 mapped itemwise on each of four muscle regions, and on a linear composite of the four regions derived from linear discriminant analysis. It can be seen that the composite function affords better separation of anger and fear items than any of the individual muscle regions. This figure demonstrates that consideration of variable conformations/patterns provides information which cannot be gleaned from any of the univariate analyses alone. Item codes: A, anger; F, fear; FRON, frontalis; CORR, corrugator; OB.OC, obicularis oculi; OB.OR, obicularis oris; DF, discriminant function. (From Fridlund *et al.*, 1984.)

All physiological responses, to varying degrees, seem to be influenced by both voluntary and involuntary processes. Skeletal muscles are strongly influenced by voluntary processes, but they are also controlled by involuntary reflex patterns elicited by particular stimuli (e.g., in response to localized pain). It now appears that visceral and glandular responses are influenced by voluntary processes more strongly than was previously recognized, though the extent of such control relative to their involuntary reflex patterns is just beginning to be determined.

There has been a paucity of studies examining autonomic patterning accompanying different emotional states. There are many reasons for this relative lack of research. They include methodological problems in recording and analyzing the data, theoretical biases that have discouraged investigators from looking for patterns or accepting evidence of patterning in the data when the patterns emerged serendipitously, and problems at a psychological level in eliciting and assessing the emotional states. However, the few studies that have attempted to address this question have come up with a surprisingly consistent pattern of findings. These studies have focused on the comparison between anger versus fear, two emotions that Ax (1953) claimed were most described as being identical physiological states. The studies prior to 1957 were reviewed by Schachter (1957). A more recent study was reported by Weerts and Roberts (1976).

Drawing on neuropsychological and neuroendocrine findings, Ax proposed that anger involved a *mixed* epinephrine and norepinephrine pattern, while fear involved a relatively pure epinephrine pattern. Schachter added that pain involved a relatively pure norepinephrine pattern, though his pain stimulus (the cold pressor test) may have pulled for this particular response because of its local vasoconstrictive effects.

Unfortunately (though understandably), no single autonomic response is a "pure" reflector of epinephrine- or norepinephrine-like patterns. Most autonomic responses are dually innervated by the sympathetic and parasympathetic branches of the autonomic nervous system, as well as by hormones. For example, an increase in heart rate can by mediated by numerous factors, including (1) an increase in peripheral sympathetic activity, (2) a decrease in peripheral parasympathetic activity, (3) an increase in circulating epinephrine (to list only one possible heart-rate-stimulating hormone), or any combination or pattern of these mechanisms.

Therefore, if on two different trials a heart rate increase of 10 beats/min is obtained, it does not follow that the two trials are showing an "identical" heart rate response, since the heart rate responses may be reflecting different patterns of neural and/or humoral mediation. Systems theory not only helps us understand this point; it also suggests a way that we can draw differential conclusions regarding underlying mechanisms. The solution is to measure patterns of processes, ideally at different levels, so as to make it possible to test differential interpretations of the data. It should be recalled that a similar point has been made previously with regard to facial EMG (e.g., corrugator activity may be increasing as a function of sadness or concentration; assessing patterns of other muscles allows one to differentiate which state, or combination of states, is being reflected by the observed corrugator activity).

Ax (1953) and Schachter (1957) dealt with this problem at the physiological level by (1) recording multiple channels of information, and (2) scoring each channel in different ways to tap different component processes imbedded in the complex response. For example, from the frontalis muscle region channel, Ax scored the data separately for (1) maximum increase in muscle tension, and (2) number of peaks in muscle tension. Ax found not only that two aspects of "muscle tension" were uncorrelated, but that the maximum muscle tension was significantly higher in anger than in fear, while the number of muscle tensions peaks was significantly higher in fear than in anger.

From the skin conductance channel, Ax scored the data separately for (1) maximum increase skin conductance, and (2) number of rises in skin conductance. Ax found not only that these two aspects of "sweat gland activity" were uncorrelated, but that the maximum increase in skin conductance was significantly higher in fear than in anger, while the number of skin conductance rises was significantly higher in anger than in fear. It seems likely that this pattern of results probably reflects some important set of underlying neuropsychological differences between anger versus fear. However, the physiological interpretation of these patterns remains to be established, and deserves to be pursued in future research.

The important discovery from these early studies was that consistent differences, especially within the cardiovascular system, were found for anger versus fear. Anger was associated with relative increases in peripheral resistance, while fear was associated with relative increases in cardiac output. If any single, easily recordable physiological parameter could be said to tap peripheral resistance, it was diastolic blood pressure. Whereas systolic blood pressure tended to be higher in fear than anger (reflecting increased cardiac output), diastolic blood pressure was significantly higher in anger than fear. In the recent Weerts and Roberts (1976) study, diastolic blood pressure was a major variable distinguishing anger versus fear elicited by imagery.

We (Schwartz et al., 1981) have recently provided an important replication and extension of these earlier findings. Thirty-two college students with a background in acting were instructed on different trials first to imagine, and then to express *nonverbally* while exercising, one of six different emotional states (happiness, sadness, anger, fear, normal exercise, and relaxation). The exercise task was a modified version of the Harvard step test, which requires subjects to walk up and down a single step.

Systolic and diastolic blood pressure were recorded with an electronic sphygmomanometer, while heart rate was recorded manually by taking the pulse. Two experimenters were used. Both were undergraduate students with no background in physiology, and were naive to the complex hypotheses of the experiment involving patterns of cardiovascular response to the different emotions.

Each trial consisted of two baseline readings taken 1 min apart; one reading taken after the 1-min imagery period (in which subjects *imagined* walking up and down the step, experiencing and expressing the requested emotion); and three readings spaced over approximately 10 min following the 1-min exercise period (in which subjects silently expressed nonverbally the different emotions while they actually walked up and down the step).

The rationale for taking only three relatively simple measures of cardiovascular function was (1) to give the subjects maximum freedom to utilize their bodies both to experience and express the emotions (the prior studies attached many electrodes sensitive to movement artifact that inhibited the subjects' overt behavior in a highly unnatural way; this may in turn have inhibited the magnitude of the cardiovascular patterns evoked in the earlier studies), and (2) to determine whether the findings would be robust enough to be clinically meaningful (and therefore detectable using standard clinical procedures for collecting cardiovascular data).

The rationale for using self-generated imagery followed by exercise was (1) to increase the likelihood that relatively pure emotions would be generated (in the prior studies it is likely that complex blends of anger and fear were evoked, at least in some subjects; also, these studies did not assess the relative emotional purity of their stimulus conditions), and (2) to determine whether allowing subjects to express their emotions overtly would lead to increased physiological patterns that would be clinically meaningful (e.g., it is possible that the style of running in terms of affective expression may have differential consequences for health, with angry running more likely to provoke heart disease and sudden death, and relaxed or happy running more likely to reduce heart disease and sudden death).

In view of the limited reliability of the cardiovascular recording procedures used in this study and the limited number of data points collected, the magnitude and consistency of the results obtained were striking. First, as can be seen in Figure 17-8, different cardiovascular patterns and levels of response were obtained following the imagery period as a function of

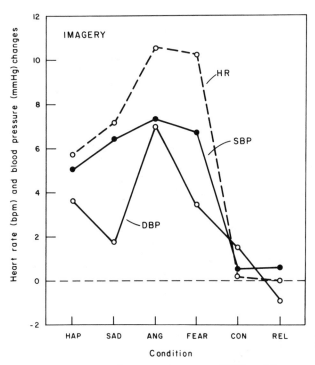

Figure 17-8. Mean changes in heart rate (HR) and in systolic (SB) and diastolic (DBP) blood pressure separately for the happiness (HAP), sadness (SAD), anger (ANG), fear (FEAR), control (CON), and relaxation (REL) conditions following seated imagery.

emotion. The classic finding of diastolic blood pressure being higher in anger than fear was replicated. In addition, both sadness and happiness were differentiated from anger and fear, which in turn were differentiated from control and relaxation.

Following the exercise, large differences in systolic blood pressure and heart rate, but not diastolic blood pressure, were found as a function of the different emotions (see Figure 17-9). Apparently, active exercise produces vasodilation in the muscles and reduces peripheral resistance, which may have overshadowed the relative differences in diastolic pressure between anger and fear. In addition, subjects expressed their anger overtly in this condition. Had subjects been instructed to express anger toward themselves (anger in), perhaps diastolic pressure would have increased after the active exercise. The important point to recognize here is that the cardiovascular patterns in emotion can vary, depending upon the skeletal behavioral state of the individual. Research is now needed that examines the generality of patterns in emotion as a function of different skeletal behavioral states.

Other findings of importance emerged from this study. For example, although systolic blood pressure response immediately following exercise was similar for anger and fear (see Figure 17-9), the *rate of recovery* of systolic blood pressure varied as a function of anger

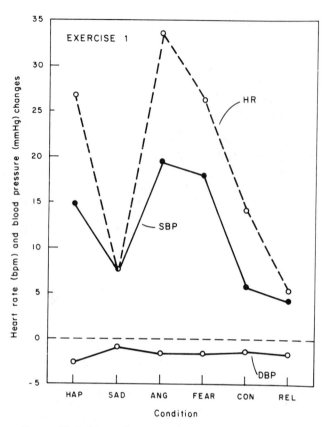

Figure 17-9. Mean changes in heart rate (HR) and in systolic (SBP) and diastolic (DBP) blood pressure separately for the happiness (HAP), sadness (SAD), anger (ANG), fear (FEAR), control (CON), and relaxation (REL) conditions during the first measurement following exercise.

versus fear. Systolic blood pressure was slower to recover following anger than following fear. The hypothesis that different emotions have different "half-lives" is important for basic as well as clinical reasons.

In a recent facial EMG study examining facial muscle patterns in response to elation versus depression self-statements, we (Sirota, Schwartz, & Kristeller, 1983), found that over the course of the experiment, EMG patterns to the elation statements did not grow over time, and EMG levels returned to baselines during rest periods interspersed throughout the experiment. However, EMG patterns to the depression statements grew in intensity over time, and the EMG levels remained high during the rest periods interspersed throughout the experiments. It will be recalled that Izard (1972) proposed that depression was a higher-order emergent emotion reflecting a particular combination of negative emotions, notably sadness and anger. Clearly, future research should record simultaneously patterns of facial muscle and cardiovascular responses as a function of emotion, skeletal behavioral state, and recovery.

Brief mention should be made of the findings obtained when multivariate procedures were applied to the Schwartz et al. (1981) data. First, multiple-regression analyses predicting systolic blood pressure from patterns of heart rate and diastolic blood pressure as a function of emotion revealed that the relationship among systolic pressure, diastolic pressure, and heart rate varied as a function of emotion. For example, during imagery, high diastolic pressure is uniquely associated with high systolic pressure during anger, and, in turn, high systolic pressure anger is uniquely associated with *lowered* heart rate. These relations may suggest that during anger the increases in systolic pressure are mediated by increases in peripheral resistance, which in turn may activate inhibition of heart rate through baroreceptor mechanisms. Moreover, discriminant analyses revealed highly significant findings deriving equations that could classify emotional state remarkably correctly as a function of cardiovascular patterning. Although the findings from the pattern classification procedures were rich and informative, space limitations preclude further discussion of these findings here.

As reported elsewhere (Schwartz, 1982), correlations were run among the physiological measures, self-reports of patterns of subjective experience for the imagery and exercise periods, and ratings by the experimenters of patterns of overt emotional expression for the imagery and exercise periods. It turned out that the physiological measures were more strongly and consistently correlated with the observers' judgments than with the subjects' own self-reports! The total set of results did not support the most obvious hypothesis—that the observers may have been using the physiological data unconsciously to make their observational ratings. On the contrary, the findings suggested that the observers were seeing relationships that the subjects themselves did not! For example, observer ratings of fear expression during fear exercise was correlated *negatively* with diastolic blood pressure ($r = .373$, $p < .05$)—a relationship that is highly counterintuitive unless one knows that diastolic pressure typically *decreases* below baseline following isotonic exercise, and that fear should potentiate this effect due to enhanced isotonic exercise. On the other hand, observer ratings of anger expression during anger exercise were correlated *positively* with diastolic blood pressure ($r = .413$, $p < .05$). Interestingly, self-ratings of fear experience during fear exercise were not correlated with diastolic blood pressure ($r = .01$, n.s.), while self-ratings of anger experience during anger exercise were correlated with diastolic blood pressure ($r = .414$, $p < .05$).

Stimulated by these findings, I (Schwartz, 1982) reviewed the original studies to see whether similar relationships among self-ratings, observer ratings, and physiological measures had been previously examined. Curiously, Schachter (1957) did obtain observer (what he called "expressed") ratings as well as self-reports. Only "mean" (a weighted average of systolic and diastolic) blood pressure correlations were presented in the paper. Schachter found that whereas *self-reports* for both fear and anger were not correlated with mean blood pressure increase, *expressed* behaviors for both fear and anger were significantly correlated with mean blood pressure.

One would hypothesize from a systems perspective that cardiovascular "behavior" and skeletal-motor "behavior" are more intimately connected with each other (both in the periphery and at the level of the brain) than they are connected with the neuropsychological systems involved in monitoring these "behaviors" and making them available to conscious experience. In other words, one's subjective experience includes both the monitoring and interpreting of cardiovascular *and* skeletal-motor processes. It therefore follows that self-report can be more readily dissociated from these two processes than the two processes can be dissociated from themselves. Note that the outside observer "sees" the manifestations of the skeletal-motor "behavior" and then tries to infer from these observations what the person *might* be feeling. In this sense, what the observer does in inferring emotion from overt behavior parallels what a physicist does in inferring the existence of subatomic particles from the "behavior" of bubbles in a cloud chamber: Both are inferences about underlying, organizing processes—an important point, which is returned to at the end of this chapter.

The subject, on the other hand, is not limited in forming and labeling his or her experience solely on the basis of peripheral cues. In fact, people probably vary (among themselves and from situation to situation) with regard to exactly how much they attend to their bodies and how they interpret these cues in forming their experience and self-reports. Because an outside observer is more attentive to overall patterns of overt behavior, an outside observer's ratings are more likely to be consistent with underlying cardiovascular patterns than will the subject's own self-reports.

I return to this issue in the section on personality and the psychophysiology of emotion. The point to emphasize here is the hypothesis that self-report and physiology should be less well connected than physiology is connected with physiology, and that the use of observer ratings can be important in clarifying this issue.

A recent study by Ekman, Levenson, and Friesen (1984) provides additional important support for the hypothesis connecting skeletal-motor behavior—in this case, that of the face—with autonomic patterning in emotion relatively dissociated from subjective experience. Following Schwartz *et al.* (1981), subjects experienced in acting were used (in this case, professional actors, $N = 12$), plus scientists who study the face ($n = 4$). Subjects were instructed to relive six emotions (happiness, sadness, anger, fear, surprise, and disgust), and also to generate overt facial expressions of emotion using instructed movements based on the anatomy of different facial expressions of emotion (Ekman & Friesen, 1978). Heart rate, skin temperature, skin resistance, and forearm flexor muscle tension were recorded. Heart rate was found to differentiate between the positive and negative emotions, while skin temperature further differentiated among the negative emotions. Interestingly, the posed facial muscle movements (which the authors claimed were associated with minimal subjective experience of emotion) led to greater autonomic patterning in emotion than did the relived emotional experiences (which the authors claimed were associated with relatively little facial movement)! The combined findings of Schwartz *et al.* (1981) and Ekman *et al.* (1984) provide important justification of conducting future research that integrates the measurement of skeletal muscle, autonomic indices, and subjective experiences of emotion over time.

CENTRAL NERVOUS SYSTEM PATTERNING AND EMOTION

The degree of subjective, skeletal, and autonomic patterning that is possible depends to a large extent on the degree of patterning of central nervous system processing that is possible. Unfortunately, difficulty in obtaining direct or even indirect electrophysiological measures of localized brain function (through depth electrodes or surface electrodes), coupled with the difficulty in interpreting overt behavior as being an indirect measure of particular neuropsychological processes, has historically led most psychophysiologists interested in the study of emotion to restrict their recording and interpretations to peripheral responses and associated levels of analysis.

However, recent theory and research on hemispheric asymmetry in cognition and emotion have made it possible to raise new questions about cognitive-affective patterning and hemispheric patterning associated with different emotional states. For example, using lateral eye movements as a relative indicator of hemispheric activation, we (Schwartz, Davidson, & Maer, 1975) demonstrated that in right-handed subjects, (1) emotional questions produced relatively more left-eye movements (indicative of right-hemispheric involvement) than nonemotional questions, (2) verbal questions produced relatively more right-eye movements (indicative of left-hemispheric involvement) than spatial questions, and (3) spatial questions produced relatively more stares and blinks than verbal questions. From these three sets of findings, it became possible to uncover discrete patterns of lateral eye movements that could distinguish among all four combinations of cognition and affect: verbal nonemotional, verbal emotional, spatial nonemotional and spatial emotional questions. In other words, not only could affective processes be distinguished from cognitive processes in terms of patterns of eye movement activity, but their interactions could be uncovered as well. It is worth noting that the concept of patterning of cognitive and affective processes at the level of the brain can become a new neuropsychological framework for reinterpreting and extending the original social-psychobiological model proposed by Schachter and Singer (1962).

From a systems perspective, the use of lateral eye movements for the purpose of inferring central nervous system patterning illustrates a changing scientific paradigm regarding the relationship among psychology, physiology, and neurology. As discussed elsewhere (Schwartz, 1978), eye movements can be defined as (1) psychological behavior (if they are simply observed by the naked eye), (2) physiological behavior (if they are recorded on a polygraph), or (3) neurological behavior (if they are interpreted as reflecting underlying neurological processes). The fact that essentially identical findings can be published in different journals reflecting different disciplines is more an indication of the particular conceptual frameworks of the investigators than the actual processes being measured. Interestingly, current research is becoming more "psychoneurophysiological," illustrating the integration and crossing of these three levels.

A major advantage in measuring lateralization of overt behavior and interpreting the findings in neurological terms is that the observations can be made unobtrusively. Thus Sackeim, Gur, and Saucy (1978) have reported that the left side of the face (controlled significantly by the right hemisphere) is more reflective of negative emotions. Their data were based on pictures taken of overt faces and shown to judges who rated left- and right-side composite photographs.

Recently, researchers have attempted to study the emotion–laterality question more closely in terms of fundamental emotions and patterns of self-report. As reviewed in Schwartz, Ahern, and Brown (1979), Tucker (1981), and Davidson (1984), it appears that the hemispheres are differentially lateralized for classes of emotion. A primary hypothesis is that the left hemisphere (in right-handed subjects) is more involved with positive emotions, and the right hemisphere is more involved with negative emotions. For example, we (Schwartz et al., 1979) reported evidence of differential lateralization for positive versus negative emotions in facial EMG recorded from the zygomatic region (which is involved with the smile) while subjects were constructing answers for questions involving positive versus negative emotions: Relatively greater zygomatic facial EMG on the right side of the

face for positive emotions was found. A different pattern (relatively greater zygomatic facial EMG on the left side of the face for both positive and negative emotions) was found when subjects were requested to produce voluntarily overt facial expressions of positive and negative emotions.

These findings were replicated and extended (Sirota & Schwartz, 1982) for elation versus depression imagery. The major right versus left zygomatic EMG difference for elation imagery occurred in pure right-handed subjects (right-handed subjects whose parents and siblings were also right-handed). Like the Schwartz et al. (1979) results, the Sirota and Schwartz (1982) finding was that voluntarily produced facial expressions did not result in a right-sided increase for positive emotions. As Fridlund and Izard (1983) point out, the interpretation of lateralized facial EMG differences are complex, due to questions of electrode placement, muscle mass, demand characteristics of the situation, and the nature of the emotion task. It is precisely because the facial laterality–emotion hypothesis raises such fundamental methodological and conceptual questions that it is such a fruitful hypothesis for further research.

Lateralized findings for positive versus negative emotions have not been restricted to facial EMG. For example, concerning lateral eye movements, we (Ahern & Schwartz, 1979) reported not only that positive emotions were associated with relatively more right-eye movements than negative emotions, but that these effects were more robust than the previously reported findings for verbal versus spatial processes. We (Ahern & Schwartz, 1979) proposed that the left–right differences in positive versus negative emotions might reflect a more basic difference in approach versus avoidance behavior. We hypothesized that these left–right processes might be mediated subcortically and therefore might be more fundamental than left–right cortical differences in verbal versus spatial processing. A similar conclusion has been proposed by Davidson and colleagues as part of their research program on cerebral laterality and emotion (see Davidson, 1984).

The hypothesis of left–right differences in positive versus negative emotions is most likely oversimplified. Current research is examining patterns of intra- as well as interhemispheric processes in different emotions. Davidson, Schwartz, Saron, Bennett, and Goleman (1979) reported findings integrating the two seemingly disparate hypotheses regarding laterality and emotion: (1) that all emotions are lateralized in the right hemisphere, and (2) that emotions are differentially lateralized depending upon their valence (or approach–avoidance tendencies). Using electroencephalogram (EEG) measures recorded from the parietal and frontal regions, they found that parietal EEG showed relatively more activation over the right hemisphere for *both* positive and negative emotions, whereas frontal EEG showed relatively more activation over the left hemisphere for positive emotions and relatively more activation over the right hemisphere for negative emotions. It is possible that the initial holistic processing of emotional stimuli (a process apparently common to all emotions) may be performed in the right parietal region, whereas the differential interpretation of positive versus negative emotions, and the expression of positive versus negative emotions, are performed by the left and right frontal regions, respectively.

An elegant study by Davidson and Fox (1982) has obtained this overall pattern of EEG findings in two samples of 10-month-old female infants. The infants sat on their mothers' laps while they watched a videotape of an actress generating happy and sad facial expressions. Davidson (1984) has recently proposed that not only are such data consistent with the hypothesis that approach versus avoidance behavior is lateralized in the infant, but moreover that the normal process of development involves the integration of these two different hemispheric styles with the maturation of the corpus callosum.

It follows that differential *intra-* versus *inter*hemispheric patterning should occur for cognitive processes as well as emotional processes. In order to validate the neuropsychological interpretation offered for the earlier lateral eye movement studies (Ahern & Schwartz, 1979; Schwartz et al., 1975) for lateralized patterns of cognitive and affective processes, we (Ahern & Schwartz, 1984) recorded EEG from the frontal and parietal regions while subjects answered affective questions. The EEG was sampled during 4-sec epochs preceding the periods when an eye movement would usually occur (in the study, subjects answered questions with their eyes closed, thus reducing actual eye movements and hence eye movement artifact). Spectral analysis was performed on the data. It was found that for the cognitive dimension, the predicted laterality was found in the posterior (parietal) region (e.g., relatively greater EEG activation for verbal versus spatial questions in the left hemisphere), with little evidence for cognitive lateralization in the anterior (frontal) region. Conversely, for the affective dimension, the predicted laterality was found in the anterior (frontal) region (e.g., relatively greater EEG activation for positive versus negative questions in the left hemisphere), with little evidence for positive-negative lateralization in the anterior (parietal) region. Furthermore, overall relative right posterior (parietal) activation was found for all emotions (replicating Davidson et al., 1979, and Davidson & Fox, 1982).

I return to the question of central nervous system patterning and emotion in the next section on personality and psychophysiological patterning. It seems likely that future research will continue to uncover organized relationships between underlying central nervous system processes and their expression in self-report, physiological activity, and overt behavior. Moreover, more sophisticated psychophysiological techniques such as neuromagnetic measurement promise to open up new vistas for exploring emotion from a biopsychosocial perspective. One challenge will be to keep the technological advances in balance with essential psychosocial advances. Sensitivity to individual differences, instructions, and the social setting will become more and more important as technologically sophisticated research on emotion develops.

INDIVIDUAL DIFFERENCES IN PSYCHOPHYSIOLOGICAL ORGANIZATION AND EMOTION

A major problem and challenge for research on the psychophysiology of emotion involves individual differences in degree of association within psychological and physiological levels and between psychological and physiological levels. The issue of association-dissociation between systems is fundamental to models of disorder within systems (Schwartz, 1983), and is often observed in the study of psychopathology. For example, in a clinical setting, Brown and colleagues (Brown, Schwartz, & Sweeney, 1978; Brown, Sweeney, & Schwartz, 1979) have reported that depressed patients and schizophrenic patients differ from each other and from normal controls in how accurately they remember expressing positive affect nonverbally with their faces and bodies. Briefly, compared to observers' ratings of actual overt facial and bodily behavior in a group situation, depressed patients reported experiencing more pleasure than they expressed, whereas schizophrenic patients reported experiencing less pleasure than they expressed.

Dissociations between self-report and behavior, and/or self-report and physiology, are not limited to hospitalized psychiatric patients. Dissociations reliably show up in random samples of relatively healthy college students, and these dissociations have important conceptual, methodogical and clinical implications. A classic example of dissociation between subjective experience and physiological activity and associated overt behavior involves repression. "Repressors" are individuals who have developed the skill of minimizing or avoiding the experience of certain negative emotions. Simply stated, repressors tend to report (and believe) that they are minimally anxious, angry, or depressed, even though their overt behavior and underlying physiology may indicate the opposite.

We (Weinberger, Schwartz, & Davidson, 1979) conducted an experiment to determine whether it was possible to distinguish between people who reported feeling little anxiety and were accurate (called "true low-anxious"), and people who reported feeling little anxiety but were self-deceptive (called "repressors"). After first splitting subjects on scores on a standard anxiety scale, the low-anxiety-reporting subjects were further split into two subgroups, based on their scores on a second personality scale hypothesized to be sensitive to defensiveness. It turns out that the "social desirability scale" (Crowne & Marlowe, 1964) is not only a measure of social desirability, but also is a reasonably good measure of defensiveness (reviewed in Weinberger et al., 1979). Thus subjects reporting low anxiety were split into a low-defensive/low-anxiety-reporting group (true low-anxiety) and a high-defensive/low-anxiety-reporting group (repressors).

In the experiment, subjects were exposed to a moderately stressful sentence completion task. Subjects were instructed to complete phrases that were neutral, sexual, or aggressive in content. Heart rate, skin resistance, and frontalis EMG from the forehead region were recorded. In addition, subjects' verbal response latencies and measures of verbal disturbance of the subjects' sentence completions were scored. Although there were some interesting patterns observed across measures, the overall findings indicated that repressors generated significantly larger physiological and overt behavioral responses (indicative of negative emotion) than true low-anxiety subjects (even though the repressors actually reported experiencing less anxiety than the true low-anxiety subjects). Furthermore, the magnitude of the repressors' physiological and psychological responses were either equal to, or even greater than, the large-magnitude responses observed in a group of high-anxiety-reporting subjects! These findings have been recently replicated and extended in an important study on "the discrepant repressor" (Asendorph & Scherer, 1984).

The combined findings provide the key for understanding why it has proven so difficult in the past to obtain consistent significant correlations between physiological responses and self-reports across subjects. If a subset of subjects generates erroneous self-report data due to such factors as defensive style (e.g., repression), then not only will correlations across a random sample of subjects below, but the correlations will ultimately be uninterpretable. From a systems point of view, we must distinguish not only among physiological parameters, observer ratings, and self-reports, but we must further distinguish among *different processes that subjects use to label their affective states and the accuracy with which they do so.* Future research on the psychophysiology of emotion must consider individual differences in defensiveness, and must include scales such as the Marlowe–Crowne, if meaningful self-report–physiology relationships are to be uncovered.

I (Schwartz, 1983a) have proposed a general systems theory of disregulation that attempts to explain how systems go out of control. Using the prefix "dis-" across terms, I have proposed that *disattention* (e.g., motivated by a repressive coping style) involves a neuropsychological *disconnection* (to varying degrees), producing a *disregulation* in the system, which is expressed as increased *disorder* in self-regulatory processes (e.g., increased responsivity to stimuli, decreased recovery from stimuli, decreased regularity of rhythms common to homeostatic processes, etc.), which in turn contributes to the development and diagnosis of *disease.* I (Schwartz, 1983a) have reviewed recent data suggesting that individual differences in lateralization to positive versus negative emotions may be related to personality measures of repression and physiological reactivity: Repressors (who may report that things are quite positive, yet express the opposite nonverbally and physiologically) appear to be *relatively functionally disconnected* between the two hemispheres, and thus suffer the consequences of a neuropsychological *disregulation.* Future research on cerebral laterality and emotion should consider the phenomenon of defensiveness, and should include such measures of defensiveness as the Marlowe–Crowne—not only to increase the likelihood of obtaining reliable results, but also the help make more meaningful interpretations of the findings (e.g., the increased laterality in repressors may reflect a conflict between approach and avoidance tendencies, with approach tendencies emphasized by the left hemisphere in right-handed individuals, and avoidance tendencies emphasized by the right hemisphere).

Recent findings (Bowen & Schwartz, in preparation a, in preparation b) provide additional information about disregulation and emotion from a systems point of view. Bowen and I discovered that when subjects are instructed simply to increase their heart rates on some trials, and to decrease their heart rates on other trials, subjects vary in the degree to which they respond physiologically in a global undifferentiated (disregulated) fashion versus a more specific, differentiated (self-regulated) fashion. Undifferentiated subjects seem to respond in a rigid manner across situations, suggesting that they emphasize individual stereotypy as described by the Laceys (Lacey & Lacey, 1958). Differentiated subjects seem to respond in a flexible manner across situations, suggesting that they emphasize situational stereotypy as described by the Laceys (Lacey & Lacey, 1958). Using four cardiovascular measures (systolic blood pressure, diastolic blood pressure, heart rate, and pulse transit time), we (Bowen & Schwartz, in preparation a) classified subjects in terms of global cardiovascular arousal (all four measures changed in the same direction in heart rate increase versus decrease trials) versus specific cardiovascular patterning (only one or two measures would change in the same direction in heart rate increase versus decrease trials).

We (Bowen & Schwartz, in preparation a) found

that by splitting subjects into undifferentiated and differentiated groups, it was possible to predict which subjects would show cardiovascular differentiation to different emotions. The undifferentiated subjects responded with overall cardiovascular arousal to imagined positive and negative emotions, whereas the differentiated subjects responded to the different imagined positive and negative emotions with differentiated patterns of cardiovascular activity. The undifferentiated subjects generated self-reports, particularly of happiness and anger, indicating a very simple, stereotypic emotional experience, whereas the differentiated subjects gave self-reports indicating a more complex, rich, blended set of emotional experiences.

In a replication and extension of these findings, we (Bowen & Schwartz, in preparation b) repeated the study using an independent sample of subjects, this time including measures of defensiveness (the Marlowe–Crowne), laterality (facial EMG), and health (self-reports of illness). Not only were the original findings replicated, but in addition the undifferentiated subjects were found to (1) score significantly higher on the Marlowe–Crowne, (2) to show evidence of increased laterality in facial EMG, and (3) to report increased illnesses.

This pattern of findings is not only consistent with the repression–cerebral disconnection–disease hypothesis (Schwartz, 1983a), but may also be related to other disattention syndromes, such as Type A behavior (discussed in Schwartz, 1983b). The important point to recognize here is that discrepancies between self-reports and physiological responses, when interpreted through the perspective of systems theory, become particularly rich and important sources of data in their own right. Patterns of discrepancies can have important implications for theory, for research, and possibly for clinical practice. Future research exploring physiological–subjective relationships in emotion will probably profit from looking closely at individual differences within and across levels of patterns of processes.

EMOTION AS BIOPSYCHOSOCIAL ORGANIZATION: METHODOLOGICAL IMPLICATIONS

The hypothesis that the concept of emotion implies not only a set of feeling states, physiological reactions, motivational expressions, and behaviors, but an *organization* of these processes to meet specific biopsychosocial goals, is a fundamental application of systems theory. A focus on organization leads us to focus our attention on the search for replicable patterns of processes within and across levels. These patterns, as indicated in the preceding section, can vary in their complexity and stability as a function of individual

differences. Viewing the individual difference variation from the perspective of levels and complexity of organization has the potential to integrate research on the psychophysiology of emotion with research on personality and psychopathology.

A focus on patterns of processes implies more than just systematically assessing patterns of subjective experience (e.g., using instruments such as the DES developed by Izard, 1972), patterns of physiological responses, or patterns of overt behavioral expression in a social context. It implies that we develop more sophisticated and meaningful ways for statistically revealing the underlying organization that is present. Multivariate statistics have been usefully applied to cardiovascular (Schwartz et al., 1981) and facial EMG (Fridlund et al., 1984) data, and it seems likely that future advances in mathematics and statistics, particularly as developed in cognitive science, artificial intelligence, and robotics research will find significant applications to future research on the psychophysiology of emotion.

Generally speaking, as noted by various authors (e.g., Fridlund & Izard, 1983; Schwartz, 1982), the concept of organization encourages one to look more precisely at psychophysiological patterns in specific stimulus–response configurations. For example, if subjects are watching a film, and are generating different facial expressions as the film unfolds, it seems prudent to examine psychophysiological patterns *as they are organized at the precise moments when particular facial expressions of emotion occur* (e.g., within a few seconds, as opposed to simply averaging all this information over minutes, or sampling responses in fixed time without regard to the flow of behavior over time). Emphasis on organization in systems terms encourages us to look for organization in meaningful biopsychosocial contexts and durations. This is clearly a challenge for future research.

Another methodological consideration clarified by a systems approach to emotion concerns the role that social variables play in the psychophysiological patterns observed in a given situation. Not only do electrodes constrain movement (and therefore emotional expression), but implicit if not explicit instructions to refrain from moving may alter the meaningfulness of the data obtained (recall that in Schwartz et al., 1981, even though patterns of cardiovascular response were found to vary in emotion following both imagery and overt exercise conditions, the *organization* of the patterns was different in the imagery and exercise conditions). The use of video cameras, the nature of the instructions used for obtaining self-reports of emotion, and the amount of self-report information sampled all have the potential to alter the psychophysiological organization obtained. This realization clearly makes research on emotion more complicated and more challenging, but the challenge can be met successfully if a biopsychosocial view of emotion is kept clearly in mind, and care is taken to design research from the perspective of biopsychosocial measurement.

The general pattern classification approach of Fridlund et al. (1984) is instructive, in that it emphasizes feature extraction as an important component of pattern analysis. From a systems perspective, "single" measures such as "corrugator EMG" are really "multiple" measures in the sense that biological signals carry complex patterns of information that can be extracted. The classic study by Ax (1953), as discussed previously, illustrates this general principle by demonstrating that it is possible to differentiate fear from anger within a "single" response (e.g., comparing maximum increase in skin conductance with number of rises in skin conductance). According to systems theory, it is possible to have patterning within individual physiological measures, since all "wholes" represent organized patterns of "parts." The recent work by Cacioppo and colleagues applying this kind of methodology to facial EMG in cognition and emotion is an important advance in this regard (Cacioppo & Petty, 1983).

EMOTION AS BIOPSYCHOSOCIAL ORGANIZATION: CONCEPTUAL IMPLICATIONS

The hypothesis that emotion reflects biopsychosocial organization has important conceptual implications that can be operationalized and put to empirical tests. One example involves the hypothesis that emotion is revealed as an emergent property of multiple interacting systems within and across levels. According to systems theory, the subjective experience of emotion should be more stable and more complete as more physiological elements are activated and organized in meaningful patterns. An approach to studying this question is to use biofeedback as a methodology for producing different combinations and patterns of physiological responses, and for examining the subjective changes that covary with the physiological patterns. For example, when subjects are taught to increase both their heart rate and frontalis muscle tension simultaneously, they report experiencing more anxiety than if they increase heart rate alone or frontalis muscle tension alone (see Schwartz, 1977).

An excellent chapter by Leventhal (1980) proposes some new aspects of emotion that are consistent with the emergent principle. Leventhal proposes that although patterns of bodily feedback contribute to the emergent experience of emotion, the emotional experience may be disrupted (if not destroyed) if subjects are instructed to attend voluntarily to specific bodily parts. This disruptive effect is predicted from systems theory. Attending to a subset of parts removes information from certain processes and alters others.

Therefore, focusing one's attention can attenuate, if not eliminate, certain emergent properties that depend upon the interaction of the multiple components for their existence. Focused attention acting as a "disemergent" may be a mechanism used by repressors to dampen their emotional experiences. An analogy would be how the perception of a forest can be disrupted or destroyed if one attends specifically to the trees.

Another implication of a systems approach to emotion involves levels of organization and the development of organization as applied to individual differences in emotional experience and expression. Our recent research (Bowen & Schwartz, in preparation a, and in preparation b) distinguishing between undifferentiated (rigid) and differentiated (flexible) cardiovascular responders suggests that subjects do vary in their ability to generate differentiated physiological and psychological patterns to different emotions. Lane and I (Lane & Schwartz, in preparation) have proposed that stages of cognitive development and stages of emotional development generally unfold in parallel and are organized by the frontal and prefrontal cortex. We have hypothesized that with increased emotional development, there is increased capacity for differentiation in biological, psychological, and social levels of functioning. The conflict in the psychophysiology literature between "arousal" versus "pattern" theorists may be caused in part by differences in subject populations sampled, who may have varied in their levels of cognitive and emotion development, and therefore in their physiological and social development as well. A challenge for future research is to view emotion from a developmental perspective (Davidson & Fox, 1984) and then to capture individual differences in the capacity to differentiate (and integrate) higher levels of physiological and psychological organization—from undifferentiated globality (e.g., being "upset") to differentiated specificity (e.g., being "disappointed"). We (Lane & Schwartz, in preparation) have proposed that a systems approach to organization and complexity may improve our capacity to understand the relationship among the psychophysiology of emotion, psychopathology, and physical disease.

This chapter has not specifically dealt with the relationship between emotion and cognition. However, since a systems approach to emotion has implications for the emotion–cognition relationship, a brief comment about this fundamental question is worth making here. As mentioned in the "Introduction and Overview," the concept of emotion is ultimately an inferred concept, not unlike inferred concepts from modern physics. There is a curious and, I believe, an important parallel between the challenges facing modern physics and those facing modern psychophysiology. In modern physics, scientists observe the behavior of meters or graphs generated by electronic machines, or the path of bubbles in cloud chambers, and attempt to infer underlying particles or forces to explain the organization or pattern of behavior observed. In psychophysiology, scientists observe the behavior of meters or graphs generated by electronic machines, or the path of behavior on a video screen, and attempt to infer underlying "particles" (thoughts) or "forces" (emotions) to explain the organization or pattern of behavior observed. Psychophysiology has one advantage over modern physics, in that its subjects can attempt to describe what they are thinking and feeling verbally (thereby providing another set of observations). But ultimately, the notion of inference becomes essential for understanding the way the science is practiced and evolves.

I believe that some of the conceptual difficulties facing modern physics have parallels in modern psychophysiology, and that we should reflect upon some of the potential implications of these parallels, since the parallels may themselves reflect systems metaprinciples (see Schwartz, 1984). For example, most behavioral and biomedical researchers view cognition and emotion as two separate, yet interacting processes, and researchers have attempted to classify some parts of the brain as more "emotional" (e.g., limbic structures) and other parts as more "cognitive" (e.g., cortical structures). However, as Zajonc (1980) has recently pointed out, all cognitive processes have affective components, and all emotional processes have cognitive components. An alternative view, one suggested by modern physics, is the hypothesis that cognition and emotion reflect two different qualities or aspects of a whole that has yet to be labeled. For example, it is now well established that light has both wave-like and particle-like properties. If an experiment is set up to measure wave properties, light will appear to function as a wave, whereas if an experiment is set up to measure particle properties, light will appear to function as a particle. However, it is difficult to conceptualize light as being both a wave and particle, shifting its relative emphasis back and forth. The concept of a "wavicle" is sometimes used to express the idea that light is not a wave versus a particle, but instead is a whole that includes wave-like and particle-like properties.

It is possible that "emotion may be to cognition as waves are to particles." In other words, it is possible that emotion and cognition are two qualities of a whole, which for lack of a better term might be called "cogmotion" (Schwartz, 1984). All levels of functioning in the nervous system from the brain stem through the prefrontal cortex, may have degrees of functioning that reflect both cognitive and affective qualities of functioning. Experiments that focus more on the cognitive versus affective qualities of functioning may emphasize and reveal the cognitive versus affective qualities of human functioning, altering the system in ways predicted by Heisenberg's uncertainty principle (which says, in essence, that if you attempt to measure one thing, not only does this influence the thing you are measuring, but it makes it difficult to assess other things because of built-in uncertainty).

Since systems theory encourages us to think about parallels between and among all levels and disciplines (including the subatomic), the reader should consider the parallel proposed here between wave–particle theory and emotion–cognition theory as a general analogy whose purpose is to stimulate new ways of thinking about the relationship between emotion and cognition, and therefore about new ways of designing experiments and interpreting data. If "cogmotion" is like "light" in the sense that the terms "cognition" and "emotion" may refer to two different qualities of the organized functioning of organisms, the relationship between thoughts and feelings may be more intimate than heretofore conceived. Psychophysiology may have the potential to uncover the implicit organization inherent in cognitive–affective integration, and thereby to provide a new window for connecting theory and research on cognition with theory and research on emotion.

ACKNOWLEDGMENTS

Preparation of this chapter was supported by a grant from the National Science Foundation. The chapter reflects an extension of Schwartz (1982).

REFERENCES

Ahern, G. L. & Schwartz, G. E. Differential lateralization for positive versus negative emotion. *Neuropsychologia*, 1979, 17, 693–697.

Ahern, G. L. & Schwartz, G. E. *Differential lateralization for positive versus negative emotion in the human brain: EEG spectral analysis.* Manuscript in preparation.

Asendorph, J. B., & Scherer, K. R. The discrepant repressor: differentiation between low anxiety, high anxiety and repression of anxiety by autonomic-facial-verbal patterns of behavior. *Journal of Personality and Social Psychology*, 1985, 45, 1334–1346.

Ax, A. F. The physiological differentiation between fear and anger in humans. *Psychosomatic Medicine*, 1953, 15, 433–442.

Basmajian, V. J. *Muscles alive: Their functions revealed by electromyography* (4th ed.). Baltimore: Williams & Wilkins, 1978.

Bowen, W., & Schwartz, G. E. Self regulated rigid & flexible cardiovascular responding: Relationship to emotion. Manuscript in preparation. (a)

Bowen, W., & Schwartz, G. E. Self regulated rigid & flexible cardiovascular responding: relationship to emotion, repression and health. Manuscript in preparation. (b)

Brown, S. L., Schwartz, G. E., & Sweeney, D. R. Dissociation of self-reported and observed pleasure in depression. *Psychosomatic Medicine*, 1978, 40, 536–548.

Brown, S. L., Sweeney, D. R., & Schwartz, G. E. Differences between self-reported and observed pleasure in depression and schizophrenia. *Journal of Nervous & Mental Disease*, 1979, 167, 410–415.

Cacioppo, J. T., & Petty, R. E. (Eds.). *Social psychophysiologyy.* New York: Guilford Press, 1983.

Cacioppo, J. T., & Petty, R. E. Electromyograms as measures of extent and affectivity of information processing. *American Psychologist*, 1981, 36, 441–456.

Crowne, D. P., & Marlowe,D. *The approval motive: Studies in evaluative dependence*. New York: Wiley, 1964.

Darwin, C. *The expression of the emotions in man and animals*. Chicago: University of Chicago Press, 1965. (Originally published 1872.)

Davidson, R. J., Schwartz, G. E., Saron, C., Bennett, J., & Goleman, D. J. Frontal versus parietal EEG asymmetry during positive and negative affect. *Psychophysiology*, 1979, 16, 202–203.

Davidson, R. J. Affective, cognition and hemispheric specialization. In C. E. Izard, J. Kagan, & R. Zajonc (Eds.), *Emotion, cognition and behavior*. New York & London: Cambridge University Press, 1984.

Davidson, R. J., & Fox, N. A. Asymmetrical brain activity discriminates between positive versus negative affective stimuli in 10-month-old human infants. *Science*, 1982, 218, 1235–1236.

Davidson, R. J., & Fox, N. A. *The psychobiology of affective development*. Hillsdale, NJ: Erlbaum, 1984.

deRosnay, J. *The macroscope*. New York: Harper & Row, 1979.

Ekman, P., Friesen, W. V., & Ellsworth, P. C. *Emotion in the human face*. Elmsford, NY: Pergamon Press, 1972.

Ekman, P., & Friesen, W. V. *Unmasking the face*. Englewood Cliffs, NJ: Prentice Hall, 1975.

Ekman, P., & Friesen, W. V. *Facial action coding system (FACS)*. Palo Alto: Consulting Psychologists Press, 1978.

Ekman, P., Levenson, R., & Friesen, W. V. Autonomic nervous system activity distinguishes among emotions. *Science*, 1984, 221, 1208–1210.

Engel, G. L. The need for a new medical model: a challenge for biomedicine. *Science*, 1977, 196, 129–136.

Fridlund, A. J., & Izard, C. E. Electromyographic studies of facial expressions of emotions. In J. T. Cacioppo & R. E. Petty (Eds.) *Social psychophysiology*. New York: Guilford Press, 1983.

Fridlund, A. J., Schwartz, G. E., & Fowler, S. C. Pattern recognition of self-reported states from multiple site facial EMG activity during affective imagery. *Psychophysiology*, 1984, 21, 622–637.

Greenfield, N. S., & Sternbach, R. A. (Eds.). *Handbook of psychophysiology*. New York: Holt, 1972.

Izard, C. E. *The face of emotion*. New York: Appleton-Century-Crofts, 1971.

Izard, C. E. *Patterns of emotions*. New York: Academic Press, 1972.

Izard, C. E. *Human emotions*. New York: Plenum Press, 1977.

James, W. What is an emotion. *Mind*, 1884, 9, 188–204.

Lacey, J. I., & Lacey, B. C. Verification and extension of the principle of autonomic response stereotyping. *American Journal of Psychology*, 1958, 71, 50–73.

Lane, R. D., & Schwartz, G. E. *A systems theory of emotional development: Integration of the biological, psychological and social perspective*. Manuscript in preparation.

Lang, P. J. A bio-informational theory of emotional imagery. *Psychophysiology*, 1979, 16, 495–512.

Lang, P. J., Miller, G. A., & Levin, D. N. Anxiety and fear: Central processing and peripheral physiology. In R. J. Davidson, G. E. Schwartz, and D. Shapiro (Eds.), *Consciousness and Self-Regulation: Advances in Research, Volume 3* (pp. 123–151). New York: Plenum, 1983.

Lang, P. J., Rice, D. G., & Sternbach, R. A. Psychophysiology of emotion. In N. S. Greenfield & R. A. Sternbach (Eds.), *Handbook of psychophysiology*. New York: Holt, 1972.

Leigh, H., Reiser, M. F. *The patient: Biological, psychological and social dimensions of medical practice*. New York: Plenum Press, 1980.

Leventhal, H. Toward a comprehensive theory of emotion. In L. Berkowitz (Ed.), *Advances in experimental social psychology*. New York: Academic Press, 1980.

McGuigan, F. J. Imagery and thinking: Covert functioning of the motor system. In G. E. Schwartz & D. Shapiro (Eds) *Consciousness and self-regulation: Advances in research and theory* (Vol. 2). New York: Plenum Press, 1978.

Miller, J. G. *Living systems*. New York: McGraw-Hill, 1978.

Phillips, D. C. *Holistic thought in social science*. Stanford University Press, 1976.

Plutchik, R. *Emotion: A psychoevolutionary synthesis*. New York: Harper & Row, 1980.

Polonsky, W. H., & Schwartz, G. E. *Facial electromyography and the self-deceptive coping style. Individual differences in the hemispheric lateralization of affect*. Manuscript submitted for publication, 1984.

Sackeim, H. A., Gur, R. C., & Saucy, M. C. Emotions are expressed more intensely on the left side of the face. *Science*, 1978, 202, 434–435.

Schachter, J. Pain, fear and anger in hypertensive and normotensives. *Psychosomatic Medicine*, 1957, 19, 17–29.

Schachter, J., & Singer, J. E. Cognitive, social and physiological determinants of emotional state. *Psychological Review*, 1962, 69, 379–399.

Schwartz, G. E. Biofeedback, self-regulation and the patterning of physiological processes. *American Scientist*, 1975, 63, 314–324.

Schwartz, G. E. Psychosomatic disorders and biofeedback: A psychobiological model of disregulation. In J. D. Maser & M. E. P. Seligman (Eds.), *Psychopathology: Theory and practice*. Baltimore: Williams & Wilkins, 1977.

Schwartz, G. E. Psychobiological foundations of psychotherapy and behavior change. In S. L. Garfield & A. E. Bergin (Eds.) *Handbook of psychotherapy and behavior change* (2nd ed.). New York: Wiley, 1978.

Schwartz, G. E. The brain as a health care system. In G. Stone, N. Adler, & F. Cohen (Eds.), *Health psychology*. San Francisco: Jossey-Bass, 1979.

Schwartz, G. E. Behavioral medicine and systems theory: A new synthesis. *National Forum*, 1980, 4, 25–30.

Schwartz, G. E. A systems analysis of psychobiology and behavior therapy: Implications for behavioral medicine. In H. Leigh (Ed.), *Psychotherapy and Psychosomatics*, 36, Special issue on behavioral medicine, 1981, 159–184.

Schwartz, G. E. Cardiovascular psychophysiology: A systems perspective. In J. T. Cacioppo & R. E. Petty (Eds.), *Focus on cardiovascular psychophysiaology*. New York: Guilford Press, 1982.

Schwartz, G. E. Disregulation theory and disease: Applications to the repression/cerebral disconnection/cardiovascular disorder hypothesis. (Special edition). *International Review of Applied Psychology*, 1983, 32, 95–118. (a)

Schwartz, G. E. Social psychophysiology and behavioral medicine: A systems perspective. In J. T. Cacioppo & R. E. Petty (Eds.), *Social psychophysiology*. New York: Guilford Press, 1983. (b)

Schwartz, G. E. Psychobiology of health: A new synthesis. In B. L. Hammonds & C. J. Scheirer (Eds.), *Psychology and health, The Master Lecture Series* (Vol. 3). Washington: American Psychological Association, 1984.

Schwartz, G. E., Ahern, G. L., & Brown, S. L. Lateralized facial muscle response to positive versus negative emotional stimuli. *Psychophysiology*, 1979, 16, 561–571.

Schwartz, G. E., & Beatty, J. (Eds.), *Biofeedback: Theory and research*. New York: Academic Press, 1977.

Schwartz, G. E., Brown, S. L., & Ahern, G. L. Facial muscle patterning and subjective experience during affective imagery: Sex differences. *Psychophysiology*, 1980, 17, 75–82.

Schwartz, G. E., Davidson, R. J., & Maer, F. Right hemisphere lateralization for emotion in the human brain: Interaction with cognition. *Science*, 1975, 190, 286–288.

Schwartz, G. E., Fair, P. L., Salt, P., Mandel, M. R., & Klerman, G. L. Facial muscle patterning to affective imagery in depressed and nondepressed subjects. *Science*, 1976, 192, 489–491. (a)

Schwartz, G. E., Fair, P. L., Salt, P., Mandel, M. R., & Klerman, G. L. Facial expression and imagery in depression: An electromyographic study. *Psychosomatic Medicine*, 1976, 38, 337–347. (b)

Schwartz, G. E., & Weinberger, D. A. Patterns of emotional responses to affective situations: Relations among happiness, sadness, anger, fear, depression and anxiety. *Motivation and Emotion*, 1980, 4, 175–191.

Schwartz, G. E., Weinberger, D. A., & Singer, J. A. Cardiovascular differentiation of happiness, sadness, anger and fear following imagery and exercise. *Psychosomatic Medicine*, 1981, 43, 343–364.

Sirota, A. D., & Schwartz, G. E. Facial muscle patterning and lateralization during elation and depression imagery. *Journal of Abnormal Psychology*, 1982, 91, 25–34.

Sirota, A. D., Schwartz, G. E., & Kristeller, J. Facial muscle activity during induced mood states: differential growth and carry over of elated versus depressed patterns. *Psychophysiology*, 1983, 20, 471.

Sternberg, R. Intelligence, information processing and analogical reasoning: The componential analysis of human abilities. Hillsdale, NJ: Erlbaum, 1977.

Tompkins, S. S. Affect as amplification: Some modifications in theory. In R. Plutchik & H. Kellerman (Eds.), *Emotion: Theory, research and experience.* New York: Academic Press, 1980.

Tucker, D. M. Lateral brain function, emotion and conceptualization. *Psychological Bulletin*, 1981, 84, 19–46.

von Bertalanffy, L. *General systems theory.* New York: Braziller, 1968.

Weerts, T. C., & Roberts, R. The physiological effects of imagining anger provoking and fear provoking scenes. *Psychophysiology*, 1976, 13, 174.

Weinberger, D. A., Schwartz, G. E., & Davidson, R. J. Low anxious, high anxious and repressive coping styles: Psychometric patterns and behavioral and physiological responses to stress. *Journal of Abnormal Psychology*, 1979, 88, 369–380.

Zajonc, R. B. Feeling and thinking: Preferences need no interferences. *American Psychologist*, 1980, 35, 151–175.

Chapter Eighteen

Sleep: Physiology and Psychophysiology

INTRODUCTION

There is a behavior whose physiological characteristics vary so greatly from those of normal wakefulness that, were it not for the pervasiveness of this behavior, it would be considered abnormal. This behavior is sleep. Associated with this state of overt physiological repose is a cognitive experience, popularly characterized as consisting of generally bizarre mentations, to which both prophetic powers and special access to the unconscious have been attributed. This cognitive experience is the dream. Since these behaviors occupy a considerable portion of our existence—a third of our lives are spent sleeping, and, by a conservative estimate of "dream time," 6–8% of our lives are spent dreaming—it is clear that an understanding of these behaviors is fundamental to a holistic comprehension of human behavior.

The extraordinary coexistence of sleep and waking behaviors would seem to suggest that we are citizens of two worlds, each with its own physiological and psychological determinants, the transition between which occurs at sleep onset. Indeed, studies of psychological and physiological processes of sleep and wakefulness can be, and have been, subjects of largely independent investigations. Although a great deal of descriptive information has been amassed for both states, an understanding of the functional significance of many processes would appear to require the integration of information gathered during both sleep and wakefulness—an approach that is receiving increasing attention (Foulkes, 1978; Foulkes, 1982; Foulkes & Kerr, 1980; Johnson, 1973; Webb, 1977).

The purpose of this chapter is to provide an overview of variations and covariations in physiological and psychological processes during sleep. This treatment is not comprehensive in the sense that an extensive cataloguing of studies covering all areas of endeavor is given. Rather, state and event correlates of sleep mentation that have emerged from psychophysiological investigations during the last 30 years are related, and some general implications of these findings for psychological processes basic to both sleep and wakefulness are discussed.

The overview of psychophysiological sleep literature begins 30 years ago, since prior to that time studies of psychophysiological relationships during sleep were virtually nonexistent. In the 1950s, a series

R. T. Pivik. Departments of Psychiatry and Physiology, School of Medicine, Faculty of Health Sciences and School of Psychology, University of Ottawa, Ottawa, Ontario, Canada.

of papers was published (Aserinsky & Kleitman, 1953, 1955; Dement, 1955; Dement & Kleitman, 1957a, 1957b; Dement & Wolpert, 1958a, 1958b) that completely altered concepts regarding both the nature of sleep and the occurrence of dreaming. The observations that so drastically changed the course and concepts in sleep and dream research were these:

1. These investigators noted the presence during sleep of episodes characterized by a high degree of physiological activation that was not wakefulness. Indeed, it has been argued that the physiological characteristics of these rapid eye movement (REM) sleep episodes differ as much from the remainder of sleep as from wakefulness, and therefore should be considered as a third state of existence (Dement, 1969b; Snyder, 1966).
2. A high proportion of arousals from these episodes were found to be associated with reports of dreaming.

These were remarkable revelations with far-reaching consequences. For example, contrary to previous thinking, sleep could no longer be considered a unitary state of repose; furthermore, in the words of Aserinsky and Kleitman (1953), it was now possible to determine "the incidence and duration of periods of dreaming" (p. 274).

Studies of psychophysiological relationships during sleep promised to significantly broaden the scope of general understanding of mind–body relationships because of several psychological and physiological features unique to sleep. For example, physiological and psychological behaviors during sleep differ from those of wakefulness in range, type, and distribution, thereby presenting a wider variety of potential psychophysiological interactions. Among physiological variables that best typify these sleep–wakefulness differences is the electroencephalogram (EEG). The EEG during normal wakefulness is characterized by fairly uniform low-voltage, nonsynchronized fast activity. Synchronized activity that is present during wakefulness is generally restricted to the alpha range (8–12 Hz). By contrast, during sleep, not only is there a greater emphasis on a wider range of EEG frequencies—ranging from those in the delta (.5- to 2-Hz) to beta (>14-Hz) bands, with 20-fold variations in amplitude (i.e., 10 μV to 200 μV)—but there is the spontaneous occurrence of EEG activities that are unique to sleep (12- to 14-Hz spindles, 4- to 7-Hz sawtooth waves, K complexes). Synchronized activity is common and is perhaps the cardinal feature of the sleep EEG. Another distinguishing feature of sleep-related EEG activity is the sustained occurrence of specific patterns over extended periods of time.

Similarly, relative to the generally unexciting nature of waking mental activity, mentation during sleep can range from the ridiculously or terrifyingly bizarre to the absolutely mundane. Furthermore, unlike general waking mentation, there are times of apparent total mental inactivity.

Relative to the physiological and psychological experiences of wakefulness, those during sleep occur under conditions in which potentially confounding variables, such as stress, expectations, and undefined variations in levels of arousal, are reduced. Such conditions—engendered by the reduction in sensory stimuli in the sleeping environment, as well as by the increased arousal thresholds characteristic of sleep (Keefe, Johnson, & Hunter, 1971; Rousey, 1979; Wilson & Zung, 1966)—enhance the possibility of observing relationships either obscured by or not present during wakefulness.

A truly remarkable feature underlying all of the observations above is the spontaneous occurrence of these physiological and psychological variations on a daily basis.

If studies of sleep psychophysiology held out great promise for understanding mind–body relationships, they also presented special methodological problems, which had to be overcome before the potential benefits could be realized. At the physiological level, these considerations consisted first of developing a technology that would permit the reliable recording of physiological variables for extended periods of time. Waking physiological studies are generally accomplished within a time frame that is brief relative to the one required for studies of sleep, and that has completely different subject demand characteristics. Studies in wakefulness gather data for a few minutes up to perhaps 2 hr, during which time subjects remain aware of physiological transducers and are instructed to avoid behaviors that might compromise the quality of the recordings (e.g., inadvertent movements, eyeblinks, etc.). The time frame for sleep recordings, by comparison, is on the order of hours—6–8 hr or more. Transducers must be securely applied to maintain skin contact for reliable recordings over such long periods of time, despite the scores of adjustments in body position that take place during the course of a normal night of sleep (Altshuler & Brebbia, 1967; Kleitman, 1963), and that are made without regard to or awareness of these transducers. Frequently, special procedures had to be developed to assess ongoing physiological variations while minimizing sleep disturbance. For example, to provide eye movement recordings devoid of superimposed EEG signals that are detected by the electrodes used to record the electrooculogram (EOG; see Figures 18-1 and 18-2), small transducers have been applied to the eyelid to detect mechanical movements of the eye (Baldridge, Whitman, & Kramer, 1963; Gross, Byrne, & Fisher, 1965); to record spinal monosynaptic reflex responses from leg musculature during sleep, a method of leg restraint was developed that prevented movement of stimulating and recording electrodes during

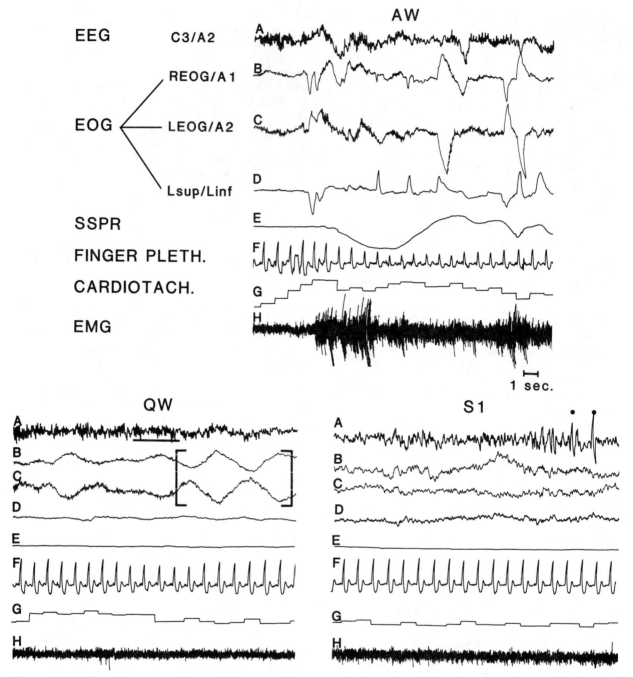

EEG — C3/A2

EOG — REOG/A1, LEOG/A2, Lsup/Linf

SSPR

FINGER PLETH.

CARDIOTACH.

EMG

AW

QW

S 1

1 sec.

Figure 18-1. Polygraphic tracings illustrating variations in physiological measures associated with variations in sleep–wakefulness. Eight channels of activity (A–H) are depicted during active and quiet wakefulness (AW and QW, respectively) and the first stage of sleep (NREM Stage 1, or S1). The recorded variables include the electroencephalogram (EEG; C3/A2, channel A), the electro-oculogram (EOG; horizontal [right and left outer canthi] and vertical [placements superior and inferior to right eye orbit] eye movement activity, channels B, C, and D, respectively), autonomic activity (spontaneous skin potential response [SSPR], channel E; finger plethysmogram, channel F; and cardiotachometer recordings, channel G), and the facial electromyogram (EMG; channel H). Electrophysiological features of note are alpha activity (underscored, channel A) and slow rolling eye movements (channels B and C) preceding sleep onset in QW, and vertex sharp waves in Stage 1 (see dots, channel A). See text for discussion of sleep stage definitions and electrophysiological composition.

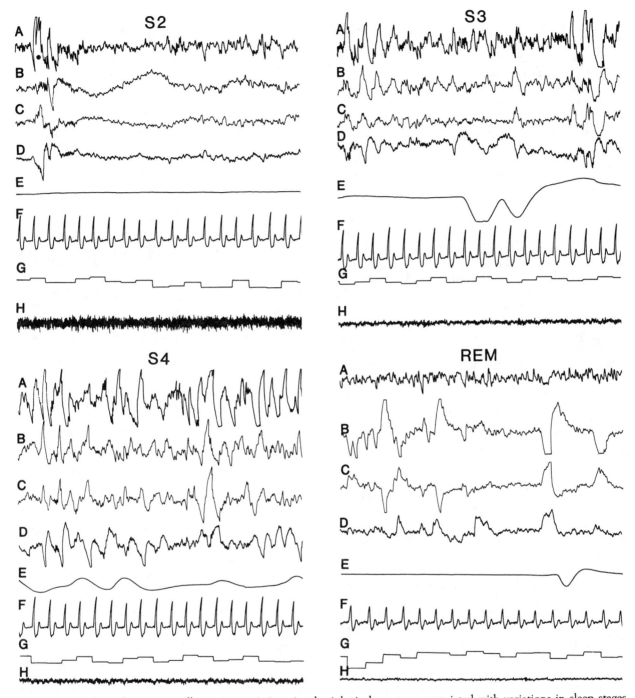

Figure 18-2. Polygraphic tracings illustrating variations in physiological measures associated with variations in sleep stages (NREM Stages 2–4 [S2–S4] and REM). For explanation of channels A–H, see Figure 18-1. Electrophysiological features of note are the K complexes in Stage 2 (see dot, channel A). See text for discussion of sleep stage definitions and electrophysiological composition.

spontaneous body movements without compromising reflex responses or sleep integrity by excessive restraint (Pivik, 1971; Pivik & Dement, 1970); and, to measure changes in middle-ear muscle activity noninvasively, a device was developed that could be in-

serted into the ear to translate changes in sound-pressure level to variations in impedance (Pessah & Roffwarg, 1972).

The wide array of physiological variables that has been recorded over long periods of time during sleep is an impressive demonstration of technological and methodological ingenuity, as well as an illustration of the ability of humans to adjust rapidly to novel environments and to sleep under less than ideal circumstances (some of these variables are discussed in greater detail later). Although sleep does occur under these conditions, there is evidence of initial sleep disturbance in the form of increased latencies to sleep onset, increased motility during sleep, and fragmentation of many sleep patterns. These influences diminish after one or two recording nights in the laboratory. This initial disruption of sleep has been termed the "first night effect" (Agnew, Webb, & Williams, 1966).

Reducing and analyzing 6–8 hr of data describing any aspect of human behavior present on a continuous basis is an awesome task. Although such analyses are somewhat simplified by the relative absence during sleep of influences from external stimuli or interactions of the sleeper with the environment, there remains a complex composition of measurements, each of which may be separately documented. For each category of physiological information, there is, over an 8-hr period, continuous data traced on a paper write-out extending .2 miles in length (assuming a paper speed of 10 mm/sec); at least two to five nights of such recordings are typically required for even the most basic sleep investigation. The application of computer techniques and procedures has somewhat eased the tasks of data reduction and analysis, but even with such aids, the amount of information acquired in the simplest sleep investigation remains formidable.

The categorization of electrophysiological recordings during sleep into stages based on the scoring of 20- to 30-sec epochs (Anders, Emde, & Parmelee, 1971; Rechtschaffen & Kales, 1968) was made in order to make such data both manageable and meaningful. It is recognized that this arbitrary division of sleep into stages based on brief segments of recordings is a smoothing of the generally continuous flux of physiological variables that occurs during sleep. Sleep is a more fluid, changing state than is suggested by the results of current scoring procedures (see Figures 18-1–18-3), and the advent of computer technology may make it practical to attend to increasingly finer distinctions in state (Hoffman, Moffitt, Shearer, Sussman, & Wells, 1979; Itil, 1969, 1970; Sussman, Moffitt, Hoffman, Wells, & Shearer, 1979). The differentiation of sleep stages into tonic and phasic components was a shift in this direction of finer state distinctions, and much of the impetus for this orientation came from investigations pursuing psychophysiological relationships.

The descriptive picture of sleep physiology has become more detailed as new methods of data acquisition and analysis have been developed, but a means of tapping into the stream of consciousness to obtain an integrated index of thought processes by decoding

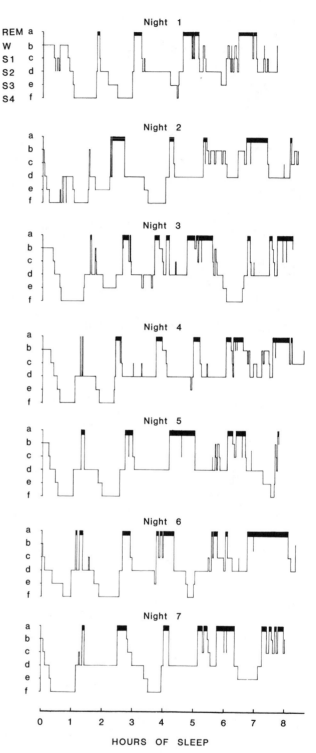

Figure 18-3. Sleep profiles depicting variations in sleep stages (ordinate) as a function of time asleep (abscissa). These profiles, based on seven consecutive nights of baseline sleep in a young adult, illustrate the stability of sleep patterns across nights, the presence of patterned oscillations between REM (darkened rectangles) and NREM sleep (i.e., sleep cycle), and the decrease in Stage 4 and increase in REM sleep as a function of sleep time within a given night.

physiological signals has not been developed. Consequently, the verbal report remains the fundamental data base for communicating psychological experiences, regardless of state. A variety of devices and techniques have been developed to deal with these reports, including rating scales and procedures for quantification of descriptive features (Winget & Kramer, 1979), free association for relating sleep to waking mentation (Foulkes, 1978; Freud, 1900/1955), and methods to quantify aspects of these reports on a grammatical basis (Foulkes, 1978).

Among behavioral states in which psychological experiences are examined—including "normal" wakefulness, drug conditions, or other altered states, such as the hypnotic trance—studies of sleep mentation are unique, in that the report of the psychological experience is obtained in a state different from that during which the experience occurs. In other words, there is a state-dependency confound inherent in sleep mentation studies. Although verbalization may occur during both REM and non-REM (NREM) sleep, intelligent dialogue has not been initiated or maintained during sleep, despite attempts to train subjects posthypnotically to relate ongoing mentation without awakening (Arkin, 1978; Arkin, Toth, Baker, & Hastey, 1970).

This state-dependent feature of sleep mentation has provoked interesting speculations regarding the origin of psychological experiences reported upon arousal from sleep. Although psychophysiological studies of sleep have been largely predicated upon the belief that the postarousal verbal reports are valid and reliable descriptions of cognitive experiences that occur during sleep, it has been considered that these reports may be generated in the process of waking up, thus reflecting hypnopompic experiences or confabulations to please the experimenter. Even if convincing arguments can be made that these experiences occur during sleep, are such experiences restricted to episodes of sustained physiological activation (as is present throughout REM sleep), or does more intermittent physiological activity (most characteristic of REM sleep, but also present during NREM sleep) correlate with dream occurrence? This issue of identifying moments of dreaming is taken up after some fundamental descriptive aspects of sleep physiology and psychology have been presented.

GENERAL FEATURES OF SLEEP PHYSIOLOGY AND PSYCHOLOGY

The classification of variations in patterns of physiological activity during sleep into stages immediately reveals a basic feature of sleep—namely, that it is not a unitary phenomenon. This was evident as early as 1937, when Loomis, Harvey, and Hobart reported a differentiation of EEG patterns during sleep. Twenty

years later, Dement and Kleitman (1957a) provided a more comprehensive differentiation, which included the newly discovered state of REM sleep. At this time, evidence of predictable variations in patterns of sleep stages across the night led to the recognition of a second fundamental characteristic of sleep—the existence of the sleep cycle (Dement & Kleitman, 1957a; see Figure 18-3). This revelation had significant implications for both the physiology and the psychology of sleep. At the physiological level, it implied the presence of active mechanisms regulating physiological variations during sleep. Moreover, since long time constants were involved in these variations, mechanisms other than those relying solely on neurophysiological processes had to be invoked; that is, sleep pattern changes had to involve neurochemical mechanisms.

In terms of cognitive functions during sleep, the implications of a sleep cycle were equally dramatic. Prior concepts of the dream as a sporadically occurring, ephemeral event were completely altered when it appeared that dream recall was associated with a physiologically identifiable state that occurred in a predictable fashion and occupied a considerable portion of each night of normal sleep.

The subsequent profusion of investigations involving sleep recordings created the need for the standardization of scoring criteria for sleep stages. The existing variety of evaluative criteria was made apparent by the systematic study of Monroe (1969), in which the unreliability then present in the application of scoring criteria was clearly illustrated. At almost the same time, a *Manual of Standardized Terminology, Techniques and Scoring for Sleep Stages of Human Subjects* (Rechtschaffen & Kales, 1968) was published, and has since served as the standard for recording and analysis of adult human sleep. The polygraphic tracings in Figures 18-1 and 18-2 illustrate typical features of physiological measures associated with sleep–wakefulness distinctions and within-sleep stage differentiations according to the Rechtschaffen and Kales (1968) manual. These tracings depict simultaneous recordings of brain waves (EEG), eye movements (EOG), autonomic activity, and muscle activity (electromyogram, or EMG) measures during active wakefulness (AW), quiet wakefulness (QW), Stages 1 through 4 of NREM sleep, and REM sleep. The basic measures suggested in the manual for sleep evaluation are EEG, EOG, and EMG (channels E, F, and G, Figures 18-1 and 18-2). The differentiation of horizontal and vertical eye movements as depicted is optional. Wakefulness (AW and QW) is characterized by a low-voltage, mixed-frequency EEG with or without prominent alpha (8- to 12-Hz) activity; blinking, rapid eye movements, and a high tonic level of EMG activity may be present.

The transition from wakefulness to sleep is accompanied by an attenuation of alpha activity (when such activity is prominent during wakefulness), a generalized slowing of EEG activity, and a prominence of activity in the theta (2- to 7-Hz) range, together with the occurrence of vertex sharp waves (see Figure 18-1, S1, tracing A). During the transition between wakefulness and Stage 1, slow horizontal eye movements occur (Figure 18-1, QW, tracings B and C), and facial muscle tonus may be reduced relative to waking levels. Stage 2 sleep (Figure 18-2, S2) is defined by the sporadic presence of two EEG wave forms—K complexes (Figure 18-2, S2, tracing A) and 12- to 14-Hz spindle activity—and the absence of delta activity (.5–2 Hz) in amounts sufficient for a Stage 3 or Stage 4 designation. Stages 3 and 4, which collectively have been termed "slow-wave sleep," are differentiated from Stage 2 and from each other by the proportion of delta activity present in the scoring epoch. Stage 3 is scored when the epoch consists of between 20% and 50% delta activity, and Stage 4 when more than half of the epoch is comprised of such activity (Figure 18-2, S3 and S4).

REM sleep is defined by the occurrence of a relatively low-voltage, mixed-frequency EEG, the absence of K complexes and spindles, the presence of sporadically occurring eye movements, and the absence of high levels of submental and facial EMG activity. Moreover, the EEG in REM sleep often contains specific features, such as sawtooth waves preceding bursts of eye movements (Berger, Olley, & Oswald, 1962), or alpha activity that is generally 1–2 Hz slower than the individual's alpha frequency during waking (Johnson, Nute, Austin, & Lubin, 1967).

The criteria above provide global descriptions of physiological patterns that have proven useful in discriminating sleep from wakefulness and investigating recurrent variations within sleep. Fundamentally, sleep–wakefulness differences include the following:

1. The presence of waveforms unique to sleep—for example, endogenously determined K complexes, 12- to 14-Hz spindle activity, vertex sharp waves, and frontal sawtooth waves.
2. The prevalence of and concentration of activities—for example, the enhancement of slower EEG frequencies (delta and theta), and the concentration of these and other activities, such as eye movements or galvanic skin responses (GSRs), at specific times of the night. With respect to EEG activity, computerized analyses have shown that on only rare instances is the EEG composed of a single frequency; even in the desynchronized low-voltage EEG of wakefulness in normal individuals, there is a small but nonetheless real component of delta activity present (Hoffman et al., 1979; Lubin, Johnson, & Austin, 1969). The shift away from the higher frequencies associated with arousal during

wakefulness and the concentration on slower activities are what make sleep unique.
3. The predictable constellations of physiological patterns that occur—for example, concentrations of delta activity are associated with high GSR activation during slow-wave sleep, and indices of cortical, ocular–motor, and autonomic arousal are associated with sustained muscular inhibition during REM sleep.

The illustrations of the different physiological measures (Figures 18-1 and 18-2) and of the unfolding of sleep patterns across the night (Figure 18-3) obscure more rapid variations that parameters of sleep physiology may undergo, either individually or in concert. Indeed, the moment of state change from wakefulness to sleep is subject to debate. The majority of investigators considers that the state change from wakefulness to sleep occurs when Stage 1 patterns appear, but arguments have been presented in support of the designation of sleep onset coincident with the appearance of Stage 2 K complexes and spindles (Agnew & Webb, 1972; Johnson, 1973; Snyder & Scott, 1972). Despite these variations in pattern, greater than 90% agreement can be achieved by independent scoring of all night sleep recordings.

Within the global patterns of state change across the night, there are still other patterns of activity characteristic of time of night or time within, preceding, or following particular stages of sleep. For example, Stage 4 is localized to the first third of the night, and proportionally greater amounts of REM sleep occur in the last third of the night (Williams, Agnew, & Webb, 1964, 1966; see Figure 18-3). Other examples of these patterns within patterns include increased frequency of body movement and endogenously evoked K complexes immediately preceding REM periods (Dement & Kleitman, 1957a; Halasz, Rajna, Pal, Kundra, Vargha, Balogh, & Kemeny, 1977; Pivik & Dement, 1968); decreased presence of K complexes and increased prominence of EEG spindle activity in the few minutes immediately following REM periods (Azumi, Shirakawa, & Takahashi, 1975; Pivik & Dement, 1968); the relative fragility of the first REM period, to the point that it may often be aborted or skipped (Berger & Oswald, 1962a; Dement & Kleitman, 1957a; Roffwarg, Muzio, & Dement, 1966); and the increase in eye movement activity, both as a function of time within a given REM period and within REM periods across the night (Aserinsky, 1969, 1971).

There are variations in other physiological measures that, although not integral to sleep stage determination, nonetheless contribute to a more complete understanding of state physiology. REM sleep, for example, is characterized by a generalized physiological upheaval, including increased activity and irregularity in respiratory (Aserinsky, 1965; Snyder, Hobson, Morrison, & Goldfrank, 1964) and cardiovascular (Snyder, Hobson, & Goldfrank, 1963; Snyder *et al.*, 1964) systems; these disturbances occur in conjunction with a centrally mediated inhibition of facial and submental musculature and spinal monosynaptic reflexes (Berger, 1961; Hodes & Dement, 1964; Jacobson, Kales, Lehmann, & Hoedemaker, 1964; Pompeiano, 1966, 1967). By contrast, with the exception of a dramatic display of electrodermal activity during Stage 4 (Asahina, 1962; Broughton, Poire, & Tassinari, 1965; Johnson & Lubin, 1966; see Figure 18-2, S4), NREM sleep is remarkably physiologically quiescent. If electrodermal activation of the intensity present during Stage 4 sleep were to occur during wakefulness, it would be indicative of a high level of arousal; however, the activity related to Stage 4 is thought to reflect a release phenomenon rather than elevated physiological arousal (Johnson, 1973). In comparison, electrodermal activity in REM sleep is typically quite limited and more similar in form to waking responses (Broughton *et al.*, 1965; Hauri & Van de Castle, 1973b). Slow-wave sleep is also notable for an associated release of growth hormone (Sassin, Parker, Mace, Gotlin, Johnson, & Rossman, 1969; Takahashi, Kipnis, & Daughaday, 1968) and is notorious for the associated occurrence of a class of sleep disorders, termed "parasomnias" (Roffwarg, 1979), which include sleep-walking, sleep-talking, enuresis, and night terrors (Arkin, 1966; Broughton, 1968; Jacobson, Kales, Lehmann, & Zweizig, 1965; Kales, Jacobson, Paulson, Kales, & Walter, 1966; Rechtschaffen, Goodenough, & Shapiro, 1962).

The initial studies of sleep psychophysiology following the discovery of REM sleep were essentially studies of state relationships. Although these states were composed of variations in several known physiological measures, they were defined primarily by sustained changes in brain wave patterns. The impetus for this first decade of psychophysiological sleep research was provided by the belief that an objective measure of dreaming (REM sleep) had been found and that dreaming was the exclusive attribute of this sleep stage. Indeed, the high incidence of recall following arousals from REM periods in some early studies was contrasted with the near-exclusion of even fragmentary reports following arousals from other stages of sleep. Implicit in such observations and in the association of dreaming with REM sleep was the assumption that the only mental activity occurring during sleep occurred during REM periods in the form of dreaming. However, within 10 years of the initial Aserinsky and Kleitman (1953, 1955) reports, evidence had begun to accumulate that seriously challenged the attribution to REM sleep of all sleep mentation. Specifically, reports of mental activity

following arousals from NREM sleep were becoming increasingly prevalent and more difficult to dismiss as artifactual (Foulkes, 1967).

In part, the failure or reluctance to appreciate the presence of mental activity during sleep outside the confines of REM sleep was based on an unstated yet seemingly universally understood concept of what constitutes a "dream." This acceptance of an intuitive understanding of the nature of dreaming was reflected in the virtual absence of a definition of "dreaming" in the early papers associating dreams with REM sleep. It was not until 1957 (Dement & Kleitman, 1957b), in a paper titled "The Relation of Eye Movements during Sleep to Dream Activity: An Objective Method for the Study of Dreaming," that the nature of what was to be accepted as a dream was made more explicit. In that study, in response to instructions to state "whether or not they had been dreaming," only subjects who "could relate a coherent, fairly detailed description of dream content" (p. 341) were considered to have been dreaming. Assertions of having dreamed "without recall of content, or vague, fragmentary impressions of content, were considered negative" (p. 341). Using these criteria, 80% of arousals from REM sleep produced recall of dreams, whereas only 7% of arousals from NREM sleep produced recall.

Initiating a postarousal interview whose opening query requires the subject to decide whether or not a dream has been occurring presupposes an implicitly understood and accepted definition of a dream experience. Although there may well be fundamental features of such experiences during sleep, which together may constitute characteristics of a "standard" dream experience, certainly all of these characteristics may not be present during each dream experience. Furthermore, the psychological experience that we collectively identify as "dreaming" may encompass quite disparate experiences on an individual basis. What one individual may term a bizarre, intense, dreamlike experience may to another seem only moderately bizarre and intense or perhaps even mundane. Nonetheless, the systematic scientific study of material related after arousal from sleep necessitates definitions of dreams. Such definitions have variously characterized the dream as a "verbal report describing an occurrence involving multisensory images and sensations, frequently of a bizarre or unreal nature and involving the narrator himself" (Berger, 1967, p. 16); "the presence of any sensory imagery with development and progression of mental activity" (Kales, Hoedemaker, Jacobson, Kales, Paulson, & Wilson, 1967, p. 556); "any occurrences with visual, auditory, or kinesthetic imagery" (Foulkes, 1962, p. 17); a "multidimensional conglomerate of an hallucinatory belief in the actual occurrence of an imagined experience which, in turn, tends to be an extended visual, sometimes bizarre, drama" (Antrobus, Fein, Jordan, Ellman, & Arkin, 1978, p. 40); or simply "thinking" (Foulkes, 1978, p. 3). When, instead of attempting to fit elicited reports into a preconceived but vaguely defined mould of the "dream," a more liberal approach was adopted in which more fragmentary, less perceptual reports of "thinking" were accepted as data, a quite different picture of the occurrence of sleep mentation emerged. Using this less restrictive approach, several studies reported recall of material subsequent to NREM sleep periods for more than 50% of the arousals (Foulkes, 1962; Goodenough, Shapiro, Holden, & Steinschriber, 1959; Molinari & Foulkes, 1969; Pivik & Foulkes, 1968).

As assessed by the incidence of recalled material subsequent to arousal from sleep, then, NREM sleep is far from being a mental void. However, there are qualitative dimensions along with REM and NREM reports differ. These differences, which were noted in the early studies of NREM mentation (Foulkes, 1962) and corroborated by subsequent investigations (Foulkes & Rechtschaffen, 1964; Pivik, 1971; Rechtschaffen, Verdone, & Wheaton, 1963), consist largely of the greater elaboration of sensory and motor dimensions in reports subsequent to REM arousals, greater correspondence to waking life in NREM reports, and the more frequent characterization of reports as "thinking" in NREM than in REM sleep. Still, NREM reports characterized as "dreaming" were reported as often as (Goodenough, Lewis, Shapiro, Jaret, & Sleser, 1965), or more often than (Bosinelli, Molinari, Bagnaresi, & Salzarulo, 1968; Foulkes, 1960, 1962; Pivik, 1971; Pivik & Foulkes, 1968; Rechtschaffen, Vogel, & Shaikun, 1963; Zimmerman, 1968) those characterized as "thinking."

Although on a paired-comparison basis REM and NREM reports can be discriminated (Bosinelli et al., 1968; Monroe, Rechtschaffen, Foulkes, & Jensen, 1965), such REM-NREM discriminability is not equally true for all NREM stage comparisons. For example, mentation elicited from arousals during the transition from wakefulness to sleep compares favorably along several dimensions (e.g., incidence, report length, and hallucinatory quality) with REM mentation (Foulkes, Spear, & Symonds, 1966; Foulkes & Vogel, 1965; Vogel, 1978; Vogel, Foulkes, & Trosman, 1966). Furthermore, a study of the discriminability between REM and sleep-onset Stage 1 reports indicated similarities in perceptual and emotional qualities that blurred the between-stage report discriminability (Vogel, Barrowclough, & Giesler, 1972).

This unique status of Stage 1 sleep reports relative to those from other NREM sleep stages was noticed early in the post-REM sleep research era. Dement and Kleitman (1957a) conducted the first study comparing recall from awakenings made at sleep onset with those made from subsequent REM periods. It is interesting that in other concurrent studies of mental activity during sleep, the opening question to the subject upon arousal was "Were you dreaming?", whereas in this particular study comparing sleep-onset mentation with REM mentation, subjects were asked to "give their impressions on what had been in their minds before the awakenings and, if possible, to differentiate between the state of mind preceding the early (sleep onset) versus later (REM) awakenings" (p. 682). Dement and Kleitman's (1957a) subjects reported that mental content at the onset of sleep was often dreamlike but differed from later reports as not being as "organized" or "real." Moreover, subjects stated they were not asleep during the initial reports as opposed to the impression of having been "really asleep" prior to the later reports. It was concluded that "no dreams were recalled after awakening during the sleep onset Stage 1, only hypnagogic reveries" (p. 689).

Dement and Kleitman (1957a) were impressed by the positive relationship between Stage 1 EEG patterns and the presence of mentation; they suggested that, with the exception of sleep onset, this EEG pattern was a better index of dreaming than were eye movements. This suggestion has been generally supported by subsequent research, which has indicated an inverse relationship between tonic background EEG activity and the incidence and qualitative aspects of material recalled following arousals from sleep. Specifically, percentages of recall are greater and reports are more vivid and bizarre following arousals from low-voltage mixed-frequency Stage 1 EEG (Dement, 1955; Dement & Kleitman, 1957b; Foulkes & Vogel, 1965; Vogel et al., 1966) than following arousals preceded by slower and higher-amplitude EEG activity (Pivik, 1971; Pivik & Foulkes, 1968). This inverse relationship between the quantity and quality of recalled material and amplitude and frequency characteristics of the EEG is also supported by observations that incidence of recall and dreamlike features of reports increase across the night (Foulkes, 1960; Goodenough et al., 1959; Shapiro, Goodenough, & Gryler, 1963; Verdone, 1963), and that high-amplitude slow EEG activity decreases and lower-voltage, fast-frequency activities increase across the night.

In addition to predominant physiological state characteristics most immediately associated with the elicited reports, there are temporal influences to be considered in evaluation studies of sleep mentation. To some extent, these temporal factors constitute intrinsic confounds that complicate attempts to correlate sleep stage independently with elicited sleep mentation. For example, elapsed time in a sleep stage prior to arousal has been shown to be a factor related to the amount and quality of recalled material. As indicated above, arousals from Stage 4 have typically produced the least recall, as well as recall that is less "dreamlike" than that elicited following arousals from other sleep stages. However, when the amount of time spent within this stage prior to awakening was controlled

(Tracy & Tracy, 1974), the difference in incidence and quality of recalled material between Stage 4 and Stage 2 became negligible. Similarly, reports elicited following arousals made early in REM periods are reduced in frequency and dreamlike quality relative to those made later (Foulkes, 1962; Kramer, Roth, & Czaya, 1975; Whitman, 1969).

In addition to these physiological and temporal influences upon sleep mentation, there is evidence suggesting that processes of memory consolidation may be impaired during sleep (Goodenough, 1967, 1968, 1978; Portnoff, Baekeland, Goodenough, Karacan, & Shapiro, 1966; Rechtschaffen, 1964; Wolpert, 1972), and that level of arousal may interact with memory processes to influence recall (Akerstedt & Gillberg, 1979; Goodenough, 1978; Koulack & Goodenough, 1976).

Although tonic background EEG activity provides a good measure of predictability regarding the incidence and quality of postsleep reports, intrastate variations and interstate similarities in incidence and cognitive features of the recalled material highlight the imprecision of this psychophysiological relationship. Clearly, tonic background EEG activity provides only a global orientation toward the identification of moments of mental activity during sleep, and definitely does not index moments of dreaming. Dreaming, whether rigidly or loosely defined, has been reported following arousals from all sleep stages. Furthermore, reports with dreamlike features have been obtained from normal individuals during relaxed wakefulness (Foulkes & Fleisher, 1975; Foulkes & Scott, 1973; Galton, 1883/1911; Spanos & Stam, 1979).

Psychophysiological studies of sleep have not been confined to the examination of EEG correlates of sleep mentation. Prominent among other physiological correlates that have been investigated in this regard are measures of autonomic and motor activities. Studies examining a variety of autonomic measures, including heart rate, respiratory rate, electrodermal activity, and penile erections, have accentuated the positive correlations between abrupt changes in these measures and amounts of recall and/or qualitative variations in recalled material; however, an outstanding positive or negative relationship has not been reported (for more extensive reviews, see Pivik, 1978; Rechtschaffen, 1973).

Certain physiological measures, conspicuous by their predictable and sustained occurrence during specific sleep stages, are impressive for the apparent absence of any influence they might exert upon concomitant mentation. Two such measures are electrodermal activity, which occurs in "storm-like" fashion during Stages 3 and 4 (Burch, 1965), and penile erections, which occur nearly exclusively in REM sleep (Fisher, Gross, & Zuch, 1965; Karacan, Goodenough, Shapiro, & Starker, 1966). The high rate of electrodermal activity during slow-wave sleep would suggest that associated mental activity would reflect the intense activation generally indicated by these levels of electrodermal activity. This is not the case. Recalled material from slow-wave sleep is either less dreamlike (Pivik, 1971) or does not differ in dreamlike quality (Tracy & Tracy, 1974) from other NREM mentation elicited at times devoid of such activity.

Similarly, if recalled REM mentation were directly influenced by background autonomic activity, 80–90% of reports following arousal from REM sleep would contain manifest sexual features, since penile tumescence (or, in the female, clitoral engorgement; Cohen & Shapiro, 1970) regularly occurs during REM sleep. Instead, the presence of overt sexual content in such reports is remarkably sparse (Fisher, 1966; Hall & Van de Castle, 1966).

Although studies relating tonic levels of autonomic activation with sleep reports have not revealed robust psychophysiological relationships, it has become apparent that better psychophysiological correlations obtain when recalled material has been elicited following moments of abrupt physiological change rather than following moments characterized by sustained tonic activity. As becomes evident in the subsequent discussion of relationships between motor phenomena during sleep and recalled mental activity, this observation remains valid for the motor system as well.

There are only two points during sleep where tonic EMG changes have been systematically related to recalled mentation—namely, during REM sleep (at which time facial and submental EMG activity are tonically reduced), and during NREM sleep, generally Stage 2, immediately preceding REM sleep onset (a time often associated with decreases in EMG activity to REM sleep levels). The REM–EMG–mentation relationships are obviously confounded with the REM-EEG results. However, the relationship of the pre-REM EMG to mentation has been studied under conditions of high and low EMG levels, with the surprising results that low-level pre-REM EMG was associated with both less recall than high-level EMG (Larson & Foulkes, 1969) and recall of less dreamlike material (Larson & Foulkes, 1969; Pivik, 1971).

As with the autonomic variations, more discrete muscle activity has been related to specific dream content from REM sleep (Grossman, Gardner, Roffwarg, Fekete, Beers, & Weiner, 1973; McGuigan & Tanner, 1970; Stoyva, 1965); the manifestation of motor activity most extensively studied in this regard is eye movement. A positive, nonspecific relationship with eye movement activity has been established for increased recall (Medoff & Foulkes, 1972; Pivik, Halper, & Dement, 1969) and increased dreamlike features, such as vividness and emotionality (Ellman, Antrobus, Arkin, Farber, Luck, Bodnar, Sanders, & Nelson, 1974; Hobson, Goldfrank, & Snyder, 1965). However, reports of increased eye movement density in association with increased activity within the dream report (Berger & Oswald, 1962b; Dement & Wolpert, 1958b; Pivik & Foulkes, 1968) have recently been questioned (Firth & Oswald, 1975; Hauri & Van de Castle, 1973a; Keenan & Krippner, 1970).

More precise relationships between eye movements and recalled mental activity have been examined in the context of what has come to be known as the "scanning" hypothesis. This hypothesis suggests that eye movements elaborated during REM sleep function to scan the visual images of the dream. The literature on this topic varies (for review, see Rechtschaffen, 1973), with reports of specific associations, but more generally with disclaimers, and the issue today remains unresolved. However, there are problems involved in assessing this particular question that underscore the general difficulties encountered in attempting to establish relationships between temporally discrete physiological measures and moment-to-moment variations in the dream experience.

The general paradigm for scanning studies requires two investigators. One investigator monitors the electrographic recordings, searches for distinctive or nondistinctive eye movement patterns, and, upon selecting a pattern, immediately arouses the subject from sleep; the second investigator, ignorant of the polygraphic tracings, interviews the subject, attempting to predict the eye movement sequence based on information related in the interview. This interviewer must be skilled in the knowledge of head–eye movement relationships and in interviewing procedures and techniques. The subject must be highly introspective and an excellent recaller. Under conditions in which these idealized characteristics of subject and interviewer have been approximated, positive results have been obtained only inconsistently.

As an adjunct to experiments of this type, an investigation was conducted (Bussel, Dement, & Pivik, 1972) in which the experimental procedures used to examine the scanning hypothesis during sleep were applied during wakefulness in an attempt to demonstrate the obvious—namely, that waking eye movements function to scan the immediate visual environment. Amazingly, this correlation could not be demonstrated. Subjects could not recall the last few seconds of their experiences and the related eye movement activity prior to the interview in sufficient detail to establish a significant relationship between eye movements and the environment—precisely the kind of psychophysiological relationship required to support the scanning hypothesis. With respect to the waking condition, surely the results derived from problems of recall and attention, and not from the absence of the relationship. Yet in the latter condition subjects were recalling waking experience while in a waking state, a situation with obvious advantages relative to subjects who must recall sleep experiences shortly after awakening from sleep while in a less-than-optimal state of wakefulness. Such demonstra-

tions underscore the difficulties intrinsic to psychophysiological studies of sleep, and serve as a reminder that experimental demands need to be carefully considered in the evaluation of negative results.

More issues were raised than resolved during the decade of psychophysiological research following the discovery of REM sleep. However, the results that were generally agreed upon pointed the way to a new direction in psychophysiological sleep research. The originally anticipated and indicated state-determined relationships (i.e., the presence of dreaming during REM sleep and the absence of mental activity at other times during sleep) were being challenged, bringing into question the validity of measures being assessed as reflections of ongoing cognitive processes. It is interesting, however, that although logically both sides of the psychophysiological coin should have been open to scrutiny, in fact it was the report of the physiological experience of dreaming, or more generally of sleep mentation, upon which the burden of validation fell. This was particularly true with respect to NREM mentation, for, unlike REM sleep, which was associated with EEG patterns compatible with those thought capable of supporting ongoing mental activity, the patterns preceding reports of NREM mentation were more similar to those more commonly associated with waking pathology (e.g., Stage 3 and 4 delta activity) or sedation (Stage 2 spindle activity).

The strongest psychophysiological association emerging from this decade of research, aside from the presence of a Stage 1 EEG pattern and the recall of dreamlike mentation, was that between eye movements and dream content in REM sleep. This relationship between aspects of recalled mental activity and transient physiological events became an integral feature of a major reorientation of physiological and psychophysiological studies of sleep. Fundamentally, this redirection consisted of a shift in focus from state to event relationships—from tonic to phasic physiological and psychophysiological correlations. The first glimmerings of such a differentiation were present in the initial Aserinsky–Dement–Kleitman papers, in which there were indications that sleep stages were not homogeneous behaviors. There were variations in all stage-related physiological measures, and although such variations were generally most pronounced during REM sleep, NREM physiology was not static. Consequently, Moruzzi's (1963, 1965) differentiation of REM sleep into tonic and phasic aspects was, to some extent, an explicit formulation of a research orientation that was already in process. However, in addition to highlighting the heterogeneous features of REM sleep, Moruzzi further suggested that REM-NREM state physiological differences were quantitative and not absolute, and that the temporally contiguous clusters of phasic events (e.g., eye movements, motor and autonomic changes) resulted from the activation of a system different and separate from that responsible for tonic state characteristics. Subsequent physiological research in humans and in other mammals (primarily the cat) substantiated these tonic–phasic distinctions (reviewed in Pivik, 1978).

At the psychophysiological interface, the new orientation was evident in increased attention to discrete physiological variables present immediately prior to content arousals, and in the search for new physiological measures of phasic activity. Interestingly, a physiological event originally described and most intensively studied in the cat became the prototype against which phasic events in the human were evaluated. There were substantive reasons why this event, termed the "PGO spike" because of the regions of the central nervous system from which it was most commonly recorded (namely, the *p*ons, the lateral geniculate bodies, and the *o*ccipital cortex), occupied so prominent a position. Those reasons had to do with the anatomical distribution and physiological correlates of this activity with respect to REM sleep physiology, as well as with the distribution of these events across the sleep cycle. Anatomically, for example, PGO activity was present in regions known to be essential for the occurrence of REM sleep (Jouvet, 1962) and was present throughout the visual system (Bizzi & Brooks, 1963; Brooks, 1967, 1968a). In terms of sleep stage distribution, this activity, although concentrated during REM sleep, occurred sporadically during NREM sleep and characteristically heralded the onset of REM sleep.

Essentially, then, PGO spike activity was most prevalent at a time when dreaming was most prevalent (i.e., during REM sleep) and was most prominent in physiological systems highly associated with dreaming (e.g., the visual system). Furthermore, the occurrence of PGO activity in NREM sleep suggested a physiological basis for reports of NREM mentation. This activity was also observed in association with hallucinatory-like behavior during wakefulness in cats (Dement, Zarcone, Ferguson, Cohen, Pivik, & Barchas, 1969; Jouvet & Delorme, 1965), thereby reinforcing the impression that PGO activation is a correlate of hallucinatory activity. Studies of phasic activity and associated sleep mentation therefore dominated the next wave of psychophysiological sleep studies. A representative overview of the variety of events examined in such studies is presented in Figure 18-4.

Studies were conducted comparing reports following phasic and tonic periods of physiological activation in both REM and NREM sleep. Differences in mentation following "phasic" and "tonic" arousals were observed, but the differences were inconsistent and did not provide a distinctive differentiation between phasic and tonic periods. These studies have been reviewed in detail (Pivik, 1978; Rechtschaffen, 1973), and it is clear that the presence of phasic activity is not a determinant of the presence of mental activity during sleep; that is, although recall may be facilitated by the presence of phasic activity preceding arousals in REM and NREM sleep, recall remains abundant in the absence of phasic events.

If phasic events are not indicative of the general presence of mental activity during sleep, then perhaps an understanding of the relevance of such activity is to be found in a consideration of particular qualitative features of the ongoing mentation. Qualitative aspects of sleep mentation that have received special attention in the context of phasic event correlates include, for example, the presence of passively received, nonintellectualized images (primary visual experiences) as opposed to the active cognitive processing of dream experiences (secondary cognitive elaboration) (Molinari & Foulkes, 1969), and discontinuity and bizarreness of mentation (Foulkes & Pope, 1973; Watson, 1972). However, phasic activity does not correlate consistently even with these more abstract qualitative features of sleep mentation.

One physiological feature of dreaming that has received only passing attention in the general psychophysiological sleep literature, and none relative to the tonic–phasic distinction, is what Rechtschaffen (1978) has termed the "single-mindedness" of dreams—that is, "the strong tendency for a single train of related thoughts and images to persist over extended periods without disruption or competition from other simultaneous thoughts and images" (p. 97). Related to this feature is a characteristic "nonreflectiveness" (Kleitman, 1967; Rechtschaffen, 1978) commonly attendant on the dream experience. This attenuation of the judgmental process is evident in the general absence of awareness during the dream that one is dreaming, as well as in the passive acceptance of events or images that, if experienced during wakefulness, would elicit quite vigorous cognitive or physical reactions. A possible relationship between phasic events and the nonreflective nature of dreams is more fully developed in a later section of this chapter.

SLEEP PSYCHOPHYSIOLOGY: APPLICATION TO ISSUES

The preceding review of psychophysiological sleep studies hints at the tremendous amount of information acquired in the post-REM sleep era and the conceptual framework within which these studies were conducted. Of the many developments prominent during this time, two general areas are singled out for more extensive discussion because they represent conceptual and methodological issues significant in the evolution of psychophysiological sleep research.

The first issue to be considered is concerned with the identification of moments of dreaming; that is, when does the cognitive experience of dreaming take

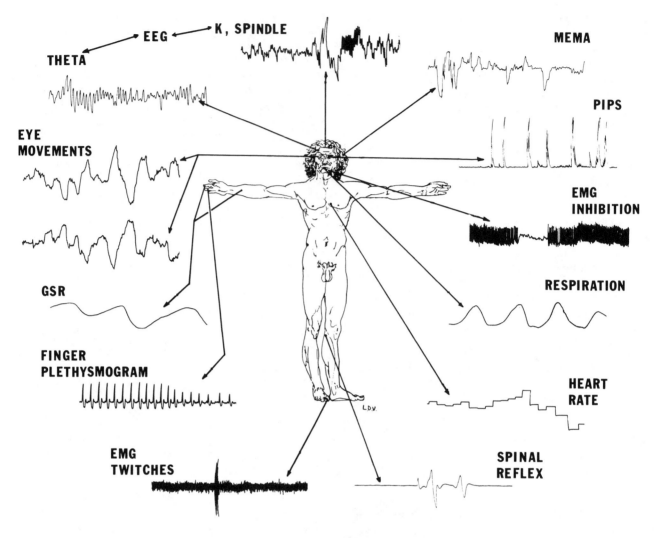

THE PHASIC PROPORTIONS OF MAN

Figure 18-4. Illustrations of various phasically occurring electrophysiological measures that have been investigated in the context of psychophysiological studies of sleep. These variables, with approximate designations of anatomical areas from which they can be recorded, include the following: EEG measures (K complex, spindle, and theta activity); various expressions of muscle activity from auditory (middle ear muscle activity [MEMA]), visual (eye movements, periorbital integrated potentials [PIPS]), and skeletal musculature (facial EMG inhibition, spinal reflexes, and EMG twitches) systems; and autonomic activity (galvanic skin response [GSR], finger plethysomogram, respiration, and heart rate). See text for a more complete listing and discussion of phasic variables.

place, and have psychophysiological studies aided in the process of identification? The second issue relates to an interpretation and possible meaning of phasic events.

Identifying Moments of Dreaming

The past quarter-century of psychophysiological sleep research has been spent either trying to identify moments of dreaming, or, assuming such moments have been identified, studying qualitative aspects of the recalled material. As previously stated, although there has been a wide range of definitions of what constitutes the dream, there is a consensus that such cognitive behavior is commonly experienced in association with sleep. However, it is not sufficient merely to loosely associate the experience of dreaming with sleep, for the nature of this association has relevance beyond our interest in dreams. The precise nature of this relationship is critical to an understanding of the full range of normal mind–body relationships, and may clarify our understanding of abnormal or pathological mind–body conditions. It is important, then, to specify the time of dream occurrence as precisely as possible, and this can only be accomplished by associating the dream report with dream physiology. But what is the dream physiology? Is it the sleep physiology preceding arousal, or is it the physiology of the postarousal (hypnopompic) period most immediately preceding the dream report? Is the dream report based on an experience that occurs during the sleep, or is it a reflection of the mind re-engaging the external environment in the process of awakening?[1] Furthermore, if dreams are a product of the mind in sleep, are there convincing logical or empirical considerations indicating that they occur only during particular stages of sleep (e.g., REM sleep), or is dreaming a more generalized phenomenon defying stage localization?

The acceptance of the dream report as the reflection of a sleep experience has been challenged primarily because the dream report is the product of the waking mind and is elicited following a period of sleep at a time when the subject is not optimally aroused (Broughton, 1968; Feltin & Broughton, 1968; Scott, 1969; Tebbs, 1972). This fundamental difference between the state in which the experience occurs and the state in which the dream report is given—that is, state dependency—has been alluded to previously. The most extreme position regarding this state-dependent feature of dream experiences and dream reports takes the stance that all dreaming takes place during the postarousal waking-up period (Goblot, 1896; Hall & Raskin, 1980), and that this postarousal mental activity results from processes functioning to effect

> a reestablishment of the cognitive structures and processes that were disestablished in falling asleep, reengagement with the world of consciousness from which we were disengaged during sleep, reorientation to a space-time world from which we were absent, and the resumption of the continuity of our waking existence which was broken by sleep.
>
> [This] theory further asserts that the sequence of cognitive activities during the period of waking up proceeds from confusion to clarity, from disorientation to orientation in time and space, and from random, fragmented, disorganized, impaired thinking to organized conceptual thinking.
>
> [This] theory also states that the elements in the postsleep reports are verbal descriptors of the cognitive processing of stimuli (immediate external and bodily, as well as past memories) acting upon us when we are waking up. (Hall & Raskin, 1980, p. 31)

Besides the attribution of sleep-related cognitive experiences to the transitional period between sleep and more complete arousal, salient features of this position are that sleep is a time of unconsciousness,

and that bodily sensations and past memories present during arousal comprise the materials from which the postarousal reports are constructed.

Is sleep a time of unconsciousness? Studies demonstrating the possibility of behavioral response during sleep (Brown & Cartwright, 1978; Evans, Gustafson, O'Connell, Orne, & Shor, 1970; Granda & Hammack, 1961; McDonald, Schicht, Fratier, Shallenberger, & Edwards, 1975; Oswald, Taylor, & Treisman, 1960; Williams, Morlock, & Morlock, 1966) and the ability to estimate elapsed time accurately over a period of sleep (Carlson, Feinberg, & Goodenough, 1978; Latash & Danilin, 1972) illustrate that sleep is not a behaviorally inert state and that mechanisms of perception and information processing are functional and functioning during sleep. However, behavioral demonstration of consciousness during sleep is not evidence that this consciousness is performing dreamwork.

Data more directly relevant to this issue, although collected in studies conducted under the assumption that mentation is an ongoing process during sleep, can nonetheless be re-evaluated in the present context. In these studies, attempts were made to influence the content of postarousal reports predictably by altering presupposed ongoing mentation via either presleep manipulations or introjections of stimuli during sleep. The presleep manipulations included distorting the waking perceptual world of subjects via visual-field-inverting prisms or colored goggles (Prevost, 1976; Roffwarg, Herman, Bowe-Anders, & Tauber, 1978) and exposing subjects to stressful films (Goodenough, Witkins, Koulack, & Cohen, 1975) or to stimuli for which they had a phobic fear (Brunette & De Koninck, 1977). However, since the imposed effects were present during wakefulness preceding sleep, their presence following arousal could be explained by a reactivation of previous waking memories not requiring active conscious processes in the intervening sleep period.

A second area of study has involved attempts to influence ongoing mentation in a more direct manner by exposing the sleeping subject to stimuli, making arousals soon after, and examining the elicited content for evidence of stimulus incorporation. These studies have involved stimulating subjects with a variety of somatic, auditory, and visual stimuli (Baldridge, 1966; Baldridge, Whitman, Kramer, Ornstein, & Lansky, 1965; Dement & Wolpert, 1958b; Foulkes, Larson, Swanson, & Rardin, 1969; Koulack, 1969). Such studies have found evidence of incorporation, but sensations evoked by the stimuli may have persisted into the postarousal period, thereby compromising the use of such demonstrations as conclusive evidence of incorporation by sleep consciousness.

To demonstrate convincingly that sleep may support mental activity demands the identification of an objective indicator of such activity without effecting

---

1. The possibility that postarousal reports are confabulated in an effort to please the experimenter is a variant of this hypnopompic hypothesis. However, on empirical (as reviewed by Foulkes, 1967) and logical (as discussed by Rechtschaffen, 1967) grounds, the contribution of active confabulation to the production of postarousal reports is minimal.

sleep disruption. This requires either remotely effecting specified variations in sleep psychology, which would be linked in a predictable way with sleep physiology, or taking advantage of spontaneously occurring physiological variations, which would distinctly reflect ongoing mental processes. Fundamental to either approach is a peripherally accessible physiological measure whose activity conveys specific information other than, and in addition to, variations along a dimension of intensity. The only measure currently available in human recordings that consistently provides such information is eye movement activity. EOG deflections reflect not only eye movement density, but directionality as well. It is not known why the extraocular musculature is spared from generalized motor inhibitory influences present during REM sleep, but the potential for psychophysiological correspondence presented by this unique feature of sleep physiology has been extensively explored.

The notion that the eye movements of REM sleep were intimately involved with dream imagery was expressed soon after the discovery of REM sleep. Aserinsky and Kleitman (1955) believed that these eye movements were "involved in the visual imagery accompanying dreaming" (p. 30), and Dement (1955) felt that they were "a direct result of visual experience, rather than merely a result of heightened nervous activity" (p. 268). The most explicit statement of this relationship is embodied in the scanning hypothesis, which, as previously discussed, remains unresolved. For the purpose of the present discussion it is not essential that the generality of a relationship between eye movement and dream content be established, for convincing instances of correspondence would provide sufficient empirical evidence that mentation does occur during sleep. A most convincing demonstration of correspondence would be the specification of eye movement patterns by predetermination of REM dream content. Two conditions in which such prespecification of dream content may occur are (1) the determination of dream content by posthypnotic suggestions made in the waking state (Barber, Walker, & Hahn, 1973; Stoyva, 1961; Tart, 1964; Tart & Dick, 1970), and (2) the spontaneous occurrence of recurrent dreams (Klein, Fiss, Shollar, Dalbeck, Warga, & Gwozdz, 1971). Despite the appropriateness and unique relevance that data from these conditions would have for the scanning issue, studies in these areas have been conducted for purposes other than demonstrating specific relationships between eye movement and dream content, and there is no mention in these reports of observations pertinent to the scanning hypothesis.

The relationship between eye movement and dream content has been most vigorously pursued in studies specifically designed to relate individual eye movements to visual sequences in the postarousal reports. During the course of these studies, instances

of remarkable correspondence have been observed. For example, an extended series of horizontal eye movements during REM was followed by a report of the subject's having observed two individuals throwing tomatoes at each other (Dement & Kleitman, 1957b). Another example of striking correspondence is depicted in Figure 18-5. The nystagmoid eye movements present in this figure were followed by a report that the subject had been viewing the painted lines extending out from the street curbing for parallel parking as he was riding by in a car (Pivik & Dement, unpublished results). The reported dream experience provided the precise perceptual situation required to elicit the observed nystagmoid eye movements!

Proponents of the Goblot (1896) hypothesis have conceded that general support for the scanning hypothesis would refute the postarousal dreaming hypothesis. Instances of correspondence such as those cited above have been dismissed with the suggestion that "direction of the eye movements [might] be one of the stimuli available to the subjects while they were waking up" (Hall & Raskin, 1980, p. 10). However, this suggestion that physiological information regarding eye movement directionality persists into the waking state is not supported by psychophysiological data, which indicate an absence of proprioceptive feedback from the extraocular musculature (Merton, 1964). This unusual feature of eye musculature excludes the possibility that information regarding eye position can be derived from muscle stretch. Consequently, the likelihood is virtually nonexistent that postarousal reports that so precisely match eye movement activity preceding arousal can be based on physiological information occurring during the process of

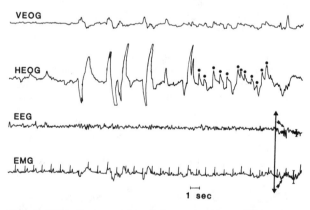

Figure 18-5. An example of the correspondence between eye movement and dream content. The figure illustrates the occurrence of horizontal nystagnoid eye movements (designated by dots) during REM sleep. Immediately following these eye movements, the subject was awakened (vertical line, lower channels) and interviewed. The subject related a dream experience (see text for elaboration) that provided the precise perceptual conditions required to elicit optokinetic nystagmus.

waking up. Whether this correspondence is true for all eye movements of all REM periods may never be demonstrated, but the fact that it can sometimes be demonstrated is very strong evidence that the associated mentation is an ongoing property of sleep.

In other instances lacking such physiological indices, the acceptance of the postarousal report as a true representation of sleep experience can be guided by logical considerations such as the following, suggested by Rechtschaffen (1967) and summarized here:

1. *Parsimony*—interpretations requiring the fewest assumptions are favored.
2. *Prevalence*—phenomena known to occur most frequently are favored over those of rare occurrence. For example, in the absence of indications of impaired memory in the recall processes in wakefulness, the subject's postarousal report is accepted as a valid representation of his or her experience, rather than questioned on the grounds of cognitive impairment.
3. *Plausibility*—an extension of the prevalence guideline, which, however, "gives special emphasis to frequency and occurrence in given situations" (Rechtschaffen, 1967, p. 7). For example, although it could be assumed that subjects are lying when questioned about the presence and details of dream experiences, on the basis of current understanding of the motivational factors promoting lying, one would consider it unlikely that subjects would lie so consistently about dream reports.
4. *Private experience*—in the absence of objective indices, there is a strong tendency to accept the existence of phenomena if they have been part of one's own experience.

On the basis of the considerations proposed by these guidelines, together with the general physiological activation present during REM sleep and the special relationship that at times exists between eye movements and postarousal reports, the conclusion seems compelling that these reports are descriptions of sleep experiences and not merely hypnopompic reveries. This is not to say that aspects of these reports are not modified by physiological and cognitive processes activated during this period of reawakening, and certainly, as Hall and Raskin (1980) suggest, the reawakening process needs further study. However, the psychophysiological data based on reports following arousals from REM sleep can be most readily explained by assuming that cognitive processes are operational during sleep.

The problems encountered in providing convincing data to place the dream experience into REM sleep are significantly compounded when attempting to validate NREM mentation similarly. Despite the high incidence of reports of mentation from NREM sleep, the demonstration of specific incorporation of audi-tory stimuli into postarousal reports presented during NREM sleep (Foulkes, 1967), and unsolicited examples such as that presented in Figure 18-6, NREM mentation remained largely rejected as a valid psychophysiological phenomenon for many years. The arguments presented by supporters of Goblot's (1896) hypothesis for the attribution of dreaming to the postarousal state were quite similar to those given by investigators who, although not questioning the veracity of dream experiences during REM sleep, were unable to accept the possibility of similar experiences during NREM sleep. As previously discussed, the validity of the NREM report was questioned not only because such reports generally differed qualitatively from those elicited following REM sleep arousals, but also because of the absence during NREM sleep of specifiable physiological indices of ongoing mentation, such as were present in REM sleep. The search for such indices to legitimize NREM mentation extended over two decades, and this research, although contributing to our knowledge of the descriptive physiology of human sleep (and, in some instances, to the cross-species comparative physiology of sleep), failed to provide the sought-after physiological justification for NREM mentation. Currently, largely on the basis of considerations contained in Rechtschaffen's (1967) logical guides, NREM mentation is generally accepted as a reliable, bona fide reflection of cognitive processes ongoing during NREM sleep (Herman, Ellman, & Roffwarg, 1978).

Since the majority of NREM reports, particularly those elicited at sleep onset, have dreamlike features, dreaming cannot be said to be an exclusive feature of REM sleep. Moreover, the previously cited reports (Foulkes & Fleisher, 1975; Foulkes & Scott, 1973; Galton, 1883/1911; Spanos & Stam, 1979) that mental experiences of normal individuals during relaxed wakefulness may also contain dreamlike features similar to those usually associated with REM sleep reports suggest that the cognitive experiences subsumed under the term "dreaming" are not even confined to sleep. Consequently, although it is possible to identify periods of time during which there is a high probability that dreaming is occurring (e.g., during REM sleep), dreaming is not the exclusive property of any stage of sleep, or even of sleep in general. A recently formulated definition of "dreaming," with slight modification to include the occurrence of mental activity with dreamlike qualities during wakefulness as well as sleep, provides the best fit to the psychophysiological sleep–wakefulness literature as it now exists. This definition considers the dream as a "form of thought, usually occurring during sleep, having specifiable properties. The quality of these properties depends on the . . . state during which this thought process occurs" (Fiss, 1979, p. 43).

Among the logical consequences that follow from the acceptance of such a broad definition of "dream-

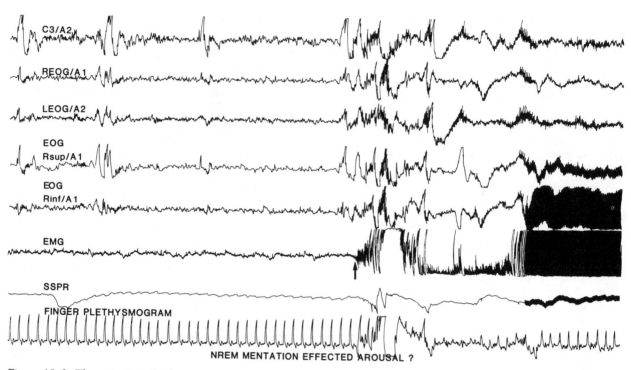

Figure 18-6. These tracings depict a spontaneous arousal (onset designated by vertical arrow, EMG channel) from Stage 2 sleep, immediately following which the subject began to remove her electrodes. High-amplitude interference in the lower tracings resulted from the removal of some electrodes before the experimenter could fully arouse the subject. Upon being asked why she was removing the electrodes, the subject replied that she dreamed the experimenter had instructed her to do so. The subject was questioned more extensively regarding the experience and was specifically asked whether she felt that the imagined instructions might have occurred while she was awakening, but she persisted in allocating the experience to a "dream" occurring during sleep.

ing" is that the curtailment or elimination of REM sleep does not constitute the elimination of dreaming. This was the premise underlying experiments of "dream deprivation" (Dement, 1960), in which it was assumed that the significance of the psychological experience of dreaming could be tested by the curtailment of REM sleep. The results of the initial experiments in this area were interpreted as indicating that REM sleep or dreaming was essential to waking psychological normality (Dement & Fisher, 1963; Sampson, 1965, 1966). However, subsequent research has not supported this interpretation of the REM deprivation data (for review, see Vogel, 1975). REM sleep deprivation not only does not entail negative consequences for waking behavior that can be attributed to the prevention of psychological experiences normally expressed during this stage of sleep, but in certain situations the curtailment of REM sleep may have beneficial effects on waking clinical symptomatology (Vogel, Thurmond, Gibbons, Sloan, Boyd, & Walker, 1975).

Perhaps there is a basic physiological substrate for hallucinations, and this substrate becomes spontaneously active during REM sleep. Dreaming, then, particularly of the type occurring during REM sleep,

might be considered as a prototypic hallucinatory experience. Such a link between dreaming and hallucinations had been postulated prior to the discovery of the relationship between REM sleep and dreaming (Freud 1900/1955; Jackson, 1958; Jung, 1944). However, if such a link exists, it is not obviously expressed, for the results of a variety of approaches attempting to reveal the nature of this postulated association between dreaming and hallucinations have been disappointing. These have included generally unremarkable findings regarding the sleep and dreams of mentally ill patients (Caldwell & Domino, 1967; Dement, 1955; Gresham, Agnew, & Williams, 1965; Kramer & Roth, 1973; Snyder, Anderson, Bunney, Kupfer, Scott, & Wyatt, 1968), and the absence of physiological signs of REM sleep during wakefulness in actively hallucinating patients (Rechtschaffen, Schulsinger, & Mednick, 1964). Although some studies (but not all; see Vogel, 1975) have reported reduced post-REM deprivation rebounds in actively ill schizophrenic patients relative to those present in normal subjects or in the same patients during remission (Azumi, Takahashi, Takahashi, Maruyama, & Kikuti, 1967; Gillin, Buchsbaum, Jacobs, Fram, Williams, Vaughn, Mellon, Snyder, & Wyatt, 1974; Zarcone, Gulevich, Pivik, &

Dement, 1968), such manipulations have not eventuated in increased adverse physiological effects during wakefulness (Hoyt & Singer, 1978; Vogel, 1975; Vogel *et al.*, 1975). Still, the results of these studies and others involving REM deprivation (Cartwright, 1966; Cartwright, Monroe, & Palmer, 1967; Cartwright & Ratzel, 1972) have been interpreted as suggesting that under certain circumstances some feature of REM sleep, perhaps related to hallucinatory behavior, may be displaced into wakefulness (Fiss, 1979).

To test this concept of displacement in normal subjects, an attempt was made (Halper, Pivik, & Dement, 1969) to experimentally recreate the conditions existing in the above-described investigations involving actively ill psychotics (i.e., REM deprivation in conjunction with the presence of waking hallucinations). Following five consecutive nights of baseline recordings, subjects ($n = 3$) were REM-deprived by arousals at the onset of each REM period for two consecutive nights, and then uninterrupted recovery sleep was recorded for the next five nights. On the day immediately following each night of deprivation, subjects were maintained in hypnotic trances for 2.5 hr—a time period approximately equivalent to the amount of REM sleep eliminated. During these trances, subjects experienced a variety of cognitive and perceptual "hallucinatory" experiences. No significant differences were found between the amount of recovery REM sleep following this procedure and that following a similar procedure in the same subjects without the waking-hypnotic manipulation. Consequently, under conditions maximizing the postulated need for displacement of hallucinatory activities attendant during REM sleep by curtailing REM sleep periods, and providing an avenue for expressing such activities by initiating hypnotic hallucinatory experiences during wakefulness, displacement could not be demonstrated. It is known that electrographic characteristics of the hypnotic state do not mimic those associated with REM sleep (Brady & Rosner, 1966; Chertok & Kramarz, 1959). However, if features of hallucinatory experiences are state-determined, then hallucinations during hypnosis and sleep might have different physiological attributes and still be functionally equivalent.

Instead of resolving issues, negative results often underscore the need for further study. The outcome of the Halper *et al.* (1969) study is a case in point. These results could indicate that the hallucinatory activity of REM sleep and hypnosis are not interchangeable, or that such a substitution is not possible in normal subjects, or perhaps that the concept of displacement is unsound and a different phenomenon underlies the rebound reduction following REM deprivation in actively ill psychotic patients. At the moment, our psychophysiological data do not provide a basis for choosing from among these alternatives. However, the application of psychophysiological techniques has provided a sound basis from which questions regarding the identification of moments of dreaming, and theories relating processes of dreaming to more general processes of hallucinations, can be more confidently and effectively approached.

Phasic Events: Implications for Consciousness

The identification of a system of phasic physiological events that becomes spontaneously active during sleep has been of immense heuristic value, but the psychological relevance of these events has remained elusive. The development of this area of psychophysiological sleep research has been influenced to an unusual degree by an animal model of PGO spike activity. The fundamental descriptive characteristics of this phasic event system have derived from studies in the cat. Furthermore, because of the brain stem origin of these events, the interrelatedness among phasic events (particularly the relationship to eye movements), and the distribution of phasic activity within sleep stages, studies of PGO activity in the cat have formed the background against which psychophysiological studies have been formulated and at times evaluated. The main features of the correspondence between the distribution of PGO spike activity in the cat and the incidence of sleep mentation have recently been summarized as follows:

1. PGO spikes are highly concentrated in REM sleep, a time when dreaming is most prominent.

2. Measured at the pontine level, spikes increase in amplitude and frequency within a REM period (Brooks, 1968 [b]), a pattern which finds a parallel in the increased intensity of dreaming as a function of REM time (Foulkes, 1966; Takeo, 1970). Interestingly enough, if the measure of spike activity were taken at the level of the lateral geniculate nucleus [LGN], the correlation would be reversed since LGN spikes decrease in frequency and amplitude as a function of REM time (Brooks, 1967).

3. Spiking during NREM sleep is most intense in the 30–60 sec preceding each REM period, but mental activity is not suddenly enhanced during ascending Stage 2, which temporally corresponds to this time of increased spike activity in the cat (Larson & Foulkes, 1969; Pivik *et al.*, 1969) and may suffer qualitatively and quantitatively relative to post-REM Stage 2 (Pivik *et al.*, 1969) which would correspond to a time marked by the virtual absence [of] spike activity in the cat.

4. Deprivation of REM sleep in the cat increases the density of spiking within REM sleep during the ensuing rebound, and increases the incidence of NREM-spike activity during the deprivation manipulation (Dement, 1969 [a]; Dement [Ferguson, Cohen, & Barchas, 1969]; Dusan-Peyrethon, [Peyrethon, & Jouvet], 1967; Ferguson, [Henriksen, McGarr, Belenky, Mitchell, Gonda, Cohen, & Dement], 1968). Correspondingly, it would be expected that REM deprivation in the human would

intensify REM dream content during the recovery period and enhance NREM mentation during the deprivation procedure. With respect to the former, both negative (Antrobus, Arkin, & Toth, 1970; Carroll, Lewis, & Oswald, 1969; Firth, 1972; Foulkes, Pivik, Ahrens, & Swanson, 1968) and positive (Greenberg, Pearlman, Fingar, Kantrowitz, & Kawliche, 1970; Pivik & Foulkes, 1966) results have been reported. Studies looking for the postulated intensification of NREM mentation during REM deprivation have been few, and the results negative (Antrobus et al., 1970; Arkin, Antrobus, Toth, & Baker, 1968; Foulkes et al., 1968), but these results are based upon either small numbers of awakenings or did not sample from all NREM sleep stages and are accordingly limited in their generality. [However, more recent investigations of this issue using larger numbers of subjects have also reported negative results; see Arkin, Antrobus, Ellman, & Farber, 1978.]

5. PGO spikes are virtually absent at sleep onset, whereas several reports (Foulkes & Vogel, 1965; Foulkes et al., 1966; Vogel et al., 1972) are consistent in demonstrating a great deal of very dreamlike activity occurring at this time in the human. (Pivik, 1978, p. 257)

It is evident that these physiological and psychological data provide only a general approximation of one another. Moreover, more detailed reviews of the relationship between moment-to-moment variations in qualitative aspects of mental activity during sleep and the occurrence of presumptive PGO analogues have not revealed consistent psychophysiological associations (Pivik, 1978; Rechtschaffen, 1973). Conceptually, the situation is further complicated by the fact that these various PGO analogues issue from different sensory and motor systems and at times, particularly in NREM sleep, occur asynchronously (Benson & Zarcone, 1979; Pessah & Roffwarg, 1972). This asynchrony, often reflected in event-specific correlations with features of mentation, has given rise to the possibility that there are multiple PGO generators acting in concert primarily at times of intense activity. Arguments made in favor of retention of a single generator theory (Pessah & Roffwarg, 1972) have the support of the lesion literature in the cat (Jouvet, 1962, 1972; Morrison & Pompeiano, 1970; Pompeiano, 1967), which suggests a primary brain stem source of phasic activity. Furthermore, there is evidence that PGO spike activity may be of fundamental significance for the REM state (Dement, 1969a; Dement, Ferguson, Cohen, & Barchas, 1969; Dement, Zarcone, Ferguson, et al., 1969). Perhaps these primary brain stem discharges have associated with them some unique cognitive correlate beyond, or in addition to, fleeting psychological activity reflecting end-organ activation. If there is a significance of such phasic activity for consciousness, then perhaps it is to be found in more general behavioral and response characteristics of PGO spike activity. Besides a relationship of PGO activity to generalized phasic in-

creases in unit activity (Hobson & McCarley, 1971), indicating that the PGO system is related to a highly excitatory process, there is little in the way of behavioral consequences of such activity that can be learned from the sleeping organism. However, through pharmacological and lesioning procedures, state and event correlates of REM sleep have been displaced into wakefulness where behavioral correlates of these activities may be investigated. For example, localized lesions in the region of the brain stem nucleus locus ceruleus (Henley & Morrison, 1974; Jouvet & Delorme, 1965; Morrison, Mann, Hendricks, & Starkweather, 1979) have been associated with the display of complex motor patterns suggesting the stalking of imaginary prey, as well as other "hallucinatory-like" behaviors. These behaviors, which occur following episodes of NREM sleep at a time when REM sleep would be expected, have been interpreted as occurring during episodes of paradoxical sleep without atonia. In another experiment involving a pharmacological manipulation (Dement, Zarcone, Ferguson, et al., 1969) in which PGO spike activity appeared during subsequent drug-induced wakefulness, animals were observed to orient abruptly toward a stimulus apparent only to the animals following spontaneous bursts of PGO spikes.

More recently, arguments have been presented that PGO activity represents a startle response to bursts of brain stem neuronal activity; furthermore, it has been shown that brain stem potentials similar in morphology to spontaneous PGO spikes may be elicited by auditory and tactile stimuli during natural wakefulness and spontaneous sleep (Bowker & Morrison, 1976, 1977). There are, however, significant differences in response characteristics differentiating the elicited potentials from spontaneously occurring PGO spikes, the most outstanding of which is the *nonhabituating quality of spontaneous PGO spike activity*. Although PGO-spike-like activity can be elicited during wakefulness or sleep, this activity tends to habituate and disappear when repetitively evoked (Morrison, 1979).

An interesting parallel can be drawn between the last-mentioned observation and the response characteristics of a human sleep phasic event, the K complex. K-complex waveforms, which are considered to be evoked potentials, occur spontaneously during sleep but may be elicited during either wakefulness or sleep (Roth, Shaw, & Green, 1956). When externally elicited, these potentials are subject to habituation (Nakagawa, Nakagawa, & Takahashi, 1966; Pampiglione, 1952). Endogenously evoked sleep K complexes, however, do not habituate. A remarkable example of this nonhabituating feature of spontaneously occurring sleep K complexes is presented in Figure 18-7. An example of spontaneously occurring PGO spike activity preceding the onset of REM sleep (comparable to the K complexes in Figure 18-7) is presented in

Figure 18-8. Although these displays of pre-REM phasic activity may eventuate in arousal, generally they do not. The ability of the central nervous system to tolerate repetitive, potentially arousing stimuli without habituation or behavioral arousal constitutes an unusual and significant feature of spontaneously occurring phasic activity.

Another feature distinguishing waking and REM PGO spike activity is the occurrence of these activities relative to eye movements. PGO spikes generally *follow* eye movements in wakefulness and *precede* REM eye movements (Brooks, 1968a, 1968b; Jeannerod & Sakai, 1970; Kiyono & Jeannerod, 1967). Moreover, waking PGO waves are influenced by retinal input, whereas PGO waves during sleep are determined by extraretinal processes (Brooks & Gershon, 1971; Jeannerod & Sakai, 1970). Although both types of PGO activity are correlated with increased brain stem neuronal activity, the consequences of each type—for example, in terms of required behavioral responses or information processing—may differ considerably. It would seem practical and perhaps essential for the organism to be able to differentiate the basis for heightened bursts of brain stem activity, particularly in view of the presence of frequently occurring, endogenously determined periodic activations of such activity as occurs in REM sleep. PGO spikes may serve this purpose by providing a neuronal signal to components of the central nervous system indicating the endogenous or exogenous source of elevated levels of brain stem activity. Such a view is in agreement with a previous suggestion that the PGO activity of wakefulness and REM reflect slightly different aspects of a common phenomenon, and that the best experimental route to understanding PGO activity during sleep would be through an understanding of PGO activity during wakefulness (Brooks, 1973).

If bursts of brain stem activity from a primary phasic event source are related to sleep mentation, how might this activity find cognitive expression? This question might be most directly answered by examining the cognitive activity accompanying instances during wakefulness when PGO-like phasic activity is present. However, such instances have not been documented in humans. Perhaps the closest approximation to a condition in which there is a sudden disruption of waking physiology by the intrusion of PGO activity occurs during REM-onset episodes in narcoleptics. The mentation accompanying these REM-onset episodes consists of a curious mix of thoughts and sensations from wakefulness and sleep, and not wild hallucinatory activity (Ribstein, 1976; Vogel, 1976). Interestingly, these narcoleptic experiences are characterized by feelings of greater control over mentation and more awareness of the environment—nonhallucinatory features that contrast with previously discussed characterizations of REM mentation as nonreflective and single-minded (Rechtschaffen, 1978b).

However, these characteristics of mental activity during REM-onset episodes suggest a basis for interpreting PGO spike activity during both wakefulness and sleep. Perhaps by conveying information regarding the source (external or internal) of activation, PGO activity provides a physiological basis for reality testing, which is expressed at the cognitive level in sleep mentation by the absence of reflectiveness. For example, the more reflective, less hallucinatory features of narcoleptic REM-onset mentation could be associated with the presence of a mix of waking and sleep PGO activity. The general nonreflective quality of REM dreams, on the other hand, would follow from the knowledge that the central nervous system activity accompanying this mentation is endogenously determined and therefore not subject to, or requiring, the cognitive evaluation and response demands as would the same experience externally generated.

Since the exception proves the rule, instances standing in apparent contradiction to the postulated relationship must be examined and evaluated. Two such examples of sleep mentation that are not characterized by the quality of nonreflectiveness are the lucid dream and the nightmare. In the lucid dream, the subject seems to be "located in a world or environment that he intellectually knows is unreal . . . while *simultaneously* experiencing the overall quality of his consciousness as having the clarity, the lucidity of his ordinary waking [consciousness]" (Tart, 1979, p. 255). Apparently, lucid dreams are often initiated when, during the dream,

> the dreamer [in ordinary dream consciousness] notices that some dream event does not make sense by ordinary consciousness standards, leading to the realization that he is dreaming. Following this realization, a major change in his pattern of mental functioning, usually quite rapid, is felt, and the dreamer wakes up in terms of his general pattern of consciousness; but he still experiences himself as located in the dream world. (Tart, 1979, p. 256)

In the nightmare or REM anxiety dream (Kahn, Fisher, & Edwards, 1978), there is complete acceptance of the reality of the ongoing mentation, as well as a strong cognitive, autonomic, and motor response to the content, which generally eventuates in arousal. In this latter situation it would be expected that information necessary to evaluate the experience as "real" or "unreal" is either lacking or misleading. It would therefore be predicted either that PGO analogues would be absent or that the temporal patterning of such events would mimic what would occur if the experience were externally generated. For example, in terms of specific PGO analogue such as the periorbital integrated potential (PIP)—which is generally considered to be an eye movement prepotential—it would be predicted that this event either would be absent or would follow eye movement activity in nightmares or REM anxiety dreams.

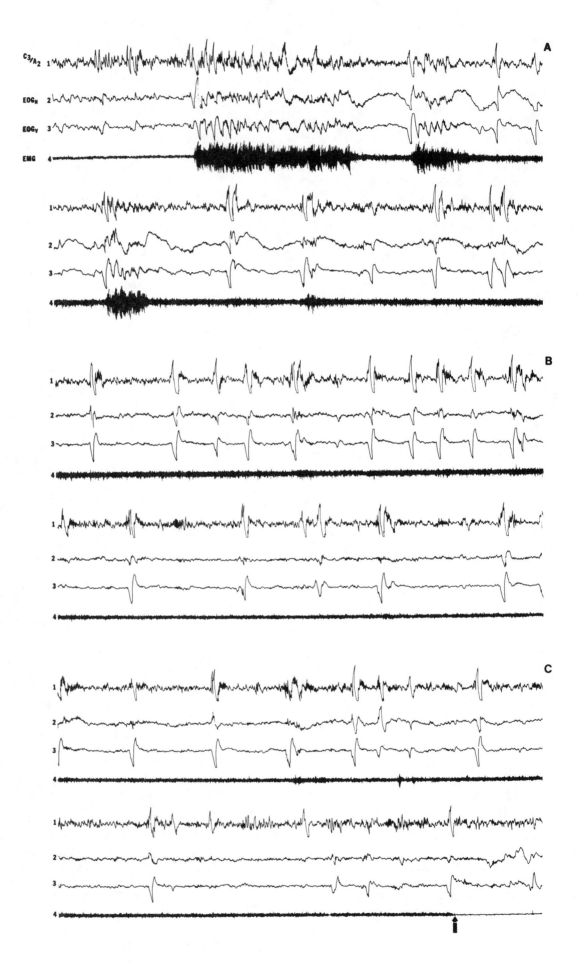

C3/A2 1

EOGH 2

EOGv 3

EMG 4

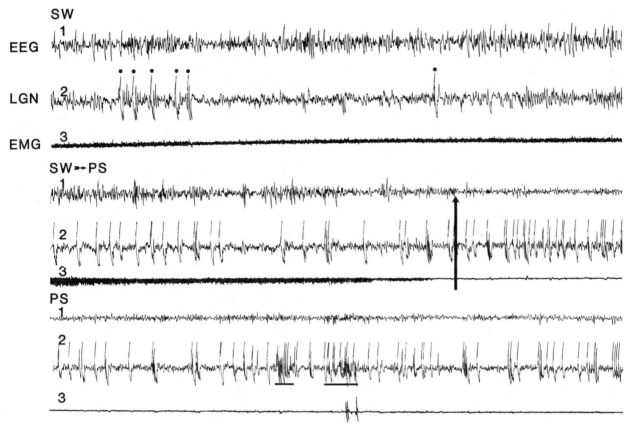

Figure 18-8. The transition between slow-wave (SW) and paradoxical sleep (PS) in the cat. Spontaneous PGO spike activity recorded from electrodes implanted in the lateral geniculate nucleus (LGN) occurred in isolated fashion (designated by dots in the upper SW tracings) preceding PS onset (vertical arrow SW → PS tracings), and singly and in clusters during PS (underscored in lower PS tracings).

The behavior of phasic events during lucid dreams is more difficult to anticipate. Unlike the situation at sleep onset in narcoleptics, where there is an admixture of stimuli from the internal and external environments, in the lucid dream the individual is aware that he or she is in the dream world and consciously reflects on events in the dream world while remaining in physiologically normal REM sleep. In terms of the postulated relationship between PGO activity and reflectiveness, the simultaneous conscious experiencing of the real and unreal in the lucid dream would suggest that the relationship of PGO analogues to ongoing sensory–motor experiences would remain in the usual sleep-related order. However, since (except in well-practiced situations) reflection and control are maximized by a reduction in sensory–motor experiences, a reduction in phasic activity might be expected. There is indirect support for such a prediction: Following arousals from REM sleep after bursts of eye movements, reports are characterized by primary visual, noncognitively elaborated experience, whereas arousals made in the absence of eye movement activity are followed by reports characterized by more secondary cognitive elaboration (Foulkes & Pope, 1973; Medoff & Foulkes, 1972; Molinari & Foulkes, 1969). Moreover, recent preliminary work by Ogilvie, Hunt, Sawicki, and McGowan (1978) suggests that during lucid dreams there is a shift toward increased alpha activity and decreased eye movement activity.

Should we expect to find any features of PGO activity during waking hallucinations or psychosis? Clearly, the physiology of waking hallucinations is not isomorphic with REM state physiology. Furthermore, phasic event physiology and the consequences and correlates of these events have not been demonstrated

Figure 18-7. An unusually long series of spontaneously occurring K complexes in Stage 2 sleep. These events, grouped in three 2-min blocks (A, B, and C) were dispersed over a 6-min period, commencing with movements (EMG tracings in the upper pair of recordings) and terminating at the onset of REM sleep (vertical arrow, lower tracings of C, designating the initial onset of the EMG inhibition and EEG desynchronization).

during wakefulness in psychotics. However, manifestations of physiological activity may be altered by state-related background activity. Consequently, even if a PGO analogue does accompany hallucinatory activity and can be recorded during REM sleep in the human, its occurrence may go unrecognized during waking hallucinatory activity, because sleep–wakefulness state differences may alter the morphological expression of the event. Still, the occurrence of endogenously determined phasic activity may be reflected in other behaviors associated with psychosis, such as difficulties in pursuit eye movement tracking performance (Holzman, Proctor, & Hughes, 1973; Pivik, 1979; Shagass, Roemer, & Amadeo, 1976), or may underlie the increased distractibility and difficulty with information processing that are characteristic of psychosis (Blum, Livingston, & Shader, 1969; Bush, 1977; Hemsley & Zawada, 1976).

SUMMARY STATEMENT

In recent psychophysiological history, there is no area where mind–body relationships have been so intensely pursued as in studies of correlations between sleep psychology and physiology. The vigor and relentlessness of this pursuit were fueled by investigators' fascination with two related behaviors, one physiological (sleep) and the other cognitive (dreaming), and ignited by Aserinsky and Kleitman's (1953) report that moments of dreaming could be identified with the occurrence of a unique constellation of physiological events during sleep. Since that seminal report, views regarding both sleep and dreaming have undergone several marked adjustments. Among the major revelations that psychophysiological sleep studies have disclosed have been the following: (1) Dreaming is a fundamental aspect of human behavior, occurring on a daily basis and in quantities, even conservatively estimated, that rival time spent in many other behaviors in which we daily engage. (2) Dreaming, even rigidly defined, is not exclusive to REM sleep, but occurs as well during NREM sleep; furthermore, dreamlike mentation may be demonstrated in normal subjects in relaxed wakefulness.

These studies, although somewhat demystifying the dream, have contributed more to an awareness of conditions under which dreamlike mentation occurs, or can occur, than to an understanding of why dreaming occurs or why we dream what we dream. The latter issues of dream function and dream process and construction would seem to require an understanding and integration of sleeping and waking cognitive processes and experiences, and such an approach is now under way and gaining momentum (Foulkes, 1978; Foulkes & Kerr, 1980). With respect to the former issue of conditions conducive to dreaming, dreamlike experiences in the "normal" individual seem to require some degree of cognitive and sensory withdrawal or disengagement from the immediate external environment; the more complete this withdrawal and the longer its occurrence, the more dreamlike the mentation. These statements are supported by empirical observations that dreamlike mentation occurs during relaxed wakefulness with eyes closed; that reports from sleep arousals increase in dreamlike quality across the night; and that REM sleep, a state characterized by increased arousal thresholds and, accordingly, a more extensive disengagement from the external environment, is characterized by the most dreamlike reports. The mentation experienced during the transition from wakefulness to sleep remains outstandingly incongruent with this general relationship between the occurrence of dreamlike mentation and the degree and duration of withdrawal from the external environment.

Since it is impossible to disentangle state-related cognitive experiences from state-related contributions to processes involved in recall and memory consolidation, it becomes possible only to speak of conditions and times during which there exists a predisposition or set of circumstances conducive to the presence of mentation. Accordingly, great emphasis and hope were placed on studies of phasic events during sleep— events that punctuate both REM and NREM sleep and that were shown to be generated by a physiological system that becomes spontaneously active only during sleep. It was thought that these special events might provide unique cues to both the detection and the distinctive features of ongoing mental processes during sleep. Consequently, during the ensuing series of psychophysiological sleep studies of phasic events, different physiological lures were tested in the stream of consciousness, in search of presumptive PGO analogues that would correlate with either the appearance or the specific features of cognitive sleep experiences. These studies were most impressive in their demonstration of the predominant absence of unusual features of, or even heightened presence of, mental activity in conjunction with phasic events. Equally impressive was the presence of mental activity, even dreamlike activity, in the absence of phasic events. As they have been measured, it is clear that phasic events do not determine sleep consciousness. It is difficult to imagine, however, that these physiological events, which are so consistently present at a time when dreamlike experiences are most commonly reported, are not without important cognitive consequences. Based on data from animal studies of phasic activity during sleep and wakefulness, together with a consideration of general qualitative characteristics of REM sleep mentation, a possible cognitive consequence of phasic activity has been explored here. It has been postulated that an important role for phasic events may be to provide orientation for consciousness by indicating whether ongoing sensory–motor experiences are endogenously or exogenously determined—thereby providing a physiological basis for the cognitive process of reality testing.

ACKNOWLEDGMENTS

Preparation of this chapter was supported by the Ontario Mental Health Foundation. I gratefully acknowledge the assistance of Mr. Fred Bylsma in the preparation of figures.

REFERENCES

Agnew, H. W., Jr., & Webb, W. B. Measurement of sleep onset by EEG criteria. *American Journal of EEG Technology*, 1972, 12, 127-134.

Agnew, H. W., Jr., Webb, W. B., & Williams, R. L. The first night effect: An EEG study of sleep. *Psychophysiology*, 1966, 2, 263-266.

Akerstedt, T., & Gillberg, M. Effects of sleep deprivation on memory and sleep latencies in connection with repeated awakenings from sleep. *Psychophysiology*, 1979, 16, 49-52.

Altshuler, K. Z., & Brebbia, D. R. Body movement artifact as a contaminant in psychophysiological studies of sleep. *Psychophysiology*, 1967, 3, 86-91.

Anders, T., Emde, R., & Parmelee, A. (Eds.). *A manual of standardized terminology, techniques and criteria for scoring of states of sleep and wakefulness in newborn infants*. Los Angeles: UCLA Brain Information, NIMDS Neurological Information Network, 1971.

Antrobus, J. S., Arkin, A. M., & Toth, M. F. The effects of REM period deprivation on sleep mentation. *Psychophysiology*, 1970, 7, 332. (Abstract)

Antrobus, J. S., Fein, G., Jordan, L., Ellman, S. J., & Arkin, A. M. Measurement and design in research on sleep reports. In A. M. Arkin, J. S. Antrobus, & S. J. Ellman (Eds.), *The mind in sleep*. Hillsdale, N.J.: Erlbaum, 1978.

Arkin, A. M. Sleep talking: A review. *Journal of Nervous and Mental Disease*. 1966, 143, 101-122.

Arkin, A. M. Sleeptalking. In A. M. Arkin, J. S. Antrobus, & S. J. Ellman (Eds.), *The mind in sleep*. Hillsdale, N.J.: Erlbaum, 1978.

Arkin, A. M., Antrobus, J. S., Ellman, S. J., & Farber, J. Sleep mentation as affected by REMP deprivation. In A. M. Arkin, J. S. Antrobus, & S. J. Ellman (Eds.), *The mind in sleep*. Hillsdale, N.J.: Erlbaum, 1978.

Arkin, A. M., Antrobus, J. S., Toth, M. F., & Baker, J. The effects of chemically induced REMP deprivation on sleep vocalization and NREM mentation: An initial exploration. *Psychophysiology*, 1968, 5, 217. (Abstract)

Arkin, A. M., Toth, M., Baker, J, & Hastey, J. M. The frequency of sleep-talking in the laboratory among chronic sleep-talkers and good dream recallers. *Journal of Nervous and Mental Disease*, 1970, 151, 369-374.

Asahina, K. Paradoxical phase and reverse paradoxical phase in human subjects. *Journal of the Physiology Society of Japan*, 1962, 24, 443-450.

Aserinsky, E. Periodic respiratory pattern occurring in conjunction with eye movements during sleep. *Science*, 1965, 150, 763-766.

Aserinsky, E. The maximal capacity for sleep: Rapid eye movement density as an index of sleep satiety. *Biological Psychiatry*, 1969, 1, 147-159.

Aserinsky, E. Rapid eye movement density and pattern in the sleep of normal young adults. *Psychophysiology*, 1971, 8, 361-375.

Aserinsky, E., & Kleitman, N. Regularly occurring periods of eye motility and concomitant phenomena during sleep. *Science*, 1953, 118, 273-274.

Aserinsky, E., & Kleitman, N. Two types of ocular motility occurring during sleep. *Journal of Applied Physiology*, 1955, 8, 1-10.

Azumi, K., Shirakawa, S., & Takahashi, S. Periodicity of sleep spindle appearance in normal adults. *Sleep Research*, 1975, 4, 263. (Abstract)

Azumi, K., Takahashi, S., Takahashi, K., Maruyama, N., & Kikuti, S. The effects of dream deprivation on chronic schizophrenics and normal adults: A comparative study. *Folia Psychiatrica et Neurologica Japonica*, 1967, 21, 205-225.

Baldridge, B. J. Physical concomitants of dreaming and the effect of stimulation on dreams. *Ohio State Medical Journal*, 1966, 62, 1273-1274.

Baldridge, B. J., Whitman, R. M., & Kramer, M. A simplified method for detecting eye movements during dreaming. *Psychosomatic Medicine*, 1963, 25, 78-82.

Baldridge, B. H., Whitman, R. M., Kramer, M. A., Ornstein, P. H., & Lansky, L. *The effect of external physical stimuli on dream content*. Paper presented at the meeting of the Association for the Psychophysiological Study of Sleep, Washington, D.C., 1965.

Barber, T. X., Walker, P. C., & Hahn, K. W., Jr. Effects of hypnotic induction and suggestions on nocturnal dreaming and thinking. *Journal of Abnormal Psychology*, 1973, 82, 414-427.

Benson, K., & Zarcone, V. P. Phasic events of REM sleep: Phenomenology of middle ear muscle activity and periorbital integrated potentials in the same normal population. *Sleep*, 1979, 2, 199-213.

Berger, R. J. Tonus of extrinsic laryngeal muscles during sleep and dreaming. *Science*, 1961, 134, 840.

Berger, R. J. When is a dream is a dream is a dream? *Experimental Neurology*, 1967, 19(Suppl. 4), 15-28.

Berger, R. J., Olley, P., & Oswald, I. The EEG, eye movements, and dreams of the blind. *Quarterly Journal of Experimental Psychology*, 1962, 14, 183-186.

Berger, R. J., & Oswald, I. Effects of sleep deprivation on behavior, subsequent sleep, and dreaming. *Journal of Mental Science*, 1962, 108, 457-465. (a)

Berger, R. J., & Oswald, I. Eye movements during active and passive dreams. *Science*, 1962, 137, 601. (b)

Bizzi, E., & Brooks, D. Functional connections between pontine recticular formation and lateral geniculate nucleus during deep sleep. *Archives Italiennes de Biologie*, 1963, 101, 648-666.

Blum, R. A., Livingston, P. B., & Shader, R. I. Changes in cognition, attention and language in acute schizophrenia. *Diseases of the Nervous System*, 1969, 30, 31-36.

Bosinelli, M., Molinari, S., Bagnaresi, G., & Salzarulo, P. Caratteristiche dell attitiva psicofisiologica durante il sonno: Un contributo alle techniche di valutazion. *Rivista Sperimentale di Freiatria*, 1968, 92, 128-150.

Bowker, R. M., & Morrison, A. R. The startle reflex and PGO spikes. *Brain Research*, 1976, 102, 185-190.

Bowker, R. M., & Morrison, A. R. The PGO spike: An indicator of hyperalertness. In W. P. Koella & P. Levin (Eds.), *Sleep, 1976*. Basel: Karger, S. 1977.

Brady, J. P., & Rosner, B. S. Rapid eye movements in hypnotically induced dreams. *Journal of Nervous and Mental Disease*, 1966, 143, 28-35.

Brooks, D. C. Localization of the lateral geniculate nucleus monophasic waves associated with paradoxical sleep in the cat. *Electroencephalography and Clinical Neurophysiology*, 1967, 23, 123-133.

Brooks, D. C. Localization and characteristics of the cortical waves associated with eye movements in the cat. *Experimental Biology*, 1968, 22, 603-613. (a)

Brooks, D. C. Waves associated with eye movement in the awake and sleeping cat. *Electroencephalography and Clinical Neurophysiology*, 1968, 24, 532-541. (b)

Brooks, D. C. Commentary. In W. B. Webb (Ed.), *Sleep: An active process*. Glenview, Ill.: Scott, Foresman, 1973.

Brooks, D. C., & Gershon, M. D. Eye movement potentials in the oculomotor and visual systems of the cat: A comparison of reserpine-induced waves with those present during wakefulness and rapid-eye-movement sleep. *Brain Research*, 1971, 27, 223–239.

Broughton, R. J. Sleep disorders: Disorders of arousal? *Science*, 1968, 159, 1070–1078.

Broughton, R. J., Poire, R., & Tassinari, C. A. The electrodermogram (Tarchanoff effect) during sleep. *Electroencephalography and Clinical Neurophysiology*, 1965, 18, 691–708.

Brown, J. N., & Cartwright, R. D. Locating NREM dreaming through instrumental responses. *Psychophysiology*, 1978, 15, 35–39.

Brunette, R., & De Koninck, J. The effect of presleep suggestions related to a phobic object on dream affect. *Sleep Research*, 1977, 6, 120. (Abstract)

Burch, N. Data processing of psychophysiological recordings. In L. D. Proctor & W. R. Adey (Eds.), *Symposium on the analysis of central nervous system and cardiovascular data using computer methods*. Washington, D.C.: National Aeronautics and Space Administration, 1965.

Bush, M. The relationship between impaired selective attention and severity of psychopathology in acute psychiatric patients. *British Journal of Medical Psychology*, 1977, 50, 251–265.

Bussel, J., Dement, W., & Pivik, R. T. The eye movement-imagery relationship in REM sleep and waking. *Sleep Research*, 1972, 1, 100. (Abstract)

Caldwell, D., & Domino, E. Electroencephalographic and eye movement patterns during sleep in chronic schizophrenic patients. *Electroencephalography and Clinical Neurophysiology*, 1967, 22, 414–420.

Carlson, V. R., Feinberg, I., & Goodenough, D. R. Perception of the duration of sleep intervals as a function of EEG sleep stage. *Physiological Psychology*, 1978, 6, 497–500.

Carroll, D., Lewis, S. A., & Oswald, I. Effect of barbiturates on dream content. *Nature*, 1969, 223, 865–866.

Cartwright, R. Dreams and drug-induced fantasy behavior. *Archives of General Psychiatry*, 1966, 15, 7–15.

Cartwright, R., Monroe, L., & Palmer, C. Individual differences in response to REM deprivation. *Archives of General Psychiatry*, 1967, 16, 297–303.

Cartwright, R., & Ratzel, R. Effects of dream loss on waking behavior. *Archives of General Psychiatry*, 1972, 27, 277–280.

Chertok, L., & Kramarz, P. Hypnosis, sleep and electro-encephalography. *Journal of Nervous and Mental Disease*, 1959, 128, 227–238.

Cohen, H. D., & Shapiro, A. Vaginal blood flow during sleep. *Psychophysiology*, 1970, 1, 338. (Abstract)

Dement, W. C. Dream recall and eye movement during sleep in schizophrenics and normals. *Journal of Nervous and Mental Disease*, 1955, 122, 263–269.

Dement, W. C. The effect of dream deprivation. *Science*, 1960, 131, 1705–1707.

Dement, W. C. The biological role of REM sleep (circa 1968). In A. Kales (Ed.), *Sleep: Physiology and pathology*. Philadelphia: J. B. Lippincott, 1969. (a)

Dement, W. C. A new look at the third state of existence. *Stanford Medical Alumni Association*, 1969, 8, 2–8. (b)

Dement, W. C., Ferguson, J., Cohen, H., & Barchas, J. Nonchemical methods and data using a biochemical model: The REM quanta. In A. Mandell & M. Mandell (Eds.), *Psychochemical research in man: Methods, strategy and theory*. New York: Academic Press, 1969.

Dement, W. C., & Fisher, C. Experimental interference with the sleep cycle. *Canadian Psychiatric Association Journal*, 1963, 8, 400–405.

Dement, W. C., & Kleitman, N. Cyclic variations in EEG during sleep and their relation to eye movements, bodily motility and dreaming. *Electroencephalography and Clinical Neurophysiology*, 1957, 9, 673–690. (a)

Dement, W. C., & Kleitman, N. The relation of eye movements

during sleep to dream activity: An objective method for the study of dreaming. *Journal of Experimental Psychology*, 1957, 53, 339–346. (b)

Dement, W., & Wolpert, E. Interrelations in the manifest content of dreams occurring on the same night. *Journal of Nervous and Mental Disease*, 1958, 126, 568–578. (a)

Dement, W., & Wolpert, E. The relation of eye movements, body motility, and external stimuli to dream content. *Journal of Experimental Psychology*, 1958, 55, 543–554. (b)

Dement, W., Zarcone, V., Ferguson, J., Cohen, H., Pivik, T., & Barchas, J. Some parallel findings in schizophrenic patients and serotonin-depleted cats. In D. V. Sankar (Ed.), *Schizophrenia: Current concepts and research*. Hicksville, N.Y.: PJD Publications, 1969.

Dusan-Peyrethon, D., Peyrethon, J., & Jouvet, M. Étude quantitative des phénomènes phasiques du sommeil paradoxale pendant et après sa déprivation instrumentale. *Comptes Rendus des Seances de la Société de Biologie et de Ses Filiales*, 1967, 161, 2530–2537.

Ellman, S. J., Antrobus, J. S., Arkin, A. M., Farber, J., Luck, D., Bodnar, R., Sanders, K., & Nelson, W. T., Jr. Sleep mentation in relation to phasic and tonic events—REMP and NREM. *Sleep Research*, 1974, 3, 115. (Abstract)

Evans, F. J., Gustafson, L. A., O'Connell, D. N., Orne, P. T., & Shor, R. E. Verbally induced behavioral responses during sleep. *Journal of Nervous and Mental Disease*, 1970, 150, 171–187.

Feltin, M., & Broughton, R. J. Differential effects of arousal from slow wave sleep versus REM sleep. *Psychophysiology*, 1968, 5, 231. (Abstract)

Ferguson, J., Henriksen, S., McGarr, K., Belenky, G., Mitchell, G., Gonda, W., Cohen, H., & Dement, W. Phasic event deprivation in the cat. *Psychophysiology*, 1968, 5, 238–239. (Abstract)

Firth, E. Eye movements, dreams and drugs. *Sleep Research*, 1972, 1, 102. (Abstract)

Firth, H., & Oswald, I. Eye movements and visually active dreams. *Psychophysiology*, 1975, 12, 602–605.

Fisher, C. Dreaming and sexuality. In R. Lowenstein, L. Newman, M. Shur, & A. Solnit (Eds.), *Psychoanalysis: A general psychology*. New York: International Universities Press, 1966.

Fisher, C., Gross, J., & Zuch, J. Cycles of penile erection synchronous with dreaming (REM) sleep. *Archives of General Psychiatry*, 1965, 12, 29–45.

Fiss, H. Current dream research: A psychobiological perspective. In B. B. Wolman (Ed.), *Handbook of dreams: Research, theories and application*. New York: Van Nostrand Reinhold, 1979.

Foulkes, D. *Dream reports from different stages of sleep*. Unpublished doctoral dissertation, University of Chicago, 1960.

Foulkes, D. Dream reports from different stages of sleep. *Journal of Abnormal Social Psychology*, 1962, 65, 14–25.

Foulkes, D. *The psychology of sleep*. New York: Scribners, 1966.

Foulkes, D. Nonrapid eye movement mentation. *Experimental Neurology*, 1967, 19(Suppl. 4), 28–38.

Foulkes, D. *A grammar of dreams*. New York: Basic Books, 1978.

Foulkes, D. *Children's dreams: Longitudinal studies*. New York: Wiley, 1982.

Foulkes, D., & Fleisher, S. Mental activity in relaxed wakefulness. *Journal of Abnormal Psychology*, 1975, 84, 66–75.

Foulkes, D., & Kerr, N. H. *Cognitive factors in REM dreaming*. Paper presented at the meeting of the international Neuropsychological Society, San Francisco, 1980.

Foulkes, D., Larson, J. D., Swanson, E. M., & Rardin, M. Two studies of childhood dreaming. *American Journal of Orthopsychiatry*, 1969, 39, 627–643.

Foulkes, D., Pivik, T., Ahrens, J., & Swanson, E. M. Effects of "dream deprivation" on dream content: An attempted cross-night replication. *Journal of Abnormal Psychology*, 1968, 73, 403–415.

Foulkes, D., & Pope, R. Primary visual experience and secondary cognitive elaboration in stage REM: A modest confirmation and an extension. *Perceptual and Motor Skills*, 1973, 37, 107–118.

Foulkes, D., & Rechtschaffen, A. Presleep determinants of dream content: Effects of two films. *Perceptual and Motor Skills*, 1964, 19, 983–1005.

Foulkes, D., & Scott, E. An above-zero waking baseline for the incidence of momentarily hallucinatory mentation. *Sleep Research*, 1973, 2, 108. (Abstract)

Foulkes, D., Spear, P. S., & Symonds, J. Individual differences in mental activity at sleep onset. *Journal of Abnormal Psychology*, 1966, 71, 280–286.

Foulkes, D., & Vogel, G. Mental activity at sleep onset. *Journal of Abnormal Psychology*, 1965, 70, 231–243.

Freud, S. *The interpretation of dreams*. New York: Basic Books, 1955. (Originally published, 1900)

Galton, F. *Inquiries into human faculty and its development*. London: J. M. Dent, 1911. (Originally published, 1883)

Gillin, J. C., Buchsbaum, M. S., Jacobs, L. S., Fram, D. H., Williams, R. B., Jr., Vaughn, T. B., Jr., Mellon, E., Snyder, F., & Wyatt, R. J. Partial REM sleep deprivation, schizophrenia and field articulation. *Archives of General Psychiatry*, 1974, 30, 653–662.

Goblot, E. Sur le souvenir des rêves. *Revue Philosophique*, 1896, 42, 288.

Goodenough, D. R. Some recent studies of dream recall. In H. A. Witkin & H. B. Lewis (Eds.), *Experimental studies of dreaming*. New York: Random House, 1967.

Goodenough, D. R. The phenomena of dream recall. In L. E. Abt & B. F. Riess (Eds.), *Progress in clinical psychology* (Vol. 8). New York: Grune & Stratton, 1968.

Goodenough, D. R. Dream recall: History and current status of the field. In A. M. Arkin, J. S. Antrobus, & S. J. Ellman (Eds.), *The mind in sleep*. Hillsdale, N.J.: Erlbaum, 1978.

Goodenough, D. R., Lewis, H. B., Shapiro, A., Jaret, & Sleser, I. Some correlates of dream reporting following laboratory awakenings. *Journal of Nervous and Mental Disease*, 1965, 140, 365–373.

Goodenough, D. R., Shapiro, A., Holden, M., & Steinschriber, L. A comparison of "dreamers" and "nondreamers": Eye movements, electroencephalograms and the recall of dreams. *Journal of Abnormal Psychology*, 1959, 59, 295–302.

Goodenough, D. R., Witkins, H. A., Koulack, D., & Cohen, H. The effects of stress films on dream affect and on respiration and eye-movement during rapid-eye movement sleep. *Psychophysiology*, 1975, 15, 313–320.

Granda, A. M., & Hammack, J. T. Operant behavior during sleep. *Science*, 1961, 133, 1485–1486.

Greenberg, R., Pearlman, C., Fingar, R., Kantrowitz, J., & Kawliche, S. The effects of dream deprivation: Implications for a theory of the psychological function of dreaming. *British Journal of Medical Psychology*, 1970, 43, 1–11.

Gresham, S. C., Agnew, H. W., Jr., & Williams, R. L. The sleep of depressed patients. An EEG and eye movement study. *Archives of General Psychiatry*, 1965, 13, 503–507.

Gross, J., Byrne, J., & Fisher, C. Eye movements during emergent stage I EEG in subjects with life-long blindness. *Journal of Nervous and Mental Disease*, 1965, 141, 365–370.

Grossman, W., Gardner, R., Roffwarg, H., Fekete, A., Beers, L., & Weiner, H. Limb movement and dream action: Are they related? *Sleep Research*, 1973, 2, 123. (Abstract)

Halasz, P., Rajna, P., Pal, I., Kundra, O., Vargha, A., Balogh, A., & Kemeny, A. K-complexes and micro-arousals as functions of the sleep process. In W. P. Koella & P. Levin (Eds.), *Sleep 1976*. Basel: S. Karger, 1977.

Hall, C. S., & Raskin, R. Do we dream during sleep? Unpublished manuscript, 1980. (Available from Calvin S. Hall, 1310 West Cliff Drive, Santa Cruz, Calif. 95060)

Hall, C., & Van de Castle, R. L. *The content analysis of dreams*. New York: Appleton-Century-Crofts, 1966.

Halper, C., Pivik, R. T., & Dement, W. C. An attempt to reduce the REM rebound following REM deprivation by the use of induced waking mentation. *Psychophysiology*, 1969, 6, 241. (Abstract)

Hauri, P., & Van de Castle, R. L. Psychophysiological parallelism in dreams. *Psychosomatic Medicine*, 1973, 35, 297–308. (a)

Hauri, P., & Van de Castle, R. L. Psychophysiological parallels in dreams. In U. J. Jovanovic (Ed.), *The nature of sleep*. Stuttgart: Fischer, 1973. (b)

Hemsley, D. R., & Zawada, S. L. 'Filtering' and the cognitive deficit in schizophrenia. *British Journal of Psychiatry*, 1976, 128, 456–461.

Henley, K., & Morrison, A. R. A reevaluation of the effects of lesions of the pontine tegmentum and locus coeruleus on phenomena of paradoxical sleep in the cat. *Acta Neurobiologiae Experimentalis*, 1974, 34, 215–232.

Herman, J. H., Ellman, S. J., & Roffwarg, H. P. The problem of NREM dream recall re-examined. In A. M. Arkin, J. S. Antrobus, & S. J. Ellman (Eds.). *The mind in sleep*. Hillsdale, N.J.: Erlbaum, 1978.

Hobson, J. A., Goldfrank, F., & Snyder, F. Respiration and mental activity in sleep. *Journal of Psychiatric Research*, 1965, 3, 79–90.

Hobson, J. A., & McCarley, R. *Neuronal activity in sleep: An annotated bibliography*. Los Angeles: UCLA Brain Information Service, 1971.

Hodes, R., & Dement, W. C. Depression of electrically induced reflexes ("H"-reflexes) in man during low voltage EEG "sleep." *Electroencephalography and Clinical Neurophysiology*, 1964, 17, 617–629.

Hoffman, R. F., Moffitt, A. R., Shearer, J. C., Sussman, P. S., & Wells, R. B. Conceptual and methodological considerations towards the development of computer-controlled research on the electro-physiology of sleep. *Waking and Sleeping*, 1979, 3, 1–16.

Holzman, P. S., Proctor, L. R., & Hughes, D. W. Eye tracking patterns in schizophrenia. *Science*, 1973, 181, 179–181.

Hoyt, M. F., & Singer, J. L. Psychological effects of REM ("dream") deprivation upon waking mentation. In A. M. Arkin, J. S. Antrobus, & S. J. Ellman (Eds.), *The mind in sleep*. Hillsdale, N.J.: Erlbaum, 1978.

Itil, T. Digital computer 'sleep prints' and psychopharmacology. *Biological Psychiatry*, 1969, 1, 91–95.

Itil, T. Digital computer analysis of the electroencephalogram during eye movement sleep state in man. *Journal of Nervous and Mental Disease*, 1970, 150, 201–208.

Jackson, H. *Selected writings* (J. Taylor, G. Holmes, & F. Walshe, Eds.). New York: Basic Books, 1958.

Jacobson, A., Kales, A., Lehmann, D., & Hoedemaker, F. S. Muscle tonus in human subjects during sleep and dreaming. *Experimental Neurology*, 1964, 10, 418–424.

Jacobson, A., Kales, A., Lehmann, D., & Zweizig, J. Somnambulism: All night electroencephalographic studies. *Science*, 1965, 148, 975–977.

Jeannerod, M., & Sakai, K. Occipital and geniculate potentials related to eye movements in the unanesthetized cat. *Brain Research*, 1970, 19, 361–377.

Johnson, L. C. Are stages of sleep related to waking behavior? *American Scientist*, 1973, 61, 326–338.

Johnson, L. C., & Lubin, A. Spontaneous electrodermal activity during waking and sleeping. *Psychophysiology*, 1966, 3, 8–17.

Johnson, L. C., Nute, C., Austin, M. J., & Lubin, A. Spectral analysis of the EEG during waking and sleeping. *Electroencephalography and Clinical Neurophysiology*, 1967, 23, 80.

Jouvet, M. Recherches sur les structures nerveuses et les mécanismes responsables des différentes phases du sommeil physiologique. *Archives Italiennes de Biologie*, 1962, 100, 125–206.

Jouvet, M. The role of monoamines and acetylcholine-containing neurons in the regulation of the sleep–waking cycle. *Ergebnisse der Physiologie*, 1972, 64, 166–307.

Jouvet, M., & Delorme, J. Locus coeruleus et sommeil paradoxal. *Comptes Rendus des Séances de la Société de Biologie et de Ses Filiales*, 1965, 159, 895–899.

Jung, C. G. *The psychology of dementia praecox*. New York: Journal of Nervous and Mental Disease Publishing Company, 1944.

Kahn, E., Fisher, C., & Edwards, A. Night terrors and anxiety dreams. In A. M. Arkin, J. S. Antrobus, & S. J. Ellman (Eds.), *The mind in sleep*. Hillsdale, N.J.: Erlbaum, 1978.

Kales, A., Hoedemaker, F., Jacobson, A., Kales, J., Paulson, M., & Wilson, T. Mentation during sleep: REM and NREM recall reports. *Perceptual and Motor Skills*, 1967, 24, 556–560.

Kales, A., Jacobson, A., Paulson, M. J., Kales, J. D., & Walter, R. D. Somnambulism: Psychophysiological correlates. I. All night EEG studies. *Archives of General Psychiatry*, 1966, 14, 586–596.

Karacan, I., Goodenough, D. R., Shapiro, A., & Starker, S. Erection cycle during sleep in relation to dream anxiety. *Archives of General Psychiatry*, 1966, 15, 183–189.

Keefe, F. B., Johnson, L. C., & Hunter, E. J. EEG and autonomic response pattern during waking and sleep stages. *Psychophysiology*, 1971, 8, 198–212.

Keenan, R., & Krippner, S. Content analysis and visual scanning in dreams. *Psychophysiology*, 1970, 7, 302–303.

Kiyono, S., & Jeannerod, M. Relations entre l'activité géniculée phasique et les mouvements oculaires chez le chat normal et sous réserpine. *Comptes Rendus des Séances de la Société de Biologie et de Ses Filiales*, 1967, 161, 1607–1611.

Klein, G. S., Fiss, H., Shollar, E., Dalbeck, R., Warga, C., & Gwozdz, F. Recurrent dream fragments and fantasies elicited in interrupted and completed REM periods. *Psychophysiology*, 1971, 7, 331–332. (Abstract)

Kleitman, N. *Sleep and wakefulness* (2nd ed.). Chicago: University of Chicago Press, 1963.

Kleitman, N. The basic rest–activity cycle and physiological correlates of dreaming. *Experimental Neurology*, 1967, 19(Suppl. 4), 2–4.

Koulack, D. Effects of somatosensory stimulation on dream content. *Archives of General Psychiatry*, 1969, 20, 718–725.

Koulack, D., & Goodenough, D. R. Dream recall and dream recall failure: An arousal–retrieval model. *Psychological Bulletin*, 1976, 83, 975–984.

Kramer, M., & Roth, T. A comparison of dream content in laboratory dream reports of schizophrenic and depressive patient groups. *Comprehensive Psychiatry*, 1973, 14, 325–329.

Kramer, M., Roth, T., & Czaya, J. Dream development within a REM period. In P. Levin & W. P. Koella (Eds.), *Sleep*. Basel: S. Karger, 1975.

Larson, J. D., & Foulkes, D. Electromyogram suppression during sleep, dream recall and orientation time. *Psychophysiology*, 1969, 5, 548–555.

Latash, L. P., & Danilin, V. P. Subjective estimation of the duration of time periods in night sleep. *Nature New Biology*, 1972, 236, 94–95.

Loomis, A. L., Harvey, E. N., & Hobart, G. A. Cerebral states during sleep as studied by human brain potentials. *Journal of Experimental Psychology*, 1937, 21, 127–144.

Lubin, A., Johnson, L. C., & Austin, M. J. Discrimination among states of consciousness using EEG spectra. *Psychophysiology*, 1969, 6, 122–132.

McDonald, D. G., Schicht, W. W., Fratier, R. B., Shallenberger, H. D., & Edwards, D. J. Studies of information processing in sleep. *Psychophysiology*, 1975, 12, 624–629.

McGuigan, F. J., & Tanner, R. G. Covert oral behavior during conversational and visual dreams. *Psychophysiology*, 1970, 7, 329. (Abstract)

Medoff, L., & Foulkes, D. "Microscopic" studies of mentation in stage REM: A preliminary report. *Psychophysiology*, 1972, 9, 114. (Abstract)

Merton, P. A. Absence of conscious position sense in the human eyes. In M. B. Bender (Ed.), *The oculomotor system*. New York: Hoeber Medical Division, Harper & Row, 1964.

Molinari, S., & Foulkes, D. Tonic and phasic events during sleep: Psychological correlates and implications. *Perceptual and Motor Skills*, 1969, 29, 343–368.

Monroe, L. J. Inter-rater reliability and the role of experience in scoring EEG sleep records: Phase I. *Psychophysiology*, 1969, 5, 376–384.

Monroe, L. J., Rechtschaffen, A., Foulkes, D., & Jensen, J. Discri-

minability of REM and NREM reports. *Journal of Personality and Social Psychology*, 1965, 2, 456–460.

Morrison, A. R. Relationships between phenomena of paradoxical sleep and their counterparts in wakefulness. *Acta Neurobiologiae Experimentalis*, 1979, 39, 567–583.

Morrison, A. R., Mann, G. Hendricks, J. C., & Starkweather, C. Release of exploratory behavior in wakefine lesions which produce paradoxical sleep without atonia. *Anatomical Record*, 1979, 193, 628. (Abstract)

Morrison, A. R., & Pompeiano, O. Vestibular influences during sleep: VI. Vestibular control of autonomic functions during the rapid eye movements of desynchronized sleep. *Archives Italiennes de Biologie*, 1970, 108, 154–180.

Moruzzi, G. Active processes in the brain stem during sleep. *Harvey Lecture Series*, 1963, 58, 233–297.

Moruzzi, G. General discussion. In *Aspects anatomo-fonctionnels de la physiologie du sommeil: Actes du Colloque International sur les Aspects Anatomo-Fontionnels de la Physiologie du Sommeil, Lyon, 1963* (Colloques Internationaux du Centre National de la Recherche Scientifique, No. 127). Paris: Centre National de la Recherche Scientifique, 1965.

Nakagawa, Y., Nakagawa, S., & Takahashi, S. Studies of K-complex (1)—On the relations between the appearances of K-complex and intensity of stimulus, interstimulus intervals and depth of sleep. In *Proceedings of the 15th Annual Meeting in Japan of the EEG Society*. Sapporo, Japan: The Research Institute of Applied Electricity, Hokkaido University, 1966.

Ogilvie, R., Hunt, H., Sawicki, C., & McGowan, K. Searching for lucid dreams. *Sleep Research*, 1978, 7, 165. (Abstract)

Oswald, I., Taylor, A. M., & Treisman, A. M. Discriminative responses to stimulation during human sleep. *Brain*, 1960, 83, 440–453.

Pampiglione, M. C. The phenomenon of adaptation in human EEG. *Review of Neurology*, 1952, 87, 197–198.

Pessah, M., & Roffwarg, H. Spontaneous middle ear muscle activity in man: A rapid eye movement phenomenon. *Science*, 1972, 178, 773–776.

Pivik, R. T. *Mental activity and phasic events during sleep*. Unpublished doctoral dissertation, Stanford University, 1971.

Pivik, R. T. Tonic states and phasic events in relation to sleep mentation. In A. M. Arkin, J. S. Antrobus, & S. J. Ellman (Eds.), *The mind in sleep*. Hillsdale, N.J.: Erlbaum, 1978.

Pivik, R. T. Smooth pursuit eye movements and attention in psychiatric patients. *Biological Psychiatry*, 1979, 14, 859–879.

Pivik, T., & Dement, W. Amphetamine, REM deprivation and K-complexes. *Psychophysiology*, 1968, 5, 241. (Abstract)

Pivik, T., & Dement, W. C. Phasic changes in muscular and reflex activity during non-REM sleep. *Experimental Neurology*, 1970, 27, 115–124.

Pivik, T., & Foulkes, D. "Dream deprivation": Effects on dream content. *Science*, 1966, 153, 1282–1284.

Pivik, T., & Foulkes, D. NREM mentation: Relation to personality, orientation time, and time of night. *Journal of Consulting and Clinical Psychology*, 1968, 37, 144–151.

Pivik, T., Halper, C., & Dement, W. Phasic events and mentation during sleep. *Psychophysiology*, 1969, 6, 215. (Abstract)

Pompeiano, O. Muscular afferents and motor control during sleep. In R. Granit (Ed.), *Muscular afferents and motor control*. Stockholm: Almquist & Siksell, 1966.

Pompeiano, O. The neurophysiological mechanism of the postural and motor events during desynchronized sleep. In S. S. Kety, E. V. Evarts, & H. L. Williams (Eds.), *Sleep and altered states of consciousness*. Baltimore: Williams & Wilkins, 1967.

Portnoff, G., Baekeland, F., Goodenough, D. R., Karacan, I., & Shapiro, A. Retention of verbal materials perceived immediately prior to onset of non-REM sleep. *Perceptual and Motor Skills*, 1966, 22, 751–758.

Prevost, F. *Les effets de l'inversion du champ visual sur le sommeil paradoxal et le contenu des rêves*. Unpublished doctoral dissertation, University of Ottawa, 1976.

Rechtschaffen, A. Discussion of *Experimental dream studies* by W. C.

Dement. In J. H. Masserman (Ed.), *Science and psychoanalysis* (Vol. 1, *Development and research*). New York: Grune & Stratton, 1964.

Rechtschaffen, A. Dream reports and dream experiences. *Experimental Neurology*, 1967, 19(Suppl. 4), 4–15.

Rechtschaffen, A. The psychophysiology of mental activity during sleep. In F. J. McGuigan & R. A. Schoonover (Eds.), *The psychophysiology of thinking*. New York: Academic Press, 1973.

Rechtschaffen, A. The single-mindedness and isolation of dreams. *Sleep*, 1978, 1, 97–109.

Rechtschaffen, A., Goodenough, D., & Shapiro, A. Patterns of sleep talking. *Archives of General Psychiatry*, 1962, 7, 418–426.

Rechtschaffen, A., & Kales, A. (Eds.). *A manual of standardized terminology, techniques and scoring system for sleep stages of human subjects* (NIH Publ. No. 204). Washington, D.C.: U.S. Government Printing Office, 1968.

Rechtschaffen, A., Schulsinger, F., & Mednick, S. A. Schizophrenia and physiological indices of dreaming. *Archives of General Psychiatry*, 1964, 10, 89–93.

Rechtschaffen, A., Verdone, P., & Wheaton, J. Reports of mental activity during sleep. *Canadian Psychiatric Association Journal*, 1963, 8, 409–414.

Rechtschaffen, A., Vogel, G., & Shaikun, G. Interrelatedness of mental activity during sleep. *Archives of General Psychiatry*, 1963, 9, 536–547.

Ribstein, M. Hypnagogic hallucinations. In C. Guilleminault, W. C. Dement, & P. Passonant (Eds.), New York: *Narcolepsy*. Spectrum, 1976.

Roffwarg, H. P. Association of sleep disorders centers (Diagnostic classification of sleep and arousal disorders, first edition, prepared by the Sleep Disorders Classification Committee, H. P. Roffwarg, Chairman). *Sleep*, 1979, 2, 1–137.

Roffwarg, H. P., Herman, J. H., Bowe-Anders, C., & Tauber, E. S. The effects of sustained alterations of waking visual input. In A. M. Arkin, J. S. Antrobus, & S. J. Ellman (Eds.), *The mind in sleep*. Hillsdale, N.J.: Erlbaum, 1978.

Roffwarg, H. P., Muzio, J. N., & Dement, W. C. Ontogenetic development of the human sleep–dream cycle. *Science*, 1966, 152, 604–619.

Roth, M., Shaw, J., & Green, J. The form, voltage distribution and physiological significance of the K-complex. *Electroencephalography and Clinical Neurophysiology*, 1956, 8, 385–402.

Rousey, C. L. Auditory acuity during sleep. *Psychophysiology*, 1979, 16, 363–366.

Sampson, H. Deprivation of dreaming sleep by two methods: 1. Compensatory REM time. *Archives of General Psychiatry*, 1965, 13, 79–86.

Sampson, H. Psychological effects of deprivation of dreaming sleep. *Journal of Nervous and Mental Disease*, 1966, 143, 305–317.

Sassin, J. F., Parker, D. C., Mace, J. W., Gotlin, R. W., Johnson, L. C., & Rossman, L. G. Human growth homore release: Relation to slow-wave sleep and sleep-waking cycles. *Science*, 1969, 165, 513–515.

Scott, J. Performance after abrupt arousal from sleep: Comparison of a simple motor, a visual-perceptual, and a cognitive task. *Proceedings of the 77th Annual Convention of the American Psychological Association*, 1969, 225–226.

Shagass, C., Roemer, R. A., & Amadeo, M. Eye-tracking performance and engagement of attention. *Archives of General Psychiatry*, 1976, 33, 121–125.

Shapiro, A., & Goodenough, D. R., & Gryler, R. B. Dream recall as a function of method of awakening. *Psychosomatic Medicine*, 1963, 25, 174–180.

Snyder, F. Toward an evolutionary theory of dreaming. *American Journal of Psychiatry*, 1966, 123, 121–142.

Snyder, F., Anderson, D., Bunney, W., Kupfer, D., Scott, J., & Wyatt, R. Longitudinal variation in the sleep of severely depressed and acutely schizophrenic patients with changing clinical status. *Psychophysiology*, 1968, 5, 235. (Abstract)

Snyder, F., Hobson, J., & Goldfrank, F. Blood pressure changes during human sleep. *Science*, 1963, 142, 1313–1314.

Snyder, F., Hobson, J., Morrison, D., & Goldfrank, F. Changes in respiration, heart rate, and systolic blood pressure in human sleep. *Journal of Applied Physiology*, 1964, 19, 417–422.

Snyder, F., & Scott, J. The psychophysiology of sleep. In N. S. Greenfield & R. A. Sternbach (Eds.), *Handbook of psychophysiology*. New York, Holt, Rinehart & Winston, 1972.

Spanos, N. P., & Stam, H. J. The elicitation of visual hallucinations via brief instructions in a normal sample. *Journal of Nervous and Mental Disease*, 1979, 167, 488–494.

Stoyva, J. *The effects of suggested dreams on the length of rapid eye movement periods*. Unpublished doctoral dissertation, University of Chicago, 1961.

Stoyva, J. M. Finger electromyographic activity during sleep: Its relation to dreaming in deaf and normal subjects. *Journal of Abnormal Psychology*, 1965, 70, 343–349.

Sussman, P., Moffitt, A., Hoffman, R., Wells, R., & Shearer, J. The description of structural and temporal characteristics of tonic electrophysiological activity during sleep. *Waking and Sleeping*, 1979, 3, 279–290.

Takahashi, Y., Kipnis, D. M., & Daughaday, W. H. Growth hormone secretion during sleep. *Journal of Clinical Investigation*, 1968, 47, 2079–2090.

Takeo, S. Relationship among physiological indices during sleep and characteristics dreams. *Psychiatria et Neurologia Japonica*, 1970, 72, 1–18.

Tart, C. T. A comparison of suggested dreams occurring in hypnosis and sleep. *International Journal of Clinical and Experimental Hypnosis*, 1964, 12, 263–289.

Tart, C. T. From spontaneous event to lucidity: A review of attempts to consciously control nocturnal dreaming. In B. B. Wolman (Ed.), *Handbook of dreams*. New York: Van Nostrand Reinhold, 1979.

Tart, C. T., & Dick, L. Conscious control of dreaming: 1. The posthypnotic dream. *Journal of Abnormal Psychology*, 1970, 76, 304–315.

Tebbs, R. B. *Post-awakening visualization performances as a function of anxiety level, REM or NREM sleep, and time of night* (USAF Academy SRI-TR-72-0005, AD-738 630). Colorado Springs, Colo: U.S. Air Force Academy, 1972.

Tracy, R. L., & Tracy, L. N. Reports of mental activity from sleep stages 2 and 4. *Perceptual and Motor Skills*, 1974, 38, 647–648.

Verdone, P. *Variables related to the temporal reference of manifest dream content*. Unpublished doctoral dissertation, University of Chicago, 1963.

Vogel, G. W. Review of REM sleep deprivation. *Archives of General Psychiatry*, 1975, 32, 749–761.

Vogel, G. W. Mentation reported from naps of narcoleptics. In C. Guilleminault, W. G. Dement, & P. Passonant (Eds.), *Narcolepsy*. New York: Spectrum, 1976.

Vogel, G. W. Sleep-onset mentation. In A. Arkin, J. Antrobus, & S. Ellman (Eds.), *The mind in sleep*. Hillsdale, N.J.: Erlbaum, 1978.

Vogel, G. W., Barrowclough, B., & Giesler, D. Limited discriminability of REM and sleep onset reports and its psychiatric implications. *Archives of General Psychiatry*, 1972, 26, 449–455.

Vogel, G. W., Foulkes, D., & Trosman, H. Ego functions and dreaming during sleep onset. *Archives of General Psychiatry*, 1966, 14, 238–248.

Vogel, G. W., Thurmond, A., Gibbons, P., Sloan, K., Boyd, M., & Walker, M. REM sleep reduction effects on depression syndromes. *Archives of General Psychiatry*, 1975, 32, 765–777.

Watson, R. K. *Mental correlates of periorbital potentials during REM sleep*. Unpublished doctoral dissertation, University of Chicago, 1972.

Webb, W. B. Schedules of work and sleep. In W. P. Koella & P. Levin (Eds.), *Sleep 1976*. Basel: S. Karger, 1976.

Whitman, R. A summary. In M. Kramer (Ed.), *Dream psychology and the new biology of sleep*. Springfield, Ill.: Charles C Thomas, 1969.

Williams, R. L., Agnew, H. W., Jr., & Webb, W. B. Sleep patterns in young adults: An EEG study. *Electroencephalography and Clinical Neurophysiology*, 1964, 17, 376–381.

Williams, H. C., Morlock, H. C., & Morlock, J. V. Instrumental behavior during sleep. *Psychophysiology*, 1966, 2, 208–216.

Williams, R. L., Agnew, H. W., Jr., & Webb, W. B. Sleep patterns in the young adult female: An EEG study. *Electroencephalography Clinical Neurophysiology*, 1966, 20, 264–266.

Wilson, W., & Zung, W. Attention, discrimination and arousal during sleep. *Archives of General Psychiatry*, 1966, 15, 523–528.

Winget, C., & Kramer, N. *Dimensions of dreaming*. Gainesville: University Presses of Florida, 1979.

Wolpert, E. A. Two classes of factors affecting dream recall. *Journal of the American Psychoanalytic Association*, 1972, 20, 45–58.

Zarcone, V., Gulevich, G., Pivik, T., & Dement, W. Partial REM phase deprivation and schizophrenia. *Archives of General Psychiatry*, 1968, 18, 194–202.

Zimmerman, W. B. Psychological and physiological differences between "light" and "deep" sleepers. *Psychophysiology*, 1968, 4, 387. (Abstract)

Chapter Nineteen

Sexuality

James H. Geer
William T. O'Donohue
Robert H. Schorman

INTRODUCTION

In this chapter, we attempt to overview the field of psychophysiology as it interfaces with human sexuality. While few would dispute the practical or theoretical importance of sex, human sexuality has nevertheless been relatively ignored by psychophysiologists. This is somewhat surprising, since sexual behavior and arousal incorporate phenomena that have traditionally been of interest to psychophysiologists. That is, many sexual responses are mediated by the autonomic nervous system, and sexual behavior falls under the general rubric of emotion. It is to increase the interaction between psychophysiology and sexuality that this chapter is dedicated.

BRIEF HISTORICAL OVERVIEW

In 1966, William Masters and Virginia Johnson published their influential book, *Human Sexual Response*. Although their model is more fully described in the "Approaches to Human Sexuality" section of this chapter, several historically relevant aspects of their

work need to be noted. Following the lead of Kinsey *et al.* (1953), Masters and Johnson described the various components of the sexual response cycle as they had observed it in their laboratory. They categorized the physiological responses that occur during the sexual response cycle into two general types. One, labeled "extragenital responses," referred to those responses that occur in other than the genital area. The other category used by Masters and Johnson was, not surprisingly, "genital responses." Prior to the pioneering work of Kurt Freund in 1963, essentially all psychophysiological measures of sexual response were measures of extragenital responding.

Masters and Johnson (1966) reported that two general physiological responses occur during sexual arousal. The first of these is myotonia, an increase in muscle activity. The second is increased vasocongestion—vasocongestion that occurs not only in the genitals, but in response sites throughout the body.

Extragenital Measures

Masters and Johnson suggested that there is a linear relationship between heart rate increases and sexual

James H. Geer. Department of Psychology, Louisiana State University, Baton Rouge, Louisiana.

William T. O'Donohue, and Robert H. Schorman. Department of Psychology, State University of New York at Stony Brook, Stony Brook, New York.

arousal. However, contradictory data have been reported. For example, Wenger, Averill, and Smith (1968) noted that heart rate decreases during early stages of sexual arousal and then increases. Also, Heiman (1977) and Hoon, Wincze, and Hoon (1976b) have questioned the proposed linear relationship between heart rate and sexual arousal.

The extragenital response measures that have proven to be the most useful in detecting and measuring sexual arousal are those that measure some aspect of vasocongestion. Based upon their evaluation of the available data concerning various extragenital measures of sexual arousal, Hoon et al. (1976b) concluded that blood pressure is the single best extragenital measure of sexual arousal.

Extragenital responses to erotic stimuli that were not reported by Masters and Johnson have also been studied. For example, pupil dilation has been reported to reflect sexual interest or arousal (Hess, 1968). There has been a limited amount of research to investigate this possibility. For example, Hamel (1974) found that female undergraduates exhibited significant pupil dilation when they viewed nude photographs of males and females. Unfortunately, in this work the relationship between pupil dilation and ratings of sexual arousal was weak. Furthermore, there were no appropriate controls for stress, excitability, anger, novelty, and other phenomena that are known to affect pupil dilation.

Other investigators have examined the relationships between electroencephalogram (EEG) phenomena and sexual arousal. Costell (1972) measured contingent negative variation (CNV) to photographs of nude members of the opposite sex. He reported that CNV amplitude increased for both men and women during stimulus presentations. However, there are a number of problems with that study. For example, heterosexual women showed greater CNV responses to slides of females—a finding that is inconsistent with the notion that CNV reflects sexual interest. In another study of EEG phenomena, Cohen, Rosen, and Goldstein (1976) reported a laterality effect associated with orgasm. However, at the present time the relationships between central nervous system events and sexual arousal are not clearly understood, and research in this area is scant.

Zuckerman (1971) reviewed the psychophysiological measures that have been taken during sexual arousal and reported that such extragenital measures as heart rate, electrodermal responses, blood pressure, and pupillary dilation have serious shortcomings as indices of sexual arousal. First, they are often responsive to nonsexual stimuli, and therefore lack the characteristic of stimulus specificity that would be desirable in an indicator response. Secondly, their association with sexual stimuli and/or subjective ratings of sexual arousal is at best weak, and thus is of limited value in the study of sexual phenomena. Other investigators have also noted low correlations between extragenital psychophysiological responses and either sexual stimulation or the subjective experience of sexual arousal (Geer, 1975; Hoon, 1979). Zuckerman (1971) suggested that if progress is to be made research on the psychophysiology of sexual phenomena should concentrate upon genital measures. Our brief review of the literature leads us to agree with Hoon's statement (1979), "Therefore, Zuckerman's (1971) conclusion that nongenital measures of sexual arousal for men and women are not clearly indicative of sexual arousal continues to hold" (p. 16).

Genital Measures

Since the early work of Freund (1963) and Masters and Johnson (1966), much effort has been concentrated on development and application of a number of methodologies for measuring genital responding. For the last 5–10 years, most work on the psychophysiology of sexual arousal has focused upon genital measures, and these studies indicate that genital measures hold promise for furthering our understanding of sexual phenomena.

As previously noted, the first report of research involving genital measures was Freund's (1963) study, in which he described the development of a device for detecting changes in the volume of the penis. Since that time, there have been developments and refinements in the methodology of measuring penile changes. Most penile measurements have typically been made with strain gauges, which measure changes in the circumference of the penis rather than changes in volume (Geer, 1975; Rosen & Keefe, 1978). The use of the strain gauge is based upon the implicit assumption that changes in penile circumference are highly correlated with changes in volume of the penis. This correlation holds at a satisfactory level.

There has been a recent interest in the measurement of additional aspects of penile responding. For example, Hatch, Heiman, and Hahn (1980) have reported using photometry[1] of the penis to assess sexual arousal. They measured penile pulse amplitude obtained by photometry, and thus proposed another psychophysiological measure to study penile changes. Bancroft and Bell (1980) have also reported using penile photometry to assess sexual arousal. This methodology holds promise for studying sexual arousal. Temperature changes of the penis and penile blood pressure have been measured in an attempt to assess vascular anomalies associated with some sexual dysfunctions (Seeley, Abramsen, Perry, Rothblatt, & Seeley, 1980). However, more data is needed before we

1. Following the suggestion of Jennings, Tahmoush, and Redmond (1980), we use the term "photometry" as a more accurate description of the procedure, rather than the term "photoplethysmograph."

can determine the utility of these measures of penile responding in assessing sexual arousal.

The first reported use of measurements of genital changes for the study of sexual arousal in women was described by Shapiro, Cohen, DiBianco, and Rosen (1968). They developed a device that measures dissipation of heat into vaginal tissues. This instrument appears to measure vaginal blood flow. However, the Shapiro *et al.* device has not been widely used, since it is relatively complicated to construct and requires individual sizing by medical personnel. Levine and Wagner (1978) have developed a device that directly measures blood flow in the vaginal wall in a highly sophisticated application of measuring the release of oxygen partial pressure (pO_2) across the vaginal mucosa. This device, which at the present time is expensive and uncomfortable to use, holds considerable promise in that it allows for the quantification of blood flow.

In 1975, Sintchak and Geer reported the development of a vaginal photometer that measured both pooled blood volume (direct current or DC component) in the vaginal walls and vaginal pulse amplitude (alternating current or AC component). Vaginal pressure pulse amplitude has proved to be sensitive to erotic stimuli and related to the subjective experience of arousal (Heiman, 1977; Rothenberg & Geer, 1980). Hoon, Wincze, and Hoon (1976) have reported successful use of the pooled blood volume measure, while others (e.g., Heiman, 1977) have not found this measure successful in indexing sexual arousal. Currently, in research involving women, the vaginal photometer is the most widely used genital response transducer.

Henson and Rubin (1978) have described a transducer for measuring labial temperature. They reported that increases in labial temperature are related to erotic stimulation. It would appear that the measurement of labial temperature holds promise as an additional methodology for measuring genital responding.

Another direction that has been taken in research involving genital measures is the attempt to develop measures that can be applied to both men and women. Thermography provides the advantage of yielding a single measure, temperature, that may be useful for both sexes. A review of the work in this area is provided by Seeley *et al.* (1980). With additional methodological improvements, thermography holds considerable promise for the study of sexual arousal. The measurement of electromyogram (EMG) activity in the genital musculature is another methodology that may allow between-sex comparisons. Finally, there have been attempts to measure vascular and muscular responses from the colon (Bohlen & Held, 1979).

There are several review articles that can be consulted by interested readers to familiarize themselves with the current methodology concerning genital measurement. Geer (1980) has presented a review of methods for assessing genital responding in both men and women. In that work, he provides a reference list that can be used to consult original sources for specification on characteristics and construction of the various devices. Hatch (1979) reviews the methodology concerning the use of vaginal photometry and also focuses upon some of the important measurement issues. Another review of genital measures in women, was done by Hoon (1979). He surveys methodology for the assessment of sexual arousal including various means of measuring subjective levels of arousal. Included in that review is a consideration of the use of such "tests" as the Sexual Arousal Inventory (Hoon, Hoon, & Wincze, 1976). Finally, Rosen and Keefe (1978) review the literature on genital measures for men. They discuss both methodological and conceptual issues in their paper. While developments continue in the field of measurement of genital responding, the cited reviews do a creditable job of describing the state of the art as it exists at the time of this writing. They provide references to the original sources on the development of genital measurement devices that can be of value to the interested researcher.

METAISSUES IN HUMAN SEXUALITY RESEARCH

There are three overall concerns in the study of human sexuality that must be addressed, due to their overwhelming importance in both defining and directing research. We refer to these as "metaissues." These concerns are not limited to psychophysiological approaches to human sexuality, but exist in all of the research methodologies in the area of psychophysiology. However, they are often more salient in human sexuality because of the sometimes sensitive nature of the field, the multidisciplinary nature of the research, and the characteristics of the researchers. The first set of these issues to which we would like to direct our readers' attention is the impact of ethics upon research in human sexuality.

Ethical Issues

Ethical issues have more impact in the study of human sexuality than perhaps in any other area of psychophysiological investigation. Although ethical considerations influence nearly every facet of the study of human sexuality, they have a particularly heavy influence upon the phenomena of sexuality itself as well as the populations studied. The impact of ethics on the selection of research topics can be illustrated with some examples. Certain topics are excluded from study because of their controversial nature. For example, under our current societal norms, it is essentially impossible to do laboratory research on human incest. This subject is forbidden because of the powerful views and values held concerning incest by both researchers and society. The theoretical or practical importance of the topic of incest is essentially irrelevant in the face of the moral issue. The study of bizarre sexual activity provides another example of topics upon which research may be restricted because society would be offended. Therefore, the study of many potentially important topics in sexuality is severely restricted, due to their value-laden nature.

There are also serious limitations on the subject populations available for study. For example, many theorists believe that the most important time period for understanding the development of sexual interest, preferences, and choices is during childhood through adolescence. Nevertheless, it is very difficult, if not impossible, to study sexuality in children or adolescents. The probability of being permitted to measure genital responses in children is essentially zero. Therefore, the full range of sexual development is not available for study using psychophysiological techniques. As another example, it is difficult to study any population of sex offenders. Issues having to do with confidentiality, threats to the individual, and possible threats to others become paramount. Thus, the populations available for study are limited not so much by the difficulty in identifying such populations as by the powerful ethical and emotional concerns that these kinds of investigations would have upon both the public and the individuals being studied.

Ethical issues also have an impact upon research funding. Investigators studying sexuality find it difficult to get funding for their research because of society's emotional views on sexuality. This occurs, in part, because funding decisions are made by public officials. These officials, sensitive to society's attitudes and feelings, are often likely to feel unsympathetic toward research in sexuality. In this indirect but powerful influence, one can clearly see the effect of values upon research in sexuality.

Levels of Analysis

Underlying all sex research are questions concerning the levels of analysis that are appropriate for understanding human sexuality. "Levels of analysis" refers to the type of phenomena studied. Psychologists have tended to focus upon one of three types of data: "(1) experiential, that is, relating to consciousness or 'mind'; (2) physiological; and (3) behavioral. The history of the study of behavioral events has been filled with controversy over which of these types or levels is most appropriate for the discipline" (Marx & Goodson, 1976, p. 393). Gewirtz (1978) suggests that

"levels of analysis" can also be construed to refer to a continuum that ranges from the macrolevel of sociological analysis to the microlevel of physiological analysis. Furthermore, Gewirtz maintains that no one level of analysis is more or less fundamental or adequate. However, many physiologists have limited their analyses of sexual phenomena to physiological activity while ignoring more moral levels of analysis.

However, in the field of sex research, one must continually pay attention to various levels of analysis. For example, in sex research, when asking questions about hormone–behavior relationships, investigators must deal with concepts from at least two levels of analysis: the physiological and the behavioral. By attending to various levels, one should be able to approach the goal of an integrated understanding of phenomena. The issue of levels of analysis becomes more obvious but also less threatening in an area where many disciplines regularly interact. In our subsequent discussion of models, the question of levels of analysis again becomes salient.

Researchers' Biases

Researchers' biases inevitably have a heavy impact upon sex research. Although this concern is relevant for any research topic, it seems more obvious and dramatic when dealing with human sexuality. In general, sex researchers have a relatively narrow subset of demographic characteristics. Most researchers in human sexuality are male, heterosexual, white, and middle-class. All of these factors have been shown to affect sexual attitude (Gagnon & Simon, 1973) and sexual behavior (Kinsey, Pomeroy, & Martin, 1948). Researchers' values and biases are often reflected in the concepts, approaches, and questions they formulate in their research. For example, views of homosexuality have undergone considerable modification in the recent past. Research has reflected this change. This change does not imply an elimination of biases, but rather the substitution of new biases. Furthermore, it often appears that we are faced with a regression of biases, in that the quality and utility of the new or old biases are judged by other biases. As Krasner and Ullmann (1973) note, "We evaluate the value of a value by another value" (p. 491).

Moreover, sex researchers are continually forced to take either explicit or implicit positions on issues that they are investigating. For example, in research on sex differences, investigators are hard pressed not to comment upon the "meaning" and implications of any differences they report. If they refuse to take an explicit position on the issues, they are even by that act taking a stance. This stance may implicitly support one position, or may even imply that there is nothing in the material that forces one to confront the issues. Of course, recognizing these concerns does not solve the issues, but it may lead us toward an appreciation of their importance.

MAJOR RESEARCH ISSUES

Any listing of the major issues in a field of study is bound to reflect the interests and biases of the enumerators. In an attempt to reduce those biases, we conducted a computer-based search of the literature. "Psychosexual," "sex," and "sexuality" were used as key words in listings in the *Psychological Abstracts* for the years 1967 through 1980.[2] The interpretation of the results of this search is problematical, since studies appear in multiple categories and key words are often assigned in an unsystematic manner. Nevertheless, from over 28,000 entries that were identified by the three key words noted above, three major topics emerged: sex differences, the development of sexuality, and applied problems.

The most common topic that resulted from the search was that of human sex differences. Listings relating to this topic occurred three times as frequently as listings for any other topic. This numerical superiority reflects the very great interest in differences between the sexes. However, in only a small proportion of the studies on the topic of sex differences did the papers refer to differences in sexual behavior. A plausible reason why sex differences have attracted so much attention is that there are very apparent major differences between the sexes. For example, it is well established that sexual behavior is strongly influenced by gender (Kinsey, Pomeroy, Martin, & Gebhard, 1953).

Psychophysiology has had an impact on this topic. For example, it has long been assumed that women are less responsive to explicit erotic stimuli than men. Schmidt and Sigusch (1970), using subjective reports as data, found that, in fact, women were more responsive to erotic stimuli than had been assumed. Heiman (1977) extended this work, using psychophysiological measures, and reported that women were quite responsive to erotic stimuli in the absence of a "romantic" context. This finding represents the type of contribution that is possible using psychophysiological methods. However, a major impediment to the psychophysiologist has been the lack of a metric that permits direct comparison of genital measures between the sexes. Since genital physiological mechanisms differ between the sexes, the development of a common metric for genital responses is a complex problem. Regardless of this complexity, we believe that psychophysiology can contribute usefully to the understanding of sex differences.

The second major research topic identified was the development of sexuality. Psychophysiology has not contributed extensively to the understanding of developmental issues. Masters and Johnson (1966) discussed the aging male and female, and Solnick and Birren (1977) have investigated genital responding in aging males. A serious problem the psychophysiologist faces, as noted above, is that societal constraints prevent using children and adolescents in studies employing genital measures. However, these constraints are eased when studying changes in older populations, and therefore psychophysiology can potentially make significant contributions to the understanding of the development of sexuality in such populations.

The third major research area identified was the study of applied issues. This topic area overlaps with those noted previously, yet is so obvious a grouping that separate discussion is warranted. Applied problems represent a very broad range of topics. For example, in addition to the obvious interest in treatment of dysfunctional and abnormal sexual behavior, there is great interest in sex education and issues relating to the regulation of reproduction. Psychophysiology's contribution to research on applied problems has tended to focus on diagnostic issues, including the assessment of progress in therapeutic programs. Because of the widespread existence of practical problems in sexuality, a continued emphasis upon applied topics can be expected.

While most research in sexuality can be identified as belonging to one of the three major areas noted above, there are other general research issues that merit comment—issues that were not obvious from the computer-based literature search. A theme that is salient in much of research on human sexuality is the relative contribution of biological versus experiential factors. Hormones, genetic factors, and the nature and role of neurological structure and function are all examples of biological factors; learning variables and such social phenomena as class and education are examples of experiential factors. As previously mentioned in the section on levels of analysis, research all too often focuses on one set of these factors while ignoring the other. However, it is likely that in most cases one is studying interactive phenomena, since much of sexual behavior results from influences of both experiential and biological factors. In fact, Storms (1981) has suggested that the development of erotic orientation results from an interaction between physiological sex drive development and social development during early adolescence. Since psychophysiology encompasses the study of both biological and experiential factors, it can make important contributions to the study of these influences and interactions in human sexuality.

Psychophysiology has typically addressed the issue of identifying main effects in the phenomena under study. Perhaps, as Cronbach (1957) has suggested,

2. The search was conducted using the *Psychological Abstracts* Computerized Data Base, State University of New York at Stony Brook.

there is a need to integrate the study of individual differences more carefully with the study of main effects. This implies that psychophysiology needs to attend more to the individual variability within main effects. Perhaps there is a need for further development of adequate models before the study of individual differences can be advanced significantly, but only time will tell for certain. It is clear, however, that at this time very little is known about individual differences in sexuality—from the perspective of psychophysiology or from those of other disciplines.

Finally, there is a great deal of interest in the topic of sex roles. It is surprising that very little is known about the impact of sex roles upon sexual behavior. As an article of faith, many believe that there is a significant relationship between these phenomena. With the possible exception of the study of atypical sex roles, such as transsexualism, little substantial has been demonstrated concerning the interaction between sex roles and sexual behavior. Theory and speculation abounds where data are almost nonexistent.

APPROACHES TO HUMAN SEXUALITY

An approach to human sexuality (or, indeed, any other field of inquiry) may be defined as a set of very general statements that attempts (1) to define what the subject matter is or ought to be, (2) to describe how this subject matter should be studied, and (3) to provide a coherent organization and interpretation of this subject matter (Marx & Hillex, 1973). In short, an approach serves as an heuristic device for the observation, description, explanation, prediction, and perhaps the control of the phenomena.

Approaches deal with many fundamental definitional issues. Definitions of the domain of investigation, the appropriate questions, and the appropriate answers are determined by the approach. For example, in the radical behavioral approach to human sexuality, sexual behavior is defined as behavior that changes in frequency as a function of sexual deprivation and satiation (Keller & Schoenfeld, 1950). In contrast, Freud (1905/1938) defined sex as pleasurable experience. These widely differing definitions lead to the study of different phenomena. Therefore, by starting from differing definitions, one often asks different questions and accepts different answers. Thus, theoretical positions are characterized by the "theory-ladenness of fact"; an approach constantly acts as a filter that heavily influences all facets of an investigation.

The quality of an approach can be evaluated on a number of dimensions. In general, it should be logically consistent, and it should accurately reflect experience. Goodson and Morgan (1976) suggest several

other relevant criteria for evaluating an approach: testability, responsiveness to new evidence, internal consistency, the extent to which the approach integrates the available empirical data, parsimony, communicability, and the extent to which it stimulates research. Space limitations do not permit us to comment on these criteria for each approach. However, it would be worthwhile for the reader to keep these criteria in mind when reading this section.

In describing the various approaches to human sexuality, we have attempted to present each approach in a positive light. Furthermore, the amount of space devoted to an approach is not meant to reflect the importance we attach to it.

Masters and Johnson's Approach

Masters and Johnson (1966) have proposed a four-phase descriptive model of the responses that occur in the human male and female during sexual arousal. We hasten to note that the model does not apply to other sexual phenomena. The four phases in the model are (1) the excitement phase, (2) the plateau phase, (3) the orgasmic phase, and (4) the resolution phase. The model describes changes in both genital and extragenital responding that are specific to each phase and to each sex. This model has provided useful signposts that may index sexual arousal in a reliable and valid manner.

The two major physiological reactions that play an important role in Masters and Johnson's sexual response cycle are myotonia and vasocongestion. It is the latter response that has been most useful to psychophysiologists studying sexual arousal.

Masters and Johnson's model is an empirical description of sexual response in men and women. The data upon which the model was based were subjective reports of the experience of sexual arousal by 382 women and 312 men, and direct observation of the 694 subjects. This model has served as a principal foundation for psychophysiological research on human sexuality. It has helped to direct researchers to the specific genital and extragenital responses accompanying sexual arousal that can be physiologically monitored. Historically, this model has served as a valuable heuristic for researchers exploring human sexuality, as it represents the first detailed description of sexual responses in humans. A brief sketch of the model follows.

The first phase of the model is the excitement phase. This phase develops in response to "effective" physical or psychological sexual stimulation. "Effective" stimulation is defined (Masters & Johnson, 1966) as stimulation that results in sexual arousal; the definition is thus circular. Sexual arousal increases in intensity during the excitement phase until the plateau phase is reached, where further stimulation maintains a constant high level of arousal. The identification of the transition point between these phases is problematical. Continued stimulation in the plateau phase results in reaching the point where orgasm is inevitable. The orgasmic stage typically lasts only a few seconds and represents the release of peak sexual tension, vasocongestion, and myotonia. It is usually longer in females than males, and there is greater individual variability in females. The final or resolution stage is characterized by a loss of tension that results in eventual return to prestimulation levels. Women may return to the orgasmic phase from any point in the resolution phase if they again receive "effective" sexual stimulation. Males, however, must pass through a refractory period of variable duration before being able to again experience orgasm. Masters and Johnson have noted that there is substantial individual variability in the timing of the phases. For the details of specific genital and extragenital changes occurring during the sexual response cycle, the reader should consult Masters and Johnson's (1966) text.

While few investigators would dispute the importance of the model, it has been subjected to serious criticism, which argues the need for revision. First, its generalizability may be limited due to subject selection biases. Masters and Johnson's sample was one of perhaps unusually sexually comfortable and liberal people. We note, parenthetically, that the same is true of much of the research using genital measures of sexual arousal. More importantly, Masters and Johnson (1966) failed to describe the methods they used to collect their psychophysiological data; hence it is impossible to replicate their studies. Furthermore, there is essentially no quantification of the data reported. Zuckerman's (1971) review of the literature revealed that nongenital measures were only weakly associated with self-reports of sexual arousal. Yet the model describes a relative invariance of some extragenital responses with sexual arousal. Research has shown that the relationships between certain extragenital responses and phases of the model, as reported by Masters and Johnson (1966), simply do not hold (e.g., heart rate; see Wenger *et al.*, 1968). Furthermore, Geer and Quartararo (1976) found a decrease in total blood volume in the genitals of human females at orgasm. This finding is at odds with the model's prediction of a peak in vasocongestion at orgasm. In addition, the universality of the model has been questioned, since there is doubt about the existence of the plateau phase (Rosen & Rosen, 1981).

Although this approach has specified the kinds of responses to be used to index sexual arousal in psychophysiological research, relatively little work has been done to refine and extend the model. Replications using psychophysiological measures could lay to rest some of the contradictory findings noted above.

Finally, psychophysiological methodologies may provide useful approaches to understanding phenomena described in the model, such as the occurrence of multiple orgasms in women.

Classical Conditioning Approach

Pavlov (1955) first described the phenomenon of classical conditioning. Rescorla (1980) has described Pavlovian conditioning "as an example of associative learning in which an organism learns the relation between two events in its environment" (p. 1). One of these events, which is usually of some importance to the animal, reliably elicits a response and is labeled the unconditioned stimulus (UCS). The other event, which is of little or no importance before learning, is labeled the conditioned stimulus (CS). As a result of exposure to some systematic relationship between these two events, the organism is changed, and this change is indexed by a modification in the animal's performance (Rescorla, 1980). After conditioning, the subject responds to the CS in a new way that is usually similar to the response to the UCS. This new response to the CS is called the conditioned response (CR). For a detailed description of the phenomena and concepts of classical conditioning, the reader should consult Beecroft (1966) or Dickinson and Mackintosh (1978).

Classical conditioning is particularly relevant to autonomically mediated behaviors and is often implicated in the acquisition of emotional responses. Since sexual arousal can be considered an emotional response, and since it is mediated by the autonomic nervous system, classical conditioning appears particularly relevant to the study of sexual arousal. Psychophysiological methods have been extensively applied to studies of autonomically mediated responses, and thus should prove useful to the study of classical conditioning as it applies to human sexuality.

Psychophysiological methodologies have been used in studies that have purported to show classical conditioning of penile tumescence (Langevin & Martin, 1975; Rachman, 1966; Rachman & Hodgson, 1968). These studies have demonstrated associative learning of sexual arousal to previously neutral stimuli (e.g., slides of boots and geometrical patterns); however, conditioning is weak. These studies can be criticized as lacking either a random or an unpaired control group; moreover, the Rachman studies were limited by small sample size. Considerable research involving classical conditioning has been concerned with the modification of atypical sexual preferences. The basis of this interest may be traced to Kinsey *et al.* (1948), who proposed that typical and atypical sexual preferences are acquired via classical conditioning. Additional work on the modification of sexual preferences has utilized aversive conditioning to modify homosexual preferences, as well as "orgasmic reconditioning," which is the pairing of sexual arousal with "appropriate" sexual stimuli (e.g., Feldman & MacCulloch, 1971; Herman, Barlow, & Agras, 1974; Marquis, 1970).

There are many interesting questions in the field of human sexuality that can be explored from the perspective of Pavlovian conditioning using psychophysiological techniques. Such issues as whether a "preparedness" dimension (Seligman, 1971) exists in the acquisition of fetishes can be studied. This would address the question of why fetishes seem to occur almost exclusively to objects that are culturally associated with women rather than to a broader range of stimuli. Furthermore, knowledge of the parameters of classical conditioning as they apply to the sexual response system might be useful for developing better treatments of sexual deviations.

Physiological Approach

The physiological approach addresses the physical and biochemical basis of human sexuality. The influences of hormonal, neural, genetic, and anatomical factors comprise the principal foci of this approach. The role of psychophysiology in the physiological approach to human sexuality is dealt with in detail in another chapter of this handbook (see Carter, Chapter 9, this volume); therefore, to avoid redundancy, only a few general points concerning this approach are mentioned here.

Psychophysiology and the physiological approach are closely related, in that they both are concerned with the study of the biological substrate of sexual behavior. The distinctions between the two are often somewhat arbitrary and equivocal. Stern (1964) differentiates the two on the basis of their independent and dependent variables. The physiological psychologist usually utilizes physiology as the independent variable and behavior as the dependent variable, while the psychophysiologist uses behavior or its environmental influences as the independent variable and some aspect of physiology as the dependent variable. Another distinction can be made according to the methodologies employed by the two approaches. In the physiological approach, the methodologies are typically more intrusive than those used in psychophysiology. That is, the biological processes occurring in the internal environment of the organism are studied more directly. For example, implantation of electrodes and the surgical removal of anatomical structures are two direct, intrusive modes of gathering information that the physiological approach utilizes.

Related to these differences in methodology are differences in the validity of the information that is gained. The physiological approach, due to its directness, allows stronger causal inferences to be made concerning the specific physiological mechanisms that influence sexual behavior. However, this directness is often gained at the expense of naturalness, which is often lost due to the reactive nature of the methodology. The relative nonintrusiveness of the psychophysiological procedures permits the behavioral researcher to study the phenomena of interest in a more natural state. However, in general, psychophysiology permits weaker causal inferences concerning the exact nature of the physiological mechanisms involved than does the physiological approach. In addition, since the level of analysis of the physiological approach is relatively molecular, this approach has to deal with the correspondence rules for the extrapolation of its findings at a molecular level to the explanation of behavioral phenomena at a more molar level.

The determination of nocturnal penile tumescence (NPT) is one example of a relatively nonintrusive mode of psychophysiological measurement that is used to aid in making inferences about the physiological basis of human sexuality. NPT is used as a diagnostic procedure for evaluating the organic basis of erectile dysfunction. If the distressed individual shows normal cyclic erections during sleep, then it is assumed that the problem is "psychological" and is not a deficit in physiological mechanisms (Karacan, Ware, Dervant, Altinel, Thoenby, Williams, Musret, & Scott; 1978). In the subsequent section on "Unique Contributions of Psychophysiology," additional interfaces between physiological theory and psychophysiological methods are described.

Radical Behavioral Approach

The radical behavioral model, derived from the research and writings of B. F. Skinner, posits that the variables that influence sexual behavior lie in the environment of the organism. The influence of the environment functions through the past and present contingencies of survival and the contingencies of reinforcement.

"Contingencies of survival" is a summary term for the selective action of the environment on the genetic endowment of the species. This construct is useful in explaining the role of sexual contact as a primary reinforcer.

At a time when the human race was periodically decimated by pestilence, famine, and war and steadily attenuated by endemic ills and unsanitary and dangerous environment, it was important that procreative behavior should be maximized. Those for whom sexual reinforcement was most powerful should have most quickly achieved copulation and should have continued to copulate most frequently. The breeders selected by sexual competition must have been not only the most powerful and skillful members of the species but those for whom sexual contact was most reinforcing. In a safer environment the same susceptibility leads to serious over-population with its attendant ills. (Skinner, 1969, pp. 50–51)

Natural selection is supplemented through selection of behaviors by consequences that cannot have evolutionary significance. This occurs because the consequences are often not stable features of the environment. This selection of behavior is called "operant conditioning"; the behaviors selected are called "operants"; and the functional relationships that exist between the responses and their environmental antecedents and consequences are called "contingencies of reinforcement." The experimental analysis of these functional relationships, using the rate of responding as the major dependent variable, is the hallmark of this approach.

The domain of "sexual" behavior can be operationally defined using this methodology. Sexual behavior is the behavior that changes in frequency as a function of sexual deprivation and satiation (Keller & Schoenfeld, 1950). Therefore, behaviors that are topographically dissimilar to obvious sexual behaviors but that prove to be functionally related by experimental manipulations of deprivation conditions can then be considered sexual in nature. Ullmann and Krasner (1975) suggest a further distinction between operant behavior in response to a sexual situation and operants required to arrive at that situation (e.g., appropriate social skills).

Within the radical behavioral model, sexual behavior is viewed as having important biological influences—both through natural selection in the evolution of the species and through the biological substrate of behavior. However, the emphasis of this model is on viewing most sexual behavior as being learned—developed and maintained through its environmental consequences.

Although it was long believed that autonomic responses were not susceptible to operant conditioning (Skinner, 1938), there have been some recent demonstrations of operant conditioning of the responses of the autonomic nervous system (e.g., Miller, 1969). However, there has been some difficulty in replicating this early work (Miller & Dworkin, 1974). Biofeedback can be construed as involving the operant conditioning of autonomic responses (Hassett, 1978). In biofeedback, physiological responses are shaped by the differential reinforcement of responses that represent movement toward the desired goal (e.g., an appropriate blood pressure). Biofeedback, according to this view, is largely a matter of contingently providing stimuli that function as reinforcers for relatively subtle changes in physiological functioning. There have been some successful attempts at operant reinforcement and maintenance of genital responding (Geer, 1979).

Research in human sexuality derived from this model has largely failed to utilize psychophysiological methodologies. This is probably due in part to the model's emphasis on overt molar behavior and on explaining that behavior at its own level (Skinner, 1950). It is argued that moving from a completely molar account of behavior to another level of analysis decreases the efficiency of the explanation, due to the residual, unexplained variance that can result from the imperfect correlations that may exist between variables at different levels of analysis (Gewirtz, 1978). Skinner (1950) criticizes "any explanation of any observed fact which appeals to events taking place somewhere else, at some other level of observation, described in different terms, and measured, if at all, in different dimensions" (p. 192). However, this *a priori* eschewal of other levels of analysis can be regarded as unnecessarily restrictive. It has been argued that the legitimacy of the use of another level of analysis should be judged on the empirical grounds of whether it can help to account further for variance in the data, instead of being ruled out because of theoretical biases (Mahoney, 1974).

The radical behavioral approach also recognizes that part of the behavior of the organism occurs beneath its skin, and that this covert behavior does not explain other (overt) behavior, but is simply more behavior to be explained. Psychophysiological techniques can, therefore, potentially play a useful role in providing reliable and valid indices of these covert behaviors in order to assess their relationships with overt behaviors and the extant environmental contingencies.

Cognitive Models

A unified cognitive theory of human sexuality does not exist. However, aspects of human sexuality have been analyzed within general cognitive models (Rook & Hammen, 1977), and there has been some use of methods borrowed from experimental cognitive psychology (e.g., Geer & Fuhr, 1976). In taking a cognitive perspective on human sexuality, the researcher focuses on the thoughts, feelings, and attributions of the subject that relate to sexual behavior.

Mahoney (1974) has described three cognitive models. The first model he terms the "covert conditioning approach." In this model, private experience is treated in the same manner as overt behavior is treated in the operant conditioning theories. Homme (1965) suggests that cognitive events are early elements in ultimately observable response chains, and therefore can be manipulated to affect the probability of observable responses. Learning principles such as reinforcement, punishment, and extinction are considered, according to this view, to be applicable to thought, images, and feelings. The second model that Mahoney describes is termed the "information-processing approach." This scheme emphasizes the acquisition, storage, and utilization of information. The third and final model described by Mahoney is called the "cognitive learning approach." The cognitive learning approach is essentially an amalgam of the views of various learning theorists and clinicians, such as Albert Bandura, George Kelly, and Albert Ellis. Perhaps the best-researched cognitive model that has been applied to human sexuality is labeling and attribution theory. Briefly stated, labeling and attribution concepts suggest that physiological arousal, no matter what its cause, will be labeled as sexual in nature if the contextual cues are sexual. This line of research stems from Schacter and Singer's (1962) model of emotion. Research in this paradigm, as it applies to human sexuality, has been thoroughly reviewed by Rook and Hammen (1977).

Psychophysiological techniques have been used to contribute to the cognitive approach to human sexuality in the work of Geer and his colleagues. For example, Geer and Fuhr (1976) used a dichotic listening task to demonstrate the relationship between attention to erotic materials and sexual arousal. They showed that distraction produced by increasingly complex cognitive tasks resulted in correspondingly less sexual arousal to a standard erotic stimulus. They measured sexual arousal with the objective methods of psychophysiology, rather than relying solely on self-reports. However, as currently structured, experimental cognitive psychology often deals with molecular concepts. Many of the procedures used in experimental cognitive research are based on events that occur in very brief periods of time—periods of time that would result in difficulty in detecting genital responses.

The Geer and Fuhr (1976) study represents the beginnings of the application of psychophysiological techniques to the study of cognitive factors in human sexuality. However, there are a number of other potential interfaces between cognitive approaches and psychophysiological methodologies. Psychophysiological measuring devices, such as the penile strain gauge, give the researcher the advantage of an objective measurement of sexual arousal that complements the subject's self-report. This on-line characteristic of psychophysiological measurements enables the researcher to study the manner in which sexual arousal covaries with reported subjective states (see Korff and Geer, 1984). This permits the study of such variables as cognitions, feelings, fantasy, and imagery. For instance, it has been demonstrated that instructions to fantasize sexual situations result in consistent changes in genital responses (e.g., Heiman, 1977; Stock & Geer, 1982). Research in the area of attribution and labeling is possible using the techniques of psychophysiology.

There have been attempts to use cognitive methods to affect sexual behavior in clinical settings (Costell, 1972). However, these clinical situations represent

applications that go beyond the models currently in vogue in experimental cognitive psychology.

The Social Learning Theory Approach

Social learning theory attempts to integrate all major principles of learning, but its defining characteristic is its focus on the social context of human behavior. As such, it involves the application of the principles of classical conditioning, operant conditioning, and observational learning to the explanation of human behavior. Since the operant and classical conditioning approaches have been covered under separate headings, this discussion is limited to observational learning.

Bandura (1969) has argued that a great deal of human learning occurs by the observation of others. Observational learning, or "modeling," according to Bandura (1969), refers to the acquisition of behavior by viewing others and the consequences of their acts. Observational learning includes not only direct observation of models, but also symbolic modeling, which may result from written materials and verbal descriptions. Relatively little work has been done on applying this approach to sexual behavior, although it has been often used to examine and explain sex role behavior. In light of this, the account that follows is largely speculative and awaits empirical confirmation.

First, one can note the various opportunities for observational learning available in this culture. Children can learn aspects of sexual behavior by observing parents or by observing models on television or in films. In addition, adults may observe explicit sexual behavior in X-rated or stag films. For the adolescent and adult, sexual behavior can also be acquired by reading sexually explicit materials. However, due to the personal and private nature of sexual behavior, probably the greatest sources of observational learning about sexuality are the verbal communications given by peers (Gebhard, 1977; Hunt, 1974). Learning from the written or spoken word is referred to by Bandura as "verbal modeling." Bandura (1977) has noted that verbal modeling occurs extensively, because words can convey an almost infinite variety of behaviors that would be inconvenient or time-consuming to model directly.

One of the major roles of modeling is in the modification of inhibitions. Research has shown that responses can be inhibited by observation of negative consequences of these responses to models, and that previously inhibited behavior can be elicited following the observation of models performing that behavior (Bandura, 1977). The literature on the effects of pornography is consistent with this view, since it has demonstrated that exposure to erotic acts does temporarily increase sexual activity (*Commission on Obscenity and Pornography*, 1970).

Despite the utility of conceptualizing some sexual behavior as learned by modeling, the limitations of the approach must be recognized. Sexual behavior is extremely complex, and while much of the behavior involved in a sexual interaction may be learned beforehand via actual or symbolic modeling, the control of learning by actual practice is probably extensive. Furthermore, social learning theory often ignores some of the important biological and developmental influences on sexual behavior. The mere presence of a model is not sufficient to result in observational learning. For example, prepubescent children may not react to models of sexual activity in a manner similar to that of the more bioligically mature individual. In addition, while a social learning approach to human sexuality has utility in conceptualizing mechanisms for the acquisition of sexual behaviors, this theory is difficult to test directly because of the private nature of sexual behavior.

Psychophysiology has not been systematically applied to a social learning approach to human sexual behavior. However, there are many possible applications. Psychophysiological techniques could be used to assess the disinhibiting or inhibiting effects of visual sexual stimuli on observers. Moreover, since it has been demonstrated that emotional responses can be acquired via modeling (Bandura, 1977), psychophysiology could be used to determine the extent to which observers have acquired emotional responses while observing modeled appropriate emotional behaviors. A potential clinical application of observational learning would be to determine whether individuals with low desire acquire desired arousal states after observing models. As Walen (1980) has noted, modeling probably sets standards as to what is regarded as erotic. Psychophysiological techniques could be used to assess the erotic value of a stimulus after individuals view models responding sexually to that stimulus.

Actuarial Approach

The strategy employed by the actuarial approach is to abandon the search for causal mechanisms and to concentrate on an account of people's sexual behavior as a function of their demographic characteristics. Probably the best-known examples of research using this approach are the studies by Kinsey and his co-workers (Kinsey *et al.*, 1948, 1953). The data in these works were gathered from detailed personal interviews and then partitioned into categories based on the personal characteristics of the subjects. The major variables that Kinsey and his colleagues found to be related to sexual behavior were age, sex, marital status, parental occupational class, religious background, education, decade of birth, age of onset of adolescence, and urban versus rural background. These variables are correlated variables that do not necessarily

identify the specific causal mechanisms involved; the actuarial approach leaves the exploration of the underlying causal mechanisms of these relationships for other approaches. However, to the extent that these indices are correlated with the behavior of interest, a univariate or multivariate prediction based on these indices is made possible—hence the use of the term "actuarial." The major strength of this approach is in determining the degree to which sexual behavior is correlated with various demographic and individual characteristics.

The nature of the information gained from this approach is illustrated in the following findings of Kinsey *et al.* (1948). The mean number of orgasms per week for white males between adolescence and 85 years of age was three. The major methods of obtaining these orgasms were masturbation, nocturnal sex dreams, heterosexual petting, coitus, homosexual relations, and relations with animals. The most sexually active males were those below the age of 30, with the frequency of orgasms declining steadily with increasing age.

Along with the advantage of allowing quantitative predictions, the actuarial method also provides a context of group membership for the further understanding of individuals' sexual behavior. Therefore, when individuals are classified into categories, a background is provided against which the individuals' behavior can be more meaningfully compared and understood.

There are a number of major problems with research using the actuarial approach. First, there is a need for continuous updating of findings to track any changes in sexual practice. Secondly, sample biases are a continuing source of error. For example, minority groups were grossly underrepresented in Kinsey's work. Stratified random sampling would be the preferred strategy for sampling subjects, but it is difficult to carry out due to subject self-selection. Furthermore, the use of self-report data has many methodological pitfalls. Distortion due to the retrospective and reactive nature of the method is an unresolved problem. Finally, the actuarial approach has the disadvantage of not providing a theoretical basis for determining which variables should be evaluated.

Psychophysiological methodologies can be utilized within the actuarial approach to develop further dimensions for classifying subjects. For example, perhaps it would be useful to categorize individuals by genital response lability. It is an empirical question whether this, or any other dimensions that might be developed from the psychophysiological methodologies can result in meaningful classifications. Furthermore, psychophysiological dimensions must prove to be sufficiently useful to justify their relatively high cost. In another application of psychophysiology to the actuarial approach, psychophysiology could be used to examine whether the traditional actuarial categories differ on any psychophysiological dimensions.

Sociological Approaches: Scripting

Most psychologists are not accustomed to thinking in terms of the more molar level of analysis that sociology employs. Sociologists have written a great deal about sexuality, especially from the vantage point of the subfield known as the sociology of deviance. These writings have described various forms of sexual deviation and their associated subcultures. This work is generally narrow in scope and is basically descriptive and explanatory in nature. Sociologists have also treated sexual behavior as one of several variables within larger theoretical frameworks. For example, a discrete form of sexual behavior, such as prostitution, is examined by functional sociological theories in terms of what functions the phenomenon performs in a given society or subculture. As an example, a function for prostitution that has been suggested is the preservation of monogamy (Lowry & Rankin, 1969).

As noted, sexuality is often treated by sociologists within broader topics of interest, such as the study of the family. However, a comprehensive sociological theory of sexual behavior has been developed by Gagnon and Simon (1973). Their theory is known as "scripting" theory; as the name would suggest, the theory has its origins in drama. Scripts are highly learned, culturally prescribed routines of behavior. As in drama, social scripts tell a person how to behave in a given situation. Gagnon and Simon assert that much of our sexual behavior consists of scripts: "Scripts are involved in learning the meaning of internal states, organizing the sequences of specifically sexual acts, decoding novel situations, setting the limits on sexual responses, and linking meanings from nonsexual aspects of life to specifically sexual experience" (1973, p. 19). These authors believe, contrary to the view of many others, that the form and meaning of sexual behavior has almost exclusively social rather than biological origins. They argue, for example, that the so-called "erogenous zones" are learned and do not reflect biological influences. Scripting theory states that there will be a particular script within each culture for the sequencing of sexual behaviors, and that the script determines what kind of stimuli will be regarded as erotic. Scripting theory is similar to social learning theory in many ways and bears some resemblance to Tolman's (1948) notion of cognitive maps. However, the theory is relatively imprecise. It does not specify conditions of acquisition, maintenance, or modification of scripts, and has few directly testable predictions.

To date, there have been no psychophysiological studies directly relevant to scripting theory. However, this methodology could contribute to the study of scripting theory. For example, the role of scripts in sexual arousal could be examined by presenting erotic stimuli that vary the sequence of sexual behavior. It follows from scripting theory that the dominant script for any one culture should produce the most intense arousal in that culture. Conversely, any sequence that varies from the dominant script—for example, intercourse occurring before sex play in most Western cultures—should yield reduced levels of arousal. Similar tests of the scripting notions are possible by manipulating scripts in a systematic manner and determining the effect of those manipulations upon sexual behavior.

Psychoanalytic Approach

Freud's definition of sexuality differs greatly from many popular conceptions and from many of the definitions provided by the other approaches in this chapter. Freud (1905/1938) distinguished "sexual activity" from "genital activity" and utilized the former as a broader concept including many activities that have little to do with the traditional conceptualizations of sex. As a result of Freudian influence, "sex" came to denote most pleasurable experiences. Furthermore, Munroe (1955) suggests that within the Freudian framework, the reduction of tension in an organ system is experienced as pleasure: "The terms 'sexuality' and 'pleasure' so easily awaken associations of wine, women and song that it is necessary to keep reminding ourselves of the almost too strictly scientific sense in which Freud used them and of his adherence to a purely biological criterion" (p. 76).

Within this enlarged definition of sex, Freud (1905/1938), in his essay "Three Contributions to the Theory of Sex," defined his major findings in sexuality as follows: (1) infantile sexuality (i.e., sexual life begins soon after birth), and (2) psychosexual development (i.e., sexual life is composed of sequential stages in which pleasures are experienced through different zones of the body). This psychosexual development usually, although not inevitably, progresses through the oral, anal, phallic, latent, and genital stages. Freud's theory of sexuality was largely based on three sources of information: (1) considerations of sexual perversions, (2) the memories of his adult patients of their childhood sexual activities, and (3) direct observation of children.

Another set of concepts with the Freudian model is concerned with the dynamics of mental functioning. Freud postulated the existence of a dynamic tension among the sexual instincts of the id operating under the pleasure principle, the ego operating under the reality principle, and the superego acting as conscience. Freud's description of the inevitable conflict between these instincts operating under different principles underwent many revisions through the years. However, the basic assertion of an unconscious conflict among the irrational, primitive, pleasure-seeking id, the more realistic and rational ego instincts, and the demands both of the extant social constraints and of the superego—a conflict resulting in various forms of compromise behavior—is regarded as one of his most important contributions (Munroe, 1955).

Freud maintained that the sexual instincts, or, as he called them, the "libido," have both mental and physical manifestations. Munroe (1955) points out that the libidinal sexual instincts are

> no more (and no less) than the tension systems presented by the organ systems of the body. Their aim is reduction of tension, which is experienced as gratification (pleasure). In so far as the body functions as a unit, the specific aims (gratification of a special organ system) may become fused, one may be substituted for another under some conditions, or some sort of coordination may be effected in the interests of the organism as a whole. (p. 74)

Freud also asserted that any problem occurring in psychosexual development as a result of either insufficient or excessive gratification of the needs of a particular stage would manifest itself in adult sexual life.

> In the first instance (insufficient gratification), as physiological maturation moves inexorably, the libido does not keep pace, as it were, and the body zone appropriate to the next phase of development does not become adequately eroticized. When gratification is excessive, then the child is reluctant to give it up. In either instance the libido becomes "fixated" at that stage. This hampers subsequent development, and the individual either fails to mature psychosexually or is at least handicapped by a tendency to "regress" to the fixation point under stress. (Katchadourian & Lunde, 1972, p. 193)

The Freudian model of sexuality was designed to help explain all behavior, not just sexual behavior. However, it is interesting to note that much less emphasis has been given to sexual behavior per se by the model than would have been expected on the basis of the central role of sexual instincts in the model.

Freudian theory has been frequently criticized for its lack of experimental verification. This deficit has been largely due to problems in providing adequate operational definitions of many Freudian constructs. However, given Freud's assertion that the libidinal instincts have direct physiological components, and his assertions concerning the psychosocial influences of these libidinal forces, it would seem that psychophysiology could play a useful role in attempting to provide operational definitions for these concepts.

Political Power Approach

The political power approach to human sexuality emanates from observations concerning the interrelationships that exist between sex and the distribution of economic and political resources. This interrelationship is such that sex (gender) has important implications for the manner in which most cultures distribute their political and economic resources; conjointly,

the allocation of political and economic resources has much to do with one's sexual behavior. Therefore, a reciprocal process occurs, in which one's sex influences the quantity and quality of resources one receives, and one's resources influences one's sexual experience. The resulting imbalances are usually in the favor of the empowered groups in society (whites, males, etc., in contemporary Western societies). It has largely been those in less advantageous positions who have created and developed this approach, which attempts to describe, understand, and rectify these inequities. Within Western society, women have made the greatest contributions toward the understanding of human sexuality within this approach. Therefore, this section concentrates on their perspective.

It is plausible that the current divisions of labor and resources can be traced back to the differential roles the two sexes play in reproduction. This becomes most apparent in primitive hunter–gatherer societies, in which the female, encumbered by pregnancy and nursing, assumes more "domestic" activities, while the physically stronger male assumes the role of the hunter (breadwinner). However, given the decreased dependence of societal functioning on biological considerations, these roles cannot currently be justified by these differential reproductive functions.

This approach proposes that the socialization process, in which members of each sex learn the "appropriate" roles, is the major mechanism that maintains and perpetuates these inequalities. The sexual socialization process is ubiquitous, operating through religion, art, literature, education, fashion, and theories of behavior. Thompson (1950), for example, suggests that many sexist biases are embodied and legitimized in Freudian theory.

Daly (1978) identifies four specific mechanisms that are essential to the "games of the fathers" (males):

> First, there is *erasure* of women. (The massacre of millions of women as witches is erased in patriarchal scholarship.) Second, there is *reversal*. (Adam gives birth to Eve, Zeus to Athena, in patriarchal myth.) Third, there is *false polarization*. (Male-defined "feminism" is set up against male-defined "sexism" in the patriarchal media.) Fourth, there is *divide and conquer*. (Token women are trained to kill off feminists in patriarchal professions.) (p. 8)

These mechanisms prevent women from escaping from the sterotyped sex roles that act to constrain them.

As already mentioned, the economic and political domination and exploitation of females by males often lead to sexual exploitation. The female is often regarded as a sexual object whose function is to give pleasure to the male, while being denied equal status in pursuing her own legitimate needs and desires. For example, in English common law until the present century, women were the property of either their fathers or their husbands. Currently, traces of this practice are found in those laws in the United States that do not admit to the existence of rape between marriage partners. Rape and pornography are thought to be further acts of contempt and aggression toward women, and illustrate the wide-ranging impact of sexism on human sexuality.

Feminists are demanding and working for change on many fronts. Daly (1978) calls for the following social changes: "*re-education* of women through the institution of Women Studies; a *rewriting* of history with a view to woman's role in it; the admission of women to vocational courses; *economic equality* through an end to job discrimination and the admission of women to trade schools and unions; *physical equality* through birth control and abortion rights; and equal representation in their government" (p. xviii).

Psychophysiology can potentially play an important role in relation to the political power approach in the area of sex differences. This area of research is discussed in another part of this chapter; however, a few points need to be made concerning research on sex differences in the context of this approach. The first point is that sex research and psychophysiology can be viewed as being male-dominated and as having unintentional and/or intentional male biases. Therefore, the theory, research, and application of these disciplines have to be viewed with these implicit or explicit biases in mind. Secondly, the ramifications of research into sex differences are particularly powerful and extensive. This makes it necessary that the researcher be sensitive to the political implications of his or her research. Finally, this approach demands recognition of the possibility that there might be very little in behavior that is uniquely and intrinsically masculine or feminine, independent of the socialization process. It may well be that only through the socialization process that "masculine" and "feminine" become defined. However, it also must be recognized that it might be in the interest of the existing power structure to perpetuate sexist distinctions by adhering to conventional definitions.

Sociobiological Approach

Sociobiology is an emerging discipline that has been based largely on the writings of Edward O. Wilson (1978). Sociobiology attempts to delineate the biological basis of the social behavior of animals; as such, it strives to account for the workings of *proximate* causal mechanisms by utilizing an *ultimate* level of analysis. By "proximate mechanisms," sociobiologists are referring to the more immediate causes of behavior, such as learning or physiological factors. The ultimate level of analysis emphasized by sociobiologists focuses upon earlier elements in the causal chain

of behavior and thereby attempts to account for these immediate or proximate causes. The ultimate level of analysis utilized in sociobiology provides an evolutionary explanation for the immediate causes of behavior (Barash, 1977). For example, learning might exist because of the role it plays in enhancing the likelihood of an organism's survival. Therefore, sociobiology often begins its analysis where other approaches end, in that it attempts to provide an evolutionary context for the findings of other approaches.

Evolution by natural selection is the most fundamental explanatory construct in this ultimate level of analysis. "Natural selection" may be thought of as differential reproduction (i.e., the tendency for some individuals in a species to produce more viable progeny than others). This difference in reproductive success is thought to be due to differences among individuals on characteristics that fit them for survival and reproduction in a given environment. If the differences that determine reproductive success reflect underlying genetic factors, then a gradual genetic shift in the population will result. This genetic change is what is commonly referred to as "evolution."

When Darwin proposed his ideas on evolution, he suggested another selective mechanism—"sexual selection," which supplements natural selection. Darwin proposed that the evolution of secondary sex differences in structure, physiology, and behavior could be conceptualized as follows:

> Darwin (1871) attributed secondary sex differences primarily to the operation of "sexual selection". He distinguished sexual from natural selection in that the latter results from the differential abilities of individuals to adapt to their "environments" while the former results specifically from the differential abilities of individuals to acquire mates. Darwin identified two types of sexual selection: intersexual selection, based on female choice of males ("the power to charm the females"), and intrasexual selection, based on male–male competition ("the power to conquer other males in battle"). The first results in the evolution of bright color and ornamentation, the second in large body size, natural weapons, and pugnacity, though both types of sexual selection can occur simultaneously (Ralls, 1976). (Symons, 1980, p. 172)

Sociobiology uses those principles that were originally developed to explain the evolution of anatomical structure and behavior patterns. This extrapolation is justified as follows:

> [C]onsider it [the correlation between genes and behavior] from a purely mechanistic viewpoint: the DNA of which genes are composed specifies the production of proteins leading to the various structures constituting an organism. These structures include bone, muscle, blood, and nerve cells. Behavior unquestionably arises as a consequence of the activity of nerve cells, which presumably are susceptible to specification by DNA, much as any other cells. Accordingly, insofar as genes specify the organization of nerve cells, just as they specify the organization of bone cells, there is every reason to accept a role

of genes in producing behavior, just as we accept the role of genes in producing structure. As phenotypes go, behavior may be somewhat more flexible or susceptible to environmental influences than most. But the relevance of genetics to behavior is undeniable, and since evolution is the primary force responsible for the genetic make-up of living things, evolution must also be relevant to behavior. (Barash, 1977, pp. 47–48)

Sexual behavior is an important area of investigation for sociobiologists, since, due to its essential role in the transmission of genes, successful reproduction becomes the ultimate goal. Sexual reproduction, despite its high cost in terms of energy expenditure and exposure to risks, has evolved because it creates genetic diversity (Wilson, 1978). In asexual reproduction, the genetic makeup of progeny is identical to that of the parent. However, in sexual reproduction, progeny share only 50% of their genes in common with each parent. This genetic diversity is the manner in which "a parent hedges its bets against an unpredictably changing environment" (Wilson, 1978, p. 122).

Two sexes, as opposed to a greater number of sexes, have become predominant because this arrangement represents the most efficient possible division of reproductive labor (Wilson, 1978). However, in the human condition this division produces a fundamental conflict of interest between the two sexes, since each sex is selected for maximization of its own fitness. This conflict can be described as follows (Wilson, 1978): Females produce fewer gametes than males and consequently have a larger investment in each of their sex cells. The costs of gestation and care for the progeny after birth are also greater for the female. On the other hand, males produce millions of sperm cells in each ejaculation, and after insemination their essential physical commitment has come to an end. Therefore, the male typically invests much less in the reproductive process than the female, although his genes profit equally. Therefore, being forward and sexually indiscriminating is often a reproductively profitable behavioral strategy for males. In contrast, it pays for the female to be selective and discriminating in order to select a male with the best genes, a male in control of the best resources, and a male more likely to remain with her after insemination.

Based on his analysis of anthropological studies of hunter–gatherer societies, Wilson (1978) suggests that sex and continuous female sexual responsiveness function to reinforce the pair-bonding that emanates from these reproductive strategies.

> It is to the advantage of each woman of the hunter-gatherer band to secure the allegiance of men who will contribute meat and hides while sharing the labor of childrearing. It is to the reciprocal advantage of each man to obtain exclusive sexual rights to women and to monopolize their economic productivity. If the evidence from hunter–gatherer life has been correctly interpreted, the exchange has resulted in near universality of the pair

bond and the prevalence of extended families with men and their wives forming the nucleus. Sexual love and the emotional satisfaction of family life can be reasonably postulated to be based on enabling mechanisms in the physiology of the brain that have been programmed to some extent through the genetic hardening of this compromise. (Wilson, 1978, pp. 139–140).

Wilson maintains that there is a "strong possibility" that homosexuality should also be viewed as biologically normal, since it also serves to strengthen bonding and since it is commonly found in many species. Furthermore, Wilson (1978) suggests that homosexuals "may be the genetic carriers of some of mankind's rare altruistic impulses" (p. 143). This statement is derived from the "kin-selection hypothesis" of homosexuality. This hypothesis is used to overcome the dilemma of how genes that predispose their carriers to become homosexuals are transmitted, since homosexuals rarely produce offspring. The reasoning is that the close relatives of homosexuals have a greater probability of successful reproduction, due to the assistance they receive from their homosexual relatives, who are freed from parental duties. Wilson (1978) asserts that this hypothesis is supported by evidence that homosexuality has a genetic component, and that homosexuals often disproportionately occupy influential roles in society. However, he fails to cite specific evidence for these assertions.

The explanatory schemes for homosexuality, continuous female responsiveness, and male promiscuity illustrate the manner in which sociobiology provides possible explanatory accounts for human sexual behavior. However, these accounts and sociobiology in general have been criticized as being largely speculative and as being difficult or impossible to test directly, particularly when applied to humans. The identification of specific genetic mechanisms underlying any phenomenon is not feasible via psychophysiology. Moreover, it is not possible to directly test the basic assertions of sociobiology using psychophysiology. Nevertheless, it is possible to test certain predictions from the approach, as well as to use this approach to help "explain" results gained from the use of psychophysiology. An example of a prediction from the approach is that novel sexual partners will be more arousing to males than to females. Psychophysiologists can, however, potentially profit by recognizing the importance of an evolutionary context provided by sociobiology.

Existential–Phenomenological Approach

Existential–phenomenological psychology can trace its roots to the philosophical position of Leibnitz, who viewed the organism as active and self-motivated. This is in opposition to traditional experimental psychology, which is heavily influenced by Locke, who viewed the organism as reactive (Matson, 1973). As its name implies, existential–phenomenological psychology is the result of the fusion of two closely related currents in philosophical thought: existentialism and phenomenology (Valle & King, 1978).

Existentialism is a broad term encompassing the thought of a variety of philosophers, including Soren Kierkegaard, Friedrich Nietzche, Feodor Dostoevski, Martin Heidegger, Jean-Paul Sartre, Maurice Merleau Ponty, and Albert Camus. Valle and King (1978) offer the following definition of existentialism:

> Existentialism, as a formal philosophical school, seeks to understand the human condition as it manifests itself in our *concrete*, *lived* situations. Its concern for these situations includes not only their physical characteristics (such as the people and places involved), but also all of our attendant moments of joy, absurdity, and indifference, as well as the range of freedom we experience as having in our responses to these various moments. (p. 6).

Phenomenology is the philosophical methodology developed by Edmund Husserl (Valle & King, 1978). Husserl was influenced by the psychologists Brentano, Stumpf, and William James, although he did not view their work as pure phenomenology (MacLeod, 1964). Valle and King (1978) define phenomenology as "a method which allows us to contact phenomena *as we actually live them out and experience them*" (p. 7). MacLeod (1964) has made the following general points about phenomenology. First, the phenomenological psychologist considers all experience as subject to inquiry. Second, the phenomenological psychologist attempts to suspend all biases in order to examine phenomena in their pure state. He or she also does this by making implicit assumptions explicit. Once these are made explicit, there is an attempt to make them inoperative. This process is known as "bracketing" and exemplifies the "transcendental attitude" of the existential phenomenologist. "Bracketing" is the attempt to experience the environment free from interpretation. The world of pure phenomena is called the *Lebenswelt* ("life-world") (Valle & King, 1978).

Valle and King (1978) define existential-phenomenological psychology as "that psychological discipline which seeks to explicate the *essence*, *structure*, or *form* of both human experience and human behavior as revealed through essentially *descriptive* techniques including disciplined reflection" (p. 7). Existential-phenomenological psychology is generally included within the larger category of humanistic psychology, although it predates the rise of humanistic psychology. Humanistic psychology, under the leadership of Abraham Maslow (Matson, 1973), arose in protest against American behaviorism in the mid-1950s. Like other humanistic psychologies, the existential-phenomenological approach rejects the notion that psychology should emulate the physical sciences. According to Georgi (1968), the fundamental insight of this approach is that human beings are not split off from the world they study. In other words, "the person is viewed as having no existence apart from the world, and the world as having no existence apart from persons" (Valle & King, 1978, p. 7). This is the concept of coconstitutionality, which is opposed to the behavioristic view of the person and the environment as separate entities.

A second important concept in existential–phenomenological psychology is the notion of dialogue. "Dialogue" is a term denoting the interaction of the person and the world. Each is seen as acting on the other. Thus people are seen as partly active and partly passive, as they both act on the world and the world acts upon them. This notion of dialogue gives rise to the key existential concept of choice. The person is seen as always having to make choices. One is not free not to choose, since not choosing is a choice in itself (Valle & King, 1978).

Finally, existential-phenomenological psychology rejects the notion of causality as it is utilized in the natural sciences. Thus traditional experimental methodology plays no part in existential–phenomenological psychology. It is replaced by description. The study of cause–effect relationships is replaced by elucidation of the "structure" of phenomena (Valle & King, 1978).

Many writers within the existential–phenomenological tradition have discussed human sexuality. Chief among them are Jean-Paul Sartre and Rollo May. Sartre's writings are primarily philosophical, and their technical nature places them beyond the scope of this chapter. However, the interested reader may refer to Friedman (1963), Russell (1979), or Sartre (1956) for detailed expositions of Sartre's philosophy of sexuality. Rollo May (1969) addresses problems in modern sexuality. He distinguishes four types of love: (1) "sex," or lust; (2) "eros," or the urge toward higher forms of being and relationships; (3) "philia," or brotherly love; and (4) "agape," or altruistic love. Every human experience of love is seen as a blending of these four types of love in varying proportions. May's thesis is that our society has overemphasized sexual love and has tended to de-emphasize the other types of love. The result of this overemphasis on sex is that sexual acts have often become meaningless and passionless. There is a preoccupation with technique, to the exclusion of the meaning of sexual activities. May (1969) refers to the result of our society's preoccupation with sex and sexual freedom as "the new puritanism" (p. 45). The new puritanism is characterized by three features: "First, a state of alienation from the body. Second, the separation of emotion from reason. And third, the use of the body as a machine" (p. 45). May (1969) believes that the solution to this "banalization" of sex is to fuse sex once again with eros. Eros is "the experiencing of the personal interactions and meaning of the act. . . . eros is a state of being" (p. 73). The reader should consult May (1969) for a full exposition of his ideas.

A major attraction of the existential–phenomenological approach is that this approach places sex in its human interpersonal context. There is an emphasis upon relationship, meaning, and values, which are often important considerations of human sexual relationships. Other approaches to sexuality tend to be more narrow in scope and to ignore these characteristics of human sexuality.

While the existential–phenomenological approach often rejects the experimental model for understanding behavior, at least some advocates (Georgi, 1968) would accept the findings of scientific methodology and attempt to integrate them into the existential-phenomenological approach. Psychophysiology has not been applied to this viewpoint, but since there is a unique emphasis on conscious experience, psychophysiology could contribute to this model by examining the correlation between sexual arousal and report of conscious experience.

It is difficult to critique this approach to sexuality, since it begins with assumptions that differ widely from those generally accepted in scientific methodology. Our proposed criteria of communicability, testability, responsiveness to new evidence, stimulation value, and so on, can be applied to this approach; however, the basic assumptions of the approach render them relatively unimportant.

UNIQUE CONTRIBUTIONS OF PSYCHOPHYSIOLOGY

Psychophysiology can make many unique and potentially powerful contributions in the field of sexuality since most psychophysiological measures can be employed directly to measure a response of interest (i.e., genital activity). In much of sexual behavior, genital activity is the response that directly interfaces with the environment, and therefore is of critical importance. It is only in the field of biofeedback that one can see as clearly the direct relationship between the response measured by psychophysiological procedures and the phenomena of interest. In much of the rest of psychophysiology, the response is often an indicator of the phenomena of interest (e.g., emotional state).

As a consequence of this characteristic of human sexuality, there are a number of important implications that can be fruitfully examined using psychophysiological techniques. One of the more obvious implications is that the measurement of genital responses at the time of erotic stimulation allows for the direct assessment of the effectiveness of stimuli and the direct assessment of the impact of experimental or environmental conditions upon the response. Freund's (1963) original studies of penile responding

to typical and atypical stimuli in subjects with atypical sexual interests utilized this property of genital measures. Clinicians find the capacity to index stimulus effectiveness valuable both for diagnostic procedures and for the assessment of treatment effectiveness. The ability to track genital responses and changes in that response system as a function of stimulus conditions continues to be one of the more important applications of psychophysiology of human sexuality (Geer, 1979).

Another major advantage of directly studying genital responses is that one can simultaneously measure genital responses and the individual's report of the subjective experience of sexual arousal. We have found that under appropriate conditions the correlation between subjective and genital measures can result in r's as high as .80 and .90 (Korff & Geer, 1983). These very high correlations facilitate the detailed study of factors that determine the relationships between subjective and physiological state. In no other area of psychophysiology is the relationship between autonomic responding and ratings of subjective experience as strong, and thus as potentially amenable to detailed study.

The powerful relationship between genital changes and subjective measures of sexual arousal can allow researchers to study fundamental theories of emotion. A common element in the theoretical views of James (1890) and Cannon (1927), as well as in the more current concepts of Schachter (1964) and Lang (1977), is the central role played by the relationship between physiological and cognitive or subjective states. Given that the emotions associated with sexual behavior follow the same "laws" as those in other emotional states, it should be possible to generate research strategies in sexuality employing psychophysiology that will have a significant payoff for the general understanding of emotions (Geer, 1980).

Since through psychophysiology the response system of interest is studied directly, there exists an opportunity and potential for the application of biofeedback (Geer, 1979). The study of biofeedback is possible not only in its usual sense of control of the response system, but also as it relates to the individual's ability to detect genital responses. The effect of that detection either upon perceived sexual arousal or upon the genital responses is of considerable interest. For example, Geer (1979) and Hoon (1979) have suggested that one of the variables influencing the occurrence of many sex differences in sexuality has to do with gender differences in ability to detect genital responding. Similarly, Barbach (1976) has suggested that the cause of sexual dysfunction in some women is their lack of attending to genital sensations. These suggestions imply that research on feedback and the interrelationship between response mechanisms is warranted.

Another unique contribution of the use of genital

measures in the study of sexual behavior is that, using these methodologies, one can investigate factors that have direct impact upon the genital response system. The types of phenomena that can be explored include effects of recreational drugs, medical conditions, and psychological phenomena that have a theoretical or empirical relationship to genital responding. As was noted in the "Approaches" section, the genital response has been used to evaluate the relative contributions of an organic or physiological factor to the development of erectile problems. Similarly, since there are a number of medications that are known to affect genital responses adversely (Kolodny, Masters, & Johnson, 1979), psychophysiology can play an important role in the study of those effects.

Since one can study the genital response directly, an evaluation of characteristics of the response system is also possible. Response system characteristics have demonstrated their importance in other areas of psychophysiology and may also do so in human sexuality. Perhaps important individual differences may be identified by studying characteristics of the genital response system. One could also examine the relationships between the genital response systems and other, more traditional psychophysiological measures. There is essentially no information available at the present time concerning response system characteristics and their impact in human sexuality. For example, there is very little known concerning basal response levels. For women, however, there appears to be a reversal of the law of initial values between resting pressure pulse amplitude and pressure pulse responding to erotic stimuli (Rothenberg & Geer, 1980; Stock & Geer, 1982). Furthermore, very little is known about response lability, response reactivity, or stability of genital responding over a time. It is likely that significant contributions to the knowledge of individual differences in human sexuality will be derived from research in psychophysiology.

In summary, the concurrent, on-line measurement of the response of interest (genital activity) provides psychophysiologists with the opportunity to study many relevant and important phenomena in sexual activity. In addition, we have suggested that psychophysiological assessment of genital responses has the potential for clarifying important theoretical and conceptual issues that range beyond sexuality to important general issues in emotional responding.

METHODOLOGICAL ISSUES

This chapter would not be complete if we did not describe some of the important methodological issues that affect the study of sexuality using psychophysiological measurements. These methodological issues provide a challenge for investigators, for, in many

instances, they severely limit both the assessment of current theoretical frameworks and the valid application of the current technology.

One of the most important methodological concerns is the obtrusiveness of most research that utilizes genital measures. Most genital measures are obtained by the placement of recording transducers in direct contact with genital tissues. The exception, thermography, requires the subject to be nude while being scanned by heat sensors. Genital recording devices are obvious to the subjects and make it clear that sexual phenomena are being evaluated. Since cognitive factors seem to play an important role in human sexuality (Geer & Fuhr, 1976), this obtrusiveness may very well provide serious impediments to valid study. The development of less obtrusive genital measures—for example, refinements in thermography that would allow the phenomena of interest to be studied in a more natural state—seems particularly important. However, there are serious ethical limitations upon the study of sexual phenomena without subjects' knowledge.

The second important methodological concern is that of subject selection biases. It seems reasonable to assume that subjects who volunteer to participate in experiments utilizing genital measures are not a truly representative sample of the general population. It must be recognized that there are selection biases toward those who feel comfortable with the experimental procedures, toward those who have liberal attitudes concerning sexuality, and toward those who are not anxious concerning their own sexuality. For example, Morokoff (1980/1981) found that volunteers from a population of college women were more liberal in attitudes and more sexually active than nonvolunteers. Thus, it must be recognized that there are subject limitations that seriously limit the generalizability of current research.

Another methodological issue is that there are severe limitations upon the behaviors that can be studied. Certain sexual behaviors cannot be studied with the transducers that measure genital responses. Movement artifacts provide a source of error variance in studying many of the common forms of sexual activity. Coitus cannot be investigated with the vaginal photoplethysmograph or with the penile strain gauges, since they would interfere with the act. As these examples illustrate, continued development of measurement devices is necessary before satisfactory study of genital responses during the full range of sexual activity is possible. At present, it is only an assumption that the study of available phenomena gives information relevant to the wider and as yet generally unavailable range of sexual activity.

Measurement problems yield another set of methodological concerns. There are unresolved issues regarding the appropriate measurement units. Investigators from different settings are using different measurement conventions. There is a need for standardization. Moreover, major problems exist in the psychophysiology of sexuality, since cross-sex comparisons are not possible, due to the lack of common measurement units. Currently the most appropriate methodology of sex comparisons is to measure both sexes on a set of variables and to determine whether the nature of relationships differ between the sexes. This type of analysis will not give direct quantitative information in terms of the strength of response, but will detect whether or not the phenomena under study follow qualitatively different functional relationships within each sex. There have, however, been attempts to develop techniques that can be used to study events that may be similar between the sexes. As noted earlier, attempts to study responses within the rectum represent such a development (Bohlen & Held, 1979). Thermographic analysis provides an identical response unit (temperature). However, since heat is generated by different tissues and perhaps by different physiological mechanisms in the sexes, one must be careful before assuming that a temperature change of, for example 1° in the penis means the same thing as a similar temperature change in the labia. The study of EMG responses in genital musculature provides another possibility for making cross-sex comparisons.

Another measurement issue concerns the fact that the measures that one obtains may not be the most appropriate for the construct of sexual arousal. In females, it may very well be that vaginal lubrication should be the principal response of interest. This is possible since lubrication facilitates coitus and, therefore, may be more directly relevant to the study of sexual phenomena. Currently, direct measures of vaginal lubrication are not employed; rather, most researchers are measuring vasocongestion. It is believed, however, that vasocongestion results in lubrication (Levine & Wagner, 1978). Similarly, in the male, the typical measure is of either penile volume changes or circumference changes. Perhaps the response of interest should be penile rigidity. The size of the erection may be of less importance than the ability of the erection to provide sufficient rigidity for penetration. Therefore, there is a need to be sensitive to evaluation of whether the operational definitions of sexual arousal currently used are definitions that validly represent the construct of interest.

Another measurement problem is response selectivity. In most studies of sexual arousal, investigators do not measure all possible response systems. There is no satisfactory measure, for example, of changes in the breast during sexual arousal. Yet it was reported by Masters and Johnson (1966) that breast changes are relevant. Likewise, in males, measures of testicular responses are not obtained, though Masters and Johnson (1966) have noted their relationship to sexual arousal. As a final example, one does not directly

measure responses in the clitoris, although much theoretical significance is attributed to the clitoris (Barbach, 1976). Perhaps clitorial measurement is important for a full and complete understanding of feminine sexuality using psychophysiological procedures. Further data are needed concerning the relationships among various responses in order to determine the appropriate measurement systems for future research.

Much of the discussion above has been predicated upon the assumption that there is a single response that best reflects sexual arousal. It may well be that concepts of patterning of responses (Schwartz, Brown, & Ahern, 1980) may prove more useful when studying sexuality. Without further research, little more can be learned concerning the possible multidimensional properties of sexual arousal and the need for multiple measures.

In sum, many of these methodological issues may be conceived of as problems in the development of appropriate constructs in the field of sexuality and in the development of adequate measures of those constructs. The methodological issues that have been described in this section are similar to many found throughout the field of psychophysiology. We do not mean to excuse them or to make light of them, but simply to point out that many of the problems in this field are analogous to those faced in the rest of psychophysiology. We hope that this chapter will contribute to a clearer understanding of how psychophysiologists can contribute to a more adequate resolution of these methodological issues, and, consequently, to a fuller understanding of human sexuality.

REFERENCES

Bancroft, J., & Bell, C. *Psychophysiological aspects of erectile dysfunctions.* Paper presented at the meeting of the International Academy of Sex Research, Tuscon, Arizona, 1980.

Bandura, A. *Principles of behavior modification.* New York: Holt, Rinehart & Winston, 1969.

Bandura, A. *Social learning theory.* Englewood Cliffs, N.J.: Prentice-Hall, 1977.

Barash, D. P. *Sociobiology and behavior.* New York: Elsevier, 1977.

Barbach, L. G. *For yourself: The fulfillment of female sexuality.* New York: Doubleday, 1976.

Beecroft, R. S. *Classical conditioning.* Goleta, Calif.: Psychonomic Press, 1966.

Bohlen, J., & Held, J. Anal probe for monitoring vascular and muscular events during sexual response. *Psychophysiology,* 1979, 16(3), 318-323.

Cannon, W. B. The James–Lange theory of emotions: A critical examination and an alternative theory. *American Journal of Psychology,* 1927, 39, 106-124.

Cohen, H. D., Rosen, R. D., & Goldstein, L. Electroencephalographic laterality changes during human sexual orgasm. *Archives of Sexual Behavior,* 1976, 5(3), 189-199.

Commission on Obscenity and Pornography. New York: Bantam, 1970.

Costell, R. Contingent negative variation as an indicator of sexual object preference. *Science,* 1972, 177, 718-720.

Cronbach, L. J. The two disciplines of scientific psychology. *American Psychologist,* 1957, 12, 671-684.

Daly, M. Gynecology: The metaethics of radical feminism. Boston: Beacon Press, 1978.

Darwin, C. The descent of man and selection in relation to sex. London: John Murray, 1871.

Dickinson, A., & Mackintosh, N. J. Classical conditioning in animals. Annual Review of Psychology, 1978, 29, 587–612.

Feldman, M. P., & MacCulloch, M. J. Homosexual behavior: Therapy and assessment. Oxford: Pergamon Press, 1971.

Freud, S. Three contributions to the theory of sex. In A. A. Bull. (Ed. and trans.), The basic writings of Sigmund Freud. New York: Modern Library, 1938. (Originally published, 1905)

Freund, K. A laboratory method for diagnosing predominance of homo- or hetero-erotic interest in the male. Behaviour Research and Therapy, 1963, 1, 85–93.

Friedman, M. Sex in Sartre and Buber. Review of Existential Psychology and Psychiatry, 1963, 3(2), 113–124.

Gagnon, J. H., & Simon, W. Sexual conduct. Chicago: Aldine, 1973.

Gebhard, P. H. The acquisition of basic information. Journal of Sex Research, 1977, 13(3), 148–169.

Geer, J. H. Direct measures of genital responding. American Psychologist, 1975, 30, 415–418.

Geer, J. H. Biofeedback in the modification of sexual dysfunctions. In R. J. Gatchel & K. P. Price (Eds.), Clinical applications of biofeedback: Appraisal and status. New York: Pergamon Press, 1979.

Geer, J. H. Measurement of genital arousal in human males and females. In I. Martin & P. H. Venables (Eds.), Techniques in psychophysiology. New York: Wiley, 1980.

Geer, J. H., & Fuhr, R. Cognitive factors in sexual arousal: The role of distraction. Journal of Consulting and Clinical Psychology, 1976, 44(2), 238–243.

Geer, J. H., & Quartararo, J. D. Vaginal blood volume responses during masturbation. Archives of Sexual Behavior, 1976, 5(5), 403–414.

Georgi, A. Existential phenomenology and the psychology of the human person. Review of Existential Psychology and Psychiatry, 1968, 8(2), 102–116.

Gewirtz, J. L. Social learning in early human development. In A. C. Catania & T. A. Bringham (Eds.), Handbook of applied behavior analysis: Social and instructional processes. New York: Irvington Press, 1978.

Goodson, F., & Morgan, G. A. Evaluation of theory. In M. H. Marx & F. E. Goodson (Eds.), Theories in contemporary psychology. New York: Macmillan, 1976.

Hamel, P. F. Female subjective and pupillary reaction to nude male and female figures. Journal of Psychology, 1974, 87(2), 171–175.

Hassett, J. A primer of psychophysiology. San Francisco: W. H. Freeman, 1978.

Hatch, J. P. Vaginal photoplethysmography: Methodological considerations, Archives of Sexual Behavior, 1979, 8(4), 357.

Hatch, J. P., Heiman, J. R., & Hahn, P. A photoplethysmographic device for measuring changes in penile blood pulse during sexual arousal in humans. Psychophysiology, 1980, 17(3), 287. (Abstract)

Heiman, J. A psychological exploration of sexual arousal patterns in females and males. Psychophysiology, 1977, 14(3), 266–273.

Henson, D. E., & Rubin, H. B. A comparison of two objective measures of sexual arousal of women. Behaviour Research and Therapy, 1978, 16, 143–151.

Herman, S. H., Barlow, D. H., & Agras, W. S. An experimental analysis of classical conditioning as a method of increasing heterosexual arousal in homosexuals. Behavior Therapy, 1974, 5, 33–47.

Hess, E. H. Pupillometric assessment. Research in Psychotherapy, 1968, 3, 573–583.

Homme, L. E. Perspectives in psychology: XIV. Control of coverants, the operants of the mind. Psychological Record, 1965, 15, 501–511.

Hoon, P. W. The assessment of sexual arousal in women. Progress in Behavior Modification, 1979, 7, 2–53.

Hoon, P. W., Hoon, E. F., & Wincze, J. P. An inventory for the measurement of female sexual arousability: The SAI. Archives of Sexual Behavior, 1976, 5(4), 291–300. (a)

Hoon, P. W., Wincze, J. P., & Hoon, E. F. Physiological assessment of sexual arousal in women. Psychophysiology, 1976, 13(3), 196–204. (b)

Hunt, M. Sexual behavior in the 1970's. Chicago: Playboy Press, 1974.

James, W. The physical basis of emotion. Psychological Review, 1980, 1, 516–529.

Jennings, J. R., Tahmoush, A. J., & Redmond, D. P. Non-invasive measurement of peripheral vascular activity. I. Martin & P. H. Venables, (Eds.), Techniques in psychophysiology. New York: Wiley, 1980.

Karacan, A., Ware, J. C., Dervant, B., Altinel, A. H., Thoenby, J. I., Williams, R. L., Musret, K., & Scott, F. B. Impotence and blood pressure in the flaccid penis: Relationship to nocturnal penile tumescence. Sleep, 1978, 1(2), 125–132.

Katchadourian, H. A., & Lunde, D. T. Fundamentals of human sexuality. New York: Holtt, Rinehart & Winston, 1972.

Keller, F. S., & Schoenfeld, W. N. Principles of psychology. New York: Appleton-Century-Crofts, 1950.

Kinsey, A. C., Pomeroy, W. B., & Martin, C. E. Sexual behavior in the human male. Philadelphia: W. B. Saunders, 1948.

Kinsey, A. C., Pomeroy, W. B., Martin, C. E., & Gebhard, P. H. Sexual behavior in the human female. Philadelphia: W. B. Saunders, 1953.

Kolodny, R. C., Masters, W. H., & Johnson, V. E. Textbook of sexual medicine. Boston: Little, Brown, 1979.

Korff, J., & Geer, J. H. Relationship between subjective sexual arousal experience and genital responses. Psychophysiology, 1983, 20, 121–127.

Krasner, L., Ullman, L. P. Behavior influence and personality. New York: Holt, Rinehart & Winston, 1973.

Lang, P. J. Imagery in therapy: An information processing analysis of fear. Behavior Therapy, 1977, 8, 862–886.

Langevin, R., & Martin, M. Can erotic response be classically conditioned? Behavior Therapy, 1975, 6, 350–355.

Levine, R. J., & Wagner, G. Haemodynamic changes of the human vagina during sexual arousal assessed by a heated oxygen electrode. Journal of Physiology, 1978, 275, 23–24.

Lowry, R. P., & Rankin, R. P. Sociology: The science of society. New York: Scribners, 1969.

MacLeod, R. B. Phenomenology: A challenge to experimental psychology. In T. Wann (Ed.), Behaviorism and phenomenology. Chicago: University of Chicago Press, 1964.

Mahoney, M. J. Cognition and behavior modification. Cambridge, Mass.: Ballinger, 1974.

Marquis, J. N. Orgasmic reconditioning: Changing sexual object choice through controlling masturbation fantasies. Journal of Behavior Therapy and Experimental Psychiatry, 1970, 1, 263–271.

Marx, M. H., & Goodson, F. (Eds.). Theories in contemporary psychology. New York: Macmillan, 1976.

Marx, M. H., & Hillex, W. A. Systems and theories in psychology. New York: McGraw-Hill, 1973.

Masters, W. H., & Johnson, V. E. Human sexual response. Boston: Little, Brown, 1966.

Matson, F. W. (Ed.). Without/within: Behaviorism and humanism. Monterey, Calif.: Brooks/Cole, 1973.

May, R. Love and will. New York: Norton, 1969.

Messé, M., & Geer, J. H. Sexual dysfunctions. In R. J. Gatchel, A. Baum, & J. E. Singer (Eds.), Behavioral medicine and clinical psychology/psychiatry: Overlapping disciplines. Hillsdale, N.J.: Erlbaum, 1982.

Miller, N. E. Learning of visceral and glandular responses. Science, 1969, 163, 434–445.

Miller, N. E., & Dworkin, B. R. Visceral learning: Recent difficulties with curarized rats and significant problem for human research. In P. A. Obrist, A. H. Black, J. Brener, & L. V. Dicara (Eds.), Cardiovascular psychophysiology. Chicago: Aldine, 1974.

Morokoff, P. J. Female sexual arousal as a function of individual differences and exposure to erotic stimuli (Doctoral dissertation, State University of New York at Stony Brook, 1980). *Dissertation Abstracts International*, 1981, 41, 4270B.

Munroe, R. L. *Schools of psychoanalytic thought*. New York: Dryden, 1955.

Pavlov, I. P. *Selected works*. Moscow: Foreign Languages Press, 1955.

Rachman, S. Sexual fetishism: An experimental analogue. *Psychological Record*, 1966, 16, 293–296.

Rachman, S., & Hodgson, R. J. Experimentally-induced "sexual fetishism": Replication and development. *Psychological Record*, 1968, 18, 25–27.

Ralls, K. Mammals in which females are larger than males. *Quarterly Review of Biology*, 1976, 51, 245–276.

Rescorla, R. A. *Pavlovian second-order conditioning*. Hillsdale, N. J.: Erlbaum, 1980.

Rook, K. S., & Hammen, C. L. A cognitive perspective on the experience of sexual arousal. *Journal of Social Issues*, 1977, 33(2), 7–29.

Rosen, R. C., & Keefe, F. J. The measurement of human penile tumescence. *Psychophysiology*, 1978, 15(4), 366–386.

Rosen, R. C., & Rosen, L. R. *Human sexuality*. New York: Knopf, 1981.

Rothenberg, G. S., & Geer, J. H. *Induced mood and sexual arousal: Some negative findings*. Paper presented at the annual meeting of the Eastern Psychological Association, Hartford, Conn., 1980.

Russell, J. M. Sartre's theory of sexuality. *Journal of Humanistic Psychology*, 1979, 19(2), 35–45.

Sartre, J. P. *Being and nothingness*. New York: Philosophical Library, 1956.

Schachter, S. The interaction of cognitive and physiological determinants of emotional state. In L. Berkowitz (Ed.), *Advances in experimental social psychology* (Vol. 1). New York: Academic Press, 1964.

Schachter, S., & Singer, J. E. Cognitive, social and physiological determinants of emotional state. *Psychological Review*, 1962, 69, 379–399.

Schmidt, G., & Sigusch, V. Sex differences in responses to psychosexual stimulation by films and slides. *Journal of Sex Research*, 1970, 6, 268–283.

Schwartz, G. E., Brown, S., & Ahern, G. L. Facial muscle patterning and subjective experience during affective imagery: Sex differences. *Psychophysiology*, 1980, 17(1), 75–82.

Seeley, F., Abramsen, P., Perry, L., Rothblatt, A., & Seeley, D.

Thermographic measures of sexual arousal: A methodological note. *Archives of Sexual Behavior*, 1980, 9(2), 77–85.

Seligman, M. E. P. Phobias and preparedness. *Behavior Therapy*, 1971, 2, 307–320.

Shapiro, A., Cohen, H., DiBianco, P., & Rosen, G. Vaginal blood flow changes during sleep and sexual arousal in women. *Psychophysiology*, 1968, 4(3), 394.

Sintchak, G., & Geer, J. H. A vaginal plethysmograph system. *Psychophysiology*, 1975, 12, 113–115.

Skinner, B. F. *The behavior of organisms: An experimental analysis*. Englewood Cliffs, N.J.: Prentice-Hall, 1938.

Skinner, B. F. Are theories of learning necessary? *Psychological Review*, 1950, 57, 192–216.

Skinner, B. F. *Contingencies of reinforcement: A theoretical analysis*. New York: Appleton-Century-Crofts, 1969.

Solnick, R., & Birren, J. E. Age and male erectile responsiveness. *Archives of Sexual Behavior*, 1977, 6(1), 1–9.

Stern, J. A. Toward a definition of psychophysiology. *Psychophysiology*, 1964, 1, 90–91.

Stock, W. E., & Geer, J. H. A study of fantasy-based sexual arousal in women. *Archives of Sexual Behavior*, 1982, 1, 33–47.

Storms, M. D. A theory of erotic orientation development. *Psychological Review*, 1981, 88(4), 340–353.

Symons, D. Précis of [the evolution of human sexuality] *Behavioral and Brain Sciences*, 1980, 3, 171–214.

Thompson, C. *Psychoanalysis: Evolution and development*. New York: Hermitage House, 1950.

Tolman, E. C. Cognitive maps in rats and men. *Psychological Review*, 1948, 55, 189–208.

Ullmann, P., & Krasner, L. *A psychological approach to abnormal behavior*. Englewood Cliffs, N.J.: Prentice-Hall, 1975.

Valle, R. S., & King, M. (Eds.). *Existential phenomenological alternatives for psychology*. Oxford: Oxford University Press, 1978.

Walen, S. R. Cognitive factors in sexual behavior. *Journal of Sex and Marital Therapy*, 1980, 6(2), 87–101.

Wenger, M. A., Averill, J. R., & Smith, D. D. B. Autonomic activity during sexual arousal. *Psychophysiology*, 1968, 4, 468–78.

Wilson, E. O. *On human nature*. Cambridge, Mass.: Harvard University Press, 1978.

Zuckerman, M. Physiological measures of sexual arousal in the human. *Psychological Bulletin*, 1971, 75(5), 329.

SECTION C
Individual Differences and
Social Processes

Chapter Twenty

Individual Differences

Anthony Gale
John A. Edwards

INTRODUCTION

When the editors invited us to contribute to this volume, they asked us *not* to provide an exhaustive review of research findings. A mere catalogue of the existing literature would not satisfy their editorial desire to obtain views on the state of the art and to force contributors to make qualitative judgments. We have, therefore, attempted to maintain a proper balance between quantity and quality. However, a difficulty for any reviewer of the psychophysiology of individual differences is that the field that exists *is* barely more than a catalogue, and a vast catalogue at that. The research is characterized by one-shot studies, is usually focused on only one variable, and rarely exceeds more sophistication in design than a correlation or two, or a 2 × 2 analysis of variance (ANOVA). A literature search reveals that few personal research careers are sustained by continuous publication in this field; the typical pattern is the odd paper or clutch of papers (and certainly barely ever more than a half-dozen), and then the author shifts to more a fashionable field, or sinks without trace. Textbooks on psychophysiology focus on other issues.

The emphasis on individual variations, if indeed more than a paragraph or two is devoted to subject variance, is very much on the side of treating psychophysiological variables as *independent* variables. Subjects differ in lability score, or response stereotypy, or range, or augmenting–reducing. Although some authorities have clearly invested effort in studying such phenomena for their own sake, the more general tendency has been to use estimates of subject variance to minimize the error term and maximize treatment effects. Few have exploited observations of individual variations in order to assist in the construction of *general* models of a psychological function. A particular difficulty is that many such workers (i.e., those who use physiological parameters as independent variables) have neglected or totally ignored the traditional psychometric approach to individual differences, where of course psychometric instruments and interview protocols have been the basis for subject group selections.

On the other hand, there has been a matching of ignorance on the part of psychometric specialists and supporters of traditional models of individual differences, who have *not* always been good psychophysiol-

Anthony Gale. Department of Psychology, University of Southampton, Southampton, England.
John A. Edwards. Department of Psychology, University of Reading, Reading, England.

ogists or competent experimentalists. They have moved from the domain of psychometric scores to that of psychophysiological indices, with an incredible indifference to problems of measurement and quantification. Given the operational differences of the two domains, in terms of sampling and measurement procedures, the probability of a successful outcome is minimal; even *within* the more closely related psychometric–behavior domain, correlations rarely exceed control over more than 10% of the variance observed. Thus it is essential that measurement reliability be as strong as possible, in order to minimize measurement error, which in any case comes from several sources in *any* study.

A strange paradox is that the psychometric tradition, in its purest and least diluted form, has been as exacting and as obsessionally forceful about methodology as any of our psychophysiological technocrats. It may be a harsh judgment, but in our view, many researchers have abused this psychometric tradition, administering questionnaires in a manner that reveals an ignorance of the nature of test theory, factor analysis, and indeed the substantive theories that have evolved hand in hand with the development of the instrument under study. Many psychophysiological investigations of traditional personality dimensions have involved experiments that, in conceptual terms, involve no more sophistication than what is implied by a purely *vernacular* interpretation of the construct under examination. Yet there *are* theories, and there have been research enterprises based upon a coherent approach.

To select some landmarks in this literature, we would point to *Pavlov's Typology*, edited by Gray (1964); *The Biological Basis of Personality* (H. J. Eysenck, 1967); *Brain Electrical Potentials and Individual Psychological Differences* (Callaway, 1975); and, more recently, *Sensation Seeking: Beyond the Optimum Level of Arousal* (Zuckerman, 1979) and *A Model for Personality*, edited by H. J. Eysenck (1981). A volume that considers many of the issues raised in the present review and that attempts to create bridges between Western and Eastern European personality constructs is *The Biological Bases of Personality and Behavior*, edited by Strelau, Farley, and Gale (1985); our own three-volume edited text, *Physiological Correlates of Human Behavior* (Gale & Edwards, 1983a), has a whole section of Volume 3 devoted to individual differences. Of recent basic texts in psychophysiology, Andreassi (1980) presents a fairly comprehensive sampling of the literature, but the earlier volumes mentioned here do represent attempts to create a rapprochement across the divide between psychophysiology and individual differences, and in some cases to provide *original* attempts to construct theories around which considerable psychophysiological experimentation *could* be established.

However, as soon becomes apparent from our review, the promise of an integrative and all-encompassing approach has yet to be realized. One fundamental reason for this is the lack of intellectual ambition in the activities of workers in the field. Our view is that *there cannot be a coherent psychophysiology of individual differences in the absence of a general and comprehensive theory of human behavior*. Such a general theory must incorporate explanations of *everyday* behavior, as well as explanations of the extreme case. If the nervous system is designed to be adaptive to and interact with the ecology of the human being, then that ecology includes day-to-day routine, interaction with others, and relaxation and tranquility in solitude, as well as extreme exhibitions of emotional behavior or performance of complex tasks under the critical and evaluative eye of the experimenter. Individual variations need to be set against a general background, within a tapestry that describes general aspects of normal behavior. There has been too much focus on the exceptional and the clinical, inducing a distorting bias on our sampling of behavior.

The desired theory must be able to handle traditional areas of concern: intellectual functioning, information processing and styles of cognition, interpersonal and social behavior, motivation, emotion and anxiety, approach–avoidance, attention and voluntary control, styles of action, and self-evaluation. These are just some of the bits and pieces that are said to be part of the makeup of the human being. We list these characteristics without any implication of priority or emphasis, and without suggestion that the domains specified are mutually exclusive or noninteractive. It is likely that such a general theory will be *hierarchical* in structure, which for us implies *process* and *dynamics* at both vertical and horizontal axes within the structure (see Royce & Powell, 1985).

Many of the elements that might contribute to such a theory are already present, and we sample these in our review. Even if the enterprise of theory building is seen to be foolhardy at this stage of our knowledge, the *weakest* possible view must be that any existing or new theory must take into account existing alternative theories and reported bodies of data. Regrettably, even this weak requirement is not satisfied. For example, electroencephalogram (EEG) characteristics have been related to anxiety, extraversion–introversion, intelligence, locus of control, primary–secondary function, and several Pavlovian dimensions. In virtually all individual cases, *other* theoretical viewpoints have been ignored or given scant mention. Yet the psychophysiological index of the function explored (in this case an alpha index of some sort) is frequently identical in each study! Thus, either the index correlates (or is expected to correlate) with everything under the sun, or what is measured is a common source of variance that has more to do with experimentation per se than the personality dimension under scrutiny. Even worse than this is the possibility that different theories make different predictions about the direction of the correlation expected, in spite of the fact that between-theory translation of the personality construct reveals *similarity* in psychological function. Similar assertions may be made in relation to the literature involving electrodermal activity (EDA) and heart rate (HR) parameters. Such a state of affairs is hardly tolerable in any discipline that seeks intellectual self-respect; unfortunately, this central criticism appears again and again in our survey. In our review, we sample bodies of data and attempt on occasion to cross-relate them. But such an endeavor is by definition post hoc; we are unable to deliver a general theory or to draw connections between areas of study with any confidence, even when they bear surface similarity.

We offer sections on intelligence, extraversion–introversion, locus of control, habituation, anxiety, sensation seeking, and some Eastern European personality dimensions. Because of limitations of space, we do not propose to consider studies that treat psychophysiological data as independent variables; such studies do constitute a viable line of inquiry, but they are referred to generally in this chapter. Nor are we able to devote attention to clinical studies, which clearly are relevant; again, such topics as psychopathy, phobias, and schizophrenia have had a fair crack of the whip so far as reviews are concerned. We offer a brief discussion of anxiety, both because it represents a variable with continuous distribution within the population and because the research on psychophysiological aspects of anxiety is illustrative of many methodological points to which we wish to draw the reader's attention. Our key focus, therefore, is upon the most frequently researched areas—namely, those derived from the psychometric tradition.

The reader may sample any of the specialized sections in any order. Unfortunately, there is much repetition between sections, because all the research is confounded by common problems of strategy and errors of measurement. We devote a section to O'Gorman's (1977) review of habituation studies, because it is a review paper that makes a major contribution on several fronts, and because the habituation paradigm has been so popular with personality researchers. The notion of "arousal" appears in some form or another across the literature; therefore, we devote a short section to problems of experimental manipulation. Further work in this field presupposes a general model of the psychology experiment and some recognition that the psychophysiological experiment constitutes a special sort of sociopsychological event; there are *prima facie* grounds for believing that personality characteristics interact with aspects of the laboratory. We therefore offer an elaboration of the laboratory arousal model of Gale (1977) and its implications for personality research.

On the basis of the special section reviews, we then list a series of guidelines for future research—reflecting, of course, the lessons that have or should have been learned from scrutinizing earlier work—with the intention of encouraging researchers to improve their *modus operandi*. Finally, we select a handful of important issues and possible growth points for the future. We believe that the psychophysiology of individual differences is not a mere appendage to some master discipline (i.e., psychophysiology or psychometrics), but has the potential for integration and evolution of theory. A severe critic might suggest that the intellectual quality of work in the field is notoriously thin; individual differences research seems like a soft option for the tender-minded, the flabby and unprotected underbelly of psychophysiology. We hope that in our consideration of existing work we may encourage the reader to venture into individual differences research or at least to graft its more potent aspects to his or her existing interests. As H. J. Eysenck has argued so often (e.g., 1976), individual differences may account for a good slice of potentially *systematic* error variance; data from individual differences are of too great heuristic value to be discarded within an uncontrolled error term. Only a very foolish and irresponsible nursemaid will cast out the baby with the bath water.

Some Preparatory Groundwork: The Four Faces of Psychophysiology

It is the very nature of psychophysiology that enforces a confrontation with the central question in psychology: What are the causal mechanisms and interactional processes that characterize the three domains of physiology, behavior, and subjective experience? Several authors have drawn attention to this tripartite distinction (Gale, 1973, 1980; Hodgson & Rachman, 1974; Lang, 1978). Other branches of psychology have managed by sleight of hand, or by the defense mechanism of denial, to stay within a single domain; yet the changing fashions in psychology constantly reflect shifts in emphasis, mirrored perhaps in a continuum that stretches from sociobiology to humanistic psychology. Yet psychophysiology can never escape from the problem; as students of the whole person, we are stuck with a problem that will never go away.

Take psychophysiological studies of schizophrenia, a field where much effort has been expended; what we *know* about schizophrenia makes it very difficult to limit our experimental investigations merely to physiological variables. It is clear that any alleged *biological* anomalies (genetically transmitted biochemical and/

or physiological dispositions) are accompanied by other causes and consequences. The patient behaves in a strange way and reports intolerable levels of sensory invasion and attentional distortions. He or she shows low levels of competence in social behavior, and ascribes meanings to words and events that seem to us to be both bizarre and yet governed by an unfathomable logic. The patient seems responsive to the environment in quite subtle ways, for he or she can adopt the institutional roles and rules and yet cast them off in other contexts. Each individual patient has developed as an individual within a family context, where the meanings of actions can only be understood in the light of their history; events that seem neutral to the outsider have deep emotional meaning for the patient. Such meanings are not only borne in the patient's mind, but are shared in the minds of intimate others. Such considerations have led psychophysiological researchers out of the laboratory and into the family home (Turpin, 1983). And yet, most psychophysiological research into schizophrenia involves presentation of simple stimuli within the laboratory. As Gale (1980) points out, "In these circumstances, what sense does it make to identify schizophrenia with a malfunction in this or that part of the brain[?] . . . my psychophysiological colleagues, in pursuit of the *biological* crock of gold . . . will never reach the end of the rainbow" (p. 72). Whatever the patient's biological predispositions, the precipitating circumstances that trigger an incident of severe breakdown involve not only the patient's biology, but his or her experience of the world and resultant personal interpretation of events.

If we shift from this extreme example to the normal population, the lessons to be learned are no different, and it is clear that studies of individual differences reflect every aspect mentioned; there are genetic theories, biological theories, biochemical theories, developmental theories, behavioral theories, cognitive theories, and social theories, as well as, of course, all-pervading psychoanalytic theories—all reflecting different aspects of the whole person. In both editions of their classic text, Hall and Lindzey (1957, 1970) present tabulations indicating the relative weights given to each facet in each major theory.

The psychophysiological worker is no stranger to the measurement of subjective report, although, given the general preoccupation with the physiological, the outsider to psychophysiology might be surprised to find a chapter of a major textbook on psychophysiology devoted to the measurement of mood by subjective techniques (Mackay, 1980). Yet data about how subjects feel or interpret experimental events have always featured in a good proportion of psychophysiological studies, while objections on the grounds of the subjects' phenomenal experience have also featured in critiques of psychophysiological research (e.g., Näätänen, 1975). Of course, psychometric instruments, the starting point for the majority of studies we report in this chapter, do ask subjects how they feel or think or believe they would act in a variety of situations. A puzzle is that few studies extend this practice *into the experiment itself*; thus a crucial facet of mental life is first exploited and then inexplicably neglected. In our view, many of the problems that arise in the interpretation of psychophysiological data might have been diminished by regular and routine sampling of subjective reports, providing indications of the subjects' interpretation of the stimuli to which they have been exposed.

Does this really matter? In the studies we review, data on the subjects' view of the procedure might have led to an improvement in both the face validity and construct validity of the experiments. Thus, studies of cortical correlates of intelligence employ stupid and mindless tasks; studies of sensation seeking employ boring and dreary stimuli; studies of locus of control provide trivial, unthreatening, inconsequential minor irritants for the subjects; studies of extraversion–introversion give poor opportunities for social contact; and studies of anxiety assume that what the experimenters take as threatening is indeed threatening for the subjects. If only these psychophysiologists had thought to treat their subjects as persons—of, if one prefers less emotive language, as scientists (Kelly, 1955) (just as the psychophysiologists themselves are persons or scientists?)—then they might have made inquiries that led to an improvement in their experimental procedures. In the case of individual differences, where the variables under examination involve interaction with and interpretation of the stimulus field, there can surely be no excuse for such indolence.

But can subjects be trusted? Will their reports just serve to make the data more messy? This is a complex problem, and we can only touch upon two aspects pertinent to our review. First, problems about subject *integrity* are used as a cop-out in some studies, in that the subject's verbal reports are said to be discrepant from observed physiological goings-on, because of the operation of defense mechanisms. While such a view is plausible and not contraintuitive, it creates a swings-and-roundabouts type of research in which *any* prediction can be confirmed. Thus the investigator must specify *in advance* under what circumstances and in which groups of individuals such dissembling (conscious or otherwise) may occur. Given the intention to relate psychometric protocol data to physiological levels and changes, such limiting conditions must surely be imposed.

This raises the second problem of mind–body relations: There are several logically possible ways in which experiential and physiological events might be related. For example, in the case of anxiety, it is frequently assumed that there is *covariation* between autonomic reactivity and experienced discomfort.

Work by Lader and Wing (1966) confirms this view. However, other alternatives are possible. Let us assume an autonomic nervous system (ANS), an experiential system (ES), and a linking connection between them (LC). The assumption made above is that there is LC fidelity and that ANS = ES. Let the subscripts $_s$ and $_{us}$ stand for two states, stable and labile, and the subscripts $_{hf}$ and $_{lf}$ for high and low fidelity, respectively. Then for LC_{hf}, $ANS_s = ES_s$ and $ANS_{us} = ES_{us}$. But for LC_{lf}, $ANS_s \neq ES_s$, and so on. The position, of course, is more complicated. For even when LC has high fidelity, the individual might have learned self-control procedures (self-talk, relaxation, and so on), such that ES, while it reflects aspects of ANS activity, is thereby robbed of its emotional quale. The self-control procedures could have a direct effect on ANS, ES, or LC. Or, in another scenario, ES (through learning) might itself be distorting, in spite of high-fidelity LC, thereby reflecting emotional quale in ES in the absence of ANS_{us}. The notion of simple parallels between autonomic reactivity and subjective report of emotional experience is therefore undermined.

A nice example is a longitudinal psychophysiological study of patients with general anxiety who were presented with stimuli ipsatized for personal fears; contrary to expectation, patients who left hospital treatment and were "cured" did *not* habituate physiological response to stimuli, while patients who stayed in treatment, because of continued anxiety, *had* habituated (Skevington, 1977). Thus, there was fractional differentiation between ANS and ES, perhaps reflecting some adaptation in LC. Indeed, it may be the very *variations* in such relations that ought to be a focal point for psychophysiological studies of individual differences. One possible resolution of the Cannon–Bard versus James–Lange controversy is that both viewpoints are correct for some individuals—that is, that people vary in the *temporal* relations and the fidelity in parallelism between autonomic change and subjective awareness. Some people run because they are afraid; some people are afraid because they run; and yet others are afraid because they think they should be running even when they are still! The majority of the studies reviewed here select only one alternative: Their starting point is the assumption that subjects' reports on their inner states and intentions, and their observations of themselves in various situations, are veridical. We believe this to be a fundamental blunder.

The next problem we raise relates to physiology–behavior relations. We have already referred to the notion of operational distance between psychometric and psychophysiological techniques of sampling, measurement, and quantification. We now consider the operational distance between individual differences theory and research practice. Although personality and intelligence theories were devised to explain

behavior, few experiments involve the observation of behavior, unless of course one regards simple reaction time (RT) studies or biofeedback studies as sampling behavior. Now most variables in individual differences theory are *dispositional* variables, defined by instances of what the individual will do in certain situations. While we need not deny that such dispositions may be tapped in the supine or even the sleeping subject, we believe we can make out a *prima facie* case for optimal sampling when the subject is actually performing those actions that the theory sets out to explain! Thus, for example, when investigating physiological correlates of intelligence, one might monitor physiological changes in bright and dull subjects while they perform an intelligence test; one might attempt to explore the *process* of problem solving, relating physiological changes to problem scanning, success, failure, perseveration, time out, frustration, sudden closure, and so on. However obvious this point might seem, such an experiment has never appeared in the psychophysiological literature on intelligence, and indeed one pair of exponents (Blinkhorn & Hendrickson, 1982) prefers "mindless paradigms." We return again and again to this issue.

Having sampled some problems relating to experience–physiology and physiology–behavior relationships, and the difficulties associated with simple-minded parallelism, we now consider yet a further source of difficulty. Given a systems point of view, there might be complementarity rather than parallelism among experience, physiology, and behavior; that is to say, individual response stereotypy may operate *among* domains as well as within domains. Given a pool of emotion that seeks discharge and that is or is not modulated, it could be expressed in skeletal behavior (facial expressions, loud outbursts of laughter, waving of arms or shuffling of feet) *or* autonomic variability, *or* verbal utterance, *or* of course any combination of these. Just as the Laceys (Lacey & Lacey, 1958) have cautioned against the use of only one physiological measure, we would caution against the use of physiological measures alone. The video camera, the tape recorder, and the fidgetometer should be part and parcel of the psychophysiological armory. Just as individuals might be maximally responsive in one physiological response system, so might they be maximally responsive in "nonphysiological" systems, in the expression of emotion. So far as the existing literature is concerned, there appear to be two data sets, one indicating covariation in indices of emotion (e.g., facial expression and HR), and the other indicating either zero correlation or a complementary relationship. Some of these studies are considered later (see "Growth Points for the Future") as bases for future research, the taxonomy of subject variation being a focus for individual differences studies. Their retrospective implications for the existing body of research are almost too far-reaching for comfort.

In the discussion so far, we have talked of three domains—physiology, behavior, and subjective experience. However, the title of this section refers to *four* faces of psychophysiology. It is difficult to characterize our fourth face, but it is orthogonal to all the other three; it is the *interaction* of the living organism with its environment. In the case of human beings, such interactions include not only other things and other persons, but interactions with the self—what the Russian tradition calls the "regulative functions of speech." Physiology, behavior, and experience are all responsive to feedback from the exterior world, but in the psychophysiology experiment everything is seen as happening *inside* the person: The subject is a prisoner not only within the soundproof cubicle, but within himself or herself. The issues are complex because the individual alters the world by acting upon it. Transactions occur, which modulate the context in which they occur. This notion of feedback, so crucial in the development of individual differentiation, is a constant feature of the individual's world view.

All the areas of concern that we consider here have explicit or implicit notions of transaction. The most explicit is the concept of locus of control, where the individual's response to the world is determined by his or her interpretation of sources of control. In the case of intelligence also, one implies a processing and reorganization of material, and, as we shall see, sensation seeking, extraversion–introversion, and anxiety also involve a filtering and reorganization of the environment on the basis of prior experience and accumulated expectation.

Such a transactional point of view has been neglected in virtually all the literature. Only the Eastern European literature, particularly the recent Polish work, has elaborated upon the notion of feedback; there, as we shall see, individuals are said to vary in terms of "style of action," which in its turn influences the nature of the information fed back to the person from the environment.

The notion of active modulation of the sensory world raises issues of awareness, conscious experience, and voluntary action. Such complex issues are dealt with elsewhere in this volume. Suffice it to say that in the psychophysiology of individual differences, the notion of *voluntary* manipulation or shaping of experience has been denied. That is to say, the experimental subject is treated as little more than a stimulus–response lump. "Acts" and "actions" have been confounded, the experimenter assuming that a stimulus is a stimulus is a stimulus. There is no recognition of the Kellian view that the subject is a scientist, testing out hunches, asking questions, or applying existing constructs to test for their range of convenience. Thus in this respect also, there is operational distance between theories of the person and the laboratory test bed in which such theories are subjected to systematic study.

Summary

In this brief discussion of crucial metatheoretical issues, we have identified the following problems that obfuscate the research to be reviewed:

1. Psychophysiology is condemned to tackling the complexity of combining the three universes of discourse: physiology, experience, and behavior.
2. In the psychophysiology of individual differences, experience is sampled to select subjects, but rarely to test them. This is one of the factors contributing to the operational gap between theory and experiment.
3. In studying physiology–experience relations, the research largely assumes only one of several logical alternatives—namely, that the two domains operate in parallel.
4. Although personality theories are about behavior, most research examines the static subject in a virtually passive and nonbehaving state, employing stimulation barely worthy of the name.
5. Emotion may not be expressed purely within physiological response systems, and, on some accounts, may work in a complementary or compensatory fashion among domains. This increases the probability of Type II errors.
6. Behavior is interactional, and all three domains are affected by feedback, both among domains and within domains in response to the environmental consequences of action.
7. Environmental stimuli, including experimental stimuli, are not definable in universal terms; each individual interprets events in terms of his or her existing repertoire of meanings; such interpretations feed back upon the external world.

The reader should now be well prepared to tackle the grim realities of research into the psychophysiology of individual differences.

EEG STUDIES OF EXTRAVERSION–INTROVERSION

This section is devoted to the analysis of EEG studies designed to test H. J. Eysenck's theory of the neurophysiological basis of extraversion–introversion and neuroticism–stability. Why devote a section to the work of one theorist? Eysenck's theory is unique because it combines within one framework a number of desirable features that are not seen together in other theories of personality. The theory bridges psychometrics, experimental psychology, neurophysiology, and psychopathology. The psychometric instruments employed were devised by Eysenck and his associates (e.g., H. J. Eysenck & Eysenck, 1964) using sound psychometric procedures, on textbook guidelines; this is apparent from the administration manual that accompanies the test, which resembles manuals devised for well-standardized tests of intelligence. After an account of the theory, the booklet gives details of the procedures adopted to establish reliability, outlines the factors that emerge from factorial analysis based on large samples, and gives the means and standard deviations for different subpopulations. The scales include a Lie scale, and while Lie scores are not wholly independent of Neuroticism scores, they do enable the researcher to exclude subjects on suspicion of faking.

One might imagine that the award of merit marks for such obvious features in a personality inventory, or for use of standard psychometric procedures, is hardly justified; unfortunately, there is reason to doubt the reliability (let alone the validity) of several scales used in personality research. Also, subject faking is sometimes used as an excuse for obtaining bland results, particularly in relation to anxiety, where the concept of defense mechanisms may be brought into play (see our discussion of locus of control research in the next section). Thus the relative purity of Eysenck's psychometrics is refreshing. Throughout the development of the theory, links have been drawn not only with animal studies of learning and conditioning, but with human studies in experimental psychology, in the fields of learning, sensation and perception, and motor behavior, and in the effects on performance of stimulant and depressant drugs.

Thus the constructs borrowed from experimental psychology have already been operationalized in many cases, or may be translated into experimental paradigms where the principle of falsifiability can be brought into action. For example, in the early experimental work, and in the case of learning theory, theorems derived from Hull's hypothetico-deductive system had already generated a coherent superstructure of parametric data. A more recent example is the exploration of individual differences in memory, where M.W. Eysenck (e.g., 1977) has combined a thorough-going Eysenckian framework in personality theory with theory and experimentation along information-processing lines. There is, of course, a clear advantage in this strategy, since there is a long tradition of carefully acquired data and theory in memory research that forces the personality theorist to be explicit about his or her experimental expectations. The unusual clarity of H. J. Eysenck's theory (so far as personality research is concerned) is both a source of strength and a weakness; the British psychological journals are strewn with articles by people who have failed to replicate studies conducted in Eysenck's laboratory, and every few years some new hero arrives to challenge the orthodox view!

The biological element has also been present during the various stages of theory construction. H. J. Eysenck claims with some justice (see also Kline, 1979) that factors resembling extraversion–introversion and neuroticism–stability are ubiquitous; that is, they emerge in some readily identifiable form from a wide variety of personality studies in different parts of the globe. This universality is important because it is taken as evidence of fundamental physiological mechanisms—basic characteristics of the nervous system—that are seen to underlie the two constructs. In his earlier work, as exemplified by *The Dynamics of Anxiety and Hysteria* (1957), Eysenck drew upon a combination of Pavlovian neurophysiology and Hullian learning theory to construct a general theory of personality, in which excitation, inhibition, conditionability, and associated constructs were used to account for a broad range of behaviors, both normal and pathological. Eysenck's neurophysiology reached its fully blown form in *The Biological Basis of Personality* (1967), in which full use was made of the discovery of arousal mechanisms by Moruzzi and Magoun (1949) and those who followed them. Extraversion-introversion was now seen to be a reflection of the threshold of excitability within the ascending reticular activating system (called "arousal" by Eysenck), while neuroticism–stability related to the threshold of excitation of the limbic system or emotional brain ("activation"). More recently, a third factor, "psychoticism," has been derived (H. J. Eysenck & Eysenck, 1976b); this is said to be a function of androgen levels.

The theory is therefore a truly psychophysiological theory because it combines neurophysiology with models of behavior, considers mechanisms as well as mere correlations, is linked to contemporary experimental psychology, and can account for differences between people. Because the theory spans both normal and abnormal behavior, it is very much a *general* theory, in the sense that psychoanalysis is a general theory. And it is clear from Eysenck's attacks upon the work of Freud (e.g., see H. J. Eysenck & Wilson, 1973) and his repeated assertions that therapies based on psychoanalytic theory, in contrast to behavioral therapies, either have no positive effect or even make patients worse (H. J. Eysenck & Rachman, 1965), that Eysenck sees his own theory as the natural contemporary heir of the grand theory tradition. Eysenck has weathered many storms; yet, as the *Festschrift* presented to him on his 65th birthday testifies (Lynn, 1981), the theory is in good enough shape to make a contribution to the current revival of interest in individual differences. (It may be a surprise to the North American reader to discover that in that book there is a contribution from Broadbent, Britian's leading theorist and experimenter in experimental psychology; however, close reading of the work of both men shows a mutuality of interest, which is not reflected in conflict between their disciplines.) Eysenck has never shirked controversy, and one particular source of confrontation has been the debate over the genetic determination of intelligence, to which we refer later in our discussion of intelligence. The notion that factors that account for the variance between individuals are inherited is, of course, extended to extraversion–introversion and neuroticism–stability. Shortage of space prevents us from reviewing in any detail psychophysiological studies of behavior genetics (for a review, see Roubertoux, 1985), but we do argue later that this is one of the potential growth points.

Summarizing, then, the theory (1) is general; (2) is founded upon sound psychometric reasoning and procedures; (3) is strongly biological in terms of genetics and of physiological and biochemical mechanisms; (4) is integrated with behavioral data; and (5) employs a number of established and well-defined paradigms, where problems of measurement have already been worked upon. One weakness in our view is the theory's failure to acknowledge in any explicit sense, or to consider the causal implications of, the phenomenal world of the individual. Thus, while the criterion measure for the majority of studies is the score obtained from responses to questions that ask subjects how they feel, think, and react in a variety of situations, there are very few studies focused upon such strategies; nor is there elaboration upon the modes of thinking or strategies used by subjects in dealing with the situations presented to them by the experimenter in the laboratory. This is strange, because the theory does extend across several areas of interest—including, for example, studies of humor, aesthetics, and sexual behavior—yet manages somehow to avoid experiential data. We see elsewhere in this chapter how studies of locus of control appear to be the one group concerned with a frankly cognitive and phenomenal approach. This is not just a matter of completeness, which is a ridiculously idealistic criterion for any theory devised by human beings about human beings. Rather, it has crucial effects upon experimentation and upon the interpretation of the experiment made by both subject and experimenter. We refer elsewhere to Averill's review of studies relating to the control of unpleasant events (Averill, 1973); there, he points out that the subject's interpretation of the stimuli presented to him or her in the laboratory may have a crucial effect upon outcome. Thus the need to explore the phenomenal world is not merely an additional optional garnish; without such considerations, data might become unnecessarily equivocal. We have further criticisms of Eysenck's theory, but we reserve these for our discussion of his neurophysiological theory in particular.

The Neurophysiological Theory

The theory of the neurophysiological basis of extraversion–introversion and neuroticism–stability as expounded by Eysenck in 1967 is quite straightforward, and is shown in schematic form in Figure 20-1.

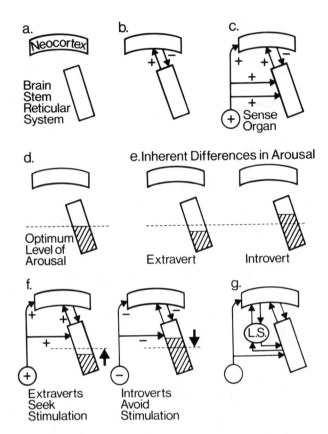

Figure 20-1. A schematic description of Eysenck's theory of the neurophysiological basis of extraversion–introversion and neuroticism–stability. (a) The brain stem reticular system (BSRF) is part of a functional system mediating arousal. (b) The BSRF and neocortex have reciprocal relations. (c) Collaterals from sense organs reach the BSRF. (d) There is an optimum level of arousal. (e) Extraverts and introverts differ in their inherent level of arousal (below and above the optimum, respectively). (f) Extraverts direct sense organs to external stimulation, thereby raising arousal level; introverts shun stimulation. (g) There are complex interactions between "arousal," mediated by the BSRF, and "activation," mediated by the limbic system (the physiological basis of neuroticism–stability).

1. Extraversion–introversion relates to the threshold of arousal of the brain stem reticular formation (BSRF).
2. This system is part of the ascending reticular activating system (ARAS) and has reciprocal relations of an inhibitory and excitatory nature with other brain areas, and with the neocortex in particular.
3. Extraverts have an inherently low level of arousal within the BSRF, and introverts have an inherently high level of arousal.
4. The BSRF, apart from inherent rhythmicity, receives sensory input through paths collateral to the classic sensory pathways; thus input from

these paths can elevate the level of arousal within the BSRF, or, in the case of monotonous stimulation, can induce habituation and lowered arousal.

5. There is an optimal level of arousal; this may be seen as a "drive" state (motivation to achieve an optimum), as an "acquired drive" (reflecting experience of specific task or functional demands), or as an experienced "hedonic" state (a correlative feeling within the individual that he or she is overaroused or underaroused, either of which induces discomfort). We should note that while these definitions are not mutually exclusive, referring as they do to different universes of description, the formal and explanatory status of each of these senses of optimum level of arousal is different, and we return to a general discussion of arousal in a later section). Some of the criticisms raised in relation to Zuckerman's trait of sensation seeking and the notion of optimal level of stimulation are equally applicable to the notion of optimal level of arousal (see "Sensation Seeking").

6. Since extraverts are born underaroused and introverts are born overaroused, the former are chronically below an optimum level, and the latter chronically above an optimum level.

7. Since extraverts and introverts share a common world, which imposes common functional demands, both must devise strategies to achieve the desired optimal state.

8. Extraverts seek additional and varied stimulation, increase sensory input, and thereby increase the level of arousal in both the BSRF and the cortex.

9. Introverts adopt the strategy of avoiding stimulation or engage in activities of a repetitive and unchanging nature; this reduces sensory input and orienting to novelty or change, thereby serving to lower the level of BSRF and cortical arousal.

10. Finally, as Figure 20-1 shows, the limbic system will contribute to overall arousal in a complex fashion: Its relationship with the BSRF and their mutual effect upon performance are seen as curvilinear, providing optimum performance at moderate levels of arousal. Excessively high levels of arousal are seen to lead to a state of negative feedback whereby the system closes down, equivalent in outcome to Pavlov's notion of "transmarginal inhibition." For Eysenck, "activation" (limbic system) is to be distinguished from "arousal" (BSRF and neocortex). He suggests that for most of our working day, neuroticism is unlikely to have effects, and the principal determinant of fluctuations in overall arousal is extraversion-introversion.

The physiological theory is consistent with the surface behavioral constellations that go with the terms "extravert" and "introvert." The extravert is happy-go-lucky, likes activity, acts before thinking, seeks the company of others, prefers variety in the satisfaction of sex and hunger drives, and laughs off life's problems. The introvert is shy, retiring, quiet in demeanor, enjoys doing things on his or her own, prefers the well-worn and familiar path, limits friendships, shuns too much contact with others or with excessive stimulation, plans ahead, and thinks before taking action. Such a link among causal mechanisms (physiology), surface behavior, and self-report is the keystone to a truly psychophysiological approach to individual differences.

We have already indicated that the theory has been subject to criticism. It is appropriate here to mention only a dozen or so criticisms!

1. The factorial purity of Eysenck's orthogonal factors and their reliability have both been challenged—for example, by Vernon (1964), who points out that the loadings obtained in different studies are not as consistent as Eysenck would have us believe.

2. The combination of *impulsivity* elements with *sociability* elements within the Extraversion–Introversion scale has been described by Guilford (1977) as a "shotgun marriage." As Schalling and Asberg (1985) argue, this means not only that subscales can yield differential effects, but that in some circumstances, they might oppose each other to give zero effects and create a Type II error.

3. While sensation seeking is clearly an important construct of Eysenck, he is again criticized (e.g., Zuckerman, 1983) for failing to acknowledge that sensation seeking can be partitioned into various aspects that do not necessarily load on each other (to provide evidence of a unitary underlying dimension) and that load on different behaviors.

4. Although Eysenck does not really acknowledge such criticisms as a virtue, he has nevertheless shifted several impulsivity items from the Extraversion–Introversion scale (in the Eysenck Personality Inventory [EPI]) to the Psychoticism scale (in the Eysenck Personality Questionnaire [EPQ]; H. J. Eysenck & Eysenck, 1976a). Such slipping of items from one place to another is worrying, since it must affect the description of the extraverted personality and, of course, the theoretical underpinning of the construct. Moreover, it means that studies using the EPQ are not strictly comparable with those using the EPI.

5. The generalizability of the scales has been questioned, since there is evidence that the use of alternative response modes (in contrast with the forced binary choice favored by Eysenck) can yield different outcomes (Jackson & Paunonen, 1980).

6. There is little direct physiological evidence that

arousal in the human is determined by the same structures as those evident in laboratory cats and rats. Eysenck (1967) acknowledges this, but suggests that the theory can be tested equally well treating its key concepts as intervening variables, and does not necessarily need hypothetical constructs embodied in actual physiology.

7. The view of the ARAS taken by Eysenck is what Thompson (1967) has described in his textbook as "the classical view" (i.e., the view prevalent in the mid-1950s); that is to say, the orderly view as conceived of by Moruzzi, Lindsley, French, and others had to be modified in the light of subsequent work.

8. A more serious concern for the present context is the difficulty of discriminating in operational terms, particularly when employing peripheral indices, between "arousal" and "activation." This is a rather important point, because, as we shall see, experimenters neglect the possible interactive effects of extraversion–introversion and neuroticism–stability at their peril.

9. The large majority of experimental work has been carried out on the extraversion–introversion dimension; a ground for neglecting neuroticism-stability in human subjects is the ethical constraint against making subjects suffer stressful conditions. Whatever the ethics, neglect of one of the two allegedly orthogonal dimensions is *logically* unwise, since it leaves open a variety of untested possibilities that have implications for the theory as a whole. Thus a number of empirical studies seem to suggest that there is really a dimension at 45° to the extraversion–introversion dimension; that is, when both extraversion and neuroticism are varied within a design, they prove not to be independent (e.g., Carlier, 1985; Coles, Gale, & Kline, 1971). Such an outcome is more compatible with the theory of Gray (1967) than that of Eysenck (see our discussion of anxiety in a later section).

10. In several controversies, where opponents have failed to replicate key findings—for example, the basic data of Franks (1956) on eyelid conditioning—Eysenck has insisted in response that inappropriate conditions were employed and that for differential conditioning to appear, very precise temporal conditions must be observed. That may well be so, but it hardly makes the theory easily applicable to real-life contexts, where events (e.g., misdemeanors followed by aversive control) are hardly preprogrammed by a laboratory microcomputer.

11. Because of his faith in his own theory and personality scales, Eysenck rarely incorporates other psychometric instruments in his research; he did in the early days, but once he had decided that many scales of interest merely reflected a large loading on his own factors, he ceased to use them. This criticism, of failing to take much practical notice of other related work, is one we lay at the door of most of the authors whose work we review in this chapter.

12. A good example of such a failure to take notice of other work is that in spite of interchanges and collaborative work between Eysenck and Zuckerman, their predictions concerning sensation seeking are quite the reverse of each other. As Feij, Orlebeke, Gazandam, and Van Zuilen (1985) point out, "in Eysenck's model, introverts are characterised by strong chronic excitation, or high arousability, but Zuckerman sees high arousability as a property of sensation seekers (i.e. extraverts)" (p. 198).

13. Feij *et al.* (1985) also comment that part of the confusion comes over the abuse of the term "arousal," which suffers from a lack of precise definition; any existing theory that makes use of such terms as "arousal," "arousability," or "activation," as Eysenck's does, is subject to this criticism.

14. Eysenck's rugged independence has led some critics to suggest that he is blind to criticism, to failure to replicate, and to theoretical niceties like the one cited under 12 above. However, those who have followed his work carefully can see that, with the passage of time, such points are absorbed into the developing theory and in some cases are used to enhance the power of the theory. This is an important observation if it is true, since some of the theories in individual differences research are very difficult to disconfirm, often because they contain their own impenetrable defense mechanisms (we make this observation in the next section in relation to studies of locus of control).

We know that more criticisms can be listed; however, when all is said and done, and given the purpose of the present review, we are obliged to conclude that of the theories of individual differences available to psychophysiologists, Eysenck's theory is not only the most comprehensive but also the most testable. Whether the criticisms are so severe that they undermine the whole enterprise is not for us to say, because if we reject this particular theory, we might as well discontinue our review at this point. Psychophysiology has had to make do with many approximations to the truth. The most recent and comprehensive critique of Eysenck's theory and its evolution is presented by Gray (1981) in a volume edited by Eysenck (yet another example, in spite of what his critics claim, of Eysenck's willingness to consider criticism!). Our empirical review is devoted to EEG studies only.

Comprehensive reviews of all psychophysiological indices and extraversion are to be found in Stelmack (1981), and Geen (1983).

EEG Studies of Eysenck's Neurophysiological Theory

We do not need to present a comprehensive review, because detailed comment on virtually all the published studies is available in reviews by Gale, Coles, and Blaydon (1969) and Gale (1973, 1981, 1983a, 1983b). Table 20-1 summarizes the studies. We propose to select a small representative sample illustrating both the strong and weak features of the research; we then offer a critique, having shown that many of the apparently contradictory findings can be reconciled by recourse to the theory itself, since so many researchers have neglected the theory.

Given the notion that extraverts are low in arousal, most researchers have made the prediction that extraverts will display a higher-amplitude, lower-frequency EEG record than introverts. Of course, in experiments of this sort, three outcomes are logically possible: The prediction that extraverts are less aroused may be confirmed; there may be no difference between the criterion groups; or the prediction might be reversed—that is, extraverts might be shown to be *more* aroused than introverts. All three outcomes are reported in the literature. The following studies (some of which did not measure extraversion–introversion directly, or were designed to test other hypotheses) have confirmed the theory: Gottlober (1938); Shagass and Kerenyi (1958); Nebylitsyn (1963); Savage (1964); Pawlik and Cattell (1965); Marton and Urban (1966); Hume (1968); Gale *et al.* (1969); Gale, Harpham, and Lucas (1972); Winter, Broadhurst, and Glass (1972); Morris and Gale (1974); Montgomery (1975); Rösler (1975); Baker (1978); Deakin and Exley (1979); Gale, Kingsley, Edwards, Porter, and Smith (reported in Gale, 1981); Gilliland, Andress, and Bracy (1981); and Venturini, de Pascalis, Imperiali, and San Martini (1981). The following are among those that have not confirmed the theory (we assume there may be other studies that were not submitted for publication, simply because they had *negative* results, and it is known that journal editors are not eager to give space to such things): Lemere (1936); Henry and Knott (1941); Claridge and Herrington (1963); Fenton and Scotton (1967); Young, Lader, and Fenton (1971); Gale, Coles, Kline, and Penfold (1971); Becker-Carus (1971); Travis, Kondo, and Knott (1974); and Strelau and Terelak (1974). There is also a group of studies that have found extraverts to be more aroused, in EEG terms: McAdam and Orme (1954); Mundy-Castle (1955); A. Glass and Broadhurst (1966); Broadhurst and Glass

(1969); and Kondo, Bean, Travis, and Knott (1978); O'Gorman and Mallise (1984).

Let us now examine a small sample of these studies in detail; we then propose a critique and a means of reconciling apparently discrepant findings.

We begin with one of the oldest studies, which, although theory-free, is remarkably sensitive from a methodological point of view and is superior in many ways to most of the studies that followed it. Lemere (1936) took 26 young adults and obtained between three and five recordings over a period of a month. This is therefore one of the few studies in the literature to measure reliability of either personality score or EEG activity, although in this case there is no formal estimate. Lemere argued that if the EEG is a measure of some fundamental aspect of the person, then it should remain stable over time. He observed that such stability did exist, but noted exceptions. Between-subject differences were maintained, even in noisy environments. Yet the quality of the alpha rhythm "deteriorated" over sessions, and in two cases was affected by external life events. Nowadays, these would be called "situational effects": One subject had an important rugby football match that day, while the other had a secret assignation with a lover! Lemere considered a number of alternative factors that might underlie individual stability of the EEG, and ruled out several possibilities by careful reasoning, including head size and skull thickness. But the EEG correlated (as stable as it was) with no general trait or characteristic (i.e., sex, personality, memory, or extraversion). It is not clear how individual differences were estimated.

Lemere's pioneer study should be read with care by all aspirants to EEG work in the field of individual differences; the paper is written with an intellectual discipline and sensitivity to sources of error that are sadly lacking in contemporary work. However, over more than 40 years, the main thrust of the work has remained the same. It amounts to the question, "If we lie people down and measure their EEG, will it relate to a questionnaire score?" This is the archetypal correlational approach, which runs right through the studies reported in this chapter and which we believe has done so much disservice to the study of individual differences in psychophysiology. It is an approach long regretted by authorities like Lindsley (1952), who urged his colleagues to stop expending their energies in searching for correlates of the alpha rhythm and to turn instead to the creation of a rapprochement with experimental psychology; this meant the use of tasks and the observation of behavior to create a coherent body of data relating to EEG to psychological process.

In the present context, the correlational approach was perhaps justifiable in the early days, and prior to the publication of Eysenck's full neurophysiological

Table 20-1

Tabulation of Published and Other Known Studies of the Relationship between Extraversion–Introversion and the EEG

Author(s), Date; Subjects; Star Rating[a]	Personality and EEG Measures Procedure[b]	Statistical Treatment and Key Results[c]	Comments
Lemere, 1936 26 normal adults ***	Good and poor alpha 3–5 recordings Lying quietly *Low arousal*	Within-subject consistency No correlation with sex, intelligence, memory *No difference between extraverts and introverts*	A classic paper raising; issues (sources of artifact) ignored by later authors. Weak on theory and personality measurement.
Gottlober, 1938 18 female and 49 male students **	Nebraska Personality Inventory (NPI) and clinical ratings Percent time alpha, mean frequency, and classed as dominant–rare Reclining, dark room, eyes closed *Low arousal*	Standard error of difference Percent extraverts with dominant alpha higher NPI alone not significant *Extraverts less aroused*	EEG scored by eye; subjects knew personality ratings in advance; clinical ratings best in prediction; neuroticism not controlled; several statistical tests; results challenged by Henry and Knott (below).
Henry & Knott, 1941 39 female and 41 male undergraduates ***	NPI Percent time alpha Lying with eyes closed *Low arousal*	Neither standard error of difference nor chi-square yielded significant effects *No difference between extraverts and introverts*	Rigorous data analysis including reworking of Gottlober's data, claiming his statistics unsatisfactory
McAdam & Orme, 1954 40 "intellectually blunted" alcoholics *	Structured interview and ranking Rorschach for neuroticism Percent time alpha, theta, and beta (index) *Low arousal*	Extraverts had high beta, low alpha, and low theta index; alpha index correlated positively with neuroticism; alpha index and frequency inversely related *Extraverts more aroused than introverts*	Existence of chi-square tables reported, but tables not presented; no test results presented; interview protocols not subjected to formal analysis; neuroticism probably confounded with extraversion (i.e., anxiety referred to in relation to dichotomized groups).
Mundy-Castle, 1955 40 clerical and technical staff, mean age 25 ****	Objective tests of primary–secondary function (e.g., tapping) 20-min, 6-channel, bipolar recording Alpha frequency hand-scored Relaxing on couch *Low arousal*	Correlations with various individual tests More secondary function correlated with lower alpha frequencies *Extraverts (i.e., primary function) more aroused*	Personality scores known in advance; unusually long recording period, but sampling frame not given; alpha claimed to be a measure of a central clock, and secondary function claimed to relate to excitability of CNS; results misinterpreted by both Savage (1964) and Eysenck (1953).
Shagass & Kerenyi, 1958 36 neurotic patients ***	Guilford Scales Frontal EEG 15–30 Hz plus integrator Amount of sodium amytal needed to induce large increase in amplitude *High arousal*	Correlation of .60 between introversion and threshold (i.e., extraverts increased abundance with lower levels of drug); hysterics had lower threshold *Extraverts less aroused*	Theory related directly to Eysenckian framework; rather than resting level being measured, change was biochemically induced.
Claridge & Herrington, 1963 47 male patients and normals **	Maudsley Personality Inventory (MPI) Hand-scoring of channel with prominent alpha Delay of alpha return after rotation of Archimedes spiral ends (eyes closed);	All correlations between questionnaire scores and EEG low and insignificant *No difference in alpha index or latency between extraverts and introverts*	Subjects tested under different conditions; aftereffect task that did yield extraversion effects used; authors claimed Savage (1964) found extraverts to have low alpha amplitude; overen-

Table 20-1
(*Continued*)

Author(s), Date; Subjects; Star Rating[a]	Personality and EEG Measures Procedure[b]	Statistical Treatment and Key Results[c]	Comments
	sedation threshold *Intermediate arousal*		thusiastic interpretation of results!
Nebylitsyn, 1963 A series of studies ***	Russian tests of excitation and inhibition in dynamism EEG conditioning, alpha orienting and habituation, photic driving *Intermediate arousal*	*Subjects equated with extraverts by Gray (1967) were less aroused*; that is, a predominance of inhibition in dynamism associated with high theta frequency, high alpha amplitude and index, high beta amplitude and index, low alpha frequency, and high beta frequency	Predominance of excitation in dynamism meant capacity to form positive conditioned responses rapidly; Gray claimed test battery showed similarity to Western measures.
Savage, 1964 20 female students ****	MPI; subjects assigned to four quadrants 4 min bipolar occipital EEG; low-frequency analyzer measuring 8–13 Hz amplitude Lying on couch with eyes closed *Low arousal*	Analysis of variance (ANOVA) showed main effect for extraversion; significant interaction gave high neurotic extraverts higher amplitude than stable extraverts; extraversion and neuroticism correlated (.24) *Extraverts less aroused than introverts*	Appropriate statistics; automated analysis, but sampling criterion not given; results claimed to be consistent with Mundy-Castle, but this untrue; lucky to get 5 subjects per cell; Gale (1981) disagreed with interpretation of interaction.
Pawlik & Cattell, 1965 26 female and 39 male undergraduates ***	Battery of behavior and personality tests Bipolar left and right hemisphere (frontal, parietal, and temporal), 20 sec selected from 2 min Alpha index, frequency, and amplitude Sitting relaxed with eyes closed or open *Low arousal*	Factor analysis on 44 variables yielded 8 factors; alpha index loaded (−.31) on extraversion, but frontoparietal with eyes shut; direction of sign changed with eyes open! *Thus extraverts less aroused, but this depended on condition*	Factor loadings universally low; correlations between alpha measures low; tiny correlations overvalued by authors; test battery items dependent on Cattell's theory.
Glass & Broadhurst, 1966 Number not given ***	MPI? Opisometric recording Percent time alpha and rate of change of potential Rest and arithmetic calculations *High arousal*	Alpha and rate of change of potential both correlated positively with introversion *Extraverts more aroused than introverts*	Personality tests given after EEG recording; a brief report, which noted abundance measures, confounded amplitude with prevalence.
Marton & Urban, 1966 40 students **	Personality measure not given Alpha index and frequency; trials to habituation Resting and conditioning trials *Intermediate arousal*	20 extraverts had alpha, but 9 introverts had none; extraverts habituated more quickly; alpha frequency for introverts higher *Extraverts less aroused than introverts*	Complete absence of measurement details for personality, EEG, and statistics; were all introverts included in measure of alpha frequency? Findings related to Hull's reactive inhibition.
Fenton & Scotton, 1967 24 females and 30 males **	MPI Hand-scoring Eyes shut for 2 min, then 60 photic stimuli	Blocking latency, index for alpha, and alpha amplitude all unrelated to either extraversion or	Rest period confounded with auditory masking noise; stimulus schedule a function of alpha, thus extraverts

Table 20-1
(*Continued*)

Author(s), Date; Subjects; Star Rating[a]	Personality and EEG Measures Procedure[b]	Statistical Treatment and Key Results[c]	Comments
	Low arousal	neuroticism; all correlations very low *No difference in EEG for extraverts and introverts*	could have shorter interstimulus interval (ISI) and finish earlier; high alpha index of 83% might indicate drowsiness; habituation score collapsed across 25 trials when EEG typically habituated in 5!
Hume, 1968 106 normals, neurotics, and psychotics ***	Eysenck Personality Inventory (EPI) and 16PF Alpha plus manual scoring of filter Variety of procedures, including two-flash threshold and habituation *Intermediate arousal?*	Principal-components analysis showing alpha index and extraversion loading on the same factor *Extraverts less aroused than introverts?*	Complex results that do not support a single arousal factor (N.B.: autonomic variables measured also); a very brief report.
Broadhurst & Glass, 1969 8 female and 43 male students ***	MPI Bipolar and transoccipital Percent time alpha; frequency, amplitude; rate of change of potential Automatic, opisometric, and hand-scoring 30-min recording with rest and mental arithmetic *High arousal*	ANOVA and correlations; extraverts had lower prevalence and amplitude than introverts, and extraversion was negatively correlated with rate of change at potential High neurotics had low amplitude but also low-frequency alpha *Extraverts more aroused than introverts*	Different sampling periods for different aspects; rest periods may not have been true rest; personality tests given after recording (2–6 months); different subjects had different treatments; experiment designed for other purposes; combination of ANOVA and correlations good, since all data used and comparison with other studies possible.
Gale, Coles, & Blaydon, 1969 19 female and 5 male students ****	EPI; high Neuroticism scorers excluded Bipolar transoccipital Eyes-closed alpha in 6 one-cycle steps to take mean dominant frequency (mdf); then theta, alpha, and beta with low-frequency analyzer; eyes-open-and-shut trials with fixed sampling schedule Lying in room with head surrounded by black screen *Intermediate arousal*	ANOVA with main effects for theta, alpha, and beta; mdf lower for extraverts; effects stronger with eyes open *Extraverts less aroused than introverts*	Study designed with theory in mind; subjects' personality scores known at time of recording and scoring; no mdf calculation for eyes open; study controlled for neuroticism, but therefore not possible to estimate effects or compare with other work; effects of opening and shutting eyes very powerful compared with small but significant personality effects.
Becker-Carus, 1971 10 male and 9 female psychology students **	Brengelman Extroversion and Neuroticism scales Measures of rigidity and field dependence; Stroop test Alpha index and frequency by zero cross in single-cycle steps Frontal, temporal, and parietal left hemisphere Hand-scoring (two raters)	Correlational analysis *No effect for extraversion* Vigilance performance correlated with alpha index Rigidity correlated with alpha frequency (negative for low frequency, positive for high) Neuroticism correlated positively with alpha index	17 subjects dropped from analysis for technical reasons; vigilance task only sampled for 6 min; no scorer reliability coefficient; only some findings given, since 150 variables were intercorrelated; no factor structure attempted; neuroticism confounded with extraversion; quite lacking in theory, and

Table 20-1
(*Continued*)

Author(s), Date; Subjects; Star Rating[a]	Personality and EEG Measures Procedure[b]	Statistical Treatment and Key Results[c]	Comments
	Eyes open and closed Mental arithmetic and visual vigilance in a 6-stage 80-min session *Intermediate and high arousal*	Good arithmetic performance correlated positively with index at rest and inversely with low alpha frequency in vigilance *No difference between extraverts and introverts*	no grounds given for the measures given or the procedure.
Young, Lader, & Fenton, 1971 64 male fraternal and identical twins **	Psychoticism, Extraversion and Neuroticism Scale (PEN) Bipolar right hemisphere 5-min record, but only last minute scored; hand-scoring 8–13 Hz but some with low-frequency analysis for delta, theta, alpha, and beta Sitting in semidark room; latter part 60 flashes for alpha attenuation and Average Evoked Potential (AEP); subjects gave reaction time (RT) to flash *Intermediate arousal*	Correlations yielded no relation between any EEG measure and personality, but intraclass correlations high for twins *No difference between extraverts and introverts*	No theoretical rationale for study; 54 correlations and none significant; did subjects know the procedure in advance? Intraclass correlations for twins indicate data were valid; variety of task conditions.
Gale, Coles, Kline, & Penfold, 1971 60 male students ***	EPI Bipolar transoccipital Low-frequency analysis Delta, theta, alpha, and beta 50 min with 5-sec auditory tones every 2 min Lying on bed with eyes shut *Low arousal*	ANOVA gave no effect for extraversion, but neuroticism associated with higher abundance; pattern of habituation to tones complex, with initial attenuation and then augmentation; response magnitude a function of prestimulus level (law of initial values) *No difference between extraverts and introverts*	Excellent methodology but unsound theoretical basis; whole experiment run blind; many faults from previous studies incorporated.
Gale, Harpham, & Lucas, 1972 20 male military personnel **	EPI Bipolar transoccipital Low-frequency analysis Alpha, theta, and beta Subjects attended on four occasions at four times of day Open and shut eyes facing a blank wall *Low arousal*	Within-subject reliability very high for all frequencies; no time-of-day effects; no amplitude correlations with extraversion, but variability across sessions correlated for both eyes open and closed *Extraverts more variable*	Study designed for other purposes; study run blind for personality scores, which were taken after testing for EEG.
Winter, Broadhurst, & Glass, 1972 7 female and 24 male medical and dental students ****	EPI Bipolar left and right hemisphere Time series analysis by computer 8–13 Hz filter Latin Square for 4 conditions: eyes open and shut	ANOVA and correlations High neurotics had low amplitude (main effect) Interaction showed that neurotic extraverts had lower amplitude than stables *Extraverts with low Neuroti-*	Personality measured months after testing; complex and well-considered data analysis, except that interaction was not tested with planned comparisons; study designed for different purpose; results for comparable group

Table 20-1
(*Continued*)

Author(s), Date; Subjects; Star Rating[a]	Personality and EEG Measures Procedure[b]	Statistical Treatment and Key Results[c]	Comments
	with and without mental arithmetic *High arousal*	cism scores were less aroused	similar to those of Gale, Coles, and Blaydon (1969).
Gale (1972, unpublished) 22 female students from 100+ sample to yield extreme groups **	EPI; high Neuroticism scorers excluded Retest of EPI after recording Low-frequency analysis 8–13 Hz filter Sitting with back to experimenter Five 2-min eyes open and eyes shut trials *Low arousal*	Because EPI scores unreliable, extraversion scores log-transformed Correlation of .45 between alpha abundance and log extraversion *Extraverts less aroused*	Only study to test reliability of EPI; 6 introverts became extraverts on retest ($p < .01$); a simple replication, but outcome worrying.
Morris & Gale, 1974 14 female and 18 male undergraduates **	EPI, Betts Questionnaire on Mental Imagery (QMI), Gordon Test of Visual Imagery Low-frequency analysis Transoccipital alpha 8–13 Hz High- and low-imagery words presented *Intermediate arousal*	Correlation matrix; extraversion correlated .45 with alpha abundance and .45 with Betts Richness of Imagery score *Extraverts less aroused than introverts*	Personality and other questionnaires administered after testing; study designed for other purposes, including incidental recall; indicates imaging could be a source of error in other studies.
Travis, Kondo, & Knott, 1974 21 female and 24 male students and employees **	EPI (mixture of A and B Forms) Central unipolar Alpha filter 8–13 Hz Five 2-min rests, following feedback trials *Intermediate arousal*	ANOVA with no effects involving extraversion High Neuroticism scorers gave higher alpha than low during feedback trials *No difference between extraverts and introverts*	Personality scores obtained after testing, but no rationale given for either biofeedback and personality or EEG and personality; sampling frame not specified; no post hoc explanation offered for neuroticism effect.
Strelau & Terelak, 1974 762 dichotomized for high–low alpha index ***	MPI, Manifest Anxiety Scale (MAS), Guilford, Thurstone, Strelau Left hemisphere hand-scored for 8–14 Hz Repeated testing up to 5 years Percent time alpha in 3-min sample Procedure not given *Low arousal?*	Extremely high retest reliability for EEG Only 2 of 24 tests were significant High neurotics and high reactives (Strelau) had low alpha index *No difference in extraversion for high and low alpha index subjects*	Report prefaced by thorough literature review; large proportion of original sample rejected; personality scores derived after EEG testing; reliability measure included for EEG scoring.
Montgomery, 1975 38 female, 38 male students *	Foulds hysteroid–obsessoid questionnaire (correlates .81 with MPI Extraversion scale) Bipolar left hemisphere Four 1-min samples 8–12 Hz filter for index, amplitude, and frequency Sitting with eyes closed *Low arousal*	Hysteroids had higher index and amplitude than obsessoids *Extraverts less aroused than introverts*	Equal numbers of males and females in two extreme groups, but use of extremes wasted data that were suited to correlation; design confounded extraversion with neuroticism; not clear if scorer blind; no fixed criterion for scoring; theta and beta measured but not reported; no rationale for study.
Rösler, 1975 32 male students	EPI, 16PF, and 14 other scales	Personality scales factor-analyzed to yield 4 fac-	Thorough review of the literature, but conditions not re-

Table 20-1
(*Continued*)

Author(s), Date; Subjects; Star Rating[a]	Personality and EEG Measures Procedure[b]	Statistical Treatment and Key Results[c]	Comments
*****	Unipolar occipital Full Fourier transform Seven conditions including rest, attentive listening, and arithmetic calculation with and without stress *Low, intermediate, and high arousal*	tors; EEG factor-analyzed to yield 4 factors; ANOVA gave modest effect for extraverts in beta, and interactions between task and personality such that among high neurotics, extraverts had higher amplitude under stress *Extraverts less aroused than introverts*	lated theoretically to extraversion–introversion; methodologically the best study to date, but with a modest yield.
Kondo, Bean, Travis, & Knott, 1978 30 female and 30 male students and employees **	EPI to compare extreme groups Unipolar, 8–13 Hz filter, for 5 min Sitting with eyes shut *Low arousal*	No effect for neuroticism, but extraverts had less integrated alpha than introverts *Extraverts more aroused than introverts*	Personality measured after testing; since extraversion the focus, extreme-group design confounded neuroticism; results contradicted earlier study, but no comment made (nevertheless, EEG–personality studies claimed to be reliable!); several names of previous authors misspelled.
Baker, 1978 16 female and 16 male pairs of same-sex friends ***	EPI Bipolar transoccipital theta, alpha, and beta Low-frequency analysis Recorded in pairs during RT task under competition *High arousal*	Extraversion positively correlated with mid-alpha baundance, and neuroticism negatively correlated to mid-alpha but positively correlated to beta *Extraverts less aroused than introverts*	Personality scores derived after testing; a social situation relevant to theory, although test made for other purposes; same author did not replicate these findings in another, similar study.
Deakin & Exley, 1979 48 female and 49 male students ****	PEN Bipolar left and right hemisphere 10 1-sec epochs scored by hand from 4 min Tested in fours, sitting in circle back-to-back *Intermediate arousal*	ANOVA and factor analysis Alpha amplitude higher for extraverts No effect for neuroticism Females had higher alpha frequency Neuroticism correlated with psychoticism score Three factors emerged that replicate ANOVA findings *Extraverts less aroused than introverts*	Very thorough in execution; high reliability coefficient for scoring; good use of statistical treatments; both hemispheres recorded, but sample source not clear; testing conditions suggested to be more arousing for neurotics, but treatment not related to theory vis-à-vis extraversion–introversion.
Gale, Kingsley, Edwards, Porter, & Smith (unpublished; reported in Gale, 1981) 24 female and 24 male undergraduates ***	PEN Bipolar left and right posterior Low-frequency analysis of theta, alpha, and beta Tested in pairs, facing each other and varying gaze under instruction *Low, intermediate, and high arousal*	ANOVA with sex, hemisphere, gaze Modest significant main effect such that introverts had lower left-hemisphere alpha abundance *Extraverts less aroused*	Extraversion findings modest compared with findings for sex and gaze; designed for other purposes but clearly related to theory; multiple experimenters to balance for subject and experimenter sex.
Gilliland, Andress, &	EPI extreme scorers; high	Extraverts had higher alpha	Brief report; not clear how

Table 20-1
(*Continued*)

Author(s), Date; Subjects; Star Rating[a]	Personality and EEG Measures Procedure[b]	Statistical Treatment and Key Results[c]	Comments
Bracy, 1981 26 males ***	Neuroticism scorers excluded Transoccipital bipolar 8–13 Hz filter Sitting with eyes open for 5 min *Low arousal*	index; when neuroticism not controlled for, differences disappeared for extraversion *Extraverts less aroused than introverts*	neuroticism handled in the design; no effect for neuroticism per se; not clear if experimenter knew personality score when recording.
Venturini, de Pascalis, Imperiali, & San Martini, 1981 10 male and 6 female university students **	Eysenck Personality Questionnaire (EPQ) (Italian version) Left and right occipital bipolar Digital analyzer for delta, theta, alpha, and beta over 8-sec epochs Reclining with eyes open for 8 min, then up to 35 auditory clicks *Low arousal*	No effect for personality for derivations or in interhemispheric asymmetry, but extraverts habituated to clicks while introverts did not Introverts desynchronized longer No effect for latency of response *Extraverts less arousible*	Possible confounding of sex with personality, since introverted group had 4 males, 1 female; very tiny groups; experimenter blind to personality scores; possible confounding of click schedule with base level, since presentation dependent; both groups contained some high Neuroticism scorers; correlation matrix for several EEG measures; Russian and Western theory used to explain findings.

[a]The number of asterisks in the first column indicates the quality of the study on a 5-point scale, taking into account quality of theory, personality measurement, EEG measurement, procedure, and execution.

[b]Italics in the second column indicate the overall arousal level of the testing conditions, following the post hoc classification of Gale (1973).

[c]Italics in the third column indicate the difference (if any) in arousal between extraverts and introverts.

theory. However, as we see from our account of the theory, the notion that there will be a straightforward correlation between extraversion score and the EEG is based on only one of the theory's assumptions. For the theory is interactive in nature; it refers to the individual's strategies for matching his or her inherent arousal level to the functional demands of the environment, in a way that helps him or her to achieve an optimal level. Now testing conditions for EEG measurement can be particularly boring and monotonous; that is to say, the laboratory is a special case of an environment that calls for an optimizing strategy. In some respects, the psychophysiological laboratory is threatening (electronic equipment, electrodes, wires, etc.); in others it is relaxing (soundproof room, bed, little stimulation, minimal demands for active response). The theory predicts differential response for extraversion–introversion and neuroticism–stability in these circumstances.

One study that did acknowledge this aspect of the theory was that by Gale *et al.* (1969). Their study had a number of novel features:

1. There were several trials with eyes open and eyes closed, giving a sample of unusual duration.

2. A wide range of EEG frequencies was sampled, and they provided both an abundance measure and a mean dominant-frequency measure.

3. Instructions to open and shut eyes were given verbally, according to a predetermined schedule.

4. The session began with an eyes-closed resting period of fixed duration.

5. Subjects lay in a soundproofed room, looking upward into a box of painted matte-black cardboard, which was, therefore, devoid of visual stimulation. It was in this last-mentioned condition (eyes open looking at a black visual field) that Gale *et al.* (1969) achieved their best effects. The rationale was that, given the absence of additional stimulation and the lack of opportunity for self-stimulation that an eyes-closed condition allows (by imagining and cogitation), the basic differences between extraverts and introverts in cortical arousal would be revealed. Virtually all studies have used an eyes-closed condition exclusively.

6. Another feature of this study was the exclusion of subjects with high Neuroticism scores, in an attempt to explore the effects of extraversion–introversion upon the EEG, independent of neuroticism–stability. Some studies that have combined

the two variables in a systematic way revealed interactions (e.g., Savage, 1964).

Gale *et al.* (1969) confirmed the theory for both amplitude and dominant-frequency measures.

A study that obtained statistically significant findings opposite to those predicted by the basic proposition of the theory (i.e., that extraverts were *more* aroused) was that by Broadhurst and Glass (1969), two workers who were particularly systematic and careful. Their subjects completed a questionnaire several months after EEG testing; thus there was no opportunity for bias during the testing session, as there was in the case of Gale *et al.* (1969) and many other studies. We should note, however, the implication that the study was not designed with this particular purpose in view; as we shall see, inattention to the need to predict from theory can indeed lead to strange results. Their subjects were required, during EEG measurement, to perform mental arithmetic calculations. Broadhurst and Glass computed both ANOVA and correlational statistics. Stable subjects had a higher alpha index than neurotics; there were no interactions between extraversion–introversion and neuroticism–stability (unlike the results from studies by Savage, 1964, and Rösler, 1975, and from a later study by the same authors, Winter *et al.*, 1972), and introverts had a significantly higher amplitude and index (alpha per unit time) than did extraverts. Another measure employed, the rate of change of potential, showed extraverts to have a higher rate of change, which Broadhurst and Glass interpreted quite reasonably as an indication of reduced cortical inhibition.

Gale (1973) has discussed the Broadhurst and Glass (1969) study at some length, pointing to eccentric methods for coping with unequal cells in an ANOVA design (these were not preselected groups) and the unusual finding that one group (neurotics) had both a low alpha amplitude and low alpha frequency, when typically these EEG measures are inversely related. However, the substantial finding—that extraverts were more aroused—cannot be challenged. Broadhurst and Glass employed more than one measure of cortical activity and more than one statistical design; both of these desirable features are unusual. They also employed an ingenious, opisometric scoring technique, whereby a cursor was run over a projected and enlarged record of the EEG trace and converted into digital data. Many of the nonmechanized studies used raters, without any indication of whether they were blind to the subjects' personality scores either at the time of scoring or recording, and in the absence of any measure of intrajudge or interjudge reliability. Since mean differences in these studies tended to be tiny, the possibility that a good proportion of the observed variance was attributable to systematic bias cannot be ruled out. The Broadhurst and Glass study is unusually competent. Unfortunately, the authors were unable to give a convincing explanation, in terms of the theory, for obtaining results apparently contrary to the theory. We return to this problem below.

Two studies by Travis *et al.* (1974) and Kondo *et al.* (1978) provide good examples of important faults. In spite of some 30 or more studies in the literature and the numerous reviews (e.g., by Brown & Klug, 1974; Eysenck, 1970, 1976; Gale, 1973; Gale *et al.*, 1969), these authors appeared to be aware of papers published in only one journal. We comment elsewhere in this chapter on the inability of researchers to conduct a standard literature review and the refusal of journal editors to insist upon a fair-minded evaluation of previous studies; it is difficult to see how theory can be advanced by selective ignorance of the facts. In the first of their studies, Travis *et al.* (1974) measured alpha during alpha feedback (provided by a signal light) and intertrial rests. Subjects with higher Neuroticism scores showed more alpha during feedback than those with lower scores. Extraversion–introversion was unrelated to either training trial or rest measures. No rationale whatever was given for believing that personality is related to the EEG or biofeedback; no evidence was shown that alpha amplitude over trials was contingent upon feedback; and not even a post hoc explanation was given for their findings, particularly in relation to effects for one dimension of personality and not the other. Travis *et al.* merely observed that their technique "presents a new approach to the examination of relationships between EEG and personality traits" (1974, p. 543). We are eager to see a new approach, but not this particular variety. This is an example of blind empiricism, which, while justifiable perhaps in certain contexts, cannot be justified when there are both theory and data with direct relevance to the hypotheses in question.

The Kondo *et al.* (1978) study obtained a resting sample of 5 min, taken from 60 subjects, while sitting with eyes closed, in a darkened soundproofed cubicle. On this occasion, the EEG did not relate to neuroticism–stability, but did show extraverts to have lowered amplitudes (i.e., to be more aroused). No attempt was made by the authors to reconcile the differences between their two studies; separate *t* tests were computed for extraversion–introversion and neuroticism–stability; and no attempt was made to consider the possibility of interaction between the two dimensions, although studies by Savage (1964), Broadhurst and Glass (1969), Gale *et al.* (1971), Winter *et al.* (1972), and Rösler (1975), to name but a few, all considered such a strategy to be important. Kondo *et al.* concluded that "further investigation would be of interest" (1978, p. 379).

Finally, two studies are reported, both of which are technically competent, and one of which (Rösler, 1975) is by far the best study in the field. A study of Deakin and Exley (1979) is somewhat limited in actual EEG measurement, but illustrates considerable care in scoring and in statistical treatment. Deakin and Exley had a total of 96 subjects, with equal numbers of males and females, whom they tested in groups of four (two males and two females) sitting in a circle with their backs to one another! No rationale is given for this strange arrangement, but it must have helped them to complete their research much more quickly. One might well ask why they did not test a whole class of students simultaneously; the answer is that they used an eight-channel EEG recorder, with two channels allocated to each subject, recording from the posterior regions of the right and left hemispheres. Subjects opened and shut their eyes upon instruction, but the data base was derived from a prolonged eyes-closed session. Since scoring was carried out by hand, some records that showed no alpha activity were discarded. Recording and scoring were carried out blind (the scorer knowing neither the sex nor personality score), and a scorer reliability coefficient of .90 was reported.

Both ANOVA and factor analysis were computed, taking amplitude and frequency of alpha separately. Neuroticism was unrelated to either EEG measure; extraverts had a higher-amplitude EEG and a tendency (not significant in the ANOVA) to lower frequency. Females had a higher frequency than males; we should note, as elsewhere in this chapter, that such sex differences are clearly a potential source for confounding in many studies, where the sex composition of the overall sample and the breakdown on sex for criterion groups are not revealed. The factor analysis revealed three factors. Factor 1 loaded highly on both neuroticism and psychoticism, but *not* on EEG measures (using the PEN scale), Factor 2 on amplitude, frequency and extraversion, and Factor 3 on frequency and sex; thus the factor analysis gave essentially the same results as the ANOVA, but the loading for extraversion on Factor 2 was particularly high (.72). Because of the laborious method used for scoring, only a total of 10 sec (10 1-sec samples) was used from a total recording time of 4 min.

The key defect in the Deakin and Exley (1979) study, which in methodological terms rates quite highly, is its theoretical naiveté. As we indicate below, Deakin and Exley were lucky to have used just about the optimal conditions for obtaining a significant effect in accordance with the theory. One irritating feature of this study is that data were scored for one hemisphere only, although recordings were taken from both. Topographical differences are important, and it is of theoretical interest that correlations between the EEG and criterion measures might *vary* from placement to placement, not only in magnitude

but in sign. It is difficult to argue that the EEG is of psychological significance and that it is a subtle discriminatory measure, and yet to ignore the established variety of waveform and frequency across the cranium. A measure that is sensitive to variation in behavior must itself be variable, by definition.

By far the most comprehensive study in the history of this topic is that of Rösler (1975). He began with a review of Eysenck's theory and previous work and then made specific predictions in attempting to relate the EEG to both extraversion–introversion and neuroticism–stability. Seven task conditions were used, involving progressive stress and active participation on the part of the subject (rest, attentive listening, mental calculation, etc.). A total of 32 subjects were tested, in the morning only, to avoid circadian effects. A battery of personality tests was administered, involving 16 scales in all; these scores were then factor-analyzed, yielding four personality factors, which Rösler named "emotional lability," "extraversion," "cyclothymia," and "sociability." Eysenck's Neuroticism and Extraversion scales loaded .91 and .70 on Factors 1 and 2, respectively; there was a *negative* but modest correlation between extraversion and the sociability factor. The EEG was recorded from one channel, digitized, subjected to fast Fourier transform, and then factor-analyzed, yielding four factors accounting for almost 80% of the variance.

The Rösler's findings, which are modestly in favor of the theory, are given in Table 20-1. The main analysis was an ANOVA for each EEG frequency factor, varying situations, extraversion, and lability. One of the problems with this study is its failure to be explicit about the effects that various combinations of neuroticism and extraversion have upon the EEG, particularly in relation to *different* frequency bands. For example, lability appeared as a significant effect for one frequency only (delta/theta) in a triple interaction with situations and extraversion. For highly labile groups, the difference between extraverts and introverts appeared only under the most stressful conditions (calculation and calculation under pressure). Now this finding is compatible with that of Deakin and Exley (1979), for although they found no relationship between neuroticism–stability and the EEG, they limited themselves to the alpha frequency. The factor to give the most robust effects was situations, and since such effects varied for different frequency bands, which themselves were shown by varimax rotation to be relatively independent, Rösler suggested that his data provide evidence for two dimensions of cortical arousal.

One problem we have with Rösler's study is that while the set of situations employed may be seen to relate to some stress factor, and therefore have face validity *prima facie* for neuroticism–stability as tasks that will induce systematic change, there is little reason to believe that they would influence extraversion–

introversion in a systematic fashion. Rösler did not employ tasks on which such differences have been found in the past. On the basis of this study and that of Savage (1964), it appears that the EEG effect of high neuroticism is additive to the extraversion dimension (i.e., it increases the range of the difference between extraverts and introverts); however, Savage and Rösler showed this for different frequency bands.

A Provisional Summary

These examples of research have been selected because they illustrate a number of typical features:

1. There is variation in personality measures employed, from clinical assessment to multibattery administration, with and without replication to ensure reliability. The retest reliability for both Eysenck's inventories and the EEG is quite high for measures of psychological interest (i.e., in the region of .70–.90); even so, that does not guarantee stability of scores for individual subjects (a) when the experimental population is small and (b) when there are probably interactive order effects for the EEG (we discuss the problem of laboratory-induced arousal below). Few studies have tried to relate the dimension in question to other personality variables of psychological interest, and most laboratories stick to their own particular favorite.

2. A range of different EEG measures has been used—of different derivation and different duration, under different conditions of testing, scored by hand or by computer, with or without repeated measurement, and with or without estimates for scorer reliability. There is no guarantee that different measures are providing a different aspect of the same process or that the process reflects a unitary aspect of "arousal," indeed, when multiple derivation is used or when different frequency bands are considered, they do not all give identical effects. When the meaning of EEG data is obscure, it is not easy to know how to interpret the results. Even when performance is involved, no study has related aspects of performance to aspects of the EEG. Thus, the best we can say is that there is or is not a *general* tendency for EEG amplitude to relate or not to relate to the personality dimensions in question.

3. Some studies have careful precautions against experimenter bias, while others provide an absolutely open invitation to systematic error. Imagine the differential response, just in the business of "wiring up," for a researcher who *knows* that one subject is highly extraverted and another is highly introverted. The more the experimenter understands the theory, the more likely is his or her behavior to be modified.

4. Some papers begin with a balanced review of the previous literature, setting the study in question

within the context both of theory and previous research; however, a large number of researchers display considerable ignorance and plunge into their experimental work as if it were the first example of its kind.

5. The experimental situations employed range from the typical clinical EEG recording (subject supine, with eyes closed, in a darkened room), through quite bizarre arrangements (for example, seating people back-to-back), to quite complex and challenging tasks (mental arithmetic under time pressure). The implications for theory of these different arrangements are rarely considered.

6. Sometimes high scorers on Neuroticism are excluded from the sample to limit measurement to EEG correlates of extraversion–introversion; neuroticism–stability is on occasion varied systematically within a factorial design; or both dimensions may be included without any realization of their possible interactive effects or the actual interactive effects revealed in previous studies.

7. Statistical treatment can range from simple cookbook statistics of extreme-group designs to correlations or to combinations of both approaches. Some of those who employ extreme groups appear not to realize (a) that such designs are wasteful of data or (b) that a significant effect for extreme groups means simply that, for it does not allow the investigator to know whether the relationship between the two variables is linear (in the absence of a central group) or curvilinear. In some correlational designs, confounding between extraversion–introversion and neuroticism–stability can occur, even though partialing-out procedures are quite straightforward. Table 20-1 illustrates the varieties of measures employed.

We must ask ourselves whether it is possible to impose order upon chaos; in spite of the limitations of this work, can we explain the discrepancies in an orderly fashion? Every student of psychology knows that different results are often obtained in different laboratories, in studies allegedly designed to put the same question to nature. But the challenge is to attempt to reconcile different findings; if the theory in question helps us to do this, then it is a more powerful theory.

A Post Hoc Hypothesis

We have seen that Eysenck's theory claims that extraverted and introverted individuals will employ different strategies to cope with excesses or deficits in stimulation. In this section we follow Gale's earlier work (1973, 1981) in classifying the experimental contexts in which the relationship between extraversion–introversion and the EEG has been explored, as "low-arousing," "moderately arousing," and "high-arousing." We then show how each of these conditions might interact with subject strategy to yield the different outcomes observed in the literature. This is a speculative and post hoc account, but there is no reason why it should not be translated ante hoc into an experimental series.

The most typical arrangement for EEG measurement is to have subjects lie on a bed, attach wires to their heads, give them nothing to do but keep their eyes closed, ask them to "keep their minds clear," and require them not to fall asleep. Gale (1973) has argued that such instructions are not easy to follow, and he provides a short descriptive essay on the subject's possible phenomenal response to such impossible instructions. Such conditions may be called "low-arousal" conditions, and given alleged excess of arousal in introverts, it will be hedonically satisfying to them to participate in such procedures. But it will not be satisfying for extraverts, whom we might expect to fall asleep because they are already hypoaroused, or to become restless in their efforts to find a means of satisfying the experimenter's instructions *not* to fall asleep. The extraverts cannot seek actively for external stimulation, because they are in a soundproofed room, with their eyes shut. Their only alternative is to cogitate, to imagine stimulation in spite of its absence. We know that the act of imaging is arousing and that extraverts report richer imagery experience than do introverts (Gale, Morris, Lucas, & Richardson, 1972; Morris & Gale, 1974). This is, of course, quite consistent with Eysenck's theory, since active imagination is a means of providing self-stimulation and should therefore be a strategy at which extraverts are adept. Given the incompatible instructions of staying awake and keeping one's mind clear, extraverts opt for the former. The strategy employed (imaging) leads to an elevation of cortical arousal. For introverts, however, the conditions are ideal; the lack of stimulation allows their inherently high level of arousal, which has probably been augmented by the very business of being prepared for recording, to subside to a satisfying level. They are used to being on their own; lack of stimulation does not make them drowsy; and they are thus not faced with instructions that are impossible to obey. Thus they become de-aroused. Under such low-arousing conditions, the EEG of extraverts and introverts might converge, coming to equality, or even allowing introverts to show *less* activated EEG than the extraverts.

"High-arousing" conditions are those involving active participation in challenging tasks. These provide extraverts with plenty of stimulation, maintain their attention, and provide no conflict. Introverts, however, may find arithmetic calculations under speed, in a laboratory that in itself is novel and stimulating, too much of a challenge; given the high arousal it induces, the challenge may be associated with a decrement in performance, which in its turn is arousing. Thus a drastic strategy is required to reduce stimulation and

to cut into this vicious spiral of positive feedback. EEG sampling in the studies that employ active tasks is typically taken during the intertrial period, to avoid muscle artifact; but this is the time-out period when introverts can relax, adopting self-calming strategies (again well practiced) that are brought with them among their behavioral repertoire to the laboratory. Thus, in such high-arousing conditions, the EEG of introverts and extraverts may again be seen to converge and possibly to cross over, under low arousal, introverts are calm and extraverts restless; under high arousal, introverts induce self-relaxation, while extraverts become stimulated and active.

As Eysenck (1976) points out, the original 1967 theory was centered upon *resting* or, rather, everyday conditions. Thus the optimal condition for showing the key effect that extraverts are less aroused than introverts is a moderately arousing condition—for example, one in which subjects have to open and shut their eyes; receive simple instructions from the experimenter; or remain in a room in a relaxed state, but with others, rather than in a soundproof box. Neither extraverts nor introverts have conflict or difficulty under such conditions. Modest task requirements and some interaction with others are sufficient to keep the extraverts relaxed and interested, yet are arousing (although not intolerably so) for the introverts. This is our post hoc hypothesis, and the implications for future experimentation are clear: Some of the conditions that have been employed in previous studies to yield contradictory results need now to be combined in a systematic fashion within one factorial design.

Design is not easy, however, for there is the possibility of asymmetrical transfer and order effects from one condition to another, particularly in a repeated-measures design; of course, independent-groups designs need to have large populations in psychophysiological research because of large between-subject variance. But these are largely technical rather than logical issues. Table 20-1 presents each of the past studies that we have located; applies our post hoc hypothesis to classify testing conditions; and, following the practice of consumer guides, gives a rating of from one to five stars for quality, together with an indication of outcome. Although this is a mosaic of findings rather than a simple balance sheet, there does seem to be some evidence for a curvilinear effect, whereby extraverts are seen to show lower arousal than introverts under moderately arousing conditions. We have accused other authors of selectivity and bias, and it could be argued that our post hoc classification is ante hoc rather than post hoc and influenced by prior knowledge of outcome. It is for the reader to decide how well the hypothesis fits the facts.

Two very recent papers by O'Gorman (1984) and O'Gorman and Mallise (1984), challenge the post hoc hypothesis. O'Gorman (1984) claims that the analysis of Gale (1973) is quite misleading because it is based on a misleading interpretation of Eysenck's theory and the conditions under which it can be confirmed or denied, and is biased in its selection and interpretation of research findings. O'Gorman (1984) supports his case with a sophisticated meta-analysis of research studies, using reliable judges both to rate the arousing qualities of individual studies and their scientific quality. O'Gorman (1984) concludes that poor personality measurement and not the arousing properties of individual procedures, account for the lack of consistency among findings. Gale (1984) attempts a rebuttal of O'Gorman's case. An excellent study by O'Gorman and Mallise (1984) failed to support the post hoc hypothesis, and indeed showed extraverts to be most aroused, in EEG terms, under the least arousing conditions. Gale (1984), while recognizing the quality of this study, claims that it is not a proper test of theory, since the tasks employed were ad hoc multicomponent tasks, and not derived from a systematic taxonomy or pretested in a systematic fashion.

Elsewhere in this chapter, we note that an actuarial or balance sheet approach ("How many studies for the hypothesis, how many against?") is no substitute for science. One careful study that reflects an understanding of the theory and that is sensitive to the sources of error already revealed in previous work would be worth its weight in gold. Regrettably, no such study has been reported. In the meanwhile, we shall have to be content with an evaluation after the fact. There are few personality theories that allow for elaborate experimentation in psychophysiology, and this is why so many straightforward by unilluminating correlational exercises exist in the literature. It is disappointing, therefore, when we have a theory like Eysenck's, which could lend itself to a systematic 2 × 2 × 3 design (extraversion–introversion, neuroticism–stability, testing conditions), that so many researchers seem content to look only for main effects (see, however, Revelle, Humphreys, Simon, & Gilliland, 1980). This is just another example of the intellectual poverty of much experimental individual differences research, in contrast with mainstream experimental psychology. Yet the potential challenge of individual differences research is no less stimulating to the inquiring mind. Indeed, it is encouraging that mainstream experimentalists are concerned with individual differences, since they recognize both that an attention to between-subjects variation can serve to account systematically for some of the error term, and also that examination of variation in strategy as revealed by individual differences can throw light on general mechanisms. The marriage between the two halves of psychology is possible if a common mode of discourse and a conviction of mutual benefit can evolve.

However, we cannot provide a confident answer about systematic effects produced by extraversion–introversion, so far as the EEG is concerned. It does look as if there is support for the theory, but the substantial demonstration is yet to come. As our summary of O'Gorman's (1977) excellent review of habituation studies indicates (see "Habituation and Individual Differences," below), it is by no means clear that Eysenck's theory is supported in relation to autonomic variables (see also Stelmack, 1981; Green, 1983).

We owe the reader an explanation for the fact that we have evaded mention of evoked potential studies. It becomes clear in our discussion of electrocortical studies of intelligence that we are even more perplexed about the interpretation of evoked potential changes than we are about the meaning of simple measures of amplitude and frequency. The reader should ensure that he or she is *au fait* with the sections of this book devoted to the interpretation of the evoked potential before he or she moves to the evoked potential studies of extraversion–introversion.

It is not our intention to be comprehensive in our review. Rather, we hope that this case study of experimental mismanagement will serve the purpose of putting the reader on guard whenever EEG studies of personality are mentioned.

SOME PSYCHOPHYSIOLOGICAL STUDIES OF LOCUS OF CONTROL

We have argued earlier that human beings are not stimulus–response lumps. They do respond to stimuli, both internal and external. But they have the capacity to observe and reflect upon the stimuli; such responses will incorporate behavioral, physiological, and experiential components. A major justification for the discipline of psychophysiology is that these components interact in a complex fashion; thus interregulation and intermodulation among these modes of response is a fact of life. Moreover, the stimulus-response system has a history and a memory for that history, so that it affects and is affected by the response to new events. Our criticism of psychophysiological studies of individual differences is that they emphasize too strongly the physiological or "biological" aspects of the person at the expense of the other aspects. The notion of "locus of control" is therefore particularly attractive for us, since it refers to the person's perception of the world and view of his or her success or failure in his or her interaction with the world.

Unfortunately, as we shall see, psychophysiologists have abused the construct of locus of control by ignoring its key notion that the person perceives the world in a particular way. Because they have imposed upon the construct traditional psychophysiological methods of study in the field of individual differences, locus of control has been oversimplified, and as a result, many important questions have been side-stepped.

Another criticism of studies in our area of concern is the self-isolation imposed by individual differences workers. Studies of locus of control intersect across several areas of psychology. There is an extensive literature covering attention, information processing, helplessness, tolerance for pain, response to threat, response to stress, risk taking, motivation, skill, response to therapy, and susceptibility to psychosomatic disease and depression. Thus psychophysiological studies of locus of control would appear to have the potential for integration and bridge building.

Yet a further criticism of the field is that although individual difference studies invariably select subjects on the basis of self-report questionnaires, the experimental procedures used rarely relate back to the processes tapped in the questionnaire. Again, locus of control studies differ in this respect, since they offer the possibility of monitoring the subject's response in the face of experimental situations involving varying degrees of control over stressful and/or rewarding events. Thus locus of control studies allow for operational proximity between constructs, psychometric measurement, and experimental manipulation, to a degree that is greater than is the case with other psychometric variables we review.

Finally, since the subject has views about the success or failure of his or her actions, locus of control studies enable us to monitor within one context, and in a meaningful and readily interpretable fashion, our three domains of description—namely, behavior, physiology, and experience. This allows for coherence and richness of interpretation within the data set.

Locus of control (e.g., Rotter, 1966) is seen as a generalized expectancy held by individuals, operating across several situations, which relates to their view of whether they have control over what happens to them. Are the rewards or punishments that occur in their world within their power to control, or are they determined by powerful others, fate, or chance, and therefore beyond their personal control (Lefcourt, 1972)? Does the world seem so complex that it is unpredictable? Such a generalized view is seen to affect an individual's response to the world in a variety of ways. Thus "external" individuals, who believe that they have relatively little control over events that influence their lives, are said to be more reactive to threat, emotionally labile, more hostile, less responsive to psychotherapy, lower in self-esteem, lower in self-control, less effective in coping with stress, more anxious, lower in motivation (particularly to avoid failure), less perceptually sensitive, less efficient in attention, failing to differentiate between relevant and irrelevant cues, less active in attention, and less skillful. The reader will detect some surface similarity with other personality constructs considered in this chapter. Indeed, locus of control has been shown to

correlate with manifest anxiety (Watson, 1967), social desirability, neuroticism, and test anxiety (e.g., Feather, 1967).

However, there is considerable danger of oversimplification, as we have seen earlier, when a construct is made into a portmanteau with extraordinary capacity for storing vernacular personality descriptions. For example, Averill (1973), in a critical review of empirical studies to that date on control over aversive stimuli, concluded that it is not always the case that a sense of personal control over impending harm will help to reduce stress reactions. There are also circumstances in which a sense of personal control may increase stress. Most control responses do not carry their own meaning with them and are defined for the individual in terms of the context in which they occur and their history. Thus the suggestion that individuals carry around with them a general strategy for coping with stress in general has to be modified, and the apparent face validity and congruity among the characteristics of the external person, as listed above, must therefore be modified. Furthermore, in relation to experimentation, Averill warns that responses that are "convenient for the experimenter" may have "little inherent significance for the subject" (p. 299). Those who wish to work in this field should read Averill's succinct analysis. Moreover, it is clear that a distinction must be drawn between estimates of the contingency of pleasant and unpleasant events, and the response to the affective quality of an event when it occurs; a great deal of subtle experimentation has weakened the apparently simple and straightforward construct of "control" (e.g., see Abramson, Alloy, & Rosoff, 1981; Alloy & Abramson, 1979).

Let it suffice to say in the present context that (1) experimental paradigms may have little face or ecological validity for the subject, and (2) it should not readily be assumed that a paradigm has the straightforward effect of reducing anxiety in certain subject groups. As always, there is a danger in personality research of borrowing constructs developed by others, without acquiring also the caution and reservations characteristic of those who have delved into the empirical literature surrounding the construct. Few of the studies we review acknowledge Averill's important contribution in either thought or deed. Nor is there much reference to many of the more contemporary developments in the study of locus of control. The old-fashioned way of treating locus of control merely as a bipolar construct has led psychophysiological researchers to neglect the possibility of differential interaction with the laboratory context for external and internal subjects. We must confess, however, that the studies we review show more sophistication than is seen in many designs for psychophysiological research, and many manage to leap beyond the constraints of univariate correlation to examine process.

Our review covers three broad categories of study: (1) correlational research, where locus of control is seen as a trait that influences psychophysiological response systems in a general way; (2) more dynamic studies, where subjects are exposed to stressors and given degrees of control; and (3) biofeedback paradigms, where the notion of control is directed to autonomic response systems. Again, our aim is to be selective in our review, the objective being to provide fuel for our characterization of individual differences research and a basis for our specification for future studies.

Correlational Studies

A study by Runcie, Graham, and Shelton (1978) is illustrative of the attempt to relate HR changes to the locus of control construct. Two experiments were reported: (1) a comparison of the effects of simple RT and mental arithmetic on HR (*qua* Lacey & Lacey, 1974), and (2) a time estimation task. Following what we consider an appropriate strategy, Runcie et al. employed an established task (i.e., the Laceys' paradigm), with an existing corpus of reliable data, for their first experiment. However, their rationale is suspect. Noting that Ray (1974; see page 459 below) obtained cardiac deceleration for externals and cardiac acceleration for internals in a conditioning task, they followed Ray in drawing a direct analogy with the classic Lacey interpretation in psychological terms, and suggested that externals attend to external stimuli and internals to internal stimuli. Thus they predicted both a task effect upon HR for RT and mental arithmetic (following Lacey and Lacey) and a differential effect for criterion groups, yielding pronounced deceleration for externals and pronounced acceleration for internals.

There are two problems here. First, identity of physiological effects need not imply identity of psychological effects; there are a variety of ways in which HR might be affected by psychological and task variables, as the literature challenging the Laceys' notion of "intake" and "rejection" amply testifies. Second, we might argue that externals, feeling as they do that they have relatively little control over external events, find external events aversive and, in the Laceys' terms, would not attend to them and would reject them. In contrast, internals with their sense of mastery, find the world rewarding and a constant source of confirmation of control, particularly when faced by the simple challenge offered by the experimenter. Davies and Phares (1967) suggested that internals do indeed tend to seek information. And again, Lefcourt (1972) concluded that internals pay attention to all types of cues, provided those cues are relevant and can be used to resolve uncertainty. These considerations would lead us to predictions contrary to those of Runcie

et al., even with a superficial inspection of the literature on locus of control. One is almost tempted to believe that Runcie et al. have fallen into the semantic trap of believing that "external" and "internal" have identical meanings for both Rotter and the Laceys!

Failing to obtain the expected cognitive style effects in their first experiment (the Laceys' paradigm), Runcie et al. (1978) then employed a time estimation task with feedback for accuracy. Here, therefore, they did attempt to consider the locus of control construct in its dynamic sense, for reinforcement could be expected to vary for the groups if indeed internals are more effective in time estimation performance. Runcie et al. argued that time estimation involves counting, is an internal task, and thus necessitates involvement with internal events; externals, therefore, because of their perceived lack of control, should show less acceleration. Having divided their HR data into five epochs per trial, Runcie et al. did obtain a modest effect, such that during the last three epochs, externals showed HR deceleration. What is not clear from their account is whether this period coincided with feedback on performance—presumably the most crucial time, in informational terms, for a locus of control study. The internal group was indeed more accurate in time estimation, but there was no differential effect for groups, in that both groups improved with trials. In attempting to impose a psychological interpretation upon these performance and HR data, Runcie et al. stretch our imaginations. They claimed that the two groups differed in their perception of the task; the internals treated feedback as more useful, exerted more effort in modifying their behavior, and therefore showed more acceleration. (Previous studies necessitating active involvement do yield such effects; e.g., see Houston, 1972.) Yet we could argue that (following Runcie et al.'s earlier hypothesis, and their data) externals showed deceleration because they did attend to the feedback provided at the end of the trials!

It may seem small-minded to subject Runcie et al.'s (1978) study to such detailed criticism, but it does contain a number of defects that typify much of individual differences research: (1) loose rationale for the study; (2) use of an ad hoc task (time estimation); (3) use of an extreme-group design, thus wasting data; and (4) post hoc explanation by exploitation of vernacular terms that are pressed into a procrustean bed in order to explain unexpected outcomes ("involvement," "effort," "task commitment," and "perception of the task"). This loose use of explanatory constructs in a quasi-formal mode could enable any interpretation of any outcome. Subjects were asked about strategy. Experiential data may of course be used to increase our confidence in a particular post hoc explanation; in the present case, subjects were asked to report on their strategy for time estimation, but no attempt was made to obtain data that might have supported interpretations in terms of "effort" and "task perception," upon which Runcie *et al.*'s explanation of their results leans so heavily.

We may note in passing that Runcie *et al.* used some 60 subjects, but failed to report the sex composition of the sample. Thus the possibility of confounding, and/or of interactions between, locus of control and sex was ignored (see Feather, 1967). This defect draws our attention to a further problem, which runs through all the individual differences literature: the failure to comment on the possibility that other personality variables were involved, but unmeasured, in the study. This is a common fault in many of the studies reviewed below. Were Runcie *et al.* measuring locus of control pure and simple, or anxiety, extraversion–introversion, sex differences, field dependence–independence, and/or engagement–involvement as well? Most of these variables have a *prima facie* case for generating differences on their tasks. Early evidence (Feather, 1967; Watson, 1967) revealed correlations between locus of control and a variety of personality measures, as well as sex. We are convinced that measurement of one simple construct in one or two simple contexts is unlikely to account for much of the variance observed, or to throw much light on the complexity of individual variations. Even so, full parametric studies should be carried out for a paradigm before it is pressed into service to enable study of individual differences. In addition, an earlier study by Williams, Poon, and Burdette (1977) found that field dependence–independence did not relate to HR or forearm blood flow (FBF), and, like Runcie *et al.*, found no difference for HR for externals and internals for intake–rejection tasks. However, while externals gave elevated FBF for all tasks, internals showed reduced FBF for an intake task.

This is not the end of our criticisms, however. In a situation where two tasks and two criterion groups are used and where changes of a bidirectional nature are predicted, discipline is required in interpreting outcomes. For it is not enough to show differences between groups or conditions if those differences do not in themselves differ significantly from a baseline measure. Thus, to say that subjects accelerated more for the rejection task (mental arithmetic) is not to show that they decelerated significantly for the intake (RT) task. Similarly, a finding that demonstrates deceleration in time estimation for externals only does not allow for an interpretation involving both externals and internals. Similar problems have arisen in studies of hemispheral differences in psychological function, where ratio effects have been interpreted as if they were necessarily absolute difference effects; a difference between two scores from one occasion to another could be due to a change in either variable or both, and the direction of the change could be positive or negtaive for either or both. Thus, in the context of a $2 \times 2 \times 2$ design, several logically possi-

ble outcomes are available, all of which may have very different implications for the appropriateness of particular interpretations. Since the simplest of individual difference studies typically involve two criterion groups and two task conditions, and temporal effects tend to be a powerful source of variance, we see that the pitfalls for the unwary are numerous. Thus the study by Runcie *et al.* provides an excellent opportunity to consider the perennial faults of psychophysiological research into personality.

Lobstein, Webb, and Edholm (1979) demonstrate how one might predict and confirm experimental findings opposite to those of Runcie *et al.* (1978). Thus they "expect[ed] internally scoring subjects to show less anxiety in response to an arousing stimulus than externally scoring subjects" (p. 13). Employing the orienting reflex (OR), they therefore expected externals to give higher accelerative HR (defensive) response to stimulation, combined with increased electrodermal responses (EDRs). There is no mention of the Laceys' hypothesis in this paper, or of the Ray (1974) and Runcie *et al.* (1978) studies. Separate locus of control scores were obtained for males and females, and subjects also completed the EPI. Data were analyzed using both ANOVA and Pearson's *r*, thereby making maximum use of the data. We select only a handful of findings: (1) Externals showed less deceleration and more acceleration in response to the first stimulus and to stimulus change (after habituation); (2) there was an interaction with neuroticism, such that stable subjects showed more acceleration than internals, yet less deceleration than externals; (3) group differences tended to dissipate as a function of time; (4) females tended to habituate EDRs quicker than males and to be less responsive to stimulus change; and finally (5) effects for EDA were consistent with those for HR, but less pronounced (i.e., externals had a higher amplitude and a longer recovery period).

Lobstein *et al.* (1979) pointed out that their experimental paradigm was passive, since subjects merely responded physiologically to nonsignificant stimuli (remember Averill's [1973] strictures about the use of stimuli that are "convenient for the experimenter"!). Where active task involvement occurs (e.g., memory performance with penalties; see Houston, 1972), elevated HR may be seen in internals because of "increased motivation." This is, of course, reminiscent of Runcie *et al.*'s interpretation, and we return to this observation in the discussion that concludes this section.

Berrgren, Öhman, and Frederikson (1977) combined data on signal and nonsignal stimuli in their report. Slow EDA habituation to nonsignal stimuli was seen to be an indication of failure to "focus attention upon relevant task cues" (a characteristic of externals), and a sign of "inefficient use of attention" (p. 714). In Experiment 1, externals showed a higher probability of responding to nonsignal stimuli. In Experiment 2, a separate subject population was used to replicate Experiment 1, while a further group was instructed to respond by pressing a microswitch at tone offset. Here Berrgren *et al.* predicted that for signal stimuli physiological effects would disappear, since externals would continue to respond willy-nilly, while internals would respond to the relevance of the stimulus. (This would lead, of course, to the perfectly reasonable prediction that the null hypothesis would not be rejected, because different effects would operate for the two groups to yield an identical result!) Again, criterion groups were distinguished for EDR to simple tones (externals taking longer to habituate), but both groups took longer to habituate to signal stimuli and were indistinguishable from each other. We should note that the differences in response to the nonsignal stimuli were due to a higher level of responding in externals, which suggested to Berrgren *et al.* that the difference was in elicitation rather than habituation; this still leaves open the question of whether the differences were due to attention or to activation—a matter considered below. They concluded

> [T]aken together these data give strong support for the hypothesis that externals have poorer control of their attention than do internals. Thus external subjects keep attending to irrelevant events and do not seem to differentiate between relevant and irrelevant cues. Internals on the other hand stop responding to irrelevant cues quite quickly, and they differentiate sharply between relevant and irrelevant cues. (1977, p. 714)

The authors then appealed to Mischel's (1968) views that situational factors will influence trait effects.

An important and unusual finding was that spontaneous responding was not related to habituation rate; thus Berrgren *et al.* (1977) concluded that differences in activation per se could not account for the obtained differences between externals and internals. They ended their report with the claim that psychophysiological data relating to locus of control are more robust and reliable than are those relating to neuroticism or extraversion–introversion (for us, all the data appear equivocal!), and they suggested that their work be extended to other contexts where habituation is related to behavior (e.g., vigilance, electrodermal conditioning, development of sleep during monotonous stimulation). Their claim for higher reliability can hardly be sustained in the absence of data from their own study demonstrating that other personality variables were not involved.

Berrgren *et al.*'s (1977) findings are in a sense worrying, because we wish to assert that it is precisely in the context of meaningful tasks that differences between criterion groups are likely to emerge. After all, the concept of locus of control is one that reflects both people's views of their success–failure in handling life's events and their coping strategies. Thus to

limit the possibility of obtaining effects only under the psychologically trivial context of the OR paradigm seems paradoxical. Indeed, Berrgren *et al.*'s claim that vigilance tasks should provide an appropriate context for future research would appear to contradict their general conclusion, unless they can demonstrate differential ORs to wanted and unwanted stimuli during a vigil—a requirement more likely to be achieved by measuring event-related potentials (ERPs) rather than EDRs. This point enables us to remind the reader of our prejudice that cognitive variables might be more likely to reveal their physiological correlates through examination of cortical processes than through study of autonomic variables, which *prima facie* would appear to be further removed from the field of consciousness and awareness.

More Dynamic Studies

An example of an experimental procedure that reflects the sort of situation in which coping strategies and individual differences may be observed in real life is provided by DeGood (1975), who measured blood pressure (BP) in a context where control over time out from an aversive shock avoidance task was either at the subject's own demand or imposed by the experimenter through a yoked control. DeGood claimed (with justice) that his procedure mimicked conditions for the development of hypertension. The group showing highest systolic BP change was the no-control/internal group (nonsignificant); for diastolic BP change, a significant interaction showed highest elevation for control/externals and no-control/internals—that is, "where personality was incongruous with experimental condition" (p. 400). A main effect for systolic BP showed no control to be more arousing than control for both personality groups (contrary to Houston, 1972). An unfortunate feature of this paper is that no specific predictions were made, nor were the findings interpreted in any detail. DeGood merely predicted that expectation of control would reduce anxiety. The results indicate that situations contrary to expectation (i.e., control for externals and no control for internals) lead to an elevation of diastolic BP. While DeGood failed to acknowledge this discrepancy between prediction and outcome, or to relate his findings to those of a similar study by Houston (1972), it does demonstrate the interactive nature of subject dispositions and prior experience with experimental context, just as Averill (1973) warns. Recognition that this is a fact of life for psychophysiological studies of individual differences would enhance the quality of research and make more explicit the need to have a theory that makes precise predictions about the interaction between traits and situations.

A complex study by Craig and Best (1977) is of relevance here, although it included no physiological

measurement. Internals were found to be more tolerant of effect on pain, as is generally expected; however, the most powerful effect on pain tolerance was
exposure to a model (tolerant, intolerant, and inactive), which persisted even after debriefing and the
model's departure. This is another example of the
mixed bag of findings for perceived control, locus of
control, and pain experience. The authors conclude
that "situational factors (modelling) are substantially
more important determinants of individual differences in pain behavior (in their findings) than personality predispositions" (p. 134). Thus trying to draw
general conclusions might be a pointless exercise unless it can be demonstrated that two different experimental paradigms make exactly the same demands of
the person: "[P]ain behavior is highly sensitive to
subtle nuances of the immediate social context"
(p. 134). Is pain behavior unique in this respect? We
doubt it.

Frankenhaeuser's laboratory has been associated
with research on responses to stress for many years,
with particular interest in the effects of personal control both in experimental and in field conditions (e.g.,
self-pacing vs. machine pacing, urban commuter
crowding). In a task involving control or no control
over noise stress during arithmetic calculations, physiological and subjective arousal (HR, catecholamine
and cortisol excretion, subjective effort, and discomfort) were lowered during control conditions (Lundberg & Frankenhaeuser, 1978). When subjects were
classified on the locus of control dimension, a crossover effect showed internals to be more aroused for
no control (*qua* DeGood, 1975). Those who are normally in control of significant reinforcers become anxious when control is lost (see Bowers, 1968). Such a
conclusion (following the "incongruence" hypothesis
of Watson & Baumal, 1967, and DeGood, 1975) are
not counterintuitive, but they do make selection of
appropriate testing conditions a complex task. Nevertheless, we believe this to be the way for future research. While the Lundberg and Frankenhaeuser
study is excellent for its combination of physiological,
performance, and experiential measures, it is unfortunate that other personality measurements were not
taken and that a correlational design was eschewed.
Also, it is disappointing that HR measures were global
and unrelated (in terms of sampling) to specific aspects of performance.

A Preliminary Summary

In summarizing this section so far, we see the following:

1. A simple intake–rejection task yields null effects
   for HR (Runcie *et al.*, 1978; Williams *et al.*,

1977), but significant effects for FBF (Williams
et al., 1977; however, see biofeedback studies
below).
2. Feedback on time estimation performance induces
   modest deceleration in externals (Runcie *et al.*,
   1978).
3. Presentation of nonsignal tones under passive conditions induces HR acceleration for externals and
   longer EDA habituation (Berrgren *et al.*, 1977;
   Lobstein *et al.*, 1979).
4. Signal stimuli in simple RT tasks remove locus of
   control effects (Berrgren *et al.*, 1977; Runcie *et al.*,
   1978).
5. Internals faced with no-control conditions in stress
   situations show elevated activation (DeGood,
   1975; Houston, 1972; Lundberg & Frankenhaeuser, 1978), while externals might show increased activation under no control (DeGood,
   1975) or decreased activation (DeGood, 1975;
   Lundberg & Frankenhaeuser, 1978).
6. Neuroticism or generalized anxiety is thought to
   have no interactive effects with locus of control
   (Berrgren *et al.*, 1977) or to have complex effects
   (Lobstein *et al.*, 1979).

Our own view is that although the OR data are
consistent, they will lead us no further unless the OR
can be shown quite unambiguously to relate to situations or contexts of direct theoretical relevance to
locus of control; in contrast, studies of avoidable and
unavoidable stress in one form or another (e.g.,
shock, noise) seem most promising for the development of the locus of control studies, allowing for
measurement of performance, physiological change,
and subjective response within one experimental
context. Moreover, such studies have greater ecological validity, given the contexts within which notions of "control" have been deployed by theorists
(D. C. Glass & Singer, 1972; Lazarus, 1966; Lefcourt,
1972). Even so, decisions made by internals and externals concerning their level of involvement in an
experimental task need systematic study, to ensure
that increases in observed activation may be reliably
linked causally to the effort or avoidance involved.

However, in view of the mixed bag of findings
relating (1) to the dependent variables selected by
researchers and (2) to other personality variables and
dimensions, future researchers would be well advised
to adopt multiple-measure, multivariate designs. This
has been achieved to a greater extent in some of the
work reported in the next subsection.

Locus of Control and Biofeedback

The notion of control and physiological responsiveness has been taken more literally in studies of bio-

feedback, where it is suggested that externals and internals might differ, both in their capacity to control physiological response and in their reaction to biofeedback; however, we should note that Williamson and Blanchard (1979), in their authoritative review of variables relating to HR and BP control, conclude that there is no evidence to suggest differential autonomic awareness between externals and internals. We review studies of locus of control and biofeedback by Fotopoulos (1970); Ray and Lamb (1974); Ray (1974); Wagner, Bourgeois, Levenson, and Denton (1974); Gatchel (1975); Blankstein and Egner (1977); Logsdon, Bourgeois, and Levenson (1978); Schneider, Sobol, Herrmann, and Cousins (1978); and—perhaps the most impressive paper in this field—R. W. Levenson and Ditto (1981). In many of these studies, it is argued that evidence as regards individual differences and biofeedback would enhance clinical application by indicating the potential value of treatment for the individual.

Fotopoulos (1970) demonstrated that internals were better able to increase HR under no-feedback conditions, but showed no difference from externals under feedback conditions (such a dissociation runs contrary to key findings in the biofeedback literature; see Williamson and Blanchard, 1979). Fotopoulos included no deceleration trials. Ray and Lamb (1974) and Ray (1974) showed externals to be superior at HR decrease and internals to be superior at HR increase, with feedback. Ray also obtained data on subjective response, which allow for a rationale for these findings: Externals "looked for objects in the room" significantly more than did internals during the HR decrease trials, and this measure was negatively correlated with performance in HR increase trials and vice versa in decrease trials. Thus, accepting environmental stimuli irrelevant to the task can cause the deceleration associated with "intake" in the Laceys' sense.

The Ray studies appear to have been conducted with care and have included the procedure of using experimenters blind to the subjects' personality score—something we consider an essential formal requirement. But as we indicate below, Ray's work has been subjected to criticism. Ray has been cautious in his conclusions and has not commited himself to an interpretation of the personality–HR–control relation. Does the strategy used imply imposition of a cognitive style, or is the style itself derived from established modes of physiological responding? This, of course, in one guise or another, is the eternal question for the psychophysiology of individual differences, and Ray has pointed to the third logically possible source of correlation—namely, that some more general aspect of organization is responsible for both physiological and cognitive modes of regulation. The implications for research into psychosomatic disorders are obvious, but how exactly one teases out the

different alternative causal chains is a challenge that has so far defeated most authorities. It may be that developmental studies of at-risk groups will reveal sequential dependencies over time.

Ray's findings that strategy affects success in HR control illustrate the naiveté of Runcie *et al.* (1978), Berrgren *et al.* (1977), and Lobstein *et al.* (1979) in attempting to devise a simple-minded model of attention in relation to locus of control. Here, "looking at objects in the room," which for Berrgren *et al.* would reflect diffuseness of attention, is in fact a more efficient strategy for the task in question—particularly when substantial decreases in HR are rare, in contrast to the more frequently obtained increases in magnitude of 15 beats or more (Williamson & Blanchard, 1979). Does Ray's finding reveal "inefficiency of attention" in externals, or does it merely indicate that the mediational processes involved in biofeedback can take on a strange and unexpected form? Just as it is difficult for the experimenter to define what is a stimulus for the subject, so is it difficult to define successful performance. Again we see the crucial problem of using such important psychological terms as "attention" in a vernacular rather than a formal, operational, and disciplined mode. (Experimenters, however scrupulous in dealing with the interpretation of hard data, lapse too easily into off-the-cuff speculation and generalization beyond the data when it comes to the indulgence of their "Discussion" section!)

Like Ray, Gatchel (1975) also demonstrated superior HR acceleration for internals and superior HR deceleration for externals. Gatchel pointed out that the Fotopoulos and Ray studies involved one session only and therefore might have confounded physiological response with individual differences in direct control of HR. Using two testing sessions, he demonstrated locus of control effects (replicating Ray and Ray & Lamb) for the first session only. Gatchel concluded that future studies should "conduct routinely a number of training sessions in order to avoid any premature statement of an association between personality measures and learned heart rate control" (1975, p. 426). Our view is that this advice misses the point, for it emphasizes trait as opposed to process variables. What is important about personality characteristics is not simple test scores for laboratory tasks, but rather the manner in which subjects achieve a score. Gatchel's study demonstrates how a dynamic and experiential exploration of change could show that, even for HR control, identical scores may be achieved by different techniques, and that the use of particular techniques is associated with particular personality traits.

Blankstein and Egner (1977) were clearly perplexed by the Ray and Lamb (1974) findings. They argued that the general mastery of the world experienced by internals should be correlated with greater control of both HR acceleration and deceleration. Providing a detailed analysis of the Ray and Lamb procedure, they suggested that the testing environment was unusual and that neither the form of feedback provided (complex array) nor the number of trials employed was appropriate to induce feedback proper, or to establish a reliable measure of control. Blankstein and Egner failed, however, in their own study to provide convincing evidence of the superiority of internals in reducing HR. As in previous studies, they showed that internals were superior in HR acceleration, both with and without feedback, and suggested that the latter condition mimics real life more accurately. Moreover, this ability improved with time and was sustained, yielding persistent individual differences (in line with other findings and contrary to Gatchel). But although there were trends toward superiority in deceleration for internals, with an accompanying improvement in ability over time, they were not statistically significant. As we have already noted, large decreases are not easily obtained (Williamson & Blanchard, 1979). Although there was covariation of respiration and HR change, subjects denied using respiration as a means of varying HR, nor did respiration measures differentiate between groups. Similarly, a posttest questionnaire provided little useful information about subject strategy, over and above the typical finding that covert verbalization and relaxing imagery were employed. In the end, Blankstein and Egner seem to have been as puzzled by their own findings as they were with those of other workers. We should note that one of their conclusions was the more sessions the better—that is, that their failure to obtain criterion group differences for deceleration was due to a lack of sufficient repeated attendances. Gatchel's advice appears to be quite the reverse! This method of compensation for unhappy results is an illustration of the "if only" syndrome in individual differences research: "If only the authors had done so and so, which might have revealed effects that were not revealed . . . and so on." Here we have two contradictory sets of advice, so it is difficult for the beginning researcher to know which "if only" to put his or her bets on.

Schneider et al. (1978) also showed internals to be superior for acceleration, but (like Blankstein and Egner) found no difference for deceleration (where no main effect was found, let alone individual differences). Their paper is important and should be read, because they have provided a methodological critique of earlier work, ensuring that their own study would be beyond criticism. Unlike Gatchel (1975) and Blankstein and Egner (1977), they used a no-feedback, feedback, no-feedback design (thus avoiding confounding with mere practice effects); unlike Ray and Lamb (1974), Ray (1974), and Gatchel (1975), they used a running baseline to compute change

scores, rather than a pre-experimental baseline. Providing detailed comparisons with previous studies, they pointed out both similarities and dissimilarities between their own findings and those of other workers. Schneider et al. gained an improvement in acceleration for internals with sessions, and an improvement with feedback. They also suggested that more extensive training might be required for successful control over deceleration, since, following Lang and Twentyman (1974), acceleration and deceleration might involve different psychophysiological processes. We should note that R. W. Levenson and Ditto (1981) (to be reviewed below) found virtually zero correlation between ability for acceleration and deceleration control, in a notably large sample.

Schneider et al. also drew an interesting distinction between chance and skill: Since experiential awareness of HR acceleration is more noticeable in real-life contexts, internals would treat control of acceleration as a skill, in contrast to the "chance" aspects of controlling deceleration, a psychophysiological process about which they have little ready information.

The Schneider et al. (1978) paper is one of the best available, since it summarizes previous research accurately, adopts a clear-cut and unambiguous design, employs rigor in data analysis, relates the data obtained back to previous studies, and eschews the exceptional use of vernacular post hoc explanation. Such papers are rare in this literature; the combination of scholarship, methodological rigor and innovative design, which is surely the ideal for our discipline, is achieved too infrequently. Perhaps research teams should be selected for the complementarity of their personality traits.

Two papers employing the H. Levenson (1973) development of the Locus of Control scales (i.e., subscales for Self, Powerful Others, and Chance) should be mentioned. Wagner et al. (1974) showed that the Self scale (I scale) predicted capacity to reduce spontaneous galvanic skin responses (GSRs), while Logsdon et al. (1978) obtained very complex findings in a study involving true and false feedback for HR control. The Logsdon et al. results were as follows:

1. Under "success" trials (false feedback indicating good performance), internals were better than externals for HR deceleration.
2. Under "failure" trials ("Helplessness"; false feedback indicating poor performance), externals were superior for deceleration. These effects held for the Chance scale only. HR acceleration data were unfortunately discarded because of strong evidence of order effects within the design (i.e., improvements over trials, independent of condition); the authors suggest that for clinical application, only HR deceleration skills are relevant.
3. A posttest questionnaire revealed no personality

differences for feelings of "helplessness"; in this connection, the authors raised the notion of the "defensive external": "Defensive blame projection could greatly reduce the level of anxiety experienced [and] thus [could] negate or at least reduce the effects of the learned helplessness manipulation" (1978, p. 543). Here then is another pitfall for the experimenter, or, looked at more optimistically, another *deus ex machina*. Logsdon *et al.* are not the only persons to refer to this concept; however, it does make the business of predicting outcome very hazardous if subjects either reveal their true nature or hide their true nature, independent of any specifiable discriminating circumstances.

Two important points arise. Logsdon *et al.* are the only workers to report crossover effects for locus of control and HR deceleration. The conditions employed are theoretically justifiable within the "learned helplessness" theory; thus other workers who have been perturbed by discrepanices in the literature may look to this paper for clarification. Unfortunately, the authors themselves did not refer to the problem, since they appear to have been oblivious of much of the literature. Secondly, it seems that the subdivision of the notion of locus of control into Self, Powerful Other, and Chance factors may give significant effects where more gross measures fail. Similar criticisms have been made of studies of extraversion–introversion, where the combination of impulsivity and sociability has been described as a "shotgun marriage" (Guilford, 1977). Although Logsdon *et al.* made the point that such discriminations are important, they neither related their own findings back to theory (i.e., showed why only Chance is the effective criterion) nor explained discrepancies between this study and the Wagner *et al.* (1974) study, although two of the authors are common to both studies.

We must emphasize an issue that is of general significance. The business of partitioning personality constructs into lower-order constructs is not just a matter of refining outcomes; there may be circumstances where characteristics relating to two subscales run contrary to each other, thus pulling the variable under study in two opposite directions and yielding a null result. To measure such effects, one needs a multicell design that allows for the partitioning of main effects and interactions. Given the Logsdon *et al.* (1978) findings, and their success in obtaining differential deceleration effects, the possibility remains open that for every study using a gross measure of locus of control and in which null results were obtained, real effects could have been there all the time, but were masked. Clearly, we are indulging in "if only" behavior, but the Logsdon *et al.* findings do give empirical support. Readers must decide themselves whether they prefer to live with Type I or Type II errors.

The study that completes this subsection is a recent and very important study by R. W. Levenson and Ditto (1981); it raises serious questions about the value of looking for correlates of HR control among traditional personality variables, and therefore challenges the entire rationale of this section. Levenson and Ditto have approached the whole problem of individual differences in HR control from a completely different perspective—that is, by starting with the fact of individual differences in control per se and then looking for correlates among a variety of measures, some of which are traditional and some of which have a more direct relevance to the business of HR control. Let us start with one of their conclusions:

"When we set out to investigate the phenomenon of individual differences (. . . large individual differences in ability to control HR . . .) several years ago, we naively expected to quickly uncover the primary variables which accounted for these differences. Three experiments and many hunches later, we have been able to rule out a number of possibilities, and find support for several others. However, the goal of identifying the essential dimension which underlies individual differences in ability to control HR (if such a thing exists) remains elusively beyond our grasp. (1981, p. 79)

Testing 100+ subjects, Levenson and Ditto employed measures of locus of control, trait anxiety, and state anxiety; posttest strategy questionnaire data; data on health and on expectations of success in the experiment; and univariate and multivariate trend analyses. Their conclusions were as follows:

1. There were wide individual differences in HR control.
2. There were powerful effects relating success and failure in control to specific strategies.
3. The correlation between ability to increase HR and decrease HR was near zero.
4. There was a modest quadratic trend relating ability to increase HR and trait anxiety, such that moderate levels of anxiety were optimal.
5. There is little future in exploring relations with conventional psychometrically established personality dimensions.
6. Among several variables unrelated to HR control were gender and some health variables (i.e., exercise and weight), but nonsmokers were superior at the ability to decrease (n for smokers was small, however).
7. One of their most positive and confident conclusions was that "subjects who most limit movement are most successful at decreasing heart rate and subjects who most increase movement are most successful at increasing heart rate" (p. 99); while the biological basis of this relationship is straightforward, few studies of HR control (and, of

course, none included in the present review) have
reported measurement of somatic activity.
8. Ability to control without feedback was positively
correlated with ability to control with feedback;
that is, subjects brought established, or at least
practiced, strategies with them to the laboratory.

Levenson and Ditto clearly see the study of personality variables and cognitive strategy as a lost cause, in
the search for the key to explaining individual differences in HR control. They have made the important
point that we emphasize elsewhere and repeatedly in
this review—that there is little prospect of relating HR
control to a psychometrically derived variable (1)
where the theoretical underpinning for that variable
has little direct relevance to HR control, and (2)
where the measurement instrument for that variable
involves processes unrelated to those apparently involved in HR control. What is particularly important
to note here is that more attention should be paid to
sorting out the variables that contribute to individual
differences in HR control (a point so firmly argued,
for example, by McCanne & Sandman, 1976) before
setting out upon an adventure to correlate differences
in such capacities to psychometric variables. Without
such clarification, confusion is likely to reign. It is just
wishful thinking to imagine that the combination of
unknown with unknown will yield order.

Summary of Feedback Studies
of Locus of Control

1. Some authors think that internals should have
more control than externals of both HR increase
and HR decrease (Blankstein & Egner, 1977;
Schneider et al., 1978), while others think
internals should be better for increase and
externals better for decrease (Gatchel, 1975; Ray,
1974; Ray & Lamb, 1974).
2. By far the most powerful finding has been that
internals are superior for HR increase (Blankstein
& Egner, 1977; Fotopoulos, 1970; Gatchel,
1975; Ray, 1974; Ray & Lamb, 1974; Schneider
et al., 1978), although this is not always the case
(R. W. Levenson & Ditto, 1981).
3. It is not clear whether this ability applies without
feedback only (Fotopoulos, 1970), with feedback
only (Ray, 1974; Ray & Lamb, 1974), or with
both feedback and no feedback (Blankstein &
Egner, 1975; Gatchel, 1975; Schneider et al.,
1978).
4. False feedback can be shown to differentiate for
locus of control for deceleration, depending on
experimental condition, and allowing for crossover effects (Logsdon et al., 1978).
5. But superior deceleration in internals has rarely
been demonstrated (Logsdon et al., 1978), while

superior deceleration in externals has occurred
on some occasions (Gatchel, 1975; Logsdon
et al., 1978; Ray, 1974; Ray & Lamb, 1974) but
not on others (Blankstein & Egner, 1977;
R. W. Levenson & Ditto, 1981; Schneider et al.,
1978).
6. Repeated sessions are thought by some to be
associated with improved differentiation (Blankstein & Egner, 1977; Schneider et al., 1978),
while others can assert the reverse (Gatchel,
1975).
7. Sometimes subjective reports explain how
internals and externals mediate HR control
differentially (Ray, 1974), while in other cases
they do not (Blankstein & Egner, 1977; Logsdon
et al., 1978).
8. Defective design and data analysis leave some
studies open to alternative explanations (Blankstein & Egner, 1977; Fotopoulos, 1970; Gatchel,
1975; Logsdon et al., 1978; Ray, 1974; Ray &
Lamb, 1974).
9. Partitioning of locus of control scales can show
differential psychophysiological effects for subscales (Logsdon et al., 1978; Wagner et al.,
1974), although even authors who have obtained
different findings from one study to another have
been unable (or unwilling?) to reconcile them.
10. Authors who reveal a knowledge of difficulties in
relation to biofeedback research designs are
exceptional (R. W. Levenson & Ditto, 1981;
Schneider et al., 1978).
11. While some workers have been scrupulous in
cross-referencing to other related studies, several
suffer from a preoccupation with a limited set of
the previous literature.
12. Some authors have expressed doubts as to
whether HR acceleration and deceleration in
feedback reflect wholly common processes of
control (Schneider et al., 1978; R. W. Levenson
and Ditto, 1981); thus it may or may not be
surprising that deceleration capacity does or does
not relate to some aspect of locus of control,
under some conditions! It should be noted
however, that internals have been reported to
be capable of decreasing the frequency of
spontaneous GSRs (Wagner et al., 1974) and
enhancing EEG alpha activity (Goesling, May,
Lavond, Barnes, & Carreira, 1974; Johnson
& Meyer, 1974). Such a capacity would appear
to be correlated *prima facie* with the ability to
reduce HR.

Thus we trust we have the reader's sympathy at this
point when we express an unwillingness to accept the
view so firmly put by Berrgren et al. (1977) that the
locus of control construct leads to the production of
reliable and consistent data. Every 10 years or so a
new construct becomes fashionable (at the time of

this writing, Type A and Type B studies are still thriving), and the full panoply of psychophysiological endeavor is applied, involving a predictable comedy of errors. We hope that the present review may go some way toward changing this regrettable state of affairs, but we are not sanguine; however high our scores on an internality scale might be, they are not high enough to make us think we can control the behavior of our colleagues.

A Conclusion for Locus of Control Studies

It is difficult to provide an audit of this work for the benefit of the newcomer. If the reader is not punch-drunk with contradictory findings, we shall attempt to bring some order to the data on psychophysiological studies of locus of control.

First, there is differential readiness to HR orienting; internals habituate more quickly. There is reason to believe that some of this variance is attributable to the intersection of externality with anxiety, since anxious subjects are similarly slower to habituate (e.g., Lader & Wing, 1966). Although Berrgren et al. (1977) obtained higher spontaneous responding in externals, the effect was not significant; since the two are normally associated, these authors argued that habituation and activation are dissociated in their study, externality being related to the former only. This is slightly circuitous reasoning, for when neuroticism is actually measured (e.g., Lobstein et al., 1979) it can interact in a complex fashion with locus of control in that it works nonadditively; low neuroticism pushes internals further away from externals (an understandable outcome), but makes externals more responsive (not easy to explain). There is a possibility here that externals may be "repressive" (i.e., may provide inaccurate self-perception data in response to questionnaires). As Weinberger, Schwartz, and Davidson (1979) point out, "persons with a repressive coping style typically deny having elevated levels of anxiety, even though they often respond nonverbally as if they were highly anxious" (p. 369). In their study of behavioral responses to stress and self-reported anxiety, they show that "repressors" and low-anxiety persons need to be distinguished if the data are to make sense. Thus locus of control studies may suffer from such inaccuracies in self-perception; the reader will recall that most well-validated personality questionnaires do have control questions for lies, social desirability, and faking. But returning to the Berrgren et al. (1977) and Lobstein et al. (1979) key finding, which is consistent across the two studies and was replicated in independent samples by Berrgren et al., it remains for locus of control theorists to determine how the association may be absorbed with mutual comfort into their theoretical frameworks. One implication is that basic mechanisms that control

the OR are innate; thus the attitude of externality could be seen to emerge as a result of the individual's experience of ready autonomic responding.

The other two points to be made can be summarized more briefly. One is that the capacity of internals to control autonomic responding is demonstrated by the several studies that give superior increase in HR for instructed and feedback conditions (but see R. W. Levenson & Ditto, 1981). The other is that when placed in certain no-control situations (i.e., when existing strategies cannot be applied), internals show increased arousal. While the feedback studies can yield reliable data, we are not clear what is to be done once it is confirmed that control of HR acceleration is superior for internals. On the other hand, the stress aversion studies show promise of further development. The raising of HR in internals in response to low-control conditions may be the first step toward an adaptation process; thus dynamic studies of adjustment are called for, involving several sessions of testing, repeated sampling of behavior (both control responses and independent, but concurrent disrupted tasks), together with experiential reports throughout (see Weinberger et al., 1979). Studies such as these hold most promise, in our view, both for development of theory and for insights into practical application. If the reader has a polygraph in search of an experimental series, and wishes to explore further the psychophysiology of locus of control, then the studies by Frankenhaeuser and associates are an excellent starting point. If signal stimuli in the OR paradigm induce null effects, then the effects for nonsignal stimuli, however replicable, will only be short-lived in more senses than one.

We have mentioned EEG studies only briefly. One ERP study is suggestive for future work. Poon, Thompson, Williams, and Marsh (1974), having shown that a late positive component (LPC) was significantly larger during acquisition in a learning task (binary choice, uncertain outcome), demonstrated that internals who were more conservative during initial stages, but increased their bets with increasing success, had larger LPCs. This study clearly has the attributes of demonstrating dynamic changes (during learning); given the discriminability of ERPs among psychologically significant events, it augurs well for future work. ERP studies are of course well placed to benefit from contemporary theories of information processing. The reader is reminded, however, that ERP interpretation is hounded by controversy and that topographical analysis is probably essential, since if topography means anything, magnitude and sign of correlation should differ for electrode placements. However, this type of paradigm does avoid the ethical problems associated with the induction of stress in the laboratory, and also the practical problem of the stress being such that the subject barely interprets it as a stress. Of course, the meaning of LPC, and the significance in psychological terms of its relationship under some conditions with locus of control, must be explained; otherwise, there will be a *déjà vu* effect of a catalogue of findings with no accompanying means of interpreting the data.

As a final caution, the reader should be warned that the very generality of the concept of locus of control (see our list of correlates at the start of this section) could lead to its downfall; the construct is clearly in danger of being overutilized, and thereby of having its explanatory power devalued. At the same time, the construct cannot stand alone. While data exist that demonstrate common variance with other psychometrically based personality variables, and while both locus of control and those other variables have common effects upon psychophysiological parameters, it makes no sense to devise studies that treat them as orthogonal. This is a theme to which we return again and again throughout this chapter.

HABITUATION AND INDIVIDUAL DIFFERENCES

Any student of the field under review has reason to be grateful to O'Gorman for his scholarly and comprehensive review, which occupied a whole issue of *Biological Psychology* (O'Gorman, 1977). The larger part of this section is a summary of O'Gorman's consideration of theoretical and methodological issues and his evaluation of the state of the art. The major part of our discussion takes us up to 1976; the last few pages are devoted to his more recent appraisal of the field (O'Gorman, 1983). Since O'Gorman's coverage is extensive, there is considerable overlap with ideas and findings considered in other sections, and appropriate cross-references are given. The two dimensions under examination by O'Gorman are anxiety (see "Anxiety" below) and extraversion–introversion (in our earlier discussion of this dimension, we have focused exclusively on EEG studies). It is not our intention to explore in any depth theoretical issues relating to habituation per se, although, in any final analysis, it is rather pointless to correlate personality with habituation measure when the mechanisms underlying habituation are not well understood. The volume edited by Kimmel, van Olst, and Orlebeke (1979) is recommended, and a succinct and lucid review by Siddle, Kuiack, and Stenfert Kroese (1983) is a good starting point.

The Ubiquity of Habituation

Habituation is observed at several levels: behavior, subjective awareness, gross physiological response, and response at the level of the individual neuron.

Thus, habituation has been studied by ethologists, psychologists, psychophysiologists, and neurophysiologists. Clearly, if all these disciplines are studying a common phenomenon, and if the phenomenon is universal, then the adaptive mechanisms involved are likely to be of considerable significance; habituation as a phenomenon provides a means of linking both theory and methods of analysis across disciplines, and such bridge-building functions may well be crucial to the evolution of our understanding. Gale (1973) has questioned the true ubiquity of the construct, suggesting that, given the failure of common patterning either *among* domains of description or *within* domains, it is difficult to assert that a common underlying mechanism is involved. O'Gorman (1977) points out that it is crucial to distinguish between theoretical and observational aspects of the phenomenon, and that the very differences in rate of response decrement are themselves of interest, particularly in the field of individual differences. Indeed, we devote a section to O'Gorman's review because of the very popularity of paradigms based upon habituation processes. O'Gorman's review was intended in part to examine the claim of Koriat, Averill, and Malmstrom (1973) that "characterized relationships between personality dimensions and indices of response habituation [are] 'will-o-the-wisps', more likely due when they are observed, to Type I errors in statistical decision-making than to any true relationship" (O'Gorman, 1977, p. 259).

Theoretical Problems

O'Gorman expresses the view, repeated so often in this chapter, that there must be a well-worked-out theory of personality *and* a well-worked-out theory of habituation, if the two are to be combined in a meaningful way to yield predictions. O'Gorman plumps for Sokolov's (e.g., 1969) neuronal model theory and its elaborated form (Groves & Thompson, 1970), while acknowledging that some 10 or more identifiable theories exist. In discussing factor-analytic studies of personality, he selects aspects of extraversion and neuroticism as a focus for his review, while concluding, "Given the uncertainty about the major dimensions of personality, a degree of arbitrariness is inevitable in the selection of dimensions to study in relation to response habituation" (1977, p. 260).

Having discussed in detail aspects of arousal, inhibition, and stimulus modeling as they relate to individual differences studies, in particular, O'Gorman then presents a table that illustrates quite clearly the lack of coherence among researchers in making *predictions* for habituation as it relates to personality. A particular problem arises when authorities disagree (1) on the alleged orthogonality of extraversion–introversion and neuroticism–stability, (2) on the effects of either factor taken separately, and (3) on their interactive effects. He shows that rationales for prediction vary in clarity, specificity, and the expected direction of effect. The reader is advised to refer to the detailed comments provided by O'Gorman (1977) and to examine the original papers detailed in his comprehensive tabulation.

Methodological Issues

Since our aim is not to be comprehensive, we now turn immediately to some fundamental issues raised by O'Gorman, which cut across all the work we consider. He makes the following points.

1. Psychometric tests and physiological response systems are distant domains, sampled by different responses and different methods of measurement. Thus the magnitude of correlation between them cannot be expected to be high. Typical relationships in personality studies rarely exceed correlations of .40; thus any sources of unreliability will reduce the *expected* degree of correlation to yield an even lower relationship. Given an expected size of correlation in the region of .30 and given also two continuously distributed variables and unselected subjects, then a sample size of 60 is essential. O'Gorman prefers contrasting-groups designs, while recognizing that they distort sampling and do not reflect the nature of the relationship (linear, curvilinear) for the population as a whole. Even so, contrasting groups assume reliability of the criterion for selection, and O'Gorman concurs with Gale (1973) that such reliability is typically assumed rather than tested for. In the case of the physiological measures employed, notions of individual response stereotypy indicate variations in the system for which any individual is maximally responsive; thus limited selection of response systems provides another potential source of unreliability.

While we accept many of O'Gorman's minimal conditions for success in this field, we wish to go further in our demands upon future researchers. In our view, only large-scale studies (populations well in excess of 100) employing multiple measures of personality and a variety of tasks, with sampling of several response systems, will yield any coherent picture. As is clear from other domains we describe, the same physiological measures are said to reflect different fundamental processes. Thus only a multifactorial design will show which factors have common loadings, will show which variables load on which factors and in which directions, and will enable factor analysis for both measures and subjects. Extreme-group designs can be imposed post hoc on factorial data, but the reverse is simply not true. The logic of psychophysiological investigations of individual differences falls far short of the logic and traditions of psychometrics. Moreover, recent comprehensive theories like that of Royce (e.g., Royce & Powell, 1985) make a multi-

variate approach essential, since within a hierarchical structure, relations need to be established both vertically and horizontally. Otherwise, process is left unexplored.

2. In the case of habituation, a variety of indices of response decrement have been employed. Correlations within and between different systems of physiological response (e.g., skin conductance response [SCR] and skin resistance response [SRR], or SCR and HR) can vary in magnitude. Indices selected vary between simple criterion scores and more elaborate regression analyses. O'Gorman concludes (a) that selection of an index is in part determined by the preferred theory of habituation, and (b) that discussion of habituation cannot be pursued in isolation from the index employed in a particular study.

3. O'Gorman then moves to consideration of experimental conditions, including stimulus characteristics, experimenter characteristics, subject state, and subject mentation. He notes that Gale (1973) drew attention to the fact that in a 30-min testing session, a subject may receive only 30 sec of actual focal stimulation; thus extraneous factors will be particularly potent in influencing the patterning of response, given the relative absence of stimulus control over the subject. In summarizing the data then available (see O'Gorman, 1977, pp. 276–287), he concludes that there is strong evidence for the influence of stimulus characteristics, sex of subject, drugs, previous experience of habituation and certain subject expectations. Other variables present a less coherent picture and yet merit further exploration.

It is not, in our view, surprising that the complexity surrounding the phenomenon of habituation (or, rather, the various phenomena of habituation) lead in turn to a very complex picture for individual differences studies. A strong line could be that researchers should *not* use habituation as a measure until all the necessary parametric studies have been completed; a weak view (which we are obliged to acknowledge, since readers are unlikely to wish to take our harsh advice!) is that workers must read O'Gorman's review to sensitize themselves before embarking upon research.

4. Finally, O'Gorman looks to the future. He recommends (a) that we retreat from one-shot studies, which lead to fragmentation of the literature rather than a cumulative increase in knowledge; (b) that this would be aided by parametric programmatic studies exploring the "conditions under which personality variables contribute a non-trivial proportion of the variance in response habituation" (p. 305); (c) that investigative studies need to be the first step along a long road; (d) that multiple systems and measures should be used with sophisticated trend analyses describing decrement rather than simple criterion measures; (e) that other personality variables should be included, while recognizing that anxiety (as opposed,

say, to extraversion–introversion or neuroticism) taken separately has yielded the most consistent findings; and finally (f) that precision in measurement must be improved.

In considering the past, O'Gorman (1977) says, "Although some potentially interesting relationships are suggested by the work to date, it must be admitted that studies of personality correlates of response habituation in non-clinical populations have provided a poor return on research investment" (p. 304). In view of the clarity and balance of O'Gorman's review, such a conclusion should surely bear a chastening message.

In his later publication, O'Gorman (1983) brings the review up to date. There is little evidence either that his principal conclusions may be overturned or that many researchers have followed up his advice in undertaking systematic and programmatic research. It is unfortunate that too many researchers seek the easy buck. O'Gorman is still able to assert the following: (1) Anxiety is positively related to number of trials to habituation for finger pulse volume (FPV) and finger blood volume (FBV), but not for EDR; (2) extraversion relates inversely to the number of trials to habituation for EDR under *certain circumstances only* (i.e., Extraversion score clearly interacts with stimulus conditions); (3) there is reason to believe that habituation as it relates to anxiety reflects *different* mechanisms from those involved in habituation and extraversion-introversion. However, while O'Gorman's 1977 paper concludes that there is little evidence that other personality variables relate systematically to habituation, in 1983 he acknowledges the work of Lobstein *et al.* (1979) and Berrgren *et al.* (1977) as indicating a relationship to locus of control (see our discussion of locus of control above). We should note here that anxiety does relate positively to locus of control scores in several psychometric studies, and it is therefore not clear whether O'Gorman needed to adjust his earlier view; anxiety and locus of control studies may be sampling common sources of variance.

An important shift in emphasis for O'Gorman between 1977 and 1983 is the general strategy to be adopted vis-à-vis habituation and individual differences. In the earlier paper, he appeals for greater methodological and conceptual order in studies involving habituation indices as dependent variables. However, in 1983, he shifts emphasis to the treatment of habituation indices as independent measures, predicting onto attentional, cognitive, and performance variables. Thus, while his earlier arguments in favor of improvements to the traditional paradigm still hold, the strategy is to move away from the traditional approach. Thus, he cites studies in which habituation indices have been shown to predict performance in vigilance, discriminative RT, and systematic desensitization. Now he concludes:

In retrospect, the use of speed or rate of habituation as an index of individual differences rather than as a dependent variable in personality research has proved the more successful strategy, to judge from the results obtained to date. More progress has been made, for example, in studying differences in performances on attentional tasks as a function of differences in speed of habituation than in attempts to account for differences in habituation in terms of extraversion and neuroticism. (1983, p. 56).

Nevertheless, O'Gorman cautions (1) that the question of what accounts for individual differences in habituation remains, and (2) that neglect of temperamental factors (which of course do influence habituation) would lead to ambiguity in the interpretation of studies. Thus "an uncritical division of subjects into rapid and slow habituators . . . may lead researchers to neglect . . . stimulus and situational factors and the attitudes and expectations of subjects . . . and the possibility . . . that it is due to the influence of temperament or to the shared meaning that subjects attribute to the experimental situations" (p. 57).

The clear lessons to be drawn from O'Gorman's two reviews are elaborated upon throughout this chapter. The multivariate approach is clearly crucial to the good health of the enterprise.

Before we move on, however, a rather important problem must be identified. Students of the OR and its habituation claim (1) that it is a ubiquitous phenomenon, (2) that it underlies many aspects of adaptation, (3) that it represents a simple form of negative learning, and (4) that there can be proximity between the phenomena observed and the theories constructed to explain them (i.e., that here we have a case of straightforward operationalization, in contrast, say, to such constructs as arousal). If we cast aside for the present the debate concerning involvement of cognitive factors, which has divided OR workers of late (e.g., Bernstein, 1979; O'Gorman, 1972), we can draw attention to two difficulties. First, lack of intercorrelation among parameters for common response systems is in a sense more worrying than the lack of covariation between systems noted by the Laceys (e.g., Lacey & Lacey, 1958). While individual response stereotypy could apply *logically* within systems, such lack of covariation *technically* makes for considerable complexity in quantification and interpretation, and must surely undermine the concept of habituation as a simple phenomenon. Secondly, as Näätänen (1985) points out, the neuronal events that accompany modeling in the Sokolovian sense occur very early in information processing. Thus, peripheral indices, with their long response latencies, represent at best a gross reflection of OR mechanisms *and* their consequences, rather than a fine discrimination of central events. If such arguments are valid—and, indeed, Näätänen supports his case with a series of elegant and carefully controlled ERP studies that demonstrate differential sensitivity of ERP components to different aspects of experimental manipulations (well *within* 1 sec of real time)—then it follows that OR work, if it is pursued, should move to measures of cortical response. The peripheral indices reviewed have barely *begun* to respond before the complex sequence of central events has completed its time course. Given the sources of error identified by O'Gorman, there is little room for further proliferation of uncertainties.

ANXIETY

Lader (1975) claims with justice that anxiety is the emotion that has received most attention in the search for autonomic and somatic correlates of arousal. In patient groups, anxiety has been conceived of as a global state of overarousal, and the experiments have been designed to demonstrate (1) greater physiological arousal in anxious persons compared with calm individuals, or (2) variations between resting and stressed conditions within individuals. Although we are not concerned in this review with the patient group studies reviewed by Lader (1975), a number of his conclusions are apposite:

1. When at rest, cardiovascular and electrodermal measures differentiate between anxiety patients and normal controls. Somatic and electrocortical measures yield less consistent findings.
2. Under conditions of stimulation, differences between patients and controls become greater, but the effects are not unidirectional. Because physiological systems are subject to Wilder's law of initial values (see Bull & Gale, 1974), ceiling effects may come into operation. For example, a patient who has high BP may show little upward change from rest to stimulation conditions, and homeostatic mechanisms may induce a paradoxical reduction in BP. Thus Lader concludes that "it is a gross oversimplification to make general assertions such as that neurotic patients are over-reactive" (p. 128). He points out that "the reactivity of patients . . . will depend on the particular physiological system, the type of 'rest' period and stimulation, [and] the test sophistication of the subject" (p. 128).
3. Patients are consistently slower than normals to react to experimental contingencies, taking longer to return to prestimulation levels. Thus not only should stimulation schedules be employed (rather than mere resting studies), but attention should be paid in their design to the measurement of *post*-stimulation periods.
4. Delayed habituation rates in anxiety patients are seen by Lader to be yet another indication of maladaptive response.

Thus we see that Lader and O'Gorman are in agreement, both in their evaluation of research findings and in their recommendations for future work. Both agree on the need for parametric studies, in view of the curvilinear relationships revealed. Moreover, O'Gorman is keener to emphasize the need for an awareness of individual response stereotypy effects, and suggests that vascular and electrodermal systems may be differentially sensitive to the aversive and novel aspects of stimulation. Thus correlations only emerge when the psychological bases of both the temperamental trait and the physiological index are congruent; this accounts for the fit between cardiovascular measures and anxiety on the one hand, and electrodermal measures and extraversion–introversion on the other. We indicate below that, for Gray, novelty and aversive properties of stimulation are not necessarily so dissociable.

A clear implication of the views of both Lader and O'Gorman is that individual variables need to be studied in great detail, both separately and in combination. It is important to note that findings relating to anxiety are more powerful than those relating to neuroticism–stability, which is consistent with the view of Gray and not, strictly speaking, compatible with the view of Eysenck that extraversion–introversion and neuroticism–stability are orthogonal; Eysenck recognizes that anxiety patients fall in the quadrant that contains high neuroticism *and* high introversion.

Two studies by Giesen and McGlynn (1977) and Holroyd, Westbrook, Wolf, and Badhorn (1978) reveal major difficulties that can arise when self-reported anxiety is related to physiological reactivity. The first study examined HR and SCR during neutral and speech-related imagery for subjects scoring high or low on self-reported anxiety for public speaking. Of interest to the present discussion is that Giesen and McGlynn used five measures of SCR and four of HR and claimed that different conclusions could be reached, depending on the response criterion specified. Holroyd *et al.* attacked the general and simple assumption that test-anxious subjects become more aroused autonomically in evaluative situations than do non-test-anxious individuals. While their highly test-anxious group performed poorly and reported higher levels of anxious arousal, performance and self-report aspects were not necessarily paralleled by autonomic changes. As we have already suggested above, Holroyd *et al.* pointed out that differences in self-reported anxiety may reflect the greater *attention* paid by test-anxious individuals to their autonomic responses, rather than actual differences in autonomic responses per se between them and the less test-anxious group.

These considerations all point to the following guidelines for studies of anxiety: (1) The context of testing (threatening–nonthreatening) is crucial; (2) the interaction of cognitive and physiological variables must be taken into account (the subject's attentional access to physiological events, their interpretation of the meaning of stimuli); and (3) the choice of the dependent physiological measure should be a function of (1) and (2).

However, the relationship between trait anxiety and anxiety that is specific to certain situations is not straightforward. Spielberger (e.g., 1966, 1972a, 1972b) argues that the failure to distinguish between *trait* and *state* anxiety leads to an arbitrary and confusing use of the term. Any general theory of anxiety must clarify the relationship between the two aspects. "State anxiety" refers to a transitory condition characterized by subjective awareness of tension and apprehension, accompanied by heightened ANS activity; "trait anxiety" is a personality trait reflecting relatively stable individual differences in the strength to respond to situations perceived as threatening, with elevations in state anxiety. Within any situation, state anxiety must be distinguished from the stimulus conditions under which it is exhibited, and from the behavioral and cognitive strategies that the individual adopts to reduce the impact of anxiety.

"Stress" must be distinguished from "threat" and "anxiety." Stress is related to external and objective stimulus conditions, which may be psychological (threat to self-esteem) or physical (warning of shock). "Threat" is defined in terms of the individual's idiosyncratic perception of the particular environment. These distinctions indicate that anxiety must be regarded as a complex process. State anxiety results from an individual's interpreting specific situations as personally threatening, but this disposition is clearly affected by his or her trait score, so that anxiety expressed in a particular situation will be a function of strength of trait combined with the personal meaning of the stimulus array.

Spielberger's work is extensive, and we have presented an unduly simple reduction of his model. However, Spielberger's approach shows how simple-minded studies of anxiety (or the related construct of locus of control) are unlikely to yield unequivocal data. Most of the psychophysiological studies reviewed by Lader and O'Gorman eschew such an analysis. They merely select an "off-the-rack" self-report measure of trait anxiety, choose an equally "off-the-rack" physiological index, and subject the experimental population to an "off-the-rack" and ecologically meaningless laboratory test. Even so, writers like Lamb (1978) are not altogether satisfied with the self-report trait scales currently available—for example, the Taylor Manifest Anxiety Scale (Taylor, 1953), the Mood Adjective Checklist (Nowlis, 1965), or the Multiple Affect Adjective Checklist (Zuckerman, 1960). Lamb suggests,

> [Self-report scales] are too idiosyncratic (having different meanings to different people) . . . are subject to a variety of response sets, and individuals . . . are not

"accurately" responding to how they feel. Although . . . various self-report measures obtained in the same experimental situation tend to correlate substantially with one another, there is typically no strong relationship between self-report and other measures of anxiety taken concurrently. (1978, p. 52)

Thus, for Lamb, it comes as no surprise that physiological measures do not differentiate reliably between subjects designated as high or low in anxiety on the basis of self-report or behavioral measures taken in either stressful or nonstressful environments (see Katkin, 1965; Martin & Sroufe, 1970).

In our earlier discussion of problems in mind–body relations, we have pointed to the need to distinguish among the autonomic system, the experiential system, and the link between them, indicating the possible number of logical combinations that empirical study may seek to sample. Anxiety research does not reflect an awareness of the range of possible outcomes. Spielberger's discussion reveals further difficulties, since few studies bother to distinguish between state and trait anxiety. Moreover, physiological activity could be thought to reflect state anxiety more than trait anxiety, and situation-specific trait anxiety measures are better predictors of elevation of state anxiety in particular situations than are general measures of trait anxiety. Thus, for example, two situations—say, fear of other persons and fear of physical harm—may have quite independent effects on state scores and identify different groups of individuals, while no distinction is drawn between them for measures of trait anxiety. In ecological terms and for purposes of clinical evaluation and therapeutic support, the distinctions provided by state measures are clearly of greater value. Thus, testing under laboratory conditions on the basis of trait score criteria can lead to confusion. A particularly sophisticated discussion of anxiety and the complexities of anxiety measurement is offered by Endler and Edwards (1982). They argue that anxiety is multidimensional and that different situations (interpersonal [ego] threat, physical danger, and ambiguous threat) can have differential effects for different A-trait persons and affect the degree to which A-state is experienced. For them anxiety can be conceptualized in at least seven ways: the proportion of situations in which an individual exhibits A-state responses; the kinds of situations; the number of anxiety responses exhibited (from among physiological, behavioral, and experiential); the prevalence of one type of response over others; the intensity of response; the duration of response; and, the relative provocativeness of situations. Within such a complex nexus, which is not far divorced from common sense, psychophysiological research has somehow to make its mark.

Lykken (1975) refers to yet another difficulty that confounds correlational work of this nature. Psychophysiological researchers choose a self-report measure of anxiety (A) seeking correlation with a physiological index (P). If A and P are indeed found to be correlated, then there is a temptation to conclude that P is either a cause or a manifestation of A. Moreover, it is suggested as a corollary that, under repeated testing conditions, P and A will continue to be correlated. However, as Lykken points out, the only time when the between-subject correlation properly estimates the within-subject covariation is when both parameters of the within-subject regression are constant *across* individuals. Given the wide variation in P across individuals, it is possible for A and P to be perfectly correlated *within* each individual over time and for between-subject correlations to be zero on any single occasion. On the other hand, a high *between*-subject correlation taken on one occasion can yield within-subject correlations about zero, when sampled on several occasions. Since anxiety shows both trait and state variation, trait components of A and P could be correlated on a particular occasion while the state components are not, and vice versa; or both sets could be correlated, or neither! Thus, a complete study of the relationship between A and P demands both a between-subject correlational design, and either a within-subject longitudinal study or an experimental manipulation of A or P. Moreover, by "replication" we mean independent replication by different laboratories upon different samples, preferably within a longitudinal framework.

Summary of Required Research Strategies

1. Since attending the psychophysiological laboratory, the application of electrodes, and most experimental tests involve encounter with another person and exposure to stressors, it is unlikely that we can measure only the effects of *trait* anxiety; at least, there will be an interaction between trait and state effects.
2. Studies of anxiety should therefore employ both state and trait measures.
3. Since individuals' perception of a situation is an important factor in their emotional response to it, studies should include probes for measuring individual differences in perception of the experimental situation.
4. Since individuals differ in the ways in which they cope with perceived threat, studies should include probes to determine individual differences in coping strategies. (Some of the studies relating to locus of control employ this precaution; see our discussion of locus of control, above.) Note that strategies differ not only *between* individuals, but also *within* individuals on different occasions.
5. Given that both the stressors themselves, and their perception as threatening or nonthreatening by subjects, are likely to affect physiological response,

research designs should be comprehensive enough to enable a distinction to be drawn between factors and levels within factors.
6. The choice of tasks should be related theoretically to the constructs of anxiety under examination.
7. On present evidence, it would appear that cardiovascular measures are those most likely to yield predicted outcomes.
8. However, in view of the curvilinearity of response, the physiological measure employed needs to be explored across a range of conditions of stimulation, so that the precise conditions under which it shows shifts in level may be determined.
9. The investigator should combine a mixture of within- and between-subject designs.

Gray's Theory of Anxiety

Although Gray's empirical work is based largely on drug studies with animals, he clearly believes that the essential characteristics of his theoretical account of anxiety apply also to humans. The temperamental characteristics of humans may be derived from factor analysis, and the factors revealed are reminiscent of those identified by Pavlov in studies of stress responses in dogs. As we have already indicated, Gray's interpretation of factorial studies varies from that of Eysenck, as he prefers a factorial solution in the form of a factor diagonal and at 45° to Eysenck's two key factors. This factor he calls "trait anxiety." While acknowledging the absence of powerful mathematical reasons for adopting either his or Eysenck's favored solution, he believes his own to represent "biological reality" more faithfully. At the same time he confesses that "much remains to be done before the present theory can be regarded as a serious alternative to Eysenck's in the field of personality" (Gray, 1983, p. 42). Gray suggests that the crucial data for making a choice between the two theories will be derived from conditioning studies; we have seen that the empirical work on correlational data tends to support Gray rather than Eysenck (see "Habituation and Individual Differences," above, and Carlier, 1985).

Gray's approach hinges on the assumption that animal studies are "virtually indispensable" once one wishes to explore the basic brain mechanisms underlying anxiety. The difficulty is that this implies that animal studies provide a direct analogue for human studies of anxiety. We have seen above that Spielberger's analysis involves a somewhat more sophisticated account than can possibly be derived from animal data. Gray's strategy is to explore the neurophysiological effects of antianxiety drugs, on the assumption that the brain mechanisms affected are those that normally underlie anxiety. Again, this implies a unitary view of the concept. But there is a further difficulty: Logically speaking, the fact that anxiety-modifying drugs are seen to affect specific brain loci in animals does *not* imply that these are the brain loci involved in human anxiety. It merely demonstrates that they are necessary but not sufficient conditions for the experiene of anxiety. Gray postulates a behavioral activation system (BAS) and a behavioral inhibition system (BIS), and personality differences are seen to reflect the relative functional dominance of the two. Anxiety reflects activation of the BIS under conditions of novelty, uncertainty, frustration, failure, and threat of punishment. It is quite conceivable that, *theoretically* speaking, Gray can achieve the degree of differentiation required by Spielberger's account; however, this clearly is not possible within the empirical domain, given the bounds of his mode of operationalizing the theory. It is also possible that Gray may be accused of an anthropomorphic circularity. Vernacular terms are used to describe human *experience*; these are then employed to label animal *behavior*; mechanisms are postulated to explain the animal's *behavior*; these mechanisms are finally claimed to underlie human *experience*!

Thus, we may conclude that although Gray and Spielberger purport to describe the same domain, there is very little overlap in functional terms. Nevertheless, in spite of some logical and many technical difficulties, Gray's theory and his careful analysis of mechanisms underlying approach and avoidance behavior have clear heuristic value for our understanding of anxiety. An introduction to the theory may be found in Gray (1983) or in more complete detail in Gray (1982). The empirical connection between psychophysiology and the theory will come when we identify those physiological indices that may be seen to reflect approach and avoidance mechanisms, respectively. For example, if the traditional hypothesis that HR is an index of human anxiety is correct, then HR increases should be associated with BIS activity, since Gray views this system as the substrate for anxiety because it responds to aversive stimuli and antianxiety drugs. However, Fowles (1980, 1982), after thorough examination of the relevant literature, argues that to assume that HR reflects anxiety is an oversimplification, and that the psychological effects on HR reflect the activity of the BAS rather than the BIS. Fowles (1982) concludes that when anxiety is induced by the threat of punishment, then anxiety is reflected in HR only to the extent that the subject is motivated to make a response to avoid the punishment. If no responses are seen as potentially effective in avoiding the punishment, then HR will not reflect anxiety. At the other extreme, if avoidance of the punishment is too easy, HR will again not reflect the potential punishment. Thus, while there is some foundation for the traditional use of HR as an index of anxiety, it is also clear that the extent of the covariance depends on the situation and is, at best, confounded with the subject's own tendency to make an active avoidance or active coping response.

Fowles (1982) suggests that HR is positively correlated with the activity of the BAS rather than the BIS. He identifies cardiac–somatic coupling and successful active avoidance and approach responses for reward as major factors controlling HR elevation; these all have in common *preparation for behavioral activation*. Moreover, HR data from classical aversive conditioning have shown mixed results, and the occurrence of HR accelerations can usually be attributed to somatic activity. Together, the evidence argues strongly against the hypothesis that HR is a direct index of anxiety. Rather than implying BIS involvement, Fowles argues that these responses are mediated by the same system, the BAS, that activates reward-seeking behavior. This would explain HR increases in the active avoidance and reward-seeking experiments and would explain why HR increases are seen in classical aversive conditioning only when the conditions provoke behvioral activation. If active avoidance is possible, the BAS activity increases, but if the subject perceives that no avoidance is possible, then the BIS is dominant. The important *theoretical* point is not whether HR can provide useful information about anxiety, but which system exerts primary control over HR.

Fowles presents a strong case for the hypothesis that the HR changes discussed above do reflect BAS activity. If he is correct, then Gray's hypothesis—that BIS activity mediates the high states of arousal or drive induced by conditioned stimuli signaling punishment—cannot be adequately tested using HR measures, because these anxiety-inducing stimuli exert their effect through a system that does not directly control HR. Fowles (1980) has proposed that EDA and not HR might be more directly related to BIS activity, but it is too early to be confident on this issue, and Gray does not specify the role (if any) of autonomic activity in human emotional behavior. Space does not permit a full description of Fowles's analysis of the problem, but the internal complexity of Gray's theory implies, as Fowles acknowledges, that the latter's particular formulation will apply only within well-defined contexts. Whatever the outcome of attempts to apply Gray's theory to human anxiety, Fowles's discussion of the psychological significance of HR already has far-reaching implications for the clinical treatment of anxiety, as well as for much published research, which has taken a simple HR–anxiety relationship for granted.

SENSATION SEEKING

A recurring theme in this review is that the human organism is not passive, merely reacting to stimuli, but is constantly interacting with the environment, searching out stimulation, appraising it, evaluating it, and acting upon it in the light of established schemas. If this is a general descriptive statement regarding human behavior, then we would expect also to find individual variations in tendencies relating to seeking stimulation, appraising and evaluating stimulation, and the degree or modes of action deployed as a consequence. We focus in this section upon the work of Zuckerman and his associates in relation to Zuckerman's Sensation Seeking Scale (SSS), and, of course, upon physiological studies in particular. "Sensation seeking is a trait defined by the need for varied, novel and complex sensations and experiences and the willingness to take physical and social risks for the sake of such experience" (Zuckerman, 1979, p. 10).

In early sensory deprivation experiments, it was evident that subjects varied in their tolerance for absence of stimulation. Zuckerman's first SSS evolved from these experiments. The basic postulate was that of a broad sensation-seeking motive—in particular, the need to maintain an optimal level of stimulation or arousal, which expresses itself in stable individual differences in behavior. As discussed below, the SSS subsequently became differentiated into four subscales, and in the light of experimental evidence, Zuckerman discarded a hypothesis of optimum arousal for one of optimum stimulation. Zuckermen, Buchsbaum, and Murphy (1980) provide a succinct review of empirical studies, and Zuckerman (1979) drew together the empirical work in a book entitled *Sensation Seeking: Beyond the Optimal Level of Arousal*. A further restatement, together with evidence from other authors, appears in Zuckerman (1983).

Zuckerman *et al.* (1980) are most complimentary about the general strategy employed by Eysenck in developing a theory based on similar constructs; nevertheless, the two approaches to sensation seeking are different. For Eysenck, sensation seeking is a lower-order construct based, as we have seen, upon more fundamental factors and structures, while for Zuckerman, sensation seeking is a fundamental construct in its own right. Thus while Eysenck has a general theory making predictions over a broad range of behavior, Zuckerman's model is more restricted in scope, and his dependent and independent variables are exclusively related operationally and theoretically to the sensation-seeking construct. Zuckerman has devoted a great deal of effort to the development of his scales, and his key data base is derived largely from correlational studies. Eysenck's strategy can be seen to be more dynamic in approach, making greater use of theoretical constructs derived from experimental psychology and exploiting associated paradigms, which involve the analysis of *process*.

While both theories may be seen to pass through successive stages, in which theoretical constructs and empirical data interlock, Zuckerman's approach involves simultaneous and interdependent evolution of the theory and the test measures. Such a strategy may be misleading, for failures to confirm theory may be due to theory, to the test measure, or both. Correla-tional studies have the perennial disadvantage of suffering from the causal directionality dilemma; thus, without a dynamic approach that predicts sequences of events, correlations may lead to a conceptual dead end. Moreover, it is one thing to show that factors relating to subscales are independent or orthogonal; it is another thing to demonstrate how such factors might interact within the fabric of behavior.

Zuckerman's justification for an almost exclusively correlational approach is not convincing to us. Zuckerman *et al.* (1980) say,

> Most of the studies discussed are correlational rather than experimental. The necessity for this rests on the difficulty, if not impossibility, of doing manipulative biological experiments on humans. The development of an animal model for sensation seeking will ultimately make such experiments possible on animals. But just as we cannot deliberately produce lung cancer in humans, we cannot drastically alter the biological traits of humans to discover the long-term behavioral effects. However, semi-experimental studies of drug effects on humans, generally those with some form of psychopathology, have given us some insights into the way CNS reactivity determines behavior. (p. 606)

There is a paradox here: If a trait is of relevance to human behavior, then it surely is instructive to observe how persons who differ on the trait differ in behavior. The notion that only extreme (pathological) groups will yield data of value undermines the range of convenience of the construct. As we argue elsewhere, a host of correlations must be shaped into a set of empirical predictions about behavior if we are to evolve a theory of behavior. Nevertheless, within the framework of the correlational approach, Zuckerman is able to prescribe conditions for satisfying the claim that sensation seeking is based in some part on biological traits: (1) Psychological and biological measures should be reliable and stable; (2) both types of measure should show strong genetic influences; (3) there should be parallels in animal behavior; (4) pathology should represent extremes of the trait; and (5) both biological and psychological traits should show characteristic age and sex effects—or, rather, if one does then the other should, and vice versa. The satisfaction of these conditions provides both the rationale and the framework for much of his research.

The SSS and the Early Theory

The 20-year development of the SSS is well documented and does not concern us here, except to say that considerable effort has been deployed both to establish reliability and to derive factor scores from large samples. Most of the psychophysiological studies employ Form IV of the scale (Zuckerman, 1971), which, in addition to the General scale, contains four subscales: (1) Thrill and Adventure Seeking

(TAS), which assesses physical risk taking, such as parachuting; (2) Experience Seeking (ES), which assesses the seeking of new sensory experience, such as music, arts, drugs, and associating with unusual people; (3) Disinhibition (Dis), which covers the hedonistic pursuit of pleasure through extraverted activities, such as social drinking, sex, and parties; and (4) Boredom Susceptibility (BS), which covers aversion to routine activity and unchanging environments. Zuckerman claims good stability for the factors underlying the scales and consistency across American and British samples, for both males and females, except for the final factor. Form V was based on the British study; it has 10 items for each of the subscales, which yield the General score (i.e., total from 40), thereby excluding the General score as a separate set of items.

An immediate question is whether the different scales load differentially on scales that measure other personality variables. A clear finding is that measures of neuroticism or other aspects of anxiety appear to have no common variance with the SSS scales. However, the pattern of correlations with other scales is rather messy. Zuckerman (1979) devotes an entire chapter to relationships between SSS and other scales, prefacing the chapter by the sort of advice that we would wish to be followed by all investigators of individual differences:

> Although correlations between trait measures are not as valuable for construct validity as correlations between a test and general experience or actual behavior in specific situations, test constructors should present the correlations between their test and existing trait measures in order to define the redundancy and the uniqueness of this measure. This approach can be abused, as in the infamous "shotgun" method of correlating one's test with every other test conceivable and overinterpreting the minimal numbers of unreplicated results, which might be due to chance. If the construct underlying a new test is well defined, it should dictate the predictions as to which kinds of tests will be related to the new measure. Factor analyses can be used to identify the dimension tapped by groups of measures and sometimes can be used to assess the relative efficiency of particular measures in identifying the basic factors. (pp. 136–137)

We quote Zuckerman at length here because we cannot put the points he makes more succinctly. What is the outcome of such an exercise for the SSS? One difficulty, of course, is that a chaotic picture of intercorrelations could reflect (1) the instability or unreliability of the SSS, (2) the instability or unreliability of the scales with which it is compared, or (3) error due to differential factorial treatment or indeed to initial population sampling. Thus while Zuckerman's strategy is logically inviolable, it is empirically uncertain and hazardous—in the best traditions of sensation seeking! We emphasize what may seem to be a psychometric nicety; however, the demonstration of

biologically significant variations between individuals must presuppose communality of findings in such endeavors.

Zuckerman's findings can be briefly summarized as follows:

1. As mentioned above, measures of anxiety and related variables, such as locus of control, share little common variance with the SSS.
2. Several measures that, unlike measures of anxiety, do have theoretical compatibility (i.e., various scales assessing experience seeking and need for change) yield several positive correlations, as do measures of extraversion. However, the highest correlations are with tests that are proximate in item content to the SSS, such that while the overall correlation with extraversion is modest, the correlation with impulsivity items is stronger.
3. Among the host of correlations reported, few reach a magnitude comparable with the retest reliability of the SSS, except for those measuring sensation seeking as such.
4. The patterning of findings varies for sex (compatible with the biological determination model), but also for different cultural groups (compatible more with some scales than others—e.g., ES more than TAS).

Zuckerman treads his way very carefully through the data he reports, and we must agree with his view that few conclusions can be drawn from his survey. The patterning of findings enables him to build up a composite picture of the sensation seeker:

> [H]igh sensation seekers are egocentrically extraverted; that is they are concerned with others as an audience or a source of stimulation, rather than in a dependent or nurturant sense. Sensation seekers maintain their autonomy through assertive relationships with others rather than through isolation. Sensation seekers are nonconformists and risk takers[,] . . . ruled by own needs rather than social conventions[, and] attracted toward a lifestyle that maximizes the opportunity for independence and hedonistic self-fulfillment with like-minded persons . . . [A high sensation seeker has] positive attitudes towards emotions and expresses . . . feelings . . . in an uninhibited fashion. . . . Sensation seeking is related to an open receptive attitude toward experience and the ability to tolerate sensations and ideas that are unusual, strange or primitive. Sensation seeking is more related to a masculine than a feminine sex role and negatively related to androgyny. (pp. 181–182)

As we indicate in the concluding sections of this chapter, the features we consider essential for the future development of research into the psychophysiology of individual differences include a sensation-seeking element. Whether this can be dissociated from a general dimension of activity or need for activity is yet to be discussed. Nevertheless, Zuckerman's psychophysiological data are sufficient for us to conclude that there is as much evidence for the existence of the sensation-seeking trait as there is for extraversion–introversion. So far as experimental testing is concerned, Zuckerman's constructs are operationally translatable into experimental tasks in a straightforward fashion; thus the issue of whether SSS components are lower-order factors within extraversion–introversion is not *necessarily* of immediate concern. As we point out below, on theoretical grounds, Zuckerman and Eysenck make contrary predictions. So far as the subscales are concerned, Zuckerman would agree with Guilford's (1977) view that Eysenck has forced impulsivity and sociability together in inappropriate wedlock. An important point to remember, however, is that sensation seeking as a general characteristic is likely on *prima facie* grounds to interact both with willingness to participate in experiments and with features of the experimental situation and task. Empirical data are available on the issue of volunteering. Cowles and Davis (1985) measured the probability of volunteering among 1421 students, and related it to personality. Stable extraverts were most willing to volunteer, and stable introverts were at least willing; yet neurotic introverts were more willing to volunteer than neurotic extraverts. They complete their report with the comment: "These data may have important implications for research in psychophysiology and personality using volunteer subjects" (1985, p. 7).

Zuckerman's initial attempt to construct a theory of sensation seeking was a simple combination of optimal-level theories (e.g., Berlyne, 1960; Hebb, 1955), whereby it was assumed that every individual has characteristic, optimal levels of stimulation and arousal for cognitive activity, motor activity, and positive affective tone. Zuckerman simply assumed a one-to-one relationship among certain qualities of stimulation—that is, intensity, novelty, complexity, and central nervous system (CNS) arousal. He further proposed that it was the capacity of these stimuli to change *tonic* levels of cortical arousal that made them rewarding: "The 'optimal level of arousal' generally means the level of cortical arousal and therefore the most pertinent studies are those utilizing the EEG" (Zuckerman, 1979, p. 59). However, Zuckerman did not make specific statements concerning the relationship between level of stimulation and level of arousal, and (like many authors) did not engage in systematic parametric study of stimulation levels and their effects, which we regard as essential in this field. Similarly, he has been particularly loose in his use of the term "arousal," which is a tantalizing construct at the best of times; we argue below that an adequate parametric exploration of the relationship between stimulation and arousal has yet to be carried out.

Zuckerman has recently rejected the basic assumption that a high sensation seeker is happiest and functions best at a high tonic level of arousal and therefore acts in a manner designed to maintain this high opti-

mum level. The data to support this view are derived from a study by one of his students (Carrol, Zuckerman, & Vogel, 1982). Carrol *et al.* selected male medical students who scored in either the top or the bottom decile on the SSS (Form V) total score. On one nondrug baseline and three treatment sessions, measures were taken of HR and BP, mood (affect adjective checklists), digit symbol substitution (cognitive task), motor performance (finger tapping and pursuit tracking), and self-rated appraisal of the effect of the three drugs—calcium carbonate (placebo), dextroamphetamine sulfate (cortical stimulant), and diazepam (cortical depressant). Sessions were at 1-week intervals with counterbalanced order. While the drug treatments produced effects on physiological arousal consistent with expectation, there were few differential effects relating to personality score. Thus Carrol *et al.* argue that such data critically injure the model of optimal level of arousal, since affective, cognitive, and motor responses to drugs that increased or decreased tonic levels of cortical arousal nevertheless generally failed to distinguish high and low sensation seekers. We see a number of problems with such a conclusion:

1. No direct measure of *cortical* arousal was taken, the measures employed being under largely autonomic control. Only a relatively small proportion of psychophysiological investigations of the SSS are devoted to cortical measures.
2. No detailed analysis is provided of the discreet relationships between performance and physiological measures; thus there may be temporal differences in the patterning of effects for the criterion groups, since strategies are employed by individuals to maintain an optimum level in spite of adverse circumstances (see our earlier discussion of EEG studies of extraversion–introversion).
3. The tasks that were employed do not appear to be overly endowed with novelty, complexity, or challenge, and in some respects may lead to confounding between sensation seeking and *activity*; that is, there is no ground for believing that these tasks will induce differential effects.

Zuckerman and colleagues' pessimistic interpretation of these findings reflects, in our view, the dangers of developing a theory so wedded to biological predispositions that it is more comfortable in the sphere of correlations than in the examination and prediction of dynamic behavior patterns during active involvement with the environment. We cannot agree with Zuckerman that this is a definitive study.

Not dissimilar criticisms may be directed at an earlier study, which Zuckerman describes as an "abortive attempt" to test the optimal-level hypothesis (1979, p. 315). Having selected visual stimuli that discriminated between high and low sensation seekers in a previous study (Zuckerman, 1972), Carrol and

Zuckerman measured SCRs (a phasic response) to these stimuli, but without empirically verifying which stimuli were *ipso generis* most stimulating (i.e., yielded largest SCRs). They were also content to analyze for response magnitude, irrespective of tonic level (supposedly the more crucial variable). Again they obtained equivocal results.

We are obliged to conclude that Zuckerman and his coworkers have yet to conduct the crucial experiment, and that they are not alone in failing to provide a careful and systematic analysis of the hypothesis of optimal level of arousal. As we argue later, this is a much-needed but particularly grueling enterprise. While it may be true that the sensation-seeking trait is not a function of optimal levels, the evidence is equivocal and does not support the rejection of Zuckerman's earlier hypothesis. We return to this issue when we consider the most recent version of the theory. First, however, we turn to a brief review of the key psychophysiological research. Zuckerman *et al.* (1980) set out findings relating to the orienting response, augmenting–reducing of the ERP, monoamine oxidase (MAO) levels, gonadal hormone levels, and genetic studies.

The OR

High sensation seekers seek stimulation and stimulation change. The OR is exhibited in response to novelty, surprise, complexity, uncertainty, and incongruity, as well as to stimuli of personal significance. The OR has also been shown to be a stable individual characteristic. Thus Zuckerman argues that there is a *prima facie* case for believing that the OR should relate to SSS score. Zuckerman's predictions are very similar to those made in the field of extraversion–introversion.

> Conceivably, high sensation seekers could have larger OR's but habituate rapidly, thereby explaining their need for novel stimuli to reach their optimal levels of arousal. Differences in basal or tonic levels of arousal might also be a factor. If sensation seekers are characterized by low levels of tonic arousal, then they might require more intense or novel stimuli to reach their optimal levels. (Zuckerman, 1979, p. 320)

Studies of sensation seeking and the OR have concentrated on EDA, using paradigms in which stimulus complexity has in fact varied very little. Neary and Zuckerman (1976) found high sensation seekers to give higher SCRs to the first presentation of a simple auditory or visual stimulus, but not to differ from low sensation seekers in resting level. Feij *et al.* (1985) have provided corroborative data, showing that within a correlation between SCR amplitude and General SSS score, the TAS subscale accounts for most of the effect, while high scorers on the Dis scale show faster habituation. Feij *et al.* suggest that the TAS score may reflect response to novelty and the Dis score may reflect response to intensity; this notion is supported by HR data showing deceleration for high sensation seekers (stimulus intake) and acceleration for low scorers (defensive reaction and/or stimulus rejection). Similar findings are reported by Cox (1977)—no basal differences (EEG, EDA, HR, digital vasomotor activity, and respiration), differential HR response, and also an interaction with tone intensity. However, Zuckerman does present findings from other studies of the OR that do not obtain significant effects.

In all the areas of research sampled in our review, contradictory findings are more the rule than the exception, and we cannot discount the sensation-seeking research on this basis. However, students of the OR will be familiar with the early study by Korn and Moyer (1968), which showed that the first trial in an OR paradigm can be sensitive to the simple instruction to attend to the stimulus, after which there is no differentiation. The stimuli used in OR research are hardly rich as a stimulation source, and we suspect that studies that do obtain significant effects are very fortunate to do so; high sensation seekers, having appraised the stimuli on the first trial, will presumably look for other things to occupy them. Moreover, since OR parameters seem to be particularly sensitive to factors relating to anxiety, and since SSS scores seem to be independent of anxiety, it is our view that the basic OR paradigm is not appropriate in attempts to elucidate the biological basis of sensation seeking. The simple approach that the OR offers has produced only weak and equivocal results, and peripheral measures are not the most straightforward means of gaining access to cortical activity.

Augmenting–Reducing of the ERP

While acknowledging the limitations of peripheral psychophysiological measures in providing direct information about CNS arousal, Zuckerman draws on only one body of evidence that attempts to evaluate the impact of a stimulus on the cortex, particularly in the sensory areas: data derived from studies of cortical augmenting–reducing. The notion that stimuli are augmented or reduced was orginated by Petrie (1967), who used kinesthetic figural aftereffect techniques to differentiate between individuals; central enhancing or diminishing processes were inferred from subjective estimates of stimulus parameters following continued stimulation. Buchsbaum and his associates have attempted to measure such cortical effects directly, by measuring the varying amplitudes of flash-evoked responses to stimuli varying in intensity (Buchsbaum, Haier, & Johnson, 1983; Buchsbaum & Pfefferbaum, 1971; Buchsbaum & Silverman, 1968). P100 and N120 have been the components measured, and the augmenting–reducing measure has been defined as the best-fit linear regression upon ERP amplitudes for stimuli of increasing intensity; augmenters have a high positive slope (i.e., increased amplitude with increasing intensity), while reducers have either a low positive slope or a negative slope, which reflects a decrement in response to higher stimulus intensities. This cortical phenomenon appears to be stable within individuals, with a test–retest reliability in the region of .70, but its physiological basis and psychological significance have yet to be established.

One fascinating study, which confirms the view that augmenting–reducing is a property of nervous systems per se involved independent, blind ratings of exploratory and behavioral traits in cats; it revealed that more exploratory, aggressive, and emotionally and behaviorally responsive cats were augmenters (Hall, Rappaport, Hopkins, Griffin, & Silverman, 1970). The correlation between SSS scores and augmenting–reducing has been studied by Zuckerman, Murtaugh, and Siegel (1974) and Coursey, Buchsbaum, and Frankel (1975). The first study (and also one by von Knorring, 1980) showed that augmenters scored more highly than reducers on the Dis subscale. In a group of chronic insomniacs, not only were high sensation seekers found to be augmenters, but SSS score was found to be the best predictor of sleep efficiency (Coursey *et al.*, 1975).

One of Zuckerman's criteria for the evaluation of biological theories is that pathology be shown to express personality traits in their extreme forms; in his report of intercorrelations between SSS and clinical scales, Zuckerman (1979) reports that sensation seeking is related to mania and character disorder of the psychopathic variety, the latter being related more to the ES and Dis scales than to the TAS scale. The most consistent clinical correlates of augmenting–reducing are found in the manic–depressive psychoses, with bipolar patients tending to be augmenters, even when in the nonmanic state. The Dis scale is the scale correlating most strongly with both augmenting–reducing and the hypomania scale of the Minnesota Multiphasic Personality Inventory (MMPI) in males. It is not surprising therefore that Zuckerman makes the link among the manic state ("sensation seeking out of control"), augmenting–reducing, and SSS scores. So far as we are aware, however, Zuckerman and his associates have not investigated these relationships within the same sample. Furthermore, while, for example, the Dis score correlates with extraversion, we need to have data concerning the multiple correlations involving the SSS, augmenting–reducing, and other personality trait measures before we can assert that any association between the SSS and augmenting–reducing is *unique* to the SSS scales. In our view, the augmenting–reducing approach, because of its close links with stimulus parameters and the fact that it may be related to behavior involving complex experimen-

tal tasks, is potentially one of the most promising lines for sensation-seeking research, with its emphasis upon cortical correlates of the dimension.

MAO Levels

Zuckerman has been one of the first personality theorists to take advantage of current developments in psychopharmacology. Zuckerman claims that the SSS provides a phenotypical measure of the reactivity of the limbic "reward" system. MAO is abundant in those areas of the limbic system (particularly the hypothalamus) where noradrenalin and serotonin are found, and MAO is one of the enzymes involved in the inactivation of noradrenalin and dopamine. The catecholamine hypothesis of depression proposes that depressed patients have a deficiency in these amines; therefore one form of treatment is administration of MAO inhibitors, which, by preventing the action of MAO, allow noradrenalin to accumulate. Since high SSS scorers are seen as tending to the manic, we might expect high scorers to exhibit *low* levels of MAO. Corroboration for this expectation comes from Schooler, Zahn, Murphy, and Buchsbaum (1978) and Schalling and Åsberg (1983). We should note that there is controversy over biochemical assay methods, and that the relationship between platelet MAO (levels in the platelet mitochondria of the blood cells, the measure employed in this type of study) and brain MAO is uncertain.

Again, these studies depend upon a straightforward correlational approach and are not task-related. However, chemicals within the brain are sensitive to a variety of variables that might relate to overall arousal level. For example, Zuckerman (1979) cites a study by Goodwin, Buchsbaum, and Muscattola, which showed that 3-methoxy-4-hydroxyphenylglycol (MHPG, a metabolite of brain noradrenalin) has different relationships with SSS scores as a function of time of day; morning samples correlated more highly with TAS scores and afternoon samples with Dis scores. This demonstrates the problem that correlations can reveal causal mechanisms, but that one needs an adequate theory to describe the directionality of cause. Do brain chemicals underlie the trait; or does behavior, as a *result* of the trait, determine brain chemicals as a by-product; or are both or either directly or indirectly affected by independent mechanisms that are responsible for circadian variations? Moreover, it has yet to be established whether these changes in brain chemicals are state- or trait-dependent, since the collection of cerebrospinal fluid, for example, is particularly stressful. We must also raise the question of why sampling of chemical products of the body should focus so much on patient samples; there appears at the time of writing to be no evidence of a relationship between MAO levels and augmenting–reducing or SSS scores in normal samples. We must emphasize that Zuckerman's use of brain biochemistry–personality correlations is not an example of the "shotgun" approach he warns against; it reflects theoretical concerns that are dealt with at the end of this section.

Gonadal Hormones

In view of sex differences in SSS scores and the possibility that hormonal levels might influence OR "arousability" as exhibited in OR and ERP paradigms, Zuckerman has turned to the study of the relationship between hormones and sensation seeking. The findings are complex and are confounded by the fact that a variety of trait measures correlate with testosterone levels in males. Daitzman and Zuckerman (1980) found such correlations for extraversion, sociability, self-acceptance, dominance, and activity. Thus the finding that high Dis scorers have higher levels of both androgens (testosterone) and estrogens (e.g., 17B estradiol) is difficult to interpret.

The Revised Theory

This is an appropriate point at which to turn to the revised theory. Put simply, gonadal hormones, whose level is determined by genetic mechanisms, regulate MAO, which regulates dopamine and noradrenalin, which in turn are involved in approach behavior and reward mechanisms; reward affects the arousal systems and positive emotions. It is approach behavior that underlies the sensation-seeking motive. Fluctuations in arousal are consequences rather than causes of approach and avoidance. Some of the things that high sensation seekers seek may have the effect of reducing arousal rather than increasing it; thus, in drug studies, what is important is the *change* in arousal induced by the drug, rather than the direction of change. Thus the new hypothesis is as follows: "[The] sensation-seeking trait is in some part a function of the levels of the catecholamines, norepinephrine and dopamine, in the reward areas of the limbic system, as well as the neuroregulators that control their availability at the synapses within these neural systems" (Zuckerman, 1979, p. 372). Thus, sensation seeking shifts from notions of cortical arousal to the concept of a limbic predisposition to seek reward. Punishment systems (following Gray) are seen to relate to anxiety, which is independent of sensation seeking. Cortical responses and, specifically, augmenting–reducing are not of course excluded from the new theory, but are seen to be some way down the causal stream.

We have some difficulty in determining (1) what implications the new theory has for data generated before the theory evolved, and (2) what implications there are for experimental studies of psychophysio-

logical and psychological aspects of sensation seeking. In the final paragraphs of his book, Zuckerman (1979) appears to be promoting what has been called a "paradigm shift," for he continues to insist that "natural behavior" rather than "trivial, and often irrelevant, laboratory experiments" should be the focus for human studies. "For experimental work, which is ultimately necessary, we must move to animal models for sensation seeking" (p. 378). Thus, in acknowledging the limitations of both correlational and laboratory data, Zuckerman looks to animal studies to find the key to brain–behavior relations. The issue of animal studies and problems of ecological validity when animals are studied in the laboratory rather than in the wild are taken up by Zuckerman (1983). While we agree that the limits of the correlational approach have been reached in Zuckerman's research, we believe that laboratory experimentation can be developed, as Eysenck and others have shown, to reveal significant aspects of the biology of individual differences. Our view is that one can learn from one's mistakes; Zuckerman appears to find experiental errors aversive.

Zuckerman (1979) is particularly critical of the arousal concept, but it is our view that he would have benefited from a more careful consideration of its various aspects in his experimental work—in particular, the distinction between trait and state and the extent to which the two might interact in dynamic situations, in which the individual acts, is affected by his or her actions, and so on. An example of this problem is seen in Zuckerman's brief discussion of diurnal variations in sensation seeking. He cites unpublished work by Hauty, who, using a state scale for sensation seeking, found temperature to follow the same curve as sensation seeking (i.e., to be lowest in the early morning and late evening, and to be higher at midday and early evening). In his discussion Zuckerman switches between trait and state concepts in a confusing fashion, shifting also between bodily states and task demands of bodily states. In the following passage, "arousal" is used in at least three senses:

> [T]he hypothesis suggested in the Zuckerman theory (1969) suggested a compensatory aspect to the diurnal variation in sensation seeking; that is[,] an individual seeks more stimulation when arousal level is low. But another factor mentioned in the postulate is task demands. In the early morning before breakfast and in the late evening before sleep task demands are usually minimal; that is, no complex cognitive activity or strenuous physical work is demanded, so that one would not expect sensation seeking state to be high. Sensation seeking state appears to be high in midday and early evening, when greater task demands coincide with arousal peaks. Therefore, sensation seeking may not be compensatory to arousal level, but may be a direct function of it. (Zuckerman, 1979, p. 319)

This is a strange debate on the part of someone with such a strong biological orientation; one might suggest that evolution arranged most of human activities to take place during daylight hours and shaped human physiology accordingly. However, the point at issue here is that Zuckerman, like many others, has difficulties in juggling with arousal constructs. This quotation also reveals the perennial problem of treating a variable as a source and a consequence of change at one and the same time; any outcome is possible. Our view is that Zuckerman rejects the value of the inverted-U hypothesis too readily.

A Summary

Zuckerman's basic ideas have led to a great deal of research. Our focus in this review is, of course, on the psychophysiological aspects. However, there are a number of issues that are relevant to studies of individual differences, whatever the mode of investigation adopted, and Zuckerman's work provides a number of illustrative examples.

1. The commitment to a sound and thorough-going psychometric approach is a sine qua non for any theorist who wishes to claim that he or she has identified a biologically significant trait; the necessary but not sufficient condition that must be satisfied is a high measure of agreement both with other well-factored trait scales and among samples derived from different cultures. This aspect of Zuckerman's work is not only rare but admirable.

2. On the basis of such work, it is not risky to assert that there is sufficient evidence to support the view that a sensation-seeking motive does exist.

3. Subjects selected on the basis of the SSS do differ on psychophysiological indices of responsiveness. The augmenting–reducing paradigm does produce consistent data, but the extent to which such data are coherent with behavior is not clear. Nevertheless, such relationships as have been observed hold for both human and nonhuman samples, again confirming of a biological link. However, the predictions based on this paradigm are not only contrary to those of Eysenck for extraversion–introversion, which is a construct both theoretically and empirically related to sensation seeking, but contrary to the data on the OR. From Zuckerman's *old* theory and Eysenck's theory, we would expect extraverts and high sensation seekers to cease to respond to stimulation rapidly, as is the case with the OR; but high sensation seekers are augmenters.

4. Such a discrepancy can be overcome by appealing to a curvilinear relationship between augmenting–reducing and stimulation intensity, such that reducers switch off when stimulation is intense, along the lines of Pavlov's construct of transmarginal inhibition. To demonstrate this, however, one needs empirical evidence based on parametric studies. Needless to say, similar difficulties arise for Eysenckian theory, but there does appear to be an internal contradiction between data generated under the parentage of Zucker-

man's old theory and data derived in conjunction with his new theory.

5. We are not convinced that Zuckerman has paid sufficient attention to the detailed analysis of the arousal construct, nor that his experimental work necessitates removal of his original theory. We see Zuckerman as someone who is more at home in the sphere of correlational work than in that of experimental work. Thus, some of his analyses of psychophysiological data are not as thorough-going as we should wish; for example, any theory that predicts both phasic and tonic differences between groups must tackle problems relating to the law of initial values.

6. The experimental paradigms that Zuckerman has employed, except for augmenting–reducing procedures, do not strike us as having direct practical relevance to his theory. If one examines the description of the sensation seeker given above on the basis of SSS correlations with a variety of scales, then a number of experiments suggest themselves, based on existing procedures—for example, vigilance studies, studies of stimulus complexity, and so on. Again, we believe Zuckerman has not exploited his theory as fully as he might within the laboratory.

7. Thus, we believe that Zuckerman's retreat to animal studies, while it might answer some questions of importance, will not answer several others. For example, where is there room in animal studies (or indeed in his new theory) for differential loadings on the four subscales of the SSS? The answer surely must be that a theory designed to explain human behavior should be focused upon studies of human behavior.

8. Moreover, mere correlations, sex differences, or age differences tell us little about process—about *how* individuals with different characteristics interact with their environment. Experimental approaches can help us to explore process, although again this is an exhortation directed at all theorists, and not just at Zuckerman and his associates.

9. Finally, while the new theory does open up exciting new territory in the form of speculation about genetic transmission of biological predispositions, there is, as in the case of intelligence and its genetic determination, the problem of assigning variance to hereditary and environmental sources and of devising a developmental–interactional model. Zuckerman (1979) does devote some discussion to family characteristics and child-rearing processes. Our verdict therefore is most positive, but we are concerned that Zuckerman might be inclined, on the basis of premature conclusions, to desert the field of traditional psychophysiology. That, in our view, would be a loss.

We do not wish to end this section by creating the false impression that Zuckerman fails to recognize problems. He presents a rare combination of careful presentation of data with an original and stimulating integrative approach. However, we believe that any theory of individual differences must in the final analysis be reducible to behavioral and psychophysiological observations, in experimental contexts wherein variables may be manipulated in a systematic and controlled fashion and specific predictions may be made. The acid test must be whether predictions can be made in specific situations. We would encourage Zuckerman to combine his data bases in one experimental series, rather than to gather together overlapping data sets from different sources. We see no reason why behavioral, physiological, and biochemical data should not be derived from experimental studies that are not trivial and that reflect the operationalization of the key constructs of the theory (i.e., where situations and task demands are varied systematically in terms of the degree of stimulation or deprivation from stimulation provided). Within such a coherent data set, Zuckerman would be able to disentangle some of the complexities to which he has drawn our attention. It is clear that the sensation-seeking motive is central to any general account of human behvior, and that the careful and systematic studies initiated by Zuckerman should be pursued further. While the correlational approach is, in our view, stultifying beyond its initial, hypothesis-suggesting stage, it need not necessarily lead to animal work as a satisfactory substitute.

INTELLIGENCE

Andreassi (1980) provides up-to-date summaries of research on intelligence employing spontaneous rhythm EEGs and evoked potentials. This is a most useful catalogue of the more recent findings. Our aim is somewhat different, since we are concerned more with the metaproblems in the field; Andreassi points out that the issues are still unresolved, in spite of a long history of inquiry, but gives little inkling of the nature of the problems, nor of the direction future research should take. Callaway (1973, 1975), in his reviews of ERP correlates of IQ, is more critical than is Andreassi; we recommend his *Brain Electrical Potentials and Individual Psychological Differences* (1975), to which we return later in this section. We propose to be selective in our approach, rather than exhaustive. The reader should return to the original papers cited by Callaway (1975) and Andreassi (1980), but he or she is also well advised to return to basic introductory texts on the nature of intelligence and its measurement, focusing in particular on the history of controversy in this field, and the problems raised over the factorial analyses of test scores (see Kline, 1979).

Without such an understanding, the reader will come nowhere near to appreciating the difficulties in the field; many of the researchers whose work we review appear to assume that intelligence is a unitary trait, that it is genetically transmitted in a straightforward manner, and that electrophysiological measurement will reveal the phenotype that reflects the genotype. They also seem to assume on occasion that *processes* involved in intellectual activity are describable in simple and reducible terms. Considerable controversy surrounds the concept of intelligence, particularly in the light of the debate over interethnic comparisons (H. J. Eysenck & Kamin, 1981). There can be no doubt that psychometrics is the most powerful psychological tool to be contributed to society so far, particularly in its capacity to predict academic performances and its uses in personnel selection and evaluation. Because of its power, its use bears responsibilities; psychologists have seen that their work can have influence on social policy, and that the issues raised by testing can be as emotive and political as those relating to nuclear energy, pollution, and armament. We are aware that the search for an electrophysiological correlate of the IQ can be seen to reinforce arguments in favor of biological differences among groups, but such an implication is false. Callaway (1973) shows his irritation with this debate:

> IQ testing has become a political issue with the resulting generation of much learned academic gibberish. People continue to argue about whether or not IQ tests are culturally biased, and some suggest [average evoked potential] AEP measures may be "culture-free". The whole argument seems absurd; as an extreme example, consider how culturally determined prenatal and perinatal nutrition can affect gross brain development. Even at the subtle psychological level we suspect that habitual modes of cognitive functioning influence AEP measures. Thus, like most other behavior, AEP's will reflect genetic, biological and social influences. (p. 557).

We quote Callaway at length because he is both right and wrong. There are few extreme hereditarians or extreme environmentalists (although there are more of the latter); most of the participants in the debate are indeed interactionists. The controversies are rarely over the two extreme positions, but over (1) the partitioning of variance among heredity, environment, and their interactions, and (2) issues relating to the nature of the interactive process and the limits of modifiability. Long ago, Anastasi (1958) identified these as the "how much" and the "how" arguments. It is certainly logically possible to separate biologically and experientially determined aspects of the ERP and to allocate differential variance. Whether ERPs are better candidates in this respect than traditional paper-and-pencil tests is, we agree, a matter of considerable doubt.

Fear of abuse of psychometric devices is matched by a concern at the use to which psychophysiological instrumentation might be put. Traditional IQ tests may be powerful, but their capacity to predict performance *other* than academic success in examinations is relatively weak. We also know from Terman's longitudinal studies that IQ alone is not the best predictor, but needs to be taken together with tests of personality and emotional stability (Terman & Oden, 1959). It is questionable whether psychophysiological measurement can *replace* paper-and-pencil tests for such purposes, particularly in the North American tradition, where subtest profiles are seen to be of more value in selection and occupational guidance than the score for *g* (general intelligence) favored by past British orthodoxy. Without wishing to question the motives of those who have set about marketing devices for measuring mental efficiency, it surely is likely in psychological terms that those who have a commercial interest in such machines are more likely to have a set to look upon their own research more favorably; commercial involvement cannot always be compatible with the disinterested view that characterizes the archetypal scientist. It is encouraging to note that Ertl (1971) has not shirked publishing nonsignificant findings.

Thus we see that there are several sources of potential bias in this field. The reader who seeks a balanced view should refer to the book of Loehlin, Lindzey, and Spuhler (1975), the proceeds of which are used to promote interethnic harmony, and whose chapters and appendices were shown to parties to the race and IQ controversy prior to publication. Another volume, by Vernon (1979), is equally objective in its evaluation of the evidence. The truth is that while there is considerable evidence of within-ethnic-group heritability of IQ and evidence of within-group relationships between IQ and variables of social significance, the logical leap to between-group comparisons simply cannot be made. And equally important, the residual variance, whatever value is placed upon the heritability estimate, is quite sufficient in an interactive model to allow for considerable variation in resultant behavior in the individual. It is social policy and not psychology that determines the resources available to ensure that all individuals develop within a psychologically satisfactory environment, and there is plenty of evidence that individuals change in a positive direction when removed from impoverished environments (Clarke & Clarke, 1976). Eaves and Young (1981) provide an excellent discussion of problems of genetic modeling in the field of individual differences, and Roubertoux (1985) reviews genetic studies relating to the transmission of psychophysiological variables.

Researchers in the field of IQ and electrocortical measures must also be familiar with the problems in psychometrics, factor analysis, test theory, and models of genetic transmission. Over and above these more tangible issues, however, is the fact that the concept of intelligence has undergone some dramatic changes in emphasis (Butcher, 1968). Just as the polygraph and the microcomputer are now commonplace in psychophysiological laboratories, so mainframe computers have taken away the mystique that surrounded factor analysis in its infancy; now thousands of test score results may be processed and infinite numbers of factorial solutions may be assessed in matters of hours rather than months or years. Thus the faith that earlier workers placed in particular factorial solutions, and the zeal and enthusiasm generated by months of hand calculation, have been diluted. The work of the Piaget school, in revealing qualitative differences in intellectual process with age, has modified notions of constancy of the IQ; the use of large computers for studies of artificial intelligence, and the growth of cognitive psychology, have shifted the emphasis to process rather than stable dispositons. Even within the psychometric tradition, Guilford (e.g., 1967) has emphasized the dynamic nature of the interaction of his 120 factors. In psychophysiology and in experimental neuropsychology, studies of hemispheric specialization clearly indicate that solutions to intellectual problems may be arrived at by very different routes. Finally, although creativity research has come to a pause if not a complete full stop, it has focused attention yet again on the need to consider *variability* in the ways in which various forms of competent behavior emerge.

Thus, although there is evidence (1) that IQ has a strong hereditary component, (2) that it has striking retest reliability, and (3) that the EEG has both reliability and strong hereditary determination, it does *not* necessarily follow that by correlating one with the other, some simple relationship will emerge. Before correlating two variables, one is well advised to know something of the *functional* significance of at least one of them! Combining the unknown with the unknown does not necessarily increase human knowledge in a systematic fashion.

We have written this lengthy introduction to the topic because we believe not only that research in this field has remained virtually stationary in conception for more than 40 years, but that psychophysiological endeavors have fallen behind parallel trends and developments in the study of intellectual process. Thus we hope that this review becomes out of date as soon as possible. Attention to our cautionary remarks is essential. Our view is that the confusion in the field, to which Andreassi and others refer quite rightly, reflects (in part at least) the refusal of researchers to tolerate complexity. The reader would be well served by referring to a classic paper by Miles (1957), which is referred to in most British texts on intelligence. Miles draws the distinction between *real* and *nominal* definitions. To list a set of attributes is not to imply that the attributes in combination form an entity. Thus "humid," "cold," "wet," and "equatorial" describe attributes of the world's weather. It is unlikely, however, that God will ever think it worthwhile to attach electrodes to the North and South Poles in order to reveal some electrophysical correlate of a thing called "the weather." The early psychometric testers claimed that their factors were only mathematical devices for characterizing clusters of related attributes. We would not be writing this chapter if we did not believe that physiology and behavior are related; this does not commit us to the view that such relationships need be simple. Indeed, since behavior is patently complex, it is likely that factors correlated with it will also be complex.

EEG and Test Intelligence

We begin our review with a quartet of papers, all published in the *Psychological Bulletin*, beginning with a major review by Ellingson (1956) and followed by a debate between Ellingson (1966) and Vogel and Broverman (1964, 1966). Ellingson has been a major critic of EEG studies and the attempt to relate the EEG to psychological processes. His 1956 review was concerned with a range of phenomena: sleep, stimulation (including photic driving), hypothesis concerning the functional characteristics of alpha activity, voluntary movement, conditioning, learning and memory, hypnosis, emotion, personality, and intellectual processes (including intelligence, mental effort, and imagery). This was, therefore, a typically impressive and wide-ranging *tour de force* of a review, which provided an authoritative background to Ellingson's observation that "The weight of evidence indicates that the alpha rhythm is unrelated to test intelligence" (1956, p. 18). The discussion of intelligence occupies only one column of a very long paper, indicating the paucity of studies in the field and the lack of coherent findings. Ellingson's conclusion was in line with earlier, more substantial reviews of the topic by Lindsley (1944) and Ostow (1950).

Vogel and Broverman (1964) set out to qualify this unanimous and negative view. They accused Ellingson and the earlier authors of selectivity, claiming that there was a continuous stream of papers that were equal in quantity and quality to those reviewed, but that reported positive results. They reviewed studies of the EEG and intelligence in the feeble-minded, children, normal adults, the aged, and those with brain disease. While pointing out that several studies might have confounded age, they concluded that EEG characteristics had been shown to relate to mental age among feeble-minded children in a majority of studies, particularly when *non*occipital placements were employed and the focus was not wholly upon simple measures of alpha activity. As regards normal children, outcomes again varied. However, they concluded that positive findings might be masked when the EEG was correlated with IQ rather than mental age; studies with null results tended not to hold chronological age constant. They cited a study by Netchine

and Lairy (1960) showing a significant negative correlation with alpha frequency at 5–6 years, which inverted sign and became significant again at 9 years through to 12 years. Studies by Lindsley and others had failed to control for age.

Among adults, only Mundy-Castle's laboratory (e.g., Mundy-Castle, 1955, 1958) had obtained significant findings; this group had been unique in using the Wechsler scales to measure intelligence. It is logically possible, of course, for the Wechsler scales to show variance with other IQ tests and with aspects of the EEG, but for the EEG not to share variance with these other tests. In relation to studies with the aged, Vogel and Broverman pointed out that the ideal study would involve controls for age, health, and pregeriatric intellectual level; no study satisfied these requirements. As with child studies, mental and chronological age were often confounded. In connection with brain disease, Vogel and Broverman cited studies indicating clear evidence of specific EEG abnormalities combined with specific intellectual loss (e.g., hemispheric differences in relation to verbal and performance scores).

Thus Vogel and Broverman (1964) concluded that, except for normal adults, the burden of evidence for an association between the EEG and measured intelligence is positive. They argued that intelligence becomes progressively differentiated and elaborated with age, making it easier to detect relationships in children, where intelligence is more unitary in nature. Moreover, if such differentiation implies differential topographical fluctuations, then occipital measurement alone (relatively successful in children) is unlikely to be successful in the case of adult subjects. The authors pleaded for a much more sophisticated approach to the analysis of the EEG, involving topography and a wide range of frequencies. Since sex differences in the EEG had been frequently reported, they cautioned against computing correlations for mixed-sex populations. (We should note that since there are established sex differences in developmental rate and attainment, even age-related sex samples cannot be compared directly, and their use might be misleading; see Tanner, 1962.) Of the several dozen studies reviewed, only one had employed an *active* task involving "intelligent" behavior; while Vogel and Broverman did not deny that correlates of mental age and EEG might be revealed at rest, they claimed that such differences as there might be would be accentuated during processes that reflect the behavior sampled by IQ tests.

Thus, with the publication of the Vogel and Broverman (1964) paper, there were two very extensive and closely argued reviews of the same subject area that came to diametrically opposed conclusions. Ellingson (1966) came back with a sharp rejoinder. He challenged the view that studies of subjects with brain damage or EEG abnormalities would illuminate problems relating to normal functioning. Abnormal EEGs and deficits in intelligence certainly can be observed in the same population, but their association implies neither correlation nor generality to other contexts. He drew attention to the fact that the EEG measures employed were often eccentric, or at least unique to the laboratory in question, unstandardized, and possibly unreliable. Few studies had employed experimenters blind to the hypothesis or to the subjects' scores on the IQ test. Retarded subjects are retarded for a variety of reasons and should not be cast indiscriminately within the same population. Ellingson then examined in detail several of the studies cited by Vogel and Broverman (1964).

Unfortunately, the Vogel and Broverman (1966) reply was equally sharp, but clearly better informed. They had little quarrel with Ellingson over methodological points, but they did take him to task over his rejection of individual studies, citing chapter and verse in a very detailed fashion. It is unfortunately clear that Ellingson had failed to read the papers in question with due care. The reader is invited to make careful scrutiny of these four papers; our view is that the Vogel and Broverman (1964, 1966) arguments and supporting data are powerful, and that Ellingson's arguments owe more to rhetoric than to reason. The key points are as follows:

1. Ellingson claimed that it was improper to include subjects with abnormal EEGs in these studies. Vogel and Broverman pointed out that estimates of abnormality can vary 15% or more in a "normal" population. Thus the definition of "abnormal EEG" is itself unreliable. (We should note that Gibbs and Gibbs's [1963] estimate of EEG abnormality in adolescents would exclude more than 30% of subjects from any study!)
2. In the studies of retarded groups, subjects were indeed selected on the basis of objective criteria, and distinctions were drawn among subcategories (i.e., subjects were not lumped together, as Ellingson alleged). This was only one of more than a dozen errors of fact of which Vogel and Broverman accused Ellingson.
3. Even so, they challenged Ellingson's view that an actuarial balance sheet is a means of deciding the truth or falsehood of a scientific assertion. If there are competent and well-designed replications with similar results, then they can only be overturned by systematic analysis: "To summarize, Ellingson's critique of Vogel and Broverman, 1964 is based almost entirely on error" (1966, p. 104).
4. Finally, Vogel and Broverman drew attention to Ellingson's conviction that "the EEG is such a primitive bioelectric function of neural tissue and as such, cannot be expected to relate to higher functions such as intelligence or personality" (Ellingson, 1966, p. 98). They charged Ellingson with the responsibility for inhibiting EEG research in

this field by asserting this *a priori* view in review articles. Presumably, this alleged prejudice limited his selection and interpretation of the existing literature.

It is refreshing to find that scientists are not free of passion. These articles are particularly angry and irritable in style, and one suspects that there were more bitter accusations before the editorial blue pencil did its work. We have devoted considerable attention to these reviews, because the issues today still remain very much the same.

List of Requirements for EEG/ERP and IQ Research

1. Care is needed in the assessment of intelligence; a global score, derived from only one IQ test, is quite unsatisfactory. Moreover, there is reason to believe that different subscales (e.g., verbal vs. performance, fluid vs. crystallized intelligence) might relate to different hemispheres, different electrode placements, and, of course, different experimental tasks and contexts.
2. Single EEG channels are insufficient. Multiple-site recording is essential, and EEG parameters should reflect reliable and well-established methods of measurement. A topographical analysis may reveal not only differential discriminability, but also differential *patterning* in terms of magnitude, sign, and the conditions under which particular effects hold.
3. Heterogeneous groups, representing the full ability range, should be used. Extreme groups may be different in a variety of ways, and special populations may give special effects; in neither case may the outcome truly reflect processes in the criterion variable.
4. Age must be controlled for or partialed out.
5. Subject sex, particularly in developmental studies, must be controlled for.
6. Subjects should perform tasks that have *prima facie* relevance to the processes underlying IQ test scores.
7. Experimenters should be blind to test scores both at the time of recording and the time of scoring, particularly if the data selection schedule is not automatic.
8. Elaborate analysis is required for determining the interrelationships between EEG parameters and IQ items and subscales.
9. Reliability estimates should be obtained of all measures employed.
10. There are always possibilities for confounding—for example, institutional life influences on experimental groups; sex and age characteristics of subjects.

11. Since most tasks employed involve experimental control of attention, and since attentional regulation is required to perform well in IQ tests, it is always possible that what is measured (particularly in extreme-group designs) is an EEG correlate of attention (i.e., it is a correlate of both IQ test performance and capacity to satisfy laboratory demands). While attentional control is clearly not unrelated to intelligent performance, few would assert that it is *synonymous* with intelligence.

All these issues of methodology and inference must be borne in mind when considering more contemporary work. Vogel and Broverman (1966) have suggested that the lack of confirmation of the EEG-IQ relation "has been due less to a failure to find relationships which have been sought than it has been due to a failure to initiate research" (p. 108).

The late 1960s and the 1970s witnessed a revival of work on this most important topic, with a shift toward evoked potential work. Regrettably, there was also a revival of the equivocal pattern of findings derived from spontaneous rhythm research, as well as of the associated errors in both method and interpretation.

More Recent Research

Traditional studies relating IQ to aspects of the EEG still appear. For example, Petersen, Sellden, and Bosaeus (1976) present a complicated study in which children who were "normal" according to a number of criteria constituted a large sample of more than 200 subjects. The study included subgroups on the basis of social class, which was its main focus; there were, in addition, subgroups classified on the basis of EEG characteristics. Generally, Petersen *et al.* found little relation between EEG and IQ, although in one case a male sample with abnormal EEG (i.e., 14- and 6-Hz wave spike) had a *higher* IQ than their normal EEG controls!

No doubt the most impressive of spontaneous EEG studies is that of Giannitrapani (1969), who explored EEG frequency and IQ, making three assumptions: (1) that frequency would be positively related to IQ; (2) that frequency would increase during mental tasks; and (3) that there would be greatest hemispheral differentiation during mental work. A sample of only 18 subjects was used, with IQ scores ranging from 93–143 (Wechsler Adult Intelligence Scale, or WAIS) and an age range of 21–45 years. Frontal, temporal, parietal, and occipital leads were sampled from both hemispheres. Conditions were rest (eyes closed) and mental multiplication. Experimenters were blind to the hypotheses; records were scored independently by two scorers, and reliability coefficients were presented. ANOVA was computed for conditions, area, period (into task), and IQ (two groups: middle and high). Also, Spearman's rho was calculated for Verbal, Performance, and full-scale IQ scores, taken separately. Strangely, conditions had no significant effect (this may have been due to fixed order), and there was no main effect for IQ and conditions; left hemisphere showed a higher frequency. Brain areas produced significant effects for IQ; there was a crossover effect, such that high-IQ subjects had higher parietal frequency in the left hemisphere and a higher occipital frequency in the right hemisphere, with the reverse holding for the middle-IQ group. Several correlations were found between IQ and (1) mathematics minus rest and (2) left-hemisphere scores for frequency, such that the higher the IQ, the *lower* the difference between conditions and the *larger* the differences between hemispheres. We shall see later that in an ERP study by Shucard and Horn (1972), it was alleged that greater *differences* between conditions for brighter subjects are evidence of greater *flexibility*; thus every possible finding can always find a plausible explanation! Some of the correlations in the Giannitrapani study are extraordinarily high, given that this was a psychophysiological study and that the number of subjects was so small; it is indeed unusual for treatment effects to be swamped by individual difference effects, since the reverse is usually the case. Thus the correlation between full-scale IQ score and a collapsed score for frontal–parietal–temporal minus occipital EEG (taking individual signs into account) was .72, and several other correlations exceeded .50, the sign varying in accordance with the crossover effects in area–IQ relations revealed in the ANOVA. Alpha index was also correlated with WAIS scores.

Does the Giannitrapani (1969) study overcome objections made to previous work? On the positive side, there was adequate topological sampling; this reveals how differences in direction of relation can occur, making it quite clear that negative findings or even positive findings based on one or two channels cannot be trusted. On this ground alone, we should be grateful for this study. Similarly, more than adequate formal requirements were satisfied for measurement and statistical analysis. The small sample and the limited choice of tasks that were employed are weaknesses. More important criticisms, on the basis of earlier studies, are as follows:

1. Age was not controlled for and might have been confounded; for example, some subjects might have been both younger and less intelligent. Younger subjects *could* have been trained nurses and older subjects established medical colleagues.
2. Was arousal controlled for? The significant correlation between alpha index and IQ suggests that high-IQ subjects were more relaxed.

3. The greater difference between hemispheres for brighter subjects indicates possibly less difficulty in mental computation (i.e., more focussed attention); this is reflected in increased differentiation of parietal activation (specific to calculation) and decreased occipital differential activation (reflecting general, nonspecific activation).

Such criticisms may seem unduly carping. The Giannitrapani study was conducted in a most scrupulous fashion and presents perhaps the most powerful set of data in the literature. Given the revival of studies of hemispheral differentiation of psychological function, this clearly represents one of the ways forward. We turn now to studies of ERPs.

ERP Studies of Test Intelligence

A study of Shucard and Horn (1972) is notable for its care and attention to detail. Referring to the early ERP work by Ertl and associates (e.g., Barry & Ertl, 1966; Ertl & Schafer, 1969), Shucard and Horn pointed out that these studies were characterized by selective subgroups (including extremes) and gross measures of the IQ, and were not integrated within a coherent theory. In contrast, they employed a wide-ranging sample in which they attempted to control for occupation, social class, age, and sex; employed a battery of 16 tests, with particular focus on the distinction between fluid and crystallized intelligence; included controls for speed; and varied attentional requirements. Their ERP measurement was limited to only one left- and one right-hemisphere channel (F3–P3 and F4–P4, the latter replicating Ertl's favored placement). Three treatments were used in fixed order: RT to a light stimulus, counting the number of light stimuli, and lying quietly and attending to the stimuli (intrinsic attention). We should note that the authors did not refer to the pitfalls of fixed-order designs.

Shucard and Horn's *general* finding (supported in terms of sign in virtually all their correlations) was that long ERP latency was associated with low ability, and short latency with high ability. This is quite in line both with Ertl's theory and his findings. The majority of their correlations were in the region of −.15 ($p < .05$ at $r = .195$ for their sample of 100). Contrary to the expectations of Vogel and Broverman (1964), the intrinsic attention condition, involving least response, yielded a higher proportion of significant correlations, which also tended to be larger in magnitude. It is not easy to make a simple verbal characterization of the mass of data presented; it does appear, however, that ERP correlations held with larger groupings of test scores (i.e., partialing out of subscales reduced the magnitude of the correlation). Shucard and Horn suggested that one might wish to interpret their task × ability finding as an indication

that "bright subjects . . . tend to maintain alertness, even during the rather boring intrinsic activation condition. . . . this implies that short evoked potential latency represents in part, intellectual alertness" (1972, p. 66). However, subjective reports indicated that brighter subjects felt less alert during the more boring tasks. This, Shucard and Horn claimed, supports the view that brighter subjects are more *flexible* (i.e., can allocate attention more appropriately to tasks making different demands on them than can duller subjects).

We find the presentation of several dozen correlations quite confusing, and cannot understand why the data were not subjected to some higher-order factor analysis to see whether a patterning of factors emerged. While Shucard and Horn were clearly and openly not satisfied with the alternative interpretations of their findings, it is difficult to see how the study constitutes a great advance in our knowledge. We should note also that correlations of about .20, whether statistically significant or not, account for less that 5% of the overall variance. It remains open whether their correlations reflect anything directly to do with intelligence, or rather, the ease with which brighter persons adapt to laboratory conditions. In a follow-up study, which procedurally appears to have been identical, Shucard and Horn (1973) examined difference scores (i.e., ERP values between conditions). Of 22 correlations, 5 were found to be significant (range .21–.25). These held only for fluid intelligence. Again, they claimed that the results indicate that brighter subjects are more "modifiable and show greater plasticity in their response" (1973, p. 66). Given the tiny size of these correlations, we are most skeptical about their bearing upon IQ. One only needs a small common variance on a factor common to IQ and ERP (capacity to relax in the laboratory?), which may be antecedent to or consequent causally upon IQ, to yield such modest evidence of a "relationship."

Such a criticism is particularly relevant to the studies of Ertl (e.g., 1971), where extreme groups were employed, for the possibility of confounding with other variables is enhanced. Indeed, in the 1971 study, Ertl failed to show an effect, for an enormous sample, in comparing high- and low-IQ subjects, but used a Fourier transform rather than his latency measure. Similar criticisms can be directed at a study by Rhodes, Dustman, and Beck (1969), which found late components of the ERP to be higher in bright children, who also showed hemispheral differences. However, as we indicate below, replications of Ertl's work by Hendrickson have yielded extremely high correlations, which are difficult to dismiss on the grounds of artifact.

A paper by Everhart, China, and Auger (1974) is of interest because it seems frankly antagonistic to Ertl. Unable to obtain a technical manual or a diagram of Ertl's commercially available Neural Efficiency Analyzer (NEA), they subjected the machine to rigorous testing to discover what exactly it measured! They reported (1) that there was relative consistency of score over six trials; (2) that the NEA measures background EEG and not visual evoked potentials (VEPs; Callaway [1975] suggests the two are in fact confounded, but in a reasonable fashion); and (3) that correlations between WAIS and NEA scores, based on two samples of 20 and 47 subjects, were as high as −.50 for Verbal scores and .54 for Digit Symbols. In all, 5 of 14 correlations were significant, with a correlation of −.43 for the full score. In view of the skepticism expressed by these authors and their reluctance to consider their findings of any value, we must conclude that this is a study clearly in support of Ertl's views and data—perhaps a reflection of ongoing EEG rather than ERP, but derived in favor of Ertl in the most hostile of circumstances. Ertl's claims are discussed below.

The Neural Efficiency Hypothesis

Callaway (1975) provides an excellent and balanced summary of the first 10 years of research on ERPs and IQ. His discussion is logical, involves rigorous analysis of previous work, and gives a detailed account of his own studies. The early work of Chalke and Ertl (1965) is characterized as being associated with a straightforward hypothesis: "[F]ast minds should have higher IQ's—fast brains should produce short-latency AEP's and fast minds should be the companions of fast brains" (1975, p. 43). Callaway then points out that the history of the research proved to be far from simple. Ertl's work is criticized on several grounds: (1) use of peculiar bipolar electrode placement (or placements, since information on location is ambiguous); (2) an unusual definition of latency ("Ertl's definition of latency can result in the identification of events that are given the same name but are quite different from subject to subject" [1975, p. 45]—Ertl's method is based on a zero-cross-type metric rather than the usual peak-type metric; (3) use of Pearson's *r* on extreme groups; and (4) insensitivity (because of a strong biological commitment) to age and arousal state of subjects. Nevertheless, in spite of these problems, Callaway finds Ertl's data impressive; he presents a table from Ertl and Schafer (1969) based on 566 schoolchildren, yielding correlations on the Wechsler Intelligence Scale For Children (WISC), PMA, and Otis in the −.35 region. Callaway cites supporting evidence from Shucard (1969), Plum (1969), Galbraith, Gliddon, and Busk (1970), Gucker (1973), Bennett (1968), and Weinberg (1969), using frequency analysis of visual evoked responses. He also presents detailed accounts of work from his own laboratories involving both visual and auditory ERPs. On the negative side are a major and

publically funded study by Davis (1971), carried out in association with Ertl, and what Callaway calls "quasi-failure to replicate" by Engel and Henderson (1973). Failure to replicate in their study could have been due to differences in electrode placements and latency measurement; an effect was found by Engel and Henderson when black and white subjects were treated within a multiple correlation. Thus we see there are data from studies using visual ERPs that both support and challenge Ertl's view—namely, that brighter subjects have shorter latency, reflecting, in his theory, faster brainpower.

However, an important difficulty arises for the theory when it comes to measurement of auditory ERPs. Callaway finds that auditory ERP measures correlated negatively with age, but correlated *positively* with IQ score. This finding undermines the neural efficiency hypothesis of Ertl, since brighter children, by definition, have higher IQ scores like those of older children. Brainpower and neural speed cannot hold for visual ERPs in one direction and auditory ERPs in the reverse direction, and at one and the same time be seen to be a fundamental property of intelligence reflected in ERPs. Hendrickson (1972) found the reverse—that is, auditory and visual effects were the same—while Rust (1975), using two samples of 84 and 212 subjects, found no relation with auditory ERPs. Callaway is unable to reconcile these contradictory findings and cites studies by Ertl himself (1969) and Straumanis, Shagass, and Overton (1973), using Down syndrome and control children, that showed *shorter* auditory ERP latencies for *duller* children.

In concluding his extensive and detailed review, Callaway rejects the neural efficiency hypothesis. Nor can a version of the Shucard and Horn boredom interpretation stand, since it fits visual ERP data but not auditory ERP data, where shorter latency goes with habituation while longer latency goes (in several studies) with higher IQ. Callaway sees studies that vary task demands, and, in particular, manipulations that cause the latency–IQ correlation to vanish, to hold most promise for future research.

The Hendrickson's Theory

We now consider two more recent studies by one group of workers that exhibit correlations of an extraordinary magnitude—in one case, barely short of the retest reliability coefficients of either IQ or EEG! These are studies by Hendrickson and Hendrickson (1980) and Blinkhorn and Hendrickson (1982). The theory is delightfully simple.

> The Hendricksons' theory proposes that higher intelligence is a function of lower error rates in the central nervous system, and that as a result of the way in which information is coded and transmitted in the brain, the effect of error is to reduce both the number and amplitude of excursions of the a.e.p. trace. Therefore, differ-

ences in IQ should be manifested in a.e.p. traces as differences in complexity, which can be determined simply by measuring the length of the trace over a standard epoch. This measure we refer to as the "string" measure, as in effect one treats an a.e.p. trace like a piece of string and measures its straightened length. (Blinkhorn & Hendrickson, 1982, p. 596)

Hendrickson and Hendrickson (1980) obtained a correlation of .77 from 254 children aged 14–16 years, using the full-scale WAIS IQ; more impressive perhaps is the study of Blinkhorn and Hendrickson (1982), using advanced students, where the correlation between score on the Advanced Progressive Matrices and the string measure was .53 for 33 subjects. Test scores were derived before the EEG study and were unknown to the experimenter. Since a variety of test scores were available, a total of 54 correlations was computed, and only 3 of these were significant. Nevertheless, Blinkhorn and Hendrickson claim that if the correlation obtained is corrected for full-range IQ score, it would be in the region of .70–.84—that is, very similar in magnitude to the one obtained in the earlier study. We should note that these data are for auditory presentation of simple tones and that Blinkhorn and Hendrickson wish to eschew the use of complex tasks. "[T]he string measurement procedure involves the subject in no decisions, makes no apparent demands on memory, involves no difficult perceptual discriminations, and uses stimulus intensities much greater than threshold . . . in a task which can perhaps best be described as mindless" (1982, p. 597).

The Neurometrics of E. Roy John

The work of E. Roy John and his associates represents a considerable contrast to the research tradition we have reviewed so far. They have sustained a prodigious research output, comprising both human and animal studies, over the last 25 years. The work is extremely complex, and it is therefore difficult to do complete justice to it within the confines of a few paragraphs; a good source of additional information is John's *Functional Neuroscience* (Vol. 2, *Neurometrics of Quantitative Electrophysiology*) (1977).

John's approach carries with it many advances in conceptualization, while sharing many of the difficulties and logical limitations of earlier work. Essentially, "neurometrics" employs powerful data acquisition and statistical techniques to derive topographical EEG profiles, which are then used to draw comparisons between criterion groups—for example, the young and the elderly, the brain-intact and the brain-damaged, and (of particular importance to the present section) normal learners and learning-retarded children. John is sharply critical of traditional psychometrics, which he claims has produced tests based on performance; performance is necessarily influenced by cultural and educational factors, both within the standardization population and within the target clinical population. It is argued that by developing taxonomies to describe brain function, neurometrics moves away from the disadvantages of cultural saturation and the potential abuse of individuals that has been made possible by paper-and-pencil tests.

The reader will anticipate our criticisms of such a view, which are not unlike the criticisms made by Callaway and referred to earlier in this section, since the view implies that the EEG reveals biologically "pure" characteristics of the nervous system, independent of cultural and educational influence. This is, of course, bizarre, since electrical potentials are worth studying because we believe them not only to reflect brain structure, but the process and content of experience. A process-oriented approach like ours finds it very difficult to partition inherent and acquired characteristics.

The key features of John's approach are as follows:

1. Routine recordings are made of EEG and ERPs from multiple recording sites and under standard testing conditions.
2. Standard testing conditions include a set of common "psychological" tests alleged to reflect resting, sensory, perceptual, and information-processing aspects of cognitive functioning. In fact, the tests are hardly surprising for the EEG buff or for those who have studied the EEG–intelligence literature, for they include eyes-open–eyes-closed, photic driving, sensory acuity, pattern exposure (including letters and simple stimuli), habituation–dishabituation, and so on.
3. These procedures are designed *not* to involve verbal interaction or overt behavioral response, in order to "substantially circumvent the developmental, linguistic and cultural limitations of psychometric tests" (John, Karmel, Corning, Easton, Brown, Ahn, John, Harmony, Prichep, Toro, Gerson, Bartlett, Thatcher, Kaye, Valdes, & Schwartz, 1977, p. 397).
4. Powerful computer programs are employed to describe EEG and ERP data. Principal–components analysis and factor analysis help to reduce the data to a manageable form, identifying profiles for electrode locations, relations between locations, and different testing conditions.
5. Group data are z-transformed to enable between-group comparisons and to enable an individual's profile to be described in terms of statistical deviation from a group norm.
6. Varimax rotation is used to achieve the best factor fit with the physiological data, enabling estimates of the amount of variance accounted for by particular factors and combinations of factors.
7. Numerical taxonomy methods allow for the grouping of data in multidimensional space. The

relative weightings of, say, different ERP factors can be assessed for different electrode locations; and any individual's weightings can be compared for relative differences against the parent population.

8. Discriminant function analysis enables comparison of test conditions and clinical treatments (e.g., drug vs. no drug), showing which aspects of the resultant factor structure are common and which are discriminating.

9. Because of the complexity of the procedures, graphic methods are used to portray individual and group profiles, enabling relatively rapid clinical evaluation.

10. Reliability is established by repeated replications, and validity is assessed—for example, by comparing false positive detections and omissions by the neurometric technique with other techniques (e.g., clinical EEG or psychometrics) in the identification of particular target populations.

John et al. (1977) claim that neurometrics is more powerful than psychometric procedures for distinguishing different subtypes of retarded learners. They end their paper with some very bold claims:

> Neurometric methods may serve to provide criteria for the efficacy of interventions. . . . The amount of damage and rate of recovery . . . may be quantitatively evaluated. . . . [Neurometrics] may also be used to assess the consequences of organic disease . . . and [to] determine the effects on human beings of drugs, food additives, toxins and environmental pollution. Once banks of data are constructed from different types of normal and abnormal individuals, and effective mass screening programs are inaugurated, neurometrics may prove useful for many of these purposes. The early detection and remediation of brain disease and cognitive disorders would reduce some of the human social and economic costs of failure to recognize these problems. (John et al., 1977, p. 1409)

Having staked their claim, they then urge caution against abuse, lest neurometrics be misused as is the case with psychometrics: "Procedures must be devised to ensure that neurometric evaluations are used to optimize the development of individuals, rather than restrict their opportunities, as has often been the case with psychometric assessment" (1977, p. 1409).

One aspect of John's work to which we have not yet referred is the integration of human and animal work. Animal studies enable John to ask questions that ethical constraints restrict in human studies. John (1980) reviews his general theory of brain functioning. He challenges the motor–sensory view, and claims that it has distorted approaches to learning and cognition, not only in laboratory but also in educational contexts. He makes trenchant criticisms of localization theories and the experiments they have spawned. Even at the level of individual neurons, he claims, the

notion of localization is untenable, since response is unpredictable and unreliable. His own theory is a statistical configuration theory, which reconciles both localizationalist and equipotentiality viewpoints and helps to make sense of existing equivocal data. "Information is represented, not by activity in a specific neuron or a selected pathway, but by the average temporal pattern of firing in anatomically extensive populations of neurons" (John, 1980, p. 131). Thus within the brain there is graded quantitative response as a representation of different functions.

In John's research, data are presented from many animal preparations, with electrodes implanted at multiple brain locations. Dynamic changes recorded in brain organization during conditioning and learning, and as stimuli acquire new meaning, are analyzed using complex computer techniques. Studies in cats have been designed to distinguish exogenous and endogenous components of ERPs recorded from different brain sites. Taking ERPs for different stimulus–response configurations, data may be derived for insertion in simultaneous equations, whose solution identifies the endogenous and exogenous components within different brain regions. Thus, relative weightings for different sites can be shown, since each region varies for endogenous *and* exogenous components. The graded contributions of different brain areas at different stages of learning can therefore be estimated. Conscious experience is thus seen as a reflection of the diffuse contributions of different brain areas under different states.

This theoretical outlook and the techniques employed to characterize brain organization are clearly related to the neurometric strategy already described. Even within the relatively limited data base available from the surface of the cranium, the same *approach* to intellectual functioning is possible, since different topographical profiles, reflecting differential graded participation of EEG and ERP factors in certain functions, may be derived for different psychological processes. Thus, the work of John is both powerful in its potential for future developments of research into cortical correlates of IQ, *and* a sound basis for criticism of all existing research reviewed so far in this section, which in contrast is typically theory-free, limited in data acquisition, limited in testing conditions, and limited in data analysis.

But John himself is not free of criticism:

1. He paints a distorted caricature of psychometrics, failing to give credit for its achievements and for the theoretical emphasis that underlies much of the work of the pioneers in this field, who were not just mere pragmatists (see Kline, 1979).

2. His accusations of psychometric abuse are unjust, since it is not the procedures themselves that lead to maltreatment of individuals, but the use to which they are put and the manner in which test findings are

misinterpreted. *Logically* speaking, neurometrics has no advantage in this respect; the spectacular claims made for its power could themselves encourage abuse; and the emphasis on biological determinants of behaviour could be seen to be compatible with a dehumanizing of people. Psychometric and neurometric procedures are strikingly similar in form.

3. John seems to be unaware of the criticisms of factor-analytic approaches to test construction and interpretation, which also have a bearing on his own work; a potential criticism is that the selection of test items (a) determines the outcome and factor structure, and (b) *excludes* alternative data bases, leading to completely different factor structures and factor loadings. It is not clear to us that John has selected the correct items or sampled the psychologically appropriate domains of behavior.

4. John's test items owe most to historical tradition, coming from the armamentarium of the EEG clinician; to a modern cognitive psychologist, they have very little to do with information processing, and they portray the individual as a passive, biologically impelled, stimulus-response lump. Thus, John is guilty of leaping from extremely simple-minded procedural paradigms to extremely complex psychological processes.

5. Mere rhetoric and assertion are not sufficient grounds for the belief that psychometric measures estimate genotype plus culture, while the EEG and neurometrics are culture- and experience-free. Given our own interactionist view, and the complicated literature on testing, we believe the partitioning of variance in any individual case to be an extremely difficult exercise. John wants to sweep away the psychometric tradition much too easily and for the wrong reasons.

6. It is somewhat strange that while in the animal work responses to learning are distinguished, the human work seems committed to a stationary and endogenous view of the brain. While John's neurometric data are already complex enough, the dynamic component must, in our view, be added and placed in the context of ecologically valid procedures, if intellectual processes and true differences—for example, between strong and weak learners—are to be captured.

7. While John's biological methods are extremely powerful, his conception of behavioral and clinical grouping seems simple-minded, for he appears to assume that clinical groupings are givens rather than human-made constructions. Research on the reliability of clinical diagnosis reveals low correlations and shifting boundaries. Yet such groupings are used as a criterion measure to assess the predictive validity of the neurometric method. This "medical model" or "disease model" of dysfunction reveals an insensitivity to the complexity of particular behavioral problems. Thus the retarded reader is likely to have a

number of associated problems, some of which arise as a *consequence* of failure. No attempt is made to partition such aspects, even though complex methods are used to distinguish components within the physiological domain. Thus, cognitive and emotional components are confounded. There also appears to be an insensitivity to the potential interactive effects of the subject–experimenter interface and consequent opportunities for confounding (see our discussion of laboratory-induced arousal in a later section).

8. Finally, the correlational and biological approach leads also to a unidirectional model of causation: Brain disorder leads to maladaptive behavior. We argue repeatedly in this review that any physiological variable worthy of study should be sensitive to patterns of multiple causation and should reflect *interactions* between nervous systems and their consequences. Paradoxically, in John's case, there appears to be a stimulus–response view in his human studies, in contrast to the very convincing and dynamic view arising from his animal work. This is the reverse of what normally occurs when animal and human models are compared!

In summary, we see John's work as a distinct break from earlier approaches in several respects. Intellectual process is seen within the framework of a general theory; multiple tasks and multiple measures are used; there are comparisons across populations using common procedures; and the data are captured and refined within a sophisticated statistical model. While we have made several criticisms, it would be improper to underestimate the clear importance and potential of this work. However, it appears to us that the work will have to be even *more* complex if it is to capture process; mere correlational data, however rich, tell us little about function. This is a fault that neurometrics, at its current stage of conceptualization and development, shares with psychometrics. As it stands, we are not convinced that neurometrics represents such a mighty advance over psychometrics, and it is much more expensive. Moreover, the potential dangers of exploitation of individuals and the danger of labeling, for which John expresses so much concern, seem to us to be equivalent. If psychophysiological methods are to replace psychometric methods, it must be appreciated that applied science occurs within a sociocultural context, where any technology may be used for good or ill.

A Conclusion

As time goes on, and more and more experimenters are dabbling with electrocortical measures and traditional IQ measures, evidence is accumulating to demonstrate a correlation between the two variables. But the position is little different from that reviewed by

Vogel and Broverman in the 1960s. Very many studies have shown modest effects, while equally competent studies show reverse findings or null effects. We are critical, in our introductory comments, of Andreassi's failure in his 1980 text to account for the discrepancies in the literature. It is clear that we ourselves have fared little better in this section. However, the signposts for future work are fairly clear. What is needed is a study involving the following: repeated measurement on a group of subjects; incorporation of spontaneous EEGs and ERPs; use of visual and auditory ERPs; standard, the Ertl and the Hendrickson measures of response; multichannel topographical recording for both EEGs and ERPs; and a variety of tasks, ranging from the Hendricksons' "mindless" tone presentations to complex problem solving. Topographical analysis would be aided by measures of coherence among locations, since Surwillo (1971) and others have suggested that the amount of brain involvement in tasks is a function of ability. Until all the existing research has been incorporated into such a common design—and such a program would not be difficult to execute—there will be lingering doubt and anxiety as to whether the EEG and IQ are correlated in a direct and simple fashion. Certainly, it seems difficult to dismiss findings like those of Giannitrapani (1969) or Hendrickson and Hendrickson (1980), with their enormous effects, on any of the grounds that have been given in relation to other studies. It must be considered remarkable that responses to a paper-and-pencil test can correlate so readily with what Ellingson called "a primitive bioelectric function of neural tissue."

On balance, time appears to show that Vogel and Broverman were correct in their predictions for the future. However, we still have a long way to go before the functional significance of these relationships is clearly understood, even if the pattern of findings becomes consistent. Correlations, yes, but process, no: Blinkhorn and Hendrickson (1982) may have generated robust data, but they have not produced sound arguments. It may well be that correlations of considerable magnitude appear under straightforward testing conditions, but it must then be shown (1) why it is they do *not* appear under complex conditions (if that indeed is the case) and (2) how evoked potential changes of this sort are involved in processes that lead to more efficient performance. Moreover, since the "string measure" of Hendrickson and Hendrickson (1980) appears to resemble at least the account of the NEA given by Everhart *et al.* (1974), it is surely incumbent upon the Hendricksons to explain to us how it is that the measure succeeds on some occasions and fails on others, and why it is that their findings for auditory potentials appear to be so different from those of authorities like Callaway and, on occasion, Ertl himself.

Finally, one feature is common to virtually all the work on this topic. Workers have set out to demonstrate that aspects of brain activity relate to a dimension of psychological significance (i.e., intelligence). But elsewhere we see that the same aspects of the EEG, for example, relate to other dimensions of psychological significance (e.g., extraversion–introversion). If all such variables are seen to correlate in a similar way with the same aspects of the electrocortical measure, then one possible logical conclusion is that they all share variance with some factor that *may* be psychologically trivial. One essential requirement if work is to progress is to include all such measures in an appropriate design, so that, at the very least, each correlated factor can be partialed out systematically—or, alternatively, so that a higher-order factor can be derived, which in turn might lead to the creation of a general model of brain function. With such a model, we shall be able to make sense of *some* findings in this review.

SOME EASTERN EUROPEAN APPROACHES TO INDIVIDUAL DIFFERENCES

We devote a section of our review to neo-Pavlovian developments in personality research, for several reasons. Such theories are frankly biological in nature, and contemporary research is very much within the psychophysiological domain. In particular, the work of Strelau and his associates in Warsaw, Poland, extends across several related research areas that are integrated within a common theoretical framework; these range from systematic studies of sensation seeking and sensation avoidance in rats to ecological studies of the behavior of high- and low-reactivity human subjects in high- and low-stimulation environments (rural and urban settings). While the physiological measures currently used in Eastern Europe are rudimentary, and their quantification and statistical treatment (even when fully reported) leave much to be desired, the basic theory and the breadth of aspiration underlying the research hold much promise. A number of Western researchers have sought to compare and contrast Western personality constructs with those of the Eastern European tradition. The emergence of common factors from such studies implies the existence of basic and universal characteristics of nervous systems per se.

Pavlov (e.g., 1957) identified various properties of the nervous system—strength, mobility, and balance—that in their various combinations yield "nervous system types." Pavlov distinguished the "genotype" (i.e., the innate nervous system type that is unalterable) and the "phenotype" (the resultant "character" that emerges from the interaction of type with environmental influences). We should note that Pavlov selected only a small proportion of the possible number of types arising from combinations of his various properties. His particular selection is seen by some (e.g., Strelau, 1985) to have been somewhat arbitrary, and this has led to some confusions. Thus the loyalty of subsequent Soviet workers to Pavlov's theory and their desire to tinker with it rather than to create a total reconstruction may perhaps have led to a standstill in conceptual development. Teplov and Nebylitsyn (see Gray, 1964) assume that investigations based upon psychophysiological and conditioned reflex methodology will enable the partitioning of innate (genotypic) and acquired factors in personality. Strelau (1985) distinguishes "temperamental" aspects of behavior, attributable to biological mechanisms common to nervous systems as such, and "personality," which is the result of interaction with the physical and social environment. Thus Strelau sees logical equivalence in the status of Pavlovian notions of weak and strong nervous systems, his own notion of reactivity, Eysenck's extraversion, Zuckerman's sensation seeking, Gray's anxiety, and so on. All are seen to reflect biological predispositions that in principle may be explored in animals as well as in humans.

Comparative studies across these dimensions have been carried out in both the East and the West, employing psychometric, psychophysiological, and experimental physiological procedures. An early attempt to build bridges between Eastern and Western constructs was Eysenck's (1966) address to the International Congress of Psychology held in Moscow, at which he proposed that strong and weak nervous systems were related to extraversion and introversion, respectively, and sought parallels between his notion of "conditionability" and Pavlovian concepts of excitation and inhibition. Earlier, Nebylitsyn (see Nebylitsyn, 1972) had related extraversion–introversion to the balance of dynamism of nervous processes (i.e., the ease of forming excitatory and inhibitory processes during the formation of conditioned reflexes). In the West, by far the greatest contribution to comparative psychophysiological studies has been made by Mangan and his associates (e.g., Paisey & Mangan, 1980).

Strelau (1983) presents a table of correlations derived from psychometric studies designed to explore the relationships among several dimensions. While much of the previous work was based upon variations of the original Russian conditioning procedures, Strelau (1972) has devised a psychometric instrument, the Strelau Temperament Inventory, which measures excitation strength, inhibition strength, mobility, and balance of nervous processes. In correlational studies, excitation strength relates to extraversion as Eysenck has claimed, with values ranging from .349 to .548; neuroticism is negatively related to excitation strength

(−.394 to −.617), which is not orthogonal in Eysenck's sense. Strength of inhibition shows no relation to extraversion–introversion, but correlates negatively with anxiety and neuroticism (−.202 to −.588), a puzzling finding. The dimension that yields highest correlations with extraversion is mobility, giving values ranging from .448 to .692; in a sense this is unfortunate, because mobility is one of the most neglected constructs both theoretically and empirically, although strength of inhibition has received even less attention.

Western workers have demonstrated similar interrelationships (e.g., Carlier, 1985; Gilliland, 1985; Paisey & Mangan, 1980, and see below). However, Carlier's study casts some doubt on the integrity of the Strelau scales and their psychometric robustness. While she shows in an elaborate factor analysis that Strelau's excitation correlates with extraversion–introversion and his inhibition with neuroticism/anxiety (Cattell's scales), she considers Strelau's scales to be poor substitutes for the Eysenck scales, for excitation *also* loads on both neuroticism and anxiety as well as inhibition and mobility! Indeed, mobility (which, as we have indicated above, correlates highly with extraversion) appears in her analysis to be a nonindependent factor, yielding loadings greater on other scales than upon itself. Balance appears to be unrelated to Western scales.

Unfortunately, Strelau's questionnaire is not based upon the procedures employed for the development of psychometric instruments as used by Eysenck and Zuckerman. There must be some doubt about its inclusion as an independent variable to empirical research. Strelau argues (Strelau, 1983) that the inventory truly reflects the Pavlovian dimensions, which do not, of course, separate out the key factors in an independent fashion. He points out that within the population at large, such factors may not truly be independent.

Strelau's Theory

For the Polish group, "temperament" is a set of relatively stable traits that are revealed in behavior by the energy level and temporal characteristics of reaction. Such traits are considered to be purely formal, since they have no content and do not have a direct effect upon behavior. Rather, temperament is a regulatory mechanism that influences behavior, but does so independently of direction or content. Energy level is an aggregate of all physiological mechanisms involved in the accumulation and release of energy—that is, at endocrinal, autonomic, and brain stem levels—including cortical mechanisms involved in the regulation of excitation by virtue of their integration with lower brain centers. "Reactivity" and "activity" are two basic features of energy level; "reactivity" is the stable pattern of an individual's response to stimulus intensity, while "activity" refers to the intensity and frequency of aspects of performance. The two dimensions are independent, yet interact in a complex fashion during the development of the individual and in response to environmental demands. Highly reactive subjects (similar to introverts) are particularly sensitive to stimulation, are deficient in those physiological mechanisms that suppress excessive stimulation, and have a high stimulation-processing coefficient. Activity refers to the relationship between optimal level of arousal and the need to increase or decrease stimulation to achieve the optimum. Here also we see a relationship with extraversion–introversion; however, the theory is more subtle than that of Eysenck, since it differentiates sensitivity from style of reaction; as we indicate below, this can lead to a process-oriented rather than a merely correlational mode of psychophysiological research.

Eliasz, one of Strelau's principal theorists, shows how in human development, reactivity and activity serve to regulate the individual's interaction with his or her physical and social environment. Such a notion of traits as regulatory mechanisms helps to create a rapprochement between trait and situational emphases, since the individual is seen (1) to *select* those aspects of the environment that match his or her temperamental characteristics and (2) to *compensate* in certain situations for excesses or deficiencies of stimulation by virtue of his or her style of action. Thus, once a goal is identified, the individual homes toward it, experiencing fluctuations in arousal as a function of inner state and stimulus input, and adopting specific and trans-situationally constant strategies to maintain his or her optimal level of arousal; behavior is seen as a complex sequence of goal-directed hunting. Such mechanisms are studied in a variety of situations. For example, foundry workers were observed at work to determine the division among key work activities, work-preparatory activities (i.e., cleaning and setting tools), and nonwork activities, which in the light of the theory *are* psychologically and physiologically work- or goal-oriented (e.g., social interaction, smoking, grooming, etc.). In another study, complex interactions were revealed among temperament, occupation, sporting activities in leisure time, and domestic accommodation, showing how the person's actions and choices and the stimulation available within the environment are in constant interplay to achieve an optimal level of arousal (Eliasz, 1985). The notion of regulatory dynamics in personality is particularly powerful and persuasive, but it takes the theory well beyond the grasp of simple empirical test.

Matysiak (1985) reports detailed parametric studies of sensation seeking in rats, in which he has been able to distinguish stimulus intensity, stimulus change, activity, and activity cost effects. This has enabled him to explore some basic issues that have never been addressed in human studies of sensation seeking: for example, how, within subjects, need for additional stimulation correlates with *reduction* of activity under overload; how different modality effects compare (i.e., whether one can construct a cross-modality intensity scale for stimulation); and what the relationships may be among stimulation intensity, change, and activity incurred in the subject's attempts to modulate sensory input. Similar points were raised in a paper by Gale (1969), in which he considered the interplay between sensation seeking and reactive inhibition effects generated by sensation-seeking activity; however, they have largely been ignored in Western work. Such issues are not treated in such a sophisticated or dynamic fashion by Zuckerman, and while Zuckerman recommends a return to animal work, the Polish school see animal and human studies progressing hand in hand. Nosal (1985) applies this complex matrix of style-of-action parameters to the study of computer programmers. Personality and cognitive variables are studied in a complex multivariate analysis in which reaction time, errors, error correction, and other performance variables are included.

Such studies have the following advantages: (1) Major individual variables are studied in interaction; (2) the tasks have ecological validity; (3) the tasks have meaning for the subject; (4) variance estimates can be assigned to dimensions taken singly or in interaction; (5) temporal analysis is possible; and (6) process is emphasized.

Such an essentially cybernetic approach to personality sets a very different model for psychophysiological research from that adopted by Western authors. It sees the individual in constant interaction with his or her environment and explores energy changes during interactional processes. For example, in the case of smoking and nicotine research, instead of examining trait differences in smoker–nonsmoker populations, or deriving correlational data from, say, vigilance performance scores, one would study the functions of nicotine and associated reactions (hand movements, respiration patterns, oral temperature variation) upon some central arousal state that the individual seeks to maintain at a stable optimum. Individuals would be seen to differ in terms of patterning of performance and the interpolation of smoking acts, or, to use Strelau's terms, their style of action. Clearly, the potential for psychophysiological studies is enormous.

Unfortunately, it has been left to Western workers (see "Growth Points for the Future," below) to follow up on this theory with psychophysiological studies of a dynamic character. The majority of such studies by Strelau and his associates have been correlational, since his laboratory appears to lack sophisticated physiological quantification and data storage capacity.

Nevertheless, the theory and the empirical studies, and the real-life observational data in particular, have clear implications for psychophysiological research.

One of the most innovative and integrative workers in the Strelau group is Klonowicz, who is particularly concerned with style of action and cost. In one psychophysiological study, coping strategies were observed in hypertensive and normal subjects. Measures of subjective activation, prostaglandin, adrenalin, and noradrenalin were taken under noise stress. Among her findings, she showed that while correct performance of arithmetic problems was equivalent for the two groups, error patterns varied both in type and in time pattern. Hypertensives performed poorly at first, were higher in subjective activation, and remained aroused; yet their adrenalin output remained high but constant. Healthy subjects began well, showed decreased activation with time, and increased adrenalin output. Such findings are interpreted within a regulatory framework in which there is interplay among established coping strategies, cognitive response, performance, and physiological reactivity (Klonowicz, Ignatowska-Switalska, & Wocial, 1985). They also reveal how traditional correlational approaches, in which total performance score is correlated with a trait measure, are in danger of compounding Type II errors, for the way in which the score is obtained (i.e., the process) is of greater interest for the psychophysiological studies of individual differences than for outcome. However, while the potential for psychophysiological data collection is rich, we should not underestimate problems of data handling; these are enormous, since they involve autocorrelation and cross-correlation across experiential, performance, and physiological domains over time. So far as we are aware, the members of the Polish school limit their analysis to simple chi-square and ANOVA statistics; factorial studies (e.g., those of Nosal) typically capture moments in time rather than complex sequences.

As Paisey and Mangan (1980) point out, Strelau's questionnaire and the empirical methods adopted in his laboratory have enabled a rapprochement between Western and Eastern work at the empirical as well as the theoretical level. The earlier tradition, as exemplified by Teplov and Nebylitsyn, involved conceptual and methodological gaps between the two disciplinary approaches. Soviet assessment of typology involved extensive ideographic studies of involuntary behavior in small subject groups, in contrast with Western large-sample, psychometric procedures. While the large-sample approach of the West can be seen to have sacrificed validity for reliability, Russian intensive studies of small groups have yielded reliable and construct-valid measures that, because of limited sample size, have had limited predictive validity. Clearly, if the complementary aspects of the two approaches can be drawn within one framework, then the chance of a revolution in individual differences research looms nearer. We regard process-oriented research as the great way forward.

A COMMENT ON THE CONCEPT OF AROUSAL AND ITS CONNECTION WITH PERFORMANCE

Any biological approach to human behavior must acknowledge that human beings are, in part at least, energy exchange systems. Energy is absorbed and utilized. In such a system, there are a number of parameters that can be described: rate of energy intake, rate of storage, leakiness of the store, and energy utilization in terms of its intensity, patterning, and time distribution. There will be thresholds at which absorption and utilization are more or less likely. As we have seen, such notions are explicitly or implicitly implicated in psychophysiological theories of personality. In the case of Strelau's theory, energy transmission is a central construct; in the case of psychophysiological measurement, the electrical activity recorded has direct or indirect connections with central energy-related physiology.

The concept of arousal has emerged as a psychological intervening variable with intimate connections with the notion of energy. In this guise, the concept of arousal can be seen to be one of the best candidates for the unification of psychology, and certainly for a rapprochement between personality theory and experimental psychology. However, its overutilization as a portmanteau, all-explaining concept has tended to inflate—and therefore to devalue—its explanatory power. It is a chastening exercise merely to list the broad range of contexts in which the concept of arousal has been used: in individual differences, extraversion–introversion, acute versus chronic schizophrenia, psychopathy, depression, autism, hyperactivity, primary–secondary function, field dependence-independence, anxiety, sensation seeking, stimulus hunger, locus of control, sex differences, and so on; in stress research, noise, loss of sleep, heat, cold, incentives, knowledge of results, and pacing; in circadian studies and biological rhythm research, time of day, menstrual cycle, sexual stimulation, hunger and postprandial states, and so forth; in social-psychological and organizational theory, social facilitation, social intimacy, personal space, evaluation apprehension, organizational climate, and so on; in experimental studies, vigilance, memory, RT, stimulus complexity, and the like; and in drug and addiction research, stimulants, depressants, alcohol, caffeine, nicotine, and so forth. The range of measurements of arousal includes questionnaires, cold pressor test, sedation threshold, EEG, ERP, HR, EDA, FPV, FBF, temperature, oxygen consumption, electromyogram (EMG), free fatty acid, urinary pH, paralinguistic and nonverbal aspects of speech, body movement, facial expression, and so on. Critics have pointed to the many contradictory data generated in the name of the construct, the lack of consistency among physiological indices of this central "unitary" phenomenon, and the manner in which its proponents use the term to describe traits, states, stimuli, circadian effects, drug effects, performance effects, and so on in a slipshod manner. Thus arousal is used by different voices as a source of stimulation, as a trait or state threshold for response, as a response to stimulation, as endogenous variation, as experienced drowsiness or alertness, as a correlate or as a consequence of action, as a measure of intensity of action, or as a drive or motivator of action.

Logically, there are a number of alternative ways of proceeding. One can treat the concept as unitary and suggest that all these uses do in fact reflect "the same thing"; in principle, therefore, an appropriate analysis should reveal a common main factor. Secondly, one may claim that the name is misleading, and that one is referring to clusters of entities, some of which are interrelated and some of which are not. Finally, one might accept a "family resemblance" view, in which some of the characteristics overlap across uses, each use being linked to other uses by direct or less direct means. One might, therefore, in the style of old theory, see arousal as a major integrating concept for psychological theory, drawing together areas of the discipline hitherto thought to be unrelated; or, alternatively, as a deceptive concept that creates confusion by creating an illusion of unity.

Our view is that the case against arousal is not yet proven. We have said earlier that in our view, authorities like Zuckerman are throwing in the towel too readily and are arguing for a paradigm shift (in Zuckerman's case, a return to animal studies) much too early. Our view is that tests of the utility of the construct have been inadequate and that most of the experimental procedures employed so far fail to capture the complexity that may be derived from even the most basic elements of arousal theory. We mention below the work of Revelle and his associates, which, in its insistence on parametric work, is some of the best in the field. For the present discussion we offer just a few comments, based on the simple diagrams in Figure 20-2. The issue of arousal–performance relations is crucial for two reasons: (1) because we argue throughout this chapter that studies of performance must be included in future research into the psychophysiology of individual differences, and (2) because we offer below a model of the sequential and cumulative sources that we believe operate in the laboratory, the context in which most research is carried out. The

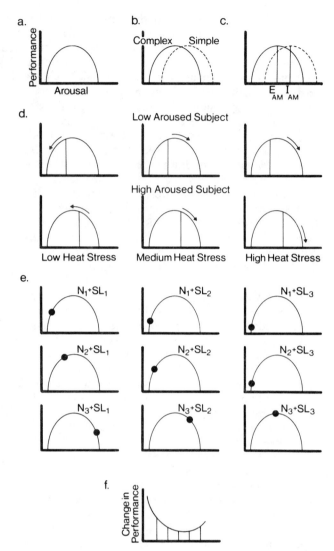

Figure 20-2. Arousal, performance, and experimental stressors. (a) The inverted-U relationship between arousal and performance. (b) Task difficulty shifts the curve. (c) Combination of two levels of task difficulty, two personality groups, and two times of day (four of the eight outcomes are shown). (d) Effects of three levels of heat stress upon a low-aroused and a high-aroused subject. Not all the effects are unidirectional. (e) Interactions among three levels of noise stress and three levels of sleep loss (low, medium, and high in both cases). (f) Change in performance induced by the application of a stressor depends upon the point of application upon the arousal continuum.

complexity of possible relationships between arousal and performance is central to the thrust of this chapter. The concept needs a fair and thorough trial before it is condemned to eternal exile.

Figure 20-2a shows the inverted-U relationship between arousal and performance; performance is best at moderate levels of arousal, is insufficiently driven to be effective at low levels, and is disrupted at high levels. Figure 20-2b presents the curves for two tasks, a simple task and a complex task; for the simple task, the curve is moved toward higher arousal values on the abscissa, since, given its simplicity, higher levels of arousal will not disrupt orderly performance. Figure 20-2c shows that with two tasks, two times of day, and two extreme personality groups (a simple $2 \times 2 \times 2$ design), one may make eight clear ante hoc predictions about performance (but see Revelle's comments below). Eight ante hoc predictions are not a bad achievement for a psychological theory. But stressors that induce variations in arousal do not operate in a simple additive fashion; loss of sleep and exposure to noise work in opposite directions under certain conditions, and their individual and combined effects upon simple and complex tasks are elaborate. Also, stressors are applied at various levels of intensity. Thus Figure 20-2d shows the hypothetical effects of three levels of heat stress on a low-aroused and a high-aroused subject. Of course, since stressors rarely appear on their own in the natural environment, and affect performance in a manner determined by their interaction with other stressors, calculation of outcome must be done with care. Figure 20-2e shows the hypothetical effects of three levels of sleep loss and three levels of noise, independent of initial subject state. Figure 20-2f shows that the increment or decrement induced by application of a stressor is dependent upon the point of application on the abscissa. Thus, a sudden loud noise will have differential effects, depending on whether it is applied against a background of drowsiness, moderate arousal, or intense arousal. And in our discussion of transmarginal inhibition, we have seen that under high-intensity stimulation there may be no observable effect and the organism may appear impervious to stimulation, if it is already at a very high resting level.

However, the account depicted in Figure 20-2 neglects temporal effects. One factor that psychophysiologists can typically guarantee to emerge in an analysis of variance is *time*. In certain tasks, such as vigilance, a decrement in arousal over time has been predicted, but in other contexts predictions about temporal changes are not part and parcel of the key hypothesis and can become neglected in the design and analysis of the experiment. However, subjects are typically exposed to new tasks, and the establishment of task mastery and the skill that comes with practice both have implications for arousal–performance relations. Established responses can benefit from higher levels of arousal; new responses need lower levels of arousal to facilitate their emission. Under the Hull–Spence drive model, established responses are higher-probability responses, which therefore occur more rapidly under conditions of high drive. Thus, depending on the task, performance might remain steady, improve,

or deteriorate over time; such effects, if collapsed by ignoring time in the analysis, can yield null effects and Type II error. As Labuc (1975) points out, possible outcomes, given two personality groups, two tasks, two stressors at only one level of intensity, and just two time periods, number 54. However, complexity does not end there. A recent paper by Revelle, Anderson, and Humphreys (1983) makes a number of penetrating observations:

1. Authors rarely sample all the possibilities in a factorial design and tend to claim ante hoc ordering of conditions, whereas they are more likely to be imposing a post hoc grouping or ordering of data. Ordering of conditions is, of course, crucial to the inverted-U hypothesis. A 2×2 design allows 24 possible orderings, 12 of which will allow for partial orderings of length 3 to be satisfied by chance! In a $2 \times 2 \times 2$ design there are 8 ways to order the cells (40,320), and 2880 ways compatible with the assumptions of a curvilinear relationship between performance and the sum of the three factors in the design. And note that Revelle *et al.* (1983) are talking of gross terminal scores and not time-dependent factors, which for a simple early–late dichotomy would yield 16 orderings.

2. In their own empirical studies, in which stressors are combined in additive rather than factorial designs, Revelle *et al.*'s findings are compatible with more than one underlying source of motivation. In studies that include extraversion, time pressure, caffeine, and time of day as key variables, they suggest that arousal, fatigue, and effort may have different effects, depending upon the task. For example, attentional and memory tasks are differentially affected by arousal (see Folkard & Monk, 1983).

3. Crossover effects in personality–arousal relations can make interpretations of findings really difficult. For example, their high-impulsive subjects were less aroused than low-impulsive subjects in morning tests, but more aroused in the evening.

4. In addition, if dichotomized personality groups are claimed to have different *optimal* levels of arousal as well as different *basal* levels, then any test of, say, Eysenck's theory can seem virtually impossible.

5. Reports of complex findings typically call upon additional and untested assumptions to cover all the data. This is necessary because insufficient attention has been paid to careful parametric work; for example, Easterbrook's (1959) cue utilization hypothesis can be superimposed on data post hoc, in the absence of separate studies that identify which cues are salient under what conditions for the particular task in question. A very useful aspect of Revelle *et al.*'s (1983) paper is that they test a number of their theories against their data (transmarginal inhibition, response competition, response criterion, cue utilization, their

two-component model), discarding some and supporting others. Such a systematic approach is most welcome in this field.

In concluding this brief discussion, we wish to make two points: (1) Given the complexity described, it is conceivable that researchers in this field could generate a host of apparently discrepant and irreconcilable data; some would argue that this is the present state of the art. (2) However, the difficulties identified above imply that, in principle, given the appropriate preparation for experimental studies, coherent data could in fact emerge. The identification of problems marks the halfway point to their solution.

An Arousal Model for the Laboratory

We have considered above the difficulties associated with temporal effects. But time in itself is not of interest—rather, the processes that occur over time are important. It is our view that there is a *prima facie* case for shifts in arousal as the experiment progresses; that is to say, there are arousal characteristics of the experiment per se, and these will interact with the specific hypotheses under test. We should remember that the experiment is not exactly a slice taken from life, but a set of social conventions enacted in a special social situation. Gale (1977) sets out the framework for a model that plots the course of arousal throughout the experiment: The subject is recruited, makes an appointment, arrives at the laboratory, is prepared for experimentation, receives instruction, undergoes the formal experimental procedure, learns new tricks, receives feedback on his or her performance, and evaluates himself or herself; the experience is then over. This sequence is pretty universal to the business of experimental psychology. Sampling of the subjects' physiological state should occur at the appropriate time or times; otherwise, the experimenters will be sampling one thing when they believe they are sampling another. If psychophysiological variables are worthwhile and are sensitive to psychological factors of significance for behavior, then they should be sensitive to the variations induced by laboratory attendance (Gale & Baker, 1981). The present discussion is, therefore, an investigation of the microstructure of the psychology experiment. Hitherto, researchers have engaged in post hoc attempts at resolving complexities within their data; given a formal framework, a model for the experiment, such interpretations may be made ante hoc and in a coherent fashion.

Our model of arousal within the laboratory has nine components: stable characteristics of the subject, cyclic rhythms, manner of recruitment, laboratory encounter, task acquisition, task mastery, task-specific arousal, situational arousal, and feedback. Note that some of these sources of arousal are in existence independent of the experiment, while some

are induced by the experiment; some persist throughout, while some appear and then are dissipated. In most psychophysiological studies, only two stages are referred to: the pretask "rest" and the task proper.

As Gale and Baker (1981) argue, the term "rest" is a misnomer that reflects the self-deception of the experimenter rather than the true state of the subject. It seems to be based upon the bizarre assumption that the longer a subject waits for the unpleasant to happen, the more relaxed he or she will feel. Even if physiological state variables are seen to subside and become less irregular during such a period, that is no guarantee either that the subject feels more relaxed or that subsequent stimulation will be interpreted in a relaxed fashion. Gale and Baker (1981) consider the various sources of arousal and the evidence for their existence. Because they treat the psychology experiment as a special social-psychological event, they are able to call upon social-psychological theories to give an account of the elements within the model. For the purposes of the present discussion, the following points are pertinent:

1. If the nine components of arousal within the laboratory are separable conceptually, it is nevertheless difficult to distinguish them empirically.
2. The components are not truly independent, and earlier aspects will have temporal and dynamic effects on later aspects (indeed, that is often the focus of the research).
3. Each source of arousal will have a threshold, rise time, peak amplitude, and recovery period, and may have overshoot to maintain homeostasis. Thus, tests focused on later stages need to acknowledge the state of the subject vis-à-vis earlier stages. For example, responses to a laboratory encounter not only might be determined by stable characteristics of the subject, but might in themselves determine the level of arousal during task mastery. This will certainly be so if responses associated with encounter have not been allowed to subside before the task is presented. The problem, therefore, is that samples derived from different subjects at even the same point in time of the procedure might be tapping different arousal sources; yet, on the other hand, a fixed and predetermined sampling schedule is often recommended.
4. Our model of laboratory arousal needs to be tested in its own right. In terms of psychophysiological research into individual differences, such a program of work is surely essential. The burgeoning literature on experimenter effects has rather passed by the psychophysiological researchers in this field, with their focus upon stable trait characteristics rather than states, situations, and their interaction with traits. One way out of this dilemma may be to shift psychophysiological research into indi-

vidual differences out of the special environment of the laboratory and into the field (e.g., Crits-Christoph & Schwartz, 1983; Turpin, 1983), but such naturalistic work itself creates new problems.

Summary

1. The concept of arousal is in need of a thoroughly conceptual analysis.
2. The concept is still alive and kicking, and should not be dismissed in the absence of appropriate tests.
3. Testing predictions in relation to arousal is a difficult business and involves complex designs.
4. Where tasks and conditions are combined, there must be antecedent parametric testing of the tasks and conditions in their own right.
5. One can conceive of the psychology experiment as a situation in which systematic and predictable changes in arousal occur in a serial fashion.
6. Research into the psychophysiology of individual differences must of necessity make use of the concept, but it must not abuse it.

The various issues we have raised, together with a comprehensive evaluation of the research literature, are reviewed by M. W. Eysenck (1982).

SEVEN DEADLY SINS: A SUMMARY OF OUR CRITICISMS

Throughout this review, we have been repetitive in identifying faults in previous research. In the following discussion, we point to seven areas of grave concern that cut across most of the topics reviewed. Our taxonomy of "deadly sins" is rather informal and is not based on a principal-components analysis of published work! Moreover, the sins we specify are not independent, for decisions in one domain influence decisions elsewhere. Some of the errors are purely technical; that is to say, they relate to equipment, computer packages, and psychometric and statistical procedures that are already available and waiting to be used. The second category, and this includes the more important sins, calls for a complete change of direction and purpose in research. Unfortunately, it is more than likely that changes will occur in the former rather than the latter, particularly since developments in technique can be used as a displacement activity to protect the individual from the harsh realities that a change of direction imposes. People build up their research lives and careers around a paradigm; to let go of the paradigm is to let go of a part of oneself.

Our deadly sins are as follows: theoretical simplemindedness; an obsession with correlation rather than process; poor psychometrics; poor physiology; trivial experimentation; procedural insensitivity; and, finally, low-level data handling and data interpretation. In each case we merely list the faults identified; the reader will have met with sufficient examples of each fault within the body of the review.

Sin Number 1: Theoretical Simplemindedness

1. Most theorists fail to set their view of individual differences within the framework of a *general theory* of behavior (i.e., about how and why people do the things they do); thus they aspire to attribute large proportions of variance to only one or two elementary constructs.
2. Other theories, even within the restricted domain of individual differences, are neglected, even when they have close identity with the preferred construct; thus many theories remain within an illusory vacuum, failing to acknowledge other constructs that affect the individual's behavior or the results of experiments. People seem to treasure their own favorite construct and stick to it.
3. The majority of personality constructs remain at a vernacular, person-in-the-street level and are not elaborated into full-fledged theory.
4. Few theories specify the rules that govern the relationships between or among key constructs; thus one cannot determine the relative importance or influence of particular factors on particular occasions.
5. The specification for operationalizing constructs to enable empirical observations is typically poor.
6. Some experimentalists set up experiments that the theory in question cannot generate, merely on the basis of surface similarities between or among ill-defined constructs.
7. Most theorists fail to recognize the operational distance between psychometric and physiological modes of measurement, and few, in devising experiments, have really attempted to close the gap; thus experiments do not even reflect the content of questionnaire test items.
8. Such vagueness ensures that contradictory predictions can be made regarding the same or similar constructs when tested in almost identical situations.
9. Some experimentalists pay no attention to theory at all and adopt a dustbowl empiricist approach, failing to recognize that "facts" in science are socially defined and cannot be truly independent of the methods and procedures employed.
10. Most theories are so strong in their positivistic and biological orientation that they neglect the possibility that individuals will develop strategies to compensate for biologically imposed characteristics and/or *consciously* shape both their

own behavior and their physiological responses. Yet this is an abuse of biology, which sees organisms adapting to their ecology and attributes the flexibility of the nervous system to this requirement.

11. Most theories, therefore, neglect the possibility that the way the subject will respond to the laboratory will be affected by a *number* of factors, not least of which will be the very variable under study. Such variables may well affect the way in which the subject interprets and copes with the demands made upon him or her by the experimenter; there is no such thing as a passive subject.

12. As a consequence, no theory has seen the necessity to construct a model of the special world of the psychophysiology experiment, within which special, tailor-made predictions need to be prepared.

13. In the face of the complexity of this order, and in search for epistemological security, some theorists slip back to the alleged comfort of animal experimentation. But such a desire to abide by Occam's razor may well be totally misleading, for animal work may have little to tell us about human experience and behavior.

If this long list of indictments is justified, is it any wonder that some authorities have claimed individual difference findings in psychophysiology to be will-o-the-wisps, or that correlations, when derived, rarely account for more than 10% of the variance observed?

Sin Number 2: The Obsession with Correlation and Not Process

This sin is really a direct consequence of Sin No. 1, but it is a sin worthy of mention in its own right.

1. Theorists slide through the sequence: genotype to phenotype to trait to behavior. Thus, genotype is seen to *determine* behavior to a large degree.

2. Developmental experiences, life adaptations, conscious reflection, and voluntary self-imposed change are ignored, because they seem to be at variance with a positivistic view.

3. Physiological characteristics are seen as phenotypic markers that identify the genotypic origins of behavior.

4. The notion that traits are in effect dispositions to behave in particular ways in particular situations, or that they might interact with other dispositions to complex ways, is eschewed.

5. Thus, the influence of environments in which the person finds himself or herself, including the environment constructed within the experimental laboratory, is not taken into account. No wonder,

therefore, that two sorts of propositions are tested: (a) Does variable X (trait) correlate with variable Y (physiological index), or (b) do subjects dichotomized for X score differ also on Y score?

6. Even where theories do focus on *process*, the experiments employed are cast in the correlational mold. This is not to say that correlation and factor analysis are not useful; they constitute powerful ways for making sense of certain types of data. But their limitations should be recognized and a rapprochement should be created with conventional experimental designs.

7. Because experimenters have prior expectations, correlations are typically interpreted in a unidirectional manner; the possibility that the Y variable is primary, or that a third variable (as yet unidentified) accounts for the common variance in X and Y, is typically neglected.

The adherence to correlation and the reluctance to shift to process-oriented research constitute the major hurdles to be overcome for the next epoch of psychophysiological studies of individual differences to begin.

Sin Number 3: Poor Psychometrics

1. Many personality scales are used that lack adequate reliability or construct validity.

2. Many authors fail to grasp the factor structure upon which assertions about constructs are based, or to acknowledge the possibility of other factor solutions to the same data. Often greater robustness is alleged in the factor structure than is warranted.

3. Some constructs are aggregated mathematical solutions, drawing together other constructs that (a) theoretically should be tested for separately; (b) can generate opposite predictions in some situations; (c) may be differentially sensitive to physiological discriminations; or (d) may be bland in effect vis-à-vis other constructs with which they are combined, and thus may mask true effects arising from such constructs by inflating the error term.

4. Most authors fail to test their own individual difference variables against other established variables; thus it is not clear how much common variance holds, or indeed whether other constructs are more fundamental and contain the construct in question as a special case.

5. Reliability for a standardizing population does not guarantee reliability for a small test population, and repeated measurement is essential.

6. Classical psychometricians call for many more subjects (200+) and many more measures than

the psychophysiological studies typically employ, if the aim is to determine the factor structure and interrelationships that hold for the population in question.

7. In such studies, both *subjects* and *measures* should be factored.

8. Apart from using personality questionnaires, researchers often use unvalidated scales of ad hoc construction to measure state variables and/or response to the experiment, rather than develop the scales following appropriate psychometric principles.

9. Sometimes people use scales or subscales developed for other purposes, without realizing that off-the-rack clothing rarely fits perfectly.

10. Scales alleging to measure the same construct do not necessarily interrelate well; thus there is an implication that (a) they are not measuring the same thing, and/or (b) their interrelationships should be explored *before* engaging in laboratory studies that involve their use.

Since the key strategy appears to be to correlate one variable or set of variables with another set, it is surely wise to ensure that the best possible groundwork is carried out in each domain separately, *before* the two domains are brought together.

Sin Number 4: Poor Physiology

Comparison of the issues raised elsewhere in this volume with the technical practices reported in the present chapter reveals the degree to which physiological measurement needs to be improved in individual differences research. Among the points we have raised are the following:

1. Neglect of the possibility of individual response stereotypy, thus raising the probability of Type II error by employing only one physiological index.

2. Failure to follow accepted practices in measuring and scoring.

3. Within even one measure (e.g., EDA, EEG), limiting measurement to single aspects without a clear rationale for so doing.

4. Using different aspects of the same measure on the false assumption that they intercorrelate.

5. Even when multiple measures are used, failing to include them within one statistical treatment.

6. Failing to appreciate that different physiological systems or aspects within systems may relate to different aspects of stimulation.

7. Assuming that a particular measure is reliable and failing to retest the same population on different occasions.

8. The almost total absence of longitudinal studies.

9. Failure to consider the effects of range and the law of initial values.

10. Selection of the physiological measure employed more as a reflection of what is available than what theory dictates; a good example is the use of HR to measure cognitive processes when measures of brain activity are available.

This list of defects has led to a state of affairs in which few comparisons can be drawn between studies, or between work carried out in different laboratories. Sins Nos. 3 and 4 may be dealt with by technical improvements in existing practice without implying a shift in overall approach. They require more sophistication in statistical treatment and in data handling than is evident in our review. At present, however, because of these failings, the correlational approach has not really had the full chance to prove itself. But a *process*-oriented approach will also need to presuppose an appropriate level of technical sophistication in the measurement of traits, states, and physiological responses, with the added dimension of time.

Sin Number 5: The Trivial Experiment

It follows from what we have said that a correlational approach will lead to simple experiments and a process-oriented approach to complex experiments. Our accusations of triviality are based on the following characteristics of tasks:

1. Many are nontasks (i.e., sitting doing nothing); we believe that human subjects in a laboratory do not do or think about nothing, and that experimenters who believe the opposite are misleading themselves.

2. Very few tasks seem to have a direct bearing on the theory in question.

3. Some tasks are devised ad hoc, lacking any parametric back-up describing the variables that influence task performance.

4. Some tasks are borrowed when their construct relationship to theory is minimal.

5. Trait statements are typically couched in terms of the person's interactions with the world, yet the tasks employed are rarely simulations of real-life events or situations and have little ecological validity. Unusual states are sampled and not everyday events. On reflection, some of the tasks employed seem simply absurd.

6. Most tasks are not reactive and do not allow the subject to reveal his or her strategies.

7. In spite of the wealth of experimentation in experimental and cognitive psychology, most paradigms in psychophysiology are home-grown. Psychophysiology lives in a vacuum.

8. It is assumed that the stimuli employed have the

same meaning for the subject as they do for the experimenter; yet the very constructs under consideration in individual differences imply that the person modulates inputs in the light of both biological predispositions and past experience.

9. Even when tasks involve measurement of performance, little attempt is made to relate performance to physiological change in a discrete manner.

10. Even simple experimental paradigms (e.g., the OR) are not as simple as personality workers contrive to believe, and have many alternative theories and data sets about them.

11. Finally, it is a remarkable observation to make, but many studies fail to make specific predictions!

Sin Number 6: Procedural Insensitivity

1. We have already referred to the need for the experimental psychologists to construct a psychological model of the psychology experiment, but no such model has yet emerged in the field reviewed.

2. We have also appealed for some recognition of the subject's phenomenology and the ways in which it might influence his or her response to the experiment; again, even in experiments related to such constructs as locus of control, which explicitly refer to the subject's view of his or her position in the world and control over events that affect him or her, no such model has emerged.

3. Such exhortations inevitably imply a temporal analysis of data, since the subject is seen as a person processing, evaluating, and coping with information.

4. Within our own model of laboratory-induced arousal, most theories of individual differences would imply differential responses of different personality dispositions to the laboratory set-up; again, such an extension of theory has not yet occurred.

5. A particular aspect of the psychophysiology laboratory is its fear-inducing properties for the newcomer. Appropriate precautions in the design of laboratories and in the experimenter's demeanor are essential. Repeated attendance will probably reveal a strong effect for number of visits as the subject adapts to aspects of the laboratory. Yet the majority of studies involve only one attendance, and even when multiple attendances are involved, we have seen that there is controversy as to whether certain effects will develop over time or dissipate over time.

6. Most studies ignore the literature on experimenter expectancy effects and experimenter–subject interactions and fail to use double-blind procedures, multiple experimenters (balanced for sex and personality), or retest methods for partitioning true subject variance.

7. In many studies, focal stimulation can occupy some 10% or less of total experimental time. This leaves the subject free from experimenter control and creates ideal conditions for uncontrolled and inflated error variance.

Experimentation is an art as well as a science, and it is not clear what makes a person a good experimenter. Good experimenters in this field will surely expose themselves to the procedures they impose upon their subjects. They will not seek to deceive themselves into thinking that either they or their subjects are stimulus–response lumps in the laboratory, rather than rational and reflective people in the outside world. An experiment needs to be a proper simulation of real-life experience and at least to have face validity for subjects to take it seriously and to cooperate enthusiastically.

Sin Number 7: Low-Level Data Handling and Interpretation

1. One-shot studies are typical; programmatic and parametric series are extremely rare.

2. Subject populations are typically too small to ensure reliability or robustness of findings.

3. Data from different laboratories are rarely comparable.

4. Extreme-group designs sample only some of the distribution, waste available information, and cannot warrant assertions about general relationships between variables (e.g., whether they are linear, monotonic, or curvilinear).

5. Balanced designs are subject to asymmetrical transfer effects, particularly when (a) changes occur *merely* as a result of passing through the laboratory procedure per se, (b) process is under investigation, and (c) subjects are thought to develop or deploy strategies.

6. Communality of physiological response does not imply communality of psychological response, and vice versa.

7. Similar terminal or gross scores could mask strong differences in the processes employed to yield such scores.

8. Relationships among the dependent variables in question (physiology, behavior, and subjective experience) can be parallel, independent, or reciprocal and complementary, and these relationships can vary within an experimental population.

9. Results from single-condition studies do not

allow the level of interpretation yielded by multifactor, multilevel studies.

10. Post hoc rationalization of data calls for follow-up studies to test the legitimacy and status of such new hypotheses.

11. Care is needed in the interpretation of crossover effects and ratio changes; significant shifts in one variable alone can induce such effects, and they need not imply shifts in both variables.

12. Effects cannot be attributed to one variable alone when there is a *prima facie* possibility that related variables might be involved, and this possibility has not yet been systematically excluded.

13. It is tempting to suggest that subjects' defense mechanisms enable them to anticipte and negate the experimenter's predictions; such a possibility is feasible and certainly not logically excluded, but only systematic study will allow such conclusions.

14. There is a danger that *any* outcome can be explained, given the appropriate seesaw constructs.

15. Sex differences can be strong sources of variation; yet they are typically neglected in basic theory construction, in the design of experiments, and in the interpretation of results.

16. Negative findings are of heuristic value and should not be discarded. In some circumstances, they are more powerful in their bearing on theory than are supportive or corroborative findings, particularly when they emerge from well-designed and theoretically derived experiments.

In concluding the case for the prosecution, we must point to a paradox. Human experience and behavior are complex, and their interrelationships with each other and with physiological events raise issues central to the whole of psychology. Yet psychophysiologists, of their own will, have chosen to deal with all three domains in spite of their complexity. If psychophysiological variables are worth studying, they must surely *reflect* the complexity of experience and behavior; otherwise they will not be sufficiently discriminating or up to the task that we set them. For example, if the EEG reflects brain processes, then it is highly unlikely that different channels of recording will interrelate in a simple fashion. Different brain areas might intercorrelate positively, negatively, or not at all, and the size of the correlation will vary from area to area, depending on the nature of the material to be processed and the strategies deployed to process it. If we add to this complexity the notion of variation among brains, the researcher must both devise adequate means of describing nature *and* tolerate the apparent confusion that nature offers. In such circumstances, very straightforward findings are hardly worth the polygraph paper they are written on.

GROWTH POINTS FOR THE FUTURE

Our review of selected topics in the psychophysiology of individual differences has revealed a *prima facie* case for the existence of biological factors that account for a significant proportion of the variance in individual behaviors. Our particular criticisms of the field amount to the accusation that such factors have not been identified in a compelling or unequivocal fashion. Weaknesses of both theory and method have become absorbed into the history of the subject, and it has proved difficult for individual researchers to escape from established tradition.

Three separable but not idependent lines of inquiry are open: (1) large-scale programmatic, multivariate studies designed to capture the full factor structure within the parent population; (2) small-scale, systematic, and repeated-measures designs, with multiple attendances by subjects, and incorporating physiological, performance, and experiential data within a process-oriented framework; and (3) studies that take individual differences in physiological parameters as independent variables, to predict variations in performance as the dependent variables.

The first strategy is recommended by O'Gorman (1977) and will, in practice, involve a persistent and continued research effort, requiring a high resource element. Since it would take a long time to complete, it is incompatible with the development of individual research careers, which depend upon regular and frequent publication. The second strategy is preferred by us, although we consider its implementation to be dependent upon progress with the first strategy. Having established the relationships that hold within the factor structure in *correlational* terms, one needs then to explore the processes and dynamics that operate to *integrate* the factors in the context of behavior proper. The first strategy benefits from the traditions of psychometrics, and the second from the traditions of experimental psychology. The third strategy (recommended by O'Gorman, 1983) suffers from its emphasis on pragmatic empiricism and its isolation from well-developed theory. It amounts to a "Let's try it and see what happens if . . ." approach to science, which may be appropriate at some stages of development within a subdiscipline, but which is not appropriate any longer in the present field. Individual differences research should not take place within a theoretical vacuum. But the absence of a *general* theory of behavior in contemporary psychology makes it very difficult to assign weightings to *any* variable, or to determine its overall significance within the flux of behavior. The psychological meaning of a variable cannot be assessed in isolation from the other variables with which it interacts or upon which it is dependent. Just as there are minitheories in individual differences research, so are there minitheories in psychology at large; thus it is perhaps unfair to demand integration of the individual differences researcher.

We have omitted in this chapter consideration of important and salient research where recent comprehensive reviews exist (e.g., extraversion–introversion and peripheral measures, Stelmack, 1981, Geen, 1983; genetic factors, Eaves & Young, 1981, Fulker, 1981, and Roubertoux, 1985; conditioning, Levey & Martin, 1981,) or where the faults we have identified in relation to other topics apply with equal force (e.g., Type A–Type B behavior, impulsivity, field dependence–independence, achievement motivation).

We conclude with some examples from the contemporary literature that, we believe, exemplify positive new approaches to this important field. Not all the studies mentioned have been concerned with personality. Nor do they all include psychophysiological measurements. In this latter case, we believe that their combination with physiological measurement would yield nonredundant information.

Some Examples of Work That Could Serve to Shift the Paradigm

In the following brief accounts of recent studies, we identify potential growth points for individual differences research from which we have extracted relevant features. Those positive characteristics that we hope may be incorporated into future research are given in italics and parentheses following each account. The reader is advised to consult the original papers for full details.

Interactions in Families and Marital Dyads

Minuchin (1974) reported differential changes in free fatty acids in family members following changes in communication patterns induced by therapy. Minuchin imposed a general systems theory approach upon family life, in which family subsystems are organized in a hierarchical structure and in which conflict is transferred from subsystems in conflict onto vulnerable individuals. Thus, individuals are described both in terms of individual attributes and in terms of the social network to which they belong. Psychophysiological measures could enable partitioning variance attributable to person–situation interaction, showing group and individual change as a function of context.

More systematic studies of interaction in marital dyads have been reported by R. W. Levenson and Gottman (1983). Here, measures of the *interaction* between the physiological systems of husband and wife and the extent to which they were locked *in phase* during neutral and conflict discussions predicted independent personal ratings of marital satisfaction. Measures of linkage alone accounted for more than 60% of the variance, and Levenson and Gottman

claim to have accounted for some 80% of the total variance by a combination of their measures. *Individual* physiological change and/or ratings of experienced emotion yielded the usual low correlations, in the region of .40. (*Ecological validity; meaning of context imposed by subjects and not experimenters; process emphasized; integration of behavioral and physiological data; partitioning of individual and interactional effects.*)

Sensation Seeking in Mixed Personality Groups

Hockey (1985) reports an elegant study in which introverts and extraverts were yoked together in various combinations, with control over the level of ambient stimulation assigned to one or another of the personality groups. Physiological measurement in such contexts could allow for independent estimates of preferred level of stimulation, response to change, tolerance of change, and level of intolerance, as measured over time. (*Group behavior; factorial design; sampling of inverted-U curve; changes over time; variation in individual and group thresholds for stimulation with and without control.*)

Type A and Type B Behavior

Research on the so-called "Type A" and "Type B" personalities suffers from many of the faults identified in our review. However, because of the interest in the prediction of serious cardiovascular illness, there is an incentive to conduct rigorously controlled studies. A recent National Institute of Mental Health (NIMH) special panel identified the development of adequate assessment procedures, proper control groups, and medically meaningful therapeutic interventions as desirable goals. Such constraints, which will influence the funding of research, could have beneficial effects on quality. Laboratory and field studies have identified differential response to situational variables *within* Type A subjects, thus creating data for a process-oriented model, including variables arising from cognitive appraisal (see Dembroski & MacDougall, 1982). In recognition of the multivariate nature of emotional expression, these studies promise to integrate task behavior, style of response, and physiological change, together with the notion of *compensatory* actions—for example, somatic responses that modulate ANS activation (see Herd, 1978; Williams, 1978). (*Integration of physiology, behavior, and cognition; task variation; identification of vulnerability factors, process measures, feedback, and compensation mechanisms.*)

Factorial Study of EEG and Performance Relations

Bodunov (1985) reported a major study in which both topographical data for the EEG and objective measures of persistence and sustained attention were subjected to factor analysis. The factors that emerged were then shown to have differential loadings for three discriminable subject groups. The data are interpreted within the framework of a general cybernetic model involving action, rhythm of response, and feedback. This is an unusual example of systematic treatment of *both* EEG and behaviorial domains. (*Multichannel recording; factor structure of objective tests; repeated measures; integrative theory.*)

Simulations of Real-Life Contexts

Schönpflug and Mundelein (1985) set up a simulation of an insurance office and used unemployed clerks as subjects, over extended periods of experimental trials. Subjects were required to work through insurance claims from clients. Data were obtained from the subject's work behavior, including routines, rest activity, and response to simulated stressors (pacing, breakdown of equipment, competition for computer time, etc.). Physiological data were obtained throughout, and subjects completed a battery of personality inventories. A study of Nosal (1985) monitored "style of action" in undergraduate chemists learning computer programming. As in the Schönpflug and Mundelein studies, subject responses were stored by the computer. Data were available not only for personality and intelligence test scores, but for perseverance, checking behavior, identification of errors, and debugging. Multivariate analysis of complex performance measures enabled partitioning of various personality factors. No physiological monitoring was included in the Nosal study. (*Simulation under controlled conditions; process; interactions between physiological state and performance variables; contexts meaningful to subjects; multivariate analysis.*)

Smoking and Personality

A series of studies by O'Connor has explored the adaptive aspects of smoking in relation to topographical changes in the ERP (e.g., O'Connor, 1980, 1982). Repeated measurements were taken from a small group of introvert and extravert smokers under conditions of cigarette smoking and sham smoking during RT and signal detection tasks. O'Connor demonstrates how extraverts and introverts use smoking and smoking acts in different ways in order to perform attentional tasks. Extraverts, he claims, smoke for the pharmacological effects, smoking aggressively to access the nicotine; introverts, on the other hand, smoke in a more integrated and smooth fashion, using the routine of smoking and associated sensory–motor behaviors to calm themselves. (*Repeated measures; topographical analysis; changes over time; process; signal detection analysis; model of attention; behavior (smoking) derived from subjects' normal repertoire of coping strategies.*)

Developmental Studies

It is hoped that discriminant analysis of physiological and other data derived in early childhood will enable the detection of individuals at risk for psychiatric disorder later in life. Recent studies within the general population also promise prediction of individual variations in behavior on the basis of physiological estimators. In a study of a wide range of behaviors, Torgersen (1985) has explored heritable and environment-induced behaviors in monozygotic and dizygotic twins at birth, 6 months of age, and 6 years of age. She employed a rigorous procedure for ensuring observer reliability. No physiological data were obtained. However, Torgersen has been able to pinpoint causal relations within the developmental process, showing the extent to which individual variables or clusters of behaviors (e.g., "the difficult child syndrome") are attributable to heredity, environment, or heredity–environment interactions. Kagan (1982, 1983) has described data in which measures of HR amplitude and variability were related to approach-avoidance behavior in nursery-age children, and has provided estimates of predictive power for HR upon target social behaviors in the first few years of life. (*Prediction of behavior from physiology; process variables; partitioning of heritability and interactive effects*).

GENERAL CONCLUSION

The psychophysiology of individual differences offers a set of very rich questions and a promise of a coherent body of integrative research. Unfortunately, there are, as yet, few acceptable answers to those questions, and the research is fragmented and lacking in integration. Researchers continue to work in isolation from one another and from mainstream experimental psychology. In this review, we have been very severe in our criticisms, just because we wish to see the promise fully realized. If we draw together the theories that exist in what we have called a "patchwork theory" (Gale & Edwards, 1983b), then the following components must be incorporated into any psychophysiological theory of individual differences: sensory preparedness, motor preparedness, modulation of input, cognitive evaluation of information, action upon and feedback from the environment, motivational systems encompassing approach and avoidance, and energy transmission. These are the components that existing theories require as a minimum condition for an integrative theory. Their combination in theory, experimental procedures, and the interpretation of data will, in our view, require a major change in research strategy. Even so, the satisfaction of such a program will constitute only a start along a highway that stretches into the distance. The full story will only be told when it is possible to integrate data on the psychophysiology of individual differences within a general theory of individual and social behavior.

REFERENCES

Abramson, L. Y., Alloy, L. B., & Rosoff, R. Depression and the generation of complex hypotheses in the judgment of contingency. *Behaviour Research and Therapy*, 1981, 19, 35–45.

Alloy, L. B., & Abramson, L. Y. Judgment of contingency in depressed and nondepressed students: Sadder but wiser? *Journal of Experimental Psychology: General*, 1979, 108, 441–485.

Anastasi, A. Heredity, environment, and the question "How?" *Psychological Review*, 1958, 65, 197–208.

Andreassi, J. L. *Psychophysiology: Human behavior and physiological response.* New York: Oxford University Press, 1980.

Averill, J. R. Personal control over aversive stimuli and its relationship to stress. *Psychological Bulletin*, 1973, 80, 286–303.

Baker, S. M. *Social facilitation, coaction and performance.* Unpublished doctoral dissertation, University of Wales, 1978.

Barry, W. M., & Ertl, J. P. Brain waves and human intelligence. In F. B. Davis (Ed.), *Modern educational developments: Another look.* New York: Educational Record Bureau, 1966.

Becker-Carus, C. H. Relationships between EEG, personality and vigilance. *Electroencephalography and Clinical Neurophysiology*, 1971, 30, 519–526.

Bennett, W. F. Human perception: A network theory approach. *Nature*, 1968, 220, 1147–1148.

Berlyne, D. E. *Conflict, arousal and curiosity.* New York: McGraw-Hill, 1960.

Bernstein, A. S. The orienting response as novelty and significance detector: Reply to O'Gorman. *Psychophysiology*, 1979, 16, 263–273.

Berrgren, T., Öhman, A. & Frederikson, M. Locus of control and habituation of the electrodermal orienting response to nonsignal and signal stimuli. *Journal of Personality and Social Psychology*, 1977, 35, 708–716.

Blankstein, K. R., & Egner, K. Relationship of the locus of control construct to the self-control of heart rate. *Journal of General Psychology*, 1977, 97, 291–306.

Blinkhorn, S. F., & Hendrickson, D. E. Averaged evoked responses and psychometric intelligence. *Nature*, 1982, 295, 596–597.

Bodunov, M. V. Typology of mental activity as a temperamental trait and the level of activation of the nervous system. In J. Strelau, F. Farley, & A. Gale (Eds.), *The biological bases of personality and behavior. Volume II. Psychophysiology, performance and applications.* New York: Hemisphere, 1985.

Bowers, K. S. Pain, anxiety and perceived control. *Journal of Consulting and Clinical Psychology*, 1968, 32, 596–602.

Broadhurst, A., & Glass, A. Relationship of personality measures to the alpha rhythm of the electroencephalogram. *British Journal of Psychiatry*, 1969, 115, 199–204.

Brown, B. B., & Klug, J. W. (Eds.). *The alpha syllabus: A handbook of human EEG alpha activity.* Springfield, Ill.: Charles C. Thomas, 1974.

Buchsbaum, M. S., Haier, R. J., & Johnson, J. Augmenting and reducing: individual differences in evoked potentials. In A. Gale & J. Edwards (Eds.), *Physiological correlates of human behaviour Volume 3, Individual differences and psychopathology.* London: Academic Press, 1983.

Buchsbaum, M. S., & Pfefferbaum, A. Individual differences in stimulus-intensity response. *Psychophysiology*, 1971, 8, 600–611.

Buchsbaum, M. S., & Silverman, J. Stimulus intensity control and the cortical evoked response. *Psychosomatic Medicine*, 1968, 30, 12–22.

Bull, R., & Gale, A. Does the law of initial values hold for G.S.R.'s? *Biological Psychology*, 1974, 1, 213–227.

Butcher, H. J. *Human intelligence: Its nature and assessment.* London: Methuen, 1968.

Callaway, E. Correlations between average evoked potentials and measures of intelligence. *Archives of General Psychiatry*, 1973, 29, 553–558.

Callaway, E. *Brain electrical potentials and individual psychological differences.* New York: Grune & Stratton, 1975.

Carlier, M. Factor analysis of Strelau's questionnaire and an attempt to validate some of the factors. In J. Strelau, F. Farley, & A. Gale (Eds.), *The biological bases of personality and behavior. Volume I. Theories, measurement techniques and development.* New York: Hemisphere, 1985.

Carrol, E. N., Zuckerman, M., & Vogel, W. H. A test of the optimal level of arousal theory of sensation seeking. *Journal of Personality and Social Psychology*, 1982, 42, 572–575.

Chalke, F. C. R., & Ertl, J. P. Evoked potentials and intelligence. *Life Sciences*, 1965, 4, 1319–1322.

Claridge, G. S., & Herrington, R. N. An EEG correlate of the Archimedes spiral after-effect and its relationship with personality. *Behavior Research and Therapy*, 1963, 1, 217–229.

Clarke, A. M., & Clarke, A. D. B. *Early experience: Myth and evidence.* London: Open Books, 1976.

Coles, M. G. H., Gale, A., & Kline, P. Personality and habituation of the orienting reaction: Tonic and response measures of electrodermal activity. *Psychophysiology*, 1971, 8, 54–63.

Coursey, R. D., Buchsbaum, M. S., & Frankel, B. L. Personality measures and evoked responses in chronic insomniacs. *Journal of Abnormal Psychology*, 1975, 84, 239–249.

Cowles, M., & Davis, C. Eysenck's personality dimensions and the volunteering subject. *Proceedings of the annual conference of the British Psychological Society*, Swansea, Wales, 1985.

Cox, D. N. *Psychophysiological correlates of sensation seeking and socialization during reduced stimulation.* Unpublished doctoral dissertation, University of British Columbia, 1977.

Craig, K. D., & Best, J. A. Perceived control over pain: Individual differences and situational determinants. *Pain*, 1977, 3, 127–135.

Crits-Christoph, P., & Schwartz, G. E. Psychophysiological contributions to psychotherapy research: A systems perspective. In A. Gale & J. Edwards (Eds.), *Physiological correlates of human behaviour Volume 3, Individual differences and psychopathology.* London: Academic Press, 1983.

Daitzman, R. J., & Zuckerman, M. Disinhibitory sensation seeking, personality, and gonadal hormones. *Personality and Individual Differences*, 1980, 1, 103–110.

Davies, W. L., & Phares, E. J. Internal–external control as a determinant of information-seeking in a social influence situation. *Journal of Personality*, 1967, 35, 547–561.

Davis, F. B. The measurement of mental capability through evoked potential recording. *Educational Records Research Bulletin*, 1971, 1.

Deakin, J. F. W., & Exley, K. A. Personality and male–female influences on the EEG alpha rhythm. *Biological Psychology*, 1979, 8, 285–290.

DeGood, D. E. Cognitive control factors in vascular stress responses. *Psychophysiology*, 1975, 12, 399–401.

Dembroski, T. M., & MacDougall, J. M. Coronary-prone behavior, social pychophysiology, and coronary heart disease. In J. R. Eiser (Ed.), *Social psychology and behavioral medicine.* New York: Wiley, 1982.

Easterbrook, J. A. The effect of emotion on cue utilization and the organization of behavior. *Psychological Review*, 1959, 66, 183–201.

Eaves, L., & Young, P. A. Genetical theory and personality differences. In R. Lynn (Ed.). *Dimensions of personality: Papers in honour of H. J. Eysenck.* Oxford: Pergamon Press, 1981.

Eliasz, A. The basic functions of the mechanisms of temperament. In J. Strelau, F. Farley, & A. Gale (Eds.), *The biological bases of personality and behavior.* New York: Hemisphere, 1983.

Ellingson, R. J. Brain waves and problems of psychology. *Psychological Bulletin*, 1956, 53, 1–34.

Ellingson, R. J. Relationship between EEG and test intelligence: A commentary. *Psychological Bulletin*, 1966, 65, 91–98.

Endler, N. S., & Edwards, J. Stress and personality. In L Goldberger & S. Breznitz (Eds.), *Handbook of stress: theoretical and clinical aspects*, New York: Free Press, 1982.

Engel, R., & Henderson, N. B. Visual evoked responses and I.Q. scores at school age. *Developmental Medicine and Child Neurology*, 1973, 15, 136–145.

Ertl, J. P. *Neural efficiency and human intelligence (Final Report, U.S. Office of Education Project No. 9-0105)*. Washington, D. C.: U.S. Office of Education, 1969.

Ertl, J. P. Fourier analysis of evoked potentials and human intelligence. *Nature*, 1971, 230, 525–526.

Ertl, J. P., & Schafer, E. W. P. Brain response correlates of psychometric intelligence. *Nature*, 1969, 223, 421–422.

Everhart, J. D., China, C. L., & Auger, R. A. Measures of EEG and verbal intelligence: An inverse relationship. *Physiological Psychology*, 1974, 2, 374–378.

Eysenck, H. J. *The structure of human personality* (1st ed.). London: Methuen, 1953.

Eysenck, H. J. *The dynamics of anxiety and hysteria*. London: Routledge & Kegan Paul, 1957.

Eysenck, H. J. Conditioning, introversion–extraversion and the strength of the nervous system. *Proceedings of the 18th International Congress of Psychology* (Moscow), 1966, 9.

Eysenck, H. J. *The biological basis of personality*. Springfield, Ill.: Charles C. Thomas, 1967.

Eysenck, H. J. *The structure of human personality*. London: Methuen, 1970.

Eysenck, H. J. (Ed.). *The measurement of personality*. Lancaster, England: Medical & Technical Publishers, 1976.

Eysenck, H. J. Models of personality. In H. J. Eysenck (Ed.), *The measurement of personality*. Lancaster, England: Medical & Technical Publishers, 1976.

Eysenck, H. J. (Ed.). *A model for personality*. Berlin: Springer-Verlag, 1981.

Eysenck, H. J., & Eysenck, S. G. B. *Manual of the Eysenck Personality Inventory*. London: University of London Press, 1964.

Eysenck, H. J., & Eysenck, S. G. B. *Eysenck Personality Questionnaire*. San Diego: Educational and Industrial Testing Service, 1976. (a)

Eysenck, H. J., & Eysenck, S. G. B. *Psychoticism as a dimension of personality*. London: Hodder & Stoughton, 1976. (b)

Eysenck, H. J., & Kamin, L. *Intelligence: The battle for the mind*. Harmondsworth, England: Penguin Books, 1981.

Eysenck, H. J., & Rachman, S. *The causes and cures of neurosis*. London: Routledge & Kegan Paul, 1965.

Eysenck, H. J., & Wilson, G. D. *The experimental study of Freudian theories*. London: Methuen, 1973.

Eysenck, M. W. *Human memory: Theory, research, and individual differences*. London: Pergamon Press, 1977.

Eysenck, M. W. *Attention and arousal: Cognition and performance*, New York & Berlin: Springer-Verlag, 1982.

Feather, N. T. Some personality correlates of external control. *Australian Journal of Psychology*, 1967, 19, 253–260.

Feij, J. A., Orlebeke, J. F., Gazandam, A., & Van Zuïlen, R. Sensation seeking: Measurement and psychophysiological correlates. In J. Strelau, F. Farley, & A. Gale (Eds.), *The biological bases of personality and behavior. Volume I. Theories, measurement techniques, and development*. New York: Hemisphere, 1985.

Fenton, G. W., & Scotton, L. Personality and the alpha rhythm. *British Journal of Psychiatry*, 1967, 113, 1283–1289.

Folkard, S., & Monk, T. Chronopsychology: Circadian rhythms and human performance. In A. Gale & J. Edwards (Eds.), *Physiological correlates of human behaviour Volume 2, Attention and performance*. London: Academic Press, 1983.

Fotopoulos, S. Internal versus external control: Increase of heart

rate by thinking under feedback and no-feedback conditions. *Dissertation Abstracts International*, 1970, 31, 3703–3704.

Fowles, D. C. The three arousal model: Implications of Gray's two factor learning theory for heart rate, electrodermal activity, and psychopathy. *Psychophysiology*, 1980, 17, 87–104.

Fowles, D. C. Heart rate as an index of anxiety: Failure of a hypothesis. In J. T. Cacioppo & R. E. Petty (Eds.), *Perspectives in cardiovascular psychophysiology*. New York: Guilford Press, 1982.

Franks, C. M. Conditioning and personality: A study of normal and neurotic subjects. *Journal of Abnormal and Social Psychology*, 1956, 52, 143–150.

Fulker, D. W. The genetic and environmental architecture of psychoticism, extraversion and neuroticism. In H. J. Eysenck (Ed.), *A model for personality*. Berlin: Springer-Verlag, 1981.

Galbraith, G. C., Gliddon, J. B., & Busk, J. Visual evoked responses in mentally retarded and nonretarded subjects. *American Journal of Mental Deficiency*, 1970, 73, 341–348.

Gale, A. 'Stimulus hunger': Individual differences in operant strategy in a button pressing task. *Behaviour Research and Therapy*, 1969, 7, 265–274.

Gale, A. EEG and extraversion: effects of changes in EPI scores over time. Unpublished study, 1972.

Gale, A. The psychophysiology of individual differences: studies of extraversion and the EEG. In P. Kline (Ed.), *New approaches in psychological measurement*. London: Wiley, 1973.

Gale, A. Some EEG correlates of sustained attention. In R. R. Mackie (Ed.), *Vigilance: Theory, operational performance and physiological correlates*. New York: Plenum Press, 1977.

Gale, A. Naive parallelism: Simply synchronize several simultaneous models. In A. J. Chapman & D. M. Jones (Eds.), *Models of man*. Leicester, England: British Psychological Society, 1980.

Gale, A. EEG studies of extraversion–introversion: What's the next step? In R. Lynn (Ed.), *Dimensions of personality: Papers in honour of H. J. Eysenck*. Oxford: Pergamon Press, 1981.

Gale, A. Electroencephalographic correlates of extraversion–introversion. In R. Sinz & M. R. Rosenweig (Eds.), *Psychophysiology 1980: Memory, motivation and event related potentials in mental operations*. Amsterdam: Elsevier Biomedical Press, 1983. (a)

Gale, A. Electroencephalographic studies of extraversion–introversion: A case study in the psychophysiology of individual differences. *Personality and Individual Differences*, 1983, 4, 371–380. (b)

Gale, A. O'Gorman versus Gale: A reply. *Biological Psychology*, 1984, 19, 129–136.

Gale, A. & Baker, S. *In vivo* or *in vitro*?: Some effects of laboratory environments with particular reference to the psychophysiology experiment. In M. J. Christie & P. Mellett (Eds.), *Foundations of psychosomatics*. Chichester: Wiley, 1981.

Gale, A., Coles, M. G. H., & Blaydon, J. Extraversion–introversion and the EEG. *British Journal of Psychology*, 1969, 60, 209–223.

Gale, A., Coles, M., Kline, P., & Penfold, V. Extraversion–introversion, neuroticism and the EEG: Basal and response measures during habituation of the orienting response. *British Journal of Psychology*, 1971, 62, 533–548.

Gale, A., & Edwards, J. (Eds.). *Physiological correlates of human behavior* (3 vols). London: Academic Press, 1983. (a)

Gale, A., & Edwards, J. A short critique of the psychophysiology of individual differences. *Personality and Individual Differences*, 1983, 4, 429–435. (b)

Gale, A., Harpham, B., & Lucas, B. Time of day and the EEG: Some negative results. *Psychonomic Science*, 1972, 28, 269–271.

Gale, A., Morris, P. E., Lucas, B., & Richardson, A. Types of imagery and imagery types. *British Journal of Psychology*, 1972, 63, 523–531.

Gatchel, R. J. Change over training sessions of relationship between locus of control and voluntary heart-rate control. *Perceptual and Motor Skills*, 1975, 40, 424–426.

Geen, R. G. The psychophysiology of extraversion-introversion. In

J. Cacioppo & R. E. Petty (Eds.), *Social psychophysiology: A sourcebook.* New York: Guilford, 1983.

Giannitrapani, D. EEG average frequency and intelligence. *Electroencephalography and Clinical Neurophysiology,* 1969, 27, 480–486.

Gibbs, F. A., & Gibbs, F. L. Fourteen and six per second positive spikes. *Electroencephalography and Clinical Neurophysiology,* 1963, 15, 553–557.

Giesen, J. M., & McGlynn, F. D. Skin conductance and heart rate responsivity to public speaking imagery among students with high and low self-reported fear: A comparative analysis of response definitions. *Journal of Clinical Psychology,* 1977, 33, 68–76.

Gilliland, K. The Temperament Inventory: Relationship to theoretically similar Western personality dimensions and construct validity. In J. Strelau, F. Farley, & A. Gale (Eds.), *The biological bases of personality and behavior. Volume I. Theories, measurement techniques, and development.* New York: Hemisphere, 1985.

Gilliland, K., Andress, D., & Bracy, S. *Differences in EEG alpha index between extraverts and introverts.* Unpublished manuscript, 1981.

Glass, A., & Broadhurst, A. Relationship between EEG as a measure of cortical activity and personality measures. *Electroencephalography and Clinical Neurophysiology,* 1966, 21, 309.

Glass, D. C., & Singer, J. E. *Urban stress: Experiments in noise and social stressors.* New York: Academic Press, 1972.

Goesling, W. J., May, C., Lavond, D., Barnes, T., & Carreira, C. Relationship between interanal and external locus of control and the operant conditioning of alpha through biofeedback training. *Perceptual and Motor Skills,* 1974, 39, 1339–1343.

Gottlober, A. The relationship between brain potentials and personality. *Journal of Experimental Psychology,* 1938, 2, 67–74.

Gray, J. A. (Ed.). *Pavlov's typology.* New York: Macmillan, 1964.

Gray, J. A. Strength of the nervous system, introversion–extraversion, conditionability and arousal. *Behaviour Research and Therapy,* 1967, 5, 151–169.

Gray, J. A. A critique of Eysenck's theory of personality. In H. J. Eysenck (Ed.), *A model for personality.* Berlin: Springer-Verlag, 1981.

Gray, J. A. *The neuropsychology of anxiety: An enquiry into the functions of the septo-hippocampal system.* Oxford: Oxford University Press, 1982.

Gray, J. A. Anxiety, personality and the brain. In A. Gale & J. Edwards (Eds.), *Physiological correlates of human behaviour* (Vol. 3, *Individual differences and psychopathology*). London: Academic Press, 1983.

Groves , P. M., & Thompson, R. F. Habituation: A dual process theory. *Psychological Review,* 1970, 77, 419–450.

Gucker, D. K. Correlating visual evoked potentials with psychometric intelligence: Variation in technique. *Perceptual and Motor Skills,* 1973, 37, 189–190.

Guilford, J. P. *The nature of human intelligence.* New York: McGraw-Hill, 1967.

Guilford, J. P. Will the real factor of extraversion–introversion please stand up?: A reply to Eysenck. *Psychological Bulletin,* 1977, 84, 412–416.

Hall, C. S., & Lindzey, G. *Theories of personality.* New York: Wiley, 1957.

Hall, C. S., & Lindzey, G. *Theories of personality.* (2nd ed.). New York: Wiley, 1970.

Hall, R. A., Rappaport, M., Hopkins, H. K., Griffin, R. B., & Silverman, J. Evoked response and behavior in cats. *Science,* 1970, 170, 998–1000.

Hebb, D. O. Drives and the C.N.S. (conceptual nervous system). *Psychological Review,* 1955, 55, 243–254.

Hendrickson, D. E. *An examination of individual differences in cortical evoked response.* Unpublished doctoral dissertation, University of London, 1972.

Hendrickson, D. E., & Hendrickson, A. E. The biological basis of individual differences in intelligence. *Personality and Individual Differences,* 1980, 1, 3–33.

Henry, L. E., & Knott, J. R. A note on the relationship between 'personality' and the alpha rhythm of the electroencephalogram. *Journal of Experimental Psychology,* 1941, 28, 362–366.

Herd, J. A. Physiological correlates of coronary prone behavior. In T. M. Dombroski, S. M. Weiss, & J. L. Shields (Eds.), *Coronary prone behavior.* New York: Springer-Verlag, 1978.

Hockey, R. Temperament differences in vigilance performance as a function of variations in the suitability of ambient noise level. In J. Strelau, F. Farley, & A. Gale (Eds.), *The biological bases of personality and behavior. Volume II. Psychophysiology, performance, and applications.* New York: Hemisphere, 1985.

Hodgson, R., & Rachman, S. II. Desynchrony in measures of fear. *Behaviour Research and Therapy,* 1974, 12, 319–326.

Holroyd, K. A., Westbrook, T., Wolf, M., & Badhorn, E. Performance, cognition, and physiological responding in test anxiety. *Journal of Abnormal Psychology,* 1978, 87, 442–451.

Houston, B. K. Control over stress, locus of control, and response to stress. *Journal of Personality and Social Psychology,* 1972, 21, 249–255.

Hume, W. I. The dimensions of central nervous arousal. *Bulletin of the British Psychological Society,* 1968, 21, 111.

Jackson, D. N., & Paunonen, S. V. Personality structure and assessment. *Annual Review of Psychology,* 1980, 31, 503–552.

John, E. R. *Functional neuroscience* (Vol. 2, *Neurometrics of quantitative electrophysiology*). Hillsdale, N.J.: Erlbaum, 1977.

John, E. R. Multipotentiality: A statistical theory of brain function—evidence and implications. In D. M. Davidson & R. J. Davidson (Eds.), *The psychobiology of consciousness.* New York: Plenum Press, 1980.

John, E. R., Karmel, B. Z., Corning, W. C., Easton, P., Brown, D., Ahn, H., John, M., Harmony, T., Prichep, L., Toro, A., Gerson, I., Bartlett, F., Thatcher, R., Kaye, H., Valdes, P., & Schwartz, E. Neurometrics. *Science,* 1977, 196, 1393–1410.

Johnson, R. K., & Meyer, R. G. The locus of control construct in EEG alpha rhythm feedback. *Journal of Consulting and Clinical Psychology,* 1974, 42, 913.

Kagan, J. *Cardiac correlates of behavioral inhibition in young children.* Paper presented at a symposium in honor of the Laceys, Minneapolis, October 1982.

Kagan, J. Stress and coping in early development. In N. Garmezy & M. Rutter (Eds.), *Stress, coping and development in children.* New York: McGraw-Hill, 1983.

Katkin, E. S. Relationship between manifest anxiety and two indices of autonomic response to stress. *Journal of Personality and Social Psychology,* 1965, 2, 324–333.

Kelly, G. A. *The psychology of personal constructs* (Vols. 1 and 2). New York: Norton, 1955.

Kimmel, H. D., van Olst, E. H., & Orlebeke, J. F. (Eds.), *The orienting reflex in humans.* Hillsdale, N.J.: Erlbaum, 1979.

Kline, P. *Psychometrics and psychology.* London: Academic Press, 1979.

Klonowicz, T., Ingatowska-Switalska, H., & Wocial, B. Hypertension and response to stress: Need for stimulation? In J. Strelau, F. Farley, & A. Gale (Eds.), *The biological bases of personality and behavior. Volume II. Psychophysiology, performance, and applications.* New York: Hemisphere, 1985.

Kondo, C. Y., Bean, J. A., Travis, T. A., & Knott, J. R. Resting levels of alpha and the Eysenck Personality Inventory. *British Journal of Psychiatry,* 1978, 132, 378–380.

Koriat, A., Averill, J. R., & Malmstrom, E. J. Individual differences in habituation: Some methodological and conceptual issues. *Journal of Research in Personality,* 1973, 7, 88–101.

Korn, J. H., & Moyer, K. E. Effects of set and sex on the electrodermal orienting response. *Psychophysiology,* 1968, 4, 453–459.

Labuc, S. *The effects of low ambient temperature on information processing.* Unpublished doctoral dissertation, University of Wales, 1975.

Lacey J. I., & Lacey, B. C. Verification and extension of the principle of autonomic response-stereotypy. *American Journal of Psychology*, 1958, 71, 50–73.

Lacey, J. I., & Lacey, B. C. On heart rate responses and behavior: A reply to Elliot. *Journal of Personality and Social Psychology*, 1974, 30, 1–18.

Lader, M. H. *The psychophysiology of mental illness*. London: Routledge & Kegan Paul, 1975.

Lader, M. H., & Wing, L. *Physiological measures, sedative drugs and morbid anxiety*. London: Oxford University Press, 1966.

Lamb, D. H. Anxiety. In H. London & J. E. Exner (Eds.), *Dimensions of personality*. New York: Wiley, 1978.

Lang, P. J. Anxiety: Toward a psychophysiological definition. In H. S. Akiskal & W. H. Webb (Eds.), *Psychiatric diagnosis: Exploration of biological predictors*. New York: Spectrum, 1978.

Lang, P. J., & Twentyman, C. T. Learning to control heart rate: Binary versus analogue feedback. *Psychophysiology*, 1974, 11, 616–629.

Lazarus, R. S. *Psychological stress and the coping process*. New York: McGraw-Hill, 1966.

Lefcourt, M. H. Recent developments in the study of locus of control. In B. Maher (Ed.) *Progress in experimental personality research* (Vol. 6). New York: Academic Press, 1972.

Lemere, F. The significance of individual differences in the Berger rhythm. *Brain*, 1936, 59, 366–375.

Levenson, H. Multidimensional locus of control in psychiatric patients. *Journal of Consulting and Clinical Psychology*, 1973, 41, 397–404.

Levenson, R. W., & Ditto, W. B. Individual differences in ability to control heart rate: Personality, strategy, physiological, and other variables. *Psychophysiology*, 1981, 18, 91–100.

Levenson, R. W., & Gottman, J. M. Marital interaction: physiological linkage and affective exchange. *Journal of Personality & Social Psychology*, 1983, 45, 587–597.

Levey, A. B., & Martin, I. Personality and conditioning. In H. J. Eysenck (Ed.), *A model for personality*. Berlin: Springer-Verlag, 1981.

Lindsley, D. B. Electroencephalography. In J. M. Hunt (Ed.), *Personality and behavior disorders* (Vol. 2). New York: Ronald Press, 1944.

Lindsley, D. B. Psychological phenomena and the electroencephalogram. *Electroencephalography and Clinical Neurophysiology*, 1952, 4, 443–456.

Lobstein, T., Webb, B., & Edholm, O. Orienting responses and locus of control. *British Journal of Social and Clinical Psychology*, 1979, 18, 13–19.

Loehlin, J. C., Lindzey, G., & Spuhler, K. P. *Race differences in intelligence*. New York: Freeman, 1975.

Logsdon, S. A., Bourgeois, A. E., & Levenson, H. Locus of control, learned helplessness, and control of heart rate using biofeedback. *Journal of Personality Assessment*, 1978, 42, 538–544.

Lundberg, U., & Frankenhaeuser, M. Psychophysiological reactions to noise as modified by personal control over noise intensity. *Biological Psychology*, 1978, 6, 51–59.

Lykken, D. T. The role of individual differences in psychophysiological research. In P. H. Venables & M. J. Christie (Eds.), *Research in psychophysiology*. London: Wiley, 1975.

Lynn, R. (Ed.), *Dimensions of personality: Papers in honour of H. J. Eysenck*. Oxford: Pergamon Press, 1981.

Mackay, C. J. The measurement of mood and psychophysiological activity using self report techniques. In I. Martin & P. H. Venables (Eds.), *Techniques in psychophysiology*. Chichester: Wiley, 1980.

Martin, B., & Sroufe, L. Anxiety. In C. Costello (Ed.), *Symptoms of psychopathology*. New York: Wiley, 1970.

Marton, M., & Urban, I. An electroencephalographic investigation of individual differences in the processes of conditioning. *Proceedings of the 18th International Congress of Psychology* (Moscow), 1966, 9, 106–109.

Matysiak, J. Self exposure to sensory stimuli in rats as activity motivated by sensory drive. In J. Strelau, F. Farley, & A. Gale

(Eds.), *The biological bases of personality and behavior*. New York: Hemisphere, 1983.

McAdam, W., & Orme, J. E. Personality traits and the normal electroencephalogram. *Journal of Mental Science*, 1954, 100, 913–921.

McCanne, T. R., & Sandman, C. A. Human operant heart rate conditioning: The importance of individual differences. *Psychological Bulletin*, 1976, 83, 587–601.

Miles, T. R. Contributions to intelligence testing and the theory of intelligence: I. On defining intelligence. *British Journal of Educational Psychology*, 1957, 27, 153–165.

Minuchin, S. *Families and family therapy*. London: Tavistock Press, 1974.

Mischel, W. *Personality and assessment*. New York: Wiley, 1968.

Montgomery, P. S. EEG alpha as an index of hysteroid and obsessoid personalities. *Psychological Reports*, 1975, 36, 431–436.

Morris, P., & Gale, A. A correlational study of variables related to imagery. *Perceptual and Motor Skills*, 1974, 38, 659–665.

Moruzzi, G., & Magoun, H. W. Brain stem reticular formation and activation of the EEG. *Electroencephalography and Clinical Neurophysiology*, 1949, 1, 455–473.

Mundy-Castle, A. C. The relationship between primary–secondary function and the alpha rhythm of the electroencephalogram. *Journal of the National Institute of Personnel Research*, 1955, 6, 95–102.

Mundy-Castle, A. C. Electrophysiological correlates of intelligence. *Journal of Personality*, 1958, 26, 184–199.

Näätänen, R. Selective attention and evoked potentials in humans: A critical review. *Biological Psychology*, 1975, 2, 237–307.

Näätänen, R. The N2 component of the evoked potential: A scalp reflection of neuronal mismatch of orienting theory? In J. Strelau, F. Farley, & A. Gale (Eds.), *The biological bases of personality and behavior. Volume II. Psychophysiology, performance, and applications*. New York: Hemisphere, 1985.

Neary, R. S., & Zuckerman, M. Sensation seeking, trait and state anxiety, and the electrodermal orienting reflex. *Psychophysiology*, 1976, 13, 205–211.

Nebylitsyn, V. D. An electro-encephalographic investigation of the properties of strength of the nervous system and equilibrium of the nervous processes in man using factor analysis. In B. M. Teplov (Ed.), *Typological features of higher nervous activity in man*. (Vol. 3). Moscow: Academy Pedagog. Nauk R.S.F.S.R., 1963.

Nebylitsyn, V. D. The problem of general and partial properties of the nervous system. In V. D. Nebylitsyn & J. A. Gray (Eds.), *Biological bases of individual behavior*. New York: Academic Press, 1972.

Netchine, S., & Lairy, G. C. Ondes cérébrales et niveau mental: Quelques aspects de l'évolution genetique du trace EEG suivant le niveau. *Enfance*, 1960, 4, 427–439.

Nosal, C. S. Temperamental and informational determinants of problem solving in the process of man–computer interaction. In J. Strelau, F. Farley, & A. Gale (Eds.), *The biological bases of personality and behavior. Volume II. Psychophysiology, performance, and applications*. New York: Hemisphere, 1985.

Nowlis, V. Research with the Mood Adjective Checklist. In S. S. Tomkins & C. E. Izard (Eds.), *Affect, cognition and personality*. New York: Springer, 1965.

O'Connor, K. The contingent negative variation and individual differences in smoking behavior. *Personality and Individual Differences*, 1980, 1, 57–72.

O'Connor, K. Individual differences in the effect of smoking on frontal–central distribution of the CNV: Some observations on smokers' control of attentional behaviour. *Personality and Individual Differences*, 1982, 3, 271–285.

O'Gorman, J. G. Electrodermal lability and recovery of habituated OR. *Australian Journal of Psychology*, 1972, 24, 241–244.

O'Gorman, J. G. Individual differences in habituation of human physiological responses: A review of theory, method and findings in the study of personality correlates of non-clinical populations. *Biological Psychology*, 1977, 5, 257–318.

O'Gorman, J. G. Habituation and personality. In A. Gale & J. Edwards (Eds.), *Physiological correlates of human behaviour Volume 3, Individual differences and psychopathology*. London, Academic Press, 1983.

O'Gorman, J. G. Extraversion and the EEG I: An evaluation of Gale's hypothesis. *Biological Psychology*, 1984, 19, 95–112.

O'Gorman, J. G. & Mallise, L. R. Extraversion and the EEG II: A test of Gale's hypothesis. *Biological Psychology*, 1984, 19, 113–127.

Ostow, M. Psychic function and the electroencephalogram. *Archives of Neurology and Psychiatry*, 1950, 64, 385–400.

Paisey ,T. J. H., & Mangan, G. L. The relationship of extraversion, neuroticism, and sensation seeking to questionnaire-derived measures of nervous system properties. *Pavlovian Journal of Biological Science*, 1980, 15, 123–130.

Pavlov, I. P. *Experimental psychology and other essays*. New York: Philosophical Library, 1957.

Pawlik K., & Cattell, R. B. The relationship between certain personality factors and measures of cortical arousal. *Neuropsychologia*, 1965, 3, 129–151.

Petersen, I., Sellden, U., & Bosaeus, E. The relationship between IQ, social class and EEG findings in healthy children investigated by child-psychiatric methods. *Scandinavian Journal of Psychology*, 1976, 17, 189–197.

Petrie, A. *Individuality in pain and suffering*. Chicago: University of Chicago Press, 1967.

Plum, A. *Visual evoked responses: Their relationship to intelligence*. Unpublished doctoral dissertation, University of Florida, 1969.

Poon, L. W., Thompson, L. W., Williams, R. B., & Marsh, G. R. Changes of anterior-posterior distribution of CNV and late positive component as a function of information processing demands. *Psychophysiology*, 1974, 11, 660–673.

Ray, W. J. The relationship of locus of control, self-report measures, and feedback to the voluntary control of heart rate. *Psychophysiology*, 1974, 11, 527–534.

Ray, W. J., & Lamb, S. B. Locus of control and the voluntary control of heart rate, *Psychosomatic Medicine*, 1974, 36, 180–182.

Revelle, W., Anderson, K. J., & Humphreys, M. S. Personality and performance: tests of the arousal model. In G. Mangan & T. Paisey (Eds.), *Contemporary approaches to temperament and personality: An East–West typology*. Oxford: Pergamon Press, 1983.

Revelle, W., Humphreys, M. S., Simon, L., & Gilliland, K. The interactive effect of personality, time of day and caffeine: A test of the arousal model. *Journal of Experimental Psychology: General*, 1980, 109, 1–31.

Rhodes, L. E., Dustman, R. E., & Beck, E. C. The visual evoked response: A comparison of bright and dull children. *Electroencephalography and Clinical Neurophysiology*, 1969, 27, 364–372.

Rösler, F. Die abhangigkeit des electroenzephalogramms von den person lichkeitsdimentionen E und N sensu Eysenck und unterschiedlich aktivierenden situationen. *Zeitschrift für Experimentelle und Angewandte Psychologie*, 1975, 12, 630–667.

Rotter, J. B. Generalized expectancies for internal versus external control of reinforcement. *Psychological Monographs*, 1966, 80, 1–28.

Roubertoux P. Genetic correlates of personality and temperament: The origins of individual differences. In J. Strelau, F. Farley, & A. Gale (Eds.), *The biological bases of personality and behavior. Volume II. Psychophysiology, performance, and applications*. New York: Hemisphere, 1985.

Royce, J. R., & Powell, A. An overview of multifactor system theory. In J. Strelau, F. Farley, & A. Gale (Eds.), *The biological bases of personality and behavior. Volume I. Theories, measurement techniques, and development*. New York: Hemisphere, 1985.

Runcie, D., Graham, J. S., & Shelton, M. L. Locus of control and cardiac response to reaction time, mental arithmetic and time estimation tasks. *Perceptual and Motor Skills*, 1978, 46, 1199–1208.

Rust, J. Cortical evoked potential, personality and intelligence. *Journal of Comparative and Physiological Psychology*, 1975, 89, 1220–1226.

Savage, R. D. Electro-cerebral activity, extraversion and neuroticism. *British Journal of Psychiatry*, 1964, 110, 98–100.

Schalling, D., & Asberg, M. Biological and psychological correlates of impulsiveness and monotony avoidance. In J. Strelau, F. Farley, & A. Gale (Eds.), *The biological bases of personality and behavior. Volume I. Theories, measurement techniques, and development*. New York: Hemisphere, 1985.

Schneider, R. D., Sobol, M. P., Herrmann, T. F., & Cousins, L. R. A re-examination of the relationship between locus of control and voluntary heart rate change. *Journal of General Psychology*, 1978, 99, 49–60.

Schönpflug, W., & Mundelein, H. Activity and reactivity: Theoretical comments and an experimental approach. In J. Strelau, F. Farley, & A. Gale (Eds.), *The biological bases of personality and behavior. Volume II. Psychophysiology, performance, and applications*. New York: Hemisphere, 1985.

Schooler, C., Zahn, T. P., Murphy, D. L., & Buchsbaum, M. S. Psychological correlates of monoamine oxidase in normals. *Journal of Nervous and Mental Disease*, 1978, 166, 177–186.

Shagass, C., & Kerenyi, A. B. Neurophysiological studies of personality. *Journal of Nervous and Mental Disease*, 1958, 126, 141–147.

Shucard, D. W. *Relationships among measures of the cortical evoked potential and abilities comprising human intelligence*. Unpublished doctoral dissertation, University of Denver, 1969.

Shucard, D. W., & Horn, J. L. Evoked cortical potentials and measurement of human abilities. *Journal of Comparative and Physiological Psychology*, 1972, 78, 59–68.

Shucard, D. W., & Horn, J. L. Evoked potential amplitude change related to intelligence and arousal. *Psychophysiology*, 1973, 10, 445–452.

Skevington, S. M. Stress and anxiety neurosis: A study of recovery. *Journal of Psychosomatic Research*, 1977, 21, 439–450.

Siddle, D. A. T., Kuiack, M., & Stenfert Kroese, B. The orienting reflex. In A. Gale & J. Edwards (Eds.), *Physiological correlates of human behaviour Volume 2, Attention and performance*. London: Academic Press, 1983.

Sokolov, E. N. The modeling properties of the nervous system. In M. Cole & I. Maltzman (Eds.), *A handbook of contemporary Soviet psychology*. London: Basic Books, 1969.

Spielberger, C. D. (Ed.). *Anxiety and behavior*. New York: Academic Press, 1966.

Spielberger, C. D. Anxiety as an emotional state. In C. D. Spielberger (Ed.), *Anxiety: Current trends in theory and research* (Vol. 1). New York: Academic Press, 1972. (a)

Spielberger, C. D. (Ed.). *Anxiety: Current trends in theory and research* (Vol. 2). New York: Academic Press, 1972. (b)

Stelmack, R. M. The psychophysiology of extraversion and neuroticism. In H. J. Eysenck (Ed.), *A model for personality*. Berlin: Springer-Verlag, 1981.

Straumanis, J. J., Shagass, C., & Overton, D. A. Auditory evoked responses in young adults with Down's syndrome and idiopathic mental retardation. *Biological Psychiatry*, 1973, 6, 75–80.

Strelau, J. A diagnosis of temperament by nonexperimental techniques. *Polish Psycholigical Bulletin*, 1972, 3, 97–105.

Strelau, J. Temperament and personality: Pavlov and beyond. In J. Strelau, F. Farley, & A. Gale (Eds.), *The biological bases of personality and behavior. Volume I. Theories, measurement techniques, and development*. New York: Hemisphere, 1985.

Strelau, J., Farley, F., & Gale, A. (Eds.). *The biological bases of personality and behavior*. (2 Volumes). New York: Hemisphere, 1985.

Strelau, J., & Terelak, J. The alpha-index in relation to temperamental traits. *Studia Psychologica*, 1974, 16, 40–50.

Surwillo, W. W. Human reaction time and period of the EEG in relation to development. *Physiological Psychology*, 1971, 8, 468–482.

Tanner, J. M. *Growth at adolescence* (2nd Ed.). Oxford: Blackwell, 1962.

Taylor, J. A. A personality scale of manifest anxiety. *Journal of Abnormal and Social Psychology*, 1953, 48, 285–290.

Terman, L. M., & Oden, M. H. *Genetic studies of genius* (Vol. 5, *The gifted group at mid-life*). Stanford, Calif.: Stanford University Press, 1959.

Thompson, R. F. *Foundations of physiological psychology*. New York: Harper & Row, 1967.

Torgersen, A. M. Temperamental differences in infants and six-year-old children: A follow-up of twins. In J. Strelau, F. Farley, & A. Gale (Eds.), *The biological bases of personality and behavior. Volume I. Theories, measurement techniques, and development*. New York: Hemisphere, 1985.

Travis, T. A., Kondo, C. Y., & Knott, J. R. Personality variables and alpha enhancement. *British Journal of Psychiatry*, 1974, 124, 542–544.

Turpin, G. Psychophysiology, psychopathology and the social environment. In A. Gale & J. Edwards (Eds.), *Physiological correlates of human behaviour Volume 3, Individual differences and psychopathology*. London: Academic Press, 1983.

Venables, P. H. The electrodermal psychophysiology of schizophrenics and children at risk for schizophrenia: Controversies and developments. *Schizophrenia Bulletin*, 1977, 3, 28–48.

Venturini, R., de Pascalis, U., Imperiali, M. G., & San Martini, P. EEG alpha reactivity and extraversion–introversion. *Personality & Individual Differences*, 1981, 2, 215–220.

Vernon, P. E. *Personality assessment: A critical survey*. London: Methuen, 1964.

Vernon, P. E. *Human intelligence: Heredity and environment*. San Francisco: W. H. Freeman, 1979.

Vogel, W., & Broverman, D. M. Relationship between EEG and test intelligene: A critical review. *Psychological Bulletin*, 1964, 62, 132–144.

Vogel, W., & Broverman, D. M. A reply to "Relationship between EEG and test intelligence: a commentary." *Psychological Bulletin*, 1966, 65, 99–109.

von Knorring, L. Visual average evoked responses and platelet monoamine oxidase in patients suffering from alcoholism. In H. Begleiter (Ed.), *The biological effects of alcohol*. New York: Plenum Press, 1980.

Wagner, C., Bourgeois, A., Levenson, H., & Denton, J. Multidimensional locus of control and voluntary control of GSR. *Perceptual and Motor Skills*, 1974, 39, 1142.

Watson, D. Relationship between locus of control and anxiety. *Journal of Personality and Social Psychology*, 1967, 6, 91–92.

Watson, D., & Baumal, E. Effects of locus of control and expectation of future control upon present performance. *Journal of Personality and Social Psychology*, 1967, 6, 212–215.

Weinberg, H. Correlation of frequency spectra of averaged visual evoked potentials with verbal intelligence. *Nature*, 1969, 224, 813–815.

Weinberger, D. A., Schwartz, G. E., & Davidson, R. J. Low anxious, high anxious and repressive coping styles: psychometric patterns and behavioral and physiological responses to stress. *Journal of Abnormal Psychology*, 1979, 88, 369–380.

Williams, R. B. Psychophysiological processes, the coronary-prone behavior pattern and coronary heart disease. In T. M. Dombroski, S. M. Weiss, & J. L. Shields (Eds.), *Coronary prone behavior*. New York: Springer-Verlag, 1978.

Williams, R. B., Poon. L. W., & Burdette, L. J. Locus of control and vasomotor response to sensory processing. *Psychosomatic Medicine*, 1977, 39, 127–133.

Williamson, D. A., & Blanchard, E. B. Heart rate and blood pressure biofeedback: I. A review of the recent experimental literature. *Biofeedback and Self-Regulation*, 1979, 4, 1–50.

Winter, K., Broadhurst, A., & Glass, A. Neuroticism, extraversion, and EEG amplitude. *Journal of Experimental Research in Personality*, 1972, 6, 44–51.

Young, J. P. R., Lader, M. H., & Fenton, G. W. The relationship of extraversion and neuroticism to the EEG. *British Journal of Psychiatry*, 1971, 119, 667–670.

Zuckerman, M. The development of an affect adjective checklist for the measurement of anxiety. *Journal of Consulting Psychology*, 1960, 24, 457–462.

Zuckerman, M. Theoretical formulations: I. In J. P. Zubek (Ed.), *Sensory deprivation: Fifteen years of research*. New York: Appleton-Century-Crofts, 1969.

Zuckerman, M. Dimensions of sensation seeking. *Journal of Consulting and Clinical Psychology*, 1971, 36, 45–52.

Zuckerman, M. *Sensation seeking: Beyond the optimum level of arousal*. Hillsdale, N.J.: Erlbaum, 1979.

Zuckerman, M. Biological foundations of the sensation seeking temperament. In J. Strelau, F. Farley, & A. Gale (Eds.), *The biological bases of personality and behavior. Volume I. Theories, measurement techniques, and development*. New York: Hemisphere, 1985.

Zuckerman, M. Animal models for personality. Paper presented at a Workshop on Individual Differences at the Annual Conference of the British Psychophysiology Society, London, England, 1983.

Zuckerman, M. (Ed.) *Biological bases of sensation seeking, impulsivity and anxiety*, Hillsdale, N.J.: Erlbaum, 1983.

Zuckerman, M., Buchsbaum, M. S., & Murphy, D. L. Sensation seeking and its biological correlates. *Psychological Bulletin*, 1980, 88, 605–632.

Zuckerman, M., Murtaugh, T. M., & Siegel, J. Sensation seeking and cortical augmenting–reducing. *Psychophysiology*, 1974, 11, 535–542.

Chapter Twenty-One

Psychophysiological Approaches to Psychopathology

Theodore P. Zahn

INTRODUCTION

This chapter reviews the more recent psychophysiological studies of psychopathology and attempts to relate them to the major conceptualizations in the field. The goals are to try to determine how such studies might help to further our understanding of the behavior disorders; to ascertain what general conclusions can be drawn from the work; to indicate where the gaps in current knowledge are; and to suggest potentially useful directions for further research.

The concept of psychopathology is, to some extent, a fuzzy one; it can be argued that since nobody is perfect, psychopathology exists in a different degree in all persons. For the most part, the subjects in the studies to be covered here are incapacitated or troublesome to a degree that they have presented themselves, or have been taken, for psychiatric treatment and have received a psychiatric diagnosis. These facts imply a "medical model" of psychopathology, complete with formal diagnostic criteria. While it may be that variations in physiological parameters are more closely related to variations in mood states, behavior, or cognitive dysfunctions, irrespective of diagnosis, than they are to the diagnostic categories themselves, virtually all of the literature uses diagnosis as the primary independent variable. So it is considered as such in this chapter as well. The functional significance of the dependent measures is, of course, critical for the interpretation of any differences found between diagnoses.

This is an appropriate place to insert the complaint about diagnoses that is almost *de rigeur* in writing on psychopathology. There is no question that lack of reliable and valid diagnoses has hindered progress in all areas of research on the behavior disorders. Recent developments of structured interview schedules and more rigorous criteria for diagnosing some disorders have helped considerably, but have not solved all the problems. Evaluation and comparison of the research done at different times and different places are especially affected, and this problem frequently presents itself in this review. One of the reasonable goals of psychophysiological research is to develop objective measures that could aid in diagnostic decision making, but such measures are not so used at present.

Theodore P. Zahn. Laboratory of Psychology and Psychopathology, National Institute of Mental Health, Bethesda, Maryland.

Goals of Psychophysiological Research in Psychopathology

In addition to establishing an efficacious nosology, the goals of the scientific study of any behavior disorder are an understanding of the psychological and biological mechanisms involved, with an eye to determining the fundamental etiology, and the development of effective treatment and prevention methods. Psychophysiological investigations have undertaken to contribute to all of these goals, but more so in some disorders than others.

Diagnostic Differentiation

The search for psychophysiological features that distinguish persons with a given diagnosis from those without it (usually normal controls) constitutes the bulk of the research in this area and can be thought to be a logical and necessary first step toward further research. Such studies frequently are done with a specific hypothesis in mind, but can be regarded also as attempts to find objective markers for the particular illness under study. The goal of this approach is to discover markers with sensitivity (i.e., present in a high proportion of cases) and specificity (i.e., present in a low proportion of nonaffected persons). The criteria for a marker lie in its empirically determined discriminative ability rather than its biological or genetic significance. Determining these is a separate problem. Markers can also be distinguished in terms of what they discriminate, such as vulnerability to a disorder, an active episode of a disorder, and so on (Zubin, 1980), and specific research strategies are necessary to address these different problems.

Investigations of specificity among major diagnostic categories are less common, but this may be partly because they presuppose adequate sensitivity. It is obvious, but frequently overlooked, that there is not enough information in a single measure to make a large number of clinical discriminations. Variables such as heart rate (HR) or contingent negative variation (CNV) amplitude can only be higher or lower in one group than another, if they differ at all. Multivariate discriminations of patterns of variables therefore are necessary to enable multiple differentiations to be made, but such discriminations have been used infrequently.

Most psychiatric disorders, especially the major psychoses, are markedly heterogeneous with respect to symptoms, clinical course, effectiveness of certain treatments, and so forth. Attempts to reduce this heterogeneity by subclassification on the basis of such attributes are necessary for progress in understanding the disorder. Such a subtyping will be more powerful to the extent that the subgroups can be differentiated by many different attributes. Psychophysiological studies have an obvious and important role here, not only to help strengthen and elucidate subclassifications based on other criteria, but also, in some cases, to form the primary basis of subtyping for which clinical and behavioral correlates can be sought.

Approaches to Interpretation of the Data

The search for psychophysiological markers is really a search for relationships or correlations between physiological variables and behavior, since diagnoses are made on the basis of behavior. Hypotheses about the meaning of such relationships are, of course, necessary to suggest new studies leading to a meaningful theoretical advance. Psychophysiological data, more so than most other kinds, admit of both psychological and biological levels of explanation. Shagass (1976) distinguishes between the psychophysiological and pathophysiological approaches in psychopathology research. In the pathophysiological approach, physiological markers are taken as having direct and primary significance for deviant behavior, independent of events at a psychological level. In the psychophysiological orientation, correlates between physiology and "psychological events" are sought. For example, depression is both a psychological state and a direct manifestation of psychopathology, but depressed mood is only one of the criteria for diagnosing primary depression. The pathophysiologist would seek correlates of the syndrome, whereas the psychophysiologist would seek correlates of the mood state. Although the distinction between pathological psychological events and pathological behavior is somewhat ambiguous in this formulation, it does make the point that some researchers interpret their data as reflecting biological processes that directly influence behavior, while others see their squiggles as reflecting symptoms or psychological processes that may be involved in symptom production. The psychophysiological orientation would seem to be more compatible with a holistic approach to behavior pathology (Engel, 1977), while the pathophysiology viewpoint would be more relevant to a disease model.

Psychological Processes

Shagass (1976) points out that a value of the psychophysiological approach is to provide objective indicators of psychological states. This may be particularly useful with patients who have trouble communicating either directly or indirectly. However, more importantly, the psychophysiological orientation leads to studies of such factors as the differential effects of particular environmental events in patients and controls on physiological activity, behavior, and (perhaps) subjective responses, or the relationships of variations in physiological variables to variations in task performance or behavior ratings. An especially fruitful area may be the study of different stages of information processing in patients using paradigms developed in "normal" cognitive psychophysiology.

Such studies possibly, but not necessarily, test hypotheses from theories of psychopathology couched in psychological terms. They may also have implications for biological theories and for what might be called psychophysiological hypotheses, involving such concepts as arousal, habituation, or conditioning, which have primarily psychophysiological referents. This viewpoint is likely to be relevant to theories that account for symptoms in terms of both biological and psychological constructs in an interactive fashion.

A thorny issue that any review of this topic must face is the concept of arousal. This term, or synonyms for it, has been used in the description of autonomic, electrocortical, and behavioral phenomena, and the concept plays a prominent role in many theories of various types of psychopathology. "Arousal" is used in this review descriptively with respect to levels of or changes in the variables traditionally associated with this concept. When these occur with considerable generality across various measures, inferences about arousal in a conceptual sense may be warranted. However, it is realized that even here this concept may have limited explanatory utility, since differences in arousal may not be isomorphic with a specific neurophysiological or neurochemical substrate. For the understanding of mechanism, differences among measures with respect to inferences about arousal are as important as their similarities. Research in psychopathology may be especially valuable in elucidating this concept, not only because a wider range of psychological and physiological states is encountered here than in normal populations, but also because of the progress being made in understanding the neurobiology of these conditions.

Biological Bases

Inferences about biological dysfunction in psychopathology made from psychophysiological data have traditionally been made in terms of the anatomical locus of the dysfunction and, to some extent, in terms of endocrine dysfunction. These types of hypotheses are still useful, of course, but in recent years much progress has been made in the understanding of the neurochemistry of the major psychoses and some neuroses. Many of the current biological hypotheses of psychopathology concern relationships between dysfunctions in neurotransmitter systems—events at the level of the individual neuron—and disordered psychological states or behavior. Since psychophysiological variables may reflect neural dysfunctions more directly than do symptoms, psychophysiological studies of psychopathology might be particularly helpful in the understanding of the intermediate steps

between the neuron and behavior (Shagass, 1976; Zahn, 1980).

These goals are hindered at present in part by an inadequate knowledge of the biological substrates of psychophysiological processes. Although researchers in psychopathology will have to look to basic research for help here, progress on this front is coming increasingly from psychophysiological studies of patients themselves in terms of the effects of drugs with more or less specific effects; it is also coming from correlational studies with enzyme activity, amines and their metabolites, and peptides as estimated from various body fluids, and with brain structure and function as determined from brain imaging techniques. Since such data are more readily available from psychiatric patients than from normal subjects, this may be one instance where research in an applied field may help in the understanding of the general processes.

If psychophysiological markers for neurochemical processes can be established, it will increase their usefulness enormously because of their noninvasive and dynamic nature. Inferences about brain events could be made on time scales not possible in studies using tissue assay or methods involving exposure to radioactivity.

Another potential use of psychophysiological indicators is as an aid to developing animal models of psychopathology. Shagass (1976) feels that no convincing animal models have been developed using behavioral criteria. Discovering how to produce electrophysiological markers in animals similar to those occurring in a given psychopathology should be of etiological significance. This is a goal for the future, since it presupposes establishing reliable and specific markers in humans.

State versus Trait Attributes

The prevailing conceptualization of the etiology of mental disorders is the diathesis–stress model. Knowledge about etiology will be incomplete without an understanding of those attributes that characterize the illness itself, as distinguished from those that are more lasting attributes or dispositions and that may play a role in the vulnerability to the disorder. This "state versus trait" issue can be investigated, in those disorders in which there are distinct exacerbations and remissions, by comparing patients with a control group when in remission as well as when they are actively symptomatic. A practical difficulty in this approach is the control of medication. However, this type of investigation probably has not received the attention that it deserves in psychophysiological studies.

Another way of attacking the same problem is the "high-risk" study, in which subjects are chosen on the basis of some established or putative marker before the onset of the illness. This approach is being used in several long-term studies, which include psychophysiological measures, in which the offspring of parents with psychopathology—usually schizophrenia—are studied. A primary purpose of this type of study is to discover vulnerability markers by comparing the premorbid data of those who eventually become ill with those of subjects who do not. The target group is chosen to increase the number of hits over what would be expected in an unselected population. Selection of target groups on the basis of other variables, including psychophysiological ones (Venables, 1978), which are thought to represent risk factors, have the additional purpose of validating that variable as a vulnerability marker. No such markers have been established to date, but this type of research is at an early stage and can be expected to increase. This approach promises, if successful, to contribute to the general goal of prevention.

A more accessible approach, which has been underutilized in psychophysiological research, is studying the relatives of patients. This will yield information on the familial nature of the variables studied, and, since many psychophysiological variables have been shown to have a significant genetic determination, may provide a clue as to the nature of the genetic predisposition to the disorder. Increased certainty about the genetic contribution will, of course, have to come from more specifically designed (and more difficult) studies using twins or adopted children.

Effects of Treatment

The use of drug effects to ascertain the biological underpinnings of psychophysiological variables has been mentioned earlier. In addition, such studies can yield information on the mechanisms involved in clinical improvement, and, by inference, the mechanisms involved in the psychopathology. Studies of psychological and other nonpharmacological treatments are also obviously germane here. This strategy will be more powerful if a placebo and/or a comparison treatment is also used and if comparisons of improved and unimproved patients in each group are possible. For practical reasons, these ideals are seldom all met in any one study. This may lead to some uncertainty in interpretation of such aspects as the difference between the concomitants of the therapeutic effects and the side effects of the treatment or the effects of repetition of the procedure.

Another use of information on treatment drug effects is to help evaluate marker-type studies in which treatment cannot be controlled.

A potentially important practical area is the prediction of treatment effects. Here only pretreatment laboratory (and clinical) data and posttreatment clinical data are necessary. However, this sort of study is fraught with problems, such as controlling for pretreatment severity of the illness, which may be correlated both with the physiological variables under study and change scores, and distinguishing between treatment-produced and spontaneous remissions. These problems are surmountable with proper design and analysis, and such studies may have important theoretical implications in terms of the differential etiology for treatment responsive and unresponsive patients.

Scope of This Review

Any review must make some arbitrary choices of what to include as both independent and dependent variables. The six groups of disorders covered here represent a wide range of types of psychopathology, but there are some notable omissions, such as substance abuse disorders, psychopathology associated with organic insults, and sexual deviations. A fairly broad definition of "psychophysiological variables" has been adopted—roughly, what can be measured with surface electrodes and transducers. One borderline area that has perhaps been given undeservedly scant attention is that of sleep research.

Virtually all of the studies covered are psychophysiological investigations of persons who have been given a psychiatric diagnosis or of their relatives. It is recognized that some hypotheses, to be covered in depth, require close attention to other types of studies, such as those on animals or nonpatient humans or those involving behavioral or neurochemical measurement. This has usually been neglected because of the length of the chapter, but references are given to papers that do adequate explorations of these areas. The intent has been to cover the published literature as thoroughly as possible, even that representing ideas that are not currently in the mainstream of thinking. Coverage of unpublished papers, papers given at meetings, and abstracts has been avoided but not absolutely eliminated. It has not been feasible to restrict the reporting of results to those for which statistical significance in the conventional sense (the .05 level) has been established, but where only nonsignificant trends exist they are indicated; otherwise the reader may assume statistical reliability. Many excellent reviews of portions of the literature exist, and where possible these are summarized. Nevertheless, it has frequently been desirable to re-evaluate some of this literature from a different perspective, and it has been attempted to bring the coverage up to date. For complete citations of the earlier literature, the reader should refer to the previous reviews.

It is assumed that the reader is knowledgeable about psychophysiological variables (or can become so from reading this volume) but not about psychopathology. Thus the beginning of each major section includes a brief description of the disorder under discussion and some of the clinical issues associated with it. The latest diagnostic criteria—those of DSM-III (American Psychiatric Association, 1980)—are used, but, of course, most of the studies reviewed have used somewhat different criteria.

SCHIZOPHRENIA

Theoretical Issues

Schizophrenia, widely considered to be the major unsolved mental health problem, has appropriately attracted more psychophysiological research than any other psychiatric disorder. This effort has been more comprehensive in scope than research has been in most other areas of psychopathology. In addition to studies directed to finding markers of schizophrenic pathology or of subgroups of patients, investigations have also evaluated treatment effects, the prediction of treatment effects, vulnerability markers, correlates of symptoms, cognitive deficits, and biological variables.

The attraction of schizophrenia for psychophysiologists stems from several sources: The disturbances in affect occurring in this syndrome would seem amenable to psychophysiological study; disorders of input regulation, attention, and cognition should be elucidated by orienting response (OR) and event-related potential (ERP) techniques; some of the neurochemical mechanisms thought to be involved in schizophrenia, such as catecholamine (and possibly opiate and peptide) systems, may also be reflected in the autonomic nervous system (ANS); and since psychophysiological variables are in part genetically determined, the possibility exists for using them to study a genetic predisposition to schizophrenia.

Yet there are formidable difficulties stemming from a number of sources in performing and evaluating research on schizophrenia. Predominant among these is the heterogeneity of the disorder. Closely allied to this is the problem of the changing criteria for the diagnosis of schizophrenia, which have decreased the heterogeneity of the classification but increased the difficulty of comparing studies done at different times. The main goals of any system of subtyping are to aid clinicians in understanding the etiological mechanisms, predicting clinical course, and choosing an effective treatment. DSM-III has taken steps toward these goals by separating out schizoaffective and schizophreniform disorders from schizophrenia proper. This continues a trend begun more than a decade ago, when it was discovered that British and American psychiatrists differed sharply on their diagnoses of patients who had both schizophrenic and affective symptoms (Cooper, Kendall, Gurland, Sharpe, Copeland, & Simon, 1972). The DSM-III format follows more closely the British custom of excluding patients from a schizophrenia diagnosis when both schizophrenia and affective disorder are present to a significant degree. This distinction has implications for prognosis and treatment. The schizophreniform distinction also follows an older European tradition, and its significance lies partly in the more recent findings that persons having these brief (less than 6 months) psychotic episodes, which may be clinically indistinguishable from "true" schizophrenia, are no more likely to have a genetic background for schizophrenia than the average person.

Even with these layers peeled off the onion, schizophrenia remains a heterogeneous category. Attempts at reducing the variance by subtyping have used both symptoms and clinical course as criteria. An example of this is the joint classification of paranoid versus nonparanoid and process versus reactive, which has shown some usefulness in reducing the heterogeneity of attention measures (Neuchterlein, 1977). Degrees of cognitive disorganization or withdrawal have also been utilized. Some of the psychophysiological research in this area has tried to cross-validate various typologies. As will become clear, this has not always been successful, and some investigators have adopted the strategem of classifying patients on the basis of a biological marker and investigating its psychological and other biological correlates.

Another source of variation comes from the clinical course of the illness. It has been proposed that schizophrenia is usually episodic (Zubin & Spring, 1977). In DSM-III, the distinction is made between symptoms that characterize an active phase of the illness, such as delusions and hallucinations (sometimes termed "florid" or "active" symptoms), and those that may precede and/or follow this phase. The latter group of symptoms includes cognitive and social impairments and strange behavior ("defect" symptoms). The term "acute schizophrenia," although usually referring to patients whose first hospitalization has been recent, has been used inconsistently with respect to the presence of active symptoms. Similarly, since episodes of active symptoms can occur throughout the course of the illness, samples of "chronic" patients may also be heterogeneous with respect to type of symptoms. The point here is that a classification on the basis of symptom type, rather than on length of illness, might be better. Studying episodic patients at different times might shed light on the determinants of the exacerbations of the psychosis, in contrast to those of more stable characteristics.

The virtually universal use of antipsychotic medication, while of great benefit to most patients, has greatly complicated research and its interpretation for the past two to three decades. Many investigators have not been able to study medication-free patients. This situation shows signs of improving, as it is increasingly being realized that medication can be ethically withheld from patients in the course of controlled investigations of new treatments, or even in order to choose the optimal treatment for a given patient in a clinical setting. However, interpretation of psychophysiological data from medicated patients entails the additional step of estimating how the drugs influence the findings, if at all. The evaluation of the effects of drugs may, of course, be a valuable undertaking in itself. Since virtually all of the most effective drugs act by blocking the effects of dopamine (DA) on its receptors, knowing their psychophysiological effects should help us understand their mechanism of action in the alleviation of symptoms.

Even studies of unmedicated patients are not without problems. For one thing, long-term use of antipsychotic drugs is thought to increase DA receptor sensitivity. This may outlast a drug-free period of even several weeks. Another complication of interpreting research findings is that in many cases there is a nonrandom selection of patients to be withheld from drugs or a selective failure to maintain drug-free status in patients who relapse quickly. This might lead to overrepresentation of less severe cases in the drug-free sample. However, sampling bias in studies of schizophrenia is almost universally present, since some patients are uncooperative, are considered untestable, or are not made available by the clinical staff. The criteria for exclusion on these grounds are variable from study to study and are, to some extent, a function of the complexity of the procedures of the study. Thus studies in baseline physiological activity and reactions to simple stimuli will usually include a higher proportion of very psychotic and disorganized patients than studies demanding complex task performance. These perhaps obvious points are made here because they are frequently overlooked in reviews.

Another side effect of pharmacotherapy is relevant to the comparison of early and later research studies. The early studies were heavily weighted with chronic patients who had been hospitalized continuously for many years. Current studies, done in the modern "revolving door" atmosphere, are likely to include a higher proportion of patients in an active phase of the illness; if long-term patients are included at all, they may be atypical, since they presumably have not responded favorably to the usual neuroleptic treatments. However, even though the earlier studies are not replicable in a strict sense, a finding that stands up over time can be regarded with some confidence as being robust and not an artifact of the particular conditions existing at a particular time.

Autonomic and Somatic Activity

Electrodermal and Cardiovascular Base Levels

Consideration of the autonomic and somatic psychophysiology of psychiatric disorders should logically start with the question of whether there are differences from normal physiological activity in the patients as a group under baseline or resting conditions. In the case of schizophrenia, some of the most interesting findings have to do with differences within the patient group, so on occasion this discussion gets ahead of itself and brings in material that is covered more fully in later sections.

Investigation of base levels has usually been undertaken with a concept of arousal in mind. By far the most widely studied system has been electrodermal activity, and within this system, skin conductance (or resistance) level (SCL) has been the favorite index of arousal. The conclusion drawn from a review of the earlier literature (Lang & Buss, 1965) is that the results are inconclusive; some studies find higher, some lower, and some about equal SCL in schizophrenics compared to normals. Many of the more recent studies have been complicated by the use of medication (or by nonreporting of medication status) and by nonrandom selection of unmedicated cases. Neuroleptic medication has been shown to lower SCL (Bernstein, 1967; Gruzelier & Hammond, 1978; Straube, 1979). Studies on drug-free patients continue to yield conflicting results. One such study (Zahn, Rosenthal, & Lawlor, 1968) observed higher SCL in chronic patients, but others, both with chronic patients (Thayer & Silber, 1971) and with acute patients (Bartfai, Levander, Edman, Schalling, & Sedvall, 1983; Straube, 1979; Zahn, Carpenter, & McGlashan, 1981a) found no differences from controls. Some studies have tested separate subgroups. Bernstein (1967) reported elevated SCL in relatively intact and coherent chronic patients, but about normal SCL in disorganized patients. Gruzelier, Eves, Connolly, and Hirsch (1981) found a marginal ($p < .06$) elevation in SCL in unmedicated, newly admitted patients, mostly due to those subjects who failed to habituate on the skin conductance orienting response (SCOR) in 15 trials. Thus, although some patient groups may have high SCL, this measure does not suggest marked arousal differences in schizophrenic patients as a whole.

The rate of spontaneous skin conductance responses (SSCRs) received little, if any, attention in the older literature. Reductions in SSCRs by drugs have been reported (Gruzelier & Hammond, 1978; Spohn, Lacoursiere, Thompson, & Coyne, 1977), but these are not always significant (Bernstein, 1967; Straube, 1979). Increased SSCRs in both chronic (Zahn et al., 1968) and acute (Bartfai, Levander, Edman, et al., 1983; Gruzelier, Eves, Connolly, & Hirsch, 1981; Zahn, Carpenter, & McGlashan, 1981a) patients have been observed, but a nonsignificant trend in the same direction (Bernstein, 1967) and no difference (Thayer & Silber, 1971) in unmedicated patients have also been reported. This variable is strongly related to SCOR frequency, irrespective of medication status (Gruzelier, Eves, Connolly, & Hirsch, 1981; Gruzelier & Venables, 1972, 1974a; Straube, 1979). Greater than normal SSCRs, even in medicated schizophrenics who also gave SCORs, were reported by Gruzelier and Venables (1972) and in remitted patients by Iacono (1982), but not by Straube (1979), while lower SSCRs in medicated SCOR nonresponders are a general finding (Gruzelier & Venables, 1972; Rubens & Lapidus, 1978; Straube, 1979). Disparate results were reported by Horvath and Meares (1979), whose unmedicated schizophrenics had slightly lower SSCRs than controls, whether or not they were SCOR habituators. The bulk of the evidence suggests a higher rate of SSCRs in schizophrenics, on average, but marked individual differences.

Other measures purporting to reflect arousal have shown even more consistent high values in schizophrenic populations. In the earlier studies, reviewed by Lang and Buss (1965), Lader (1975), and Spohn and Patterson (1979), resting HR was consistently higher in unmedicated schizophrenics, a result confirmed in later studies (Bartfai, Levander, Edman, et al., 1983; Kelly, 1980; Zahn, Carpenter, & McGlashan, 1981a). Since neuroleptic medication increases HR (Spohn et al., 1977; Tecce & Cole, 1972), it is not surprising that studies of medicated patients are in agreement with this conclusion (Spohn & Patterson, 1979). Patients who gave SCORs had higher HR than nonresponders, despite equal amounts of medication (Gruzelier & Venables, 1975a). Although Tarrier, Cooke, and Lader (1978) found higher than normal HR in patients in partial remission, most of whom were medicated, my colleagues and I (Zahn, Carpenter, & McGlashan, 1981b) observed that HR decreased to normal levels in unmedicated acute patients when they remitted.

Several other cardiovascular variables have been shown consistently to be elevated in schizophrenia. Reduced cutaneous blood flow (vasoconstriction) has been found (Lang & Buss, 1965; Lader, 1975), as well as increased forearm (muscle) blood flow (FBF) (Kelly, 1980), a measure that increases markedly under stress. Low finger blood flow (which decreased with stress) and low finger temperature (FT) in unmedicated schizophrenics was reported by Maricq and Weinrich (1980), and medicated patients were higher than unmedicated patients on these two variables.

Visibility of the capillary bed of the nailfold plexus was high in a significantly greater proportion of schizophrenics than controls, particularly those who were chronic and had a familial history of schizophrenia and early onset (Maricq, 1963). This was interpreted as reflecting high tonic vasoconstriction, and there is some evidence that it is genetically controlled (Maricq & Jones, 1976). Schizophrenics with high plexus visibility had reduced finger blood flow and FT and marginally slower skin conductance response (SCR) recovery time (Maricq & Weinrich, 1980), but normals had the opposite relationship between these variables. Higher plexus visibility in schizophrenia, as well

as its association with low FT, was also reported by Sendi, Beckett, Caldwell, Grisell, and Gottlieb (1969); these investigators found some, but inconclusive, evidence that visibility could be increased or lowered (only in the high-visibility group) by cooling or warming the hands, and that these subjects showed slow recovery of FT from the experimental changes. These results are interpreted in terms of a failure of autonomic control over temperature changes in the high-plexus-visibility subjects. Some confirmation of a clinical relationship with tonic vasoconstriction was found in another study (Zahn, Carpenter, & McGlashan, 1981b). Acute schizophrenics with a poor clinical course had lower FT than patients who remitted during a short hospitalization, who, in turn, had higher FT than controls.

The FT of schizophrenics who gave SCORs was higher than in nonresponders, and nonsignificantly lower in more chronic patients (Gruzelier & Venables, 1975a). The high FT in SCOR responders is apparently inconsistent with a simple model of arousal, since these patients were high on other indices. However, we (Zahn, Carpenters, & McGlashan, 1981b) found high SSCRs and HR in the group with low FT. Since, in contrast to our patients, the patients of Gruzelier and Venables (1975a) were medicated, this factor might be invoked as an explanation, but the mechanism is obscure. These authors cite "inhibitory" and "homeostatic" factors in a general way to account for this unexpected result. It is possible that neuroleptics alter these in some complex way.

Although the early literature permitted a conclusion of higher diastolic blood pressure (DBP) in schizophrenics (Lang & Buss, 1965), later studies have not found significantly elevated blood pressure in schizophrenics as a group (Kelly, 1980; Lader, 1975). Gruzelier and Venables (1975a) found significantly higher systolic blood pressure (SBP) but not DBP in SCOR responders than in nonresponders.

Pupillary Activity

Pupillary activity should be an especially valuable tool for studying the ANS, since a physiological model based on reciprocal sympathetic and parasympathetic influences has been proposed (Hakerem & Lidsky, 1975). Hakerem, Sutton, and Zubin (1964) reported unmedicated acute schizophrenics to have smaller dark-adapted pupils than chronic patients or normals, and although there were no differences from normal in extent or speed of constrictions to a series of 1-sec light flashes, the time of constriction was shorter in the patients. These results are interpreted in terms of low sympathetic tone in the patients, especially the acute patients. A similarity between these data and data from Lowenstein and Westphal (cited by Hakerem et al., 1964) on catatonic schizophrenics and in patients with disorders of the basal ganglia is suggested. In a second study from this laboratory (Lidsky, Hakerem, & Sutton, 1971), unmedicated recent admissions, most of whom were diagnosed as schizophrenic, had smaller initial diameters and markedly lower constriction to 30-sec light pulses even when differences in initial diameter were controlled.

Some confirmation of these findings is provided by Rubin and Barry (1972b), who found abnormally small constrictions (defined as being outside the 95% confidence limit for controls) in 37% of unmedicated active schizophrenics and in 44% of remitted patients, half of whom were drug-free. Abnormally reduced dilation during 10-sec dark periods was present in 78% of symptomatic and 63% of remitted patients. Rubin and Barry (1976) confirmed the earlier findings of smaller dark-adapted pupils in schizophrenics. In addition, 65% of the patients had an abnormally high threshold for the minimum intensity to produce a discernible constriction, and this group evidenced smaller constrictions at higher intensities as well. Schizophrenics as a group had smaller increases in constriction with increased stimulus intensity, and these were independent of threshold and initial diameter.

Smaller pupillary constriction in medicated schizophrenics has also been reported by Patterson (1976b). This difference was accounted for primarily by the patients who did not give SCORs, and this group also showed less and slower dilation in dark periods. An interesting but puzzling finding was that the patients, SCOR responders in particular, showed more constriction in the first 500 msec poststimulus. A further breakdown of the SCOR responder group on the basis of SCOR recovery-halftime showed that patients with slow SCOR recovery had less responsive pupils in terms of both dilation and constriction (Patterson, 1976a). No differences in pupil size were obtained in these studies, but apparently only data for the light-adapted pupil were reported—a measure that Rubin and Barry (1972b) also found not to differentiate patients from controls. Since dilation was small in patients with absent or slow-recovery SCORs, small dark-adapted pupils can be assumed for these groups. Smaller pupillary constriction in unmedicated schizophrenics who gave less than three SCORs compared to controls was also reported by Straube (1980).

The results from these different laboratories are remarkably consistent, especially for schizophrenia research. The conventional interpretation in terms of reciprocal sympathetic nervous system (SNS) and parasympathetic nervous system (PNS) influences would attribute the smaller initial diameter and reduced dilation in schizophrenics to a relative PNS or cholinergic dominance, and the smaller constriction to a relative SNS or adrenergic dominance (Lidsky et al., 1971; Rubin & Barry, 1976). Similar difficulties are found for the model in interpreting the data of Patterson (1976a). Drug studies have produced different and inconsistent conclusions. Amphetamine, which increases catecholamine activity, was found to attenuate constriction but not to alter pupil size (Lowenfeld, cited in Lidsky et al., 1971), while drugs that block catecholamine receptors had very similar effects (Patterson & Venables, 1981). Only scopolamine, an anticholinergic drug, produced results consistent with the reciprocal-effects model: It decreased extent of constriction and increased pupil size (Patterson & Venables, 1981). Thus the evidence from both the schizophrenia and the pharmacological studies is inconsistent with the traditional model of pupillary activity, suggesting that inferences about autonomic balance made from pupil data are hazardous at best.

Greater use of concurrent recording of other ANS parameters might help resolve the paradoxical findings, but it should be kept in mind that pupil measurement is not performed under true resting conditions. The subject must sit upright and maintain a fixation using a headrest—in effect, must perform a task. As indicated below, the ANS response to task performance may be low in schizophrenia, so that results obtained under resting conditions cannot be generalized to task conditions. Therefore, the concurrent measures should be taken during the actual pupil measurement to be interpretable. Some confirmation of this point comes from a study of the effects of a cold pressor stress on pupil diameter and the light reflex (Rubin & Barry, 1972a). Normal subjects showed the expected results of increased diameter and reduced constriction to light during cold pressor stimulation, followed by recovery to initial levels in a minute or two. Most patients showed little effect of the stress, and many showed large SNS reactions during the recovery period. The authors attribute the results to a defect in SNS-PNS in interaction. An alternative hypothesis of atypical ANS reactions by the schizophrenics to the procedures may be equally tenable.

A more definitive conclusion about relative SNS-PNS balance in schizophrenia was made by Wenger (1966) on the basis of his standardized battery of a dozen or so ANS variables measured under resting conditions. This battery includes salivary output, respiratory frequency, and sublingual temperature, as well as electrodermal and cardiovascular variables; a standardized profile was determined by means of principal-components analysis. Studies using this technique consistently show marked SNS dominance in unmedicated schizophrenics, more so than in any other group studied with this method (Wenger, 1966).

In summary, although the literature on base levels of ANS variables is somewhat inconclusive, mean differences between schizophrenics and controls are generally in the direction of higher SNS activity in schizophrenics than in normal controls. The evidence for this conclusion seems somewhat stronger for cardiovascular variables than for the electrodermal system. Pupillographic data, while showing quite reliable and replicable differences between patients and controls, have eluded interpretation. There is also evidence of considerable heterogeneity among schizophrenic patients. This heterogeneity appears to be positively skewed, such that deviations in the direction of higher levels are more extreme than those in the opposite direction, thus accounting for the overall mean difference.

An obvious possible interpretation of these results is that some patients may be unusually disturbed by the test situation because of paranoid ideation about the electrodes and wires, or because of the strange surroundings in the laboratory or social interaction with the experimenters. The question can be rephrased as to whether the results obtained in the laboratory generalize to ordinary or familiar nonlaboratory settings. There is little direct evidence bearing on this point. This problem could be addressed by telemetering data from patients in their familiar surroundings, by collecting data during sleep, or by simply taking the pulse manually at the same time each day. The less direct evidence that does exist from repeated baseline measurements suggests that the schizophrenic versus normal differences are maintained across repeated test sessions (Zahn, 1964; Zahn, Carpenter, & McGlashan, 1981a). Further, studies reporting changes in measures (usually SCL) during nontask periods have found that while normal subjects show the expected decline in level, many patients, particularly those with higher levels initially, show a smaller decline or even an increase in level with time in the session (Bernstein, 1967; Bernstein, Taylor, Starkey, Juni, Lubowsky, & Paley, 1981; Gruzelier, Eves, Connolly, & Hirsch, 1981; Straube, 1979; Zahn, 1964), so that the groups are more different at the end than at the beginning of the session. Although these results may be subject to various interpretations, they suggest that neither the novelty of the situation nor the necessity for social interaction (since subjects are usually left by themselves during recording periods) can account for the differences in baseline levels.

The OR

No experimental paradigm has been more widely used in schizophrenia research than the simple presentation of a series of stimuli and concurrent measurement of the physiological response. Unfortunately, the size of this literature is due as much to conflicting results among laboratories as to the inherent importance of the problem. The paradigm has the intrinsic advantages of simplicity: Nothing is required of the patient except willingness to tolerate the procedure and to stay awake. Thus, very cognitively impaired subjects can be studied. Despite this simplicity, however, a number of methodological variations are possible in the procedure itself, in addition to variations in the population studied. This literature is prototypic of the difficulties in obtaining true replication in this area, and, indeed, in evaluating the results from even a simple paradigm.

A comprehensive review of this literature has been made by Öhman (1981); a more detailed review of results from six laboratories appears in Bernstein, Frith, Gruzelier, Patterson, Straube, Venables, and Zahn (1982), in which all the data have been analyzed in exactly the same way. This is useful because investigators have tended to report different parameters and to highlight different aspects of their data, depending on their theoretical persuasions and on which differences seem most striking to them.

NONRESPONDING

The parameter that has received the most recent attention is response frequency, or number of trials to habituation. Perhaps the most consistent finding among these studies is that "nonresponding," defined as failure to respond to the first two or three stimuli, is greater among schizophrenic samples than among normal or nonschizophrenic patient samples (Bernstein et al., 1982; Levinson, Edelberg, & Bridger, 1984; Öhman, 1981). Yet there is considerable heterogeneity in this variable, the proportion of nonresponders ranging from 0% to 75% among schizophrenics and from 0% to 40% among control samples. Two sources of the variability are suggested by Bernstein's studies (Bernstein, 1970; Bernstein et al., 1981). Stimulus intensity and modality and clinical differences markedly affected nonresponding and, more importantly, the differences between groups. The results for intensity generalized to the finger pulse volume orienting response (FPVOR) as well (Bernstein et al., 1981). Greater SCOR nonresponding was found among "confused" schizophrenics than normals only to visual stimuli and to weak (60-dB) auditory stimuli, but not among "clear" schizophrenics nor for more intense (75- to 90-dB) auditory stimuli.

A similar result is reported by Gruzelier, Eves, Connolly, and Hirsch (1981) in a study in which a series of 90-dB tones followed a series of 13 70-dB tones. Stimulus intensity influenced nonresponding in Bernstein's confused schizophrenics and in the Gruzelier group's patients more than in controls, but in a combined analysis of 18 samples of schizophrenics from six laboratories, auditory stimulus intensity correlated only .30 with percentage of nonresponding patients, while for nine samples of nomals, the correlation was .80. This suggests a considerable variance due to clinical and methodological variations. Thus

Patterson (cited in Bernstein *et al.*, 1982) found almost twice the porportion of nonresponders at one hospital than at two others (62% vs. 35%), despite similar selection and methodological procedures. It does appear that nonresponding is likely to be rather low in unmedicated newly admitted patients. Three studies of such samples reported 0% to 28% nonresponders to moderate-intensity auditory stimuli (Bartfai, Levander, Edman *et al.*, 1983; Frith, Stevens, Johnstone, & Crow, 1982; Zahn, Carpenter, & McGlashan, 1981a).

TRIALS TO HABITUATION

Similar or even greater variability of results is seen when the rest of the trials-to-habituation distribution is considered. Various studies report that schizophrenic responders take either fewer, equal, or more trials to habituate than controls. As in the case of nonresponding, different studies from the same laboratory tend to be consistent. Thus Bernstein (Bernstein, 1970; Bernstein *et al.*, 1981) found fewer trials to habituation in all his schizophrenic groups, compared to controls, for all intensities of visual or auditory stimuli, and in FPVOR as well as SCOR. Similarly, Patterson and Straube (cited in Bernstein *et al.*, 1982) obtained fast SCOR habituation by this criterion in more than one sample of patients. On the other hand, Gruzelier (Gruzelier, Connolly, Eves, Hirsch, Zaki, Weller, & Yorkston, 1981; Gruzelier, Eves, Connolly, & Hirsch, 1981; Gruzelier & Venables, 1972) has consistently found schizophrenic responders to take more trials to habituate than control responders, and in combination with the high proportion of nonresponders in these studies (54–70%), the patients' trials-to-habituation curve is bimodal or U-shaped. A striking confirmation of this bimodality was found by Rubens and Lapidus (1978): SCOR frequencies of all patients were either less than or greater than those of the controls, without overlap. A variant on this type of finding was obtained (Zahn, cited in Bernstein *et al.*, 1982) in which the proportion of chronic schizophrenics at either extreme of the trials-to-habituation distribution was greater than that for normals, but in which many patients had intermediate values. These data are more congruent with a hypothesis of greater variability in schizophrenics than with a bimodal distribution.

Other distributions have also been reported. Iacono (1982) observed greater nonresponding in remitted patients than in controls, but responders in the two groups did not differ. Frith *et al.*, 1982, and Deakin, Baker, Frith, Joseph, and Johnstone (1979) found schizophrenics to be mostly responders to 85-dB tones or to fail to habituate in 14 trials, but they did not test a normal group. Horvath and Meares (1979) reported only nonhabituation in nonparanoid schizophrenics to 10 100-dB tones, but paranoid patients habituated like normals. Similarly, Gruzelier, Connolly, Eves, *et al.* (1981) found more slow or nonhabituation in schizophrenics than in controls to a 90-dB tone, whereas the same patients showed the bimodal distribution typical of studies from that laboratory to a 70-dB tone series.

MEASURES OF HABITUATION

Measures of habituation that take amplitude into account might be expected to provide more information than response frequency, but they do not completely remove the conflicting results. Using a range-corrected measure, Zahn *et al.* (1968) found that schizophrenic responders habituated at a slower rate than normals—a result that agreed with an analysis of the frequency of SCORs per block of eight trials. In this study, the overall mean amplitudes of the schizophrenics were larger than those of controls. In a later study on acute schizophrenics, whose overall SCR amplitudes were lower than those of controls (Zahn, Carpenter, & McGlashan, 1981a), the responding patients also had a significantly slower rate of habituation, in agreement with similar analyses based on SCOR frequency. The transformation thus seems to have had the desired effect of producing an index of habituation rate unconfounded by differences in level of responding. It should be noted that in neither of these studies did trials to criterion differentiate the groups. Other investigators have not similarly transformed the data. Gruzelier, Connolly, Eves, *et al.* (1981), Gruzelier and Venables (1972), and Horvath and Meares (1979) reported slower habituation; Gruzelier, Eves, Connolly, and Hirsch (1981), Iacono (1982), and Tarrier *et al.* (1978) reported no difference; and Bernstein *et al.* (1981) reported faster habituation in their responding patients—results similar to those with response frequency (and similarly conflicting). Robinson, Rosenthal, and Rasmussen (1977), studying an unusual sample of nonpatient adoptees, compared those who had been given a diagnosis falling within the schizophrenia spectrum to closely matched adoptees without such a diagnosis, and found slower SCOR habituation in the spectrum cases.

We (Zahn *et al.*, 1968; Zahn, Carpenter, & McGlashan, 1981b) also developed a measure of responding irregularity, based on the number of switches between responding and nonresponding over the series of trials; we found more such runs in the patients in both studies. This could account for the disparity between the trials-to-habituation and slope measures. This result was not confirmed by Bernstein, Taylor, Starkey, Lubowsky, Juni, and Paley (1983) who found much lower posthabituation responding in chronic schizophrenics than in normal or patient controls using a 70-trial OR paradigm. However, Bartfai, Levander, Edman, *et al.* (1983) reported just the opposite results in an acute unmedicated sample. Along the same lines, Gruzelier, Eves, Connolly, and Hirsch (1981) observed marked irregularity of response amplitudes in schizophrenics. This was not evaluated statistically, however.

DISHABITUATION

One of the possible interpretations of the irregularity of SCOR responding in schizophrenics is that of spontaneous dishabituation. Attempts to study dishabituation in schizophrenia have been made, but the dishabituating stimuli used (changes in intensity, frequency, or duration of tones) seem to have been ineffectual in producing dishabituation in either schizophrenics or controls when this is defined as an increment in responding to the trial after the novel stimulus (Frith et al., 1982; Gruzelier, Eves, Connolly, & Hirsch, 1981; Iacono, 1982). Only Horvath and Meares (1979) obtained a clear difference in responding to the dishabituating stimulus itself: Paranoid schizophrenics gave smaller SCRs than controls.

ATTEMPTS TO ACCOUNT FOR DIFFERENCES AMONG STUDIES

Considerable thought and discussion have been given to the reasons for the discrepancies in OR studies of schizophrenia (Bernstein et al., 1982; Öhman, 1981; Venables, 1977; Zahn, 1976). Instructions, response criteria, subject sampling, and medication have been considered as relevant variables, in addition to stimulus intensity. It has been proposed that the usual neutral instructions given in OR studies are ambiguous and might lead to differing attributions of stimulus significance by schizophrenics (Iacono & Lykken, 1979). This hypothesis does not receive much support, since low OR incidence in schizophrenics occurs in studies using neutral instructions (Bernstein et al., 1981), as well as in those that instructed subjects explicitly not to attend to the tones (Iacono, 1982; Straube, 1979). A direct test of this hypothesis has not been made.

Levinson et al. (1984) argue that the usual latency window and habituation criterion are too liberal. Reducing the window from .8–5 sec to 1–2.4 sec increased the nonresponders in their chronic medicated schizophrenics from 56% to 75% and decreased the slow habituators from 19% to 0%. More importantly, the SSCR rate within the subtracted portion of the window did not exceed the intertrial SSCR rate. This suggestion also has merit because it increased the discriminative power of nonresponding as a diagnostic marker, but even 56% nonresponding is higher than many studies and needs explanation.

There is abundant evidence that symptomatology and prognosis are related to OR responsivity. Schizophrenics labeled "confused" differed from "clear" schizophrenics and controls in showing more nonresponding (Bernstein, 1970). Similarly, nonresponders were rated higher than responders on The Brief Psy-

chiatric Rating Scale (BPRS) subscales of conceptual disorganization and emotional withdrawal and lower on excitement in the studies of Bernstein et al. (1981) and Straube (1979), and the latter study reported more depressive symptoms (depressed mood, somatic concern, and motor retardation) in nonresponders as well. Similarly, schizophrenics showing relatively few or no posthabituation SCORs in an extended OR paradigm had higher rated emotional withdrawal and lower suspiciousness on the BPRS than more responsive patients (Bernstein et al., 1983). Gruzelier (1976) found slow habituators to be rated higher than nonresponders on anxiety, manic state, psychotic belligerence, and assaultive behaviors, but these differences occurred only in less chronic patients. In contrast, Deakin et al. (1979) reported nonhabituators in a chronic sample not to have high anxiety ratings, but to have flat and incongruous affect, delusions, and hallucinations. Overresponding patients in the Rubens and Lapidus (1978) study had more rated and self-reported anxiety than underresponders and controls; similarly, they had the most extreme scores on "stimulus barrier functioning," defined as "a measure of ego strength in regulating and responding to internal and external stimulation" (Rubens & Lapidus, 1978, p. 201). Nonhabituation occurred in nonparanoid, but not in paranoid patients (Horvath & Meares, 1979). The results of these studies are seemingly in conflict with the generally "sicker" clinical picture seen in nonresponders than in responders by Bernstein and Straube. This point must be qualified, however, because of the different clinical measures involved and the fact that Bernstein's and Straube's less disorganized patients were habituators rather than overresponders.

The data do suggest that, compared to global severity, a more relevant clinical dimension for OR frequency might be activity versus withdrawal, or positive versus negative symptoms. Support for this idea comes from the Frith, Stevens, Johnstone, and Crow (1979) study, which excluded patients with only negative symptoms and from the Bartfai, Levander, Edman, et al. (1983) study which included only patients with positive symptoms. Both of these studies found few nonresponders. However, the picture is complicated by the finding of the latter study that habituators had higher ratings on active psychotic symptoms than nonhabituators (Bartfai, Edman, Levander, Schalling, & Sedvall, 1984) suggesting a nonlinear relationship between active symptoms and SCOR responding. However, it may be that highly aggressive/anxious patients or those with very active symptomatology did not find their way into the studies in which low responding was the predominant schizophrenic feature, while the bimodal studies missed patients who were neither particularly withdrawn nor affectively labile. Another relevant dimension may be prognosis: Slow habituation was associated with poor outcome of an acute schizophrenic episode in two studies (Frith *et al.*, 1979; Zahn, Carpenter, & McGlashan, 1981b). In the latter study, good- and poor-outcome patients were no different in global psychopathology at the time of the test. Thus, even in the absence of a common metric of clinical evaluation, a consensus seems to be developing about clinical variables affecting the OR. A detailed clinical assessment of subjects would appear to be a valuable part of future studies.

More careful attention has been given to the possibility that the conflicting results in this area are due to differences in medication, particularly on the basis of the early findings of slow habituation in unmedicated chronic patients (Zahn *et al.*, 1968) but nonresponding in medicated schizophrenics (Bernstein, 1970; Gruzelier & Venables, 1972). The consensus is that maintenance dosages of neuroleptic drugs do not appreciably affect OR frequency (Bernstein *et al.*, 1982; Öhman, 1981; Zahn, 1976). This conclusion is based largely on similar medication regimens in responders and nonresponders (Gruzelier & Venables, 1972), lack of significant changes in responder status with medication withdrawal (Gruzelier & Hammond, 1978), and failure to find differences between medicated and unmedicated subjects in the same study (Bernstein, 1970; Bernstein *et al.*, 1981; Gruzelier, Connolly, Eves, *et al.*, 1981; Straube, 1979). Indeed, the differences between studies reporting only low responding in patients and those reporting bimodal distributions cannot be so explained, since both findings are on medicated subjects (assuming equal compliance with medication regimens).

Other data both strengthen and restrict this conclusion. An objection to the evidence against the drug hypothesis, based on similar results in medicated and unmedicated patients, is that the determinants of drug status are nonrandom, so that the drug-free subjects may be the quiet, untroublesome patients likely to have low ANS activity. Studies showing a relatively low proportion of nonresponders but slow habituation in their patients (Deakin *et al.*, 1979; Frith *et al.*, 1979; Horvath & Meares, 1979; Zahn *et al.*, 1968) have tended to be done in a context in which all patients were taken off medication. However, with one exception, these studies used 85-dB to 100-dB stimuli with uncontrolled rise time, characteristics widely assumed to enhance the production of defensive reactions (DRs) rather than true ORs. (Although Zahn *et al.* [1968] used 72-dB stimuli, there was a noticeable click-transient, which may have increased the effective intensity.)

Studies that have varied stimulus intensity in unmedicated patients help to clarify this point. When stimulus intensity was increased from 60 dB to 80 dB, normalization of the SCOR in newly admitted adolescent schizophrenics was reported by Bernstein and Taylor (1976). Comparing SCORs to 70-dB and 90-

dB tones with controlled rise time in new admissions routinely kept off drugs, Gruzelier, Eves, Connolly, *et al.* (1981) obtained the expected (for that laboratory) bimodal distribution of responding in the schizophrenics for only the 70-dB tone. The more intense stimulus produced slower habituation in the patients than in controls. This finding is similar to those obtained in other studies with comparable sampling, medication, and stimulus parameters, and dissimilar to those from other studies using intense stimuli with medicated patients (Bernstein, 1970; Bernstein *et al.*, 1981; Gruzelier & Venables, 1972). This suggests that hyperreactivity and/or slow habituation of DRs (or startle reactions) is found in schizophrenics, and that this phenomenon can be attenuated by neuroleptic drugs.

The first part of this conclusion is supported by a finding of slower habituation of the startle reflex as measured by eyeblinks in schizophrenic compared to nonschizophrenic patients and normal controls (Geyer & Braff, 1982). The second part of the conclusion receives direct support from Gruzelier and Hammond (1978), who found attenuation by chlorpromazine of SCORs to "subjectively loud and unpleasant noise" stimuli of 75 dB but no consistent effects on SCORs to benign 70-dB tones. Further evidence for a lack of effect of a phenothiazine on the SCOR to moderate tones comes from Gruzelier, Connolly, Eves, *et al.* (1981), where in both cross-sectional and longitudinal open drug trials (all subjects were tested off, then on, drugs), bimodal distributions of trials to habituation to 70-dB tones were obtained for both drug-free patients and those on chlorpromazine. SCORs to a series of 90-dB tones (250-msec rise time) were reduced in frequency and amplitude by chlorpromazine, but not significantly. The evidence, then, suggests differential neuroleptic effects on the SCOR to stimuli of different intensities. This can account for some of the conflicting results in the literature. Whether only DRs rather than ORs are attenuated by these drugs can be determined only by studies using measures that differentiate between these two classes of responses, such as HR and, perhaps, eyeblinks.

Gruzelier, Connolly, Eves, *et al.* (1981) did find marked effects of propranolol on the OR when that drug was either given alone or in combination with chlorpromazine. This usually took the form of a reduction in SCOR frequency, especially to the loud tones, but about half of the nonresponders to the mild tones increased responding. Thus propranolol tended to normalize SCOR frequency, and it also produced a clinical benefit. There were no significant effects on SCL or SSCRs, although the latter were reduced by 50% or more in two studies. Evidence of similar effects on SCORs in a small group of patients given dextro-propranolol, a form with less beta-adrenergic blocking action, suggests that the effects of the drug are central rather than peripheral and possibly occur in the limbic system (Gruzelier, Hirsch, Weller, & Murphy, 1979).

HEART RATE ORIENTING RESPONSES

Only a small modern literature exists on the heart rate orienting response (HROR). In addition to its importance for determining the generality of the results obtained from the overworked electrodermal system, study of the HROR might permit more definitive conclusions about whether ORs (deceleration) or DRs (acceleration) are elicited under some conditions. We (Zahn et al., 1968) observed greater acceleration in the first nine poststimulus beats but no differences in deceleration in chronic unmedicated patients compared to controls, suggesting a greater DR in the patients. Acute patients had less deceleration than controls, but this was significant only on the first trial (Zahn, Carpenter, & McGlashan, 1981a). Gruzelier (1975) reported greater acceleration in schizophrenic SCOR responders compared to nonpsychotic psychiatric controls. SCOR nonresponders in both groups had flat HR curves, whereas nonschizophrenic responders showed deceleration. Thus, these studies tend to agree in finding smaller or fewer decelerative HRORs and more of an accelerative tendency in schizophrenics. This might be interpreted as a tendency for schizophrenics to show DRs or to manifest an active process of stimulus rejection. However, Bartfai, Levander, Edman, et al. (1983) did not find HR acceleration in their schizophrenics; but they did find deceleration in both patients and controls. The evidence as a whole is rather meager, and the problem requires further study.

OTHER SCOR CHARACTERISTICS

The literature on other SCOR characteristics has been reviewed comprehensively by Öhman (1981). Where differences exist, the data for SCOR amplitudes roughly parallel that for frequency: Studies finding slow habituation in responders also tend to find higher amplitudes in schizophrenic versus control responders (e.g., Gruzelier & Venables, 1972), and the converse is true for studies finding fast habituation in responders (e.g., Bernstein et al., 1981), but many reports of no difference exist. These studies add up to an inconclusive total, and the same sources of variability (clinical differences, intensity, medication) probably influence both amplitude and frequency in about the same way.

Latency and rise times of SCORs, in the few studies that measured them, have shown equivocal results. In studies reporting significant differences in recovery half-time, shorter recovery half-time in schizophrenics was observed (Öhman, 1981). This result was independent of SCOR amplitude (Öhman, 1981; Zahn, Carpenter, & McGlasham, 1981a). Marginal conflicting evidence on this point was reported by

Maricq and Edelberg (1975), but when only drug-free patients were considered, the difference, although still in the direction of longer recovery half-time in the patients, was clearly not significant (Maricq & Weinrich, 1980). Patterson and Venables (1978) found a subgroup of schizophrenics with one to two trials to habituation whose SCORs had slower recovery half-times and also longer rise times and latencies than those of controls, suggesting that these SCOR attributes have similar sources of variation as response frequency.

Effects of Significance

In an earlier review, it was concluded that both phasic and tonic ANS reactivity to meaningful or significant stimuli and situations were impaired in unmedicated schizophrenics (Zahn, 1975). More recent data qualify this conclusion, although there is also more support for it.

PHASIC SCRs

Gruzelier and Venables (1973) found SCOR nonresponding schizophrenics to be about as reactive as responders and nonschizophrenic patients to signal stimuli in a discrimination task to which a key press was required. However, the nonresponders' deficit remained to the nonsignal stimuli in the task. Similarly, Bernstein and Taylor (1976) reported unmedicated adolescent schizophrenics to be significantly hyporesponsive both to simple tones and to nonsignal tones in a discrimination task, but to be only nonsignificantly hyporesponsive when a motor response was required to the tones. This study also found that the SCORs of schizophrenics to either praising or scolding messages were at normal levels. "Priming" subjects with a scolding message just before a 60-dB tone normalized SCORs to that tone in schizophrenics, but they were hyporeactive after a praising message. In a later study, Bernstein, Schneider, Juni, Pope, and Starkey (1980) observed medicated adult schizophrenics to be hyporeactive to verbal stimuli under nontask conditions, but to react at normal levels when the stimuli were part of a task. SCRs and HR accelerative responses to tones with and without task significance were found by A. L. Gray (1975) not to differentiate schizophrenics and controls.

Thus, these studies suggest essentially normal phasic ANS reactions in schizophrenics under some conditions. The relevant condition would appear to require a motor response rather than significance per se, since the evidence suggests impairment in schizophrenics in "no-go" trials in a discrimination task (Gruzelier & Venables, 1973). However, there is an apparent conflict with data from my laboratory (Zahn, 1964, 1975; Zahn, Carpenter, & McGlashan, 1981a), which consistently show schizophrenic impairment in SCRs to the imperative stimuli in a reaction time task. One difference that might be relevant is that the studies cited above, finding minimal schizophrenic impairment, used key or button presses as motor responses, while the studies from my laboratory used the release of a previously depressed key. This might seem a trivial difference, but, in fact, I (Zahn, 1964, 1975) found minimal schizophrenic impairment in SCRs under conditions where either a "casual" key press was required to a tone or when the key press initiated the foreperiod of an RT trial, although this was not as clearly shown later (Zahn, Carpenter, & McGlashan, 1981a). In addition, I (Zahn, 1964) reported greater key pressure in schizophrenics than in controls, suggesting that the effective stimulus complex may have been more intense for the patients. None of the more recent studies has measured motor responses. However, a more direct conflict in results occurs in the case of verbal responses: Bernstein *et al.* (1980) found normal reactions in schizophrenics to task-related verbal stimuli, but I (Zahn, 1975) found impaired SCRs in schizophrenics to a word association task.

Patient characteristics and medication might also contribute to the variance in ANS reactions to meaningful stimuli. Evidence of lower reactivity in poor premorbid or chronic patients or in acute patients with a poor clinical outcome, as compared to good premorbid, acute, or good-outcome patients, has been presented in several studies (Fowles, Watt, Maher, & Grinspoon, 1970; Magaro, 1973; Zahn, Carpenter, & McGlashan, 1981b). The very interesting finding that drugs attenuated phasic skin conductance and tonic skin conductance (SC) reactivity in poor premorbid patients, but had the opposite effects in good premorbids (M. J. Goldstein, 1970), has been replicated (Magaro, 1973) but not further followed up.

In a Soviet study apparently uninfluenced by the recent Western literature (a situation that has been reciprocated), Saarma (1974) found no differences between unmedicated schizophrenics and controls in the frequency of SC, HR, or respiratory reactions to signal stimuli, but the patients had lower SCR amplitudes, as well as fewer trials on which all three measures were responsive to the stimuli. The last of these variables has not been studied as such by other investigators in this type of situation.

Many of the more recent results cited above contradict the generalization that phasic ANS reactions to demanding stimuli are disproportionately low in schizophrenics or that their ANS is "not well-modulated by the demands of the environment" (Zahn, 1975, p. 120). In fact, in some of these studies, schizophrenics showed more of an effect from changes in the environment than did controls; a similar conclusion has been drawn from the SCOR studies in terms of stimulus intensity. Further study of the conditions that differentially affect ANS responding in schizophrenics and controls is particularly important for

understanding of the role of ANS activity in disordered behavior.

ANTICIPATORY ACTIVITY

There is evidence of poor autonomic conditioning in schizophrenics (Ax, Bamford, Beckett, Fretz, & Gottlieb, 1970; Gorham, Novelly, Ax, & Frohman, 1978) from studies using a delay-discriminative classical conditioning procedure in which the conditioned response (CR) is anticipatory to an aversive stimulus, but the role of awareness of the contingencies in this paradigm clouds its interpretation (J. A. Stern & Janes, 1973). Studies taking awareness into account, however, have produced conflicting results. Ax *et al.* (1970), Baer and Fuhrer (1969), and Rist, Baumann, and Cohen (1981) all found that schizophrenics could not verbalize the stimulus contingencies adequately in a differential conditioning paradigm. Fuhrer and Baer (1970) observed that, when given information about the contingencies, schizophrenics acquired conditioning as well as controls, but Rist *et al.* (1981) found that only normals responded to such information. However, in a second study in which only consistent SCR responders to the unconditioned stimulus (UCS) were included, Rist *et al.* (1981) obtained evidence of normal or better conditioning and effects of information in schizophrenics for both SCR and HR deceleration. Similarly, Robinson *et al.* (1977) reported better SCR trace conditioning in schizophrenia-spectrum cases than in controls when only SCR responders were included. The Rist *et al.* (1981) paper suggests that sex, length of hospitalization, and responder status of the subjects, as well as instructions, the type of UCS, and the physiological measure, can all affect the results.

In contrast to both Fuhrer and Baer (1970) and Rist *et al.* (1981), who found normal or greater ANS anticipatory activity in aware schizophrenics when the UCS was an imperative stimulus for an RT response, a number of studies using a similar but nondiscriminative warned RT paradigm, in which awareness is not an issue, have obtained different results. A. L. Gray (1975) found less SCR anticipatory activity and less HR slowing prior to an RT imperative stimulus in chronic schizophrenics than in controls. My colleagues and I have obtained partial replication of these results (Zahn, 1964; and Zahn, Carpenter, & McGlashan, 1981a, 1981b); we reported fewer anticipatory SCRs late in the RT foreperiod in unmedicated chronic and acute schizophrenics, and attenuated HR slowing in the foreperiod in acute patients with a poor clinical course. Besides making use of a nondiscriminative procedure, our studies also tested unmedicated patients. However, impairment in anticipatory HR slowing was obtained in medicated patients by Waddington, MacCulloch, Schalken, and Sambrooks (1978), using an RT task with aversive stimuli. This suggests the rather surprising hypothesis that the addition of a discrimination task (if subjects are made aware of the contingencies) abolishes the deficit in anticipatory ANS responding in schizophrenics.

Studies on anticipatory activity would seem to have implications for theories of deficits in attention in schizophrenia. They provide some support for the idea that slow RT in schizophrenia may be due, in part, to inadequate preparation to respond (Shakow, 1962). Physiological activity during RT foreperiods may index such preparation. Although there is some evidence that subjects with inadequate anticipatory activity show the most severe deficits in RT (Baer & Fuhrer, 1969; Zahn, Carpenter, & McGlashan, 1981b), a definite relationship between these variables has not been established. Investigations of the effects on RT of procedures that alter anticipatory activity may be one useful approach to this problem. In view of the absence of a clear understanding of bradycardia and attention, this may be one area where studies of psychopathology may shed light on the normal process, because of the large variations in both the behavioral and physiological responses in schizophrenics.

Some investigators using conditioning techniques treat them like psychometric tests. Thus Ax (1975) considers classical ANS differential conditioning as a test of motivational aptitude or aptitude for limbic learning. Similarly, Ban, Ananth, and Lehmann (1979) have developed a battery of autonomic and skeletal orienting and conditioning techniques for use in classifying schizophrenics. The performances of 80 medicated schizophrenics were distributed over 97% of the 117 possible categories. Although "impairment" was noted in almost all chronic schizophrenic patients, no comparison data or relationship with meaningful clinical variables are presented; thus the utility of this technique remains to be shown.

TONIC ANS CHANGES

Investigations and/or reports of tonic ANS changes to stress in schizophrenia have declined in recent years, perhaps as a function of the decline in respectability of the arousal concept. Earlier studies have been reviewed elsewhere (Zahn, 1975). That many conflicting findings exist should surprise no one. However, it has been pointed out that while the literature prior to 1950 generally indicated tonic ANS hyporeactivity in schizophrenics to both physiological and psychological stressors, some important later studies found no difference or the opposite result. For example, tonic hyperreactivity in acute psychotics and normal reactivity in chronic schizophrenics to painful stimuli and task performance was reported by Malmo and Shagass (1952). Greater electromyogram (EMG) response to 1 min of presumably noxious white noise stimulation was found in psychotics (mostly "early" schizophrenics), as compared to neurotics, patients

with character disorders, and normals (I. B. Goldstein, 1965). Many other studies found attenuated tonic reactions to task performance in schizophrenics, although there were many negative results as well. Prognosis, chronicity, and medication may all affect tonic changes, as detailed above. (See pp. 513–514.)

Among the more recent studies, A. L. Gray (1975) found normal increments in SCL due to RT task performance in schizophrenics, but the patients showed a paradoxical decrease in both SCL and HR when the stimuli presented were 110-dB tones compared to 70-dB tones. I (Zahn, 1964, 1975, 1977) have consistently observed attenuated SCL reactions to task performance in schizophrenics, and we (Zahn, Carpenter, & McGlasdhan, 1981a) found low reactivity in acute schizophrenics to a mental arithmetic task in terms of SSCR, SCL, HR, and skin temperature, although their tonic response to an RT task was not different from controls. Poor-outcome patients were significantly more impaired than those who remitted quickly on only the SSCR measure (Zahn, Carpenter, & McGlashan, 1981b). Attenuated cardiovascular responses to a mental arithmetic procedure in schizophrenics was found by Kelly (1980), who measured FBF, HR, SBP, and DBP. This study included patients with eight different affective and neurotic disorders, most of whom had attenuated stress reactions. The schizophrenics were lowest on all variables except SBP, although statistical comparisons were reported only with normals. Albus, Ackenheil, Engel, and Muller (1982) compared 12 drug-free acute schizophrenics with 53 controls on the responses of several physiological variables to four procedures including cold pressor and mental arithmetic. The patients had low HR reactivity but a greater trapezius EMG response to the stressors.

In general, the evidence continues to support the hypothesis of low tonic ANS reactivity to the mild stress of task performance in schizophrenia. In conjunction with the (rather sparse) evidence of overreactivity in situations involving pain, the tonic results bear a similarity to the results on the phasic SCR to moderate and aversive stimuli: schizophrenic hyporeactivity to mild or moderate stimulation, and hyperreactivity to intense stimulation. Alternative hypotheses based on motivation and incentive are possible, especially in view of the impairment in interpersonal relationships generally attributed to schizophrenics. For example, hyperreactivity in the pain–stress situations might be attributable to a fear of really being harmed, and hyporesponsivity to mental arithmetic tasks might be attributable to low motivation. On the other hand, the atypical ANS reactions of schizophrenics may play a significant role in their psychological state in these situations. Progress in understanding the mechanisms of tonic ANS changes in schizophrenia might come from manipulating motivation and incentive, and from measuring ANS reactions to nonpsychological stressors (such as physical activity or pharmacological agents) in both patients and controls.

Relationships of ANS Activity to Task Performance

An important question is whether psychophysiological variables can aid in understanding the pervasive deficits in task performance found in schizophrenia. An affirmative answer to this question would imply that these variables reflect underlying processes that also affect performance. In the absence of a clear understanding of the processes reflected by either the physiological or the behavioral variables, a definitive answer to the question is impossible at present; however, establishing empirical relationships between variables in these two domains would seem of critical importance in furthering the understanding of their relationships to a common process.

Historically, the hypothesis that has most often guided thinking in this area is that of an "inverted-U" relationship between arousal and performance. Although this idea has face validity—it is easy to imagine having difficulty tying one's shoelaces when either half asleep or in a state of panic—evidence of its validity with respect to the behavior deficits in schizophrenia and under the less extreme states found in laboratory conditions is harder to come by. More importantly, there is a conceptual difficulty with the hypothesis, since neither arousal nor performance is a unitary concept; different indices of each may be essentially unrelated. For example, Kornetsky and Mirsky (1966) and Mirsky (1969) present evidence from pharmacological and behavioral studies that the hypothesis has explanatory value in schizophrenia for tests of sustained attention, but not for other tests.

The best tests of the hypothesis should come from studies in which psychophysiological data are collected in conjunction with behavioral data. In an earlier review of this area (Zahn, 1975), it was concluded that a "strong" form of the hypothesis—namely, that arousal indices should be higher in schizophrenics during performance of a task on which they exhibited impairment—is not well supported by the data. A weaker form, which proposes that the peak of the inverted U is reached at lower levels of activation in schizophrenics, fares somewhat better; however, supporting evidence for this model, based on negative correlations between arousal indices during the task and performance, is inconsistent. There is better evidence that high resting levels on ANS measures and low specific reactivity during the task are related to impairment.

The most powerful new evidence in support of the inverted-U hypothesis comes from the well-designed study of Spohn *et al.* (1977), in which phenothiazines reduced some base SCLs during both rest and task

periods; reduced SCR and HR response amplitudes to task-related stimuli; and improved performance on attention and information-processing tasks, but not on tests of thought disorder. These results are quite consistent with the ideas of Kornetsky and Mirsky (1966).

The separation of schizophrenics on the basis of the SCOR should be a useful tool in investigating relationships to attention and information-processing measures, since SCOR responders and nonresponders differ generally in arousal indices. Straube (1979) observed that SCOR nonresponders made more errors on a dichotic shadowing task than responders, due chiefly to omissions. Since some baseline measures were very low in the nonresponders compared to controls, this finding provides tentative support for the inverted-U hypothesis at the low end. However, Patterson and Venables (1980) reported about equal impairment in both SCOR responders and nonresponders of sensitivity in a signal detection task, while a group with one or two trials to habituation performed at normal levels. This result can also be fit to a weak inverted-U model, since the group with unimpaired performance had intermediate SCL during the OR series, although no schizophrenic group exceeded the controls in SCL.

That the type of task as well as medication may be critical variables is shown by Gruzelier and Hammond (1978), who found that in auditory signal detection, responders were more impaired than nonresponders when on placebo and when the measures were false positives or when the stimulus presentation rate was fast. Nonresponders showed more errors of omission when on chlorpromazine. Similarly, Weiner (1981), who had chronic schizophrenics with either high or low resting frontalis EMG levels press a button for monetary rewards, found that low-EMG patients were more impaired on tasks requiring fast response rates (fixed interval and fixed ratio schedules), while high-EMG patients were impaired when reinforcements were given for slow response rates.

Finally, we (Zahn, Carpenter, & McGlashan, 1981b) found that acute unmedicated patients with poor outcome, who had higher SSCRs and HR during both rest and an RT task than either good-outcome patients or controls, showed the most impairment on RT. Similarly, Bartfai, Levander, and Sedvall (1983) reported poorer eye tracking in SCOR nonhabituators than in habituators. These results are also consistent with the inverted-U model, and are unique in that there was a clear behavior deficit in schizophrenics as compared to controls. However, other variables, such as attenuated anticipatory HR slowing and fewer and longer-latency SCRs elicited by the RT stimuli—variables clearly not indicating high arousal—also characterized the group with slow RT. More evidence of between- and within-subject covariation of physiolog-

ical and performance variables will be needed to clarify this issue.

The difficulties in establishing a relationship between arousal and performance, even when these are
specifically defined, is pointed out by several studies
that have investigated the two-flash threshold (TFT)
in relation to skin potential level (SPL) or SCL. The
TFT has sometimes been considered to reflect "cortical arousal" (Venables, 1963). The earlier investigations showed SPL and TFT to be intercorrelated in
the opposite direction in some schizophrenics compared to controls, but the directionality differed in
different studies (Lykken & Maley, 1968; Venables,
1963). In a complex series of experiments, Gruzelier,
Lykken, and Venables (1972) confirmed the opposite
directionality of the ANS-TFT relationship and
showed that this was dependent to some extent on the
type and level of the ANS variables and perhaps the
method of measuring TFT. At low to moderate levels
of SPL or SCL, the relationship between level and
TFT was positive for controls and negative for nonparanoid schizophrenics. At high levels, either under
nonactivated conditions or when physically stressed
by a bicycle ergometer, controls showed a negative
relationship between activation and TFT, while the
nonparanoid group showed either no effect or a positive relationship. The data for the controls thus fit an
upright-U relationship, while those for the nonpara-
noids are consistent with an inverted-U relationship.
A paradoxical finding of increased HR but decreased
SCL during activation was obtained for the nonparanoid group. Paranoid patients were generally more
similar to controls, particularly under the activation
conditions. Apparently there were some differences
between results obtained with two different psychophysical methods of determining TFT, but these are
not detailed. Gruzelier et al. (1972) interpret their
results in terms of inhibitory processes (possibly mediated by the hippocampus) protecting the nonparanoid patients against high somatic arousal (possibly
mediated by the reticular activating system), thus suggesting a neurophysiological substrate for the inverted-U relationship.

In contrast, Claridge and Clark (1982) found evidence in acute unmedicated schizophrenics of an upright-U relationship between TFT and range-corrected SCL. This result was obtained, however, by
plotting three daily observations for each subject, and
omitting a third of the patients who could not be kept
off medication for 3 days. A similar procedure on the
patients when medicated produced no discernible
trends between SCL and TFT. Upright-U curves were
also reported for subjects given LSD-25 and subjects
high on the Eysenck Psychoticism scale, while control
subjects showed an inverted-U relationship (Claridge,
1978). Claridge also proposes hippocampal regulation of reticular-mediated activation as a mechanism,

but suggests that this process has broken down in
schizophrenics. The directly opposite results of Claridge (1978; Claridge & Clark, 1982) and Gruzelier
et al. (1972) for both schizophrenics and controls are
probably due to some of the many methodological
differences between the two sets of studies. Discovering these would seem to be imperative for further
theoretical development to occur.

Differences in limbic control over the SCOR have
also been suggested to underlie the dichotomy between nonresponders and slow habituators that was
found by Gruzelier and Venables (1972). Schizophrenics so classified differed on TFT in the expected direction—lower TFT in the SCOR responder group
(Gruzelier & Venables, 1974b). However, correlations between SCL during the task and TFT were
negative in both groups, despite much higher and
more labile SCL in the responders (Gruzelier & Venables, 1975b). Normal controls, who were intermediate on SCL, also showed negative correlations when
TFT was measured by the method of limits (as was
used in most of the previous research), but had nonsignificantly positive correlations when TFT was measured by the more sophisticated constant-stimulus
method. Through the use of the latter procedure, it
was found that, compared to controls, both schizophrenic groups had a lower criterion (greater probability of reporting "two" to a single flash) and lower
sensitivity. Criterion and sensitivity were positively
correlated with SCL in the patient group as a whole.
Similar positive correlations were obtained for controls with sensitivity, but SCL correlated negatively
with the criterion measure in this group.

Despite the apparently chaotic nature of the data
from these studies, a possible pattern can be discerned
for the schizophrenics when medication status is considered. The findings that medicated schizophrenics
with high SCL have low TFT and high criterion and
sensitivity scores (Gruzelier & Venables, 1974b,
1975b) are consistent with the findings of Gruzelier
et al. (1972) for TFT and with those of Straube
(1979) and Gruzelier and Hammond (1978) showing
better performance on signal detection measures in
medicated SCOR responders than in nonresponders.
On the other hand, studies on unmedicated patients
have tended to show superior performance (Gruzelier
& Hammond, 1978; Zahn, 1975; Zahn, Carpenter, &
McGlashan, 1981b) and low TFT (Claridge, 1978) in
patients with evidence of lower arousal. Although
there are some exceptions (Claridge & Clark, 1982),
the data for medicated patients generally seem to fit
on the ascending limb of the inverted-U function, and
the data for unmedicated patients seem to fit on the
descending limb. Paradoxically, the data for normal
controls in the TFT-SCL studies show a greater lack
of consistency than those for the schizophrenics. This
might not be unexpected, however, given the usual

assumption that normals are close to an optimal level of activation, so that a slight variation in conditions might move them to one limb or the other.

SC Laterality

Interest in asymmetry of electrodermal activity in schizophrenia has increased, in part because of the general increase of interest in hemispheric specialization of function and in part because of the influential ideas of Flor-Henry (1969), who associated schizophrenia with left-hemisphere dysfunction and affective disorders with right-hemisphere dysfunction, based on studies of temporal lobe epilepsy.

The data on this topic have been reviewed by Öhman (1981). Results obtained for SCL have been particularly difficult to interpret, because the few positive results that have been obtained are contaminated by confounding the SCOR responder status and diagnosis, as well as an interaction of responder status and length of hospitalization. The positive results show higher right-hand versus left-hand SCL in schizophrenic responders (Gruzelier & Venables, 1974a; Rippon, 1979), but many negative results exist as well (Bartfai, Levander, Edman, et al., 1983; Bernstein et al., 1981; Gruzelier, Eves, Connolly, & Hirsch, 1981; Iacono, 1982; Schneider, 1982; Straube, 1979).

Greater SCOR reactivity from the right versus left hand in schizophrenics is perhaps a somewhat better confirmed finding: Several British studies report higher right-hand response frequency and/or amplitude in schizophrenics but not in controls, or more schizophrenics showing right-hand superiority than controls (Gruzelier, 1973; Gruzelier & Venables, 1974a; Gruzelier, Connolly, Eves, et al., 1981). A similar difference between patients and controls in SCOR amplitude was found by Patterson and Venables (1978), mostly due to greater left-hand values in controls. Several other recent studies have not shown schizophrenics and controls to differ Bartfai, Levander, Edman, et al., 1983; Bernstein et al., 1981; Gruzelier, Eves, Connolly, & Hirsch, 1981; Iacono, 1982; Schneider, 1982; Straube, 1979; Tarrier et al., 1978). Bernstein et al. (1981) also investigated FPVOR bilaterally, with negative results.

It is possible that these results might merely reflect overall differences in responding (Öhman, 1981). In most of the studies showing larger right-hand SCORs in schizophrenics, the responders were slow habituators, while in the negative studies the responders tended to show faster habituation than controls. Gruzelier and his colleagues (see Gruzelier, 1981) showed that normals who had slow habituation also had a right-side advantage in SCOR. Although this was not the case among schizophrenics, too few cases with fast or moderate habituation have appeared in

Gruzelier's studies for the hypothesis to have been tested properly (Öhman, 1981). In addition, Gruzelier, Connolly, Eves, et al. (1981) found that propranolol both normalized habituation rates and eliminated the asymmetry.

Data from the unmedicated acute cases provide evidence of two subgroups of patients based on SCOR laterality and clinical ratings: an L > R group, characterized predominantly by florid manic and paranoid symptoms, and a R > L group, which is high on defect symptoms of withdrawal, motor retardation, and blunted affect (Gruzelier, 1981). Thus the patients with predominantly florid symptoms had SCR laterality similar to that of patients with affective disorders (Gruzelier & Venables, 1973; Myslobodsky & Horesh, 1978).

Although the positive evidence suggests higher right-sided electrodermal activity in schizophrenia, there are many conflicting results. Further studies examining the influences of such variables as chronicity, drug status, and clinical state, as well as situational and task influences, are needed. The latter class of variables has been virtually ignored in schizophrenia laterality research, with focus being almost exclusively on the SCOR, yet they have been the most interesting source of results in studies on normal humans. There also remains the problem of interpretation. Gruzelier (1979) argues that the right-side advantage is schizophrenics indicates a left-hemisphere dysfunction, probably in the frontal temporo-limbic region, and Öhman (1981) suggests that this dysfunction may be of the nature of reduced left-hemisphere inhibition. Other writers have different views (Myslobodsky & Horesh, 1978). A detailed examination of this issue is beyond the scope of this chapter, but it is to be hoped (and expected) that the newer tomographic techniques of examining brain structure and function will help provide a more definitive answer.

Electrocortical Studies

The Electroencephalogram

Several early (Mirsky, 1969) and recent comprehensive reviews of the electroencephalogram (EEG) literature exist (Buchsbaum, 1979a; Itil, 1977; Saletu, 1980; Shagass, 1976), so this topic need not be covered in detail here. It is customary to distinguish between qualitative EEG findings or abnormalities and quantitative differences in frequency, amplitude, and variability.

QUALITATIVE FINDINGS

EEG abnormalities are frequently reported in schizophrenic samples, but the incidence has ranged from 5% to 80% in different studies, suggesting considerable variability in sampling or in the thresholds for detecting abnormalities. Among the many abnormalities detected have been spikes, spike-and-wave patterns, sharp waves (especially from the temporal lobes), "choppy" records, dysrhythmia, and diffuse slowing. Although most of these abnormalities have not been associated with individual differences in behavior, a few such relationships have been found. Soviet investigators have reported some EEG differences among subtypes of schizophrenia, most notably that the nuclear, long-lasting form is characterized by more pathological EEG signs than are episodic or paranoid forms (Mirsky, 1969). A "B-mitten" EEG pattern recorded in sleep appeared more often in reactive than in process patients, while process patients, who are resistant to neuroleptic treatment, frequently showed a "hypernormal" stability of the alpha rhythm. Suicide and aggressive behavior may be associated with a 14 and 6 spike-and-wave pattern. Thus certain subgroups of cases presenting as schizophrenic may have a fairly specific brain dysfunction. A recent large-scale study (Small, Milstein, Sharpley, Klapper, & Small, 1984) concluded that prognosis may be better if the EEG is abnormal and that many "schizophrenics" with abnormal EEGs are misdiagnosed.

QUANTITATIVE FINDINGS

Although much of the early work in evaluating EEG frequency and amplitude was done by eye, this field has benefited from the introduction of many analog and digital techniques for computing these parameters automatically. Using an early technique of integrating the EEG voltage, schizophrenics consistently showed less variability in that measure, suggesting sustained hyperarousal (Mirsky, 1969). Itil, Saletu, and Davis (1972) compared 100 drug-free schizophrenics with 100 controls using a visual analysis, an analog frequency analyzer, and digital period analysis. All three methods showed less fast alpha (10–13 Hz), less slow beta, and more fast activity in schizophrenics. Excess slow activity in the patients was also shown by the automatic techniques. A discriminant analysis of the combined methods classified 87.5% of patients and controls correctly. In addition, visual analysis showed that controls has less dysrhythmia, higher amplitudes, more sleep-like patterns, and occipito-frontal synchronization.

The confirmation, by more sophisticated techniques, of the early observations of more low-voltage, fast activity and less well-organized alpha in schizophrenics compared to controls is thought by Itil (1977) to be the most important recent set of findings in this area. Artifactual interpretations having been discounted (Itil, 1977; Shagass, 1976), interpretations in terms of arousal have been made (Itil, 1977; Saletu, 1980), and these are consistent with the general flavor of the ANS baseline data. Similarly, evidence of less within-subject variability in schizoph-

renics' EEGs, which has been attributed to less drowsiness than in controls, is consistent with the less rapid decline in their baseline measures (such as SCL) that is frequently found.

Also consistent with this interpretation is evidence that neuroleptic drugs reduce fast and increase slow activity, and that these changes seem correlated with therapeutic effects (Saletu, 1980). The finding that therapy-resistant patients have more slow activity than good responders when drug-free fits well with the EEG neuroleptic data (Itil, 1977; Saletu, 1980).

Shagass (1976) considers the lower alpha abundance found in schizophrenics as possibly secondary to emotional disturbance and of little interest. He considers lower alpha peak frequency and EEG hyperstability, which he feels are both reliable and specific markers for chronic schizophrenia, as more important. However, evidence that EEG frequency deviance may have biological significance comes from evidence that excessive fast beta is also seen during sleep (Itil, 1977) and that schizophrenics with excess slow activity, chiefly in the theta band, are less likely to have a family history of mental illness (Hays, 1977).

In a large study which did not analyze separate frequency bands, Shagass, Roemer, and Straumanis (1982) found lower EEG amplitude variability, higher frequency variability, less effects of eye opening and more waveshape symmetry and lower variability of symmetry in schizophrenics. The major interpretation of these findings is higher cortical activation in schizophrenics, confirming much of the previous literature.

Most recent studies have examined frequencies using Fourier transform spectral analysis and have provided some confirmation of the earlier evidence. A sophisticated geometric analysis of the frequency spectrum was used by Kemali, Vacca, Marciano, Nolfe, and Iorio (1981) with a heterogeneous group of 67 unmedicated schizophrenics and a similar number of controls. The relative power of alpha was lower and that of beta was higher in the patients at all leads, and delta power was higher in anterior right leads. Mean frequency in the beta range was faster and more variable in the schizophrenics. Depressives and heroin abusers were clearly different. Subgroups based on chronicity or paranoid status were quite similar. Similarly, Morihisa, Duffy, and Wyatt (1983) reported more delta and fast beta (20 to 31.5 Hz) and less alpha in the EEGs of both unmedicated and medicated chronic schizophrenics than in controls. However the differences in delta were the most widely distributed. Shaw, Brooks, Colter, and O'Connor (1979) reported less power for 4- to 20-Hz frequencies in medicated schizophrenics. This is not inconsistent with the previously mentioned studies despite the use of a midfrontal reference and poor age and sex matching of subjects.

Bernstein et al. (1981) found slower alpha frequencies and nonsignificantly more nonalpha power in medicated patients than in controls, while Iacono (1982) reported less alpha and more delta in medicated patients who were in remission and nonsignificantly slower alpha only in schizophrenic SCOR responders. Both of these studies showed an independence of EEG frequency distributions and ANS levels. Medication status (Bernstein *et al.*, 1981) and SCOR responder status (Iacono, 1982) were both related to ANS base levels in the expected direction but were unrelated to the EEG. Although confirmation on unmedicated patients is needed, this evidence, in addition to the similarities found between medicated and unmedicated patients (Morihisa *et al.*, 1983), casts doubt on attributions of the EEG findings to emotional disturbance or a general concept of arousal.

Independence of EEG and ANS indices of orienting is suggested by the findings of Bernstein *et al.* (1981) that schizophrenics did not differ from controls in alpha-blocking frequency to tones but, as reported earlier, were hyporesponsive on ANS indices. However, there is some evidence of slow habituation of alpha-blocking duration to light flashes (Milstein, Stevens, & Sachdev, 1969). Earlier evidence that alpha-blocking latency is faster in schizophrenics (Buchsbaum, 1979a) has been confirmed recently (J. R. Davis, Glaros, & Davidson, 1981). This result is not observed with ANS measures.

Some investigators have studied changes in frequency spectra as a function of parameters stimulation. Spratt and Gale (1979) used stimuli varying in the number and variety of geometrical figures presented. Normal subjects, as in previous work, showed reductions in alpha and beta power as a function of increasing stimulus complexity. Schizophrenics did not show this effect under neutral instructions, but instructions to count the stimuli normalized their EEG responses to increases in number but not variety. There was some evidence that performance on a recognition task given later was related to the alpha attenuation during the initial stimulation period in the patients. This suggests that the patients, unlike the controls, were inattentive to irrelevant stimulus attributes but appropriately responsive to instructions—a conclusion not compatible with a segmental set theory of attention in schizophrenia (Shakow, 1962). Basically negative results for differential power-spectral response to spatial imagery and mental arithmetic tasks were reported by Shaw *et al.* (1979); however, the coherence between pairs of leads was higher in the arithmetic task than in the spatial task for schizophrenics, while the reverse held for normal and neurotic subjects. The meaning of this result is not clear.

In a study by Koukkou (1982), the peak frequencies of the power spectra in the 2- to 8-Hz, 8- to 13-Hz, and 13- to 26-Hz ranges were computed before and after various signal stimuli (e.g., sentences to remember, signal tones). Acute and remitted schizophrenics, all unmedicated, were compared to controls. Controls showed an increase in peak alpha frequency and a decrease in theta frequency following stimulation. Acute patients, but not the remitted group, showed a diminished alpha response under all conditions. Less marked was a smaller theta response in both patient groups. These results are interpreted as indicating a defect in the later (postfilter) stages of information processing in acute patients, which disappears with symptomatic recovery. This finding bears some similarity to that of diminished ANS response to meaningful stimuli in acute patients, especially those with poor outcome (Zahn, Carpenter, & McGlashan, 1981b). Since the remitted patients were not tested while acutely psychotic, it is not possible to know whether their data reflect a state change or a prognostic marker.

Thus, there seem to be some replicable diagnostic markers in the EEGs of schizophrenics, some of which seem appropriately treatment-predictive and treatment-responsive. The functional significance of these markers, however, is not clear. Interpretations of EEG frequency data in terms of a general concept of arousal are not supported by direct comparisons with ANS data. It may be that some of the findings reflect state differences, but these may turn out to be better described in terms of attention or other cognitive processes than in terms of arousal.

Attempts to relate transient behavioral abnormalities with EEG abnormalities were made by Stevens, Bigelow, Denney, Lipkin, Livermore, Rauscher, and Wyatt (1979) and by Stevens and Livermore (1982), who telemetered EEG from freely moving schizophrenic patients and controls. In the 1979 study, many abnormalities in temporal regions were found, but it was concluded that these were not associated with abnormal behaviors. In the later study, which analyzed power spectra, a "ramp" pattern thought to reflect spike activity in deep structures was seen only in patients, twice as often during "abnormal" events as during normal behavior. The authors reported other EEG correlates of abnormal behaviors, such as hallucinations and blocking, many involving increased slow activity and reduced alpha and most supported statistically. This study is perhaps unique in demonstrating a direct connection between pathological brain activity and abnormal behavior, even though a specific abnormality in schizophrenics has not been found.

ERPs

Since the basic dysfunction in schizophrenics may begin at the initial stages of processing stimuli, it has seemed reasonable that ERP techniques might provide more valuable data than those from the EEG as markers of psychopathology. Psychophysiological studies of schizophrenia have begun to take advantage of the recent developments in using ERP techniques to study various stages of information processing.

MIDDLE ERPs

A preponderance of the evidence in this literature up to the late 1970s indicates that ERPs to stimuli in various modalities with latencies greater than 100 msec are smaller in schizophrenics than in controls (reviews by Buchsbaum, 1977; Saletu, 1980; Shagass, 1979). This does not appear to be due to medication. Some recent data, however, may question the generality of this finding for ERPs in the 100- to 200-msec range. Pfefferbaum, Horvath, Roth, Tinklenberg, and Kopell (1980) reported larger P200 to tone pips of various intensities in schizophrenics. The patients had marginally smaller N120 ERPs as well. In the same subjects, Roth, Horvath, Pfefferbaum, and Kopell (1980) found larger N120 in controls only when the interstimulus interval (ISI) was long (6.25 sec); however, in a paradigm with mixed noise and tones of varying intensity, the patients had generally smaller ERPs than controls.

One possible source of the differences among these studies is the instructions with respect to attention to the stimuli. In Pfefferbaum et al. (1980), subjects were asked to read a book and ignore the stimuli, while in Roth, Horvath, Pfefferbaum, and Kopell (1980), they were asked merely to sit quietly with eyes open. Another study from the same laboratory, in which subjects were asked not to attend to the tones, no significant differences were obtained for ISIs ranging from .75 to 3 sec (Roth, Horvath, Pfefferbaum, Tinklenberg, Mezzich, & Kopell, 1979). Similarly, Roth, Pfefferbaum, Kelly, Berger, and Kopell (1981) failed to find differences between schizophrenics and controls in paradigms with either single-intensity tones and 8-sec ISI or variable-intensity tones and a 4-sec ISI with instructions to ignore the stimuli. However, in paradigms in which attention was directed to the stimuli by means of task requirements, attentuation of N120 (Roth, Horvath, Pfefferbaum, & Kopell, 1980; Roth et al., 1981) and P200 (Roth, Horvath, Pfefferbaum, & Kopell, 1980) in schizophrenics was observed. Thus in this group of studies, the schizophrenic deficit in ERP amplitude is roughly proportional to the extent to which attention is directed to the stimuli by the instructions. However, the most striking differences are between the task and nontask conditions, so the "arousing" effects of task demands may also play a role (Buchsbaum, 1977). A paradigm to control attention, in which ERPs to mixed tones and lights of four intensities were recorded when subjects were asked to count repetitions of the same intensity in either modality, was used in schizophrenics by G. C. Davis, Buchsbaum, and Bunney (1980). Attention enhanced N120 to only low-intensity stim-

uli in normals, but not in the patient group. This supports the idea of a disproportionate schizophrenic ERP deficit to attended stimuli, although verification of appropriate task performance is lacking.

In a similar paradigm R. Cohen, Sommer, and Hermanutz (1981) recorded ERPs to rare clicks in subjects who counted either the clicks or interspersed visual stimuli. Attention to the clicks increased N90 in controls but decreased it in schizophrenics. Counting performance was indeed poorer in schizophrenics, suggesting an inability to follow instructions completely. R. Cohen et al. (1981) suggest that the counting instructions may have produced interferences in the patients. P340 and N220 to attended clicks were also reduced in the schizophrenics. A unique facet of this study is that the subjects were separated on the basis of the SCOR into nonresponders, habituators, and nonhabituators. The main result pertaining to this breakdown was that with directed attention N220 was decreased in the nonresponders, unchanged in habituators, and increased in nonhabituators.

A somewhat different result was obtained for a dichotic listening paradigm by Baribeau-Braun, Picton, and Gosselin (1983). They found that when the ISI was relatively long, N1 was smaller than normal in schizophrenics for noncritical stimuli presented to the attended ear but not for stimuli to the unattended ear. For short ISIs, the patients had small N1s to unattended stimuli but equally small N1s under conditions of divided attention. Thus schizophrenics seem to have trouble with channel selectivity under some conditions and with divided attention under other conditions.

Another paradigm with implications for attention was used by Braff, Callaway, and Naylor (1977), who compared the click ERPs of schizophrenic and nonschizophrenic patients when the stimuli were self-produced by release of a button, with systematic variation of the delay between button release and click. Both groups showed attenuated ERPs with shorter delays, but the maximum attenuation was reached at a shorter delay in the nonschizophrenics (250 msec, compared to 500 msec in schizophrenics). On the assumption that reduced ERPs in this paradigm are due to reductions in time uncertainty at the shorter warning intervals, it is hypothesized that this is interfered with in schizophrenics due to a persistence of the effects of the initiating stimulus (button release) in "very short-term memory."

A difference between the group of studies from Roth's laboratory and many of the other studies in this area is that, for at least some of the paradigms used, control over various sources of artifact from ocular and muscle sources by Roth's group was attempted. This was also done by R. Cohen et al. (1981) and Baribeau-Braun et al. (1983). However, it would be premature to attribute the earlier consistent finding of low schizophrenic ERP amplitudes to inadequate control over sources of artifact. Studies from Shagass's laboratory (Shagass, 1979) have shown small ERPs in schizophrenics but no difference from ocular channels. A direct comparison of the effects of the background EEG was made by Lifshitz, Susswein, and Lee (1979), who compared the auditory ERPs of schizophrenics and controls on unselected trials (although stimuli were omitted during periods with a "noisy" EEG) and on trials in which the prestimulus period had low power in the delta band, as determined by Fourier analysis. Schizophrenics had smaller N120–P200 ERPs than controls under both conditions, but the results were much more significant under the low delta selection, despite fewer trials in the averaged data. This shows that reducing a possible source of variability may enhance weaker trends rather than weaken them further.

The possibility that small ERPs in schizophrenics may be due to drug effects has been given only a little attention. Straumanis, Shagass, and Roemer (1982) tested patients shortly after admission (after at least a week of no treatment) and before discharge when either on antipsychotic drugs or unmedicated. They concluded that where significant effects occurred, the drugs tended to normalize somatosensory and auditory ERPs (increased middle components) but worsen visual (pattern) ERPs.

Depression of visual ERP amplitude (most reliably for P90–N110) and increases in latency following performance of a 15-min arithmetic task were reported for unmedicated schizophrenics but not for normal, neurotic, or affective-disorder subjects by Kadobayashi, Nakamura, and Kato (1977). Further, this group observed a remarkable correlation between the time of the minimum ERP and clinical subtype (Kadobayashi, Mori, Arima, & Kato, 1978). This peaked at 1, 3, and 5 min posttask for paranoid, hebephrenic, and simple schizophrenics, respectively, with only 10 exceptions in 72 cases. The results suggest marked state effects on the ERP, but just what they are cannot be determined without replication with ancillary background EEG and/or ANS measures.

EFFECTS OF STIMULUS INTENSITY

Some differences between schizophrenics and controls in the effects of stimulus intensity have been found (Buchsbaum, 1977; Shagass, 1977), the best confirmed being that acute patients tend to show a small or even negative relationship ("reducing") between amplitude of an early peak (P100–N140 for visual ERP) and intensity. This has been replicated for the somatosensory modality (G.C. Davis *et al.*, 1980). Steeper than normal positive slopes ("augmenting") for chronic schizophrenics (Asarnow, Cromwell, & Rennick, 1978) and relative augmenting in chronic (compared with acute) patients and in paranoid schizophrenics (Schooler, Buchsbaum, & Carpenter, 1976) have been reported. Smaller effects of the in-

tensity of a noise stimulus in schizophrenics (not necessarily acute) for N120, P200, and P300 peaks measured from baseline was reported by Roth, Pfefferbaum, Horvath, Berger, and Kopell (1980), but no significant differences were obtained when pure tones were the stimuli (Pfefferbaum *et al.*, 1980; Roth, Pfefferbaum, Horvath, Berger, & Kopell, 1980; Roth *et al.* 1981). The stimulus intensity effect has been tied to a concept of "stimulus intensity control," a perceptual style by which the impact of intense stimulation on the nervous system is regulated (Buchsbaum, 1975). Reducing may serve a protective function in schizophrenics if they are prone to disorganization by high stimulus input. The augmenting in chronic patients has been attributed to a failure of this reducing mechanism, and that in paranoid patients has been attributed to enhanced vigilance (Schooler *et al.*, 1976). A more biological hypothesis of reducing has been prompted by the finding that naltrexone, a narcotic antagonist that may reduce hallucinations in some schizophrenics, increased the amplitude–intensity slope of somatosensory and visual N120 to normal levels in a small group of schizophrenics, although the results were of marginal significance (G. C. Davis *et al.*, 1980). This has been taken to support the concept of an endorphin basis for attention dysfunction in schizophrenia.

LATE ERPs

A very consistent finding in schizophrenia research is that P300 is smaller in these patients than in controls (Roth, 1977). This difference has appeared using paradigms not specifically designed to elicit P300 and when subjects were instructed to ignore the stimuli, but in each case some stimulus uncertainty was present. This has been twice confirmed recently by Roth's group (Roth, Horvath, Pfefferbaum, & Kopell, 1980; Roth *et al.*, 1981), whose subjects responded as quickly as possible to rare tones that differed in pitch from frequent tones, and by R. Cohen *et al.* (1981), whose subjects counted infrequent clicks. In the latter study, counting accuracy was correlated with P340 amplitude in the schizophrenic group. Similar results were obtained by Pass, Klorman, Salzman, Klein, and Kaskey (1980) using a continuous performance task (CPT) with acute schizophrenics. The patients had a disproportionate deficit in P300 (called "late positive component") following target stimuli as compared to nontarget stimuli. This type of effect was also reported for an auditory discrimination task (Hiramatsu, Kameyama, Niwa, Saitoh, Rymar, & Itoh, 1983). Reduced P300 (termed "P400") in a mixed group of psychiatric patients, including schizophrenics, was reported by Josiassen, Shagass, Roemer, and Straumanis (1981) using somatosensory ERPs and a counting task. These investigators questioned the specificity of this deficit to schizophrenia; they showed that it was related to severity of psychopathology, irrespective of diagnosis, and not correlated with counting accuracy.

These paradigms confound stimulus frequency with signal value; however, smaller than normal increments in P300 due to uncertainty and modality shifts in paradigms where signal value is not an issue have been reported for schizophrenics (Levit, Sutton, & Zubin, 1973; Verleger & Cohen, 1978). Roth et al. (1981) used two infrequent tones, each presented 10% of the time, requiring a response to just one of them. The patients showed impairment in P300 to both rare tones, but this ERP was potentiated in both groups to an equal degree when the response was required to the rare stimulus. Thus the schizophrenics had an attenuated response to the delivery of information, but were normally reactive to the addition of a motor response requirement. A similar conclusion for P3 may be drawn from the Baribeau-Braun et al. (1983) study of dichotic listening. Similarly, Duncan-Johnson, Roth, and Kopell (1984), in a study of the effects of different sequences of two equiprobable tones in a choice RT paradigm, reported similar effects of sequence on P300 amplitude in schizophrenics and controls, but a generally attenuated P300 in the patients. However, Brecher and Begleiter (1983) found that introducing a monetary incentive for correct responses increased the deficit in P300 of unmedicated schizophrenics. This was due to an increase in P300 under incentive conditions in normals but not in the patients.

Habituation of ERPs has not been extensively studied in schizophrenia. However, two studies suggest that P300 habituated in schizophrenics but not in normals, while N120 habituated only in normals (Levit et al., 1973; Verleger & Cohen, 1978). "Slow waves" and "sustained potentials," defined as the mean voltage (with respect to baseline) of some variously defined period 350 msec poststimulus or later, have also been studied. Pfefferbaum et al. (1980) observed diminished negative sustained potentials in schizophrenics in a tone intensity paradigm—a finding that they speculate might account, in part, for the larger positive and smaller negative ERPs observed in their study. This finding was not replicated in later tests with similar paradigms, but Roth et al. (1981) showed schizophrenics to have smaller (less positive) slow waves after infrequent stimuli in an RT paradigm, and interpreted this as reflecting poor selective attention. In a similar paradigm, R. Cohen et al. (1981) found a diminished (less negative) sustained potential at the frontal lead in schizophrenics only under conditions of active attention. This was more pronounced in SC nonresponders.

Reduced late slow activity after auditory stimuli in schizophrenics was found by Lifshitz et al. (1979), but only from a bipolar derivation near the vertex. This wave was a better discriminator of schizophrenics from controls (including a psychiatric control group) than vertex N120–P200. However, electro-oculogram (EOG) activity for the same time band discriminated almost as well, although Lifshitz et al. (1979) believe it not to be a cause of the slow potential.

The earlier literature on the CNV, well reviewed by Roth (1977), suggests attenuation in schizophrenics. This was not confirmed by Roth et al. (1979), but schizophrenics with hallucinations had smaller CNVs than nonhallucinating patients—a finding in some agreement with earlier reports that CNV deficits are confined to patients with Schneider's "first rank" symptoms (Roth, 1977). Reduced CNV in schizophrenics has recently been confirmed in three studies (Briling, 1980; Rizzo, Albani, Spadaro, & Morocutti, 1983; van den Bosch, 1983), but Bachneff and Engelsman (1983) obtained basically negative results. Briling (1980) attempted to manipulate attention within the CNV paradigm. For controls, CNVs were larger when the first stimulus was one of three words and the second was a tone than they were when those stimuli were in the reverse order, and CNVs were attenuated when the words (as the first stimulus) were counted. The patients did not show those changes, but performance was not verified. Diminished CNV has been reported in schizophrenics even after clinical recovery (Roth, 1977), suggesting that it may reflect a trait. The earlier literature suggested that CNV deficits do not appear to be specific to schizophrenia. In a large study, however, van den Bosch (1983) found CNV deficits in DSM III diagnosed schizophrenics, and not in several other diagnostic groups, including nonschizophrenic psychotics. Unfortunately patients with major affective disorders were excluded, so specificity has not been completely established.

Slow recovery of the CNV (termed "postimperative negative variation," or PINV) in psychotics in general, including schizophrenics, is somewhat better confirmed than the low CNV (Roth, 1977). The PINV findings were confirmed by Briling (1980) and marginally confirmed by Bachneff and Engelsmann (1983) and Roth et al. (1979) but also questioned, due to the susceptibility to artifact of this wave and the possibility that the findings may merely reflect slow RT in the patients. Reduction of PINV duration (but no change in DNV amplitude) by neuroleptic medication was reported by Rizzo et al. (1983).

EARLY ERPs

In contrast to the rather general findings of smaller middle and late ERPs in schizophrenics, the data on early ERPs indicate negative or even the converse findings. A study of the very early auditory brain stem evoked potentials (BSEPs) in schizophrenia (Pfefferbaum et al., 1980) produced negative results. However, Josiassen, Busk, Hart, and Vanderploeg (1980) found that 3 of 9 schizophrenics were beyond the range of normals and depressed patients in the latency of BSEP peaks V–VI, and delayed peak V in a set of monzygotic schizophrenic quadruplets was reported by Buchsbaum, Mirsky, DeLisi, Morihisa, Karson,

Mendelson, King, Johnson, and Kessler (1984), leaving open the possibility of abnormal BSEPs in a subset of schizophrenics.

Pfefferbaum et al. (1980) found marginally greater amplitude in the patients of a later peak (P50) in a variable tone intensity paradigm. Shagass (1979) reviewed evidence from his studies of a larger somatosensory N60 from central leads contralateral to the stimulation in chronic schizophrenics. This finding is thought to reflect "altered topography" in the patients, since it is claimed that the generator for this wave is more frontal. Larger N60 is tentatively attributed to a reduction in inhibition of the spread of the discharge from the primary generator (Shagass, Roemer, Straumanis, & Amadeo, 1978). This has led Shagass (1976, 1979) to postulate a defective filtering or gating of input, which leads, by some unspecified mechanism, to impaired information processing as reflected in the attenuated later ERPs.

Much of the earlier ERP work in psychopathology measured recovery functions in which ERP amplitude to the second of two closely paired stimuli (S2) is plotted as a function of the ISI or the intensity of the first stimulus (S1) Reviews by Shagass (1976, 1977, 1979) suggest that schizophrenics, but also patients with other disorders, consistently show reduced amplitude recovery, up to ISIs of 100 msec. and that this is independent of stimulus modality. Shagass (1977) believes this measure may reflect cortical excitability.

Very striking results of a different nature have been reported by Adler, Pachtman, Franks, Pecevich, Waldo, and Freedman (1982). First, in apparent contrast to previous work P50 to clicks was smaller in schizophrenics. More importantly, for paired clicks, when the ISI was .5 to 2 sec, P50 to the second stimulus was attenuated markedly (compared to the first) in controls but minimally in unmedicated schizophrenics. Percentage recovery at the .5-sec ISI discriminated the groups with 96% accuracy. P50 recovery in a group of medicated patients was very similar to that in the drug-free patients (Freedman, Adler, Waldo, Pachtman, & Franks, 1983). As Adler et al. (1982) point out, the larger early ERPs found by other investigators may be due to the short ISIs in those studies which would cause attenuation in the controls. For just schizophrenics, P50 suppression was highly correlated with P50 amplitude and latency to unpaired stimuli, suggesting a failure of the first stimulus to induce an inhibitory process. The authors favor a simple failure of inhibition hypothesis. This seems to be a very promising new lead. Replication attempts in other laboratories and parametric variations will no doubt be forthcoming.

LATENCY

There are no general and consistent findings with respect to ERP latency in schizophrenia. However, Saletu (1980) cites some evidence of faster latencies in the middle range for auditory and visual ERPs in schizophrenics. Shagass (1979) has failed to find latency differences in any modality in the middle peaks, but did find shorter latency in an early visual potential (P45). Similarly, faster auditory P50 latency in unmedicated schizophrenics but not in medicated patients was reported by Freedman et al. (1983). The recent group of studies by Roth and his colleagues reports conflicting results for ERP latencies to nonattended tones, with significant findings of only faster P200 for patients in one study (Pfefferbaum et al., 1980), only slower N120 in another (Roth et al., 1981) and no differences in a third (Roth, Horvath, Pfefferbaum, & Kopell, 1980). However, in RT paradigms, these investigators have found consistently that P200 latency is faster to nontarget frequent tones in schizophrenics. On the basis of the general literature on selective attention, the short P200 latency, together with the lower amplitude of N120 in the schizophrenics, is thought to be compatible with a selective attention impairment in these subjects, but other interpretations are not ruled out (Roth et al., 1981).

The latency of P300 has not been found to be abnormal in schizophrenics, except in the case of nontarget rare tones, to which it was faster than in controls (Roth, Horvath, Pfefferbaum, & Kopell, 1980; Roth et al., 1981). This is taken to indicate that stimulus evaluation time is not prolonged in schizophrenics.

VARIABILITY

In view of the evidence of greater perceptual and behavioral variability in schizophrenic individuals, it should not come as a surprise that a consistent finding is greater ERP variability as measured by correlating data points for different averages from the same lead or for different leads (Buchsbaum, 1977; Shagass, 1976). A potentially important exception is Shagass's finding that for somatosensory ERPs, stability of waveshape within the first 100 msec is higher in schizophrenics (particularly those with high psychosis and low depression ratings) than in controls or other patients (Shagass, 1976, 1979). This is taken as support for the hypothesis of defective filtering outlined above. The early reduced variability is assumed to be causally related to the increased variability after 100 msec. A more recent study only partially confirmed the hypothesis (Shagass, Roemer, Straumanis, & Amadeo, 1980). Although reduced early variability and increased later variability were again present in chronic schizophrenics, reduced early variability occurred as well for a mixed group of psychiatric patients who had normal late variability. In addition, the variability of auditory and visual ERPs was greater for schizophrenics, even for the early portion of the curve. Thus reduced variability of ERPs under 100 msec does not necessarily lead to greater variability of later epochs. Furthermore, the result may be specific to somatosensory stimulation, although the possibility that the analogous stages of visual and auditory signal processing were not reflected in the recordings cannot be ruled out.

It might be thought the greater ERP variability would, of necessity, produce smaller ERPs, especially if there were variability in latency characteristics. As mentioned earlier, Roth, Pfefferbaum, Horvath, Berger, and Kopell (1980) showed that this did not account for reduced P300, but the same latency adjustment techniques have not been tried with other potentials. It has been proposed that ERP waveshape variability is a function of the signal-to-noise ratio of the ERP to the background EEG (Buchsbaum, 1977), and low signal-to-noise ratios in schizophrenics were reported by Buchsbaum and Coppola (1979). It is clear that high variability of the background EEG is not responsible for the high ERP variability in schizophrenics. First, high EEG variability is not usually found in these patients; second, the independence of background and waveshape variability has been demonstrated directly (R. T. Jones & Callaway, 1970); finally, both higher variability and lower variability have been shown in different epochs (Shagass, 1977). Thus, high variability in schizophrenics, according to this view, would be due solely to their smaller ERPs. The literature does indeed suggest a general negative correlation between amplitude and variability. To determine whether the variability of ERP waveshapes provides any information independent of amplitude, researchers should investigate it in situations that produce minimal amplitude differences. Better still, methods of assessing individual trials should be utilized.

Hemispheric Differences and Topography

Electrocortical investigations of lateral asymmetry have usually started with the working hypothesis of dominant-hemisphere dysfunction in schizophrenia, based on the ideas of Flor-Henry (1969) and the general idea that cognitive dysfunction should be localized in the dominant hemisphere.

EEGs

Qualitative studies have not found a unilateral predominance of EEG abnormalities in schizophrenia (Abrams & Taylor, 1979; Stevens et al., 1979). Studies of EEG spectra have produced more positive results. Flor-Henry, Koles, Howarth, and Burton (1979) compared schizophrenics with affective-disorder patients and normal controls. Only the schizophrenics had increased power in the beta band over the left temporal area (referred to vertex). However, muscle artifacts were also strongly lateralized to the left in the schizophrenics. Flor-Henry's group concluded that although their final spectra included the contribution of muscle activity, this activity reflects the same central process as the EEG. The role of EMG artifacts in producing spurious results was nicely demonstrated by Volavka, Abrams, Taylor, and Recker

(1981). They found schizophrenics (but not depressives) to have a predominance of fast beta from right versus left temporal leads (referred to linked earlobes) when the data were screened for EMG artifacts. As with Flor-Henry, Koles, Howarth, and Burton (1979), however, the results were in the opposite direction with unedited data. In later reports, presumably on new cases, each of these groups replicated their previous results (Abrams, Taylor, & Volavka, 1983; Flor-Henry & Koles, 1983). Nevertheless, even studies that have screened the raw data for artifacts have produced conflicting results on this point: While Coger, Dymond, and Serafetinides (1979) reported greater beta power in schizophrenics specifically from a left temporal lead referred to left frontal, and Morihisa et al. (1983) found the maximal excess of fast beta in schizophrenics in a left posterior region, Shaw et al. (1979) reported generally negative results. In unmedicated patients, Kemali et al. (1981) observed no hemispheric differences in relative power of any band; indeed, these investigators consider schizophrenics to have "hypersymmetric" EEG records. A similar conclusion, namely, that schizophrenics have a less lateralized brain organization than controls, was based on findings of a decrease in interhemispheric alpha coherence during visual imagery in schizophrenics, but an increase in coherence in controls (Shaw et al., 1979; Shaw, Coulter, & Resek, 1983). That some of the conflicting results might be due to heterogeneity among schizophrenics is suggested by a study by Serafetinides, Coger, Martin, and Dymond (1981), in which only a subgroup of patients with high ratings on thought disorder and paranoid symptoms had an excess of fast beta (24–30 Hz) from left frontotemporal leads compared to homologous right leads.

Despite the inconsistencies, the preceding evidence on beta activity hints weakly at a left temporal focus in schizophrenia. Low left-hemisphere EEG amplitude (ignoring frequency components) has been reported in two studies (Matousek, Capone, & Okawa, 1981; Shagass et al., 1982). However, Etevenon (1984) reported lower right than left alpha power in just "residual" schizophrenics and Flor-Henry and Koles (1984) reported low alpha power from a right temporal locus in schizophrenics in general. Stevens and Livermore (1982) found an excess of slow activity in schizophrenics' right temporal regions during all abnormal behaviors except hallucinating, for which there was excess delta activity in left central–parietal regions.

Shaw et al. (1979) did find that, in general, intrahemispheric coherence was higher on the left than on the right side in schizophrenics and higher on the right side in normals and neurotics. Left-hemisphere coherence was generally higher in schizophrenics than in controls, especially neurotics. This result is hypothesized to reflect a more diffuse organization of the functioning of the dominant hemisphere in schizophrenics. Flor-Henry, Koles, Howarth, and Burton (1979) reported bilateral low intrahemispheric coherence in unmedicated schizophrenics. In a later study, however (Flor-Henry & Koles, 1984), this was confined to the right hemisphere. All three studies reported reduced interhemispheric coherence in their patients, suggesting to Shaw *et al.* an impairment of callosal transfer of information. Flor-Henry's group also concluded that their schizophrenics had more right-hemisphere involvement in a verbal task than controls, based on decreases in power from right leads. Shaw *et al.* (1979) did not replicate this result.

In sum, to the extent that the observations presented in this section are reliable they do not point to a definite locus of abnormal brain activity. The location of abnormality seems to depend on the phenomenon being measured and on the type of behavior coincident with the EEG measurement. The data seem more consistent with hypotheses implicating a subcortical abnormality or the functional organization of brain activity as a whole rather than with hypotheses concerning a specific cortical region.

ERPs

An increasing amount of attention is being given to hemispheric asymmetries of ERPs. In earlier studies from Shagass's laboratory, the positive results concerned waveshape stability. Roemer, Shagass, Straumanis, and Amadeo (1978) found low stability of visual ERPs in schizophrenics *vs.* both patient and nonpatient controls from left-hemisphere leads only. A direct comparison between homologous leads in the two hemispheres showed significantly lower stability on the left side. These authors conclude that left-hemisphere responsiveness undergoes greater moment-to-moment fluctuations in schizophrenics than in controls. Neuroleptic medication reduced stability only in the right hemisphere, thus making the two sides more equal. Assuming that there was clinical improvement, this would suggest that the asymmetry, rather than low stability per se, was the pathognomonic feature. These results were partially confirmed for the auditory ERP (Roemer, Shagass, Straumanis, & Amadeo, 1979) by the finding of unilateral low left-hemisphere stability in schizophrenics for the early part of the ERP (15–100 msec), but bilateral lower values for schizophrenics under all other conditions. Thus these studies suggests a left-hemisphere dysfunction in schizophrenics, but it may not be manifested under all conditions.

Several recent studies have also suggested a left-hemisphere problem in schizophrenia on the basis of ERP amplitudes. Serafetinides *et al.* (1981) found a right-hemisphere advantage in visual P100–N140 in schizophrenics, but this was significant only in patients with high anxiety–depression ratings. Smaller left temporal than right temporal N100 and P200 in an attention task for schizophrenics but not controls was reported by Hiramatsu, Kameyama, Saitoh, Niwa, Rymar, and Itoh (1984), but they could not replicate this in a second study. Connolly, Gruzelier, Man-

chanda, and Hirsch (1983) reported similar results for P100–N120 when simply measuring peaks, but using spectral analyses of the same data (Jutai, Gruzelier, Connolly, Manchanda, & Hirsch, 1984), this result was not clear. In fact, the most significant patient–control differences were found from right-hemisphere placements. Using a factor-analytic approach on a large data set, Shagass, Roemer, and Straumanis (1983) found visual ERP asymmetries that favored the right hemisphere in their various schizophrenic groups but favored the left hemisphere in controls and subjects with major depression. This held for latency bands of 50–249 msec. In a topographic analysis of P300 with a brain mapping technique, Morstyn, Duffy, and McCarley (1983) observed the maximal schizophrenic deficit in the left temporal region. In another study using that technique (Morihisa *et al.*, 1983), lateral differences in ERPs were reported but they are difficult to interpret because they were not analyzed in terms of conventional peaks.

Thus the ERP evidence in general points to a left-hemisphere abnormality in schizophrenics, perhaps most strongly exhibited in components relevant to attention in the paradigms used. That this is not a drug-produced artifact is suggested by similar findings in medicated and unmedicated patients in the studies reviewed. However, Mintz, Tomer, and Myslobodsky (1982) presented evidence of selective potentiation of right hemisphere late ERPs from neuroleptics of the piperazine class, so the question of medication-influence is still open.

In a study designed to measure the transmission of information across the corpus callosum, Tress, Kugler, and Caudrey (1979) recorded early ERPs (20–100 msec) bilaterally to tactile stimulation on each arm. The latency of a negative peak at about 50 msec (N50) was delayed in ipsilateral recordings in controls, but schizophrenics had about equal ipsilateral and contralateral latencies to right-arm stimulation. This result has been replicated by the same group (Tress, Caudrey, & Mehta, 1983), who also found similar effects for P25 and N35. Similar and striking results were reported by G. H. Jones and Miller (1981), using a comparable technique and blind scoring of records. Again, the latency of ipsilateral N50 was delayed in controls but not in schizophrenics. Similar results were obtained for the preceding and following positive peaks, and for all three peaks the differences between contralateral and ipsilateral latencies separated 12 patients from 12 controls without overlap. Differential effects due to which hand was stimulated did not occur. These authors were able to rule out medication as a factor in the results.

However, Shagass, Josiassen, Roemer, Straumanis, and Slepner (1983), attempting to replicate G. H. Jones and Miller (1981), using the same bipolar montage, could not identify the relevant peaks sufficiently well to test the hypothesis. This problem was also encountered in a similar study by Gulmann, Wild-schiodtz, and Orbaek (1982), who felt a negative peak at about 70–80 msec was the first one that could be measured reliably. Their results for this peak, however, were similar to those of G. H. Jones and Miller except that the effect held for just left-arm stimulation.

Despite these apparent replications, problems of interpretation remain. Both Tress *et al.* (1983) and Shagass, Josiassen, *et al.* (1983) argue, on different grounds, that the ipsilateral–contralateral latency differences in controls do not represent callosal transmission time. Questions about EMG artifacts and the use of bipolar recordings have also been raised.

A different approach was used by Buchsbaum, Carpenter, Fedio, Goodwin, Murphy, and Post (1979), who compared ERPs in each hemisphere to visual stimuli to each hemiretina under conditions of attention or inattention to the stimuli. Since it showed significant attention effects in normals, N120 from a temporo-parietal (Wernicke) area was chosen for study. Schizophrenics showed a disproportionately small effect of attention in left-hemisphere N120 amplitude when stimuli were delivered to the right retina. The specificity of this finding seems to rule out most of the usual sources of artifact. Since under this condition the signal must cross the corpus callosum, the results point to a rather specific deficit in the right-to-left transfer of information into the left temporo-parietal area. Whether this particular finding bears a direct relationship to the somatosensory studies is problematical, but it is clear that alternative methods of studying the callosal transmission problem will be necessary for more definitive interpretations of the results. Other explanations are doubtless possible, including failure of some inhibitory mechanism in the brain stem. This problem seems worth further exploration.

Using a comprehensive 16-lead montage over just the left hemisphere, Buchsbaum, King, Cappelletti, Coppola, and Van Kammen (1982) presented cortical maps indicating a schizophrenic deficit in N120 and P200 to attended (i.e., counted) light flashes over the entire hemisphere. However, the differences in N120 reached maximal significance in the temporal and parietal areas. The patients showed particular attenuation of P200 in frontal and parietal regions but, like the controls, had a realtive "hot spot" for P200 at the vertex. Interest in ERP and EEG topography differences should increase with the spread of these sophisticated mapping techniques.

Motor and Muscle Activity

In contrast to studies of skeletal muscle tension (reviewed in an earlier section), which have not been pursued to a great extent in recent years, several techniques involving recording of motor and muscle activity have been extensively studied recently in schizophrenia. Although these techniques are grouped under one heading, there are wide differences in conceptual approach behind them.

Smooth Pursuit Eye Movements

The initial modern observation of disturbed smooth pursuit eye movements (SPEMs) in schizophrenia was made by Holzman, Proctor, and Hughes (1973), and this finding has survived a number of independent replications with variations in methodology. Holzman and his colleagues have described two principal types of SPEM difficulty in schizophrenics—one in which SPEMs are replaced by saccades, and one in which SPEMs are overlaid by small movements ("cogwheeling") (Holzman & Levy, 1977). Later studies using improved recording techniques have characterized SPEM impairment as either saccadic intrusions, which also occur during fixation, or saccadic smooth pursuit (Stark, 1983). Holzman and Levy (1977) found that SPEM dysfunction was specific to schizophrenia (although this depended somewhat on the method of diagnosis) and was present in first-degree relatives of schizophrenics. Moreover, two studies of twins in which at least one member of each pair was schizophrenic showed signigicantly greater concordance for SPEM dysfunction in monozygotic than in dizygotic pairs (Holzman, Kringlen, Levy, & Haberman, 1980; Holzman & Levy, 1977). In addition, impaired SPEMs were observed in remitted schizophrenics (Iacono, Tuason, & Johnson, 1981). This evidence would seem to make SPEM dysfunction a prime candidate for a genetic marker of schizophrenia.

However, there are problems with ready acceptance of this hypothesis. Not all schizophrenics show deviant SPEMs—50–85%, according to Holzman *et al.* (1980). Similar discordance between a diagnosis of schizophrenia and SPEMs was present in the twin studies. A more serious problem is that Shagass, Amadeo, and Overton (1974) reported SPEM dysfunction in psychotic depressives. Later studies (reviewed by Lipton, Holzman, Levy, & Levin, 1984; Spohn, 1984) have shown that about 50% of "functional psychotics" showed impaired SPEMs. In a group of mixed schizophrenic and nonschizophrenic patients in remission, diagnosis had no effect on SPEMs, but patients with higher psychosis ratings in their previous hospitalization had more impaired tracking (Salzman, Klein, & Strauss, 1978). This supports the trait notion of SPEMs, but not the specificity hypothesis. In another study of remitted patients (Iacono, Peloquin, Lumry, Valentine, & Tuason, 1982), unipolar and bipolar depressives did not show any SPEM impairment that could not be shown to be due to lithium medication. This evidence, plus that of Holzman, Solomon, Levin, and Waternaux (1984) that SPEM dysfunction runs in families of schizophrenics but not in families of manic–depressives, supports Spohn's (1983) conclusion that SPEM dysfunction may be a genetic trait marker for just chronic schizophrenia but a less specific marker for psychosis. In addition, similar SPEM problems are present in a wide variety of opthalmological and neurological conditions (Stark, 1983).

Another important question is the nature of the deficit leading to poor SPEMs. That psychological factors are involved was first demonstrated by Shagass, Roemer, and Amadeo (1976), who found improved tracking in schizophrenics when they were asked to read constantly changing numbers on a swinging pendulum. This has been replicated with the observations that the schizophrenic deficit remains significant under these conditions and that focused attention improves saccadic SPEM deficits but not cogwheeling (Holzman & Levy, 1977). On the basis of these data and the observation that subjects are unaware of either their SPEM dysfunction or its improvement by focusing attention, Holzman, Levy, and Proctor (1978) conclude that the SPEM deficit is one of involuntary attention or a failure of "cognitive centering." A somewhat similar view is implicit in the idea that number reading improves tracking by providing feedback, since, in order to be read, the numbers must occupy foveal vision (Shagass *et al.*, 1976).

Many investigators have considered the possibility of an oculomotor dysfunction. Some abnormalities of saccadic eye movements have been found in schizophrenics—such as bursts of 4- to 6-Hz saccadic oscillations (Cegalis & Sweeney, 1979), slow saccade velocity during fixation tasks (Cegalis, Sweeney, & Dellis, 1982), and saccade overshoot (Mather & Putchat, 1983)—but these have been attributed to faulty attention or information processing rather than to oculomotor dysfunction. Studies of saccadic reaction time (Iacono *et al.*, 1981; Levin, Jones, Stark, Merrin, & Holzman, 1982) and oculomotor reflexes (Latham, Holzman, Manshreck, & Tole, 1981) have not shown impairment in subjects showing SPEM dysfunction. This evidence and studies of optokinetic nystagmus are taken to rule out motivation and voluntary attention, on the one hand, and brain-stem mechanisms, on the other, as explanatory factors (Levin *et al.*, 1983). A different point of view is taken by Cegalis, Hafez, and Wang (1983). On the basis of their finding of an increased frequency and velocity of saccades during SPEM by schizophrenics and the other saccadic abnormalities mentioned earlier, they feel that hypotheses implicating brain stem and cerebellar mechanisms cannot be ruled out at present.

Two studies have attempted to produce SPEM deficits in normals. Although Brezinova and Kendell (1977) reported only a trend for a competing task to impair SPEMs as assessed by blind ratings, Pass, Salzman, Klorman, Kaskey, and Klein (1978) found that a competing task produced increases in velocity arrests in normals to the level of acute schizophrenics under baseline conditions. The patients showed significantly more impairment from the distraction than did the controls. Brezinova and Kendell (1977) did observe schizophrenic-like SPEMs in normals after a prolonged (1-hr) session of continuous tracking. These studies provide further support for the role of focused attention in SPEM dysfunction.

Much of the recent research in this area is concerned with problems of measurement. Cegalis and Sweeney (1981) and Iacono and Koenig (1983), for example, have developed a number of measures, some of which seem to be affected differentially by variations in attention in the schizophrenic group, which differ in their ability to discriminate nonschizophrenic patients from controls and from schizophrenics. Surprisingly, there are few studies of individual differences among schizophrenics and of the psychological and biological correlates of SPEM performance. However, van den Bosch (1984) reported correlations indicating that schizophrenics with deviant SPEMs also had slow reaction time and small CNVs, consistent with a general attention impairment.

The Hoffmann Reflex

Recent studies of muscle electrophysiology were initiated primarily on the basis of prior evidence suggesting enzyme and morphological abnormalities of the skeletal muscle system (Goode, Meltzer, Crayton, & Mazura, 1977). These authors found evidence of slower nerve conduction velocity in chronically hospitalized schizophrenics, and evidence of a low number of functional motor units in a small foot muscle in chronic schizophrenics in general.

Most of the recent studies have been on the recovery function of the Hoffmann reflex, a monosynaptic reflex whose amplitude is taken to reflect the excitability of the alpha motoneuron. When two stimuli are presented with an ISI of less than 1 sec, the Hoffmann reflex to the second stimulus is diminished. However, the recovery curve is bimodal: Almost complete recovery occurs at an ISI of about 200 msec, but inhibition reappears for ISIs in the range of 300–1000 msec. The parameter that has been of major interest to investigators is maximum early recovery.

Early reports of diminished Hoffmann reflex recovery in schizophrenics have been replicated, but this finding holds only for acute schizophrenics (Goode, Meltzer, & Mazura, 1979; Metz, Goode, & Meltzer, 1980). Chronic schizophrenics, on the other hand, are likely to have augmented recovery curves. This feature is not specific to schizophrenia; schizoaffective and affective-disorder patients, whether manic or depressed, also tend to show higher recovery functions than controls. However, this variable in unmedicated patients was correlated with the number of primary symptoms for schizophrenia (Goode, Manning, & Middleton, 1981). In this study, the amount by which reflex recovery on the right leg exceeded that on the left correlated positively with withdrawal–retardation ratings and negatively with anxiety–depression ratings from the BPRS in right-handed subjects. This is seemingly consistent with the idea of left-hemisphere problems in more schizophrenic subjects and right-hemisphere deficit in more depressed patients. However, these positive findings are based on data from fewer than a third (10 or 11 out of 36) of the patients in the study, indicating much unexplained loss of data. Neuroleptic drugs attenuated recovery, but a drug that blocks serotonin (5-HT) uptake (fluoxetine) augmented it (Metz et al., 1980).

Although the Hoffmann reflex results seem replicable, it is clear from the data that there is considerable overlap of all groups with controls, and that only a relatively small number of patients are extremely deviant. Some attempt has been made to relate the findings to altered DA functioning, but it is recognized that the diagnostic nonspecificity of the impairment and the opposite results obtained in acute and chronic patients are not suggestive of a simple relationship with a single neurotransmitter (Goode et al., 1979; Metz et al., 1980). Nevertheless, the data do suggest a possible skeletal muscle abnormality in some schizophrenics, which may have implications for such psychomotor impairments as slow RT or poor eye tracking.

Blinking and the Blink Reflex

Stevens (1978), in tests on 44 drug-free schizophrenics in various settings, observed high spontaneous blink rates in 20 patients and either an absence of the glabellar reflex (blinking to a light tap on the forehead), bursts of rapid blinking to the tap, or failure of habituation of this reflex in a majority of patients. Pharmacological evidence and data from patients with Parkinson disease were cited to support the relation of some of these data to increased DA activity, but the contribution of tardive dyskinesia consequent to drug withdrawal could not be ruled out.

A more systematic and controlled study showing reduced habituation of the blink reflex to loud sounds in schizophrenics has been cited earlier (Geyer & Braff, 1982). These authors, however, apparently did not find a disproportionate number of nonresponders in the schizophrenic group, but this could be due to stimulus intensity. Braff, Stone, Callaway, Geyer, Glick, and Bali (1978) reported no amplitude or latency differences in the blink reflex to loud noise stimuli in schizophrenics compared to controls. However, the main interest in this study was the effects of warning stimuli presented 30–2000 msec prestimulus.

The blink amplitude reduction and latency facilitation customarily found in this procedure were reduced in the schizophrenics at the 60-msec ISI. This was taken to reflect a defect in a preattentive filter mechanism in the patients.

Systematic study of spontaneous blink rates in schizophrenics has been undertaken by Karson and his colleagues (summarized in Karson, Kleinman, Freed, Bigelow, Weinberger, & Wyatt, 1982). Higher blink rates in unmedicated schizophrenics than in controls occurred, except in a group of patients who had never been on neuroleptic drugs. However, such drugs reduced blink rates to about control levels, suggesting that this variable is influenced by DA. This hypothesis has received some support from subsequent findings that elevated blink rates and their reduction by drugs that block DA receptors are more marked in patients without enlarged lateral ventricles, as determined by computerized tomography (CT) scan. These patients are clinically more responsive to neuroleptic drugs than patients with large ventricles, and are considered to have a DA-related illness. In addition, improvement in rated clinical state correlated significantly with the reduction in blink rate only in patients with normal ventricles (Karson, Bigelow, Kleinman, Weinberger, & Wyatt, 1982). This group found that blink rates were not associated with symptoms of tardive dyskinesia (Karson, Kleinman, Freed, et al., 1982). A much lower than normal blink rate in medicated schizophrenics was reported by Kitamura, Kahn, Kumar, and Mackintosh (1984), who also found negative correlations between blink rate and both drug dosage and BPRS ratings of blunted affect. This supports the DA hypothesis and increases the similarity of blink rate and some ANS arousal measures.

The case for regarding eyeblink frequency as a marker for schizophrenia is weakened by observations presented by Tecce, Savignano-Bowman, and Cole (1978) of even higher rates in aged subjects and psychosurgery patients than in schizophrenics, although details of the studies are not given. These investigators regard blink frequency as a nonspecific stress indicator or an index of "negative hedonic tone." The data in the studies by Karson and his colleagues were collected during clinical interviews, frequently when subjects were speaking—a condition that increases blink rates. Although controls were tested under similar conditions, it is not known how much this interpersonal situation contributed to the results that were obtained. In addition, drug trials always followed placebo trials and may not have been double-blind. However, blink rate can be measured under various conditions in and out of the laboratory, and such data are readily available in recordings of EEG, eye tracking, and the like. Thus this measure seems worthy of further study.

Prediction of Clinical Outcome

Among the attempts to cope with the heterogeneity of schizophrenia by subclassification, those based on clinical course or response to treatment are of major practical importance. The distinction between process and reactive schizophrenia, based on case history data, has prognostic implications and has been in use for some time. A similar distinction is that between chronic and episodic forms of the disorder (Zubin & Spring, 1977). The fact that patients vary in their response to neuroleptic medication has prompted investigators to look for differences between responders and nonresponders to treatment. Since virtually all the drugs used to treat schizophrenia reduce DA activity, the distinction based on treatment response has implications for the biological etiology of this classification. The findings that patients with abnormal CT scans, chiefly enlarged lateral ventricles, tend to be unresponsive to neuroleptic treatment has led to a model of two major forms of schizophrenia—one primarily dopaminergic in etiology, and one in which strutural brain damage is involved.

Despite its practical and etiological importance, few psychophysiological studies of treatment outcome exist. There is a literature on differences between process and reactive schizophrenics (reviewed by Klorman, Strauss, & Kokes, 1977), but few consistent findings have emerged. Many of the studies can be faulted on methodological grounds, such as using only chronic patients (who should not be reactive if the prediction of clinical course had been accurate) or failure to control for medication. As indicated above (see page 521), however, two studies that did control for these factors reported higher ANS base levels and lowered reactivity in patients with a poor prognosis, similar to results with chronic schizophrenics (Fowles et al., 1970; Magaro, 1973). In any case, this is an indirect approach. Comparisons based on actual outcome would be preferable.

Computerized EEG predictors of outcome from treatment in chronic schizophrenics with three different antipsychotic drugs were studied by Itil, Marasa, Saletu, Davis, and Mucciardi (1975). Only two modest ($<.4$) correlations between predrug EEG parameters and changes in global psychopathology were found, indicating greater clinical improvement in patients with higher mean frequencies and more very fast activity. Comparing groups selected on the basis of degree of improvement, there were nonsignificant trends for subjects who improved to have had less slow activity and more fast activity in their predrug EEGs. The treatments did increase theta and decrease beta activity, and these changes, as well as the decrease in mean frequency, were significantly correlated with global improvement. Thus, while predrug prediction of improvement was marginal, there was a good correspondence between clinical and EEG changes. Further, the EEG changes can be considered to be in the normal direction. However, alpha activity was not changed much by the drugs.

A study of the electrodermal responses to tones and words in newly admitted patients in relation to the length of hospitalization (longer or shorter than 7 weeks) was reported by Stern, Surphlis, and Koff (1965). No differences between groups were found. However, two studies using ANS measures have found predictors of clinical outcome. Frith *et al.* (1979) measured the SCORs to a series of tones before and after treatment with either a DA blocker or inactive drugs in newly admitted, acutely psychotic patients. In about half of the patients the SCORs failed to habituate, and this group showed significantly less clinical improvement than did habituators. This result was independent of the type of treatment received, and habituation status was a slightly better predictor of outcome than either type of treatment or acute versus insidious onset of symptoms. Habituators had lower SCL and SSCR rates and slower recovery half-time, but the relationship of these variables to clinical improvement is not given. Interestingly, although the active drug reduced the incidence of SCORS, clinical improvement was not accompanied by such a reduction. Thus, in contrast to the EEG findings (Itil et al., 1975), pretreatment SCORS were a good predictor of clinical improvement, but this was independent of whether an antipsychotic drug was given; and although the active drug "normalized" the SCORs, this was not correlated with clinical improvement.

We (Zahn, Carpenter, & McGlashan, 1981b) obtained somewhat similar results when we tested unmedicated acute schizophrenics shortly after hospital admission and also after about a 3-month treatment period. Medication was not varied systematically, as it was by Itil *et al.* (1975) and Frith et al. (1979). Compared to patients who showed minimal improvement, those with definite improvement had lower resting HR and SSCRs, faster SCOR habituation (as indicated by several range-corrected measures), and greater tonic and phasic ANS reactions to tasks and to task-related stimuli. These measures were all closer to normal control values in the improved group. The results were independent of treatment with neuroleptics. A discriminant analysis classified 84% of the patients correctly with respect to clinical improvement. The posttreatment data showed very few ANS changes to accompany clinical improvement; only a reduction in HR was significant. These findings confirm and extend those of Frith *et al.* (1979) with respect to the predictors of clinical improvement, their independence of the use of medication, and the lack of change with improvement in unmedicated patients.

However, a study of the SCOR in very chronic (>20 years hospitalization) older (55–67) schizophrenics tested after only a 1-week drug-free period (Schneider, 1982) obtained quite different results. The patients who later improved on a controlled drug trial had a higher SCL and SSCR rate and took more trials to habituate than nonimprovers. Although controls were not tested, the values of these variables seem low compared to those in other studies. This suggests, as was true in our study (Zahn, Carpenter, & McGlashan, 1981b), the more deviant subjects had the worse prognosis. The results might be due to subtle neurological deficits in the drug resistant subjects.

A study by Landau, Buchsbaum, Carpenter, Strauss, and Sacks (1975) tested a sample that overlapped with ours (Zahn, Carpenter & McGlashan, 1981b), using the augmenting–reducing paradigm with visual ERPs. Subjects who later improved were mostly reducers, while unimproved subjects were augmenters. There was a nonsignificant trend toward less reducing with clinical improvement, which was independent of medication usage between tests. Unlike our findings (Zahn, Carpenter, & McGlashan, 1981b), however, the curve for the improved group differed substantially from that for controls (who showed augmenting).

The differences among the results of these studies can be seen to have some consistency when chronicity is taken into account. The two studies on chronic patients (Itil et al., 1975; Schneider, 1982) found relationships between high indices of arousal and good prognosis, whereas the three studies on acute patients reported lower reactivity in patients with better outcome. The stability of the ANS measures in the presence of clinical change suggests that they have the nature of traits, a point compatible to some extent with twin studies (Zahn, 1977); however, the data are also not incompatible with the idea that ANS changes may precede clinical changes (Zahn, 1980).

An innovative study related to the last point addresses the role of ANS activity in the relapse of discharged schizophrenics (Tarrier, Vaughn, Lader, & Leff, 1979). Previous work had shown that the probability of relapse was increased by living with a relative who had a high degree of "expressed emotion" (EE) and by the occurrence of significant "life events." In this study, subjects were tested in their homes while only the experimenter was present and also while talking with their key relatives. Subjects with high-EE relatives had a higher rate of SSCRs only when interacting with their relatives and had a greater increase in DBP in the presence of the relatives than low-EE subjects, although these results occurred only on the first of three tests given at 3- to 6-month intervals. Subjects tested within 3 weeks following a life event showed a large SSCR increase in the presence of their relatives. A replication on subjects during an acute psychotic episode showed markedly higher SSCR rates in patients from high-EE families throughout the session (Sturgeon, Turpin, Kuipers, Berkowitz, & Leff, 1984). There was not a large difference in response to the relative, perhaps partly due to the initial difference. Comparisons with the earlier data and with followup data showed higher SSCR rates in the acutely ill patients than in remitted patients only for those from high-EE families, suggesting that this variable is state-related in only some patients. Familial EE and SSCR rate during a psychotic episode were also both shown to be independent predictors of relapse. This study confirms and extends the hypothesis that high ANS activity during an acute schizophrenic episode is predictive of a poor clinical course.

High-Risk Studies

Starting with Mednick and Schulsinger (1973), several studies of children at risk for schizophrenia (by virtue of having a schizophrenic parent) have been undertaken. Many of these include psychophysiological measurement as an integral part of the study. The general aim of much of this research is to study the development of persons who later are diagnosed as schizophrenic. Using offspring of schizophrenic parents increases the number of such cases in the sample.

ANS Studies

The early findings on the ANS were reviewed by me (Zahn, 1977) and by Öhman (1981). Following the lead of Mednick and Schulsinger (1973), most high-risk studies have included ANS orienting and conditioning procedures. The initial results in that study, comparing all high-risk subjects ($N = 207$) to control subjects ($N = 104$), found high SCL, large SCR amplitudes to most stimuli, evidence of greater conditioning, and fast SCR latencies and recovery times in the high-risk group. An initial clinical follow-up found these features, except for high SCL, to be more deviant in general in 20 subjects who developed some sort of psychopathology. However, in a later followup using better diagnostic procedures, only fast recovery rate on the early test was predictive of the later development of schizophrenia.

The more recent studies have differed in significant ways from the Mednick and Schulsinger (1973) study, and none has obtained results as dramatic. Janes, Hesselbrock, and Stern (1978), who counted skin potential responses in a conditioning procedure in which the stimuli were cool and warm air applied to the back of the wrist, obtained completely negative results. Their only positive finding was that children of psychotic parents had more movement artifacts than control children. Preliminary results from another high-risk study (G. Fein, Tursky, & Erlenmeyer-Kimling, 1975) were also negative.

However, Prentky, Salzman, and Klein (1981), using a procedure similar to that of Mednick and Schulsinger (1973), did obtain some positive results similar to those of the earlier study. This study compared range-corrected SC measurements from orienting, conditioning, extinction, and generalization procedures in 7- and 10-year-old children whose parents had diagnoses of schizophrenia or affective psychosis or were nonpsychotic (neurosis, personality disorder). The offspring of schizophrenics showed greater generalization and larger third-interval SCRs on trials where the UCS (95-dB white noise) was omitted and during extinction. These results were more marked in the 10-year-old group. This group also showed evidence of greater conditioning, a nonsignificant trend for slower habituation of the SCOR (particularly on early trials), and a smaller increase in SCL during the experiment. The SCR results are similar to those found by Mednick and Schulsinger (1973), but those for SCL are different, as is the lack of differences in SCR latency or recovery. Prentky *et al.* (1981) point out that the more marked results for their 10-year-old sample compared to the younger one, together with the more dramatic results obtained by Mednick and Schulsinger (1973), whose subjects were older, suggest increasingly deviant ANS activity with increasing age. However, one might question the lack of a normal control group in the Prentky *et al.* (1981) study, since the children in their comparison groups might be deviant in their own ways.

A test of the genetically determined ANS characteristics in the offspring of schizophrenic parents (Van Dyke, Rosenthal, & Rasmussen, 1974) compared adults, one of whose biological parents was schizophrenic, but who had been adopted at an early age, with matched control adoptees. Using an SCR conditioning procedure similar to that of Mednick and Schulsinger (1973), evidence of larger and more frequent SCRs, slower habituation, and superior conditioning was found in the index group, although the differences were not as large as those found by Mednick and Schulsinger. Furthermore, no SCR latency or recovery differences were found.

Although the failure of later studies to obtain as clear-cut results as the earlier ones may be due to methodological and sampling differences (Mednick, 1978; Zahn, 1977), the positive results that have been obtained are probably about as consistent as might be expected, given the facts that almost 90% of the high-risk subjects can be expected not to become schizophrenic, and that the genetic diathesis is probably present in well under half of the subjects, depending on which genetic model is accepted. One of the most interesting aspects of this group of studies is that, of the replicated results, only slow habituation is a common (but not universal) finding in adult schizophrenics; large SCR amplitudes and superior conditioning are definitely not the rule. Other evidence of large SCR amplitudes in persons with a schizophrenic genotype comes from a report (Zahn, 1975) on nonschizophrenic monozygotic twins of schizophrenic probands. This evidence leads to the intriguing model of a premorbid ANS hyperactivity in such cases, which becomes overregulated or inhibited with the development of overt schizophrenic symptomatology. This model is subject to empirical test in the longitudinal studies in progress.

Some of these findings receive support from a study using a quite different method of selecting high risk subjects (Valone, Goldstein, & Norton, 1984). The subjects were disturbed nonpsychotic adolescents. Those who had a high-EE parent were more likely to receive a schizophrenia spectrum diagnosis on a 5-year follow-up examination. During a laboratory confrontation designed to be stressful, the increment in SCL for both the adolescent and the parent was greater for high-EE parents than for low-EE parents. These results are taken to show that high-EE marks a familial emotional climate accompanied by mutually high ANS activity and predisposing to schizophrenia spectrum disorders in this type of sample. Genetic factors may also play a role. The role of the ANS in the predisposition to schizophrenia would be more directly established if it were shown that high ANS activity was itself related to a future spectrum diagnosis.

EEG and ERP Studies

This area has received less attention than the ANS area and has not been extensively reported. EEGs from a subsample of the Mednick and Schulsinger (1973) cases were computer-analyzed by Itil (1977). The high-risk subjects had significantly less alpha, more fast beta, and greater variability than controls; these results are similar to some findings in schizophrenics. A period analysis showed more delta activity in the index group as well.

Auditory ERPs from this study are reported by Saletu, Saletu, Marasa, Mednick, and Schulsinger (1975). The high-risk group demonstrated faster latencies, especially for those peaks after about 170 msec, and no differences in amplitude. The findings for latency are similar to, but much smaller in magnitude than, those reported for schizophrenics from that laboratory (Saletu, 1980); however, fast latency is not a general finding in schizophrenia. In contrast, a study on small groups of high-risk children and controls found larger ERP amplitudes to both CPT stimuli and single photic stimuli in the high-risk group, as well as longer latencies to the task stimuli (Herman, Mirsky,

Ricks, & Gallant, 1977). A study on early ERPs to paired clicks in parents of schizophrenics (Siegel, Waldo, Mizner, Adler, & Freedman, 1984) reported a failure of inhibition in the ERP to the second click (similar to findings in the patients) in about half of the parents.

In a larger study, D. Friedman, Frosch, and Erlenmeyer-Kimling (1979) did not obtain significant or consistent differences in ERPs to clicks in high-risk versus control children across three age ranges. However, using an "oddball" task paradigm, differences in late positive components between high-risk and normal control subjects were found (Friedman, Vaughn, & Erlenmeyer-Kimling, 1982). The direction of these differences depends to some extent on electrode location, but in general P350 and P400 favor the controls. Minimal differences in task performance were found, suggesting that deviant neural organization may antedate attention disorders in high-risk subjects.

Deficits in attention-related ERPs in well siblings of schizophrenics have been reported by Saitoh, Niwa, Hiramatsu, Kameyama, Rymar, and Itoh (1984). In a dichotic discrimination task, high-risk siblings, like schizophrenics, showed low N100 amplitude to all stimuli, but unlike schizophrenics, the siblings showed a normal increase to attended stimuli. However, the late positive component did not increase to the target stimuli in the siblings (or in schizophrenics) as it did in the controls. The siblings' performance was also impaired.

These studies give further support to the importance of attention-related ERPs in investigations of schizophrenia and are consistent with a hypothesis that these are reflecting brain activity related to a genetic predisposition to schizophrenia. Much further replication and exploration remains to be done before this hypothesis can be accepted, including follow-up evaluation of the high-risk groups.

Summary and Conclusions

Empirical Summary

In the preceding review, much attention has been given to apparently conflicting findings, with attempts sometimes made to resolve the conflicts. In the following summary, emphasis is on the general trends in the data, integration of data from different areas, and the implications of the data for the major theoretical conceptualizations of schizophrenia.

The recent evidence on ANS base levels supports the earlier conclusions of higher sympathetic activity in schizophrenics as a group than in controls, but it is important that it also points to marked individual differences among patients. Less impressive evidence of the group difference comes from SCL, perhaps the most widely used measure, than from many other

purported indices of ANS arousal, particularly indices of cardiovascular functioning. This underscores the importance of measuring several indices. A system producing replicated findings, but conflicting evidence with respect to SNS versus PNS activity, is pupil diameter: The baseline data indicate PNS dominance, and the light reflex data indicate SNS dominance in schizophrenics. These observations suggest that the model on which these inferences are based is oversimplified. Again, concurrent measurement of other ANS indices might help clarify these findings.

Quantitative analyses of the EEG have shown lower integrated activity, lower amplitude variability, less alpha power, lower alpha peak frequency, and more slow and fast activity in schizophrenics than in controls. Many of these findings have been attributed to high arousal, but studies that have recorded ANS variables along with the EEG have shown no correspondence between the two sets of measures.

Recent data on the SCOR have shown a large proportion of schizophrenics who are unresponsive or hyporesponsive to moderate-intensity stimuli. Some, but not all, studies have found a subgroup of patients with excessively slow habituation. These individual differences in the SCOR have been related consistently to corresponding differences in both electrodermal and cardiovascular base levels and to differences in symptomatology within the patient group. This, along with evidence of similar electrodermal and cardiovascular differences in the OR, strongly suggests a central origin of the SCOR differences. However, in a study that measured alpha blocking along with ANS indices of the OR (Bernstein et al., 1981), the cortical index did not show the hyporeactivity that was a prominent feature of the ANS in the schizophrenics. In general, EEG studies have focused less on individual differences among patients than have many of the more recent ANS studies. Perhaps there are indeed fewer such differences in EEG activity.

Workers in this area have tended to regard differences in the SCOR in terms of information-processing concepts, such as input gating (Venables, 1977) or a sensory filter (Horvath & Meares, 1979; see Ohman, 1981, for a review). Other theories of the SCOR take slow habituation to be an indicator of anxiety or arousal (Lader & Wing, 1969; see also "Anxiety, Neuroses, and Miscellaneous Conditions," below). These theories are not necessarily incompatible, but the emphasis in the latter group is on the OR as determined by the general state of the ANS, whereas the former group emphasizes the mechansims that provide modulation or control over stimulus input.

If, as seems likely, the OR is determined by both these components, it would be useful to be able to estimate the contribution of each of them separately. One such attempt has been made by use of a ratio of SCORs to SSCRs (Zahn et al., 1968; Zahn, Carpenter, & McGlashan, 1981a); this measure provided maximal separation between schizophrenics and controls in both studies (the schizophrenics having lower ratios), despite a greater mean SCOR frequency in the chronic patients in the earlier study. Although the measure used may not have ideal psychometric properties, and techniques based on regression analysis might be superior, the results suggest that when differences in the lability of the electrodermal system are taken into account, the SCORs of schizophrenics are even more attenuated than they might appear otherwise, perhaps reflecting severe gating or attention impairment.

In this review, it has been seen that, in general, hyperresponsivity (i.e., slow habituation) for schizophrenics as a group occurred consistently only in studies of unmedicated patients that used stimuli with characteristics likely to elicit DRs rather than true ORs. The conclusion of hyporeactivity to moderate stimuli and hyperreactivity to intense stimuli in schizophrenia is just the opposite of the "transmarginal inhibition" hypotheses frequently proposed.

Indirect evidence also suggests that neuroleptic drugs attenuate ORs (or DRs) to intense stimuli, at least in some patients, but not to moderate stimuli. In terms of the two-component model of the OR proposed above, it can be speculated that the lack of a clear drug effect on moderate-stimulus ORs is due to the expected reduction of the OR, by virtue of the lowered ANS activation's being offset by potentiation of the OR from improved attention capacity (Spohn et al., 1977). For intense stimuli, the attention or gating mechanism may play less of a role—such stimuli will "get through" any barrier—so that only the attenuation due to lowered activation results from the medication in this case. More direct evidence on this and the related question of whether schizophrenics have an altered threshold for elicitation of DRs is needed. Although the proposed model accounts for some of the conflicting results on the OR, it does not explain why some studies have found unimodal and some have found bimodal SCOR distributions. Equally puzzling is the observation that the beta-adrenergic receptor blocker propranolol, either alone or in combination with phenothiazines, reduced the frequency of both nonresponding and nonhabituation in schizophrenics.

On a similar issue, support for the generalization that schizophrenics are disproportionately hyporeactive to significant stimuli (Zahn, 1964, 1975) has been equivocal, with some studies confirming it and some showing even greater increments in responding to significant versus nonsignificant stimuli in patients than in controls. The conditions determining these disparate results are not clear. The evidence is more supportive of reduced ANS anticipatory activity in schizophrenia, providing a possible bridge to theories of impaired preparatory sets. Diminished tonic ANS

reactions to performance stress continues to be supported.

The analysis of the ERP literature presented earlier has pointed up the critical role of attention in such studies. Even with rather subtle variations in the instructions, schizophrenic attenuation in middle and late ERPs may be present only when at least passive attention is directed toward the stimuli. When attention effects have been made more explicit or active by use of task-related stimuli, the schizophrenic deficit in ERPs (especially those thought to be most affected by attention, such as P300 and the CNV) has been more consistent. There is a parallel here with some, but not all, of the ANS findings, indicating a specific deficit in responding to task-related (attended) stimuli. Unlike the case with the SCOR, increases in stimulus intensity seem to produce relatively less of an increment in the ERPs of schizophrenics than in those of controls; this phenomenon is most striking in acute patients. However, this conflict may be only apparent, since the conditions producing the ANS results—intense auditory stimuli and unmedicated patients—have not occurred simultaneously in ERP studies.

Apparently independently of attention, larger early ERPs have been reported in schizophrenics, possibly due to a failure of sequential inhibition when ISIs are short. Latencies of these early peaks in somatosensory ERPs do not appear to show the same delay in ipsilateral versus contralateral recordings. The interpretation of this finding is unclear.

EEG evidence for a hypothesized left-hemisphere dysfunction is confused. However, replicated findings of low interhemispheric coherence of EEG frequency spectra suggest a defect in transmission of signals across the corpus callosum. Several ERP studies have indicated a left-hemisphere problem in schizophrenics which may be more likely to be manifested during attention tasks.

Dysfunction in pendulum eye tracking meets many of the criteria for a genetic marker of schizophrenia, such as reasonably good sensitivity, specificity, and familial concordance. There is much evidence that relates this dysfunction closely to disturbances of involuntary attention rather than to a neurological or oculomotor defect.

Studies of treatment outcome have shown that chronic schizophrenics who are more likely to benefit from neuroleptics have higher EEG and ANS indices of arousal than drug-resistant patients. Poor-prognosis acute schizophrenics, however, have higher ANS base levels and slower SCOR habituation than patients with good outcome, and this is independent of drug treatment. Poor-outcome patients also showed inadequate phasic, tonic, and anticipatory reactions during task performance, but less ERP "reducing" to visual stimuli of different intensities. These features were largely independent of clinical state, suggesting that they may reflect longer-lasting dispositions or traits. There is also evidence that high ANS activity and high responsivity to family interactions is related to a generally stressful familial environment and other life stresses and to poor clinical course.

The possible genetic basis or such traits has been investigated more directly by high-risk studies of the offspring of schizophrenic parents. Although the long-term results of these studies are not in, and there is much conflicting evidence, the data suggest that a genetic risk for schizophrenia may be accompanied by an ANS hyperresponsivity and slow habituation (perhaps more so to aversive stimuli) and by deviant late positive ERPs in an attention paradigm. These results are only partially congruent with those obtained on schizophrenic patients, suggesting changes with the onset and/or development of the illness. There is some evidence that high-risk children become more deviant with age, and it is unfortunate that these studies have not done periodic reassessments to check on developmental trends. The familial issue can be attacked simply and cheaply by studies of patients' relatives. Such studies of eye tracking and of attention-related ERPs suggest familial concordance for these measures. More purely genetic strategies, in addition to twin studies, that have not been explored are comparisons of full and half siblings of patients and studies of biological and adoptive parents, although these may take a considerable effort at case finding.

Research on the important question of possible physiological determinants of performance has been inadequate in scope and conflicting in outcome. This area has suffered from failure to study tasks that measure processes representing key deficits, such as selective attention. However, support for the detrimental role of high arousal on performance comes from evidence that phenothiazines reduce ANS activation and improve performance, specifically on attention and information-processing tasks. Moreover, much of the conflicting correlational evidence can be reconciled when the use of medication is taken into account. ANS indices of arousal seem to be positively related to performance in medicated patients, but negatively related in drug-free patients. These data can be fit to a model of a change from the descending to the ascending limbs of an inverted-U function when patients are given neuroleptics.

Theoretical Summary

BIOCHEMICAL HYPOTHESES

The hypothesis that excessive DA activity is involved in schizophrenia was developed from pharmacological evidence, especially evidence that the effective antipsychotic drugs all block DA receptors. Psychophysiological studies as a rule have not been conducted from this perspective. Development of psychophysiological indicators of DA activity could be extremely valuable in both practical and scientific developments.

One line of inquiry comes from the study of the effects of neuroleptic drugs. The evidence suggests that neuroleptic drugs produce ANS deactivation, protect schizophrenics from disorganization from task-related or demanding stimuli, and increase habituation rates to intense stimuli. Neuroleptics may also reduce EEG fast activity, increase slow activity, and reduce blink rates. Evidence relevant to a DA model comes from two studies that measured the ANS effects of drugs that increase DA activity: L-dopa given to Parkinson patients (Horvath & Meares, 1974), and D-amphetamine given to normal males (Zahn, Rapoport, & Thompson, 1981). Both studies reported increases in ANS base levels and reduced habituation, although only D-amphetamine increased HR. The pattern of ANS effects of amphetamine, including reduced HR slowing in the RT foreperiod and reduced ANS responding (specifically to signal stimuli), matched rather closely the differences between schizophrenics and controls tested on similar procedures. In this context, the effect of amphetamine in reducing the pupillary light reflex cited earlier, which is similar to findings with schizophrenics, is also relevant. Horvath and Meares (1979) point out that their L-dopa results do not match their schizophrenia results, in that their patients did not show elevated SSCRs, and paranoids habituated normally. These observations are taken as evidence against the DA hypothesis. However, their data may be atypical with respect to both the SSCR and the paranoid–nonparanoid findings.

Caution in accepting a DA model of the ANS activity of schizophrenics is advisable on several other grounds. First, the drugs used are not specific: They also block norepinephrine (NE) activity, and may alter cholinergic activity as well. Comparative studies of drugs with different effects will be necessary in order to pin down the observed effects to a given neurotransmitter. Second, there is puzzling evidence of negative correlations between some indices of ANS activity that are high in schizophrenics and urinary catecholamine metabolities (Deakin et al., 1979; Zahn, 1980). Third, similar ANS effects might be produced by other drugs that have different effects on neurotransmitters (e.g., Patterson & Venables, 1981). Claridge (1978) has proposed LSD, a drug without clear effects on DA, as a better model for schizophrenia than amphetamine, partly on the basis of data showing the same SCL versus TFT relationships in normals given LSD as in schizophrenics. The possible involvement of cholinergic hypoactivity in some of the schizophrenia findings has been stressed by Patterson (1976a, 1976b) and Spohn and Patterson (1979). These ideas are compatible with the general feeling that a DA disorder may not be the primary or sole cause of schizophrenia, or may not be present in all cases (Haracz, 1982). More pharmacological studies on both patients and controls are needed to determine whether patterns of psychophysiological activity can be associated reliably with the activity of different neurotransmitters. Other strategies with the same goal would include correlations of psychophysiological variables with amines and their metabolites from blood, urine, and cerebrospinal fluid, and comparison of patients who are thought to differ in dopaminergic activity on the basis of other biological markers or of treatment response. The latter strategy has produced evidence of dopaminergic involvement in blink rates in schizophrenia.

It is possible that psychophysiological predictors of therapeutic outcome from neuroleptic drugs can be discovered. However, an EEG study attempting this was basically unsuccessful; and in one ANS study on this problem, although the drug increased habituation rate and habituation rate predicted outcome, this was independent of drug treatment. Thus the antipsychotic effects of drugs may not be related to their effects on habituation.

NEUROPHYSIOLOGICAL HYPOTHESES

Only a few psychophysiologists have made serious proposals about specific areas in the brain that are dysfunctional in schizophrenia. It is, of course, possible that no specific location or lesion is involved; the dysfunction may be in the functional organization of the brain as a whole. Alternatively, the heterogeneity of this syndrome is such that various areas may be involved. Mirsky (1969) concluded, largely on the basis of electrophysiological evidence, that schizophrenics as a group were overaroused, and hypothesized that this reflected dysfunctional brain stem mechanisms. Schizophrenic heterogeneity was attributed to defects in various cortical areas. The negative findings on schizophrenics' BSEPs provide no support for this hypothesis but do not refute it.

It has been proposed, largely on the basis of indirect evidence from animal studies, that the SCOR differences among schizophrenics and between patients and controls reflect limbic dysfunction (Gruzelier & Venables, 1972; Venables, 1977). In this view, impairment of hippocampal inhibition of arousal accounts for the slow habituation found in some schizophrenics, and amygdaloid dysfunction accounts for nonresponding. At another point, on the basis of TFT and SCOR recovery data, these authors (Gruzelier & Venables, 1974b, 1975b) propose that hippocampal dysfunction may be characteristic of all schizophrenics and that differences in the OR are determined by the intactness of the amygdala. Additional support, on a general level, for hippocampal involvement in some of the psychophysiological features of schizophrenia is suggested by the evidence that this structure has acetylcholine (ACh) as its principal transmitter (Drachman, 1978). Arguments suggesting inadequate ACh functioning in schizophrenia were presented earlier. Since the hippocampus is involved in short-term memory, its dysfunction might impair formation of a Sokolovian neuronal model and retard habituation. It has been suggested previously that reduced cholinergic activity may account for SCOR hyporesponding and several other findings in schizophrenia; indeed, direct evidence for this possibility exists (Patterson & Venables, 1981). It is unlikely that both extremes of SCOR responding are due to the same mechanism, although a threshold model is possible. Dose–response studies of cholinergic drugs might help clarify this.

However, a defect in the hippocampal–cholinergic system by itself is doubtless inadequate to account for even the SCOR data. The hypothesized involvement of the amygdala fits with the idea of a DA influence, since the amygdala receives projections from the mesolimbic DA system (Bunney & Aghajanian, 1978). Thus the concept of an altered DA-ACh balance in schizophrenia can be seen as having an anatomical counterpart in the limbic system. Although some of the results may be contaminated by muscle artifacts, much of the topological EEG and ERP evidence implicates the temporal lobe, and some suggests parietal involvement (possibly more pronounced in the dominant hemisphere). However, some evidence suggests that the two hemispheres may be out of synchrony in schizophrenia, due to impairment of callosal transmission. Further development of mapping techniques and artifact control, along with attention to differences among patients, should help clarify some of these issues. Limitations on their effectiveness, however, come from inadequate knowledge about where the various potentials are generated, and the consequent problem of discriminating cortical from subcortical influences.

Most of the work on laterality is based on explicit or implicit hypotheses about lateralized dysfunction. A more detailed theory has been proposed by Venables (1984), in a closely reasoned paper, who interprets the research findings as indicating an overactive left hemisphere in adult process schizophrenics. He goes on to speculate that this is due to a long-standing right-hemisphere dysfunction, thereby attempting to account for some of the apparently conflicting findings with respect to laterality. Another recent hypothesis (Levin, 1984), based mainly on an interpretation of the eye tracking data as indicating a failure of schizophrenics to inhibit saccades, proposes frontal lobe dysfunction in some schizophrenics. Although both Venables (1984) and Levin (1984), of course, lean heavily on various kinds of data to support their theories, the impetus for them came directly from psychophysiological data.

PSYCHOLOGICAL HYPOTHESES

Most of the speculations about the meaning of psychophysiological data have focused on their relationship to psychological constructs, rather than on their relationship to clinical symptomatology or to the implications for the biological etiology of the disorder. Thus there have been few attempts to "explain" hallucinations, delusions, thought disorder, and the like by psychophysiological results. Rather, such data have been referred to defects of perception and information processing, which are assumed to be basic to the clinical symptoms.

Much of the thinking in this area has been influenced by the phenomenological picture presented by McGhie and Chapman (1961), in which schizophrenics are seen as confused and overwhelmed by ordinary environmental stimuli. A failure to inhibit reactions to irrelevant stimuli thus interferes with responses to relevant stimuli. This has played a part in the development of the hypothesis of a defective filter in the early stages of information processing in schizophrenia, leading to defects in selective attention and signal detection.

What does the psychophysiological evidence tell us about such a filter? If it is assumed that the operation of the filter is indicated by physiological responses to stimuli, then the answer to this question depends on the type of response measured and the situation. The ERP literature suggests, in schizophrenics, a gating out of stimuli to which subjects are asked to attend, but perhaps no differences in reactions to unattended stimuli. This result seems to hold for the later peaks, which may reflect subsequent information processing, as well as for the earlier peaks. Thus, while ERPs are not larger in schizophrenics, the reactions to attended and nonattended stimuli are more similar.

One exception to this comes from Shagass's (1979) finding of a larger somatosensory peak (N60) in schizophrenics, indicating a "too open" filter in an early processing stage. The relation of this to the attenuation of later ERPs is problematical. The interpretation of larger N60 in schizophrenics is also uncertain in view of the evidence that the opposite result may occur with a longer ISI (Adler et al., 1982) suggesting defective inhibition in schizophrenia. This would seem a plausible physiological mechanism for a defective filter. Investigation of ERPs of less than 100 msec, along with later ERPs, to stimuli of various modalities under controlled conditions of attention and variations in the ISI, might help answer these questions.

A defective early-stage ("preattentive") filter is also implied by the finding of reduced inhibition of the blink reflex by prestimulation at 60 msec. Studies of the blink reflex and its inhibition and facilitation have been underexploited in schizophrenia research.

A related and consistent finding relevant to this problem is the higher waveshape variability after 100 msec poststimulus, not attributable to variability in background EEG, in schizophrenia. It has not been determined whether the low average amplitude occurs because of the high variability or whether the converse is true, but the low signal-to-noise ratio implied

could be related to impaired selectivity in signal processing.

The ANS data present a less consistent picture. Low signal-to-noise ratios in schizophrenia are also implied by the low SCOR:SSCR ratios obtained in some studies. The high rate of SSCRs found in many schizophrenics is frequently interpreted as reactivity to internal and irrelevant external stimuli. These observations can be seen as consistent with an overly permeable filter. On the other hand, low reactivity or nonresponding to nonsignal stimuli of moderate intensity is a prominent feature in schizophrenia, and ANS reactions to signal stimuli are at or below normal levels, suggesting, like the ERP findings, an overly "closed" gate. Overresponding in schizophrenics usually takes the form of failure of habituation rather than large response amplitudes, indicating involvement of a later stage of processing rather than an input filter that is "too open." This analysis suggests that dysfunctions in selective attention could be due to weak reactions to both signal and nonsignal stimuli in a noisy background. The filter in many schizophrenics might be said to be nonselectively impermeable, rather than nonselectively permeable, as is frequently assumed. In most cases, the behavioral effects of these two alternatives will be indistinguishable. It has been stated earlier (see page 523) that SCOR nonresponders were more prone than responders to errors of omission in signal detection tasks, while nonhabituators were more prone to errors of commission. Further studies along these lines, counterbalancing signal detection and response requirements (i.e., responses to nondetection of the critical stimulus) and recording physiological data during the procedure, might provide a more definitive test.

The filter idea is also implicit in the interpretation of low ERP amplitudes, especially to intense stimuli, as reflecting a mechanism that protects schizophrenics against the disrupting effects of stimulation (e.g., Schooler et al., 1976). This appears to be more pronounced in patients who are less chronic and who have good prognosis, suggesting a breakdown in this mechanism in chronic patients. SCOR nonresponding has also been interpreted as reflecting a protective mechanism (Straube, 1979). However, while there is some apparent similarity of the association between slow habituation and poor prognosis with the ERP reducing data, SCOR nonresponding may be most common in more disorganized and withdrawn patients, suggesting a different mechanism.

A more sophisticated version of the impaired filter idea has been proposed recently by Callaway and Naghdi (1982). The evidence in schizophrenia for short latency of alpha blocking and of some ERPs, larger and more stable early somatosensory ERPs, and prolonged effects of prior stimulation on early ERPs and on the PINV are taken to indicate fast and persistent operation of automatic or parallel processes of handling information. The high efficiency of this mode may interfere with the controlled or limited channel capacity processes of schizophrenics, which are manifested by, say, small and variable later ERPs and impaired behavior. While the categorization of some of the variables into one or another type of processing seems somewhat arbitrary, this theory suggests some interesting studies that will test its main assumptions.

Inferences about other stages of information processing have also been made from psychophysiological data. Smaller P300 has been interpreted in terms of "response set" (Josiassen et al., 1981), but Roth et al. (1981) showed that requiring a motor response to an improbable stimulus produced equal increments of P300 in schizophrenics and controls. The normal latency of P300 in schizophrenics is interpreted as showing normal stimulus evaluation time, at least in a rather simple paradigm (Roth et al., 1981). Reduced anticipatory SCRs, HR slowing, and CNV have been attributed to inadequate preparation.

However, the data at hand do not permit us to specify a particular stage of processing as especially vulnerable to schizophrenic deficit. Indeed, it is still quite possible to attribute most results to a general factor of preoccupation or distraction (Mannuzza, 1980). If a more specific dysfunction exists, studies in which stimulus and response uncertainty, stimulus probability, and task difficulty are varied independently and systematically, as well as some of the paradigms suggested by Callaway and Naghdi (1982), might elucidate it.

AFFECTIVE DISORDERS

Theoretical Considerations

Affective disorders come in many varieties, virtually all of which feature depressed mood as a fundamental attribute. There is little agreement on the subclassification that might facilitate understanding of etiology and optimize treatment decisions, or even on whether different symptom patterns should be treated as types or as variations along several dimensions. Psychophysiological studies might be expected to be useful in the search for clinically meaningful classifications or dimensions, and, indeed, many of the studies that are reviewed below have addressed this problem.

The best-supported subclassification is the "unipolar" versus "bipolar" dichotomy (Kendell, 1976). Not only is this based on the obvious clinical distinction between patients who suffer only periods of depression and those who have periods of mania as well (unipolar mania is quite rare), but the two disorders tend to "breed true." Bipolar relatives are more likely to be found in the families of bipolar probands, and

unipolar relatives are more frequent in the families of unipolar probands than would be expected in the general population. In addition, bipolar illness tends to have an earlier onset and has a sex distribution less weighted with females than unipolar depression. Moreover, there is evidence favoring lithium carbonate as a treatment for bipolar illness and tricyclic antidepressants for unipolar patients (Katz & Hirschfeld, 1978). Yet even here, the separation between groups may not be as clean as necessary to support the idea of a separate etiology, since bipolar patients may also have a higher than expected number of unipolar relatives, and vice versa (Taylor, Abrams, & Hayman, 1980), and the evidence suggests that lithium and electroconvulsive therapy (ECT) may be effective in both groups. In addition, there is a problem in diagnosis stemming from the fact that several depressive episodes may occur before the first clear episode of mania.

Another widely used clinical distinction is "endogenous" versus "nonendogenous" (or reactive) depression. This distinction in current usage is not based on the presence of a precipitating life event, but on a "characteristic complex of current clinical psychopathology involving early morning awakening, anorexia and weight loss, psychomotor disturbance, diurnal mood variation, severe depressed mood, and lack of reactivity to external stimuli" (Katz & Hirschfeld, 1978, p. 1189). This is similar to the category of "major depression" in DSM-III. However, it should be remembered that the disregard for precipitating factors in this distinction is a fairly recent development, and the usage of this term in the literature is somewhat inconsistent.

A similar distinction is that between "psychotic" and "neurotic" depression. These terms have also been used inconsistently, sometimes referring to the presence or absence, respectively, of delusions, hallucinations, or gross loss of insight, and sometimes as alternate names for the endogenous–nonendogenous distinction outlined above. However, the severity or incapacitating nature of the symptoms seems to be the critical feature here, rather than the pattern of symptoms per se. There is disagreement about whether this is a continuum or whether psychotic and neurotic types represent distinct illnesses with separate etiologies. Neurotic depression can also be considered a heterogeneous category (Katz & Hirschfeld, 1978). "Primary" versus "secondary" depression is another categorization. This one cuts across some of the other dichotomies and simply refers to the absence or presence of other types of psychiatric disorders. Depression is frequently associated with schizophrenia (schizoaffective) or anxiety states, and it is not always agreed to which class these disorders belong. It is recognized, however, that anxiety and agitation frequently accompany primary depression, and some writers have given "agitated" depression separate subtype status, contrasted with "retarded" depression. Similarly, some have split "hostile" depression off as a separate subtype distinct from the agitated and retarded varieties (Kendell, 1976).

This confusing array of diagnostic schemes makes for severe difficulties in conducting and interpreting research in this area. Although there are several semi-structured interview schedules in wide use that have increased the objectivity and reliability of diagnoses (Katz & Hirschfeld, 1978), as well as a growing consensus on some of the critical dimensions by which to classify patients, the validity of these systems has not clearly been established. It is not unreasonable to think that psychophysiological investigations may be of some value in this enterprise.

It is a bit surprising that more psychophysiological research has not been performed on affective disorders, since they have many inherent features that should facilitate research. Despite the many clinical variations by which depressive illness presents itself, the ubiquitous dysphoric mood state, including feelings of helplessness and hopelessness, suggests common underlying physiological concomitants. These may occur as well in subclinical or "normal" depressed states. Thus, unlike many other psychopathological conditions, a potential model exists for studying an essential part of the condition in the absence of gross psychopathology. Moreover, since most types of depressive illness are episodic, the investigation of state and trait aspects of the disorders should be possible. In addition, the major hypotheses of the biological etiology of affective disorders implicate low activity of monoaminergic systems, in terms of either 5-HT (Murphy, Campbell, & Costa, 1978) or NE (Schildkraut, 1978), and these systems may also be involved in the control of psychophysiological processes. Thus, psychophysiological investigations may be expected to contribute to study of the classification, phenomenology, and etiology of affective disorders.

Autonomic and Somatic Activity

Base Levels

The relatively small literature on the psychophysiology of affective disorders has been reviewed by Christie, Little, and Gordon (1980) and Lader (1975), and that on electrodermal variables by J. A. Stern and Janes (1973). For SC variables, the findings more often than not suggest low baseline activity in depression. Many of these studies assessed the effects of depressed mood in a mixed sample of psychiatric patients rather than comparing diagnostic groups. Several recent studies have confirmed this result. Low SCL in depressives diagnosed by contemporary methods, compared to normal controls, was observed in

medicated unipolar depressives (Dawson, Schell, & Catania, 1977) and in endogenous depressives who were unmedicated 3–7 days (Lapierre & Butter, 1980; Mirkin & Coppen, 1980; Storrie, Doerr, & Johnson, 1981; Ward, Doerr, & Storrie, 1983). Similar results in mostly medicated unipolar and bipolar patients in remission were reported by Iacono, Lykken, Peloquin, Lumry, Valentine, and Tuason (1983) and Iacono, Lykken, Haroian, Peloquin, Valentine, and Tuason (1984). There is also negative evidence. Lapierre and Butter (1980) found no differences between depressed groups and controls in SSCRs, and Toone, Cooke, and Lader (1981), with patients unmedicated 2 weeks minimum, obtained no differences on either SCL or SSCRs, the latter measure being slightly higher in depressives than in controls. Similarly, Albus, Engel, Muller, Zander, and Ackenheil (1982) found slightly higher SCL in endogenous depressives drug free for 4 weeks.

That a diagnosis of depression does not necessarily imply low SC activity is shown by a report of a dramatic difference between agitated and retarded depressed patients on both SCL and SSCRs, the agitated group having much higher, and the retarded group much lower, values than normal controls or an intermediate depressed group (Lader & Wing, 1969). Although Noble and Lader (1971d) confirmed this result for SSCRs (but not SCL), the results were not as dramatic. More recent attempts at confirmation have not been successful (Dawson et al., 1977; Lapierre & Butter, 1980; Toone et al., 1981). The failure to replicate has been attributed to difficulties in obtaining severely depressed unmedicated cases (Noble & Lader, 1971d; Toone et al., 1981).

However, significant heterogeneity within the depressive group has been shown in studies using different subclassifications. Thus, Byrne (1975) found SSCRs to be lower than those of controls in psychotic depressives and higher than those of controls in neurotic depressives, and Mirkin and Coppen (1980) obtained comparable results on SCL with the endogenous versus nonendogenous distinction. Frith et al. (1982) reported neurotic depressives to be very similar to patients with anxiety disorders on SCL and SSCRs. Noble and Lader (1972) reported similar differences for SCL and SSCRs when their subjects were divided by endogenous versus reactive criteria, but they believe that the critical variable is retardation, which is correlated with the endogenous classification.

Cardiovascular variables have been even less intensively studies than SC. Many of the reported results for HR are suspect since antidepressant drugs increase HR (Iacono, Lykken, Peloquin, et al., 1983; Zahn, Insel, & Murphy, 1984). In three studies, patients were unmedicated for a sufficient period. Lader and Wing (1969) found higher HR than normal in agitated but not retarded patients. Bruno, Myers, and

Glassman (1983) correlated cardiovascular variables with global depression ratings. The results for HR and blood pressure were not significant but the length of the pre-ejection period was positively correlated with depression, indicating lower beta-adrenergic activity with increasing depression. Nonsignificantly elevated resting HR was reported by Albus, Engel, Muller *et al.* (1982).

Elevated resting SBP was found in depressives by I. B. Goldstein (1965). Kelly (1980) found SBP to be high in agitated patients, but not markedly so in non-agitated patients. Similarly, Heine (1970) reported that elevated blood pressure was associated with anxiety and agitation in depressed subjects more than with severity of depression. It should be pointed out that Kelly's (1980) nonagitated group had self-ratings of trait and state anxiety almost as high as those in the agitated group, so the critical variable may be agitation rather than anxiety per se. Although there is some evidence of a high incidence of hypertension in older individuals who have suffered from periodic depressive episodes, M. J. Friedman and Bennet (1977) did not find either the diagnoses of depression or self-ratings of depression in a series of admissions to a psychiatric clinic to be related to hypertension (as defined by a DBP greater than 90).

FBF, a measure that has been shown to have a strong direct relationship to stress and anxiety, was observed by Kelly (1980) to be markedly elevated in agitated depressives, but slightly lower than that of controls in nonagitated depressives. Similarly, Noble and Lader (1971c) reported an inverse correlation between retardation and FBF. Bruno *et al.* (1983) reported that global depression ratings were negatively correlated with resting FBF and positively correlated with forearm vascular resistance, suggesting to them that sympathetic cholinergic activity decreases with increased depression. As was the case with blood pressure, it has been pointed out that FBF is disproportionately low in depressives in relation to their high rated anxiety.

An area that has attracted particular attention in the affective disorders is that of salivation. In general, saliva output is low in depressed patients as a whole (Lader, 1975), but there is less agreement on relationships with subtypes. Noble and Lader (1971a) found lower salivary flow in retarded than in agitated patients, using the same classification in which the retarded group had lower resting SSCRs. This suggests low PNS activity in the retarded group, since that branch of the ANS stimulates salivary output.

Another psychophysiological variable that has been investigated for some time is the EMG. Several studies have shown increased resting EMG levels in depressed patients (Albus, Engel, Muller *et al.*, 1982; Lader, 1975). Interestingly, a study with negative results is that of Lader and Wing (1969), which reported such dramatic differences between agitated and retarded depressives on ANS variables. However, Noble and Lader (1971b) reported higher forearm extensor EMG to correlate with severity of depression and with a number of somatic symptoms accompanying depression. Theoretically, one might expect relationships between forearm EMG activity and FBF, but these two variables showed different patterns of correlations with clinical variables.

An interesting use of EMG of facial muscles as an objective measure of facial expression was made by Schwartz, Fair, Salt, Mandel, and Klerman (1976). Happy and sad imagery produced distinct patterns of EMG activity in several facial locations, and the pattern accompanying happy imagery was attenuated in depressed patients. Using a similar technique, Teasdale and Bancroft (1977) replicated the Schwartz *et al.* (1976) finding that EMG from corrugator supercilii differentiates between happy and unhappy thoughts, and they found significant within-subject correlations averaging about .70 between depressive mood ratings and corrugator EMG in all five of their depressed patients. However, with a larger group of subjects, Carney, Hong, O'Connell, and Amado (1981) failed to replicate this result. Although this technique may yield a more sensitive measure of facial expression than clinical observation, as claimed, the differentiation between depressed patients and controls needs further validation.

Responsivity and Habituation

The earlier literature on SC reactivity to discrete stimuli and stressors yields the rather consistent conclusion that this system is less responsive in patients with depression than in normals (Lader, 1975). The Lader and Wing (1969) study provides an exception, in that the agitated depressives failed to habituate to a series of 20 nonsignal tones while retarded depressives were almost completely unresponsive, but the depressive group as a whole had a smaller SCR amplitude to the first tone than controls. However, Byrne (1975) reported larger than normal SCR amplitudes to signal stimuli in neurotic depressives, but smaller than normal SCRs in psychotic depressives. Habituation was marginally slower in the neurotic as compared to the psychotic group. Somewhat similarly, Frith *et al.* (1982) reported similar habituation curves in neurotic depressives and anxiety disorders. Low reactivity in depressives has been confirmed more recently by Storrie *et al.* (1981), who used a Valsalva maneuver as the stimulus, and by Dawson *et al.* (1977), who found diminished SCRs with longer latencies in depressives to a variety of signal, nonsignal, and conditioning stimuli. Similar results were reported for remitted unipolar and bipolar patients (Iacono, Lykken, Peloquin *et al.*, 1983; Iacono, Peloquin, Lykken, *et al.*, 1984). Bipolars were in between unipolars and controls on all variables. Dawson *et al.* (1977) also observed that low SCR magnitude and longer latencies were correlated with severity of depression. Mirkin and Coppen (1980) found more SCOR nonresponders to tones among unmedicated depressed patients (67%), especially when subtyped as endogenous (82%), compared to controls (13%). Of importance was the finding that the nonresponding patients had lower uptake of 5-HT by platelets, a measure that may be a biological marker for depressive illness. On the other hand, Toone et al. (1981) reported no SCOR differences in their depressives compared to controls. Lapierre and Butter (1980) also found no SCOR amplitude or frequency differences between agitated or retarded depressives and controls, but longer SCR latencies occurred in both patient groups, and retarded patients "manifested a reverberation of responsivity, namely, that the number of bursts following stimulation was greater in number but of lower magnitude" (p. 222). This aspect of SC responding has not been widely studied, but a similar finding has been reported by Japanese investigators in patients with "atypical psychosis" (Shirafuji & Nareta, 1962).

Marked and highly significant differences among large samples of normal controls, neurotic depressives, and psychotic depressives were obtained using a "sedation threshold" technique, which determines the amount of intravenous sodium thiopental necessary to inhibit SCRs to signal stimuli completely (Perez-Reyes, 1972). The neurotic depressive group, which included cases of depression with anxiety, had the highest threshold, and the psychotic depressive group, which included bipolar and agitated depressives, had the lowest threshold. The results were attributed to differences in the balance of excitatory and inhibitory influences on SC activity. Problems with this research are the lack of consideration of the effects of baseline values on responsivity and the absence of a placebo control, so that the specific effects of the barbiturate infusion are not clear.

Cardiovascular reactivity has been studied relatively little in relation to depression. I. B. Goldstein (1965) found depressives to have at least as large a HR and SBP response to noise stress as either patient or normal controls, and their SBP response may have been larger, but it was not analyzed statistically. Contrasted with these findings are those of Kelly and Walter (1969) and Kelly (1980) that both agitated and nonagitated depressives had lower FBF, HR, and SBP reactions to a stressful mental arithmetic procedure than controls. In contrast, Dawson et al. (1977) reported a nonsignificantly greater increment in HR from a rest to a task period, despite higher initial levels in depressives than in controls. However, phasic HR responsivity, both decelerative and accelerative, to a variety of stimuli was lower in the depressed group. Similarly, retarded depressives had reduced vasoconstrictive ORs compared to controls, with agitated patients in between (Lapierre & Butter, 1980).

Many of these findings may have been influenced by current or recent antidepressant drug treatment. However, depressives who were unmedicated for 4 weeks had a small HR response to mental arithmetic compared to controls (Albus, Engel, Muller, et al., 1982).

Other measures of reactivity have been neglected in this area. The most notable finding is a much greater EMG response to noise stress in depressed as compared to nondepressed patients and controls (I. B. Goldstein, 1965).

Smooth Pursuit Eye Movements

Some evidence of impaired SPEM in affective disorders exists. Holzman and Levy (1977) reported some increase in velocity arrests in manic–depressive patients. This impairment was not as great as in chronic schizophrenics. It was dependent on the method of diagnosis, and the proportion of these patients classified as poor trackers was not high. However, Shagass et al. (1974) found impaired tracking in psychotic depressives, and Levin, Lipton, and Holzman (1981) and Iacono et al. (1982) found impairment in bipolar patients almost equal to that of schizophrenics. Iacono et al. (1982), whose patients were in remission, were able to show that lithium had an adverse effect on SPEMs. Remitted unipolar patients were not impaired. Thus, if patients with affective disorders show a SPEM deficit, it is likely to be confined to bipolar, manic–depressive, or psychotic patients and to be less extreme than that shown by schizophrenics. Moreover, SPEM dysfunction appears not to run in the families of affective-disorder patients as it does in families of schizophrenics (Holzman et al., 1984).

Lateral Asymmetry of Electrodermal Activity

Interest in laterality of physiological activity in depression stems in large part from the ideas of Flor-Henry (1969) that depression is related to dysfunction in the nondominant hemisphere. This hypothesis was tested by Gruzelier and Venables (1973, 1974a) by analyses of bilateral SCORs to nonsignal and signal tones. During both tone series, SCL from the left hand was higher ($p < .06$) than that on the right for the depressed subjects, while right-hand superiority occurred in schizophrenics and patients with personality disorders. Depressives had significantly lower SCOR amplitudes to nonsignal tones on the right hand, but showed nonsignificant differences in the opposite direction in SCORs to signal tones.

Partial confirmation of these results has been obtained by Myslobodsky and Horesh (1978), who found lower right-hand SC activity in endogenous depressives during a neutral tone series and during visual and verbal tasks. Reactive depressives had no consistent laterality differences, and the laterality of controls varied with the type of task. In addition, both depressed subgroups had significantly more left-going eye movements while answering various types of questions. Myslobodsky and Horesh attribute both findings to hyperactivity in the nondominant (right) hemisphere, a position exactly opposite to that taken by Gruzelier and Venables (1974a).

Schneider (1983) also reported higher SCL and SCOR amplitudes from the left versus the right hand in depressives, who were different from controls in that respect. However, three recent studies have failed to confirm the laterality difference in SCL or SCRs in depressives (Iacono & Tuason, 1983; Storrie et al., 1981; Toone et al., 1981). Toone et al. (1981) did find a greater change in SCL during the rest and tones periods from the left hand in only the depressed group, suggesting a greater tonic SCR to session onset on the left hand in that group. The positive results are all in the direction of higher left than right SC activity in depressives, but the reasons for the discrepencies among these studies is not too clear, nor is it clear how the lateralized control of SC activity is accomplished by the brain.

Effects of Clinical Changes

Affective disorders present a valuable opportunity to study correlated changes in physiological and mood states because of their episodic nature. Most studies of intrasubject somatic and ANS changes have been studies of treatment effects in unipolar depressives.

Some earlier studies reported that ECT increased the number of active sweat glands (Lader, 1975) or increased elicited SCR frequency or amplitude (J. A. Stern & Janes, 1973). However Noble and Lader (1971d) failed to find any changes in electrodermal activity in depressed subjects following a course of ECT, despite clinical improvement. Similarly, Dawson et al. (1977) obtained rather clear-cut negative results on the effects of ECT on a number of SC and HR variables in a study that also included a retest of a matched control group. No effects of ECT on HR at rest or during task performance were found by Noble and Lader (1971c), but a significant increase in resting FBF occurred after ECT, despite a modest decrease in anxiety ratings. This is an unexpected result because of the high FBF reported in some unmedicated depressives (Kelly, 1980).

Less paradoxical results have been reported for EMG where levels were found to be decreased after ECT (Noble & Lader, 1971b). Similarly, there have been reports of increased salivary flow in depressives in remission, although there are negative findings on this point as well (Lader, 1975). Noble and Lader (1971c) found an increase in salivary flow in retarded depressives (who were low prior to treatment) after a course of ECT, but a decrease in flow in nonretarded

patients. Since there was no differential effect of treatment in these same two groups on other psychophysiological variables (Noble & Lader, 1971a, 1971b, 1971d), this effect may be specific to salivary output, or it may be due to chance. However, it does point to the possible utility of examining clinical differences among patients who respond physiologically in different ways to the same treatments.

Amitriptyline in depressives was reported to reduce a factor score called "activation," which was loaded by several SCR variables (Heimann, 1978); similarly, it was reported to reduce SCL and SSCR rate and to increase speed of SCOR habituation and HR (Breyer-Pfaff, Gaertner, & Giedke, 1982). In the latter study, SCR maximum amplitude and range of SCL increased after 2 weeks of medication but decreased to predrug levels at 4 weeks. On the other hand, Storrie et al. (1981) were unable to demonstrate effects of tricyclic or antipsychotic medication on SCL or SCR, despite clinical improvement. However, the patients were drug-free only 3 days and their drug history was uncontrolled, so this may have contributed to the negative results.

In a placebo-controlled study, Johnstone, Bourne, Crow, Frith, Gamble, Lofthouse, Owen, Owens, Robinson, and Stevens (1981) tested a mixed group of depressed and anxious neurotic outpatients in an SCOR paradigm at baseline and after 3 weeks on placebo, amitriptyline, diazepam, or both active drugs. Significant reductions in SCL and in SCOR and SSCR frequency occurred on placebo, and they were only slightly more pronounced on amitriptyline. Diazepam and the combined treatment reduced these variables somewhat more. There were marked reductions in rated depression after all treatments, including placebo. Correlations between changes in depression (at 4 weeks) and changes in the SC variables indicated, surprisingly, that patients whose SCL and SCOR frequency decreased the most on placebo had the least reduction in depression, whereas for amitriptyline, SCL decrease and recovery time increase were positively related to improvement. Such a result could be due to differences in initial level between placebo responders and drug responders, but this was apparently not investigated; nor are possible differences between patients who were predominantly anxious or depressed mentioned. This study does, importantly, demonstrate large placebo and/or habituation effects in both clinical and physiological variables.

The results for amitriptyline are similar to those for another tricyclic—clomipramine—in obsessive-compulsive patients (Zahn, Insel, & Murphy, 1984) which will be described in a later section (page 587).

The relationship between clinical changes and physiological changes was investigated by Escobar, Gomez, and Tuason (1977), who compared patients with primary versus secondary depression on blood pressure changes during chlorimipramine treatment. Depression ratings and SBP declined at a faster rate over the 14-day drug trial in the primary group than in the secondary group. There is also some evidence that greater increases in HR are associated with greater antidepressant effects of tricyclics (Asberg, 1974) and that HR is related to both clinical effects and plasma levels of the drug in a different fashion than are anticholinergic side effects. This suggests that the cardiovascular effects of antidepressant drugs are related to the therapeutic action of the drugs rather than to their side effects.

The mechanism of the antidepressant action of tricyclic drugs has frequently been assumed to be the blockade of the re-uptake of neurotransmitters, resulting in an increase in their circulating levels. One of the problems with this hypothesis is that clinical improvement occurs gradually over a 2- to 4-week period, whereas the effects on neurotransmitters are immediate. An alternate hypothesis based on changes in receptor sensitivity has been tested by comparing the effects of clonidine, a drug that stimulates presynaptic alpha-adrenergic autoreceptors, on SBP in patients when they were on a chronic regimen of desipramine or on placebo (Charney, Heninger, Sternberg, Redmond, Leckman, Maas, & Roth, 1981). Results showed that the hypotensive effects of clonidine were attenuated by chronic tricyclic treatment. Similar effects occurred with a metabolite of NE, but there were no effects on HR. The implications of these findings are that chronic drug treatment lowers the sensitivity of the presynaptic receptors, and thus that supersensitivity of these receptors may play a role in the etiology of some cases of depression. Changes in receptor sensitivity may have played a role in the nonmonotonic changes in SC lability over a 4-week period of medication cited above (Breyer-Pfaff et al., 1982) and in the decline in tricyclic-produced elevations in HR with continued treatment (Glassman & Bigger, 1981).

Very little work on pretreatment somatic or ANS predictors of treatment response has been reported. Dawson et al. (1977) found that patients showing the least improvement from ECT had low tonic and phasic HR reactions and low SCL prior to treatment. It should be noted that these are not really pretreatment predictors, since the patients were taking antidepressant medication. Possibly a poor response to ECT occurred in patients showing the greatest ANS effects of the drugs. Breyer-Pfaff et al. (1982) reported poor clinical response to amitriptyline in slow pretreatment SCOR habituators, but only in patients with high plasma drug levels. These results hint at the possibility of different ANS predictors for different types of treatment; however, comparative, placebo-controlled studies will be necessary to give more life to this hope. This possibility may not be too far-fetched, since there has been some success using biochemical and electrophysiological predictors (Goodwin, Cowdry & Webster, 1978).

Two studies (Carney et al., 1981; Schwartz, Fair, Mandel, Salt, Mieske, & Klerman, 1978) reported that high resting corrugator EMG activity was predictive of good 2-week outcome in depressed patients, most of whom were currently or recently medicated on the pretreatment test. A similar study on drug-free patients found nonsignificant effects for corrugator EMG, but high zygomatic EMG predicted good outcome (Greden, Price, Genero, Feinberg, & Levine, 1984). Carney et al. (1981) found a similar relationship with zygomatic EMG, but this group failed to replicate the results of Schwartz et al. (1978) that reductions in EMG were related to clinical change.

EEG and ERPs

Resting EEG

No specific EEG abnormality has been found in any type of affective disorder, but a number of studies have reported differences from controls in the distribution of EEG frequencies (see Perris, 1980, and Shagass, 1975, for reviews). A great divergence of findings exists, many of which have been attributed to age differences or muscle artifact. One specific pattern that was found in 20% of manic and involutional depressed patients is the "mitten pattern," a slow wave-and-spike pattern that occurs only in sleep. A confirmed finding is that alpha frequency is slower in depressed than in manic patients. Interestingly, EEG abnormalities, chiefly in excessive slow-wave activity, were found to be more likely to occur in bipolar patients without a family history of affective disorder than in those with a positive history (Kadrmas & Winokur, 1979); this finding confirms earlier studies and is similar to findings in schizophrenia (Hays, 1977).

There has been some recent interest in the topography of EEG abnormalities. Abrams and Taylor (1979) found that, compared to schizophrenics, affective-disorder patients had more abnormalities (predominantly slow waves) from parieto-occipital and occipital leads and fewer from the temporal region, and more of them tended to show a right-hemisphere locus.

Studies of the effects of visual stimulation on the EEG have found prolonged alpha blocking in depressed patients and more pronounced photic driving from repetitive light flashes in manic patients than in controls. These findings contrast with the low ANS responsivity frequently found in depressives, as described earlier.

Quantified EEG and Hemispheric Asymmetries

Several groups of investigators have been studying EEG using quantitative methods. The focus of these studies is often on lateralized differences that it is impossible to separate these two topics. The interest in laterality has been stimulated largely by the Flor-Henry's (1969) hypothesis of nondominant-hemisphere involvement in affective disorders. Aside from this, most studies seem to have been undertaken only with the notion that the EEG techniques used reflect functional states of the brain that may be related to affective illness in some way.

The mean integrated amplitude of the EEG was found by d'Elia and Perris (1973) not to be lateralized in depressed patients, but the within-subjects variance on this measure was lower on the left side, and the lower left-side mean and variability of amplitude correlated with rated depression. Although data from normal controls are not presented, these authors conclude that low mean and variability of integrated amplitudes are related to depression. It will be recalled that such findings have also been obtained in schizophrenics. These results were replicated by the same group (Perris, 1980). Shagass *et al.* (1982) found depressives to have larger EEG amplitudes than controls, suggesting low activation in the patients. Similarly, the mean amplitude in the alpha band was reported to be high in depressives (von Knorring, Perris, Goldstein, Kemali, Monakhov, & Vacca, 1983). Unlike Shagass *et al.* (1982), von Knorring *et al.* (1983) found greater within-patient variability and a right-side advantage for amplitude in depressives, suggesting lower right brain activation in that group. Another finding reported by von Knorring (1984) is that more depressives than controls have polymodal distributions of mean integrated amplitude for just the right hemisphere, indicating more disorganization of that hemisphere.

Several studies have looked at the frequency and amplitude of different bandwidths at different locations. A "systemic structural analysis," which is a complex transformation of these basic variables, was developed by Perris, Monakhov, von Knorring, Botskarev, and Nikiforov (1978). Unmedicated depressed patients scoring high on an anxiety–depression scale were shown to have a predominance of beta, particularly in the left percentral area, and little alpha or theta, whereas the low group showed a more variable spectral pattern in different areas. Intercorrelations of the transformed variables showed many significant correlations involving the left precentral area but few elsewhere in high anxiety–depression patients, whereas low scorers had many significant correlations in all areas except left precentral. No statistical analyses are presented in this paper, however. A replication of the latter finding was made by Monakhov, Perris, Botskarev, von Knorring, and Nikiforov (1979), who conclude that more severely ill patients have more left precentral involvement. However since a similar pattern of correlations did not occur with untransformed variables and since it was not shown that the same transformed variables were similarly correlated in the two studies, this conclusion must be regarded with caution. Patients with symptoms (retrospectively determined) suggesting agitated or anxious depression had an excess of beta activity (not particularly localized), and those with symptoms of retarded depression had more alpha and theta (Monakhov & Perris, 1980).

Using a somewhat different method, this time with a normal control group, Perris, von Knorring, Cumberbatch, and Marciano (1981) reported that controls had more theta activity bilaterally than depressives. The two groups also differed in the hemispheric differences of various frequency components, most markedly at central leads. Whereas in controls alpha and beta activity was lateralized to the left and delta and theta to the right, the opposite distribution was present in depressives. Kemali *et al.* (1981) obtained different results with the same method. Their main positive results concerned the variability of the frequency distribution within a given band. Depressives had a lower variability of delta frequencies in most leads and a higher variability of alpha at two locations. In contrast to the results of Perris *et al.* (1981), more beta activity occurred in the left frontal region in the depressives than in controls.

A predominantly left-sided distribution of beta in depressives as compared to controls was found by Matousek, Capone, and Okawa (1981), although statistical reliability was present only for bipolar temporal and parieto-occipital leads. A similar result for monopolar temporal recording in depressives compared to schizophrenics was obtained by Volavka *et al.* (1981), who also showed that the finding was reversed when muscle artifacts were not edited out. However, Flor-Henry and Koles (1984) obtained a similar result with unedited records, but an even more extreme left predominance for beta in schizophrenics. Thus, higher beta activity from left-sided leads is one quantitative EEG feature that has met the test of cross-laboratory replication, although there are opposite results (Flor-Henry, Koles, Howarth, & Burton, 1979; Perris *et al.*, 1981). High left frontal beta activity, it may be recalled, also characterized only those depressives who scored high on an anxiety–depression index (Perris *et al.*, 1978). Thus, the differences in results could be due to clinical differences among samples, as well as to methodological differences.

In a major study on several diagnostic groups, Shagass, Roemer, and Straumanis (1982) have considered several indices of amplitude, frequency, and variability as indices of activation. They conclude that under an eyes-closed condition manics, like schizophrenics, are higher in activation than normals, whereas depressives are lower than normals. The response to eye opening, however, is large for depressives, normal for manics, and small for schizophrenics. Thus some diagnostic specificity is achieved by combining markers. No laterality differences are reported, but only a preliminary analysis of that aspect is reported. Somewhat similar findings were obtained by Flor-Henry and Koles (1984) in that alpha power was low, indicating activation, in manics but not in depressives.

The previous studies described in this section have been in resting subjects. Flor-Henry and Koles (1980) compared EEG spectra of normals, depressives, manics, and schizophrenics during rest (eyes open) and during verbal and spatial processing. At rest, manics and depressives had lower right parietal alpha power than controls. During the tasks normals showed greater left- than right-hemisphere activation during verbal versus spatial tasks, while the patients showed a reduced laterality (or even a trend toward reversed laterality in manics). The authors conclude that the right hemisphere is abnormally activated in affective disorders. These findings, apparently were not replicated in a later study (Flor-Henry & Koles, 1984).

ERPs

As with most work on the EEG, the primary motivation of at least the earlier work using ERP techniques in affective disorders was atheoretical; it was mainly intended to investigate the possibility of some brain dysfunction in these disorders. Interpretation and comparison of these studies is difficult because of many variations in technique, such as type of recording, stimulus parameters, recording site, and measurement technique, not to mention the lack of screening of the raw data for sources of artifact in many studies.

Much of the earlier work was done by Shagass and his collaborators (summarized in Shagass, 1972), who examined the early components of somatosensory ERPs using bipolar recording. Psychotic depressed subjects, along with other nonneurotic patients, showed a larger early peak (30 msec) than normal, and this peak showed greater increases in amplitude with increases in stimulus intensity in these patients than in the other groups. However, with a larger series of patients using a single stimulus intensity, there were no significant differences between any of the various patient groups and controls. Several other early studies, which focused on the middle range of ERPs, produced conflicting results; some found smaller and some larger ERPs in affective-disorder patients (Buchsbaum, 1979b; Lader, 1975).

In the ERP recovery technique, stimuli are paired at intervals from 2 to 200 msec, and the amplitude of the ERP to the second stimulus relative to the first stimulus is plotted as a function of the ISI. The amplitude of early potentials (20–30 msec) has consistently shown diminished recovery in psychotic depressives, particularly in the 2 to 20 msec range of ISIs (Shagass, 1972). In early studies, using somatosensory stimuli, psychotics of all kinds had impaired recovery compared to nonpsychotics, but in later studies, neurotics with depression and/or anxiety and a group labeled "personality disorder" also showed slower recovery

than controls. Although there has been some confirmation of this finding with visual stimuli (Lader, 1975), the recovery technique is not in general use, perhaps because of its lack of diagnostic specificity or its many technical complications.

However, using a more recently developed recovery technique in which clicks are separated by .5 to 2 sec., acute manics exhibited a lack of inhibition in P50 to the second click similar to that shown by schizophrenics (Franks, Adler, Waldo, Alpert, & Freedman, 1983; see page 531). Patients diagnosed bipolar affective disorder who were euthymic at the time of the test showed a normal amount of inhibition.

In recent work (Shagass et al., 1980), using monopolar recording, drug-free psychotic depressives (85% were diagnosed manic–depressive, depressed, but 48% were diagnosed bipolar) were compared with controls and other patients (age and sex-matched) on ERPs to stimuli in three modalities from 15 lead locations. The main differences between the patients and controls were a larger somatosensory P90 but smaller N130 at frontal leads and smaller P185 and P290 in the depressives. To auditory stimuli, depressives had larger P50 and P90 but smaller N75 and N110. Shagass et al. (1980) were not able to discount EOG influences completely from the P90 results. The data for N130 are more clearly interpretable in terms of attention. This peak was clearly larger in frontal leads in controls, but not in the depressed group, and it was even smaller in schizophrenics. The ordering of the groups in this regard was about the same as for cognitive impairment. Shagass et al. (1980) suggest that paradigms designed to elicit middle and late components might enhance these differences.

Buchsbaum, Carpenter, Fedio, et al. (1979) reported larger increases in N120 from temporo-parietal leads under conditions of attention in patients with affective disorders than in normals or schizophrenics—just the opposite of what might be expected. However, this peak was larger in affective patients under conditions of inattention, so the group difference was enhanced by directing attention to the stimulus. On the other hand, Roth et al. (1981), in a carefully controlled study, found smaller P200 in unipolar depressives only to nonattended tones and smaller N120 only to infrequent nontarget stimuli in a discrimination task. Thus, manipulation of attention and task requirements may have differential ERP effects in affective patients compared to controls, but much more work will be needed for these effects to be clarified.

In contrast to previous studies, Shagass et al. (1980) found a number of differences between psychotic depressives and schizophrenics. In particular, early somatosensory peaks P15, P45, and N60 were smaller and P90 and N130 were larger in depressives. Visual peak P90 was larger and P200 was smaller in that group as well. The P15 peak is taken to reflect activity in the thalamus, and, as with P45, the difference was found only in the left-hemisphere-to-right-side stimulation. Fewer differences were found between psychotic and neurotic depressives, possibly due in part to a small sample size. Visual P90 from right leads and P200 were particularly large in neurotic depressives as compared to both psychotic depressives and normal controls. Aside from the instances mentioned, Shagass *et al.* (1980) do not attempt an interpretation of the results in terms of brain dysfunction or psychological functioning.

Buchsbaum, Goodwin, Murphy, and Borge (1971) found patients with bipolar affective disorder, whether manic or depressed, to have a larger-amplitude visual P100–N140 component that also increased more rapidly with increased stimulus intensity (augmenting), compared to normal controls, while unipolars had smaller amplitudes and less positive amplitude–intensity slopes than controls. In a later study (Buchsbaum, Landau, Murphy, & Goodwin, 1973), these differences, especially for unipolars, depended partly on gender; male unipolars had relatively high ERP amplitudes and were reducers, whereas female unipolars had low amplitudes and augmented more than controls but less than female bipolars. Unipolar patients (especially males) tended to have the fastest latencies for all peaks, with bipolars next, and controls slowest. Augmenting in bipolars was present, whether they were in the manic or depressed state. This was also shown by similar slopes of P100 during both manic and depressed phases in a rapidly cycling bipolar patient (Buchsbaum, Post, & Bunney, 1977), but there were some state changes in P200, and the P100 slope seemed to decrease 8–10 days prior to a switch into mania. Rated severity of depression has been consistently associated with reducing to visual stimuli by this group (Buchsbaum *et al.*, 1971, 1973; Rey, Savard, Silber, Buchsbaum, & Post, 1979).

Although Gershon and Buchsbaum (1977) conclude that reducing in unipolar patients has not generally been confirmed, there seems to be more support for it than for augmenting in bipolar patients, but only under certain conditions. Thus von Knorring (1978) reported that psychotic depressives were more often reducers and had higher rated depression than nonpsychotic depressives, but bipolar patients were not more likely to be augmenters than unipolars. J. Friedman and Meares (1979) found reducing for visual P100–N140 in unipolar patients, but augmenting for later components and when auditory ERPs were measured. However, Roth *et al.* (1981) found augmenting of auditory N120 to about the same degree in unipolar depressives and controls, but the depressed group showed less augmenting of P200 than schizophrenics. Individual differences in augmenting–reducing may be modality-specific (Raine, Mitchell, & Venables, 1981) and component-specific. Thus, Buchsbaum,

Davis, Goodwin, Murphy, and Post (1980) failed to find differences between bipolar patients and controls in vertex P100 slope to somatosensory stimuli. On N120 both bipolar and unipolar patients showed less augmenting than controls, and bipolar patients who were manic showed a reducing pattern—quite different results than were obtained for visual P100 in the earlier studies. The connection between reducing and depression is strengthened by a report of negative correlations of somatosensory N140–P200 amplitude with poor appetite and indecisiveness and between P100–N140 slope and negative evaluation symptoms in depressives (Agren, Osterberg, & Franzen, 1983). In general the more depressed patients had small ERPs and lower slopes.

Buchsbaum (1975, 1979b) has interpreted the visual ERP results in terms of a psychological construct of stimulation seeking or stimulus intensity modulation, and has attempted to support this by relating ERP data to other relevant psychological and biological parameters. In work relevant to this section, studies on pain tolerance in normals had shown that visual reducers were relatively pain-tolerant; however, in affective patients, both bipolar patients who were visual augmenters and unipolar patients who were reducers showed low pain sensitivity compared to controls (Buchsbaum, 1979b). These results were interpreted as suggesting differences in regulating mechanisms. However, von Knorring, Epsvall, and Perris (1974) and von Knorring (1978) found reducing to be related to pain tolerance in depressives of all types, suggesting similar mechanisms in patients and in controls. Similarly, Buchsbaum *et al.* (1980) reported pain-insensitive bipolars and normals to have less somatosensory N120 augmenting than pain-sensitive subjects. A recent related finding is that subjects with major depression who were nonsuppressors in the dexamethasone suppression test were visual augmenters, whereas suppressors were not (Haier, 1983). Although these groups did not differ in pain sensitivity, there was a negative correlation between pain sensitivity and augmenting in just the nonsuppressors.

Evidence on biological markers includes findings that P100–N140 amplitude correlated positively with urinary cortisol levels in a small group of bipolar patients and negatively with platelet monoamine oxidase (MAO) activity in a mixed sample (Buchsbaum, 1979b). The latter result is taken to support the hypothesis that bipolar patients are high on sensation seeking, on the basis of similar relationships of MAO activity and augmenting with sensation seeking in normal males. In other studies, however, middle visual ERP amplitudes and latencies were positively correlated with MAO activity in depressed patients (Perris, 1980; Perris & Eisemann, 1980), but these relationships could have been due to age. A metabolite of 5-HT in cerebrospinal fluid correlated positively with ERP amplitude and negatively with latency (Perris,

1980). This result, if confirmed, could be interesting in view of the low 5-HT theory of depression and the negative correlations between ERP amplitude and depression ratings mentioned earlier.

A small amount of work exists on later ERP components and slow potentials. Levit et al. (1973) found smaller P300 in a guessing task in medicated depressives than in normals, but it was larger in depressives than in schizophrenics. However, as in schizophrenics, the increase in P300 due to stimulus uncertainty was below normal. Similar but nonsignificant results for P300 amplitude were obtained by Roth et al. (1981) and Baribeau-Braun and Lesevre (1983) reported reduced P300 (only at frontal leads) and reduced slow wave in retarded depressives. However, using a similar paradigm, Giedke, Thier, and Bolz (1981) did not find amplitude or latency differences in P300 between depressives and controls despite slow RT in the patients. Most of their patients had been unmedicated for 6 days or more, raising the possibility that the conflicting results might be due to this factor.

The PINV appears to be more abnormal than the CNV in depressives. Abnormal prolongation of the PINV has been reported in mixed groups of neurotic and psychotic patients (Perris, 1980); however, it was more likely in psychotic than in neurotic depressives or controls (Dongier, Dubrovsky, & Engelsmann, 1977), although it did not discriminate between the psychoses. This process has been attributed to "cortical inhibition" by Dongier et al. Timset-Berthier and Timset (1981) found depressed subjects with either a flat or a prolonged CNV to be more likely to be diagnosed as primary than as secondary depressives and to have depression rated as more severe. These subjects also had smaller P300, less reduction in alpha during the period between the first and second stimuli, and slower RT than depressives with normal CNVs. Their results are also attributed to inhibitory processes and possibly to low 5-HT activity. This group of results also might be associated with attention deficits, which may be likely in depressives, especially those diagnosed as primary and/or psychotic.

There is some evidence of lateralized ERP brain differences in affective disorders. Perris (1974) reported that psychotic depressives had smaller left-than right-hemisphere early ERPs (<50 msec) to light flashes. Schizophrenics did not show this difference and neurotic depressives showed it less clearly, but there were no controls and the measurement techniques are unclear. In a study using the maximum amplitude of the visual ERP as a measure (Perris & Eisemann, 1980), no differences in lateralization occurred between depressives and controls, but patients with a left-hemisphere deficit had poorer clinical ratings. Confirmatory evidence of a left-hemisphere deficit in depressives was reported by Shagass et al. (1980), in which some ERP amplitudes were higher on the right side in the patients and higher on the left side in controls. More striking evidence comes from analyses of ERP waveshape stability, in which several significant differences were found; these were all in the direction of lower stability in the left hemisphere in depressives relative to controls. This pattern is similar to findings in schizophrenics. In a more recent and major study focusing only on amplitudes and using a factor-analytic approach to reduce the data, Shagass, Roemer, and Straumanis (1984) did not find major depressives and controls to show differently lateralized ERPs, but both groups differed from schizophrenics.

Many of these ERP findings, like many (but not all) of the EEG findings, suggest a left-hemisphere deficit in patients with affective disorders—the converse of the original hypothesis (Flor-Henry, 1969). However, different aspects of the EEG and of ERPs may reflect processes that may have different lateral foci. The conflicting evidence that exists may reflect a situation in which dysfunction may not be attributed exclusively or even primarily to one side of the brain.

Treatment Effects on EEG and ERPs

Lithium carbonate has been the most extensively studied treatment of affective illness, and several replicated findings exist. At therapeutic doses, lithium has been found to increase density at delta and theta wave bands and to slow the peak alpha frequency (Heninger, 1978). The latter finding is interesting in relation to the faster alpha frequency observed in untreated manics as compared to depressives (Shagass, 1977). These changes correlated with clinical changes of reduced symptoms of mania and more symptoms of depression within the patient group.

The most consistent effects of lithium on ERPs is to increase the amplitude of the early positive components in the case of somatosensory and auditory ERPs (Heninger, 1978). Heninger also reported increased latency of peaks at N150 for somatosensory and at N85 for auditory ERPs, but this result has not been replicated (Shagass & Straumanis, 1978). A recent study by Straumanis, Shagass, Roemer, Mendels, and Ramsey (1981) found that in general, for stimuli in three modalities, lithium increased the amplitude of positive peaks at both short and long latencies and, to a lesser extent, decreased the amplitude of negative peaks. Topography of the peaks was not altered by lithium, and there were few relationships between ERP changes and clinical changes—a result also obtained by Heninger (1978). The effects of lithium on somatosensory ERP recovery function were complex: Recovery was either increased or decreased, depending on the intensity of the first stimulus.

Very few of the effects of lithium just described can be construed as "normalization." In fact, some, like the increase in the amplitude of early peaks (which may already be greater in depressed patients than in controls), go in the opposite direction. Straumanis *et al.* (1981) make the observation that similar effects of lithium have been observed in both depressed and manic patients so that "they may be pharmacological effects at a tissue level and not directly related to the therapeutic effects of lithium" (p. 126).

One of the peaks of the visual ERP found by Straumanis *et al.* (1981) to be increased by lithium was P300, even though the paradigm used was not optimal for maximizing that wave. The effects of lithium on P300 in CPTs in manic patients were studied by Kaskey, Salzman, Ciccone, and Klorman (1980). Although lithium did not increase P300 to all stimuli, it increased the difference in P300 to critical and noncritical stimuli. This finding, along with a decrease in commission errors, is interpreted as indicating that lithium enhances selective attention—a conclusion supported by a possible enhancement of the CNV by lithium (Tecce *et al.*, 1978).

Findings with respect to lithium on other visual ERPs have been inconsistent (Heninger, 1978; Straumanis *et al.*, 1981). That this may be due to differences in stimulus intensity and type of patient is suggested by the results of Buchsbaum *et al.* (1971) that the augmenting shown in visual P100–N140 at the vertex in bipolar patients was attenuated by lithium. However, increased augmenting of visual ERPs during chronic lithium treatment in a group largely composed of bipolar patients was reported for an N120 component from occipital leads (Buchsbaum, Gerner, & Post, 1981), and no consistent effects were observed for somatosensory ERP augmenting from parietal or vertex leads (Buchsbaum, Lavine, Davis, Goodwin, Murphy, & Post, 1979). The situation is further complicated by a report that mere repetition of the procedure without clinical or treatment changes markedly attenuated augmenting just in bipolar patients (Buchsbaum, 1979b). However, the slope of P100 for both visual and somatosensory ERPs predicted clinical response to lithium: Augmenters were significantly more likely to show a clinical improvement than were reducers (Baron, Gershon, Rudy, Jones, & Buchsbaum, 1975; Buchsbaum, Lavine, Davis, *et al.*, 1979).

Tricyclic antidepressants in acute studies have been found to increase EEG power at fast and slow frequencies and to reduce it in an alpha band (Fink, 1974; Itil, 1974). Chronic administration may produce less pronounced effects on slow and middle bands and may reduce beta activity. This has been interpreted as a central inhibitory effect (Itil, 1974).

These drugs seem generally to reduce amplitudes of early, middle, and late ERP components, irrespective of stimulus modality (Shagass & Straumanis, 1978). Exceptions to this are findings of increased amplitude of visual P100–N140 by amitriptyline (J. Friedman, McCallum, & Meares, 1980) and increased CNV

(Timset-Berthier & Timset, 1981). Tricyclics also reduced the amplitude–intensity slopes of auditory but not visual ERPs (J. Friedman & Meares, 1979). However, a very similar reduction in augmenting occurred in patients who improved clinically during a placebo trial. Since greater reducing on a repeat test can occur even in the absence of clinical changes (Buchsbaum, 1979b), the effects of either the drug or clinical changes per se are not clear. A night of sleep deprivation has been found to reduce depression in endogenous patients. The effects of this on the visual ERPs of depressed patients (mostly bipolars) was to increase augmenting of just vertex P100; other leads did not show this effect (Buchsbaum *et al.*, 1981). This result conflicts with the J. Friedman and Meares (1979) result and suggests that the effect of clinical improvement is dependent on the type of subject or the particular treatment used.

Two recent studies from Shagass's laboratory obtained basically negative results with respect to the effects of tricyclic medication on ERPs in three modalities (Straumanis, Shagass, & Roemer, 1982) and on somatosensory P400 (Josiassen, Shagass, Straumanis, & Roemer, 1984). However, these studies were not done as placebo-controlled trials, subjects were drug-free as few as 4 days, and the numbers of subjects were small, so they leave something to be desired methodologically.

That increased NE activity might be associated with reducing was proposed by Buchsbaum, Post, and Bunney (1977). The evidence from the J. Friedman and Meares (1979) study is consistent with this hypothesis, at least for auditory ERPs. However, administration of L-dopa to depressed subjects increased augmenting in unipolar patients and produced weak reducing, probably nonsignificant, in bipolar patients (Henry, Buchsbaum, & Murphy, 1976). These changes are in the direction of "normalization," but the drug had no beneficial clinical changes. On the assumption that L-dopa increases NE, as well as DA, these data are inconsistent with the hypothesis but suggest different regulating mechanisms in unipolar and bipolar patients. Oral amphetamine, given to a group of depressed patients (mostly unipolar), did not affect the amplitude–intensity slopes but did increase P200 amplitude (Buchsbaum, Van Kammen, & Murphy, 1977).

Summary and Conclusions

The evidence on ANS base levels suggests considerable heterogeneity in patients with depressive diagnoses, and this seems correlated with the diagnostic subclassifications currently in use. Patients labeled "retarded," "psychotic," and "endogenous" are likely to have below-normal SCL and low SCORs while "agitated," "neurotic," and "nonendogenous" patients may be above normal on these variables. Electrodermal and cardiovascular reactivity to signal stimuli and stressors is usually low in depressive samples. There also may be similar subtype differences, but these have not been explored adequately. Many of these findings seem to be state independent, making them candidates for genetic markers.

Thus much of the evidence might seem consistent with the low NE hypothesis of affective disorders (Schildkraut, 1978). There is a further parallel in the large amount of heterogeneity in both the ANS and NE measures, but no studies have correlated these two sets of measures in depressives. However, studies of schizophrenics cited earlier (Deakin et al., 1979; Zahn, 1980) showed negative relationships between urinary NE metabolites and ANS activity.

Contrasted with the SC findings is the evidence that base levels of cardiovascular variables are frequently higher than normal in depressives, particularly, but not exclusively, in the agitated type. There are no reports of significantly lower values. These findings seem inconsistent with the low NE hypothesis. However, HR, like SCL, was negatively correlated with urinary MHPG in chronic schizophrenics (Deakin et al., 1979), suggesting that the HR findings in depression may be less paradoxical. Some of these paradoxical results might be clarified by studies of the relationships of ANS activity to monoamine metabolites from body fluids, especially cerebrospinal fluid in affective patients.

Although the ANS findings are probably not due entirely to drug effects, the fact that antidepressant drugs reduce SC activity and increase HR together with the frequent use of patients either on medication or off medication for an inadequate period militates caution in interpreting the data. However, the ANS findings do seem compatible with the recent hypothesis of increased presynaptic alpha-adrenergic receptor sensitivity. However, evidence against that hypothesis comes from a finding that clonidine reduces blood pressure in unmedicated depressives no less than in controls (Charney, Hafstad, Giddings, & Landis, 1982). Other evidence from that study suggests decreased postsynaptic alpha receptor sensitivity in depression. This hypothesis seems consistent with low ANS activity and also with the ANS-NE correlations if it is assumed that the decreased receptor sensitivity is produced by an excess of neurotransmitter. The low 5-HT hypothesis (Murphy et al. 1978) fares well, since there is direct evidence of a relationship of low SC activity to low 5-HT activity in depressives. This might be thought surprising, since 5-HT is frequently considered to be an "inhibitory" neurotransmitter, but such an interpretation is probably oversimplified.

Since cardiovascular variables are regulated by the balance of SNS and PNS influences, the data are consistent with a hypothesis of low PNS or cholinergic activity in depression. This hypothesis has been entertained above on the basis of the data on salivary output in depression. More direct tests of this hypothesis using HR data are possible (Akselrod, Gordon, Ubel, Shannon, Barger, & Cohen, 1981; Porges, 1976) but have not been performed.

Another consideration is the high subjective anxiety that frequently accompanies depression, perhaps more frequently in nonendogenous types. This would be expected to be related positively to ANS base levels and might account for some of the conflicting findings there. Ratings of subjective anxiety should be a routine part of studies in this area.

Although the clinical EEG does not suggest cerebral pathology as a major feature of affective illness, these patients may be prone to more slow and fast activity, differences in alpha frequency, prolonged alpha blocking, and more photic driving than controls. The clinical distinctions that relate to many of the EEG findings are "mania" versus "depression" or "manic-depressive" versus "depressive," but the agitation-retardation dimension and simply the severity of the symptoms may be important as well. Much of the ERP literature also focuses on unipolar and bipolar patients, for whom the evidence suggests reducing and augmenting, respectively, although many of these studies have not been well controlled for ocular influences. These ERP characteristics may be related to other biological systems that are abnormal in some patients, such as MAO activity, cortisol levels, and pain tolerance. In Shagass's studies, which have attempted to find empirical markers of diagnosis, psychotic depressives could be discriminated from neurotic depressives, but manic-depressives were heavily represented in the psychotic group. These studies have typically found neurotic depressives to be similar to controls and psychotic depressives to resemble schizophrenics; in recent work, however, each of the two depressive groups seems to have its own pattern. Recent EEG and ERP studies have reported definite schizophrenic-like abnormalities in manics with depressives either different from normal in the opposite direction or similar to normals.

Unlike the ANS data, there are many findings of larger than normal ERPs in affective disorders. However, ERP components thought to reflect attention or information processing have been found to be smaller in depressives, but not to the same extent as in schizophrenics. Similarly, eye-tracking impairment in psychotic or bipolar affective-disorder patients may be present, but this may be due to lithium treatment. These findings might all reflect a moderate amount of cognitive dysfunction. Some evidence of greater left hemisphere impairment exists in both EEG and ERP studies; this may or may not be consistent with the electrodermal data, but may also reflect cognitive dysfunction. The findings of prolonged alpha blocking, large PINV, prolonged poststimulus SC responding, and (on a shorter time scale) impaired ERP recovery functions, suggest problems in inhibitory control.

The ANS literature divides the affective disorders into two groups: hypoactive (endogenous, retarded, etc.) and hyperactive (or normoactive) (reactive, agitated, etc.). None of the studies has investigated the unipolar–bipolar distinction or the mania–depression distinction. The EEG and ERP literature, conversely, seems to have focused mainly on the unipolar–bipolar and psychotic–neurotic distinctions at the expense of the endogenous–nonendogenous and retarded–agitated distinctions. Since investigators do not usually publish negative results or always mention all the unsuccessful analyses they run, it is possible that ANS measures can make only the one distinction and EEG and ERP the other. However, there is apparently a large gap in the data base at this point.

Studies of treatment are flawed by the lack of placebo (or untreated) controls. Most of the literature on ANS effects of treatment is on ECT. The positive findings that exist are that ECT increases SC activity, blood flow, and salivation and reduces EMG, but there are many negative findings. Except for blood flow, these are reversals of the pretreatment deficits and suggest that the deficits are state-related. However, the evidence is still weak on this point. The episodic nature of depressive illness is ideally suited to the investigation of the state versus trait issue. Studies of psychophysiological concomitants of clinical improvement and relapse are sorely needed. These would ideally involve patients who are unmedicated at the times of testing and would include a normal control group. Clinically diagnosable depressive episodes may, in some persons, be time-locked to the menstrual cycle, childbirth, or personal loss, providing good research possibilities. Studies of nonpathological mood and physiological changes during the menstrual cycle and postpartum periods suggest the potential fruitfulness of this approach (Christie et al., 1980).

The sparse evidence on tricyclic antidepressants suggests that this treatment decreases SC activity and may increase HR and decrease SBP. Most of this evidence comes from studies of amitriptyline, which has its effects primarily on 5-HT (Goodwin et al., 1978). This confirms the involvement of 5-HT in SC activity, but these effects seem to be in the direction of increasing rather than decreasing the differences between depressive and controls. However, the one placebo-controlled study, on a mixed depressed–anxious neurotic group, showed almost as much effect from placebo. Whether this would hold for a purer sample of endogenous cases remains to be seen. The lack of specificity in the biological effects of tricyclics makes it difficult to attribute somatic effects to a specific neurochemical process in a given study. Since the drugs in use vary in anticholinergic ("side") effects, as well as in the extent to which target neurotransmitters (NE or 5-HT) are affected, comparative studies of different drugs might increase understanding of the neurochemical mechanisms underlying psychophysiological systems and perhaps their role in affective illness. The technique of using the SBP response to clonidine as an indicator of the sensitivity of noradrenergic autoreceptors is a promising new approach, which shows the potential usefulness of psychophysiological measures as markers of neurochemical processes.

The study of psychophysiological predictors of treatment response has been grossly neglected. Augmenting–reducing of the visual ERP has been found to predict the relative efficacy of lithium versus tricyclic treatment, but whether this reflects more than the bipolar–unipolar dichotomy is not known (Goodwin et al., 1978). Preliminary data suggesting that the presence and type of CNV abnormality may predict outcome and clinical response to different tricyclic drugs is presented by Timset-Berthier and Timset (1981). Urinary and cerebrospinal fluid metabolites of NE and 5-HT are predictive of which tricyclic drug is likely to be effective. Clinical predictors are less certain, but there is evidence that endogenous depressives respond better to tricyclics as a class than nonendogenous patients (Goodwin et al., 1978). The psychophysiological differences found between endogenous or primary depressives and other types suggest a possible predictive utility of these measures.

As in the case of ANS activity, different clinically effective treatments produce different electrocortical changes. The long-term effects of ECT seem to be EEG normalization—an increase in alpha and a decrease in fast and slow activity. Lithium slows alpha and increases delta and theta activity; these changes have been related to shifts in affect away from mania and toward depression. Generally, lithium has been found to increase ERP amplitudes without correlated changes in affect, and some of these changes may be related to improved attention. Tricyclic antidepressants, on the other hand, seem generally to reduce ERP amplitudes. Both lithium and tricyclics have been found to reduce amplitude–intensity slopes, along with clinical improvement and reversal of preexisting ERP abnormalities, but lack of proper controls makes interpretation of these promising findings difficult.

Psychophysiological investigations of affective disorders have produced some promising leads; as a whole, however, this effort has been characterized by the application of circumscribed methodologies to patients selected by clinical criteria that vary from study to study. Further progress may come from attempts to discover biologically defined subtypes of affective disorders by relating the various measures (e.g., somatic and electrocortical) to one another, to carefully determined clinical dimensions or classifications, and to indicators of biological activity in other systems, such as 5-HT, NE, and endocrine systems. Well-replicated (but by no means perfect) biological state markers include high cortisol levels, the failure of dexamethasone to suppress plasma cortisol (Carrol, Curtis, & Mendels, 1976), and sleep phenomena, especially reduced rapid eye movement (REM) latency (Kupfer, 1976). Comparison of somatic and electrocortical activity with these markers in the same subjects should help reduce the biological and behavioral heterogeneity of this complex group of disorders to manageable proportions.

CRIMINALITY AND PSYCHOPATHY

Theoretical Issues

A biological conception of the etiology of habitual antisocial and criminal behavior has been popular since antiquity, and it is no surprise that a genetic etiology has been hypothesized. There is evidence from twin and adoption studies for a genetic basis (D. Rosenthal, 1975); however, as Rosenthal points out, such evidence is inconclusive because of the many nonspecific genetically influenced factors (such as low IQ) that are correlated with criminal convictions but are not considered aspects of criminality. These would artificially inflate the heritability estimates. That environmental factors play a crucial role in the development of criminality is, of course, uncontestable.

What has interested psychophysiologists in this area, however, is not so much criminality per se, but a conception of a personality disorder leading to habitual antisocial behavior—one that is independent of other forms of psychopathology or low IQ, and that includes atypical emotional reactions as key features. The psychopath (or sociopath) has been most influentially conceptualized by Cleckley (1976) as a person who is fundamentally unsocialized; is incapable of emotional relationships with others; is unable to feel guilt or to learn from (punishing) experience; has low frustration tolerance; is relatively free from anxiety; and is aggressive, impulsive, and irresponsible. Quay (1965) proposed that some of these characteristics are attributable to pathological "stimulus seeking," due to a lack of responsiveness to the usual range of environmental stimuli. Most psychophysiological investigations have been concerned with the hypothesis, in one form or another, that psychopaths have a disorder of low ANS or central nervous system (CNS) arousal and/or responsivity, either directly to or in anticipation of aversive stimulation or to stimuli in general. This defect might explain many of the characteristics, particularly the shallow affect and in-

effectiveness of punishment, that are attributed to these individuals.

Subjects in these studies have come from a variety of settings, such as ordinary prisons, prisons for "abnormal offenders," and an organization for voluntary treatment of compulsive gambling. This is not a drawback, since the concept of psychopathy does not necessarily imply criminality in a legal sense, nor does unlawful behavior imply psychopathy. Similar findings in subjects from a variety of sources would give the conclusions more generality. Various "diagnostic" methods have been used to distinguish the psychopaths in the larger prison population. Hare (1970), who has been the most active investigator in this field, uses a rating scale based on the classical Cleckley description, the information coming from case records. Other methods are ratings based on interviews and self-report scales. Of these, the most widely used have been the Minnesota Multiphasic Personality Inventory (MMPI) Psychopathic Deviate (Pd) scale, sometimes in combination with Mania (Ma) and the Socialization scale from the California Personality Inventory. The choice of a comparison group has also been variable among studies. Relatively few have included a normal control group. One reason for this may be that many studies on psychopaths have involved fairly strong aversive stimuli to which investigators may be reluctant to expose normal volunteers.

Another distinct approach to the study of criminals has focused on the investigation of the EEG correlates of pathological aggression. One of the basic ideas behind this approach is that, since aggressive and violent behavior sometimes accompany temporal lobe or psychomotor seizures, a proportion of aggressive criminals may suffer from a form of temporal lobe epilepsy. Although the evidence is unclear as to whether there is a higher proportion of genuine temporal lobe epileptics in prison than in the general population (Monroe, 1978), and although at best such patients comprise only a small proportion of even very aggressive prisoners, the evidence of temporal lobe and limbic system involvement in aggressive behavior from neurophysiological studies on animals has led to a search for abnormalities in this area. These investigations almost exclusively use a clinical EEG approach, and the target symptom is aggression.

Given all these differences in methodology, it might be surprising to find any similarities in results across laboratories. Yet some findings seem to have stood up quite well, as is evident from the following survey of the literature.

Baseline Physiological Activity

ANS Activity

Early theorizing (Hare, 1970; Quay, 1965) hypothesized low autonomic and cortical arousal, levels below a hypothetical optimal level, as a factor in the impulsive and stimulus seeking behavior of psychopaths. Studies of resting tonic SCL have generally failed to confirm this hypothesis, although Hare (1978a) points out that nonsignificant differences in eight studies, when combined, yield a significantly lower mean SCL in primary psychopaths. However, even if this is true, the theoretical significance of the difference cannot be large. Similarly, resting SSCR frequency has sometimes, but not consistently, been lower in primary psychopaths than various comparison groups (Hare, 1978a). A study (Blackburn, 1979) from Broadmoor, a hospital for "abnormal offenders," found primary psychopaths to emit more SSCRs than secondary psychopaths. The distinction between these groups was based on more extraneous symptoms, such as anxiety, social withdrawal, and dysphoria in the secondary group. However, in another study from Broadmoor (Hinton, O'Neill, Dishman, & Webster, 1979), "primary psychopaths," defined as recidivists who committed multiple types of crimes against strangers, had lower SSCR rates than nonpsychopathic inmates (domestic crimes only). No consistent differences in HR have been found among subgroups of criminals or between psychopaths and controls, although in several studies spontaneous HR variability was smaller in psychopaths (Hare, 1978a).

Several studies have reported that for both SCL and SSCRs the differences between groups increase over the course of a monotonous experimental session, either due to an increase in control levels or decrease in levels for the psychopaths (Hare, 1978a). This suggests a difference in or a differential response to boredom, and may reflect a tendency sometimes noted (Hare, 1975; Mawson & Mawson, 1977) for psychopaths to become drowsy in such situations.

EEG Activity

Clinical EEG studies typically find that over 50% of their samples have EEG abnormalities, but frequently the population sampled is selected on some nonrandom basis, and control groups are not always included. This rate of abnormal EEGs is similar to that found in schizophrenics but different from that reported for controls and some other patient groups, such as alcoholics and neurotics. However, some studies that have used normal controls have not obtained differences (Syndulko, 1978). The abnormalities found consist mainly of diffuse or frontal slow activity.

A more interesting question is whether there is any relationship between the EEG abnormalities and behavior. There are several studies with negative results on this question (Syndulko, 1978); however, in a mixed group of patients, Monroe and Mickle (1967) reported a relationship between "negativism, destruc-

tive behavior, and anger" and EEG abnormalities (usually frontal 3- to 4-Hz activity) under alpha-chloralose activation. D. Williams (1969) compared 206 habitually aggressive prisoners with 127 who had committed only one crime of violence, and found some abnormality in 65% of the former and 24% of the latter group with blind clinical scoring. The figures were 57% versus 12% when subjects with known head injury, mental retardation, and epilepsy were excluded. Williams states that abnormal EEGs are present in 12% of the (unspecified) "general population." Theta activity, mainly from anterior leads, was found in over 80% of each group who had abnormal EEGs. Frontal lobe disorders occurred in 57% of the habitual offenders versus 19% of the single offenders. Thus, frontal lobe abnormalities seem more strongly related to habitual violence in prisoners than other abnormalities. Investigations of the relationship between theta abundance and aggression has produced only modest results in other studies. Monroe (1978) reported that of prisoners who showed high theta activity (in alpha-chloralose-activated EEG records), 68% had an "episodic dyscontrol" disorder, while 49% with low theta showed this syndrome. Correlations of theta activity were significantly but weakly (about .20) related to ratings of aggressiveness from case material.

Conflicting results were reported by Blackburn (1975). Aggression was not correlated with EEG abundance from posterior leads in any frequency band, but aggressive inmates tended to have a faster dominant EEG frequency and to show a slower increase in theta during an OR procedure.

Variables other than aggression may influence EEG activity. In Blackburn's (1979) study, secondary psychopaths had low SC indices of arousal, as well as high alpha and theta abundance. From questionnaire data, ratings, and comparisons with nonpsychopathic inmates, Blackburn concludes that "aggressive offenders who are also socially withdrawn and anxious (secondary psychopaths) do display high levels of theta activity in their resting records while those who are less anxious or withdrawn (primary psychopaths) are characterized by relatively little theta and high arousal" (1979, pp. 148–149). This may be a partial replication of the Monroe (1978) findings, since MMPI profiles of his episodic dyscontrol patients were similar to those of the secondary psychopaths (generally elevated scores), and both these studies tested inmates at special institutions rather than regular prisons.

These findings were partially confirmed in another study of Broadmoor patients (Howard, 1984), which separated drug-free patients on the basis of Welch's A scale of the MMPI. High A patients had an excess of "atypical" EEGs most marked in excess theta from fronto-temporal areas. This study also found that those inmates with prominent posterior temporal slow activity were very likely to be high on classical Cleckley-type psychopathy ratings.

A quite different group of subjects—compulsive gamblers in a treatment program—was reported by Syndulko, Parker, Jens, Maltzman, and Ziskind (1975) to have less delta power from posterior leads than controls during a postexperimental rest period.

It is difficult to draw firm conclusions from this set of studies, particularly in view of the paucity of normal or nonpsychopath data. However, variations in slow-wave activity seem to distinguish subgroups of psychopaths, even if the relevant personality or clinical dimensions associated with this cannot be specified. There is at least a superficial conceptual similarity of the EEG data with the SC data. Inclusion of both sets of measures and careful and comprehensive clinical evaluation should help clarify these relationships in future studies.

Conditioning and Anticipation

Electrodermal Responses

Great impetus to the investigation of psychopathy by psychophysiological techniques was given by Lykken (1957), who showed poorer classical conditioning of anticipatory electrodermal responses and poorer avoidance learning to shock in sociopathic subjects defined by the Cleckley criteria, compared to normal controls. This was taken to relate to the psychopaths' inability to profit from aversive experiences. Since that time, replications and many variations on the original theme have occurred, showing less anticipatory electrodermal activity in primary psychopaths, such as prison inmates (Hare, 1978a) or compulsive gamblers (Ziskind, Syndulko, & Maltzman, 1977), compared to normals and sometimes to prison inmates judged to be nonpsychopathic. However, Hare (1982) found a negative association between psychopathy and anticipatory SC responding only when subjects could avoid the noxious stimulus and not when it was unavoidable. That learning of the CS-UCS contingency is not what is impaired in these studies is shown by similar findings when subjects are told the contingency ahead of time and when a countdown procedure is used to minimize errors of time estimation (Hare, Frazelle, & Cox, 1978; Tharp, Maltzman, Syndulko, & Ziskind, 1980). Some studies have investigated the anticipatory responses of psychopaths to shocking another person or to the sight of another person being shocked (vicarious conditioning), with somewhat mixed results. Hare and Craigen (1974) found no differences in vicarious anticipatory SCRs, but Aniskiewicz (1979) reported fewer conditioned anticipatory and orienting SCRs in both primary and secondary psychopaths than in controls, and Dengerink and Bertilson (1975) obtained progressively

lower SCL during the task in psychopaths compared with controls.

An obvious question is whether these results reflect a general insensitivity to noxious UCSs. Primary psychopaths gave smaller SCRs to shock or loud tones than nonpsychopathic criminals (Hare, 1978b; Hare & Craigen, 1974), but only psychopaths who also had low socialization scores were unresponsive to 120-dB tones. Tharp et al. (1980), however, obtained no differences in SC unconditioned response (UCR) magnitude, despite a difference in anticipatory activity between compulsive gamblers and controls. Aniskiewicz (1979) found primary psychopaths to be at low levels but secondary psychopaths to be at normal levels on a vicarious UCR, while both groups showed low anticipation of this. Blackburn (1979) found no differences in response to a cold pressor task. Thus, psychopaths may or may not be electrodermally hyporeactive to aversive stimuli, and this seems independent of the differences usually found in anticipatory stimuli.

Surprisingly little work has been done using the conditioning paradigm with UCSs other than aversive physical stimuli. Schmauk (1970) reported almost as marked anticipatory SC activity in primary psychopaths as in normal controls when loss of money for errors in a maze-learning task was used, but significantly smaller SCRs in the psychopaths when either shock or social censure was the reinforcer. Similarly, Hare and Quinn (1971) found nonsignificant differences in conditioned orienting and anticipatory SCRs in psychopaths compared to nonpsychopath prisoners when the UCS was a picture of a nude woman. This result contrasts with that for a shock UCS. Interpretation of these results is difficult, since the psychopaths also had a nonsignificantly smaller UCS to the nude woman than the nonpsychopaths did, and both groups reacted less to this UCS than to the shock. Thus the main hypothesis did not receive a good test. Such a test will require finding a nonaversive UCS that produces large SCRs, at least in controls. It is surprising that RT stimuli have not been tried as a UCS. With appropriate reinforcement contingencies, the conditioning method could also be used to compare the physiological effects of reward, avoidance, and escape stiuations. Such studies would have theoretical relevance, as becomes evident below.

Other Measures

The findings of less electrodermal anticipation of aversive events in psychopaths seem impressively consistent, despite a variety of methodological and subject (both experimental and control) differences. However, this general result seems to hold only for SC and not for other autonomic indices. HR has been the most widely studied of the other measures. Hare and Quinn (1971) found differential HR and vasomotor conditioning to be no different in psychopaths and controls. However, Dengerink and Bertilson (1975) reported higher tonic HR in psychopaths in a task where they shocked another person, and Hare and Craigen (1974) obtained a significantly greater anticipatory acceleration–deceleration pattern in psychopaths than in prisoner controls when the subjects were either receiving the shocks or giving them in a vicarious conditioning paradigm. Hare et al. (1978) observed a pattern of HR acceleration in psychopaths and small deceleration in nonpsychopaths in a countdown procedure. In a similar paradigm, Tharp et al. (1980) found only deceleration in both groups. Finally, Hare (1982) found both marginally significant greater HR acceleration and deceleration in psychopathic versus nonpsychopathic prisoners, depending on the conditions. Hare (1982) believes the results were due to differences in the direction of attention, and indeed, this variable may have played a role in some of the previous results. However, these conflicting results do not alter the conclusion that the deficit in anticipation of noxious stimulation in psychopaths is specific to electrodermal activity.

There have been some studies of the CNV in RT settings. An early study by McCallum (1973) showed smaller CNVs in sociopaths compared to controls, but subsequent studies have not replicated this result (Dongier et al., 1977; Fenton, Fenwick, Ferguson, & Lam, 1978; Syndulko et al., 1975). However, Syndulko et al. (1975) did observe that the CNVs of older psychopaths (gamblers) failed to increase when the intensity of the second stimulus was increased from 70 to 95 dB, as did the CNVs of controls or younger psychopaths. In addition, N150 in the ERP to the first stimulus failed to show the normal increase with increased intensity of the second stimulus for the psychopaths as a whole, but no other differences in N150 or P300 were found. This is the only nonelectrodermal finding of its kind. It is potentially important and deserves further exploration.

Other Studies of Physiological Responsivity

Although, as mentioned earlier, there is some (but inconsistent) evidence of smaller SCRs to strong stimuli in psychopaths than controls, there seem to be no consistent differences in responsivity to nonaversive stimuli. This suggests a relatively flat amplitude–intensity function in these subjects. A direct test provided suggestive evidence for this hypothesis (Hare, 1978b). The SCOR to the first of a series of moderate-intensity tones was smaller in delinquent boys than in controls (Borkovec, 1970), and smaller in those with more offenses than in less delinquent subjects (Siddle, Nicol, & Foggitt, 1973); however, only marginal differences in habituation were found. Blackburn's (1979) secondary psychopaths showed smaller

SCRs and faster SCR habituation to 94-dB tones than his primary group, but HR habituation was slower in the secondary group. The consistent reversal of results from this study compared to others (see page 559) suggests that the group labels might be reversed.

Larger positive skin potential responses and larger HR responses (acceleration–deceleration) to relevant questions in a lie detection situation were observed in psychopaths than in controls by D. C. Raskin and Hare (1978). They also found a greater SCR differentiation between control and relevant questions by "guilty" psychopaths with low socialization scores. Since these results occurred in the context of a mock crime rather than a real one, the situation can be thought of as more interesting or challenging than the usual conditioning or habituation study, but not as threatening or aversive. However, this study shows that there are conditions under which psychopaths have relatively high ANS activity.

Blackburn (1975) reported that aggressive prisoners had a markedly larger reduction in alpha abundance in a cold pressor test than nonaggressive prisoners. No differences in a tonic alpha or theta OR to a tone series were observed, nor did differences in theta responses relate to aggression. The positive finding seems not to have been replicated (Blackburn, 1979), and ANS responses to a cold pressor task did not discriminate more from less aggressive prisoners. However, the separation on the aggression variable may not have been as extreme in the later study.

SCOR recovery half-time has been shown fairly consistently to be slow in more severely (compared to less severely) delinquent juveniles (Siddle, Mednick, Nicol, & Foggitt, 1976) and adults (Hinton et al., 1979); in less socialized criminals (Levander, Schalling, Lidberg, Bartfai, & Lidberg, 1980); and in primary compared to secondary psychopaths, but only for intense (120-dB) stimuli (Hare, 1978b). Mednick and Hutchings (1978) report, from a prospective study, slow recovery half-times of SCORs in subjects who later were convicted of a crime. They also found slow recovery half-times, slow rise times, and fewer SCORs in children of criminal fathers, and particularly slow recovery times in males with criminal records whose fathers did *not* have criminal records, but fast recovery times in noncriminal sons of the criminal fathers. Mednick and Hutchings take these data to suggest that where the behavior of the son goes against the home environmental influence, the operation of genetic (or at least biological) factors in the etiology of criminality is more critical.

Summary and Conclusions

First, for the criminal population as a whole, it would appear from the EEG evidence at first blush that a substantial proportion suffers from some kind of brain pathology. However, as Syndulko (1978) points out, the studies have not had adequate controls over the state of the subjects, and it is possible to argue that the "abnormalities" seen—largely anterior slow-wave activity—are consequences of a proneness to become drowsy in boring experiments; this conclusion is supported by some of the electrodermal literature. Conversely, it is possible to attribute the drowsiness to brain pathology. More studies are needed in which autonomic and electrocortical data are obtained on the same subjects and in which there is careful control or observation of behavioral states. The clinical EEG and ANS studies have emerged from separate theoretical contexts, and it is difficult to tell from the literature whether the two types of studies are dealing with the same kinds of people. One could speculate that there are aggressively impulsive criminals for whom clinical signs of brain pathology are more likely, and a separate group of classical psychopaths with unremarkable EEGs and sluggish electrodermal activity; however, the evidence for this distinction is incomplete. On the other hand, a hypothesis of frontal lobe pathology would seem to be consistent with the impulsivity and poor anticipation of punishment shown behaviorally and electrodermally by psychopaths.

As for theories of classical psychopathy, the strikingly consistent findings of low anticipatory electrodermal activity from various populations considered to be psychopathic support the original notion by Lykken (1957) of inadequate avoidance learning because of a diminished anticipatory fear response. A new twist on this basic idea has been proposed by Mednick and Hutchings (1978) on the assumption that SCR recovery time reflects the speed of fear reduction. Since avoidance learning may be facilitated by rapid fear reduction, the consistent evidence of slow recovery time in criminal populations suggests slow fear reduction, and thus poor avoidance learning. On the basis of his family studies, Mednick proposes slow recovery time as a marker for the genetic etiology of criminality. This is an appealing notion, particularly when it is considered in combination with the low anticipatory SCR findings, but it needs testing in an actual avoidance learning paradigm.

The hypothesis that psychopaths have a steeper gradient of fear as threat of punishment becomes temporally less remote (Hare, 1970) has not been refuted, but the generally lower responsivity to intense stimuli in psychopathy and its specificity to the electrodermal system are not accounted for by this theory. Similarly, the sensation-seeking hypothesis (Quay, 1965) receives support from evidence that greater stimulation levels are needed to produce the same electrodermal response in psychopaths (Hare, 1978a), but it is clear that the psychophysiology of psychopathy is dissimilar to that of high sensation seekers in the general

population. For example, high sensation seekers seem to give large first trial SCORs (Zuckerman, 1978), whereas there is some evidence that psychopaths show the opposite trend.

One problem with these theories is that they take into account only one or another of the reasonably well-established psychophysiological findings. A more comprehensive hypothesis is that of Venables (1974), who points out that slow SCR recovery and HR acceleration have both been related to a "closed-gate" (sensory rejection) mode of input regulation and to defensive reactions. This might attenuate the influence of the social environment on behavior. The gating mechanism is attributed to limbic system functioning on the basis of animal evidence that hippocampal lesions lead to fast-recovery SCORs and facilitate active avoidance, while amygdala lesions produce SCOR nonresponding and impair active avoidance.

A set of constructs that deals explicitly with the apparently conflicting results from SC and HR anticipatory responses has been proposed by Fowles (1980). This model proposes three separate but interrelated arousal systems: a behavioral inhibition system (BIS), which is indexed by electrodermal activity and activated by stimuli conditioned by aversive UCSs; a behavior-activating system (BAS), indexed by HR speeding and activated by rewarded CSs; and finally a general arousal system (A), which is similar to the older arousal concept and mediated by the reticular activating system. The BIS is considered to be the substrate for anxiety and mediates passive avoidance, while the BAS mediates active avoidance. The assumption of a weak BIS in psychopaths allows Fowles to account for much of the clinical data in psychopathy, such as impulsivity, ineffectiveness of punishment, poor socialization, and weak affective attachments, as well as the deficits in SC anticipation of punishment. Since the BIS has not particular relevance for HR, Fowles makes the additional assumption of an overactive BAS to account for the findings of greater HR anticipatory acceleration. It should be recalled, however, that this response may not always occur. It is possible that it is related to the aggressive behavior common in some psychopaths. J. A. Gray (1977), on the basis of pharmacological studies in animals, hypothesizes a medial septal and hippocampal substrate for the BIS and speculates that its inhibition will either increase or decrease hippocampal theta activity, depending on the specific bandwidth within the theta range. It is assumed that NE, 5-HT, and ACh are the neurotransmitters in this system. It should be noted that this approach, while providing a link between autonomic, electrocortical, and behavioral data, implies hippocampal hypofunction in psychopaths—exactly the opposite conclusion from the one reached by Venables (1974) in his interpretation of the recovery time data—and is seemingly in conflict with the empirical base for Venable's hypothesis. Different predictions about active avoidance in psychopathy are also implied by these two theories. Obviously, there are some complexities in the limbic conrol of the ANS that have not been dealt with.

Two theories of psychopathy based on alterations in neurotransmitter functioning have been proposed, both based on the concept of SNS-PNS balance. Porges (1976) hypothesizes that low catecholaminergic activity or relative cholinergic dominance could explain limited reactivity to environmental stimuli, poor avoidance learning, and weak affective systems in psychopaths. While this is a plausible explanation for some of the psychopathy data, this theory would seem to have trouble explaining the specificity of the deficits in reactivity that have been demonstrated earlier, and there is no mechanism proposed for how cholinergic dominance would mediate impulsivity. Mawson and Mawson (1977) also propose a PNS dominance in psychopathy, related to the activity of 5-HT and ACh, but they propose that this alternates with periods of SNS dominance mediated by NE and DA activity. This argument is based in part on the assumptions that the two arousal systems are mutually inhibitory, and that swings from SNS dominance to PNS dominance are both larger and more rapid in psychopaths than in controls. This theory would make the same predictions as Hare's "steep gradient of fear" hypothesis, and is also consistent with the data showing increasingly lower SCL in psychopaths than in controls as a function of time in a boring situation. The greater impulsivity and aggressiveness of psychopathic behavior are taken to reflect greater and more rapid shifts to SNS dominance. This theory, however, is based in large part on an interpretation of the evidence as showing either higher or lower arousal in psychopaths. It is inconsistent with the data showing that low SC activity and HR speeding can occur simultaneously in psychopathy.

All of these attempts to elucidate a biological substrate for primary psychopathic behavior are partially successful, but none accounts adequately for all of the major behavioral and psychophysiological findings. As in research on other behavior disorders, this is due in part to a lack of understanding of the basic neurophysiological and neurochemical mechanisms mediating psychophysiological variables. No attempt to add yet another theory to the list is made here, but it might be pointed out that the apparent specificity of the major psychophysiological differences between primary psychopaths and various controls of situations involving reactions to aversive stimulation (and also, perhaps, to boring situations) might suggest an involvement of the endogenous opiates, or perhaps an interaction of these opiates with catecholaminergic systems. Interest in the endorphins in neuroscience is relatively recent, and it will predictably be only a

matter of time before a more articulated theory is proposed. Such a theory would be testable using the narcotic antagonist naloxone. If primary psychopaths have an overactive endorphin system (or opiate receptor supersensitivity), naloxone, of course, should reduce their differences from controls in anticipatory ANS responses to aversive stimuli and in SC recovery time.

HYPERACTIVITY IN CHILDREN

Theoretical Issues

"Hyperactivity," also known as "hyperkinesis of childhood" or "minimal brain dysfunction," is commonly diagnosed on the basis of impulsivity, motor restlessness, short attention span, and learning difficulties. Most of these criteria have been used in selecting subjects for virtually all the studies to be covered later. Yet the concept has undergone a change in DSM-III. The major entry for the syndrome is called "attentional deficit disorder, with or without hyperactivity." This change reflects the opinion of many clinicians that attention problems and impulsivity are primary and that some children who show these symptoms may be hypoactive or normoactive. Some of the symptoms previously called "hyperkinetic" may be included in "oppositional disorders" and "conduct disorder." In addition, there is evidence from a large prospective study that the symptoms listed above "do not associate enough to warrant the designation of a syndrome" (Nichols & Chen, 1981, p. 51). Nevertheless, the syndrome is frequently diagnosed and, as psychiatric disorders go, is considered not uncommon, particularly in boys. Estimates of prevalence range from 5% to 15% of the population of grade-school children. Because most of the research to be examined here has been done on subjects more or less fitting the DSM-II definition of "hyperactivity," this review continues to use that term, but the clinical heterogeneity of this diagnosis should be kept in mind.

Hyperactivity is commonly believed to have a biological basis: There is good evidence for several biological etiologies, but each of them accounts for only a small amount of variance, and their specificity to the hyperactive (HA) syndrome can be questioned (Rapoport & Ferguson, 1981). Associations with HA-type behavior disorders have been found for prenatal and perinatal risk factors; minor physical anomalies (which are presumed to develop *in utero*); genetic factors (specifically alcoholism, sociopathy, or hysteria in the biological parents); and toxins in the physical environment, such as food additives and lead. The evidence shows that toxic reactions to food additives may affect at best only a small number of HA children, but high lead levels have been found in a larger number. Poor social and home environment may potentiate the effects of perinatal stress, but not specifically for hyperactivity (Rapoport & Ferguson, 1981).

Most HA children cannot be shown to have been exposed to any of these risk factors, however, and psychophysiological and other biological investigations have been undertaken, in part, to obtain current evidence of biological pathology. The dramatic behavioral improvements in many or most HA children that have been produced by stimulant drugs, such as dextroamphetamine and methylphenidate, have been taken to be evidence of a specific biological basis for hyperactivity, and a positive response to stimulants has frequently been taken to validate the diagnosis. Many theories of hyperactivity have taken this drug effect as a starting point, assuming that the pharmcological action is to correct a deficiency of arousal or of catecholamine activity. Although it does not disconfirm these theories, the recent findings that dextroamphetamine produces similar "paradoxical" motor quieting and improvements in attention and memory in normal children, as well as in HA children (Rapoport, Buchsbaum, Weingartner, Zahn, Ludlow, & Mikkelsen, 1980), invalidates diagnostic conclusions made from a positive drug response.

However, some HA children are not improved by stimulant drugs, and a minority seem to have a negative clinical response. One of the areas of psychophysiological investigation has been to try to predict clinical response from biological measures under placebo conditions and/or from the physiological response to the stimulant medication. Of course, most research has dealt with comparisons of HA subjects and controls, and with the effects of stimulant medication.

Baseline Studies

Autonomic Activity

An early report (Satterfield & Dawson, 1971) of significantly lower SCL and marginally lower SSCR frequency in HA children compared to controls stimulated much interest in using autonomic measures to test the low-arousal hypothesis of hyperactivity. Unfortunately, nine other investigations (reviewed in Hastings & Barkley, 1978) have shown remarkable unanimity in failing to replicate this result: Almost all of them found no differences, although one study (Spring, Greenberg, Scott, & Hopwood, 1974) found SSCR frequency to be marginally lower in the HA group. A later study from Satterfield's group (Satterfield, Atonian, Brashears, Burleigh, & Dawson, 1974) reported higher SCL in HA children, a result attributed to a more stimulating experimental setting. We (Zahn, Little, & Wender, 1978) obtained a similar result for SCL in a retest of children who had been seen earlier in a less stimulating atmosphere (Zahn, Abate, Little, & Wender, 1975), in which no arousal differences were observed. In the retest, the subjects were required to sit upright and fixate a spot so that pupil size could be recorded. The HA group had significantly higher SCL and marginally greater pupil size than controls, but the groups did not differ in HR. These results suggest a greater tonic SCL response to environmental stimulation in HA subjects—a suggestion that is dealt with later.

No evidence for low resting arousal in drug-free HA children has been found in cardiovascular variables. In fact, slightly higher HR and SBP have been reported in some studies (Hastings & Barkley, 1978), but this is not a consistent finding. A study of pupil size during a 10-min dark period (Yoss, 1970) showed that 25–35% of HA children had a "drowsy" pattern of many spontaneous fluctuations and gradual pupillary constriction, similar to what is seen in narcolepsy. However, no control data were reported. In an attempted replication, we (Zahn et al., 1978) found that a proportion of HA children showed this pattern, but that a similar number of controls also showed it. Thus, a varied group of indices has not shown abnormal baseline ANS arousal in HA children.

Resting EEG

Studies from a clinical EEG perspective have reported from 15% to 45% of the records of HA children to be "abnormal" or "borderline," but control data are generally not presented. The abnormalities consist mainly of excess slow-wave activity with some spiking (Hastings & Barkley, 1978). Less power in the alpha band (Montagu, 1975), and larger and more abundant alpha waves (Grunewald-Zuberbier, Grunewald, & Rasche, 1975), have been reported in HA children compared to controls. In the last-mentioned study there was less beta activity and lower beta mean frequency in the HA group; however, the controls in this study were not normals, but behaviorally disturbed children with low activity levels.

Using quantitative techniques, Dykman, Holcomb, Oglesby, and Ackerman (1982) found low beta power in learning disabled (LD) and a similar, but nonsignificant, trend in HA children. Low power at all frequency bands in young (<90 months) HA children was reported by Satterfield, Schell, Backs, and Hidaka (1984), but older HA children had higher alpha and beta power compared to age-matched controls. This result was due to negative correlations between age and power in just the controls. In contrast, Callaway, Halliday, and Naylor (1983) observed low alpha and markedly low beta power in an older HA group, and a positive correlation between beta power and age in just the controls. The marked differences in the results of these studies may be due to differences in attention. Satterfield et al. (1984) had their subjects watch television cartoons during a click ERP procedure while the subjects of Callaway *et al.* (1983) were resting with eyes open and closed. In any case, there seems not to be a simple answer to the question of whether there is a characteristic EEG pattern in HA children.

ANS Responsivity

One point for which there is considerable agreement among studies is that HA children show a deficiency in ANS responding to stimuli. This has been widely replicated for phasic SCR amplitude (Hastings & Barkley, 1978). Most studies report smaller SCRs in HA children for both signal (task-related) and nonsignal (orienting) stimuli (usually tones), but two studies did not observe differences in the amplitudes of SCORs (N. J. Cohen & Douglas, 1972; Rugel & Rosenthal, 1974), although Cohen and Douglas found smaller SCORs on the first trial in the HA group. Spontaneous SCRs seem not to be significantly smaller in HA children (Satterfield & Dawson, 1971; Zahn *et al.*, 1975). Thus, it may be that the HA deficit on SCR amplitude increases in relation to the importance or meaningfulness of the stimuli. This conclusion is suggested also by Conners's (1975) finding that SCR and vasoconstrictive response amplitudes did not increase to "response" tones compared to "no-response" tones in HA children, but did increase in controls. In fact, the HA children gave larger SCRs to the no-response stimuli—the only difference of this kind that has been reported.

We (Zahn *et al.*, 1975) examined various SCR parameters. Our HA subjects, in addition to smaller amplitudes, also had longer SCR onset latencies, rise times, and recovery times than controls. The increased rise and recovery times occurred only for SSCRs and ORs and not for SCRs to stimuli in an RT task. The result needs replicating, but explanations of this "sluggish" SCR topography in terms of peripheral factors seem unlikely, since the groups did not differ in overall SCR frequency, skin temperature, or SCL. On the basis of the current model of SCRs as dually determined by duct filling and a faster change in membrane potential, the data suggest less influence of the membrane mechanism on the SCRs of the HA children.

Consistent with the lower electrodermal responsivity, smaller pupillary dilation was reported in HA children to RT stimuli (Zahn *et al.*, 1978), but this difference disappeared when baseline pupil size was covaried out. No differences in pupillary constriction or in its recovery to light stimuli were found, but another parasympathetically mediated response, the decelerative component of the HROR, was smaller in HA children (Zahn *et al.*, 1975, 1978). More importantly, perhaps, smaller anticipatory HR deceleration

during RT foreperiods was observed in LD (Sroufe, Sonies, West, & Wright, 1973) and HA (Zahn *et al.*, 1978) children compared to controls; we did not obtain this result in our earlier study (Zahn *et al.*, 1975), perhaps because of nonoptimal foreperiods. This can be thought to be a fairly direct physiological manifestation of the attentional problems in HA children. However, it can also be seen as another manifestation of a general lack of autonomic responsivity to the environment, which has also been amply documented in electrodermal variables.

Habituation of the SCOR to simple stimuli using a trials-to-criterion measure has been reported to be faster in HA children in several studies (R. H. Rosenthal & Allen, 1978); however, since this measure is confounded with initial responsivity, as pointed out earlier, conclusions about habituation per se are not possible. Conners (1975) reported *slower* habituation of SCR and vasoconstrictive response amplitudes in HA children even when initial amplitudes were covaried out, but no statistics are given. The data from most of these studies show that normals give greater OR amplitudes than HA children on early trials, and that there is very little difference on later trials. This supports the generalization of greater autonomic response deficits in HA children to more "attention-getting" stimuli as much as any concept of an habituation difference.

ERPs

Given the importance of attention problems in HA children, and given that some aspects of ERPs are influenced by attentional variables, ERPs would seem to be a fruitful area of study. Since HA children are characterized by short attention span and low and sluggish ANS responsivity, it might be hypothesized that ERP amplitudes would be lower and latencies longer in these subjects. Such findings were obtained by Satterfield, Lesser, Saul, and Cantwell (1973), whose subjects received 90-dB click stimuli at .4-Hz and 2-Hz rates while watching television and were told to ignore the stimuli. Smaller N120–P180 and P180–N280 amplitudes at both stimulation rates and smaller P180 from baseline for the 2-Hz rate were found in the HA group. Latency effects were variable: Controls had shorter N120 and longer N280 latencies. The results were interpreted in terms of delayed CNS maturation in the HA group.

Quite different results were obtained by Buchsbaum and Wender (1973), who used light flashes of four intensities at a 1-Hz rate. Subjects were told to watch the lights but also to monitor their EEG on an oscilloscope and try to minimize artifacts. This study found larger N140–P200 amplitudes and shorter P100, N140, and P200 latencies in the HA children at all intensities. The HA group also had a greater amplitude–intensity slope ("augmenting"). An auditory ERP variability procedure showed that HA children had more variable ERPs. These authors also attributed their results to a "neurophysiological maturational lag" in the HA subjects.

The reasons for the conflicting results of these studies are not readily apparent, since they differed in so many methodological details. If the amplitudes of middle components of the ERP do vary directly and latencies vary inversely with attention, insofar as the Satterfield et al. subjects were told to ignore the clicks and the Buchsbaum and Wender subjects told to watch the flashes, it might be concluded that the HA subjects followed the instructions better than the controls! Although this explanation seems implausible, variations in attentional requirements might be expected to influence ERPs differently in HA and normal subjects. Hall, Griffin, Moyer, Hopkins, and Rapoport (1976) attempted to compare differences in attentional demands by having subjects watch for a green flash, to which they were to respond in one condition and not in another. Four intensities of light flashes were presented in both conditions. This study tested original and replication samples of HA children and controls, and subjects with abnormal EEGs were screened out. Results were conflicting: For the first sample, amplitude differences were similar to those in the Satterfield et al. (1973) study, while in the replication sample, they were similar to those in Buschbaum and Wender (1973). No differences in amplitude–intensity slopes were found, and the attention manipulation did not affect the results. Similarly, Callaway et al. (1983) did not find differential attention effects on visual ERPs. HA children had larger ERPs under both conditions. Both smaller (Conners, 1970) and larger (Sobotka & May, 1977) middle ERPs in an attention condition in LD children versus controls have been reported. However, Dykman, Holcomb, Ackerman, and McCray (1983) found greater auditory ERP augmenting and larger amplitudes in HA compared to LD boys using an attention paradigm. These studies suggest considerable variability in results using this method.

One source of variability is suggested by Satterfield and Braley (1977) and Satterfield et al. (1984), who compared HA and control children in three age groups using the Satterfield et al. (1973) technique. Younger HA subjects tended to have smaller ERP amplitudes than controls, especially for the later peaks, while older HAs had larger amplitudes of the earlier peaks when compared to age-matched controls (Satterfield & Braley, 1977) or were no different (Satterfield et al., 1984). This was due generally to positive correlations of amplitude with age in the HA group and negative correlations in the controls.

In contrast, in a longitudinal study (Satterfield et al., 1984), HA children showed either no age effects on amplitude or a negative trend similar to (but less extreme than) controls. In addition, Callaway et al. (1983) failed to find differential age effects on ERP amplitudes. Thus, age may or may not play a critical role in HA versus normal differences in ERPs. A more important reason for the variability in results of the reviewed studies above may be the differences in attention. Several studies have attempted to control attention to the stimulus by manipulating the task demands of the stimulus.

Effects of uncertainty of single and double clicks were studied by Prichep, Sutton, and Hakerem (1976). In an "uncertain" condition, subjects guessed whether a single or double click would be presented and were rewarded for correct guesses. This was compared to a "certain" condition. Compared to controls, HA children had larger P300 amplitudes to the second click in the certain condition and smaller P186 and larger N250 amplitudes to the second click in the uncertain condition (all measured from baseline). The authors point out that in general the HA group showed smaller positive and larger negative peaks under uncertainty and that the difference between ERPs under the two conditions was larger in the controls. On the basis of the literature on normal adults, the authors interpret the data as indicating inappropriate response to task demands, low attention to the stimuli, and low task-specific arousal in the HA subjects.

Different manipulations of attention have produced other differences between HA and control children, but the basic trend of smaller differences between attended and nonattended stimuli is similar. Loiselle, Stamm, Maitinsky, and Whipple (1980) used a paradigm in which a different set of frequent and rare tones was presented to each ear, but only the rare tones to one ear were counted. In normal children, both N100 to the frequent tones and P300 to the rare stimuli in the attended ear were larger than the homologous components to unattended-ear stimuli, as expected, but there were no significant effects of attention in HA children. A striking finding in this study was that P300 amplitude to the attended stimuli correlated .8 with correct detections in both HA and control subjects. It should be noted that the boys in this study were aged 12 and 13. Similar results for N100 were obtained for 14-year-old subjects (Zambelli, Stamm, Maitinsky, & Loiselle, 1977). The early component is attributed to a stimulus evaluation process and P300 to a response set; this explanation suggests that HA boys are deficient in both of these processes, possibly due to a difficulty in maintaining attention to the relevant ear.

Another examination of P300 was made by Klorman, Salzman, Pass, Borgstedt, and Dainer (1979), using a CPT. The procedure was run under both a passive condition ("attend only") and an active condition ("respond quickly to the letter X"). P300 to both target and nontarget stimuli was smaller in HA boys only in the active condition. This was accompanied by, but not significantly correlated with, the usual HA performance deficits. However, normals showed nonsignificantly greater amplitudes in the passive condition, and the difference between passive and active conditions was not significant. In a later study (Michael, Klorman, Salzman, Borgstedt, & Dainer, 1981), the P300 deficit in the CPT was present only in HA children below age 9 compared to age-matched controls. With a more complex "BX" version of the CPT ("respond to X only if preceded by B"), a P300 deficit was found for HA children as a whole, and no significant interactions with age were found. A similar study on nonhyperactive LD children found lower P300 in the LD group only on the critical (following B) stimuli of the "BX" task and no age interactions (Dainer, Klorman, Salzman, Hess, Davidson, & Michael, 1981); these results suggest that LD children have the same types of deficits as HA children, but perhaps not to the same degree. These findings conflict with those of an earlier study (Musso & Harter, 1978), whose LD children showed greater effects of attention on P300 than controls. Both studies found longer P300 latencies in their LD groups, however.

This last group of studies has provided encouraging evidence that there may be consistent electrophysiological correlates of attention dysfunction in hyperactivity, but that the specific correlates depend on the attention paradigm used. Attention-related ERP deficits seem to be present into adolescence, but it takes sufficiently challenging tasks to elicit them.

Studies of another attention-related potential, the CNV, have produced conflicting results. Absent CNVs in six of seven HA boys versus two of seven controls was reported by Andreasen, Peters, and Knott (1976) in a study in which artifacts were carefully controlled, but scoring was not done blindly with respect to diagnosis. Negative results for CNV were reported by Prichep et al. (1976), but their paradigm may not have been optimal for eliciting this potential. Similar conflicting results exist in the LD literature (Dainer et al., 1981). This area has not as yet profited from the careful attention to age and methodological variables that has been given to the P300 studies.

Since the most consistent findings have been from studies where active attention was demanded, the results of these studies cannot be said to reflect gross (or even minimal) brain pathology. Evidence of neuropathology in HA children has come from a study of the very early ERP components using the brain stem evoked potential (BSEP) technique (Sohmer & Student, 1978). These investigators found delayed latency of the first response wave and very significant delayed transmission time (difference between wave I and wave IV) in HA children compared to controls. In fact, their HA subjects showed significantly longer transmission time than did autistic and retarded children. This study needs replication, especially in view of technical difficulties experienced by that laboratory (Student & Sohmer, 1979).

Prediction of Treatment Response

One of the popular attempted uses of psychophysiological data in studies of HA children is to predict the effects of stimulant drug therapy. One source of this interest has stemmed from the idea that the "paradoxical" effects of stimulants are unique to this particular subgroup of children and that a favorable response is indicative of a "true" biologically based HA syndrome. Now that the nonspecificity of the quieting and attentional effects of the drugs has been shown, this approach is less useful. It would seem more appropriate to think of children with a minimal response to the drugs as perhaps receiving a nonoptimal dose. However, the small number of children whose behavior is clearly worsened by the drugs may have been misdiagnosed as HA when their true condition is, say, schizophrenia or anxiety neurosis. This suggests that large and important sources of variance in outcome studies would be the number and types of misdiagnosed subjects and the care taken to optimize dose level. Another source of variation is the amount of impairment on off-drug or placebo conditions. Finally, since different behaviors have been shown to have different dose–response relationships (Sprague & Sleator, 1977), the type of behavior used to index the clinical change in another important source of variation. Evaluating changes in psychophysiology with respect to outcome has different theoretical implications. Only drug-free predictors are considered in this section.

ANS Studies

Conflicting results have been reported for SC predictors of treatment outcome. In one study (Satterfield, Cantwell, Lesser, & Podosin, 1972), the six best and five worst clinical responders out of a total subject group of 31 were compared. Placebo SCL was significantly lower for good than for poor drug responders, the two groups falling on either side of controls. Similarly, Satterfield, Atonian, Brashears, Burleigh, and Dawson (1974) found SCL to be negatively correlated with the severity of HA symptoms and with the amount of improvement on medication. Quite different results were obtained by our group (Zahn et al., 1975); we compared 22 good with 18 moderate responders or nonresponders and found only a chance number of differences in off-drug variables. However, when on- and off-drug values were combined, a clear pattern of lower SCL, fewer and smaller elicited SCRs, and more "sluggish" SCRs characterized the *poor* responders. The off-drug differences were similar but not significant. The medication appeared to enhance the differences somewhat, but did not have a differential effect on the two groups. Further clouding the issue was the finding that the poor responders had higher anxiety ratings—a result that makes some intuitive sense but seems inconsistent with the autonomic data.

These conflicting results may indicate the existence of subgroups of good drug responders who are either high or low in ANS activity. Such a finding using pupillary response to light was reported by Knopp, Arnold, Andras, and Smeltzer (1973), whose good responders gave either larger or smaller pupillary constrictions to light compared to (unspecified) controls; these responses were normalized by drugs. Poor responders showed smaller changes. A formula using both the predrug values and the changes predicted clinical response. Using the same formula, we (Zahn et al., 1978) obtained nonsignificant results in the same direction.

Another explanation of findings of both high and low arousal in good drug responders is suggested by the study of Barkley and Jackson (1977), in which high predrug respiratory rate was negatively correlated with improvement in motor activity and attention, but positively correlated with improvement in play activity. The relevance of this finding for the previous conflicting results lies in the criteria for improvement. Satterfield et al. (1972) and Satterfield, Atonian, Brashears, Burleigh, and Dawson (1974), who found negative correlations between arousal and improvement, used teacher's ratings (the drug dosage level was determined by the physician), while we (Zahn et al., 1975) used parent and psychiatrist ratings. Thus, off-drug ANS activity may differ in predictions of improvement, depending on the behaviors or contexts involved. This hypothesis would seem to be worthy of more study.

EEG and ERP Studies

Various EEG and ERP predictors of good treatment response have been found by Satterfield's group (summarized in Satterfield, Cantwell, & Satterfield, 1974). These include high EEG amplitude and excessive slow-wave activity, large P180–N280 ERPs to clicks, and slow ERP recovery (not defined further). These markers are taken as evidence of low CNS arousal in drug responders, but the data are somewhat equivocal on the question of whether HA children showing the most deviant CNS functioning are most likely to improve on drugs. The ERP amplitude differences have not been confirmed in other studies (Buchsbaum & Wender, 1973; Halliday, Callaway, & Rosenthal, 1984; McIntyre, Firemark, Cho, Bodner, & Gomez, 1981), and the results of Hall et al. (1976) are in the opposite direction. Some evidence of large amplitudes in better amphetamine responders, most consistently

on ratings of conduct problems, is presented by Saletu, Saletu, Simeon, Viamontes, and Itil (1975); however, as in the Hall et al. (1976) study, pretreatment variations in ratings were not controlled. No significant differenes in EEG power at any bandwidth were reported by McIntyre et al. (1981), although drug responders had more theta power and also significantly faster peak frequency in the beta range.

ERP latency has been examined in several studies, also with conflicting results. Hall et al. (1976) found good drug response to be predictable from long N140 latencies under conditions of inattention and a small increase with attention, while McIntyre et al. (1981) reported fast latencies in peaks of over 200 msec for auditory and visual stimuli in drug responders. Saletu, Saletu, Simeon, Viamontes, and Itil (1975) obtained fewer than a chance number of significant correlations between improvement on specific symptoms after amphetamine therapy and pretreatment ERP latencies. The data of Buchsbaum and Wender (1973) suggest an interaction with age: In the 6- to 9-year-old group, responders had the faster latencies, while the reverse held for the 10- to 12-year-old group. However, these differences depended on stimulus intensity. Good responders showed a less mature pattern of a smaller decrease in latency with increasing stimulus intensity. High ERP variability was related to a good drug response by both Buchsbaum and Wender (1973) and Hall et al. (1976). Buchsbaum and Wender (1973) also observed reversed hemispheric asymmetry in good drug responders.

Like the autonomic data, the ERP findings on predicting treatment outcome are rife with contradictory findings. This may be due to the large number of methodological differences between studies, but it also may be that these variables are not predictors of outcome for the "true" HA group as a whole. However, intensive clinical and experimental study of the relatively small number of children who have a definite negative or worsening response to stimulant drug therapy might lead to a clearer diagnostic description and might elucidate underlying mechansims as well.

There is one report of the long-term prediction of delinquency independent of drug treatment (Satterfield & Schell, 1984). The childhood EEG and ERPs of HA boys who became delinquent as teenagers were *less* abnormal than that of nondelinquent HA boys. The most discriminating variables were alpha and beta[2] power, which were larger, and N2 amplitude, which was smaller in nondelinquent HA subjects than in delinquent and control subjects. The data suggest a meaningful physiological subgrouping of HA children which may find clinical expression in the DSM III distinction between attention deficit and conduct disorders. Whether they are interpretable in terms of lower arousal in the delinquent group than in the nondelinquent group, as the authors suggest, is questionable.

Effects of Stimulant Drugs

In no other disorder has there been as much interest in studying the effects of the effective medication with laboratory measures of behavior and psychophysiological techniques as in hyperactivity. This is in part due to the relative ease of performing such studies. It is not considered unethical to withhold medication. In fact, many physicians recommend drug holidays periodically. The effects of stimulant medication, usually dextroamphetamine or methylphenidate, have a rapid onset and a relatively short half-life, which make acute studies possible in a short period of time. The dramatic and "paradoxical" quieting effects of the stimulants pose a fascinating scientific problem. Since the drugs are effective in reversing the major symptoms of hyperactivity, impulsivity, and inattention, an understanding of the mechanisms of their effects might provide a key to understanding the condition itself. Coupled with this idea has been the notion that the effects are "paradoxical" in the sense of "specific to HA children," so that a favorable therapeutic response to the drugs is taken as confirmatory of the diagnosis. The recent evidence of similar amphetamine effects in normal and HA children has somewhat invalidated this idea, but the other reasons, for studying drug effects are justification enough.

ANS Effects of Drugs

Since stimulant drugs reduce some aspects of behavioral arousal, and because ANS (and CNS) arousal has sometimes been thought to be low in HA children, it is natural that arousal measures should be a prime target for investigation. Not surprisingly, most studies have found various measures thought to reflect ANS arousal to be increased by stimulant drugs (Barkley, 1977), although there have been some exceptions. Increases in blood pressure and HR are the rule. A decrease in skin temperature, attributed to peripheral vasoconstriction, occurred in three studies (Solanto & Conners, 1982; Zahn et al., 1975; Zahn, Rapoport, & Thompson, 1980) but not in another (Zahn et al., 1978). Electrodermal variables—SCL and the SSCR frequency—have also produced fairly consistent results; in over half of the studies, increases in these variables due to stimulant drug medication have been reported, while, with one exception, the negative results have been marginal in the same direction or nonsignificant. The exception was a decrease in skin "admittance" (Montagu & Swarbrick, 1975), a measure of AC conductance. The little that is known about this variable makes interpretation of the result difficult. Pupillary size (Zahn et al., 1978) and respiration rate (Barkley, 1977) were not affected by stimulants.

Most of the evidence, then, suggests a nonparadoxical increase in baseline sympathetic activity following stimulant drug intake in HA children, and thus permits speculation that this increased arousal may be beneficial to behavior in these children. Since these measures have not been shown to be abnormally low in HA as compared to control subjects, the data support the position that the "optimal" arousal point may be higher in HA children than in controls (Zentall, 1975), and that only at this relatively high level will the child cease attempts to raise it further by disruptive behavior. Doubts about this model come from a study that tested acute effects of D-amphetamine and placebo on both normal and HA children using a conventional double-blind crossover design, preceded by an initial off-drug test (Zahn et al., 1980). The active drug produced increases in HR and decreases in skin temperature in both groups (along with improvements in target symptoms of motor activity, attention, and impulsivity in both groups), but significant changes in SCL and SSCRs were not found. However, compared to the first (no-drug) day, subjects in both groups on placebo had higher levels of the two electrodermal measures, as well as higher HR. These indices of high arousal on the placebo day were *not* generally accompanied by behavioral improvements. Motor activity *increased* under placebo, and one measure of impulsivity decreased for just the normal group. This study thus shows a dissociation between arousal and behavioral improvement, suggesting that some other effect of stimulant medication is responsible for improving HA symptoms.

An effect of stimulant drugs on the cholinergic system has been suggested by Porges (1976) as a possibly important mediator of the symptomatic improvement. One line of evidence for this hypothesis comes from studies showing that stimulant medication potentiates HR deceleration and reduces HR variability in RT foreperiods (Porges, Walter, Korb, & Sprague, 1975; Sroufe et al., 1973). Although we (Zahn et al., 1975, 1978) reported equivocal results in early studies, D-amphetamine in a later study (Zahn et al., 1980) increased HR deceleration significantly in normal boys and marginally ($p < .10$) in HA boys. However, we (Zahn, Rapoport, & Thompson, 1981) obtained the opposite effects in normal men—significantly different for the boys' results—and also found greater SNS activation in terms of SC measures in the men than in the boys. Although this indicates a different effect of amphetamine on the SNS-PNS balance of men and boys, the lack of an improvement in attention in the men is consistent with the hypothesis.

Porges (1976) developed another measure of the vagal–parasympathetic–cholinergic system—the coherence between respiratory and HR fluctuations over the range of expected respiration frequencies. This was lower in HA than in to control children, and it was elevated by a moderate (.5 mg/kg) dose of methylphenidate, but not by 1.0 mg/kg of methylphenidate or by low doses of D-amphetamine. Recently, this result has been replicated (Porges, Bohrer, Keren, Cheung, Franks, & Drasgow, 1981) and extended. Again, the coherence measure peaked at a .5 mg/kg dose of methylphenidate and decreased (nonsignificantly) at 1.0 mg/kg. In addition, a measure of "vagal tone," which is the sum of spectral density estimates of heart period over the respiratory frequency bandwidth, was, like heart period, a monotonically decreasing function of drug dosage. These findings are especially interesting in view of evidence that methylphenidate at the 1.0 mg/kg dose led to a decrement in performance on a cognitive task compared to enhanced performance at .5 mg/kg, but that ratings of disruptive classroom behavior decreased further at the high dose (Sprague & Sleator, 1977). These parallel dose–response curves for cognition and the coherence measure on the one hand, and for disruptive behavior and vagal tone on the other, are suggestive of independent physiological mediation of these two types of behavior—a hypothesis supported also by a lack of correlation between the two physiological measures.

As Porges *et al.* (1981) note, there are some problems in interpreting these data. Earlier, Porges (1976) interpreted HR–respiratory coherence as an inverse function of SNS-PNS balance, suggesting that, in concordance with the HR deceleration data, moderate doses of stimulants alter this balance in the PNS (cholinergic) direction. Porges *et al.* (1981) have reinterpreted coherence as indicative of the temporal stability of the brain stem system by which respiratory activity influences beat-to-beat HR. Autonomic balance is indicated by HR and vagal tone, both of which show that methylphenidate tilts the system toward SNS dominance. This is a radical departure from the earlier interpretation; however, it is not necessarily in conflict with attributing greater HR deceleration to a stronger cholinergic influence, since this occurred during periods of focused attention, whereas the other measures were taken in resting periods. The data suggest that these spectral-analytic methods may be potentially very useful, not only in the study of hyperactivity but in other disorders as well. Their interpretation will depend on other studies, such as those of the direct effects of motor activity and of changes in sympathetic balance produced by methods other than stimulant drug administration.

Another method of comparing physiological and behavioral effects of drugs is to compare the time course of a single administration. Solanto and Conners (1982) showed that HR increases and skin temperature decreases followed a time course for 6 hours after a dose of methylphenidate that paralleled improved attention more closely than it paralleled decreased motor activity. This supports the idea of separate mechanisms for attention and motor activity, but unlike the Sprague and Sleator (1977) results, it couples HR with attention rather than with activity.

So far, the physiological effects described for stimulants have been nonparadoxical; they are what might be expected from stimulants or from drugs that enhance attentional ability. The effects reported for other measures of autonomic responsivity, however, are not so easily digested. N. J. Cohen, Douglas, and Morgenstern (1971) found a decrease in SCOR amplitude after methylphenidate compared to placebo, but no change in response to signal stimuli. A smaller increase in SCL from nontask to task conditions was also observed. The OR result was not replicated by Spring *et al.* (1974), but we (Zahn *et al.*, 1975) found a generalized reduction of amplitudes of SSCRs, SCORs, and SCRs to signal stimuli in HA subjects taking drugs, as well as decreased rise rates and increased latency of SCORs. These results may be attributable in part to peripheral factors: When the changes in both base SCL and skin temperature were simultaneously covaried out, only the amplitudes of elicited SCRs showed a significant drug effect, but at reduced levels. Similarly, the drugs attenuated the pupil dilation response to signal stimuli (pupil constriction to light was not affected), but this effect was reduced to nonsignificance when change in baseline pupil size was covaried. In another study (Conners & Rothschild, 1973), which measured FPVOR amplitude using a measure that corrects for prestimulus FPV, found marginally lower FPVOR amplitude after D-amphetamine treatment compared to placebo. However, habituation was much faster after drug treatment. Thus, stimulant drugs appear to attenuate phasic sympathetic response amplitudes, but it is not always clear how robust this effect is when changes in base levels are controlled.

In a comparison of drug effects in normal and HA boys (Zahn *et al.*, 1980), both groups showed some evidence of SCR attenuation due to D-amphetamine, despite minimal changes in base SCL, but in different parts of the test. Normals' responses to signal stimuli were attenuated, while for HA boys, only SCOR and SSCR amplitude were attenuated. These results are similar to the N. J. Cohen *et al.* (1971) data, and they generally confirm the previous results showing some, but inconsistent, attenuation of phasic responses independent of baseline changes. This can be considered paradoxical, since the drugs seem to increase the difference from normal children.

If the nature of the stimuli is considered, these data do not seem quite so paradoxical. Both N. J. Cohen *et al.* (1971) and our group (Zahn *et al.*, 1980) found the SCORs in HA children to be more attenuated by drugs than were SCRs to imperative stimuli, and our earlier data (Zahn *et al.*, 1975) reveal a similar trend. Thus, it may be that while the drugs tend to attenuate SCR amplitude in general, possibly due to peripheral mechanisms, the attenuation is greater for nonsignal stimuli, thus increasing the specificity of SCRs in favor of more demanding stimuli. This feature of

SCR specificity may be what is more closely related to the behavioral improvement, rather than amplitude per se. Studies need to be designed (and analyzed) to focus on this aspect of the data.

ERP Effects of Drugs

Many ERP studies of drugs have not reported overall drug effects, but rather have focused on differential effects in good and poor drug responders. Satterfield *et al.* (1973) reported increases in ERPs to 90-dB clicks in poor drug responders and slight decreases in ERPs of good responders after methylphenidate treatment. These changes represent normalization for only the poor drug responders. Buchsbaum and Wender (1973) reported similar results of N140–P200 to high-intensity stimuli and noted that augmenting increased on amphetamine for the drug nonresponders but slightly decreased in responders. ERP latencies tended to decrease for nonresponders and increase for responders. In contrast to Satterfield *et al.* (1972), these results all represent trends toward normalization in the responders and the opposite trends in nonresponders. Amphetamine reduced ERP variability in the HA group as a whole. Saletu, Saletu, Simeon, Viamontes, and Itil (1975) found only nonsignificant trends for increases in latency and amplitude of peaks in the 100–250 msec range elicited by light flashes (occipital leads) after D-amphetamine treatment in HA children as a group. However, good stimulant drug responders showed a greater latency increase of P100. The most consistent trend in these studies, none of which used an attention-controlling task, seems to be that the good drug responders failed to show any drug effects on ERP amplitude and that poor responders showed amplitude increases. Thus the effects of stimulant drugs on HA children as a group might be a modest increase in amplitude. There were two findings of increased latency in good responders, however.

In a study that compared an attention condition (counting occasional dim flashes) with a passive procedure, Halliday, Rosenthal, Naylor, and Callaway (1976) did find two discriminators between good and poor responders, which were replicated in two separate samples. One was a methylphenidate-produced increase in N145–P190 in the attention task in responders, but a decrease in nonresponders; the other was a decrease in ERP variability in attention compared to passive conditions in responders while on the medication, but an increase in variability in nonresponders. These findings are suggestive of "better" or more efficient ERPs in medicated responders. These results were, remarkably, repeated almost precisely in a prospective replication (Halliday, Callaway, & Rosenthal, 1984). However, these findings, as well as those of Buchsbaum and Wender (1973), were not replicated by Hall *et al.* (1976).

Four studies with task-induced attentional control have reported significant drug effects on ERP components for HA children as a whole. Prichep *et al.* (1976) found no effects of methylphenidate to either the first or the second of two clicks when the occurrence of the second click was certain; however, effects were found under conditions of uncertainty. To the first click, P186 and P295 were smaller and N103 was larger under drug than under placebo. These effects were relatively small compared to the effects on the second (uncertain) click, for which the drug produced larger P186 and smaller N250. In general, methylphenidate increased the "positivity" of the ERP to the uncertain clicks—an effect that, as may be recalled, is in the direction of normalization. Similarly, Klorman *et al.* (1979) showed that methylphenidate increased P300 amplitude in a CPT, also suggesting normalization. This effect was about the same for the target stimuli as for the nontarget stimuli. In a replication and extension of this study (Michael *et al.*, 1981), clear drug enhancement of P300 occurred only with recordings from parietal electrode placements. For both parietal and vertex recordings, the drug ameliorated the decline in P300 amplitude over the course of the sessions. Similar effects were observed during the more complex "BX" version of the CPT, but the overall drug effect on P300 was less marked and depended on the sequence of conditions. Improvement in task performance from the drug was marked in both of these studies. Thus the performance effects match, in a general way, the trend for enhanced ERP amplitude. However, unlike P300, the performance effects of the drug were not influenced by sequence or time course. This suggests that there is greater robustness in the effects of stimulant drugs on behavior and that the ERPs are mediated by somewhat different processes.

Using a paradigm similar to that of Halliday *et al.* (1976), but computing peak amplitudes from baseline rather than peak-to-peak values, Halliday, Callaway, Rosenthal, and Naylor (1979) found that methylphenidate decreased the amplitude of P228 in the attention condition in HA boys. Effects of the drug on N159 depended on age, task, and dose. Boys under 10 years of age showed a linear increase in N159 with increasing drug dose for just the passive condition, while boys over 10 showed a nonmonotonic increase–decrease in N159 with increasing drug dose in just the active condition. N159 latency decreased for the older boys and increased in the younger boys on drugs. Different results were obtained when principal components rather than the raw data were analyzed. A notable negative finding is that a component identified as P300 showed only effects of type of task. In a recent study using the same attention paradigm, however, Halliday, Callaway, and Naylor (1983) emphasize the paucity of drug effects on ERP amplitude and their interaction with age and attention conditions.

The main simple effect was an increase in negativity in the 100–250-msec range with increasing methylphenidate dosage. No latency effects were found, despite a large decrease in RT.

Some of the drug effects found may not be specific to HA children. In a study on young adults, Coons, Peloquin, Klorman, Bauer, Ryan, Pearlmutter, and Salzman (1981) found no effects of methylphenidate on the "X" or "BX" versions of the CPT on either performance or P300 (where placebo performance was nearly perfect); however, on a still more difficult version, the drug enhanced both dependent variables. Thus, positive drug effects were obtained only under conditions of attentional demand.

Neither Prichep *et al.* (1976) nor Michael *et al.* (1981) found drug effects on the CNV. However, Andreasen *et al.* (1976) reported some CNV enhancement due to methylphenidate medication in HA children, and similar effects have been reported in normal adults (Coons *et al.*, 1981).

Most of the positive findings of drug effects on ERP seem to be confined to changes in amplitude of those ERP components that are also affected by attention in the particular task used. It is interesting that both increases and decreases in amplitude and latency have been found as a consequence of stimulant drug administration. The data are consistent with a model of a drug-produced increase in ability to focus attention, which is manifested by changes in attention-related ERP components. These studies, along with the studies on the effects of diagnosis in drug-free subjects, provide encouragment that ERP techniques can be used to help elucidate the nature of the attention deficit in these attention deficit disorders. This will not be an easy undertaking, however, since these studies have revealed a number of variables that influence the ERP results. Especially puzzling are the effects of age found in some studies, especially since the behavioral effects of stimulant drugs are similar for younger and older HA children. It seems likely that differences in the amount of the subjects' capacity required to perform the task might mediate age differences in drug effects on ERPs. Although most studies adjust dose levels for body weight, this might not be appropriate for wide variations in weight (Rapoport *et al.*, 1980) and might lead to nonoptimal doses for some subjects. Use of a dose–response paradigm and tasks whose parameters can be adjusted to produce the same (nonzero) error rates would seem desirable in future studies. Prior studies on normal subjects to work out methodological details and age effects would seem to be a prerequisite of studies on HA children and the effects of drugs.

Summary and Conclusions

One of the more consistent findings is that HA and normal children do not differ in autonomic base levels. Thus an early and interesting hypothesis of low ANS arousal in these children has not been supported. However, some EEG studies have suggested that a minority of HA children may have excessive slow-wave activity. This is evidence of a biological abnormality in some children, but better-controlled studies are needed. Several recent studies have found relatively large middle ERP amplitudes and/or amplitude–intensity augmenting in HA groups. These findings seem independent of attention and arousal and suggest a possible lack of inhibitory control at some stage of processing.

Another consistent finding is smaller ANS responses in HA versus normal children. The findings from various studies are most consistent for responses to signal stimuli and for the early trials in an OR series, suggesting a disproportionate deficit for more significant stimuli. Habituation has been reported to be faster in some studies, but this could be a function of the small initial amplitudes. Smaller HR deceleration during RT foreperiods has also been reported in more than one study. Since physiological responses mediated by both the SNS and PNS are small in HA children, and the deficit is greater when significant stimuli are presented, these findings would seem to be related to the attention deficits that characterize these children. Virtually no evidence of this beyond the presence of both deficits in the same group exists, however. From a biological standpoint, these findings are more consistent with a disturbance in some part of the nervous system utilizing cholinergic neurotransmission than with a monoaminergic deficit.

Many conflicting results with respect to ERP amplitude have been reported, most notably in the earlier studies. The source of these differences might be ascribed to age of the subjects, methodological differences between studies, and lack of control over attention to the stimuli and to ocular and muscular sources of artifact. Other EEG evidence suggests high alpha and beta power and small N2 amplitudes in those HA children who are at low risk for future delinquency. The interpretation of this is problematic. Other recent studies, however, utilizing various methods of attentional control and tasks that produce performance deficits in HA children, have agreed in finding that HA children have attenuated differences in P300 and/or late positive components to irrelevant versus attended task-relevant stimuli. Small N100 in HA groups has been consistently reported from one laboratory. This result may depend on the particular task. The question of whether ERPs to irrelevant stimuli are larger or those to relevant stimuli are smaller in HA children is moot. These ERP differences persist into adolescence but are demonstrable only with sufficiently challenging tasks. These studies show that interpretations of data in terms of "maturational lag" can arise from inappropriate experimental paradigms for a given age group. The data can be said to be a manifestation of a selective attention deficit in hyperactivity, but it may be premature to attribute this to a specific processing stage.

Although the literature on the middle and late ERPs does not point to a biological etiology of hyperactivity, a report of delayed brain stem transmission in HA children does suggest a neurogenic dysfunction, perhaps involving the auditory system. Attempted replication of this should be of high priority. An implication of this is that there may be selective deficits in auditory signal precessing—a hypothesis that is testable by other ERP techniques.

The theoretical importance of studies of pretreatment predictors of stimulant drug response has been diminished by findings that normal and non-HA children are similarly affected by drugs, although prediction studies may have practical utility. Early findings that good treatment response may be predictable from low SCL, high EEG amplitude, excessive EEG slow-wave activity, and large ERPs have not been generally confirmed, but the early studies used an extreme-groups design while others have investigated the entire sample. The possibility remains that a subgroup of apparently HA children, for whom stimulant drugs are contraindicated, can be identified on the basis of physiological measures. However, recent evidence is consistent with the hypothesis that the major source of individual differences in medication effects is in the metabolism of the drugs.

Many of the prediction studies suffer from methodological problems, such as failure to control for pretreatment differences in severity of target symptoms. More interesting are indications that different target symptoms may differ in their predictability from a given physiological marker. This has serious implications for the design of prediction studies. Many of them evaluate outcome while the subjects are on an "optimal" dose of stimulant medication which has been determined by each child's doctor, based on unspecified criteria of clinical change. Determination of optimum dosage using the same well-validated rating scales and other measures that are used as outcome criteria would permit dose–response relationships for different classes of symptoms to be established, might help establish reliable physiological predictors of treatment response, and would seem to be clinically beneficial.

The effects of stimulant drugs, long considered paradoxical in terms of behavioral quieting, are non-paradoxical with respect to ANS base levels. Increases in arousal indices are quite reliably found. The independence of these changes from behavioral improvement has been shown by a report that placebo-induced increases in base levels were not accompanied by favorable behavioral changes.

More paradoxical results of drugs are attenuation of already low SCR amplitudes and further increases in their rise and recovery times. These changes are related to the changes in base levels, but cannot be completely accounted for by them. However, one less puzzling feature of these data is that attenuation of SCRs to nonsignal stimuli seems to be greater than that to signal stimuli—results consistent with improvements in attention.

An effect even more closely related to attention improvements is potentiation of HR deceleration and reduction in HR variability during RT foreperiods. These findings have led to speculations about the role of the cholinergic and parasympathetic systems in stimulant drug effects, especially since there is evidence from animal studies of an increase in cholinergic activity after low doses of amphetamine. This, in turn, has led to dose–response studies of the effects of methylphenidate on measures of HR-respiratory coherence and "vagal tone." Coherence seems to parallel cognitive performance, peaking at a moderate dosage of stimulant and then declining, while vagal tone parallels heart period and ratings of conduct problems in showing a monotonic decrease with increasing drug dosage. This is an important finding, suggesting independent physiological control over two of the key symptoms of hyperactivity. Interpretations in terms of SNS-PNS balance have not been completely satisfactory in explaining these two dose–response curves, although with sufficient post hoc assumptions a model along these lines might be possible. An alternate interpretation of the HR–respiratory coherence data implicates brain stem dysfunction. This idea would be supported if the prolonged brain stem transmission found in HA children responded to stimulant drugs in a similar fashion.

More often than not, when stimulant drug effects on ERP amplitudes have been reported, they have been increases. In studies without explicit controls for attention and artifacts, however, this result is somewhat more likely for poor drug responders. These studies are equivocal as to whether drugs normalize ERPs.

Studies using various attention paradigms have fairly consistently obtained results that are interpretable as improvements, although in some instances this represents smaller ERPs on drug. The specific drug effects obtained are dependent on the paradigm used. As in the comparisons with normal children, positive results have been obtained only with sufficiently challenging tasks for the age group studied. Drug effects similar to those found for HA children (enhancement of P300) were reported for adults when a difficult task was used. In general, drug effects on ERPs are consistent with increased ability for focused and/or selective attention. A task for future research is to determine whether there are selective and perhaps dose-dependent effects on ERPs related to different stages of processing.

In conclusion, although there are some promising leads, psychophysiological studies have not pointed to a specific biological etiology of hyperactivity. The hypothesis of low catecholamine functioning may be supported by the low ANS responsivity findings, but in the absence of more definitive knowledge about the relationships between these two systems, this hypothesis remains speculative at present. Also, it is difficult to account for effects of stimulant drugs on this basis. Some of the data suggest cholinergic involvement as a definite possibility. The data in general have not supported a theory of maturational lag, although some support is thought to exist in a few studies. Finally, although results of studies of LD children have not been covered comprehensively in this review, the similarities to the results of the HA studies that have been covered suggest a spectrum of disorders involving these groups.

AUTISM AND OTHER CHILDHOOD PSYCHOSES

Theoretical Issues

A variety of terminologies has been used to describe autism and other severe developmental disorders (Ornitz & Ritvo, 1976). "Early infantile autism," referred to in this chapter simply as "autism," has been fairly well defined, as psychiatric syndromes go. "Childhood psychosis," "early-onset psychosis," and "childhood schizophrenia" have been used in a confusing fashion to refer to a variety of disorders, including autism itself, as well as conditions other than autism. One of the unfortunate consequences of this semantic confusion is that it promotes conceptualization of these disorders as childhood versions of more familiar adult psychoses, especially schizophrenia. Many investigators (e.g., Fish, 1977), in fact, believe this to be the case. However, many (e.g., Rutter, 1972) see autism as phenomenologically and etiologically distinct from adult schizophrenia. DSM-III takes this latter position in categorizing "infantile autism" under "pervasive developmental disorders." Childhood schizophrenia, in which hallucinations, delusions, and loose associations are common, is not recognized as a separate diagnosis, but simply as schizophrenia with an early onset. One of the themes of research in this area is the comparison of findings in autistic children with those from schizophrenia studies.

Research on psychotic children, when it is focused on a subgroup, has looked at autistic children. However, even "true" autism is quite heterogeneous with respect to symptoms. These children have been observed to be alternatively hyporeactive or hyperreactive to environmental stimuli. Loud sounds may elicit no response at some times, but at other times an autistic child may show heightened awareness of, or sensitivity to, ordinary stimuli of low intensity. Speech and language development is severely retarded, as is development of social skills. Develop-

ment is characterized by unevenness, with sudden spurts and "islands" of particular competence in some areas. Stereotyped motor activities, such as rocking, head banging, and especially hand flapping in front of the face, are common autistic behaviors. These may alternate with periods of posturing or staring into space. The most characteristic symptom of autism is a disturbance of interpersonal relatedness, in which other persons in the environment are responded to more as objects than as people. Ornitz and Ritvo (1976) regard many of these symptoms as manifestations of a desire to maintain sameness in the environment, due to a profound aversion to changes in perceptual set.

Although autism is associated only sometimes with a known physical illness, such as phenylketonuria or rubella, it is widely regarded as being organic and possibly genetic in etiology. Infantile autism is defined in DSM-III as having an onset within the first 30 months of life. The early onset is of diagnostic importance in distingishing it from the phenotypically similar but less severe "childhood-onset pervasive developmental disorder." Prognosis is guarded, and no successful pharmacotherapy is available. Much of the psychophysiological research on autism is directed specifically toward discovering a basic neuropathology.

Other forms of childhood psychoses are apparently more rare, have not been described as precisely, and are not studied as separate groups. Frequently, studies will lump together true autistics with other children who show bizarre behavior, making interpretations of the results difficult. Many other methodological problems present themselves in research in this area. Severe difficulties in achieving and maintaining cooperation have been addressed in various ways. These include using several adaptation sessions, enlisting a parent or teacher to stay with or hold a child during testing, giving children a sedative, testing during sleep, or testing only more cooperative and/or older subjects. Autistic children usually score in the retarded range on intelligence tests, so some studies have included a comparison group matched on IQ or mental age. Because of the methodological problems, sample sizes in experimental studies tend to be quite small. Despite these difficulties, several replicated psychophysiological findings have emerged, and there seems to have been some progress in understanding autism.

Autonomic Measures

Few studies have been reported on electrodermal activity in autistic children. Bernal and Miller (1970) studied the SCOR to 15 68-dB tones in 20 children who met the criteria for autism and 20 controls. The autistics had smaller SCORs on the first block of three trials but were not different on later trials, by which time habituation was nearly complete for both groups. Similar results were obtained with SCORs to a series of visual stimuli (raising the room illumination), to a series of tones of different intensities, and to photic stimuli. No differences occurred in response to novel stimuli presented after the habituation trials, nor were there differences in SCL, SSCRs, or slope of SCL during the series of stimuli. Quite different results were obtained by Palkovitz and Wiesenfeld (1980). They found very significantly higher SCL and SSCR frequency in their 10 autistics as compared to normal children, despite several sessions of adaptation to the situation for the patients. No SCOR differences were found to any of the stimuli.

Still different results are reported by James and Barry (1981) in a study of 40 unmedicated autistic children, diagnosed by the perhaps overinclusive Coleman (1976) criteria. The investigators found very striking ($p < .001$) slow SCOR habituation to both auditory and visual stimulation in autistics as compared to age- and IQ-matched retardates and to age-matched normals. A respiratory OR—increase in period of the respiratory cycle containing the stimulus—showed similar results. Cephalic and peripheral vasomotor responses were larger in autistics, but failed to habituate in any group (James & Barry, 1980b, 1981). These authors emphasize the perceptual or stimulus registration aspects of their results. Excessively slow habituation has also been considered as an arousal index (Lader, 1975). Unfortunately, James and Barry (1980b) do not report base levels. In any event, these clear-cut results suggest that there is a definable group of psychotic children (diagnosed by relatively inclusive criteria) for whom slow habituation, at least under some testing conditions, is a prominent feature.

Using more conservative diagnostic criteria, Stevens and Gruzelier (1984) found some evidence of slowed habituation in autistics compared to either normals or retarded subjects with careful matching for chronological and mental age. Although a trials-to-habituation measure did not differentiate the groups, the statistics showed trends for slower reductions in amplitude over trials. SCL was not higher than normal in the autistics. Autistic children diagnosed by similar criteria were compared with normals, retardates, and child psychiatric patients using an SCOR paradigm by van Engeland (1984). The major finding was that the autistic group had significantly more SCOR nonresponders (about 30%) to 85 dB tones than the other groups (<5%). There was also some evidence of larger amplitude SCORs and fast recovery half-time in the autistics but no differences in SSCR rate or trials to habituation. Thus, there is much disagreement among even studies with similar diagnostic criteria.

Several studies have found higher HR in at least some autistic children. Walter, Aldridge, Cooper, O'Gorman, McCallum, and Winter (1971) reported tachycardia in some autistics. D. J. Cohen and Johnson (1977) reported tachycardia in a majority of autistics, and Kootz and Cohen (1981) also found significantly high HR in autistics. Kootz, Marinelli, and Cohen (1982) found a subgroup of low functioning autistics to have a significant decrease in HR with repeated testing, suggesting that tachycardia may be elicited by the test situation in some subjects. Lake, Ziegler, and Murphy (1977) found marginally ($p < .10$) higher HR in an autistic group than in controls. This study also obtained higher DBP and plasma NE levels in autistics.

In a study of the HROR, Miller and Bernal (1971) found some evidence of a smaller HR decelerative response in their autistic subjects, but different measurement techniques produced different results, depending on the type of stimulus. Palkovitz and Wiesenfeld (1980) report significant HR deceleration following each of their three types of stimuli in controls, but a small tendency for acceleration was shown in the autistics. Paradoxically, the HROR seemed to differentiate the stimulus types better in the patients than in the controls.

A finding of a lack of correlation between different physiological indices of orienting in a heterogeneous group of disturbed children with autistic features was reported by Walter et al. (1971). They noted that 13 out of 30 of their subjects failed to give "nonspecific" electrocortical responses to auditory or visual stimuli. However, in most of these, an autonomic (SC or HR) response was present. Two cases with cortical responses failed to give autonomic responses. This is an unsystematic report that does not present the actual data, but it points to an area of possible importance that warrants systematic study.

These studies suggest that if a difference between autistic and control children is to be found, it will be in the direction of higher ANS base levels in the autistic group. Strikingly conflicting results have been obtained on the OR. However, different indices are likely to give different results in the same children at the same time. Clinical observations emphasize marked within-subject variability in states of activity, attention deployment, and behavioral reactions of stimuli in autistic children. It would seem critical in future research to investigate the effects of state or concurrent activity on physiological baselines and ORs, or at least to attempt to control it.

The problem of control of activity level is especially critical in interpreting one of the well-replicated findings in autism: greater HR variability. This finding was originally reported by MacCulloch and Williams (1971), using telemetered HR in freely moving autistic, retarded, and normal children. Autistics showed significantly higher HR variability than the other two groups, and retardates showed significantly higher variability than the normal controls. A strong argument is advanced for interpretation of this finding in terms of brain stem pathology, but the question of the lack of concurrent measurement of motor activity is also raised.

An attempt to control state was made in a study of HR and HR variability by C. Hutt, Forrest, and Richer (1975). Telemetered HR was recorded during task performance, other activity, and stereotyped behaviors in nine autistic children and under the first two conditions in two normal control groups, one of which consisted of 2-year-olds. The mean age of the autistics was 8.8 years. The autistics had higher HR variability than the controls under the two conditions common to all groups. Variability of HR decreased during task performance in all groups, but significantly more in the autistic group, a finding attributed to the effects of workload. Interestingly, HR variability was much greater in the autistic group during stereotyped activities, and the authors noted that HR level dropped significantly after an episode of stereotypy. This is taken to support the position, based on other evidence, that stereotypies are more likely to occur in threatening situations and that they function to reduce arousal.

The finding of higher HR variability in autistic children than in retarded controls was confirmed using telemetered HR in a classroom setting (Graveling & Brooke, 1978). Lowering the environmental stimulation was reported to have increased HR and HR variability in only the autistic group, but the statistical analyses are questionable.

A study of the portion of HR variability that is controlled by respiratory activity was done in a mixed group of psychotic children by Piggott, Ax, Bamford, and Fetzner (1973). HR and respiration were measured under conditions of spontaneous breathing and controlled breathing to various depths. Spontaneous respiration was faster and shallower in the psychotic group. The major findings were that HR acceleration was not sustained as long with increasing depth of respiration for the psychotic group as for the controls, and that the duration of the lags between respiratory changes and HR changes was less consistent in the psychotic group. The conclusion that the regulating mechanism of sinus arrhythmia is less well coordinated in the psychotic group is consistent with the conclusion of a general dysfunction in HR control from the HR variability findings.

It will be recalled that C. Hutt et al. (1975) interpreted their HR variability data in terms of "workload"—a concept that is similar or perhaps identical to "attention." Autistic children unquestionably have a severe disorder of attention. An attempt to study this psychophysiologically was made by D. J. Cohen and Johnson (1977), by means of the idea that during sensory intake tasks FBF decreases and forearm vascular resistance (FVR) increases, while the opposite reactions occur during tasks in which rejection of sensory stimuli facilitates performance (R. B. Williams, Bittker, Buchsbaum, & Wynne, 1975). Autistic children were compared with normal adults and children and with a heterogeneous group of nonpsychotic, atypical children. Great difficulty was reported in involving the autistics in the tasks. On the two tasks performed by all children (both of the sensory intake variety), no significant changes were found in any group, with the values for the autistics very similar to those for controls. When all tasks actually done were averaged, however, FBF was higher and FVR lower for both disturbed groups than for controls; these results indicate more sensory rejection, even though the autistics did not do any sensory rejection tasks. Kootz and Cohen (1981) reported that autistics did not respond to the sensory intake task of reaction time in the expected direction as did the controls. However, RT was very poor, indicating a lack of cooperation. Kootz et al. (1982) found more of a sensory rejection pattern in low-functioning autistics compared to high-functioning autistics who had fairly good RT.

A conclusion supported by these studies and by C. Hutt et al. (1975) is that when autistic children are able to perform a task, they have a normal cardiovascular response. However, Lake et al. (1977) found that autistics had a significantly smaller HR increment than controls to a postural change from supine to standing; D. J. Cohen and Johnson (1977) noted that the high HR in autistics was, unlike that of controls, unrelated to environmental demands, but no statistical comparisons were given. Similarly, Kootz and Cohen (1981) reported small HR responses to tasks in autistics. These studies do not refute the generalization since high base levels in autistics have not been compensated for and/or task performance is grossly impaired.

Electrocortical Studies

Continuous EEG

Clinical EEG findings in autism have been reviewed by Small (1975) and by James and Barry (1980a). The incidence of abnormal EEGs in autism has ranged from 10% to 81%, with an average of 51%; significantly more abnormalities were reported in autistic children than in controls in the five studies where controls were tested (Small, 1975). These appear to be usually bilateral and independent of handedness (Tsai & Stewart, 1982). There are several reports of spike, spike-and-wave, and other epileptiform abnormalities (James & Barry, 1980a), most notably from a large series of patients diagnosed and tested by DeMyer, Barton, DeMyer, Norton, Allen, and Steele

(1973). These findings are noteworthy, since about 25% of autistic children are reported to develop seizure disorders by late adolescence (Ornitz & Ritvo, 1973). However, this group also found abnormal EEGs in 54% of nonautistic "hospitalized mentally ill" children and in 40% of nonpsychotic retardates, compared to 64% of autistic children (Small, 1975). This type of abnormality is by no means a universal finding in studies of autism.

Similarly, conflicting evidence exists on characteristic EEG frequency: S. J. Hutt, Hutt, Lee, and Ounsted (1965) reported less alpha and more low-voltage fast activity in psychotic children than in controls, while Stevens and Milstein (1970) found unusually persistent alpha in the target group. Itil, Simeon, and Coffin (1976) confirmed the S. J. Hutt *et al.* findings in a mixed group of psychotic children (only 36% of whom were autistic), using a computerized frequency analysis, but they also found more slow activity in the psychotic group. EEG frequency analysis may reflect state differences more than neuropathology; this is reflected in the observations of S. J. Hutt *et al.* (1965) that desynchronization was less in an unstructured environment (an empty room) and greatest when performing a task with an adult and during episodes of stereotypic behavior. However, Small (1975) summarizes several observations indicating that the EEGs of autistics are less variable, less subject to environmental influences, and more symmetrical than normal. More careful attention to state variables may help resolve some of the conflicting findings. The effects of stimulus modality on alpha abundance were studied by Hermelin and O'Connor (1968). Autistics had more adaption of alpha than controls or children with Down's syndrome after 2 min of intermittent light stimulation, but less alpha during either continuous or intermittent tone stimulation; these results suggest more arousal from sounds than from lights in autistics. This modality difference is in apparent conflict with the Bernal and Miller (1970) study of the SCOR, but it may be due to methodological differences.

One state that has received some attention is that of sleep. However, findings have been mostly negative with respect to either the distribution of sleep stages or the detection of EEG abnormalities (Ornitz, Ritvo, & Walter, 1965), although, as pointed out by Small (1975), clinical EEG abnormalities are best detected at this time.

ERPs

Given the susceptibility of ERPs to artifact from muscle activity and eye movements, and the need for subjects to cooperate over a period of several minutes, it is not surprising that there are few studies reported of ERPs in childhood psychosis. There is agreement among the published studies that psychotic children have impaired ERPs, but less agreement as to the specifics.

Small (1971), emphasizing the difficulty in obtaining valid data, found autistics to have discernible visual ERPs, but they were of low amplitude. Auditory ERPs were even more impaired. Walter *et al.* (1971) noted the absence of "nonspecific responses" to visual and auditory stimuli in a minority of children with autistic features. This suggests that the majority did give responses. No amplitude comparisons were given. In two studies of conditioning, Lelord, Laffont, Jusseaume, and Stephant (1973) and Martineau, Laffont, Bruneau, Roux, and Lelord (1980) found smaller auditory ERPs in autistic and retarded children than in controls, whether or not the auditory stimulus was paired with light.

Two studies (Novick, Kurtzberg, & Vaughan, 1979; Novick, Vaughan, Kurtzberg, & Simon, 1980) used the strategem of testing adolescent subjects with a history of autistic traits in order to obtain data reliable enough for precise analysis of waveforms. There were no deficits in early components (P60 and N100), but the autistic subjects had small auditory P200 as compared to age-matched controls. In two paradigms designed to elicit P300 (pitch discrimination and missing stimulus), the autistics performed the tasks adequately but had markedly smaller P300s. Both P200 and P300 for combined conditions separated the five patients from the five controls without overlap. These findings are attributed to a defect in the inferior parietal cortex, and the similarity with data in adult schizophrenia is described. However, in a study on adolescents (Niwa, Ohta, & Yamazaki, 1983), all four autistic subjects showed an increment in P300 to the rare stimuli in an oddball paradigm and no gross abnormalities in amplitude.

ERP studies during sleep have been carried out by Ornitz and his colleagues. Using a two-click ERP procedure, Ornitz, Forsythe, Tanguay, Ritvo, de la Pena, and Ghahremani (1974) failed to find differences in recovery functions during REM sleep in autistic and normal children. However, in another study from this group (Tanguay, 1976), controls consistently had larger ERPs over the right hemisphere, whereas autistics as a group did not; these results suggest an absence or delay of hemispheric specialization.

Studies of the CNV have been plagued by technical difficulties (Small, 1971). However, Small, DeMyer, and Milstein (1971) were able to obtain normal CNVs in their autistic subjects, although they did not vary with stimulus familiarity, as was true of controls. In contrast, Walter *et al.* (1971) noted the absence of CNV in many of their cases. These tended to be the patients with pronounced autonomic excitement and anxious behavior. Lelord *et al.* (1973) and Martineau *et al.* (1980) observed that autistics were more likely to show a CNV-like slow negative potential following a tone during and after tone–light pairing (with no task requirement) than were normals or retarded subjects. In the Martineau *et al.* study, eye movements were recorded and ruled out as a source of artifact. Thus, the CNV is not necessarily impaired in autism, but it may be elicited in atypical situations.

In a study of schizophrenic children (Strandburg, Marsh, Brown, Asarnow, & Guthrie, 1984), ERPs to a span of apprehension task were studied using a principal component analysis. The patients, who were impaired on the task, were also impaired on CNV, N1, P3 and slow wave components and showed fewer changes as a function of task difficulty than controls. This pattern of impairment seems closer to that of adult schizophrenics than to that of autistic children.

BSEPs

The hypothesis of brain stem dysfunction as an important etiological factor in autism has been entertained for some time, due largely to the well-confirmed findings of vestibular dysfunction, as evidenced by the lack of postrotational nystagmus in these children (Colbert, Koegler, & Markham, 1959). Recently several studies have used the BSEP to test this hypothesis more directly. The first reported study using this technique (Student & Sohmer, 1978) found an abnormally long latency for wave I, which reflects activity in the auditory (eighth) nerve. They also reported significantly longer brain stem transmission times (difference between waves I and IV) in autistics; however, in a reanalysis of their data prompted by discovery of technical difficulties, (Student & Sohmer, 1979), this difference, while still present, was no longer significant. However, Rosenblum, Arick, Krug, Stubbs, Young, and Pelson (1980) found significantly longer latencies of waves II and IV in six autistics than in six age-matched controls (age range 5–16 years), as well as longer transmission time between waves I and V.

Similar findings have been reported by Skoff, Mirsky, and Turner (1980), who recorded BSEPs from stimuli to each ear in 19 autistic and 20 control children. The autistics had significantly longer transmission time for stimuli delivered to each ear and longer III–V interpeak latencies for the left ear. On a case-by-case basis, 56% of the autistic sample had one or more abnormally long latency, most of them for left-ear stimulation. A further analysis of clinical data for these cases (D. Fein, Skoff, & Mirsky, 1981) showed that the patients with abnormal BSEPs were significantly more likely to be socially aloof, have long attention spans, attempt to maintain environmental sameness, exhibit ritualistic or compulsive behavior, and have "islands of good functioning." No differences were found in language, perception, or motor behavior. Thus, the subjects with evidence of brain

stem dysfunction were more typically autistic (i.e., they met narrower diagnostic criteria for this syndrome).

Further confirmation of delayed BSEP peaks has been reported in a carefully controlled study by Tanguay, Edwards, Buchwald, Schwafel, and Allen (1982). Increased latency for wave I was present in only the right ear. Slow transmission time occurred in both ears, but this was rarely abnormal for both ears in the same subject. Of 14 patients, 8 had at least one clearly abnormal transmission time. The latest confirmation of delayed BSEP in autism (Gillberg, Rosenhall, & Johansson, 1983) reported that 33% of autistic patients had abnormal wave V latencies but that they were not lateralized. There was an association of delayed BSEP with muscular hypotonia which may be related to vestibular damage.

Summary and Conclusions

Research on autism and childhood psychoses is perhaps more difficult than in any other type of psychopathology, because of the difficulties in obtaining clean data from subjects whose behavior is difficult to control and because of problems in diagnosing and subtyping this heterogeneous group of children. Nevertheless, there are certain findings that receive a modest or better amount of support.

Electrodermal and HR indices of arousal have sometimes been found to be high in these children. Although there are negative findings in this area, lower than normal values have not been reported. Thus most autistic and psychotic children may have chronically high levels of autonomic activity, but a subgroup may be at a normal level. Alternatively, it may be hypothesized that these children exhibit high ANS activity some of the time. Both of these hypotheses might suggest a dysfunction in inhibitory control mediated by the reticular formation or limbic mechanisms. A more conservative interpretation of the data, however, is that a subject who has aversive reactions to other people and who does not understand what is being done to him or her might be expected to exhibit high arousal. In support of this latter view is the evidence that none of the three studies that telemetered HR in free settings found a difference in mean HR between autistics and controls. While the latter hypothesis would be very difficult to refute, because of the problem of proving that subjects are not upset merely by the experimental situation itself, more studies of the effects of different spontaneous and induced behavioral states on tonic ANS levels would seem indicated, using telemetry of HR and other variables if possible.

One twice-replicated finding with no conflicting evidence to date is that of high spontaneous HR variability in autism; this suggests, at one level, a diffuse attentional focus, and, at another, a dysfunction in brain stem or peripheral regulating mechanisms. Although differences in concurrent activity levels cannot be entirely ruled out as contributing to these results, it might be expected that activity would raise tonic HR as well as variability. This was not the case in the studies finding high variability. In addition, studies on HA children, a group high in motor activity, have found no differences in HR levels or variability under resting conditions (Zahn et al., 1975). This high spontaneous HR variability stands in contrast to the evidence from other studies of sluggish responsivity of tonic HR to postural and of HR and respiratory changes and to task performance. Direct comparison of spontaneous and elicited HR changes in the same subjects would seem indicated. It would seem especially important to study the frequency components of HR variability in these children, since differential sympathetic and parasympathetic influences on different frequency components have been demonstrated (Akselrod et al., 1981). The related method of cross-spectral analysis of HR and respiration (Porges et al., 1981) should be useful in testing hypotheses about brain stem dysfunction.

Studies of physiological responding to discrete sensory stimuli have produced conflicting results; however, with one major exception (James & Barry, 1980b), the positive results that have been obtained have been in the direction of either lower or atypical responding in autistic subjects. This holds for both autonomic and ERP measures. Very little can be said about stimulus modality differences in responsivity, since the small amount of evidence on this topic is mostly negative. The data are somewhat inconsistent with clinical reports (1) that autistics swing between hyporeactivity and hyperreactivity to stimuli, and (2) that they are particularly prone to deficits in auditory perception. Despite clinical reports of the lack of a startle response in these children, no systematic research on this has been done. Studies in which stimulus parameters (intensity, duration, quality, and modality) are varied while children are in different behavior states are needed to determine relationships between physiological and behavioral effects of stimuli.

Clinical EEG findings are so varied as to permit no definite conclusions. Some of the findings, such as reduced alpha abundance, may reflect state differences rather than indicating neuropathology per se. However, brain abnormalities (localizable lesions and enlarged lateral ventricles) were found on CT scans for 53% of 17 autistic subjects by Damasio, Maurer, Damasio, and Chui (1980), and several "normal" scans were found to have unusual hemispheric asymmetries. These findings are roughly similar to those in adult schizophrenia. Damasio et al. (1980) have concluded, "If there is a relation between the autism syndrome and brain structure, the pathogenesis of autism must depend on different causes and mechanisms, albeit acting on the same neural system and rendering it dysfunctional" (p. 508). This could apply as well to the EEG findings. However, Hier, LeMay, and Rosenberger (1979) report only lateral asymmetries in CT scans: Over twice as many autistic subjects (57%) as retarded or neurological controls had a larger right than left parieto-occipital region. Although this may or may not relate to language difficulties, as the authors claim, it does suggest more attention to lateral electrocortical and ANS differences in these subjects—research area that has received practically no attention except BSEP studies. The CT scan findings, however, stand in marked contrast to the bilateral EEG abnormalities and symmetrical EEG patterns reported.

The best-confirmed findings on autism (vestibular dysfunction, greater HR variability, and longer brain stem transmission time) all implicate neuropathology of the brain stem as an etiological factor. Brain stem dysfunction could also be responsible for the disturbances of perception, modulation of sensory input, motility, and perhaps arousal seen in autism. The finding that autistics with abnormal BSEPs had the more classical "Kanner" pattern of symptomotology (D. Fein et al., 1981) suggests a specific relationship between a neurological deficit in the auditory pathway and a behavior pattern, but it also shows severe autistic-type behavior pathology in subjects without demostrated dysfunction in this area. It would be important to confirm this result and to determine whether other evidence of brain stem dysfunction—say, in the vestibular or cardiovascular regulatory systems—is related to a different clinical picture.

The research and clinical findings on autism can be seen as compatible with a model of brain stem dysfunction in which different patterns of regulating centers are affected in different children. However, there may be subtypes of this syndrome without brain stem involvement.

Progress in understanding the phenomenology and etiology of autism may be faciliated by studies on adolescent and older subejcts who have clear histories of infantile autism. Such studies are likely to produce clean data and to permit study of the psychophysiology of higher cognitive functioning. However, the validity of using older age groups should be established by replication of some of the key studies, such as those on vestibular functioning and brain stem transmission time, to see whether these dysfunctions are still present.

One great problem appearing in the studies reviewed here as a whole is the lack of direct comparison between autism (in the classical sense of early infantile autism) and nonautistic early-onset psychosis. This lack points up the difficulties of differential diagnosis in this area. It may be that there are too few children who meet the criteria for psychosis, and who

have few autistic features and few or no evident organic signs, to make up a separate study group. There
seems to be some agreement that autism is present
within the first 2 years of life (Ornitz & Ritvo, 1976)
and that infantile and later-onset child psychoses have
different genetic relationships to adult schizophrenia
(Fish, 1977), so that simply an age-of-onset breakdown might provide a meaningful basis of group separation.

Psychophysiological investigations should certainly
have a role in validating any subtype classification
made on case history or clinical grounds. Alternatively, subgroups could be formed on the basis of one
or another biological marker, such as was done using
the BSEP by D. Fein *et al.* (1981). Clinical and physiological differences between the subgroups would indicate the validity of the marker. Both of these strategies suggest a multivariate approach and larger sample
sizes than are usually found in research in autism.
Enough progress has been made in this field to suggest
that such an approach is not premature.

ANXIETY, NEUROSES, AND MISCELLANEOUS CONDITIONS

Theoretical Considerations

In no other group of disorders has the study of autonomic and somatic functioning played as prominent a
role as in anxiety states and those neuroses in which
anxiety is a prominent symptom. This importance
starts at the diagnostic level. In DSM-III, motor tension and autonomic hyperactivity, along with subjective and behavioral signs, are the categories of symptoms listed for a positive diagnosis of "generalized
anxiety disorder." Three of the four categories are
necessary for a definite diagnosis.

"Panic disorder" is also diagnosed in part by a
number of somatic symptoms, but the list is different
from that given for "anxiety disorder." It should be
kept in mind that clinically, for both disorders, the
assessment of the psychophysiological symptoms is
made from the subjective experiences of the patient
and/or behavioral observation, rather than by direct
measurement. Thus, the distinction between anxiety
states and panic attacks seems based not only on
intensity or duration, but on a qualitative difference
in the phenomenology of the disorders. This is further
complicated in that some persons with frequent panic
attacks also develop agoraphobia. The question of
whether the somatic manifestations of these disorders
are also qualitatively different is amenable to objective
psychophysiological investigation.

Anxiety, of course, plays an important role in
many other neurotic disorders. Investigations of ANS
activity in various neuroses have been undertaken,

with the idea that the findings could throw light on
the role of anxiety and fear in these disorders. The
question of the generality or situational specificity of
high ANS activity is particularly germane here. Similarly, investigation of changes in ANS activity during
treatment, especially behavioral treatment, has been a
popular area, since it bears on the theoretical formulations underlying various therapeutic approaches. In
addition, it might be possible to use psychophysiological measures as objective indices of the course or
outcome of treatment.

The use of such methods to investigate the role of
anxiety in a given disorder, or in treatment, is not
without conceptual problems. It is sometimes assumed by non-psychophysiologists that indices of
ANS activity are measures of anxiety. However, the
quite imperfect correlations among different autonomic measures and between these and subjective and
behavioral states makes this assumption questionable.
The DSM-III criteria for diagnosing anxiety disorder
recognize this in requiring that only three of the four
manifestations be met, so that a positive diagnosis
may be made in the absence of extreme ANS activity
(as assessed subjectively and behaviorally). This
scheme is consistent with the increasingly popular
notion of anxiety as a multifaceted state, having behavioral, subjective and somatic aspects that are
loosely tied together. Such a conceptualization is consistent with the lack of strong relationships among the
various components of anxiety and is also consistent
with the obvious fact that high levels of ANS activity
can accompany states other than anxiety (although the
patterning may be somewhat different in different
states). The subjective report has usually been given
criterion status (Lader, 1975), in part because of the
nonspecificity of the other indicators, and will probably continue to have that role despite the equal weighting given the four components by DSM-III.

The psychophysiological study of anxiety and fear
disorders is important also because of the light it can
shed on the normal and subclinical manifestations of
these emotions. In no other form of psychopathology
can a continuum between normal and pathological
states be conceptualized as clearly. This is especially
important because of the key roles of anxiety and fear
in personality theories and as explanatory constructs
in many areas of normal psychology. This problem is
beyond the scope of the present discussion, however.
This section, like previous sections, focuses on psychophysiological investigations in patients and on the
effects of various treatments–pharmacological, surgical, and behavioral.

Psychophysiology of Anxiety Neurosis

Somatic aspects of neuroses have been studied intensively since the early part of this century. The litera-

ture before 1975 has been reviewed by Lader (1975), who points out that many of these studies are unsatisfactory: They lump a heterogeneous set of conditions under the rubric of "psychoneurosis," so that possible correlations with specific clinical features, such as anxiety, are not obtainable. However, there are also many studies in which it is possible to ascertain the influence of anxiety on a wide variety of somatic measures.

Baseline Studies

The literature on baseline measures holds few surprises. Electrodermal measures have been among the most widely studied, and although there have been some exceptions, the evidence is generally in favor of increased palmar sweat gland activity, measured both directly and electrically, in anxiety neurotics compared to normal controls and to other types of patients where they have been included for comparison. The best-confirmed index is the frequency of SSCRs. High SCL, slow habituation of the OR, and slower decline of SCL during rest periods are also well confirmed.

Among cardiovascular measures, HR has frequently, but not always, been found to be higher (but not lower) and sometimes more variable in anxiety states. Similar results have been obtained with blood pressure. The HR level difference, along with higher SSCRs, may persist during sleep (Monti, Altier, Prandro, & Gil, 1975). Reduced cutaneous blood flow (greater peripheral vasoconstriction) has been shown in anxiety states, and a series of studies (Kelly, 1980; Kelly, Brown, & Shaffer, 1970; Kelly & Martin, 1969) has shown that increased FBF (increased blood supply to the forearm muscles) is a strong correlate of anxiety in a variety of neurotic conditions. These studies have typically found FBF to be superior to other cardiovascular and electrodermal variables in this regard. Surprisingly little work has been reported on other ANS measures. In particular, pupillometry would seem to be a useful technique; however, only one study of 11 mixed neurotic patients appears to have been reported, with negative results for resting or stressed pupil size (Rubin, 1964). However, Wenger's (1966) studies on psychoneurotic samples using his extensive battery of ANS indices, which yields a score on autonomic balance, showed that these groups—"selected to include patients who manifested anxiety" (p. 179)—had scores significantly in the sympathetic direction as compared to controls.

Among other somatic measures, EMG has been most extensively studied. Predictably, anxiety patients have been found to have higher muscle tension than controls, but in some studies, this was only apparent during periods of extra environmental stimulation with white noise. Respiration has been reported to be more irregular and faster in neurotic patients.

Analyses of EEG frequency have typically shown less alpha and more beta in anxiety patients. Bond, James, and Lader (1974a), using a frequency analyzer, reported higher voltage at all frequencies for anxious patients, but the greatest difference was for the beta band. However, relative to the total voltage, alpha was reduced in the neurotics. Higher-amplitude EEGs in unspecified psychoneurotics were also found by Shagass, Straumanis, and Overton (1979). No difference in mean EEG frequency occurred, but frequency variability was lower in the patients. EEG spectra during an RT task were studied in unspecified neurotic patients and controls by Mantanus, Timset-Berthier, Gerono, and Von Frenckell (1981). The patients had slightly but significantly more beta and less theta and delta during the 1-sec foreperiods, but in pretrial recordings only the difference in beta was significant. However, Flor-Henry, Yeudall, Koles, and Howarth (1979) reported only minimal differences in EEG spectra between obsessional patients and controls.

ORs

As in other areas, one of the more popular paradigms in studying anxiety states has been habituation of the SCOR. The usual finding, over the years, has been slower habituation in patients with anxiety states than in controls (Lader, 1975). In an intensive examination of this paradigm using 100-dB tones, Lader and Wing (1966) found smaller SCRs in anxiety neurotics than in controls to the first five stimuli, but smaller SCRs in the controls on the later trials. Habituation rate, measured as the slope of the function relating log stimulus number to SCR amplitude, was greatly reduced in the patients, even when corrected for the initial amplitude as measured by the intercept of the function. The controls had a more rapid decline over time in SCL, but there were no differences in the course of SSCRs, HR, or EMG. FPVORs also failed to differentiate the clinical groups. More recently, the result of slow SCOR habituation in anxiety states has been replicated by Lader (1967), Horvath and Meares (1979), and M. Raskin (1975). These studies all presented 100-dB stimuli to their subjects. It may be noteworthy that in one of the failures to find slow SCOR habituation in anxious patients (Tan, 1964), only moderately intense stimuli were used; however, all the patients also carried a diagnosis of depression, so this is not a "clean" disconfirmation. On the other hand, significant correlations between rated anxiety and SCOR frequency were reported in a large mixed sample of anxious and depressed patients (Johnstone et al., 1981). However, negative results in SCOR habituation were reported by Hart (1974), who presented anxious patients and control subjects with 30 1000-Hz tones, 10 each at 50, 75 or 100 dB. The patients did not differ from controls in SCOR amplitude or habituation, although their SSCR rate was higher. Hart did find a component of the HROR, the initial deceleration, to habituate in normals for the two low-intensity tones but not in the patients. Methodological differences that might account for these disparate results include the exclusively male composition of the sample, the intermixture of different intensity tones in the same series, or, more importantly, the use of an adaptation session prior to the main experiment. Unfortunately, no data are reported from the adaptation session. Hart (1974) attributes his results to slower habituation in his controls, compared to those of Lader and Wing (1966), rather than to faster habituation in his patients.

Some work exists on other indices of habituation. A unique method was used by Brierley (1969), who measured FBF during periods of stimulation by a "ticking clock" amplified to 80–85 dB and during interspersed quiet periods. Similar to the SCR results, he found a significantly diminished response to the first few stimuli and slow habituation of the FBF during stimulus periods in agoraphobic patients as compared to controls. Chattopadhyay, Cooke, Toone, and Lader (1980) investigated ERPs to frequent and rare tones and SCRs and alpha attentuation to visual stimuli. There were no significant differences in habituation in anxiety neurotics compared to controls, but when subjects were separated on the basis of state anxiety, irrespective of diagnosis, high-anxiety subjects habituated the most slowly on N180, alpha attenuation, and SCR, but not on P300 or on the other ERPs. Thus, there seems to be some generality to the slow-habituation finding, if not complete replicability. Aside from Hart's (1974) study, there seem to have been no attempts to adapt subjects to the experimental situation by preceding it with adaptation sessions. However, Chattopadhyay et al. (1980) tried the reverse procedure with normal subjects by testing them under a threat of a strong shock. This strategem increased baseline arousal measures, compared to a control session, without affecting habituation.

Establishing the generality of the slow-habituation finding is especially important, since it is a critical underpinning of the Lader and Wing theory of the etiology of anxiety states. One assumption of this theory is that ANS activation and habituation rate vary inversely. This is shown by comparisons of patients and controls and by similar dose–response effects of a benzodiazepine drug and a barbiturate. On the basis of data from a study of monozygotic and dizygotic twins, habituation rate is also assumed to be a genetically influenced trait. The notion is that if a slow habituator is exposed to high levels of environmental stimulation, habituation will be reduced to nil and the high activation will be perpetuated indefinitely through a positive feedback process, even after removal of the original eliciting stimulation. It is speculated that enhanced conditioning and generalization in states of high activation lead to triggering of an anxiety reaction by many stimuli.

An extension of these views is made by Beech and Perigault (1977) in a theory of obsessional disorders. This theory makes the assumption, based primarily on the authors' clinical experience, that obsessionals show marked fluctations in arousal, rather than being in a steady state of high arousal, as implied by the Lader and Wing theory of anxiety states. Beech and Perigault speculate that when arousal reaches a critical high level, a person may invent a "reason" for the accompanying subjective state of intense discomfort. Obsessive ruminations and rituals are learned on the basis of fortuitous connections accompanying spontaneous waning of the high activation state. The particular features of ANS activity characteristic of obsessionals that make them prone to this disorder are thought to be (in addition to ANS lability) rapid (one-trial) conditionability, which would facilitate establishment of the initial connection, and slow habituation, which should strengthen resistance to extinction of the obsessive behavior. Although the point is not explicitly stated, if the obsessive behavior is paired only sometimes with arousal reductions, this, too, should favor its maintenance through partial reinforcement. Beech and Perigault present only minimal objective evidence for their theory. On the basis of data on a small number of cases, it is their impression that obsessives show slower SC habituation and better one-trial conditioning than either controls or severely ill phobic patients, but may not differ from the phobics on activation. The latter finding is supported by other evidence in the literature that is reviewed in the next section, but there are no controlled studies that address the other points.

Both of the theories described above give a central role to a biological trait of slow habituation. Other theories of anxiety neurosis emphasize cognitive factors as primary. An attempt to test the role of cognition in the Lader and Wing habituation paradigm was made by M. Raskin (1975). The thoughts and feelings of the subjects during the procedure were assessed by means of a postsession questionnaire and interview. The Lader and Wing electrodermal results were replicated. The questionnaire produced negative results, but the interview revealed that many subjects (significantly more in the anxiety group than in the normal controls) attributed signal value to the tones. Of these subjects, none in either groups habituated. However, of three formerly anxious patients who had remitted, none habituated, nor did they attribute signal value to the tones. This study suggests that unrealistic cognitions about the stimuli may be important but not necessary to retard habituation. However, the discrepancy between the inquiry via questionnaire and interview is puzzling, and suggests that the question may have been asked in the wrong way by one or the other method. It is possible also that under the pressure of the interview, post hoc attributions of significance were made by some subjects to "explain" the discomfort the stimuli produced. This explanation is similar to the idea proposed by Beech and Perigault (1977) for obsessives. However, a cognitive rather than an arousal explanation of slow habituation is also consistent with the finding of Chattopadhyay et al. (1980) that increased activation per se produced by the threat of a shock may not retard habituation.

Aside from the classical OR paradigm, few data on phasic ANS responses to discrete stimuli seem to exist. No significant differences in SCRs to eyelid conditioning stimuli were found in anxiety neurotics compared to controls by Kelly and Martin (1969). In view of the questions raised earlier about the effects of significance attributed to OR stimuli by anxious subjects, it would be useful to try to exert some control over this by using stimuli with explicit signal value. In Hart's (1974) study, no differences in SCRs to signal stimuli (tone discrimination task) were found between anxiety patients and controls, but the patients showed less initial HR deceleration on just the first trial block. These results are similar to those obtained with nonsignal stimuli, suggesting that significance had little effect. Chattopadhyay, Bond, and Lader (1975) compared drug-free anxiety-state patients and controls on several SC variables during presentation of 64 clicks (passive condition), followed by 32 clicks to which a fast motor response was required (active condition). The patients had a significantly greater number of SCRs only in the passive condition, suggesting a smaller effect of significance in this group, but no distinction between spontaneous and elicited SCRs was made. This is perhaps the only study on anxiety states to measure SCR characteristics, but this was done for only four "clear and typical" SCRs for each condition. Amplitudes and onset angle of these SCRs were significantly greater in controls for just the active condition; offset angle was greater in controls for both conditions; and recovery half-time was nonsignificantly longer in the patients under the passive condition. Thus, the SCRs of the patients were more "sluggish," despite their higher SCL. In fact, high positive correlations (.70–.80) were obtained between SCL and recovery time for both groups in both conditions—a result that is inconsistent with the model of fast recovery associated with full sweat glands.

The small amount of ERP research on neurosis has not produced consistent findings. Shorter latencies for peaks between 100 and 280 msec, and a smaller amplitude for just P200–N280 for click ERPs, were reported for anxiety patients by Bond, James, and Lader (1974a), while Chattopadhyay et al. (1980) found no latency differences and large P300 in subjects with high state anxiety, independent of diagnosis. On the other hand, Crighel, Predescu, Matei, Nica, and Prica (1976), averaging after just 15 photic stimuli, found generally smaller and delayed peaks (except for P300) in neurotics, independent of whether they were high on anxiety and/or depression. However, P300 and N220 were both found to be smaller and of shorter latency in obsessional patients than in con-

trols (Beech, Ciesielski, & Gordon, 1983), partially confirming previous results. However, Shagass, Roemer, and Straumanis (1981) observed larger somatosensory ERPs in a mixed sample of neurotic patients than in controls in 2 of 18 comparisons, both from frontal leads. The emphasis in the Shagass et al. study is on the correlations between ERP and EEG amplitudes. For ERPs less than 100 msec, these were significantly positive for controls and insignificantly negative for neurotics—a confirmation of a previous finding. The authors speculate that a hypothetical process common to both the EEG and ERPs may be defective in neurosis.

The CNV in anxiety states has received some attention, chiefly from Walter's laboratory (Tecce, 1972). The CNV was smaller, more subject to reduction by distraction, and slower to be re-established after extinction in anxiety cases, all of whom were on anxiolytic drugs, than in controls. Since distracted normal subjects and nondistracted anxiety patients had about the same CNV amplitude (McCallum & Walter, 1968), an attentional difference between groups might be hypothesized as a critical factor in these results. However, similar results have not been obtained in obsessive patients, whose anxiety may be lower than that of patients in anxiety states (McCallum & Walter, 1968; Tecce, 1972. Sartory and Master (1984) in fact reported larger late CNVs and prolonged negativity in obsessives under some conditions. Negative results for the CNV in unspecified neurotics were obtained by Mantanus et al. (1984), although these patients had a reduced PINV.

That the role of anxiety may not be straightforward is suggested by two studies that involved presenting pictures of phobic objects to phobic patients. In one study (Dubrovsky, Solyom, & Barbas, 1978), the phobic scene was the imperative stimulus itself, which was switched off by the subject's response. In this case, phobic scenes elicited larger CNVs, longer PINVs, and faster RT than neutral scenes. In a study by Rizzo, Spadaro, Albani, and Morocutti (1983), the phobic stimulus was presented 5 sec before the CNV warning stimulus. In this case, CNV amplitude was reduced and PINV prolonged by phobic scenes. Assuming that in both studies the phobic scene condition was anxiety producing, then the one consistent effect of anxiety is PINV enhancement; the CNV apparently depended on task and incentive factors.

Reactions to Stress

Slow habituation implies a defective regulating mechanism of some sort. A defect in the regulation of physiological responses to stress was proposed some years ago by Malmo and Shagass (1952) on the basis of studies showing that psychoneurotic patients, most of whom had prominent anxiety symptoms, were equal to or higher than controls on cardiovascular and EMG reactions to pain and performance stresses, and that their response frequently tended to continue to increase under some conditions when that of controls began to decline. There are also a few reports in the older literature of a slow recovery from stress in neurotics (Lader, 1975), but there seems to have been surprisingly little work done on this.

More recent studies would question the empirical base of the Malmo–Shagass theory of poor regulation. Bond, James, and Lader (1974a) reported a lower tonic increase in SCL to an RT task in anxious patients than in controls. Kelly (1980) has consistently found lower cardiovascular response to mental arithmetic with harassment in a large number of patients with anxiety as a major or prominent symptom. In both these studies, however, stress increased the level of ANS activity in the controls up to the stressed level of the patients, so that the major difference in stress response could be accounted for by the high prestress values for the patients. These studies did not attempt to correct or control for differences in base level; indeed, the base-level differences were so great as to make such a correction dubious. However, the patients with monosymptomatic phobias studied by Kelly (1980) were not greatly different in their baseline measures from controls, yet their low stress response was similar to that of chronic anxiety patients who had high base levels of cardiovascular activity. This argues for the independence of base levels and stress response, at least in this case, but no further evidence of this is presented.

Independence of stressor effects and base levels is also suggested by a study on the effects of an injection of sodium lactate, a drug that produces severe anxiety or panic attacks in most anxiety patients (Kelly, Mitchell-Heggs, & Sherman, 1971). The infusion produced somewhat larger increases in FBF and HR in anxious patients than in controls, despite significantly higher baseline values for the patients; however, a mental arithmetic test, given later in the same session, produced greater increases in controls. This evidence is only suggestive, since differences between groups in change scores were not tested statistically, and it is possible that the greater response to the drug by the patients occurred despite an initial levels effect. These findings appear to cast doubt on the widely held view of an exaggerated response to stress in anxiety states. On the other hand, it could be argued that the general test situation is so stressful for these patients that the addition of a task does not make that much difference. Thus, the hypothesis of an exaggerated response to stress in anxiety states has not really been refuted by the stress studies. To do so, it will be necessary to show that psychophysiological recording procedures are not atypical with respect to their stressfulness in these patients. One approach to answering this question might be to give patients several sessions of adaptation to the recording procedure before introducing specific stimuli or stressful tasks. Patients might be tested in familiar surroundings rather than in a strange laboratory. Telemetry might be usefully employed in naturalistic settings to investigate the situation specificity of high ANS activation. Other techniques aimed to reduce baseline activation fall into the category of therapy and are discussed in a later section.

Comparisons of Diagnostic Groups

In many of the early studies, there was a distressing tendency to lump patients with a number of diagnoses into one group of "psychoneurotics" for comparison with controls. To the extent that there are real differences in psychophysiological functioning among different diagnostic groups, this strategy will, of course, produce different results, depending on the proportion of one or another type of patient in the total sample. Many of the more recent studies have avoided this pitfall either by focusing on patients with a specific diagnosis or by comparing several groups.

Two large-scale studies compared several groups. Lader (1967) compared patients ($N = 90$) with five diagnoses: anxiety with depression, anxiety state, agoraphobia, social phobia, and specific phobia. The last group consisted of patients terrified mainly of one or another small animal. Lader found that the first four groups were all similar in showing a high rate of SSCRs and slow habituation, while the specific phobics were at control levels. There was somewhat more differentiation among the groups on various anxiety ratings, but the specific phobics were clearly the lowest on nonspecific anxiety and the overt anxiety displayed in the test situation. Overt anxiety was also the only rating to correlate appreciably with the SC measures.

Using a somewhat different diagnostic breakdown, Kelly (1980) has reported differences in baseline cardiovascular functioning in several groups (total $N = 361$). He obtained results that were similar to Lader's (1967) findings with electrodermal variables, in that patients with diagnoses of chronic anxiety and agitated depression were the highest groups on all four dependent variables: FBF, HR, SBP, and DBP. A group labeled as displaying "phobic anxiety" was not significantly different from controls on any of the variables. These subjects were described as anxious only in certain situations (e.g., restaurants, small spaces), and not at other times (Kelly & Walter, (1969). Thus, this finding can be considered a limited confirmation and generalization of the Lader study. Interesting results were also obtained with other patient groups; unfortunately, statistical comparisons were made only between patient groups and controls, and not among different patient groups. Patients with obsessional neuroses, although appreciably lower than the highest two groups, were higher than controls at significant or marginally significant levels on all four variables. This finding gives some support to one of the assumptions on the Beech and Perigault (1977) theory of obsessions. However, no baseline physiological differences were found between a group of obsessive adolescents and age-matched controls (Rapoport, Elkins, Langer, Sceery, Buchsbaum, Gillin, Murphy, Zahn, Lake, Ludlow, & Mendelson, 1981), although the patients had smaller SCL changes due to task performance.

Another group in the intermediate range on some of Kelly's measures was that of patients with hysteria. The patients were slightly higher on FBF, significantly higher on HR, and no different on blood pressure than controls. This contrasts with other studies in the literature. Lader and Sartorius (1968) found hysterics who had conversion symptoms at the time of testing to be even higher on their electrodermal activation measures than anxious patients. These conflicting results may be due to clinical differences in the patients tested, since only a minority of Kelly's patients had conversion symptoms; the remainder had histrionic personalities (Kelly & Walter, 1968). Meares and Horvath (1972) made the distinction between acute hysterics with good premorbid adjustment and short-lived conversion symptoms, and patients whose hysterical symptoms were part of a long-term pattern of difficulties and were resistant to treatment. Acute hysterics were similar to controls, but the chronic hysterics had nonsignificantly higher HR and slower habituation than even patients with anxiety states (Horvath & Meares, 1979). The clinical distinction between acute and chronic hysteria received some confirmation in Lader's (1969) data, in that subjects with higher arousal indices and anxiety ratings showed poorer 3-year outcomes. These findings are important, because they would not be predicted from the classical clinical description of conversion hysteria as manifested by *la belle indifférence* (an apparent unconcern with one's condition). In this context, it is interesting that Lader and Sartorius found self-ratings of anxiety in their hysteria group to be significantly higher than those for patients with anxiety states, while on the experimenters' ratings, the hysterics were significantly lower in anxiety than the anxiety-state patients. Thus, the ANS results agreed with subjective ratings of anxiety better than with its behavioral expression. The similarity in the results of Lader and Sartorius, whose patients had conversion symptoms, and those of Meares and Horvath, whose patients were in remission, suggests a revision of the classical psychoanalytic idea that conversion symptoms protect against anxiety. This is a good example of how psychophysiological investigation, along with careful clinical ratings and case history material, can be used to test clinical hypotheses.

Evoked response techniques are used clinically to help diagnose hysterical sensory defects. There were some early reports of failure to obtain discernible ERPs to stimulation of sites affected by hysterical anesthesia, but these were not confirmed (Lader, 1975). Levy and Mashin (1973) showed that somatosensory ERPs to sites affected by hysterical anesthesia, compared to homologous unaffected areas, were attenuated in all nine of their cases if the stimulation was just suprathreshold or not directly over a sensory nerve, although ERPs were usually not absent. With supramaximal stimulation over a nerve, the two sites gave similar ERPs, but subjects did not perceive the stimuli on the affected side. These authors hypothesize that hysterical anesthesia involves both a reduction in sensory receptor sensitivity and a central mechanism that attenuates afferent input over a limited range of intensities. However, this mechanism may not hold for other sensory modalities (Lader, 1975).

Another interesting condition that has been studied psychophysiologically is depersonalization. However, this comes in several varieties: It can be secondary to such disorders as schizophrenia or temporal lobe epilepsy; it is sometimes diagnosed as a disorder in its own right when it is the primary symptom; or it can be a temporary state accompanying anxiety disorders. Lader (1975) gives two examples of episodes of depersonalization in patients with severe anxiety. Dramatic reductions in ANS arousal indices occurred during this state, accompanied by marked subjective changes. In addition to feelings of unreality, the subjects reported attenuation of sensory input, leading Lader to speculate that this state "may be linked to some emergency physiological mechanism, which counteracts excess arousal from sensory input by blocking that sensory input" (Lader, 1975, p. 192).

Patients with a diagnosis of primary idiopathic depersonalization were studied by Kelly (1980). In contrast to Lader's acute cases, these patients were suffering from a chronic condition with a poor prognosis (Kelly & Walter, 1968). They were found to be significantly higher than normals on state and trait anxiety measures but only moderately higher on FBF and blood pressure, although having significantly elevated HR. These dissimilar findings suggest that the acute and chronic forms of depersonalization are fundamentally different disorders, although there is a partial similarity between these results and those found in acute and chronic hysteria, and, to some extent, those for quickly remitting and chronic schizophrenia. In all three cases, the chronic forms show disturbances of autonomic functioning, while the episodic form does not. However, only in the transient depersonalization is there evidence that the symptoms have protective function.

The psychophysiology of another dissociative disorder—multiple personality—has been studied. One objective of this type of study is to test the hypothesis that these cases are "for real" (i.e., to rule out faking as an explanation). However, this type of case may also permit studying the somatic accompaniments of mood and personality differences within the same body, as well as the role of awareness. In one case (Ludwig, Brandsma, Wilbur, Bendfeldt, & Jameson, 1972), four different personalities each produced a different set of emotionally toned words. Later, SCRs were recorded from each personality to all the emotional words, as well as neutral words. The "main" personality gave larger SCRs only to his own emotional words, and each alternate responded just to his own words plus those of the main personality. This result corresponded fairly well with the degree of awareness or amnesia of one personality for another. Rather large differences occurred among personalities in alpha and theta abundance, effects of opening the eyes on alpha blocking, and the visual ERP. In a study of a second case (Larmore, Ludwig & Cain, 1977), using a different paradigm, there were differences in alpha blocking as well as in ERP "reducing," and some differences in EMG and blood pressure among personalities. These were thought to correspond to differences in the personality types of the alternates. Both studies suggest physiological differences among the personalities marked enough to rule out the faking hypothesis, but they could have been improved by replications to test the between-personality variability compared to the within-personality variability. Such an approach as well as the use of controls who simulate personality changes has been tried in some recent ERP research, reviewed by Putnam (1984). Results so far are mixed regarding reliable differences among personalities.

Very little psychophysiological research has been done on anorexia nervosa, but one of the studies is particularly interesting, because a well-established finding of clinical psychophysiology was used to test a specific hypothesis (Salkind, Fincham, & Silverstone, 1980). The hypothesis was that anorexia is a phobic disorder, and the test measured the changes in SCL to imagining food-related, weight-related, and body image stimuli and stimuli related to vomiting. It was found that SC responses to these stimuli were very small and frequently absent, a quite different result from that obtained in phobic subjects when imagining feared stimuli. Although this study lacks the controls to determine whether anorexics differ from normals in autonomic activity, the disconfirmation of the main hypothesis seems rather clear. The hypothesis that anorexia may have an organic basis is suggested by findings of close to 50% abnormal EEGs in these patients, manifested by diffuse slowing and wave-spike transients (Nell, Merlkangas, Foster, Merlkangas, Spiker, & Kupfer, 1980). Thus, the psychophysiological data suggest that anorexia nervosa is more similar to organic or affective disorders than to phobias, but the effects of secondary depression cannot be ignored.

Interest in the biological basis of panic attacks has been stimulated by findings that about half the patients suffering from these attacks also have mitral valve prolapse (MVP) (Gorman, Fyer, Gliklich, King, & Klein, 1981), and that these two groups are indistinguishable clinically. Conversely, 50% to 60% of MVP patients were found to exhibit psychiatric symptoms, compared to 18% with more serious cardiovascular conditions (Szmuilowicz & Flannery, 1980). The MVP syndrome has been found to be accompanied by ANS dysfunctions (Gaffney, Karlsson, Campbell, Schutte, Nixon, Willerson, & Blomquist, 1979). Whether these differ in MVP cases with and without panic states has not been determined, nor has ANS activity in anxiety and panic patients with and without MVP been compared. However, HR and blood pressure are being studied in conjunction with pharmacologic challenges in patients with panic disorder in order to help determine the roles of catecholamines and adrenergic receptor sensitivity in this disorder (e.g., Charney, Heninger, & Breier, 1984).

Treatment Effects

Somatic Treatments

ANXIOLYTIC DRUGS

A number of drugs have been used to provide symptomatic relief of anxiety states, and a small amount of research exists on their autonomic effects, mostly using electrodermal dependent variables. Meprobamate has been reported to decrease SCL and to decrease SC responsivity to various events, including painful stimuli (Lader & Wing, 1966). In a methodologically sophisticated comparison of the effects of a barbiturate (amylobarbitone) and chlordiazepoxide (Librium) on physiological indices in anxiety-state patients, Lader and Wing (1966) found linear dose-response curves for both drugs on several SC variables. The drugs potentiated the decrease in SCL over the course of the experiment, increased the rate of habituation of the SCOR, and decreased the SSCR rate. Amylobarbitone decreased HR, but not in a dose-dependent manner, and chlordiazepoxide increased HR slightly. No effects on EMG were found. Both drugs also reduced rated anxiety in a dose-dependent manner. Thus, the SC measures were generally associated with the subjective measures better than the other physiological variables studied. In another study of the effects of chlordiazepoxide on anxiety patients (Kelly et al., 1970), the effects on SSCRs, SCL, and anxiety self-ratings were in the predicted direction but not significant, but significantly reduced resting FBF was obtained. This study used a different design, in that half of the 30 subjects were tested on active medication and half on placebo (double-blind), rather than each subject serving as his or her own control, as in the Lader and Wing (1966) study. Thus, the method may not have been as sensitive.

The effects of an acute intravenous administration of diazepam on a variety of ANS measures in 15 anxiety-state patients were reported by Kelly, Pik, and Chen (1973). Although the design included a placebo injection, in addition to rest and stress periods, the placebo was always given first, so that it is impossible to separate temporal from pharmacological effects. Nevertheless, during nonstress periods there were significant declines in FBF and HR and an increase in finger pulse amplitude that seemed to accelerate after the diazepam injection. Similar but nonsignificant trends were evident for SC measures.

Bond, James, and Lader (1974b) compared the effects of three benzodiazepines with amylobarbitone and placebo in 20 anxiety patients in a clinical trial design, in which dosage was adjusted for optimal clinical response for each patient. The subjects sat through presentation of 64 clicks (passive condition) and then received 32 more clicks to which a quick response was required (active condition). All drugs produced nonsignificant decreases in SCL in both conditions. The benzodiazepines reduced SSCRs in the passive condition and attenuated all middle ERP amplitudes under both conditions; these changes correlated significantly with decreases in rated anxiety. A frequency analysis of the EEG showed, surprisingly, that under both conditions, the benzodiazepines decreased voltage in the delta and alpha wavebands and increased it in the beta band. Correlational analyses showed that decreased slow-wave activity and increased fast-wave activity were related to decreased SSCRs and to lower anxiety ratings—just the opposite of the usual interpretation of EEG frequency in terms of arousal. However, it is important to note that, unlike their effects on SC, the benzodiazepines did not reduce the anxiety versus normal differences on EEG and ERP. Compared to controls, drug-free anxious patients had more beta and less relative alpha activity and equal or smaller ERPs. Thus, some of the differences were significantly increased by the drugs. This may be related to the inconsistent but largely absent effects of these drugs on cognitive functioning.

Tricyclic drugs used mainly as antidepressants are also beneficial for patients with anxiety-spectrum disorders, a situation which adds to the lack of a clear distinction between the two types of disorders. Obsessive–compulsive disorder is especially ambiguous in that it has features of both anxiety and depressive disorders. We (Zahn, Insel, & Murphy, 1984) studied the effects of clorgyline, a MAO inhibitor, and clomipramine, a tricyclic, on obsessives using a placebo-controlled crossover design. Clorgyline, which was not clinically effective, reduced baseline SSCRs and tended to reduce SCL throughout the session compared to placebo, but did not affect reactivity. Clomipramine, which produced marked clinical improvement, not only reduced SC arousal indices, but attenuated SC reactivity to tones and to task performance and reduced HR acceleration to loud tones. This suggests that high ANS reactivity, but not high arousal per se may be necessary for the maintenance of obses-

sive behavior. These results are generally confirmatory of those for amitriptyline described earlier (pp. 549–550).

Diminution of the CNV by benzodiazepines has been reported for normal subjects (Tecce et al., 1978), a result also apparently inconsistent with what might be expected to accompany clinical improvement. Tecce et al. (1978) speculate that the opposite result migh be obtained with anxiety patients, whose CNVs may be already depressed by virtue of their distracted clinical state. However, attenuation of the middle ERP components from benzodiazepines has also been found in normals (Shagass, 1974), similar to the findings in anxiety patients; thus it seems as if ERP diminution may be a general result of these drugs, independent of clincial state.

PSYCHOSURGERY

The effects of psychosurgery on the cardiovascular activity of heterogeneous groups of patients suffering from anxiety, depression, and obsessions, plus a few schizophrenics, has been studied by Kelly and his colleagues using Kelly's test procedures as described above. In the earlier studies, a standard frontal leucotomy and a modified leucotomy were compared (Kelly, 1972; Kelly, Walter, Mitchell-Heggs, & Sargent, 1972). At a 6-week follow-up, significant reductions in FBF, HR, and blood pressure were obtained under both "basal" and stress conditions. Only the standard operation was evaluated at an 18-month follow-up. The declines in FBF and HR were maintained. State and trait anxiety scores were generally reduced significantly only 6 weeks after the standard leucotomy. A regression analysis showed that high preoperative stress and basal FBF combined predicted good outcome, but accounted for only 11.5% of the variance.

Another surgical technique was investigated by this group—"stereotoxic limbic leucotomy," in which small lesions are made bilaterally in the lower medial quadrant of the frontal lobes and additional lesions are made in the cingulum bundle (Kelly, Richardson, Mitchell-Heggs, Greenup, Chen, & Hafner, 1973). Despite marked and lasting improvements in symptomatology and anxiety over a 16-month period, the ANS changes in 57 patients were rather small and transient (Mitchell-Heggs, Kelly, and Richardson, 1976). The decrease in FBF was not significant, HR decreased only 4–5 beats/min, and the maximum SBP decrease was 7 mm Hg.

Interpretation of these studies is difficult because of the lack of nonoperated patient controls or normal controls. Since the patients selected for these procedures were chronic and had not responded to less invasive treatments, the clinical results seem reasonably clear. Although there is some concordance among symptomatic, subjective, and ANS changes, the ANS changes are too small and inconsistent to account for the clinical changes.

An important use of psychophysiological recordings was made by Kelly (1980) during surgical procedures to assist in the final placement of the electrodes. Stimulation of the anterior cyngulate gyrus and lower medial quadrant of the frontal lobe produced similar ANS reactions. Most pronounced and consistent was a severe decrease in respiratory amplitude, usually to the point of blockage (apnea). Increased SC, HR, blood pressure, and FBF occurred, but finger pulse volume was sometimes increased, was sometimes decreased, and sometimes showed a biphasic decrease-increase pattern. Biphasic effects on FBF were less common. These result suggest compensatory feedback mechanisms operating in the case of the cardiovascular variables. Since the studies were done under general anesthesia, the ANS effects could not be secondary to subjective effects. In one patient tested under a local anesthetic, similar results for cingulate stimulation were found, except for an increase in respiration rate rather than apnea, and no subjective changes were reported from the stimulation. In this patient, when this area was destroyed by freezing, an increase in respiration rate was also produced, but SC, HR, and FBF decreased.

Apnea and tachycardia were also found to follow from stimulation of medial amygdaloid nucleus in patients lesioned in that area for aggressive behavior. Kelly (1980) takes this as evidence that these lesions are interrupting the frontal lobe connections with the limbic mechanisms mediating emotional behavior. Evidence that this circuit also includes the posteromedial hypothalamus is suggested by Sano and his coworkers (cited in Kelly, 1980), who found that stimulation of this area increased ANS indices, and that its destruction reduced pathological anxiety. However, stimulation also produced marked subjective feelings of horror. This suggests a difference in function of this area, but the parameters of the stimulation applied may have been different.

Thus, lesions in areas that produce ANS changes on stimulation are frequently successful in reducing anxiety, depression, and obsessive behavior. Long-term reductions in indices of ANS activity under laboratory conditions, however, are not marked. Findings that these reductions are somewhat more robust at 6 weeks than later suggest a recovery of these functions—a well-known process in other types of functioning after brain injury. Kelly (1980) emphasizes that these operations do not produce a generalized emotional blunting, but reduce the pathological affective symptoms. He suggests that there is an increased suppression of old learning, allowing new learning to occur. This hypothesis is not inconsistent with the ideas proposed by Lader and Wing (1966) and by Beech and Perigault (1977), which implicate slow habituation (or extinction) in the maintenance of anxiety and obsessive disorders. The (temporary) disruption of the brain mechanisms mediating autonomic and affective reactions would allow extinction of the pathological responses to occur. Even if there were no permanent reduction in ANS–affective reactivity, the reduction in pathological behavior would be permanent unless conditions optimal for its relearning occurred. The model based on extinction receives support from the recent work using behavior therapy, which is described in the next section.

Behavior Therapy

The most exciting developments in recent years in the treatment of neuroses are the behaviorally based therapies, which have been applied successfully to specific phobias and obsessive–compulsive disorders, among others. It is natural that psychophysiological techniques would be intimately involved in studies of the therapeutic process, along with subjective and behavioral measures; in fact, the contemporary conceptualization of anxiety as incorporating all three of these functions owes a great deal to the contribution of investigators in this area.

SYSTEMATIC DESENSITIZATION

Although there had been a few earlier psychophysiological studies on the psychotherapeutic process, it was not until Wolpe (1958) introduced the method of systematic desensitization and the associated theory of reciprocal inhibition of anxiety by relaxation, in which ANS activity was hypothesized to play an important mediating role, that research in this area began to intensify. This research has had several goals: verification of the effects of the therapy, study of the components of the therapeutic process, prediction of individual differences in treatment outcome, and inquiry into the mechanisms of therapeutic change. Reviews by Mathews (1971, 1978) and Katkin and Deitz (1973) have contributed to the following summary.

The desensitization technique involves the repeated presentation of fear-related items in ascending order of threat to a relaxed patient (Van Egeren, Feather, & Hein, 1971). In most treatment and laboratory situations, the fear stimuli are suggested by the therapist and imagined by the client, the hierarchy of items along a threat continuum having been worked out beforehand. To the extent that physiological activity is involved in this process, it should roughly parallel the elicitation of fear by the stimuli and its reduction with relaxation and repetition.

Many studies have shown an increase in ANS activity accompanying imagery or similar presentation of fear-related items (Mathews, 1971). Work with nonpatient phobics selected by questionnaire has shown that this has the characteristics of a DR rather than an OR (Fredrikson, 1981; Hare & Blevings, 1975; Klorman, Weissberg, & Wiesenfeld, 1977). Lang, Melamed, and Hart (1970) reported that subjects with sepcific phobias gave significantly larger HR, SCR, and respiration rate responses to visualized scenes eliciting a subjective fear response than to hierarchy scenes not eliciting such a response. Moreover, the evidence suggests that for group data, the physiological response parallels the subjective response to items along the hierarchy (Mathews, 1971). For example, Van Egeren et al. (1971) obtained this result for SC and vasomotor responses, but not for HR or respiratory rate while Lang et al. (1970) observed it for SC and HR but not respiratory rate. In addition, this group found a correlation of .65 between the HR response and anxiety ratings to hierarchy items.

The reciprocal inhibition or counterconditioning conceptualization of the desensitization method presupposes deep relaxation. Several studies have addressed the question of whether special training is superior in lowering baseline ANS and EMG levels, compared to control or self-instructed relaxation. Although some superiority of training in muscular relaxation has been found, there are many negative results as well. It is not clear whether this is due to the particular procedures used or whether, in fact, many subjects are able to achieve low baseline levels without special training.

A more germane question is whether relaxation training affects the ANS response to phobic stimuli and its decline with repetition. Van Egeren et al. (1971), studying public-speaking phobias, obtained some moderate support for the effectiveness of relaxation in attenuating SCRs to hierarchy items and speeding the extinction of vasomotor responses with repeated presentation; in each case, however, the result held just for that one measure. However, Waters, McDonald, and Koresko (1972) reported that relaxation training did not affect the physiological habituation and behavioral improvement consequent upon simple exposure. O'Brien and Borkovec (1977) found that socially anxious women given both imagery and relaxation training had lower HR before and during an imagery procedure than subjects given either type of training alone, but this did not hold for behavioral or subjective responses. Mere repetition of a phobic slide led to disappearance of DRs (HR increase) and the appearance of ORs (HR decrease) in phobic subjects (selected by questionnaire) in one study (Klorman et al., 1977) but not in another (Fredrikson, 1981). In general, however, this type of study has produced inconsistent results (Borkovec & O'Brien, 1976), and thus provides little support for the counterconditioning theory of desensitization. However, this may be due to differences in the responses of subjects to the relaxation procedure. Physiological and behavioral assessment of relaxation achieved in these situations might lead to better predictors of treatment response.

The equivocal effects of relaxation training also provide little support for the hypothesis proposed by Lader, Gelder, and Marks (1967) that desensitization is a habituation process that is facilitated by a low state of arousal. This hypothesis is supported by the inverse relationship between arousal and habituation rate (Lader & Wing, 1966), and the finding of Lader et al. (1967) that habituation of the SCOR to tones and spontaneous SC fluctuations correlated .49 and − .42, respectively, with improvement in phobic patients subsequently treated by desensitization. These findings may reflect differences in the specificity of the phobias of the patients. Specific phobics seem generally not to have high levels of anxiety or of physiological activity outside the phobic situation, and they are treated more successfully by behavioral techniques.

Striking evidence of an association between rapid habituation to phobic items and good treatment response was found by Lang et al. (1970). The rate of decline of the HR response to hierarchy items held in imagery correlated .91 with treatment success. In addition, the pretreatment HR response to items eliciting a fear signal correlated .75 with outcome; this is consistent with the ideas that specificity of the arousal response or that concordance between subjective and ANS components of fear is conducive to clinical improvement. However, other physiological measures did not significantly relate to outcome.

Evidence confirmatory of the specificity notion comes from a study by Öst, Jerremalm, and Johansson (1981), who divided subjects with social phobias into two groups, based on whether their response to a social challenge was predominantly in behavioral inadequacies or a large increase in HR, but not both. Half of each group was given social skills training and half an applied muscular relaxation technique. Although no direct comparisons were made, the high-HR reactors appeared to have a better outcome from relaxation than the behavioral reactors (who were low-HR reactors), while the opposite held for social skills training. A similar result was obtained in a study of claustrophobic subjects (Öst, Johansson, & Jerremalm, 1982) in which exposure therapy and relaxation were compared. However, in an attempted replication on agoraphobic patients (Öst, Jerremalm, & Johansson, 1984), exposure and relaxation treatments were equally effective for subjects who were primarily HR or behavioral reactors to a phobic challenge. Öst et al. (1984) think classifying and rating agoraphobic subjects may present special methodological problems. However, the more generalized anxiety and arousal in agoraphobia than in specific phobias may preclude specificity in the effectiveness of different therapeutic approaches.

Marks, Boulougouris, and Marset (1971) found that higher pretreatment SSCR and HR levels during imagery predicted a worse clinical outcome of desensitization therapy. These results are not in direct conflict with those of Lang et al. (1970), since levels rather than responses were used as predictors, and significant correlations were more often obtained under conditions of neutral or low-fear imagery than under high-fear conditions. Moreover, the subjects were patients suffering from agoraphobia or social phobias, conditions that can be assumed to be characterized by much higher generalized anxiety than the student volunteers with circumscribed phobias used by Lang et al. (1970). It is also relevant to note that desensitization was not a particularly effective treatment for these subjects. A tentative conclusion from these studies is that low generalized anxiety, reflected in part by fast habituation, specificity of ANS reactivity to phobic imagery, and low nonspecific ANS responses, promotes successful desensitization. Whether the critical mechanism is faster habituation of the fear response; achievement of lower levels of arousal, which are more conducive to counterconditioning; achievement of more vivid, and hence more effective, imagery; or some combination of these is not clear at this point.

FLOODING

The predictors for the effectiveness of the other major behavioral treatment for phobic disorders—flooding or "implosion"—seem to be quite different. The Marks et al. (1971) study described above compared flooding with desensitization and found good outcome from flooding to be positively correlated with pretreatment SSCRs and HR during imagery. These results were confirmed in subsequent studies from this group (R. Stern & Marks, 1972; Watson & Marks, 1971) and recently by Vermilyea, Boice, and Barlow (1984). As was the case for desensitization, the predictor variables were as likely to come from neutral or low-fear imagery as from phobic imagery settings. In addition, although there were some instances in which the physiological variables predicted outcome as defined by therapist or patient ratings, most of the significant correlations were with posttreatment physiological activity, which this group also includes as criteria of outcome. For example, the highest correlations reported were between initial SSCRs and outcome HR (.97) and initial HR versus outcome SSCRs (.84), all of which measures were taken during the phobic imagery. The use of physiological variables as outcome criteria may be justified on the grounds that in these studies they paralleled the clinical rating data for the group as a whole (although correlations with clinical ratings are not given) and showed similar effects of different treatments.

These promising results were not replicated in a similar study by another British group (Gelder, Bancroft, Gath, Johnston, Mathews, & Shaw, 1973; Mathews, Johnston, Shaw, & Gelder, 1974). Neither HR nor SCL responses (SSCRs were not measured) were significantly related to clinical outcome for either flooding or desensitization, nor was pretreatment anxiety. This negative result may be partly due to the fact that physiological measures were not used as criteria

of outcome. There were also no clinical outcome differences between these treatments, although both were superior to a control treatment. The only psychophysiological difference found in this study was lower baseline HR after both active treatments versus no change after the control treatment. Thus, there was some physiological parallel to clinical results, but of a somewhat different nature than that found by the Marks et al. studies. Another study (Mathews, Johnston, Lancashire, Munby, Shaw, & Gelder, 1976), comparing flooding in imagery with flooding in vivo (exposure to threatening situations), also failed to find ANS predictors. This study did find higher HR during phobic versus neutral imagery, and a greater decline in HR during phobic compared to neutral imagery across treatment sessions—results that paralleled subjective anxiety.

Further positive evidence for a relationship between pretreatment physiological activity and outcome of flooding comes from a study on 12 obsessive–compulsive patients (Boulougouris, Rabavilas, & Stefanis, 1977) using methods quite similar to those used by Marks and his colleagues with phobic patients. As in those studies, the most consistent relationships were found with physiological outcome variables; however, some were found with outcome ratings as well, and these were as likely to be with responses to neutral fantasies as to obsessive ones, suggesting a generalized reaction. Treatment effects on reductions of HR and the maximum SCR to flooding in vivo were similar to those produced on anxiety ratings.

The success of both desensitization and flooding treatments in reducing phobic anxiety—success that persists beyond the treatment situation—raises questions about how these two apparently different procedures produce similar results. One line of inquiry comes from physiological recording during the procedures. R. Stern and Marks (1973) recorded HR with a portable device from subjects during a 2-hour session of flooding in vivo; they found that after an initial increase, there was a marked decrease during the second hour to a level significantly below baseline. A series of four 30-min exposures separated by 30-min "safe" periods produced a less regular HR decline and was less effective therapeutically. Less dramatic effects of a similar nature during flooding in imagery have been reported for HR (Mathews et al., 1974). This study also found that the initial increase in HR disappeared in later stages of treatment. A similar nonmonotonic course of SSCRs was reported by McCutcheon and Adams (1975), but Mathews et al. (1974, 1976) found only linear decreases in SCL during phobic imagery flooding. A reason for some of these apparently conflicting results is suggested by the early finding that flooding in imagery is more likely to produce an exponential decay function than flooding in vivo (Watson, Gaind, & Marks, 1972).

More recently Lande (1982) found an increase-decrease pattern for HR and subjective anxiety for imagery flooding sessions of 24–48 min. HR frequently, but not always, ended below baseline. However, Mavissakalian and Michelson (1982), who had agoraphobics navigate a .4-mile course in a downtown area, observed that HR remained elevated while subjective anxiety increased and then decreased. Problems with this study are that the time of exposure is uncontrolled and half or more of the patients were taking imipramine. Another HR pattern was observed by Öst, Sterner, and Lindahl (1984), who studied the HR and blood pressure reactions of blood phobics to a gory film. Physiological increases during the film were followed by profound decreases below baseline after the film was stopped, most markedly in subjects who fainted or nearly fainted. This reaction may be specific to blood phobia, but the results suggest that continuing measurements beyond the duration of the exposure might be informative.

Thus, the evidence is that flooding, like desensitization, produces decreased physiological activity along with decreased fear if sessions are long enough, although the time course may differ in the two treatments. The question of the process by which this decline in anxiety and ANS activity comes about has been the subject of speculation. Hodgson and Rachman (1974) found that flooding with a horrific theme not related to the patients' phobia produced desensitization of the main phobia when the phobic imagery was given immediately after the irrelevant flooding, but that sensitization occurred when the two sessions were separated by 24 hr. This suggests the development of some inhibitory process during prolonged flooding that attenuates the fear response. Possibly some biological mechanism, such as the endorphin system, is involved here.

However, the question of the mechanism of the reduction of anxiety and ANS activity during flooding is separate from hypothesis that achieving a state of low arousal is a necessary or a beneficial condition of clinical improvement. Evidence in support of this hypothesis comes from studies (reviewed in Mathews, 1978) showing that anxiolytic drugs given in conjunction with exposure therapy usually produce better outcomes than placebo trials. An alternative hypothesis is that the effects of the drugs may not be relevant per se, but may facilitate approach to phobic stimuli (Mathews, 1978), and thus may facilitate extinction or habituation. Mathews argues against the hypothesis of the necessity of anxiety reduction as a critical factor, largely on the basis of negative evidence for the beneficial effects of diazepam found in one study (Hafner & Marks, 1976), and the finding that flooding with imagery and *in vivo* had similar long-term effects, despite a significantly greater reduction in anxiety ratings in the *in vivo* sessions themselves (Johnston, Lancashire, Mathews, Munby, Shaw, & Gelder,

1976). Interpretation of these studies is complicated by the testing of subjects in groups in the Hafner and Marks (1976) study, which may have reduced differences in exposure to the phobic situation, and by uncontrolled intersession practice by the subjects. Since exposure to the phobic situation in real life or in imagination is unquestionably a necessary condition for improvement, the virtually inevitable lack of control over this variable in long-term outcome studies makes it difficult to assess the role of arousal in the process of change.

A related problem is whether reduction of the ANS component reduces anxiety as manifested subjectively or behaviorally. Gatchel and Proctor (1976) reported that biofeedback training for HR slowing led to lower observer and self-anxiety ratings and lower SCL during speaking in speech-anxious students, compared to a control group who performed a tracking task instead of the HR training. However, Nunes and Marks (1976) found no effect of HR biofeedback in subjective anxiety, SSCRs, or respiration rate during exposure sessions in patients with specific phobias. Similarly, Rupert and Holmes (1978) observed no effect of HR biofeedback on anxiety levels of anxious inpatients, although they were able only to achieve significant HR increases. It is possible that these conflicting results are due to differences in severity of psychopathology in the studies, or to the fact that in the Gatchel and Proctor (1976) study only the biofeedback group was given instructions to try to keep their HR low while speaking. A difference in attention deployment might have been the critical factor, rather than the slower HR. It is also relevant to note that reductions in HR accomplished with beta-adrenergic receptor blocking agents have not been effective in reducing phobic (Bernadt, Silverstone, & Singleton, 1980) or obsessive (Rabavilas, Boulougouris, Perissaki, & Stefanis, 1979) behavior. This contrasts with the positive effects generally obtained for the benzodiazepines, which probably act more generally and more centrally. These results suggest that reducing just one part of the ANS component of anxiety may not change the other components.

Summary and Conclusions

Research on ANS activity in anxiety states and other neuroses has shown such an intimate connection between the physiological and psychological manifestations of these disorders that investigators in this area define anxiety in terms of loosely coupled physiological, subjective, and behavioral aspects. Patients with anxiety disorders have been shown to have higher baseline levels than controls on a wide variety of physiological measures considered to reflect arousal. Slow habituation of the OR has also been found to be a diagnostic marker, but there is some evidence of powerful influence by cognitive factors. Attenuated response to stressful tasks also occurs in these patients, but there has been inadequate control of the effects of initial levels, and some early conflicting evidence exists. Slower reductions in base levels during initial rest periods or after stress may also distinguish anxiety patients from controls.

Studies of separate diagnostic groups have shown that electrodermal and cardiovascular indices are highest in patients diagnosed as suffering from anxiety state, agitated depression (or depression with anxiety), and agoraphobia, but they are not particularly high in patients with specific phobias. For other neurotic disorders, there is less agreement, but this may be due to differences in diagnosis or to clinical differences among subgroups. For example, a clinical distinction between chronic and acute hysteria has been shown to parallel a physiological difference between these subtypes and to have implications for prognosis. In these studies, there has generally been a reasonably good concordance between the physiological measures and subjective anxiety. Not surprisingly, these relationships appear to be better for state anxiety in the testing situation than for measures of trait anxiety. Drugs that reduce subjective anxiety and fear also reduce the ANS indicators. A similar finding exists for the short-term effects of psychosurgery, while long-term follow-up studies suggest considerable recovery of ANS function but continued clinical benefit. Behavioral treatments also reduce ANS, behavioral, and subjective indicators of situational anxiety, but generalized effects on ANS activity (as defined by base levels in the test situation) have been less well studied.

In general, the tripartite notion of anxiety is well supported by the data; that is, this conception has proved useful to researchers studying these problems. However, the idea that the three manifestations of anxiety are loosely coupled, implying imperfect correlation, is also well supported. Conditions affecting the degree of relationship among indices, termed "synchrony" by Hodgson and Rachman (1974), can be studied in their own right. It is obvious that the considerable synchrony of various ANS and subjective indices in the group data in the anxiety studies is due to the large variations in anxiety being dealt with, in relation to individual differences in extraneous influences on ANS measures (e.g., sweat gland density, physical condition, age).

The same reasoning is relevant to the concept of ANS arousal. It is probably no accident that some psychophysiologists who espouse the concept of ANS arousal most vigorously, such as Malmo and Lader, have studied anxiety neuroses. Lader (1975) takes the position that low correlations among physiological indices occur because different measures are maximally sensitive over different ranges of arousal and have different triggering thresholds and ceilings. Thus,

large group differences in anxiety will produce synchronous changes in most ANS measures, as the literature reviewed would suggest, whereas within-group correlations or assessment of the effects of laboratory stressors would imply much less synchrony. This view does not deny directional fractionation, but merely sets limits on its occurrence. This model would account for the differences in perception of somatic effects accompanying anxiety and panic states mentioned earlier, also in terms of activation of new, high-threshold somatic systems during panic states.

The problem of synchrony is more critical in the studies of behavior therapy, where individual differences in fear may be relatively small and where within-group correlations among different outcome criteria or between predictors and outcome criteria are wanted. This literature as a whole is rather disappointing in its neglect of such concepts as individual response specificity and individual differences in the range of ANS variables, as well as in a rather cursory treatment of ANS data in general. The best studies from a psychophysiological standpoint, with some exceptions, have been those using college-student volunteers rather than clinically defined patients as subjects. This topic is extremely complex; there is a need to consider differences in patient type, treatment type, and parameters of treatment, not to mention lack of control over activity outside of treatment. While these factors make it difficult to compare studies, one cannot help speculating that more definitive results might be obtained by recording several ANS parameters and assessing changes for each subject in terms of activity on his or her maximally reactive parameter. Alternatively, or in addition, range correction procedures might be fruitfully employed in these studies. Differences among studies in what was measured (e.g., levels during exposure or changes from baseline) and differences in the amount of control over base-line influences on response also hinder comparison and interpretation of the data. These points are emphasized, because knowledge of how ANS activity before, during, and after treatment relates to therapeutic reduction in fear might tell us much about the process by which it is reduced and might suggest hypotheses about its acquisition.

GENERAL DISCUSSION

Perhaps the most striking attribute of the topic of this chapter is the variety of problems addressed and methods used by researchers who employ psychophsiological techniques to study psychopathology. A general summary of the field as a whole would not be very useful at this point, given that a summary and conclusions about each diagnostic group covered have already been attempted. However, some tentative conclusions about the progress of the field with respect to the issues raised at the outset, as well as selected comparisons of various separate diagnostic groupings, are presented here.

Similarity among Diagnostic Groups

Consideration of the several types of psychopathology discussed here shows certain broad similarities in some aspects of psychophysiological functioning in two or more groups. In other cases, similarities have been proposed on clinical and/or genetic grounds. In these cases, we may inquire whether the psychophysiological data suggest a biological similarity among the groups.

Schizophrenia, Depression, and Anxiety States

In studies using the SCOR paradigm, electrodermal nonresponding is seen not only in a large proportion of schizophrenics, but in a significant number of depressives as well—perhaps most frequently in those diagnosed as endogenous, retarded, or psychotic. This is congruent, to some extent, with the overlapping symptomatology of these groups: Some depressives have cognitive impairment, delusions, and so on; some schizophrenics are depressed; and anhedonia is present in both groups. There is some evidence that depressive affect is related to nonresponding in schizophrenia, suggesting that nonresponding may be linked more closely to a symptom cluster that overlaps diagnoses than to a specific syndrome.

Slow habituation is seen in some schizophrenics and depressives, but in a higher proportion of patients with some sort of anxiety disorder. The depressives in this group are likely to be classified as agitated or neurotic. For the nonschizophrenic groups, these findings are congruent with the finding of a similar clinical response to treatment in neurotic patients, whether they were either primarily anxious or depressed (Johnstone *et al.*, 1981). Some direct evidence associates SCOR responsivity with behavioral agitation and anxiety in schizophrenics, again showing a closer relationship of SCOR responding to symptoms than to diagnoses.

Although baseline measures, especially SSCRs, are correlated with SCOR responsivity, the data show that, in general, schizophrenics and anxiety patients are more likely to have elevated SSCRs than depressives. Thus schizophrenics are likely to have more nonspecific and less specific electrodermal reactivity than the nonschizophrenic groups. If a diagnostic marker is to be found with the SCOR paradigm, it might be in this sort of combination of variables. Other SCOR characteristics, such as recovery time, might also participate in the equation, but these have not been well studied in anxiety and depression.

Cardiovascular indices of activation also show similarities among patients with schizophrenia, depression, and various anxiety disorders. Although these groups all showed higher base levels and lower reactivity to stress than controls (Kelly, 1980), quantitative differentiation of the groups was possible. Schizophrenics and nonanxious depressives had lower base levels than patients with anxiety, and schizophrenics had the lowest response to the stressor. The combination of base levels and reactivity seems to sort out these groups in the same way as the SSCR-SCOR data.

The ordering of these three groups on ANS reactivity also mirrors that based on middle and especially late ERP amplitudes, on which schizophrenics are more impaired than depressives, and the sparse evidence on neurotic patients, although not completely consistent, indicates normal or larger ERPs. There is evidence of less alpha and more beta in the resting EEGs of these groups; however, this evidence is equivocal, particularly for depressed subjects. In fact, recent evidence suggests that depressives and schizophrenics may deviate from normal in different directions in EEG activation, but manics and schizophrenics are similar on several EEG and ERP markers. EEG frequency may not be related to the ANS data.

Further evidence for a similarity among these groups is that the drugs most commonly used to treat them—neuroleptics, tricyclic antidepressants, and benzodiazapines—all seem to have the effect of ANS "deactivation," despite differences in the neurochemical mode of action. This raises some serious questions about the role of ANS activation in these disorders and the mechanism by which it occurs. One possible explanation of this is that, in some of these disorders at least, the arousal indices reflect a state such as stress that is secondary to the major symptoms. When the symptoms are reduced, in a manner specific to a given treatment, the reduction in stress produces a decrease in arousal. Since high ANS activity seems to be part and parcel of anxiety states, suggesting that the effective drugs for these may have a direct role in the reduction of activation, the secondary-effect hypothesis would be most likely for schizophrenia and the affective disorders.

However, evidence has been presented earlier that in schizophrenia, the ANS effects of neuroleptics are immediate while the clinical changes are gradual; this is not what would be predicted from the hypothesis. This suggests that if there is a causal link between lowered ANS activity and clinical improvement, it goes in the opposite direction: Lowered activation might be beneficial itself and/or permit more beneficial effects of whatever therapeutic influences are present in the environment. Clinical effects of antidepressants are also gradual, but the relevant ANS studies have not been done. Schizophrenics with active or positive symptoms are more likely to have high ANS indices and also to respond to neuroleptics, suggesting a direct role of activation. However, these two lines of evidence come from separate studies, and there is no direct positive evidence on this point. For affective disorders, on the other hand, patients with either psychomotor agitation or retardation seem likely to respond to tricyclics as long as they fit the endogenous classification (Goodwin *et al.*, 1978).

Thus, while reductions in ANS activity are probably not secondary to decreases in the major symptoms of the psychoses, it has not been established that they are primary. They could be irrelevant side effects, or, perhaps more likely, could be directly beneficial to some patients but not to others. Evidence relevant to this problem could come from correlating ANS changes with clinical changes during treatment. Such studies would have to control pretreatment levels, and it might also be necessary to monitor drug levels in plasma or other body fluids in order to protect against spurious correlations due to differences in the metabolism of the drug. Some evidence using these techniques (see pp. 549–550) suggests that high pretreatment ANS base levels and large declines in ANS activity with treatment are related to clinical improvement.

It may be that the similarity among the effects of various drugs is more apparent than real, since detailed comparative studies have not been done. Investigations of various aspects of ANS activity besides activation levels, and similarly comprehensive evaluation of electrocortical effects, will be necessary before such a conclusion is justified. For example, there is recent evidence that two drugs used for depression differ markedly in effects on ANS reactivity but have similar effects on base levels. Given the close relationship of ERPs and attention, studies relating ERP changes to changes in attention and clinical state might be useful interpreting the drug effects and might help elucidate the psychopathological significance of different ERPs.

The evidence of the quantitative EEG, on the other hand, points to different effects of different drugs; perhaps the best-confirmed of those are a reduction in beta from neuroleptics and tricyclics and an increase from diazepam. Specificity of the effects of drugs is claimed for EEG frequency spectra (Fink, 1974; Itil, 1974). The functional significance of such changes is not clear, but, with comparisons of EEG and ANS data in the same subjects, an interpretation based on arousal does not fit the data.

Depression, Psychopathy, and Hyperactivity

On the basis of a study of familial risk, Winokur (1978) has proposed that depressives having relatives with alcoholism or antisocial personality may consti-

tute a clinically distinct group. Although there is no good support for this connection from the psychophysiological studies on affective disorders and psychopathy, a significant proportion of depressives and primary psychopaths as a group show low electrodermal base levels and responsivity; this finding, at least, is not inconsistent with the hypothesis. Positive support for the clinical distinction could come from psychophysiological studies of subgroups of depressives chosen on the basis of the familial marker, but such studies have not been done.

A link between hyperactivity in children and psychopathy has been proposed on the clinical grounds of the occurrence of impulsivity and aggression in some HA children, bolstered by findings of low electrodermal arousal indices in both groups. In addition, an excess of alcoholism and sociopathy in the fathers and hysteria in the mothers of the biological (but not the adoptive) parents of HA children has been reported (see Rapoport & Ferguson, 1981). The review of hyperactivity in this chapter provides no support for ANS hypoarousal in HA children in terms of base levels, but low-amplitude, slow-recovery SCORs may occur in these children, as well as in delinquent adolescents and perhaps in adult psychopaths. The data base for these conclusions was established before the diagnostic refinements of DSM-III, where the distinction between children with attention deficits and those with conduct disorders is made. Thus, it is possible that only impulsive-aggressive children may be physiologically similar to adolescent and adult delinquents. ERP studies of delinquents using attention paradigms might also be useful here, since reasonably consistent findings in HA children have been established with these methods.

The literature on hysteria gives absolutely no support for a genetic relationship of hysteria with hyperactivity. High ANS base levels and slow habituation occur in patients with hysteria (see page 585). Although there is some variation in results associated with clinical differences, low values have not been reported. The reasons for this apparent conflict are obscure.

Markers

It should be clear by now that precious few diagnostic markers meeting adequate criteria of sensitivity and specficity have been established for the major diagnostic groupings. Perhaps the best candidate for a genetic marker is pendulum eye-tracking dysfunction in schizophrenia, which seems to have reasonably good specificity in comparison to other "functional" disorders (but possibly not for some organic conditions) and familial concordance. The fact that this marker is subject to influence by attention does not refute its status as a marker, but does have implications for its functional significance. Similar comments apply to low middle and late ERP amplitudes, but in this case, the role of attention is even greater. Furthermore, only quantitative differences between schizophrenics and psychotic depressives seem to exist, and family studies remain to be done. This suggests a closer relationship of these markers to a functional deficit for which there is overlap among diagnostic groups than to diagnosis itself. However, studies that carefully control and manipulate specific demands on attention might turn up more specific markers.

These examples illustrate the intimate connection between the functional state of the subject and psychophysiological markers. Although the empirical adequacy of markers is evaluated by the statistical criteria of sensitivity and specificity, their pathophysiological significance (Shagass, 1976) depends on assumptions regarding their direct biological determinants—assumptions that should not be taken on faith. The main point here is that the pathophysiological significance of a marker cannot be established without an understanding of its psychophysiological significance. This caveat may apply as well to neurochemical and other biological phenomena as it does to psychophysiological ones. To deal with this problem, it will be necessary to develop and use research strategies to tease out the interplay between psychological and biological determinants of psychophysiological variables.

A number of other reasonably consistent findings have been reported in this chapter, such as ERP reducing in depressed patients, impaired electrodermal anticipation of aversive stimulation in primary psychopaths, small SCRs in hyperactive children, delayed BSERs in autistic children, and impaired habituation in patients with anxiety disorders, just as examples. Adequate specificity of these putative diagnostic markers remains to be established, but such findings seem to be of more interest in terms of what they suggest about the nature and etiology of the disorders than as empirical markers.

It may be unrealistic to expect to find markers for global syndromes such as the ones represented by the section headings of this chapter because of the marked within-diagnosis heterogeneity of symptoms and possibly of etiology in virtually all disorders. Most of the "consistent findings" listed in the last paragraph, for example, as well as many other of the more interesting results reported, are present in only a proportion of the populations studied. The point has been made that in such a case a substantial proportion of studies comparing samples of patients with controls will yield results that are not statistically significant (Buchsbaum & Rieder, 1979). Therefore group comparisons by parametric statistics may obscure the true situation, which might be better revealed by plotting frequency distributions—a practice that, fortunately, is becoming increasingly common. However, even the demonstration of a substantial number of outliers in the patient group will not be too meaningful in most cases, unless these differ in some clinical, behavioral, or biological way from patients with more normal values. This suggests that the most fruitful approach in future work may be to correlate the psychophysiological data with specific symptoms and with behavioral and biological variables, rather than with global diagnoses.

Function

Interpretation of psychophysiological data in terms of their functional significance has generally proved more satisfactory than regarding them simply as markers of diagnosis. For example, through the use of appropriate ERP paradigms, attention dysfunction in schizophrenia, hyperactivity, autism, and (to a lesser extent) affective disorders has been analyzed. The ERP research has begun to tell us a little more about the nature of the attention deficits in these groups, and about the similarities and differences between them, than is known (or suspected) from strictly behavioral research. Distinctions between different disorders in terms of the general degree of cognitive impairment on the basis of SCOR and SSCR relationships have been pointed out earlier. ANS base levels, responsivity, and habituation seem to vary in a reasonable fashion with the affective states of depression and anxiety, at least at pathological extremes. Many other examples are indicated in the preceding sections.

However, it is obvious that these psychophysiological relationships are not commutative. We cannot yet be mind readers. A given physiological state cannot be attributed to any particular psychological state. For example, it would be premature to attribute the SCOR nonresponding found both in schizophrenia and in endogenous depression to a common psychological state. It might be said that this marker reflects a lack of interest in the environment in both conditions, but this interpretation, while not completely trivial, hardly goes beyond the data. The psychological processes leading to lack of environmental interest are not revealed by nonresponding alone. To make an analogy with markers of diagnosis, a given psychophysiological variable may have good sensitivity with respect to a psychological process, but few variables, if any, have specificity for a single process.

I have pointed out with respect to diagnosis, it might be possible to obtain more specificity by considering several variables at once. For example, the interpretation of SCOR nonresponding might be different for subjects with many or few SSCRs, or subjects with high or low HR, or subjects giving adequate or deficient SCRs to signal stimuli. Such patterning has rarely been studied as such in psychopathology, despite the availability of multivariate computer programs.

Up to now, psychophysiological variables have been considered as indicators of (read: factors caused by) psychological processes. The points made could apply equally in the more exciting (to a psychophysiologist) case in which the psychological processes are a more or less direct consequence of the physiological processes measured. However, little evidence for causal relationships in this direction exists at present. Such evidence might be forthcoming from some of the longitudinal high-risk studies in progress and could come from longitudinal studies of patients who have periods of remission and exacerbation, but these studies are infrequent and difficult. Repeated studies of ANS activity during behavior therapy of phobic and obsessive patients have suggested that both systematic desensitization and flooding, when successful, are accompanied by reduction in ANS reactions to the critical stimuli. This suggests that a common mechanism of extinction (or fatigue) underlies these apparently dissimilar treatments.

Biological Substrates

Progress in understanding the neurobiology of psychiatric disorders from psychophysiological studies has been disappointingly slow. Perhaps the best evidence pointing to a specific etiology is in autism, where the BSEP, HR variability, and nystagmus findings all seem to point to brain stem dysfunction. The question raised about nonpsychotic disorders is usually whether they have a biological basis at all. The recent psychophysiological evidence is supportive of biological involvement in anxiety disorders and psychopathy. The role of physiological activity here might be best conceptualized in terms of increasing vulnerability. For hyperactivity, on the other hand, although there seem to be replicable physiological markers, the demonstration of the nonparadoxical nature of stimulant drug effects has removed a strong support of a biological hypothesis.

Although a prominent role for biology in the etiology of the major psychoses is infrequently questioned at present, determining its nature from the psychophysiological data is proving difficult. This may be due to the marked heterogeneity of these disorders; schizophrenia and the affective disorders are regarded as composed of several rather distinct subdisorders, each possibly with a separate etiology. A number of promising hypotheses and findings have been described in the preceding sections, and progress is definitely being made.

One of the strategies mentioned in this chapter is that of studying the neurobiological bases of physiological measures by the comparative effects of different treatment drugs. The apparent similarity, as mentioned earlier, of the effects of ANS arousal indices and on some ERPs of the drugs used to treat schizophrenia, affective disorders, and anxiety disorders suggests that simple one-to-one inferences about mechanism are not valid from such variables. This is not surprising. For example, at the peripheral level, the SNS has both cholinergic and adrenergic synapses, so that dysfunction at either site might affect SNS activity similarly. Interactions between neurotransmitters occur centrally as well. Drugs not only have more than one effect on neurotransmitters and neuromodulators; with chronic administration, they may also alter receptor sensitivity. Thus similar effects of different drugs could be attributable to similar or different mechanisms, and resolving this question is not a simple matter. Multivariate comparative studies of acute and chronic effects of different drugs under the same conditions might help narrow the possibilities with respect to mechanism. Thus this strategy is still viable, but the problem may be more complex than anticipated.

It has been the aim of this chapter to show the many ways in which psychophysiology has contributed and might contribute to the understanding of psychiatric disorders. It can be concluded that this contribution has been considerable and that future progress should occur at an increasing rate, determined largely by the imagination and skill of the scientists involved.

ACKNOWLEDGMENTS

I am indebted to many persons whose help facilitated the production of this chapter. The quality of portions of the manuscript has been improved considerably by the critical comments of Connie Duncan-Johnson, Deborah Fein, Judith Rapoport, Judith Rumsey, and Carmi Schooler. Bibliographic assistance was provided by Elisabeth Evensen, and Marie Elliott provided expert editorial assistance. Finally, the many words herein were processed by Nancy Garritt, Betty Dodson, Mary LaPadula, and Patricia Burgess.

REFERENCES

Abrams, R., & Taylor, M. A. Differential EEG patterns in affective disorder and schizophrenia. *Archives of General Psychiatry*, 1979, 36, 1355–1358.

Abrams, R., Taylor, M. A., & Volavka, J. Interhemispheric power ratios in schizophrenia and affective disorder. In P. Flor-Henry & J. Gruzelier (Eds.), *Laterality and psychopathology*. Amsterdam: Elsevier Science Publishers, 1983.

Adler, L. E., Pachtman, E., Franks, R. D., Pecevich, M., Waldo, M. C., & Freedman, R. Neurophysiological evidence for a defect in neuronal mechanisms involved in sensory gating in schizophrenia. *Biological Psychiatry*, 1982, 17, 639–654.

Ågren, H., Osterberg, B., & Franzen, O. Depression and somatosensory evoked potentials: II. Correlations between SEP and depressive phenomenology. *Biological Psychiatry*, 1983, 18, 651–659.

Ågren, H., Osterberg, B., Niklasson, F., & Franzen, O. Depression and somatosensory evoked potentials: I. Correlations between SEP and monoamine and purine metabolites in CSF. *Biological Psychiatry*, 1983, 18, 635–649.

Akselrod, S., Gordon, D., Ubel, F. A., Shannon, D. C., Barger, A. C., & Cohen, R. J. Power spectrum analysis of heart rate fluctuation: A quantitative probe of beat-to-beat cardiovascular control. *Science*, 1981, 213, 220–222.

Albus, M., Engel, R. R., Muller, F., Zander, K.-J., & Ackenheil, M. Experimental stress situations and the state of autonomic arousal in schizophrenic and depressive patients. *International Pharmacopsychiatry*, 1982, 17, 129–135.

Albus, M., Ackenheil, M., Engel, R. R., & Muller, F. Situational reactivity of autonomic functions in schizophrenic patients. *Psychiatry Research*, 1982, 6, 361–370.

American Psychiatric Association. *Diagnostic and statistical manual of mental disorders* (3rd ed.). Washington, D.C.: Author, 1980.

Andreasen, N. J. C., Peters, J. F., & Knott, J. R. CNV's in hyperactive children: Effects of chemotherapy. In W. C. McCallum & J. R. Knott (Eds.), *The responsive brain*. Bristol, England: J. Wright, 1976.

Aniskiewicz, A. S. Autonomic components of vicarious conditioning and psychopathy. *Journal of Clinical Psychology*, 1979, 35(1), 60–67.

Asberg, M. Plasma nortriptyline levels—relationship to clinical effects. *Clinical Pharmacology and Therapeutics*, 1974, 16, 215–229.

Asarnow, R. F., Cromwell, R. L., & Rennick, P. M. Cognitive and evoked response measures of information processing in schizophrenics with and without a family history of schizophrenia. *Journal of Nervous and Mental Disease*, 1978, 116, 719–730.

Ax, A. F. Emotional learning deficiency in schizophrenia. In M. L. Kietzman, S. Sutton, & J. Zubin (Eds.), *Experimental approaches to psychopathology*. New York: Academic Press, 1975.

Ax, A. F., Bamford, J. L., Beckett, P. G. S., Fretz, N. F., & Gottlieb, J. S. Autonomic conditioning in chronic schizophrenics. *Journal of Abnormal Psychology*, 1970, 76, 140–154.

Bachneff, S. A., & Engelsmann, F. Correlates of cerebral event-related slow potentials and psychopathology. *Psychological Medicine*, 1983, 13, 763–770.

Baer, P. E., & Fuhrer, M. J. Cognitive factors in differential conditioning of the GSR: Use of a reaction time task as the UCS with normals and schizophrenics. *Journal of Abnormal Psychology*, 1969, 74, 544–552.

Ban, T. A., Ananth, J. V., & Lehmann, H. E. Conditioning and the classification of the chronic schizophrenic patient. *Pavlovian Journal of Biological Science*, 1979, 14, 44–60.

Baribeau-Braun, J., Picton, T. W., & Gosselin, J.-Y. Schizophrenia: A neurophysiological evaluation of abnormal information processing. *Science*, 1983, 219, 874–876.

Baribeau-Braun, J., & Lesevre, N. Event-related potential assessment of psychomotor retardation in depressives. In J. Mendlewicz & H. M. van Praag (Eds.), *Advances in biological psychiatry*, Vol 13. New York: S. Karger, 1983.

Barkley, R. A. A review of stimulant drug research with hyperactive children. *Journal of Child Psychology and Psychiatry*, 1977, 18, 137–165.

Barkley, R. A., & Jackson, T. L., Jr. Hyperkinesis, autonomic nervous system activity and stimulant drug effects. *Journal of Child Psychology and Psychiatry*, 1977, 18, 347–357.

Baron, M., Gershon, E. S., Rudy, V., Jones, W. Z., & Buchsbaum, M. S. Lithium carbonate response in depression. *Archives of General Psychiatry*, 1975, 32, 1107–1111.

Bartfai, A., Edman, G., Levander, S. E., Schalling, D., & Sedvall, G. Bilateral skin conductance activity, clinical symptoms and CSF monoamine metabolite levels in unmedicated schizophrenics, differing in rate of habituation. *Biological Psychology*, 1984, 18, 201–218.

Bartfai, A., Levander, S., Edman, G., Schalling, D., & Sedvall, G. Skin conductance responses in unmedicated recently admitted schizophrenic patients. *Psychophysiology*, 1983, 20, 180–187.

Bartfai, A., Levander, S. E., & Sedvall, G. Smooth pursuit eye movements, clinical symptoms, CSF metabolites, and skin conductance habituation in schizophrenic patients. *Biological Psychiatry*, 1983, 18, 971–987.

Beech, H. R., & Perigault, J. Toward a theory of obsessional disorder. In H. R. Beech (Ed.), *Obsessional states*. London: Methuen 1977.

Beech, H. R., Ciesielski, K. T., & Gordon, P. K. Further observations of evoked potentials in obsessional patients. *British Journal of Psychiatry*, 1983, 142, 605–609.

Bernadt, M. W., Silverstone, T., & Singleton, W. Behavioural and subjective effects of beta-adrenergic blockade in phobic subjects. *British Journal of Psychiatry*, 1980, 137, 452–457.

Bernal, M. E., & Miller, W. H. Electrodermal and cardiac responses of schizophrenic children to sensory stimuli. *Psychophysiology*, 1970, 1, 155–168.

Bernstein, A. S. Electrodermal base level, tonic arousal, and adaptation in chronic schizophrenics. *Journal of Abnormal Psychology*, 1967, 72, 221–232.

Bernstein, A. S. Phasic electrodermal orienting response in chronic schizophrenics: II. Response to auditory signals of varying intensity. *Journal of Abnormal Psychology*, 1970, 75, 146–156.

Bernstein, A. S., Frith, C. D., Gruzelier, J. H., Patterson, T., Straube, E. R., Venables, P. H., & Zahn, T. P. An analysis of skin conductance orienting responses in samples of British, American, and German schizophrenics. *Biological Psychology*, 1982, 14, 155–211.

Bernstein, A. S., Schneider, S. J., Juni, S., Pope, A. T., & Starkey, P. W. The effect of stimulus significance on the electrodermal response in chronic schizophrenia. *Journal of Abnormal Psychology*, 1980, 89, 93–97.

Bernstein, A. S., & Taylor, K. W. Stimulus significance and the phasic electrodermal orienting response in schizophrenic and nonschizophrenic adolescents: A preliminary report. In D. V. Siva Sankar (Ed.), *Mental health in children* (Vol. 2). Westbury, N.Y.: PJD Publications, 1976.

Bernstein, A. S., Taylor, K. W., Starkey, P., Juni, S., Lubowsky, J., & Paley, H. Bilateral skin conductance, finger pulse volume and EEG orienting response to tones of differing intensities in chronic schizophrenics and controls. *Journal of Nervous and Mental Disease*, 1981, 169, 513–528.

Bernstein, A. S., Taylor, K. W., Starkey, P., Lubowsky, J., Juni, S., & Herbert, P. The effect of prolonged stimulus repetition on autonomic response and EEG activity in normal subjects, schizophrenic, and nonschizophrenic patients. *Psychophysiology*, 1983, 20, 332–342.

Blackburn, R. Aggression and the EEG: A quantitative analysis. *Journal of Abnormal Psychology*, 1975, 84, 358–365.

Blackburn, R. Cortical and autonomic arousal in primary and secondary psychopaths. *Psychophysiology*, 1979, 16, 143–150.

Bond, A. J., James, D. C., & Lader, M. H. Physiological and psychological measures in anxious patients. *Psychological Medicine*, 1974, 4, 364–373. (a)

Bond, A. J., James, D. C., & Lader, M. H. Sedative effects on physiological and psychological measures in anxious patients. *Psychological Medicine*, 1974, 4, 374–380. (b)

Borkovec, T. D. Autonomic reactivity to sensory stimulation in psychopathic, neurotic and normal juvenile delinquents. *Journal of Consulting and Clinical Psychology*, 1970, 35, 217–222.

Borkovec, T. D., & O'Brien, G. T. Methodological and target behavior issues in analogue therapy research. In M. Hersen, R. M. Eisler, & P. M. Miller (Eds.), *Progress in behavior modification*. New York: Academic Press, 1976.

Boulougouris, J. C., Rabavilas, A. D., & Stefanis, C. Psychophysiological responses in obsessive compulsive patients. *Behaviour Research and Therapy*, 1977, 15, 221–230.

Braff, D. L., Callaway, E., & Naylor, H. Very short-term memory (VSTM) dysfunction in schizophrenia. *Archives of General Psychiatry*, 1977, 34, 25–30.

Braff, D. L., Stone, C., Callaway, E., Geyer, M., Glick, I., & Bali, L. Prestimulus effects in human startle reflex in normals and schizophrenics. *Psychophysiology*, 1978, 15, 339–343.

Brecher, M., & Begleiter, H. Event-related brain potentials to high-incentive stimuli in unmedicated schizophrenic patients. *Biological Psychiatry*, 1983, 18, 661–674.

Breyer-Pfaff, U., Gaertner, H. J., & Giedke, H. Plasma levels, psychophysiological variables, and clinical response to amitriptyline. *Psychiatry Research*, 1982, 6, 223–234.

Brezinova, V., & Kendell, R. E. Smooth pursuit eye movements of schizophrenics and normal people under stress. *British Journal of Psychiatry*, 1977, 130, 59–63.

Brierley, H. The habituation of forearm muscle blood flow in phobic subjects. *Journal of Neurology, Neurosurgery and Psychiatry*, 1969, 32, 15–20.

Briling, E. G. Active attention and the conditioned slow negative potential in schizophrenics. *Neuroscience and Behavioral Physiology*, 1980, 10, 328–332.

Bruno, R. L., Myers, S. J., & Glassman, A. H. A correlational study of cardiovascular autonomic functioning and unipolar depression. *Biological Psychiatry*, 1983, 18, 227–235.

Buchsbaum, M. S. Average evoked response augmenting/reducing in schizophrenia and affective disorders. In D. X. Freedman (Ed.), *The biology of the major psychoses: A comparative analysis.* New York: Raven Press, 1975.

Buchsbaum, M. S. The middle evoked response components and schizophrenia. *Schizophrenia Bulletin*, 1977, 3, 93–104.

Buchsbaum, M. S. Neurophysiological aspects of the schizophrenic syndrome. In L. Bellak (Ed.), *Disorders of the schizophrenic syndrome.* New York: Basic Books, 1979. (a)

Buchsbaum, M. S. Neurophysiological reactivity, stimulus intensity modulation and the depressive disorders. In R. A. Depue (Ed.), *The psychobiology of the depressive disorders.* New York: Academic Press, 1979. (b)

Buchsbaum, M. S., Carpenter, W. T., Fedio, P., Goodwin, F. K., Murphy, D. L., & Post, R. M. Hemispheric differences in evoked potential enhancement by selective attention to hemiretinally presented stimuli in schizophrenic, affective and posttemporal lobectomy patients. In J. Gruzelier & P. Flor-Henry (Eds.), *Hemispheric asymmetries of function in psychopathology.* Amsterdam: Elsevier, 1979.

Buchsbaum, M. S., & Coppola, R. Signal-to-noise ratio and response variability in affective disorders and schizophrenia. In H. Begleiter (Ed.), *Evoked brain potentials and behavior,* New York: Plenum Press, 1979.

Buchsbaum, M. S., Davis, G. C., Goodwin, F. K., Murphy, D. L., & Post R. M. Psychophysical pain judgments and somatosensory evoked potentials in patients with affective illness and in normal adults. *Advances in Biological Psychiatry*, 1980, 4, 63–72.

Buchsbaum, M. S., Gerner, R., & Post, R. M. The effects of sleep deprivation on average evoked responses in depressed patients and normals. *Biological Psychiatry*, 1981, 16, 351–363.

Buchsbaum, M. S., Goodwin, F. K., Murphy, D. L., & Borge, G. F. AER in effective disorders. *American Journal of Psychiatry*, 1971, 128, 19–25.

Buchsbaum, M. S., King, A. C., Cappelletti, J., Coppola, R., & Van Kammen, D. P. Visual evoked potential topography in patients with schizophrenia and normal controls. *Advances in Biological Psychiatry*, 1982, 9, 50–56.

Buchsbaum, M. S., Landau, S., Murphy, D. L., & Goodwin, F. K. Average evoked response in bipolar and unipolar affective disorders: Relationship to sex, age of onset and monoamine oxidase. *Biological Psychiatry*, 1973, 7, 199–212.

Buchsbaum, M. S., Lavine, R. A., Davis, G. C., Goodwin, F. K., Murphy, D. L., & Post, R. M. Effects of lithium on somatosensory evoked potentials and prediction of clinical response in patients with affective illness. In T. B. Cooper, S. Gershon, N. S. Kline, & M. Schou (Eds.), *Lithium: Controversies and unresolved issues.* Amsterdam: Excerpta Medica, 1979.

Buchsbaum, M. S., Mirsky, A. F., DeLisi, L. E., Morihisa, J., Kar-

son, C. N., Mendelson, W. B., King, A. C., Johnson, J., & Kessler, R. The Genain Quadruplets: Electrophysiological, positron emission, and x-ray tomographic studies. *Psychiatry Research*, 1984, 13, 95–108.

Buchsbaum, M. S., Post, R. M., & Bunney, W. E. Average evoked responses in a rapidly cycling manic–depressive patient. *Biological Psychiatry*, 1977, 12, 83–99.

Buchsbaum, M. S., & Rieder, R. O. Biologic heterogeniety and psychiatric research. *Archives of General Psychiatry*, 1979, 36, 1163–1169.

Buchsbaum, M. S., Van Kammen, D. P., & Murphy, D. L. Individual differences in average evoked responses to d- and l-amphetamine with and without lithium carbonate in depressed patients. *Psychopharmacology*, 1977, 51, 129–135.

Buchsbaum, M. S., & Wender, P. Average evoked responses in normal and minimally brain dysfunctioned children treated with amphetamine: A preliminary report. *Archives of General Psychiatry*, 1973, 29, 764–770.

Bunney, B. S., & Aghajanian, G. K. Mesolimbic and mesocortical dopaminergic systems: Physiology and pharmacology. In M. A. Lipton, A. DiMascio, & K. F. Killam (Eds.), *Psychopharmacology: A generation of progress.* New York: Raven Press, 1978.

Byrne, D. G. A psychophysiological distinction between types of depressive states. *Australian and New Zealand Journal of Psychiatry*, 1975, 9, 181–185.

Callaway, E., Halliday, R., & Naylor, H. Hyperactive children's event-related potentials fail to support underarousal and maturational-lag theories. *Archives of General Psychiatry*, 1983, 40, 1243–1248.

Callaway, E., & Naghdi, S. An information processing model for schizophrenia. *Archives of General Psychiatry*, 1982, 39, 339–347.

Carney, R. M., Hong, B. A., O'Connell, M. F., & Amado, H. Facial electromyography as a predictor of treatment outcome in depression. *British Journal of Psychiatry*, 1981, 138, 485–489.

Carroll, B. J., Curtis, G. L., & Mendels, J. Neuroendocrine regulation in depression: II. Discrimination of depressed from nondepressed patients. *Archives of General Psychiatry*, 1976, 33, 1051–1058.

Cegalis, J. A., Hafez, H., & Wong, P. S. What is deviant about deviant smooth pursuit eye movements in schizophrenia? *Psychiatry Research*, 1983, 10, 47–58.

Cegalis, J. A., & Sweeney, J. A. Eye movements in schizophrenia: A quantitative analysis. *Biological Psychiatry*, 1979, 14, 13–26.

Cegalis, J. A., & Sweeney, J. A. The effects of attention on smooth pursuit eye movements of schizophrenics. *Journal of Psychiatric Research*, 1981, 16, 145–162.

Cegalis, J. A., Sweeney, J. A., & Dellis, E. M. Reflex saccades and attention in schizophrenia. *Psychiatry Research*, 1982, 7, 189–198.

Charney, D. S., Heninger, G. R., & Breier, A. Noradrenergic function in panic anxiety. *Archives of General Psychiatry*, 1984, 41, 751–763.

Charney, D. S., Heninger, G. R., Sternberg, D. E., Redmond, D. E., Leckman, J. F., Maas, J. W., & Roth, R. H. Presynaptic adrenergic receptor sensitivity in depression. *Archives of General Psychiatry*, 1981, 38, 1334–1340.

Charney, D. S., Heninger, G. R., Sternberg, D. E., Hafstad, K. M., Giddings, S., & Landis, D. H. Adrenergic receptor sensitivity in depression: Effects of clonidine in depressed patients and healthy subjects. *Archives of General Psychiatry*, 1982, 39, 290–294.

Chattopadhyay, P. K., Bond, A. J., & Lader, M. H. Characteristics of galvanic skin response in anxiety states. *Journal of Psychiatric Research*, 1975, 12, 265–270.

Chattopadhyay, P. K., Cooke, E., Toone, B., & Lader, M. Habituation of physiological responses in anxiety. *Biological Psychiatry*, 1980, 15, 711–721.

Christie, M. J., Little, B. C., & Gordon, A. M. Peripheral indices of depressive states. In H. M. Van Praag, M. H. Lader, O. J.

Rafaelsen, & E. J. Sachar (Eds.), *Handbook of biological psychiatry: Part II. Brain mechanisms and abnormal behavior—Psychophysiology.* New York: Marcel Dekker, 1980.

Ciesielski, K. T., Beech, H. R., & Gordon, P. K. Some electrophysiological observations in obsessional states. *British Journal of Psychiatry,* 1981, 138, 479–484.

Claridge, G. Animal models of schizophrenia: The case for LSD-25. *Schizophrenia Bulletin,* 1978, 4, 186–210.

Claridge, G., & Clark, K. Covariation between two-flash threshold and skin conductance level in first-breakdown schizophrenics: Relationships in drug-free patients and effects of treatment. *Psychiatry Research,* 1982, 6, 371–380.

Cleckley, H. *The mask of sanity* (5th ed.). St. Louis: C. V. Mosby, 1976.

Coger, R. W., Dymond, A. M., & Serafetinides, E. A. Electroencephalographic similarities between chronic alcoholics and chronic, nonparanoid schizophrenics. *Archives of General Psychiatry,* 1979, 36, 91–94.

Cohen, D. J., & Johnson, W. T. Cardiovascular correlates of attention in normal and psychiatrically disturbed children. *Archives of General Psychiatry,* 1977, 34, 561–567.

Cohen, N. J., & Douglas, V. I. Characteristics of the orienting response in hyperactive and normal children. *Psychophysiology,* 1972, 9, 238–245.

Cohen, N. J., Douglas, V. I., & Morgenstern, G. The effect of methylphenidate on attentive behavior and autonomic activity in hyperactive children. *Psychopharmacologia,* 1971, 22, 282–294.

Cohen, R., Sommer, W., & Hermanutz, M. Auditory event related potentials in chronic schizophrenics: Effects of electrodermal response type and demands on selective attention. *Advances in Biological Psychiatry,* 1981, 6, 180–185.

Colbert, E. G., Koegler, R. R., & Markham, C. H. Vestibular dysfunction in childhood schizophrenia. *Archives of General Psychiatry,* 1959, 1, 600–617.

Coleman, M. (Ed.). *The autistic syndromes.* Amsterdam: North-Holland, 1976.

Conners, C. K. Symptom patterns in hyperkinetic, neurotic and normal children. *Child Development,* 1970, 41, 669–682.

Conners, C. K. Minimal brain dysfunction and psychopathology in children. In A. Davids (Ed.), *Child personality and psychopathology: Current topics* (Vol. 2). New York: Wiley, 1975.

Conners, C. K., & Rothschild, G. H. The effect of dextroamphetamine on habituation of peripheral vascular response in children. *Journal of Abnormal Child Psychology,* 1973, 1, 16–25.

Connolly, J. F., Gruzelier, J. H., Manchanda, R., & Hirsch, S. R. Visual evoked potentials in schizophrenia. Intensity effects and hemispheric asymmetry. *British Journal of Psychiatry,* 1983, 142, 152–155.

Coons, H. W., Peloquin, L., Klorman, R., Bauer, L. O., Ryan, R. M., Pearlmutter, K. A., & Salzman, L. F. Effect of methylphenidate on young adults' vigilance and event-related potentials. *Electroencephalography and Clinical Neurophysiology,* 1981, 51, 373–387.

Cooper, J. E., Kendall, R. E., Gurland, B. J., Sharpe, L., Copeland, J. R. M., & Simon, R. J. *Psychiatric diagnosis in New York and London: A comparative study of mental hospital admissions* (Maudsley Monograph No. 20) London: Oxford University Press, 1972.

Crighel, E., Predescu, V., Matei, M., Nica, S., & Prica, A. Neocortical reactivity to peripheral stimuli in neurotics. *Neuropsychobiology,* 1976, 2, 258–268.

Dainer, K. B., Klorman, R., Salzman, L. F., Hess, D. W., Davidson, P. W., & Michael, R. L. Learning-disordered children's evoked potentials during sustained attention. *Journal of Abnormal Child Psychology,* 1981, 9, 79–94.

Damasio, H., Maurer, R. G., Damasio, A. R., & Chui, H. C. Computerized tomographic scan findings in patients with autistic behavior. *Archives of Neurology,* 1980, 37, 504–510.

Davis, G. C., Buchsbaum, M. S., & Bunney, W. E. Alterations of evoked potentials link research in attention dysfunction to pep-

tide response symptoms of schizophrenia. In E. Costa & M. Trabucchi (Eds.), *Neural peptides and neuronal communication.* New York: Raven Press, 1980.

Davis, J. R., Glaros, A. G., & Davidson, G. S. Visual information processing and alpha blocking in schizophrenics and normals. *Journal of Psychiatric Research,* 1981, 16, 95–102.

Dawson, M. E., Schell, A. M., & Catania, J. J. Autonomic correlates of depression and clinical improvement following electroconvulsive shock therapy. *Psychophysiology,* 1977, 14, 569–578.

Deakin, J. F. W., Baker, H. F., Frith, C. D., Joseph, M. H., & Johnstone, E. C. Arousal related to excretion of noradrenaline metabolites and clinical aspects of unmedicated chronic schizophrenic patients. *Journal of Psychiatric Research,* 1979, 15, 57–65.

d'Elia, G., & Perris, C. Cerebral functional dominance and depression. *Acta Psychiatrica Scandinavica,* 1973, 49, 191–197.

DeMyer, M. K., Barton, S., DeMyer, W. E., Norton, J. A., Allen, J., & Steele, R. Prognosis in autism: A followup study. *Journal of Autism and Childhood Schizophrenia,* 1973, 3, 199–246.

Dengerink, H. A., & Bertilson, H. S. Psychopathy and physiological arousal in an aggressive task. *Psychophysiology,* 1975, 12, 682–684.

Dongier, M., Dubrovsky, B., & Englesmann, F. Event-related slow potentials in psychiatry. In C. Shagass, S. Gershon, & A. J. Friedhoff (Eds.), *Psychopathology and brain dysfunction.* New York: Raven Press, 1977.

Drachman, D. Central cholinergic system and memory. In M. A. Lipton, A. DiMascio, & K. F. Killam (Eds.), *Psychopharmacology: A generation of progress.* New York: Raven Press, 1978.

Dubrovsky, B., Solyom, L., & Barbas, H. Characteristics of the contingent negative variation in patients suffering from specific phobias. *Biological Psychiatry,* 1978, 13, 531–540.

Duncan-Johnson, C. C., Roth, W. T., & Kopell, B. S. Effects of stimulus sequence on P300 and reaction time in schizophrenics. In R. Karrer, J. Cohen, & P. Tueting (Eds.), *Brain and information: Event-related potentials,* Vol. 425. New York: The New York Academy of Sciences, 1984.

Dykman, R. A., Holcomb, P. J., Ackerman, P. T., & McCray, D. S. Auditory ERP augmentation–reduction and methylphenidate dosage needs in attention and reading disordered children. *Psychiatry Research,* 1983, 9, 255–269.

Dykman, R. A., Holcomb, P. J., Oglesby, D. M., & Ackerman, P. T. Electrocortical frequencies in hyperactive, learning-disabled, mixed, and normal children. *Biological Psychiatry,* 1982, 17, 675–685.

Engle, G. L. The need for a new medical model: A challenge for biomedicine. *Science,* 1977, 196, 129–136.

Escobar, J. I., Gomez, O., & Tuason, V. B. Depressive subtypes, blood pressure changes, and response to treatment. *Diseases of the Nervous System,* 1977, 38, 76–79.

Etevenon, P. Intra and inter-hemispheric changes in alpha intensities in EEGs of schizophrenic patients versus matched controls. *Biological Psychology,* 1984, 19, 247–256.

Fein, D., Skoff, B. F., & Mirsky, A. F. Clinical correlates of brainstem dysfunction in autistic children. *Journal of Autism and Childhood Schizophrenia,* 1981, 11, 303–315.

Fein, G., Tursky, B., & Erlenmeyer-Kimling, L. Stimulus sensivity and reactivity in children at high risk for schizophrenia. *Psychophysiology,* 1975, 12, 226.

Fenton, G. W., Fenwick, P. B., Ferguson, W., & Lam, C. T. The contingent negative variation in antisocial behaviour: A pilot study of Broadmoor patients. *British Journal of Psychiatry,* 1978, 132, 368–377.

Fink, M. EEG profiles and bioavailability measures of psychoactive drugs. In T. M. Itil (Ed.), *Modern problems of pharmacopsychiatry* (Vol. 8, *Psychotropic drugs and the human EEG*). Basel: Karger, 1974.

Fish, B. Neurobiologic antecedents of schizophrenia in children. *Archives of General Psychiatry,* 1977, 34, 1297–1313.

Flor-Henry, P. Psychosis and temporal lobe epilepsy: A controlled investigation. *Epilepsia*, 1969, 10, 363–395.

Flor-Henry, P., & Koles, Z. J. EEG studies in depression, mania and normals: Evidence for partial shifts of laterality in the affective psychoses. *Advances in Biological Psychiatry*, 1980, 4, 21–43.

Flor-Henry, P., & Koles, Z. J. Statistical quantitative EEG studies of depression, mania, schizophrenia and normals. *Biological Psychology*, 1984, 19, 257–279.

Flor-Henry, P., Koles, Z. J., Howarth, B. G., & Burton, L. Neurophysiological studies of schizophrenia, mania and depression. In J. Gruzelier & P. Flor-Henry (Eds.), *Hemispheric asymmetries of function in psychopathology*. Amsterdam: Elsevier, 1979.

Flor-Henry, P., Yeudall, L. T., Koles, Z. J., & Howarth, B. G. Neuropsychological and power spectral EEG investigations of the obsessive–compulsive syndrome. *Biological Psychiatry*, 1979, 14, 119–130.

Fowles, D. C. The three arousal model: Implications of Gray's two-factor learning theory for heart rate, electrodermal activity, and psychopathy. *Psychophysiology*, 1980, 17, 87–104.

Fowles, D. C., Watt, N. F., Maher, B. A., & Grinspoon, L. Autonomic arousal in good and poor premorbid schizophrenics. *British Journal of Social and Clinical Psychology*, 1970, 9, 135–147.

Fredrikson, M. Orienting and defensive reactions to phobic and conditioned fear stimuli in phobics and normals. *Psychophysiology*, 1981, 18, 456–465.

Freedman, R., Adler, L. E., Waldo, M. C., Pachtman, E., & Franks, R. D. Neurophysiological evidence for a defect in inhibitory pathways in schizophrenia: Comparison of medicated and drug-free patients. *Biological Psychiatry*, 1983, 18, 537–551.

Friedman, D., Frosch, A., & Erlenmeyer-Kimling, L. Auditory evoked potentials in children at high risk for schizophrenia. In H. Begleiter (Ed.), *Evoked brain potentials and behavior* (Vol. 2). New York: Plenum, 1979.

Friedman, D., Vaughan, H. G., Jr., & Erlenmeyer-Kimling, L. Cognitive brain potentials in children at risk for schizophrenia: Preliminary findings. *Schizophrenia Bulletin*, 1982, 8, 514–531.

Friedman, J., McCallum, P., & Meares, R. Stimulus intensity control in depression: A study of the comparative effect of doxepin and amitriptyline on cortical evoked potentials. *Australian and New Zealand Journal of Psychiatry*, 1980, 14, 115–119.

Friedman, J., & Meares, R. The effects of placebo and tricyclic antidepressants on cortical evoked potentials in depressed patients. *Biological Psychology*, 1979, 8, 291–302.

Friedman, M. J., & Bennet, P. L. Depression and hypertension. *Psychosomatic Medicine*, 1977, 39, 134–142.

Frith, C. D., Stevens, M., Johnstone, E. C., & Crow, T. J. Skin conductance responsivity during acute episodes of schizophrenia as a predictor of symptomatic improvement. *Psychological Medicine*, 1979, 8, 1–6.

Frith, C.D., Stevens, M., Johnstone, E. C., & Crow, T. J. Skin conductance habituation during acute episodes of schizophrenia: Qualitative differences from anxious and depressed patients. *Psychological Medicine*, 1982, 12, 575–583.

Fuhrer, M. J., & Baer, P. E. Preparatory instructions in the differential conditioning of the galvanic skin response of schizophrenics and normals. *Journal of Abnormal Psychology*, 1970, 76, 482–484.

Gaffney, F. A., Karlsson, E. S., Campbell, W., Schutte, J. E., Nixon, J. V., Willerson, J. T., & Blomquist, C. G. Autonomic dysfunction in women with mitral valve prolapse syndrome. *Circulation*, 1979, 59, 894–901.

Gatchel, R. J., & Proctor, J. D. Effectiveness of voluntary heart rate control in reducing speech anxiety. *Journal of Consulting and Clinical Psychology*, 1976, 44, 381–389.

Gelder, M. G., Bancroft, J. H. J., Gath, D., Johnston, D. W., Mathews, A. M., & Shaw, P. M. Specific and non-specific factors in behaviour therapy. *British Journal of Psychiatry*, 1973, 123, 445–462.

Gershon, E. S., & Buchsbaum, M. S. A genetic study of average evoked response augmentation/reduction in affective disorders. In C. Shagass, S. Gershon, & A. J. Friedhoff (Eds.), *Psychopathology and brain dysfunction*. New York: Raven Press, 1977.

Geyer, M. A., & Braff, D. L. Habituation of the blink reflex in normals and schizophrenic patients. *Psychophysiology*, 1982, 19, 1–6.

Giedke, H., Thier, P., & Bolz, J. The relationship between P_3-latency and reaction time in depression. *Biological Psychology*, 1981, 13, 31–49.

Gillberg, C., Rosenhall, U., & Johansson, E. Auditory brainstem responses in childhood psychosis. *Journal of Autism and Developmental Disorders*, 1983, 13, 181–195.

Glassman, A. H., & Bigger, J. T. Cardiovascular effects of therapeutic doses of tricyclic antidepressants: A review. *Archives of General Psychiatry*, 1981, 38, 815–820.

Goldstein, I. B. The relationship of muscle tension and autonomic activity to psychiatric disorders. *Psychosomatic Medicine*, 1965, 27, 39–52.

Goldstein, M. J. Premorbid adjustment, paranoid status, and patterns of response to phenothiazine in acute schizophrenia. *Schizophrenia Bulletin*, 1970, 3, 24–37.

Goode, D. J., Manning, A. A., & Middleton, J. F. Cortical laterality and asymmetry of the Hoffman reflex in psychiatric patients. *Biological Psychiatry*, 1981, 16, 1137–1152.

Goode, D. J., Meltzer, H. Y., Crayton, J. W., & Mazura, T. A. Physiological abnormalities of the neuromuscular systems in schizophrenia. *Schizophrenia Bulletin*, 1977, 3, 121–138.

Goode, D. J., Meltzer, H. Y., & Mazura, T. A. Hoffman reflex abnormalities in psychotic patients. *Biological Psychiatry*, 1979, 14, 95–110.

Goodwin, F. K., Cowdry, R. W., & Webster, M. K. Predictors of drug response in the affective disorders: Toward an integrated approach. In M. A. Lipton, A. DiMascio, & K. F. Killam (Eds.), *Psychopharmacology: A generation of progress*. New York: Raven Press, 1978.

Gorham, J. C., Novelly, R. A., Ax, A. F., & Frohman, C. E. Classically conditioned autonomic discrimination and tryptophan uptake in chronic schizophrenia. *Psychophysiology*, 1978, 15, 158–164.

Gorman, J. M., Fyer, A. F., Gliklich, J., King, D., & Klein, D. F. Effect of sodium lactate on patients with panic disorder and mitral valve prolapse. *American Journal of Psychiatry*, 1981, 138, 247–249.

Graveling, R. A., & Brooke, J. D. Hormonal and cardiac response of autistic children to changes in environmental stimulation. *Journal of Autism and Childhood Schizophrenia*, 1978, 8, 441–455.

Gray, A. L. Autonomic correlates of chronic schizophrenia: A reaction time paradigm. *Journal of Abnormal Psychology*, 1975, 84, 189–196.

Gray, J. A. Drug effects on fear and frustration: Possible limbic site of action of minor tranquilizers. In L. L. Iversen, S. D. Iversen, & S. H. Snyder (Eds.) *Handbook of psychopharmacology* (Vol. 8, *Drugs, neurotransmitters, and behavior*). New York: Plenum, 1977.

Greden, J. F., Price, H. L., Genero, N., Feinberg, M., & Levine, S. Facial EMG activity levels predict treatment outcome in depression. *Psychiatry Research*, 1984, 13, 345–352.

Grunewald-Zuberbier, E., Grunewald, G., & Rasche, A. Hyperactive behavior and EEG arousal reactions in children. *Electroencephalography and Clinical Neurophysiology*, 1975, 38, 149–159.

Gruzelier, J. H. Bilateral asymmetry of skin conductance orienting activity and levels in schizophrenics. *Biological Psychology*, 1973, 1, 21–41.

Gruzelier, J. H. The cardiac responses of schizophrenics to orienting, signal, and non-signal tones. *Biological Psychology*, 1975, 3, 143–155.

Gruzelier, J. H. Clinical attributes of schizophrenia skin conductance responders and non-responders. *Psychological Medicine*, 1976, 6, 245–249.

Gruzelier, J. H. Lateral asymmetries in electrodermal activity and psychosis. In J. Gruzelier & P. Flor-Henry (Eds.), *Hemispheric asymmetries of function in psychopathology*. Amsterdam: Elsevier, 1979.

Gruzelier, J. H. Hemispheric imbalances masquerading as paranoid and nonparanoid syndromes: A speculative reinterpretation. *Schizophrenia Bulletin*, 1981, 7, 662–673.

Gruzelier, J. H., Connolly, J., Eves, F., Hirsch, S., Zaki, S., Weller, M., & Yorkston, N. Effect of propanalol and phenothiazines on electrodermal orienting and habituation in schizophrenia. *Psychological Medicine*, 1981, 11, 1–16.

Gruzelier, J. H., Eves, F., Connolly, J., & Hirsch, S. Orienting, habituation, sensitization, and dishabituation in the electrodermal system of consecutive, drug free, admissions for schizophrenia. *Biological Psychology*, 1981, 12, 187–209.

Gruzelier, J. H., & Hammond, N. V. The effect of chlorpromazine upon psychophysiological, endocrine and information processing measures in schizophrenia. *Journal of Psychiatric Research*, 1978, 14, 167–182.

Gruzelier, J. H., Hirsch, S. R., Weller, M., & Murphy, C. The influence of D- or DL-propanalol and chlorpromazine on habituation of phasic electrodermal responses in schizophrenia. *Acta Psychiatrica Scandinavica*, 1979, 60, 241–248.

Gruzelier, J. H., Lykken, D. T., and Venables, P. H. Schizophrenia and arousal revisited. *Archives of General Psychiatry*, 1972, 26, 427–432.

Gruzelier, J. H., & Venables, P. H. Skin conductance orienting activity in a heterogeneous sample of schizophrenics: Possible evidence of limbic dysfunction. *Journal of Nervous and Mental Disease*, 1972, 155, 277–287.

Gruzelier, J. H., & Venables, P. H. Skin conductance responses to tones with and without attentional significance in schizophrenic and nonschizophrenic psychiatric patients. *Neuropsychologia*, 1973, 11, 221–230.

Gruzelier, J. H., & Venables, P. H. Bimodality and lateral asymmetry of skin conductance orienting activity in schizophrenics: Replication and evidence of lateral asymmetry in patients with depression and disorders of personality. *Biological Psychiatry*, 1974, 8, 55–73. (a)

Gruzelier, J. H., & Venables, P. H. Two-flash threshold, sensitivity and beta in normal subjects and schizophrenics. *Quarterly Journal of Experimental Psychology*, 1974, 26, 594–604. (b)

Gruzelier, J. H., & Venables, P. H. Evidence in high and low arousal in schizophrenia. *Psychophysiology*, 1975, 12, 66–73. (a)

Gruzelier, J. H., & Venables, P. H. Relations between two-flash discrimination and electrodermal activity, re-examined in schizophrenics and normals. *Journal of Psychiatric Research*, 1975, 12, 73–85. (b)

Gulmann, N. C., Wildschiodtz, G., & Orbaek, K. Alteration of interhemisphere conduction through corpus callosum in chronic schizophrenia. *Biological Psychiatry*, 1982, 17, 585–594.

Hafner, J., & Marks, I. M. Exposure *in vivo* of agoraphobics: The contributions of diazepam, group exposure, and anxiety evocation. *Psychological Medicine*, 1976, 6, 71–88.

Haier, R. J. Pain sensitivity, evoked potentials, and the dexamethasone suppression test in depressed patients. *Psychiatry Research*, 1983, 10, 201–206.

Hakerem, G., & Lidsky, A. Characteristics of pupillary reactivity in psychiatric patients and normal controls. In M. L. Kietzman, S. Sutton, & J. Zubin (Eds.), *Experimental approaches to psychopathology*. New York: Academic Press, 1975.

Hakerem, G., Sutton, S., & Zubin, J. Pupillary reactions to light in schizophrenic patients and normals. *Annals of the New York Academy of Sciences*, 1964, 105, 820–831.

Hall, R. A., Griffin, R. B., Moyer, D. L., Hopkins, K. H., & Rapoport, M. Evoked potential, stimulus intensity, and drug treatment in hyperkinesis. *Psychophysiology*, 1976, 13, 405–415.

Halliday, R., Callaway, E., & Naylor, H. Visual evoked potential changes induced by methyphenidate in hyperactive children:

Dose/response effects. *Electroencephalography and Clinical Neurophysiology*, 1983, 55, 258–267.

Halliday, R., Callaway, E., Rosenthal, J., & Naylor, H. The effects of methylphenidate dosage on the visual event related potential of hyperactive children. In D. Lehmann & E. Callaway (Eds.), *Human evoked potentials*. New York: Plenum Press, 1979.

Halliday, R., Callaway, E., & Rosenthal, J. H. The visual ERP predicts clinical response to methylphenidate in hyperactive children. *Psychophysiology*, 1984, 21, 114–121.

Halliday, R., Rosenthal, J. H., Naylor, H., & Callaway, E. Averaged evoked potential predictors of clinical improvement in hyperactive children treated with methylphenidate: An initial study and replication. *Psychophysiology*, 1976, 13, 429–439.

Haracz, J. L. The dopamine hypothesis: An overview of studies with schizophrenic patients. *Schizophrenia Bulletin*, 1982, 8, 438–469.

Hare, R. D. *Psychopathy: Theory and research*. New York: Wiley, 1970.

Hare, R. D. Psychopathy. In P. Venables & M. Christie (Eds.), *Research in psychophysiology*. New York: Wiley, 1975.

Hare, R. D. Electrodermal and cardiovascular correlates of psychopathy. In R. D. Hare & D. Schalling (Eds.), *Psychopathic behavior: Approaches to research*. New York: Wiley, 1978. (a)

Hare, R. D. Psychopathy and electrodermal responses to nonsignal stimulation. *Biological Psychology*, 1978, 6, 237–246. (b)

Hare, R. D. Psychopathy and physiological activity during anticipation of an aversive stimulus in a distraction paradigm. *Psychophysiology*, 1982, 19, 266–271.

Hare, R. D., & Blevings, G. Defensive responses to phobic stimuli. *Biological Psychology*, 1975, 3, 1–13.

Hare, R. D., & Craigen, D. Psychopathy and physiological activity in a mixed-motive game situation. *Psychophysiology*, 1974, 11, 197–206.

Hare, R. D., Frazelle, J., & Cox, D. N. Psychopathy and physiological responses to threat of an aversive stimulus. *Psychophysiology*, 1978, 15, 165–172.

Hare, R. D., & Quinn, M. Psychopathy and autonomic conditioning. *Journal of Abnormal Psychology*, 1971, 77, 223–239.

Hart, J. D. Physiological responses of anxious and normal subjects to simple signal and nonsignal auditory stimuli. *Psychophysiology*, 1974, 11, 443–451.

Hastings, J. E., & Barkley, R. A. A review of psychophysiological research with hyperactive children. *Journal of Abnormal Child Psychology*, 1978, 6, 413–447.

Hays, P. Electroencephalographic variants and genetic predisposition to schizophrenia. *Journal of Neurology, Neurosurgery and Psychiatry*, 1977, 40, 753–755.

Heimann, H. Changes of psychophysiological reactivity in affective disorders. *Archiv für Psychiatrie und Nervenkrankheiten*, 1978, 225, 223–231.

Heninger, G. R. Lithium carbonate and brain function. *Archives of General Psychiatry*, 1978, 35, 228–233.

Henry, G. M., Buchsbaum, M., & Murphy, D. L. Intravenous L-DOPA plus carbidopa in depressed patients: Average evoked response, learning and behavioral changes. *Psychosomatic Medicine*, 1976, 38, 95–105.

Herman, J., Mirsky, A. F., Ricks, N. L., & Gallant, D. Behavioral and electrographic measures of attention in children at risk for schizophrenia. *Journal of Abnormal Psychology*, 1977, 86, 27–33.

Hermelin, B., & O'Connor, N. Measures of the occipital alpha rhythm in normal, subnormal and autistic children. *British Journal of Psychiatry*, 1968, 114, 603–610.

Hier, D. B., LeMay, M., & Rosenberger, P. B. Autism and unfavorable left–right brain asymmetries of the brain. *Journal of Autism and Developmental Disorders*, 1979, 9, 153–159

Hinton, J. W., O'Neill, M., Dishman, J., & Webster, S. Electrodermal indices of public offending and recidivism. *Biological Psychology*, 1979, 9, 297–310.

Hiramatsu, K., Kameyama, T., Saitoh, O., Niwa, S., Rymar, K., & Itoh, K. Correlations of event-related potentials with schizophrenic deficits in information processing and hemispheric dysfunction. *Biological Psychology*, 1984, 19, 281–294.

Hodgson, R., & Rachman, S. Desynchrony in measures of fear. *Behaviour Research and Therapy*, 1974, 12, 319–326.

Holzman, P. S., Kringlen, E., Levy, D. L., & Haberman, S. J. Deviant eye tracking in twins discordant for psychosis: A replication. *Archives of General Psychiatry*, 1980, 37, 627–631.

Holzman, P. S., & Levy, D. L. Smooth pursuit eye movements and functional psychoses: A review. *Schizophrenia Bulletin*, 1977, 3, 15–27.

Holzman, P. S., Levy, D. L., & Proctor, L. R. The several qualities of attention in schizophrenia. *Journal of Psychiatric Research*, 1978, 14, 99–110.

Holzman, P. S., Proctor, L R., & Hughes, D. W. Eye tracking patterns in schizophrenia. *Science*, 1973, 181, 179–181.

Holzman, P. S., Solomon, C. M., Levin, S., & Waternaux, C. S. Pursuit eye movement dysfunctions in schizophrenia. *Archives of General Psychiatry*, 1984, 41, 136–139.

Horvath, T. B., & Meares, R. A. L-dopa and arousal. *Journal of Neurology, Neurosurgery and Psychiatry*, 1974, 37, 416–421.

Horvath, T., & Meares, R. The sensory filter in schizophrenia: A study of habituation, arousal and the dopamine hypothesis. *British Journal of Psychiatry*, 1979, 134, 39–45.

Howard, R. C. The clinical EEG and personality in mentally abnormal offenders. *Psychological Medicine*, 1984, 14, 569–580.

Hutt, C., Forrest, S. J., & Richer, J. Cardiac arrhythmia and behaviour in autistic children. *Acta Psychiatria Scandanavica*, 1975, 51, 361–372.

Hutt, S. J., Hutt, C., Lee, D., & Ounsted, C. A behavioral and electroencephalographic study of autistic children. *Journal of Psychiatric Research*, 1965, 3, 181–198.

Iacono, W. G. Bilateral electrodermal habituation–dishabituation and resting EEG in remitted schizophrenics. *Journal of Nervous and Mental Disease*, 1982, 170, 91–101.

Iacono, W. G., & Koenig, W. G. R. Features that distinguish the smooth-pursuit eye-tracking performance of schizophrenic, affective-disorder, and normal individuals. *Journal of Abnormal Psychology*, 1983, 92, 29–41.

Iacono, W. G., & Lykken, D. T. The orienting response: Importance of instructions. *Schizophrenia Bulletin*, 1979, 5, 11–14.

Iacono, W. G., Lykken, D. T., Peloquin, L. J., Lumry, A. E., Valentine, R. H., & Tuason, V. B. Electrodermal activity in euthymic unipolar and bipolar affective disorders. *Archives of General Psychiatry*, 1983, 40, 557–565.

Iacono, W. G., Peloquin, L. J., Lumry A. E., Valentine, R. H., & Tuason, V. B. Eye tracking in patients with unipolar and bipolar affective disorders in remission. *Journal of Abnormal Psychology*, 1982, 91, 35–44.

Iacono, W. G., Peloquin, L. J., Lykken, D. T., Haroian, K. P., Valentine, R. H., & Tuason, V. B. Electrodermal activity in euthymic patients with affective disorders: One-year retest stability and the effects of stimulus intensity and significance. *Journal of Abnormal Psychology*, 1984, 93, 304–311.

Iacono, W. G., & Tuason, V. B. Bilateral electrodermal asymmetry in euthymic patients with unipolar and bipolar affective disorders. *Biological Psychiatry*, 1983, 18, 303–316.

Iacono, W. G., Tuason, V. B., & Johnson, R. A. Dissociation of smooth-pursuit and saccadic eye tracking in remitted schizophrenics. *Archives of General Psychiatry*, 1981, 38, 991–996.

Itil, T. M. Quantative pharmaco-electroencephalography. Use of computerized cerebral biopotentials in psychotropic drug research. In T. M. Itil (Ed.), *Modern problems of pharmacopsychiatry* (Vol. 8,*Psychotropic drugs and the human EEG*). Basel: Karger, 1974.

Itil, T. M. Qualitative and quantitative EEG findings in schizophrenia. *Schizophrenia Bulletin*, 1977, 3, 61–79.

Itil, T. M., Marasa, J., Saletu, B., Davis, S., & Mucciardi, A. N. Computerized EEG: Predictor of outcome in schizophrenia. *Journal of Nervous and Mental Disease*, 1975, 160, 188–203.

Itil, T. M., Saletu, B., & Davis, S. EEG findings in chronic schizophrenia based on digital computer period analysis and analog power spectra. *Biological Psychiatry*, 1972, 5, 1–13.

Itil, T. M., Simeon, J., & Coffin, C. Qualitative and quantitative EEG in psychotic children. *Diseases of the Nervous System*, 1976, 37, 247–252.

James, A. L., & Barry, R. J. Respiratory and vascular responses to simple visual stimuli in autistics, retardates and normals. *Psychophysiology*, 1980, 17, 541–547. (a)

James, A. L., & Barry, R. J. A review of psychophysiology in early onset psychosis. *Schizophrenia Bulletin*, 1980, 6, 506–525. (b)

James, A. L., & Barry, R. J. *Impaired habituation in early-onset psychosis*. Paper presented at the 21st Annual Meeting of the Society for Psychophysiological Research, Washington, D.C., October 1981.

Janes, C. L., Hesselbrock, V., & Stern, J. A. Parental psychopathology, age, and race as related to electrodermal activity of children. *Psychophysiology*, 1978, 15, 24–34.

Johnston, D. W., Lancashire, M., Mathews, A. M., Munby, M., Shaw, P. M., & Gelder, M. G. Imaginal flooding and exposure to real phobic situations: Changes during treatment. *British Journal of Psychiatry*, 1976, 129, 372–377.

Johnstone, E. C., Bourne, R. C., Crow, T. J., Frith, C. D., Gamble, S., Lofthouse, R., Owen, F., Owens, D. G .C., Robinson, J., & Stevens, M. The relationship between clinical response, psychophysiological variables and plasma levels of amitriptyline and diazepam in neurotic outpatients. *Psychopharmacology*, 1981, 72, 233–240

Jones, G. H., & Miller, J. J. Functional tests of the corpus callosum in schizophrenia. *British Journal of Psychiatry*, 1981, 139, 553–557.

Jones, R. T., & Callaway, E. Auditory evoked responses in schizophrenia—A reassessment. *Biological Psychiatry*, 1970, 2, 291–298.

Josiassen, R. C., Busk, J., Hart, A. D., & Vanderploeg, R. Early auditory information processing in schizophrenia: A preliminary report. *Biological Psychology*, 1980, 10, 225–234.

Josiassen, R. C., Shagass, C., Roemer, R. A., & Straumanis, J. J. The attention-related somatosensory evoked potential late positive wave in psychiatric patients. *Psychiatry Research*, 1981, 5, 147–155.

Josiassen, R. C., Shagass, C., Straumanis, J. J., & Roemer, R. C. Psychiatric drugs and the somatosensory P400 wave. *Psychiatry Research*, 1984, 11, 151–162.

Jutai, J. W., Gruzelier, J. H., Connolly, J. F., Manchanda, R., & Hirsch, S. R. Schizophrenia and spectral analysis of the visual evoked potential. *British Journal of Psychiatry*, 1984, 145, 496–501.

Kadobayashi, I., Nakamura, M., & Kato, N. Changes in visual evoked potentials of schizophrenics after addition test. *Electroencephalography and Clinical Neurophysiology*, 1977, 43, 837–845.

Kadobayashi, I., Mori, M., Arima, S., & Kato, N. Visual evoked potential characteristics and subtypes of schizophrenia. *Journal of Nervous and Mental Disease*, 1978, 166, 775–780.

Kadrmas, A., & Winokur, G. Manic depressive illness and EEG abnormalities. *Journal of Clinical Psychiatry*, 1979, 35, 306–307.

Karson, C. N., Bigelow, L.B., Kleinman, J. E., Weinberger, D. R., & Wyatt, R. J. Haloperidol-induced changes in blink rates correlate with changes in BPRS score. *British Journal of Psychiatry*, 1982, 140, 503–507.

Karson, C. N., Kleinman, J. E., Freed, W. J., Bigelow, L. B., Weinberger, D. R., & Wyatt, R. J. Blink rates in schizophrenia. In E. Usdin & I. Hanin, (Eds.), *Biological markers in psychiatry and neurology*. New York: Pergamon Press, 1982.

Kaskey, G. B., Salzman, L. F., Ciccone, J. R., & Klorman, R. Effects of lithium on evoked potentials and performance during sustained attention. *Psychiatry Research*, 1980, 3, 281–289.

Katkin, E. S., & Deitz, S. R. Systematic desensitization. In W. F. Prokasy & D. C. Raskin (Eds.), *Electrodermal activity in psychological research*. New York: Academic Press, 1973.

Katz, M. M., & Hirschfeld, R. M. A. Phenomenology and classification of depression. In M. A. Lipton, A. DiMascio, & K.F. Killam (Eds.), *Psychopharmacology: A generation of progress*. New York: Raven Press, 1978.

Kelly, D. Physiological changes during operations on the limbic system in man. *Conditional Reflex*, 1972, 7, 127–138.

Kelly, D. *Anxiety and emotions*. Springfield, Ill.: Charles C Thomas, 1980.

Kelly, D., Brown, C. C., & Shaffer, J. W. A comparison of physiological and psychological measurements on anxious patients and normal controls. *Psychophysiology*, 1970, 6, 429–441.

Kelly, D., & Martin, I. Autonomic reactivity, eyelid conditioning and their relationship to neuroticism and extraversion. *Behaviour Research and Therapy*, 1969, 7, 233–244.

Kelly, D., Mitchell-Heggs, N., & Sherman, D. Anxiety and the effects of sodium lactate assessed clinically and physiologically. *British Journal of Psychiatry*, 1971, 119, 129–141.

Kelly, D., Pik, R., & Chen, C. A psychological and physiological evaluation of the effects of intravenous diazepam. *British Journal of Psychiatry*, 1973, 122, 419–426.

Kelly, D., Richardson, A., Mitchell-Heggs, N., Greenup, C., Chen, C., & Hafner, J. Stereotoxic limbic leucotomy: A preliminary report on forty patients. *British Journal of Psychiatry*, 1973, 123, 141–148.

Kelly, D., & Walter, C. J. S. The relationship between clinical diagnosis and anxiety assessed by forearm blood flow and other measurements. *British Journal of Psychiatry*, 1968, 114, 611–666.

Kelly, D., & Walter, C. J. S. A clinical and physiological relationship between anxiety and depression. *British Journal of Psychiatry*, 1969, 115, 401–406.

Kelly, D., Walter, C. J. S., Mitchell-Heggs, N., & Sargent, W. Modified leucotomy assessed clinically, physiologically and psychologically at six weeks and eighteen months. *British Journal of Psychiatry*, 1972, 120, 19–29.

Kemali, D., Vacca, L., Marciano, F., Nolfe, G., & Iorio, C. CEEG findings in schizophrenics, depressives, obsessives, heroin addicts and normals. *Advances in Biological Psychiatry*, 1981, 6, 17–28.

Kendell, R. E. The classification of depressions: A review of contemporary confusion. *British Journal of Psychiatry*, 1976, 129, 15–28.

Kitamura, T., Kahn, A., Kumar, R., & Mackintosh, J. H. Blink rate and blunted affect among chronic schizophrenic patients. *Biological Psychiatry*, 1984, 19, 429–434.

Klorman, R., Salzman, L. F., Pass, H. L., Borgstedt, A. D., & Dainer, K. B. Effects of methylphenidate on hyperactive children's evoked responses during passive and active attention. *Psychophysiology*, 1979, 16, 23–29.

Klorman, R., Strauss, J. S., & Kokes, R. F. Premorbid adjustment in schizophrenia: Concepts, measures, and implications (Part IV). *Schizophrenia Bulletin*, 1977, 3, 226–239.

Klorman, R., Weissberg, R. P., & Wiesenfeld, A. R. Individual differences in fear and autonomic reactions to affective stimulation. *Psychophysiology*, 1977, 14, 45–51.

Knopp, W., Arnold, L. E., Andras, R. L., & Smeltzer, D. J. Predicting amphetamine response in hyperkinetic children by electronic pupillography. *Pharmakopsychiatry*, 1973, 6, 158–166.

Kootz, J. P., Marinelli, B., & Cohen, D. J. Modulation of response to environmental stimulation in autistic children. *Journal of Autism and Developmental Disorders*, 1982, 12, 185–193.

Kootz, J. P., & Cohen, D. J. Modulation of sensory intake in autistic children. *Journal of the American Academy of Child Psychiatry*, 1981, 20, 692–701.

Kornetsky, C., & Mirsky, A. F. On certain psychopharmacological and physiological differences between schizophrenics and normal persons. *Psychopharmacologia*, 1966, 8, 309–318.

Koukkou, M. EEG states of the brain, information processing and schizophrenic primary systems. *Psychiatry Research*, 1982, 6, 235–244.

Kupfer, D. J. REM latency: A psychobiologic marker for primary depressive disease. *Biological Psychiatry*, 1976, 11, 159–174.

Lader, M. H. Palmar skin conductance measures anxiety and phobic states. *Journal of Psychosomatic Research*, 1967, 11, 271–28.

Lader, M. H. *The psychophysiology of mental illness*. London: Routledge & Kegan Paul, 1975.

Lader, M. H., Gelder, M. G., & Marks, I. M. Palmar skin conductance measures as predictors or response to desensitization. *Journal of Psychosomatic Response*, 1967, 11, 283–290.

Lader, M. H., & Sartorius, N. Anxiety in patients with hysterical conversion symptoms. *Journal of Neurology, Neurosurgery and Psychiatry*, 1968, 31, 490–497.

Lader, M. H., & Wing, L. *Physiological measures, sedative drugs, and morbid anxiety*. London: Oxford University Press, 1966.

Lader, M. H., & Wing, L. Physiological measures in agitated and retarded depressed patients. *Journal of Psychiatric Research*, 1969, 7, 89–95.

Lake, C. R., Ziegler, M. G., & Murphy, D. L. Increased norepinephrine levels and decreased dopamine-B-hydroxylase activity in primary autism. *Archives of General Psychiatry*, 1977, 34, 553–556.

Landau, S. G., Buchsbaum, M. S., Carpenter, W., Strauss, J., & Sacks, M., Schizophrenia and stimulus intensity control. *Archives of General Psychiatry*, 1975, 32, 1239–1245.

Lande, S. D. Physiological and subjective measures of anxiety during flooding. *Behaviour Research and Therapy*, 1982, 20, 81–88.

Lang, P. J., & Buss, A. H. Psychological deficit in schizophrenia: II. Interference and activation. *Journal of Abnormal Psychology*, 1965, 70, 77–126.

Lang, P. J., Melamed, B. G., & Hart, J. A psychophysiological analysis of fear modification using an automated desensitization procedure. *Journal of Abnormal Psychology*, 1970, 76, 220–234.

Lapierre, Y. D., & Butter, H. J. Agitated and retarded depression: A clinical psychophysiological evaluation. *Neuropsychobiology*, 1980, 6, 217–223.

Larmore, K., Ludwig, A. M., & Cain, R. L. Multiple personality—An objective case study. *British Journal of Psychiatry*, 1977, 131, 35–40.

Latham, C., Holzman, P. S., Manshreck, T. C., & Tole, J. Optokinetic nystagmus and pursuit eye movement in schizophrenia. *Archives of General Psychiatry*, 1981, 38, 997–1003.

Lelord, G., Laffont, F., Jusseaume, P., & Stephant, J. L. Comparative study of conditioning of averaged evoked responses by coupling sound and light in normal and autistic children. *Psychophysiology*, 1973, 10, 415–425.

Levander, S. E., Schalling, D. S., Lidberg, L., Bartfai, A., & Lidberg, Y. Skin conductance recovery time and personality in a group of criminals. *Psychophysiology*, 1980, 17, 105–111.

Levin, S. Frontal lobe dysfunctions in schizophrenia—I. Eye movement impairments. *Journal of Psychiatric Research*, 1984, 18, 27–55.

Levin, S., Jones, A., Stark, L., Merrin, E. L., & Holzman, P. S. Saccadic eye movements of schizophrenic patients measured by reflected light technique. *Biological Psychiatry*, 1982, 17, 1277–1287.

Levin, S., Lipton, R. B., & Holzman, P. S. Pursuit eye movements in psychopathology: Effects of target characteristics. *Biological Psychiatry*, 1981, 16, 255–267.

Levinson, D. F., Edelberg, R., & Bridger, W. H. The orienting response in schizophrenia: Proposed resolution of a controversy. *Biological Psychiatry*, 1984, 19, 489–507.

Levit, A. L., Sutton, S., & Zubin, J. Evoked potential correlates information processing in psychiatric patients. *Psychological Medicine*, 1973, 3, 487–494.

Levy, R., & Mashin, J. The somatosensory evoked response in patients with hysterical anaesthesia. *Journal of Psychosomatic Research*, 1973, 71, 81–84.

Lidsky, A., Hakerem, G., & Sutton, S. Pupillary reactions to single light pulses in psychiatric patients and normals. *Journal of Nervous and Mental Disease*, 1971, 153, 286–291.

Lifshitz, K., Susswein, S., & Lee, K. Auditory evoked potentials and psychopathology. In H. Begleiter (Ed.), *Evoked brain potentials and behavior*. New York: Plenum Press, 1979.

Lipton, R. B., Levy, D. L., Holzman, P. S., & Levin, S. Eye movement dysfunctions in psychiatric patients: A review. *Schizophrenia Bulletin*, 1983, 9, 13–32.

Loiselle, D. L., Stamm, J. S., Maitinsky, S., & Whipple, S. C. Evoked potential and behavioral signs of attentive dysfunction in hyperactive boys. *Psychophysiology*, 1980, 17, 193–201.

Ludwig, A. M., Brandsma, J. M., Wilbur, C. B., Bendfeldt, F., & Jameson, D. H. The objective study of a multiple personality: Or, are four heads better than one? *Archives of General Psychiatry*, 1972, 26, 298–310.

Lykken, D. T. A study of anxiety in the sociopathic personality. *Journal of Abnormal Social Psychology*, 1957, 55, 6–10.

Lykken, D. T., & Maley, M. Autonomic versus cortical arousal in schizophrenics and non-psychotics. *Journal of Psychiatric Research*, 1968, 6, 21–33.

MacCulloch, M. J., & Williams, C. On the nature of infantile autism. *Acta Psychiatrica Scandinavica*, 1971, 47, 295–314.

Magaro, P. A. Skin conductance basal level and reactivity in schizophrenia as a function of chronicity, premorbid adjustment, diagnosis, and medication. *Journal of Abnormal Psychology*, 1973, 81, 270–281.

Malmo, R. B., & Shagass, C. Studies of blood pressure in psychiatric patients under stress. *Psychosomatic Medicine*, 1952, 14, 82–93.

Mannuzza, S. Cross-modal reaction time and schizophrenic attentional deficit: A critical review. *Schizophrenia Bulletin*, 1980, 6, 654–675.

Mantanus, H., Timset-Berthier, M., Gerono, A., & Von Frenckell, R. A correlation study of contingent negative variation, reaction time, and EEG power spectrum in control and psychopathological populations. *Biological Psychology*, 1981, 13, 227–237.

Maricq, H. R. Familial schizophrenia as defined by nailfold capillary pattern and selected psychiatric traits. *Journal of Nervous and Mental Disease*, 1963, 136, 216–226.

Maricq, H. R., & Edelberg, R. Electrodermal recovery rate in a schizophrenic population. *Psychophysiology*, 1975, 12, 630–641.

Maricq, H. R., & Jones, M. B. Visibility of the nailfold plexus and heredity. *Biological Psychiatry*, 1976, 11, 205–215.

Maricq, H. R., & Weinrich, M. C. Psychophysiological studies in schizophrenic patients seleted on the basis of a "genetic marker." *Acta Psychiatrica Scandanavica*, 1980, 61, 185–208.

Marks, I. M., Boulougouris, J., & Marset, P. Flooding versus desensitization in the treatment of phobic patients. A crossover study. *British Journal of Psychiatry*, 1971, 119, 353–375.

Martineau, J., Laffont, F., Bruneau, N., Roux, S., & Lelord, G. Event related potentials evoked by sensory stimulation in normal, mentally retarded and autistic children. *Electroencephalography and Clinical Neurophysiology*, 1980, 48, 140–153.

Mather, J. A., & Putchat, C. Motor control of schizophrenics—I. Oculomotor control of schizophrenics: A deficit in sensory processing, not strictly in motor control. *Journal of Psychiatric Research*, 1982/83, 17, 343–360.

Mathews, A. Psychophysiological approaches to the investigation of desensitization and related procedures. *Psychological Bulletin*, 1971, 76, 73–91.

Mathews, A. Fear-reduction research and clinical phobias. *Psychological Bulletin*, 1978, 85, 390–404.

Mathews, A. M., Johnston, D. W., Lancashire, M., Munby, M., Shaw, P. M., & Gelder, M. G. Imaginal flooding and exposure to real phobic situations: Treatment outcome with agoraphobic patients. *British Journal of Psychiatry*, 1976, 129, 362–371.

Mathews, A. M., Johnston, D. W., Shaw, P. M., & Gelder, M. G. Process variables and the prediction of outcome in behaviour therapy. *British Journal of Psychiatry*, 1974, 25, 256–264.

Matousek, M., Capone, C., & Okawa, M. Measurement of the interhemispheral differences as a diagnostic tool in psychiatry. *Advances in Biological Psychiatry*, 1981, 6, 76–80.

Mavissakalian, M., & Michelson, L. Patterns of psychophysiological change in the treatment of agoraphobia. *Behaviour Research and Therapy*, 1982, 20, 347–356.

Mawson, A. R., & Mawson, C. Psychopathy and arousal: A new interpretation of the psychophysiological literature. *Biological Psychiatry*, 1977, 12, 49–74.

McCallum, W. C. The CNV and conditionability in psychopaths. *Electroencephalography and Clinical Neurophysiology*, 1973, (Suppl. 33), 337–343.

McCallum, W. C., & Walter, W. G. The effects of attention and distraction in the contingent negative variation in normal and neurotic subjects. *Electroencephalography and Clinical Neurophysiology*, 1968, 25, 319–329.

McCutcheon, B. A., & Adams, H. E. The physiological basis of implosive therapy. *Behaviour Research and Therapy*, 1975, 13, 93–100.

McGhie, A., & Chapman, J. Disorders of attention and perception in early schizophrenia. *British Journal of Medical Psychology*, 1961, 34, 103–116.

McIntyre, H. B., Firemark, H. M., Cho, A. K., Bodner, L., & Gomez, M. Computer analyzed EEG in amphetamine-responsive hyperactive children. *Psychiatry Research*, 1981, 4, 189–197.

Meares, R., & Horvath, T. 'Acute' and 'chronic' hysteria. *British Journal of Psychiatry*, 1972, 121, 653–657.

Mednick, S. A. Berkson's fallacy and high risk research. In L. C. Wynne, R. L. Cromwell, & S. Matthysse (Eds.), *The nature of schizophrenia*. New York: Wiley, 1978.

Mednick, S. A., & Hutchings, B. Genetic and psychophysiological factors in antisocial behavior. In R. D. Hare & D. Schalling (Eds.), *Psychopathic behavior: Approaches to research*. New York: Wiley, 1978.

Mednick, S. A., & Schulsinger, F. Studies of children at high risk for schizophrenia. In S. R. Dean (Ed.), *Schizophrenia: The first ten Dean Award lectures*. New York: MSS Information Corp., 1973.

Metz, J., Goode, D. J., & Meltzer, H. Y. Descriptive studies of H-reflex recovery curves in psychiatric patients. *Psychological Medicine*, 1980, 10, 541–548.

Michael, R. L., Klorman, R., Salzman, L. F., Borgstedt, A. D., & Danier, K. B. Normalizing effects of methylphenidate on hyperactive children's viligance performance and evoked potentials. *Psychophysiology*, 1981, 18, 665–677.

Miller, W. H., & Bernal, M. E. Measurement of the cardiac response in schizophrenic and normal children. *Psychophysiology*, 1971, 8, 533–537.

Milstein, V., Stevens, J., & Sachdev, K. Habituation of the alpha attenuation response in children and adults with psychiatric disorders. *Electroencephalography and Clinical Neurophysiology*, 1969, 26, 12–18.

Mintz, M., Tomer, R., & Myslobodsky, M. S. Neuroleptic-induced lateral asymmetry of visual evoked potentials in schizophrenia. *Biological Psychiatry*, 1982, 17, 815–828.

Mirkin, A. M., & Coppen, A. Electrodermal activity in depression: Clinical and biochemical correlates. *British Journal of Psychiatry*, 1980, 137, 93–97.

Mirsky, A. F. Neuropsychological bases of schizophrenia. *Annual Review of Psychology*, 1969, 20, 321–348.

Mitchell-Heggs, N., Kelly, D., & Richardson, A. Stereotaxic limbic leucotomy—A follow-up at 16 months. *British Journal of Psychiatry*, 1976, 128, 226–240.

Monakhov, K., & Perris, C. Neurophysiological correlates of depressive symptomatology. *Neuropsychobiology*, 1980, 6, 268–279.

Monakhov, K., Perris, C., Botskarev, V. K., von Knorring, L., & Nikiforov, A. I. Functional interhemispheric differences in relation to various psychopathological components of the depressive syndromes. *Neuropsychobiology*, 1979, 5, 143–155.

Monroe, R. R. *Brain dysfunction in aggressive criminals.* Lexington, Mass.: Lexington Books, 1978.

Monroe, R. R., & Mickle, W. A. Alpha chloralose-activated electroencephalograms in psychiatric patients. *Journal of Nervous and Mental Disease,* 1967, 144, 59–68.

Montagu, J. D. The hyperkinetic child: A behavioral, electrodermal and EEG investigation. *Developmental Medicine and Child Neurology,* 1975, 17, 299–305.

Montagu, J. D., & Swarbrick, L. Effect of amphetamines in hyperkinetic children: Stimulant or sedative? A pilot study. *Developmental Medicine and Child Neurology,* 1975, 17, 293–298.

Monti, J. M., Altier, H., Prandro, M., & Gil, J. L. The actions of flunitrazepam (Rohypnol) on heart and respiratory rates and skin potential fluctuations during the sleep cycle in normal volunteers and neurotic patients with insomnia. *Psychopharmacologia,* 1975, 43, 187–190.

Morihisa, J. M., Duffy, F. H., & Wyatt, R. J. Brain electrical activity mapping (BEAM) in schizophrenic patients. *Archives of General Psychiatry,* 1983, 40, 719–728.

Morstyn, R., Duffy, F. H., & McCarley, R. W. Altered P300 topography in schizophrenia. *Archives of General Psychiatry,* 1983, 40, 729–734.

Murphy, D. L., Campbell, I., & Costa, J. L. Current status of the indoleamine hypothesis of the affective disorders. In M. A. Lipton, A. DiMascio, & K. F. Killam (Eds.), *Psychopharmacology: A generation of progress.* New York: Raven Press, 1978.

Musso, M. F., & Harter, M. R. Contingent negative variation, evoked potential, and psychophysical measures of selective attention in children with learning disabilities. In D A. Otto (Ed.), *Multidisciplinary perspectives in event-related brain potential research.* Washington, D.C.: U.S. Environmental Protection Agency, 1978.

Myslobodsky, M. S., & Horesh, N. Bilateral electrodermal activity in depressive patients. *Biological Psychology,* 1978, 6, 111–120.

Nell, J. F., Merlkangas, J. R., Foster, F. G., Merlkangas, K. R., Spiker, D. G., & Kupfer, D. J. Waking and all-night sleep EEG's in anorexia nervosa. *Clinical Electroencephalography,* 1980, 11, 9–15.

Neuchterlein, K. H. Reaction time and attention in schizophrenia: A critical evaluation of the data and theories. *Schizophrenia Bulletin,* 1977, 3, 373–428.

Nichols, P. L., & Chen, T. C. *Minimal brain dysfunction: A prospective study.* Hillsdale, N.J.: Erlbaum, 1981.

Niwa, S., Ohta, M., & Yamazaki, K. P300 and stimulus evaluation process in autistic subjects. *Journal of Autism and Developmental Disorders,* 1983, 13, 33–42.

Noble, P. J., & Lader, M. H. Depressive illness, pulse rate and forearm blood flow. *British Journal of Psychiatry,* 1971, 119, 261–266. (a)

Noble, P. J., & Lader, M. H. An electromyograph study of depressed patients. *Journal of Psychosomatic Research,* 1971, 15, 233–239. (b)

Noble, P. J., & Lader, M. H. Salivary secretion and depressive illness: A physiological and psychometric study. *Psychological Medicine,* 1971, 1, 372–376. (c)

Noble, P. J., & Lader, M. H. The symptomatic correlates of skin conductance changes in depression. *Journal of Psychiatric Research,* 1971, 9, 61–69. (d)

Noble, P. J., & Lader, M. H. A physiological comparison of "endogenous" and "reactive" depression. *British Journal of Psychiatry,* 1972, 120, 541–542.

Novick, B., Kurtzberg, D., & Vaughan, H. G. An electrophysiologic indication of defective information storage in childhood autism. *Psychiatry Research,* 1979, 1, 101–108.

Novick, B., Vaughan, H. G., Kurtzberg, D., & Simson, R. An electrophysiologic indication of auditory processing defects in autism. *Psychiatry Research,* 1980, 3, 107–114.

Nunes, J. S., & Marks, I. M. Feedback of true heart rate during response in vivo. *Archives of General Psychiatry,* 1976, 33, 1346–1350.

O'Brien, G. T., & Borkovec, T. D. The role of relaxation in systematic desensitization: Revisiting and unresolved issues. *Journal of Behavioral Therapy and Experimental Psychiatry,* 1977, 8, 359–364.

Öhman, A. Electrodermal activity and vulnerability to schizophrenia: A review. *Biological Psychology,* 1981, 12, 87–145.

Ornitz, E. M., Forsythe, A. G., Tanguay, P. E., Ritvo, E. R., de la Pena, A., & Ghahremani, J. The recovery cycle of the averaged auditory evoked response during sleep in autistic children. *Electroencephalography and Clinical Neurophysiology,* 1974, 37, 173–174.

Ornitz, E. M., & Ritvo, E. R. The syndrome of autism: A critical review. *American Journal of Psychiatry,* 1976, 133, 609–621.

Ornitz, E. M., Ritvo, E. R., & Walter, R. D. Dreaming sleep in autistic and schizophrenic children. *American Journal of Psychiatry,* 1965, 122, 419–424.

Öst, L., Jerremalm, A., & Jansson, L. Individual response patterns and the effects of different behavioral methods in the treatment of agoraphobia. *Behaviour Research and Therapy,* 1984, 22, 697–707.

Öst, L.-G., Jerremalm, A., & Johansson, J. Individual response patterns and the effects of different behavioral methods in the treatment of social phobia. *Behaviour Research and Therapy,* 1981, 19, 1–16.

Öst, L., Johansson, J., & Jerremalm, A. Individual response patterns and the effects of different behavioral methods in the treatment of claustrophobia. *Behaviour Research and Therapy,* 1982, 20, 445–460.

Öst, L., Sterner, V., & Lindahl, I. Physiological responses in blood phobics. *Behaviour Research and Therapy,* 1984, 22, 109–117.

Palkovitz, R. J., & Wiesenfeld, A. R. Differential autonomic responses of autistic and normal children. *Journal of Autism and Developmental Disorders,* 1980, 10, 347–360.

Pass, H. L., Klorman, R., Salzman, L. F., Klein, R. H., & Kaskey, G. B. The late positive component of the evoked response in acute schizophrenics during a test of sustained attention. *Biological Psychiatry,* 1980, 15, 9–20.

Pass, H. L., Salzman, L. F., Klorman, R., Kaskey, G. B., & Klein, R. H. The effect of distraction in acute schizophrenics' visual tracking. *Biological Psychiatry,* 1978, 13, 587–593.

Patterson, T. Skin conductance recovery and pupillometrics in chronic schizophrenia. *Psychophysiology,* 1976, 13, 189–195. (a)

Patterson, T. Skin conductance responding/nonresponding and pupillometrics in chronic schizophrenia: A confirmation of Gruzelier and Venables. *Journal of Nervous and Mental Disease,* 1976, 163, 200–209. (b)

Patterson, T., & Venables, P. H. Bilateral skin conductance and skin potential in schizophrenic and normal subjects: The identification of the fast habituator group of schizophrenics. *Psychophysiology,* 1978, 15, 556–560.

Patterson, T., & Venables, P. H. Auditory vigilance: Normals compared to schizophrenic subjects defined by skin conductance variables. *Psychiatry Research,* 1980, 2, 107–112.

Patterson, T., & Venables, P. H. Bilateral skin conductance and the pupillary light–dark reflex: Manipulation by chlorpromazine, haloperidol, scopolamine, and placebo. *Psychopharmacology,* 1981, 73, 63–69.

Perez-Reyes, M. Differences in sedative susceptibility between types of depression: Clinical and neurophysiological significance. In T. A. Williams, M. M. Katz, & J. A. Shield (Eds.), *Recent advances in the psychobiology of the depressive illnesses.* Washington, D.C.: U.S. Government Printing Office, 1972.

Perris, C. Averaged evoked responses (AER) in patients with affective disorders. *Acta Psychiatrica Scandinavica,* 1974 (Suppl. 255), 89–97.

Perris, C. Central measures of depression. In H. M. van Praag, M. H. Lader, O. H. Rafaelsen, & E. J. Sachar (Eds.), *Handbook of bioligical psychiatry: Part II. Brain mechanisms and abnormal behavior—Psychophysiology.* New York: Marcel Dekker, 1980.

Perris, C., & Eisemann, M. Further studies of averaged evoked potentials in depressed patients with special reference to possible interhemispheric asymmetries. *Advances in Biological Psychiatry*, 1980, 4, 44–54.

Perris, C., Monokhov, K., von Knorring, L., Botskarev, V., & Nikiforov, A. Systemic structural analysis of the electroencephalogram of depressed patients: General principles and preliminary results of an international collaborative study. *Neuropsychobiology*, 1978, 4, 207–228.

Perris, C., von Knorring, L., Cumberbatch, J., & Marciano, F. Further studies of depressed patients by means of computerized EEG. *Advances in Biological Psychiatry*, 1981, 6, 41–49.

Pfefferbaum, A., Horvath, T. B., Roth, W. T., Tinklenberg, J. R., & Kopell, B. S. Auditory brain stem and cortical evoked potentials in schizophrenia. *Biological Psychiatry*, 1980, 15, 209.

Piggott, L. R., Ax, A. F., Bamford, J. L., & Fetzner, J. M. Respiration sinus arrhythmia in psychotic children. *Psychophysiology*, 1973, 10, 401–414.

Porges, S. W. Peripheral and neurochemical parallels of psychopathology: A psychophysiological model relating autonomic imbalance of hyperactivity, psychopathy and autism. In H. Reese (Ed.), *Advances in child development and behavior* (Vol. 11). New York: Academic Press, 1976.

Porges, S. W., Bohrer, R. E., Keren, G., Cheung, M. N., Franks, G. J., & Dragsow, F. The influence of methylphenidate on spontaneous autonomic activity and behavior in children diagnosed as hyperactive. *Psychophysiology*, 1981, 18, 42–48.

Porges, S. W., Walter, G. F., Korb, R. J., & Sprague, R. L. The influences of methylphenidate on heart rate and behavioral measures of attention in hyperactive children. *Child Development*, 1975, 46, 727–733.

Prentky, R. A., Salzman, L. F., & Klein, R. H. Habituation and conditioning of skin conductance responses in children at risk. *Schizophrenia Bulletin*, 1981, 7, 281–291.

Prichep, L. S., Sutton, S., & Hakerem, G. Evoked potentials in hyperkinetic and normal children under certainty and uncertainty: A placebo and methylphenidate study. *Psychophysiology*, 1976, 13, 419–428.

Putnam, F. W. The psychophysiologic investigation of multiple personality disorder. *Psychiatric Clinics of North America*, 1984, 7, 31–39.

Quay, H. C. Psychopathic personality as pathological stimulation seeking. *American Journal of Psychiatry*, 1965, 122, 180–183.

Rabavilas, A. O., Boulougouris, J. C., Perissaki, C., & Stefanis, C. The effect of peripheral beta-blockade on psychophysiologic responses in obsessional neurotics. *Comprehensive Psychiatry*, 1979, 20, 378–383.

Rabavilas, A. D., Stefanis, C. N., Liappos, J., Perissaki, C., & Rinieris, P. Synchrony of subjective and psychophysiological responses in involutional depression. *Neuropsychobiology*, 1982, 8, 156–161.

Raine, A., Mitchell, D. A., & Venables, P. H. Cortical augmenting-reducing—modality specific? *Psychophysiology*, 1981, 18, 700–708.

Rapoport, J. L., Buchsbaum, M. S., Weingartner, H., Zahn, T. P., Ludlow, C., & Mikkelsen, E. J. Dextroamphetamine: Cognitive and behavioral effects in normal and hyperactive children and normal adults. *Archives of General Psychiatry*, 1980, 37, 933–943.

Rapoport, J. L., Elkins, R., Langer, D. H., Sceery, W., Buchsbaum, M. S., Gillin, J. C., Murphy, D. L., Zahn, T. P., Lake, C. R., Ludlow, C., & Mendelson, W. Childhood obsessive-compulsive disorder. *American Journal of Psychiatry*, 1981, 138, 1545–1454.

Rapoport, J. L., & Ferguson, H. B. Biological validation of the hyperkinetic syndrome. *Developmental Medicine and Child Neurology*, 1981, 23, 667–682.

Raskin, D. C., & Hare, R. D. Psychopathy and detection of deception in a prison population. *Psychophysiology*, 1978, 15, 126–136.

Raskin, M. Decreased skin conductance response habituation in

chronically anxious patients. *Biological Psychology*, 1975, 2, 309–319.

Rey, A. C., Savard, R. J., Silber, E., Buchsbaum, M., & Post, R. Cognitive changes and the averaged evoked response in depression. *Cognitive Therapy and Research*, 1979, 3, 263–267.

Rippon, G. Bilateral differences in skin conductance level in schizophrenic patients. In J. Gruzelier & P. Flor-Henry (Eds.), *Hemispheric asymmetries of function in psychopathology*. Amsterdam: Elsevier, 1979.

Rist, F., Baumann, W., & Cohen, R. Effects of awareness and motor involvement on autonomic conditioning in chronic schizophrenics. *Pavlovian Journal of Biological Science*, 1981, 16, 8–17.

Rizzo, P. A., Albani, G. F., Spadaro, M., & Morocutti, C. Brain slow potentials (CNV), prolactin, and schizophrenia. *Biological Psychiatry*, 1983, 18, 175–183.

Rizzo, P. A., Spadaro, M., Albani, G., & Morocutti, C. Contingent negative variation and phobic disorders. *Neuropsychobiology*, 1983, 9, 73–77.

Robinson, T. N., Rosenthal, D., & Rasmussen, P. V. Spectrum diagnosis and ego strength functioning as related to electrodermal activity in a conditioning paradigm. *Journal of Psychiatric Research*, 1977, 13, 257–272.

Roemer, R. A., Shagass, C., Straumanis, J. J., & Amadeo, M. Pattern evoked potential measurements suggesting lateralized hemispheric dysfunction in chronic schizophrenics. *Biological Psychiatry*, 1978, 13, 185–202.

Roemer, R. A., Shagass, C., Straumanis, J. J., & Amadeo, M. Somatosensory and auditory evoked potential studies of functional differences between the cerebral hemispheres in psychosis. *Biological Psychiatry*, 1979, 14, 357–374.

Rosenblum, S. M., Arick, J. R., Krug, D. A., Stubbs, E. G., Young, N. B., & Pelson, R. O. Auditory brainstem evoked responses in autistic children. *Journal of Autism and Developmental Disorders*, 1980, 10, 215–226.

Rosenthal, D. Heredity in criminality. *Criminal Justice and Behavior*, 1975, 2, 3–21.

Rosenthal, R. H., & Allen, T. W. An examination of attention, arousal, and learning dysfunctions of hyperkinetic children. *Psychological Bulletin*, 1978, 85, 689–715.

Roth, W. T. Late event-related potentials and psychopathology. *Schizophrenia Bulletin*, 1977, 3, 105–120.

Roth, W. T., Horvath, T. B., Pfefferbaum, A., & Kopell, B. S. Event-related potentials in schizophrenics. *Electroencephalography and Clinical Neurophysiology*, 1980, 48, 127–139.

Roth, W. T., Horvath, T. B., Pfefferbaum, A., Tinklenberg, S. R., Mezzich, J. E., & Kopell, B. S. Late event-related potentials and schizophrenia. In H. Begleiter (Ed.), *Evoked brain potentials and behavior* (Vol. 2). New York: Plenum Press, 1979.

Roth, W. T., Pfefferbaum, A., Horvath, T. B., Berger, P. A., & Kopell, B. S. P3 reduction in auditory evoked potentials of schizophrenics. *Electroencephalography and Clinical Neurophysiology*, 1980, 49, 497–505.

Roth, W. T., Pfefferbaum, A., Kelly, A. F., Berger, P. A., & Kopell, B. S. Auditory event-related potentials in schizophrenia and depression. *Psychiatry Research*, 1981, 4, 199–121.

Rubens, R. L., & Lapidus, L. B. Schizophrenic patterns of arousal and stimulus barrier functioning. *Journal of Abnormal Psychology*, 1978, 87, 199–211.

Rubin, L. S. Autonomic dysfunction as a concomitant of neurotic behavior. *Journal of Nervous and Mental Disease*, 1964, 138, 558–574.

Rubin, L. S., & Barry, T. J. The effect of the cold pressor test on pupillary reactivity of schizophrenics in remission. *Biological Psychiatry*, 1972, 5, 181–197. (a)

Rubin, L. S., & Barry, T. J. The reactivity of the iris muscles as an index of autonomic dysfunction in schizophrenic remission. *Journal of Nervous and Mental Disease*, 1972, 155, 265–276. (b)

Rubin, L. S., & Barry, T. J. Amplitude of pupillary contraction as a function of intensity of illumination in schizophrenia. *Biological Psychiatry*, 1976, 11, 267–282.

Rugel, R. P., & Rosenthal, R. Skin conductance, reaction time, and observational ratings in learning-disabled children. *Journal of Abnormal Child Psychology*, 1974, 2, 183–192.

Rupert, P. A., & Holmes, D. S. Effects of multiple sessions of true and placebo heart rate biofeedback training on the heart rates and anxiety levels of anxious patients during and following treatment. *Psychophysiology*, 1978, 15, 582–590.

Rutter, M. Childhood schizophrenia reconsidered. *Journal of Autism and Childhood Schizophrenia*, 1972, 2, 315–337.

Saarma, J. Autonomic component of the orienting reflex in schizophrenics. *Biological Psychiatry*, 1974, 9, 55–60.

Saitoh, O., Niwa, S.-I., Hiramatsu, K.-I., Kameyama, T., Rymar, K., & Itoh, K. Abnormalities in late positive components of event-related potentials may reflect a genetic predisposition to schizophrenia. *Biological Psychiatry*, 1984, 19, 293–303.

Saletu, B. Central measures in schizophrenia. In H. M. Van Praag, M. H. Lader, O. J. Rafaelsen, & E. J. Sachar (Eds.), *Handbook of biological psychiatry: Part II. Brain mechanisms and abnormal behavior—Psychophysiology*. New York: Marcel Dekker, 1980.

Saletu, B., Saletu, M., Marasa, J., Mednick, S., & Schulsinger, F. Acoustic evoked potentials in offspring of schizophrenic mothers ("high risk children for schizophrenia"). *Clinical Electroencephalography*, 1975, 6, 92–102.

Saletu, B., Saletu, M., Simeon, J., Viamontes, G., & Itil, T. M. Comparative symptomatological and evoked potential studies with d-amphetamine, thiordazine, and placebo in hyperkinetic children. *Biological Psychiatry*, 1975, 10, 253–276.

Salkind, M. R., Fincham, J., & Silverstone, T. Is anorexia nervosa a phobic disorder?: A psychophysiologic enquiry. *Biological Psychiatry*, 1980, 15, 803–808.

Salzman, L. F., Klein, R. H., & Strauss, J. S. Pendulum eye-tracking in remitted psychiatric patients. *Journal of Psychiatric Research*, 1978, 14, 121–126.

Sartory, G., & Master, D. Contingent negative variation in obsessional–compulsive patients. *Biological Psychology*, 1984, 18, 253–267.

Satterfield, J. H., Atonian, G., Brashears, G. C., Burleigh, A. C., & Dawson, M. E. Electrodermal studies of minimal brain dysfunction children. In C. K. Conners (Ed.), *Clinical use of stimulant drugs in children* (No. 313). Amsterdam: Excerpta Medica International Congress Series, 1974.

Satterfield, J. H., & Braley, B. W. Evoked potentials and brain maturation in hyperactive and normal children. *Electroencephalography and Clinical Neurophysiology*, 1977, 43, 43–51.

Satterfield, J. H., Cantwell, D. P., Lesser, L. I., & Podosin, R. L. Physiological studies of the hyperkinetic child: I. *American Journal of Psychiatry*, 1972, 128, 1418–1424.

Satterfield, J. H., Cantwell, D. P., & Satterfield, B. T. Pathophysiology of the hyperactive child syndrome. *Archives of General Psychiatry*, 1974, 31, 839–844.

Satterfield, J. H., & Dawson, M. E. Electrodermal correlates of hyperactivity in children. *Psychophysiology*, 1971, 8, 191–197.

Satterfield, J. H., Lesser, L. I., Saul, R. E., & Cantwell, D. P. EEG aspects in the diagnosis and treatment of minimal brain dysfunction. *Annals of the New York Academy of Sciences*, 1973, 205, 274–282.

Satterfield, J. H., & Schell, A. M. Childhood brain function differences in delinquent and non-delinquent hyperactive boys. *Electroencephalography and Clinical Neurophysiology*, 1984, 57, 199–207.

Satterfield, J. H., Schell, A. M., Backs, R. W., & Hidaka, K. C. A cross-sectional and longitudinal study of age effects of electrophysiological measures in hyperactive and normal children. *Biological Psychiatry*, 1984, 19, 973–990.

Schildkraut, J. J. Current status of the catecholamine hypothesis of affective disorders. In M. A. Lipton, A. DiMascio, & K. F. Killam (Eds.), *Psychopharmacology: A generation of progress*, New York: Raven Press, 1978.

Schmauk, F. J. Punishment, arousal, and avoidance learning in sociopaths. *Journal of Abnormal Psychology*, 2970, 76, 325–335.

Schneider, S. J. Electrodermal activity and therapeutic response to neuroleptic treatment in chronic schizophrenic in-patients. *Psychological Medicine*, 1982, 12, 607–613.

Schneider, S. J. Multiple measures of hemispheric dysfunction in schizophrenia and depression. *Psychological Medicine*, 1983, 13, 287–297.

Schooler, C., Buchsbaum, M. S., & Carpenter, W. T. Evoked response and kinesthetic measures of augmenting/reducing in schizophrenics: Replications and extensions. *Journal of Nervous and Mental Disease*, 1976, 163, 221–232.

Schwartz, G. E., Fair, P. L., Mandel, M. R., Salt, P., Mieske, M., & Klerman, G. L. Facial electromyography in the assessment of improvement in depression. *Psychosomatic Medicine*, 1978, 40, 355–360.

Schwartz, G. E., Fair, P. L., Salt, P., Mandel, M. R., & Klerman, G. L. Facial expression and imagery in depression: An electromyographic study. *Psychosomatic Medicine*, 1976, 38, 337–347.

Sendi, S. B., Beckett, P. G. S., Caldwell, D. F., Grisell, J., & Gottlieb, J. S. Nailfold capillary structure and skin temperature in schizophrenia. *Diseases of the Nervous System*, 1969, 30, 138–144.

Serafetinides, E. A., Coger, R. W., Martin, J., & Dymond, A. M. Schizophrenic symptomatology and cerebral dominance patterns: A comparison of EEG, AER, and BPRS measures. *Comprehensive Psychiatry*, 1981, 22, 218–225.

Shagass, C. *Evoked brain potentials in psychiatry*. New York: Plenum Press, 1972.

Shagass, C. Effects of psychotropic drugs on human evoked potentials. In T. M. Itil (Ed.), *Modern problems of pharmacopsychiatry* (Vol. 8, *Psychotropic drugs and the human EEG*). Basel: Karger, 1974.

Shagass, C. EEG and evoked potentials in the psychoses. In D. X. Freedman (Ed.), *Biology of the major psychoses: A comparative analysis*. New York: Raven Press, 1975.

Shagass, C. An electrophysiological view of schizophrenia. *Biological Psychiatry*, 1976, 11, 3–30.

Shagass, C. Twisted thoughts, twisted brain waves? In C. Shagass, E. Gershon, & A. Friedhoff (Eds.), *Psychopathology and brain dysfunction*. New York: Raven Press, 1977.

Shagass, C. Sensory evoked potentials in psychosis. In H. Begleiter (Ed.), *Evoked brain potentials and behavior* (Vol. 2). New York: Plenum, 1979.

Shagass, C., Amadeo, M., & Overton, D. A. Eye-tracking performance in psychiatric patients. *Biological Psychiatry*, 1974, 9, 245–260.

Shagass, E., Roemer, R. A., & Amadeo, M. Eye-tracking performance and engagement of attention. *Archives of General Psychiatry*, 1976, 33, 121–125.

Shagass, C., Roemer, R. A., & Straumanis, J. J. Confirmation of deviant EEG–evoked potential relationships in the neuroses. *Biological Psychiatry*, 1981, 16, 1153–1161.

Shagass, C., Roemer, R. A., Straumanis, J. J. Relationships between psychiatric diagnosis and some quantitative EEG variables. *Archives of General Psychiatry*, 1982, 39, 1423–1435.

Shagass, C., Roemer, R. A., Straumanis, J. J. Evoked potential studies of topographic correlates of psychopathology. In P. Flor-Henry & J. Gruzelier (Eds.), *Laterality and psychopathology*. Amsterdam: Elsevier Science Publishers, 1983.

Shagass, C., Roemer, R. A., Straumanis, J. J., & Josiassen, R. C. Psychiatric diagnostic discriminations with combinations of quantitative EEG variables. *British Journal of Psychiatry*, 1984, 144, 581–592.

Shagass, C., Roemer, R. A., Straumanis, J. J., & Amadeo, M. Evoked potential correlates of psychosis. *Biological Psychiatry*, 1978, 13, 163–184.

Shagass, C., Roemer, R. A., Straumanis, J. J., & Amadeo, M.

Topography of sensory evoked potentials in depressive disorders. *Biological Psychiatry*, 1980, 15, 183–207.

Shagass, C., & Straumanis, J. J. Drugs and human sensory evoked potentials. In M. A. Lipton, A. DiMascio, & K. F. Killam (Eds.), *Psychopharmacology: A generation of progress*. New York: Raven Press, 1978.

Shagass, C., Straumanis, J. J., & Overton, D. A. Correlations between psychiatric diagnosis and some quantitative EEG variables. *Neuropsychobiology*, 1979, 5, 16–26.

Shakow, D. Segmental set: A theory of the formal psychological deficit in schizophrenia. *Archives of General Psychiatry*, 1962, 6, 1–17.

Shaw, J. C., Brooks, S., Colter, N., & O'Connor, K. P. A comparison of schizophrenic and neurotic patients using EEG power and coherence spectra. In J. Gruzelier & P. Flor-Henry (Eds.), *Hemispheric asymmetries of function in psychopathology*. Amsterdam: Elsevier, 1979.

Shaw, J. C., Colter, N., & Resek, G. EEG coherence, lateral preference and schizophrenia. *Psychological Medicine*, 1983, 13, 299–306.

Shirafuji, Y., & Nareta, T. Galvanic skin response of atypical psychosis. *Folia Psychiatrica et Neurologica Japonica*, 1962, 16, 225–235.

Siddle, D. A. T., Mednick, S. A., Nicol, A. R., & Foggitt, R. H. Skin conductance recovery in antisocial adolescents. *British Journal of Social and Clinical Psychology*, 1976, 15, 425–428.

Siddle, D. A., Nicol, A. R., & Foggitt, R. H. Habituation and overextinction of the GSR component of the orienting response in antisocial adolescents. *British Journal of Social and Clinical Psychology*, 1973, 12, 303.

Siegel, C., Waldo, M., Mizner, B., Adler, L. E., & Freedman, R. Deficits in sensory gating in schizophrenic patients and their relatives. *Archives of General Psychiatry*, 1984, 41, 607–612.

Skoff, B. F., Mirsky, A. F., & Turner, D. Prolonged brainstem transmission time in autism. *Psychiatry Research*, 1980, 2, 157–166.

Small, J. G. Sensory and evoked responses of autistic children. In D. W. Churchill, G. D. Alpern, & M. K. DeMyer (Eds.), *Infantile autism*. Springfield, Ill.: Charles C Thomas, 1971.

Small, J. G. EEG and neurophysiological studies of early infantile autism. *Biological Psychiatry*, 1975, 10, 385–397.

Small, J. G., DeMyer, M. K., & Milstein, V. CNV responses of autistic and normal children. *Journal of Autism and Childhood Schizophrenia*, 1971, 215–231.

Small, J. G., Milstein, V., Sharpley, P. H., Klapper, M., & Small, I. F. Electroencephalographic findings in relation to diagnostic constructs in psychiatry. *Biological Psychiatry*, 1984, 19, 471–487.

Sobotka, K. R., & May, J. G. Visual evoked potentials and reaction time in normal and dyslexic children. *Psychophysiology*, 1977, 14, 18–24.

Sohmer, H., & Student, M. Auditory nerve and brain-stem evoked responses in normal, autistic, minimal brain dysfunction and psychomotor retarded children. *Electroencephalography and Clinical Neurophysiology*, 1978, 44, 380–386.

Solanto, M. V., & Conners, C. K. A dose-response and time-action analysis of autonomic and behavioral effects of methylphenidate in attention deficit disorder with hyperactivity. *Psychophysiology*, 1982, 19, 658–667.

Spohn, H. E., Lacoursiere, R. B., Thompson, K., & Coyne, L. Phenothiazine effects on psychological and psychophysiological dysfunction in chronic schizophrenics. *Archives of General Psychiatry*, 1977, 34, 633–644.

Spohn, H. E., & Larson, J. Is eye tracking dysfunction specific to schizophrenia? *Schizophrenia Bulletin*, 1983, 9, 50–55.

Spohn, H. E., & Patterson, T. Recent studies of psychophysiology in schizophrenia. *Schizophrenia Bulletin*, 1979, 5, 581–611.

Sprague, R. L., & Sleator, E. K. Methylphenidate in hyperkinetic children: Differences in dose effects on learning and social behavior. *Science*, 1977, 198, 1274–1276.

Spratt, G., & Gale, A. An EEG study of visual attention in schizo-

phrenic patients and normal controls. *Biological Psychology*, 1979, 9, 249–269.

Spring, C., Greenberg, L., Scott, J., & Hopwood, J. Electrodermal activity in hyperactive boys who are methylphenidate responders. *Psychophysiology*, 1974, 11, 436–442.

Sroufe, L. A., Sonies, B. C., West, W. D., & Wright, F. S. Anticipatory heart rate deceleration and reaction time in children with and without referral for learning disability. *Child Development*, 1973, 44, 267–273.

Stark, L. Abnormal patterns of normal eye movements in schizophrenia. *Schizophrenia Bulletin*, 1983, 9, 55–72.

Stern, J. A., & Janes, C. L. Personality and psychopathology. In W. F. Prokasy & D. C. Raskin (Eds.), *Electrodermal activity in psychological research*. New York: Academic Press, 1973.

Stern, J. A., Surphlis, W., & Koff, E. Electrodermal responsiveness as related to psychiatric diagnosis and prognosis. *Psychophysiology*, 1965, 2, 51–61.

Stern, R., & Marks, I. Brief and prolonged flooding: A comparison of agoraphobic patients. *Archives of General Psychiatry*, 1973, 28, 270–276.

Stevens, J. R. Eye blink and schizophrenia: Psychosis or tardive dyskinesia? *American Journal of Psychiatry*, 1978, 35, 223–226.

Stevens, J. R., Bigelow, L., Denney, D., Lipkin, J., Livermore, A. H., Rauscher, F., & Wyatt, R. J. Telemetered EEG-EOG during psychotic behaviors of schizophrenia. *Archives of General Psychiatry*, 1979, 36, 251–262.

Stevens, J. R., & Livermore, S. Telemetered EEG in schizophrenia: spectral analysis during abnormal behavior episodes. *Journal of Neurology, Neurosurgery, and Psychiatry*, 1982, 45, 385–395.

Stevens, J. R., & Milstein, V. Severe psychiatric disorders of childhood. Electroencephalogram and clinical correlates. *American Journal of Diseases of Children*, 1970, 120, 182–192.

Stevens, S., & Gruzelier, J. Electrodermal activity to auditory stimuli in autistic, retarded, and normal children. *Journal of Autism and Developmental Disorders*, 1984, 14, 245–260.

Storrie, M. C., Doerr, H. O., & Johnson, M. H. Skin conductance characteristics of depressed subjects before and after therapeutic intervention. *Journal of Nervous and Mental Disease*, 1981, 169, 176–179.

Strandburg, R. J., Marsh, J. T., Brown, W. S., Asarnow, R. F., & Guthrie, D. Event-related potential concomitants of information processing dysfunction in schizophrenic children. *Electroencephalography and Clinical Neurophysiology*, 1984, 57, 236–253.

Straube, E. R. On the meaning of electrodermal nonresponding in schizophrenia. *Journal of Nervous and Mental Disease*, 1979, 167, 601–611.

Straube, E. R. Reduced reactivity and psychopathology—Examples from research on schizophrenia. In J. Koukkou, D. Lehmann, & J. Angst (Eds.), *Functional states of the brain: Their determinants*. Amsterdam: Elsevier, 1980.

Straumanis, J. J., Shagass, C., & Roemer, R. A. Influence of antipsychotic and antidepressant drugs on evoked potential correlates of psychosis. *Biological Psychiatry*, 1982, 17, 1101–1122.

Straumanis, J. J., Shagass, C., Roemer, R. A., Mendels, J., & Ramsey, T. A. Cerebral evoked potential changes produced by treatment with lithium carbonate. *Biological Psychiatry*, 1981, 16, 113–129.

Student, M., & Sohmer, H. Evidence from auditory nerve and brainstem evoked responses for an organic brain lesion in children with autistic traits. *Journal of Autism and Childhood Schizophrenia*, 1978, 8, 13–20.

Student, M., & Sohmer, H. Erratum. *Journal of Autism and Childhood Schizophrenia*, 1979, 9, 309.

Sturgeon, D., Turpin, G., Kuipers, L., Berkowitz, R., & Leff, J. Psychophysiological responses of schizophrenic patients to high and low expressed emotion relatives: A follow-up study. *British Journal of Psychiatry*, 1984, 145, 62–69.

Syndulko, K. Electrocortical investigations of sociopathy. In R. D. Hare & S. Schalling (Eds.), *Psychopathic behavior: Approaches to research*. New York: Wiley, 1978.

Syndulko, K., Parker, D. A., Jens, R., Maltzman, I., & Ziskind, E. Psychophysiology of sociopathy: Electrocortical measures. *Biological Psychology*, 1975, 3, 185–200.

Szmuilowicz, J., & Flannery, M. B. Mitral valve prolapse syndrome and psychological disturbance. *Psychosomatics*, 1980, 21, 419–421.

Tan, B. K. Physiological correlates of anxiety. *Canadian Psychiatric Journal*, 1964, 9, 63–71.

Tanguay, P. E. Clinical and electrophysiological research. In E. R. Ritvo, B. J. Freeman, E. M. Ornitz, & P. E. Tanguay (Eds.), *Autism: Diagnosis, current research and management*. New York: Spectrum, 1976.

Tanguay, P. E., Edwards, R. M., Buchwald, J., Schwafel, J., & Allen, V. Auditory brainstem evoked responses in autistic children. *Archives of General Psychiatry*, 1982, 39, 174–180.

Tarrier, N., Cooke, G., & Lader, M. Electrodermal and heart rate measurements in chronic and partially remitted schizophrenic patients. *Acta Psychiatrica Scandinavica*, 1978, 57, 369–376.

Tarrier, N., Vaughn, C., Lader, M. H., & Leff, J. P. Bodily reactions to people and events in schizophrenics. *Archives of General Psychiatry*, 1979, 36, 311–315.

Taylor, M. A., Abrams, R., & Hayman, M. A. The classification of affective disorders—A reassessment of the bipolar–unipolar dichotomy. *Journal of Affective Disorders*, 1980, 2, 95–109.

Teasdale, D., & Bancroft, J. Manipulation of thought content as a determinant of mood and corrugator electromyographic activity in depressed patients. *Journal of Abnormal Psychology*, 1977, 86, 235–241.

Tecce, J. J. Contingent negative variation (CNV) and psychological processes in man. *Psychological Bulletin*, 1972, 77, 73–108.

Tecce, J. J., & Cole, J. O. Psychophysiologic responses of schizophrenics to drugs. *Psychopharmacologia*, 1972, 24, 159–200.

Tecce, J. J., Savignano-Bowman, J., & Cole, J. O. Drug effects on contingent negative variation and eyeblinks: The distraction-arousal hypothesis. In M. A. Lipton, A. DiMascio, & K. F. Killam (Eds.), *Psychopharmacology: A generation of progress*. New York: Raven Press, 1978.

Tharp, V. K., Maltzman, I., Syndulko, K., & Ziskind, E. Autonomic activity during anticipation of an aversive tone in non-institutionalized sociopaths. *Psychophysiology*, 1980, 17, 123–128.

Thayer, J., & Silber, D. E. Relationship between levels of arousal and responsiveness among schizophrenic and normal subjects. *Journal of Abnormal Psychology*, 1971, 77, 162–173.

Timset-Berthier, M., & Timset, M. Toward a neurochemical interpretation of CNV in psychiatry. Some preliminary results in depressive patients. *Advances in Biological Psychiatry*, 1981, 6, 165–172.

Toone, B. K., Cooke, E., & Lader, M. H. Electrodermal activity in the affective disorders and schizophrenia. *Psychological Medicine*, 1981, 11, 497–508.

Tress, K. H., Caudrey, D. J., & Mehta, B. Tactile-evoked potentials in schizophrenia: Interhemispheric transfer and drug effects. *British Journal of Psychiatry*, 1983, 143, 156–164.

Tress, K. H., Kugler, D. J., & Caudrey, D. J. Interhemispheric integration in schizophrenia. In J. Gruzelier & P. Flor-Henry (Eds.), *Hemispheric asymmetries of function in psychopathology*. Amsterdam: Elsevier, 1979.

Tsai, L. Y., & Stewart, M. A. Handedness and EEG correlation in autistic children. *Biological Psychiatry*, 1982, 17, 595–598.

Valone, K., Goldstein, M. J., & Norton, J. P. Parental expressed emotion and psychophysiological reactivity in an adolescent sample at risk for schizophrenia spectrum disorders. *Journal of Abnormal Psychology*, 1984, 93, 448–457.

van den Bosch, R. J. Contingent negative variation and psychopathology: Frontal-central distribution, and association with performance measures. *Biological Psychiatry*, 1983, 18, 615–634.

van den Bosch, R. J. Eye tracking impairment: Attentional and psychometric correlates in psychiatric patients. *Journal of Psychiatric Research*, 1984, 18, 277–286.

Van Dyke, J. L., Rosenthal, D., & Rasmussen, P. V. Electrodermal functioning in adopted-away offspring of schizophrenics. *Journal of Psychiatric Research*, 1974, 10, 199–215.

Van Egeren, L. F., Feather, B. W., & Hein, P. L. Desensitization of phobias: Some psychophysiological propositions. *Psychophysiology*, 1971, 8, 213–228.

van Engeland, H. The electrodermal orienting response to auditive stimuli in autistic children, normal children, mentally retarded children, and child psychiatric patients. *Journal of Autism and Devleopmental Disorders*, 1984, 14, 261–279.

Venables, P. H. The relationship between level of skin potential and fusion of paired light flashes in schizophrenic and normal subjects. *Journal of Psychiatric Research*, 1963, 1, 279–287.

Venables, P. H. The recovery limb of the skin conductance response in "high-risk" research. In S. A. Mednick, F. Schulsinger, J. Higgins, & B. Bell (Eds.), *Genetics, environment, and psychopathology*. New York: American Elsevier, 1974.

Venables, P. H. The electrodermal psychophysiology of schizophrenics and children at risk for schizophrenia: Controversies and developments. *Schizophrenia Bulletin*, 1977, 3, 28–48.

Venables, P. H. Psychophysiology and psychometrics. *Psychophysiology*, 1978, 15, 302–315.

Venables, P. H. Cerebral mechanisms, autonomic responsiveness and attention in schizophrenia. In W. D. Spaulding, & J. K. Cole (Eds.), *Nebraska Symposium on Motivation, 1983, Vol. 31: Theories of schizophrenia and psychosis*. Lincoln: University of Nebraska, Press, 1984.

Verleger, R., & Cohen, R. Effects of certainty, modality shift and guess outcome on evoked potentials and reaction time in chronic schizophrenics. *Psychological Medicine*, 1978, 8, 81–93.

Vermilyea, J. A., Boice, R., & Barlow, D. H. Rachman and Hodgson (1974) a decade later: How do desynchronous response systems relate to the treatment of agoraphobia. *Behaviour Research and Therapy*, 1984, 22, 615–621.

Volavka, J., Abrams, R., Taylor, M. A., & Recker, D. Hemispheric lateralization of fast EEG activity in schizophrenia and endogenous depression. *Advances in Biological Psychiatry*, 1981, 6, 72–75.

von Knorring, L. An experimental study of visual averaged evoked responses (V.AER) and pain measures (PM) in patients with depressive disorders. *Biological Psychology*, 1978, 6, 27–38.

von Knorring, L., Epsvall, M., & Perris, C. Averaged evoked responses, pain measures, and personality variables in patients with depressive disorders. *Acta Psychiatrica Scandinavica*, 1974, (Suppl. 255), 99–108.

von Knorring, L. Interhemispheric EEG differences in affective disorders. In P. Flor-Henry, & J. Gruzelier (Eds.), *Laterality and psychopathology*. Amsterdam: Elsevier Science Publishers, 1983.

von Knorring, L., Perris, C., Goldstein, L., Kemali, D., Monakhov, K. & Vacca, L. Intercorrelations between different computer-based measures of the EEG alpha amplitude and its variability over time and their validity in differentiating healthy volunteers from depressed patients. In J. Mendlewicz & H. M. Van Praag (Eds.), *Advances in biological psychiatry*, Vol. 13. New York: S. Karger, 1983.

Waddington, J. L., MacCulloch, M., Schalken, M. L., & Sambrooks, J. E. Absence of cardiac deceleration in a singalled escape paradigm: A psychophysiological deficit in chronic schizophrenia. *Psychological Medicine*, 1978, 8, 157–162.

Walter, W. G., Aldridge, V. J., Cooper, R., O'Gorman, G., McCallum, C., & Winter, A. L. Neurophysiological correlates of apparent defects of sensori-motor integration in autistic children. In D. W. Churchill, G. D. Alpern, & M. K. DeMyer (Eds.), *Infantile autism*. Springfield, Ill.: Charles C Thomas, 1971.

Waters, W. F., McDonald, D. G., & Koresko, K. C. Psychophysiological responses during analogue systematic desensitization and non-relaxation control procedures. *Behaviour Research and Therapy*, 1972, 10, 381–393.

Watson, J. P., & Marks, I. M. Relevant and irrelevant fear in flooding—a crossover study of phobic patients. *Behavior Therapy*, 1971, 2, 275–293.

Watson, J. P., Gaind, R., & Marks, I. M. Physiological habituation to continuous phobic stimulation. *Behaviour Research and Therapy*, 1972, 10, 269–278.

Weiner, H. Baseline muscle tensions and motoric responding of schizophrenics. *British Journal of Clinical Psychology*, 1981, 20, 25–33.

Wenger, M. A. Studies of autonomic balance: A summary. *Psychophysiology*, 1966, 2, 173–186.

Williams, D. Neural factors related to habitual aggression. *Brain*, 1969, 92, 503–520.

Williams, R. B., Bittker, T. E., Buchsbaum, M., & Wynne, L. C. Cardiovascular and neurophysiologic correlates of sensory intake and rejection: I. Effect of cognitive tasks. *Psychophysiology*, 1975, 12, 427–433.

Winokur, G. Mania and depression: Family studies and genetics in relation to treatment. In M. A. Lipton, A. DiMascio, & K. F. Killam (Eds.), *Psychopharmacology: A generation of progress*. New York: Raven Press, 1978.

Wolpe, J. *Psychotherapy by reciprocal inhibition*. Stanford, Calif.: Stanford University Press, 1958.

Yoss, R. E. The inheritance of diurnal sleepiness as measured by pupillography. *Mayo Clinic Proceedings*, 1970, 45, 426–437.

Zahn, T. P. *Autonomic reactivity and behavior in schizophrenia* (Psychiatric Research Report 19). Washington, D.C.: American Psychiatric Association, 1964.

Zahn, T. P. Psychophysiological concomitants of task performance in schizophrenia. In M. L. Kietzman, S. Sutton, & J. Zubin (Eds.), *Experimental approaches to psychopathology*. New York: Academic Press, 1975.

Zahn, T. P. On the bimodality of the distribution of electrodermal orienting responses in schizophrenic patients. *Journal of Nervous and Mental Disease*, 1976, 162, 195–199.

Zahn, T. P. Autonomic nervous system characteristics possibly related to a genetic predisposition to schizophrenia. *Schizophrenia Bulletin*, 1977, 3, 49–60.

Zahn, T. P. Predicting outcome from measures of attention and autonomic functioning. In C. Baxter & T. Melnechuk (Eds.), *Perspectives in schizophrenia research*. New York: Raven Press, 1980.

Zahn, T. P., Abate, F., Little, B. C., & Wender, P. H. Minimal brain dysfunction, stimulant drugs and autonomic nervous system activity. *Archives of General Psychiatry*, 1975, 32, 381–387.

Zahn, T. P., Carpenter, W. T., & McGlashan, T. H. Autonomic nervous system activity in acute schizophrenia: I. Method and comparison with normal controls. *Archives of General Psychiatry*, 1981, 38, 251–258. (a)

Zahn, T. P., Carpenter, W. T., & McGlashan, T. H. Autonomic nervous system activity in acute schizophrenia: II. Relationships to short-term prognosis and clinical state. *Archives of General Psychiatry*, 1981, 38, 260–266. (b)

Zahn, T. P., Insel, T. R., & Murphy, D. L. Psychophysiological changes during pharmacological treatment of patients with obsessive compulsive disorder. *British Journal of Psychiatry*, 1984, 145, 39–44.

Zahn, T. P., Little, B. C., & Wender, P. H. Pupillary and heart rate reactivity in children with minimal brain dysfunction. *Journal of Abnormal Child Psychology*, 1978, 6, 135–147.

Zahn, T. P., Rapoport, J. L., & Thompson, C. L. Autonomic and behavioral effects of dextroamphetamine and placebo in normal and hyperactive prepubertal boys. *Journal of Abnormal Child Psychology*, 1980, 8, 145–160.

Zahn, T. P., Rapoport, J. L., & Thompson, C. L. Autonomic effects of dextroamphetamine in normal men: Implications for hyperactivity and schizophrenia. *Psychiatry Research*, 1981, 4, 39–47.

Zahn, T. P., Rosenthal, D., & Lawlor, W. G. Electrodermal and heart rate orienting reactions in chronic schizophrenia. *Journal of Psychiatric Research*, 1968, 6, 117–134.

Zambelli, A. J., Stamm, J. S., Maitinsky, S., & Loiselle, D. L. Auditory evoked potentials and selective attention in formerly hyperactive adolescent boys. *American Journal of Psychiatry*, 1977, 134, 742–747.

Zentall, S. Optimal stimulation as theoretical basis of hyperactivity. *American Journal of Orthopsychiatry*, 1975, 45, 549–563.

Ziskind, E., Syndulko, K., & Maltzman, I. Evidence for a neurologic disorder in the sociopath syndrome: Aversive conditioning and recidivism. In C. Shagass, S. Gershon, & A. J. Friedhoff (Eds.), *Psychopathology and brain dysfunction*. New York: Raven Press, 1977.

Zubin, J. Chronic schizophrenia from the standpoint of vulnerability. In C. F. Baxter & T. Melnechuk (Eds.), *Perspectives in schizophrenia research*. New York: Raven Press, 1980.

Zubin, J., & Spring, B. Vulnerability: A new view of schizophrenia. *Journal of Abnormal Psychology*, 1977, 86, 103–126.

Zuckerman, M. Sensation seeking and psychopathy. In R. D. Hare & D. Schalling (Eds.), *Psychopathic behavior: Approaches to research*. New York: Wiley, 1978.

Chapter Twenty-Two
Developmental Psychophysiology

Stephen W. Porges
Nathan A. Fox

DEVELOPMENTAL PSYCHOPHYSIOLOGY: A DEFINITION

Developmental psychophysiology as a discipline can approach age and maturational influences on a variety of empirical and theoretical levels. Research can investigate the sensory input apparatus, the neural effector apparatus, and the central integrative process. Most psychophysiologists infer that the observed developmental differences are a function of changing central integrative capacities linked to cognitive and sensory processing. Thus, many researchers assume that the sensory input and motor output systems are developmentally invariant. Contributing to this assumption has been the difficulty in assessing both the sensory efferent and central integrative processes with noninvasive methods. Recent knowledge, regarding the ontogeny of effector systems (e.g., myelination) and the development of methods to extract central neuroregulatory processes from peripheral physiological activity, is forcing a reconceptualization of the approaches available to study developmental processes. Consistent with these recent scientific advances, this chapter focuses on the observed developmental shifts in response parameters that may be determined by at least two measurable sources of variance: the maturation of the effector system, and the maturation of the central integrative processes controlling the effector system.

Developmental psychophysiology assumes that there is a dynamic interplay between the continuously changing nervous system and the changing effector system. Therefore, to interpret the response profiles of a given subject accurately, it is necessary to have an understanding of the maturation of the central control and morphology of the effector systems. Since excellent sources are available for integrated literature reviews (e.g., Berg & Berg, 1979), this chapter does not contain a comprehensive review of developmental research. Rather, it focuses on specific responses systems as illustrative examples of a developmental approach that incorporates a knowledge of the changing morphology of the effector system and the changing neuroregulatory influences of the central nervous system on the effector system. Electrodermal, cardiovascular, and electroencephalogram (EEG) response systems are used as examples.

Stephen W. Porges and Nathan A. Fox. Department of Human Development, University of Maryland, College Park, Maryland.

THE AGING PROCESS: INFLUENCES ON PHYSIOLOGICAL ACTIVITY

There are many indications that functional changes occur in physiological mechanisms during aging. However, the literature is fragmentary, and the majority of studies are insufficiently controlled for age-related diseases. Disease may contribute to a complex interaction in which age may function to maximize or minimize the probability of disease.

The effect of age is biphasic. During early development, the peripheral physiological systems mature and become more "integrated" with central control systems. During the later years, the physiological systems exhibit various levels of attenuated output and dysfunction. In this chapter, we use the term "development" when we are discussing the maturation of the physiological response systems during the early phases; we use the term "aging" when we are discussing the "postmature" period.

The response systems studied by psychophysiologists exhibit massive physiological changes as a function of age. Generally, by about 60 years of age, most individuals exhibit a gradual decline in the functional capability of a variety of bodily systems. For example, the aging process results in the following:

1. Decline in speed of conduction of nerve impulses.
2. Decline in cardiac output.
3. Decline in basal metabolism.
4. Decline in vital capacity.
5. Decline in maximum breathing capacity.
6. Decline in gonadal endocrine secretion.
7. Decline in muscular strength and speed of motion.
8. Increase in cerebrovascular resistance.
9. Increase in blood pressure.
10. Increase in peripheral vascular resistance.

Age does not affect all physiological systems to the same degree, nor does age similarly affect the same systems in two chronologically matched individuals. However, regardless of individual differences, there is a decline in functional capability as humans age. This decline affects the physiological response systems that are often used to index psychological processes in psychophysiological research. The developmental psychophysiologist, who is primarily interested in the cardiovascular, respiratory, electrodermal, and cortical response systems, must understand the ontogeny of these systems in order to interpret developmental differences in both physiological levels and reactivity.

The developmental shifts in the nervous system suggest that the developmental psychophysiologist consider two classes of response variables. The first involves a change in level or variability in response to an external physical stimulus; the second involves neurally mediated mechanisms of physiological state. The heart rate change during a reaction time task would be an example of the first class. The spontaneous oscillations in heart rate would be an example of the second.

According to theories relating psychological arousal to physiological state (e.g., Duffy, 1962; Lindsley, 1951), the base levels of such physiological variables as skin potential, skin resistance, cortical activity, and heart rate may be used as indices of arousal. From the clear evidence of age differences in these variables, this view would imply that arousal varies developmentally in parallel with the physiological measures. It is now known that the peripheral systems may change independently of the state of central arousal. For example, diabetes produces a peripheral neuropathy that results in attenuated electrodermal and heart rate reactivity, independently of central arousal.

Although the fallacy of defining individual psychological arousal levels solely in terms of autonomic base levels is quite obvious, neural control of the various physiological response systems may be extracted from base-level measurements. For example, the vagus contributes to the neural control of specific endogenous rhythms in the heart rate pattern (e.g., respiratory sinus arrhythmia). Thus, it may be possible to extract a measure of vagal tone from spontaneous heart rate activity (see Porges, McCabe, & Yongue, 1982). Since the evoked heart rate response is primarily mediated by the vagus, the age changes in the topography of the evoked heart rate response may be directly related to age changes in vagal cardioinhibitory tone.

It behooves developmental psychophysiologists to acknowledge that the responses that they monitor are directly influenced by central neural pathways. Although it has been convenient, for heuristic purposes, to partition the nervous system into central and peripheral components, the two are merely components of an integrated system. If the autonomic nervous system is viewed as manifesting neurophysiological continuity with the central nervous system, the autonomic measures may be more meaningful (Porges, 1984). Developmental psychophysiologists must, therefore, consider the physiological state (e.g., components determined by homeostatic regulation, maturation, external stimulation, and disease) in the complex interpretation of response parameters.

ELECTRODERMAL SYSTEM

Overview

The study of electrodermal activity parallels the history of psychophysiology. In the 1800s, Galvani discovered that nerve and muscle actions were related to electrical processes. It was generally accepted by the mid-1800s that the body's electrical characteristics provided not only a basis for a theory of disease, but a window for diagnosis and intervention. Thus, it was believed that diseases of the nervous system could be diagnosed by measuring changes in the distribution of the electrical activity in the body and the sensitivity of various areas of the body to electrical stimulation. Although careful and sensitive measurement procedures were not available, theoretical positions evolved that are still influencing psychophysiological research and medical treatment.

Underlying the electrical activity on the surface of the skin is a complex physiological response system. In this section, we discuss the developmental shifts in terms of the sweat glands, neural control, and the observable psychophysiological response.

Sweat Glands: Density and Reactivity

There are two classes of sweat glands: apocrine and eccrine. Apocrine glands are found primarily in the armpits and genital areas. These glands respond primarily to stressful stimuli and are not primarily involved in heat regulation. Eccrine sweat glands are found over most of the body. Although the eccrine sweat glands are primarily involved in thermoregulation, there are populations of eccrine glands concentrated on the palms of the hands and soles of the feet that are less responsive to heat changes and more responsive to external stimuli and states of alertness. Psychophysiologists are primarily interested in the subset of eccrine sweat glands located on the palms.

The action of the sweat glands (i.e., eccrine) in most areas of the body is primarily to regulate temperature by increasing evaporative water loss in response to environmental overheating. Verbov and Baxter (1974) have expressed doubt that the newborn infant, particularly the infant with low birth weight, is capable of sweating. Although the density of active sweat glands on the thigh of the baby at term is more than six times that of the adult, the mean peak sweat rate following intradermal acetylcholine stimulation is only one-third of the maximum rate recorded in adults (Foster, Hey, & Katz, 1969). The sweat response to thermal stimulation in the first 10 days after birth is lower than in later life, and is not governed by glandular limitations in the full-term infant. In the premature infant, the inability to sweat in response to either thermal or acetylcholine stimulation may be a function of incomplete development and differentiation of the sweat glands.

The action of the eccrine sweat glands located on the palm of the hand and the sole of the foot is determined primarily by emotional factors and is virtually unaffected by changes in ambient temperature. Harpin and Rutter (1982) have used the palmar water loss technique to evaluate emotional sweating in new-

borns. In newborns at least 37 weeks of gestational age, there was a relation between palmar water loss and state of arousal from the day of birth. Premature infants did not exhibit reliable palmar sweat responses until they were the equivalent of 36 to 37 weeks of conceptional age (i.e., gestational age plus postpartum period equivalent to 36 to 37 weeks).

The aging process also changes the condition and density of the sweat glands. Catania, Thompson, Michalewski, and Bowman (1980) reported significant differences in sweat gland count between young adults (mean age = 25.3 years) and old adults (mean age = 69.5 years). Similarly, there have been several reports of a marked decrease with age in the number of active eccrine sweat glands on palmar surfaces (Juniper & Dykman, 1967; MacKinnon, 1954; Silver, Montagna, & Karacan, 1964), as well as decreased output per sweat gland (Silver *et al.*, 1964). It thus becomes clear that there are developmental shifts in the state and reactivity of the sweat glands, which may influence both basal and evoked electrodermal responses.

Basal Electrodermal Activity

Given the description above of age-related changes in sweat gland density and reactivity, it would seem likely that electrodermal activity would change developmentally. There have been few studies evaluating the age differences in skin conductance level and skin potential level. These studies have reported consistent effects of increased basal skin resistance (Shmavonian, Miller, & Cohen, 1968; Shmavonian, Yarmat, & Cohen, 1965) or decreased basal skin conductance levels (Garwood, Engel, & Quilter, 1979; Plouffe & Stelmack, 1984) with increased age. Surwillo and Quilter (1965) reported that aging influenced the frequency of spontaneous skin potential responses during vigilance. Although the range of basal skin potential (i.e., the differential voltage between an active palmar lead and a referent forearm lead) was not different between a young adult group (i.e., aged 22–53 years) and an old adult group (i.e., aged 54–85 years), the number of spontaneous skin potential responses during a vigilance task decreased monotonically as a function of age group (Group 1, 22–47 years; Group 2, 48–67 years; Group 3, 68–85 years).

In the infant, basal electrodermal levels have been reported to be a function of behavioral state. Bell (1970) recorded skin potential in neonates and observed sleep cycles. Skin potential declined (i.e., negative potential decreased) from the waking level, continued to decrease in level throughout sleep, increased in variability during rapid eye movement (REM) sleep, and increased in level when the neonate awoke. Of interest is the finding that skin potential did not differ between non-REM (NREM) and REM periods. In adults, it has been reported (Koumans, Tursky, & Soloman, 1968) that skin potential was lower during sleeping than waking states.

Curzi-Dascalova, Pajot, and Dreyfus-Brisac (1973) have reported more frequent spontaneous skin potential responses in infants during REM than NREM. This finding is inconsistent with the adult pattern (Johnson & Lubin, 1966; Koumans *et al.*, 1968), which is characterized by greater spontaneous electrodermal activity during NREM than REM states. Curzi-Dascalova and Dreyfus-Brisac (1976) have reported that the frequency of spontaneous skin potential responses during active sleep in the infant is at a higher level than that of adults during REM and remains at that level during the first 6 months of age.

Evoked Electrodermal Responses

Crowell, Davis, Chun, and Spellacy (1965) reported skin conductance changes in the neonate to light, sound, tactile, and olfactory stimuli. Of the total of 306 stimulations (across subjects), 54 conductance changes met the criteria set by the authors. The most potent elicitors were auditory clicks (5 Hz at 50 dB) and glacial acetic acid presented with a cotton swab 5 mm from the infants' nares for 2 sec. These stimuli produced conductance changes in 10 out of 18 presentations. Stechler, Bradford, and Levy (1966) reported skin potential changes in the neonate while attending to a visual target. The responses were similar in topography to adult skin potential changes. Baseline shifts in the negative direction tended to parallel an increased level of alertness and activity. In the Crowell *et al.* (1965) study, 11% of the stimuli produced criterion responses. Stechler *et al.* reported that 63% of the total of 180 puffs of nitrogen directed just above the umbilicus produced skin potential responses. The puffs were presented only if the neonate had gazed at the target for at least 10 sec. In contrast, it has been reported that reactive sweating does not occur in the human until the second month of life.

In attempts to collect skin potential and skin resistance data on neonates, one of us (Porges) noted many technical problems. First, even with the use of small-diameter electrodes, the recording of electrodermal activity was very sensitive to movement artifact when the electrodes were placed on the palms or the soles. In preliminary research, it was difficult to decipher whether apparent electrodermal activity was a function of pressure on the electrode (i.e., the Ebbecke effect; see Edelberg, 1967) or an indication of a reflex of central origin. Second, when using the skin resistance procedure with small-diameter electrodes, it was necessary to assess the current density, because many bridge circuits produce a current density high enough to produce an irritating electrical stimulation of skin.

Although the literature abounds with numerous examples of electrodermal reactivity in the adult and aging populations, there are few studies of children. Janes, Hesselbrock, and Stern (1978) reported that younger children were more responsive than older children on a variety of electrodermal responses, including conditioning, habituation, and spontaneous responding between trials.

When a broad range of age groups were tested in a study of skin resistance conditioning, age differences were observed in the magnitude of the responses, although all groups exhibited differential conditioning (Morrow, Boring, Keough, & Haesly, 1969). In this study, children (mean age = 11 years, 2 months), young adults (mean age = 20 years, 6 months), and aged adults (mean age = 68 years, 3 months) were tested. The responses to both the positive and the negative conditioned stimuli were greater in the younger groups than in the aged. There were no differences in magnitude of responding between the children and the young adults. Convergent findings of greater skin resistance reactivity in younger subjects have been reported (Botwinick & Kornetsky, 1960; Shmavonian *et al.*, 1965, 1968). However, in these studies it was inferred that the aged population exhibited poorer conditionability. In fact, aged males (mean age = 66 years) in the Shmavonian *et al.* (1968) study did not appear to respond at all.

It is obvious from the review above that the aging process influences the number of sweat glands and the neurally mediated reactivity of the sweat glands. These influences are manifested in psychophysiological research both in differences in basal state (i.e., level and frequency) and in magnitude of stimulus-elicited electrodermal responses. The age differences in the "effector" system, on the level of the end organ (i.e., the sweat gland), make it difficult to interpret developmental differences in electrodermal activity as a valid index of differential psychological processing. Thus, developmental differences in such psychological processes as orienting, habituation, and conditioning may not be accurately manifested in developmental differences in electrodermal activity.

Unfortunately, there are few studies investigating the neural modulation of the sweat glands. A better understanding of the neural mediation of sweat gland activity may provide insight into quantitative strategies that may be less affected by the age-influenced magnitude differences. For example, one of us (Porges) has studied the rhythmic characteristics of skin potential as a function of task demands. Instead of quantifying spontaneous skin potential activity by counting fluctuations or measuring the average electrical potential, spectral analysis was applied to evaluate rhythmicity. This analysis approach identified a dominant rhythm of approximately .1 Hz. The amplitude and regularity of this rhythm were enhanced while the subject was on an attention-demanding task, relative to the intertrial interval. The .1-Hz rhythm has been observed in other physiological response systems and has been theoretically assumed to parallel blood pressure oscillations associated with the baroreceptor reflex. Perhaps the study of electrodermal rhythmicity will provide a more sensitive index of neural modulation, which will be less sensitive to the massive developmental differences observed in the magnitude of the evoked response.

CARDIOVASCULAR SYSTEM

Overview

The cardiovascular system is, perhaps, the first integrated autonomic system to function in the prenatal development of the human. Like the electrodermal system, described above, the cardiovascular system exhibits massive age-related changes that reflect maturation of both end-organ and neural components. Aging influences the cardiovascular system by reducing both the plasticity and pliability of the end organs and the impact of centrally mediated neural influences.

The heart and the supportive vascular system are influenced by the aging process. The status of cells and tissues in all parts of the body is dependent upon the vascular system, since oxygenation is a function of adequate circulation. The aging process in the cardiovascular system includes a decrease in heart rate reactivity, decreased efficiency of the heart as a pump, decreased velocity of contraction and relaxation of heart muscle, and decreased rate of cardiac hypertrophy. The arteries are less plastic, and there is decreased baroreceptor sensitivity. Peripheral vascular resistance increases, and organ perfusion in general decreases. Blood pressure tends to rise. Moreover, atherosclerosis and essential hypertension are more frequent with the aged population.

Exercise and Resting Heart Rate

Aging reduces the influence of maximal exercise on heart rate. Londeree and Moeschberger (1982) surveyed a literature based upon 388 sources and over 23,000 subjects aged 5–81. Their findings may be summarized as follows:

1. Maximum heart rate declines with age.
2. There is considerable variability in maximum heart rate among individuals.
3. There is no sex or race difference in maximum heart rate.

With aging, the cardiovascular function at rest and during exercise changes (Astrand & Rodahl, 1970;

Brandfonbrener, Landowne, & Shock, 1955; Marshall & Shepherd, 1968); cardiac function becomes depressed, arterial blood pressure becomes higher, and heart rate, cardiac output, and oxygen uptake during maximal exercise become lower. Sato, Hasegawa, Takahashi, Hirata, Shimomura, and Hotta (1981) have inferred from their data that the exercise mediate changes in the neural control of the heart changes with aging. They have suggested that the relative neural influences of the sympathetics and the vagus change with aging: Sympathetic influences increase, and vagal influences decrease.

Neural Control of the Heart

The study of the neural control of the heart may be approached via invasive or noninvasive methods. Regardless of the method, the approaches are dependent upon a basic understanding of neurophysiological reflexes. Within psychophysiology, the baroreceptor reflex is commonly cited. The term "baroreceptor reflex" refers to the neurophysiological mediation of the vagal control of the heart when the baroreceptors are stimulated during increased blood pressure. The reflex is characterized by an increase in cardiac vagal tone, which results in a rapid decrease in heart rate. Baroreceptor reflexes may be studied through manipulation of blood pressure with pharmacological agents, through orthostatic stimulation (i.e., body tilt), and through direct electrical stimulation of the afferent branch of the reflex. Rothbaum, Shaw, Angell, and Shock (1974) studied the effects of aging on the baroreceptor reflex of rats. Baroreceptor reactivity was measured by the decrease in heart rate in response to a 55 mm Hg increase in systolic blood pressure induced by the continuous infusion of phenylephrine. The baroreceptor reflex was significantly greater in the young group (12 months old) than the old group (24 months old). In both groups there was a significant baroreceptor reflex, which was abolished by cholinergic blockade with atropine. These data support the view that the decreased baroreceptor reflex is primarily due to decreases in parasympathetic influences (i.e., vagal activity). The mechanisms underlying the decreased vagal efferent influence of the heart are not totally understood. The decrease may be due to a decrease in the number of baroreceptor stretch receptors or to a decreased compliance of the arterial wall in pressoreceptor areas, resulting in a distortion of stretch receptors in response to a given blood pressure increase. The reduced baroreceptor reactivity in the aged rats studied by Rothbaum *et al.* was not due to an increase in sympathetic activity, since reduction in heart rate following beta-adrenergic blockade was similar for both groups.

A study similar to the Rothbaum *et al.* (1974) study was conducted with humans. Gribbin, Pickering, Sleight, and Peto (1971) assessed the baroreceptor reflex in untreated subjects who ranged in age from 19 to 66 years. Blood pressure was manipulated by infusing phenylephrine to elicit the baroreceptor reflex. Prior to infusion, the range of mean arterial pressure varied from 70 to 150 mm Hg, and there was no correlation between age and arterial pressure. Baroreceptor sensitivity was related to age and to the pretreatment blood pressure. Hypertensives under 40 years of age had significantly faster heart rate than age-matched normotensives, but not older hypertensives. The authors suggest that their findings may be explained by decrease in arterial distensibility due to the aging process or to hypertension. The authors claim that there is no evidence in humans or animals of selective baroreceptor degeneration during the aging process.

The aging process results in a progressive increase in rigidity of the aorta and peripheral arteries (Dustan, 1974; Hollander, 1976). Several processes are involved in this mechanical change. The elastic fibers of the media uncoil and fracture, while the collagenous matrix increases. Calcium is deposited in substantial quantities in the media. There is a degeneration of the small arteries and arterioles of the kidney (Heptinstall, 1974). These changes result in a developmental shift toward systolic hypertension in the elderly and a reduction in adaptability of the circulation to stress. Reductions in arterial baroreceptor sensitivity, responsiveness of the renin–angiotensin system, and the capacity to conserve sodium may also play a role (Swales, 1979).

There are other neural influences on the heart, including chemoreceptor reflexes and the modulation of the neural tone by respiration. By studying developmentally the strength of these influences, it is possible to infer the ontogeny of the vagal control of the heart. Since the vagal control of the heart is a primary determinant of the evoked heart rate response, we focus here on developmental shifts in vagal tone. Since prospective studies with humans are rare and cross-sectional studies are often confounded with disease and other intervening factors, many of the studies reviewed here focus on animal preparations.

Animal preparations have been used to study the development of neural influences on the heart for the following reasons: First, invasive techniques, including surgical and pharmacological manipulations, are often necessary to determine the physiological mechanisms of the neural control of the heart; second, the human infant matures less rapidly than other animals; third, some animals (such as the rat) develop neural control of the heart virtually totally postpartum. Adolph (1971) studied the ontogeny of heart rate control in the hamster, rat, and guinea pig. By pharmacologically manipulating the sympathetics and the vagus, he was able to evaluate the neural control of the

heart at different ages for the different species. Heart rate increased with age in the three species. After peak heart rate was reached, blocking of the vagus was more effective in producing even higher heart rates.

The development of neural control in such animals as the rat is not accurately extracted from the average heart rate level. For example, in the study of the rat preparation, resting heart rate in the infant rat has been found to increase during two periods: first, within the first 3 days following birth; and second, after 14 days of age (Adolph, 1967; Ashida, 1972; Hofer & Reiser, 1969). The increase in heart rate that occurs during the first 3 days is not prevented by antisympathetic agents (e.g., reserpine, propranolol, pentolinium, or chlorisondamine). However, the later increase in heart rate is eliminated by the antisympathetics. These findings suggest that the sympathetic input does not contribute to the increase in postnatal heart rate until about 2 weeks postpartum.

Parasympathetic control via the vagus has been studied in the rat via nerve stimulation and blockade. Vagal nerve stimulation has been reported to decrease heart rate on the day of birth (Adolph, 1967; Mills, 1978) and even 1 day prior to birth (Adolph, 1967). Vagal blockade by atropine has been observed to have little or no effect on basal heart rate in rats prior to 16 days of age (Adolph, 1967, 1971). On the basis of this literature, it appears that the development of evoked vagal influences precedes the development of more tonic vagal influences on the heart.

Larson and Porges (1982) approached the question of ontogeny of the vagal control of the heart in the rat preparation by studying changes in the amplitude of respiration sinus arrhythmia. Through the use of the Porges method (see Bohrer & Porges, 1982; Porges, Bohrer, Keren, Cheung, Franks, & Drasgow, 1981), an accurate measure of the amplitudes of respiratory sinus arrhythmia was derived and used as an estimate of vagal tone. In the Larson and Porges (1982) study, rat pups were studied longitudinally for the first 24 days postpartum. Vagal tone exhibited a monotonic pattern of increases from Day 1 to Day 18 and a monotonic pattern of slight decreases from Day 18 to Day 24. The adult levels were approximately in the Day 18 to Day 24 range. Values of vagal tone were low during the first few weeks postpartum, when vagal blockage by atropine has been reported to have little effect. The peak in vagal tone during the third week postpartum corresponded to the time when vagal blockade by atropine has been reported to be effective on basal heart rate. These data suggest that even though vagal influences during the first 2 weeks postpartum are not sensitive to atropine manipulations, the amplitude of respiratory sinus arrhythmia indexes the maturational trend in vagal tone.

Other researchers have demonstrated the developmental shifts in the neural tone of the heart. Egbert and Katona (1980) demonstrated increased vagal control over the first few months in cats. Mace and Levy (1983) demonstrated that puppies exhibited smaller changes in heart rate than adult dogs to both vagal and sympathetic stimulation.

Mace and Levy (1983) reported that changes in heart rate were much greater with right-sided stimulation of the vagal and sympathetic nerves. In some of their subjects (11% of the adult dogs and almost 50% of the puppies), left-sided sympathetic stimulation did not increase heart rate. This asymmetry in reactivity provides important information regarding the higher-order control of the nerves mediating heart rate changes. It is important to note that the sinoatrial node, which mediates most of the chronotropic influences to the heart, is stimulated by the right vagus. Moreover, sensory input from cortex into the cells of origin of the vagus is crossed. Thus, the higher-order input that mediates medullary control of heart rate comes from the left side of the brain. In research with human neonates, one of us (Porges) has observed a higher probability of low vagal tone (i.e., low-amplitude respiratory sinus arrhythmia) in infants who were born right occipital anterior (ROA) than infants who were born left occipital anterior (LOA). Being born ROA is a risk factor associated with more difficult delivery. These findings suggest the possibility that some ROA infants experience compression of the left hemisphere, which reduces the higher neural input to the cells of origin of the vagus and results in a lower vagal tone. Support for this speculation may be derived from Krasney and Koehler (1976), who studied the effects of elevating intracranial pressure on heart rate and rhythm in anesthetized dogs. Raising intracranial pressure by left-sided intracranial balloon inflation produced cardiac dysrhythmias in 9 of 12 dogs.

There are other methods of deriving information regarding cardiac vagal tone. Instantaneous heart rate changes with forced breathing and in response to the transition from lying to standing have been used as simple tests to assess cardiac vagal control. Wieling, van Brederode, de Rijk, Borst, and Dunning (1982) examined heart changes induced by forced breathing and posture changes in humans between the ages of 10 and 65. Test results declined with age, implying that cardiac vagal tone degenerated with the aging process. Although the two tests have been assumed to reflect vagal tone, the heart rate changes elicited by the two tests were not correlated.

Neuroanatomy of the Vagus

Neuroanatomical studies support many of the contentions stated above regarding the development of vagal control of the heart. Marlot and Duron (1979) studied the histological maturation of the phrenic and vagus nerves in the kitten. The number of myelinated fibers in the phrenic and vagus nerves was lower in young kittens than in adult cats. This suggests that less information, which depends upon number of fibers, is carried by the vagus in the young than in the adult cat.

Similar findings have been reported with human infants. Sachis, Armstrong, Becker, and Bryan (1982) reported a developmental trend in the total number of myelinated vagus fibers in infants who died from causes other than sudden infant death syndrome (SIDS). The developmental trend was characterized by most of the increase in myelinated fibers occurring during the 24th through the 50th week postconception. Most of their subjects were premature infants. Total myelinated vagus fibers increased linearly with postconceptional age. By 40 weeks postconception, the total counts of myelinated fibers were comparable to those in the adolescent group. Preterm infants (i.e., less than or equal to 38 weeks postconception) showed significantly fewer total myelinated vagus fibers than the full-term or adolescent groups. The frequency of small-diameter myelinated fibers was related to postconceptional age for only the premature infants (Sachis et al., 1982). In other research, Sachis, Armstrong, Becker, and Bryan (1981) noted that infants who died of SIDS had fewer small myelinated vagus fibers than infants who died from other causes. These findings suggest the possibility of perinatal hypoxia as being causal in destroying the vulnerable small-diameter fibers of the vagus and functionally changing the cardiopulmonary control system.

Not only is hypoxia potentially responsible for damaging the medullary control system of cardiopulmonary function, but reduced oxygen tension may influence all electrical activity of the nervous system. Speckmann and Caspers (1974) have reported that during progressive asphyxia three phases of I-neuron activity can be identified: an initial depolarization in response to an initial fall of the partial oxygen pressure, an intermediate repolarization or hyperpolarization in response to increasing partial carbon dioxide pressure, and a terminal depolarization in response to an insufficient oxygen supply. Monitoring of the vagal tone to the heart may provide an important window to the changing neuronal activity as a function of oxygen and carbon dioxide tensions.

In summary, there are developmental trends in myelination and diameter of the vagus. In the human, most of the developmental changes occur during the last trimester of gestation. The histological research suggests only minor postterm changes. Moreover, the neurophysiological literature implies that central changes, such as reduced oxygen tensions or increased intracranial pressure, will have immediate consequences in the vagal control of the heart. Similarly, damage to central structures that have neural input to the cells of origin of the vagus may have peripheral manifestation in the vagal drive to the heart. This suggests that the monitoring of the cardiovagal control of the heart will provide an important noninvasive window to the function and state of higher central processes.

Evoked Heart Rate Responses

An understanding of the development of the neural control of the heart is an important prerequisite to the study of evoked heart rate responses in psychophysiological paradigms. Since the latency, direction, and magnitude of the heart rate response to experimental manipulations are, in part, determined by the neural control of the heart, it is important to have information regarding the maturational (i.e., age postconception) and perinatal (e.g., hypoxia, medication, etc.) influences on the neural control of the heart.

A strong argument may be made that the evoked heart rate response is related to the tonic state of neural control of the heart. More specifically, the chronotropic changes in tonic heart rate are primarily determined by the vagal control on the heart. Thus, transitory manipulation of vagal efferent influences will result in a transient change in base-level heart rate and the magnitude of the evoked response. Theoretically, this is produced by a modulation of central and perhaps cortical influences on the medullary centers that control vagal output to the heart. Many cortical areas have neural projections that reach the medullary centers within a few synapses. Neurophysiological changes in many of the cortical areas thus have almost immediate consequences on the vagal outflow to the heart. Of course, from the vantage point of most psychophysiologists, the change in electrophysiological and biochemical conditions may only be assessed on the level of the heart as changes in rate. Thus, although the changes may manifest within a couple of hundred milliseconds, it may take one or two heart beats for the heart rate to be influenced.

The evoked heart rate response is determined by supramedullary influences as well as vagal influences. The heart rate provides a noninvasive window to the changing central states that parallel cognitive activity. The evoked heart rate response is not merely a peripheral indicator of global state or emotion, but may reflect in "real time" the processing demands placed on the higher levels of the central nervous system.

Although the evoked heart rate response has been used as an index of attention (e.g., heart rate deceleration), the topography of the response (e.g., magnitude, direction, and latency) is not an isomorphic manifestation of the cognitive process. The topography of the response is determined by the complex interaction among the situational demands (e.g., external stimulus, contextual cues, and task demands), condition of the tonic neural influences on the heart (primarily the cardiac vagal tone), and the higher-level

neural inputs that modulate the vagal output. The functional neural states described above are, in part, determined by the morphology of the nervous system (e.g., myelination).

Developmentally, in response to simple physical stimuli such as auditory signals, there is a shift in the primary direction of the response from acceleration to deceleration (Graham, Berg, Berg, Jackson, Hatton, & Kantrowitz, 1970). This developmental shift has often been interpreted (Graham & Jackson, 1970) to suggest that very young infants, who primarily respond with heart rate acceleration, are responding with a protective/defensive system, while older infants, who respond with heart rate deceleration, are attending or orienting to the stimulus.

The analysis of the cognitive correlates of the heart rate response is more complicated than the accelerative–decelerative dichotomy. When information regarding the development of the neural control of the autonomic nervous system is considered, the interpretation of the evoked heart rate response may change. The developmental shift in vagal control of the heart may predispose infants at different ages to respond with heart rate response patterns of different topographies. For example, the directionality of the heart rate response may not reflect the same psychological properties as have been observed in the adult (e.g., acceleration associated with startle or defense and deceleration associated with attention or orienting). However, if the shift in the neural control of the heart actually parallels a psychological shift from defensive to orienting behavior, then the directionality of the heart rate response could be used as an important indicator of psychological activity. To test this assumption would be extremely difficult, since it would necessitate a criterion measure of the psychological process—an elusive if not impossible task with a preverbal infant.

The developmental shift in response topography of the evoked heart rate response is not a simple manifestation of developmental shifts in cognitive processing. The shift in response topography is a manifestation of the changing functional and morphological status of the "brain–vagus–heart" axis. Thus, although there are reports of age-related changes in the heart rate response pattern, explanations of these changes must incorporate information regarding maturational shifts in neurophysiological modulation of the heart. In general, these points have been avoided, and it has been assumed that the efferent output (i.e., brain–vagus–heart connections) and the afferent input are unaffected by maturational and aging influences. The observed developmental shifts have, therefore, been attributed to maturational shifts in the central processing of information within the brain, and more specifically the cortex.

The evoked heart rate responses, often used to monitor cognitive activity, are often mapped into the sympathetic and parasympathetic nervous systems. Heart rate acceleration is assumed to be a manifestation of excitatory sympathetic influences, and heart rate deceleration is assumed to be a manifestation of the inhibitory parasympathetic influences via the vagus. However, in virtually every situation in which the developmental psychophysiologist may monitor heart rate, the changes are primarily mediated by the vagus. Heart rate acceleration is determined by reduced vagal input, and heart rate deceleration is determined by inhanced vagal input. Even the heart rate accelerations associated with motor activity have been linked to changing vagal tone (Gelsema, de Groot, & Bouman, 1983). Thus, although the mean heart rate is determined by the additive input of the tonic sympathetic and vagal system, the evoked heart rate response is primarily mediated by the vagus. Thus, methods that evaluate the tonic vagal tone may be useful in predicting subsequent heart rate reactivity. In fact, Linnemeyer and Porges (in press) have reported a relationship between an estimate of tonic vagal tone derived from respiratory sinus arrhythmia and evoked heart rate response in human infants.

Although this chapter has not attempted to survey the literature on the evoked heart rate response, it is clear that there are some developmental trends. Human neonates are less likely than other individuals to exhibit heart rate decelerations to auditory and visual stimuli. However, when the neonate is tested in a quiet alert state, the heart rate response, although smaller than in more mature infants, is often decelerative (Berg & Berg, 1979; Porges, 1974; Stamps & Porges, 1975). The magnitude and the direction of the heart rate response have been used as indicators of psychological processes. The topographic differences between the neonate's and the older infant's heart rate response have been used as confirmation of the differential maturational status of the central information-processing mechanisms. One can argue, based upon the information presented in this chapter, that developmental shifts in both the myelination of the vagus and the tonic influence of the vagus on the heart could modulate the evoked heart rate response and could account for the observed developmental differences. A more complicated explanation would include the possible developmental shifts in the central regulation of the efferent output system.

EEG

Overview

The EEG has been used for diagnostic purposes in clinical settings. Isoelectric activity has been used as a sign of brain death, and patterns of EEG activity have been used in the localization of focal epileptic seizures

and tumors (Tharp, Cukier, & Monod, 1981). Since Berger (1931) reported age differences in the frequency distribution of the EEG, many studies have detailed the EEG development in normal children (e.g., Ellingson, 1967; Lindsley, 1939).

Dreyfus-Brisac (1964, 1968) recorded from the scalp of very young premature infants. She found that it was possible to record electrical activity in prematures as young as 4 months postconception. EEG activity appeared to take on a normal-term pattern by 8 months postconception. Researchers have utilized the EEG to investigate the maturation of sleep and the basic sleep–wake cycle in both preterm and normal-term infants. Parmelee and colleagues (Parmelee, Akiyama, Shultz, Wenner, Shultz, & Stern, 1968; Parmelee & Stern, 1972) studied the differentiation of sleep patterns in infants and noted that the maturation of certain EEG parameters paralleled the ontogeny of infant state differentiation.

Basic to the EEG is the question of the precise origin and interpretation of the electrical activity recorded from the scalp. While the mechanisms for generation of the EEG are still unknown, there is speculation that maintenance and regulation of rhythmic activity are subcortical in origin and possibly located in nonspecific nuclei of the thalamus. In a comprehensive review of the development of brain activity, Woodruff (1978) has speculated that the maturation of rhythmic EEG activity, particularly alpha rhythm, reflects neuroanatomical changes in the brain, such as dendritic branching and myelination. These changes may be reflected in such behavioral developments as the maturation of the visual system and the disappearance of "primitive" subcortical responses. The precise age-related changes in frequency, both at infancy and in older adult periods, and their possible physiological correlates are outlined below.

Development of the EEG

Frequency Characteristics

A large number of studies document change in EEG activity during the first year of life (Ellingson, 1958, 1967; Hagne, 1968, 1972; Mizuno, Yamauchi, Watanabe, Komatshshiro, Takasi, Iinuma, & Arakawa, 1970; Eeg-Olofsson, 1971). These studies of sleeping and awake infants describe a pattern that involves the maturation of fast frequencies during the first year. The EEG during the first 3 months of life is generally of low voltage and slow rhythmic quality, showing a predominance of delta activity (.5–5.0 Hz). Woodruff (1978) has documented changes in both the EEG rhythm over the first months of life and notes that at about 3 months of age the dominant rhythm increases to 6–7 Hz (i.e., theta range). During the next few months, high-voltage activity appears, and faster-frequency activity may be recorded. By the end of the first year of life, the EEG recorded from central and posterior regions appears similar to an adult pattern. Changes in the EEG past the first year are more gradual and less dramatic as periods of alertness predominate and as periods of drowsiness and frequent state change, so prevalent in the young infant, decrease. With these changes come a decrease in delta and theta activity and an increase in faster activity. Surwillo (1961) demonstrated a linear increase in alpha frequency during childhood (46–140 months). However, if the pattern that occurs during the first year is added to Surwillo's data, the rapid changes in EEG maturation are more accurately described as a logarithmic function (Woodruff, 1978).

Behavioral Significance

A number of researchers have attempted to relate changes in frequency of the EEG over the first year of life to changes in behavior. Among them, Hagne (1972) followed 26 newborn infants through the first year of life. EEG was recorded, as well as measures of neurological and sensory–motor development. She computed a delta:theta ratio score and examined the peak frequency of the EEG at each age point. These measures were correlated with neurological and developmental status. Her results revealed significant correlations between 4-month delta:theta ratio and developmental status, as well as between peak frequency and development. The delta:theta ratio was negatively correlated with the developmental status. The ratio decreased with age. The peak frequency, however, was positively correlated with maturation. The peak frequency increased with age. These data suggest that the age-dependent development of the EEG spectrum reflects the relative decrease in slow rhythmic activity over the first year.

A clearer demonstration of behavioral changes coincident with changes in the EEG during the first year of life was provided by Woodruff and colleagues (Woodruff, Klitsch, & Gerrity, 1981). Sixteen infants were examined at 2, 5, 8, 11, 13, 15, and 17 weeks of age. At each age, measures of visual preference and neuromotor maturation were collected. Woodruff et al. reported that by the eighth week postpartum, infants displayed a change from quantitative to qualitative visual preference. In addition, in 15 of the infants, this change in preference was accompanied by neuromotor changes (decrease in primitive reflexes) indicative of a shift from subcortical to cortical control. The EEG data (for one infant) recorded at each assessment point demonstrated that the onset of occipital alpha occurred at approximately the same time that the change in visual preference and disappearance of primitive reflexes occurred. Woodruff et al. (1981) subsequently confirmed this pattern with a large sample in a cross-sectional study.

In a longitudinal study of the development of emotional responses over the first year of life, Emde, Gaensbauer, and Harmon (1976) recorded EEG during sleep in a group of infants over the first year of life. These infants were subsequently seen in a laboratory setting, where their behavioral response to a number of affect-eliciting situations was recorded. The authors found changes in EEG activity to parallel shifts in early state organization at about 2–3 months. They also noted changes in specific EEG parameters at about 7–9 months, which they suggest parallel a biobehavioral shift in emotional response of the infant.

Two EEG parameters—hypersynchronous drowsy activity and K complexes—appear in the sleep recordings of infants during the latter part of the first year. Both patterns are absent at birth, but continue throughout life once they appear. Hypersynchronous drowsy activity is seen during the transition from wakefulness to sleep and consists of high-amplitude 4- to 6-Hz activity with generalized synchrony. K complexes are well-defined negative sharp waves followed by positive waves. In the Emde et al. (1976) study, 11 of 14 infants developed K complexes prior to the onset of stranger distress, and 12 of 14 infants developed hypersynchronous drowsy activity before the onset of stranger distress. Since correlations between these two events were low, the authors caution against any causal link between these phenomena. Indeed, little physiological explanation for the appearance, significance, or origin of these EEG parameters is offered, and the above-mentioned data may reflect an unknown mediating process that determines both the appearance of the EEG parameters and the change in emotion. Fox and Davidson (1984) have speculated that the ontogeny of affect may involve the development of neural connections between discrete brain regions, rather than the maturation of only specific areas. The Fox and Davidson (1984) study evaluated the asymmetrical activation of different brain regions during the expression of emotion at birth in human neonates. Fox and Davidson speculate that asymmetry of activation may decrease with age as greater interhemispheric connections are completed.

Aging

There are a number of studies in the EEG literature which have reported changes in EEG frequency with aging. For example, Obrist (1954; Obrist & Busse, 1965) documented the progressive slowing of alpha activity in elderly subjects, as well as increases in slow-wave activity. However, more recent studies, which have carefully controlled for cerebrovascular differences, medication, and psychiatric illness, have reported results inconsistent with those of Obrist. For example, Katz and Horowitz (1982) and Prinz, Peskind, Vitaliano, Raskind, Eisdorfer, Zencuznikov, and

Gerber (1982) both found that the dominant frequency in elderly subjects remained above 9 Hz. Torres, Faora, Loewenson, and Johnson (1983) found that elderly subjects had a mean alpha frequency of 9.7 Hz, significantly greater than that of hospitalized elderly subjects.

The studies that have reported relative decreases in alpha and increases in slow-wave theta and delta activity have attempted to correlate these frequency changes with changes in behavior. Researchers have examined changes in memory, reaction time, and affect and have attempted to relate changes that occur in these domains to changes in EEG frequency. Perhaps the most widely examined relation is between changes in the EEG and changes in reaction time. Much of this work is based upon Surwillo's excitability hypothesis, which relates alpha rhythm to the timing of behavior (Surwillo, 1975). Essentially, Surwillo argues that a subject's reaction time will be a function of the timing of the alpha rhythm and stimulus presentation. According to this model, stimuli are sampled at discrete intervals in the alpha phase; longer reaction time will occur if a stimulus is presented when a new sample is just beginning. The alpha cycle (approximately 100 msec) is thought to be related to the points where samples occur. Thus, there should be a strong relation between the phase of alpha when the stimulus is presented and reaction time. Attempts to confirm this model, however, have not been successful (Woodruff, 1978), and its applicability to the geriatric population is in doubt (Thompson & Wilson, 1966).

Among the results of studies that examine EEG in the elderly are data indicating increases in fast-frequency activity with age (Wang & Busse, 1969). A number of studies have reported that with age the amplitude of the upper part of the beta band increases while the lower part of beta and alpha decrease. Roubicek (1977) argued that the increase in beta activity is associated with physiological well-being and increased attention span, although the evidence relating these phenomena is scant.

There are reports that mood changes and affect disorders in clinical populations are related to changes in EEG frequency. Researchers have noted that among populations of depressed individuals there is a marked increase in upper-band beta activity. Flor-Henry (1979) observed fast-frequency activity in the right temporal region in depressed patients and bilateral high-frequency activity in mania. Flor-Henry (1979) also reported focal slow-wave activity in depressed individuals. A similar pattern has been reported in the geriatric literature. Thus, it is possible that the pattern of EEG activity reported in the elderly may have behavioral significance in terms of the reported changes in affect often observed in large portions of the elderly population.

A recent study on EEG correlates of elderly dementia and depressed populations may lend insight into the physiological bases for the various affective disorders. Reynolds, Spiker, Hanin, and Kupfer (1983) recorded EEG during sleep in a population of elderly depressed and elderly demented patients. They reported that patients with dementia had less sleep continuity and longer REM density than depressed elderly patients. These authors speculate that the differences in REM may be controlled by cholinergic mechanisms. Their hypothesis is based upon research demonstrating that cholinergic agonists induce REM and anticholinergic agents block REM. Thus, the differences in REM sleep distribution may be related to deficits in acetylcholine production in dementia (leading to diminished REM) and to increased cholinergic input in depression (affecting mood and the timing of REM, and perhaps contributions to the high-frequency EEG activity).

Affect and Cerebral Asymmetry

The differential role of the two cerebral hemispheres in emotion has theoretical origins in the early observations of brain-damaged patients. Clinical reports noted that following unilateral left-hemisphere damage, patients displayed a high incidence of negative affect characterized by pessimism about the future (Goldstein, 1939). Following right-hemisphere damage, a different affective profile emerged: Patients with unilateral right-hemisphere damage expressed indifference about their state or euphoria. Recent studies have evaluated the effects of the caudality of lesion (i.e., the anterior–posterior plane) on the affective response of the patient. Depressive reactions associated with left-hemisphere damage also tend to be associated with damage to the left frontal region (e.g., Robinson & Szetela, 1981).

Hemispheric differences in the control of positive and negative emotion have been examined extensively in depressed patients. These individuals can be assumed to be tonically in a negative affective state. Various reports indicate that depressed patients have greater right-hemisphere activation in temporal central and frontal leads (e.g., Flor-Henry, Kokes, Howath, & Burton, 1979; Schaffer, Davidson, & Saron, 1983). However, some findings suggest that activation asymmetry varies as a function of the nature of the depressive symptomatology (Perris & Monakhov, 1979). Schaffer *et al.* (1983) found that subclinically depressed subjects were reliably distinguished from matched controls on the basis of a 1-min sample of resting eyes-closed EEG. The depressed subjects exhibited significantly greater right frontal activation compared with controls. No group differences were found on parietal activation asymmetry for the same epochs.

Electrophysiological studies of activation asymmetries associated with emotion in adults have helped to identify the regions exhibiting differential lateralization for positive and negative emotion. For example, Davidson, Schwartz, Saron, Bennett, and Goleman (1979) reported that frontal activation asymmetery discriminated between epochs of self-rated positive versus negative emotion. Subjects were exposed to video segments designed to elicit a range of emotions. The positive epochs were associated with significantly greater left frontal activation than the negative epochs. Parietal asymmetry from the same points in time did not discriminate between segments. Other research (e.g., Tucker, Stenslie, Roth, & Shearer, 1981) has replicated this pattern of findings.

Davidson and Fox (1982) attempted to extend the adult findings on differences in frontal EEG asymmetry between positive and negative affective stimuli to infants. EEG was recorded from left and right frontal and parietal regions referred to a common vertex (the cephalic site) in 10-month-old female infants. EEG was evaluated in response to "positive" (laughing and smiling) and "negative" (frowning and crying) video segments. The results indicated that infants displayed greater relative left frontal activation in response to the "positive" video segment. Moreover, 83% of the infants showed equal or greater relative left frontal activation during the "positive" segment. Parietal asymmetry did not discriminate between conditions.

A subsequent study (Fox et al., 1983) explored the origins of this brain asymmetry for affect. EEG was recorded in response to liquid tastes in newborn infants. EEG was recorded while the infants were awake and alert immediately after feeding. Four stimuli were presented: distilled water; sucrose solution (25%, .73 M); citric acid solution (2.5%, .12 c); and quinine sulfate solution (.25%, .0003 M). The sucrose condition elicited higher frontal ratio scores than the citric acid condition, although there were no overall differences in arousal across hemispheres among conditions. Examination of the infant facial data indicated that the newborns reliably displayed facial expressions of disgust to the citric acid solution and interest to the sucrose solution. These facial behaviors may reflect general withdrawal or approach responses to the liquid tastes. Thus, the data seem to indicate that brain electrical activation asymmetry is present at birth in response to a certain set of stimuli eliciting approach or withdrawal.

EEG in the Infant: Methodological Issues

Electrode Placement

EEG recordings in adults use the standard International 10-20 system, in which scalp electrodes are topographically located across the skull and are assumed to record brain activity from regions underneath the site. Although there may be age differences in skull thickness, the localization of an electrode site is determined on the basis of skull geometry. While there are limited data on the neuronal maturation of the cerebral cortex over the first year of life, little is known about variations in brain structure or skull geometry. Since the skull shape changes dramatically over the first year as the fontanelles grow and fuse, precise placement of scalp electrodes even using the International 10-20 system may be problematic.

Behavioral State

Studies of adult brain electrical activity usually record a resting eyes-open–eyes-closed baseline period and compare task-responsive EEG to these baseline epochs. Other researchers have investigated individual differences in the resting EEG (cf. Schaffer, Davidson, & Saron, 1983). The recording of a resting eyes-open–eyes-closed baseline period in an infant is not feasible, since periods of quiet alertness in young infants are usually accompanied by perceptual motor and cognitive activity of an undetermined nature. Indeed, the majority of studies of infant EEG involve recording of the brain electrical activity while the infant is asleep or sedated. Psychophysiologists have been skeptical about the use of task-responsive EEG in alert, awake infants, because these periods of alertness are hard to maintain and because there is no "appropriate" baseline period for comparison.

Scalp Preparation

Preparation of the scalp and electrode placement cannot be easily completed on an alert, moving infant. Movement artifact occurs in an awake, alert infant during an EEG recording. Recent research (Fox & Davidson, 1984) has utilized a cap especially designed for infants. Electrodes are sewn into the cap, and the cap itself comes in a range of head circumferences to accommodate infants over the first year. Use of the cap seems to eliminate some of the problems that researchers have had with EEG recordings with infants.

Reference Electrode

There are a number of studies that have utilized the cephalic site as a reference in EEG recording. These studies have examined asymmetries in brain electrical activity between homologous scalp leads (Davidson & Fox, 1982). However, use of the cephalic site may be problematic if electrical activity at the site varies as a function of changes in arousal. This would confound the interpretation of the activity recorded from the lateral scalp regions. Most evoked potential studies utilize a noncephalic reference (linked ears or mastoids) to circumvent this problem. However, it has been suggested that the linked-ears reference artifactually attenuates the magnitude of asymmetries in brain electrical activity by acting like a low-resistance shunt across the head (Nunez, 1981). Thus, while the linked-ears reference avoids some of the problems associated with the cephalic site, it introduces others.

CONCLUSIONS

Many psychophysiologists monitor physiological responses that they assume are sensitive indicators of the development of cognition and affect. The following assumptions are inherent in this approach:

1. That physiological responses are reliable indicators of psychological processes.
2. That physiological responses identified as reliable indicators of psychological processes in older, verbal individuals reflect the same psychological processes in young infants.
3. That maturation selectively influences only the physiological response components that index or are mediated by developmental changes in cognition (the psychological process).

Violations of these assumptions may not create a serious problem, if the investigator is merely attempting to identify indicators of responsiveness to various stimulus dimensions. For example, a reliable response of any topography (e.g., heart rate acceleration, deceleration, or change in variability) may be interpreted to reflect the subject's detection of the stimulus. However, violations of these assumptions limit the specific interpretation of the response. For example, one could not determine whether the response is an orienting or a defensive response. Furthermore, given the changing neural control of physiological response systems during development, the same stimulus array presented at various stages of maturation is only interpretable as an indicator of stimulus detection. Interpreting the response as the manifestation of a specific cognitive or affective process may be difficult.

This chapter has strongly suggested that the elicited responses that many psychophysiologists study are determined by the following factors:

1. The stimulus conditions, including the subject's previous history with the stimulus.
2. The behavioral state of the subject.
3. The condition of the sensory apparatus determined by maturation, injury, or normal range of individual differences.
4. The central processing of the afferent information.
5. The status of the central afferent–efferent integration.
6. The neuroregulation of the effector system.
7. The status of the end organ of the efferent output system.
8. The recording technology.
9. The quantitative methodology.

It is obvious from the present discussion that statements regarding developmental shifts in physiological response topography are not simply related to shifts in psychological processing. Inferences regarding developmental shifts in psychological processes must be made cautiously within the context of neurophysiological maturation. Research must be conducted within a theoretical context that includes an understanding of the multiple determinants of the responses we study. For example, even on the level of defining a response, the parameters must be consistent with the underlying neurophysiological mechanisms. One must be careful to be sensitive to the latency and magnitude of the response. It is necessary to sample rapidly enough to detect rapid changes and long enough to characterize the total response pattern. With electrical potentials, it will be necessary to have a neurophysiological reason for selecting specific amplifier and filter settings that may determine the shape of the response pattern.

REFERENCES

Adolph, E. F. Ranges of heart rates and their regulations at various ages (rat). *American Journal of Physiology*, 1967, 212, 595–602.

Adolph, E. F. Ontogeny of heart-rate controls in hamster, rat and guinea pig. *American Journal of Physiology*, 1971, 220, 1896–1902.

Ashida, S. Developmental changes in the basal and evoked heart rate in neonatal rats. *Journal of Comparative and Physiological Psychology*, 1972, 78, 368–374.

Astrand, P. O., & Rodahl, K. *Textbook of work physiology.* New York: McGraw-Hill, 1970.

Bell, R. Q. Sleep cycles and skin potential in newborns studied with a simplified observation and recording system. *Psychophysiology*, 1970, 6, 778–786.

Berg, W. K., & Berg, K. M. Psychophysiological development in infancy: State, sensory function and attention. In J. Osofsky (Ed.), *Handbook of infant development.* New York: Wiley, 1979.

Berger, H. Uber das electroencephalogram das menschen. III. *Archives of Psychiatry Nervenkr.*, 1931, 94, 16–60.

Bohrer, R. E., & Porges, S. W. The application of time-series statistics to psychological research: An introduction. In G. Keren (Ed.), *Statistical and methodological issues in psychology and social science research.* Hillsdale, N.J.: Erlbaum, 1982.

Botwinick, J., & Kornetsky, C. Age differences in the acquisition and extinction of the GSR. *Journal of Gerontology*, 1960, 15, 83–84.

Brandfonbrener, M., Landowne, M., & Shock, N. W. Changes in cardiac output with age. *Circulation*, 1955, 12, 557–566.

Catania, J. L., Thompson, L. W., Michalewski, H. A., & Bowman, T. E. Comparisons of sweat gland counts, electrodermal activity, and habituation behavior in young and old groups of subjects. *Psychophysiology*, 1980, 17, 146–152.

Crowell, D. H., Davis, C. M., Chun, B. J., & Spellacy, F. J. Galvinic skin reflex in newborn humans. *Science*, 1965, 148, 1108–1111.

Curzi-Dascalova, L., & Dreyfus-Brisac, C. Distribution of skin potential responses according to states of sleep during the first months of life in human babies. *Electroencephalography and Clinical Neurophysiology*, 1976, 41, 399–407.

Curzi-Dascalova, L., Pajot, N., & Dreyfus-Brisac, C. Spontaneous skin potential responses in sleeping infants between 24 and

41 weeks of conceptional age. *Psychophysiology*, 1973, 10, 478–486.

Davidson, R. J., & Fox, N. A. Asymmetrical brain activity discriminates between positive and negative stimuli in human infants. *Science*, 1982, 218, 1235–1237.

Davidson, R. J., Schwartz, G. E., Saron, C., Bennett, J., & Goleman, D. J. Frontal versus parietal EEG asymmetry during positive versus negative affect. *Psychophysiology*, 1979, 16, 202–203.

Dreyfus-Brisac, C. The electroencephalogram of the premature infant and full term newborn: Normal and abnormal development of waking and sleeping patterns. In P. Kellaway & I. Petersen (Eds.), *Neurological and electroencephalographic correlative studies in infancy*. New York: Grune & Stratton, 1964.

Dreyfus-Brisac, C. Sleep ontogenesis in early human prematures from 24 to 27 weeks conceptional age. *Developmental Psychobiology*, 1968, 1, 162–169.

Duffy, E. *Activation and behavior*. New York: Wiley, 1962.

Dustan, H. P. Atherosclerosis complicating chronic hypertension. *Circulation*, 1974, 50, 871–879.

Edelberg, R. Electrical properties of the skin. In C. C. Brown (Ed.), *Methods of psychophysiology*. Baltimore: Williams & Wilkins, 1967.

Eeg-Olofsson, O. The development of the electroencephalogram in normal children and adolescents from the age of 1 through 21 years. *Acta Paediatrica Scandinavica*, 1971, 209 (Suppl.), 1–46.

Egbert, J. R., & Katona, P. G. Development of autonomic heart rate control in the kitten during sleep. *American Journal of Physiology: Heart and Circulation Physiology*, 1980, 238, 829–835.

Ellingson, R. J. Electroencephalograms of normal full term newborns immediately after birth with observations on arousal and visual evoked responses. *Electroencephalography and Clinical Neurophysiology*, 1958, 10, 31–50.

Ellingson, R. J. The study of brain electrical activity in infants. In L. P. Lipsitt & C. C. Spiker (Eds.), *Advances in child development and behavior* (Vol. 3). New York: Academic Press, 1967.

Emde, R., Gaensbauer, R., & Harmon, R. Emotional expression in infancy: A bio-behavioral study. *Psychological Issues Monograph Series*, 1976, 10(No. 37).

Flor-Henry, P. On certain aspects of the localization of the cerebral systems regulating and determining emotion. *Biological Psychiatry*, 1979, 14, 677–697.

Flor-Henry, P., Kokes, Z. J., Howath, B. G., & Burton, L. Neurophysiological studies of schizophrenia, mania, and depression. In J. Gruzelier & P. Flor-Henry (Eds.), *Hemispheric asymmetries of function in psychopathology*. 1979.

Foster, K. G., Hey, E. N., & Katz, G. The response of the sweat glands of the newborn baby to thermal stimuli and to intradermal acetylcholine. *Journal of Physiology*, 1969, 203, 13–29.

Fox, N. A., & Davidson, R. J. Hemispheric asymmetries and the development of affect: A developmental model. In N. A. Fox & R. J. Davidson (Eds.), *The psychobiology of affective development*. Hillsdale, N.J.: Erlbaum, 1984.

Fox, N. A., Davidson, R. J., Schaffer, C. E., Saron, C., & Gelles, M. EEG asymmetries in newborn infants in response to tastes differing in affective valence. *Psychophysiology*, 1983, 20, 440 (abstract).

Garwood, M. K., Engel, B. T., & Quilter, R. E. Age differences in the effect of epidermal hydration on electrodermal activity. *Psychophysiology*, 1979, 16, 311–317.

Gelsema, A. J., de Groot, G., & Bouman, L. N. Instantaneous cardiac acceleration in the cat elicited by peripheral nerve stimulation. *Journal of Applied Physiology: Respiration, Environment, Exercise Physiology*, 1983, 55, 703–710.

Goldstein, K. *The Organism*. New York: Academic Book Publishers, 1939.

Graham, F. K., & Jackson, J. C. Arousal systems and infant heart rate responses. In H. W. Reese & L. P. Lipsitt (Eds.), *Advances in child development and behavior*. New York: Academic Press, 1970.

Graham, F. K., Berg, K. M., Berg, W. K., Jackson, J. C., Hatton, H. M., & Kantrowitz, S. R. Cardiac orienting response as a function of age. *Psychonomic Science*, 1970, 19, 363–365.

Gribbin, B., Pickering, T. G., Sleight, P., & Peto, R. Effect of age and high blood pressure on baroreflex sensitivity in man. *Circulation Research*, 1971, 29, 424–431.

Hagne, I. Development of the waking EEG in normal infants during the first year of life. In P. Kellaway & I. Peterson (Eds.), *Clinical electroencephalography in children*. New York: Grune & Stratton, 1968.

Hagne, I. Development of the EEG in normal infants during the first year of life. *Acta Paediatrica Scandinavica*, 1972, (Suppl. 232), 97–118.

Harpin, V. A., & Rutter, N. Development of emotional sweating in the newborn infant. *Archives of Disease in Childhood*, 1982, 57, 691–695.

Heptinstall, R. H. *Pathology of the kidney*. Boston: Little, Brown, 1974.

Hofer, M. A., & Reiser, M. F. The development of cardiac rate regulation in preweanling rats. *Psychosomatic Medicine*, 1969, 31, 372–388.

Hollander, W. Roles of hypertension in atherosclerosis and cardiovascular disease. *American Journal of Cardiology*, 1976, 38, 786–800.

Janes, C. L., Hesselbrock, V., & Stern, J. A. Parental psychopathology, age, and race as related to electrodermal activity of children. *Psychophysiology*, 1978, 15, 24–34.

Johnson, L. C., & Lubin, A. Spontaneous electrodermal activity during sleeping and waking. *Psychophysiology*, 1966, 3, 8–17.

Juniper, K., & Dykman, R. A. Skin resistance, sweat gland counts, salivary flow, and gastric secretion: Age, race and sex differences and intercorrelations. *Psychophysiology*, 1967, 4, 216–222.

Katz, R. I., & Horowitz, G. R. Electroencephalogram in the septuagenarian: Studies in a normal geriatric population. *Journal of the American Geriatric Society*, 1982, 30, 273–275.

Koumans, A. J. R., Tursky, B., & Soloman, P. Electrodermal levels and fluctuations during normal sleep. *Psychophysiology*, 1968, 5, 300–306.

Krasney, J. A., & Koehler, R. C. Heart rate and rhythm and intracranial pressure. *American Journal of Physiology*, 1976, 230, 1695–1700.

Larson, S. K., & Porges, S. W. The ontogeny of heart period patterning in the rat. *Developmental Psychobiology*, 1982, 15, 519–528.

Lindsley, D. B. A longitudinal study of the occipital alpha rhythm in normal children: Frequency and amplitude standards. *Journal of Genetic Psychology*, 1939, 55, 197–213.

Lindsley, D. B. Emotion. In S. S. Stevens (Ed.), *Handbook of experimental psychology*. New York: Wiley, 1951.

Linnemeyer, S. A., & Porges, S. W. Psychophysiology of visual recognition memory. *Infant Behavior & Development*. (in press)

Londeree, B. R., & Moeschberger, M. L. Effect of age and other factors on maximal heart rate. *Research Quarterly for Exercise and Sport*, 1982, 55, 297–304.

Mace, S. E., & Levy, M. N. Neural control of heart rate: A comparison between puppies and adult animals. *Pediatric Research*, 1983, 17, 491–495.

MacKinnon, D. C. B. Variation with age in the number of active plamar digital sweat glands. *Journal of Neurology, Neurosurgery and Psychiatry*, 1954, 17, 124–126.

Marlot, D., & Duron, B. Postnatal maturation of phrenic, vagus, and intercostal nerves in the kitten. *Biology of the Neonate*, 1979, 36, 264–272.

Marshall, R. J., & Shepherd, J. T. *Cardiac function in health and disease*. Philadelphia: W. B. Saunders, 1968.

Mills, E. Time course for development of vagal inhibition of the heart in neonatal rats. *Life Sciences*, 1978, 23, 2717–2720.

Mizuno, T., Yamauchi, N., Watanabe, A., Komatshshiro, M., Takasi, T., Iinuma, K., & Arakawa, T. Maturation patterns of EEG basic waves of healthy infants under twelve months of age. *Tokyo Journal of Experimental Medicine*, 1970, 102, 91–98.

Morrow, M. C., Boring, F. W., Keough, T. E., & Haesly, R. R. Differential GSR conditioning as a function of age. *Developmental Psychology*, 1969, 1, 299–302.

Nunez, P. L. *Electrical fields of the brain*. New York: Oxford University Press, 1981.

Obrist, W. D. The electroencephalogram of normal aged adults. *Electroencephalography and Clinical Neurophysiology*, 1954, 6, 235–244.

Obrist, W. D., & Busse, E. W. The electroencephalogram in old age. In W. P. Wilson (Ed.), *Applications of electroencephalography in psychiatry*. Durham, N.C.: Duke University Press, 1965.

Parmelee, A. H., Akiyama, Y., Shultz, M. A., Wenner, W. H., Shultz, F. J., & Stern, E. The electroencephalogram in active and quiet sleep in infants. In P. Kellaway & I. Petersen (Eds.), *Clinical electroencephalography in children*. New York: Grune & Stratton, 1968.

Parmelee, A. H., & Stern, E. Development of states in infants. In C. B. Clemente, D. P. Purpura, & F. E. Mayer (Eds.), *Sleep and the maturing nervous system*. New York: Academic Press, 1972.

Perris, C., & Monakhov, K. Depressive symptomatology and systemic structural analysis of the EEG. In J. Gruzelier & P. Flor-Henry (Eds.), *Hemispheric asymmetries of function in psychopathology*. New York: Elsevier/North Holland, 1979.

Plouffe, L., & Stelmack, R. M. The electrodermal orienting response and memory: An analysis of age differences in picture recall. *Psychophysiology*, 1984, 21, 191–198.

Porges, S. W. Heart rate oscillation: An index of neural mediation. In M. Coles, J. R. Jennings, & J. A. Stern (Eds.), *Psychophysiological perspectives*. New York: Van Nostrand Reinhold, 1984.

Porges, S. W. Heart rate indices of newborn attentional responsivity. *Merrill–Palmer Quarterly*, 1974, 20, 231–254.

Porges, S. W. Heart rate patterns in neonates: A potential diagnostic window to the brain. In T. Field & A. Sostek (Eds.), *Infants born at risk: Physiological, perceptual, and cognitive processes*. New York: Grune & Stratton, 1983.

Porges, S. W., Bohrer, R. E., Keren, G., Cheung, M. N., Franks, G. J., & Drasgow, F. The influence of methylphenidate on spontaneous autonomic activity and behavior in children diagnosed as hyperactive. *Psychophysiology*, 1981, 18, 42–48.

Porges, S. W., McCabe, P. M., & Yongue, B. G. Respiratory-heart rate interactions: Psychophysiological implications for pathophysiology and behavior. In J. T. Cacioppo & R. E. Petty (Eds.), *Perspectives in cardiovascular psychophysiology*. New York: Guilford Press, 1982.

Prinz, P. N., Peskind, E. R., Vitaliano, P. P., Raskind, M. A., Eisdorfer, C., Zencuznikov, N., & Gerber, C. V. Changes in sleep and waking EEG of non-demented and demented elderly subjects. *Journal of the American Geriatric Society*, 1982, 30, 86–93.

Reynolds, C. F., Spiker, D. G., Hanin, I., & Kupfer, D. J. Electroencephalography in sleep, aging, and psychopathology: New data and state of the art. *Biological Psychiatry*, 1983, 18, 139–153.

Robinson, R. G., & Szetela, B. Mood change following left hemisphere brain injury. *Annals of Neurology*, 1981, 9, 447–453.

Rothbaum, D. A., Shaw, D. J., Angell, C. S., & Shock, N. W. Age differences in the baroreceptor response of rats. *Journal of Gerontology*, 1974, 29, 488–492.

Roubicek, J. The electroencephalogram in the middle aged and the elderly. *Journal of the American Geriatrics Society*, 1977, 25, 145–152.

Sachis, P. N., Armstrong, D. L., Becker, L. E., & Bryan, A. C. The vagus nerve and sudden infant death syndrome: A morphometric study. *Journal of Pediatrics*, 1981, 98, 278–280.

Sachis, P. N., Armstrong, D. L., Becker, L. E., & Bryan, A. C. Myelination of the human vagus nerve from 24 weeks postconceptional age to adolescence. *Journal of Neuropathology and Experimental Neurology*, 1982, 41, 466–472.

Sato, I., Hasegawa, Y., Takahashi, N., Hirata, Y., Shimomura, K., & Hotta, K. Age-related changes of cardiac control function in man with special reference to heart rate control at rest and during exercise. *Journal of Gerontology*, 1981, 36, 564–572.

Schaffer, K., Davidson, R. J., & Saron, C. Frontal and parietal EEG asymmetry in depressed and non-depressed subjects. *Biological Psychiatry*, 1983, 18, 753–762.

Shmavonian, B. M., Miller, L. H., & Cohen, S. I. Differences among age and sex groups in electrodermal conditioning. *Psychophysiology*, 1968, 5, 119–131.

Shmavonian, B. M., Yarmat, A. J., & Cohen, S. I. Relationships between the autonomic nervous system and central nervous system in age differences in behavior. In A. T. Welford & J. E. Birren (Eds.), *Behavior, aging and the nervous system*. Springfield, Ill.: Charles C Thomas, 1965.

Silver, A., Montagna, A., & Karacan, I. Age and sex differences in spontaneous adrenergic and cholinergic human sweating. *Journal of Investigative Dermatology*, 1964, 43, 255–265.

Speckmann, E. J., & Caspers, H. The effect of O_2 and CO_2 tensions in the nervous system tissue on neuronal activity and DC potentials. In A. Remond (Ed.), *Handbook of EEG clinical neurophysiology* (Vol. 2C). Amsterdam: Elsevier, 1974.

Stamps, L. E., & Porges, S. W. Heart rate conditioning in newborn infants: Relationships among conditionability, heart rate variability, and sex. *Developmental Psychology*, 1975, 11, 424–431.

Stechler, G., Bradford, S., & Levy, H. Attention in the newborn: Effect on mobility and skin potential. *Science*, 1966, 151, 1246–1248.

Surwillo, W. W. Frequency of the "alpha" rhythm, reaction time, and age. *Nature*, 1961, 191, 823–824.

Surwillo, W. W. Reaction time variability, periodicities in reaction time distribution and the EEG sating-signal hypothesis. *Biological Psychology*, 1975, 3, 197, 247–261.

Surwillo, W. W., & Quilter, R. E. The relation of frequency of spontaneous skin potential responses to vigilance and to age. *Psychophysiology*, 1965, 1, 272–276.

Swales, J. D. Pathophysiology of blood pressure in the elderly. *Age and Angina*, 1979, 8, 104–109.

Tharp, B. R., Cukier, F., & Monod, N. The prognostic value of the electroencephalogram in premature infants. *Electroencephalography and Clinical Neurophysiology*, 1981, 51, 219–236.

Thompson, L. W., & Wilson, S. Electrocortical reactivity and learning in the elderly. *Journal of Gerontology*, 1966, 21, 45–51.

Torres, F., Faora, A., Loewenson, R., & Johnson, E. The electroencephalogram of elderly subjects revisited. *Electroencephalography and Clinical Neurophysiology*, 1983, 56, 391–398.

Tucker, D. M., Stenslie, C. E., Roth, R. S., & Shearer, S. L. Right frontal activation and right hemisphere performance decrement during a depressed mood. *Archives of General Psychiatry*, 1981, 38, 169–174.

Verbov, J., & Baxter, J. Onset of palmar sweating in the newborn infant. *British Journal of Dermatology*, 1974, 90, 269–276.

Wang, H. S., & Busse, E. W. EEG of healthy old persons—A longitudinal study: I. Dominant background activity and occipital rhythm. *Journal of Gerontology*, 1969, 24, 419–426.

Wieling, W., van Brederode, J. F. M., de Rijk, L. G., Borst, C., & Dunning, A. J. Reflex control of heart rate in normal subjects in relation to age: A data base for cardiac vagal neuropathy. *Diabetologia*, 1982, 22, 163–166.

Woodruff, D. S. Brain electrical activity and behavior: Relationships over the life span. In P. Baltes (Ed.), *Life span development and behavior* (Vol. 1). New York: Academic Press, 1978.

Woodruff, D. S., Klitsch, E. N. S., & Gerrity, K. M. *EEG as a measure of cortical maturation in the first four months of life*. Paper presented at the meeting of the Society for Research in Child Development, Boston, April 1981.

Chapter Twenty-Three
Psychosomatics

Paul A. Obrist
Kathleen C. Light
Alan W. Langer
John P. Koepke

INTRODUCTION

Our goal in this chapter is to describe a mechanistic psychophysiological strategy for studying a common derangement of human biological function, essential hypertension. But a few initial clarifications are necessary. First, while the chapter's title is "Psychosomatics" and the volume's title is *Psychophysiology*, we use the terms "psychosomatics" and "psychophysiology" only in broad description of research that attempts to decipher how various aspects of our biological functioning—including behavior—interact. We do not adhere to dualistic viewpoints (McMahon & Hastrup, 1980) or classic reductionistic approaches (see Dubos, 1959, on the "doctrine of specific etiology"), but prefer inductionistic strategies (Ader, 1980). Second, we avoid using the term "stress" where possible because of its circular nature (Obrist, 1981); also, as Ader (1980) has pointed out, it lacks explanatory power. Third, although hypertension is our focus, the underlying principles of the research strategy we advocate should apply equally well to some other diseases of visceral function, such as those of the gastrointestinal system (J. M. Weiss, 1977). Fourth, a

detailed review of the topic of hypertension as a psychosomatic disorder is not attempted; the reader is referred to other sources (Brady, Anderson & Harris, 1972; Frumkin, Nathan, Prout & Cohen, 1978; Graham, 1972; Guttman & Benson, 1971; Henry & Cassel, 1969; Shapiro, Mainardi, & Surwit, 1977; Shapiro, Schwartz, Ferguson, Redmond, & Weiss, 1977; H. Weiner, 1977a, 1977b). It is the intention of this chapter to advocate a research strategy that emphasizes going beyond demonstrating a concomitance between behavioral states and blood pressure (BP) to one that seeks to delineate the means (mechanisms) by which these aspects of our biology interact. To elucidate these mechanisms, we must first consider how cardiovascular activity subserves metabolic function. From this vantage, diseases of the cardiovascular system appear as regulatory disorders (Page & McCubbin, 1966; H. Weiner, 1977a) that arise when the system adapts ineffectively or inefficiently to the demands created by its surroundings.

One difficulty elaborated below is that BP is not a static event in anyone, but is quite labile. Sometimes, its elevation appears clearly necessary and without pathophysiological consequences, as during exercise,

Paul A. Obrist, Kathleen C. Light, Alan W. Langer, and John P. Koepke. Department of Psychiatry, Medical School, University of North Carolina at Chapel Hill, Chapel Hill, North Carolina.

where an elevated BP facilitates metabolic activity. A transient elevation of the BP does not therefore make a *prima facie* case that we are dealing with events critical to the etiology of hypertension. Our problem, then, is to decipher when gross elevations of BP warn of lethal consequences. To do so, we must recognize that the BP is a derived value; its level represents shifts in highly complex mechanisms, with pathological elevations reflecting faults in those mechanisms. We also point out that hypertension is a progressive disease, probably originating early in life, so that insight into its etiology requires a prospective strategy.

With these guidelines established, we describe some working hypotheses so as to illustrate how a psychophysiological research strategy might shed light on the etiological process. These hypotheses are intended to move us beyond the demonstration that BP is subject to behavioral influences (the "behavioral–cardiovascular interaction") to the elucidation of mechanisms that could have pathophysiological importance. Finally, we review some research on humans that has been guided by our working hypothesis. It concerns the behavioral–cardiovascular interaction and appears to be making some inroads into our understanding of the etiological process of hypertension. Admittedly, we are dealing speculatively with the etiological process, and our focus is deliberately narrow. It is well to remember that there are probably numerous etiological routes, some interacting, others not (see Page, 1977, on the mosaic model).

SOME GUIDELINES

Our efforts to conceptualize the problem of hypertension are facilitated by several guiding principles, the more important of which are as follows.

Blood Pressure Is a Variable Event

In all humans, regardless of the status of their health, and in several other mammalian species, the BP has been shown to vary appreciably within individuals across differing conditions. The BP may rise acutely or even chronically in a variety of environmental circumstances, which implies that behavioral factors contribute to the hypertensive process. While evidence of this type is a necessary starting point for our efforts, it is not especially informative with regard to mechanisms, or the particular qualities of the behavioral–cardiovascular interaction that are of significance, or the prediction of who in the population will become hypertensive. In Dahl's (1970) words,

> the important question is not whether blood pressure goes up under various psychological stresses or whether it can be conditioned to respond to one thing or another.

The central issue is the relevance of these phenomena to chronic hypertension. And here the waters become murky indeed. (p. 132)

More recently, writing from the viewpoint of an epidemiologist, Paul (1977) was similarly cautious: "it is not established that repetitive or continuous psychological stress leads to sustained elevation of blood pressure in anyone" (p. 624). Thus, our task is not the mere demonstration of the BP's lability. It is to advance our understanding of the disease process itself, and ultimately to decipher the influence of the behavioral–cardiovascular interaction.

The lability of the BP can be seen in different ways. Exercise offers an extreme example: Carlsten and Grimby (1966) showed that at intense levels of human activity, the systolic blood pressure (SBP) can exceed 180 mm Hg. This was 50 mm Hg above their subjects' resting levels—no trifling change. In dogs, SBP increases average 25 mm Hg at moderate levels of treadmill exercise (Langer, 1978; Langer, Obrist, & McCubbin, 1979). Such elevated pressures result from an increased cardiac output necessitated by the increased metabolic activity of the active muscles. The consequence is an increase in muscle blood flow, so the elevated BP is in this instance a useful event.[1]

An appreciable degree of variability in the BP has also been observed in normotensive adult humans under circumstances that are not as metabolically demanding as exercise and do not appear particularly threatening. This is most clearly seen when the BP is measured continuously with invasive procedures. In one study (Bevan, Honour, & Stott, 1969) of eight normotensive subjects monitored over 14 to 22 consecutive hr, both the SBP and the diastolic blood pressure (DBP) showed considerable variability during waking hours. For example, in one subject SBP values ranged from about 80 to 150 mm Hg, and the DBP from about 50 to 90 mm Hg. This degree of variability even surprised the investigators, who were led to comment:

> The range in each subject was huge, despite the absence of activity that was in any way out of the ordinary. In most subjects, the highest pressure was more than twice the lowest. Considering 150 mmHg systolic pressure as a popular division, every subject was hypertensive at some time . . . (p. 343)

We have also measured the BP invasively, but for briefer periods of time, in the course of evaluating

---

1. It could be argued that elevated BP during exercise is not an appropriate example of BP lability for our purposes, since it occurs in the face of a decreased vascular resistance, contrary to what is found in established hypertension. Furthermore, the myocardial and vascular effects of exercise involve mechanisms that do not perpetuate the elevated BP once the exercise is terminated. The example serves, nonetheless, to reinforce two major points we tend to ignore: that BP is not a static event, even in healthy people, and that its elevation can serve a useful purpose, probably without pathological consequences.

some noninvasive methodologies. The BP obtained from 25 young adults at rest as well as during several experimental tasks was again strikingly variable. For example, in one study using nine medical students (Pollak & Obrist, 1983), the range of *resting* values average 31 mm Hg SBP ($SD = 7.5$) and 22 mm Hg DBP ($SD = 4.7$).

What is important to underscore is, first, that the BP is variable (although not as much as the cardiac output and heart rate [HR] can be; see Ferrario & Page, 1978); and, second, that an elevation of the BP per se is not necessarily an omen of an eventual hypertension, even when no metabolic necessity (e.g., exercise) is apparent. At least it does not seem reasonable to propose that the wide range of values occurring in thse nonexercising normotensives is a forerunner of hypertension in all such individuals. There is evidence that even individuals considered hypertensive demonstrate a considerably labile BP and present normotensive values in a variety of circumstances (Julius, Ellis, Pascual, Matice, Hansson, Hunyor, & Sandler, 1974; Sokolow, Werdegar, Perloff, Cowan, & Brenenstuhl, 1970; Surwit & Shapiro, 1977; Watson, Stallard, Flinn, & Littler, 1980; see Obrist, 1981 and 1982, for reviews). The lability problem is thus not unique to "normotensives" and raises still other questions, such as those concerning the accuracy of our diagnostic procedures. In any case, it should be kept in mind that an elevation of the BP can serve an important metabolic function and, under less demanding metabolic situations, can have unknown consequences. What is important to ascertain, then, is when or under what conditions an elevation of the BP is of particular significance with regard to hypertension.

The Blood Pressure Is a Derived Value

Any given BP reflects the interaction of the cardiac output and vascular resistance (Guyton, 1980b, p. 24). Since these are the only two determinants of the BP, it would appear to be a rather simple derived event. Yet the controls affecting both determinants are complex and only partially understood. The output and resistance are both subject to intrinsic and extrinsic (neurohumoral) influences. The intrinsic mechanism can be illustrated by the cardiovascular exercise response, wherein the elevated cardiac output is facilitated by an increase in venous return resulting from, among other things, the mechanical action of the exercising muscles (Berne & Levy, 1977). The decreased vascular resistance of the active muscles also largely reflects the direct action of their increased metabolic activity (Shepherd & Vanhoutte, 1975; Skinner, 1975). In fact, there is probably no more powerful control of the vasculature than that exerted by intrinsic mechanisms in response to metabolic demands,

whether in exercising muscles or in other vital organs, such as the brain (Scheinberg, 1975), myocardium (Berne, 1975), and kidneys (Hollenberg, 1975). Intrinsically controlled increases in vascular resistance also may be pertinent to established hypertension; such vasoconstriction is proposed to derive from pressure-induced structural (Folkow, Hallback, Lundgren, Sivertsson, & Weiss, 1973) and cardiac-output-induced autoregulatory (Guyton, 1980b) changes in the arterioles.

Extrinsically, a wide range of neurohumoral factors must be considered. Particular attention has been paid to the catecholamines (i.e., norepinephrine and epinephrine), but their effects are not simple, because adrenergic receptor sites differ (the alpha–beta distinction; see Ahlquist, 1976a, 1976b). Norepinephrine, for instance, can evoke increased myocardial rate, contractility, and vasoconstriction, while epinephrine can evoke similar myocardial and vasacular changes, as well as vasodilation (Mayer, 1980; N. Weiner, 1980). Other humoral agents are also known to influence cardiovascular events, particularly vascular resistance. Besides the well-publicized renin–angiotensin mechanism, which has a powerful vasoconstrictor influence (Guyton, Cowley, Coleman, McCaa, & Young, 1980; Page & Bumpus, 1974), other vasoconstrictors exist, such as antidiuretic hormone (ADH or vasopressin; Hays, 1980). There are also vasodilator substances, such as prostaglandins (Lee, 1977; Moncada, Flower, & Vane, 1980), prolactin (Horrobin, 1977), and kallikrein (Croxatto, Albertini, Corthorn, & Rusas, 1977). Other agents, like aldosterone (Reid & Ganong, 1977), influence BP less directly, exerting their control on the blood volume (Guyton, 1980a). Numerous other factors (e.g., additional hormonal substances, cations, bodily states like alkalosis, etc.) can also influence the BP through vascular mechanisms (see Frohlich, 1977b). The influence of these factors in the etiology of hypertension remains largely obscure, but their numbers alone should warn us that simple explanations involving BP control mechanisms are unlikely.

The fact that the BP is a derived value, and a complex one at that, should make us aware of several problems posed by hypertension. For one thing, hypertension may be a reflection not of some single etiological event, but rather of multiple interacting events, as the mosaic model proposes (Page, 1977; Page & McCubbin, 1966). The interactive nature of BP control can be illustrated through, again, the cardiovascular response to exercise, where we see the myocardium as well as the vasculature influenced by both intrinsic and extrinsic factors (Obrist, 1981). The increased cardiac output reflects, for example, neurogenic influences on HR, as well as both neurogenic and intrinsic influences on cardiac contractility, stroke volume, and venous return (Braunwald, Sonnenblick, Ross, Glick, & Epstein, 1967; E. E. Smith, Guyton, Manning, & White, 1976). The vascular adjustments reflect a similar interactive influence, with the intrinsically mediated vasodilation in the active muscles complemented by neurogenically mediated increases in vascular resistance in nonactive muscles and areas of the viscera, shunting blood to the working muscles (Shepherd & Vanhoutte, 1975; Skinner, 1975; E. E. Smith *et al.*, 1976).

It is reasonable to assume, therefore, that interactive mechanisms are probably involved in hypertension, and that an elevated BP might arise from impairment of any of the many factors involved in controlling BP. As we propose later, one such factor subject to a behavioral influence would be the complex interplay between the cardiac output and the kidneys' handling of sodium; they can act in concert to raise the vascular resistance and hence the BP. This proposed etiological route is only one of several possible ways in which BP control mechanisms can be influenced. Recent interest in endogenous vasodilating substances, such as prostaglandin, reflects this appreciation:

> The principal underlying theory is that high blood pressure is not necessarily due solely to agents or mechanisms which raise the blood pressure but may be a deficiency disorder of agents or mechanisms which are antihypertensive and vasodilatory in nature. (Lee, 1977, p. 373)

Regardless of the particular merit of these hypotheses, they underscore the possibility that since the control of the BP is complex, its pathological elevation may involve several etiological processes or routes. In turn, the significance of behavioral influences may vary as a function of the etiological route. In some cases, behavior may be paramount, such as when we see neurally mediated influences on the cardiac output and the renal handling of sodium. In others, behavior would be secondary or insignificant—if, say, it were shown that some hypertensions involved a deficiency in compensatory vasodilatory mechanisms that was genetic in basis. In short, an elevated BP is a symptom, just like an elevated body temperature, and as such it is uninformative about the etiological basis of the disorder.

This raises a second point. Despite the daunting complexity of BP mechanisms, we must shift our focus from the symptom itself to the way in which the BP is controlled, and must determine how the behavioral–cardiovascular interaction is involved. This will require singling out just a few such mechanisms to study, with the understanding that even these few are not simple and that even if our efforts bear fruit, we shall not yet have solved the problem of hypertension.

A final point to emphasize is that psychophysiological research must move away from a view of the BP as an independent entity, subject to control by various behavioral operations (e.g., biofeedback), to an orientation that seeks to evaluate its control mechanisms. The nonmechanistic approach was quite common in the early research on biofeedback and visceral learning (Katkin & Murray, 1968; Miller, 1969), notably in efforts to demonstrate an absence of mediating mechanisms. Even in more recent literature (Miller & Brucker, 1979) dealing with "learned" increases of the BP in paralyzed humans, the emphasis is on what the BP changes are *not* due to, rather than the mediating mechanism.

In summary, while the control of the BP is complex and the likely causes of hypertension are many, there is no reason why a psychophysiological strategy cannot shed some light on these processes, provided that we study the BP in terms of the mechanisms that control it.

Hypertension Is a Progressive Condition

It is indisputable that established hypertension develops over a period of years, as evidenced by the progressively greater incidence of elevated BPs with age (Geddes, 1970; Pickering, 1968). Furthermore, the etiological process probably originates some decades before the point when the BP is considered hypertensive, since follow-up studies observe a modest degree of correlation among BP values over periods as long as 20 years (Kuller, Crook, Almes, Detre, Reese, & Rutan, 1980). It has also been reported that BP is higher in adolescents whose parents are hypertensive (Falkner, Onesti, Angelakos, Fernandes, & Langman, 1979; Higgins, Keller, Metzner, Moore, & Ostrander, 1980). Such observations suggest that if we are to understand the etiological process, we must begin its study before the BP becomes noticeably elevated, preferably when normotensive values are still evident. Such a prospective strategy becomes even more advisable in view of the proposal that events initially active in the etiological process become less significant in time, with other factors emerging as the individual ages (see below). For instance, neurogenic mechanisms involving primarily the myocardium and sodium balance may gradually engage the vasculature through intrinsic mechanisms, thus superseding the initial autonomic influence. Another possibility is that the nature of the behavioral–cardiovascular interaction changes with age, with the significant behavioral influences dissipating over time. Does the 50-year-old interact with his or her environment in the same manner as the 20-year-old? In any case, efforts focusing on the etiological process once the hypertension has clearly emerged may misinform us about the etiological process, in regard both to BP control mechanisms and to the manner in which they are influenced by the individual's interaction with his or her environment.

SOME WORKING HYPOTHESES

Over the past several years, our thinking has been shaped by some working hypotheses about the nature of the etiological process, based on a variety of data and following the above-mentioned guidelines. Our task is not only to evaluate the merit of these hypotheses, but simultaneously to link them to the behavioral–cardiovascular interaction. The role of the latter in hypertension remains a disputed point, as indicated by Dahl's (1970) and Paul's (1977) remarks that the behavioral influence is arguably minimal and certainly not established. In keeping with our guidelines, we do not consider our working model applicable to all hypertensive conditions; rather, it is one possible route for hypertension that interests us because it implicates a behavioral influence. Before taking up the behavioral factors, we discuss two means by which BP control mechanisms could be modified so as to result in hypertensive disease. They involve a complex interplay among myocardial, renal, and vascular processes. Next, we consider the concept of metabolic inappropriateness, which suggests that an elevation of the BP be considered symptomatic of eventual hypertension if it reflects a breakdown in the efficiency with which certain fundamental metabolic processes are maintained. Finally, some behavioral data are presented to incorporate the behavioral–cardiovascular interaction.

Myocardial, Vascular, and Renal Mechanisms

In established hypertension, there is consistently observed an elevated vascular resistance, but an either normal or subnormal cardiac output (Freis, 1960; Lund-Johansen, 1967; Page & McCubbin, 1966); this observation suggests that vascular control mechanisms are the source of the problem. However, this may prove misleading, because some individuals who are only marginally hypertensive demonstrate an elevated cardiac output, while vascular influences are less obvious (Frohlich, 1977b; Lund-Johansen, 1967, 1973, 1979; Safar, Weiss, Levenson, London, & Milliez, 1973). Since this marginally hypertensive group is noticeably younger, it suggests that myocardial involvement may be an early precursor to a more elevated BP, with an elevated vascular resistance being secondary to the myocardial influence.

Certain follow-up (longitudinal) data suggest such a transition. Among individuals evidencing an initial elevated cardiac output, some demonstrate an elevated peripheral resistance and normal output anywhere from 2 to 10 years later (Birkenhager & Schalekamp, 1976; Eich, Cuddy, Smulyan, & Lyons, 1966; Lund-Johansen, 1979). A similar transition has been demonstrated in spontaneously hypertensive rats

(Pfeffer & Frohlich, 1973). In addition, similar but vastly accelerated shifts in the hemodynamic picture have also been seen in monkeys over a 72-hr shock avoidance task (Forsyth, 1971) and in conscious dogs within 6 hr of continuous stellate ganglion stimulation (Laird, Tarazi, Ferrario, & Manger, 1975). These latter effects demonstrate the facility of the cardiovascular system to vary the means by which BP is controlled even under more or less constant conditions, and suggest the potential of the cardiac output actually to trigger changes in vascular resistance. Finally, where evaluated, the cardiac output has been observed to result from neurogenic (beta-adrenergic)[2] influences on the heart in humans (Frohlich, 1977b; Julius & Esler, 1975), monkeys (Forsyth, 1976), and spontaneously hypertensive rats (SHR) (L. Weiss, Lundgren, & Folkow, 1974).

Three mechanisms have been suggested that could account for this hemodynamic shift; these could act singly or in concert. Two involve intrinsically mediated increases in vascular resistance resulting from an elevated output. One proposes that the elevated pressure associated with the increased output eventually results in vascular smooth muscle hypertrophy (Folkow et al., 1973). The second proposes that the increased output triggers autoregulation of vascular resistance because of excessive tissue perfusion (blood flow) (Coleman, Granger, & Guyton, 1971; Guyton, 1980b). Both mechanisms increase vascular resistance, and thus would not only sustain or even increase the elevated pressure, but would also reduce the cardiac output because of the reduction of venous return.

A third mechanism has been proposed to involve blunted beta-adrenergic receptor sensitivity in established hypertension (Bertel, Buhler, Kiowski, & Lutold, 1980; Buhler, Kiowski, van Brummelen, Amann, Bertel, Landmann, Lutold, & Bolli, 1980). In this case, decreased responsiveness of beta receptors in the myocardium would result in at least a normalizing of the cardiac output, while their blunted beta-adrenergic vasodilatory action would result in an increased vascular resistance, which would be even more pronounced should there be an increase in alpha-adrenergic drive. Thus, such a vascular mechanism working in conjunction with structural or auto-

2. At least two types of adrenergic (sympathetic) receptors are held to exist. Those referred to as "beta-adrenergic" receptors are found on the myocardium and in some vascular beds. Their excitation results in increased myocardial rate and contractility, but vascular dilation. The second type, "alpha-adrenergic" receptors, are found primarily in various vascular beds, and their excitation results in vascular constriction. The important distinction, then, is with respect to sympathetic influences on the vascular system; that is, increases in sympathetic excitation can result in both vasodilation and vasoconstriction, with the net effect on vascular resistance dependent on the relative contribution of each (see later discussion).

regulatory changes would act to enhance increases in vascular resistance.

In passing, the importance of keeping in mind these possible transition mechanisms is twofold. One, without some reasonable possibilities, the neurogenic-mediated increased cardiac output observed in borderline hypertension stands as an epiphenomenon. That is, if the elevated output has no possible consequences, then it has no significance—why pursue the problem? Second, such proposed mechanisms provide a perspective on the significance of neurogenic factors in sustaining hypertension. This is important even if the proposed mechanisms are not as yet definitively ascertained, since it guides behavioral treatment or preventive efforts until such time as the etiological pathways are better understood. For example, since these proposed mechanisms suggest a lesser neurogenic influence in established than in borderline hypertension, it suggests our efforts might be most beneficial if aimed at the latter condition, particularly as a preventive measure.

Therefore, one route that the hypertensive process might involve is an initial sympathetically mediated myocardial contribution, which over time could alter vascular resistance through intrinsically mediated vascular change, and/or which could become blunted over time and permits the manifestation of vasoconstrictor influences on peripheral resistance (see Frohlich, 1977a).

We are also considering a second means by which BP control mechanisms can be influenced. This involves the renal handling of the balance between sodium ingestion and excretion. Since the plasma level of sodium is quite stable,[3] any failure to balance intake with output can have serious consequences (e.g., excessive hydration or dehydration). In fact, balance is usually achieved but, in certain instances, at some expense to certain bodily processes, of which the BP is proposed to be one. Several investigators (Brown, Fraser, Lever, Morton, Robertson, & Schalekamp, 1977; Dahl, 1972, 1977; Freis, 1976; Guyton, 1977, 1980a; Tobian, 1978) have proposed that the kidneys' inability to handle excesses of ingested sodium (which in Western society usually far exceeds bodily needs; Dahl, 1972, 1977) constitutes the basis of established hypertension. Guyton's position illustrates the point. He suggests that over time a kidney

abnormality develops that requires an elevation of BP to achieve balance. The elevated BP thus acts as a natriuretic; or, as Brown et al. (1977) remark, "the rise in pressure is the price paid to maintain sodium balance" (p. 539). In this case, then, the elevated BP is indicative of a failure by the kidneys to maintain balance at normotensive levels of pressure, and the elevated pressure thus acts to attain this end (see also Doyle, Mendelsohn, & Morgan, 1980, Vol. 1, pp. 17–23).

While there is abundant evidence suggesting renal involvement in BP control and hence in the etiology of hypertension, the specific mechanisms remain obscure and controversial. Brown et al. (1977) suggest that the development of such a kidney abnormality would involve, among other things, sympathetic hyperreactivity: "It has been . . . suggested that the initial rise of pressure in essential hypertension is produced by a non-renal mechanism, possibly autonomic nervous system overactivity; . . . the kidney is affected by the resulting hypertension thereafter" (p. 538). Consistent with this proposal is the recent report (Grim, Luft, Miller, Rose, Christian, & Weinberger, 1980) that young normotensives with a family history of hypertension excrete a sodium load less efficiently than age-matched normotensives with no such family history, and that this blunted natriuresis correlates with elevated plasma renin values. Since a family history of hypertension is one of our better (but far from perfect) predictors (Grim et al., 1980; Schweitzer, Gearing, & Perera, 1967), and since plasma renin is controlled partly by sympathetic activity (Zanchetti & Bartorelli, 1977), these data implicate sympathetically mediated renal activity in the etiological process.

In regard to renal functioning, Guyton (1977, 1980b) has proposed a sequence of events that result in an elevation of BP. He refers to this as a "cascade effect," since each step amplifies the next. Here sodium retention first involves an expansion of the plasma volume. This in turn increases the cardiac output, which then acts to raise the vascular resistance via autoregulatory mechanisms. Sodium retention has also been reported to enhance reactivity to vasoconstrictive agents (Brown et al., 1977; Doyle et al., 1980, Vol. 2) and thus could complement other mechanisms acting to elevate the vascular resistance. Finally, a role for behavioral influences is possible in the light of the neurogenic influence on renin release, as well as other aspects of kidney functioning (Bello-Reuss, Trevino, & Gottschalk, 1976; Grignolo, 1980). In summary, renal influences on the cardiac output and vascular resistance mediated via adrenergic mechanisms could influence the BP; the action would resemble the direct neurogenic influence on the cardiac output suggested earlier. In principle, these could well be complementary processes, since

---

3. We have first-hand knowledge of this from a recent study (Grignolo, 1980; Grignolo, Koepke, & Obrist, 1982) where plasma sodium was assessed repeatedly (up to 68 occasions) on six dogs. The group and individual values were strikingly alike, rarely deviating over 1–2%. No other biological function assessed in our studies has shown such constancy, and we find it all the more dramatic when one considers how much sodium ingestion can vary. Since it is the kidney that is responsible for fine-tuning plasma sodium levels (Dahl, 1977), this constancy is a reminder that the kidneys possess potent means and can exert far-reaching effects.

both involve adrenergic mechanisms (see later discussion).

Our working hypotheses thus concern two routes by which the hypertensive process might evolve. Admittedly, there is some dispute about this scheme. Not all borderline hypertensives display an elevated cardiac output, nor is a marginally elevated pressure in early adulthood a particularly powerful predictor of eventual hypertension (Julius, 1977a; Julius & Schork, 1971). Moreover, evidence exists that questions the neurogenic mechanisms (e.g., Frohlich, 1977b; Touw, Haywood, Shaffer, & Brody, 1980). Nonetheless, our scheme remains plausible as one of admittedly many possible means whereby an established hypertension might evolve. In Page's (1977) words, "The causes are many because of the interrelatedness of the many dynamic regulatory mechanisms" (p. 587). Our model at least provides a framework within which we can evaluate the etiological process, including behavioral influences. The importance of the behavioral influences should become more apparent below when we present data from behavioral paradigms. The model has the further advantage of depicting hypertension as a progressive condition and moving us away from viewing the BP in isolation from its control mechanisms.

The Issue of Metabolic Inappropriateness

There is still another aspect to our conceptual scheme, which addresses a problem created by the lability of the BP and which further reinforces the necessity to evaluate BP control mechanisms. Since it appears that transient elevations of the BP, or for that matter of the cardiac output or of renal retention of sodium, do not constitute the invariant forerunners of an established hypertension, it is necessary to decipher cirumstances where they are. We propose that these events have an ominous flavor with respect to pathophysiology when they are a reflection of metabolically inappropriate adjustments or a breakdown in the efficiency in which metabolic homeostasis is being maintained. That is to say, while metabolic processes through most people's lives are not compromised, the efficiency with which they are being maintained can be. This is seen, for example, when the cardiac output overperfuses the tissues, or the kidneys retain sodium when sodium is not necessary. In such instances, any elevation of the BP is symptomatic of these inefficient homeostatic adjustments. With overperfusion, it reflects the attempt by the tissues to regulate blood flow to more appropriate levels. With sodium retention, it reflects a means by which sodium balance might be achieved.

In the remainder of this section, we would like to review some evidence indicative of how behavioral influences can result in such inappropriate adjust-

ments by the myocardium and kidneys. The best evidence we have is from chronically prepared conscious dogs. There is also suggestive evidence from young adult humans, but only with respect to myocardial events. Finally, it is pointed out that there are circumstances where transient increases in the BP appear of little significance, since they reflect mechanisms that reflect no compromise in metabolic efficiency.

One problem with this hypothesis is determining whether a given myocardial or renal adjustment is inefficient. For myocardial processes, we used the normal cardiovascular adjustment to exercise as our yardstick, since the cardiovascular exercise response usually is not considered to have pathophysiological consequences. It is well documented that during exercise, HR, cardiac output, SBP, and blood flow in the active muscles all increase more or less linearly with such metabolic demands as oxygen consumption (e.g., Carlsten & Grimby, 1966). Our behavioral challenges (e.g., shock avoidance) required a minimal level of exercise, and if the relation between cardiac output and oxygen consumption were to deviate from the exercise norm, it would indicate an inefficient adjustment. A deviant renal response would be characterized by a disruption in the sodium balance, as indicated by excretion rates falling acutely relative to ingestion. Normative values were ascertained during both the resting state and exercise response, since if the behavioral challenge were to have no effect on sodium balance, the excretion rate should be constant under all conditions.

Nonmetabolic Influences on the Myocardium

Evidence accumulated over the years suggests that in certain situations a cardiovascular exercise-like response can be evoked when the organism is not exercising, or when oxygen consumption and other aspects of metabolic activity associated with exercise are only minimally elevated. For example, Brod (1963) reported an increase in cardiac output and forearm blood flow during a difficult mental arithmetic task, even though oxygen consumption in the musculature of the forearm did not noticeably change. A similar disproportionate increase in HR and cardiac output relative to oxygen consumption has also been suggested in differing behavioral paradigms with dogs (Barger, Richards, Metcalfe, & Gunther, 1956), rats (Brener, Phillips, & Connally, 1977; Sherwood, Brener & Moncur, 1983), and humans (Blix, Stromme, & Ursin, 1974; Gliner, Bedi, & Horvath, 1979; Gorlin, Brachfeld, Turner, Messer, & Salazar, 1959; Grollman, 1929; Hickman, Cargill, & Golden, 1948; Stead, Warren, Merrill, & Brannon, 1945; Stromme, Wikeby, Blix, & Ursin, 1978).

When we began looking at these events (Langer, 1978; Langer et al., 1979), a disproportionate relationship was observed between cardiac output and HR on the one hand, and oxygen consumption on the other (assessed by the arteriovenous blood oxygen content difference). For example, one dog evidenced similar levels of cardiac output and HR during shock avoidance as during intermediate levels of exercise (treadmill), yet oxygen consumption rose 50% during avoidance versus 150% in exercise.

Until recently, our data on humans were less definitive. Initially, we observed that the relationship between HR and several aspects of somatic activity can be disrupted under certain conditions. Data suggesting this possibility emerged from studies where the influence of the cardiac innervations was evaluated pharmacologically. Using a shock avoidance task, both phasic (measured over seconds) and tonic (measured over minutes) increases in sympathetically (beta-adrenergic) mediated increases in HR and carotid dP/dt[4] were not found to covary directly with several aspects of somatic–motor activity (Obrist, Lawler, Howard, Smithson, Martin, & Manning, 1974; Obrist, Gaebelein, Shanks-Teller, Langer, Grignolo, Light, & McCubbin, 1978). We interpreted these results to reflect a disruption in the myocardial–somatic relationship, because with earlier work using the classical aversive conditioning paradigm and signaled reaction time tasks, HR changes (both increases and decreases) were found to covary directionally with somatic–motor activity; in this case, however, the HR changes were mediated by vagal (parasympathetic) influences (Obrist, Webb, & Sutterer, 1969; Obrist, Webb, Sutterer, & Howard, 1970a; Obrist, Wood, & Perez-Reyes, 1965). These latter effects were proposed (Obrist, 1976, 1981; Obrist, Howard, Lawler, Galosy, Meyers, & Gaebelein, 1974; Obrist, Langer, Grignolo, Light, & McCubbin, 1980; Obrist, Webb, Sutterer, & Howard, 1970b) to reflect a common central nervous system mechanism integrating somatic–motor and cardiovascular events, such as occurs during exercise. As such, they would reflect a metabolically appropriate change. Furthermore, where we see a disruption of the myocardial–somatic relationship, the dominance of sympathetic over vagal influences is consistent with our scheme implicating beta-adrenergic influences. Finally, where we observe sympathetic influences, particularly on tonic levels of

HR, there are individuals who evidence HR increases of 40 beats per min (bpm) or more while quietly sitting awaiting signals to execute a simple sensory-motor task that requires little or *no* effort. With HR changes of this magnitude, there are probably appreciable increases in the cardiac output (Anderson, Yingling, & Sagawa, 1979; Gliner *et al.*, 1979; Langer *et al.*, 1979), yet oxygen consumption has probably changed little.

Following the development of a respiratory gas analysis system (Langer, Hutcheson, Charlton, McCubbin, Obrist & Stoney, 1985a), we have more recently been able to evaluate carefully behavioral influences upon the relationship between cardiovascular and metabolic adjustments in humans. In an initial study (Langer, McCubbin, Stoney, Hutcheson, Charlton, & Obrist, 1985b) conducted on 34 healthy young men, responses to the physical demands of bicycle exercise (300 kpm min^{-1}) were compared to those evoked by an aversive reaction time (RT) task. The beta-adrenergic innervations were blocked in 14 of these subjects who were pretreated with 4 mg of propranolol, administered intravenously. For the remaining 20 subjects, the autonomic innervations were left intact. In the absence of pharmacological intervention, exercise led to substantial increases in both heart rate and oxygen consumption, indicating an integrated cardiovascular–metabolic response pattern. In contrast, heart rate increased significantly during the RT task while oxygen consumption remained unchanged from resting levels. In the beta-blocked group, heart rate still increased substantially in response to exercise, but showed no change from resting baseline during the RT task. Oxygen consumption adjustments for the two tasks were not affected by beta-blockade. These findings indicate that the behavioral responses evoked by the RT task were associated with an augmentation of beta-adrenergic influences upon the myocardium which were apparently responsible for metabolically excessive adjustments in cardiac activity.

In our continuing efforts to understand the overall hemodynamic changes produced by such behaviorally evoked sympathetic responses, we have most recently completed a study using the technique of impedance cardiography to measure cardiac output, which represents the functionally most significant aspect of myocardial performance. An additional advantage is that the concomitant monitoring of arterial pressure permits the derivation of changes in the total peripheral resistance to blood flow in the systemic circulation. This study (Sherwood, Allen, Langer, & Obrist, in press) involved testing 28 healthy young men during two experimental sessions, one with no invasive procedures and a second in which half the men received propranolol to block the beta-adrenergic receptors while the other half received a saline placebo. Responses to bicycle exercise, a cold pressor task, and a

---

4. "Carotid dP/dt" refers to the rate of change of pressure in the carotid pulse wave, a measure that has been shown to have a certain sensitivity to sympathetic influences on myocardial contractility (Obrist, Gaebelein, Shanks-Teller, Langer, Grignolo, Light, & McCubbin, 1978; Obrist, Lawler, Howard, Smithson, Martin, & Manning, 1974). However, it has certain undesirable features (e.g., it cannot be calibrated); in more recent studies, it has been replaced by measurements utilizing the pre-ejection period of the heart, such as the R-wave-to-pulse-wave interval (Obrist, 1981; Obrist & Light, 1980; Obrist, Light, McCubbin, Hutcheson, & Hoffer, 1979; Pollak & Obrist, 1983).

similar aversive RT task across the two sessions were compared. The results for RT and exercise provided a basic replication of those found by Langer *et al.* (1985b), with the additional evidence that the heart rate responses during RT were primarily responsible for proportionate elevations in cardiac output which, relative to the exercise condition, were in excess of the concurrent metabolic demands. However, the responses observed to the cold pressor task emphasize that heart rate may not always provide a reliable index of cardiac output changes. In response to the cold pressor task, both heart rate and oxygen consumption increased to similar levels as for RT, but stroke volume decreased such that the significantly less pronounced net adjustments in cardiac output were consistent with metabolic demands. Furthermore, indices of myocardial contractility showed that in addition to the chronotropic effects, sympathetic mechanisms were also responsible for pronounced positive inotropic influences on the heart during the RT task. Vascular resistance was found to decrease during RT as during exercise, but it increased during the cold pressor task. However, the effects of propranolol revealed that while the vascular responses during RT were beta-adrenergically mediated, the directionally similar exercise effects were apparently dependent upon intrinsic vascular autoregulation.

The studies described above provide evidence which demonstrates that certain behavioral responses may evoke metabolically inappropriate cardiovascular adjustments. How might such responses relate to pathophysiology? The autoregulation hypothesis mentioned earlier is one possibility. A closer look at its details will help clarify the BP effects in question. When the cardiac output is disproportionately higher than is normally required by changes in oxygen consumption and related metabolic activities, the tissues are being overperfused. Overperfusion probably has no immediate effect on vascular processes, unlike underperfusion, where powerful mechanisms act in seconds to protect vital organs from an inadequate blood supply (e.g., the baroreceptors; see McCubbin & Ferrario, 1977; Peart, 1977). However, evidence of vascular autoregulation in response to excessive blood flow suggests that the tissues do not tolerate this luxury of riches for long and can in a matter of time (somewhere between minutes and hours) decrease flow via an elevation of vascular resistance (Guyton, 1980a, pp. 78–83). As a consequence, an already elevated BP due to an increased cardiac output is sustained and elevated even more. The correction thus perpetuates the problem.

This scheme of events illustrates the issue of metabolic inappropriateness and its consequences. Note that the initial elevation of the BP indicates a metabolically inappropriate adjustment of the myocardium to tissue demands. In time, the elevated BP reflects the tissue response in correcting the myocardial excess. If

the autoregulation is not reversed, then, over time, the concomitant elevated BP can have pathophysiological consequences. A sustained elevation of the BP can thus be symptomatic of the tissues' attempt to correct for the myocardium's metabolically inappropriate response.

Sodium Balance and the Kidneys

Besides the evidence that the kidneys' handling of sodium balance involves neurohumoral mechanisms, there is evidence that behavioral factors can alter various aspects of renal functioning (Grignolo, 1980). These include renal blood flow (Brod, 1963; O. A. Smith, Hohimer, Astley, & Taylor, 1979), plasma renin (Blair, Feigl, & Smith, 1976), and water and sodium excretion (Corson, 1963; Schottstaedt, Grace, & Wolff, 1956). While these studies are consistent with the possibility that a renal abnormality could result from behaviorally induced autonomic influences, they have as yet shed little insight into the means by which it could do so, particularly sodium balance. Two studies we initiated bear more directly on this question and offer encouraging results.

Both studies evaluated the renal handling of sodium by measuring the excretion rates of sodium and water during a shock avoidance procedure. These dependent measures were selected because they demonstrate in the most direct way possible any disruption of renal functioning in maintaining sodium balance. Other aspects of kidney functioning, such as renal blood flow or glomular filtration rate, can be less sensitive to the renal handling of sodium, and thus to the behavioral influences. After saline loading, which amplifies excretion rates and thus permits the more ready detection of any influence exerted by the experimental procedures, sodium excretion rates were allowed to stabilize. The first study (Grignolo, 1980; Grignolo, Koepke, & Obrist, 1982) examined the influence of treadmill exercise and shock avoidance on sodium excretion rates. Relative to baseline, shock avoidance resulted in a retention of both water and sodium, whereas exercise increased the excretion rates. The retention during avoidance was most pronounced when HR was most accelerated. For example, in the dog whose HR accelerated most (average increase of 68 bpm), water and sodium excretion decreased by 44% and 49%, respectively. Even though exercise produced a similar increase in this animal's HR (mean change 64 bpm), excretion rate rose by 54% for water and 33% for sodium. The second study (Koepke, Grignolo, Light, & Obrist, 1983; Koepke, Light, & Obrist, 1983) employed beta-adrenergic blockade, following which sodium and water excretion were no longer modified by the shock avoidance task. In short, a behavioral challenge (shock avoidance) evoked retention of sodium and water (thus imbalancing intake and output), which involved, among other things, beta-adrenergic mechanisms. This retention of sodium was a particularly deviant metabolic response, since it occurred in a saline-loaded preparation whose excretion rates were already high.

These data throw only a little light on the development of the "abnormal" kidney believed to be a necessary condition for the development of established hypertension. They do serve as a starting point and implicate behavior as a significant link in the chain of events.

Comment

We have now observed in chronically prepared dogs the disruption of two basic metabolic processes in conjunction with a behavioral task. In one case, the cardiac output rose to a disproportionately greater extent than the oxygen consumption. In the second, sodium excretion decreased, and this acted to augment an imbalance created by saline loading. It is likely that both processes have a common neurogenic mechanism. We have not yet examined beta-adrenergic influences on sodium excretion *with* the cardiac output and oxygen consumption during shock avoidance, but data from another study (Grignolo, Light, & Obrist, 1981) indicates that in the dog, shock avoidance can evoke appreciable beta-adrenergic influences on the myocardium, which are apparent in intraventricular dP/dt and HR (see also Anderson & Brady, 1976; Forsyth, 1976). Given that beta-adrenergic blockade countered the behaviorally evoked retention of sodium and water, it seems likely that conditions that evoke beta-adrenergic activation involve the myocardium and kidneys simultaneously. If so, the cardiac output could be influenced in two ways: directly, via the expression of increased adrenergic drive on the myocardium; and less directly, through the renal retention of sodium. As a result of these cardiac output changes and the proposed vascular sequelae, the BP is influenced. Elevated BP would in this case reflect a chain of events triggered by inappropriate adjustments by two vital organs involved in the maintenance of homeostasis.

In other circumstances, we believe that changes in BP control mechanisms (and the ensuing BP elevation) do not reflect any significant disruption of metabolic efficiency and hence are not significant to the etiological process. An example is the lability of the BP in normotensive individuals (which most of us are) who never evidence hypertension; consider too the elevated BP that accompanies exercise. In the latter case, it is obvious why the BP increases have no ominous consequences. The peripheral resistance decreases because of the autoregulated and metabolically appropriate increase of blood flow in the active muscles, avoiding vascular changes that would unduly elevate the BP much beyond the exercise period. Any

renal retention of sodium during exercise, which has been reported under some circumstances, probably creates no imbalance because sodium is excreted via the sweat glands. In effect, the myocardial and renal changes are accompanied by vascular and excretory changes that protect us from any lethal consequences of the elevated cardiac output and BP. There is "metabolic burn-off," in the words of Folkow and Neil (1971, p. 348).

There are still other circumstances more common to psychophysiological endeavors in which the lability of the BP is reported (see Bevan et al., 1969). Of what significance are these? Not much can be said until their control mechanisms are delineated. Some of them may involve only direct neurogenic (alpha-adrenergic) influences on vascular resistance. For example, we have observed anticipatory phasic increases in BP during both classical conditioning (Obrist et al., 1965) and the foreperiod of a reaction time task (Obrist, Lawler, Howard, et al., 1974) while the HR was under vagal control. Similarly, we (Obrist et al., 1978) have seen tonic increases in BP without appreciable myocardial involvement, as with cold pressor (see next section). While we can rule out a myocardial contribution to these BP changes, we cannot say much about renal influences, though they would be unlikely if beta-adrenergic mechanisms are the primary mediator of the renal effect. As things stand, the BP changes that reflect a direct vascular influence strike us as etiologically insignificant, since it is hard to make a case that they reflect any disruption of important metabolic processes. Granted, the alpha-adrenergic innervation of the vasculature is important in controlling blood flow during exercise and in thermoregulation, but such adjustments do not seem relevant to hypertension. We appear to be endowed with vascular control mechanisms that are responsive to a variety of events even when there is no obvious metabolic necessity to alter blood flow, but they do not appear to reflect potentially pathogenic processes. Until we can link them to such processes, it does not seem justified to consider vascular events of this nature to be relevant to the etiological process.

In line with this reasoning, it is not surprising that procedures that involve primarily vascular mechanisms, such as the cold pressor, are poor prognosticators of an eventual hypertension. Admittedly, hypertensives (Engel & Bickford, 1961) as well as siblings of hypertensives (Falkner et al., 1979) evidence exaggerated cold pressor responses to a variety of behavioral challenges and stimuli. Such data do not define control mechanisms, however. Nor, in the case of established hypertensives, is it clear whether the vascular hyperreactivity is a precursor or a consequence of the hypertension. The latter might result from structural changes, as proposed by Folkow et al. (1973), or from electrolyte (e.g., sodium) changes within the vasculature (Doyle et al., 1980).

In summary, our position is that because acute elevations of BP are but symptoms of the operation of a variety of control mechanisms, their significance to the etiological process cannot be known until the particular mechanism or mechanisms responsible are delineated. We have proposed two possibly interacting control mechanisms that may be of importance. Our data base is primarily restricted to dogs, but additional evidence from humans, demonstrating beta-adrenergic influences on the myocardium in BP control, likewise suggests their relevance to the etiological process. This evidence is presented in the next section.

THE BEHAVIORAL–CARDIAC INTERACTION AND BP CONTROL

It is well established that the BP and several other aspects of cardiovascular function can be modified by behavioral events. Yet only recently have efforts been initiated to evaluate the pertinent BP control mechanisms. For example, the BP elevations observed during shock avoidance have been found to accompany an elevated cardiac output in both dogs (Anderson & Tosheff, 1973; Langer et al., 1979; Lawler, Obrist, & Lawler, 1975) and monkeys (Forsyth, 1971), and this involves beta-adrenergic mechanisms (Anderson & Brady, 1976; Forsyth, 1976; Grignolo et al., 1981). In humans, an elevation of cardiac output mediates the pressor response evoked by a challenging mental arithmetic task (Brod, 1963). Such reports clearly indicate that the cardiac output is subject to behavioral modification and, at least in dogs and monkeys, the participation of beta-adrenergic mechanisms.

The remainder of this section presents data from humans that likewise implicate the behavioral–cardiovascular interaction in the etiological process, and that are consistent with the proposal implicating beta-adrenergic influences on the myocardium. The data are from our laboratory, using young adult normotensives as subjects; established hypertension is rarely seen in this age group. Beta-adrenergic influences on HR and myocardial force have been evaluated pharmacologically, thus enabling us to comment on the neurogenic mechanism. Since the cardiac output and oxygen consumption were not measured, some caution is necessary in relating these results to our working hypothesis of metabolic inappropriateness. Nonetheless, the results suggest that beta-adrenergic myocardial hyperreactivity is an early marker of the hypertensive disease process. Further confirmation of this point, however, will require an evaluation of the cardiac output and of renal functioning, as well as longer-term prospective studies.

Beta-Adrenergic Myocardial Control and BP

Our first step in deciphering behavioral influences on the etiological process was to evaluate the respective influence of the two cardiac innervations within our behavioral paradigms—specifically, to determine whether these paradigms evoke beta-adrenergic effects. Such a demonstration might appear to be proving the obvious, but it should be kept in mind that in certain situations, such as classical aversive conditioning, vagal influences on the heart have been observed to be the primary neurogenic mechanism in regard to phasic anticipatory decreases and increases in HR, and have acted to mask sympathetic effects (Obrist et al., 1965; Obrist et al., 1970a; Obrist, Lawler, Howard, et al., 1974). However, and as previously indicated, beta-adrenergic influences were observed once the individuals were given some control of the experimental contingencies, with tonic levels of change evidencing the most pronounced effects. For example, the average increase in HR during the first 2 min of an unsignaled shock avoidance task was 22 bpm above the pretask baseline. With a pharmacologically blocked sympathetic innervation, the HR change averaged only 7 bpm. Beta-adrenergic myocardial influences were also observable with the indirect measures of contractility (i.e., carotid dP/dt and R-wave-to-pulse-wave interval) (Obrist et al., 1978; Obrist, Light, McCubbin, Hutcheson, & Hoffer, 1979). Thus, we see two aspects of myocardial performance that are subject to a behavioral influence, which is mediated in turn by beta-adrenergic mechanisms (see also Light & Obrist, 1980b). Clearly, increased beta-adrenergic drive can be evoked by some behavioral events—a necessary first step in implicating the behavioral–cardiovascular interaction in the etiological process.

The next step in evaluating our working hypothesis was to determine the relationship between beta-adrenergically mediated myocardial events and BP—specifically, to establish whether the BP was influenced by our experimental procedures in a like manner as the myocardium. This work also focused on tonic levels of BP.

A distinct, direct, myocardial influence on SBP was apparent, most clearly in the shock avoidance study, where beta-adrenergic influences were evaluated pharmacologically. As with HR and the myocardial contractile measures, there was an appreciable increase in SBP during the early minutes of the task, which was significantly attenuated by the blocking agent (i.e., mean increase 23 vs. 14 mm Hg). The myocardial contribution to the SBP stood in contrast to tasks that evoked a lesser beta-adrenergic effect on the myocardium (e.g., the cold pressor and viewing a pornographic movie). These conditions evoked smaller SBP increases, which were minimally affected by pharmacological blockade; in other words, under these conditions, vascular control dominated the SBP (Obrist et al., 1978; Obrist et al., 1979).

These differential myocardial and vascular effects on the SBP were also seen with DBP, but they were evidenced in a different manner. During shock avoidance, the DBP changed appreciably less than the SBP (average change 3 mm Hg DBP vs. 23 mm Hg SBP). In fact, they were inversely related events: The subjects with the greatest SBP increases tended to have the smallest DBP increases. Beta-adrenergic blockade, on the other hand, which attenuated the SBP increase, potentiated the DBP increase (average change 3 mm Hg vs. 13 mm Hg DBP for intact vs. blocked). The other tasks (cold pressor and film) evoked larger increases in DBP than shock avoidance, and they were not influenced by pharmacological blockade (see Obrist et al., 1978). We infer from these results that beta-adrenergic vascular receptors (primarily in striate and cardiac muscle) are more active during avoidance. Upon stimulation, these receptors elicit vasodilation, which counteracts any alpha-adrenergically mediated vascular constriction. The vascular resistance either does not change or even decreases; hence the minimal change in DBP. However, once these beta-adrenergic vascular receptors are blocked, the alpha-adrenergic constriction (which is always present under these conditions) is now manifested, and DBP increases more.[5]

Thus, vascular influences on BP appear to have been minimal during shock avoidance, the increased SBP being accounted for by such myocardial events as increased contractility and (presumably) increased cardiac output. By contrast, vascular influences were more dominant during the cold pressor and the film, as indicated by the larger increase in DBP and by the failure of beta-adrenergic blockade to influence either the DBP or the SBP.

The differential vascular influences have been observed more directly in rhesus monkeys by Forsyth (1976), who measured regional blood flows during shock avoidance as well as cardiac output. With an intact beta-adrenergic innervation, cardiac output increased while peripheral resistance decreased, whereas

following beta-adrenergic blockade, cardiac output fell significantly but vascular resistance significantly rose. The differential vascular effects were restricted to striate and cardiac muscle. A similar interaction between beta-adrenergic vasodilation and alpha-adrenergic vasoconstriction has also been reported in normotensive rats (control) as well as SHR injected with epinephrine, although the vasodilative effect was blunted in the SHR (Kopin, McCarty, & Yamaguchi, 1980).

Therefore, some behavioral tasks evoke appreciable increases in beta-adrenergic excitation of the heart. In the vasculature, beta adrenergic activity leads to decreased resistance. The result is an appreciable increase in SBP, but little or no change in DBP. These efforts represent a second step in spelling out how the behavioral–cardiovascular interaction may be etiologically relevant. They suggest in the course of its development that when hypertension involves an initial myocardial component, it will first be seen as an elevated SBP but not an elevated DBP. This interpretation is consistent with the observation in young borderline hypertensives of an elevated SBP but a normotensive DBP (Safar et al., 1973).

Individual Differences in Beta-Adrenergic Reactivity

Although the data above establish that beta-adrenergic mechanisms can be engaged by the behavioral tasks and can in turn influence the BP, they are not informative as to who in the population may become hypertensive. Hypertension is a common medical problem, yet affects something less than 20% of the adult population between 40 and 60 years of age (U.S. National Center for Health Statistics, 1964). Any prospective effort needs guidelines to determine on whom to focus its efforts. One common, although not too successful, approach is a symptomatic one: limiting observations to the BP per se in seeking a predictor of eventual hypertension. Both marginally elevated BP (borderline hypertension) in young adulthood and the BP response to noxious stimuli or other challenging events have been studied, without yielding much insight into matters. Julius (1977a), in a review of the literature concerning the predictive worth of borderline values, concluded, "The subsequent development of established hypertension in patients with previous borderline hypertension is noted in a minority only, the highest proportion being 26%" (p. 631). BP reactivity as a predictor has led to a similar cautious conclusion. H. Weiner (1970) notes, for example, that "tests such as the cold pressor . . . produce different results in the hands of different investigators and are, therefore, not reliable predictor variables" (p. 59). Julius and Schork (1971) likewise warn: "If

---

5. These small DBP effects associated with beta-adrenergic excitation suggest that vasoconstrictive influences are not exaggerated (i.e., hyperresponsive); some (e.g., Doyle et al., 1980) hold such hyperresponsivity to be a precursor and then a hallmark of established hypertension. Thus, one could question whether these behaviorally evoked beta-adrenergic effects are of particular relevance to the etiology. However, in a recent study (Light, 1981), we have obtained our first evidence that beta-adrenergically reactive subjects also have a propensity to vasoconstrictive hyperreactivity (alpha-adrenergic), except that it goes undetected because of the greater vasodilatory effects resulting from beta-adrenergic excitation. This was revealed when subjects were exposed to the experimental tasks, first with an intact innervation and then following beta-adrenergic blockade. Subjects evidencing the greatest effect (attenuation) of pharmacological blockade on HR and SBP demonstrated the greatest increase in DBP. Thus, blockade uncovered a more pronounced alpha-adrenergically mediated vasoconstriction.

exposed to different pressure raising stimuli, patients with borderline hypertension do not show a stereotyped 'hyperreactive' response" (p. 740).

Such inconclusive results are not surprising. As we have remarked earlier, efforts that measure BP but fail to evaluate BP control mechanisms are superficial, since a marginally elevated pressure or BP hyperreactivity is not necessarily indicative of more fundamental disruptions of metabolic processes.

Our work evaluating beta-adrenergic control mechanisms has given us a different perspective on the problem, and one clear lead to follow: the observation that there are appreciable individual differences in beta-adrenergic reactivity. This raises the question of whether the more reactive individuals are more at risk of developing established hypertension. The data presented below bear on this question.

The extent of the individual differences was not too apparent until some studies were launched that obtained two types of baselines. One was the usual resting period obtained on the first occasion a subject came to the laboratory. This occurred just prior to exposure to the laboratory-imposed tasks and stimuli; henceforth it was called the "pretask baseline." The second baseline also involved a resting state but was obtained usually 1 to 2 weeks later. On this occasion, the individual was specifically instructed that only rest was required and no tasks or arousing stimuli were involved; henceforth it was called the "relaxation baseline." The latter baseline most clearly revealed the extent of the individual differences, as the following case shows. With HR as our index of beta-adrenergic reactivity for one group of 56 subjects, it was noted that during the first 2 min of a shock avoidance task, the 14 most reactive subjects (uppermost quartile) increased their HR by an average of 57 bpm (i.e., from a relaxation baseline of 63 bpm to 120 bpm). In contrast, the 14 least reactive subjects evidenced an increase averaging only 9 bpm (i.e., from a relaxation baseline of 67 bpm to 76 bpm). While the shock avoidance task evoked the greater HR increases from the most reactive subjects, their HR was also more accelerated than that of the other subjects during the pretask baseline (as compared to the relaxation baseline) and during two other procedures, the cold pressor and a pornographic movie. Paralleling this uniform hyperreactivity, the least reactive group was uniformly unreactive under all conditions. Since the relaxation baselines for all quartiles of reactivity were very similar, we can conclude that hyperreactivity occurs under several qualitatively distinct conditions, including the resting state that anticipates exposure to the experimental procedures. It appears, therefore, that hyperreactivity is evoked by any novel and/or challenging circumstance.

We have since replicated these baseline effects and have further demonstrated that one's degree of reactivity is fairly characteristic in a variety of circum-

stances, from challenging mental arithmetic tasks to competitive sensory–motor tasks (motivated by financial rewards rather than aversive events) to the less contrived task of preparing and then making a short speech before a videotape camera (Hastrup, Swaney, Obrist, Beeler, & Chaska, 1981; Light, 1981; Light & Obrist, 1983). Clearly, individuals differ appreciably in their beta-adrenergic reactivity, and characteristically high and low reactivity are reliable phenomena. Both types of observations are necessary preconditions if we are to implicate sympathetically mediated myocardial activity in the etiological process.

Similarly, individual differences in SBP reactivity are seen across several conditions and relate directly to the HR effects. This is illustrated in the above-mentioned study of 56 subjects, where both types of baseline were obtained and the individuals were exposed to three experimental tasks. The quartile of highest HR reactivity also had the highest SBP levels during the pretask baseline, as well as during the cold pressor, film, and shock avoidance tasks; the last of these again evoked the greatest changes. But, as with HR, all subjects had essentially the same SBP at the relaxation baseline. For example, the average SBP values for the most and least reactive HR quartiles were 124 and 121 mm Hg, respectively, during the relaxation baseline, but 170 and 137 mm Hg, respectively, early in the shock avoidance task. Apparently myocardial reactivity and SBP responsiveness are linked under several circumstances. We cannot claim with authority that these HR effects reflect an involvement of the cardiac output, but the magnitude of the effects in the most reactive subjects makes a contribution of the cardiac output a likelihood (see Gliner et al., 1979). We have more confidence that beta-adrenergic influences are involved, since pharmacological blockade appreciably reduces HR reactivity (and, in the process, individual differences), and provides baseline values comparable to those obtained when subjects are resting during the follow-up or relaxation baseline (66 vs. 67 bpm).

These observations advance us another step toward implicating behaviorally evoked beta-adrenergic effects in the etiological process. Two other observations that further strengthen this association follow.

Beta-Adrenergic Reactivity and Parental History of Hypertension

Hypertension has been shown to have familial trends, such that hypertensive parents are more apt to have hypertensive offspring than normotensive parents (Grim et al., 1980; Schweitzer et al., 1967). In the light of this relationship, it was reasoned that if beta-adrenergic reactivity is of significance in the etiological process, we might expect to find a greater incidence of hypertension in the parents of our more reactive than in the parents of our less reactive subjects. Such a relationship was found. But, before we describe these data, we should point out that the research strategy characterized by this effort is only a temporary short cut to long-term prospective studies, which evaluate not only beta-adrenergic reactivity but other events that might contribute to the predictive equation. These other events could range from renal functioning to one's life style. For present purposes, positive results serve to reinforce the pursuit of myocardial reactivity, but not at the expense of ignoring other possible contributing variables.

We have assessed the relationship between beta-adrenergic reactivity (as assessed by HR) and parental hypertension in three separate efforts. In the first and most extensive of these (Hastrup, Light, & Obrist, 1982), usable histories were obtained from the parents of 104 subjects (i.e., 208 parents) after the subjects (offspring) had participated in the laboratory studies. Both HR reactivity to the shock avoidance task and the absolute levels of HR during the early minutes of the task proved directly related to hypertension in the parents. For example, of the 34 parents we classified as hypertensive, 30 had sons who were above the median HR levels during shock avoidance. A somewhat reverse strategy was employed in the next two efforts (Obrist, 1981). Subjects were first selected on the basis of either having or not having a hypertensive parent (in about equal numbers) and then exposed to the experimental procedures. Both studies used a reaction time task with financial rather than aversive incentives, and one also used the task of preparing and delivering a short (2- to 3-min) video-taped speech. Again, HR reactivity under all conditions was found to be significantly greater in the sons of hypertensive parents. Therefore, in three independent evaluations using different laboratory procedures, we have been able to demonstrate a greater incidence of parental hypertension in subjects who evidence greater HR reactivity.

SBP was found to relate to family history in a similar manner as HR. However, we do not feel this observation to be as significant as those dealing with myocardial events, for two reasons. First, the HR effects bear more directly on the etiological process (i.e., beta-adrenergic reactivity). Second, a relationship between SBP in parents and siblings could exist for any number of reasons. In fact, it would be expected on the basis of the reports of a weak but statistically significant relationship between the BP of parents and their siblings (Feinleib, 1979; Higgins *et al.*, 1980). Evidence of such a nature (i.e., familial trends) does not provide much insight into etiological mechanisms.

The importance of beta-adrenergic mechanisms is further supported by two other aspects of the data. One is that HR changes evoked by a task that evokes less appreciable beta-adrenergic effects (namely, the cold pressor) were *not* found to relate to parental history, nor were the HR changes associated with isometric hand grip exercise. The latter does evoke an appreciable HR response involving a synergistic interaction among the innervations, including increased beta-adrenergic excitation (Pollak, Obrist, & Godaert, 1981), but it is a procedure that probably involves a more metabolically appropriate response than would a shock avoidance task. These data thus reinforce the significance of beta-adrenergic mechanisms, since when they were minimal (cold pressor) or appropriate to metabolic requirements (hand grip), the resulting HR changes were unrelated to parental hypertension.

The second relevant observation relates parental history to casual SBP levels[6] and beta-adrenergic mechanisms (Light & Obrist, 1980a). In a group of about 60 subjects, nearly half showed a casual SBP of 135 mm Hg or more on at least one occasion. These casual values were obtained from the relaxation baseline previously described, their student health records, or a campus BP screening procedure. The presence of marginally elevated casual SBP values was not found to relate to HR reactivity during shock avoidance. That is to say, equal numbers of high and low HR reactors had marginally elevated casual pressures. However, the presence of the marginally elevated SBP values related to hypertension in the parent, primarily in those subjects who were high HR reactors. This result indicates that mere lability of the casual SBP is not a particularly good predictor of eventual hypertension, unless it occurs in individuals who are beta-adrenergically hyperreactive. Put another way, insight into BP control mechanisms provides a necessary condition to make casual SBP values an informative event about potential consequences.

Behavioral–Cardiac Interaction and Borderline Hypertension

In the previously cited studies evaluating the resting state hemodynamics of borderline hypertension (e.g., Lund-Johansen, 1967), the influence of behavioral factors was largely unknown. Although neurogenic influences on the myocardium under these circumstances have been shown via pharmacological intervention (Julius & Esler, 1975), there is no way of determining what (if any) contribution the diagnostic procedure or still other behavioral events may have made. While we tend to equate neurogenic with behavioral influences, it is always possible that the neurogenic contribution is triggered by some disruption in homeostasis where the behavioral influence is irrelevant or at best secondary.

---

6. "Casual" SBP levels are SBP values obtained when the subjects were not intentionally provoked by or anticipating any specific laboratory task. We believe they are comparable to values clinically obtained for diagnostic purposes.

We too have encountered similarly elevated resting state (pretask baseline) SBP values in some of our subjects. But in this instance, a better case can be made that behavioral influences are of significance—specifically, the novelty of the circumstances or the uncertainty they generate. Furthermore, beta-adrenergic mechanisms appear to be involved. In short, such data counter arguments (e.g., Dahl, 1970) that the influence of the behavioral cardiac interaction is minimal, at least in borderline hypertension.

Of the initial 138 subjects for whom we obtained both types of baseline measurements, 33 had pretask resting baseline SBP values of 140 mm Hg or greater, averaging 146 mm Hg. According to some criteria (e.g., Julius, 1977b), this would be termed borderline hypertension. At follow-up or relaxation baseline, 27 of the 33 had SBP values below 140 mm Hg, averaging 131 mm Hg. A behavioral influence is indicated in these resting state baseline differences, because the first measurement immediately preceded experimental procedures like the cold pressor and shock avoidance, and was taken on each subject's first visit to the laboratory. The follow-up baseline, on the other hand, represented the second or, commonly, the third visit to the laboratory and was taken when the subject should not have been expecting involvement in any laboratory procedures, other than resting. A beta-adrenergic influence is inferred, since HR also decreased between the baselines, and the magnitude of the HR decrease was directly related to that of the SBP decrease ($r = .52$, $p < .001$). Keeping in mind that the difference in SBP and HR between baselines was noticeably less in the remaining subjects, whose BP values were normotensive on both occasions, these results suggest that we demonstrated during the first baseline a beta-adrenergically mediated borderline hypertension, which was triggered by behavioral events. Another aspect of the significance of these elevated baseline values is that these 33 subjects were more responsive (in terms of both HR and SBP) to the shock avoidance task; in addition, the incidence of hypertension in their parents was noticeably greater.

These data thus underscore several points about the behavioral–cardiovascular interaction. Its influence is seen when borderline hypertension values are encountered; it involves beta-adrenergic mechanisms; and it may reflect the beginnings of (or at least the propensity to develop) a future hypertension. But a note of caution is necessary. We do not suggest examining borderline hypertensive values in isolation from their causal mechanisms; that would be to retreat from our guidelines and our opposition to a symptomatic approach. Rather, we cite these data to underscore the possibility that marginally elevated SBP values, which others consider indicative of borderline hypertension, can reflect a behavioral influence mediated by beta-adrenergic mechanisms.

COMMENTARY AND SUMMARY

This chapter has several qualities that deserve comment. First, it sometimes resorts to the "rediscovery" of observations previously reported in the literature. For example, the observation that individuals respond in a quantitatively similar manner to qualitatively different events, as well as to repetitions of the same event, is reminiscent of reports made over 20 years ago in which the Laceys (Lacey, 1959; Lacey & Lacey, 1958, 1962) described individual response stereotypy. They even suggested that evidence of stereotyped autonomic responding ("autonomic constitution") may reflect a predisposition to psychosomatic disorders (Lacey & Lacey, 1958, 1962), much as we hypothesize that myocardial beta-adrenergic hyperreactivity predisposes individuals to hypertension. Though not directly referred to, individual differences in autonomic activity must have been evident in these earlier studies; how else could one obtain reliable stereotyped responding? There have also been reports over the years of an influence of behavioral factors on both myocardial and renal functioning, suggestive of an acute impairment in metabolic efficiency (see Grignolo, 1980; Langer, 1978). Unfortunately, like the symptomatic studies of hypertension, these earlier efforts did not much advance our understanding of the etiology. Part of the problem was that they lacked a conceptual framework anchored on some understanding of BP control mechanisms and the manner in which they interact with an organism's behavior.

It is this sort of situation that we believe justifies a second quality of this chapter—namely, its speculative nature. What we have attempted to do is to tie together some of these empirical observations into a network of working hypotheses. Whatever their ultimate merit, our speculations will have served the purpose of generating questions that have broadened our data base and have shed light on the mechanisms of BP control and how they are influenced by the individual's social milieu and behavior. Such data should enable us to develop more valid conceptual schemes, and should also enable us as behavioral scientists to treat and even prevent hypertension in more rational ways than are now common to such current techniques as biofeedback, or, for that matter, procedures more common to medical practice.

A third quality of this chapter is its mechanistic bias. We would like to reinforce the importance of this strategy, because it is alien to many psychophysiological endeavors. It is more than just a reductionistic approach. As Page (1977) has said, also referring to hypertension research: "Reductionism has been, and always will be, essential, but true understanding of living organisms also requires synthesis based on what has been learned from jumbles of isolated facts" (p. 587). (Also see Ader, 1980.) The importance of a mechanistic strategy can be seen in the following example: There is now abundant evidence of an association between hypertension and salt ingestion (Dahl, 1972; Freis, 1976; Tobian, 1978). To some, hypertension is the price we pay in Western society for our way of life with its reliance on packaged, salt-laden foods. Yet the basis of this association is not understood (Page, 1977; Paul, 1977), so the role of sodium can be causal or an aggravation of the hypertensive process, or both. Certainly many of us can ingest vast amounts of sodium, yet remain in sodium balance and suffer no pathological consequences (Tobian, 1978). Thus, in order to understand how sodium ingestion bears on hypertension, we must decipher why some people's kidneys seem unable to handle salt intake without producing or aggravating pathophysiological events. This, in turn, requires insight into the mechanism by which renal functioning is impaired. Failure to achieve this shall leave us with an association between two events without an ability to predict with much certainty which individuals cannot handle high-salt diets without some costs to their health.

This is the same position we are in when we demonstrate a relationship between hypertension (or, for that matter, any other risk factor) in parents and in their offspring; the association represents only the beginning of our endeavors to understand the process. We cannot expect progress until we begin to spell out the basis of the association between the events; this includes, among other things, the mechanisms. It is for this reason that we have focused our energies on beta-adrenergic influences on myocardial and renal functioning, since this is one conceivable route (mechanisms) relating life events and hypertensive disease. In effect, as we spell out the basis of such associations, we shall be better able to predict the individual at risk.

Finally, some comment appears warranted with respect to our research strategy and one other contemporary research effort in health-related research—namely, the work on the Type A (coronary-prone) behavior pattern and atherosclerosis (Dembroski, Weiss, Shields, Haynes, & Feinleib, 1978). This effort, as is true of those looking for the "hypertensive personality," first looks for a relationship between some behavioral dimension and a disease state. In the case of the Type A research, where such a relationship has now been quite consistently found, the question is then raised as to what the mechanisms are. Our strategy, on the other hand, is to look first at mechanisms (in our case, BP control mechanisms), and to determine whether they relate to any aspect of the organism–environment interaction, without immediate concern for the disease state. Our approach is illustrated by our interest in beta-adrenergic influences on the myocardium, vasculature, and kidneys. We have made some efforts to determine whether individual differences in beta-adrenergic myocardial reactivity

relate to specific behavioral dimensions such as Types A and B, but without success. Our apparent failure in this regard is not understood. The observation that beta-adrenergic hyperreactivity is characteristic of some individuals in a variety of conditions with distinct qualitative differences (e.g., the resting state vs. competitive games) suggests that there is probably no one simple behavioral dimension that shall prove of overriding importance.

The last word is not in on this matter; nonetheless, caution is warranted in our search for the coronary-prone or hypertensive personality. Considering what is probably a very complex etiology for any of these degenerative disease states, with the possibility that the etiological route may differ among individuals, it seems unwise to invest excessive energies in evaluating particular behavioral dimensions until the mechanisms are better understood. This line of reasoning does not explain why a relationship is found between, say, Type A behavior and atherosclerosis. It does argue, though, for the likelihood that such a relationship only reflects the tip of the iceberg and that our understanding of these disease states will advance only as rapidly as we elucidate the means (mechanisms) by which any behavioral state is translated into cardiovascular activity.

Our data and position can be summarized as follows. We know that everyone's BP is labile to varying degrees, and that its elevation is sometimes essential to insure adequate tissue perfusion, such as when one exercises or when the blood supply to critical organs is impaired. While the lability of the BP is common to all individuals, only a certain percentage ever develop hypertension. Thus, there must be circumstances in which and individuals in whom elevated BP—even if only acutely so—reflects processes that over time sustain the heightened BP. Several lines of evidence converge to suggest that one fault may lie in disruptions of at least two major processes involved in the control of metabolic homeostasis: the myocardial control of the cardiac output, and the renal control of sodium balance. The net effect of their disruption is to alter BP control mechanisms, such that over time the BP becomes established at elevated levels. In either case, an acute (transient) or more permanent elevation of the BP is symptomatic of the disruption in the efficiency with which the myocardium and kidneys maintain homeostasis.

One line of evidence implicating these mechanisms comes from individuals with a marginally elevated BP who evidence an elevated cardiac output; some longitudinal data and observations with varying types of animal preparations suggest that this combination of events represents the beginnings of the hypertensive process. Renal involvement is deduced from a consideration of the mechanisms involved in sodium balance. One possibility is that an elevated BP may gradually become necessary to achieve balance; that is, a BP natriuresis may arise.

That behavioral factors can influence these mechanisms is seen in different ways. First, both the myocardial control of the cardiac output and the renal control of sodium balance are subject to neurohumoral influences. Second, various types of behavioral paradigms can disrupt both functions. The most conclusive behavioral data derive from dogs in a shock avoidance procedure, where beta-adrenergic influences on the heart can be marked, the cardiac output rises disproportionately higher than any increase in oxygen consumption, and beta-adrenergic mechanisms mediate the renal retention of sodium.

In humans, the evidence is less complete, but it still suggests that behaviorally evoked beta-adrenergic influences on the heart are important. In young adult males, a shock avoidance paradigm evokes beta-adrenergic influences on both phasic and tonic HR and two indirect indices of cardiac contractility. The SBP is similarly influenced, while the DBP relates inversely, if anything, to these effects. Appreciable individual differences in beta-adrenergic reactivity, in association with SBP responsiveness, are seen. High reactivity is common to a variety of circumstances and relates to a parental history of hypertension. Still to be evaluated in this population are renal functioning and the cardiac output, as well as their relationship to metabolic processes.

ACKNOWLEDGMENTS

Our research was supported by the following research grants: MH 07995, National Institute of Mental Health; HL 18976, HL 23718, HL 24643, and National Service Award F-32-HL 05531, National Heart, Lung and Blood Institute.

REFERENCES

Ader, R. Psychosomatic and psychoimmunologic research. *Psychosomatic Medicine*, 1980, 42, 307–321.

Ahlquist, R. P. Present state of alpha and beta-adrenergic drugs: I. The adrenergic receptor. *American Heart Journal*, 1976, 92, 661–644. (a)

Ahlquist, R. P. Present state of alpha and beta-adrenergic drugs: II. The adrenergic blocking agents. *American Heart Journal*, 1976, 92, 804–807. (b)

Anderson, D. E., & Brady, J. V. Cardiovascular responses to avoidance conditioning in the dog. *Psychosomatic Medicine*, 1976, 38, 181–189.

Anderson, D. E., & Tosheff, J. G. Cardiac output and total peripheral resistance changes during pre avoidance periods in dogs. *Journal of Applied Physiology*, 1973, 34, 650–654.

Anderson, D. E., Yingling, J. E., & Sagawa, K. Minute to minute covariations in cardiovascular activity of conscious dogs. *American Journal of Physiology: Heart and Circulatory Physiology*, 1979, 5, H434–H439.

Barger, A. C., Richards, V., Metcalfe, J., & Gunther, B. Regulation of the circulation during exercise: Cardiac output (direct Fick) and metabolic adjustments in the normal dog. *American Journal of Physiology*, 1956, 184, 613–623.

Bello-Reuss, E., Trevino, D. L., & Gottschalk, C. W. Effect of renal sympathetic nerve stimulation on proximal water and sodium transport. *Journal of Clinical Investigation*, 1976, 57, 1104–1107.

Bertel, O., Buhler, F. R., Kiowski, W., & Lutold, B. Decreased beta-adrenoreceptor responsiveness as related to age, blood pressure and plasma catecholamines in patients with essential hypertension. *Hypertension*, 1980, 2, 130–138.

Berne, R. M. Myocardial blood flow: Metabolic determinants. In R. Zelis (Ed.), *The peripheral circulations*. New York: Grune & Stratton, 1975.

Berne, R. M., & Levy, M. N. *Cardiovascular physiology* (3rd ed.). St. Louis: C. V. Mosby, 1977.

Bevan, A. T., Honour, A. J., & Stott, F. H. Direct arterial pressure recording in unrestricted man. *Clinical Science*, 1969, 36, 329–344.

Birkenhager, W. H., & Schalekamp, M. A. D. H. *Control mechanisms in essential hypertension*. New York: American Elsevier, 1976.

Blair, M. L., Feigl, E. O., & Smith, O. A. Elevations of plasma renin activity during avoidance performance in baboons. *American Journal of Physiology*, 1976, 231, 772–776.

Blix, A. S., Stromme, S. B., & Ursin, H. Additional heart rate—an indicator of psychological activation. *Aerospace Medicine*, 1974, 45, 1219–1222.

Brady, J. V., Anderson, D. E., & Harris, A. H. Behavior and the cardiovascular system in experimental animals. In C. Bartorelli & A. Zanchetti (Eds.), *Neural and psychological mechanisms in cardiovascular disease*. Milan, Italy: Il Ponte, 1972.

Braunwald, E., Sonnenblick, E. H., Ross, J., Glick, G., & Epstein, S. F. An analysis of the cardiac response to exercise. *Circulation Research*, 1967, 20–21(Suppl. 1), I44–I58.

Brener, J., Phillips, K., & Connally, S. Oxygen consumption and ambulation during operant conditioning of heart rate increases and decreases in rats. *Psychophysiology*, 1977, 14, 483–491.

Brod, J. Hemodynamic basis of acute pressor reactions and hypertension. *British Heart Journal*, 1963, 25, 227–245.

Brown, J. J., Fraser, R., Lever, A. F., Morton, J. J., Robertson, J. I. S., & Schalekamp, M. A. D. H. Mechanisms in hypertension: A personal view. In J. Genest, E. Koiw, & O. Kuchel (Eds.), *Hypertension: Physiopathology and treatment*. New York: McGraw-Hill, 1977.

Buhler, F. R., Kiowski, W., van Brummelen, P., Amann, F. W., Bertel, O., Landmann, R., Lutold, B. E., & Bolli, P. Plasma catecholamines and cardiac renal and peripheral vascular adrenoceptor-mediated responses in different age groups of normal and hypertensive subjects. *Clinical and Experimental Hypertension*, 1980, 2, 409–426.

Carlsten, A., & Grimby, G. *The circulatory response to muscular exercise in man*. Springfield, Ill.: Charles C Thomas, 1966.

Coleman, T. G., Granger, H. J., & Guyton, A. C. Whole body circulatory, autoregulation and hypertension. *Circulation Research*, 1971, 29(Suppl. 2), I176–I186.

Corson, S. A. Conditioning of water and electrolyte excretion. In R. Levine (Ed.), *Endocrines and the central nervous system*. Baltimore: Williams & Wilkins, 1963.

Croxatto, H. R., Albertini, R., Corthorn, J., & Rusas, R. Kallikrein and kinins in hypertension. In J. Genest, E. Koiw, & O. Kuchel (Eds.), *Hypertension: Physiopathology and treatment*. New York: McGraw-Hill, 1977.

Dahl, L. K. Mechanisms of hypertension. *Circulation Research*, 1970, 27(Suppl. 1), 132–136.

Dahl, L. K. Salt and hypertension. *American Journal of Clinical Nutrition*, 1972, 25, 231–244.

Dahl, L. K. Salt intake and hypertension. In J. Genest, E. Koiw, & O. Kuchel (Eds.), *Hypertension: Physiopathology and treatment*. New York: McGraw-Hill, 1977.

Dembroski, T. M., Weiss, S. M., Shields, J. L., Haynes, S. G., & Feinleib, M. (Eds.). *Coronary prone behavior*. New York: Springer-Verlag, 1978.

Doyle, A. E., Mendelsohn, F. A. O., & Morgan, T. O. *Pharmaco-

logical and therapeutic aspects of hypertension (Vols. 1–2). Boca Raton, Fla.: CRC Press, 1980.

Dubos, R. *Mirage of health*. New York: Harper & Brothers, 1959.

Eich, R. H., Cuddy, R. P., Smulyan, H., & Lyons, R. H. Hemodynamics in labile hypertension: A follow up study. *Circulation*, 1966, 34, 299–307.

Engel, B. T., & Bickford, A. F. Response specificity. *Archives of General Psychiatry*, 1961, 5, 478–489.

Falkner, B., Onesti, G., Angelakos, E. T., Fernandes, M., & Langman, C. Cardiovascular response to mental stress in normal adolescents with hypertensive parents: Hemodynamics and mental stress in adolescents. *Hypertension*, 1979, 1, 23–30.

Feinleib, M. Genetics and familial aggregation of blood pressure. In G. Onesti & C. R. Klimt (Eds.), *Hypertension—determinants, complications and intervention*. New York: Grune & Stratton, 1979.

Ferrario, C. M., & Page, I. H. Current views concerning cardiac output in the genesis of experimental hypertension. *Circulation Research*, 1978, 43, 821–831.

Folkow, B. U. B., Hallback, M. I. L., Lundgren, Y., Sivertsson, R., & Weiss, L. Importance of adaptive changes in vascular design for establishment of primary hypertension, studies in man and in spontaneously hypertensive rat. *Circulation Research*, 1973, 32–33(Suppl.), I2–I16.

Folkow, B., & Neil, E. *Circulation*. New York: Oxford University Press, 1971.

Forsyth, R. P. Regional blood flow changes during 72 hour avoidance schedules in monkeys. *Science*, 1971, 173, 546–548.

Forsyth, R. P. Effect of propranolol on stress-induced hemodynamic changes in monkeys. In P. R. Saxena & R. P. Forsyth (Eds.), *Beta-adrenoceptor blocking agents*. Amsterdam: North-Holland, 1976.

Freis, E. D. Hemodynamics of hypertension. *Physiological Reviews*, 1960, 40, 27–53.

Freis, E. D. Salt, volume and the prevention of hypertension. *Circulation*, 1976, 53, 589–594.

Frohlich, E. D. Cardiac participation in hypertension. *Cardiovascular Medicine*, 1977, 2, 109–110. (a)

Frohlich, E. D. Hemodynamics of hypertension. In J. Genest, E. Koiw, & O. Kuchel (Eds.), *Hypertension: Physiopathology and treatment*. New York: McGraw-Hill, 1977.

Frumkin, K., Nathan, R. J., Prout, M. F., & Cohen, M. L. Nonpharmacological control of essential hypertension in man: A critical review of the experimental literature. *Psychosomatic Medicine*, 1978, 40, 294–320.

Geddes, L. A. *The direct and indirect measurement of blood pressure*. Chicago: Year Book Medical Publishers, 1970.

Gliner, J. A., Bedi, J. F., & Horvath, S. M. Somatic and nonsomatic influences on the heart: Hemodynamic changes. *Psychophysiology*, 1979, 16, 358–362.

Gorlin, R., Brachfeld, N., Turner, J. D., Messer, J. V., & Salazar, E. The idiopathic high cardiac output state. *Journal of Clinical Investigation*, 1959, 38, 2144–2153.

Graham, D. T. Psychosomatic medicine. In N. S. Greenfield & R. A. Sternbach (Eds.), *Handbook of psychophysiology*. New York: Holt, Rinehart & Winston, 1972.

Grignolo, A. *Renal function and cardiovascular dynamics during treadmill exercise and shock-avoidance in dogs*. Unpublished doctoral dissertation, University of North Carolina at Chapel Hill, 1980.

Grignolo, A., Koepke, J. P., & Obrist, P. A. Renal function and cardiovascular dynamics during treadmill exercise and shock avoidance in dogs. *American Journal of Physiology: Regulatory Integrative and Comparative Physiology*, II, 1982, 242, R482–R490.

Grignolo, A., Light, K. C., & Obrist, P. A. Beta-adrenergic influences on cardiac dynamics during shock avoidance in dogs. *Pharmacology, Biochemistry and Behavior*, 1981, 5, 313–329.

Grim, C. E., Luft, F. C., Miller, J. Z., Rose, R. J., Christian, J. C., & Weinberger, M. H. An approach to the evaluation of genetic influences on factors that regulate arterial blood pressure in man. *Hypertension*, 1980, 2(Part 2), I34–I42.

Grollman, A. Physiological variations in the cardiac output of man: The effect of psychic disturbances on the cardiac output, pulse, blood pressure and O_2 consumption of man. *American Journal of Physiology*, 1929, 89, 584–588.

Guttman, M. C., & Benson, H. Interaction of environmental factors and systemic arterial blood pressure: A review. *Medicine*, 1971, 50, 543–553.

Guyton, A. C. Personal views on mechanisms of hypertension. In J. Genest, E. Koiw, & O. Kuchel (Eds.), *Hypertension: Physiopathology and treatment*. New York: McGraw-Hill, 1977.

Guyton, A. C. (Ed.). *Arterial blood pressure and hypertension*. Philadelphia: W. B. Saunders, 1980. (a)

Guyton, A. C. Qualitative schemas of the principle of arterial pressure and control mechanisms. In A. C. Guyton (Ed.), *Arterial blood pressure and hypertension*. Philadelphia: W. B. Saunders, 1980. (b)

Guyton, A. C., Cowley, A. A., Coleman, T. G., McCaa, R. E., & Young, D. B. The renin-angiotensin system: Its vasoconstrictor function. In A. C. Guyton (Ed.), *Arterial blood pressure and hypertension*. Philadelphia: W. B. Saunders, 1980.

Hastrup, J. L., Light, K. C., & Obrist, P. A. Parental hypertension and cardiovascular response to stress in healthy young adults. *Psychophysiology*, 1982, 19, 615–622.

Hastrup, J. L., Swaney, K., Obrist, P. A., Beeler, C., & Chaska, L. Relationship of parental history of hypertension to cardiovascular reactivity: Public speaking and reaction time task. *Psychophysiology*, 1981, 18, 186. (Abstract)

Hays, R. M. Agents affecting the renal conservation of water. In A. G. Goodman, L. S. Goodman, & A. Gilman (Eds.), *Goodman and Gilman's The pharmacological basis of therapeutics*. New York: Macmillan, 1980.

Henry, J. P., & Cassel, J. C. Psychosocial factors in essential hypertension: Recent epidemiologic and animal literature evidence. *American Journal of Epidemiology*, 1969, 90, 171–200.

Hickman, J. B., Cargill, W. H., & Golden, A. Cardiovascular reactions to emotional stimuli: Effect on the cardiac output arteriovenous oxygen difference, arterial pressure and peripheral resistance. *Journal of Clinical Investigation*, 1948, 27, 290–298.

Higgins, M. W., Keller, J. B., Metzner, H. L., Moore, F. E., & Ostrander, L. D. Studies of blood pressure in Tecumseh, Michigan: II. Antecedents in childhood of high blood pressure in young adults. *Hypertension*, 1980, 2(Part 2), I117–I123.

Hollenberg, N. K. The renal circulation. In R. Zelis (Ed.), *The peripheral circulations*. New York: Grune & Stratton, 1975.

Horrobin, D. F. Prolactin: Effects on fluid and electrolyte balance and on the cardiovascular system. In J. Genest, E. Koiw, & O. Kuchel (Eds.), *Hypertension: Physiopathology and treatment*. New York: McGraw-Hill, 1977.

Julius, S. Borderline hypertension: Epidemiologic and clinical implications. In J. Genest, E. Koiw, & O. Kuchel (Eds.), *Hypertension: Physiopathology and treatment*. New York: McGraw-Hill, 1977. (a)

Julius, S. Classification of hypertension. In J. Genest, E. Koiw, & O. Kuchel (Eds.), *Hypertension: Physiopathology and treatment*. New York: McGraw-Hill, 1977. (b)

Julius, S., Ellis, C. N., Pascual, A. V., Matice, M., Hansson, L., Hunyor, S. N., & Sandler, L. N. Home blood pressure determination. *Journal of the American Medical Association*, 1974, 229, 663–666.

Julius, S., & Esler, M. D. Autonomic nervous cardiovascular regulation in borderline hypertension. *American Journal of Cardiology*, 1975, 36, 685–696.

Julius, S., & Schork, M. A. Borderline hypertension: A critical review. *Journal of Chronic Disease*, 1971, 23, 723–754.

Katkin, E. S., & Murray, E. N. Instrumental conditioning of autonomically mediated behavior: Theoretical and methodological issues. *Psychological Bulletin*, 1968, 70, 52–68.

Koepke, K. P., Grignolo, A., Light, K. C., & Obrist, P. A. Central beta adrenoceptor mediation of the antinatriuretic response to behavioral stress in conscious dogs. *Journal of Pharmacology and Experimental Therapeutics*, 1983, 227, 73–77.

Koepke, K. P., Light, K. C., & Obrist, P. A. Neural control of renal excretory function during behavioral stress in conscious dogs. *American Journal of Physiology*, 1983, 245, R251–R258.

Kopin, I. J., McCarty, R., & Yamaguchi, I. Plasma Catecholamines in human and experimental hypertension. *Clinical and Experimental Hypertension*, 1980, 2(3&4), 379–394.

Kuller, L. H., Crook, M., Almes, M. J., Detre, K., Reese, G., & Rutan, G. Dormont High School (Pittsburgh, Pennsylvania) blood pressure study. *Hypertension*, 1980, 2, I109–I116.

Lacey, J. I. Psychophysiological approaches to the evaluation of psychotherapeutic process and outcome. In E. A. Rubenstein & M. B. Parloff (Eds.), *Research in psychotherapy*. Washington, D.C.: American Psychological Association, 1959.

Lacey, J. I., & Lacey, B. C. Verification and extension of the principle of autonomic response-stereotypy. *American Journal of Psychology*, 1958, 71, 50–73.

Lacey, J. I., & Lacey, B. C. The law of initial value in the longitudinal study of autonomic constitution: Reproducibility of autonomic responses and response patterns over a four year interval. *Annals of the New York Academy of Sciences*, 1962, 98, 1257–1290, 1322–1326.

Laird, J. F., Tarazi, R. C., Ferrario, C. M., & Manger, W. M. Hemodynamic and humoral characteristics of hypertension induced by prolonged stellate ganglion stimulation in conscious dogs. *Circulation Research*, 1975, 36, 455–464.

Langer, A. W. *A comparison of the effect of the treadmill exercise and signaled shock avoidance training on hemodynamic processes and the arterial–mixed venous oxygen content difference in conscious dogs.* Unpublished doctoral dissertation, University of North Carolina, Chapel Hill, 1978.

Langer, A. W., Hutcheson, J. S., Charlton, J. D., McCubbin, J. A., Obrist, P. A., & Stoney, C. M. On-line minicomputerized measurement of cardiopulmonary function on a breath-by-breath basis. *Psychophysiology*, 1985a, 22, 50–58.

Langer, A. W., McCubbin, J. A., Stoney, C. M., Hutcheson, J. S., Charlton, J. D., & Obrist, P. A. Cardiopulmonary adjustments during exercise and an aversive reaction time task: Effects of beta-adrenoceptor blockade. *Psychophysiology*, 1985b, 22, 59–68.

Langer, A. W., Obrist, P. A., & McCubbin, J. A. Hemodynamic and metabolic adjustments during exercise and shock avoidance in dogs. *American Journal of Physiology: Heart and Circulatory Physiology*, 1979, 5, H225–H230.

Lee, J. B. Prostaglandins, neutral lipids, renal interstitial cells, and hypertension. In J. Genest, E. Koiw, & O. Kuchel (Eds.), *Hypertension: Physiopathology and treatment*. New York: McGraw-Hill, 1977.

Lawler, J. E., Obrist, P. A., & Lawler, K. A. Cardiovascular functions during pre-avoidance, avoidance and post-avoidance in dogs. *Psychophysiology*, 1975, 12, 4–11.

Light, K. C. Cardiovascular responses to effortful active coping: Implications for the role of stress in hypertension development. *Psychophysiology*, 1981, 18, 216–225.

Light, K. C., & Obrist, P. A. Cardiovascular reactivity to behavioral stress in young males with and without marginally elevated systolic pressure: A comparison of clinic, home and laboratory measures. *Hypertension*, 1980, 2, 802–808. (a)

Light, K. C., & Obrist, P. A. Cardiovascular response to stress: Effects of opportunity to avoid, shock experience and performance feedback. *Psychophysiology*, 1980, 17, 243–252. (b)

Light, K. C., & Obrist, P. A. Task difficulty, heart rate reactivity and cardiovasacular response to an appetitive reaction time task. *Psychophysiology*, 1983, 20, 301–311.

Lund-Johansen, P. Hemodynamics in early essential hypertension. *Acta Medica Scandinavica*, 1967, 182(Suppl. 482), 8–101.

Lund-Johansen, P. Hemodynamic alterations in essential hypertension. In A. Onesti, K. E. Kim, & J. H. Moyer (Eds.), *Hypertension: Mechanisms and management*. New York: Grune and Stratton, 1973.

Lund-Johansen, P. Spontaneous changes in central hemodynamics in essential hypertension—a 10 year follow up study. In G. On-

esti & C. R. Klimt (Eds.), *Hypertension—determinants, complications and intervention*. New York: Grune & Stratton, 1979.

Mayer, S. E. Neurohumoral transmission and the autonomic nervous system. In A. G. Goodman, L. S. Goodman, & A. Gilman (Eds.), *Goodman and Gilman's The pharmacological basis of therapeutics*. New York: Macmillan, 1980, 56–90.

McCubbin, J. W., & Ferrario, C. M. Baroreceptor reflexes and hypertension. In J. Genest, E. Koiw, & O. Kuchel (Eds.), *Hypertension: Physiopathology and treatment*. New York: McGraw-Hill, 1977.

McMahon, C. E., & Hastrup, J. L. The role of imagination in the disease process: Post-Cartesian history. *Journal of Behavioral Medicine*, 1980, 3, 205–217.

Miller, N. E. Learning of visceral and glandular responses. *Science*, 1969, 163, 434–445.

Miller, N. E., & Brucker, B. S. A learned visceral response apparently independent of skeletal ones in patients paralyzed by spinal lesions. In N. Birbaumer & H. D. Kimmel (Eds.), *Biofeedback and self regulations*. Hillside, N.J.: Erlbaum, 1979.

Moncada, S., Flower, R. J., & Vane, J. R. Prostaglandins, prostacylin and thromboxane A_2. In A. G. Goodman, L. S. Goodman, & A. Gilman (Eds.), *Goodman and Gilman's The pharmacological basis of therapeutics*. New York: Macmillan, 1980.

Obrist, P. A. The cardiovascular–behavioral interaction—as it appears today. *Psychophysiology*, 1976, 13, 85–107.

Obrist, P. A. *Cardiovascular psychophysiology—a perspective*. New York: Plenum, 1981.

Obrist, P. A. Cardiovascular functioning: An appraisal of biofeedback procedures. In L. White & B. Tursky (Eds.), *Clinical biofeedback: Efficacy and mechanisms*. New York: Guilford Press, 1982.

Obrist, P. A., Gaebelein, C. J., Shanks-Teller, E., Langer, A. W., Grignolo, A., Light, K. C., & McCubbin, J. A. The relationship between heart rate, carotid dP/dt, and blood pressure in humans as a function of the type of stress. *Psychophysiology*, 1978, 15, 102–115.

Obrist, P. A., Howard, J. L., Lawler, J. E., Galosy, R., Meyers, K., & Gaebelein, C. J. Cardiac–somatic interaction. In P. A. Obrist, A. H. Black, J. Brener, & L. DiCara (Eds.), *Cardiovascular psychophysiology—current issues in response mechanisms, biofeedback and methodology*. Chicago: Aldine, 1974.

Obrist, P. A., Langer, A. W., Grignolo, A., Light, K. C., & McCubbin, J. A. The cardiac–behavioral interaction. In P. Venables & I. Martin (Eds.), *Techniques in psychophysiology*. Chichester: Wiley, 1980.

Obrist, P. A., Lawler, J. E., Howard, J. L., Smithson, K. W., Martin, P. L., & Manning, J. Sympathetic influences on the heart in humans: Effects on contractility and heart rate of acute stress. *Psychophysiology*, 1974, 11, 405–427.

Obrist, P. A., & Light, K. C. Comments on the Ronald J. Haslegrave and John J. Furedy article "Carotid dP/dt as a psychophysiological index of sympathetic myocardial effects: Some considerations." *Psychophysiology*, 1980, 17, 495–498.

Obrist, P. A., Light, K. C., McCubbin, J. A., Hutcheson, J. S., & Hoffer, J. L. Pulse transit time: Relationship to blood pressure and myocardial performance. *Psychophysiology*, 1979, 16, 292–301.

Obrist, P. A., Webb, R. A., & Sutterer, J. R. Heart rate and somatic changes during aversive conditioning and a simple reaction time task. *Psychophysiology*, 1969, 5, 696–723.

Obrist, P. A., Webb, R. A., Sutterer, J. R., & Howard, J. L. Cardiac deceleration and reaction time: An evaluation of two hypotheses. *Psychophysiology*, 1970, 6, 695–706. (a)

Obrist, P. A., Webb, R. A., Sutterer, J. R., & Howard, J. L. The cardiac–somatic relationship: Some reformulations. *Psychophysiology*, 1970, 6, 569–587. (b)

Obrist, P. A., Wood, D. M., & Perez-Reyes, M. Heart rate during conditioning in humans: Effects of UCS intensity, vagal blockade, and adrenergic block of vasomotor activity. *Journal of Experimental Psychology*, 1965, 70, 32–42.

Page, I. H. Some regulatory mechanisms of renovascular and essential arterial hypertension. In J. Genest, E. Koiw, & O. Kuchel (Eds.), *Hypertension: Physiopathology and treatment.* New York: McGraw-Hill, 1977.

Page, I. H., & Bumpus, F. M. (Eds.). *Angiotensin.* New York: Springer-Verlag, 1974.

Page, I. H., & McCubbin, J. W. The physiology of arterial hypertension. In W. F. Hamilton & P. Dow (Eds.), *Handbook of physiology: Circulation* (Section 2, Vol. 1). Washington, D.C.: American Physiological Society, 1966.

Paul, O. Epidemiology of hypertension. In J. Genest, E. Koiw, & O. Kuchel (Eds.), *Hypertension: Physiopathology and treatment.* New York: McGraw-Hill, 1977.

Peart, W. S. Personal views on mechanisms of hypertension. In J. Genest, E. Koiw, & O. Kuchel (Eds.), *Hypertension: Physiopathology and treatment.* New York: McGraw-Hill, 1977.

Pfeffer, M. A., & Frohlich, E. D. Hemodynamic and myocardial function in young and old normotensive and spontaneously hypertensive rats. *Circulation Research,* 1973, 32(Suppl. 1), I28–I38.

Pickering, R. G. *High blood pressure.* New York: Grune & Stratton, 1968.

Pollak, M. H., & Obrist, P. A. Aortic-radial pulse transit time and ECG Q-wave to radial pulse wave interval as indices of beat-by-beat blood pressure changes. *Psychophysiology,* 1983, 20, 21–28.

Pollak, M. H., Obrist, P. A., & Godaert, G. Individual differences in cardiovascular lability and response: Variations during unrestricted daily activity and autonomic mechanisms underlying response to laboratory tasks. *Psychophysiology,* 1981, 18, 169. (Abstract)

Reid, I. A., & Ganong, W. F. Control of aldosterone secretion. In J. Genest, E. Koiw, & O. Kuchel (Eds.), *Hypertension: Physiopathology and treatment.* New York: McGraw-Hill, 1977.

Safar, M. E., Weiss, Y. A., Levenson, J. A., London, G. M., & Milliez, P. L. Hemodynamic study of 85 patients with borderline hypertension. *American Journal of Cardiology,* 1973, 31, 315–319.

Schottstaedt, W. W., Grace, W. J., & Wolff, H. G. Life situations, behavior, attitudes, emotions and renal excretion of fluid and electrolytes. *Journal of Psychosomatic Research,* 1956, 1, 75–83; 147–159; 203–211; 287–291; 292–298.

Scheinberg, P. The cerebral circulation. In R. Zelis (Ed.), *The peripheral circulations.* New York: Grune & Stratton, 1975.

Schweitzer, M. D., Gearing, F. R., & Perera, G. A. Family studies of primary hypertension: Their contributions to the understanding of genetic factors. In J. Stamler, R. Stamler, & T. N. Pullman (Eds.), *The epidemiology of hypertension.* New York: Grune & Stratton, 1967.

Shapiro, D., Mainardi, J. A., & Surwit, R. S. Biofeedback and self regulation in essential hypertension. In G. E. Schwartz & J. Beatty (Eds.), *Biofeedback: Theory and research.* New York: Academic, 1977.

Shapiro, A. P., Schwartz, G. E., Ferguson, D. C. E., Redmond, D. P., & Weiss, S. M. Behavioral methods in the treatment of hypertension—I. Review of their clinical status. *Annals of Internal Medicine,* 1977, 86, 626–636.

Shepherd, J. T., & Vanhoutte, P. M. Skeletal muscle blood flow: neurogenic determinants. In R. Zelis (Ed.), *The peripheral circulations.* New York: Grune & Stratton, 1975.

Sherwood, A., Allen, M. T., Obrist, P. A., & Langer, A. W. Evaluation of beta-adrenergic influences on cardiovascular and metabolic adjustments to physical and psychological stress. *Psychophysiology,* in press.

Sherwood, A., Brener, J., & Moncur, D. Information and states of motor readiness: Their effects on the covariation of heart rate and energy expenditure. *Psychophysiology,* 1983, 20, 513–529.

Skinner, N. S. Skeletal muscle blood flow: Metabolic determinants. In R. Zelis (Ed.), *The peripheral circulations.* New York: Grune & Stratton, 1975.

Smith, E. E., Guyton, A. C., Manning, R. D., & White, R. J. Integrated mechanisms of cardiovascular response and control during exercise in the normal human. *Progress in Cardiovascular Disease,* 1976, 18, 421–443.

Smith, O. A., Hohimer, A. R., Astley, C. A., & Taylor, D. J. Renal and hind limb vascular control during acute emotion in the baboon. *American Journal of Physiology,* 1979, 236, R198–R205.

Sokolow, M., Werdegar, D., Perloff, D. B., Cowan, R. M., & Brenenstuhl, H. Preliminary studies relating portably recorded blood pressure to daily life events in patients with essential hypertension. In M. Koster, H. Musaph, & P. Visser (Eds.), *Psychosomatics in essential hypertension* (Bibliotheca Psychiatica No. 144). White Plains, N.Y.: S. Karger, 1970.

Stead, E. A., Warren, J. V., Merrill, A. J., & Brannon, E. S. The cardiac output in male subjects as measured by the technique of atrial catherization: Normal values with observations on the effects of anxiety and tilting. *Journal of Clinical Investigation,* 1945, 24, 326–331.

Stromme, S. B., Wikeby, P. C., Blix, A. S., & Ursin, H. Additional heart rate. In H. Ursin, E. Baade, & S. Levine (Eds.), *Psychobiology of stress: A study of coping men.* New York: Academic Press, 1978.

Surwit, R. S., & Shapiro, D. Biofeedback and meditation in the treatment of borderline hypertension. In J. Beatty & H. Legewie (Eds.), *Biofeedback and behavior.* New York: Plenum, 1977.

Tobian, L. Salt and hypertension. *Annals of the New York Academy of Sciences,* 1978, 304, 178–195.

Touw, K. B., Haywood, J. R., Shaffer, R. A., & Brody, M. J. Contribution of the sympathetic nervous system to vascular resistance in conscious young and adult spontaneously hypertensive rats. *Hypertension,* 1980, 2, 408–418.

U.S. National Center for Health Statistics. Vital and health statistics. In *Heart disease in adults: United States 1960–1962* (PHS Publ. No. 1000, Series 11, No. 6). Washington, D.C.: U.S. Government Printing Office, 1964.

Watson, R. D. S., Stallard, T. J., Flinn, R. M., & Littler, W. A. Factors determining direct arterial pressure and its variability in hypertensive man. *Hypertension,* 1980, 2, 333–341.

Weiner, H. Psychosomatic research in essential hypertension. In M. Koster, H. Musaph, & P. Viser (Eds.), *Psychosomatics in essential hypertension* (Bibliotheca Psychiatica No. 144). White Plains, N.Y.: S. Karger, 1970.

Weiner, H. Personality factors and the importance of emotional stresses in hypertension. In J. Genest, E. Koiw, & O. Kuchel (Eds.), *Hypertension: Physiopathology and treatment.* New York: McGraw-Hill, 1977. (a)

Weiner, H. *Psychobiology and human disease.* New York: Elsevier, 1977. (b)

Weiner, N. Norepinephrine, epinephrine and the sympathomimetic amines. In A. G. Goodman, L. S. Goodman, & A. Gilman (Eds.), *Goodman and Gilman's The pharmacological basis of therapeutics.* New York: Macmillan, 1980.

Weiss, J. M. Psychological and behavioral influences on gastrointestinal lesions in animal models. In J. D. Maser & M. E. P. Seligman (Eds.), *Psychopathology: Experimental model.* San Francisco: W. H. Freeman, 1977.

Weiss, L., Lundgren, Y., & Folkow, B. Effects of prolonged treatment with adrenergic β-receptor antagonists on blood pressure, cardiovascular design and reactivity in spontaneously hypertensive rates (SHR). *Acta Physiologica Scandinavica,* 1974, 91, 447–451.

Zanchetti, A., & Bartorelli, C. Central nervous mechanisms in arterial hypertension: Experimental and clinical evidence. In J. Genest, E. Koiw, & O. Kuchel (Eds.), *Hypertension: Physiopathology and treatment.* New York: McGraw-Hill, 1977.

Chapter Twenty-Four
Social Processes

John T. Cacioppo
Richard E. Petty

INTRODUCTION

Different strategies can be employed to study social behavior. One, for instance, involves the use of gross observational procedures to catalog the vagaries of social behavior and to begin identifying the eliciting conditions. In a second, the emphasis is not on discovering yet more categories of social behavior, but rather on specifying the *processes* underlying the behaviors that gross observations have already catalogued. Choice of strategy will be dependent on the question that a particular investigator seeks to answer. Some strategies (and tools) are better suited for cataloguing social behaviors, whereas others are better suited for studying the rudimentary processes underlying these behaviors. The application of psychophysiological recording techniques, for example, can be, and has often been, overly complicated and cumbersome when used as a means of discovering, describing, and cataloguing social behavior.

In the present chapter, we are concerned with the task of delineating the *foundations of social processes.* Our premise is that social processes are composed of a finite number of distinct subprocesses, or "stages." A

stage, in turn, is viewed as consisting of a limited number of elements, or "constructs." Finally, each stage is viewed as possessing identifiable properties and propensities for combining to yield social behavior. We propose that psychophysiology can be useful in helping to identify these stages.

The present approach to the study of social processes is not unlike the chemist's approach to the study of chemical processes. In this conception, processing stages roughly correspond to chemical elements; social processes correspond to chemical substances. A finite number of chemical elements combine in an orderly sequence to yield an almost infinite number of substances, and a finite number of elementary processing stages are assumed to combine in an orderly sequence to yield an almost infinite variety of social processes. Moreover, just as early investigations in chemistry sometimes revealed that isolated "elements" were in fact combinations of smaller elements, the isolation of certain fundamental processing stages does not preclude, but rather facilitates, the subsequent division of these components into yet more elementary stages. Finally, just as the total number of distinct chemical elements that exists

John T. Cacioppo. Department of Psychology, University of Iowa, Iowa City, Iowa.
Richard E. Petty. Department of Psychology, University of Missouri–Columbia, Columbia, Missouri.

is empirically defined, with the presumption being only that the total is finite, the total number of processing stages is defined empirically and is assumed to be finite.

With few exceptions, the stages of social processes have been viewed as being conscious, though not necessarily reportable (Nisbett & Wilson, 1977; cf. Zajonc, 1980b). These conceptions are due partially to the predominant paradigm in the social sciences. Generally, this research relies on people's self-reports to assess the efficacy of the experimental manipulations, the effects of these manipulations on verbal or overt behavioral responses, and the operation of some assumed intervening operation (Gerard, 1964). This methodology may provide details about those aspects of social processes that involve short-term memory (see Ericcson & Simon, 1980), but may be less sensitive to rudimentary elements and stages that are not conscious, only briefly conscious, or conscious but excised by subjects in experiments or interviews. In addition, inferences about the stages comprising social processes that are based solely on the study of subsequent verbal or behavioral responses may suffer, because these responses reflect upon an entire sequence of stages and lag differentially behind these constituent stages. Thus, although a number of informative functional relationships have been documented in the social sciences, the successful specification of the foundations of these relationships has been more elusive. This is in part because these individual elements and stages may have no overt behavioral component, and in part because the similar behavioral outcomes that emerge do not always derive from the same set and sequence of stages (e.g., Fazio, Zanna, & Cooper, 1977).

Continuous recordings of physiological responses, though not without problems, can provide concurrent and independent data regarding social processes. Our aims in the present chapter are (1) to trace the history of psychophysiological applications to the study of social processes and behavior; (2) to outline two analytical frameworks for collecting and interpreting physiological data to study the rudiments of social processes; and (3) to illustrate these interpretive frameworks in a brief review of studies of social processes in which psychophysiological measures have been obtained. Most of the studies that we review are from social psychology or psychophysiology, but the analytical frameworks outlined and the principles described in this chapter are obviously applicable generally to the social sciences. Finally, it should be emphasized that the physiological data obtained in these studies are not viewed here as mere correlates of, or alternative expressions for, social processes. Rather, they are viewed as harboring information (limited only by the logic of the experimental design) with which to (1) isolate candidates for the fundamental stages and elements of social processes, (2) identify

their properties, and (3) explore the manner in which they combine. We begin by reviewing the historical roots of psychophysiological research on social processes.

HISTORICAL BACKGROUND

Traditionally, psychophysiological investigations of social processes were defined by the use of a social factor as an independent variable and of a polygraph to obtain at least one of the dependent measures. This most often meant recording galvanic skin responses (GSRs) during what in all other respects would be regarded as a traditional social-psychological study (Schwartz & Shapiro, 1973). Research of this kind has gone by various names over the years, including "interpersonal physiology" (DiMascio, Boyd, & Greenblatt, 1957), "sociophysiology" (Boyd & DiMascio, 1954; Waid, 1984), "the psychobiology of social psychology" (Leiderman & Shapiro, 1964), and "social psychophysiology" (Cacioppo, 1982; Cacioppo & Petty, 1983b; Schwartz & Shapiro, 1973). The application of psychophysiology to the study of social processes, however, can no longer be characterized by any single measure or measurement instrument. The relationships between social processes and bodily states have now been advanced using misattribution procedures (e.g., Zanna & Cooper, 1976; Zillmann, 1978), cardiac pacemakers (Cacioppo, 1979), drugs (e.g., J. Cooper, Zanna, & Taves, 1978; Schachter & Singer, 1962), hypnosis (Maslach, 1979), expressive and postural manipulations (e.g., Laird, 1974; Petty, Wells, Heesacker, Brock, & Cacioppo, 1983; Vaughan & Lanzetta, 1981), operant training procedures for shaping physiological activity (Cacioppo, Sandman, & Walker, 1978), and exercise (e.g., Pennebaker & Lightner, 1980; Zillmann, 1983). Moreover, a full array of psychophysiological measures, ranging from heart rate (HR) to electrocortical activity, has been employed (see Cacioppo & Petty, 1983a; Shapiro & Crider, 1969).

The utility of adopting a psychophysiological perspective as well as a developed methodology to delineate social processes is in part responsible for this broader conception. For example, although most social psychologists have focused on the role of situational factors in shaping social behavior, it is now evident that human association can markedly influence the organismic environment (Christie & Mellett, 1981; Kaplan, 1979) and that physiological factors are important determinants of people's exchanges and interactions with one another (Cacioppo & Petty, 1983b; Waid, 1984). We use the term "social psychophysiology" to refer to this area of research in the present chapter, because it best reflects the origins of much of the early research; it is the term most commonly used in the contemporary literature; and, most importantly, it is defined more generally than its alternatives to include any use of noninvasive procedures to study the relationships between actual and perceived physiological events (i.e., signs, symptoms, undetected physiological responses) and social cognition and behavior (Cacioppo & Petty, 1983a).

Early Observations

The perspective on human behavior epitomized by social psychophysiology is quite old, dating back at least to the third century B.C., when a young man named Antiochus had the fortune of being the son of one of Alexander the Great's leading generals and the misfortune of falling in love with his father's young and beautiful bride (Mesulam & Perry, 1972). The son knew that his love for his stepmother should never be realized. He tried to control his manner when in her presence, but apparently wished privately to lapse. The young man soon began manifesting what appeared to be a mysterious illness. He would on occasion suffer from debilitating attacks, characterized by changes including increased heart beat variability, stammering speech, profuse perspiring, weakening muscles, and pallor. Several local physicians had unsuccessfully attended to the young man when the well-known Greek physician Erasistratos arrived. To isolate what particular stimulus triggered the attacks, Erasistratos observed the peripheral physiological responses of the young man during the course of the day. Based upon the distinctive syndrome of physiological responses that was evoked by the stepmother's visits to the young man, Erasistratos deduced that the young man suffered from lovesickness. The father gave up his new bride, and the son recovered. This case is, to our knowledge, the first recorded "social-psychophysiological" inquiry.

Articles bearing this perspective began appearing in the psychological literature in the 1920s. For example, Riddle (1925) studied the changes in people's breathing when they were bluffing during a game of poker. For the next 35 years, most of the empirical investigations were conducted by psychiatrists interested in obtaining "objective" measures of therapeutic effectiveness (Shapiro & Crider, 1969). One study, however, conducted by C. E. Smith in 1936 and reported in the *Journal of Abnormal and Social Psychology*, is quite contemporary in its attempt to focus on the foundations of social processes using psychophysiology (cf. Crider, 1983). Smith began by administering a questionnaire in a class of college students. The questionnaire was designed to assess each student's attitudes and strength of conviction on 20 different and, at that time, controversial issues (e.g., "Divorce should be granted only in the case of grave offense," "Modernistic art should be enthusias-

tically encouraged"). Four weeks later, subjects were asked to participate in an experiment. Subjects (all males) were tested individually, and GSR recordings were obtained. For half of the issues, a subject was led to believe that the majority of his peers agreed with him, whereas he was led to believe that the majority disagreed with him on the other half. Smith found that (1) disagreement with an opinion statement was accompanied by greater GSRs than was agreement; (2) the responses of subjects who knew they were in the minority rather than the majority were accompanied by greater GSRs; (3) the magnitude of the GSRs varied with the degree of conviction reported, excluding indifference and absolute conviction; and (4) the GSRs accompanying absolute conviction tended to be smaller than the response accompanying the degree of conviction immediately preceding the absolute. Thus, Smith compared the GSRs obtained across clearly constructed experimental conditions to generate hypotheses regarding the processes underlying conformity, and in so doing, developed the notion that unless individuals have a very strong conviction in an attitude, they undergo conflict when they realize that they hold a deviant (i.e., nonnormative) position on an issue (see also Murray, 1938).

The first summary of empirical research in social psychophysiology was published by Kaplan and Bloom in 1960. This review focused on the psychophysiological concomitants of social status, social sanction, definition of the situation, and empathy. Kaplan and Bloom expressed an optimism that this approach had come of age: "In recent years sociological and social psychological concepts have been applied in physiological studies at an ever increasing rate. The acceptance and utilization of such concepts have been said to form the basis for a relatively new field of inquiry" (Kaplan & Bloom, 1960, p. 133). Their review appeared in the *Journal of Nervous and Mental Diseases* rather than a social science journal, perhaps in part because most of the research reviewed by Kaplan and Bloom was conducted to assess therapeutic effectiveness. For example, neither the study by Riddle (1925) nor any of C. E. Smith's studies (C. E. Smith, 1936; C. E. Smith & Diven, cited in Murray, 1938) was discussed. At about the same point in time, John Lacey's seminal critique of psychophysiological measures of therapeutic effectiveness appeared in a volume on research in psychotherapy. Lacey (1959) argued that there was little consistency in the literature upon which to build bridges between psychophysiological data and therapeutic outcomes. He went on to argue that the phenomena of individual and stimulus–response stereotypies were largely responsible for the apparent inconsistencies in the psychophysiological data, and that these stereotypies were so pervasive that they, rather than complex therapeutic factors, should be the focus of research in the coming years (cf. Coles, Jennings, & Stern, 1984). Not surprisingly, the search for psychophysiological indices of psychotherapeutic effectiveness slowed following Lacey's review.

Investigations of the reciprocal influence between social and physiological systems, however, began to broaden in scope and increase in number. In 1962, Schachter and Singer published their influential paper, "Cognitive, Social, and Physiological Determinants of Emotional State." The thrust of their two-factor theory of emotions was that the sensations derived from a large and unexpected increase in diffuse physiological arousal could be experienced as widely different emotions, depending upon the circumstances covarying with these sensations.[1] Two years later, Leiderman and Shapiro (1964) published a small edited book, *Psychobiological Approaches to Social Behavior*, which generally depicted a different vein of research: Evidence was presented for the dramatic impact that social factors such as conformity pressures and group interactions can have on physiological responding. The book was interesting and informative, but has been overlooked by most social psychologists. Moreover, psychophysiologists who were aware of this research apparently concluded that social factors were potentially powerful contaminants in psychophysiological studies (cf. Schwartz & Shapiro, 1973; Shapiro & Crider, 1969). Hence, much of the research in psychophysiology during the 1960s was conducted with care in eliminating potentially complicating social factors from empirical studies and, consequently, from psychophysiological theorizing.

By the next decade, psychophysiological recording had become relatively standardized. The discipline of psychophysiology had its own textbook (Sternbach, 1966), handbook (Greenfield & Sternbach, 1972), journal, and society. The second edition of *The Handbook of Social Psychology* was published at about this point in time, containing an interesting chapter by Shapiro and Crider (1969) on "Psychophysiological Approaches to Social Psychology"; a year later, in the *Annual Review of Psychology*, a chapter entitled "Psychophysiological Contributions to Social Psychology" (Shapiro & Schwartz, 1970) appeared. This coverage of social-psychophysiological research was not directed solely to a social-psychological audience,

either, as a chapter entitled "Social Psychophysiology" (Schwartz & Shapiro, 1973) appeared early in this decade in an edited book on electrodermal activity (EDA) that was compiled largely for a psychophysiological audience (Prokasy & Raskin, 1973). Also, Kaplan (1972, 1979) reviewed early research in the area for the field of medical sociology.

Early Obstacles

A major emphasis in these reviews was on applying psychophysiological procedures to validate social-psychological constructs and measures. Their utility in this endeavor proved considerable:

> At the very simplest methodological level, the attraction of social psychologists to physiological techniques is not hard to understand. The techniques provide nonverbal, objective [and] relatively bias-free indices of human reaction that have some of the same appeal as gestural, postural, and other indicators of overt response. (Shapiro & Schwartz, 1970, pp. 88–89)

However, the attractiveness of applying psychophysiological procedures to help isolate and identify the elementary constructs and stages of social processes was tempered, it would appear, by three barriers: (1) the physiological background, technical sophistication, and elaborate instrumentation that are necessary for collecting, reducing, and analyzing interpretable psychophysiological data in already complex social-psychological paradigms; (2) the absence of analytical frameworks within which to create treatment comparisons and interpret physiological data bearing upon social processes, resulting in a paucity of conceptual links with clear ranges of validity between the physiological data and social-psychological constructs; and (3) the inevitable pitting of social-psychological and psychophysiological procedures against each other in studies of construct validation (Cacioppo, 1982; Shapiro & Crider, 1969).

Three distinct responses to these barriers can be found in the literature: (1) the simple dismissal of physiological factors as being irrelevant, at least at present, to the study of social processes, and the dismissal of the study of social factors as too molar to contribute to an understanding of psychophysiological relationships; (2) adoption of the view that diffuse and perceptible changes in physiological arousal are the major physiological processes relevant to social cognition and behavior; and (3) the narrowing of the breadth of the social issue under investigation while increasing the depth (levels) of the analysis to entertain highly specific, potentially reciprocal, and biologically aptive (i.e., adaptive and exaptive; cf. Gould & Vrba, 1982) influences between social and physiological systems.

---

1. According to Schachter (1964), "the present formulation . . . maintains simply that cognitive and situational factors determine the labels applied to any of a variety of states of physiological arousal" (p. 71). The physiological features of these arousal states were never explicitly specified, but investigators came to focus on the following prerequisite reportable features of this physiological state: (1) the *perception* of a state of diffuse physiological arousal, (2) experienced immediately as being neither pleasant nor unpleasant, and (3) emerging in the absence of an immediate and plausible cause. Recent reviews of the present status of this formulation can be found in Cotton (1981), Manstead and Wagner (1981), Cacioppo and Petty (in press), and Zillmann (1978).

Dismissal of Social-Psychophysiological Influences

When physiological data have been used successfully to validate a social-psychological construct, it has occasionally been reasoned that there is no further utility in using psychophysiological procedures to investigate the phenomena involving the construct, since the simpler, less expensive, and less time-consuming verbal or behavioral measures traditionally used by social psychologists have been documented to be generally just as informative. On the other hand, when application of a psychophysiological perspective has failed to confirm the validity of a verbal or behavioral measure of a social construct, the theoretical inclination of the investigator has influenced the decision as to whether the theoretical construct, the verbal or behavioral measure, or the psychophysiological validation procedure is suspect.

Moreover, in pointing to powerful situational determinants and consequences of social behavior, investigators have occasionally deemphasized the role of organismic factors. Valins (1966), for example, proposed a modification of Schachter and Singer's (1962) theory of emotions when he argued that the actual sensation of a change in physiological arousal is unimportant; rather, the simple belief that a change has occurred is both necessary and sufficient to initiate an emotional reaction by evoking the search for an emotional label. Several years later, Bem (1972) argued more generally that people are typically insensitive to internal sources of information and reasoned that people infer their feelings toward issues and events by observing their overt behavior just as an observer would do. These theoretical stances, of course, imply that there is no need to try to surmount the obstacles to social-psychophysiological research.

Focus on Arousal

The second and perhaps predominant response, however, has been to view the physiological factor important in the study of social processes as consisting of diffuse, perceptible changes in physiological arousal. In its simplest form, this view has provided the justification for research being conducted with little or no psychophysiological recording equipment and expertise, since it is reasoned that any single physiological response (e.g., see Krugman, 1981), or even simple self-reports of bodily sensations, can index a person's physiological arousal at that moment in time (e.g., Thayer, 1970). Hence, psychophysiological procedures as simple as occasionally palpating the radial artery in a subject's wrist to measure HR or monitoring any one of a number of electrodermal responses (EDRs) have been used in various studies as if they were equivalent measures of physiological functioning.

Interestingly, this viewpoint has led to the development or refinement of assessment procedures (e.g., misattribution paradigms) that allow researchers to consider the influence of perceived physiological events (e.g., "felt arousal") on social processes without the use of psychophysiological recording equipment. For instance, in the misattribution paradigm, subjects ingest a placebo that they believe has specific experimenter-specified side effects. This assessment procedure is based upon the notion that people search for the cause of an unexplained change in their bodily sensations, such as a sudden feeling of tension or arousal (cf. Zanna & Cooper, 1976). In their search, people consider external as well as internal causes and sometimes misattribute the true cause of a felt bodily reaction (e.g., increased sympathetic activity due to a transgression they have committed) to something that seems to be a reasonable cause at the time (e.g., a pill they have recently ingested). Of course, only when a stimulus is believed to have the same or nearly the same effects on individuals as they are experiencing at the moment will misattribution to the stimulus be likely (cf. Zillmann, 1983). Thus, in the misattribution paradigm, subjects are either exposed or not exposed to social conditions that are believed to affect physiological responding, and are either exposed or not exposed to a possible external cause for experiencing specific bodily sensations. The nature of the internal state that people are experiencing in the various social conditions is then inferred indirectly by determining what type of "side effect" elicits misattribution.

In an illustrative experiment by Higgins, Rhodewalt, and Zanna (1979), subjects were given a drug and were told that the experiment concerned the effects of the drug on learning. Subjects were instructed that the pill might cause them to feel "unpleasantly sedated" (unpleasant–unaroused), "relaxed" (pleasant–unaroused), "tense" (unpleasant–aroused), "pleasantly excited" (pleasant–aroused), or nothing in particular (no-side-effects control group). Subjects were also told that any side effects would occur quickly (e.g., 5 min), and that the effects of the drug on learning would not occur fully for some time (e.g., 30 min). Subjects were asked to assist the experimenter in another "unrelated" study to allow time for the drug's possible effect on learning to take full effect.

Subjects in this study had, in fact, been given a placebo, a pill made of milk powder, which had absolutely no perceptible physiological effects. While subjects were "waiting" for the pill to reach its full effect, they were induced to write a counterattitudinal message under conditions designed to arouse cognitive dissonance (see pp. 670–673). Higgins et al. (1979) replicated previous research findings that a pill described as having the side effect of making the person feel "tense," in contrast to a pill with no side effects, attenuated attitude change. This suggests that subjects misattributed the sensations aroused by cognitive dissonance to the pill, rather than resolving the dissonance by changing their attitudes (cf. Zanna &

Cooper, 1974). Importantly, Higgins *et al.* (1979) found that the pill described as possibly causing a feeling of unpleasant sedation blocked attitude change, too. Overall, the feature of felt unpleasantness was significantly more effective in eliciting the misattribution of cognitive dissonance to the pill than was the feature of felt physiological arousal. These data suggest that the social conditions postulated to instigate cognitive dissonance create a perceptible organismic reaction that is felt to be unpleasant.

Perhaps the oldest and most straightforward procedure, however, is to ask subjects to describe their bodily sensations, and this procedure has also been employed in research on social processes. For example, Shaffer (1975) was interested in assessing the symptomatological effects characterizing cognitive dissonance; however, rather than employing a misattribution paradigm, he simply asked subjects to report how much "frustration/mental discomfort" they felt. Some subjects had written an essay consonant with their initial attitude (low-dissonance group), and others had written an essay dissonant with their initial attitude (high-dissonance group). Shaffer found that subjects who had written the counterattitudinal essay reported feeling more frustration and mental discomfort than subjects who had written the proattitudinal essay. Moreover, the within-cell correlation between reported frustration/mental discomfort and attitude evidenced a strong association ($r = .57$); this is consistent with the notion that cognitive dissonance is subjectively perceived as an unpleasant state that is followed by the modification of attitudes in an attempt to eliminate the conditions (e.g., attitude–behavior discrepancy) that have caused the dissonance.

Verbal reports have been promoted as measures of specific physiological changes as well. The James–Lange theory of emotions, for instance, assumed that people can at a minimum distinguish the idiosyncratic bodily reactions that accompany divergent emotional reactions. However, studies of the relationship between the physiological and verbal covariants of emotion revealed large discrepancies, and the accuracy and validity of verbal reports were called into question (e.g., Syz, 1926).

Nisbett and Wilson (1977) have argued more recently that people cannot accurately report the causes (antecedents) of their emotions or behaviors. Their critique of verbal reports as data about psychological processes applies to stimuli arising from within an individual's body as well as to those emanating from the external environment. Although the experiments and interpretations offered by Nisbett and Wilson (1977) have been criticized on various grounds (see Ericcson & Simon, 1980; Sabini & Silver, 1981; E. R. Smith & Miller, 1978; White, 1980), their caveat regarding the interpretation of verbal reports nevertheless has important implications. Specifically, verbal reports concerning an individual's bodily sensations or states may best be viewed as symptomatology data whose relationship to physiological reactions is open to empirical study. In a review of relevant literature, Blascovich and Katkin (1983) indicated that verbal reports of *specific* bodily states (e.g., resting HR) and reactions (e.g., increased HR) are generally inaccurate, and Pennebaker (1982) concluded that the causes of bodily reactions are typically reported incorrectly by people. Thus, verbal reports of specific physiological activity cannot be assumed to be redundant with actual physiological measures.

Although the apparent dissociation between verbal and psychophysiological measures of specific bodily reactions quelled research in this area for decades, the recent spate of investigations on the operant conditioning of visceral activity has led to a renewed interest in the relationship between proprioception or interoception and physiological reactions (Brener, 1977). From the point of view of operant conditioning theorists, an individual's detection of a specific physiological change need not be accurate, as long as a perceptible event is correlated with the physiological change of interest to the investigator. For instance, individuals may not be able to discriminate between large changes in HR during mild exertion, but nevertheless may reliably detect increases in HR from momentarily correlated and perceptible changes in cardiac stroke volume.

More recently, Mackay (1980) has contended that adjective checklists (e.g., the stress–arousal checklist) provide an integrative measure of physiological activity that is more representative of general physiological arousal than any single psychophysiological measure. In a review of verbal measures of physiological activity, Mackay (1980) cites two lines of evidence for this proposition. The first derives from research showing that verbal reports of arousal (e.g., as assessed using adjective checklists) correlate more highly with physiological composites (e.g., HR and skin conductance) than do pairs of physiological variables. The second line of evidence comes from a deductive rather than an inductive research strategy: Subjects are exposed to discernible external stimuli (e.g., noise) that are hypothesized to alter physiological arousal, and verbal measures of physiological arousal are administered. Generally, self-reports of arousal have covaried with the expected effects of the independent variables on physiological activation.

The validity and sensitivity of verbal measures of general physiological arousal are still questionable for two reasons, however. First, self-report measures of arousal may be more highly correlated with the average of several physiological measures of arousal than with any single physiological measure of arousal, or than with any two physiological measures of arousal, because of reduction in measurement error that accompanies the use of multiple measures to gauge a single construct. Second, Zillmann and his colleagues

(Zillmann, 1979) have clearly demonstrated that reported arousal subsides more quickly following exercise than do changes in blood pressure and HR. Hence, independent variables that excite specific effector systems may also alter verbal reports of arousal, but this convergence is apparently lost soon afterward in most instances (see also Cacioppo, Marshall-Goodell, & Gormezano, 1983; Lang, 1971; Mewborn & Rogers, 1979).

Finally, even if the change in reportable states is assumed to be based in a physiological change, it would be an error to equate the two, since numerous physiological changes go unnoticed (e.g., Cacioppo & Petty, 1982a). Furthermore, situational and social factors can alter the bodily sensations that are heeded and encoded (Scheier, Carver, & Matthews, 1983), and the same reportable state may be accompanied by a variety of physiological changes (e.g., Schwartz, 1982). Hence, the validity of self-report and misattribution measures of *actual* physiological activity in studies of social processes cannot be accepted without strong reservations at present.

In sum, the view that arousal is the sine qua non of physiological influences on social processes has stimulated interesting research on nonelectrophysiological measures of bodily processes. The accumulated research suggests that verbal measures of physiological activity (or activation), as well as assessments derived from the use of the misattribution paradigm, cannot be taken as indices of physiological activity per se; rather, they stand as indices of a reportable state that may or may not be highly related to the targeted physiological process. Thus, the low intercorrelations among physiological, reportable, and behavioral responses to experimental treatments suggest that each of these types of responses harbors distinctive information that must be tied empirically and theoretically to social processes.

Focus on Response Syndromes and Systems

The third major response to the barriers to psychophysiological investigations of social processes emerged from research attacking the presumed pervasiveness and influence of general and diffuse physiological arousal. One of the major conceptions of physiological arousal derived from Cannon's early work on the flight-or-fight response. Cannon observed that organisms exhibit generalized discharges in the sympathetic nervous system in response to threatening stimuli. In part from Cannon's (1927) observations, Duffy (e.g., 1951, 1972) developed notions about stressors, autonomic arousal, and (adaptive) behavioral activation. According to Duffy (1957),

> Measurement of the physiological indicants of arousal affords, when other factors are constant, a direct measure of the "motivating" or "emotional" value of the situation of the individual. The concept serves to break

down the distinction between the arousal aspect of "drives" or "motives" and that of "emotion," and to suggest instead a continuum in the degree of activation of the individual. (p. 273)

Malmo (1958) made a similar proposal, and both he and Duffy viewed the relationship between drive/arousal and performance as being in the form of an inverted U.

Lindsley (1951) noted the electroencephalogram (EEG) activity obtained during sleeping and waking states roughly mirrors the behavioral activity of the organism. He suggested that the general arousal system of the brain may serve as the basis for behavioral arousal. The early research on the reticular activating system (RAS) indicated that this diffuse subcortical tract was intimately related to electrocortical activity; it was considered to be the instrument of the brain's arousal system (Moruzzi & Magoun, 1949; but see Vanderwolf & Robinson, 1981). Hebb (1955) related the RAS to generalized drive states, arguing that the former represented an anatomical mechanism for energizing behavior in a nonspecific fashion, whereas the latter was a hypothetical construct representing the same nonspecific energization of behavior. Hence, Hebb (1955) suggested that the neural basis of generalized drive was the RAS. Physiological responses (e.g., the EEG) were believed to reflect the level of activity in the RAS, and therefore an individual's level of drive at any given moment in time.

Research spearheaded by the Laceys (cf. Lacey, 1967), however, indicated that the extent of covariation is low between indices of autonomic and behavioral activity, and between measures of autonomic and electrocortical excitation. Specifically, electrocortical, autonomic, and behavioral measures tend not to act in a unitary fashion except across vast differences in activity levels (e.g., deep sleep to ecstatic states), following highly unusual and salient external events (e.g., following an unexpected gunshot), or in metabolically demanding situations (e.g., during strenuous exercise). Even physiological measures obtained during physically nondemanding tasks from effectors within a single system (e.g., the autonomic or somatic nervous system) do not covary highly (Cacioppo & Petty, 1981a; Fridlund, Cottam, & Fowler, 1982; Lacey, Kagan, Lacey, & Moss, 1963). Finally, as noted above, there can be large discrepancies between the facts of and the feelings arising from physiological changes. The same physiological reaction in two people can lead to distinctive reports (symptoms), because the individuals differ in their sensitivity and attention to detectable physiological reactions (L. C. Miller, Murphy, & Buss, 1981), the aspects of the detectable physiological responses they heed (Pennebaker & Skelton, 1981), their allocation of attention to detectable physiological reactions and external demands when performing a task (Scheier et al., 1983), and the hypotheses they carry about what internal sensations represent physiological changes such as "arousal" and "hypertension" (Leventhal & Nerenz, 1981).

Psychophysiologists and social psychologists alike have wrestled with integrating these viewpoints:

> The effect of attempting to assimilate all of these traditions to a single arousal theory was to create a model in which the reticular activating system was assumed to serve as a generalized arousal mechanism which responded to sensory input of all kinds, energized behavior, and produced both EEG and sympathetic nervous system activation. . . . As is well-known, this model failed the empirical test rather badly. (Fowles, 1980, p. 88)

The reactions of many frustrated investigators are represented in Kiesler and Pallak's (1976) comments:

> We use the terms *motivation* (drive) and *arousal* loosely and interchangeably. . . . We recognize the continuing controversy regarding these concepts in the literature. . . . Our simplistic use of the terms does not imply a theoretical stance on our part, but rather reflects the state of the art in social psychology. (p. 1015)

Multicomponent arousal models emerged to account for these nuances (e.g., Fowles, 1980, 1982; Routtenberg, 1968), and the conceptualizations of independent dimensions of physiological activation accent the dubious nature of using single physiological indices in social-psychological studies to assess "physiological arousal."

Therefore, despite the past importance of the nonspecific, unidimensional concept of arousal in psychophysiological studies of social processes, there is a decreasing tendency for investigators to assume that general physiological arousal, specific physiological measures, reportable levels of felt arousal, and overt behavioral intensity necessarily or typically covary. Instead, these constructs are increasingly being treated as elements of perhaps independent stages whose interrelationships, and whose positions in social processes, are subject to empirical and theoretical investigation. Studies of the incipient and transient patterning of facial muscles during social interaction (e.g., see reviews by Fridlund & Izard, 1983; Schwartz, 1975) and excitation transfer (e.g., see Zillmann, 1979, 1984) are illustrative.

Convergence of Approaches

There is already evidence of a convergence among the three research strategies outlined above. Schachter (1978), for example, has recently explained that the essential point of his early position on emotion and arousal was that "most complex behavior cannot yet be understood in purely biological terms" (p. 433); however, he has come to believe "that there are areas about which we know sufficient biology to render the

continued use of psychological explanatory constructs both superfluous and misleading" (p. 434). Although we do not anticipate the rejection of psychological constructs in favor of biological constructs to explain social processes, at least in the foreseeable future, there has been a clear decline in the dismissal of physiological factors as irrelevant. Moreover, the non-electrophysiological procedures developed by investigators to study the effects of diffuse and perceptible physiological arousal on social processes have raised interesting questions regarding the actual physiological basis for the obtained data and observed individual differences. In turn, such questions have stimulated research, for example, on the symptoms and sensations people associate with various patterns of somatic and autonomic responses (Blascovich & Katkin, 1983; Leventhal & Mosbach, 1983; Pennebaker, 1982; Scheier et al., 1983).

Finally, it should be noted that psychophysiologists are taking an increasing interest in social factors not because they necessarily want to identify rudimentary social processes, but rather because of the dramatic effects social factors can exert on an organism's reactions to nonsocial stimuli (e.g., Gantt, Newton, Royer, & Stephens, 1966; Lynch & McCarthy, 1969; cf. Pribram, 1962). This interest has grown for two reasons. First, since social factors may alter the psychophysiological reactions to nonsocial stimuli, comprehensive psychophysiological models must deal with these factors (Cacioppo & Petty, 1983c). Second, consideration of social factors has contributed to the construction of more sensitive, artifact-free psychophysiological experimentation. Gale and his colleagues, for instance, have consistently emphasized the importance of creating a comfortable psychosocial environment for psychophysiological experimentation—one that is free of demand characteristics, experimenter effects, and evaluation apprehension (Gale, 1973; Gale & Baker, 1981; Gale & Smith, 1980). Since this research represents more the application of social psychology to psychophysiological experimentation than the application of psychophysiology to the study of social processes, it is not reviewed here. Interested readers may wish to consult discussions of this work in Christie and Todd (1975) and Gale and Baker (1981).

ANALYTIC FRAMEWORKS

Although a social-psychophysiological perspective is not a privileged pathway to understanding social or physiological processes, contemporary research has highlighted several advantages that the applications of psychophysiological procedures can yield when used in clearly conceived experimental studies of social processes. First, social-psychophysiological research has helped to advance our understanding of the determinants of people's physiological responses and the operation of physiological mechanisms by expanding the set of independent and dependent variables in psychophysiology to include powerful social factors (e.g., Cacioppo & Petty, 1983a; Shapiro & Crider, 1969). Second, this viewpoint can lead to the discovery and ultimately to the explanation of instances of complex human behavior that are shaped by a combination of social, dispositional, and physiological factors (e.g., Leventhal, 1980). Third psychophysiological procedures can provide means for assessing the construct validity of theoretical concepts in the social sciences (e.g., Cook & Selltiz, 1964; Tursky & Jamner, 1983). Fourth, a general social-psychophysiological perspective can lead to discoveries in applied areas—for example, behavioral medicine—as the regulation (or deregulation) of the human organism is viewed within a broader social context (Henry & Stephens, 1977; Schwartz, 1983; Spitzer & Rodin, 1983). Finally, this orientation can lead to a greater specification and refinement of existing theories of social processes and to the development of new theories as the elementary stages of social processes are isolated and identified. As we have noted, it is this last focus with which we are primarily concerned in this chapter.

In Search of Elementary Stages of Social Processes

Psychophysiology as Description: The Molar Method

In one of the earliest empirical studies of social interaction, Boyd and DiMascio (1954) evaluated a psychotherapeutic interview of a single patient (diagnosed "schizophrenic, paranoid type") using the Bales Interaction Scoring System and measures of HR, GSR, and facial temperature. Boyd and DiMascio reported that positive and negative verbal exchanges increased while neutral exchanges decreased as the interview proceeded. They also noted that skin resistance dropped; HR increased, then slowed; and facial temperature rose, then dropped during the interview. The investigators suggested,

> At the beginning of the interview sympathetic tension was elevated immediately and was accompanied by profuse "neutral" interaction: as the interview proceeded the patient expressed more feelings (cf. less neutral) and these were accompanied by reduced productivity and sympathetic relaxation. (Boyd & DiMascio, 1954, p. 211)

However, these physiological changes were not clearly related to changes in the behavioral interaction as the interview progressed, and no comparison conditions were included to determine what aspects of the social interaction caused particular physiological and behavioral responses, what aspects were reliable, or what

aspects were unique to persons with thought disorders. The significance of these data for understanding the rudimentary processes operating in psychotherapeutic interviews (or social exchanges generally) is meager, although these data do furnish a description of the psychophysiology of a highly limited and possibly idiosyncratic event.

How, then, are the constituent stages of various social processes to be analyzed? Note, first, that the term "stage" is used here in an operational rather than a functional sense (cf. A. F. Sanders, 1980). Although any complex social process is assumed to consist of more than one sequentially ordered processing stage, it is always possible that a stage is, in fact, comprised of a set of yet more elementary operations (e.g., unidentified substages), which may or may not be ordered sequentially. Hence, a stage can be viewed as an empirically identified link in a chain of intervening components of a social process.

Not surprisingly, the identification of the fundamental stages of various social processes through the application of psychophysiological concepts and techniques depends upon the reigning experimental logic. For example, randomization, replication, and multiple operationalization are as fundamental to social-psychophysiological investigations as they are to social and behavioral experimentation (cf. Campbell & Stanley, 1963). Investigators may wish to interpret an observed physiological response as "a nonreactive index," "the physiological basis," or "an integral component" of a social process. However, because social constructs, stages, and processes are abstractions based upon observable (e.g., physiological, verbal, behavioral) events, it is generally necessary to utilize an experimental design that includes several conditions, none of which uniquely identifies the effect of the stage under study, but which taken together define such an effect (cf. Pachella, 1974).

In this section, two general analytic frameworks are outlined for designing and interpreting psychophysiological investigations of the stages of social processes. With regard to the design of the experiments, the first framework, based upon the subtractive method, begins with a theoretical sequence of stages that is thought to influence some social behavior. The second framework, based upon the additive-factors method, makes no assumptions about the nature of the constituent stages of a social process. It is possible, however, that one might design an experiment using one framework, but interpret the obtained data using another. For example, even though the logic of the subtractive method may have been used to construct the conditions in a multifactor experiment, the logic of the additive-factors method could be used to search for possible differences in processing stages should no apparent differences be obtained on the verbal or behavioral outcome variable of interest (e.g., recall, percentage of correct responses on a task, attitude change). Alternatively, if differences between two conditions emerge on the outcome variable of interest, then the logic of the subtractive method may be invoked to help interpret the significance of the accompanying psychophysiological data. Hence, these analytic frameworks serve as complementing heuristic aids.

The Comparison of n with n − 1 Stages: The Subtractive Method

At the simplest level, experimental design begins with an experimental and a control condition. The experimental condition represents the presence of some factor, and the control condition represents the absence of this factor. The experimental factor might be selected because it is theoretically believed to harbor *n* stages of a social process; the construction of the control condition, on the other hand, is guided theoretically to incorporate *n* − 1 stages of the social process, and hence to yield a different impact on social cognition (e.g., attitudes) or behavior (e.g., supportive action).

The principle underlying the inclusion of physiological measures in these designs is that the physiological character, or "markers," of the various constituent stages of a social process might be deduced through the systematic application of the procedure of stage deletion. Thus, this approach is sometimes termed the "subtractive method" (Donders, 1868). If, for example, differences in performance result when individuals perform a task while observed versus unobserved, then the presence of an observer can be conceived as introducing one or more additional processing stages. If a theory including this stage or stages is posited to explain people's performances, then comparison conditions can be constructed and physiological measures obtained to determine the physiological markers of this and each of the accompanying processing stages.

When, in a subsequent study, one of these stages is thought to be responsible for the differential impact of two conditions on behavior (e.g., in a study of social influence), then analyses of the concomitant physiological activity can again be informative, in one of two ways.

1. If the patterns of physiological activity resulting from the isolation of presumably identical stages are dissimilar, then the similarity of the stages is challenged, even though there may be similarities between the subsequent behavioral outcomes. The greater the evidence from multiple operationalizations that a particular stage is accompanied by a specific profile of physiological responses across the ranges of the stimuli employed in the investigations, the more challenging is the dissimilarity in obtained physiological profiles (i.e., the failure of this template matching when two possibly similar stages are isolated and compared).

2. If, on the other hand, the patterns of physiological activity resulting from the isolation of these presumably identical stages of processing are similar, then convergent evidence is obtained that the same fundamental stage is a part of both processes, although these data do not prove that the stages are the same. The more peculiar the physiological profile is to a given stage within a particular experimental context, however, the greater the value of the convergent evidence conferred. Monitoring phasic changes in skin resistance alone, for example, provides weak convergent evidence for a particular psychological stage, since it is characteristic of so many divergent stages (e.g., see Schwartz & Shapiro, 1973).

There are two additional concerns that should be considered when using this framework to investigate an elementary stage of a social process. First, the subtractive method contains the implicit assumption that a stage can be inserted or deleted without changing the nature of the other constituent stages. But this method has long been criticized for ignoring the possibility that manipulating a factor to insert or delete a processing stage might introduce a completely different processing structure (Külpe, 1895). This problem can be attenuated by using multiple operationalizations to insert or delete a stage. If each operational insertion or deletion of a stage alters the processing structure of the task differently, then no distinctive features attributable to the conceptual processing stage of interest should be observed across operationalizations, and alternative experimental operations and means for isolating the stage will have to be devised.

Parametric studies of a processing stage can also provide important information about the range over which a stage is manifested as a particular physiological profile, thereby improving an investigator's ability to generate appropriate comparison conditions and predictions, and to draw clear interpretations. A failure to find the same profile of physiological response across a wide range of levels of a social stimulus believed to invoke a given processing stage does not in itself indicate whether a new stage is invoked or whether the old stage is manifested differently within the organism at various levels of stimulation; it *does* clearly indicate an important limitation when one is interpreting the physiological profile obtained in a subsequent study of this processing stage. As Donchin (1982) suggests, "each hypothesis so tested generates predictions for its own specific range of validity. The observed relations may or may not be universally applicable" (p. 460).

Second, in order to construct the set of comparison tasks using the subtractive method, one must already have a clearly articulated hypothesis about the sequence of events that transpires between stimulus and overt response. This assumption renders the subtractive method particularly useful in testing an existing theory about the stages constituting a social process and in determining whether a given stage is among the set constituting two separate social processes. Note, however, that confirmatory evidence can still be questioned by the assertion that the addition or deletion of a particular stage results in an essentially different set of stages. Again, the inclusion of several experimental and comparison tasks (i.e., multiple operationalizations) appears to be the judicious action regarding this criticism, which can always be applied and can never be disproven (cf. Pachella, 1974).

The subtractive method can also yield data that is helpful in deriving comprehensive, empirically based models of the foundations of social processes. Again, assume that the comparison is between experimental conditions with differential impacts on behavior as a function of some social stimulus. If the physiological profile that differentiates these conditions is similar to a distinctive physiological profile that has been found previously to characterize a particular processing stage, then the possibility is raised that the same processing stage has been detected in another context, although one cannot logically conclude that this stage has definitely been detected. The stronger and more distinctive the link between a physiological profile and a processing stage within the ranges of stimuli employed, however, the stronger this possibility. Finally, if other (e.g., behavioral) sources of converging evidence are also obtained in the experiment or from subsequent experimental research, then the plausibility of this inference is enhanced. Similarly, if the sequence of physiological activity differentiating two conditions can be modeled by concatenating the physiological responses found previously to characterize even more rudimentary types or stages of a social process, then a model of a set of stages distinguishing these two conditions would be suggested, though certainly not confirmed. Again, converging evidence for this empirically derived model could be marshaled from other (e.g., observational, verbal) measures obtained in the experiment and from subsequent experimental studies. Monitoring incipient somatic activity at sites that have been associated with distinctive dimensions of information processing (e.g., affective, linguistic) in a persuasion experiment, for example, does not guarantee that these types of processes are reflected in the activity at the respective recording sites (e.g., corrugator or zygomatic muscle regions, perioral muscle region), but it does potentiate a more informative assessment than is provided by relying solely upon self-reports and/or subsequent behavioral measures (Cacioppo & Petty, 1981a).

Generating Candidates for Stages: The Additive-Factors Method

An analytic framework adapted from the additive-factors method for isolating stages of informational flow (Sternberg, 1969; see reviews, critiques, and suggestions by Pachella, 1974; A. F. Sanders, 1980; Schweickert, 1980) is particularly helpful in conceptualizing the potential set and sequence of stages constituting a social process when one is (1) designing a study with no strong *a priori* notion of what the constituent stages might be, or (2) interpreting psychophysiological data from conditions that yield similar results on the verbal or behavioral measure of interest (e.g., performance, aggression, attitude change). The basic assumption of this analytic framework, like that underlying the subtractive method, is that the recording interval during which a given social process unfolds is filled with a sequence of independent processing stages. Each stage receives the input from a previous step and performs a particular transformation on this input before passing it on to the next stage of the sequence. Differences in the output of a stage are interpreted as possibly being due to differences in the input from the preceding stage, which in turn can derive from either a different input to the inaugural stage or a different set of preceding stages. Thus, a stage is assumed to perform a constant function (e.g., informational transformation), regardless of the nature or duration of the stages preceding or following it.

Recall that the operational definition of a "stage" that we have adopted structures the social process such that (1) all the stages of a social process are executed in a sequence (although concurrent operations may be executed within a processing stage—cf. A. F. Sanders, 1980)[2]; and (2) each stage has an impact on physiological, verbal, and/or behavioral responses (otherwise, it has yet to qualify as a processing stage). The psychophysiological profile obtained during a social process is viewed simply as the aggregate of the profiles characterizing each constituent stage plus noise (e.g., measurement error, individual differences, irrelevant physiological processes).

Several interesting propositions can be derived from these assumptions. First, if the manipulation of an independent variable affects a specific processing stage with physiological manifestations, then the aggregate of the physiological profiles is expected to change accordingly. Second, if two (or more) independent variables affect different processing stages, each with physiological manifestations, then the independent variables are expected to produce independent effects on physiological activity. Finally, if two (or more) independent variables modify each other's effects on a processing stage (or set of stages), then the independent variables are expected to contribute interactively to the profile of physiological activity. Thus, the effect of the experimental factors on psy-

---

2. Schweickert (1980) has discussed a method for identifying the separate paths of concurrent processes using reaction times, but application of his concept of "critical-path scheduling" is beyond the scope of the present chapter.

tasks whose correct response is not dominant for the performer). The term "social facilitation" came to be used generically to refer to the facilitatory and inhibitory effects of conspecifics on task performance.

Mere Presence and Arousal

Zajonc (1965) based his analysis upon the notion that the mere presence of conspecifics increases an organism's level of general drive, which in the Hull–Spence formulation (Spence, 1956) increases the likelihood of the performer's emitting the dominant response to a task. Zajonc suggested that the mechanism by which the presence of others increases a person's general level of drive is physiological arousal. Zajonc (1965) acknowledged, however, that his postulate about the underlying physiological mechanism was a speculation based primarily on a few studies of the effects of population density on the secretion of adrenal corticosteroids in animals. More recently, Zajonc (1980a) has suggested that the presence of conspecifics introduces more uncertainty into the situation, and that increased physiological arousal and drive are innate responses to uncertainty. Zajonc has maintained throughout that it is "the *mere* presence of others that is the sufficient condition bringing these effects about" (Zajonc, 1980a, p. 38).

This formulation led to a spate of research (e.g., see recent reviews by Borden, 1980; Geen & Gange, 1977; Moore & Baron, 1983; G. S. Sanders, 1981; Zajonc, 1980a). In a demonstrative study, Zajonc and Sales (1966) presented lists of words to subjects, whose task it was to identify each word as it was presented. Some of the words were presented repeatedly, whereas others were infrequently presented. This was done to manipulate the habit strength associated with each word. Zajonc and Sales (1966), who were working within the Hullian model of "response potential = drive $\times$ habit," then asked subjects to identify which word was presented tachistoscopically; some subjects were observed and others were not. In fact, no word was actually presented to subjects on the tachistoscope, but Zajonc and Sales found, as they had expected, that subjects who were observed during this task reported seeing words with high habit strength (i.e., those seen frequently before the pseudorecognition task) more frequently and words with low habit strength less frequently than did subjects working alone. Other behavioral investigations have found that the physical presence of an observer (1) interferes with short-term recall in paired-associate learning but aids long-term recall; (2) improves performance on simple tasks and impairs the initial performance on complex tasks; and (3) facilitates rather than inhibits task performance following practice and mastery of these tasks (Geen & Gange, 1977).

Physiological responses have been monitored in only a few of these experiments, and the most popular physiological measure has been palmar sweating, obtained using either the palmar sweat index (which provides a rough indication of the number of active sweat glands at the finger tips; see Dabbs, Johnson, & Leventhal, 1968) or the sweat bottle technique (which involves measuring the conductivity of distilled water following the immersion of the hand in it for a few seconds; see Strahan, Todd, & Inglis, 1974). These measures are somewhat crude, but they have revealed increased palmar sweating immediately before or following the task in just over half of the published studies in which it has been obtained (cf. Geen, 1980; Moore & Baron, 1983).

Geen (1977) provides an illustrative experiment. Eighty female subjects performed a set of eight difficult anagrams. Subjects performed the task either alone or while being observed by the experimenter. Of those being observed, some were told that the experimenter was watching "in order to evaluate the subject's task performance" (p. 715); others were told that the observations were being made "so that the experimenter would have a basis for advising the subject on ways to improve performance on a subsequent task" (p. 715); and still others were not told anything about the reason for the experimenter's observations. Time to solve the anagrams and change in palmar sweating from before to after the task served as the dependent measures. Geen found that subjects performed the task fastest when working unobserved, next fastest when observed by a "helpful" experimenter, and slowest when observed by an evaluative or unexplained experimenter. Palmar sweating was affected similarly, with the highest levels found when an evaluative observer was present and the lowest levels exhibited when no observer was present.

The physical versus concealed (but acknowledged) presence of an observer has seldom been manipulated in the same experiment. Instead, in the majority of the experiments documenting increased palmar sweating prior to the task, observers have been in the test situation with the subject (e.g., Carver & Scheier, 1981; Droppleman & McNair, 1971; Martens, 1969a, 1969b, 1969c); conversely, in the majority of the studies failing to find greater palmar sweating, observers have been concealed (Bargh & Cohen, 1978; Cohen, 1979; Cohen & Davis, 1973). In the only study in which palmar sweating was monitored before and *during* the performance of a task (copying German prose), the presence of an observer (the experimenter), who was seated clearly in view several feet in front of the subject, resulted in more palmar sweating prior to the onset of the task, but slightly less palmar sweating during the performance of the task (Carver & Scheier, 1981).

In a study in which several measures of autonomic activity were monitored, Geen (1979) gave subjects success or failure feedback on a preliminary task, which they performed either alone or while being observed by the experimenter, who was standing several feet behind them. Next, subjects performed a difficult paired-associates learning task. Subjects who were observed during the preliminary task were again observed, and those who completed the preliminary task alone performed the paired-associates task unobserved. Geen found that subjects who were with an observer performed more poorly on the difficult paired-associates task and displayed more spontaneous skin resistance responses (SSRRs) following failure feedback than did subjects who received failure feedback but performed the tasks alone; no differences were observed on the measures of HR or maximum skin conductance level (SCL), however. Whether subjects were observed or alone had no effect on performance or on either physiological measure when subjects had received success feedback following the preliminary task.

SCL and HR have been monitored simultaneously in similar experiments employing tasks ranging from listening to a persuasive communication (Borden, Hendrick, & Walker, 1976) to a pseudorecognition task (Henchy & Glass, 1968) and a reaction time task (Moore, 1977). In each of these investigations, the presence of observers failed to influence SCL or tonic HR. Kissel (1965), who only monitored SCL, found that it was actually lower when subjects worked on four insoluble tasks in the presence of a friend (who was working on an unrelated task in the same room) than when subjects worked on the insoluble tasks alone or in the presence of a stranger. The SCLs of subjects in these latter conditions did not differ significantly; this finding replicates those of Geen (1979), Borden et al. (1976), Henchy and Glass (1968), and Moore (1977), all of whom employed strangers rather than friends (see also Shapiro & Leiderman, 1967; Shapiro, Leiderman, & Morningstar, 1964).[4]

The influence of observers on forehead (frontalis region) electromyogram (EMG) activity has been examined in at least three other experiments (cf. Moore

& Baron, 1983). In two studies, subjects were placed in a supine position and were instructed to keep their eyes open while listening to a recording of a humorous (Chapman, 1972; cf. Chapman, 1973) or mystery (Chapman, 1974) story. Wallerstein (1954) had previously found that attentive listening to recorded stories caused forehead tension to increase, and Chapman replicated this effect. Furthermore, Chapman (1974) varied whether or not the subject was observed, and in the latter condition whether the observer was physically present or concealed. He found that subjects exhibited steeper forehead EMG gradients when observers were either present or concealed than when subjects listened to a story unobserved. There was also a nonsignificant tendency for the physically present observer to evoke higher levels of forehead EMG activity than did the concealed observer. In another study, Musante and Anker (1972) instructed subjects that their task was to inhibit all movements when three tones were sounded. Subjects were then exposed to the tones either while the experimenter watched or while alone. Under these conditions, Musante and Anker (1972) observed lower levels of forehead EMG activity following the tones when in the presence of another than when alone.

These physiological data have been somewhat difficult to characterize, for the following reasons: (1) No study has been designed specifically to isolate the elementary stages of the process underlying the effects on performance of being observed; (2) few studies have simultaneously recorded multiple measures of physiological activity; (3) no study has reported the intermeasure correlations between physiological and performance variables[5]; and (4) most studies have been conducted under the assumption that one physiological measure is as good as another (or several) when indexing physiological activity. Nevertheless, these studies do not support the conception that the behavioral effects of being observed are mediated by general physiological or autonomic arousal (cf. Vanderwolf & Robinson, 1981). Furthermore, no study has ever explicitly tested Zajonc's (1965) original speculation that the mere presence of others influences behavior through its effects on adrenocortical activity. Indeed, the adrenomedullary complex, which is innervated by and affects the sympathetic branch of the autonomic nervous system, appears a more likely candidate for the underlying physiological mechanism of

---

4. A few additional studies are tangentially relevant to the present discussion. In an unpublished study, Shapiro (cited in Schwartz & Shapiro, 1973) periodically recorded the skin potential level of subjects during a 15-min rest period, which they knew would be followed by a simple task. Schwartz and Shapiro (1973) note that "these subjects were known to each other, not friends but costudents in a nursing school" (p. 400). Some subjects were seated alone, and others were seated in groups of three. Subjects in triads were asked to refrain from interacting, though they were in visual contact with one another. Shapiro found larger decrements in skin potential level in subjects who anticipated the task in the presence of others rather than alone—a result reminiscent of Kissel's (1965; see also Back & Bogdonoff, 1964). Finally, Latane and Cappell (1972), who monitored only HR, found that solitary rats exhibited higher HRs when a conspecific was temporarily placed in the openfield situation with them. However, if the placement of another rat in the situation increased the somatic activity of the subject, then the increased HR could be attributable to the increased somatic activity of the subject, rather than the physical presence of a conspecific (see Obrist, 1976, 1981).

5. In one of the few related studies in which a physiological index and performance were correlated, Church (1962) tested 92 subjects in a simple reaction time task under competitive and noncompetitive testing conditions. Church found that subjects responded more quickly, reported being more alert, and exhibited higher SCLs when tested under competitive conditions. These measures were not correlated, however. "Put simply, the physiology does not seem to 'mediate' the overt performance, while both are separately affected by the nature of the social setting" (Schwartz & Shapiro, 1973, p. 399).

"social facilitation effects" than the hypothalamic–pituitary–adrenal cortex axis posited by Zajonc (1965). Zajonc based his speculations upon evidence that crowded conditions in animal colonies lead to increased secretion of adrenocortical steroids. But the actions of the hypothalamic–pituitary–adrenal cortex mechanism are tonic rather than phasic: The physiological and behavioral effects of adrenocortical steroids are slow to develop, are slow to dissipate, and operate primarily to increase an organism's *readiness* for energy expenditure ("arousability") rather than present activity at sympathetically innervated effectors (Zillmann, 1984). The release of catecholamines (i.e., epinephrine) from the adrenomedullary complex, on the other hand, occurs more quickly in response to a stimulus, has been associated with psychological stressors (in contrast to norepinephrine, which has been associated more with physical stressors), contributes to elevated activity in the sympathetic nervous system, and dissipates within a short period of time. As Zillmann (1984) has noted,

> . . . the level of adrenomedullary activity may vary quasi-tonically throughout the day (rising during work periods and declining during recumbency . . .), the energizing hyperglycemic effect of medullary secretion is essentially phasic. Generally speaking, the energy supplied is absorbed by one episode of vigorous, strenuous action—or by just a few such episodes at the most. (p. 112)

No published study has explicitly addressed the notion that the presence of others affects the phasic actions of the adrenomedullary system or of the hypothalamic–pituitary–adrenal cortex mechanism. Nevertheless, what is known at present about the behavioral effects of these endocrinological mechanisms points to the adrenomedullary system as more likely than the hypothalamic–pituitary–adrenal cortex system to be involved in producing the short-latency behavioral effects observed in social facilitation research. Consistent with this reasoning, Singer, Lundberg, and Frankenhaeuser (1978) found that perceptions of control were related to catecholamine response to crowding on commuter trains.

Reconsideration

The behavioral data that have accrued since Zajonc's (1965) conceptualization of "social facilitation" have also led to a spate of theoretical work. A number of alternative explanations have now been proposed to account for the inhibitory and excitatory effects of observers, including learned drive (Cottrell, 1972), a modified conception of learned drive (Geen, 1980; Weiss & Miller, 1971), objective self-awareness (Duval & Wicklund, 1972), distraction/conflict (Baron, Moore, & Sanders, 1978; G. S. Sanders, 1981), self-presentation (Bond, 1982; Borden, 1980), self-consciousness (Carver & Scheier, 1981), and in-

hibition of overt practice (Berger, Carli, Garcia, & Brady, 1982; Berger, Hamptom, Carli, Grandmaison, Sadow, Donath, & Herschlag, 1981). Moreover, the notion that the mere presence of conspecifics is sufficient to produce these behavioral effects by enhancing drive remains a fundamental postulate in several of these formulations (Markus, 1981; Zajonc, 1980). Do the accumulated physiological data do anything more than question Zajonc's (1965) initial speculations regarding the physiological mechanism underlying the facilitatory and inhibitory effects of observed performances? We believe so. Since most of these models do not make or differ in their psychophysiological predictions, we do not begin this analysis with any preconceptions regarding the component processing stages that may emerge from a reconsideration of the accumulated physiological data in light of the heuristics outlined above (see the discussion of analytic frameworks).

To begin with, recall that although the presence of an observer was not found to affect HR, it was found that palmar sweating and time to perform a difficult task were greatest when an observer was described as evaluative, moderate in levels when the observer was described as watching in order to offer helpful suggestions later, and least when there was no observer present during task performance (Geen, 1977). Consider also the conceptually similar finding that SSRRs and errors on a difficult task were more frequent when the subject was observed performing a task associated with failure than when the subject was alone or observed performing a task associated with success, and that measures from these latter two conditions did not differ (Geen, 1979). These experimental conditions, when viewed as converging operations yielding similar physiological results, suggest a fundamental stage in social facilitation. In adducing the characteristics of this stage, it is of interest to note that "EDA responds to threatening stimuli, that this response is not attributable to somatic activity, and that—at least in many cases—HR does not respond to these stimuli" (Fowles, 1980, p. 93). Katkin and his colleagues (Hirschman & Katkin, 1971; Katkin, 1965, 1966, 1975; Rappaport & Katkin, 1972), for example, report finding that "the creation of psychologically stressful situations results in a substantial increase in the frequency of spontaneous electrodermal responses" (Masling, Price, Goldband, & Katkin, 1981, p. 396). The link between the EDRs and the punitive consequences of a stimulus is unlikely to be invariant (e.g., novel stimuli also elicit EDRs; cf. Venables & Christie, 1980), and the appearance of the consequence (e.g., SCRs, SSRRs) does not prove the presence of the antecedent (threats of punishment). The link between EDRs under similar conditions (e.g., Block, 1981; Masling *et al.*, 1981; Szpiler & Epstein, 1976) simply raises the possibility that the processing stage invoked by the introduction of an observer gauges the potential punitive consequences aroused by this intrusion upon the organism's environment. The characterization of this processing stage as threat assessment gains plausibility only when consideration is given to the nature of the experimental conditions that led to these and related physiological results (e.g., Kissel, 1965, concerning SCL and the presence of friends vs. strangers; Fowles, 1982, concerning HR and positive incentives). It seems more plausible, for example, that the presence of an evaluative experimenter is more threatening but no more novel to a subject than the presence of an experimenter who is observing a subject's performance in order to be helpful. Moreover, the finding that an experimenter who simply watched subjects perform had the same physiological and behavioral effects as an observer who was explicitly described as being evaluative suggests that observers in an experimental context are assumed to be evaluative (Geen, 1977).

The palmar sweating data associated with the salience of the observer, on the other hand, may simply illustrate the limitation of inferring processing stages from insensitive physiological data. The notion of an early threat assessment stage in social facilitation leads to an expectation regarding the effects of concealed versus unconcealed observers: The more threatening the observer, the clearer the physiological effects should be, and the stronger the behavioral effects should be. Thus, the presence of the observer may serve as a weaker manipulation affecting the same processing stage as the description of the observer as evaluative versus helpful.

The data are not in complete accord with this expectation. Palmar sweating was generally higher and facilitatory–inhibitory behavioral effects were obtained when a subject performed a task while observed by someone present rather than while alone. However, no differences in palmar sweating were generally obtained (even though the behavioral effects emerged) when subjects performed the task while being watched by a concealed observer rather than while alone. There are two obvious but very different interpretations for these results: (1) Given that the patterns of physiological activity resulting from the isolation of what are presumably identical processing stages appear dissimilar, one might conclude that the processing stages are, in fact, dissimilar. (2) Alternatively, the experimental conditions may have isolated different levels of the same processing stage, but the physiological "index" for gradations in the processing stage may have been insensitive or invalid across this range (see pp. 655–656).[6]

6. The same argument applies to the inconsistent results regarding SCLs. Nonspecific fluctuations and electrodermal levels are viewed as being relatively independent (Katkin, 1965; Szpiler & Epstein, 1976). In reviewing these data, however, Fowles (1980) suggested that SCL may simply be less sensitive: "[I]t seems more likely that electrodermal level is inconsistently related to anticipation of punishment because of peripheral physiological limitations" (p. 95).

Which interpretation is to be favored? Unlike the first, the second interpretation hinges on the assumption that because of the gross nature of the palmar sweating index, small differences induced by the (less threatening) presence of a concealed (in contrast to unconcealed) observer may not have been noticeable. That is, palmar sweating, which reflects surface sweating on the palms, may not have been a sufficiently sensitive index to gauge small but behaviorally significant changes in perceived threat. Two additional predictions follow uniquely from the second explanation: (1) More sensitive physiological measures should differentiate the conditions where subjects were observed by an unconcealed versus concealed observer; and (2) social facilitation effects should be stronger when the observer is unconcealed than concealed.

In an experiment pertinent to the former hypothesis, Chapman (1974) monitored forehead EMG activity as subjects listened to a story while unobserved, watched by a concealed observer, or watched by an unconcealed observer. As would be expected if palmar sweating were simply insensitive to subtle differences in the potential punitive consequences aroused by the observer, Chapman found forehead EMG activity to be higher during the story when the subject was observed than when unobserved, and slightly though not significantly higher when the observer was present than when concealed.

Whether an observer is concealed or not has not generally been viewed as informative, since the facilitatory or inhibitory effects of being observed have emerged in both instances (Markus, 1978; cf. Geen, 1980). Unfortunately, no performance data were provided by Chapman (1974), and it is uncertain from the existing psychophysiological studies whether the behavioral effects on performance would be strengthened if a physically present observer were contrasted with a concealed observer. Several experiments, however, provide tentative evidence for a related prediction: that the "attentiveness" of an observer influences the behavioral effects of observed performances. Strube, Miles, and Finch (1981) recorded the running speed of joggers who were in the presence of an attentive or an inattentive observer. They found that the joggers with an attentive observer ran around the track more quickly than did the joggers with an inattentive observer. In another study, subjects performed a pseudorecognition task alone, in the presence of two inattentive and blindfolded persons, or in the presence of two observers (Cottrell, Wack, Sekerak, & Rittle, 1968). Subjects in the presence of the blindfolded observers performed similarly to the subjects who were alone, whereas subjects in the presence of observers reported seeing stimuli with higher habit strength than those in the other conditions. Finally, Cohen and Davis (1973) taught subjects to solve hidden-word problems in a particular manner and then shifted the test items so that a more efficient problem-solving strategy became available.

Subjects in some of the conditions in their experiment performed the task unobserved or while being watched through a one-way mirror by nonevaluative or evaluative observers. Cohen and Davis (1973) found that the concealed observer described as being evaluative inhibited subjects most from finding this new problem-solving strategy, that the concealed but less evaluative observer inhibited subjects less often, and that unobserved subjects were the most likely to find the more efficient problem-solving strategy (see also Henchy & Glass, 1968; Sasfy & Okun, 1974). At present, therefore, parsimony would appear to favor the adduction from these data of one stage, which functions to gauge the potential punitive consequences aroused by the introduction of a conspecific.

The remaining physiological data suggest a second processing stage bearing upon energy expenditure (e.g., efforts to emit socially valued behaviors for personal advancement within the group). The existence of this second processing stage is suggested by the experiments in which somatic activity was monitored. Chapman's (1973, 1974) experiments, for instance, demonstrated that a somatic response previously found to covary with the performance of a task (listening to a story) was found to be of greater magnitude when the subject was observed than when not observed. Moreover, Musante and Anker (1972) provided evidence that when trying harder to perform a task meant relaxing a specific muscle region, then the one somatic measure obtained (frontalis EMG) was lower when the subject was observed than when not observed. Finally, the somatic changes obtained by Chapman (1973, 1974) and Musante and Anker (1972) were exhibited at the onset of the task rather than in anticipation of the task; this result further suggests that the presence of the observer affects how hard subjects strive to perform a specific behavior, rather than how tense or generally aroused they become. Thus, this processing stage may not reflect a change in the generalized drive (see criticisms of this concept by Bond, 1982; Zillmann, 1984), but rather a stage of effortful striving, based in heightened sympathetic activity and catecholamine circulation, that fosters short-term demands for vigorous activity (e.g., fight, flight, or task performance). In other words, it is possible that the presence of observers heightens sympathetic tonus and efforts to deal with sometimes conflicting environmental demands.[7] Evidence that the underlying processing stage may be better characterized as "effortful striving" than as generalized drive is provided by several recent experiments (e.g., Bond, 1982; Groff, Baron, & Moore, 1983). For example, Bond (1982) found that subjects who were observed performed better on difficult tasks embedded within the context of simple tasks when observed than when unobserved, whereas subjects performed simple tasks embedded in a pool of difficult tasks more poorly when observed than when unobserved. Note, too, that given both the timing of the physiological changes (see also Carver & Scheier, 1981) and the nature of threat assessment and effortful striving, it seems reasonable to suggest that (1) these two stages have a special propensity for combining, and (2) the decision regarding the potential punitive consequence (or threat) aroused by the presence of the observer precedes and influences the mobilization of temporary energy resources (i.e., effortful striving).[8]

Finally, although these stages have been derived from research that typically appears under the rubric of "social facilitation," the ultimate value of the application of psychophysiological research to social processes lies in the identification of the finite set of fundamental stages that exist in various combinations to yield a wide range of social processes. Thus, the present stages are assumed to be among the total set of elementary building blocks that make up other social processes, such as social inhibition. It is of interest, therefore, that Latane, Williams, and Harkins (1979) found that subjects expended more physical effort (i.e., clapped and shouted more loudly) when they believed that they were personally accountable for their performance; if the presence of others made it possible to diffuse the responsibility for their performance, then each individual's personal efforts declined. Petty, Harkins, Williams, and Latane (1977) found that this effect applied to cognitive as well as physical efforts. Are the preceding stages involved in producing this social inhibition? There are no experiments on social inhibition to our knowledge that have included psychophysiological measures, but if social inhibition (i.e., individuals expending less effort to perform a task) emerges at least in part as a result of the presence of conspecifics' lowering the potential punitive consequences for a performer, psychophysiological research on this issue may prove interesting (e.g., diffusion of responsibility would be expected to be associated with lower levels of SSRRs).

Summary

The proposed stages of the social process described above are undeniably crude, but their derivation should serve to illustrate the application of psychophysiological procedures to delineate the building blocks of social processes. Moreover, these stages provide a starting point from which to construct com-

---

7. This processing stage may correspond to the excitatory component in Zillmann's (1983, 1984) three-factor theory of emotion.

8. The wording used here is not meant to suggest that subjects are aware of either stage. That is, subjects are not viewed as *necessarily* being consciously involved in, or able to report on, their decision regarding the threat value of an observer or their allocation of effort to emit socially valued behaviors. Indeed, it seems more probable to us that human subjects will be able to provide verbal data that are products of rather than first-hand reports on these processing stages, whereas these processes in subhuman species may be evident in a more primitive form (cf. Uetz et al., 1982).

parison conditions (e.g., concealed vs. unconcealed observers) and select physiological measures (e.g., task-relevant and task-irrelevant EMG, SCRs, SCL, and/or SSRRs) in future research.

It is somewhat encouraging, nevertheless, that behavioral predictions can be derived from the analysis of the existing psychophysiological data (e.g., regarding concealed vs. unconcealed observers), and that the various competing models of social facilitation are compatible with the existence of the stages that have been derived. Some of the current formulations suggest that the presence of conspecifics has an innate threat value (Markus, 1981; Zajonc, 1980); others suggest that this threat value is learned (Cottrell, 1972); and still others suggest that what has been learned is that the presence of others in specific conditions poses a threat (e.g., Geen, 1981). There are existing formulations that emphasize the role played by the stage of threat assessment (e.g., evaluation apprehension), others that emphasize the stage of effortful striving (e.g., drive conceptions), and still others that straddle the two (e.g., self-presentation).

Indeed, in light of recent controversies in the area (cf. Geen, 1981; Markus, 1981; G. S. Sanders, 1981), psychophysiological studies may help distinguish between operational and conceptual differences among theories. For example, Zajonc, Heingarner, and Herman (1969) demonstrated that the photophobic cockroach (*Blatta orientalis*) runs a simple maze more quickly and a complex maze more slowly when conspecifics are present and the context is punitive (i.e., when the maze is illuminated). They suggested that the presence of conspecifics is innately threatening. Of course, this study, while interesting, cannot be taken as evidence that the presence of conspecifics is *always* threatening, arousing, or energizing. Ethological research on territorial instincts clearly suggests that the presence of conspecifics is innately threatening only within specific environmental contexts (e.g., during feeding).

The observations by Uetz, Kane, and Stratton (1982) of the normally inhospitable spider (*Metepeira spinipes*) provide a case in point. Spiders share the part of the web that forms the suprastructure (i.e., the "space web") for their individual retreats and prey-catching spirals. These spiders individually reconstruct their sticky prey-catching spirals daily, whereas they work cooperatively, though not daily, to maintain the communal space web. Uetz *et al.* (1982) found that these spiders adjusted group size and territorial distances to match the availability of valued resources (i.e., foodstuff). For example, they found that the distance to the nearest conspecific within a colony was correlated ($r = -.97$) with the availability of prey. When they manipulated the availability of prey (e.g., by moving the colony, or by attracting prey to the area of the colony), the spiders adjusted this nearest-neighbor distance. Uetz *et al.* (1982) concluded,

The combination of solitary and communal behavior exhibited by this species suggests that it represents an intermediate stage in the evolution of social behavior in spiders. . . . the advantages of group living—exploitation of habitats free of competing species, increased prey capture efficiency, architectual stability of webs, and so on—would usually outweigh the advantages gained by maintaining maximum distances from conspecifics at the cost of aggressive behavior. (p. 542)

Finally, the various demonstrations that more cogitative threats can be posed by humans (e.g., embarrassment, evaluation apprehension) and can produce facilitatory or inhibitory effects on performance should come as no surprise, given humans' greater capacity to learn, employ symbols, and make controlled assessments of impending threats.

Attitude Formation, Maintenance, and Change

The concept of "attitude" has long been central to disciplines within the social sciences, including social psychology (e.g., Allport, 1935; McGuire, 1969), clinical and counseling psychology (Corrigan, Dell, Lewis, & Schmidt, 1980; Strong, 1978), political science (e.g., Oskamp, 1977; Tursky & Jamner, 1983), communications (e.g., Roloff & Miller, 1980; M. J. Smith, 1982), and consumer behavior and marketing (Kassarjian & Robertson, 1981). There are perhaps more social-psychophysiological studies dealing with attitudes and attitude change than any other topic. Unlike the situation in social facilitation research, verbal rather than behavioral measures have been the more common outcome variable in attitude studies. An exhaustive survey of this research is not attempted here, although interested readers may wish to consult reviews of this literature in Cacioppo and Petty (1983b) and Waid (1984). Our aim in this section is to provide descriptions of the psychophysiological data pertaining to a few of the distinctive processing stages in attitude change.

An "attitude" represents a general and enduring favorable or unfavorable feeling about a person, object, or issue. Ever since Thurstone (1928) developed the first attitude scale, attitude measurement techniques have tended to focus on the assessment of a general evaluation of, or affective reaction to, a stimulus. For example, the respected scaling techniques of Thurstone (1928), Likert (1932), and Guttman (1944), as well as the more popular and contemporary semantic differential (Osgood, Suci, & Tannenbaum, 1957) and single-item rating scales, are all designed to gauge how much one likes or dislikes, promotes or detracts from, or feels generally favorable or unfavorable toward a stimulus (cf. Cacioppo, Harkins, & Petty, 1981).

Different theories of attitude formation, maintenance, and change postulate different intervening processes between intitial exposure to some attitude-relevant stimulus (e.g., a persuasive message) and the subsequent attitudinal response (e.g., resistance, yielding; see Petty & Cacioppo, 1981, for a review). Only recently, however, have psychophysiological procedures been applied to the study of the underlying attitudinal processes. Psychophysiological investigations designed to measure attitudes are far more common than those designed to explore attitudinal processes. The rationale for searching for a psychophysiological index of attitudes is the understandable concern that people may not report their true attitudes, either because they are not aware of how they really feel or because they are not willing to disclose these feelings (Cook & Selltiz, 1964). Although these studies in and of themselves are not particularly informative about the rudimentary processes underlying attitude formation, maintenance, and change, they do furnish data about the physiological response profiles characterizing an elementary component of these processes—namely, affective (i.e., favorable–unfavorable) reactions.

Initially, one may think that the affective reaction *is* the attitude or the fundamental process underlying attitude formation and change. After all, attitude development and change are conceived of as involving the arousal of new positive or negative feelings about the attitude stimulus. This conceptualization, however, simply suggests that an affective reaction is *a* fundamental stage in attitude development and change; it does not mean that other stages are not involved. That is, the notion of a general feeling of liking or disliking accompanied by bodily responses (i.e., an affective reaction) should not be viewed as synonymous with the notion of an attitude. Consider a person whose attitude toward some object was developed long ago and has not undergone change recently (e.g., an attitude toward one's favorite Bogart movie or one's first love). It is conceivable that should this person be asked to indicate his or her attitude toward the object, the person would not have to re-experience the feelings once associated with it; recalling the evaluation of the object should be sufficient. The individual might even recall that he or she had once felt a strong affection for the object, but this memory could be accessed without also accessing (or re-experiencing) these feelings. In these instances, the attitude is akin to a bit of knowledge regarding one's evaluation of the object, rather than to a nonspecific feeling of liking or disliking accompanied by bodily responses. In sum, then, it seems reasonable that most attitudes are maintained as general beliefs or memories of one's evaluations of and affective reactions to stimuli, rather than in the form of affective reactions per se. In this way, people can hold many attitudes simultaneously (which they must in this complex world if attitudes endure), even though they cannot possibly maintain as many feelings (affects) simultaneously as they retain attitudes.

One important implication of this distinction is that psychophysiological assessments designed to tap the affective "roots" of an attitude may generally be insensitive (cf. Cacioppo & Sandman, 1981; Petty & Cacioppo, 1983), unless a physiological index of an evaluative belief is formed artificially—for instance, through semantic conditioning (cf. Tursky & Jamner, 1983). Second, attitude development and change may involve a stage representing an affective reaction, but, depending upon the antecedent conditions, this stage may be preceded by others, such as the instigation and reduction of cognitive dissonance (Fazio *et al.*, 1977; Festinger, 1957) or fear (Janis & Feshbach, 1953; Leventhal, 1970); by attention, comprehension, and cognitive elaboration (Cacioppo & Petty, 1981a; Petty & Cacioppo, 1981); or by surprisingly little else (Wilson, 1979). As in the discussion of observed versus unobserved performance, it is assumed that the various theories of attitude formation, maintenance, and change can ultimately be viewed as unique subsets and sequences of a finite number of elementary stages in which these particular stages may be included.

Affective Reactions

In one of the earliest studies relevant to our search for physiological profiles of affective reactions, Dysinger (1931) monitored SRRs as subjects were exposed to words that varied in the pleasantness ratings they elicited (cf. McCurdy, 1950). Dysinger found that the SRRs were correlated with the extremity of the ratings, but were unrelated to the direction of the reaction: The more pleasant *or* unpleasant the word, the larger the SRR it elicited. A slightly different finding emerges when complete attitude statements (e.g., Dickson & McGinnies, 1966), attitude objects (e.g., J. B. Cooper & Singer, 1956), or people (e.g., Rankin & Campbell, 1955) are presented, rather than individual words. Generally, the more discrepant the attitude stimulus from an individual's own position, the larger the SRR. For example, recall that C. E. Smith (1936) found that students showed the largest SRRs when they disagreed with the statement presented and they believed their own position was in conflict with group norms. Two decades later, J. B. Cooper and Singer (1956) demonstrated a similar effect. They asked 126 students to rate and rank 20 ethnic and national groups. Of these 126 subjects, 20 who had extreme attitudes toward their most liked and disliked groups subsequently served in a laboratory study in which skin resistance was monitored while the experimenter complimented the most disliked nationality, derogated the most liked nationality, complimented a neutral nationality, and derogated a neutral nationality. Subjects emitted the largest SRRs to derogatory statements about the most liked nationalities and to complimentary statements about the most disliked nationalities, and the SRRs to these two types of statements were equivalent.

It has been suggested that SRRs reflect the extremity but not the direction of an attitude (e.g., Lemon, 1973). This inference is based upon the notion that the SRRs are reflecting the emotional arousal elicited by the stimulus. Although this inference has been appealing to some because of the utility of such a measure (cf. J. B. Cooper, 1959), the support is equivocal. Specifically, the presentation of pleasant versus unpleasant words and of attitude statements that are consistent versus inconsistent with subjects' own attitudes might initially be thought to isolate the same fundamental stage—namely, an affective reaction. The effects of these manipulations on SRRs, however, are different. The former manipulation leads to similar increases in SRRs, whereas the latter does not. These different effects are sometimes interpreted as signaling that exposure to consistent attitude statements does not elicit an affective reaction, but this interpretation lacks independent support. Hence, alternative interpretations should also be considered. For instance, the experimental conditions eliciting SRRs in these studies resemble the conditions necessary to elicit an orienting response (e.g., novelty, signal value—cf. Cacioppo & Sandman, 1981; Petty & Cacioppo, 1983; Shapiro & Crider, 1969). Shapiro and Crider (1969) noted over a decade ago that statements conflicting with a person's attitude may elicit SRRs because "this inconsistency may be seen as a source of novelty, incongruity, or violation of expectancy and thereby a determinant of orienting reactions in the individual exposed to the communication" (p. 22). Alternatively, if subjects are stressed or frustrated when exposed to a subset of the attitudinal stimuli in the experimental setting (e.g., by being exposed to taboo words or by having others disagree with them), then the SRRs may not reflect the affective reaction to the attitude stimulus per se, but rather the reaction to the context in which it appears. Thus, although SRRs have been one of the most commonly employed physiological indices of attitudes (cf. Schwartz & Shapiro, 1973), these responses are elicited by such a variety of physical and psychological stimuli that they have provided an ambiguous marker for the processing stage representing an affective reaction.

A very different physiological assessment of this processing stage was advanced by Hess (1965), who argued that the pupillary response to a stimulus that has been repeatedly presented covaries with the person's attitude. According to Hess, the more liked the stimulus, the more pupillary dilation; the more disliked the stimulus, the more pupillary constriction. This bidirectional physiological index of attitudes is not necessarily evident when the stimulus is first presented, presumably because of other influences on pupil size (e.g., interest, novelty, mental load); rather, in Hess's view, this relationship emerges after multiple exposures to the stimulus.

A recent experiment by Metalis and Hess (1982)

illustrates this relationship. Male and female undergraduates were shown a series of pictures depicting either normal people in neutral settings, people with grotesque skin diseases, or nude men and/or women in erotic postures. Each photograph was preceded by a control slide of comparable overall luminance. The pupillary response was defined as the average change in pupil size to the picture slide following the control slide; these slides were paired and presented three times (but sampled only twice—the first and third presentations). They reported finding pupillary dilation by men and women to the erotic photographs, and the largest dilations were evoked by the photographs of men and women in erotic poses. Subjects also displayed pupillary constriction to photographs of skin diseases, and pupillary responses to the neutral photographs fell between those evoked by the erotic and disease pictures.

The association between pupillary responses and affective reactions to stimuli has also been assailed, however, and definitive responses to the concerns expressed by critics have not been forthcoming. One concern expressed has been methodological and notes that many nonpsychological factors can affect pupil size (e.g., the wavelength of the visual stimulus—see Goldwater, 1972; Woodmansee, 1970). For example, Janisse and Peavler (1974) suggested that different visual fixation points may account for the effect in Hess's original research, wherein females were found to show larger pupillary responses to male pin-ups than males. The same criticism can be leveled against Metalis and Hess (1982). For example, Metalis and Hess obtained subjects' evaluations of each photograph in addition to assessing their pupillary reactions, and found that these measures were not correlated except when diseases were depicted. Unfortunately, it is uncertain whether pupillary constriction evoked by pictures of skin diseases reflected a negative affective reaction or a focusing on the lighter area of the photograph. In particular, the more a person disliked a given photograph in this set, the more likely he or she may have been to fixate on an area of normal rather than diseased skin. It is noteworthy, therefore, that no investigator has documented a significant relationship between attitudes and pupillary responses when auditory, olfactory, or tactile stimuli have been employed (Goldwater, 1972).

Another concern that has been expressed is that pupillary responses may reflect a processing stage under certain test conditions, but that this stage is not necessarily related to affective or evaluative reactions. Beatty (1982), for example, reviews research demonstrating that pupil size varies systematically with overall cognitive load, a point to which we return below (see pp. 669–670). Hence, although pupil size is occasionally cited as a bidirectional measure of attitudes or as a marker for affective reactions, the accumulated evidence is at present more in accord with the conclusion reached by Woodmansee (1970): "[T]he pupil does not measure attitude or qualitatively different affective states. There is ample evidence, however, that the pupil, in its reflex dilation reaction may be used to indicate . . . attentiveness, interest, and perceptual orienting" (p. 532).

A more recent attempt to obtain, under circumscribed testing conditions, a physiological marker of the affective reactions to attitudinal stimuli relies upon one of the oldest sets of scientific observations (and one of the most commonly employed naturalistic assessment procedures) of bodily responses and emotions: subtle changes in facial expression. Darwin (1872/1904) linked affective reactions directly to facial expressions and argued that different facial expressions were biologically adaptive. Both Izard (1971) and Ekman (1972) have provided evidence that different emotions can be linked to unique facial expressions across a wide variety of situations and cultures, and they too suggest that these distinctive facial displays have functional significance (e.g., as a form of communication).

Clearly, facial expressions can be used in deceptive as well as veridical communication in social settings (Kraut, 1982; Zuckerman, Larrance, Spiegel, & Klorman, 1981). Ekman and Friesen (1975) have argued that cultural differences in the facial expression of emotion are due to cultural differences in "display rules." These observations limit the conditions under which changes in facial expression can be used to mark an affective reaction during attitudinal processing (i.e., subjects should not be aware that facial expressions are being monitored). Moreover, between-subject comparisons of facial expressiveness to gauge the intensity of affective reactions may be misleading, since several studies suggest that intense facial displays may actually help relieve some of the potency of an emotional reaction (cf. Buck, 1980; Notarious, Wemple, Ingraham, Burns, & Kollar, 1982). Particularly informative for studying the affective processing stage, however, may be spontaneous facial expressions obtained in a within-subjects design; through the use of EMG techniques, these "expressions" include (or concern primarily) those that are so subtle that neither the person nor an observer can detect them in a videotape replay.[9]

Schwartz and his colleagues (e.g., S. L. Brown & Schwartz, 1980; Schwartz, 1975; Schwartz, Fair, Mandel, Salt, Mieske, & Klerman, 1978; Schwartz, Fair,

Salt, Mandel, & Klerman, 1976a, 1976b), for instance, reasoned that different affective reactions should be identifiable in changes in the EMG activity of facial muscles when subjects are overtly inactive. In an early experiment, Schwartz et al. (1976b) asked people to imagine positive or negative events in their lives. In their observations of changes in the mean amplitude of integrated EMG (IEMG) activity over facial muscle regions, Schwartz et al. found that people generally responded with higher IEMG activity over the depressor annuli oris and zygomatic major muscle regions and lower IEMG activity over the corrugator supercilii muscle region when imagining happy, in contrast to sad, events. In another study, changes in mean-amplitude IEMG activity were monitored over the corrugator supercilii and zygomatic major muscle regions of the face while subjects engaged in emotional imagery (e.g., "Picture the last situation in which you laughed," "Picture the last funeral you went to"). Again, the changes in mean-amplitude IEMG activity indicated elevated activity over the zygomatic major region and lowered activity over the corrugator supercilii region when subjects engaged in pleasant, in contrast to unpleasant, emotional imagery (see S. L. Brown & Schwartz, 1980; Fridlund & Izard, 1983).

We (Cacioppo & Petty, 1979a, Experiment 2) reasoned that patterns of low-amplitude EMG activity over facial muscles might distinguish positive from negative affective reactions to a persuasive communication. Changes in the mean-amplitude IEMG activity were recorded over the corrugator supercilii, depressor anguli oris, and zygomatic major muscle regions using miniature surface electrodes while undergraduate students anticipated and then listened to either an involving proattitudinal communication (e.g., recommending more lenient visitation hours in dormitory rooms) or an involving counterattitudinal communication (e.g., recommending stricter visitation hours in dormitory rooms). A control group was forewarned only that they would hear a message and subsequently heard a news story about an archeological expedition in Asia. The observed patterns of subtle facial IEMG activity and reported evaluations of the messages were consistent. Subjects who were exposed to the proattitudinal message showed slightly higher mean-amplitude IEMG activity over the zygomatic major and depressor anguli oris muscle regions and lower mean-amplitude IEMG activity over the corrugator supercilii muscle region than subjects who were exposed to the counterattitudinal message. The neutral message was rated by subjects as being relatively pleasant, and the pattern of IEMG activity over these muscle regions during the message more closely matched that found during the proattitudinal than during the counterattitudinal communication.

In another study (Cacioppo, Petty, & Marshall-Goodell, 1984), IEMG activity was recorded over the

---

9. We are not suggesting, however, that covert facial expressions always reflect veridical affective reactions. The presentation of a stimulus that has been associated repeatedly with deceptive facial expressions might elicit covertly deceptive expressions, and covert expressions of emotion that are evinced while an individual is being scrutinized by an observer might be subject to the same display rules as are overt expressions of emotion in these conditions.

zygomatic major, corrugator supercilii, levator labii superioris, masseter, orbicularis oris, and superficial forearm flexors muscle regions while subjects imagined or performed simple physical or attitudinal tasks. In the physical tasks, subjects either imagined or actually lifted a 16-kg or a 35-kg weight. In the attitudinal tasks, subjects adopted an attitudinal set of either agreement or disagreement as they silently read neutral text or imagined reading an editorial. The tasks were ordered randomly, and subjects were focused on the distinction between imagining and performing tasks rather than the distinction between physical and attitudinal tasks. Multivariate analyses of the topographical features of the IEMG responses over each muscle region were performed to determine the effects of the tasks on changes in IEMG response waveforms, and univariate analyses were conducted to isolate the features of the waveform (e.g., mean amplitude, variance time) that were altered by tasks (cf. Cacioppo, Marshall-Goodell, & Dorfman, 1983). Results for the physical tasks showed that the form of the IEMG response over the forearm was dramatically affected by the parameters of the tasks, whereas the IEMG waveforms obtained from facial muscles were not. Results for the attitudinal tasks showed that the parameters of the tasks influenced the form of the responses over facial muscles previously associated with affective processing in similar paradigms (e.g., corrugator supercilii, zygomatic major), whereas the form of the IEMG responses over the forearm and facial muscles not implicated previously in low-level affective processing (e.g., orbicularis oris) were not differentiated by the attitudinal tasks. These data support the notion of temporal and spatial specificity in incipient skeletal–motor activity during low-level affective processing, given that subjects are relaxed, unobtrusively observed, and involved in the tasks. Finally, subsequent analyses of covariance suggested that the analyses of the topography of phasic IEMG responses provided significantly better differentiation of the antecedent conditions than did analyses of mean amplitude alone.

Lanzetta and his colleagues have also found that subtle changes in the mean amplitude of IEMG activity over facial muscles accompany affective reactions in social settings. In one study, subjects viewed a videotape of a confederate who was ostensibly receiving an electric shock (Vaughan & Lanzetta, 1980). With each delivery of an electric shock, the confederate grimaced in pain. EMG recordings over the medial frontalis, masseter, and orbicularis oculi muscle regions, which were selected because of their possible involvement in expressions of pain, revealed that higher mean-amplitude IEMG activity was present over the latter two sites in subjects immediately after the confederate's grimace as compared to preceding levels.

In a follow-up study, Englis, Vaughan, and Lanzetta (1982) constructed a stock market game that subjects ostensibly played with another person. Subjects tried to guess which market indices would rise or decline and were rewarded with money for correct guesses but punished with mild finger shock for incorrect guesses. During the game, subjects viewed another "subject" on a video monitor. (All subjects actually were exposed to a videotape of a confederate.) Some subjects found that when the confederate smiled, their own guess was correct and they were rewarded, and when the confederate expressed pain, their own guess was incorrect and they were punished. Other subjects observed the opposite: When the confederate smiled, their own guess was incorrect and they were punished, but when the confederate expressed pain, their own guess was correct and they received a reward. After completing the game, subjects simply watched a videotape of the confederate. Surface EMG over the corrugator supercilii, masseter, and orbicularis oculi muscle regions, as well as skin conductance and HR, were monitored continuously during the game and postgame periods. Consistent with the previous findings using surface EMG recordings, Englis et al. (1982) reported that when the confederate and subject shared outcomes, mean amplitude of the IEMG activity over the monitored regions was higher in both phases of the experiment when the confederate exhibited a pained than when he or she exhibited a happy facial expression. On the other hand, when the outcomes of the confederate and subject were asymmetrical, this profile tended to be reversed. Thus, the incipient changes in facial muscle activity appeared to mark subjects' affective reaction to, rather than mimicry of, the confederate's overt facial expression.

In sum, preliminary evidence suggests that subtle facial muscle changes may reflect the general nature of subjects' affective reactions to attitudinal stimuli as long as the subject is generally relaxed, inactive, involved in the task, and unobtrusively observed so that display rules or deceptive expressions are not invoked and the small muscular signals of interest are not masked by background somatic activity. It has not yet been determined, however, whether changes in the mean amplitude of IEMG activity over facial muscles reflect the specific nature of simple positive or negative evaluations (e.g., mild anger vs. sadness), whether they are sensitive to the intensity as well as to the direction (i.e., positive or negative) of affective reactions (cf. Schwartz et al., 1976a), or whether additional features of the IEMG response (e.g., variance amplitude, mean time) will improve the value of subtle facial IEMG profiles as markers of this processing stage (cf. Cacioppo, Marshall-Goodell, & Dorfman, 1983). Finally, the ease with which subjects can control their facial expressions heightens concerns about demand charcacteristics in this type of research. Interested readers may wish to consult Fridlund and Izard (1983), who review methodological concerns and offer suggestions for securing interpretable data.

Message Processing

Research on persuasive communications has recently moved from focusing on how well people learn and subsequently recall externally provided message arguments (e.g., Eagly, 1974; N. Miller & Campbell, 1959) to what people understand to be the meaning, personal implications, and merits of these message arguments (cf. Cialdini, Petty, & Cacioppo, 1981; Eagly & Himmelfarb, 1978). Thus, the emphasis in much of the recent research on persuasion has moved from the preliminary stages of message reception to succeeding stages, such as issue-relevant thinking (e.g., message elaboration). In this section, we examine the psychophysiological markers of one stage of this sequence, issue-relevant thinking. Psychophysiological applications to the study of attentional processes and learning are reviewed elsewhere in this volume.

Before proceeding, we should clarify that not all instances of resistance or susceptibility to persuasive communications are predicated on issue-relevant thinking, or what we have characterized as the "central route" to persuasion (Cacioppo & Petty, 1982b; Petty & Cacioppo, 1981). A recent estimate places the average person at the receiving end of hundreds of persuasive messages a day from advertisers alone (Will, 1982), and when the virtual deluge of appeals, prompts, suggestions, and counsels that an individual receives daily from personal contacts (e.g., friends, sales clerks, physicians) is considered, it is obvious that people do not have the luxury of either considering or rejecting every recommendation to which they are exposed. Recommendations that have important personal consequences, for instance, are more likely to elicit extensive issue-relevant thinking that is then instrumental in determining their susceptibility or resistance to an appeal (Petty & Cacioppo, 1979), whereas acceptance of recommendations that have no personal consequences and/or on topics about which individuals know little is likely to be determined by peripheral cues (cf. Cacioppo & Petty, 1982b; Petty & Cacioppo, 1981). Extensive issue-relevant thinking, therefore, is likely to be a fundamental stage of some, but certainly not all, attitudinal processes.

In an early study to determine the physiological profiles of issue-relevant thinking, subjects were told the topic and position of an audio communication that they were to hear later in the experimental session, and subjects were instructed to take the next 60 sec to "collect their thoughts" on the issue (Cacioppo & Petty, 1979a). Mean-amplitude IEMG activity over the perioral (e.g., orbicularis oris) muscle region and over the trapezius muscle region, HR, breathing rate, and cephalic pulse amplitude were calculated for the 60 sec immediately preceding and following the forewarning and instruction to subjects to collect their thoughts on the issue. Persuasive messages were not presented, in order to avoid confounding the reception of message arguments with the issue-relevant thinking that subjects produced in response to the forewarning and experimental instruction. Results indicated that the mean amplitude of perioral IEMG activity, HR, and breathing rate were heightened during the "collect thoughts" interval. Moreover, the mean amplitude of non-oral IEMG activity and cephalic pulse amplitude were unchanged, suggesting that subjects were not simply more generally aroused during this interval.

The discrepancy between subjects' initial attitudes and the impending recommendation was varied in this study to be low, moderate, or high (e.g., advocating that tuition be raised from 5.5% to 100% per quarter when subjects wanted no tuition increase). This manipulation had profound effects on the number of favorable and unfavorable thoughts listed and the agreement with the recommendation that they reported, but it had no effect on any of the physiological measures obtained. Correlational analyses also indicated that neither the autonomic measures monitored nor somatic measures of activity over the perioral or trapezius muscle regions reflected the affective tone of the issue-relevant thinking (as assessed using the thought-listing technique; see Cacioppo & Petty, 1981c, for a review of this procedure). In combination with the studies of physiological markers described in the preceding section, these data suggest that the processing stages of issue-relevant thinking and affective reactions have distinctive physiological consequences in the persuasion paradigm (Cacioppo & Petty, 1981a).

Further evidence that silent linguistic processing results in changes in EMG activity localized over the perioral muscle region was obtained in two experiments using the well-researched orienting task paradigm developed by cognitive psychologists to study encoding operations (see Cermak & Craik, 1978; Craik & Lockhart, 1972). In the first experiment, subjects were asked in half of the trials to determine whether or not a trait adjective was self-descriptive, and in the other half to determine whether or not the trait adjective was printed in upper-case letters (Cacioppo & Petty, 1979b). HR and the mean amplitude of the IEMG activity over the perioral region and over the nonpreferred forearm (superficial forearm flexors) were recorded during the first few seconds following the presentation of the trait adjective. Finally, subjects were asked to recall as many of the trait adjectives as possible at the completion of the study. Results revealed that subjects could recall more of the traits whose meaning and self-reference had to be determined than whose orthographic appearance was judged. In addition, the former task led to higher mean-amplitude IEMG activity over the perioral region than the latter task, but similar levels of HR and mean-amplitude IEMG activity over the non-oral muscle region. This finding has been conceptually replicated in a follow-up study using a wider variety of orienting tasks and a different presentation modality (Cacioppo & Petty, 1981b).

Finally, although changes in mean-amplitude IEMG activity over the perioral region can mark major differences in the extent of such types of linguistic processing as issue-relevant thinking, they can also reflect reading, recalling information, and problem solving (see reviews by Garrity, 1977; McGuigan, 1978) and listening to persuasive communications (Cacioppo & Petty, 1979a, Experiment 2). Recall that in this latter experiment, subjects were told that they would hear a communication in 1 min, and following this period all subjects were exposed to a tape-recorded message. Some subjects anticipated and heard a proattitudinal message; others anticipated and heard a counterattitudinal message; and still others anticipated only hearing some unspecified message that, as it turned out, was judged to be an enjoyable news story. Changes in HR and changes in mean-amplitude IEMG activity over the perioral and over selected facial muscle regions were monitored. (The results of the latter measures have been described in the preceding section and are not repeated here.) Previous experimental work had indicated that subjects engage in extensive topic-relevant thinking when anticipating an involving counterattitudinal appeal (Petty & Cacioppo, 1977); as expected, higher mean-amplitude IEMG activity over the perioral region was observed when subjects anticipated the counterattitudinal message, but not the proattitudinal or undescribed communication. Moreover, comparable elevations in mean-amplitude IEMG activity over the perioral region were observed during the presentation of these messages. Thus, although substantial differences in the extent of issue-relevant thinking can lead to localized differences in IEMG activity over the perioral muscle region, so too may message comprehension or extensive issue-irrelevant thinking.[10]

10. HR in this study was not found to change during the anticipatory interval; this result contrasts with the increased HR observed following the forewarning of a counterattitudinal appeal when subjects were explicitly instructed to "collect their thoughts" on the issue (Cacioppo & Petty, 1979a). As outlined above (see pp. 655–656), this result can be interpreted in several ways. First, differences in processing stages may have existed across the two studies. For example, the increases in HR observed when subjects were instructed to "collect their thoughts" perhaps reflect an additional processing stage concerning the presence of a social incentive (cf. Fowles, 1982). Alternatively, changes in HR may have simply been insensitive to the relatively small differences in covert verbalizations (Johnson & Campos, 1967; Lynch, Thomas, Long, Malinow, &

It should be noted that although changes in the IEMG activity localized over the perioral muscle region appear to vary with substantial differences in the extent of linguistic processing in the persuasion paradigm, these changes may not reflect rudimentary differences in imagery or in general cognitive load if *linguistic* processing is constant across conditions (B. B. Brown, 1968; Totten, 1935; cf. McGuigan, 1978). Beatty (1982) has contended that task-evoked pupillary responses provide a sensitive measure of the overall information-processing load on an individual. Although to date no experiment has documented the course of the pupillary response during the presentation of persuasive communications or documented its utility in gauging the cognitive load on a recipient of a persuasive message, the pupillary response may prove to be a sensitive marker of this attitudinal processing component. According to Beatty (1982; see also Chapter 3, this volume), the pupillary response

> provides a reliable and sensitive indication of within-task variations in processing load. It generates a reasonable and orderly index of between-task variations in processing load. It reflects differences in processing load between individuals who differ in psychometric ability when performing the same objective task. (1982, p. 291)

Thus, if an attempt at social influence causes individuals to think about the verbal arguments with which they can respond, parallel increases in pupillary and perioral EMG activity can reasonably be expected; however, if the influence attempt primarily evokes images rather than verbal consideration, then divergences in pupillary and perioral EMG responses can occur. When investigations of pupillary responses in a persuasion context are conducted, it is of course important to control for potentially confounding features of the persuasive message and context, such as novelty, the luminosity of the material in the setting, and the person's focal point during the presentation (e.g., by using audiotaped messages).

Cognitive Dissonance

"Attitude-discrepant behavior" refers to actions people take that they know are inconsistent with their attitudes toward the target of their actions. For instance, if a person is opposed to being assertive but finds himself or herself voluntarily being extraordinarily assertive in a social setting, then the person is engaging in an attitude-discrepant action. One may initially think that people would seldom do such a thing, but a voluminous literature in social psychology demonstrates that people are often "induced" to

Katcher, 1981) or mental concentration (cf. Coles & Duncan-Johnson, 1975; Lacey et al., 1963) normally elicited by the anticipation of or exposure to a persuasive communication. Additional research is required to determine the reliability and psychological significance of this difference in HR response.

perform an attitude-discrepant behavior when interacting with others. The theory of cognitive dissonance, which has stimulated more research in social psychology than any other formulation, addresses the consequences of this kind of social behavior.

According to Festinger (1957), two elements of information (cognitions) are dissonant for an individual when the individual knows that one suggests the opposite of the other. Exceptions to this general postulate were soon found, and the theory of cognitive dissonance underwent a series of changes and refinements (Aronson, 1969; Brehm & Cohen, 1962; Wicklund & Brehm, 1976; cf. Greenwald & Ronis, 1978). At present, cognitive dissonance is thought to develop when an individual accepts personal responsibility for an action associated with negative consequences that were foreseeable or that should have been foreseeable (cf. Cialdini *et al.*, 1981). According to dissonance theory, the reduction of cognitive dissonance can occur in one of several ways, including (1) denying responsibility for, control over, or negative consequences from the behavior; (2) changing the attitude to make it more consistent with the behavior; or (3) misattributing the dissonant state to a cause that is either temporary and self-correcting or beyond one's control (e.g., a pill whose "side effects" are described as making one feel unpleasant). Finally, the mode selected for dissonance reduction is thought to follow the path of least resistance. Hence, denial of responsibility for one's actions or misattributing the cause of a dissonant state to an external agent is usually preferable to changing one's attitude, since the latter requires more cognitive reorganization and effort.

The spate of research generated by cognitive dissonance theory has led to the emergence of a number of alternative theories, such as Bem's (1965, 1972) self-perception theory and Tedeschi, Schlenker, and Bonoma's (1971) theory of impression management. The distinctive feature of dissonance theory is the postulated internal state of dissonance. Unfortunately, Festinger (1957) was not very explicit about this internal state. He described the presence of cognitive dissonance as physiologically discomforting (p. 2), for which "one can substitute other notions similar in nature, such as 'hunger,' 'frustration,' or 'disequilibrium,'" (p. 3); he also described dissonance as a drive-like state (p. 18).

Despite the proliferation of theories, published psychophysiological studies of dissonance arousal are uncommon (see Fazio & Cooper, 1983). The first and only published study for over a decade on the physiological responses to dissonance arousal was reported by Gerard (1967). Subjects were exposed to several paintings and were asked to rank the paintings from their most to least liked. Subsequently, subjects were given a choice between two paintings they liked about equally well (the stimuli the subject had ranked third and fourth) or between two that were not nearly

equally liked (the stimuli the subject had ranked third and eighth). Deciding between two similarly attractive alternatives, in contrast to one attractive and one unattractive alternative, is thought to create more cognitive dissonance, since when two alternatives are relatively equal in their attractiveness the individual foregoes more attractive features in the unchosen alternative and/or accepts more unattractive features in the chosen alternative than when the alternatives are very different in their attractiveness. Indeed, Gerard (1967) observed a constriction of the blood vessels in the fingers of 10 of the 12 subjects who had chosen between the two attractive paintings, whereas he observed digital vasoconstriction in only 1 of the 12 subjects following the choice between an attractive and an unattractive painting. Unfortunately, the normal attitudinal effects of choosing between two attractive, in contrast to attractive and unattractive, alternatives were not observed. Moreover, this same paradigm has been found to cause subjects who have made a difficult rather than a simple choice to attend more carefully to the chosen alternative. Since digital vasoconstriction is a component of the orienting response, there is some question whether the vasoconstriction observed by Gerard (1967) is attributable to the arousal of cognitive dissonance or to possibly more pronounced orientations to the paintings by subjects in the "high-dissonance" conditions.

Fazio and Cooper (1983) review several conceptually similar but unpublished studies. Buck (1970), for example, in a doctoral dissertation, reported a study in which subjects were induced, under conditions of high choice, to deliver a series of audio tones, mild electric shocks, or painful shocks to another individual. Since harming an innocent victim is typically counterattitudinal for people, the delivery of intense electric shocks by subjects to their partners was assumed to constitute an attitude-discrepant action for which they were personally responsible and that had clear and foreseeable negative consequences. Buck, who monitored HR and SCRs, found that subjects who delivered intense shocks showed the largest SCRs and subjects who delivered harmless tones exhibited the smallest SCRs. No differences in HR were found, however.[11]

---

11. Fazio and Cooper (1983) review a second study in which HR and SCRs were recorded, by Gleason and Katkin (1978). Subjects were instructed to spend 5 min thinking of arguments either supporting or attacking the recommendation that average grades at their university be lowered (a counterattitudinal appeal). Gleason and Katkin found that subjects who were trying to think of arguments favoring the counterattitudinal appeal exhibited higher HR and more SSCRs than subjects trying to think of arguments attacking the appeal. As Fazio and Cooper (1983) note, however, there is no reason to believe that Gleason and Katkin's manipulations created different levels of dissonance arousal, since it is unclear whether subjects had any choice in this activity or anticipated negative consequences from preparing their speeches.

Croyle and Cooper (1983) provide an interesting and informative set of observations in this area. They note that in previous dissonance research in which physiological measures were obtained, the typical dissonance effects on attitudes were not observed (e.g., Buck, 1970; Gerard, 1967). They suggest that subjects may have been misattributing the dissonance to the electronic gadgetry associated with physiological recordings, thereby rendering attitude change unnecessary. Croyle and Cooper dealt with this problem by conducting two experiments. The first was designed to validate that a given set of procedures induced cognitive dissonance. Subjects were induced under the perception of high choice to write an essay either supporting or attacking the recommendation, "Alcohol use should be totally banned from the university campus and eating clubs"; another group of subjects were induced under the perception of low choice to write an essay favoring this recommendation. Only the subjects who perceived that they had high choice *and* who wrote the essay favoring this counterattitudinal recommendation were expected to experience dissonance as a result of their decision. No physiological measures were obtained; rather, subjects were simply asked their attitude toward the recommendation after they had written the essay. As would be expected, subjects in the high-choice/counterattitudinal-essay condition showed more attitude change than subjects in the remaining conditions.

In a follow-up study, different groups of subjects were exposed to the same experimental manipulations while spontaneous SCRs (SSCRs) were measured "to examine the impact of simple mental and physical tasks on the electrical activity of the skin." Following the composition of their essays, subjects were given a 3-min rest period. An analysis of covariance was conducted using the number of SSCRs emitted during this rest period as the criterion and the number of SSCRs displayed during the pre-essay period as the covariate. As expected, Croyle and Cooper found higher levels of SSCR activity in the high-dissonance than in the low-dissonance conditions.

Even though the sparse data on the physiological characteristics of dissonance have not consistently indicated that dissonance arousal initiates a diffuse and unitary increase in physiological arousal (e.g., Buck, 1970), the physiological data are consistent with the view that the instigation of dissonance leads to heightened activity in the sympathetic nervous system (cf. J. Cooper et al., 1978; Fazio & Cooper, 1983), and they provide an interesting picture of dissonance as an attitudinal processing stage.

Specifically, the observation of increased EDRs in the high-dissonance condition while HR remains constant across high- and low-dissonance conditions is the same pattern found to characterize the threat assessment stage involved in observed performances (see the earlier discussion of observed vs. unobserved performance). It is particularly interesting to note,

therefore, that cognitive dissonance is *not* aroused if individuals believe (1) that there is no choice but to act as they do (Linder, Cooper, & Johes, 1967; Sherman, 1970); (2) that no one can identify them with the discrepant behavior, so they can deny that they seriously mean what they say or do (Brehm & Cohen, 1962; Riess & Schlenker, 1977); or (3) that the actions for which they are personally responsible cause no harm to themselves or significant others (Calder, Ross, & Insko, 1973; Collins & Hoyt, 1972; J. Cooper & Worchel, 1970; Goethals & Cooper, 1975). Dissonance is aroused only when a person is forced to conclude that he or she is the willing causal agent of some discrepant decision or action that leads predictably to negative consequences that are (or can be) recognized by others. In other words, a fundamental feature of cognitive dissonance is social dissonance (cf. Fazio & Cooper, 1983; Schlenker, 1980). The logic of the experimental conditions that give rise to cognitive dissonance, therefore, is in accord with the "stage" suggested by perusing the physiological data: A criterial, and probably early, processing stage involves determining the potential punitive consequences for oneself as a result of one's decision (see footnote 8).

At present, there is insufficient psychophysiological data on dissonance arousal and reduction using various operationalizations and measures to permit us to derive candidates for other processing stages. Another finding from behavioral studies of dissonance, however, is pertinent here, given the commonality between the threat assessment stage that possibly underlies both social facilitation and cognitive dissonance phenomena. It will be recalled that the presence of an observer was found to facilitate the performance of sets of simple tasks and to impair the performance of sets of difficult tasks. The arousal of cognitive dissonance apparently has the same facilitatory–inhibitory effects on performance (Kiesler & Pallak, 1976). In an illustrative study, Pallak and Pittman (1972) examined the performance of subjects under conditions of high versus low dissonance on simple and difficult Stroop tests. Subjects performed a boring task that involved pronouncing words as they appeared on a memory drum. After 5 min of this boring task, subjects were told that they were to perform the same task using the same words for an additional 30 min. The experimenter subtly induced half of the subjects to agree to perform this task while maintaining the impression that subjects were personally responsible for choosing to perform the task (high-dissonance group), whereas the other subjects were given no choice but to perform the task (low-dissonance group). Immediately following this "decision" by subjects, but prior to the continuation of work on the boring pronunciation task, subjects performed either the simple (i.e., low-response-competition) or difficult (i.e., high-response-competition) Stroop test. Pallak and Pittman (1972) found that subjects from the high-dissonance, in contrast to the low-dissonance, group increased the number of correct responses they made on the simple test and increased the number of errors they made on the difficult test across the trials of the test. This suggests that effortful striving may be a second processing stage underlying dissonance as well as social facilitation processes. Further research is needed to determine the similarities and differences in the processing stages underlying these two very different social processes, of course; however, psychophysiological recordings may contribute importantly to the delineation of their respective processing stages and to the specification of common elementary stages.

Summary

We have reviewed a variety of ways in which psychophysiological procedures have been related to attitudes and attitude change. Studies have typically measured only one bodily response (e.g., SRR or pupillary dilation) to assess attitudes, and these studies have been vulnerable to the criticisms that attention, interest, distress, or cognitive load was being measured, rather than positive or negative feelings about the stimulus per se. Assessments of facial EMG activity may prove to be a valid, though possibly insensitive, physiological *index* of attitudes, but the benefits of such a measure may not outweigh the costs in most instances.

The application of psychophysiological procedures, including the assessment of skin conductance and facial EMG, to investigate the underlying processing stages appears to us to be a more useful and promising endeavor. Psychophysiological studies of attitudinal processes are still uncommon, and it is clear even from a casual perusal of this literature that many more processing stages may exist than the ones that have been studied. Moreover, the physiological data pertaining to these stages are themselves so sparse that the conceptualizations of these stages are likely to undergo considerable revision and refinement as more data accrue. The commonality in a processing stage suggested by psychophysiological studies of social facilitation and cognitive dissonance, however, is encouraging, given the thesis that psychophysiological investigations of social processes should uncover commonalities between and distinctions among the constituent stages underlying social processes.

CONCLUSION

Social scientists are chagrined when people see as "obvious" scientific propositions regarding the role of situational factors in social behavior or regarding the effects of human association on the behavior of individuals (cf. Holden, 1982; Lazarsfeld, 1949). For example, in a variation of an analysis provided by Lazarsfeld (1949), we recently presented individuals with several statements about social behavior (e.g., "A bystander is more likely to offer help when witnessing an emergency with others than when alone"). Our respondents assured us that many of these claims were so apparent as to warrant neither empirical documentation nor theoretical investigation. Despite the apparently self-evident nature of the principles of social processes when unveiled, people are in fact quite poor at specifying these principles correctly. The interesting aspect of the propositions that we gave to the participants in our inquiry was that in every instance we presented a general "principle" that had been disconfirmed in empirical research. That is, social processes appear more obvious than they are. In this chapter, we have outlined (1) the history of the application of psychophysiological procedures to study social processes; (2) the means by which psychophysiological procedures can contribute to the delineation of the *foundations* of social processes; and (3) selected candidates for the elementary processing stages underlying selected interpersonal and intrapersonal processes.

Specifically, we have advanced the position that social processes are constituted by the concatenation of unique combinations of a finite number of elementary and generally sequential processing stages. In applying psychophysiology to isolate and identify these elementary stages, we have argued against the general search for universal physiological descriptions (or "correlates") of social processes; rather, we have emphasized how these procedures can be employed within limits to delineate the rudimentary building blocks of social processes. Our review suggests that (1) the application of psychophysiological concepts and procedures to investigate the stages of social processes need not be reductionistic or incompatible with the use of social paradigms and methodologies; (2) the selection of psychophysiological measures and procedures and the construction of comparison conditions should be specifically linked to the theoretical question being posed; (3) at least some elementary processing stages, like some chemical elements, show an affinity for one another; and (4) differences among very different social processes may indeed ultimately be understood in terms of the differences in the concatenation of a subset of a finite number of processing stages, though a great deal needs to be accomplished before these fundamental stages are identified and their positions in various social processes are understood.

ACKNOWLEDGMENTS

We wish to thank Barbara L. Andersen, Robert S. Baron, and Marcia Ward for comments on an earlier draft of this chapter. Preparation of this chapter was supported by National Science Foundation Grant Nos. BNS 80-23589, BNS 82-17096 & BNS 8444909.

REFERENCES

Allport, G. W. Attitudes. In C. Murchison (Ed.), *Handbook of social psychology* (Vol. 2). Worcester, Mass.: Clark University Press, 1935.

Aronson, E. The theory of cognitive dissonance: A current perspective. In L. Berkowitz (Ed.), *Advances in experimental social psychology* (Vol. 4). New York: Academic Press, 1969.

Back, K. W., & Bogdonoff, M. D. Plasma lipid responses to leadership, conformity, and deviation. In P. H. Leiderman & D. Shapiro (Eds.), *Psychobiological approaches to social behavior*. Stanford, Calif.: Stanford University Press, 1964.

Bargh, J. A., & Cohen, J. L. Mediating factors in the arousal-performance relationship. *Motivation and Emotion*, 1978, 2, 243–257.

Baron, R. S., Moore, D., & Sanders, G. S. Distraction as a source of drive in social facilitation research. *Journal of Personality and Social Psychology*, 1978, 36, 816–824.

Beatty, J. Task-evoked pupillary responses, processing load, and the structure of processing resources. *Psychological Bulletin*, 1982, 91, 276–292.

Bem, D. J. An example analysis of self-persuasion. *Journal of Experimental Social Psychology*, 1965, 1, 199–218.

Bem, D. J. Self-perception theory. In L. Berkowitz (Ed.), *Advances in experimental social psychology* (Vol. 6). New York: Academic Press, 1972.

Berger, S. M., Carli, L. L., Garcia, R., & Brady, J. J., Jr. Audience affects and anticipatory learning: A comparison of drive and practice-inhibition analyses. *Journal of Personality and Social Psychology*, 1982, 42, 478–486.

Berger, S. M., Hamptom, K. L., Carli, L. L., Grandmaison, P. S., Sadow, J. S., Donath, C. H., & Herschlag, L. R. Audience-induced inhibition of overt practice during learning. *Journal of Personality and Social Psychology*, 1981, 40, 479–491.

Blascovich, J., & Katkin, E. S. Visceral perception and social behavior. In J. T. Cacioppo & R. E. Petty (Eds.), *Social psychophysiology: A sourcebook*. New York: Guilford Press, 1983.

Block, A. R. An investigation of the response of the spouse to chronic pain behavior. *Psychosomatic Medicine*, 1981, 43, 415–422.

Bond, C. F., Jr. Social facilitation: A self-presentational view. *Journal of Personality and Social Psychology*, 1982, 42, 1042–1050.

Borden, R. J. Audience influence. In P. B. Paulis (Ed.), *Psychology of group influence*. Hillsdale, N.J.: Erlbaum, 1980.

Borden, R. J., Hendrick, C., & Walker, J. W. Affective physiological, and attitudinal consequences of audience presence. *Bulletin of the Psychonomic Society*, 1976, 7, 33–36.

Boyd, R. W., & DiMascio, A. Social behavior and autonomic physiology: A sociophysiologic study. *Journal of Nervous and Mental Disease*, 1954, 120, 207–212.

Brehm, J. W., & Cohen, A. R. *Explorations in cognitive dissonance*. New York: Wiley, 1962.

Brener, J. Sensory and perceptual determinants of voluntary visceral control. In G. E. Schwartz & J. Beatty (Eds.), *Biofeedback: Theory and research*. New York: Academic Press, 1977.

Brown, B. B. Visual recall ability and eye movements. *Psychophysiology*, 1968, 4, 300–306.

Brown, S. L., & Schwartz, G. E. Relationships between facial electromyography and subjective experience during affective imagery. *Biological Psychology*, 1980, 11, 49–62.

Buck, R. Nonverbal behavior and the theory of emotion: The facial feedback hypothesis. *Journal of Personality and Social Psychology*, 1980, 38, 811–824.

Buck, R. W., Jr. *Relationships between dissonance-reducing behavior and tension measures following aggression*. Unpublished doctoral dissertation, University of Pittsburgh, 1970.

Cacioppo, J. T. Effects of exogenous changes in heart rate on facilitation of thought and resistance to persuasion. *Journal of Personality and Social Psychology*, 1979, 37, 489–498.

Cacioppo, J. T. Social psychophysiology: A classic perspective and contemporary approach. *Psychophysiology*, 1982, 19, 241–251.

Cacioppo, J. T., Harkins, S. G., & Petty, R. E. The nature of attitudes and cognitive responses and their relationships to behavior. In R. Petty, T. Ostrom, & T. Brock (Eds.), *Cognitive responses in persuasion*. Hillsdale, N.J.: Erlbaum, 1981.

Cacioppo, J. T., Marshall-Goodell, B., & Dorfman, D. Skeletomuscular patterning: Topographical analysis of the integrated electromyogram. *Psychophysiology*, 1983, 20, 269–283.

Cacioppo, J. T., Marshall-Goodell, B., & Gormezano, I. Social psychophysiology: Bioelectrical measurement, experimental control, and analog/digital data acquisition. In J. T. Cacioppo & R. E. Petty (Eds.), *Social psychophysiology: A sourcebook*. New York: Guilford Press, 1983.

Cacioppo, J. T., & Petty, R. E. Attitudes and cognitive response: An electrophysiological approach. *Journal of Personality and Social Psychology*, 1979, 37, 2181–2199. (a)

Cacioppo, J. T., & Petty, R. E. Lip and nonpreferred forearm EMG activity as a function of orienting task. *Journal of Biological Psychology*, 1979, 9, 103–113. (b)

Cacioppo, J. T., & Petty, R. E. Electromyograms as measures of extent affectivity of information processing. *American Psychologist*, 1981, 36, 441–456. (a)

Cacioppo, J. T., & Petty, R. E. Electromyographic specificity during covert information processing. *Psychophysiology*, 1981, 18, 518–523. (b)

Cacioppo, J. T., & Petty, R. E. Social psychological procedures for cognitive response assessment: The thought-listing technique. In T. V. Merluzzi, C. R. Glass, & M. Genest (Eds.), *Cognitive assessment*. New York: Guilford Press, 1981. (c)

Cacioppo, J. T., & Petty, R. E. A biosocial model of attitude change: Signs, symptoms, and undetected physiological responses. In J. T. Cacioppo & R. E. Petty (Eds.), *Perspectives in cardiovascular psychophysiology*. New York: Guilford Press, 1982. (a)

Cacioppo, J. T., & Petty, R. E. Language variables, attitudes, and persuasion. In E. B. Ryan & H. Giles (Eds.), *Attitudes towards language variation: Social and applied contexts*. London: Edward Arnold, 1982. (b)

Cacioppo, J. T., & Petty, R. E. Foundations of social psychophysiology. In J. T. Cacioppo & R. E. Petty (Eds.), *Social psychophysiology: A sourcebook*. New York: Guilford Press, 1983. (a)

Cacioppo, J. T., & Petty, R. E. (Eds.). *Social psychophysiology: A sourcebook*. New York: Guilford Press, 1983. (b)

Cacioppo, J. T., & Petty, R. E. Soviet contributions to social psychophysiology. In J. T. Cacioppo & R. E. Petty (Eds.), *Social psychophysiology: A sourcebook*. New York: Guilford Press, 1983. (c)

Cacioppo, J. T., & Petty, R. E. Social psychophysiology. In L. Stegagno (Ed.), *Psychophysiology*. Turin, Italy: Boringhieri Publishers, in press.

Cacioppo, J. T., Petty, R. E., & Marshall-Goodell, B. Electromyographic specificity during simple physical and attitudinal tasks: Location and topographical features of integrated EMG responses. *Biological Psychology*, 1984, 18, 85–121.

Cacioppo, J. T., & Sandman, C. A. Psychophysiological functioning, cognitive responding, and attitudes. In R. E. Petty, T. M. Ostrom, & T. C. Brock (Eds.), *Cognitive responses in persuasion*. Hillsdale, N. J.: Erlbaum, 1981.

Cacioppo, J. T., Sandman, C. A., & Walker, B. B. The effects of operant heart rate conditioning on cognitive elaboration and attitude change. *Psychophysiology*, 1978, 15, 330–338.

Calder, B. J., Ross, M., & Insko, C. A. Attitude change and attitude attribution: Effects of incentive, choice, and consequences. *Journal of Personality and Social Psychology*, 1973, 25, 84–99.

Campbell, D. T., & Stanley, J. C. *Experimental and quasi-experimental designs for research*. Chicago: Rand McNally, 1963.

Cannon, W. B. The James–Lange theory of emotions: A critical examination and an alternative theory. *American Journal of Psychology*, 1927, 39, 106–124.

Carver, C. S., & Scheier, M. F. The self-attention-induced feedback loop and social facilitation. *Journal of Experimental Social Psychology*, 1981, 17, 545–568.

Cermak, L. S., & Craik, F. I. M. (Eds.). *Levels of processing in human memory.* Hillsdale, N.J.: Erlbaum, 1978.

Chapman, A. J. *Some aspects of the social facilitation of "humorous laughter" in children.* Unpublished doctoral dissertation, University of Leicester, 1972.

Chapman, A. J. An electromyographic study of apprehension about evaluation. *Psychological Reports,* 1973, 33, 811–814.

Chapman, A. J. An electromyographic study of social facilitation: A test of the "mere presence" hypothesis. *British Journal of Psychology,* 1974, 65, 123–128.

Christie, M. J., & Mellett, P. G. *Foundations of psychosomatics.* Chichester, England: Wiley, 1981.

Christie, M. J., & Todd, J. L. Experimenter-subject-situational interactions. In P. H. Venables & M. J. Christie (Eds.), *Research in psychophysiology.* London: Wiley, 1975.

Church, R. M. The effect of competition on reaction time and palmar skin conductance. *Journal of Abnormal and Social Psychology,* 1962, 65, 32–40.

Cialdini, R. B., Petty, R. E., & Cacioppo, J. T. Attitudes and attitude change. *Annual Review of Psychology,* 1981, 32, 357–404.

Cohen, J. L. Social facilitation increased evaluation apprehension through permanency of record. *Motivation and Emotion,* 1979, 3, 19–33.

Cohen, J. L., & Davis, J. H. Affects of audience status, evaluation, and time of action on performance with hidden-word problems. *Journal of Personality and Social Psychology,* 1973, 27, 74–85.

Coles, M. G. H., & Duncan-Johnson, C. C. Cardiac activity and information processing: The effects of stimulus significance, detection, and response requirements. *Journal of Experimental Psychology: Human Perception and Performance,* 1975, 1, 418–428.

Coles, M. G. H., Jennings, J. R., & Stern, J. A. (Eds.). *Psychophysiological perspectives: Festschrift for Beatrice and John Lacey.* New York: Van Nostrand Reinhold, 1984.

Collins, B. E., & Hoyt, M. G. Personal responsibility for consequences: An integration and extension of the "forced compliance" literature. *Journal of Experimental Social Psychology,* 1972, 8, 558–593.

Cook, S. W., & Selltiz, C. A multiple-indicator approach to attitude measurement. *Psychological Bulletin,* 1964, 62, 36–55.

Cooper, J., & Worchel, S. Role of undesired consequences in arousing cognitive dissonance. *Journal of Personality and Social Psychology,* 1970, 16, 199–206.

Cooper, J., Zanna, M. P., & Taves, P. A. Arousal as a necessary condition for attitude change following induced compliance. *Journal of Personality and Social Psychology,* 1978, 36, 1101–1106.

Cooper, J. B., & Singer, D. N. The role of emotion and prejudice. *Journal of Social Psychology,* 1956, 44, 241–247.

Cooper, J. B. Emotion and prejudice. *Science,* 1959, 130, 314–318.

Corrigan, J. D., Dell, D. M., Lewis, K. N., & Schmidt, L. D. Counseling as a social influence process: A review. *Journal of Counseling Psychology Monograph,* 1980, 27, 395–441.

Cotton, J. L. A review of research on Schachter's theory of emotion and the misattribution of arousal. *European Journal of Social Psychology,* 1981, 11, 365–397.

Cottrell, N. B. Social facilitation. In C. G. McClintock (Ed.), *Experimental social psychology.* New York: Holt, Rinehart & Winston, 1972.

Cottrell, N. B., Wack, D. L., Sekerak, G. J., & Rittle, R. H. Social facilitation of dominant responses by the presence of an audience and the mere presence of others. *Journal of Personality and Social Psychology,* 1968, 9, 245–250.

Craik, F. M., & Lockhart, R. S. Levels of processing: A framework for memory research. *Journal of Verbal Learning and Verbal Behavior,* 1972, 11, 671–684.

Crider, A. The promise of social psychophysiology. In J. T. Cacioppo & R. E. Petty (Eds.), *Social psychophysiology: A sourcebook.* New York: Guilford Press, 1983.

Croyle, R. T., & Cooper, J. Dissonance arousal: Physiological evidence. *Journal of Personality and Social Psychology,* 1983, 45, 782–791.

Dabbs, J. M., Jr., Johnson, J. E., & Leventhal, H. Palmar sweating: A quick and simple measure. *Journal of Experimental Psychology,* 1968, 78, 347–350.

Darwin, C. *The expression of the emotions in man and animals.* London: Murray, 1904. (Originally published, 1872)

Dickson, H. W., & McGinnies, E. Affectivity and the arousal of attitudes as measured by galvanic skin response. *American Journal of Psychology,* 1966, 79, 584–587.

DiMascio, A., Boyd, R. W., & Greenblatt, M. Physiological correlates of tension and antagonism during psychotherapy: A study of "interpersonal physiology." *Psychosomatic Medicine,* 1957, 19, 99–104.

Donchin, E. The relevance of dissociations and the irrelevance of dissociationism: A reply to Schwartz and Pritchard. *Psychophysiology,* 1982, 19, 457–463.

Donders, F. C. Die schnelligkeit psychischer Prozesse. *Archive für Anatomie und Physiologie,* 1868, 657–681.

Droppleman, L. F., & McNair, D. M. An experimental analog of public speaking. *Journal of Consulting and Clinical Psychology,* 1971, 36, 91–96.

Duffy, E. The concept of energy mobilization. *Psychological Review,* 1951, 58, 30–40.

Duffy, E. The psychological significance of the concept of "arousal" or "activation." *Psychological Review,* 1957, 64, 265–275.

Duffy, E. Activation. In N. S. Greenfield & R. A. Sternbach (Eds.), *Handbook of psychophysiology.* New York: Holt, Rinehart & Winston, 1972.

Duval, S., & Wicklund, R. A. *A theory of objective self-awareness.* New York: Academic Press, 1972.

Dysinger, D. W. A comparative study of affective responses by means of the impressive and expressive methods. *Psychological Monographs,* 1931, 41(No. 187).

Eagly, A. H. Comprehensibility of persuasive arguments as a determinant of opinion change. *Journal of Personality and Social Psychology,* 1974, 29, 758–773.

Eagly, A. H., & Himmelfarb, S. Attitudes and opinions. In M. Rosenzweig & L. Porter (Eds.), *Annual review of psychology* (Vol. 29). Palo Alto, Calif.: Annual Reviews, 1978.

Ekman, P. Universal and cultural differences in facial expression of emotion. In J. R. Cole (Ed.), *Nebraska Symposium on Motivation* (Vol. 19). Lincoln: University of Nebraska Press, 1972.

Ekman, P., & Friesen, W. V. *Unmasking the face.* Englewood Cliffs, N.J.: Prentice-Hall, 1975.

Ekman, P., & Friesen, W. V. *Facial action coding system.* Palo Alto, Calif.: Consulting Psychologists Corporation, 1978.

Englis, B. G., Vaughan, K. B., & Lanzetta, J. T. Conditioning of counterempathic emotional responses. *Journal of Experimental Social Psychology,* 1982, 18, 375–391.

Ericcson, K. A., & Simon, H. A. Verbal reports as data. *Psychological Review,* 1980, 87, 215–251.

Fazio, R. H., & Cooper, J. Arousal in the dissonance process. In J. T. Cacioppo & R. E. Petty (Eds.), *Social psychophysiology: A sourcebook.* New York: Guilford Press, 1983.

Fazio, R. H., Zanna, M. P., & Cooper, J. Dissonance and self-perception: An integrative view of each theory's proper domain of application. *Journal of Experimental Social Psychology,* 1977, 13, 464–479.

Festinger, L. *A theory of cognitive dissonance.* Stanford, Calif.: Stanford University Press, 1957.

Fowles, D. C. The three arousal model: Implications of Gray's two-factor learning theory for heart rate, electrodermal activity, and psychopathy. *Psychophysiology,* 1980, 17, 87–104.

Fowles, D. C. Heart rate as an index of anxiety: Failure of a hypothesis. In J. T. Cacioppo & R. E. Petty (Eds.), *Perspectives in cardiovascular psychophysiology.* New York: Guilford Press, 1982.

Fridlund, A. J., Cottam, G. L., & Fowler, S. C. In search of the general tension factor: Tensional patterning during auditory stimulation. *Psychophysiology,* 1982, 19, 136–145.

Fridlund, A. J., & Izard, C. E. Electromyographic studies of facial expressions of emotions and patterns of emotion. In J. T. Cacioppo & R. E. Petty (Eds.), *Social psychophysiology: A sourcebook.* New York: Guilford Press, 1983.

Gale, A. The psychophysiology of individual differences: Studies in extraversion and EEG. In P. Kline (Ed.), *New approaches to psychological measurements.* London: Wiley, 1973.

Gale, A., & Baker, S. In vivo or in vitro?: Some effects of laboratory environments, with particular reference to the psychophysiological experiment. In M. J. Christie & P. G. Mellet (Eds.), *Foundations of psychosomatics.* Chichester, England: Wiley, 1981.

Gale, A., & Smith, D. On setting up a psychophysiological laboratory. In I. Martin & P. Venables (Eds.), *Techniques in psychophysiology.* Chichester, England: Wiley, 1980.

Gantt, W. H., Newton, J. E. O., Royer, F. L., & Stephens, J. H. Affect of person. *Conditional Reflex,* 1966, 1, 18–35.

Garrity, L. I. Electromyography: A review of the current status of subvocal speech research. *Memory and Cognition,* 1977, 5, 615–622.

Geen, R. G. Affects of anticipation of positive and negative outcomes on audience anxiety. *Journal of Consulting and Clinical Psychology,* 1977, 45, 715–716.

Geen, R. G. Affects of being observed on learning following success and failure experiences. *Motivation and Emotion,* 1979, 3, 355–371.

Geen, R. G. The effects of being observed on performance. In P. B. Paulis (Ed.), *Psychology of group influence.* Hillsdale, N.J.: Erlbaum, 1980.

Geen, R. G. Evaluation apprehension and social facilitation: A reply to Sanders. *Journal of Experimental Social Psychology,* 1981, 17, 252–256.

Geen, R. G., & Gange, J. J. Drive theory of social facilitation: Twelve years of theory and research. *Psychological Bulletin,* 1977, 84, 1267–1288.

Gerard, H. B. Physiological measurement in social psychological research. In P. H. Leiderman & D. Shapiro (Eds.), *Psychobiological approaches to social behavior.* Stanford, Calif.: Stanford University Press, 1964.

Gerard, H. B. Choice difficulty, dissonance, and the decision sequence. *Journal of Personality,* 1967, 35, 91–108.

Gleason, J. M., & Katkin, E. S. *The effects of cognitive dissonance on heart rate and electrodermal response.* Paper presented at the Society for Psychophysiological Research, Madison, Wisconsin, 1978.

Goethals, G. R., & Cooper, J. When dissonance is reduced: The timing of self-justificatory attitude change. *Journal of Personality and Social Psychology,* 1975, 32, 361–387.

Goldwater, B. C. Psychological significance of pupillary movements. *Psychological Bulletin,* 1972, 77, 340–355.

Gould, S. J., & Vrba, E. S. Exaptation—a missing term in the science of form. *Paleobiology,* 1982, 8, 4–15.

Greenfield, N. S., & Sternbach, R. A. (Eds.). *Handbook of psychophysiology.* New York: Holt, Rinehart & Winston, 1972.

Greenwald, A. G., & Ronis, D. L. Twenty years of cognitive dissonance: Case study of the evolution of a theory. *Psychological Review,* 1978, 85, 53–57.

Groff, B. D., Baron, R. S., & Moore, D. L. Distraction, attentional conflict, and drivelike behavior. *Journal of Experimental Social Psychology,* 1983, 19, 359–380.

Guttman, L. A basis for scaling qualitative data. *American Sociological Review,* 1944, 9, 139–150.

Hebb, D. O. Drives and the C.N.S. (conceptual nervous system). *Psychological Review,* 1955, 62, 243–254.

Henchy, T., & Glass, D. C. Evaluation apprehension and the social facilitation of dominant and subordinate responses. *Journal of Personality and Social Psychology,* 1968, 10, 446–454.

Henry, J. P., & Stephens, P. M. *Stress, help, and the social environment: A sociobiologic approach to medicine.* New York: Springer-Verlag, 1977.

Hess, E. H. Attitude and pupil size. *Scientific American,* 1965, 212, 46–54.

Higgins, E. T., Rhodewalt, F., & Zanna, M. P. Dissonance motiva-

tion: Its nature, persistence, and reinstatement. *Journal of Experimental Social Psychology,* 1979, 15, 16–34.

Hirschman, R. D., & Katkin, E. S. Relationships among attention, GSR activity, and perceived similarity of self and others. *Journal of Personality,* 1971, 39, 277–288.

Holden, C. Academy boosts social sciences. *Science,* 1982, 217, 133.

Hord, D. J., Johnson, L. G., & Lubin, A. Differential affect of the law of initial value (LIV) on autonomic variables. *Psychophysiology,* 1964, 1, 79–87.

Izard, C. E. *The face of emotion.* New York: Appleton-Century-Crofts, 1971.

Janis, I. L., & Feshbach, S. Effects of fear-arousing communications. *Journal of Abnormal and Social Psychology,* 1953, 48, 78–92.

Janisse, M. P., & Peavler, W. S. Pupillary research today: Emotion in the eye. *Psychology Today,* February, 1974, pp. 60–63.

Johnson, H. J., & Campos, J. J. The effect of cognitive tasks and verbalization instruction on heart rate and skin conductance. *Psychophysiology,* 1967, 4, 143–150.

Kaplan, H. B. Studies in sociophysiology. In E. Gartly Jaco (Ed.), *Patients, physicians, and illness.* New York: Free Press, 1972.

Kaplan, H. B. Social psychology of disease. In H. E. Freeman, S. Levine, & L. G. Reeder (Eds.), *Handbook of medical sociology* (3rd ed.). Englewood Cliffs, N.J.: Prentice-Hall, 1979.

Kaplan, H. B., & Bloom, S. W. The use of sociological and social-psychological concepts in physiological research: A review of selected experimental studies. *Journal of Nervous and Mental Disease,* 1960, 131, 128–134.

Kassarjian, H. H., & Robertson, T. S. *Perspectives in consumer behavior.* Glenview, Ill.: Scott-Foresman, 1981.

Katkin, E. S. Relationship between manifest anxiety and two indices of autonomic responses to stress. *Journal of Personality and Social Psychology,* 1965, 2, 324–333.

Katkin, E. S. The relationship between a measure of transitory anxiety and spontaneous autonomic activity. *Journal of Abnormal Psychology,* 1966, 71, 142–146.

Katkin, E. S. Electrodermal lability: A psychophysiological analysis of individual differences in response to stress. In I. G. Sarason & C. D. Spielberger (Eds.), *Stress and anxiety* (Vol. 2). Washington, D.C.: Hemisphere, 1975.

Kiesler, C. A., & Pallak, M. S. Arousal properties of dissonance manipulations. *Psychological Bulletin,* 1976, 83, 1014–1025.

Kissel, S. Stress-reducing properties of social stimuli. *Journal of Personality and Social Psychology,* 1965, 2, 378–384.

Kraut, R. E. Social presence, facial feedback, and emotion. *Journal of Personality and Social Psychology,* 1982, 42, 853–863.

Krugman, H. E. *The effective use of physiological measurement in advertising research.* Paper presented at the 12th Annual Attitude Research Conference of the American Marketing Association, Hot Springs, Virginia, 1981.

Kulpe, O. *Outlines of psychology.* New York: Macmillan, 1895.

Lacey, J. I. Psychophysiological approaches to the evaluation of psychotherapeutic process and outcome. In E. A. Rubinstein & M. B. Parloff (Eds.), *Research in psychotherapy* (Vol. 1). Washington, D.C.: American Psychological Association, 1959.

Lacey, J. I. Somatic response patterning and stress: Some revisions of activation theory. In M. H. Appley & R. Trumbull (Eds.), *Psychological stress: Issues in research.* New York: Appleton-Century-Crofts, 1967.

Lacey, J. I., Kagan, J., Lacey, B. C., & Moss, M. A. H. The visceral level: Situational determinants and behavioral correlates of autonomic response patterns. In P. N. Knapp (Ed.), *Expression of the emotions in man.* New York: International Universities Press, 1963.

Laird, J. D. Self-attribution of emotion: The effects of expressive behavior on the quality of emotional experience. *Journal of Personality and Social Psychology,* 1974, 29, 475–486.

Lang, P. J. The application of psychophysiological methods to the study of psychotherapy and behavior modification. In A. E.

Bergin & S. L. Garfield (Eds.), *Handbook of psychotherapy and behavior change*. New York: Wiley, 1971.

Latane, B., & Cappell, H. The effects of togetherness on heart rate in rats. *Psychonomic Science*, 1972, 29, 177–179.

Latane, B., Williams, K. D., & Harkins, S. G. Many hands make light the work: The causes and consequences of social loafing. *Journal of Personality and Social Psychology*, 1979, 37, 822–832.

Lazarsfeld, P. F. The American soldier—an expository review. *Public Opinion Quarterly*, 1949, 13, 377–404.

Leiderman, P. H., & Shapiro, D. (Eds.). *Psychobiological approaches to social behavior*. Stanford, Calif.: Stanford University Press, 1964.

Lemon, N. *Attitudes and their measurement*. New York: Wiley, 1973.

Leventhal, H. Findings and theory in the study of fear communications. In L. Berkowitz (Ed.), *Advances in experimental social psychology* (Vol. 5). New York: Academic Press, 1970.

Leventhal, H. Toward a comprehensive theory of emotion. In L. Berkowitz (Ed.), *Advances in experimental social psychology* (Vol. 13). New York: Academic Press, 1980.

Leventhal, H., & Mosbach, P. The perceptual–motor theory of emotion. In J. T. Cacioppo & R. E. Petty (Eds.), *Social psychophysiology: A sourcebook*. New York: Guilford Press, 1983.

Leventhal, H., & Nerenz, D. R. *Illness cognitions as a source of distress in treatment*. Paper presented at the annual meeting of the American Psychological Association, Los Angeles, August 1981.

Likert, R. A technique for the measurement of attitudes. *Archives of Psychology*, 1932, 140, 1–55(Whole).

Linder, D. E., Cooper, J., & Johes, E. E. Decision freedom as a determinant of the role of incentive magnitude in attitude change. *Journal of Personality and Social Psychology*, 1967, 6, 245–254.

Lindsley, D. B. Emotion. In S. S. Stevens (Ed.), *Handbook of experimental psychology*. New York: Wiley, 1951.

Lynch, J. J., Long, J. M., Thomas, S. A., Malinow, K. L., & Katcher, A. H. The effects of talking on blood pressure of hypertensive and normotensive individuals. *Psychosomatic Medicine*, 1981, 43, 25–33.

Lynch, J. J., & McCarthy, J. F. Social responding in dogs: Heart rate changes to a person. *Psychophysiology*, 1969, 5, 389–393.

Mackay, C. J. The measurement of mood and psychophysiological activity using self-report techniques. In I. Martin & P. H. Venables (Eds.), *Techniques in psychophysiology*. Chichester, England: Wiley, 1980.

Malmo, R. B. Measurement of drive: An unresolved problem in psychology. In M. R. Jones (Ed.), *Nebraska Symposium on Motivation* (Vol. 6). Lincoln: University of Nebraska Press, 1958.

Manstead, A. S. R., & Wagner, H. L. Arousal-cognition and emotion: An appraisal of two-factor theory. *Current Psychological Reviews*, 1981, 1, 35–54.

Markus, H. The effects of mere presence on social facilitation: An unobtrusive test. *Journal of Experimental Social Psychology*, 1978, 14, 389–397.

Markus, H. The drive for integration: Some comments. *Journal of Experimental Social Psychology*, 1981, 17, 257–261.

Martens, R. Effect of an audience on learning and performance of a complex motor skill. *Journal of Personality and Social Psychology*, 1969, 12, 252–260. (a)

Martens, R. Affect on performance of learning a complex motor task in the presence of spectators. *Research Quarterly*, 1969, 40, 733–737. (b)

Martens, R. Palmar sweating in the presence of an audience. *Journal of Experimental Social Psychology*, 1969, 5, 371–374. (c)

Maslach, C. Negative emotional biasing of unexplained arousal. *Journal of Personality and Social Psychology*, 1979, 37, 953–969.

Masling, J., Price, J., Goldband, S., & Katkin, E. S. Oral imagery and autonomic arousal in social isolation. *Journal of Personality and Social Psychology*, 1981, 40, 395–400.

McCurdy, H. G. Consciousness and the galvanometer. *Psychological Review*, 1950, 57, 322–327.

McGuigan, F. J. *Cognitive psychophysiology: Principles of covert behavior*. Englewood Cliffs, N.J.: Prentice-Hall, 1978.

McGuire, W. J. The nature of attitudes and attitude change. In G. Lindzey & E. Aronson (Eds.), *The handbook of social psychology* (2nd ed., Vol. 3). Reading, Mass.: Addison-Wesley, 1969.

Mesulam, M., & Perry, J. The diagnosis of lovesickness: Experimental psychophysiology without the polygraph. *Psychophysiology*, 1972, 9, 546–551.

Metalis, S. A., & Hess, E. H., Pupillary response/semantic differential scale relationships. *Journal of Research in Personality*, 1982, 16, 201–216.

Mewborn, C. R., & Rogers, R. W. Affects of threatening and reassuring components of fear appeals on physiological and verbal measures of emotion and attitudes. *Journal of Experimental Social Psychology*, 1979, 15, 242–253.

Miller, L. C., Murphy, R., & Buss, A. H. Consciousness of body: Private and public. *Journal of Personality and Social Psychology*, 1981, 41, 397–406.

Miller, N., & Campbell, D. T. Recency and primacy in persuasion as a function of the timing of speeches and measurements. *Journal of Abnormal and Social Psychology*, 1959, 59, 1–9.

Moore, D. L. *Are audiences distracting?: Behavioral and physiological data*. Unpublished master's thesis, University of Iowa, 1977.

Moore, D. L., & Baron, R. S. Social facilitation: A psychophysiological analysis. In J. T. Cacioppo & R. E. Petty (Eds.), *Social psychophysiology: A sourcebook*. New York: Guilford Press, 1983.

Moruzzi, G., & Magoun, H. W. Brainstem reticular formation and activation of the EEG. *Electroencephalography and Clinical Neurophysiology*, 1949, 1, 455–473.

Murray, H. A. *Explorations in personality: A clinical and experimental study of fifty men of college age*. New York: Oxford University Press, 1938.

Musante, G., & Anker, J. M. Experimenter's presence: Effects on subject's performance. *Psychological Reports*, 1972, 30, 903–904.

Nisbett, R. E., & Wilson, T. D. Telling more than we can know: Verbal reports on mental processes. *Psychological Review*, 1977, 84, 231–259.

Notarious, C. I., Wemple, C., Ingraham, L. J., Burns, T. J., & Kollar, E. Multichannel responses to an interpersonal stressor: Interrelationships among facial display, heart rate, self-report of emotion, and threat appraisal. *Journal of Personality and Social Psychology*, 1982, 43, 400–408.

Obrist, P. A. The cardiovascular–behavioral interaction—as it appears today. *Psychophysiology*, 1976, 13, 95–107.

Obrist, P. A. *Cardiovascular psychophysiology: A perspective*. New York: Plenum Press, 1981.

Osgood, C. E., Suci, G. J., & Tannenbaum, P. H. *The measurement of meaning*. Urbana: University of Illinois Press, 1957.

Oskamp, S. *Attitudes and opinions*. Englewood Cliffs, N.J.: Prentice-Hall, 1977.

Pachella, R. G. The interpretation of reaction time in information-processing research. In B. Y. Kantowitz (Ed.), *Human information processes: Tutorials in performance and cognition*. Hillsdale, N.J.: Erlbaum, 1974.

Pallak, M. S., & Pittman, E. S. General motivation effects of dissonance arousal. *Journal of Personality and Social Psychology*, 1972, 21, 349–358.

Pennebaker, J. W. Accuracy of symptom perception. In A. Baum, J. E. Singer, & S. E. Taylor (Eds.), *Handbook of psychology in health* (Vol. 4). Hillsdale, N.J.: Erlbaum, 1982.

Pennebaker, J. W. Physical symptoms and sensations: Psychological caruses and correlates. In J. T. Cacioppo & R. E. Petty (Eds.), *Social psychophysiology: A sourcebook*. New York: Guilford Press, 1983.

Pennebaker, J. W., & Lightner, J. M. Competition of internal and external information in an exercise setting. *Journal of Personality and Social Psychology*, 1980, 39, 165–174.

Pennebaker, J. W., & Skelton, J. A. Selective monitoring of physical sensations. *Journal of Personality and Social Psychology*, 1981, 41, 213–223.

Petty, R. E., & Cacioppo, J. T. Forewarning, cognitive responding and resistance to persuasion. *Journal of Personality and Social Psychology*, 1977, 35, 645–655.

Petty, R. E., & Cacioppo, J. T. Issue-involvement can increase or decrease persuasion by enhancing message-relevant cognitive responses. *Journal of Personality and Social Psychology*, 1979, 37, 1915–1926.

Petty, R. E., & Cacioppo, J. T. *Attitudes and persuasion: Classic and contemporary approaches.* Dubuque, Ia.: Wm. C. Brown, 1981.

Petty, R. E., & Cacioppo, J. T. The role of bodily responses in attitude measurement and change. In J. T. Cacioppo & R. E. Petty (Eds.), *Social psychophysiology: A sourcebook.* New York: Guilford Press, 1983.

Petty, R. E., Harkins, S. G., Williams, K. D., & Latane, B. The effects of group size on cognitive effort and evaluation. *Personality and Social Psychology Bulletin*, 1977, 3, 579–582.

Petty, R. E., Wells, G. L., Heesacker, M., Brock, T. C., & Cacioppo, J. T. The effects of recipient posture on persuasion: A cognitive response analysis. *Personality and Social Psychology Bulletin*, 1983, 9, 209–222.

Pribram, K. H. Interrelations of psychology and the neurological disciplines. In S. Koch (Ed.), *Psychology: A study of a science* (Vol. 4). New York: McGraw-Hill, 1962.

Prokasy, W. F., & Raskin, D. C. (Eds.). *Electrodermal activity in psychological research.* New York: Academic Press, 1973.

Rankin, R. E., & Campbell, D. T. Galvanic skin responses to Negro and white experimenters. *Journal of Abnormal and Social Psychology*, 1955, 51, 30–33.

Rappaport, H., & Katkin, E. S. Relationships among manifest anxiety, responses to stress, and perception of autonomic activity. *Journal of Consulting and Clinical Psychology*, 1972, 38, 219–224.

Riddle, E. M. Aggressive behavior in a small social group. *Archives of Psychology*, 1925 (No. 78).

Riess, M., & Schlenker, B. R. Attitude change and responsibility avoidance as modes of dilemma resolution in forced-compliance situations. *Journal of Personality and Social Psychology*, 1977, 35, 21–30.

Roloff, M. E., & Miller, G. R. *Persuasion: New directions in theory and research.* Beverly Hills, Calif.: Sage, 1980.

Routtenberg, A. The two-arousal hypothesis: Reticular formation and limbic systems. *Psychological Review*, 1968, 75, 51–80.

Sabini, J., & Silver, M. Introspection and causal accounts. *Journal of Personality and Social Psychology*, 1981, 40, 171–179.

Sanders, A. F. Stage analysis of reaction processes. In G. E. Stelmach & J. Requin (Eds.), *Tutorials in motor behavior.* Amsterdam: North-Holland, 1980.

Sanders, G. S. Driven by distraction: An integrative review of social facilitation theory and research. *Journal of Experimental Social Psychology*, 1981, 17, 227–251.

Sasfy, J., & Okun, M. Form evaluation and audience expertness as joint determinants of audience effects. *Journal of Experimental Social Psychology*, 1974, 10, 461–467.

Schachter, S. The interaction of cognitive and physiological determinants of emotion. In P. H. Leiderman & D. Shapiro (Eds.), *Psychobiological approaches to social behavior.* Stanford, Calif.: Stanford University Press, 1964.

Schachter, S. Second thoughts on biological and physiological explanations of behavior. In L. Berkowitz (Ed.), *Cognitive theories in social psychology.* New York: Academic Press, 1978.

Schachter, S., & Singer, J. E. Cognitive, social, and physiological determinants of emotional state. *Psychological Review*, 1962, 69, 379–399.

Scheier, M. F., Carver, C. S., & Matthews, K. Attentional factors in the perception of bodily states. In J. T. Cacioppo & R. E. Petty (Eds.), *Social psychophysiology: A sourcebook.* New York: Guilford Press, 1983.

Schlenker, B. R. *Impression management: The self-concept, social identity, and interpersonal relations.* Monterey, Calif.: Brooks/Cole, 1980.

Schwartz, G. E. Biofeedback, self-regulation, and the patterning of physiological processes. *American Scientist*, 1975, 63, 314–324.

Schwartz, G. E. Cardiovascular psychophysiology: A systems perspective. In J. T. Cacioppo & R. E. Petty (Eds.), *Perspectives in cardiovascular psychophysiology.* New York: Guilford Press, 1982.

Schwartz, G. E. Social psychophysiology and behavioral medicine: A systems perspective. In J. T. Cacioppo & R. E. Petty (Eds.), *Social psychophysiology: A sourcebook.* New York: Guilford Press, 1983.

Schwartz, G. E., Fair, P. L., Mandel, M. R., Salt, P., Mieske, M., & Klerman, G. L. Facial electromyography in the assessment of improvement in depression. *Psychosomatic Medicine*, 1978, 40, 355–360.

Schwartz, G. E., Fair, P. L., Salt, P., Mandel, M. R., & Klerman, G. L. Facial expressions and imagery in depression: An electromyographic study. *Psychosomatic Medicine*, 1976, 38, 337–347. (a)

Schwartz, G. E., Fair, P. L., Salt, P., Mandel, M. R., & Klerman, G. L. Facial muscle patterning to affective imagery in depressed and nondepressed subjects. *Science*, 1976, 192, 489–491. (b)

Schwartz, G. E., & Shapiro, D. Social psychophysiology. In W. F. Prokasy & D. C. Raskin (Eds.), *Electrodermal activity in psychological research.* New York: Academic Press, 1973.

Schweickert, R. Critical-path scheduling of mental processes in a dual task. *Science*, 1980, 209, 704–706.

Shaffer, D. R. Some effects of consonant and dissonant attitudinal advocacy on initial attitude salience and attitude change. *Journal of Personality and Social Psychology*, 1975, 32, 160–168.

Shapiro, D., & Crider, A. Psychophysiological approaches to social psychology. In G. Lindzey & E. Aronson (Eds.), *The handbook of social psychology* (2nd ed., Vol. 3). Reading, Mass.: Addison-Wesley, 1969.

Shapiro, D., & Leiderman, P. H. Arousal correlates of task role and group setting. *Journal of Personality and Social Psychology*, 1967, 5, 103–107.

Shapiro, D., Leiderman, P. H., & Morningstar, M. E. Social isolation and social interaction: A behavioral and physiological comparison. In P. H. Leiderman & D. Shapiro (Eds.), *Psychobiological approaches to social behavior.* Stanford, Calif.: Stanford University Press, 1964.

Shapiro, D., & Schwartz, G. E. Psychophysiological contributions to social psychology. *Annual Review of Psychology*, 1970, 21, 87–112.

Sherman, S. J. Effects of choice and incentive on attitude change in a discrepant behavior situation. *Journal of Personality and Social Psychology*, 1970, 15, 245–252.

Singer, J. E., Lundberg, U., & Frankenhaeuser, M. Stress on the train: A study of urban commuting. In A. Baum, J. E. Singer, & S. Valins (Eds.), *Advances in environmental psychology* (Vol. 1). Hillsdale, N.J.: Erlbaum, 1978.

Smith, C. E. The autonomic excitation resulting from the interaction of individual opinion and group opinion. *Journal of Abnormal and Social Psychology*, 1936, 30, 138–164.

Smith, E. R., & Miller, F. D. Limits on perception of cognitive processes: A reply to Nisbett and Wilson. *Psychological Review*, 1978, 85, 355–362.

Smith, M. J. *Persuasion and human action.* Belmont, Calif.: Wadsworth, 1982.

Spence, K. W. *Behavior theory and conditioning.* New Haven, Conn.: Yale University Press, 1956.

Spitzer, L., & Rodin, J. Arousal-induced eating: Conventional wisdom or empirical finding? In J. T. Cacioppo & R. E. Petty (Eds.), *Social psychophysiology: A sourcebook.* New York: Guilford Press, 1983.

Sternbach, R. A. *Principles of psychophysiology.* New York: Academic Press, 1966.

Sternberg, S. The discovery of processing stages: Extensions of Donders' method. *Acta Psychologia*, 1969, 30, 276–315.

Strahan, R. F., Todd, J. B., & Inglis, G. B. A palmar sweat measure particularly suited for naturalistic research. *Psychophysiology*, 1974, 11, 715–720.

Strong, S. R. Social psychological approach to psychotherapy research. In S. L. Garfield & A. E. Bergin (Eds.), *Handbook of psychotherapy and behavior change* (2nd ed.). New York: Wiley, 1978.

Strube, N. G., Miles, M. E., & Finch, W. H. The social facilitation of a simple task: Field tests of alternative explanations. *Personality and Social Psychology Bulletin*, 1981, 7, 701–707.

Syz, H. C. Observations on the unreliability of subjective reports of emotional reactions. *British Journal of Psychology*, 1926, 17, 119–126.

Szpiler, J. A., & Epstein, S. Availability of an avoidance response as related to autonomic arousal. *Journal of Abnormal Psychology*, 1976, 85, 72–82.

Tedeschi, J. T., Schlenker, B. R., & Bonoma, T. V. Cognitive dissonance: Private ratiocination or public spectacle? *American Psychologist*, 1971, 26, 685–695.

Thayer, R. E. Activation states as assessed by verbal report and four psychophysiological variables. *Psychophysiology*, 1970, 7, 86–94.

Thurstone, L. L. Attitudes can be measured. *American Journal of Sociology*, 1928, 33, 529–544.

Totten, E. Eye movement during visual imagery. *Comparative Psychology Monographs*, 1935, 11, 1–46.

Triplett, N. The dynamogenic factors in pacemaking and competition. *American Journal of Psychology*, 1898, 9, 507–533.

Tursky, B., & Jamner, L. Evaluation of social and political beliefs: A psychophysiological approach. In J. T. Cacioppo & R. E. Petty (Eds.), *Social psychophysiology: A sourcebook*. New York: Guilford Press, 1983.

Uetz, G. W., Kane, T. C., & Stratton, G. E. Variation in the social grouping tendency of a communal web-building spider. *Science*, 1982, 217, 547–549.

Valins, S. Cognitive effects of false heart rate feedback. *Journal of Personality and Social Psychology*, 1966, 4, 400–408.

Vanderwolf, C. H., & Robinson, T. E. Reticulo-cortical activity and behavior: A critique of the arousal theory and a new synthesis. *Behavioral and Brain Sciences*, 1981, 4, 459–514.

Vaughan, K. D., & Lanzetta, J. T. Vicarious instigation and conditioning of facial expression in autonomic responses to a model's display of pain. *Journal of Personality and Social Psychology*, 1980, 38, 909–923.

Vaughan, K. D., & Lanzetta, J. T. The effect of modification of expressive displays on vicarious emotional arousal. *Journal of Experimental Social Psychology*, 1981, 17, 16–30.

Venables, P. H., & Christie, M. J. Electrodermal activity. In I. Martin & P. H. Venables (Eds.), *Techniques in psychophysiology*. Chichester, England: Wiley, 1980.

Waid, W. *Sociophysiology*. New York: Springer-Verlag, 1984.

Wallerstein, H. An electromyographic study of attention listening. *Canadian Journal of Psychology*, 1954, 8, 228–238.

Weiss, R. F., & Miller, F. G. The drive theory of social facilitation. *Psychological Review*, 1971, 78, 44–57.

White, P. Limitations on verbal reports of internal events: A refutation of Nisbett and Wilson and of Bem. *Psychological Review*, 1980, 87, 105–112.

Wicklund, R. A., & Brehm, J. W. *Perspectives on cognitive dissonance*. Hillsdale, N.J.: Erlbaum, 1976.

Will, G. F. But first, a message from . . . *Newsweek*, May 10, 1982, p. 98.

Wilson, W. R. Feeling more than we can know: Exposure effects without learning. *Journal of Personality and Social Psychology*, 1979, 37, 811–821.

Woodmansee, J. J. The pupil response as a measure of social attitudes. In G. F. Summers (Ed.), *Attitude measurement*. Chicago: Rand McNally, 1970.

Zajonc, R. B. Social facilitation. *Science*, 1965, 149, 269–274.

Zajonc, R. B. Compresence. In P. B. Paulis (Ed.), *Psychology of group influence*. Hillsdale, N.J.: Erlbaum, 1980. (a)

Zajonc, R. B. Feeling and thinking: Preferences need no inferences. *American Psychologist*, 1980, 35, 151–175. (b)

Zajonc, R. B., Heingarner, A., & Herman, E. M. Social enhancement and impairment in performance in the cockroach. *Journal of Personality and Social Psychology*, 1969, 13, 83–92.

Zajonc, R. B., & Sales, S. M. Social facilitation of dominant and subordinate responses. *Journal of Experimental Social Psychology*, 1966, 2, 160–168.

Zanna, M. P., & Cooper, J. Dissonance and the pill: An attribution approach to studying the arousal properties of dissonance. *Journal of Personality and Social Psychology*, 1974, 29, 703–709.

Zanna, M. P., & Cooper, J. Dissonance and the attribution process. In J. H. Harvey, W. J. Ickes, & R. F. Kidd (Eds.), *New directions in attribution research*. Hillsdale, N.J.: Erlbaum, 1976.

Zillmann, D. Attribution and the misattribution of excitatory reaction. In J. H. Harvey, W. J. Ickes, & R. F. Kidd (Eds.), *New directions in attribution research* (Vol. 2). Hillsdale, N.J.: Erlbaum, 1978.

Zillmann, D. *Hostility and aggression*. Hillsdale, N.J.: Erlbaum, 1979.

Zillmann, D. Transfer of excitation in emotional behavior. In J. T. Cacioppo & R. E. Petty (Eds.), *Social psychophysiology: A sourcebook*. New York: Guilford Press, 1983.

Zillmann, D. *Connections between sex and aggression*. Hillsdale, N.J.: Erlbaum, 1984.

Zuckerman, M., Larrance, D. T., Spiegel, N. A., & Klorman, R. Controlling nonverbal cues: Facial expressions and tone of voice. *Journal of Experimental Social Psychology*, 1981, 17, 506–524.

PART THREE
APPLICATIONS

Chapter Twenty-Five

Lie Detection as Psychophysiological Differentiation: Some Fine Lines

John J. Furedy

INTRODUCTION

Lie detection is a complex and emotional topic. Much of the complexity arises from the fact that it is both of scientific interest and of practical value. Extreme supporters of current lie detection techniques appear to view them as the only route to truth and justice. Polygraphy has extreme opponents, however, who see it as the way to perdition, coercion, and an overall loss of human rights and freedoms.

In controversies of this sort, important (though subtle) distinctions are often ignored, both because of the complexities inherent in the problem and because of the emotions that tend to blind the participants. The aim of this chapter, as suggested by its title, is to make some conceptual distinctions that are relevant for a rational understanding of lie detection. These distinctions or "fine lines" will be drawn with a view to clarifying the issues under dispute.

With that in mind, I begin with a discussion of the key terms in the chapter title, to clarify the terms of reference.

Definitions

The most critical term to be defined from the title is "lie." There is little dispute about the meaning of a lie, although the term is sometimes loosely used. Definitions of a lie that depend on how accurately the communication reflects reality are inadequate. To make a statement that is false is not necessarily to lie. For example, an untrue communication can occur by mistake or accident, such as slips of the tongue or errors as described by Freud, or more simply because of a lack of accurate knowledge of the reality being communicated. These situations would generally not be classified as lies on the part of the communicator, even though such a communication is untrue. Conversely, a lie can occur even when an untrue communication has not been conveyed but the communication is misinterpreted. For example, if significant omissions are made in the communication with respect to the truth, and the result is a false interpretation by the receiver of the communication, then it would generally be agreed that a lie has occurred. In

John J. Furedy. Department of Psychology, University of Toronto, Toronto, Ontario, Canada.

this case, deception is achieved without the communication of untrue information: Such a communication may leave out significant portions of a completely truthful communication; or the communication may be completely truthful, but the communicator, through circumstance and/or nonverbal communication, leads the receiver of the communication to disbelieve the communication independently of the information contained therein.

The essence of lying is in the intent to deceive on the part of the communicator. This has indeed led many to adopt the term "deception," rather than "lying," because of that term's emphasis on the intent to deceive. Thus any definition of a lie must center on the *communicator* and his or her intentions, rather than on the veracity of the communication. Lykken (1981) has adopted Webster's definition in defining a lie as "a falsehood acted or uttered with the intention to deceive" (p. 24). Podlesny and Raskin (1977) have defined deception as "an act or state designed to conceal or distort the truth for the purpose of misleading others" (p. 782). However, a more complete definition comes from the early writings of Duprat, who defined a lie as follows: "A psycho-sociological act of suggestion, oral or not, by which one tends more or less intentionally to introduce into the mind of another a belief, positive or negative, which is not in harmony with that which the author supposes to be the truth" (Duprat, 1903, p. 30). This definition incorporates the necessary emphasis on the communicator's intention. In addition, it eliminates the need for the act to be oral, and explicitly states that the belief suggested by the communicator can alter the communicator's veracity by invention or exaggeration (positive lies) or by omission or attenuation (negative lies). From these definitions, it should be clear that the critical aspect of lying is the intent to deceive.

In speaking of the *accuracy* of the detection of deception or lying, it is common to specify a single percentage detection rate. However, this practice ignores a distinction that is important when the object of detection is not a physical "thing" but a psychological process. In the case of a physical object like the proverbial needle in a haystack, the most common error is the false negative—not finding the needle when it is, in fact, there. Therefore, a single percentage detection estimate is, for all practical purposes, quite sufficient for expressing accuracy. With a psychological process like lying, errors of the false positive type (i.e., deciding, wrongly, that lying has occurred) are equally plausible. In fact, research indicates that false positive errors in lie detection are actually more frequent than are false negatives (e.g., Barland & Raskin, 1975; Horvath, 1977). In addition, except for habitual criminals, it is also at least arguable that false positive errors are more serious than are false negative errors (cf. Lykken, 1981). For the detection of deception, then, an accuracy rating expressed only in terms

of false negative rates is seriously misleading, because it ignores a distinction of empirical and ethical importance. In other words, the detection of deception is not like looking for physical objects. It is more a problem of *differentiation* between two psychological processes—lying and not lying.

The differentiation involved is of a *psychophysiological* sort, because the indicators used for the detection are physiological changes in such functions as skin conductance, blood pressure, respiration, and heart rate.[1] Such functions are recordable through surface electrodes, and the changes involved are so small that they are not detectable by the individual from whom the recordings are made.

Implicit in this use of the term "psychophysiological" is a definition of "psychophysiology" as the field that studies "psychological processes in the organism as a whole by means of unobtrusively measured physiological processes" (Furedy, 1983, p. 16). As has been argued in more detail elsewhere (Furedy, 1983), neither this particular definition nor, indeed, the need for genuine, objectively evaluatable definitions has been universally accepted. In particular, the definition is not favored by those who wish to view psychophysiology from a more "biological" perspective (e.g., Obrist, 1976, 1981), and to eschew the indexing-of-psychological-processes notion that is implied by the definition. Although I have argued that even for cardiovascular psychophysiology the indexing view has merit (Furedy, 1983), it appears that the definition of "psychophysiology" offered here is particularly apt for lie detection, as long as it is recognized that the definition does not isolate the areas of psychophysiology and physiology "from one another, but rather brings them into a more scientifically meaningful relationship" (Furedy, 1983, p. 17). In other words, the psychophysiologist studying lie detection is primarily concerned with the degree to which dif-

---

1. In fact, the standard polygraph as used by members of the American Polygraph Association records the following four functions: "GSR," "cardio," respiration, and peripheral vasomotor activity. The last two of these measures require no further comment, but the first two need some. The "GSR" is the phasic skin resistance or conductance response, and was earlier regarded by field polygraphers as relatively insensitive, in contrast to laboratory experience. However, this particular field–lab discrepancy was due to inadequate instrumentation and measurement in the field. Current scientific polygraphers (e.g., Raskin, Barland, & Podlesny, 1977) agree with the evidence of laboratory workers (e.g., Curtow, Parks, Lucas, & Thomas, 1972) that the "GSR" is the most sensitive of the four measures, although a composite of the four may be slightly more sensitive still (Curtow *et al.*, 1972). The "cardio" is actually a measure of blood pressure, and is, moreover, one that does not distinguish between systolic and diastolic pressures. Rather it is a "relative" measure that gives a beat-by-beat indication of changes in the approximate mean of the systolic and diastolic pressures. Because the cuff needs to be kept inflated above diastolic pressure during the polygraphic examination, this index is not as unobtrusive as one might wish from a psychophysiological point of view (see Furedy, 1983), and may, indeed, produce some additional strain in the examinee.

ferentiation occurs, but is also concerned with the underlying physiological mechanisms of the differentiation phenomenon.

The differentiation between lying and not lying does not necessarily have to be psychophysiological, but other modes of differentiation, such as those involving introspection and behavioral observation, appear to be less promising. Introspection, indeed, seems to be of no relevance, because the context is one in which the person being examined may not wish to provide accurate information through the introspective mode (if he or she is deceptive). Behavioral indices of deception may be more plausible, and attempts have been made to examine the behavioral correlates of lying. Indices of this sort that have been investigated include measures of reaction time (e.g., Crosland, 1929; Ellson, Davis, Saltzman, & Burke, 1952; Marston, 1921); interference with motor behavior (Luria, 1932); changes in voice quality (Alpert, Kurtzberg & Friedhoff, 1963); and changes in frequency of other nonverbal behaviors, such as postural changes, eye contact, eye movements, gestures, facial expressions, and speech hesitation (e.g., Ekman & Friesen, 1969, 1974; McClintock & Hunt, 1975; Mehrabian, 1971).

But, like introspective reports, behavioral indices are under voluntary control to a significant degree, and this severely limits their usefulness for lie detection. In contrast, it is a property of psychophysiological measures that the subject is unaware of them. This minimizes the potential problems associated with the subject's awareness of both his or her intention to deceive, and of what behaviors (e.g., looking someone straight in the eye) are normally associated with veridical responding. Hence, by elimination, psychophysiology appears to offer the only sound way to differentiate deception from honesty. To the extent that this differentiation is possible, we can move toward an understanding of the psychological process of deception.

Origins of Lie Detection: Historical Background[2]

In this section, I briefly review the prescientific origins of lie detection, as well as the period from the 19th century up to the 1940s that preceded the current profession of polygraphy—today's most commonly used method of lie detection.

Human society has always been interested in detecting deception, although the question of guilt rather than the process of deception itself has been the matter of central concern, as is the case today among polygraphers. The earliest recorded instance of the

2. This section and the next one are based on a more extended account by Heslegrave (1981).

use of both behavioral and psychophysiological measures in the enterprise of detecting deception/guilt is from a Hindu medical source of about 900 B.C., in which persons falsely denying being poisoners were said to manifest such physiological changes as blushing, and such behaviors as rubbing the roots of their hair with their fingers (Wise, 1845, p. 394). The most impressive instance of prescientific detection comes from about the beginning of the third century B.C., in the story of Alexander the Great's physician, Erasistratus. This famed anatomist used the "tumultuous rhythm" of the heart (Trovillo, 1939, p. 850) to determine that the crown prince of the Seleucid court in Syria was deceptive about his impious—and hence guilty—love for his newly acquired stepmother. In this instance, the later birth of a daughter to the (now unhappy) pair confirmed these early polygraphic efforts of Erasistratus; the path of true (or any other sort of) love seldom runs smooth.

The instances above illustrate relatively unobtrusive, observational methods for determining guilt. More obtrusive methods that were popular, especially in the Middle Ages in Europe, included trial by combat, trial by ordeal, and physical torture. Torture, in particular, was designed to detect guilt by eliciting confession, and this confession-eliciting function is regarded by modern polygraphers as an important adjunct of their technique. It is for this reason that opponents of modern polygraphy have referred to it as the "fourth degree" (Lykken, 1981). As in the case of the third degree (i.e., physical torture), one problem is that the confession so induced may be false, being given only to stop the interrogation process.

The basis for modern polygraphy began in the late 19th century, with the development of equipment that would measure psychophysiological functions relatively unobtrusively. Lombroso (1895) reported data from practical applications of the measurement of blood pressure and peripheral vasomotor activity in the interrogation of criminal suspects. Over a decade later, the application of psychophysiological measurement techniques to forensic problems received approbation from a no less influential source than Munsterberg (1908), whose student Marston (1917) began the era of modern polygraphy by reporting a 96% accuracy rate using blood pressure as the single measure. Other workers during the same period (e.g., Benoussi, 1914) used respiration as their measure, and reported similarly high rates of accuracy. These high rates, needless to say, did not go unchallenged by other workers of that era (e.g., Landis & Gullette, 1925), and in general it is fair to say that the conditions of these early experiments were highly variable. However, enthusiasts were not deterred, and Marston (1938) is credited by Lykken (1981) as being the first to introduce the notion of a "specific lie response" that could be detected by a unique psychophysiological pattern of responding. Many modern practicing polygraphers believe in such qualitative "lie pattern" specificity, although the evidence for this belief is notably lacking. On the other hand, in their more cautious moments, even severe critics of polygraphy admit that, quantitatively, it performs at a level of accuracy better than chance (for this qualitative–quantitative distinction, see Furedy, 1982).

Lie Detection Today: Techniques and Theoretical Background

There are a variety of lie detection techniques. Podlesny and Raskin (1977) identified five different techniques, while Lykken (1981) has listed nine different techniques. These techniques differ in many ways, including the purpose of each test (see Lykken, 1979, and Raskin & Podlesny, 1979), its vulnerability to countermeasures (see Barland & Raskin, 1973, for a detailed account of possible countermeasures and research on their effectiveness; see also Kubis, 1962; Lykken, 1960; Rovner, Raskin, & Kircher, 1979), and the theory underlying each test (Barland & Raskin, 1973; Lykken, 1974, 1978, 1979; Podlesny & Raskin, 1977, 1978; Raskin, 1978). For the purposes of this chapter, however, the techniques can be considered essentially equivalent, since all of them compare the subjects' responses to questions relevant to the issue under investigation to the subjects' responses to questions that are meant to act as control questions. The nature of these control questions is the primary dimension of difference among these techniques. The control questions can range from (1) being irrelevant to the matter under investigation (Relevant/Irrelevant technique) through (2) being related to, but less serious than, the matter under investigation ("control question" technique) to (3) being as serious as the relevant question, but being related to a fictitious matter (Truth Control [Lykken, 1981] or Guilt Complex technique). If autonomic responses to relevant questions are greater than those to control questions, deception is indicated; if autonomic responses to relevant questions are less than to control questions, honesty is indicated; with slight differences, the examiner classifies the case as "inconclusive." In situations where the relevant question is unknown to the examiner, as in the case where knowledge of the matter under investigation is incomplete (Searching Peak of Tension technique), the largest autonomic response indicates deception.

In order for these lie detection techniques to detect deception, two basic assumptions must be true: (1) Deception is detectable through greater increases in autonomic arousal during deception than during honest responding; (2) the most salient property of the detection-of-deception paradigm that could account for the greater arousal associated with relevant questions is that an act of deception has occurred. Let us, in the light of these two assumptions, consider two of the primary techniques used in lie detection: the Control Question and Guilty Knowledge techniques.

The Control Question method is the most commonly used field and laboratory questioning technique. In this technique, the control questions are paired with the relevant questions by being temporally adjacent in the question series; the temporal proximity minimizes differential habituation effects. The control questions are designed in a pretest interview and deal with similar circumstances to those covered by the relevant questions "so that the subject is very likely to be deceptive to them or very concerned about them" (Podlesny & Raskin, 1977, p. 786). Although there is some dispute over the exact theoretical formulation underlying the Control Question method (Lykken, 1978, 1979; Raskin, 1978; Raskin & Podlesny, 1979), in general the theory of the method is that guilty subjects will reply deceptively to relevant questions and will show stronger autonomic responding to the relevant than to the control questions. In contrast, the control questions are meant to be "a stronger stimulus for the innocent subject because he knows he is truthful to the relevant questions; he has been led to believe that the control questions are also very important in assessing his veracity . . . and he is either deceptive in his answers, very concerned about his answers, or unsure of his truthfulness because of the vagueness of the questions and problems in recalling the events" (Raskin & Podlesny, 1979, p. 54).

A number of problems with the Control Question technique have been identified by Lykken (1974, 1978, 1979). For example, the identification of control and relevant questions is not too difficult, and therefore control questions may still be of less concern to the subject than relevant questions. Furthermore, the relevant questions are more arousing than the control questions, so that the greater affect associated with the relevant questions remains a problem. Lykken has also raised questions about whether the purpose of the control questions can ever be fulfilled, especially since the subject is instructed to respond honestly to all questions. Lykken (1979, p. 49) argues that it is impossible to discover whether a subject would be more concerned with the relevant or with the control questions, whether a subject might be unsure of his or her answers to the control questions, or whether a subject is being honest or deceptive in replying to control questions.

Lykken (1979) has also criticized the control aspect of this test, since the responses to the control questions, in his view, do not provide a reasonable estimate of what the relevant responses would be if the answer to the relevant questions were honest. However, Raskin and Podlesny (1979) have stated that the control questions are not meant as a scientific control for deception. Rather, they are meant as a stronger emotional stimulus than the relevant questions for innocent subjects. Therefore, they are meant as "emotional standard" questions (Barland & Raskin, 1973, p. 430) to enhance the innocent subjects' responses. In fact, in Raskin and Podlesny's terms (1979), quoted above, the control questions are meant to be of great concern to all subjects (since guilty and innocent subjects cannot be discriminated beforehand). More importantly, however, the purpose of the control questions is to elicit deception or at least to make a subject unsure that he or she has answered truthfully.

Indeed, further considerations of the rationale of the Control Question technique seem to imply that the deception that is detected is not in the guilty but in the innocent subjects. This strange conclusion appears to follow if one grants the assumption that the control questions do in fact elicit deception, as Podlesny and Raskin (1977) and Raskin and Podlesny (1979) have suggested. In that case, it would seem that a guilty subject would not be detected by the technique, since he or she would respond deceptively both to the control questions (by instructions) and to the relevant questions (by reason of guilt), so that no differentiation would ensue. The differentiation, rather, would ensue in the case of the innocent subject, who would respond deceptively only to the control questions. This differentiation, of course, would be in a direction opposite to that expected by the advocates of the Control Question technique (i.e., larger responses to the control questions), as well as occurring for the wrong target population (i.e., for the innocent rather than for the guilty or "deceptive"). Nevertheless, if the detection of the process of deception is really the issue, one would seem forced to interpret the larger autonomic responses to the control relative to the relevant questions in the innocent subject (classified as "nondeceptive" by the polygrapher) as the "detection of deception"!

These considerations suggest that the Control Question technique is not really designed to detect deception. Rather, the technique appears to rest on the notion of picking up the greater significance and affective value of the relevant questions for the guilty relative to the innocent. Deception itself, as the previous analysis shows, may occur in replies to both relevant and control questions, and may in fact be detected with greater frequency in the innocent than in the guilty. In view of these difficulties, the "guilty knowledge" technique was developed by Lykken (1959, 1960, 1974) in an attempt to generate a detection-of-deception procedure with improved scientific and experimental focus on the deception process itself in the guilty person.

The Guilty Knowledge technique seeks to provide a genuine control comparison that is a reasonable estimate of the honest subject's responses to the relevant questions. In this technique, the subject is asked

a question and given alternative answers in a multiple-choice format, with the relevant answer embedded among other alternative plausible answers (usually four). A laboratory example of this procedure is the common card-test procedure. Here the subject selects a card from a number of alternatives, and then the examiner questions the subject about each alternative in the set of cards. For example, the examiner may ask: "Did you select number 1? Did you select number 2? . . . Did you select number 5?" All alternatives are equally plausible. This procedure can also be used in real crime situations. For example, if the crime involved murder through a stabbing with a knife, the questions might be: "Did you kill Mr. Chiu with a gun? Did you kill Mr. Chiu with a rope? Did you kill Mr. Chiu with a knife? Did you kill Mr. Chiu with a rock? [or] Did you kill Mr. Chiu with a hammer?" (Regina vs. Wong, 1977, p. 515; see also Lykken, 1979, 1981, for the Control Question version of this test). Therefore, each alternative or question should be equally plausible to the innocent subject, but the guilty subject should show a stronger autonomic response to the third alternative. Control is achieved because the other alternative questions on the same topic provide a reasonable estimate of the honest subject's response to the relevant question. If care is taken in the construction of the test, then the problem of stimulus characteristics associated with the control alternatives can be handled adequately. In addition, if desired, the test can be biased in favor of false negative errors by making the control alternative more emotionally arousing than the relevant alternative—a procedure not unlike the control question technique.

One distinct advantage of this technique is that, as the number of different questions increases, the probability that the subject will show the largest response to the relevant alternative on each question will be the product of the probabilities of each question independently. Therefore, if there are five alternatives to each question, the probability that an innocent subject will show the largest response to the relevant item in one question is .20. However, over three questions, the probability that an innocent subject will show the largest response to all three relevant alternatives will be .008. By employing a large number of questions, one can theoretically guard against false positive outcomes as Lykken suggests (1974), and the evidence supports this suggestion (Davidson, 1968; Lykken, 1959, 1960; Podlesny & Raskin, 1977).

However, the Guilty Knowledge technique, which is the major alternative to the Control Question technique, also appears *not* to detect deception itself. This emerges from considering the following theoretical basis for the tests, as stated by Lykken:

> [T]he basic assumption of the guilty knowledge test is that the guilty subject will show [a] stronger autonomic response to what he recognizes as the significant alterna-

tive than he would have shown without such guilty knowledge. . . . In the language of psychophysiology, all of the guilty knowledge test alternatives can be expected to produce orienting reflexes that will vary in amplitude from subject to subject for a number of reasons, of which guilt [or deception] is only one. However, for the guilty subject only, the "correct" alternative will have special significance, and added "signal value" (Berlyne, 1960), which will tend to produce a stronger orienting reflex than that subject will show to other alternatives. (Lykken, 1974, p. 727)

This quotation indicates that the basic assumption is not that the guilty knowledge test will detect deception, but rather that there will be a differentially greater orienting reflex (and thus autonomic arousal) associated with the identification of the relevant alternative because of its greater signal value or attention-getting quality. Subjects will orient toward the correct alternative if it is known to them (i.e., if they are guilty subjects) and will produce a stronger orienting reflex than they would if the orienting reflex were merely a product of the content of the question. This analysis is in line with Berlyne's (1960) view of stronger orienting reflexes when the stimulus has a single value, and also with the Bernstein's (1979) position that the magnitude of the orienting reflex can be shown to be directly related to the significance of the stimulus. Bernstein's analysis also suggests that arousal can be enhanced by any manipulation that assigns greater significance to the relevant questions. For example, the performance of some prior relevant behavior (i.e., choosing a card) would be one way of assigning greater significance to the relevant question, and no process of deception per se need be involved.

Janisse and Bradley (1980) conducted a study to determine whether deception is a critical feature of the Guilty Knowledge technique. They ran three groups of subjects in a card-test situation, and all subjects selected one card out of five. One group concealed their choice and were instructed to respond "no" to each question; a second group concealed their choice and were instructed to attempt to deceive the experimenter but remain silent; and the final group *revealed* their choice to the experimenter and were instructed simply to sit and listen to the questions, since they were not attempting to conceal information. The results showed that the choice of card in *all* groups was detected at rates significantly better than chance. There were also no statistical differences among groups, but the verbal "no" and silent groups appeared to be consistently more detectable over various dependent measures. These results demonstrate that merely performing some behavior that is made relevant through instructions is a sufficient condition for the detection of that behavior.

Careful consideration of so-called detection-of-deception techniques therefore suggests that these techniques are designed not to detect deception, but

rather to detect greater emotional or orienting responses. Deception, then, does not appear to be a critical feature of current lie detection techniques. In fact, it can be argued that there has not been an adequate demonstration that deception is even a *sufficient* condition for the enhancement of autonomic responsivity.

Polygraphic, Psychological, and Psychophysiological Perspectives on Lie Detection

Some of the implications of viewing lie detection as psychophysiological differentiation have been explored already. The concern of this section is to distinguish among three perspectives of lie detection: polygraphic, psychological, and psychophysiological.

The applied polygraphic approach to lie detection focuses on the global lie detection "package," and is primarily concerned with this question: Do lie detection techniques detect guilty persons? The global package includes a number of factors that may each be of considerable importance in determining the success rate, but that are typically quite difficult to specify in ways that allow replication for further research. One such factor is the interviewing skill of the polygrapher, which includes as an important component his or her ability to convince the interviewee of the infallibility of the lie detection procedure. Although polygraphers are trained to increase this ability, it is obvious that many important aspects of it still are not specifiable, but rather are gained through osmosis.

Consistent with this Gestalt-like, subjective perspective is the fact that most professional polygraphers interpret their physiological records in an unquantified, subjective way. Thus, although there has been some emphasis on quantified methods by such scientifically trained polygraphers as D. C. Raskin, most professional polygraphers make their decision according to the overall look or patterning of the various measures, rather than a more quantifiable (and hence specifiable) index. In addition, rather than having the scorer of the records be independent of the examiner (i.e., "blind" scoring), most polygraphers inspect their own recordings, and therefore have already formed opinions about whether those records are those of a "deceptive" or an "honest" subject.

It is important to recognize that from a more scientific, psychological perspective, the main problem with the polygrapher's subjective approach is not so much that it is less effective (although that too appears to be the case; cf. discussion in section 1.4.4 of Szucko & Kleinmuntz, 1981), but that it cannot be objectively investigated. Any phenomenon that is unspecifiable independently of the skill of some highly successful practitioner is not one that can be examined in a scientific way, whereby the factors responsible for the phenomenon are identified and analyzed. In this connection, it also bears emphasis that according to professional polygraphers an important function of the procedure, in addition to detecting deception, is that of eliciting confessions. The confession-eliciting function of polygraphy can interfere with its deception-detecting function unless it is assumed that such elicited confessions are always true. Professional polygraphers do make this very strong assumption either implicitly or explicitly, but anyone familiar with the principles of social psychology can recognize that the assumption is false. People can, under some circumstances, confess to crimes they have not committed, even when not being subjected to any physical torture or "third degree." The fact that psychological pressure, or the "fourth degree" (Lykken, 1981), can sometimes elicit false confessions as a means of relieving this pressure is one that is ignored by professional polygraphers, perhaps because their training in psychology is usually minimal.

From the perspective of the science of psychology, lie detection is considered as a phenomenon like any other. The primary focus of this perspective is on the empirical and systematic study of those factors or processes that influence how well lie detection techniques differentiate deceptive from honest persons. From this perspective, the concern is with such issues as (1) the influence of variables that might affect confessions, (2) the examination of the value of specific components of the polygraphic package in detecting deception or identifying guilty persons, (3) the role of individual differences in detectability, and (4) the legal questions surrounding lie detection. However, the focus of such research is not primarily on effects of these factors on autonomic responses. Rather, the focus is on more general psychological issues, and need not be concerned with the psychophysiological issues relevant to the autonomic measures. For example, research from the psychological perspective has provided valuable data showing that the experience of professional polygraphers plays a role in making reliable decisions. Horvath and Reid (1972) showed that, for examiners with more than 1 year of experience, correct decisions on blindly read charts constituted 91.4% of all decisions, whereas for examiners with less than 6 months of experience, correct decisions averaged 79.1%.

From the perspective of psychophysiology, the focus is on that aspect of lie detection in which physiological measures are employed. However, unlike the polygrapher, the psychophysiologist's interest is primarily in the measures themselves (and the underlying psychological processes that they reflect), rather than their utility in detecting the guilty. Moreover, because this interest is scientific, the measures need to be expressed in objective, quantifiable terms, rather than in terms of the Gestalt-like, subjective methods used by many professional polygraphers.

Accordingly, there are two classes of studies that are of no direct interest to the psychophysiologist. One such class consists of studies that focus on the detection of deception through the global and subjective assessment of both the polygraphic records and other facts, such as the "facts" (in the legal sense) of the case. The other such class consists of studies that detect deception through the measurement of nonphysiological responses, such as the reaction time to word associations (e.g., Crosland, 1929) and other nonverbal behavioral symptoms (e.g., Ekman & Friesen, 1969, 1974; McClintock & Hunt, 1975; Mehrabian, 1971). The former class of studies really deals with the effectiveness of the "art" of employing the total polygraphic package. In ruling out this area from our inquiry, it is important to note that the line being drawn is not evaluative but demarcative (Popper, 1959). This recognizes the possibility that under some circumstances art may be more effective than science, but also makes it clear that art and science need to be distinguished. On the other hand, the latter class of studies, which deals with nonphysiological variables, is scientific in orientation. However, the orientation is toward the (scientific) application of a technology, rather than the (scientific) study of phenomena. In addition, from a psychophysiological perspective, these studies are excluded simply because the dependent variables used are not physiological.

Some Fine Lines in Looking at Lie Detection as Psychophysiological Differentiation

In this subsection, I briefly consider a number of distinctions that have often had an implicit influence on various controversies. These distinctions are also examined in more detail in later sections.

A Closer Look at the Discriminandum

The process to be discriminated is deception, as distinct from telling the truth. As argued above (see pp. 687–688), the techniques currently used really appear to be designed to detect greater emotional responses or orienting responses, rather than deception itself. While it is probably true that deception produces greater arousal than telling the truth, it does not follow that deception is the only source of arousal in lie detection paradigms. Therefore, when psychophysiological measures are used as the criteria for making a decision between truth telling and deception, two assumptions are implicitly made: (1) Deception is detectable through greater increases in autonomic arousal than during honest responding; (2) the most salient property of the detection-of-deception paradigm responsible for this greater arousal is the occurrence of an act of deception. To test the second assumption adequately, it is necessary first to determine whether deception can be differentiated from other sources of arousal, and then to distinguish between the arousal produced by deception and by other sources. As noted earlier in the discussion of the Guilty Person and Guilty Knowledge techniques, two important nondeception sources of arousal are emotionality and the (significance-enhanced) orienting reflex.

Group-Based Data versus Individual-Based Decisions

The conclusions drawn from psychophysiological research are almost uniformly statistical (i.e., based on groups). This is so even if the comparison is within subjects, as is the case in lie detection. Thus the conclusion of a study may be that lying was detected in $X\%$ of the individuals at a Y level of significance, where X is greater than 50 and Y less than .05. This is an entirely useful piece of information about a class of individuals tested under a specified set of conditions, and to the extent that X and Y are, respectively, high and low, our confidence in generalizing from these results is properly increased. However, these group-based results do not have strong implications for the individual-based decisions that are made in the field, where the polygrapher has to decide whether a given individual is lying. More precisely, the leap from group-based data to individual-based decisions is impossible unless the detection rate is virtually error-free (i.e., $X = 100$). Not even the most enthusiastic proponents of polygraphy argue for such a rate, although the polygrapher does try to convince the examinee that, for the particular sort of case for which he or she is being tested, the polygraph is error-free.

False Positive versus False Negative Errors

As noted before, polygraphers tend to speak only in terms of false negative errors when stating accuracy figures; however, this position rests on a false analogy with the discovery of physical objects. In lie detection, the possibility of false positive errors is a very real one. Moreover, the two sorts of errors have consequences that are radically different, as a function both of specifiable features of the situation and of differing ethical values.

If we hold conventional ethical views, it follows that a false positive error would be very serious in the case of a person without a criminal record accused of even the relatively minor offence of stealing. Conversely, a false negative would be very serious in the case of a convicted murderer/rapist, whereas one would be prepared to tolerate false positives (i.e., wrongfully accusing the person of that particular rape/murder) in that case. In such extreme cases, it is clear that to talk of a percentage error rate without specifying the sort of error involved is to provide little information. Moreover, comparison of the two sorts

of error rates in percentage terms becomes difficult if not impossible. Thus we can say that one sort of error is worse than the other, but we are hard put to quantify the extent of this difference.

The situation becomes even more complicated if conventional ethical views are abandoned and we take less orthodox ethical positions. It could be argued, for example, that to accuse a convicted (but reformed) rapist of a rape that he has not perpetrated is not only intrinsically evil, but may also produce a reaction against law and order in the (reformed) individual, who may now feel justified in going back to his old ways. Similarly, it could be argued that to fail to bring a previously honest but now criminal thief to justice is reprehensible because of the breakdown in the concept of law and order that this error causes. The fact that these arguments lack plausibility for most of us only points to the fact that most of us accept conventional ethical views. Such a lack of plausibility, however, is no justification for not considering those sorts of arguments, or for dismissing them out of hand. Accordingly, while it is an advance to specify the two sorts of error rates in percentage terms over the method of simply stating a single figure as if there were only one error rate, it is not clear that the percentages can be validly compared to each other, or even assessed in absolute terms. Is a 5% false positive rate acceptable for individuals with previously clear records who are accused of thievery? The answer to such a question depends not only on objectively specifiable circumstances, but also on the ethical values held by society.

Psychophysiological Differentiation versus Polygraphic Package

The distinction between the polygraphic package (PP) and psychophysiological differentiation (PD) is not binary, but represents more of a continuum. At the PP end, the decision is made by the examiner, who interprets the recordings in the light of the full context of what is known about the examinee both before and during the interview, as well as of the examiner's own experience. At this Gestalt level, it is quite reasonable to speak of the "art" of polygraphy. At the PD end, the decision is made using conventional scientific psychophysiological methods. That is, the decision maker is ignorant of anything about the examinee except the psychophysiological recordings. Moreover, there is no judgment involved even in the assessment of the recordings. Rather, the decision is derivable from quantified rules of measurement, so that, in principle, the decision could be reached by a computer.

One type of case that falls somewhere in the middle between PD and PP as here defined is that in which only the records are used to make the decision, but the decision itself is made in subjective terms rather than in terms of some formula. It is because there are, then, at least three sorts of cases that it is not enough to make such binary distinctions as clinical versus statistical predictions (Meehl, 1954; Szucko & Kleinmuntz, 1981), or clinical lie test versus polygraph lie control test per se (Lykken, 1981).

Moreover, the PD versus PP contrast is associated with two issues rather than one. One of these issues, to which most attention has been paid, is how well a given procedure works. For example, Szucko and Kleinmuntz's (1981) recent study suggests that when only the records are available, the more PD-oriented approach of basing the decision on the actuarial, formula-based method is generally superior to the intuitive, experience-based method. This result is contrary to the expectations of polygraphers, but in line with the analogous results in clinical-psychological diagnosis (e.g., Meehl, 1965). However, this instance of the "formula" being better than the "head" (Meehl, 1965) for lie detection would probably be disputed by polygraphers, who could argue that for the art of polygraphy to reach its full flower, not only the recordings but also the full context must be available. It will be noted that for a head–formula comparison of this sort, the specification of the overall context would be a difficult task. Nevertheless, at least in principle, this head–formula, intuitive–actuarial comparison is also resoluble empirically.

However, it should also be noted that even if this comparison is resolved in favor of the head/intuitive/PP approach—that is, it is resolved that "art" works better than "science"—there is still a second issue to be faced: that of communicability. The term "communicability" should be understood in its declarative, propositional sense, such that a method is "communicable" only if it can be stated as a set of propositional rules. There is a sense of communication between artists or craftspeople, whereby the art or craft can be passed on from teacher to pupil in a relatively efficient way. To the extent that this passing on is not propositional, however, it is not communication in the scientific sense. Nor, indeed, is it communication in the technological sense, because no sound technology can depend on intuitive, artistic methods. Therefore, even if it were found that in the hands of a first-rate and highly experienced polygrapher, a full-blown PP procedure was superior to a formula-based, PD procedure, this would not mean that in a strict technological sense the PP *procedure* worked better than the PD *procedure*. To the extent that there is an artistic component to a procedure—a component that cannot be propositionally specified and depends, therefore, on the artistic skills of the person applying it—the procedure cannot be said to be technologically efficient, simply because it cannot be communicated from practitioner to practitioner. By analogy, it is quite possible that there are individual faith healers who effect greater cures than does orthodox science-based medi-cine, but because of the great dependence of the efficiency of faith healing on the characteristics of the practitioner, faith healing is not only scientifically, but also technologically, inferior to orthodox medical procedures. This inferiority stems from the difference in communicability between the two technologies.

Personal/Political versus Scientific Aspects of the Disputes among the Experts

An important contributing factor to scientific and technological advance is the presence of opposing points of view. Ideally, such disputes are strictly scientific in the sense of being resolved solely in terms of internal consistency, or consistency with matters of fact. Such ideal, purely scientific disputes are rare even in the pure sciences. Personal and political aspects played a large part in the Leibnitz–Newton dispute, since even the greatest minds not only think but also feel. These feelings, moreover, affect not only the principals but also their respective followers, so that what may have started out as a factual, scientific dispute can quickly become thoroughly politicized.

The amount of politicization is increased if the contending parties not only have their own theories to protect, but also have other vested interests in those theories. In an area of applied and ethical relevance, such as lie detection, other vested interests obviously exist to a marked degree. Polygraphers who believe their lie detection procedures to be valid have more at stake than just protecting their beliefs: Their livelihood is also at stake. On the other hand, those who disagree with polygraphers concerning the validity of lie detection procedures also often have strong views on the ethics of employing those procedures, even if the procedures are reasonably valid. So the disagreements are fueled not only by a conflict concerning a matter of fact (the degree of validity of lie detection procedures), but also by (often unstated) conflicts concerning job security, protection of individual rights, views about the importance of catching criminals, and so on. And it goes without saying that the passions aroused by these political considerations lead to negative emotions that add to, and are probably qualitatively different from, the emotions aroused by the scientific passion for truth.

The main detrimental feature of the politicization process is not the ill feelings that it produces, but rather a product of these feelings. This product is that the internal logic of each position and its consistency with evidence become more and more irrelevant for the settling of the dispute. In purely scientific terms, this means that understanding cannot advance, so that there is no genuine epistemological advance; in some cases, indeed, there may even be an epistemological regression. An example of such a regression is provided by the dispute in astronomy about whether the earth moves around the sun. Although Aristotle denied this, there were a number of ancient Greek theorists who held the contrary, and correct, heliocentric position. Up to some time after Galileo's death, the Aristotelian, terracentric position held sway. From an epistemological point of view, this was regressive—not so much because of the incorrectness of the terracentric position, but because the grounds adduced to support it were based on vested (religious and political) interests rather than on logic and evidence.

The settling of factual disputes through political means also produces technological, practical regressions, although this sort of regression is often long-term rather than short-term. Thus it is doubtful whether the adoption of the heliocentric position actually improved navigation, as was claimed during Copernicus's and Galileo's time by the adherents of this position. But there is little doubt that in the end a technology that is based on politics rather than science will fail; ship navigation may have been just as efficient when based on the false terracentric position, but clearly rocket navigation to the moon could not be effective if based on that position.

These general points about the personal/political aspects of disputes are made not through any desire to eradicate them through some reform; human nature prevents such a reform. Rather, the aim in making the points is to suggest that in any dispute it is important to try, as clearly as possible, to distinguish between the scientific and the personal/political aspects. Making this sort of distinction is usually difficult, because proponents of positions seldom characterize their positions as political, but rather try to maintain as disinterestedly "scientific" a tone as possible. Nevertheless, the way in which a proponent will defend his or her position in the light of criticism will often reveal more about underlying political influences than the way in which the position is originally stated. However, it bears emphasis at the outset that even if the scientific–political distinction can validly be made, the process of analysis is itself somewhat subjective, and hence open to error. But then the possibility of error is present in any empirical enquiry.

PROBLEMS

This section comments on four sorts of problems that I consider important in lie detection as viewed from a PD perspective. The treatment is brief, because many aspects of each sort of problem have already been discussed above.

Reliability

Random errors of measurement are significantly present in any biological preparation, and they probably increase when social factors (i.e., pertaining to interaction between organisms) are introduced, as is the case in lie detection. Two of the most common ways of increasing reliability are to increase the number of observations per subject and to increase the number of subjects observed. Many areas in basic psychophysiology are such that both these moves are feasible, but this is not the case in lie detection. Thus polygraphers would not be willing to repeat critical questions over and over to the examinee in the way that experimenters can repeat stimuli to subjects. In the case of increasing subjects, the difficulty is not just practical but logical. As discussed before (see page 690), the critical reliability is that concerned with the decision about single individuals and not groups. Increasing the size of the sample, therefore, is logically irrelevant to improving reliability, and would in fact give a false picture of it. In this regard, however, it should be emphasized that the focus is on lie detection itself, rather than on the also pertinent issue of the factors that may or may not improve it. The latter issue is open to investigation using group data, and the reliability of results bearing on it may legitimately be increased by increasing sample size.

Validity

Problems of validity may be defined as systematic errors of measurement, which mean that the instrument in question does not measure what it is meant to measure. Also of relevance is the consideration of the sorts of systematic errors that may arise. Finally, I comment on the extent to which perfect validity should be sought.

Concerning systematic errors, the main source of these is the possibility that the lie detection procedure may be measuring anxiety rather than lying. The control question procedure—which is most convenient for polygraphers to use, and which therefore is in almost universal usage among them—is particularly open to this source of error. Somewhat ironically, it is probably the case that the more knowledgeable the innocent subject is about polygraphy when being examined, the more likely the subject is found to be wrongly guilty. That is, knowing the fallibility of polygraphy is itself likely to induce anxiety, which may be overly manifest when the subject is faced with the critical question. In PD terms, then, the problem is that although it is probably the case that lying leads to anxiety, the fact that the converse does not follow means that discrimination between the anxious guilty subject and the anxious innocent subject may not be present, no matter how effective may be the discrimination between the anxious and the less so.

The two sorts of systematic errors, as noted above, are false positives and false negatives. In this connection, it bears recognition that lie detection is essentially a problem in psychophysics, and that this field was markedly affected a few decades ago by the advent of signal detection theory (SDT). According to some proponents of SDT, the whole aim of psychophysics—the determination of thresholds—had to be abandoned, to be replaced by the sensitivity measurement of the distance (d') between the signal and noise distributions. This extreme version of SDT seems to me, however, to smack of picayune positivism: One cannot ignore the problem of determining what a threshold is simply by abolishing the term and replacing it by an incommensurable term like d' (incommensurable because the abscissa of the signal–noise distributions is unspecifiable in physical units). Similarly, the accuracy of the lie detection procedure cannot adequately be specified in terms of d', but must be stated in terms of (commensurable) percentages.

The valuable contribution of the SDT approach is both to draw attention to the distinction between the two sorts of errors, and to remind us of how (response) bias against committing one or the other error can affect the overall decision. Thus if one values the detrimental effects of false positives greatly, one will tend to detect fewer liars (and hence to increase the false negative rate). Conversely, if one is mainly concerned to avoid false negatives (the example of the murderer/rapist given above is a likely case in point), the rate of detection will rise, but so will the false positive rate. It will be noted that SDT cannot specify what the correct values are for the two sorts of errors, that being an ethical (and most would say, subjective) matter. It can, however, give an indication of what values or "response biases" are operating over a series of lie detection decisions. Moreover, SDT is also useful for comparing the *relative* validities or sensitivities of different sorts of lie detection procedures with the d' index, and this is useful for both scientific and technological purposes.

The consideration of relative validities raises the question of whether perfect validity should be sought. The notion that such a quest is reasonable appears to follow from one reason that has been given for banning polygraphy as evidence in court cases—the reason that polygraphy is not perfectly accurate.[3] However, perfect validity is an unrealistic aim both in science and in technology. In science any empirical assertion is open to doubt, and this extends even to the so-called "laws" in the hardest of sciences. For example, Newton's laws have been shown to be false by 20th-century physical observations. From a technological point of view, which in the present case is the legal context, it is the case that all sources of evidence are open to doubt. Eyewitness observation is commonly erroneous, and even technologies (such as ballistics) that are based on "harder" sciences provide inferences from one "expert" that are disputed by

another. At the other end of the continuum of admissible evidence is psychiatric testimony, which almost always is in marked dispute among the experts. Rejection of polygraphic evidence solely because that evidence is not guaranteed to be 100% accurate, then, would seem to be unjustified.

Communicability

As with reliability and validity, the more communicability a procedure possesses, the better it is for both scientific and technological purposes. The term "communicable" is here used in its declarative, propositional sense, as specified above (see pp. 690–691). Scientific activity, therefore, will inevitably include important uncommunicable components, such as the creativity that is responsible for the generation of new theories. However, the *evaluation* of theories can only proceed if they are communicable. Similarly, exciting new phenomena may well be obtained through uncommunicable means, such as serendipity and an intuitive feeling for what to do next—that is, through what we might call the "art" of science. However, unless the phenomena are communicable in the sense of having a set of rules that specify the conditions under which they may be obtained, they are not of genuine scientific utility. The situation in the case of technological efficiency, as argued above (see page 691), is the same: No matter how powerful a procedure may be, it is of no general technological use if it is not communicable.

In the case of lie detection, especially as it is currently used in the field by polygraphers, there are at least two factors that reduce communicability. One factor is the relative lack of quantification and specification of the psychophysiological measures that are used to make decisions in the field. The other is the lack of specification of the independent variables. In particular, the 30- to 60-min interview that precedes the psychophysiological measurement is a rich and complex social interaction that is probably impossible to specify (and hence to reproduce). To the extent that these two factors are present, the whole procedure depends on extraordinary polygraphic skill or experience. The question of whether this skill is really so great is itself an empirical one, and one to which some negative answers have been given recently (e.g., Szucko & Kleinmuntz, 1981). What is clear, however, is that, real or not, this sort of skill is very difficult to communicate in the sense defined here.

The Laboratory–Field Gap

Psychophysiologists are often urged to do experimental research on lie detection because of the relevance of their findings for field practices. Yet the transition from laboratory findings to conclusions relevant for

---

3. Another and more valid argument against the use of polygraphy, at least in jury trials, is the claim that many (lay) jurors believe polygraphy to be perfect, and hence attribute too much weight to evidence based on it. However, for evidence contrary to this claim, see Cavoukian and Heslegrave (1980).

the field is a logically perilous enterprise. The gap between research and applications is considerable in all areas, but lie detection is one in which there are additional complications that bear emphasis. One such complication is that the emotional tone of the laboratory has, of necessity, to be radically different from that in the field. Even quasi-realistic experiments in which subjects do actually steal some money (e.g., Podlesny & Raskin, 1978) are very different from field situations, where the crimes are usually much graver and—perhaps more importantly—the consequences of being detected are of an entirely different order of severity.

Some light could be shed on this issue by varying the severity of the deception or "crime" in the laboratory to determine its effects on the accuracy of detection. However, that light would again, of necessity, be indirect. Suppose that the degree-of-severity manipulation did not affect detection accuracy. This would not allow the conclusion that variation in emotional tone between laboratory and field makes no difference, because that variation is over a much wider range (and may, indeed, be on a different dimension or quality of affect) than the range investigated in the laboratory study.

In the end, therefore, evaluation of lie detection in the field can only be researched in the field itself. Unfortunately, the execution of evaluative research in the field of lie detection is fraught with special difficulties. The most obvious and quite serious one is that the field setting is highly uncontrolled, not only from the point of view of experimentation (i.e., manipulation of independent variables), but also from that of observation (i.e., ability to specify the conditions under which the dependent variables are measured). The full polygraphic procedure, including the lengthy prerecording interview as well as the information that the examiner has about the examinee, is as richly unique as any clinical interview. It is influenced by the nature of the examinee, the skill and experience of the examiner, and the specific relationship between the two. Generalizing from a studied sample to the population, therefore, is very risky.

Another difficulty, and one unique to lie detection, is that the criterion for validation is itself uncertain. The two most commonly used criteria (and probably the only reasonable ones available) are confession and jury findings; obviously, both are open not only to considerable random error, but also probably to systematic error. For example, during a period of conservatism, it is quite possible that the rate of false convictions (and perhaps even of false confessions) increases. On the other hand, this difficulty is severe only if the aim of the evaluation is absolute rather than relative. That is, if the aim is to find out the absolute accuracy of a given lie detection procedure, then it is doubtful whether the figure obtained can be regarded with confidence. If, however, the aim is to compare the relative validities of different procedures, the fact that the criterion of validity is not error-free will not matter, as long as the source of systematic error does not confound the comparison.

However, aside from these technological issues, it is also the case that evaluation in field lie detection raises ethical or value judgment problems. Even if research could supply us with valid figures on accuracy, valid figures cannot by themselves be used to make what are essentially ethical decisions. For example, a 5% false positive rate may appear to be an excellent testimonial for a particular lie detection procedure, but many would *evaluate* it as unsatisfactory if the procedure was used in *repeated* checks on the employees of a bank whenever money was missing. This evaluation would be supported partly by the gravity of the consequences of any false positive error, and partly by the fact that to the extent that the checks are repeated, the 5% value for the false positive rate is an underestimate. On the other hand, there would be others in whose opinion this usage of the procedure with the 5% false positive error rate would be quite justified. The justification would consist of arguments like that of the importance in our society of making sure that at least people who work in a bank are honest. It is obvious, then, that this sort of dispute is not only technical but ethical. The fact that it is part and parcel of the general problem of the evaluation of field lie detection renders that problem even more complex.

This chapter has so far dealt in generalities, with various examples used in a brief way to illustrate the points. In the next section, I focus on a specific, current, and still ongoing controversy over the value of lie detection.

WHERE EXPERTS DISAGREE: COMMENTS ON THE LYKKEN-RASKIN CONTROVERSY

There are some controversies that are open to resolution by superior authority. Some may consider legal controversies to be of this sort, with the judge and/or jury acting as the superior, resolving authority. Another example of such a resoluble controversy might be the question of when life begins. In principle although probably not in fact, biological scientists can be appealed to for a ruling on the basis of their scientific authority.

On the other hand, there are controversies that, even on the face of it, are not open to resolution. There are the disputes between or among people who are expert in the *same* field. In such controversies the experts have the same facts available to them (i.e., their background training is the same), and yet they disagree. The controversy to be discussed in this sec-

tion is of the latter sort. Accordingly, I offer no resolution, but only comments on the dispute.

What Is the Dispute?

In the most general of terms, one may describe
Lykken's (1974, 1981) position as being against polygraphy, and Raskin's (1978) as being for it. However,
the dispute looks different, depending on the perspectives discussed above (see pp. 688–689). In particular, from an overall polygraphic perspective (which
includes considerations of the social good), the dispute is a multifaceted one. In summary, one side
writes about polygraphy as an unethical, charlatan
procedure, while to the other side it is an effective
modern technology for getting at the truth.

From the more specific scientific perspective of
psychophysiology, it is at least arguable that there is
only one point of disagreement between the two sides.
This point is whether polygraphy is only about 70%
accurate (the claim Lykken defends), or whether, in
the hands of a competent polygrapher using quantified methods, its accuracy is on the order of 90% (the
claim Raskin defends). This is not to say that Lykken
and Raskin do not diverge on other issues, or even
that in all their writings they do not give different
impressions of their positions. For example, I have
elsewhere suggested that Lykken's (1981) book often
gives the impression that polygraphy is no better than
chance, rather than having some (i.e., 70%) degree of
accuracy (Furedy, 1982). Again, for someone well
trained in scientific methodology and familiar with
the normal concept of experimental control, Raskin's
acceptance of the logic of the control question methodology in polygraphy seems questionable. Moreover, the marked difference between the activities of
the two disputants strongly suggests that there is more
to the dispute between them than whether the correct
accuracy figure is 70% or 90%. On the one hand,
Raskin has become an experienced professional polygrapher, and has contributed toward the quantification of record scoring. On the other hand, Lykken has
never administered a polygraph, and has confined his
empirical research to the Guilty Knowledge technique, which is not used by professional polygraphers. Nevertheless, the scientific bone of contention between the two appears to be reducible to the
argument about relative accuracy.

To say that the scientific aspect of the dispute is a
single issue is not to say, of course, that the resolution
of the issue is itself simple. Indeed, as we shall see, the
arguments for and against the two positions are complex and multifaceted. They often involve considerations that, on examination, turn out to be irrelevant
from a scientific point of view. Nevertheless, the distinction between the polygraphic and the psychophysiological perspectives suggested here does serve to
reduce complexity and to contribute toward an ultimate scientific resolution of the dispute.

Why Take Up This Dispute?

We may begin by asking why any dispute should be
taken up. In the case of purely political disputes, the
more people who take them up, the more trouble
tends to develop. Indeed, because even scientific disputes have nonintellectual, political components,
there is a lot to be said for not actually getting into the
dispute by becoming a disputant.

Fortunately, disputes can be taken up not only by
becoming a disputant, but also by becoming a nonpar-
ticipating listener. The benefits gained from taking up
disputes in the listener mode are, of course, epistemological or informational. Much valuable information
can be gleaned from examining those often ingenious
arguments that participants in the scientific dispute
bring up. The aim of the disputant is to use these
arguments to undermine the position of the opponent. There may also be an aim to change the mind of
the opponent, but such an aim is not realistic. The
arguments seldom change the minds of the participants themselves. One reason is that the participants
are too familiar with, or expert in, the issues under
discussion to make it likely that they will learn anything new. However, a more compelling reason is that
because of the political components that are inevitable
even in all scientific disputes (carried on, as they must
be, between or among human beings), the participants
themselves are frequently too prejudiced to gain any
epistemological benefits from the dispute. These two
factors, however, do not apply to the listener, who
can employ the (often heated) dispute between (often
prejudiced) experts to sharpen the epistemological
issues, as well as learn some previously unknown
facts. Moreover, these gains are available to listeners
without the political costs involved in becoming an
active participant in the dispute.

These considerations apply to taking up any dispute in the nonparticipatory, listening mode. This
dispute is important to psychophysiologists for a
number of reasons. First, as argued at the outset,
research into lie detection (at least from a PD perspective) is of particular interest to psychophysiology. The
second major reason for looking at the Lykken–Raskin dispute is that the psychophysiological credentials
of both protagonists are excellent. Both have made
significant contributions to psychophysiology, and
both are highly regarded experimental researchers. To
the extent that examining disputes advances our understanding, the Lykken-Raskin dispute is an ideal
choice. It is superior, for instance, to such (hypothetical) alternatives as a dispute between a civil libertarian
with a humanistic rather than scientific background
arguing with a practicing polygrapher, because, for an

intellectual argument to be profitable, the disputants must share as much common background as possible.

There are also two reasons why I am interested in acting as a "listener" in this case. The first is that I am in a relatively disinterested position with respect to the dispute, not having published any empirical research in this area. The second and more important reason stems from my general interest in the nature of scientific controversy—an interest in what is common to such disputes. It is on these communal elements that my remaining comments concentrate.[4]

Scientific versus Nonscientific Aspects of Disputes

It is important to recognize that even in the purest of scientific disputes among the most eminent scientists, nonscientific aspects do play a part: All humans not only cognize, they also emote. Sometimes the points in dispute may be quite esoteric to the outside observer, as was the case in the Leibnitz–Newton controversy. On other occasions, although the arguments themselves may be esoteric, the point at issue can capture the attention of the public. This was the case in the dispute over terracentrism, in which Galileo and the scholars who opposed him were the active participants, and again in the dispute over evolution, which is still going on in at least the public, if not the scientific, domain. There is little doubt that perceived social relevance tends to increase the role of the nonscientific, personal/political aspects of controversies. However, there are other contributing factors. One such factor is the degree of technical complexity involved in the dispute. This usually increases as the dispute develops, and one of the effects is drastically to reduce the number of people who are not only able, but also willing, to follow the intricacies of the arguments being offered. With an ever-decreasing number prepared to follow the merits of the argument, the remainder base their decision on emotional/political considerations; this remainder can come to include scientists who are well qualified in areas related to the dispute.

At the same time, it becomes more and more difficult to identify particular concerns in terms of their

scientific status. This is because the arguments are almost always put forward as impersonal, rational ones by their proponents. The task of the listener to a scientific dispute is that of distinguishing between those arguments that stand on their own merits and those that stem from (implicit) appeals to authority, emotion, and even prejudice. This task is not an easy one, but it is one that should nevertheless be undertaken.

Some Elements of the Dispute

A marked feature of the Lykken–Raskin dispute is that it is a scientific one with immediate and highly significant technological and social implications. This is especially the case in North America, where the use of polygraphy is increasing. This close link to applications has the obvious effect of increasing interest in the controversy, with more and more people taking sides on the issues. One point that bears emphasis is that this increased degree of emotional commitment occurs not only among those who are laypersons with respect to the dispute (this group includes not only nonscientists, but also all those scientists who are not actively studying the particular issues under dispute), but also among the expert disputants. Whenever disputes heat up in this manner, it is useful to remember various (often implicit) elements that can contribute to the explicitly stated arguments. My characterization here of the subjective, nonscientific elements is deliberately general, with no attempt to illustrate these elements by drawing on examples from the dispute itself. Such an attempt would automatically result in the loss of "listener" status on my part. More importantly, it would be subject to error, with grave consequences. It is for the reader to decide which cap fits what wearer; my task is only to indicate the sorts of caps that are at hand.

Legalism

The focus of a scientific dispute should be the issues and not the personalities. Indeed, it is this that distinguishes scientific from other sorts of disputes. Nevertheless, once the human factors emerging from the adversary situation that develops begin to exercise their influence, the element of legalism enters the picture. That is, from what the problem *is*, the focus shifts to what the opponents have *said*. This shift is especially important when the opponents have said something that is demonstrably wrong. In terms of advancing understanding of the issues under consideration, such wrong statements are useless and should be ignored. However, in terms of a legalistic adversary system, these misstatements are of critical value for advancing the cause of one adversary. Nor will the

---

4. Another reason for believing that my comments as a "listener" to the Lykken–Raskin dispute may be of value is that I have been a participant in other, different disputes, such as those concerning GSR measurement (e.g., Furedy, 1969), Emmert's law (e.g., Furedy & Stanley, 1971), validity of measures of preception (e.g., Furedy & Klajner, 1974), random control methodology in Pavlovian conditioning (e.g., Furedy, Poulos, & Schiffman, 1975), role of orienting reaction in autonomic conditioning (e.g., Furedy & Poulos, 1977), alternative measures of heart rate variability (e.g., Heslegrave, Ogilvie, & Furedy, 1979), and validity of carotid dP/dt as a measure of myocardial sympathetic influence (e.g., Furedy & Heslegrave, 1983).

party who has originally made the misstatement be inclined to admit to error. This means that much energy will be spent on the misstatement, instead of getting on to other issues that are more relevant to a better understanding of the problem. Again, however, this energy is wasted only in terms of advancing understanding; in terms of a legalistic framework, the time spent either attacking or defending a misstatement is valuable, even critical, for helping either to defeat one's adversary or to defend one's own position.

On the other hand, the question of whether a particular dispute has shifted from a scientific to a legalistic one is often not easy to answer. There is a fine line between thoroughly examining the assumptions of a given position, and legalistically attacking the statements made by an adversary. Both activities involve detailed arguments over technical and often intrinsically uninteresting aspects. Needless to say, a legalistically motivated attack will not be stated to be explicitly so, because it is in everyone's interests to seem as objective and detached as possible. In the end it is up to the reader of, or listener to, a dispute to make the decision about this fine line for himself or herself. As a fellow listener, but not a judge, I can do no more than alert the reader to the consequences of legalism; I cannot identify specific cases to which it applies.

Misrepresentation

Misrepresentation is obviously related to legalism. Such cruder forms of misrepresentation as stating the opposite of what one's opponent has said are rare in the scientific, refereed-journal literature. However, there are more subtle forms of misrepresentation that can be equally effective, if not more so. Taking a statement out of context is one such form. Another is reinterpreting a statement or a position in such a way that the audience can be convinced that the reinterpretation has absurd consequences. Yet another is to take an opponent's assertion that is clearly meant as an analogy to state a testable theory; usually one can then derive consequences from this theory that are palpably false.

One problem with such more subtle misrepresentations is that in current scholarly disputes they are becoming harder and harder to correct. Except for the relatively new *Brain and Behavioral Sciences* journal and a few others, most journals in psychology are not set up for a discussion, point–counterpoint mode of publication. Instead, such point–counterpart affairs have lags of years between point and counterpoint. Partly because of this long latency, there is a considerable loss of interest by the audience in listening further to the problem, and editors often reflect this loss of interest by refusing to publish pieces that, on their own admission, do in fact correct a significant error in a paper previously published in the journal. This means that if one is skillful enough or lucky enough to get a misrepresentation past an editor and the one or two consultants who review the paper, the misrepresentation can come to acquire a face validity that is almost unimpeachable. For legalistic purposes, this, of course, is a highly desirable result; for advancing scientific (or, for that matter, practical) understanding of the problem, it is a less attractive one.

However, as with the more general influence of legalism, so with misrepresentation: There are fine lines that need to be drawn. Thus what may seem to one observer to be a misrepresentation of a position may seem to another observer to be simply a clarificatory logical analysis of the position—a clarification that results in bringing out implicit assumptions that are patently false. It must also be remembered that there can be multiple interpretations of what may look like a single position. The most common sort of such ambiguity is that between a position put forward as a genuine theory that makes assertions about the way things are, and one put forward as a model, approach, or thought-organizing instrument for looking at the world. To pick relatively current and well-known examples of this ambiguity, consider the levels-of-processing position in memory put forward by Craik and Lockhart (1972). Later critics of the position, such as Eysenck (1978), represented it and attacked it as a theory, and pointed to many consequences that were false. In their response, Lockhart and Craik (1978) cited their original paper to emphasize the view that they had put forward the position not as a theory but as an approach—in other words, that their critics had misrepresented their original position.

As with all disputes, I do not wish to proffer judgment. However, it is the case that there are aspects of the original paper that support the Lockhart-Craik "strict approach" interpretation, in which case their critics would indeed be misrepresenting their position and attacking a much more vulnerable position that they never espoused. However, to the extent that the original paper (Craik & Lockhart, 1972) does refer to predictions from the position that had been confirmed, and uses these confirmations to support the position, it could at least be argued that a plausible interpretation of their position is one of a theory that stands or falls strictly on the basis of evidence. In the end, as with most disputes, it comes down to a matter of judgment. The judgment is of the degree to which the position (in this example) was originally put forward as an approach only (in which case there has been misrepresentation), or as a genuine theory (in which case there has been no misrepresentation, but only clarificatory logical analysis). Moreover, because of the general lack of point–counterpoint publication format, that judgment can be made only by the listener to, or reader of, the dispute.

Political Factors

The presence of these factors in all scientific activity has already been noted. Political factors gain in importance during disputes, because the loss of a dispute can mean a loss not only of reputation, but also of research support. In the North American system, such support is almost completely external to the universities, and is judged by one's peers (i.e., experts within one's own area). It is obvious that there are considerable pressures to survive a dispute at all costs, and to ignore the possibility that, through losing some political point, one may gain epistemologically by learning something new—for that learning may well cost one the practical possibility of doing further research. Under these conditions, the investigatory motive that, in theory, fuels all scientific activity can be easily submerged in such practical motives as not only wishing to keep one's own reputation, but in not wishing to have to close down one's laboratory through lack of funding.

With regard to the dispute under consideration, there is also another set of political factors or vested interests that is operating. The operation of vested interests on the side of the polygraphers is obvious, and Lykken often uses this argument to attack their credibility. However, it bears emphasis that opponents of polygraphy may also have interests that are vested against the use of lie detection techniques. Both sets of interests are at least partially based on such personal/political considerations as one's views concerning the relative value of individual liberty versus that of so-called "law and order." It is these views that determine the value that is placed on false positive and false negative errors, and it is these views that at least play a part in determining positions taken in the dispute.

The Scientific Center of the Dispute and Research Implications

As stated above (see page 698), the scientific center of this dispute is simply that of the accuracy of the PD afforded by the polygraphic charts alone scored "blind"—that is, by one who has not conducted the interview and knows nothing about the interviewee. Lykken places this accuracy at about 70% (against a 50% baseline of chance), with the additional claim that the rate of false positives (classifying truthful as deceptive) is appreciably higher than that of false negatives. This accuracy rate is unimpressive, according to Lykken (1981), because it is not clearly higher than that achieved by good clinical diagnostic methods—that is, by simply interviewing the suspect (possibly in a polygraphic setting) but not using the psychophysiological data.

Raskin (1978) places the accuracy rate at about 90%, provided that the polygrapher is competent. The term "competent" includes not only interviewing expertise, but also the employment of objective scoring methods to the development of which Raskin has contributed (cf. reference notes in Raskin & Podlesny, 1979). The difference of 20% is of obvious technological significance. In the courtroom, a 90% accuracy rate would provide strong support for the general use of polygraphy, given that no source of evidence is perfect and that many are below the 90% level. Even in noncriminal uses (which both Lykken and Raskin oppose), there could be some argument made for the use of such an accurate instrument, especially if there were fewer false positives than false negatives. The 20% difference is also of scientific significance, both for psychological testing in general and for psychophysiology in particular. A 90% accuracy rate for a differentiator is well above that of most psychological tests and/or PD measures. Hence, such an accuracy rate would suggest a rather marked effect due to the psychological phenomenon of deception. On the other hand, a 70% accuracy rate would warrant much less scientific enthusiasm for lie detection, although there would still be a phenomenon there worthy of investigation.

Accordingly, there does appear to be a scientific center of the dispute that is of significance and that is not overly complex. Answering the issue in dispute is, of course, a more complex enterprise, but it is at least clear that the accuracy issue, unlike the other more political aspects of the dispute mentioned above, is open to empirical investigation.

In addition, there are other research implications that arise from considering the Lykken–Raskin dispute, given that it is the case (as both disputants appear to agree) that lie detection does differentiate subjects at levels better than chance. The first of such implications comprises the question of what the factors are that affect accuracy. Like the question of overall accuracy, the question of relevant factors has an answer that, in principle, can be obtained through research. However, it bears emphasis that the research needs to be of the field variety.

On the other hand, there is also a set of relevant issues that may be investigated in the more artificial setting of the laboratory. Laboratory studies may be useful for providing hints or hypotheses about those factors that may improve accuracy in the field, even though evaluation of those hypotheses needs to be done in the field itself. Again, the laboratory can be useful in providing information about possible psychological as well as physiological mechanisms that may underlie the process of deception. Thus, it has recently been argued on the basis of a laboratory study that the psychological mechanisms appear to be those related to conflict rather than mental load, and that the physiological mechanisms appear to involve parasympathetic rather than sympathetic activation or "inhibitory arousal" (Heslegrave, 1981).

The significance of a given piece of research, then, is also an issue concerning which fine lines must be drawn. The distinction between field and laboratory research is critical. Results from the latter can only serve to suggest hypotheses concerning, but never as validation for, assertions made about the field. Nevertheless, laboratory research should not be viewed as a mere adjunct (and only a suggestive one at that) to field research. Such a view is correct from a techno-logical, society-oriented perspective, the concern of which is over the desirability of using polygraphy. I take Lykken's (1981) recent book to have this as its central concern, and it is this issue that, in my view, provides most of the fuel for the heat in the dispute between Lykken and Raskin. However, as indicated at the outset, the investigation of the psychological pro-cess of deception through unobtrusive physiological indices is a fascinating problem in its own right; it belongs to the field of psychophysiology, and is best attacked through experiments (i.e., in the laboratory). Although the scientific center of the Lykken–Raskin dispute concerns the field only, it is clear that the dispute has also led some laboratory researchers to see research implications of which some at least are resol-uble not in the field but in the laboratory (e.g., Ben-Shakhar, Lieblich, & Kugelmass, 1975; Dawson, 1980; Gustafson & Orne, 1965; Hemsley, 1977; Heslegrave, 1981; Janisse & Bradley, 1980; Kugel-mass & Lieblich, 1966; Thackray & Orne, 1968; Waid, Orne, & Wilson, 1979). Most importantly, however, research relevant to the center of the dispute and to the scientific implications can result in a reso-lution of the dispute that is empirical rather than evaluative, and that psychophysiologists are best fit-ted to carry out. The main long-term value of the Lykken–Raskin controversy, in my view, is that it has been instrumental in shedding light on the problems. This light comprises not only the arguments of the participants, but also, and more importantly, the im-plications that research psychophysiologists see in the dispute—implications that can be subjected to empiri-cal and more disinterested investigation by them.

The psychophysiologist who decides to conduct research in lie detection may well feel nervous about working in such an obviously controversial area. I have also felt nervous about writing this chapter for the same reason, and I suspect I have offered far fewer answers than authors of other chapters in this volume, who can write with more authority on their areas. This lack of willingness to provide definitive answers is nowhere more apparent than in my discussion of the Lykken–Raskin controversy. Here, I have sought

only to note some general trends of such controver-sies without trying to identify a given trend with the argument of a given participant. Such identification in a controversial context is a judgment that no authority can give; the reader alone can decide.

These feelings of uncertainty and doubt, however, may be viewed in a more positive light from the point of view of research. Research, after all, has the resolv-ing of doubt as its ultimate *raison d'être*. The area of lie detection, moreover, is one that would greatly benefit from psychophysiological research. Those benefits are both scientific and technological. The latter benefits are present even if, as Lykken (1981) advocates, the ultimate decision is more or less to abandon poly-graphic techniques in society. The abandoning of an unsound technique is as much of a technological ad-vance as the development of a sound one. Both scien-tific and technological benefits can only come, how-ever, if we are prepared both to "draw the fine lines" and to consider the controversies. Controversies are inevitable, and must be considered in sufficient detail so as to strip away the irrelevant emotional/political components, and to leave the issues that are empirical and therefore open to resolution through research.

ACKNOWLEDGMENTS

The preparation of this chapter was facilitated by a grant from the National Science and Engineering Council of Canada. I am indebted for critical comments on an earlier draft to Diane Riley, with whom I have coauthored papers in other areas of psychophysiology. For stylistic help in clarifying my writing, I acknowledge the aid of a nonpsychophysiologist, Christine Furedy, with whom I have pub-lished papers in higher education and the history of psychology. My greatest intellectual debt, however, is to Ron Heslegrave, with whom I have published papers on the noninvasive measurement of myocardial sympathetic influence and on the measurement of heart rate variability.

The debt to Ron Heslegrave in this chapter is particularly great, because it was only through his deciding to investigate lie detection for his PhD (Heslegrave, 1981), which I supervised, that I became interested in the topic. Our original intention was to author the present chapter jointly, but this proved impracticable because of the idiosyncratic way in which the manuscript developed, with its emphasis on the general nature of controversy in science. However, as regards the specific content on lie detection, my debt to Ron is considerable, and this debt is also specifically referenced in those parts of the chapter where appropriate.

REFERENCES

Alpert, M., Kurtzberg, R. L., & Friedhoff, A. J. Transient voice changes associated with emotional stimuli. *Archives of General Psychiatry*, 1963, 8, 362–365.

Barland, G. H., & Raskin, D. C. Detection of deception. In W. F. Prokasy & D. C. Raskin (Eds.), *Electrodermal activity in psycho-logical research*. New York: Academic Press, 1973.

Barland, G. H., & Raskin, D. C. An evaluation of field techniques in detection of deception. *Psychophysiology*, 1975, 12, 321–330.

Ben-Shakhar, G., Lieblich, I., & Kugelmass, S. Detection of infor-mation and GSR habituation: An attempt to derive detection efficiency from two habituation curves. *Psychophysiology*, 1975, 12, 283–288.

Benoussi, V. Die Atmungsymptome der Luge. *Archive für die Gesampte Psychologie*, 1914, 31, 244–273.

Berlyne, D. E. *Conflict, arousal and curiosity.* New York: McGraw-Hill, 1960.

Bernstein, A. S. The orienting reflex as novelty and significance detector: Reply to O'Gorman. *Psychophysiology*, 1979, 16, 263–273.

Cavoukian, A., & Heslegrave, R. J. The admissability of polygraph evidence in court: Some empirical findings. *Law and Human Behaviour*, 1980, 4, 117–131.

Craik, F., & Lockhart, R. Levels of processing: A framework for memory research. *Journal of Verbal Learning and Verbal Behaviour*, 1972, 11, 671–684.

Crosland, H. R. *The psychological methods of word association and reaction time as tests of deception* (University of Oregon Publications in Psychology Series, Vol. 1, No. 1). Eugene: University of Oregon, 1929.

Curtow, R. J., Parks, A., Lucas, N., & Thomas, K. The objective use of multiple physiological indices in the detection of deception. *Psychophysiology*, 1972, 9, 578–588.

Davidson, P. O. Validity of the guilty-knowledge technique: The effects of motivation. *Journal of Applied Psychology*, 1968, 52, 62–65.

Dawson, M. E. Physiological detection of deception: Measurement of responses to questions and answers during countermeasure maneuvers. *Psychophysiology*, 1980, 17, 8–17.

Duprat, G. L. *Le mensonge: Étude de psychosociologie et pathologie.* Paris: Felix Alcan, 1903.

Ekman, A., & Friesen, W. V. Non-verbal leakage and clues to deception. *Psychiatry*, 1969, 32, 88–106.

Ekman, A., & Friesen, W. V. Detecting deception from the body or face. *Journal of Personality and Social Psychology*, 1974, 29, 288–298.

Ellson, D. G., Davis, R. C., Saltzman, I. J., & Burke, C. J. *A report of research on detection of deception* (Technical report prepared under Contract N6ONR-18011 for the Office of Naval Research). Bloomington: Indiana University, 1952.

Eysenck, M. W. Levels of processing: A critique. *British Journal of Psychology*, 1978, 69, 157–169.

Furedy, J. J. Some uses and abuses of electrodermal measures. *Psychonomic Science*, 1969, 15, 98–99.

Furedy, J. J. [Review of D. T. Lykken's *A tremor in the blood: Uses and abuses of the lie detector*]. *Criminal Justice and Behavior*, 1982, 9, 501–508.

Furedy, J. J. Operational, analogical, and genuine definition of psychophysiology. *International Journal of Psychophysiology*, 1983, 1, 13–19.

Furedy, J. J., & Heslegrave, R. J. A consideration of recent criticisms of the T-wave amplitude index of myocardial sympathetic activity. *Psychophysiology*, 1983, 13, 204–211.

Furedy, J. J., & Klajner, F. On evaluating autonomic and verbal indices of negative preception. *Psychophysiology*, 1974, 11, 121–124.

Furedy, J. J., & Poulos, C. X. Short-interval classical SCR conditioning and the stimulus-sequence-change-elicited OR: The case of the empirical red herring. *Psychophysiology*, 1977, 14, 351–359.

Furedy, J. J., Poulos, C. X., & Schiffman, K. Logical problems with Prokasy's assessment of contingency relations in classical skin conductance conditioning. *Behavior, Research Method and Instrumentation*, 1975, 7, 521–523.

Furedy, J. J., & Stanley, G. More data and arguments for partial failure of Emmert's law under conditions of size constancy and veridical distance perception: Rejoinder to Teghtsoonian's comments. *Perception and Psychophysics*, 1971, 10, 99–100.

Gustafson, L. A., & Orne, M. T. Effects of perceived role and role success on the detection of deception. *Journal of Applied Psychology*, 1965, 49, 412–417.

Hemsley, G. D. *Experimental studies in the behavioral indicants of deception.* Unpublished doctoral dissertation, University of Toronto, 1977.

Heslegrave, R. J. *A psychophysiological analysis of the detection of deception: The role of information, retrieval, novelty and conflict mechanisms.* Unpublished doctoral dissertation, University of Toronto, 1981.

Heslegrave, R. J., Ogilvie, J. C., and Furedy, J. J. Measuring baseline–treatment differences in heart rate variability: Variance versus successive difference mean square and beats per minute versus interbeat intervals. *Psychophysiology*, 1979, 16, 151–157.

Horvath, F. S. The effect of selected variables on interpretation of polygraph records. *Journal of Applied Psychology*, 1977, 62, 127–136.

Horvath, F. S., & Reid, J. E. The polygraph silent answer test. *Journal of Criminal Law, Criminology, and Police Science*, 1972, 63, 285–293.

Janisse, M. P., & Bradley, M. T. Deception, information and the pupillary response. *Perceptual and Motor Skills*, 1980, 50, 748–750.

Kubis, J. F. *Studies in lie detection: Computer feasibility considerations* (Technical Report 62-205, prepared for Air Force Systems Command, Contract No. AF 30(602)-2270, Project No. 5534). Bronx, N.Y.: Fordham University, 1962.

Kugelmass, S., & Lieblich, I. Effects of realistic stress and procedural interference in experimental lie detection. *Journal of Applied Psychology*, 1966, 50, 211–216.

Landis, C., & Gullette, R. Studies of emotional reations: III. Systolic blood pressure and inspiration–expiration ratios. *Journal of Comparative Psychology*, 1925, 5, 221–253.

Lockhart, R., & Craik, F. Levels of processing: A reply to Eysenck. *British Journal of Psychology*, 1978, 69, 171–175.

Lombroso, C. *L'homme criminel* (2nd ed.). Paris: Felix Alcan, 1895.

Luria, A. R. *The nature of human conflicts: Or emotion, conflict and will* (W. H. Gantt, trans.). New York: Liveright, 1932.

Lykken, D. T. The GSR in the detection of guilty. *Journal of Applied Psychology*, 1959, 43, 385–388.

Lykken, D. T. The validity of the guilty knowledge technique: The effects of faking. *Journal of Applied Psychology*, 1960, 44, 258–262.

Lykken, D. T. Psychology and the lie detector industry. *American Psychologist*, 1974, 29, 725–739.

Lykken, D. T. The psychopath and the lie detector. *Psychophysiology*, 1978, 15, 137–142.

Lykken, D. T. The detection of deception. *Psychological Bulletin*, 1979, 86, 47–53.

Lykken, D. T. *A tremor in the blood: Uses and abuses of the lie detector.* New York: McGraw-Hill, 1981.

Marston, W. M. Systolic blood pressure symptoms of deception. *Journal of Experimental Psychology*, 1917, 2, 117–163.

Marston, W. M. Psychological possibilities in the deception test. *Journal of Criminal Law, Criminology, and Police Science*, 1921, 11, 551–570.

Marston, W. M. *The lie detector test.* New York: R. K. Smith, 1938.

McClintock, C. C., & Hunt, R. G. Non-verbal indicators of affect and deception in an interview setting. *Journal of Applied Social Psychology*, 1975, 5, 54–67.

Meehl, P. E. *Clinical versus statistical prediction: A theoretical analysis and a review of the evidence.* Minneapolis: University of Minnesota Press, 1954.

Meehl, P. E. Seer over sign: The first sound example. *Journal of Experimental Research in Personality*, 1965, 1, 27–32.

Mehrabian, A. Non-verbal betrayal of feeling. *Journal of Experimental Research in Personality*, 1971, 5, 64–73.

Munsterberg, H. *On the witness stand.* New York: Doubleday, 1908.

Obrist, P. A. The cardiovascular–behavioral interaction—as it appears today. *Psychophysiology*, 1976, 13, 95–107.

Obrist, P. A. *Cardiovascular psychophysiology: A perspective.* New York: Plenum Press, 1981.

Podlesny, J. A., & Raskin, D. C. Physiological measures and the detection of deception. *Psychological Bulletin*, 1977, 84, 782–799.

Podlesny, J. A., & Raskin, D. C. Effectiveness of techniques and physiological measures in the detection of deception. *Psychophysiology*, 1978, 15, 344–359.

Popper, K. R. *The logic of scientific discovery.* London: Hutchinson, 1959.

Raskin, D. C. Scientific assessment of the accuracy of detection of deception: A reply to Lykken. *Psychophysiology*, 1978, 15, 143–147.

Raskin, D. C., Barland, G. H., & Podlesny, J. A. Validity and reliability of detection of deception. *Polygraph*, 1977, 6, 1–39.

Raskin, D. C., & Podlesny, J. A. Truth and deception: A reply to Lykken. *Psychological Bulletin*, 1979, 86, 54–59.

Regina versus Wong. *Criminal Cases*, 1977, 33, 515.

Rovner, L. I., Raskin, D. C., & Kircher, J. C. Effects of informa-

tion and practice on detection of deception. *Psychophysiology*, 1979, 16, 197–198.

Szucko, J. J., & Kleinmuntz, B. Statistical versus clinical lie-detection. *American Psychologist*, 1981, 36, 488–496.

Thackray, R. I., & Orne, M. T. A comparison of physiological indices in detection of deception. *Psychophysiology*, 1968, 4, 329–339.

Trovillo, P. V. A history of lie detection. *Journal of Criminal Law, Criminology, and Police Science*, 1939, 29, 848–881; 30, 104–119.

Waid, W. M., Orne, M. T., & Wilson, S. T. Effects of level of socialization on electrodermal detection of deception. *Psychophysiology*, 1979, 16, 15–22.

Wise, T. A. *Commentaries on the Hindu Bengal Medical Service of Calcutta.* Calcutta: Thacker, 1845.

Chapter Twenty-Six

Applications of Brain Event-Related Potentials to Problems in Engineering Psychology

Emanuel Donchin
Arthur F. Kramer
Christopher Wickens

INTRODUCTION

We review in this chapter evidence suggesting that the brain event-related potential (ERP) can be incorporated into the collection of tools of engineering psychology. The utility of the ERP as a tool in the study of cognitive science has been discussed elsewhere (Donchin, 1979, 1981; Donchin, Karis, Bashore, Coles, & Gratton, Chapter 12, this volume; Wickens, 1979). As the human factors that must be addressed by the engineer are increasingly "cognitive" in nature (Rasmussen, 1981; Sheridan, 1981), there is an increasing need for enriching the repertoire of techniques for the assessment of cognitive function. We believe that psychophysiological techniques, in particular ERP-based procedures, can serve this function. We realize that this proposition is not self-evident to the engineering psychology profession. The recording of the ERP is cumbersome. Electrodes must be placed on the subject's scalp. Special equipment is needed for analyzing, digitizing, averaging, and displaying the data. The physiological nature of the signals is essentially unknown, and the functional significance of the ERP components is a subject of controversy. What

benefits would accrue to the system designers as they encumber themselves with this exotic technique? Is it likely to help in the assessment of cognitive workload? After all, there is a strong tendency to trust the *subjective* reports of operators in assessing workload. These reports appear to be preferred even to the seemingly simpler techniques proposed by the experimental psychologist. Sheridan and his coworkers concluded (Sheridan, 1980; Sheridan & Simpson, 1979) that it is possible to obtain a reliable and valid measure of workload by administering a rather simple questionnaire. Why should one bother with more costly, elaborate, and indirect measurements of workload?

The question is reasonable, and the answer is clear. If nothing is gained by complicating the measurement process, it is best to avoid the complications. We claim, however, that there are circumstances in which subjective reports may need augmentation, and that in a subset of these circumstances, the ERPs may be very useful.

Consider, for example, the following task. In Figure 26-1 are displayed four pairs of words. The task is to write "yes" next to the pair if the words rhyme, and to write "no" next to the pair if the words do not

Emanuel Donchin, Arthur F. Kramer, and Christopher Wickens. Cognitive Psychophysiology Laboratory, Department of Psychology, University of Illinois, Champaign, Illinois.

Match — Catch

Make — Ache

Catch — Watch

Shirt — Witch

Figure 26-1. A sample of word pairs presented to subjects in a phonological judgment task.

rhyme. Most subjects report that the decision requires the same effort regardless of the pair used, and are quite surprised when they find that their subjective assessment of the workload imposed by these simple judgments does not reflect objective measures of performance.

Note that the four word pairs in Figure 26-1 are instances of four possible relationships between the two words in the pair, as follows:

1. (RO) The two words rhyme and look alike ("Match–Catch").
2. (R-) The two words rhyme but do not look alike ("Make–Ache").
3. (WO) The two words look alike but do not rhyme ("Catch–Watch").
4. (W-) The two words neither rhyme nor look alike ("Shirt–Witch").

We label these pairs with an R to indicate a phonological match, with an O to indicate an orthographic match, with a W to indicate a phonological mismatch, and with a hyphen (-) to indicate an orthographic mismatch. Thus, for the RO and W- pairs, the phonological and the orthographic information agree, and for the R- and WO pairs, there is a conflict between the phonological and the orthographic information. While it is easy to analyze the stimuli in Figure 26-1 and see that they do indeed differ in these attributes, subjects do not usually perceive themselves as having greater difficulty in deciding that the words "Catch–Watch" do *not* rhyme than they do in deciding that the words "Shirt–Witch" do not rhyme.

But these subjective impressions are somewhat misleading. Polich, McCarthy, Wang, and Donchin (1983) and Kramer, Ross, and Donchin (1982) presented subjects with the two words of each pair in succession and required them to indicate their judgments by pressing one of two buttons immediately after the appearance of the second word. The reaction times belied the subjective reports. This can be seen in Figure 26-2, where the reaction time for each of the classes is shown. It is clear that a conflict between phonology and orthography retarded the subjects' reactions by a considerable number of milliseconds. The average delay was about 300 msec when the second word "looked like" the first word but did *not* rhyme with it (the WO pairs, such as "Catch–Watch"). In other words, an individual's subjective assessment may not reveal a processing delay that may cost an operator up to 300 msec in responding to a display change!

What we find, then, is that when tasks place demands on the human information-processing system that affect, or depend on, interactions between or among the automatically activated elements of the

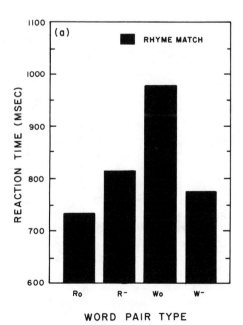

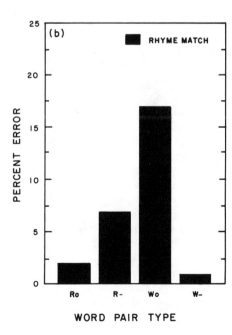

Figure 26-2. Mean reaction times for correct responses and percentage of errors averaged across 40 subjects in the phonological judgment task. (Adapted from Kramer, Ross, & Donchin, 1982.)

processing machinery, loads may be imposed on the system that directly affect its performance, even though they are not available to the internal monitors that yield subjective reports.

This phase of the analysis illustrates the need to supplement subjective reports by accurate and detailed measures of performance. Where, though, can psychophysiology help? We submit that its most effective role is, when properly used, in carrying the analysis beyond the limits imposed by the examination of the more overt responses. Thus, for example, the data in Figure 26-2 indicate that a phonology–orthography conflict delayed the subjects' reactions. But these data do not permit unequivocal conclusions regarding the functional locus of the delay. Did the conflict cause reprocessing of the signal? Were the subjects more cautious when they detected the conflict, or did they require more time to encode the stimuli? Why was the cost of conflict lower for the R-pair than it was for the WO pair? These and similar questions are important not merely for their theoretical significance, but also because our understanding of the nature of the interference is necessary if we are to develop systematic guidelines for improving the design of displays and related systems. The analysis supported by the ERPs may be especially helpful when there is a need to resolve conflicting theories. There are those who suggest that phonological and orthographic codes interact at the encoding stage (Meyer, Schvaneveldt, & Ruddy, 1975; Shulman, Hornak, & Sanders, 1978). Others have suggested that the interference occurs at a response selection stage (Conrad, 1978).

Kramer *et al.*'s (1982) ERP data, shown in part in Figure 26-3, provide information that complements the reaction time data. The waveforms shown in Figure 26-3 are of ERPs averaged over 40 subjects. These data were recorded at the parietal electrode, and each of the lines represents an average over one of the four classes of pairs (RO, R-, WO, W-). As usual, the ERP appears as a sequence of peaks and troughs (often referred to as "components"). It is evident that the waveforms for the four ERPs are congruent until the point of presentation of the second stimulus. The subjects, of course, did not know which of the four pair classes would be used on any trial until the appearance of the second stimulus. Once this happened, the waveforms diverged. It is quite evident that the ERP that was elicited by the WO pair type is different from the other three ERPs. It is characterized by a substantial delay in the elicitation of a large positive (downward-going) component, relative to the appearance of a similar component in the other three ERPs. In our terminology, the latency of this peak, labeled the "P300" for reasons that become apparent later, is increased in the ERP elicited by the WO pairs. Thus, the ERP provides additional data on the two types of orthography–phonology conflict that occurred in this

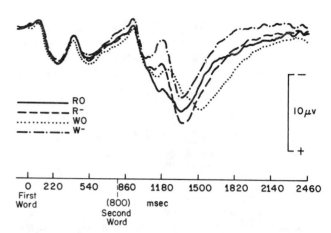

Figure 26-3. Grand average ERPs recorded at the parietal electrode in the phonological judgment task. The data span an epoch that began 100 msec prior to the presentation of the first of a pair of words and ended 1460 msec after the presentation of the second stimulus. The first word was presented at 0 msec, as indicated in the figure. The second word in the pair was presented at 800 msec. Each stimulus was displayed for 200 msec. (Adapted from Kramer, Ross, & Donchin, 1982.)

experiment. If we can interpret these ERP changes, we may be able to gain a better understanding of the process. In fact, since the latency of the P300 component of the ERP provides a measure of mental processing time that is unaffected by response selection and execution processes (McCarthy & Donchin, 1981), the data of Figure 26-3 suggest that at least some of the effect of the orthography–phonology conflict operates prior to the response selection stage. It is interesting to note that the differences obtained in the reaction times were larger than the P300 difference. This suggests that interference, which begins prior to the response selection stage, is amplified during later processing and therefore may reflect a cascading process (McClelland, 1979).

Further examination of Figure 26-3 reveals that the four ERPs differ also in the disposition of a negative (upward-going) peak that just precedes the P300. This peak is labeled "N200." The differences in the amplitude of the N200 component may serve to clarify some issues concerning the detection of orthographic and phonological mismatches. As can be seen in Figure 26-3, the largest N200s were elicited by the W-pairs, in which both the orthography and the phonology of the pair members mismatch. The R- list (phonological match, orthographic mismatch) also elicited a relatively large N200. Thus the R- and W- pair types, which both involve orthographic mismatches, elicited an N200. This suggests that the detection of an orthograpic mismatch may occur automatically. In fact, in an experimental condition not shown here, the subjects were instructed to report "yes" if the words matched visually, regardless of the phonology. The N200 elicited in that condition by the R- and W- pairs was identical to that elicited during the rhyme condition. On the other hand, the WO pairs (orthographic match, phonological mismatch) elicited an N200 only when the subjects were instructed to detect rhymes. This suggests that a phonological mismatch may be detected only when the phonology of the task is relevant. In other words, the ERP data indicate that a phonological comparator was involved solely in the rhyme condition, even though orthographic comparators were involved regardless of the task. Thus both the latency of the P300 component and the amplitude of the N200 component provide information that complements introspection and traditional overt response analysis.

We discuss these data because they illustrate our basic contention: Subjective reports, while valuable, do have limitations. In assessing the demands that a system places on an operator, it is particularly unwise to trust introspective claims that *deny* differences in workload between the systems under comparison. This is especially so when the demands imposed by the system operate at levels of processing that are not normally open to examination by introspection. It is in this domain that the human factors expert is most likely to benefit from the models and techniques of the experimental psychologist. On occasion it will be found that the assessment can be augmented by utilizing ERPs. This is particularly true when there is an interest in developing a theoretical account for the differences between the demands imposed on the operator by different systems. The theoretical models that can be adduced abound in references to internal processing entities. As the ERP components are manifestations of such processing entities, their study is of use.

In the remainder of this chapter, we illustrate these concepts by reviewing a series of studies demonstrating that the amplitude of the P300 can serve as a measure of "workload." We precede this discussion with a brief overview of the study of ERPs. For more details, the reader is referred to Callaway, Tueting, and Koslow (1978), Otto (1978), and Donchin *et al.* (Chapter 12, this volume).

Introductory Comments on the P300 Component

The ERP is a transient series of voltage oscillations in the brain that can be recorded from the scalp in response to the occurrence of a discrete event (Donchin, 1975; Regan, 1972). The ERP is viewed as a sequence of components commonly labeled with an "N" or a "P," which denotes polarity, and a number, which indicates minimal latency measured from the onset of the eliciting event (e.g., "N100" is a negative-

going component that occurs at least 100 msec after a stimulus). Since ERPs are relatively small, relative to the ongoing EEG (2–20 μV for the ERPs vs. 50–100 μV for the EEG), their study became practical only after the development of reliable signal averagers (Clynes & Kohn, 1960). These capitalize on the fact that the ERP is, by definition, time-locked to the eliciting event.

It is crucial to recognize the componential nature of the ERP. Early studies of the ERP, which treated the waveform as a unitary entity and measured the amplitude over the entire recording epoch (Satterfield, 1965), were difficult to interpret. The effects of the experimental manipulations tend to be quite specific to a few components, and a combination of the measures of the entire epoch may obscure the relevant variance. There is a degree of controversy as to the proper identification and definition of components (Donchin, Ritter, & McCallum, 1978; Picton & Stuss, 1980). In this chapter, however, we follow Donchin *et al.*'s (1978) definition of an ERP component in terms of the responsiveness of the waveforms to specific experimental manipulations. A component is thus mapped into a cognitive space populated by psychological concepts, such as decisions, expectations, plans, strategies, associations, and memories. Specific components are associated with particular entities in this cognitive space in much the same manner in which cells in the periphery of the visual system are mapped into a field in the visual cortex. The subset of elements in cognitive space associated with a particular component thus contributes to the definition of the ERP component.

The specific attributes of a waveform that are examined in defining a "component" are the amplitude, latency, and scalp distribution. It is the sensitivity of these attributes to experimental manipulations that defines an ERP component. Although no reference has been made to the underlying neural source of components, it is generally assumed that a scalp distribution that is invariant across repeated stimulus presentations implies a specific and fixed set of neural generators (Goff, Allison, & Vaughan, 1978; Wood & Allison, 1981). Thus the scalp distribution, which is related to the underlying neural population responsible for the generation of the component, is assumed to be a crucial defining characteristic.

The ERP components we discuss in this chapter are "endogenous" and are distinct from another class of ERPs called "exogenous" (Donchin *et al.*, 1978; Sutton, Braren, Zubin, & John, 1965). The exogenous components represent an obligatory response of the brain to the presentation of a stimulus. These components are primarily sensitive to such physical attributes of the stimuli as intensity, modality, and rate. The seven peaks or "bumps" that occur in the first 8–10 msec after the presentation of an auditory or somatosensory stimulus are a prototypical example of the exogenous category (Jewett, Romano, & Williston, 1970).

Endogenous components, typically, are not sensitive to changes in the physical characteristics of the eliciting stimuli. On the other hand, these components are very sensitive to changes in the processing demands of the task imposed on the subject. The endogenous components are nonobligatory responses to stimuli. The strategies and expectancies of the subject, as well as other psychological aspects of the task, account for the variance in the endogenous components. A typical example, and one to which we devote the remainder of this chapter, is the P300 component.

This ERP component is elicited by rare, task-relevant stimuli. A task in which it is readily elicited is often called the "oddball" paradigm. In a study by Duncan-Johnson and Donchin (1977), using this paradigm, the subjects were instructed to count covertly the total number of higher-pitched tones in a Bernoulli series. In different blocks of trials, the relative probability of the two tones was manipulated. It can be seen in Figure 26-4 that the amplitude of the P300 increased monotonically as the probability of the stimulus decreased. This occurred regardless of which of the two stimuli was being counted. When the subjects were solving a word puzzle and were not required to process the tones, the P300s were not elicited. Note that the ERPs in Figure 26-4 that were obtained in this "ignore" condition showed no P300 at all levels of probability. Thus, the amplitude of P300 is determined by a combination of the task relevance and the subjective probability of the eliciting event. This basic finding plays a crucial role in the use of P300 in the assessment of workload.

The demonstration that P300 is elicited by unexpected, task-relevant stimuli led Donchin, McCarthy, Kutas, and Ritter (1983) to suggest that "the P300 is a manifestation, at the scalp, of neural action that is invoked whenever the need arises to update the 'neuronal model' (Sokolov, 1969) that seems to underlie the ability of the nervous system to control behavior" (p. 105). The neural or mental model is continually assessed for deviations from inputs and revised when the discrepancies exceed some criterion value. The frequency with which the mental model is revised is based on the surprise value and task relevance of the stimuli. Donchin (1981) also argued that the concept of a subroutine is an appropriate metaphor for the activity of ERP components (Donchin, 1975; Donchin, Kubovy, Kutas, Johnson, & Herning, 1973). In software applications, subroutines represent algorithms that are designed to accomplish a specific task and which can be employed in a variety of different programs. ERP components may be associated with specific information-processing functions that are activated in a variety of different tasks. In the case of the P300, the subroutine may be invoked whenever there

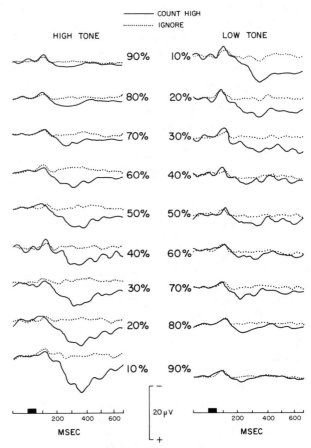

Figure 26-4. Averaged ERPs elicited by high and low tones presented in a Bernoulli series. The waveforms represent experimental conditions in which subjects counted the high tones (solid lines) or solved a word puzzle as the words were presented. (Copyright 1977, The Society for Psychophysiological Research. Reprinted with permission of the publisher from "On Quantifying Surprise: The Variation in Event-Related Potentials with Subjective Probability" by C. C. Duncan-Johnson and E. Donchin. *Psychophysiology*, 1977, 14, 456–467.)

is a need to evaluate surprising, task-relevant events. This interpretation of the changes in P300 amplitude is strengthened by the evidence that has accumulated in the past decade regarding the factors that control the latency of the P300. As the use we make of P300 in the analysis of human–machine interaction depends strongly on our theoretical interpretation of the component, it is useful to provide a brief review of the latency data and their interpretation.

The Latency of the P300 Component

The peak latency of the P300 component appears to depend on the time required to recognize and evaluate a task-relevant event. The latency ranges between 300 and 750 msec following the presentation of a discrete stimulus. In fairly simple tasks calling, for example, for a discrimination between two tones that differ in pitch (i.e., 1000–1600 Hz), the stimuli elicit relatively short-latency P300s. More difficult discriminations (e.g., semantic analysis) result in increases in the latency of P300.

Assuming that manual or vocal reaction time terminates processing, and that P300 is a manifestation of a process that precedes the response, then it would be expected the P300 latency and reaction time should positively covary. This prediction has been supported by numerous studies (Bostock & Jarvis, 1970; Rohrbaugh, Donchin, & Eriksen, 1974; Wilkinson & Morlock, 1967). Other investigations, however, have failed to detect a relationship between P300 latency and reaction time (Karlin & Martz, 1973; Karlin, Martz, & Mordkoff, 1970).

Donchin *et al.* (1978) proposed an interpretation of the processes underlying the P300 that may reconcile these contradictory findings. They suggested that P300 latency is determined by the time required to evaluate the stimulus, but is largely independent of response selection and execution time. The correlation between reaction time and P300 latency would accordingly vary as a function of the percentage of reaction time variance that is accounted for by stimulus evaluation processes. This percentage would be affected by the strategies employed by the subject. The strategies, therefore, should influence the relationship between P300 latency and reaction time (see also Ritter, Simson, & Vaughan, 1972). Evidence that P300 is determined by the amount of time required to recognize and evaluate a stimulus has been reported by several investigators who have employed Sternberg's (1966, 1969a, 1969b) additive-factors methodology (Ford, Mohs, Pfefferbaum, & Kopell, 1980; Ford, Roth, Mohs, Hopkins, & Kopell, 1979; Gomer, Spicuzza, & O'Donnell, 1976; Kramer, Fisk, & Schneider, 1983). Sternberg's paradigm involves the factorial manipulation of two or more experimental variables that are expected to differentially affect the durations of specific stages of processing. For example, the superimposition of a mask over a display is assumed to influence processing in an early, perceptual stage. On the other hand, reduction of the compatibility between the stimulus and the response would be expected to affect the selection and the execution of the response. In the studies mentioned above, both P300 latency and reaction time increased monotonically with increasing memory load.

Other investigators, employing different paradigms, also report that P300 latency and reaction time are positively correlated when stimulus evaluation time is manipulated. Squires, Donchin, Squires, and Grossberg (1977) found that P300 latency and reaction time covaried with the difficulty of auditory and visual discriminations. Furthermore, P300 latency varied with the manipulation of stimulus discriminability, while reaction time was influenced by both stimulus evaluation and response selection factors. Heffley, Wickens, and Donchin (1978) performed an experiment in which subjects were required to monitor a dynamic visual display for intensifications of one of two classes of targets. P300 latency was found to increase monotonically with the number of elements on the display. Since subjects were not required to make an overt response, the differences in P300 latency were attributed to stimulus evaluation processes.

If P300 latency is determined by stimulus evaluation time and is largely independent of the time required for response selection and execution, then experimental variables that have a different effect on processing time in the two stages should influence the relationship between P300 latency and reaction time. For example, when subjects are instructed to respond quickly with a low regard for accuracy, their responses are probably emitted without full evaluation of the stimulus (Wickelgren, 1977). On the other hand, if subjects are instructed to respond accurately, they are likely to perform a more thorough analysis of the stimuli prior to responding. This analysis leads to the prediction that the correlation between P300 latency and reaction time will vary with the subject's strategies. Specifically, it is predicted that the correlation will be high and positive when the subjects are instructed to be accurate, while low correlations will be observed under speed instructions.

Kutas, McCarthy, and Donchin (1977) tested this hypothesis by requiring subjects to distinguish between two stimuli under both speed and accuracy instructions. In one experimental condition, subjects were required to discriminate between two names, "Nancy" and "David," presented on a CRT (with relative frequencies of 20% and 80%, respectively). In a second condition, female names comprised 20% of the items and male names 80%. In the third condition, subjects were required to discriminate between synonyms of the word "Prod" that occurred with a relative probability of 20% and unrelated words that were presented with the complementary probability. The average P300 latency was shortest for the first condition, intermediate for the second, and longest for the third condition. The more complex the discrimination, the longer the P300 latency. A detailed analysis of the single trials (Woody, 1967) revealed that the correlation between P300 latency and reaction time was larger for the accuracy condition (.617) than the speed condition (.257). Kutas *et al.* (1977) concluded that the data supported the hypothesis that P300 latency reflects the termination of a stimulus evaluation process, while reaction time indexes the entire sequence of processing from encoding to response selection and execution. Thus, under the accuracy condition, when response selection was contingent on stimulus evaluation processes, P300 latency and reaction time were tightly coupled. However, when subjects performed the discrimination under the speed instructions, the processes of stimulus evaluation and response selection were more loosely coupled, and hence the relationship between P300 latency and reaction time was not as high.

Additional evidence bearing on the issue of the P300's sensitivity to the manipulation of stimulus evaluation processes has been obtained in a study by McCarthy and Donchin (1981), who manipulated orthogonally two independent variables in an additive-factors design (Sternberg, 1969a). One factor, stimulus discriminability, has been shown to affect an early encoding stage of processing, while the second factor, stimulus response incompatibility, influences the later stages of response selection and execution (Bertelson, 1963; Sanders, 1970; Schwartz, Pomerantz, & Egeth, 1977). The subjects' task was to decide which of two target stimuli, the words "RIGHT" or "LEFT," were presented in a matrix of characters on a CRT. The characters were either presented within a 4×4 matrix of # (number) signs (no-noise condition) or in a 4×4 matrix of letters chosen randomly from the alphabet (noise condition). Stimulus response incompatibility was manipulated by preceding the target matrix either with the cue "SAME" or with the cue "OPPOSITE." "SAME" signaled a compatible response. The cue "OPPOSITE" indicated an incompatible response: The right hand would respond to the word "LEFT" and the left hand to the cue "RIGHT." Reaction time increased when the command word was embedded in noise and when the response was incompatible with the stimulus. The effect of the two variables on the reaction time was additive, implying that these manipulations influenced different stages of processing. P300 latency was increased by the addition of the noise to the target matrix, but was not affected by the incompatibility between the stimulus and the response. These results support the conclusion that P300 latency is affected by a subset of the set of processes that affect reaction time. The P300 is elicited only after the stimulus has been evaluated. Subsequent processing required for the selection and execution of the response does not appear to influence the latency of the P300.

The P300 component of the ERP provides a metric for the decomposition of stages of information processing that complements the traditional behavioral measures. In terms of applications to system design and workload evaluation, ERPs used in conjunction with behavioral and subjective measures permit the assessment of stage-specific task interference effects. For example, if two time-shared tasks interfere with each other, it is usually desirable to know the locus of

this interaction. Only by discovering the stage at which tasks interact can systems be designed that minimize operator workload.

THE P300 AND HUMAN ENGINEERING

P300 and Perceptual–Central Processing Resources

The studies reviewed above provide evidence that the P300 component is a manifestation at the scalp of a processing entity, or a subroutine, that is invoked whenever surprising, task-relevant stimuli are present. The routine appears to be performing a role in the context-updating activities that occur whenever an event calls for the revision of the neuronal model or schema of the environment. It is noteworthy that this subroutine is invoked only if the stimuli are associated with a task that requires that they be processed. Ignored stimuli do not elicit a P300. But what if the stimuli are only partially ignored? What if the subject is instructed to perform the oddball task concurrently with another task? Would the amplitude of the P300 reflect the centrality of the oddball task? Would it, perhaps, change with the amount of resources allocated to the oddball task? Clearly, if it would change in this manner, the P300 might serve as a very useful measure of the amount of resources demanded by the two tasks. It is this series of questions that lies at the core of the usage that can be made of P300 in the assessment of workload.

The study of cognitive workload and of the allocation of processing resources to several tasks performed concurrently is, in fact, the area of research that has profited most from the incorporation of ERP measures. The research reviewed here has been performed within the framework of resource allocation theory. This class of models suggests that it is useful to conceptualize human capacity as represented by a finite pool of "resources" available for sharing among concurrently performed tasks (Kahneman, 1973; Moray, 1967; Norman & Bobrow, 1975). In the Kahneman (1973) model, these processing resources are undifferentiated, implying that all tasks draw resources from the same pool. The general model predicts that when two tasks are time-shared, their levels of performance should decrease relative to single-task levels.

This model underlies the secondary-task technique, a method that is commonly employed in the assessment of the workload associated with a task; the workload is viewed as reflected by the amount of processing resources consumed by a task (Knowles, 1963; Rolfe, 1971; Wickens, 1979). In the secondary-task technique, the subject is assigned two tasks—

a "primary" task, which is to be performed as well as possible, and a "secondary" task, which need be performed only to the extent that primary-task performance remains stable. It is assumed that the demands imposed upon the subjects by the primary task can be assessed by monitoring performance on the secondary task. An easy primary task will require a minimal amount of processing resources, leaving an ample supply for the performance of a secondary task, while a difficult primary task will require the majority of processing resources, leaving an insufficient supply for the performance of the secondary task. Thus, the better the performance of the *secondary* task, the less demanding the primary task.

Although the secondary-task procedure has been extensively used, it presents a number of practical problems (Brown, 1978; Ogden, Levine, & Eisner, 1979). Particularly unfortunate is the fact that secondary-task responses often intrude upon primary-task performance. Of course, fluctuations in primary-task performance make the interpretation of the resource tradeoff extremely difficult. Evidently, it would be useful to have a secondary task that is sensitive to changes in primary task difficulty but that does not require an overt response.

It has been the basic assumption of our research program that the oddball task can be used as a nonintrusive secondary task, since the ERP-eliciting tones occur intermittently, are easily discriminable, and do not require an overt response. Another advantage of this procedure is that it can be applied uniformly across different operational settings. In other words, the oddball task can be inserted into virtually any operational setting without requiring modifications in the system associated with the primary task. Wickens, Isreal, and Donchin (1977) reported one of the first studies in the series, using a compensatory tracking task as the primary task and the oddball paradigm as the secondary task.

Figure 26-5 illustrates the experimental procedures used in this and several other studies to be discussed. The subjects sat in front of a CRT and were instructed to cancel computer-generated cursor movements by keeping the cursor superimposed on a target in the center of the display. This was accomplished by movement of a joystick mounted on the right-hand side of the subject's chair. Levels of tracking difficulty were manipulated by requiring the subject to track in either one or two dimensions (horizontal and/or vertical). The compensatory tracking task was defined as the primary task. In addition to the tracking, the subjects were also instructed to count one of two tones presented in a Bernoulli series of high- and low-pitched tones. Control conditions were also included in which the subjects performed each of the two tasks separately.

The data indicate that the introduction of the tracking task drastically diminished the amplitude of the P300. However, no further reduction in P300 amplitude could be observed as tracking difficulty increased by requiring tracking in two dimensions. Even though tracking difficulty—assessed by root mean square

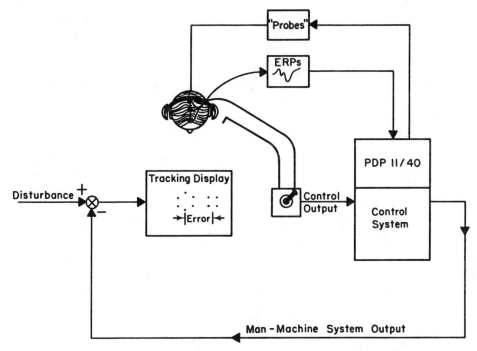

Figure 26-5. An illustration of the experimental paradigm employed in the analysis of the utility of the ERP as a workload measure.

(RMS) error as well as by reaction time to the tones—definitely increased with the addition of a tracking dimension, P300 amplitude did not change.

Isreal, Chesney, Wickens, and Donchin (1980) conducted a similar study requiring subjects to perform a compensatory tracking task concurrently with a counting task. In this case, however, the bandwidth of the random forcing function, rather than the dimensionality of the tracking task, was manipulated. The bandwidth was increased gradually until the cursor's speed reached the highest level the subject could tolerate without exceeding a preset error criterion.

The results are shown in Figure 26-6. Again, P300 amplitude was diminished by the introduction of the tracking task, but increases in the bandwidth of the forcing function did not produce systematic changes in the amplitude of the P300. These results cannot be explained easily within the framework of an undifferentiated capacity theory if we assume that P300 amplitude indexes the demands placed on the subject by the primary task. Increasing the bandwidth clearly affects the performance of overt secondary tasks (McDonald, 1973; Wierwille, Gutmann, Hicks, & Muto, 1977). The fact that P300 did not change, even though a dramatic drop in amplitude was observed with the introduction of the task, requires explanation.

One interpretation of the results is that the P300 is not sensitive to the processing demands of the task, but instead reflects the motor activity required by tracking. This hypothesis was tested by Isreal, Chesney, Wickens, and Donchin (1980) by instructing subjects to manipulate a joystick with one hand concurrently with the oddball task. The amplitude of the P300 component elicited by the tones was not affected by the motor demand. Thus, it would seem that hand movements per se did not decrease the amplitude of the P300.

Another interpretation of the results is that the resources that are tapped when the dimensionality, or the bandwidth of the target, is increased are not the resources reqwuired by the oddball task. Several investigators have proposed that processing resources are not undifferentiated, but, rather, are structured according to various information-processing stages (Kantowitz & Knight, 1976; Kinsbourne & Hicks, 1978; Navon & Gopher, 1979, 1980; Sanders, 1979). Wickens (1980) has identified hypothetical processing structures on the basis of input and output modalities (visual–auditory, manual–vocal), stages of information processing (encoding and central processing, response selection and execution), and codes of processing (verbal, spatial). In this framework, dual tasks are expected to interfere to the extent that they share overlapping resources. For example, two tasks that both require substantial central processing will interfere with each other to a greater extent than a task with central processing demands and another with

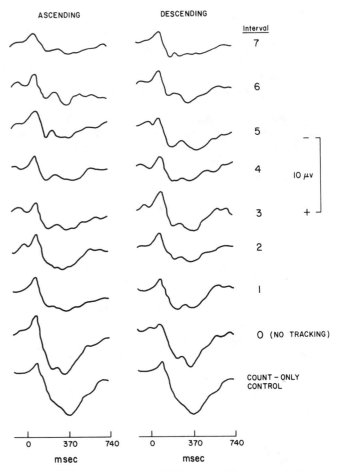

Figure 26-6. Average parietal ERPs, elicited by equiprobable counted tones, for each bandwidth interval and count-only control conditions, for ascending and descending blocks of trials. Bandwidth increases from 1 to 7. (Copyright 1980, The Society for Psychophysiological Research. Reprinted with permission of the publisher from "P300 and Tracking Difficulty: Evidence for Multiple Resources in Dual-Task Performance" by J. B. Isreal, G. L. Chesney, C. D. Wickens, and E. Donchin. *Psychophysiology*, 1980, 17, 259–273.)

heavy demands for response processes. This view of the allocation of processing resources is consistent with studies that show little or no decrement in performance when two difficult tasks are time-shared (Allport, Antonis, & Reynolds, 1972; North, 1977; Wickens & Kessel, 1979).

The notion that P300 is sensitive to a specific aspect of information processing is consistent with the data, reviewed above, regarding the relation between P300 latency and reaction time, P300 latency appears to be sensitive to a *subset* of the processes that determine reaction time. Furthermore, P300 latency is influenced by manipulations of factors that are assumed to affect relatively early processes of stimulus evaluation, while being insensitive to changes in variables that produce their effect on the later processes of response selection and execution. If the manipulation of the dimensionality and bandwidth of the tracking task demands resources associated largely with response selection and execution processes, then P300 amplitude should not reflect fluctuations in performance. On the other hand, if the perceptual aspects of a task are manipulated, the amplitude of the P300 elicited by a secondary task can be expected to covary with primary-task difficulty.

Isreal, Wickens, Chesney, and Donchin (1980) tested the latter hypothesis by combining the oddball task as a secondary task with a visual monitoring task that served as the primary task. The subjects were instructed to monitor a simulated air traffic control display either for course changes or for intensifications of one of two classes of stimuli (triangles or squares). Primary-task difficulty was manipulated by increasing the number of elements traversing the CRT (Sperando, 1978). The numerosity variable did have a systematic effect on reaction time to the tones when subjects were monitoring for course changes. Reaction time increased monotonically from the control condition to the condition in which subjects were required to monitor eight elements simultaneously. However, in the flash detection condition, reaction time did not increase significantly as a function of the number of elements displayed.

As can be seen in Figure 26-7, the P300 elicited by the counted tones decreased monotonically with increases in difficulty in the monitoring task when subjects were detecting course changes. In the flash detection condition, P300s decreased with the introduction of the monitoring task, but increases in the number of display elements failed to attenuate P300 amplitude further. This result is also consistent with the reaction time data. Since the primary task did not require a response, the data of Isreal, Wickens, Chesney, and Donchin (1980) have demonstrated that P300 amplitude is sensitive to the perceptual demands of a primary task.

The Use of P300 in Task Analysis

This structure-specific conception of processing resources has several implications for the study of human–machine systems. One area that might benefit from the use of the structure-specific analysis of human information-processing resources is task analysis. Traditionally, the analysis of operator performance in complex systems has been conducted by detailing the observable aspects of tasks and task sequences (Kidd & Van Cott, 1972). This analysis has usually taken the form of elaborate flow charts, which outline such aspects of operator behavior as information input, decisions, and required actions (Coakley & Fucigna, 1955; Folley, Altman, Graser, Preston, & Weislogel, 1960). Although these procedures provide

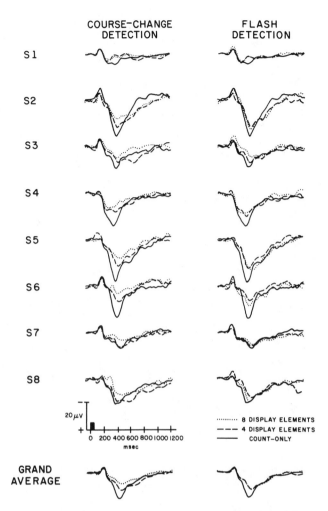

Figure 26-7. Single-subject and average ERPs elicited by infrequent, counted tones presented concurrently with each of two monitoring tasks. Two monitoring conditions as well as a count-only control condition are presented. All waveforms displayed were recorded at the parietal electrode. (From "The Event-Related Brain Potential as an Index of Display Monitoring Workload" by J. B. Isreal, C. D. Wickens, G. L. Chesney, and E. Donchin. *Human Factors*, 1980, 22, 212–224. Copyright 1980, by The Human Factors Society, Inc. and reproduced by permission.)

an accurate description of the behavior exhibited by the operators, they do not enable a microanalysis of the task that could provide the system designer with information on the resources required by different subtask sequences. It would be useful to examine a breakdown in performance under high-workload conditions for their relation to resource competition. For example, it would be advantageous to know whether the operator is required to perform tasks that demand a great deal of response processing but little perceptual analysis.

We (Kramer, Wickens, & Donchin, 1983) performed a componential analysis of the demands of controlling higher-order systems. By "order of control," we refer to the number of time integrations of the output of a controller (i.e., joystick) and the output of the system. In a first-order or velocity-driven system, a deflection of the joystick corresponds to a change in the velocity of the controlled element. A second-order or acceleration-driven system produces a change in the acceleration of the controlled element proportional to the movement of the control stick. The increase in system order appears to increase the demand for both perceptual resources (Wickens, Derrick, Micallizi, & Berringer, 1980) and response-related resources (North, 1977; Trumbo, Noble, & Swink, 1967; Vidulich & Wickens, 1981). Effective control over second-order dynamics requires a large degree of perceptual anticipation, as well as a modified response strategy. Assuming that P300 amplitude is sensitive to the perceptual aspects of a task, then a reduction in P300 amplitude by higher-order control should localize some of the influence of the order variable at the earlier processing stages.

Figure 26-8 illustrates the subjects' task. The target appeared on the screen and moved in a straight line at a randomly selected angle. The subjects had to move the cursor into the neighborhood of the target. The time between the appearance of the target and its acquisition by the cursor was called the "acquisition phase." Acquisition was accomplished by manipulating the two-axis joystick mounted on the right side of the chair in which subjects sat. Successful acquisition

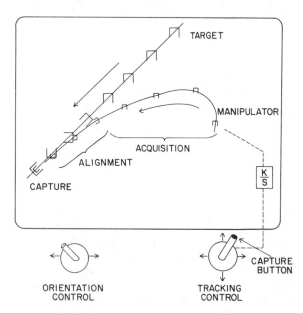

Figure 26-8. The temporal sequence of the target acquisition task (from upper right to lower left). (From "An Analysis of the Processing Demands of a Complex Perceptual–Motor Task" by A. F. Kramer, C. D. Wickens, and E. Donchin. *Human Factors*, 1983, 25. Copyright 1983, by The Human Factors Society, Inc. and reproduced by permission.)

initiated the alignment phase. The target began to rotate at a constant velocity in either a clockwise or a counterclockwise direction. The subjects had to rotate the cursor at the same velocity as the target, while also keeping the two elements superimposed. The rotation was accomplished by manipulating the single-axis joystick mounted on the left side of the chair. A deflection of the stick to the right produced a clockwise rotation of the cursor at an angular velocity proportional to the angle of deflection; a deflection to the left produced a counterclockwise rotation. Deviation from the initial acquisition criterion for more than 1000 msec necessitated a realignment of the elements. Once the subjects decided that all of the criteria had been satisfied and that the target and cursor were aligned, they could press a capture button, and the trial was terminated.

We assumed that the alignment phase would be more difficult than the acquisition phase, due to increased perceptual demands imposed by the requirement to control the additional rotational axis. We predicted, therefore, that the P300 elicited by the intensifications of the target and cursor, associated with an oddball task run concurrently with the tracking task, would be larger during the acquisition than during the alignment phase.

The ERP results presented in Figure 26-9 confirm these predictions. The P300 amplitude was attenuated as a function of phase, larger-amplitude P300s elicited in the acquisition phase, and of system order; larger P300s were elicited during the easier, first-order tracking. Another study employing a compensatory tracking task also found a systematic relationship between P300 amplitude and system order (Wickens, Gill, Kramer, Ross, & Donchin, 1981). These studies, along with additive-factors investigators of manual control parameters, have provided converging evidence that system order has a salient perceptual–central processing component (Wickens & Derrick, 1981; Wickens, Derrick, Micallizi, & Berringer, 1980). The results might also be useful in the design and evaluation of complex tracking tasks. If operators are required to perform a tracking task with higher-order system dynamics, then concurrently performed tasks should be designed so as to minimize perceptual–central processing load. We see here, again, how the ERPs provide data that increase the theoretical depth with which one can draw conclsuions about the human information-processing system.

P300 and Resource Reciprocity

The studies cited above have demonstrated a robust relationship between P300 amplitude and the allocation of processing resources in a secondary task. P300s elicited by secondary-task probes decrease in amplitude with increases in the perceptual–central pro-

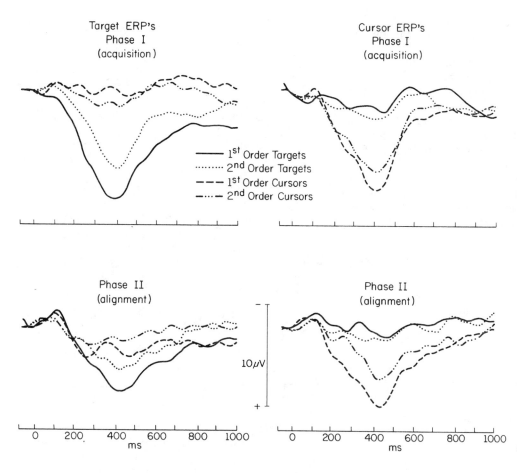

Target ERP's
Phase I
(acquisition)

Cursor ERP's
Phase I
(acquisition)

——— 1st Order Targets
·········· 2nd Order Targets
– – – 1st Order Cursors
–··–··– 2nd Order Cursors

Phase II
(alignment)

Phase II
(alignment)

10μV

0   200   400   600   800   1000
ms

0   200   400   600   800   1000
ms

Figure 26-9. Average parietal waveforms elicited by intensifications of the tracking elements. The left panel presents waveforms recorded when the intensity of the target was the relevant event. The right panel displays waveforms collected when the intensity of the cursor was relevant. The top panels display waveforms recorded during the acquisition phase; the bottom panels present waveforms collected during the alignment phase of the target acquisition task. (From "An Analysis of the Processing Demands of a Complex Perceptual–Motor Task" by A. F. Kramer, C. D. Wickens, and E. Donchin. *Human Factors*, 1983, 25. Copyright 1983, by The Human Factors Society, Inc. Reproduced by permission.)

cessing difficulty of primary tasks. As outlined previously, one of the basic assumptions of the secondary-task technique is that increases in primary-task difficulty divert processing resources from the secondary task. The decrement in secondary-task performance is believed to reflect this shift of resources from the secondary to the primary task. Thus, it is assumed that there is a reciprocal relationship between the resources allocated to the primary and secondary tasks. If this assumption is correct, then it should be possible to demonstrate that P300s elicited by task-relevant, discrete events embedded within the primary task are directly related to primary-task difficulty.

We (Kramer, Wickens, Vanasse, Heffley, & Donchin, 1981) conducted an experiment in which ERPs were elicited by task-relevant events embedded within a tracking task. The subjects were required to perform a single-axis pursuit step-tracking task with either first-order (velocity) or second-order (acceleration) control dynamics. In this task, the horizontal position of a target was determined by a random series of step displacements occurring at 3-sec intervals. The subjects' task was to keep the cursor superimposed on the target. Difficulty was varied by manipulating two variables: the degree of predictability of the series of steps, and the system order. In the high-predictability condition, the step changes alternated in a regular right–left pattern. In the low-predictability condition, the sequence of step changes was random. The magnitude of the changes was unpredictable in both conditions. The two dimensions of difficulty, system order and input predictability, were crossed to create three conditions of increasing difficulty: first-order control of predictable input, first-order control of unpredictable input, and second-order control of unpredictable input.

Three different types of probes were employed as ERP-eliciting events. In one condition, subjects performed the tracking task while also counting the number of occurrences of a low-pitched tone from a Bernoulli series of high- and low-pitched tones. In the second condition, subjects counted the dimmer of two flashes in a Bernoulli sequence. The flash appeared as a horizontal bar along the path traversed by the target. In the primary-task probe condition, subjects counted the total number of step changes to the left. Two control conditions were also included: one in which the subjects counted the probes but did not track, and a second in which subjects performed the tracking task without counting the probes.

The important findings to note in the data presented in Figure 26-10 are the monotonic relations between the tracking difficulty manipulations and the subjects' perceived ratings of difficulty, as well as those between tracking difficulty and RMS error. Both the subjective and the behavioral indices converge on the same ordering of task difficulty. However, these measures do not provide information concerning the underlying resource structure of the task.

The effect of tracking difficulty on P300 amplitude in the auditory condition (see Figure 26-11) provided results consistent with previous research (Isreal,

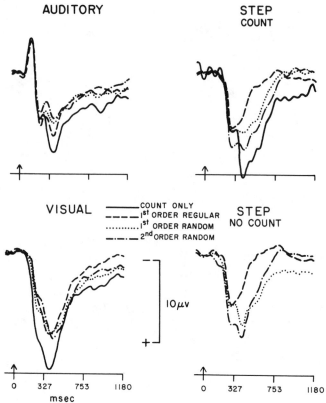

Figure 26-11. Average parietal ERPs elicited by visual, auditory, and spatial probes presented concurrently with a pursuit step-tracking task at each level of difficulty. Also shown are the ERPs elicited during single-task count conditions. (From "Primary and Secondary Task Analysis of Step Tracking: An Event-Related Potentials Approach," by A. Kramer, C. D. Wickens, L. Vanasse, E. F. Heffley, and E. Donchin. In R. C. Sugerman (Ed.), *Proceedings of the 25th Annual Meeting of the Human Factors Society, Rochester, New York*. Rochester: Human Factors Society, 1981.)

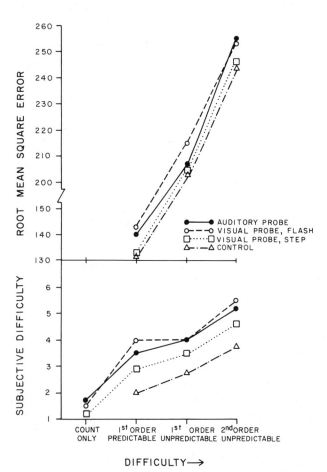

Figure 26-10. Average root mean square error and subjective difficulty ratings recorded for each condition in a pursuit step-tracking task. (From "Primary and Secondary Task Analysis of Step Tracking: An Event-Related Potentials Approach," by A. Kramer, C. D. Wickens, L. Vanasse, E. F. Heffley, and E. Donchin. In R. C. Sugerman (Ed.), *Proceedings of the 25th Annual Meeting of the Human Factors Society, Rochester, New York*. Rochester: Human Factors Society, 1981.)

Wickens, Chesney, & Donchin, 1980; Wickens, Heffley, Kramer, & Donchin, 1980). Thus, in the auditory condition, an increase in the difficulty of the primary task resulted in a decrease in the amplitude of the P300 elicited by the secondary-task probes. In the visual condition, the introduction of the tracking task resulted in a reduction in the amplitude of the P300. However, increases in tracking difficulty failed to produce any further attenuation. In the step conditions, the amplitude of the P300 elicited by the discrete changes in the spatial position of the controlled element increased with increments in the difficulty of the primary task. Thus, the hypothesis of resource reciprocity between the primary and secondary tasks was confirmed.

One final aspect of the step-tracking study has considerable potential practical utility. The sensitivity of the P300 elicited by visual steps to resource allocation was observed, independently of whether or not the subjects were required to count the stimuli. These data suggest that inferences from the P300 about resource allocation, and therefore about workload, can be made in the total absence of a secondary-task requirement—a considerable advantage if workload is to be assessed unobtrusively in real-time environments.

P300 and Skill Development

Another area in which ERPs (the P300 in particular) have provided useful converging evidence of a hypothetical process is the development of skill. Whether one conceptualizes the development of a skilled behavior as being a discrete two-stage process (Schneider & Shiffrin, 1977; Shiffrin & Schneider, 1977) or a continuous process (Hirst, Spelke, Reaves, Caharack, & Neisser, 1980; Spelke, Hirst, & Neisser, 1976), the modulation of some hypothetical resources are usually believed to underlie the overt, measurable improvement in performance. Norman and Bobrow (1975) have argued persuasively that there are at least two distinct limits on the performance of complex tasks. The performance of resource-limited processes can benefit from an increase in the amount of processing resources allocated to the task, while the performance level attained with a data-limited process is independent of the quantity of processing resources. The performance of a data-limited process may be improved by increasing the quality of the input stimuli (signal detection limits) or by improving the memory representation of the task (mem-

ory data limits). If the P300 amplitude does in fact index the quantity of perceptual resources allocated to the performance of a task, then the modulation of resources presumed to underlie the development of a skilled behavior should be reflected in the amplitude of the P300. With increasing automaticity of a well-practiced task, the structure of the task should change from primarily resource-limited to data-limited. In terms of a single-task situation, P300s elicited by task-relevant events embedded within the primary task embedded within the primary task should decrease in should decrease in amplitude, reflecting less of a demand for resources. Rosler (1981) found a sytematic decrease in P300 amplitude as subjects' performance improved during a multiblock stimulus-discrimination-learning task.

In terms of a secondary-task paradigm, P300s elicited by secondary-task probes should increase in amplitude as the primary task becomes progressively more data-limited. This variation in the amplitude of the P300 would presumably result from the increased quantity of processing resources which can be allocated to the secondary task. The target acquisition study outlined previously has found results that are consistent with this hypothesis (Kramer *et al.*, 1983). In this experiment, two groups of subjects received different levels of practice on the task: One group received 120 practice trials and the other 520 practice trials prior to ERP recording.

Behavioral indices of target acquisition performance confirmed that the highly practiced group performed substantially better than the less practiced group. As can be seen from Figure 26-12, when subjects were relatively inexperienced with the task, both

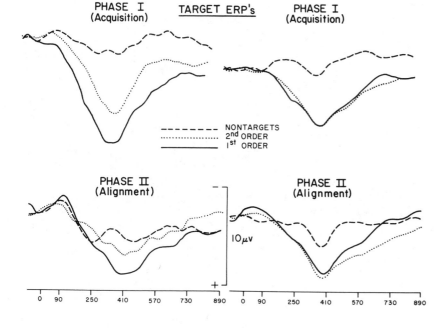

Figure 26-12. Average parietal ERPs elicited by intensifications of the tracking elements. The left panels present waveforms elicited after 120 practice trials, while the right panels present waveforms elicited after 520 practice trials. (From "An Analysis of the Processing Demands of a Complex Perceptual–Motor Task" by A. F. Kramer, C. D. Wickens, and E. Donchin. *Human Factors*, 1983, 25. Reprinted by permission.)

manipulations of primary-task difficulty attenuated the amplitude of the P300, with smaller-amplitude P300s elicited in the alignment phase and in the second-order condition. However, when subjects were thoroughly practiced on the task, the P300s elicited by secondary-task probes were the same for different levels of workload. Thus both performance and ERP measures provide evidence for a modulation in the demand for processing resources with practice.

Similar results were obtained in a study of operator workload conducted in a part-task aircraft simulator (Natani & Gomer, 1981). In this case, subjects were required to fly a command flight profile and maintain air speed while concurrently performing threat avoidance and target acquisition tasks. Workload was manipulated by varying the bandwidth of the pitch- and roll-forcing functions. On the first day of the experiment, both behavioral (composite RMS error) and ERP measures indicated a substantial difference between the two workload conditions. P300 amplitude elicited by auditory probes was significantly larger in the low-workload condition. However, on the second day, subjects' performance as well as P300 amplitude indicated no differences between the two workload levels.

In both single-task and dual-task situations, P300 amplitude has been found to react systematically to changes in the skill level of the subjects. The modulation in resource requirements inferred from P300 amplitude may be useful in monitoring the skill development of human operators in complex systems. Furthermore, the sensitivity of P300 to perceptual resources provides information on a selective aspect of resource changes over practice.

SUMMARY AND CONCLUSIONS

The investigations reported above demonstrate that the P300 elicited by a secondary task can diagnostically reflect primary-task workload variations of a perceptual–cognitive nature, uncontaminated by response factors. The absence of overt response requirements provide the P300 eliciting oddball task with a considerable advantage over secondary tasks, which require frequent responses.

As a secondary task, however, the probe task is not entirely unobtrusive, and interpretation of the measures still requires the investigator to make certain assumptions about the nature of the interaction between the primary and secondary tasks in order to make inferences concerning operator workload. It is for this reason that our most recent observations that the P300 elicited by primary-task stimuli also reflects resource allocation are particularly encouraging to the utility of the ERP as a measure of workload in extra-laboratory environments.

We have reviewed in this chapter studies of the ERP that have, we think, one characteristic in common. In each case, the ERP has served as a source of information on the timing or the "intensity" of an information-processing activity whose behavior is not easily monitored by means of observations on overt responses. It would seem that a science of engineering psychology that is interested in developing and testing hypotheses about the internal structure and the operating modes of the human operator would benefit from this additional information. We advocate here the use of the ERP as an analytical tool that can usefully aid in deepening our understanding of, and the measurement of, mental workload.

ACKNOWLEDGMENTS

The work conducted at the Cognitive Psychophysiology Laboratory would not have been possible without the assistance of numerous members of the scientific and technical staff. We would like to thank Mike Anderson, Brian Foote, and Dave McWilliams for their invaluable programming and engineering help. Members of the scientific staff who have been instrumental in the research reported here include Jack Isreal, Daniel Gopher, Greg Chesney, Connie Duncan-Johnson, John Polich, Greg McCarthy, and Earle Heffley.

The research has been supported under the Office of Naval Research (Contract No. N00014-76-C-0002) with funds provided by the Defense Advanced Research Projects Agency; the Air Force Office of Scientific Research under Contract No. F49620-79C-0233; Wright-Patterson Air Force Base under Contract No. F33615-79C-0512; and the U.S. Environmental Protection Agency under Contract No. R805628010. The support of Drs. Craig Fields, Judith Daly, Al Fregley, Don Woodward, Bob O'Donnell, and Dave Otto is gratefully acknowledged.

Part of this chapter was presented at the AIAA Workshop on Flight Testing to Identify Pilot Workload and Pilot Dynamics, Edwards Air Force Base, California, January 1982.

REFERENCES

Allport, D. A., Antonis, B., & Reynolds, P. On the division of attention: A disproof of the single channel hypothesis. *Quarterly Journal of Experimental Psychology*, 1972, 24, 225–235.

Bertelson, P. S-R relationships and reaction time to new versus repeated signals in a serial task. *Journal of Experimental Psychology*, 1963, 65, 478–484.

Bostock, H., & Jarvis, M. J. Changes in the form of the cerebral evoked response related to the speed of simple reaction time. *Electroencephalography and Clinical Neurophysiology*, 1970, 29, 137–145.

Brown, I. D. Dual task methods of assessing workload. *Ergonomics*, 1978, 21, 221–224.

Callaway, E., Tueting, P., & Koslow, S. (Eds.). *Brain event-related potentials in man*. New York: Academic Press, 1978.

Coakley, J. D., & Fucigna, J. T. *Human engineering recommendations for the instrumentation of radar* (Report No. AN/FPS-16 [Xn-2]). Moorestown, N.J.: Radio Corporation of America, 1955.

Clynes, M., & Kohn, M. The use of Mnemotron for biological data storage, reproduction, and for an average transient computer. In *Abstracts of the 4th Annual Meeting of the Biophysics Society, Philadelphia, Pennsylvania.* 1960.

Conrad, C. Some factors involved in the recognition of words. In J. W. Cotton & R. W. Klatzky (Eds.), *Semantic factors in cognition*. Hillsdale, N.J.: Erlbaum, 1978.

Donchin, E. Brain electrical correlates of pattern recognition. In G. F. Inbar (Ed.), *Signal analysis and pattern recognition in biomedical engineering*. New York: Wiley, 1975.

Donchin, E. Event-related brain potentials: A tool in the study of human information processing. In H. Begleiter (Ed.), *Evoked brain potentials and behavior*. New York: Plenum Press, 1979.

Donchin, E. Surprise! . . . Surprise? *Psychophysiology*, 1981, 18, 493–513.

Donchin, E., & Isreal, J. B. Event-related potentials and psychological theory. In H. H. Kornhuber & L. Deecke (Eds.), *Motivation, motor and sensory processes of the brain: Electrical Potentials, behavioral and clinical use*. Amsterdam: North-Holland Biomedical Press, 1980.

Donchin, E., Kubovy, M., Kutas, M., Johnson, R., Jr., & Herning, R. I. Graded changes in evoked response (P300) amplitude as a function of cognitive activity. *Perception and Psychophysics*, 1973, 14, 319–324.

Donchin, E., McCarthy, G., Kutas, M., & Ritter, W. Event-related brain potentials in the study of consciousness. In R. J. Davidson, G. E. Schwartz, & D. Shapiro (Eds.), *Consciousness and self regulation*. New York: Plenum Press, 1983.

Donchin, E., Ritter, W., & McCallum, C. Cognitive psychophysiology: The endogenous components of the ERP. In E. Callaway, P. Tueting, & S. Koslow (Eds.), *Brain event-related potentials in man*. New York: Academic Press, 1978.

Duncan-Johnson, C. C., & Donchin, E. On quantifying surprise: The variation in event-related potentials with subjective probability. *Psychophysiology*, 1977, 14, 456–467.

Folley, Jr., J. D., Altman, J. W., Graser, R., Preston, H. O., & Weislogel, R. C. *Human factors methods for system design* (Report No. AIR-B90-60-FR-225). Pittsburgh: The American Institutes for Research, 1960.

Ford, J. M., Roth, W. T., Mohs, R. C., Hopkins, W. F., & Kopell, B. S. Event-related potentials recorded from young and old adults during a memory retrieval task. *Electroencephalography and Clinical Neurophysiology*, 1979, 47, 450–454.

Ford, M. M., Mohs, R. C., Pfefferbaum, A., & Kopell, B. S. On the utility of P300 latency and reaction time for studying cognitive processes. In H. H. Kornhuber & L. Deecke (Eds.), *Motivation, motor and sensory processes of the brain: Electrical potentials, behavioral and clinical use*. Amsterdam: North-Holland Biomedical Press, 1980.

Goff, W. R., Allison, T., & Vaughan, Jr., H. G. The functional neuroanatomy of the event-related potentials. In E. Callaway, P. Tueting, & S. Koslow (Eds.), *Brain event-related potentials in man*. New York: Academic Press, 1978.

Gomer, F. E., Spicuzza, R. J., & O'Donnell, R. D. Evoked potential correlates of visual item recognition during memory scanning tasks. *Physiological Psychology*, 1976, 4, 61–65.

Heffley, E., Wickens, C. D., & Donchin, E. Intramodality selective attention and P300—reexamination in a visual monitoring task. *Psychophysiology*, 1978, 15, 269–270.

Hirst, W., Spelke, E. S., Reaves, C. C., Caharack, G., & Neisser, U. Dividing attention without alternation or automaticity. *Journal of Experimental Psychology: General*, 1980, 109, 98–117.

Isreal, J. B., Chesney, G. L., Wickens, C. D., & Donchin, E. P300 and tracking difficulty: Evidence for multiple resources in dual-task performance. *Psychophysiology*, 1980, 17, 259–273.

Isreal, J. B., Wickens, C. D., Chesney, G. L., & Donchin, E. The event-related brain potential as an index of display monitoring workload. *Human Factors*, 1980, 22, 212–224.

Jewett, D., Romano, H. W., & Williston, J. S. Human auditory evoked responses: Possible brain stem components detected on the scalp. *Science*, 1970, 167, 1517–1518.

Kahneman, D. *Attention and effort*. Englewood Cliffs, N.J.: Prentice-Hall, 1973.

Kantowitz, B. H., & Knight, J. L. On experimenter limited processes. *Psychological Review*, 1976, 83, 502–507.

Karlin, L., & Martz, M. J. Response probability and sensory evoked potentials. In S. Kornblum (Ed.), *Attention and performance IV*. New York: Academic Press, 1973.

Karlin, L., Martz, M. J., & Mordkoff, A. M. Motor performance and sensory evoked potentials. *Electroencephalography and Clinical Neurophysiology*, 1970, 28, 307–313.

Kidd, J. S., & Van Cott, H. P. System and human engineering analysis. In H. P. Van Cott & R. G. Kinkade (Eds.), *Human engineering guide to equipment design*. Washington, D.C.: U.S. Government Printing Office, 1972.

Kinsbourne, M., & Hicks, R. E. Functional cerebral space: A model for overflow, transfer and interference effects in human performance. In J. Requin (Ed.), *Attention and performance VII*. New York: Academic Press, 1978.

Knowles, W. B. Operator loading tasks. *Human Factors*, 1963, 5, 155–161.

Kramer, A. F., Fisk, A., & Schneider, W. P300, consistency and visual search. *Psychophysiology*, 1983, 20, 453–454.

Kramer, A., Ross, W., & Donchin, E. A chronometric analysis of the role of orthographic and phonological cues in a non-lexical decision task. *Psychophysiology*, 1982, 19, 330–331. (Abstract)

Kramer, A. F., Wickens, C. D., & Donchin, E. An analysis of the processing demands of a complex perceptual–motor task. *Human Factors*, 1983, 25, 597–621.

Kramer, A., Wickens, C. D., Vanasse, L., Heffley, E. F., & Donchin, E. Primary and secondary task analysis of step tracking: An event-related potentials approach. In R. C. Sugarman (Ed.), *Proceedings of the 25th Annual Meeting of the Human Factors Society, Rochester, New York*. Rochester: Human Factors Society, 1981.

Kutas, M., McCarthy, G., & Donchin, E. Augmenting mental chronometry: The P300 as a measure of stimulus evaluation time. *Science*, 1977, 197, 792–795.

McCarthy, G., & Donchin, E. A metric for thought: A comparison of P300 latency and reaction time. *Science*, 1981, 211, 77–80.

McClelland, J. L. On time relations of mental processes: A framework for analyzing processes in cascade. *Psychological Review*, 1979, 86, 287–330.

McDonald, L. B. *A model for predicting driver workload in the freeway environment: A feasibility study*. Unpublished doctoral dissertation, Texas A & M University, 1973.

Meyer, D. E., Schvaneveldt, R. W., & Ruddy, M. G. Loci of contextual effects on visual word recognition. In P. Rabbit & S. Dornic (Eds.), *Attention and performance V*. New York: Academic Press, 1975.

Moray, N. Where is capacity limited?: A survey and a model. In A. F. Sanders (Ed.), *Attention and performance I*. Amsterdam: North-Holland, 1967.

Natani, K., & Gomer, F. E. *Electrocortical activity and operator workload: A comparison of changes in the electroencephalogram and in event-related potentials* (McDonnell Douglas Technical Report, MDC E2427). St. Louis: McDonnell Douglas Astronautics Company, 1981.

Navon, D., & Gopher, D. On the economy of the human processing system. *Psychological Review*, 1979, 86, 214–255.

Navon, D., & Gopher, D. Interpretations of task difficulty in terms of resources: Efficiency, load, demand and cost composition. In R. Nickerson & R. Pew (Eds.), *Attention and performance VIII*. Hillsdale, N.J.: Erlbaum, 1980.

Norman, D., & Bobrow, D. On data-limited and resource-limited processes. *Cognitive Psychology*, 1975, 7, 44–64.

North, R. Task functional demands as factors in dual-task performance. In *Proceedings of the 21st Annual Meeting of the Human Factors Society, Santa Monica, California*. Santa Monica: Human Factors Society, 1977.

Ogden, G. D., Levine, J. W., & Eisner, E. J. Measurement of workload by secondary tasks. *Human Factors*, 1979, 21, 529–548.

Otto, D. A. (Ed.). *Multidisciplinary perspectives in event-related brain potential research* (EPA 600/9-77-043). Washington, D.C.: U.S. Government Printing Office, 1978.

Picton, T. W., & Stuss, D. T. The component structure of the human event-related potentials. In H. H. Kornhuber & L. Deecke (Eds.), *Motivation, motdor and sensory processes of the brain: Electrical potentials, behavioral and clinical use.* Amsterdam: North-Holland Biomedical Press, 1980.

Polich, J. M., McCarthy, G., Wang, W. S., & Donchin, E. When words collide: Orthographic and phonological interference during word processing. *Biological Psychology,* 1983, 16, 155–180.

Rasmussen, J. Models of mental strategies in process plant diagnosis. In J. Rasmussen & W. B. Rouse (Eds.), *Human detection and diagnosis of system failures.* New York: Plenum Press, 1981.

Regan, D. *Evoked potentials in psychology, sensory physiology and clinical medicine.* London: Chapman & Hall, 1972.

Ritter, W., Simson, R., & Vaughan, H. G., Jr. Association cortex potentials and reaction time in auditory discriminations. *Electroencephalography and Clinical Neurophysiology,* 1972, 33, 547–557.

Rohrbaugh, J. W., Donchin, E., & Eriksen, C. W. Decision making and the P300 component of the cortical evoked response. *Perception and Psychophysics,* 1974, 15, 368–374.

Rolfe, J. M. The secondary task as a measure of mental load. In W. T. Singleton, J. G. Fox, & D. Witfield (Eds.), *Measurements of man at work.* London: Taylor & Francis, 1971.

Rösler, F. Event-related brain potentials in a stimulus discrimination learning paradigm. *Physiological Psychology,* 1981, 18, 447–455.

Sanders, A. F. Some variables affecting the relation between relative stimulus frequency and choice reaction time. In A. F. Sanders (Ed.), *Attention and performance III.* Amsterdam: North-Holland, 1970.

Sanders, A. F. Some remarks on mental load. In N. Moray (Ed.), *Mental workload: Its theory and measurement.* New York: Plenum Press, 1979.

Satterfield, J. H. Evoked cortical response enhancement and attention in man: A study of responses to auditory and shock stimuli. *Electroencephalography and Clinical Neurophysiology,* 1965, 19, 470–475.

Schneider, W., & Shiffrin, R. M. Controlled and automatic human information processing: I. Detection, search and attention. *Psychological Review,* 1977, 84, 1–66.

Schwartz, S. P., Pomerantz, J. R., & Egeth, H. E. State and process limitations in information processing: An additive factors analysis. *Journal of Experimental Psychology: Human Perception and Performance,* 1977, 3, 402–410.

Sheridan, T. B. Mental workload—What is it? Why bother with it? *Human Factors Society Bulletin,* 1980, 23, 1–2.

Sheridan, T. B. Understanding human error and aiding human diagnostic behavior in nuclear power plants. In J. Rasmussen & W. B. Rouse (Eds.), *Human detection and diagnosis of system failures.* New York: Plenum Press, 1981.

Sheridan, T. B., & Simpson, R. W. *Toward the definition and measurement of mental workload of transport pilots* (FTL Report R79-4). Cambridge, Mass.: Massachusetts Institute of Technology Flight Transportation Laboratory, 1979.

Shiffrin, R. M., & Schneider, W. Controlled and automatic human information processing: II. Perceptual learning, automatic attending and a general theory. *Psychological Review,* 1977, 84, 127–190.

Shulman, H. G., Hornak, R., & Sanders, E. The effects of graphemic, phonetic and semantic relationships on access to lexical structures. *Memory and Cognition,* 1978, 6, 115–123.

Sokolov, E. N. The modeling properties of the nervous system. In I. Maltzman & K. Cole (Eds.), *Handbook of contemporary Soviet psychology.* New York: Basic Books, 1969.

Spelke, E. S., Hirst, W. C., & Neisser, U. Skills of divided attention. *Cognition,* 1976, 4, 215–230.

Sperando, J. C. The regulation of working methods as a function of workload among air traffic controllers. *Ergonomics,* 1978, 21, 193–202.

Squires, N. K., Donchin, E., Squires, K. C., & Grossberg, S. Bisensory stimulation: Inferring decision related processes from the P300 component. *Journal of Experimental Psychology: Human Perception and Performance,* 1977, 3, 299–315.

Sternberg, S. High speed scanning in human memory. *Science,* 1966, 153, 652–654.

Sternberg, S. The discovery of processing stages: Extensions of Donders' method. *Acta Psychologica,* 1969, 30, 276–315. (a)

Sternberg, S. Memory scanning: Mental processes revealed by reaction time experiments. *American Scientist,* 1969, 57, 421–457. (b)

Sutton, S., Braren, M., Zubin, J., & John, E. R. Evoked potential correlates of stimulus uncertainty. *Science,* 1965, 150, 1187–1188.

Trumbo, D., Noble, M., & Swink, J. Secondary task interference in the performance of tracking tasks. *Journal of Experimental Psychology,* 1967, 73, 232–240.

Vidulich, M., & Wickens, C. D. *Time-sharing, manual control and memory search: The joint effects of input and output modality competition, priorities and control order* (Technical Report EPL-81-4/ONR-81-4). Urbana–Champaign: Engineering Psychology Research Laboratory, University of Illinois, 1981.

Wickelgren, W. Speed accuracy tradeoff and information processing dynamics. *Acta Psychologica,* 1977, 41, 67–85.

Wickens, C. D. Human workload measurement. In N. Moray (Ed.), *Mental workload: Its theory and measurement.* New York: Plenum Press, 1979.

Wickens, C. D. The structure of attentional resources. In R. Nickerson & R. Pew (Eds.), *Attention and performance VIII.* Hillsdale, N.J.: Erlbaum, 1980.

Wickens, C. D., & Derrick, W. *The processing demands of higher order manual control: Application of additive factors methodology* (Technical Report EPL-81-1/ONR-81-1). Urbana–Champaign: Engineering Psychology Research Laboratory, University of Illinois, 1981.

Wickens, C. D., Derrick, W. D., Micallizi, J., & Berringer, D. The structure of processing resources. In R. E. Corrick, E. C. Haseltine, & R. T. Durst (Eds.), *Proceedings of the 24th Annual Meeting of the Human Factors Society, Los Angeles, California.* Los Angeles: Human Factors Society, 1980.

Wickens, C. D., Gill, R., Kramer, A., Ross, W., & Donchin, E. The cognitive demands of second order manual control: Applications of the event-related brain potential. In *Proceedings of the 17th Annual NASA Conference on Manual Control* (NASA TM). Washington, D.C.: National Aeronautics and Space Administration, 1981.

Wickens, C. D., Heffley, E. F., Kramer, A. F., & Donchin, E. The event-related brain potential as an index of attention allocation in complex displays. In G. E. Corrick, E. C. Haseltine, & R. T. Durst (Eds.), *Proceedings of the 24th Annual Meeting of the Human Factors Society, Los Angeles, California.* Los Angeles: Human Factors Society, 1980.

Wickens, C. D., Isreal, J. B., & Donchin, E. The event-related cortical potential as an index of task workload. In *Proceedings of the 21st Annual Meeting of the Human Factors Society, Santa Monica, California.* Santa Monica: Human Factors Society, 1977.

Wickens, C. D., & Kessel, D. The effect of participatory mode and task workload on the detection of dynamic system failures. *IEEE Transactions on Systems, Man and Cybernetics,* 1979, SMC-13, 24–34.

Wierwille, W. W., Gutmann, J. C., Hicks, T. G., & Muto, W. H. Secondary task measurements of workload as a function of simulated vehicle dynamics and driving conditions. *Human Factors,* 1977, 19, 557–566.

Wilkinson, R. T., & Morlock, Jr., H. C. Auditory evoked response and reaction time. *Electroencephalography and Clinical Neurophysiology,* 1967, 23, 50–56.

Williges, R. C., & Wierwille, W. W. Behavioral measures of aircrew mental workload. *Human Factors,* 1979, 21, 549–574.

Wood, C. C., & Allison, T. Interpretation of evoked potentials: A neurophysiological perspective. *Canadian Journal of Psychology,* 1981, 35, 113–135.

Woody, C. D. Characterization of an adaptive filter for the analysis of variable latency neuroelectric signals. *Medical and Biological Engineering,* 1967, 5, 539–553.

Author Index

Numbers in italic indicate pages on which the complete references can be found.

Subject Index